America

Past and Present

Revised Seventh Edition
AP* Edition

ROBERT A. DIVINE
University of Texas

T. H. BREEN
Northwestern University

GEORGE M. FREDRICKSON
Stanford University

R. HAL WILLIAMS
Southern Methodist University

ARIELA J. GROSS
University of Southern California

H. W. BRANDS
Texas A&M University

PEARSON
Longman

New York San Francisco Boston
London Toronto Sydney Tokyo Singapore Madrid
Mexico City Munich Paris Cape Town Hong Kong Montreal

Vice President and Publisher: Priscilla McGeehon
Development Manager: Betty Slack
Development Editor: Karen Helfrich
Executive Marketing Manager: Sue Westmoreland
Media Editor: Patrick McCarthy
Supplements Editor: Kristi Olson
Production Manager: Douglas Bell
Project Coordination, Text Design, and Electronic Page Makeup: Elm Street Publishing Services, Inc.
Cover Image: A pieced cotton coverlet, circa 1920. Copyright © Christie's Images/CORBIS.
Art Studio: Maps.com and Burmar Technical Corporation
Photo Research: Photosearch, Inc.
Senior Manufacturing Buyer: Alfred C. Dorsey
Printer and Binder: Quebecor World/Versailles
Cover Printer: The Lehigh Press, Inc.

For permission to use copyrighted material, grateful acknowledgment is made to the following copyright holders and to those on pp. C1–C5, which are hereby made part of this copyright page.

Text credits: p. 529, Arthur Miller, *The Price.* New York, New York: Viking Penguin, 1968; p. 868, from "I Have a Dream" by Martin Luther King, Jr. Copyright © 1963 by Martin Luther King, Jr., copyright renewed © 1991 by Coretta Scott King. Reprinted by arrangement with the Heirs to the Estate of Martin Luther King, Jr., c/o Writer's House, Inc. as agent for the proprietor.

Library of Congress Cataloging-in-Publication Data

America, past and present / Robert A. Divine . . . [et al.].—AP ed.
p. cm.
Includes bibliographical references and index.
ISBN 0-321-24380-3
1. United States—History. I. Divine, Robert A.
E178.1.A4894 2005b
973—dc22

2004002037

Please visit our website at http://www.ablongman.com/divine

ISBN 0-321-18309-6 (Complete Edition)
ISBN 0-321-18308-8 (Volume I)
ISBN 0-321-18307-X (Volume II)
ISBN 0-321-24380-3 (Advanced Placement Edition)

6 7 8 9 10—QWV—07 06

Brief Contents

Detailed Contents

Maps

BACK ENDPAPER

MAPS (CONTINUED)

Figures and Tables

FIGURES

TABLES

Features

FEATURE ESSAYS

A two-page essay in each chapter provides in-depth information on historical topics.

LAW AND SOCIETY ESSAYS

Nine essays offer detailed discussions of significant, provocative legal cases in U.S. history.

A Look at the Past

Examples of artifacts, paintings, drawings, lithographs, architecture, political cartoons, and photographs—all with detailed captions—help students to understand how historians study history.

Preface

The seventh edition of *America Past and Present* is a major revision that strives to achieve the shared goal of the previous editions: to present a clear, relevant, and balanced history of the United States as an unfolding story of national development, from the days of the earliest inhabitants to the present. We emphasize the story because we strongly believe in the value of historical narrative in providing a vivid sense of the past. In each chapter, we seek to blend the excitement and drama of the American experience with insights about the social, economic, and cultural issues that underlie it.

Revisions for the Seventh Edition

In this edition, we have reviewed each chapter carefully to take account of recent scholarly work, to offer new perspectives, and to sharpen the analysis and the prose. In many cases, we have adopted the suggestions offered by those who used the previous editions in their classrooms.

Throughout this edition, as in previous editions, we pay particular attention to the roles that women and minority groups have played in the development of American society and the American nation. These people appear throughout the text, not as witnesses to the historical narrative but as principal actors in its evolution. New and additional material in this edition includes the following:

- Chapter 1, ecological transformation and the impact of the environment on human encounters during the contact era.
- Chapter 6, new opening vignette highlighting the search for balance between public morality and private freedom in the new republic; additional coverage of treaties and western lands after the Revolutionary War.
- Chapter 7, scientific debate and the spirit of nationalism in the post–revolutionary era.
- Chapter 9, expanded discussion of treaties negotiated with Great Britain following the War of 1812.
- Chapter 11, revised and reorganized to enhance and emphasize coverage of the lives and lifestyles of slaves and their experience of slavery.
- Chapter 12, expanded discussion of black abolitionists and women's rights reformers.
- Chapter 16, restructured and revised to devote greater attention to lives of former slaves during Reconstruction; includes new sections on Black Codes and Jim Crow laws.
- Chapter 17, new opening vignette exploring a Native American's experience of conquest and exploitation of the American West.
- Chapter 26, new opening vignette highlighting personal experiences of hardship during the Great Depression; revised discussion of the stock market crash of 1929.
- Chapter 29, expanded discussion of early civil rights leaders.
- Chapter 31, shifts in the labor movement in the 1970s, including the rise of public employee

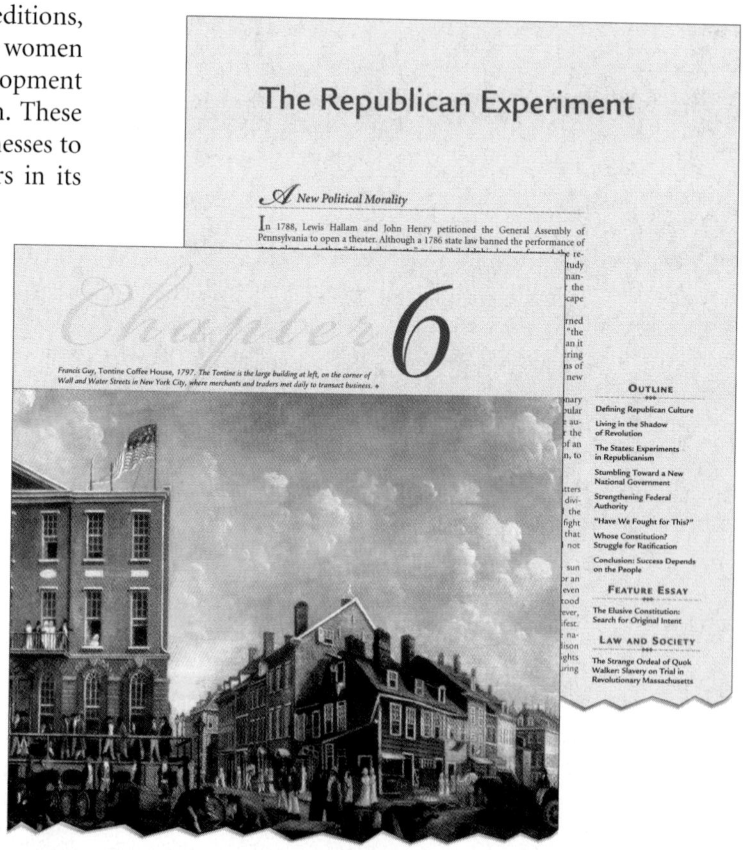

unions; the changing American family at the turn of the century.

- Chapter 33, revised and restructured to concentrate on the shifting economy of the 1990s to the present and the role of government policy in shaping American economy; updated with new discussion of foreign policy and homeland defense post–September 11, including new sections on the war on terrorism and war in Iraq.

Approach and Themes

As the title suggests, our book is a blend of the traditional and the new. The strong narrative emphasis and chronological organization are traditional; the incorporation of the many fresh insights that historians have gained from social sciences in the past quarter century is new. We have used significant incidents and episodes to reflect the dilemmas, the choices, and the decisions made by the people as well as by their leaders. After discussion of the colonial period, most of the chapters examine shorter time periods, usually about a decade, permitting us to view major political and public events as points of reference and orientation around which social themes are integrated. This approach gives unity and direction to the text.

In recounting the story of the American past, we see a nation in flux. The early Africans and Europeans developed complex agrarian folkways that blended Old World customs and New World experiences; as cultural identities evolved, the idea of political independence became more acceptable. People who had been subjects of the British crown created a system of government that challenged later Americans to work out the full implications of theories of social and economic equality.

The growing sectional rift between the North and South, revolving around divergent models of economic growth and conflicting social values, culminated in civil war. In the post–Civil War period, the development of a more industrialized economy severely tested the values of an agrarian society, engendering a Populist reform movement. In the early twentieth century, Progressive reformers sought to infuse the industrial order with social justice. World War I demonstrated the extent of American power in the world. The Great Depression and World War II tested the resiliency of the maturing American nation. The Cold War ushered in an era of crises, foreign and domestic, that revealed both the strengths and the weaknesses of modern America. Although the Cold War ended with the break-up of the Soviet Union in the early 1990s, new threats to world peace in Africa, the Balkans, and the Middle East, and attacks on the World Trade Center and the Pentagon on September 11, 2001, led to the war on terrorism rather than to a new era of peace and tranquility.

Our story of American history goes beyond the major events that have helped to shape the nation—the wars fought, the presidents elected, the legislation enacted, the treaties signed. The impact of change on human lives adds a vital dimension to our understanding of history. How did the American Revolution affect the lives of ordinary citizens? What was it like for both blacks and whites to live in a plantation society? How did the shift from an agrarian to an industrial economy affect both men and women? What impact has technology, in the form of the automobile and the computer, had on patterns of life in the twentieth century? Our narrative explores these issues as well.

Our commitment is not to any particular ideology or point of view; rather, we hope to challenge our readers to rediscover the fascination of the American past and reach their own conclusions about its significance in their lives. At the same time, we have not avoided controversial issues; instead, we have tried to offer reasoned judgments on such morally charged subjects as the nature of slavery and the advent of nuclear weapons. We believe that while history rarely repeats itself, the story of the American past is relevant to the problems and dilemmas facing the nation today, and we have therefore sought to stress themes and ideas that continue to shape our national culture.

Structure and Features

The structure and features of the book are intended to stimulate student interest and to reinforce learning. Each chapter begins with a vignette that introduces the chapter themes and previews the topics to be discussed. The chapter chronology serves as a summary of the key events covered in the chapter. The recommended readings and suggested Web sites at the end of each chapter are sources students can consult for further information on many topics.

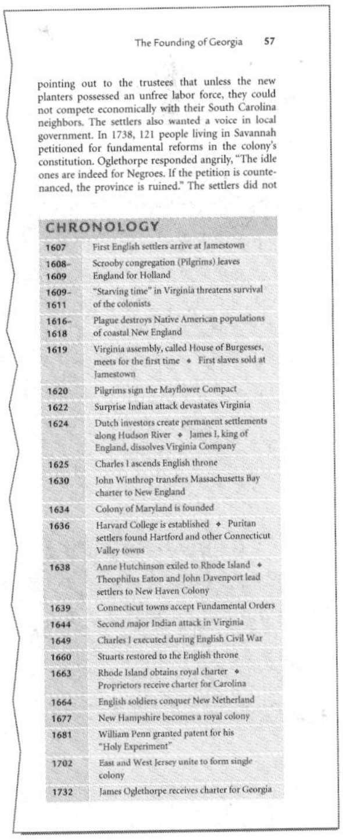
The Founding of Georgia 57

pointing out to the trustees that unless the new planters possessed an unfree labor force, they could not compete economically with their South Carolina neighbors. The settlers also wanted a voice in local government. In 1738, 121 people living in Savannah petitioned for fundamental reforms in the colony's constitution. Oglethorpe responded angrily, "The idle ones are indeed for Negroes. If the petition is countenanced, the province is ruined." The settlers did not

CHRONOLOGY	
1607	First English settlers arrive at Jamestown
1608–1609	Scrooby congregation (Pilgrims) leaves England for Holland
1609–1611	"Starving time" in Virginia threatens survival of the colonists
1616–1618	Plague destroys Native American populations of coastal New England
1619	Virginia assembly, called House of Burgesses, meets for the first time ◆ First slaves sold at Jamestown
1620	Pilgrims sign the Mayflower Compact
1622	Surprise Indian attack devastates Virginia
1624	Dutch investors create permanent settlements along Hudson River ◆ James I, king of England, dissolves Virginia Company
1625	Charles I ascends English throne
1630	John Winthrop transfers Massachusetts Bay charter to New England
1634	Colony of Maryland is founded
1636	Harvard College is established ◆ Puritan settlers found Hartford and other Connecticut Valley towns
1638	Anne Hutchinson exiled to Rhode Island ◆ Theophilus Eaton and John Davenport lead settlers to New Haven Colony
1639	Connecticut towns accept Fundamental Orders
1644	Second major Indian attack in Virginia
1649	Charles I executed during English Civil War
1660	Stuarts restored to the English throne
1663	Rhode Island obtains royal charter ◆ Proprietors receive charter for Carolina
1664	English soldiers conquer New Netherland
1677	New Hampshire becomes a royal colony
1681	William Penn granted patent for his "Holy Experiment"
1702	East and West Jersey unite to form single colony
1732	James Oglethorpe receives charter for Georgia

The feature essay in each chapter offers an examination of a high-interest topic related to the chapters themes and topics. Key terms, highlighted in boldface type in the chapter text, are defined in the new end-of-text glossary, pp. G1–G14.

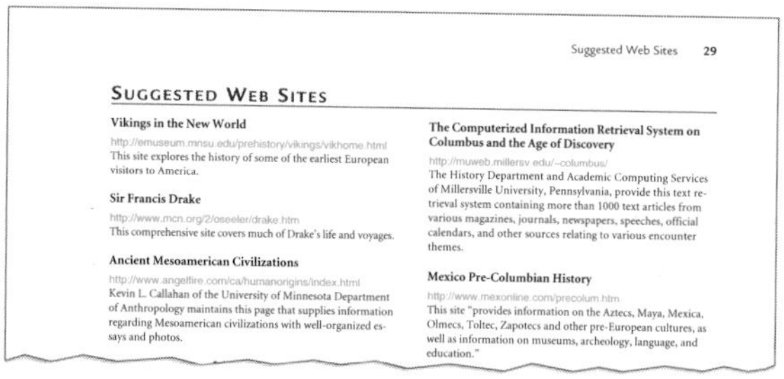
Suggested Web Sites 29

SUGGESTED WEB SITES

Vikings in the New World
http://emuseum.mnsu.edu/prehistory/vikings/vikhome.html
This site explores the history of some of the earliest European visitors to America.

Sir Francis Drake
http://www.mcn.org/2/oseeler/drake.htm
This comprehensive site covers much of Drake's life and voyages.

Ancient Mesoamerican Civilizations
http://www.angelfire.com/ca/humanorigins/index.html
Kevin L. Callahan of the University of Minnesota Department of Anthropology maintains this page that supplies information regarding Mesoamerican civilizations with well-organized essays and photos.

The Computerized Information Retrieval System on Columbus and the Age of Discovery
http://muweb.millersv.edu/~columbus/
The History Department and Academic Computing Services of Millersville University, Pennsylvania, provide this text retrieval system containing more than 1000 text articles from various magazines, journals, newspapers, speeches, official calendars, and other sources relating to various encounter themes.

Mexico Pre-Columbian History
http://www.mexonline.com/precolum.htm
This site "provides information on the Aztecs, Maya, Mexica, Olmecs, Toltec, Zapotecs and other pre-European cultures, as well as information on museums, archeology, language, and education."

Feature Essays

There are eight new "Feature Essays" in the seventh edition, four of them focusing on aspects of peoples' relationships with and impact on the natural world throughout American history. The new essays are:

- Chapter 7, "Defense of Superiority: Science in the Service of Nationalism in the Early Republic"
- Chapter 8, "Barbary Pirates and American Captives: The Nation's First Hostage Crisis"
- Chapter 9, "Confronting New Land"
- Chapter 11, "Harriet Jacobs and Maria Norcom: Women of Southern Households"
- Chapter 18, "Chicago's 'Second Nature'"
- Chapter 19, "Ellis Island: Isle of Hope, Isle of Tears"
- Chapter 31, "Three Mile Island and Chernobyl: The Promise and Peril of Nuclear Power"
- Chapter 33, "The Dot.com Boom and Bust"

Law and Society Essays

Nine "Law and Society" essays appear in the text. Each of these essays focuses on a significant legal case or legal problem in American history and includes a discussion of the background of the case, excerpts from the trial transcript or other relevant primary source material, and coverage of the case in the news media of the period. The introductory section establishes the context for the case and the concluding paragraphs of each essay invite students to explore the legal contest from the perspective of social/cultural historians. New discussion questions are included to spark class discussion. The seventh edition includes two new "Law and Society" essays:

- Chapter 12, "The Legal Rights of Married Women: Reforming the Law of Coverture"
- Chapter 25, "The Scopes "Monkey" Trial: Contesting Cultural Differences"

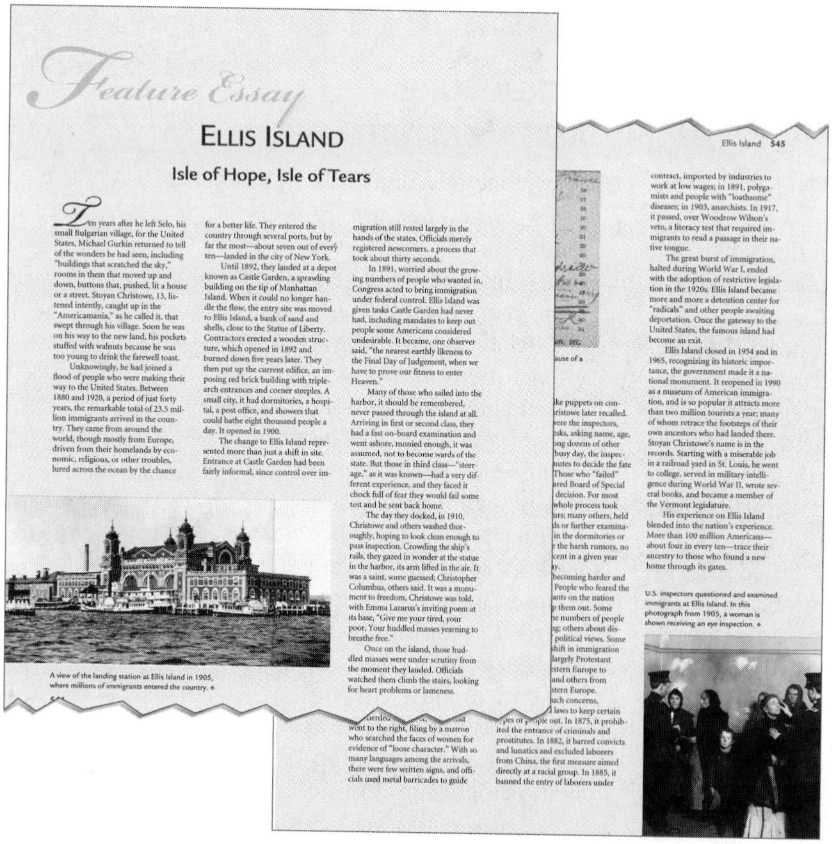
Feature Essay

ELLIS ISLAND

Isle of Hope, Isle of Tears

Ten years after he left Selo, his small Bulgarian village, for the United States, Michael Gurkin returned to tell of the wonders he had seen, including "buildings that scratched the sky," rooms in them that moved up and down, buttons that, pushed, lit a house or a street. Stoyan Christowe, 13, listened intently, caught up in the "Americamania," as he called it, that swept through his village. Soon he was on his way to the new land, his pockets stuffed with walnuts because he was too young to drink the farewell toast.

Unknowingly, he had joined a flood of people who were making their way to the United States. Between 1880 and 1920, a period of just forty years, the remarkable total of 23.5 million immigrants arrived in the country. They came from around the world, though mostly from Europe, driven from their homelands by economic, religious, or other troubles, lured across the ocean by the chance for a better life. They entered the country through several ports, but by far the most—about seven out of every ten—landed in the city of New York.

Until 1892, they landed at a depot known as Castle Garden, a sprawling building on the tip of Manhattan Island. When it could no longer handle the flow, the entry site was moved to Ellis Island, a bank of sand and shells, close to the Statue of Liberty. Contractors erected a wooden structure, which opened in 1892 and burned down five years later. They then put up the current edifice, an imposing red brick building with triple-arch entrances and corner steeples. A small city, it had dormitories, a hospital, a post office, and showers that could bathe eight thousand people a day. It opened in 1900.

The change to Ellis Island represented more than just a shift in site. Entrance at Castle Garden had been fairly informal, since control over immigration still rested largely in the hands of the states. Officials merely registered newcomers, a process that took about thirty seconds.

In 1891, worried about the growing numbers of people who wanted in, Congress acted to bring immigration under federal control. Ellis Island was given tasks Castle Garden had never had, including mandates to keep out people some Americans considered undesirable. It became, one observer said, "the nearest earthly likeness to the Final Day of Judgement, when we have to prove our fitness to enter Heaven."

Many of those who sailed into the harbor, it should be remembered, never passed through the island at all. Arriving in first or second class, they had a fast on-board examination and went ashore, monied enough, it was assumed, not to become wards of the state. But those in third class—"steerage," as it was known—had a very different experience, and they faced it chock full of fear they would fail some test and be sent back home.

The day they docked, in 1910, Christowe and others washed thoroughly, hoping to look clean enough to pass inspection. Crowding the ship's rails, they gazed in wonder at the statue in the harbor, its arm lifted in the air. It was a saint, some guessed; Christopher Columbus, others said. It was a monument to freedom, Christowe was told, with Emma Lazarus's inviting poem at its base, "Give me your tired, your poor, Your huddled masses yearning to breathe free."

Once on the island, those huddled masses were under scrutiny from the moment they landed. Officials watched them climb the stairs, looking for heart problems or lameness.

A view of the landing station at Ellis Island in 1905, where millions of immigrants entered the country.

went to the right, filing by a matron who searched the faces of women for evidence of "loose character." With so many languages among the arrivals, there were few written signs, and officials used metal barricades to guide

ause of a

ke puppets on con-
ristowe later recalled.
ere the inspectors,
sks, asking name, age,
ng dozens of other
busy day, the inspec-
nutes to decide the fate
Those who "failed"
red Board of Special
decision. For most
whole process took
urs; many others, held
ds or further examina-
in the dormitories or
the harsh rumors, no
cent in a given year
y.
becoming harder and
People who feared the
ants on the nation
p them out. Some
e numbers of people
g; others about dis-
political views. Some
hift in immigration
largely Protestant
stern Europe to
and others from
stern Europe.
uch concerns,
laws to keep certain

ple out. In 1875, it prohibited the entrance of criminals and prostitutes. In 1882, it barred convicts and lunatics and excluded laborers from China, the first measure aimed directly at a racial group. In 1885, it banned the entry of laborers under

Ellis Island 545

contract, imported by industries to work at low wages; in 1891, polygamists and people with "loathsome" diseases; in 1903, anarchists. In 1917, it passed, over Woodrow Wilson's veto, a literacy test that required immigrants to read a passage in their native tongue.

The great burst of immigration, halted during World War I, ended with the adoption of restrictive legislation in the 1920s. Ellis Island became more and more a detention center for "radicals" and other people awaiting deportation. Once the gateway to the United States, the famous island had become an exit.

Ellis Island closed in 1954 and in 1965, recognizing its historic importance, the government made it a national monument. It reopened in 1990 as a museum of American immigration, and is so popular it attracts more than two million tourists a year; many of whom retrace the footsteps of their own ancestors who had landed there. Stoyan Christowe's name is in the records. Starting with a miserable job in a railroad yard in St. Louis, he went to college, served in military intelligence during World War II, wrote several books, and became a member of the Vermont legislature.

His experience on Ellis Island blended into the nation's experience. More than 100 million Americans—about four in every ten—trace their ancestry to those who found a new home through its gates.

U.S. inspectors questioned and examined immigrants at Ellis Island. In this photograph from 1905, a woman is shown receiving an eye inspection.

Visual Program

The extensive full-color map program has been improved with several new and revised maps. Each map includes a caption to help students identify the purpose and significance of the map. New charts, graphs, and tables—many with a capsulized format for convenient review of factual information—relate to social and economic change. The rich, full-color illustration program, bearing directly on the narrative, advances and expands the themes, provides elaboration and contrast, tells more of the story, and generally adds another dimension of learning. "Look at the Past" photographs are illustrations of artifacts that present students with a material record of America's past. Captions invite them to consider the historical significance of the artifacts and make connections with similar materials they encounter today.

Author Responsibility

Although this book is a joint effort, each author took primary responsibility for writing one section. T. H. Breen contributed the first eight chapters, going from the earliest Native American period to the second decade of the nineteenth century. George M. Fredrickson wrote Chapters 9 through 16, carrying the narrative through the Reconstruction era. Ariela J. Gross revised Chapters 11 and 16 and contributed the Law and Society feature in Chapter 12. R. Hal Williams was responsible for Chapters 17 through 24, focusing on the industrial transformation, urbanization, and the events culminating in World War I. The final nine chapters, bringing the story through the Great Depression, World War II, and the Cold War and its aftermath, were the work of H. W. Brands, especially Chapters 25 through 27, and Robert A. Divine, primarily Chapters 28 through 33. Each contributor reviewed and revised the work of his or her colleagues and helped shape the material into its final form.

Supplements

For Instructors

Companion Website, www.PHSchool.com/advanced (www.ablongman.com/divineap)

The Companion Website provides a wealth of resources for students and instructors using *America Past and Present, AP* Edition.* Instructors will have access to portions of the instructor's manual, teaching links, source documents, and photos and will be able to download maps and figures that appear in the text.

Instructor's Resources

This teacher's resource manual includes chapter summaries; lesson and discussion suggestions; chapter-specific review questions in different formats; reproducible map and graph worksheets; a graph correlation guide based on The College Board topic outline; practice Document-Based Questions (DBQs) and free response questions; and skills worksheets to teach students how to read and interpret maps and graphs, analyze documents, form a coherent argument, and provide evidence to support it in an essay.

Test Bank

This test bank contains more than 1,200 multiple-choice, true/false, matching, and completion questions. All of the multiple-choice questions include five answer choices, conforming to the format of the AP* exam.

TestGen-EQ Computerized Testing System

This flexible, easy-to-master computer test bank includes all the test items in the printed test bank. The software allows instructors to edit existing questions and add their own items. Tests can be printed in several different formats and can include figures such as graphs and tables.

Visual Aids

Map Transparencies

The set includes four-color map transparency acetates drawn from the text.

For Students

Companion Website, www.PHSchool.com/advanced (www.ablongman.com/divineap)

The Companion Website provides a wealth of resources for students and instructors using *America Past and Present, AP* Edition.* Students will find chapter summaries, primary sources, practice tests, web activities, multimedia resources, research and writing guides, and much more. The practice tests and study questions feature on-line scoring to give students immediate feedback.

AP* Exam Text Plus Test Workbook

A number of instructors have created this supplement, including Michael Barbour, Tony Jones, Len Rabinowitz, and Gordon Utz. This supplement is aimed to help students achieve success on the Advanced Placement* exam. Key features include: an overview of the AP* program and AP* exam for U.S. History; correlations between key AP* test topics and *America Past and Present, AP* Edition;* a chapter summary and hundreds of practice study questions with detailed answers and explanations for each chapter of the text; two full practice exams with answers and explanations; and strategies and samples of Document-Based Questions.

Document-Based Question Booklet

Created by Gordon Utz, this student booklet is geared toward providing additional practice on the Document-Based Question portion of the AP* Exam. This guide contains twelve Document-Based Questions in addition to step-by-step instructions on how to tackle a DBQ question and the Dos and Don'ts of DBQ writing. In addition, each DBQ includes a thorough explanation, model thesis statement, fact sheet based on *America Past and Present, AP* Edition,* grading rubric, examples of good analysis level writing, and samples of facts from the source document that could be useful in the essay.

Correlation Guide

AP* United States History Topics Correlated to *America Past and Present*, Seventh Edition

AP* Topics	*America Past and Present*, Seventh Edition
1. Discovery and Settlement of the New World, 1492–1650	Chapters 1, 2
Europe in the sixteenth century	pp. 11–16
Spanish, English, and French exploration	pp. 17–25
First English settlements	pp. 34–41
Jamestown	pp. 34–36
Plymouth	p. 41
Spanish and French settlements and long-term influence	pp. 19–22
American Indians	pp. 4–10
2. America and the British Empire, 1650–1754	Chapters 2, 3
Chesapeake country	pp. 33–40
Growth of New England	pp. 41–48
Restoration Colonies	pp. 54–56
Mercantilism; the Dominion of New England	p. 77
Origins of Slavery	pp. 71–76
3. Colonial Society in the Mid-Eighteenth Century	Chapters 4, 5
Social Structure	pp. 62–71
Family	pp. 62–69
Farm and town life; the economy	pp. 68–72
Culture	pp. 62–63, 104–11
Great Awakening	pp. 108–11
The American Mind	pp. 104–06
"Folkways"	pp. 62–63
New Immigrants	pp. 95–97
4. Road to Revolution, 1754–1775	Chapters 4, 5
Anglo-French rivalries and Seven Years' War	pp. 118–21
Imperial reorganization of 1763	p. 120
Stamp Act	pp. 132–34
Declaratory Act	pp. 134, 138, 141
Townshend Act	pp. 134–35
Boston Tea Party	pp. 140–42
Philosophy of the American Revolution	pp. 125–36
5. The American Revolution, 1775–1783	Chapters 5, 6
Continental Congress	pp. 142–44
Declaration of Independence	p. 144
The War	pp. 145–52
French alliance	pp. 149–50
War and society; Loyalists	pp. 152–53
War economy	pp. 171–72
Articles of Confederation	pp. 166–67
Peace of Paris	pp. 153–54
Creating state governments	pp. 164–66
Political organization	pp. 164–66
Social reform: women, slavery	pp. 160–62
6. Constitution and New Republic, 1776–1800	Chapters 6, 7
Philadelphia Convention: drafting the Constitution	pp. 175–76
Federalists versus Anti-Federalists	pp. 181–83
Bill of Rights	pp. 183–84
Washington's presidency	pp. 191–92
Hamilton's financial program	pp. 196–99
Foreign and domestic difficulties	pp. 207–08
Beginnings of political parties	pp. 191–92
John Adams' presidency	pp. 208–13
Alien and Sedition Acts	pp. 210–12
XYZ Affair	pp. 209–10
Election of 1800	pp. 213–15

AP* Topics	*America Past and Present,* **Seventh Edition**
7. The Age of Jefferson, 1800–1816	Chapter 8
Jefferson's presidency	pp. 213–29
The Louisiana Purchase	pp. 226–28
Burr Conspiracy	pp. 234–35
The Supreme Court under John Marshall	pp. 229–33
Neutral rights, impressments, embargo	pp. 236–38
Madison	pp. 233–39
War of 1812	pp. 240–42, 247–48
Causes	pp. 238–39
Invasion of Canada	pp. 239–41
Hartford Convention	p. 242
Conduct of the war	pp. 240–42
Treaty of Ghent	pp. 242–44
New Orleans	pp. 241–43
8. Nationalism and Economic Expansion	Chapter 9
James Monroe; Era of Good Feelings	pp. 263–64
Panic of 1819	pp. 251, 260, 264, 269
Settlement of the West	pp. 248, 252–54
Missouri Compromise	pp. 264–66
Foreign affairs: Canada, Florida, the Monroe Doctrine	pp. 267–68
Election of 1824: end of Virginia dynasty	pp. 279–81
Economic revolution	pp. 256–62
Early railroads and canals	pp. 259, 374–75
Expansion of business	pp. 261–62, 267
Beginnings of factory system	pp. 261–62
Early labor movement; women	pp. 261–62
Social mobility; extremes of wealth	p. 279
The cotton revolution in the South	pp. 259–60
Commercial agriculture	pp. 259–60
9. Sectionalism	Chapters 9, 11, 13
The South	pp. 301–03, 322–24
Cotton Kingdom	pp. 322–24
Southern trade and industry	pp. 303–05
Southern society and culture	pp. 302–03, 312–21
Gradations of White society	pp. 312–21
Nature of Slavery: "peculiar institution"	pp. 303–17
The mind of the South	pp. 321–26
The North	pp. 399–411
The Northeast industry	pp. 375–78
Labor	p. 382
Immigration	pp. 380–81
Urban slums	p. 381
Northwest agriculture	pp. 379–80
Westward expansion	pp. 251–56, 367–69
Advance of agricultural frontier	p. 251
Significance of the frontier	pp. 367–69
Life on the frontier; squatters	pp. 254–56
Removal of American Indians	pp. 252–53, 284–86
10. The Age of Jackson, 1828–1848	Chapter 10
Democracy and the "common man"	p. 274
Expansion of Suffrage	p. 279
Rotation in office	pp. 283–84
Second party system	pp. 296–97
Democratic Party	pp. 282–83, 294–95
Whig Party	pp. 291–92, 296–97
Internal improvements and states' rights: the Maysville Road veto	p. 287
The Nullification Crisis	pp. 286–88
Tariff issue	p. 288
The Union: Calhoun and Jackson	pp. 281–82, 286–88
The Bank War: Jackson and Biddle	pp. 288–91
Martin Van Buren	pp. 291–96
Independent treasury system	p. 292
Panic of 1837	pp. 291–92
11. Territorial Expansion and Sectional Crisis	Chapter 13
Manifest Destiny and mission	pp. 367–69
Texas annexation, the Oregon boundary, and California	pp. 367–70
James K. Polk and the Mexican War; slavery and Wilmot Proviso	pp. 370–73, 388–89
Later expansionist efforts	pp. 360–66
12. Creating an American Culture	Chapters 9, 12
Cultural nationalism	pp. 243–44, 266–67
Education reform/professionalism	pp. 280, 338–40
Religion; revivalism	pp. 329–33
Utopian experiments: Mormons, Oneida Community	pp. 346–47, 365–66

AP* Topics	*America Past and Present,* Seventh Edition
Transcendentalists	pp. 347–50
National literature, art, architecture	pp. 276–78, 347–50
Reform crusades	pp. 351–52
Feminism; roles of women in the nineteenth century	pp. 335–36
Abolitionism	pp. 343–45
Temperance	pp. 333–34
Criminals and the insane	pp. 340–41
13. The 1850's: Decade of Crisis	Chapter 14
The Compromise of 1850	pp. 391–93
Fugitive Slave Act and *Uncle Tom's Cabin*	pp. 391–92, 400–401
Kansas-Nebraska Act and realignment of parties	pp. 393–95
Demise of the Whig Party	p. 395
Emergence of the Republican Party	pp. 397–98
Dred Scott decision and Lecompton crisis	pp. 401–03, 414–16
Lincoln-Douglas debates, 1858	pp. 403–04
John Brown's raid	pp. 404, 406–07
The election of 1860; Abraham Lincoln	pp. 405, 408–09, 419–20
The secession crisis	pp. 421–23
14. Civil War	Chapters 15, 16
The Union	pp. 427–31
Mobilization and finance	pp. 430–31
Civil Liberties	p. 431
Election of 1864	pp. 443–44
The South	pp. 427–31
Confederate constitution	pp. 421–22
Mobilization and finance	pp. 430–31
States' rights and the Confederacy	pp. 421–25
Foreign affairs and diplomacy	pp. 436–37
Military strategy, campaigns, and battles	pp. 432–44
The abolition of slavery	pp. 438–39
Confiscation Acts	pp. 438–39
Emancipation Proclamation	pp. 437–38
Freedmen's Bureau	pp. 461–65
Thirteenth Amendment	p. 454
Effects of war on society	pp. 444–46, 478
Inflation and public debt	pp. 430–31
Role of women	pp. 444–46
Devastation of the South	pp. 471–75
Changing labor patterns	pp. 460–61
15. Reconstruction to 1877	Chapter 16
Presidential Plans: Lincoln and Johnson	pp. 453–56
Radical (congressional) plans	pp. 457–58
Civil rights and the Fourteenth Amendment	pp. 456–57
Military reconstruction	pp. 457–58, 462
Impeachment of Johnson	pp. 459–60
African American suffrage: the Fifteenth Amendment	pp. 466–68
Southern state governments: problems, achievements, weakness	pp. 458, 476–77
Compromise of 1877 and the end of Reconstruction	pp. 471–72
16. New South and the Last West	Chapters 16, 17
Politics in the New South	pp. 471–75
The Redeemers	pp. 472–73
Whites and African Americans in the New South	pp. 460–65
Subordination of freed slaves: Jim Crow	pp. 473–75
Southern economy; colonial status of the South	p. 460
Sharecropping	pp. 461–62
Industrial stirrings	pp. 472–73
Cattle Kingdom	pp. 499–502
Open-range ranching	pp. 494, 499–502
Day of the cowboy	pp. 499–500
Building the Western railroad	pp. 512–18
Subordination of American Indians: dispersal of tribes	pp. 485–91
Farming the plains; problems in agriculture	pp. 504–05
Mining bonanza	pp. 496–99
17. Industrialization and Corporate Consolidation	Chapters 18, 19
Industrial growth: railroads, iron, coal, electricity, steel, oil, banks	pp. 510–36
Laissez-faire conservatism	pp. 578–79
Gospel of Wealth	p. 531
Myth of the "self-made man"	pp. 531, 589
Social Darwinism; survival of the fittest	p. 560
Social Critics and dissenters	pp. 552, 560–65
Effects of technological developments on worker-workplace	pp. 512, 516, 522–24
Union movement	pp. 531–33
Knights of Labor and American Federation of Labor	pp. 532–33
Haymarket, Homestead, and Pullman	pp. 532, 535, 585

AP* Topics	*America Past and Present,* Seventh Edition
18. Urban Society	Chapter 19
Lure of the city	pp. 550–60
Immigration	pp. 543–48
City problems	pp. 564–65
Slums	pp. 562–63
Machine politics	pp. 548–50
Awakening conscience; reforms	pp. 560–65, 664–65
Social legislation	pp. 562, 564–65
Settlement houses: Jane Addams and Lillian Wald	pp. 562–63
Structural reforms in government	pp. 664–67
19. Intellectual and Cultural Movements	Chapters 19, 20
Education	pp. 555–57
Colleges and universities	pp. 557–60
Scientific advances	p. 557
Professionalism and the social sciences	pp. 657–58
Realism in literature and art	pp. 589–91
Mass culture	pp. 550–60
Use of leisure	pp. 552–53
Publishing and Journalism	pp. 614–15
20. National Politics, 1877–1896: The Gilded Age	Chapter 20
A conservative presidency	pp. 575–76, 587–88, 596
Issues	pp. 578–79
Tariff controversy	pp. 606–08
Railroad regulation	pp. 576, 584, 673–74
Trusts	pp. 578–79
Agrarian discontent	pp. 580–81
Crisis of 1890s	pp. 579–96
Populism	pp. 579–83, 595–96
Silver questions	pp. 577–79, 594–95
Election of 1896: McKinley versus Bryan	pp. 591, 594–96
21. Foreign Policy, 1865–1914	Chapters 21, 24
Seward and the purchase of Alaska	p. 607
The new imperialism	pp. 603–09, 617–21
Blaine and Latin America	p. 607
International Darwinism: missionaries, politicians, and naval expansionists	pp. 606–09
Spanish-American War	pp. 611–20
Cuban independence	pp. 601–02, 611–17
Debate on Philippines	pp. 620–22
The Far East: John Hay and the Open Door	pp. 623–24, 693–94
Theodore Roosevelt	pp. 669–72, 691–92
The Panama Canal	pp. 691–92
Roosevelt Corollary	pp. 692–93
Far East	p. 693
Taft and dollar diplomacy	p. 693
Wilson and moral diplomacy	p. 694
22. Progressive Era	Chapters 22, 23
Origins of Progressivism	pp. 627–28
Progressive attitudes and motives	pp. 627–28
Muckrakers	pp. 627–28
Social Gospel	pp. 658–59
Municipal, state, and national reforms	pp. 664–67
Political suffrage	pp. 660–62
Social and economic: regulations	p. 669
Socialism: alternatives	p. 662
Black America	pp. 558–59, 638–39
Washington, Du Bois, and Garvey	pp. 558–59, 638–39
Urban migration	p. 539
Civil rights organizations	pp. 582, 638–39, 660
Women's role: family, work, education, unionization, and suffrage	pp. 660–62
Roosevelt's Square Deal	pp. 668–69
Managing the trusts	pp. 667–68
Conservation	pp. 665–66, 671–72
Taft	pp. 673–75
Pinchot-Ballinger controversy	p. 673
Payne-Aldrich Tariff	p. 673
Wilson's New Freedom	pp. 675–78
Tariffs	pp. 676–78
Banking reform	p. 678
Antitrust Act of 1914	pp. 667–68, 677
23. The First World War	Chapter 24
Problems of neutrality	pp. 696–697
Submarines	pp. 668–69, 689–90, 697–99
Economic ties	pp. 696–97, 702

AP* Topics	*America Past and Present*, Seventh Edition
Psychological and ethnic ties	pp. 696–97
Preparedness and pacifism	pp. 696–97, 699, 702
Mobilization	p. 701
Fighting the war	pp. 700–703
Financing the war	p. 708
War boards	pp. 709, 722
Propaganda, public opinion, civil liberties	pp. 688, 696-97, 706–08
Wilson's Fourteen Points	pp. 712–14
Treaty of Versailles	pp. 712–16
Ratification fight	pp. 713–15
Postwar demobilization	pp. 730, 736
Red Scare	pp. 732–34
Labor strife	pp. 722, 733
24. New Era: The 1920's	Chapter 25
Republican governments	pp. 721–22, 737–38
Business creed	pp. 721–22
Harding scandals	pp. 737–38
Economic development	pp. 721–23
Prosperity and wealth	pp. 720–23
Farm and labor problems	pp. 722, 739
New culture	pp. 720–23
Consumerism: automobile, radio, movies	pp. 719–23
Women, the family	pp. 724–25
Modern religion	pp. 732–37
Literature of alienation	pp. 727–32
Jazz age	pp. 723–29
Harlem Renaissance	pp. 729–32
Conflict of cultures	pp. 732–37
Prohibition, bootlegging	pp. 734–35
Nativism	pp. 736–37
Ku Klux Klan	pp. 735–36
Religious fundamentalism versus modernists	pp. 732–37
Myth of isolation	pp. 737–41
Replacing the League of Nations	pp. 713–15, 737–38
Business and diplomacy	pp. 737–41
25. Depression, 1929–1933	Chapter 26
Wall Street crash	p. 751
Depression economy	pp. 773–74
Moods of despair	pp. 750–61
Agrarian unrest	pp. 758–59, 766
Bonus march	p. 754
Hoover-Stimson diplomacy; Japan	pp. 779–81
26. New Deal	Chapter 26
Franklin D. Roosevelt	pp. 754–55, 761–62, 772–74
Background, ideas	pp. 754–55
Philosophy of New Deal	pp. 761–64
100 Days; "alphabet agencies"	pp. 755–57
Second New Deal	pp. 768–69
Critics; left and right	pp. 762, 764, 768
Rise of CIO; labor strikes	pp. 764–56
Supreme Court fight	pp. 772–73
Recession of 1938	p. 773
American people in the Depression	pp. 749–61
Social values, women, ethnic groups	pp. 766–68
Indian Reorganization Act	p. 767
Mexican American deportation	pp. 753, 766–67
The racial issue	p. 753
27. Diplomacy in the 1930s	Chapter 27
Good Neighbor Policy: Montevideo, Buenos Aires	pp. 779–80
London Economic Conference	pp. 784–85
Disarmament	pp. 783–84
Isolationism: neutrality legislation	pp. 782–83
Aggressors: Japan, Italy, and Germany	pp. 781, 784
Appeasement	pp. 783–84
Rearmament; Blitzkrieg; Lend-Lease	pp. 780, 784–85
Atlantic Charter	pp. 784–85
Pearl Harbor	pp. 787–88
28. The Second World War	Chapters 27, 28
Organizing for war	pp. 784–88
Mobilizing production	pp. 792, 798
Propaganda	pp. 792–94
Internment of Japanese Americans	pp. 796–97
The war in Europe, Africa, and the Mediterranean; D Day	pp. 783–86, 788–92, 798
The war in the Pacific: Hiroshima, Nagasaki	pp. 786–88, 791–92, 802–03

AP* Topics	*America Past and Present,* Seventh Edition
Diplomacy	pp. 780–81, 788–89
War aims	pp. 790–91
Wartime conferences: Tehran, Yalta, Potsdam	pp. 799, 802, 807–08
Postwar atmospheres; the United Nations	pp. 808–10
29. Truman and the Cold War	Chapter 28
Postwar economic adjustments	pp. 822–23
The Taft-Hartley Act	p. 822
Civil Rights and the election of 1948	pp. 814, 822, 850
Containment in Europe and the Middle East	pp. 811–15
Truman Doctrine	pp. 811–12
Marshall Plan	pp. 812–13
Berlin Crisis	pp. 814–15
NATO	pp. 813–14
Revolution in China	pp. 816–17
Limited War: Korea, MacArthur	pp. 817–21
30. Eisenhower and Modern Republicanism	Chapters 28, 29, 30
Domestic frustrations; McCarthyism	pp. 824–27
Civil rights movement	pp. 851–52
The Warren Court and *Brown v. Board of Education*	pp. 850–52
Montgomery bus boycott	pp. 852–53
Greensboro sit-in	pp. 853–54
John Foster Dulles' foreign policy	pp. 828–31
Crisis in Southeast Asia	pp. 829–30
Massive retaliation	pp. 828–30
Nationalism in Southeast Asia, the Middle East, Latin America	pp. 828–31
Khrushchev and Berlin	pp. 831–33
American people: homogenized society	pp. 836–39
Prosperity: economic consolidation	pp. 839–41
Consumer Culture	pp. 838–41
Consensus of values	pp. 840–41
Space Race	pp. 846–47
31. Kennedy's New Frontier; Johnson's Great Society	Chapter 30
New domestic programs	pp. 864–69, 872–73
Tax Cut	pp. 865–66
War on Poverty	p. 871
Affirmative Action	pp. 956–959
Civil Rights and civil liberties	pp. 866–68, 872–73
African Americans: political, cultural, and economic roles	pp. 866–68, 872
The leadership of Martin Luther King, Jr.	pp. 867–68
Resurgence of feminism	pp. 871, 885
The New Left and the Counterculture	pp. 880–81
Emergence of the Republican Party in the South	pp. 888–89, 900
The Supreme Court and the Miranda decision	p. 868
Foreign Policy	pp. 859–62, 876–77, 885–87
Bay of Pigs	pp. 861–62
Cuban missile crisis	pp. 862–64
Vietnam quagmire	pp. 876–80, 885–89
32. Nixon	Chapter 31
Election of 1968	pp. 885, 888–89
Nixon-Kissinger foreign policy	pp. 897–99
Vietnam: escalation and pullout	pp. 898–99
China: restoring relations	pp. 897–98
Soviet Union: détente	pp. 897–98
New Federalism	pp. 895–97
Supreme Court and *Roe v. Wade*	pp. 910, 920–924
Watergate Crisis and resignation	pp. 893-94, 900–901
33. The United States since 1974	Chapters 32, 33
The New Right and the conservative social agenda	pp. 895–96, 927–28, 949
Ford and Rockefeller	pp. 912–13
Carter	pp. 913–14
Deregulation	p. 932
Energy and Inflation	pp. 901–04
Camp David Accords	pp. 916, 940
Iranian hostage crisis	pp. 916–17
Reagan	pp. 929–44
Tax cuts and budgets deficits	933-36
Defense buildup	pp. 933, 939, 944
New disarmament treaties	pp. 943–44
Foreign crises: the Persian Gulf and Central America	pp. 942–43, 952–53
Society	pp. 963–69
Old and new urban problems	pp. 963–64
Asian and Hispanic immigrants	pp. 962, 965–66
Resurgent fundamentalism	p. 928
African Americans and local, state, and national politics	pp. 929–30, 932

Acknowledgments

The authors acknowledge with special gratitude the contribution of Professor Jeanne Whitney of Salisbury State University for her work in selecting many of the featured "Look at the Past" illustrations and writing the informative and thought-provoking captions to accompany these photos. We are also most grateful to our consultants and reviewers whose thoughtful and constructive work contributed greatly to this edition. Their many helpful suggestions led to significant improvements in the final product.

Elizabeth Ansnes, *San Jose State University*
Donald Scott Barton, *East Central University*
Chad Berry, *Maryville College*
Kent Blaser, *Wayne State College*
Eric J. Bolsterli, *University of Texas at Arlington*
Kathleen S. Carter, *High Point University*
Yvonne Sutton Cornelius, *Nashville State Community College*
Edward R. Crowther, *Adams State University*
Roger P. Davis, *University of Nebraska at Kearney*
Patricia Norred Derr, *Kutztown University*
Wallace Hettle, *University of Northern Iowa*
Virginia G. Jelatis, *Western Illinois University*
Sandra Wagner-Wright, *University of Hawaii at Hilo*

This book owes much to the many conscientious historians who reviewed previous editions and offered valuable suggestions that led to many improvements in the text. We acknowledge with gratitude the contributions of the following:

Frank W. Abbott, *University of Houston*
Joseph L. Adams, *St. Louis Community College at Meramec*
Frank Alduino, *Anne Arundel Community College*
Kenneth G. Alfers, *Mountain View College*
Thomas Archdeacon, *University of Wisconsin*
James Axtell, *College of William and Mary*
Kenneth R. Bain, *Northwestern University*
James Banks, *Cuyahoga Community College*
Lois W. Banner, *Hamilton College*
David Bernstein, *California State University, Long Beach*
James D. Border, *Berkshire Community College*
Alexander O. Boulton, *Villa Julie College*
Mary C. Brennan, *Ohio State University*
Blanche Brick, *Blinn College*
Daniel Patrick Brown, *Moorpark College*
Thomas Camfield, *Sam Houston State University*
Clayborne Carson, *Stanford University*
Kathleen S. Carter, *High Point University*
Raphael Cassimere, Jr., *University of New Orleans*
Francis Coan, *Central Connecticut State University*
Charles L. Cohen, *University of Wisconsin*
Jerald Combs, *San Francisco State University*
John Cooper, *University of Wisconsin*
Nancy F. Cott, *Yale University*
Virginia Crane, *University of Wisconsin, Oshkosh*
James C. Curtis, *University of Delaware*
Bruce J. Dierenfield, *Canisius College*
Charles Douglass, *Florida Community College at Jacksonville*
Thomas Dublin, *State University of New York at Binghamton*
Perry R. Duis, *University of Illinois at Chicago*
Richard Ellis, *State University of New York at Buffalo*
John P. Farr, *Chattanooga State Technical Community College*
James E. Fell, Jr., *University of Colorado, Denver*
Eric Foner, *Columbia University*
Stephen Foster, *Northern Illinois University*
William W. Freehling, *Johns Hopkins University*
Fred E. Freidel, *Bellevue Community College*
Richard Frey, *Southern Oregon State College*
Gary W. Gallagher, *Pennsylvania State University*
Sara E. Gallaway, *Oxnard College*
Don R. Gerlach, *University of Akron*
August W. Giebelhaus, *Georgia Institute of Technology*
Louis S. Gomolak, *Southwest Texas State University*
Lewis L. Gould, *University of Texas*
Lawrence Grear, *Langston University*
Richard C. Haney, *University of Wisconsin, Whitewater*
George Harrison, *Jones County Junior College*
Edward F. Hass, *Wright State University*
Tim Heinrichs, *Bellevue Community College*
Mary Ann Heiss, *Kent State University*
Kenneth E. Hendrickson, *Sam Houston State University*
Sondra Herman, *De Anza Community College*
Anne Hickling, *San Jose City College*
James Hollingsworth, *Pasco-Hernando Community College*
Ranford Hopkins, *Moorpark College*
Brian Hosmer, *University of Delaware*
John R. Howe, *University of Minnesota*
Nathan I. Huggins, *Harvard University*
Susan Hult, *Houston Community College*
James A. Hurst, *Northwest Missouri State University*

Wallace S. Hutcheon, *Northern Virginia Community College*
Robert M. Ireland, *University of Kentucky*
Carol E. Jenson, *University of Wisconsin, La Crosse*
Juli A. Jones, *St. Charles County Community College*
Robert R. Jones, *University of Southwestern Louisiana*
John Kelley, *Shawnee State Community College*
Richard S. Kirkendall, *University of Washington*
I. E. Kirkpatrick, *Tyler Junior College*
Fred Koestler, *Tarleton State University*
Lawrence F. Kohl, *University of Alabama*
Steven Lawson, *Rutgers University*
Edward Lee, *Winthrop University*
Kathy Long, *Chattanooga State Technical Community College*
Henry Louis, *Kansas City Kansas Community College*
Warren Mackey, *Chattanooga State Technical Community College*
Thomas R. Mandeville, *Clinton Community College*
Karen Marcotte, *Palo Alto College*
Herbert F. Margulies, *University of Hawaii*
Myron Marty, *National Endowment for the Humanities*
Robert C. McMath, Jr., *Georgia Institute of Technology*
T. Ronald Melton, *Brewton-Parker College*
James H. Merrell, *Vassar College*
Joseph C. Miller, *University of Virginia*
William G. Morris, *Midland College*
Harmon Mothershead, *Northwest Missouri State University*
Timothy Moy, *University of New Mexico*
Peter Murray, *Methodist College*
John M. Murrin, *Princeton University*
John K. Nelson, *University of North Carolina*
Roger L. Nichols, *University of Arizona*
Elizabeth R. Osborne, *Indiana University–Purdue University at Indianapolis*
Elliot Pasternack, *Middlesex County College*
J'Nell L. Pate, *Tarrant County Junior College*
Michael Perman, *University of Illinois, Chicago*
Charles A. Pilant, *Cumberland College*
Nora Ramirez, *San Antonio Community College*
Marlette Rebhorn, *Austin Community College*
Douglas W. Richmond, *University of Texas, Arlington*
Andrew W. Robertson, *Louisiana State University*
David Sandoval, *University of Southern Colorado*
Howard Schonberger, *University of Maine*
Ingrid Winther Scobie, *Texas Women's University*
Rebecca S. Shoemaker, *Indiana State University*
Kathryn Kish Sklar, *State University of New York at Binghamton*
Allan Spetter, *Wright State University*
Cherry L. Spruill, *Indiana University–Purdue University at Indianapolis*
Mark J. Stegmaier, *Cameron University*
George G. Suggs, Jr., *Southeast Missouri State University*
H. Micheal Tarver, *McNeese State University*
Paul F. Taylor, *Augusta College*
Michael E. Thompson, *South Seattle Community College*
George Torok, *El Paso Community College*
Clyde D. Tyson, *Niagara County Community College*
Nancy C. Unger, *San Francisco State University*
Richard Vanderpool, *Umpqua Community College*
Donna L. VanRaaphorst, *Cuyahoga Community College*
Russell Veeder, *Dickinson State University*
Daniel C. Vogt, *Jackson State University*
Forrest A. Walker, *Eastern New Mexico State University*
James P. Walsh, *Central Connecticut State University*
Ronald Walters, *Johns Hopkins University*
Marli Weiner, *University of Maine*
Frank Wetta, *Galveston Community College*
James C. Williams, *De Anza College*
James M. Woods, *Georgia Southern University*
David Yancey, *San Jose City College*
Rosemarie Zagarri, *Catholic University*
Robert F. Zeidel, *University of Wisconsin, Stout*

The staff at Longman continued its generous support and assistance for our efforts. We thank Acquisitions Editor Ashley Dodge for her attention, support, and thoughtful guidance throughout this revision; Development Manager Betty Slack and Development Editor Karen Helfrich, who helped us augment and enhance the appeal of the text; and Executive Marketing Manager Sue Westmoreland, who worked zealously to convey the message and vision of the authors to the Longman sales force and to the marketplace. Production Manager Douglas Bell, Cover Design Manager/Cover Designer Nancy Danahy, and Project Editor Heather Johnson and the staff at Elm Street Publishing Services put the finishing touches on this new edition and deftly guided it through the many phases of production.

Finally, each author received aid and encouragement from many colleagues, friends, and family members. Bob Divine extends special thanks to Mitch Lerner for research assistance and editorial suggestions. T. H. Breen thanks Bradley S. Schlager, Seth Cotlar, Timothy Hall, Christopher Hodson, and Patrick Griffin for their help with this edition. George Fredrickson acknowledges with gratitude the research and assistance of Jared Farmer. Hal Williams extends thanks to Carole S. Cohen, Jacqueline Bradley, Lisa R. Henry, and Susan Harper-Bisso for their help with revisions for this edition. Ariela Gross extends thanks to Lori Martinez, John Acevedo, and especially Stephen Andrews for invaluable help with this edition.

The Authors

About the Authors

ROBERT A. DIVINE

Robert A. Divine, George W. Littlefield Professor Emeritus in American History at the University of Texas at Austin, received his Ph.D. from Yale University in 1954. A specialist in American diplomatic history, he taught from 1954 to 1996 at the University of Texas, where he was honored by both the student association and the graduate school for teaching excellence. His extensive published work includes *The Illusion of Neutrality* (1962); *Second Chance: The Triumph of Internationalism in America During World War II* (1967); and *Blowing on the Wind* (1978). His most recent work is *Perpetual War for Perpetual Peace* (2000), a comparative analysis of twentieth-century American wars. He is also the author of *Eisenhower and the Cold War* (1981) and editor of three volumes of essays on the presidency of Lyndon Johnson. His book, *The Sputnik Challenge* (1993), won the Eugene E. Emme Astronautical Literature Award for 1993. He has been a fellow at the Center for Advanced Study in the Behavioral Sciences and has given the Albert Shaw Lectures in Diplomatic History at Johns Hopkins University.

T. H. BREEN

T. H. Breen, William Smith Mason Professor of American History at Northwestern University, received his Ph.D. from Yale University in 1968. He has taught at Northwestern since 1970. Breen's major books include *The Character of the Good Ruler: A Study of Puritan Political Ideas in New England* (1974); *Puritans and Adventurers: Change and Persistence in Early America* (1980); *Tobacco Culture: The Mentality of the Great Tidewater Planters on the Eve of Revolution* (1985); and, with Stephen Innes of the University of Virginia, *"Myne Owne Ground": Race and Freedom on Virginia's Eastern Shore* (1980). His *Imagining the Past* (1989) won the 1990 Historic Preservation Book Award. His most recent book is *Common Goods: Revolutionary Markets on the Eve of American Independence* (2003). In addition to receiving several awards for outstanding teaching at Northwestern, Breen has been the recipient of research grants from the American Council of Learned Societies, the Guggenheim Foundation, the Institute for Advanced Study (Princeton), the National Humanities Center, and the Huntington Library. For his article "Narrative of Commercial Life: Consumption, Ideology, and Community on the Eve of the American Revolution," which appeared in the July 1993 issue of *William and Mary Quarterly*, Breen received an award from the National Society, Daughters of Colonial Wars, for best article published in the quarterly in 1993 and the Douglass Adair Memorial Prize for best article published in the quarterly during the 1988–1993 period. He has served as the Fowler Hamilton Fellow at Christ Church, Oxford University (1987–1988), the Pitt Professor of American History and Institutions, Cambridge University (1990–1991), and the Harmsworth Professor of American History at Oxford University (2000–2001). He is currently working on an opera based on an essay he wrote on the wrongful execution of an African American in 1768.

GEORGE M. FREDRICKSON

George M. Fredrickson is Edgar E. Robinson Professor Emeritus of United States History at Stanford University. He is the author or editor of several books, including *The Inner Civil War* (1965), *The Black Image in the White Mind* (1971), and *White Supremacy: A Comparative Study in American and South African History* (1981), which won both the Ralph Waldo Emerson Award from Phi Beta Kappa and the Merle Curti Award from the Organization of American Historians. His most recent books are *Black Liberation: A Comparative History of Black Ideologies in the United States and South Africa* (1995); *The Comparative Imagination: Racism, Nationalism, and Social Movements* (1997); and *Racism: A Short History* (2002). He received his A.B. and Ph.D. from Harvard and has been the recipient of a Guggenheim Fellowship, two National Endowment for the Humanities Senior Fellowships, and a fellowship from the Center for Advanced Studies in the Behavioral Sciences. Before coming to Stanford in 1984, he taught at Northwestern. He has also served as Fulbright lecturer in American History at Moscow University and as the Harmsworth Professor of American History at Oxford. He served as president of the Organization of American Historians in 1997–1998.

R. HAL WILLIAMS

R. Hal Williams is professor of history at Southern Methodist University. He received his A.B. from Princeton University in 1963 and his Ph.D. from Yale University in 1968. His books include *The Democratic Party and California Politics, 1880–1896* (1973); *Years of Decision: American Politics in the 1890s* (1978); and *The Manhattan Project: A Documentary Introduction to the Atomic Age* (1990). A specialist in American political history, he taught at Yale University from 1968 to 1975 and came to SMU in 1975 as chair of the Department of History. From 1980 to 1988, he served as dean of Dedman College, the school of humanities and sciences, at SMU. In 1980, he was a visiting professor at University College, Oxford University. Williams has received grants from the American Philosophical Society and the National Endowment for the Humanities, and he has served on the Texas Committee for the Humanities. He is currently working on a biography of James G. Blaine, the late-nineteenth-century speaker of the House, secretary of state, and Republican presidential candidate.

ARIELA J. GROSS

Ariela J. Gross is professor of law and history at the University of Southern California. She received her B.A. from Harvard University, her J.D. from Stanford Law School, and her Ph.D. from Stanford University. She is the author of *Double Character: Slavery and Mastery in the Antebellum Southern Courtroom* (2000) and numerous law review articles and book chapters. Her current work in progress, a history of racial identity on trial in the United States to be published by Farrar, Straus & Giroux, is supported by fellowships from the Guggenheim Foundation, the National Endowment for the Humanities, and the American Council for Learned Societies.

H. W. BRANDS

H. W. Brands is University Distinguished Professor and Melbern G. Glasscock Chair in American History at Texas A&M University, where he has taught since 1987. He is the author of numerous works of history and international affairs, including *The Devil We Knew: Americans and the Cold War* (1993), *What America Owes the World: The Struggle for the Soul of Foreign Policy* (1998), *Into the Labyrinth: The United States and the Middle East* (1994), *The Reckless Decade: America in the 1890s* (1995), *TR: The Last Romantic* (a biography of Theodore Roosevelt) (1997), *The First American: The Life and Times of Benjamin Franklin* (2000), *The Strange Death of American Liberalism* (2001), *The Age of Gold: The California Gold Rush and the New American Dream* (2002), and *Woodrow Wilson* (2003). His writing has received critical and popular acclaim; *The First American* was a finalist for the Pulitzer Prize and a national bestseller. He lectures frequently across North America and in Europe. His essays and reviews have appeared in the *New York Times*, the *Wall Street Journal*, the *Washington Post*, the *Los Angeles Times*, and *Atlantic Monthly*. He is a regular guest on radio and television, and has participated in several historical documentary films.

Chapter 1

Europeans imagined a New World that often bore little relation to reality. This early engraving depicts the coast of North America as a dangerous place where hostile Indians, navigational hazards, and sea monsters greeted English sailors. ❖

New World Encounters

Clash of Cultures: Interpreting Murder in Early Maryland

New World conquest sparked unexpected, often embarrassing contests over the alleged superiority of European culture. Not surprisingly, the colonizers insisted they brought the benefits of civilization to the primitive and savage peoples of North America. Native Americans never shared this perspective, voicing a strong preference for their own values and institutions. In early seventeenth-century Maryland the struggle over cultural superiority turned dramatically on how best to punish the crime of murder, an issue about which both Native Americans and Europeans had firm opinions.

The actual events that occurred at Captain William Claiborne's trading post in 1635 may never be known. Surviving records indicate that several young Native American males identified as Wicomesses apparently traveled to Claiborne's on business, but to their great annoyance, they found the proprietor entertaining Susquehannocks, their most hated enemies. The situation deteriorated rapidly after the Susquehannocks ridiculed the Wicomesses, "whereat some of Claiborne's people that saw it, did laugh." Unwilling to endure public humiliation, the Wicomesses later ambushed the Susquehannocks, killing five, and then returned to the trading post where they murdered three Englishmen.

Wicomess leaders realized immediately that something had to be done. They dispatched a trusted messenger to inform the governor of Maryland that they intended "to offer satisfaction for the harm . . . done to the English." The murder of the Susquehannocks was another matter, best addressed by the Native Americans themselves. The governor praised the Wicomesses for coming forward, announcing that "I expect that those men, who have done this outrage, should be delivered unto me, to do with them as I shall think fit."

The Wicomess spokesman was dumbfounded. The governor surely did not understand basic Native American legal procedure. "It is the manner amongst us Indians, that if any such like accident happens," he explained, "we do redeem the life of a man that is so slain with a 100 Arms length of *Roanoke* (which is a sort of Beads that they make, and use for money.)" The governor's demand for prisoners seemed doubly impertinent, "since you [English settlers] are here strangers, and coming into our Country, you should rather conform your selves to the Customs of our Country, than impose yours upon us." At this point the governor hastily ended the conversation, perhaps uncomfortably aware that if the legal tables had been turned and the murders committed in England, he would be the one loudly defending "the Customs of our Country."

EUROPEANS SAILING IN THE WAKE of Admiral Christopher Columbus constructed a narrative of superiority that survived long after the Wicomesses had been dispersed—a fate that befell them in the late seventeenth century. The story recounted first in Europe and then in the United States depicted heroic adventures, missionaries, and soldiers sharing Western civilization with the peoples of the New World and opening a vast virgin land to economic development. The familiar tale celebrated material progress, the inevitable spread of European values, and the taming of frontiers.

OUTLINE

FEATURE ESSAY

It was a history crafted by the victors—usually by white leaders such as Maryland's governor—and by the children of the victors to explain how they had come to inherit the land.

This narrative of events no longer provides an adequate explanation for European conquest and settlement. It is not so much wrong as partisan, incomplete, even offensive. History recounted from the perspective of the victors inevitably silences the voices of the victims, the peoples who, in the victors' view, foolishly resisted economic and technological progress. Heroic tales of the advance of Western values only serve to deflect modern attention away from the rich cultural and racial diversity that characterized North American societies for a very long time. More disturbing, traditional tales of European conquest also obscure the sufferings of the millions of Native Americans who perished, as well as the huge numbers of Africans sold in the New World as slaves.

By placing these complex, often unsettling, experiences within an interpretive framework of *creative adaptations*—rather than of *exploration* or *settlement*—we go a long way toward recapturing the full human dimensions of conquest and resistance. While the New World often witnessed tragic violence and systematic betrayal, it allowed ordinary people of three different races and many different ethnic identities opportunities to shape their own lives as best they could within diverse, often hostile environments.

It should be remembered that neither the Native Americans nor the Africans were passive victims of European exploitation. Within their own families and communities they made choices, sometimes rebelling, sometimes accommodating, but always trying to make sense in terms of their own cultures of what was happening to them. Of course, that was precisely what the Wicomess messenger tried to tell the governor of Maryland.

Native American Histories Before Conquest

As almost any Native American could have informed the first European adventurers, the peopling of America did not begin in 1492. In fact, although Spanish invaders such as Columbus proclaimed the discovery of a "New World," they really brought into contact three worlds—Europe, Africa, and America—that in the fifteenth century were already old. Indeed, the first migrants reached the North American continent some fifteen to twenty thousand years ago. The precise dating of this great human trek remains a hotly contested topic. Although some archaeologists maintain that settlement began as early as thirty thousand years ago, the scientific evidence in support of this thesis currently is not persuasive. However this debate eventually resolves itself, no one doubts that Native Americans have recorded a very long history in North America. Their social and cultural development over the period was as complex as any encountered in the so-called Old World.

Environmental conditions played a major part in the story. Twenty thousand years ago the earth's climate was considerably colder than it is today. Huge glaciers, often more than a mile thick, extended as far south as the present states of Illinois and Ohio and covered broad sections of western Canada. Much of the world's moisture was transformed into ice, and the oceans dropped hundreds of feet below their current levels. The receding waters created a land bridge connecting Asia and North America, a region now submerged beneath the Bering Sea that modern archaeologists named Beringia.

Even at the height of the last Ice Age, much of the far North remained free of glaciers. Small bands of spear-throwing Paleo-Indians pursued giant mammals (megafauna)—woolly mammoths and mastodons, for example—across the vast tundra of Beringia. These hunters were the first human beings to set foot on a vast, uninhabited continent. Because these migrations took place over a long period of time and involved small, independent bands of highly nomadic people, the Paleo-Indians never developed a sense of common identity. Each group focused on its own immediate survival, adjusting to the opportunities presented by various microenvironments.

The material culture of the Paleo-Indians differed little from that of other Stone Age peoples found in Asia, Africa, and Europe. In terms of human health, however, something occurred on the Beringian tundra that forever altered the history of Native Americans. For reasons that remain obscure, the members of these small migrating groups stopped hosting a number of communicative diseases—smallpox and measles being the deadliest—and although Native Americans experienced illnesses such as tuberculosis, they no longer suffered the major epidemics that under normal conditions would have killed a large percentage of their population every year. The physical isolation of the various bands may have protected them from the spread of contagious disease. Another theory notes that epidemics have frequently been associated with prolonged contact with domestic animals such as cattle and pigs. Since the Paleo-Indians did not domesticate animals, not even horses, they may have avoided the microbes that caused virulent European and African

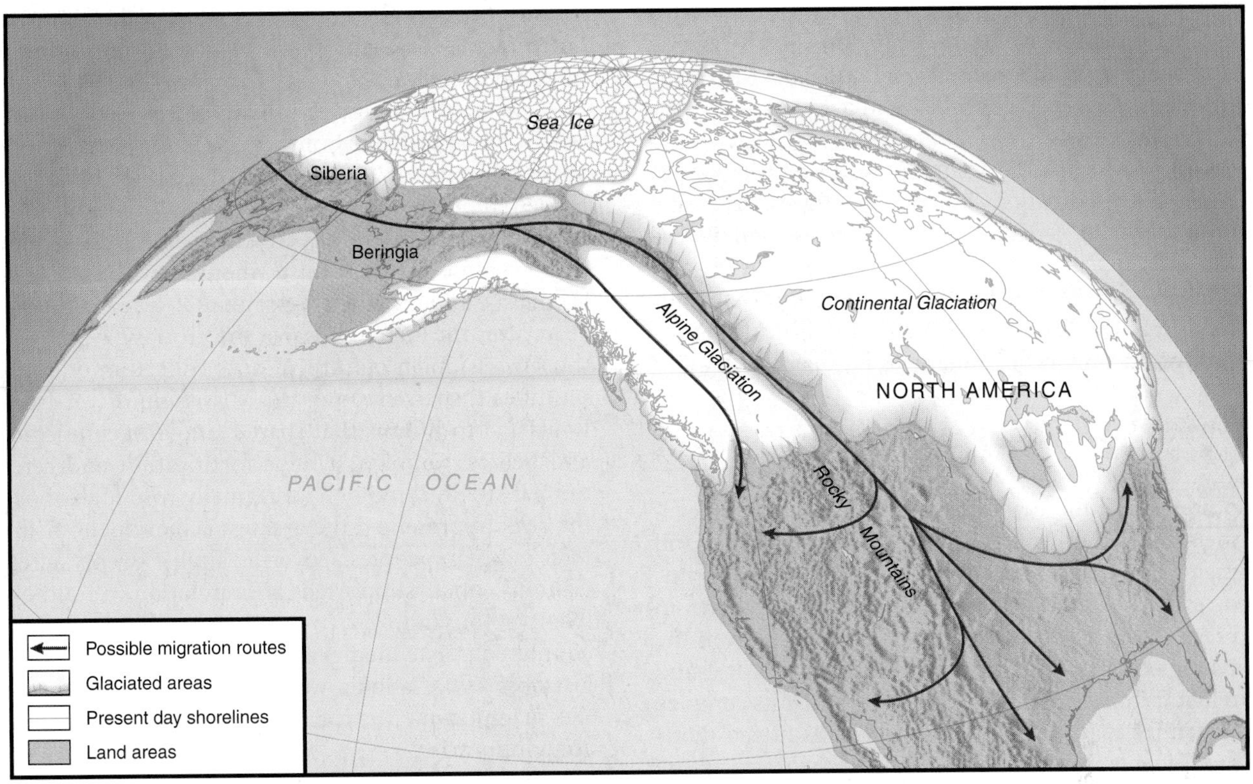

ROUTES OF THE FIRST AMERICANS *The peopling of North America began about 20,000 years ago, during an Ice Age, and continued for many millennia. Land bridges created by lower sea levels during glaciation formed a tundra coastal plain over what is now the Bering Strait, between Asia and North America.* ❖

diseases. Whatever the explanation for this curious epidemiological record, Native Americans lost inherited immunities that later might have protected them from many contagious germs. Thus, when they first came into contact with Europeans and Africans, Native Americans had no defense against the great killers of the Early Modern world.

The Environmental Challenge: Food, Climate, and Culture

Some twelve thousand years ago global warming substantially reduced the glaciers, allowing nomadic hunters to pour into the heart of the North American continent. Within just a few thousand years, Native Americans had journeyed from Colorado to the southern tip of South America. Blessed with a seemingly inexhaustible supply of meat, the early migrants experienced rapid population growth. As archaeologists have discovered, however, the sudden expansion of human population coincided with the loss of scores of large mammals, many of them the spear-throwers' favorite sources of food. The animals that died out during this period included mammoths and mastodons; camels and, amazingly, horses were eradicated from the land. The peoples of the Great Plains did not obtain horses until the Spanish reintroduced them in the New World in 1547. Some archaeologists have suggested that the early Paleo-Indian hunters bear responsibility for the mass extinction of so many animals. It is more probable that climatic warming, which transformed well-watered regions into arid territories, put the large mammals under severe stress, and the early humans simply contributed to an ecological process over which they ultimately had little control.

The Indian peoples adjusted to the changing environmental conditions. As they dispersed across the North American continent, they developed new food sources, at first smaller mammals and fish, nuts and berries, and then about five thousand years ago, they discovered how to cultivate certain plants. Knowledge of maize (corn), squash, and beans spread north from central Mexico. The peoples living in the Southwest acquired cultivation skills long before the bands living along the Atlantic Coast. The shift to basic crops—a transformation that is sometimes termed the **Agricultural Revolution**—profoundly altered Native American societies. The availability of a more reliable store of food helped liberate nomadic groups from the insecurities of hunting and gathering. It was during this period that Native Americans began to produce ceramics, a valuable technology for the storage of grain. The vegetable harvest made possible the establishment of permanent villages, that often were governed by clearly defined hierarchies of elders and kings, and as the food supply increased, the Native American population greatly expanded, especially around urban centers in the Southwest and in the Mississippi Valley. Although the evidence is patchy, scholars currently estimate that approximately four million Native Americans lived north of Mexico at the time of the initial encounter with Europeans.

Mysterious Disappearances

Several magnificent sites in North America provide powerful testimony to the cultural and social achievements of native peoples during the final two thousand years before European conquest. One of the more impressive is Chaco Canyon on the San Juan River in present-day New Mexico. The massive pueblo was the center of Anasazi culture, serving both political and religious functions, and it is estimated that its complex structures may have housed as many as fifteen thousand people. The Anasazis sustained their agriculture through a huge, technologically sophisticated network of irrigation canals that carried water long distances. They also constructed a transportation system connecting Chaco Canyon by road to more than seventy outlying villages. Some of the highways were almost a hundred miles long.

The center of the Anasazi culture was Chaco Canyon. Pueblo Bonita was the largest of Chaco's twelve towns. The pueblo rose five stories high on walls made of adobe and faced with sandstone slabs. More than 650 living quarters and storage rooms surrounded the central plaza. Roads extending some four hundred miles linked Pueblo Bonita to outlying pueblos. ❖

During this period equally impressive urban centers developed throughout the Ohio and Mississippi Valleys. In present-day southern Ohio, the Adena and Hopewell peoples—names assigned by archaeologists to distinguish differences in material culture—built large ceremonial mounds, where they buried the families of local elites. Approximately a thousand years after the birth of Christ, the groups gave way to the Mississippian culture, a loose collection of communities dispersed along the Mississippi River from Louisiana to Illinois that shared similar technologies and beliefs. Cahokia, a huge fortification and ceremonial site in Illinois that originally rose high above the river, represented the greatest achievement of the Mississippian peoples. Covering almost twenty acres, Cahokia once supported a population of almost twenty-thousand, a city rivaling in size many encountered in late medieval Europe. As one archaeologist observed, Cahokia was "as spectacular as any of the magnificent Mexican civilizations that were its contemporaries."

Recent research reveals that the various Native American peoples did not live in isolated communities. To be sure, over the millennia they developed many different cultural and social practices, reflecting the specific constraints of local ecologies. More than three hundred separate languages had evolved in North America before European conquest. But members of the groups traded goods over extremely long distances. Burial mounds found in the Ohio Valley, for example, have yielded obsidian from western Wyoming, shells from Florida, mica quarried in North Carolina and Tennessee, and copper found near Lake Superior.

Yet however advanced the Native American cultures of the southwest and Mississippi Valley may have been, both cultures disappeared mysteriously just before the arrival of the Europeans. No one knows what events brought down the great city of Cahokia or persuaded the Anasazis to abandon Chaco Canyon. Some scholars have suggested that climatic changes coupled with continuing population growth put too much pressure on food supplies; others insist that chronic warfare destabilized the social order. It has even been argued that diseases carried to the New World by the first European adventurers ravaged the cultures. About one point modern commentators are in full agreement: The breakdown of Mississippian culture caused smaller bands to disperse, construct new identities, and establish different political structures. They were the peoples who first encountered the Europeans along the Atlantic Coast and who seemed to the newcomers to have lived in the same places and followed the same patterns of behavior since the dawn of time.

Aztec Dominance

The stability resulting from the Agricultural Revolution allowed the Indians of Mexico and Central America to structure their societies in more complex ways. Like the Incas who lived in what is now known as Peru, the Mayan and Toltec peoples of Central Mexico built vast cities, formed government bureaucracies that dominated large tributary populations, and developed hieroglyphic writing as well as an accurate solar calendar. Their cities, which housed several hundred thousand people, greatly impressed the Spanish conquerors. Bernal Díaz del Castillo reported, "When we saw all those [Aztec] towns and villages built in the water, and other great towns on dry land, and that straight and level causeway leading to Mexico, we were astounded. . . . Indeed, some of our soldiers asked whether it was not all a dream."

Not long before Columbus began his first voyage across the Atlantic, the Aztecs, an aggressive, warlike people, swept through the Valley of Mexico, conquering the great cities that their enemies had constructed. Aztec warriors ruled by force, reducing defeated rivals to tributary status. In 1519, the Aztecs' main ceremonial center, Tenochtitlán, contained as many as 250,000 people as compared with only 50,000 in Seville, the port from which the early Spaniards had sailed. Elaborate human sacrifice associated with Huitzilopochtli, the Aztec sun god, horrified Europeans, who apparently did not find the savagery of their own civilization so objectionable. The Aztec ritual killings were connected to the agricultural cycle, and the Indians believed the blood of their victims possessed extraordinary fertility powers. A fragment of an Aztec song-poem captures the indomitable spirit that once pervaded this militant culture:

> Proud of itself
> is the city of Mexico-Tenochtitlán.
> Here no one fears to die in war.
> This is our glory. . . .
>
> Who could conquer Tenochtitlán?
> Who could shake the foundation of heaven?

Aztec human sacrifice depicted in the Codex Magliabechiano, *a sixteenth-century Spanish account of the lives of the native Mexicans. The ritual sacrifices performed by Aztec priests were associated with worship of the sun god—each offering was considered a sacred debt payment.* ❖

❖ A Look at the Past ❖

Effigy Jar

Clay effigy jars suggest the complexity of Mississippian society. Members of the culture built large earthen temple mounds, practiced elaborate burials, and made clay jars depicting the faces of respected dead members. What do these customs, particularly the effigy jars, reveal about the Mississippian attitude toward death?

Eastern Woodland Cultures

In the northeast region along the Atlantic coast, the Indians did not practice intensive agriculture. These peoples, numbering less than a million at the time of conquest, generally supplemented farming with seasonal hunting and gathering. Most belonged to what ethnographers term the Eastern Woodland Cultures. Small bands formed villages during the warm summer months. The women cultivated maize and other crops while the men hunted and fished. During the winter, difficulties associated with feeding so many people forced the communities to disperse. Each family lived off the land as best it could.

Seventeenth-century English settlers were most likely to have encountered the Algonquian-speaking peoples who occupied much of the territory along the Atlantic coast from North Carolina to Maine. Included in this large linguistic family were the Powhatans of Tidewater Virginia, the Narragansetts of Rhode Island, and the Abenakis of northern New England.

Despite common linguistic roots, however, the scattered Algonquian communities would have found communication extremely difficult. They had developed very different dialects. A sixteenth-century Narragansett, for example, would have found it hard to comprehend a Powhatan. The major groups of the Southeast, such as the Creeks, belonged to a separate language group (Muskogean); the Indians of the eastern Great Lakes region and upper St. Lawrence Valley generally spoke Iroquoian dialects.

Linguistic ties had little effect on Indian politics. Algonquian groups who lived in different regions, exploited different resources, and spoke different dialects did not develop strong ties of mutual identity, and when their own interests were involved, they were more than willing to ally themselves with Europeans or "foreign" Indians against other Algonquian speakers. Divisions among Indian groups would in time facilitate European conquest. Local Native American peoples greatly outnumbered the first settlers, and had the Europeans not forged alliances with the Indians, they could not so easily have gained a foothold on the continent.

However divided the Indians of eastern North America may have been, they shared many cultural values and assumptions. Most Native Americans, for example, defined their place in society through kinship. Such personal bonds determined the character of economic and political relations. The farming bands living in areas eventually claimed by England were often matrilineal, which meant in effect that the women owned the planting fields and houses, maintained tribal customs, and had a role in tribal government. Among the native communities of Canada and the northern Great Lakes, patrilineal forms were much more common. In these groups, the men owned the hunting grounds that the family needed to survive.

Eastern Woodland communities organized diplomacy, trade, and war around reciprocal relationships that impressed Europeans as being extraordinarily egalitarian, even democratic. Chains of native author-

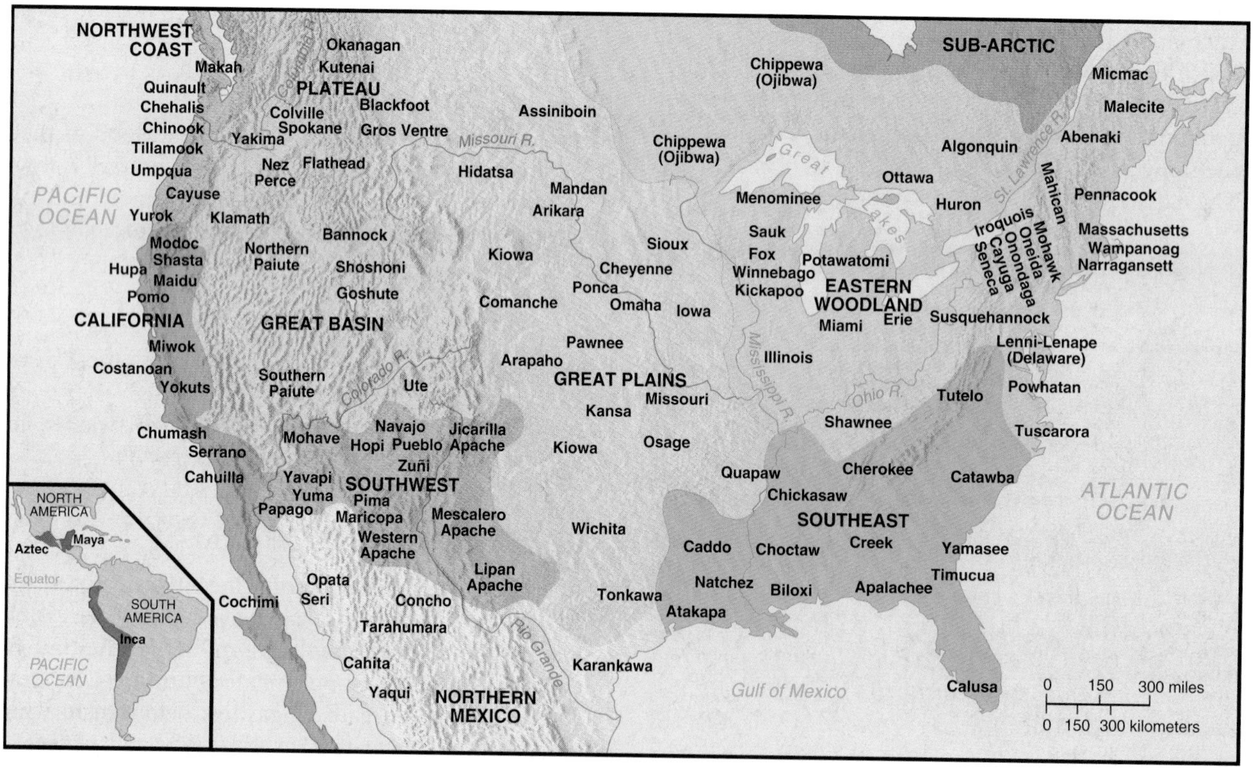

THE FIRST AMERICANS: LOCATION OF MAJOR INDIAN GROUPS AND CULTURE AREAS IN THE 1600s *Native Americans had complex social structures, religious systems, and a sophisticated agricultural technology when they came into initial contact with Europeans.* ❖

ity were loosely structured. Native leaders were such renowned public speakers because persuasive rhetoric was often their only effective source of power. It required considerable oratorical skills for an Indian leader to persuade independent-minded warriors to support a certain policy.

Before the arrival of the white settlers, Indian wars were seldom very lethal. Young warriors attacked neighboring bands largely to exact revenge for a previous insult or the death of a relative, or to secure captives. Fatalities, when they did occur, sparked cycles of revenge. Some captives were tortured to death; others were adopted into the community as replacements for fallen relatives.

A World Transformed

The arrival of large numbers of white men and women on the North American continent profoundly altered Native American cultures. Change did not occur at the same rates in all places. Indian villages located on the Atlantic coast came under severe pressure almost immediately; inland groups had more time to adjust. Wherever they lived, however, Indians discovered that conquest strained traditional ways of life, and as daily patterns of experience changed almost beyond recognition, native peoples had to devise new answers, new responses, and new ways to survive in physical and social environments that eroded tradition. Historian James Merrell reminded us the Indians found themselves living in a world that from their perspective was just as "new" as that which greeted the European invaders.

Cultural Negotiations

Native Americans were not passive victims of geopolitical forces beyond their control. So long as they remained healthy, they held their own in the early exchanges, and although they eagerly accepted certain trade goods, they generally resisted other aspects of European cultures. The earliest recorded contacts between Indians and explorers suggest curiosity and surprise rather than hostility. A Southeastern Indian who encountered Hernando de Soto in 1540 expressed awe (at least that is what a Spanish witness recorded): "The things that seldom happen bring astonishment. Think, then, what must be the effect on me and mine, the sight of you and your people, whom we have at no time seen . . . things so altogether new, as to strike awe and terror to our hearts."

What Indians desired most was peaceful trade. The earliest French explorers reported that natives waved from shore, urging the Europeans to exchange metal items for beaver skins. In fact, the Indians did not perceive themselves at a disadvantage in these dealings. They could readily see the technological advantage of guns over bows and arrows. Metal knives made daily tasks much easier. And to acquire such goods they gave up pelts, which to them seemed in abundant supply. "The English have no sense," one Indian informed a French priest. "They give us twenty knives like this for one Beaver skin." Another native announced that "the Beaver does everything perfectly well: it makes kettles, hatchets, swords, knives, bread . . . in short, it makes everything." The man who recorded these observations reminded French readers—in case they had missed the point—that the Indian was "making sport of us Europeans."

Trading sessions along the eastern frontier were really cultural seminars. The Europeans tried to make sense out of Indian customs, and although they may have called the natives "savages," they quickly discovered that the Indians drove hard bargains. They demanded gifts; they set the time and place of trade.

The Indians used the occasions to study the newcomers. They formed opinions about the Europeans, some flattering, some less so, but they never concluded from their observations that Indian culture was inferior to that of the colonizers. They regarded the beards worn by European men as particularly revolting. As an eighteenth-century Englishman said of the Iroquois, "They seem always to have Looked upon themselves as far Superior to the rest of Mankind and accordingly Call themselves *Ongwehoenwe,* i.e., Men Surpassing all other men."

For Europeans, communicating with the Indians was always an ordeal. The invaders reported having gained deep insight into Native American cultures through sign languages. How much accurate information explorers and traders took from these crude improvised exchanges is a matter of conjecture. In a letter written in 1493, Columbus expressed frustration: "I did not understand those people nor they me, except for what common sense dictated, although they were saddened and I much more so, because I wanted to have good information concerning everything."

In the absence of meaningful conversation, Europeans often concluded that the Indians held them in high regard, perhaps seeing the newcomers as gods. Such one-sided encounters involved a good deal of projection, a mental process of translating alien sounds and gestures into messages that Europeans wanted to hear. Sometimes the adventurers did not even try to communicate, assuming from superficial observation—as did the sixteenth-century explorer Giovanni da Verrazzano—"that they have no religion, and that they live in absolute freedom, and that everything they do proceeds from Ignorance."

Ethnocentric Europeans tried repeatedly to "civilize" the Indians. In practice that meant persuading natives to dress like the colonists, attend white schools, live in permanent structures, and, most important, accept Christianity. The Indians listened more or less patiently, but in the end, they usually rejected European values. One South Carolina trader explained that when Indians were asked to become more English, they said no, "for they thought it hard, that we should desire them to change their manners and customs, since they did not desire us to turn Indians."

To be sure, some Indians were strongly attracted to Christianity, but most paid it lip service or found it irrelevant to their needs. As one Huron told a French priest, "It would be useless for me to repent having sinned, seeing that I never have sinned." Another Huron announced that he did not fear punishment after death since "we cannot tell whether everything that appears faulty to Men, is so in the Eyes of God."

Among some Indian groups, gender figured significantly in a person's willingness to convert to Christianity. Native men who traded animal skins for European goods had more frequent contact with the whites, and they proved more receptive to the arguments of missionaries. But native women jealously guarded traditional culture, a system that often sanctioned polygamy—a husband having several wives—and gave women substantial authority over the distribution of food within the village. French Jesuits seemed especially eager to undermine the independence of Native American women. Among other demands, missionaries insisted on monogamous marriages, an institution based on Christian values but that made little sense in Indian societies where constant warfare killed off large numbers of young males and increasingly left native women without sufficient marriage partners.

The white settlers' educational system proved no more successful than their religion was in winning cultural converts. Young Indian scholars deserted stuffy classrooms at the first chance. In 1744, Virginia offered several Iroquois boys a free education at the College of William and Mary. The Iroquois leaders rejected the invitation because they found that boys who had gone to college "were absolutely good for nothing being neither acquainted with the true methods of killing deer, catching Beaver, or surprising an enemy."

Even matrimony seldom eroded the Indians' attachment to their own customs. When Native Americans and whites married—unions the English found less desirable than did the French or Spanish—the European partner usually elected to live among the Indians. Impatient settlers who regarded the Indians simply as an obstruction to progress sometimes developed more coercive methods, such as enslavement, to achieve cultural conversion. Again, from the white perspective, the results were disappointing. Indian slaves ran away or died. In either case, they did not become Europeans.

Threats to Survival: Trade and Disease

Over time, cooperative encounters between the Native Americans and Europeans became less frequent. The Europeans found it almost impossible to understand the Indians' relation to the land and other natural resources. English planters cleared the forests and fenced the fields and, in the process, radically altered the ecological systems on which the Indians depended. The European system of land use inevitably reduced the supply of deer and other animals essential to traditional native cultures.

Dependency also came in more subtle forms. The Indians welcomed European commerce, but like so many consumers throughout recorded history, they discovered that the objects they most coveted inevitably brought them into debt. To pay for the trade goods, the Indians hunted more aggressively and even further reduced the population of fur-bearing mammals.

Commerce eroded Indian independence in other ways. After several disastrous wars—the Yamasee War in South Carolina (1715), for example—the natives learned that demonstrations of force usually resulted in the suspension of normal trade, on which the Indians had grown quite dependent for guns and ammunition, among other things. A hardened English businessman made the point quite bluntly. When asked if the Catawbas would harm his traders, he responded that "the danger would be . . . little from them, because they are too fond of our trade to lose it for the pleasure of shedding a little English blood."

It was disease, however, that ultimately destroyed the cultural integrity of many North American tribes. European adventurers exposed the Indians to bacteria and viruses against which they possessed no natural immunity. Smallpox, measles, and influenza decimated the Native American population. Other diseases such as alcoholism took a terrible toll.

Within a generation of initial contact with Europeans, the Caribs, who gave the Caribbean its name, were virtually extinct. The decimation of Native American peoples was an aspect of ecological transformation known as the **Columbian Exchange.** European conquerors exposed the Indians to several new fatal diseases; the Indians introduced the invaders to marvelous plants such as corn and potatoes, which altered the course of European history. (See the Feature Essay, "The Columbian Exchange: Ecological Revolution," pp. 12–13.)

The Algonquian communities of New England experienced appalling rates of death. One Massachusetts colonist reported in 1630 that the Indian peoples of his region "above twelve years since were swept away by a great & grievous Plague . . . so that there are verie few left to inhabite the Country." Settlers possessed no knowledge of germ theory—it was not formulated until the mid-nineteenth century—and speculated that a Christian God had providentially cleared the wilderness of heathens.

Historical demographers now estimate that some tribes suffered a 90 to 95 percent population loss within the first century of European contact. The death of so many Indians decreased the supply of indigenous laborers, who were needed by the Europeans to work the mines and to grow staple crops such as sugar and tobacco. The decimation of native populations may have persuaded colonists throughout the New World to seek a substitute labor force in Africa. Indeed, the enslavement of blacks has been described as an effort by Europeans to "repopulate" the New World.

Indians who survived the epidemics often found that the fabric of traditional culture had come unraveled. The enormity of the death toll and the agony that accompanied it called traditional religious beliefs and practices into question. The survivors lost not only members of their families, but also elders who might have told them how properly to bury the dead and give spiritual comfort to the living.

Some native peoples, such as the Iroquois, who lived a long way from the coast and thus had more time to adjust to the challenge, withstood the crisis better than did those who immediately confronted the Europeans and Africans. Refugee Indians from the hardest hit eastern communities were absorbed into healthier western groups. However horrific the crisis may have been, it demonstrated powerfully just how much the environment—a source of opportunity as well as devastation—shaped human encounters throughout the New World.

West Africa: Ancient and Complex Societies

During the era of the European slave trade, roughly from the late fifteenth through the mid-nineteenth centuries, a number of enduring myths about sub-Saharan West Africa were propagated. Even today, commentators claim that the people who inhabited this region four hundred years ago were isolated from the rest of the world and had a simple, self-sufficient economy. Indeed, some scholars still depict the vast region stretching from the Senegal River south to modern Angola as a single cultural unit, as if at one time all the men and women living there must have shared a common set of African political, religious, and social values.

Sub-Saharan West Africa defies such easy generalizations. The first Portuguese who explored the African coast during the fifteenth century encountered a great variety of political and religious cultures. Many hundreds of years earlier, Africans living in this region had come into contact with Islam, the religion founded by the Prophet Muhammad during the seventh century. Islam spread slowly from Arabia into West Africa. Not until A.D. 1030 did a kingdom located in the Senegal Valley accept the Muslim religion. Many other West Africans, such as those in ancient Ghana, resisted Islam and continued to observe traditional religions.

As Muslim traders from North Africa and the Middle East brought a new religion to parts of West Africa, they expanded sophisticated trade networks that linked the villagers of Senegambia with urban centers in northwest Africa, Morocco, Tunisia, and Cyrenaica. Great camel caravans regularly crossed the Sahara carrying trade goods that were exchanged for gold and slaves. Sub-Saharan Africa's well-developed links with Islam surprised a French priest who in 1686 observed African pilgrims going "to visit Mecca to visit Mahomet's tomb, although they are eleven or twelve hundred leagues distance from it."

West Africans spoke many languages and organized themselves into diverse political systems. Several populous states, sometimes termed "empires," exercised loose control over large areas. Ancient African empires such as Ghana were vulnerable to external attack as well as internal rebellion, and the oral and written histories of this region record the rise and fall of several large kingdoms. When European traders first arrived, the list of major states would have included Mali, Benin, and Kongo. Many other Africans lived in what are known as stateless societies, really largely autonomous communities organized around lineage structures. In these respects, African and Native American cultures had much in common.

Whatever the form of government, men and women constructed their primary social identity within well-defined lineage groups, which consisted of persons claiming descent from a common ancestor. Disputes among members of lineage groups were generally settled by clan elders. The senior leaders allocated economic and human resources. They determined who received land and who might take a wife—critical decisions because within the villages of West Africa, women and children cultivated the fields. The communities were economically self-sufficient. Not only were they able to grow enough food to feed themselves, but they also produced trade goods, such as iron, kola, and gum.

The first Europeans to reach the West African coast by sail were the Portuguese. Strong winds and

Feature Essay

The Columbian Exchange

Ecological Revolution

Modern Americans often speak of the degradation of the global environment in apocalyptic terms, as if the current generation confronts a unique challenge in world history. No doubt, many chemical compounds produced during the twentieth century have proved far more toxic than their inventors ever imagined. But contemporary concerns about the future of the planet should not cause us to lose sight of the historical sweep of these problems. We are certainly not the first society to experience a massive ecological transformation caused by the inevitable intervention of human beings into the processes of nature. Recapturing an earlier moment of environmental history—known as the Columbian Exchange—reminds us that the moral dimensions of change are often a matter of perspective. What one group proclaims as providential progress may strike others as utter disaster.

The first major "ecological revolution" occurred as a direct result of New World exploration during the fifteenth and sixteenth centuries. The earliest explorers had expected America to be an extension of Europe, a place inhabited by familiar plants and animals. They were surprised. The exotic flora of the New World, sketched here from sixteenth-century drawings, included the food staple maize and the succulent pineapple. Equally strange to European eyes were buffalo, rattlesnakes, catfish, and the peculiar absence of horses and cattle. No domestic animal was common to both sides of the Atlantic except the dog. And perhaps the most striking difference was between the people themselves. Both Native Americans and Europeans found each other to be the most exotic people they had ever encountered.

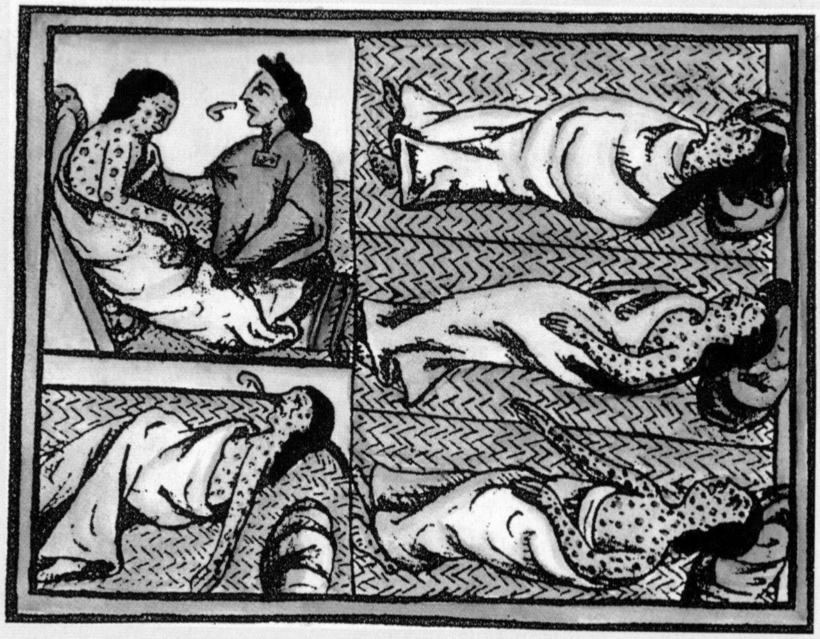

As Native Americans were exposed to common Old World diseases, particularly smallpox, they died by the millions. ❖

The most immediate biological consequence of contact between the people of Europe, Africa, and the New World was the transfer of disease. Within a year of Columbus's return from the Caribbean, syphilis appeared in Europe for the first time and became identified as the American disease, even though as we now know, it came originally from West Africa. By 1505, syphilis had spread all the way to China.

The effect of Old World diseases in the Americas was catastrophic. Native Americans had little natural immunity to common African and European diseases because America remained biologically isolated after the reimmersion of the Bering land bridge. When they were exposed to influenza, typhus, measles, and especially smallpox, they died by the millions. Indeed, European exploration of America set off the worst demographic disaster in world history. Within fifty years of the first contact, epidemics had virtually exterminated the native population of Hispaniola and devastated the densely populated Valley of Mexico.

Also unsettling but by no means as destructive was the transfer of plants and animals from the Old World to the New. Spanish colonizers carried sugar

Two examples of Old World–New World species exchange. Maize (corn) became a European dietary staple in the centuries after contact with America, while the Old World dandelion stepped off invaders' ships in the crusted mud of English or Spanish boots and spread far beyond the newcomers' initial cultural dominions, becoming today's most familiar "weed." ❖

and bananas across the Atlantic, and in time these crops transformed the economies of Latin America. Even more spectacular was the success of European animals in America. During the sixteenth century, pigs, sheep, and cattle arrived as passengers on European ships, and in the fertile New World environment, they multiplied more rapidly than they had in Europe. Some animals survived shipwrecks. On Sable Island, a small, desolate island off the coast of Nova Scotia, one can still see the small, longhaired cattle, the successors of the earliest cattle transported to America. Other animals escaped from the ranches of New Spain, generating new breeds such as the fabled Texas longhorn.

No European animal more profoundly affected Native American life than the horse. Once common in North America, the horse mysteriously disappeared from the continent sometime during the last Ice Age. The early Spanish explorers reintroduced the horse to North America, and the sight of this large, powerful animal at first terrified the Indians. Mounted conquistadores discovered that if they could not frighten Indian foes into submission, they could simply outmaneuver them on horseback. The Native Americans of the Southwest quickly adapted the horse to their own use. Sedentary farmers acquired new hunting skills, and soon the Indians were riding across the Great Plains in pursuit of buffalo. The Comanche, Apache, Sioux, and Blackfoot tribes—just to name a few—became dependent on the horse. Mounted Indian warriors galloped into battle, unaware that it was their white adversaries who had brought the horse to America.

Equally dramatic was the effect of American crops on European and African societies. From his first trip to the New World, Columbus brought back a plant that revolutionized the diets of both humans and animals—maize. During the next century, American beans, squash, and sweet potatoes appeared on European tables. The pepper and tomato, other New World discoveries, added a distinctive flavor to Mediterranean cooking. Despite strong prohibitions on the use of tobacco (in Russia, a user might have his nose amputated), European demand for tobacco grew astronomically during the seventeenth century. The potato caught on more slowly in Europe because of a widespread fear that root crops caused disease. The most rapid acceptance of the white potato came in Ireland, where it became a diet staple in the 1600s. Irish immigrants—unaware of the genealogy of this native American crop—reintroduced the potato into Massachusetts Bay in 1718. And in West Africa, corn gradually replaced traditional animal feeds of low yield.

These sweeping changes in agriculture and diet helped reshape the Old World economies. Partly because of the rich new sources of nutrition from America, the population of Europe, which had long been relatively stable, nearly doubled in the eighteenth century. Even as cities swelled and industries flourished, European farmers were able to feed the growing population. In many ways, the seeds and plants of the New World were far more valuable in Western economic development than all the silver of Mexico and Peru.

Europeans brought animals such as domestic cattle and horses to the New World. The reintroduction of the horse to North America, where it had once thrived and then disappeared, had a profound impact on Native Americans. ❖

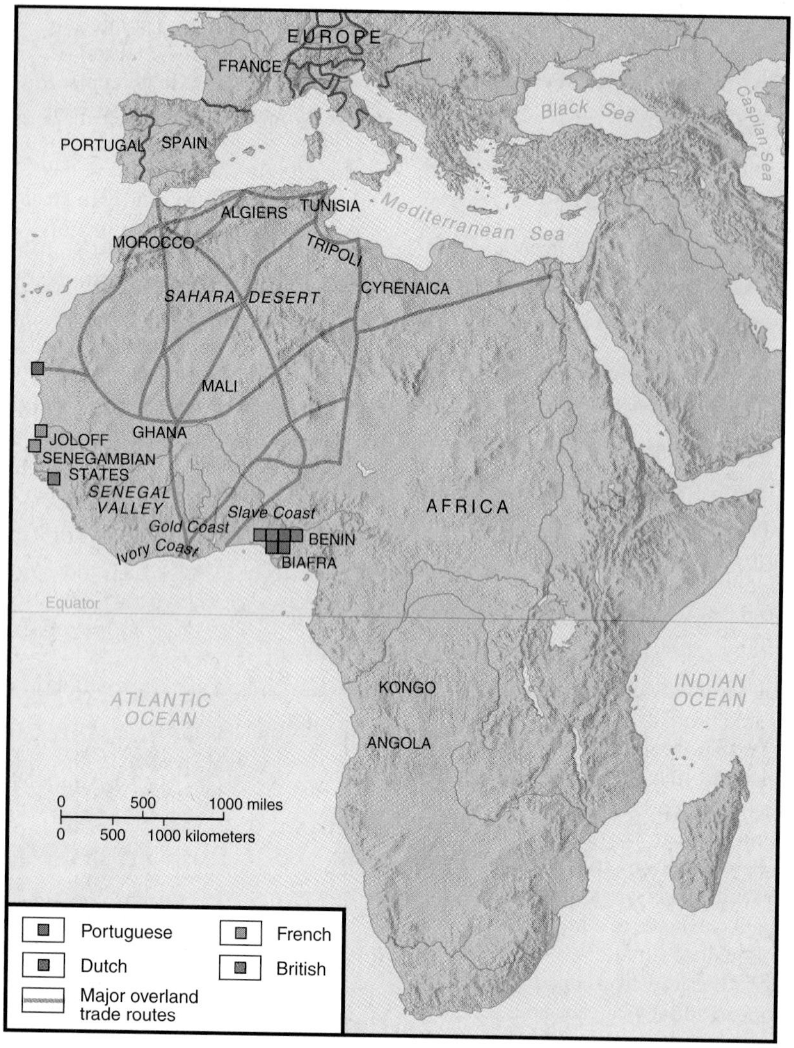

TRADE ROUTES IN AFRICA *African trade routes were well established by the late 1600s. Trade restrictions—and a deadly disease environment—confined European settlements primarily to coastal regions.*

currents along the Atlantic coast moved southward, which meant a ship could sail with the wind from Portugal to West Africa without difficulty. The problem was returning. Advances in maritime technology allowed the Portuguese to overcome these difficulties. By constructing a new type of ship, one uniting European hull design with lateen (triangular) sails from the Middle East, Portuguese caravels were able to navigate successfully against African winds and currents. During the fifteenth century, Portuguese sailors discovered that by sailing far to the west, often as far as the Azores, they could, on their return trips to Europe, catch a reliable westerly wind. Columbus was evidently familiar with the technique. Before attempting to cross the Atlantic Ocean, he sailed to the Gold Coast, and on the way, he undoubtedly studied the wind patterns that would carry his famed caravels to the New World and back again.

The Portuguese journeyed to Africa in search of gold and slaves. Mali and Joloff officials were willing partners in this commerce but insisted that Europeans respect trade regulations established by Africans. They required the Europeans to pay tolls and other fees and restricted the foreign traders to conducting their business in small forts or castles located at the mouths of the major rivers. Local merchants acquired some slaves and gold in the interior and transported them to the coast, where they were exchanged for European manufactures. Transactions were calculated in terms of local African currencies: A slave would be offered to a European trader for so many bars of iron or ounces of gold.

European slave traders accepted these terms largely because they had no other choice. The African states fielded formidable armies, and outsiders soon discovered they could not impose their will on the region simply by demonstrations of force. Moreover, local diseases proved so lethal for Europeans—six out of ten of whom would die within a single year's stay in Africa—that they were happy to avoid dangerous trips to the interior. The slaves were usually men and women taken captive during wars; others were victims of judicial practices designed specifically to supply the growing American

Local African rulers allowed European traders to build compounds along the West African coast. Constructed to expedite the slave trade, each of these so-called "slave factories" served a different European interest. Cape Coast Castle, which changed hands several times as rival nations fought for its control, became one of the largest slave trading posts in the world after the British captured and reinforced it in 1665. ❖

market. By 1650, most West African slaves were destined for the New World rather than the Middle East.

Even before Europeans colonized the New World, the Portuguese were purchasing almost a thousand slaves a year on the West African coast. The slaves were frequently forced to work on the sugar plantations of Madeira (Portuguese) and the Canaries (Spanish), Atlantic islands on which Europeans experimented with forms of unfree labor that would later be more fully and more ruthlessly established in the American colonies. It is currently estimated that approximately 10.7 million Africans were taken to the New World as slaves. The figure for the eighteenth century alone is about 5.5 million, of which more than one-third came from West Central Africa. The Bight of Benin, the Bight of Biafra, and the Gold Coast supplied most of the others.

The peopling of the New World is usually seen as a story of European migrations. But in fact, during every year between 1650 and 1831, more Africans than Europeans came to the Americas. As historian Davis Eltis wrote, "In terms of immigration alone . . . America was an extension of Africa rather than Europe until late in the nineteenth century."

Europe on the Eve of Conquest

In ancient times, the West possessed a mythical appeal to people living along the shores of the Mediterranean Sea. Classical writers speculated about the fate of Atlantis, a fabled Western civilization that was said to have sunk beneath the ocean. Fallen Greek heroes allegedly spent eternity in an uncharted western paradise. But because the ships of Greece and Rome were ill designed to sail the open ocean, the lands to the west remained the stuff of legend and fantasy. In the fifth century, an intrepid Irish monk, St. Brendan, reported finding enchanted islands far out in the Atlantic. He even claimed to have met a talking whale named Jasconius, who allowed the famished voyager to cook a meal on his back.

In the tenth century, Scandinavian seafarers known as Norsemen or Vikings actually established settlements in the New World, but almost a thousand years passed before they received credit for their accomplishment. In the year 984, a band of Vikings led by Eric the Red sailed west from Iceland to a large island in the North Atlantic. Eric, who possessed a fine sense of public relations, named the island Greenland, reasoning that others would more willingly colonize the icebound region "if the country had a good name." A few years later, Eric's son Leif founded a small settlement he named Vinland at a location in northern Newfoundland now called L'Anse aux Meadows. At the time, the Norse voyages went unnoticed by other Europeans. The hostility of Native Americans, poor lines of communication, climatic cooling, and political upheavals in Scandinavia made maintenance of these distant outposts impossible. At the time of his first voyage in 1492, Columbus seemed to have been unaware of these earlier exploits.

Building New Nation-States

At the time of the Viking settlement, other Europeans were unprepared to sponsor transatlantic exploration. Nor would they be in a position to do so for several more centuries. Medieval kingdoms were loosely organized, and until the early fifteenth century, fierce provincial loyalties, widespread ignorance of classical learning, and dreadful plagues such as the Black Death discouraged people from thinking expansively about the world beyond their own immediate communities.

In the fifteenth century, however, these conditions began to change. Europe became more prosperous, political authority was more centralized, and the **Renaissance** fostered a more expansive outlook

Materials excavated at L'Anse aux Meadows, on the northernmost tip of Newfoundland, provide evidence of a Viking settlement in North America. Using the materials excavated at the site, archaeologists have reconstructed the typically Norse dwellings, which had turf walls and roofs, wooden doors and doorframes. ❖

among literate people in the arts and sciences, the Renaissance encouraged—first in Italy and later throughout Europe—bold new creative thinking which challenged the orthodoxies of the Middle Ages. A major element in the shift was the slow but steady growth of population after 1450. Historians are uncertain about the cause of the increase—after all, neither the quality of medicine nor sanitation improved much—but the result was a substantial rise in the price of land, since there were more mouths to feed. Landlords profited from these trends, and as their income expanded, they demanded more of the luxury items, such as spices, silks, and jewels, that came from distant Asian ports. Economic prosperity created powerful new incentives for exploration and trade.

This period also witnessed the centralization of political authority under a group of rulers whom historians refer to collectively as the New Monarchs. Before the mid-fifteenth century, feudal nobles dominated small districts throughout Europe. Conceding only nominal allegiance to larger territorial leaders, the local barons taxed the peasants and waged war pretty much as they pleased. They also dispensed what passed for justice. The New Monarchs challenged the nobles' autonomy. The changes that accompanied the challenges came slowly, and in many areas violently, but the results altered traditional political relationships between the nobility and the crown, and between the citizen and the state. The New Monarchs of Europe recruited armies and supported these expensive organizations with revenues from national taxes. They created effective national courts. While these monarchs were often despotic, they personified the emergent nation-states of Europe and brought a measure of peace to local communities weary of chronic feudal war.

The story was the same throughout most of western Europe. The Tudors of England, represented by Henry VII (r. 1485–1509), ended a long civil war known as the War of the Roses. Louis XI, the French monarch (r. 1461–1483), strengthened royal authority by reorganizing state finances. The political unification of Spain began in 1469 with the marriage of Ferdinand of Aragon and Isabella of Castile, setting off a nation-building process that involved driving both the Jews and Muslims out of Spain. These strong-willed monarchs forged nations out of groups of independent kingdoms. If political centralization had not occurred, the major European countries could not possibly have generated the financial and military resources necessary for worldwide exploration.

A final prerequisite to exploration was reliable technical knowledge. Ptolemy (second century A.D.) and other ancient geographers had mapped the known world and had even demonstrated that the world was round. During the Middle Ages, however, Europeans lost effective contact with classical tradition. Within Arab societies, the old learning had survived, indeed flourished, and when Europeans eventually rediscovered the classical texts during the Renaissance, they drew heavily on the work of Arab scholars. This "new" learning generated great intellectual curiosity about the globe and about the world that existed beyond the Mediterranean.

The invention of printing from movable type by Johann Gutenberg in the 1440s greatly facilitated the spread of technical knowledge. Indeed, printing sparked a communications revolution whose impact on the lives of ordinary people was as far-reaching as that caused by telephones, television, and computers in modern times. Sea captains published their findings as quickly as they could engage a printer, and by the beginning of the sixteenth century, a small, though growing, number of educated readers throughout Europe were well informed about the exploration of the New World. The printing press invited Europeans to imagine exciting opportunities that they had hardly perceived when the Vikings sailed the North Atlantic.

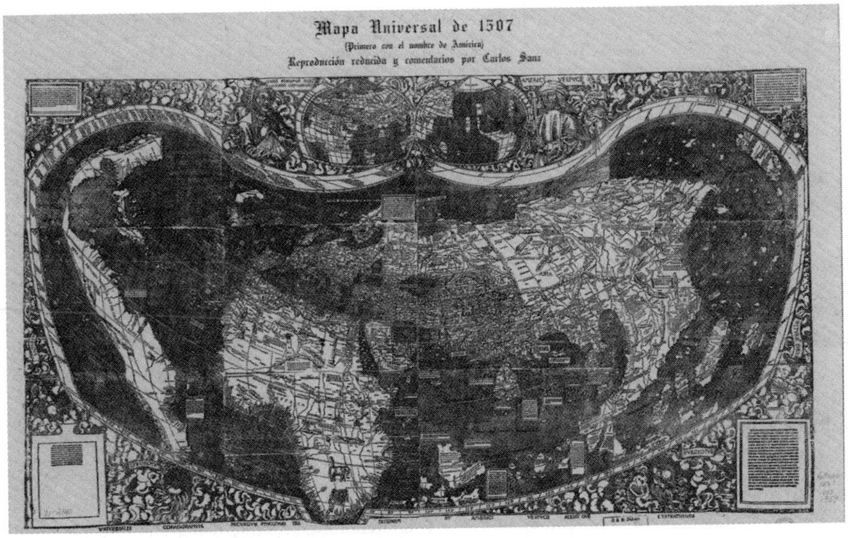

This 1507 map of the world drawn by Martin Waldseemüller incorporated data from the voyages of Italian adventurer Amerigo Vespucci, who asserted that the New World was a separate continent. Waldseemüller gave Vespucci more credit than he deserved and named the continent "America," rather than Columbia in honor of Christopher Columbus ❖

Imagining a New World

By 1500, centralization of political authority and advances in geographic knowledge brought Spain to the first rank as a world power. In the early fifteenth century, though, Spain consisted of several autonomous kingdoms. It lacked rich natural resources and possessed few good seaports. In fact, there was little about this land to suggest its people would take the lead in conquering and colonizing the New World.

By the end of the century, however, Spain suddenly came alive with creative energy. The union of Ferdinand and Isabella sparked a drive for political consolidation that, because of the monarchs' fervid Catholicism, took on the characteristics of a religious crusade. Spurred by the militant faith of their monarchs, the armies of Castile and Aragon waged holy war—known as the *Reconquista*—against the independent states in southern Spain that earlier had been captured by Muslims. In 1492, the Moorish (Islamic) kingdom of Granada fell, and, for the first time in centuries, the entire Iberian peninsula was united under Christian rulers. Spanish authorities showed no tolerance for people who rejected the Catholic faith.

During the Reconquista, thousands of Jews and Moors were driven from the country. Indeed, Columbus undoubtedly encountered such refugees as he was preparing for his famous voyage. From this volatile social and political environment came the **conquistadores,** men eager for personal glory and material gain, uncompromising in matters of religion, and unswerving in their loyalty to the crown. They were prepared to employ fire and sword in any cause sanctioned by God and king, and these adventurers carried European culture to the most populous regions of the New World.

Long before Spaniards ever reached the West Indies, they conquered the indigenous peoples of the Canary Islands, a strategically located archipelago in the eastern Atlantic. The harsh labor systems the Spanish developed in the Canaries served as models of subjugation in America. Indeed, the Spanish experience paralleled that of the English in Ireland (see "English Conquest of Ireland," p. 25). An early-fifteenth-century Spanish chronicle described the Canary natives as "miscreants . . . [who] do not acknowledge their creator and live in part like beasts." Many islanders quickly died of disease; others were killed in battle or enslaved. The new Spanish landholders introduced sugar, a labor-intensive plantation crop. The landowners forced slaves captured in Africa to provide the labor. This oppressive process was driven by dreams of great wealth, and would be repeated many times by European colonists through the centuries.

Myths and Reality

If it had not been for Christopher Columbus (Cristoforo Colombo), of course, Spain might never have gained an American empire. Little is known about his early life. Born in Genoa in 1451 of humble parentage, Columbus soon devoured the classical learning that had so recently been rediscovered and made available in printed form. He mastered geography, and—perhaps while sailing the coast of West Africa—he became obsessed with the idea of voyaging west across the Atlantic Ocean to reach Cathay, as China was then known.

In 1484, Columbus presented his plan to the king of Portugal. However, while the Portuguese were just as interested as Columbus in reaching Cathay, they elected to voyage around the continent of Africa instead of following the route suggested by Columbus. They suspected that Columbus had substantially underestimated the circumference of the earth and that for all his enthusiasm, he would almost certainly starve before reaching Asia. The Portuguese decision eventually paid off quite handsomely. In 1498, one of their captains, Vasco da Gama, returned from the coast of India carrying a fortune in spices and other luxury goods.

Undaunted by rejection, Columbus petitioned Isabella and Ferdinand for financial backing. They were initially no more interested in his grand design than the Portuguese had been. But time was on Columbus's side. Spain's aggressive New Monarchs envied the success of their neighbor, Portugal. Columbus boldly played on the rivalry between the countries, talking of wealth and empire. Indeed, for a person with little success or apparent support, he was supremely confident. One contemporary reported that when Columbus "made up his mind, he was as sure he would discover what he did discover, and find what he did find, as if he held it in a chamber under lock and key."

Columbus's stubborn lobbying on behalf of the "Enterprise of the Indies" gradually wore down opposition in the Spanish court, and the two sovereigns provided him with a small fleet that contained two of the most famous caravels ever constructed, the *Niña* and the *Pinta,* as well as the square-rigged *nao Santa Maria.* The indomitable admiral set sail for Cathay in August 1492, the year of Spain's unification.

Educated Europeans of the fifteenth century knew the world was round. No one seriously believed that Columbus and his crew would tumble off the edge of the earth. The concern was with size, not shape. Columbus estimated the distance to the mainland of Asia to be about 3,000 nautical miles, a voyage his small ships would have no difficulty completing. The actual distance is 10,600 nautical miles, however, and had the New World not been in his way, he and his crew would have run out of food and water long before they reached China, as the Portuguese had predicted.

After stopping in the Canary Islands to refit the ships, Columbus continued his westward voyage in early September. When the tiny Spanish fleet sighted an island in the Bahamas after only thirty-three days at sea, the admiral concluded he had reached Asia. Since his mathematical calculations had obviously been correct, he assumed he would soon encounter the Chinese. It never occurred to Columbus that he had stumbled upon a new world. He assured his men, his patrons, and perhaps himself that the islands were indeed part of the fabled "Indies." Or if not the Indies themselves, then they were surely an extension of the great Asian landmass. He searched for the splendid cities Marco Polo had described, but instead of meeting wealthy Chinese, Columbus encountered Native Americans, whom he appropriately, if mistakenly, called "Indians."

After his first voyage of discovery, Columbus returned to the New World three more times. But despite his considerable courage and ingenuity, he could never find the treasure his financial supporters in Spain angrily demanded. Columbus died in 1506 a frustrated but wealthy entrepreneur, unaware that he had reached a previously unknown continent separating Asia from Europe. The final disgrace came in December 1500 when an ambitious falsifier, Amerigo Vespucci, published a sensational account of his travels across the Atlantic that convinced German mapmakers he had proved America was distinct from Asia. Before the misconception could be corrected, the name *America* gained general acceptance throughout Europe.

Only two years after Columbus's first voyage, Spain and Portugal almost went to war over the anticipated treasure of Asia. Pope Alexander VI negotiated a settlement that pleased both kingdoms. Portugal wanted to exclude the Spanish from the west coast of Africa and, what was more important, from Columbus's new route to "India." Spain insisted on maintaining complete control over lands discovered by Columbus, which then still were regarded as extensions of China. The **Treaty of Tordesillas** (1494) divided the entire world along a line located 270 leagues west of the Azores. Any new lands discovered west of the line belonged to Spain. At the time, no European had ever seen Brazil, which turned out to be on Portugal's side of the line. (To this day, Brazilians speak Portuguese.) The treaty failed to discourage future English, Dutch, and French adventurers from trying their luck in the New World.

The Conquistadores: Faith and Greed

Spain's new discoveries unleashed a horde of conquistadores on the Caribbean. These independent adventurers carved out small settlements on Cuba, Hispaniola, Jamaica, and Puerto Rico in the 1490s and early 1500s. They were not interested in creating a permanent society in the New World. Rather, they came for instant wealth, preferably in gold, and were not squeamish about the means they used to obtain it. Bernal Díaz, one of the first Spaniards to migrate to the region, explained he had traveled to America "to serve God and His Majesty, to give light to those who were in darkness, and to grow rich, as all men desire to do." In less than two decades, the Indians who had inhabited the Caribbean islands had been exterminated, victims of exploitation and disease.

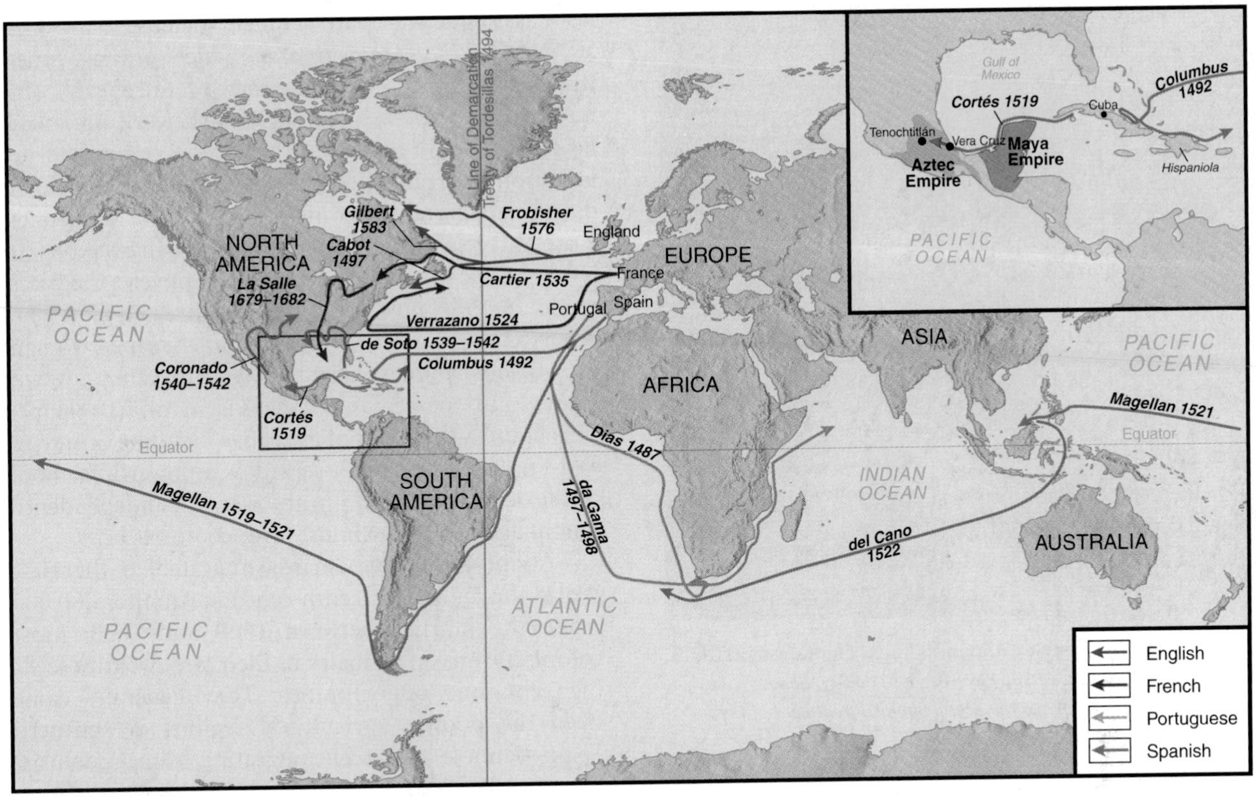

VOYAGES OF EUROPEAN EXPLORATION *The routes of the major voyagers to the New World and Asia. Early explorers established land claims for the competing European states.*

For a quarter century, the conquistadores concentrated their energies on the major islands that Columbus had discovered. Rumors of fabulous wealth in Mexico, however, aroused the interest of many Spaniards, including Hernán Cortés, a minor government functionary in Cuba. Like so many members of his class, he dreamed of glory, military adventure, and riches that would transform him from an ambitious court clerk into an honored *hidalgo.* On November 18, 1518, Cortés and a small army left Cuba to verify the stories of Mexico's treasure. Events soon demonstrated that Cortés was a leader of extraordinary ability.

His adversary was the legendary Aztec emperor, Montezuma. The confrontation between the two powerful personalities is one of the more dramatic of early American history. A fear of competition from rival conquistadores coupled with a burning desire to conquer a vast new empire drove Cortés forward. Determined to push his men through any obstacle, he scuttled the ships that had carried them to Mexico in order to prevent them from retreating. Cortés led his band of six hundred followers across rugged mountains and on the way gathered allies from among the Tlaxcalans, a tributary people eager to free themselves from Aztec domination.

In matters of war, Cortés possessed obvious technological superiority over the Aztecs. The sound of gunfire initially frightened the Indians. Moreover, Aztec troops had never seen horses, much less armored horses carrying sword-wielding Spaniards. But these elements would have counted for little had Cortés not also gained a psychological advantage over his opponents. At first, Montezuma thought that the Spaniards were gods, representatives of the fearful plumed serpent, Quetzalcoatl. Instead of resisting immediately, the emperor hesitated. When Montezuma's resolve hardened, it was too late. Cortés's victory in Mexico, coupled with other conquests in South America, transformed Spain, at least temporarily, into the wealthiest state in Europe.

From Plunder to Settlement

Following the conquest of Mexico, renamed New Spain, the Spanish crown confronted a difficult problem. Ambitious conquistadores, interested chiefly in their own wealth and glory, had to be brought under royal authority, a task easier imagined than accomplished. Adventurers like Cortés were stubbornly independent, quick to take offense, and thousands of miles away from the seat of imperial government.

The crown found a partial solution in the ***encomienda* system.** The monarch rewarded the leaders of the conquest with Indian villages. The people who

Indian Slaves Working at a Spanish Sugar Plantation on the Island of Hispaniola *(1595) by Theodore de Bry. Some contemporaries condemned the brutal Spanish treatment of the Native Americans.* ❖

lived in the settlements provided the *encomenderos* with labor tribute in exchange for legal protection and religious guidance. The system, of course, cruelly exploited Indian laborers. One historian concluded, "The first encomenderos, without known exception, understood Spanish authority as provision for unlimited personal opportunism." Cortés alone was granted the services of more than twenty-three thousand Indian workers. The encomienda system made the colonizers more dependent on the king, for it was he who legitimized their title. In the words of one scholar, the new economic structure helped to transform "a frontier of plunder into a frontier of settlement."

Spain's rulers attempted to maintain tight personal control over their American possessions. The volume of correspondence between the two continents, much of it concerning mundane matters, was staggering. All documents were duplicated several times by hand. Because the trip to Madrid took many months, a year often passed before receipt of an answer to a simple request. But somehow the cumbersome system worked. In Mexico, officials appointed in Spain established a rigid hierarchical order, directing the affairs of the countryside from urban centers.

The Spanish also brought Catholicism to the New World. The Dominicans and Franciscans, the two largest religious orders, established Indian missions throughout New Spain. Some friars tried to protect the Native Americans from the worst forms of exploitation. One courageous Dominican, Fra Bartolomé de las Casas, published an eloquent defense of Indian rights, *Historia de las Indias,* which among other things questioned the legitimacy of European conquest of the New World. Las Casas's work provoked heated debate in Spain, and while the crown had no intention of repudiating the vast American empire, it did initiate certain reforms designed to bring greater "love and moderation" to Spanish-Indian relations. It is impossible to ascertain how many converts the friars made. In 1531, however, a newly converted Christian reported a vision of the Virgin, a dark-skinned woman of obvious Indian ancestry, who became known throughout the region as the Virgin of Guadalupe. This figure—the result of a creative blending of Indian and European cultures—served as a powerful symbol of Mexican nationalism in the wars for independence fought against Spain almost three centuries later.

About 250,000 Spaniards migrated to the New World during the sixteenth century. Another 200,000 made the journey between 1600 and 1650. Most colonists were single males in their late twenties seeking economic opportunities. They generally came from the poorest agricultural regions of southern Spain—almost 40 percent migrating from Andalusia. Since so few Spanish women migrated, especially in the sixteenth century, the men often married Indians and blacks, unions which produced *mestizos* and *mulattos.* The frequency of interracial marriage indicated that, among other things, the people of New Spain were more tolerant of racial differences than were the English who settled in North America. For the people of New Spain, social standing was affected as much, or more, by economic worth as it was by color. Persons born in the New World, even those of Spanish parentage (*criollos*), were regarded as socially inferior to natives of the mother country (*peninsulares*).

Spain claimed far more of the New World than it could possibly manage. Spain's rulers regarded the American colonies primarily as a source of precious metal, and between 1500 and 1650, an estimated 200 tons of gold and 16,000 tons of silver were shipped back to the Spanish treasury in Madrid. This great wealth, however, proved a mixed blessing. The sudden acquisition of so much money stimulated a horrendous inflation that hurt ordinary Spaniards. They were hurt further by long, debilitating European wars funded by American gold and silver. Moreover, instead of developing its own industry, Spain became dependent on the annual shipment of bullion from America, and in 1603, one insightful Spaniard declared, "The New World conquered by you, has conquered you in its turn." This somewhat weakened, although still formidable, empire would eventually extend its territorial claims north to California and the Southwest (see Chapter 4).

The Virgin of Guadalupe is perhaps the best-known religious symbol of Mexico. The image reflects the sixteenth-century encounter between Europeans and Indians. The Virgin Mary was already an important religious figure among the Spanish when they arrived in America. Like the Indian Juan Diego to whom she is said to have appeared and offered hope, comfort, and protection, the Virgin is dark-skinned. This 1531 representation shows her clothed in a robe adorned with stars and surrounded by a crown of sunrays. Each year hundreds of thousands of people visit the shrine of the Virgin at Tepeyac, outside Mexico City. ❖

THE FRENCH CLAIM CANADA

French interest in the New World developed slowly. More than three decades after Columbus's discovery, King Francis I sponsored the unsuccessful efforts of Giovanni da Verrazzano to find a short water route to China, via a northwest passage around or through North America. In 1534, the king sent Jacques Cartier on a similar quest. The rocky, barren coast of Labrador depressed the explorer. He grumbled, "I am rather inclined to believe that this is the land God gave to Cain."

Discovery of a large, promising waterway the following year raised Cartier's spirits. He reconnoitered the Gulf of Saint Lawrence, traveling up the magnificent river as far as modern Montreal. Despite his high expectations, however, Cartier got no closer to China, and discouraged by the harsh winters, he headed home in 1542. Not until sixty-five years later did Samuel de Champlain resettle this region for France. He founded Quebec in 1608.

As was the case with other colonial powers, the French declared they had migrated to the New World in search of wealth as well as in hopes of converting the Indians to Christianity. As it turned out, these economic and spiritual goals required full cooperation between the French and the Native Americans. In contrast to the English settlers, who established independent farms and who regarded the Indians at best as obstacles in the path of civilization, the French viewed the natives as necessary economic partners. Furs were Canada's most valuable export, and to obtain the pelts of beaver and other animals, the French were absolutely dependent on Indian hunters and trappers. French traders lived among the Indians, often taking native wives and studying local cultures.

Frenchmen known as *coureurs de bois* (forest runners), following Canada's great river networks, paddled deep into the heart of the continent in search of fresh sources of furs. Some intrepid traders penetrated beyond the Great Lakes into the Mississippi Valley. In 1673, Père Jacques Marquette journeyed down the Mississippi River, and nine years later, Sieur de La Salle traveled all the way to the Gulf of Mexico. In the early eighteenth century, the French established small settlements in Louisiana, the most important being New Orleans. The spreading French influence worried English colonists living along the Atlantic coast, for it appeared the French were about to cut them off from the trans-Appalachian west.

Catholic missionaries also depended on Indian cooperation. Canadian priests were drawn from two orders, the Jesuits and the Recollects, and although measuring their success in the New World is difficult, it seems they converted more Indians to Christianity than did their English Protestant counterparts to the south. Like the fur traders, the missionaries lived among the Indians and learned to speak their languages.

The French dream of a vast American empire suffered from serious flaws. The crown remained largely indifferent to Canadian affairs. Royal officials stationed in New France received limited and sporadic support from Paris. An even greater problem was the decision to settle what seemed to many rural peasants and urban artisans a cold, inhospitable land. Throughout the colonial period, Canada's European population remained small. A census of 1663

A French coureur de bois, *or forest runner, is shown equipped with a rifle, a pipe, and snowshoes to track new sources of fur in the wilderness of New France.* ❖

recorded a mere 3035 French residents. By 1700, the figure had reached only 15,000. Moreover, because of the colony's geography, all exports and imports had to go through Quebec. It was relatively easy, therefore, for crown officials to control that traffic, usually by awarding fur-trading monopolies to court favorites. Such practices created political tensions and hindered economic growth.

The English Enter the Competition

The first English visit to North America remains shrouded in mystery. Fishermen working out of Bristol and other western English ports may have landed in Nova Scotia and Newfoundland as early as the 1480s. The codfish of the Grand Banks undoubtedly drew vessels of all nations, and during the summer months some sailors probably dried and salted their catches on Canada's convenient shores. John Cabot (Giovanni Caboto), a Venetian sea captain, completed the first recorded transatlantic voyage by an English vessel in 1497, while attempting to find a northwest passage to Asia.

Cabot died during a second attempt to find a direct route to Cathay in 1498. Although Sebastian Cabot continued his father's explorations in the Hudson Bay region in 1508–1509, England's interest in the New World waned. For the next three-quarters of a century, the English people were preoccupied with more pressing domestic and religious concerns. When curiosity about the New World revived, however, Cabot's voyages established England's belated claim to American territory.

Birth of English Protestantism

At the time of Cabot's death, England was not prepared to compete with Spain and Portugal for the riches of the Orient. Although Henry VII, the first Tudor monarch, brought peace to England after a bitter civil war, the country still contained too many "over-mighty subjects," powerful local magnates who maintained armed retainers and who often paid little attention to royal authority. Henry possessed no standing army; his small navy intimidated no one. To be sure, the Tudors gave nominal allegiance to the pope in Rome, but unlike the rulers of Spain, they were not crusaders for Catholicism.

A complex web of international diplomacy also worked against England's early entry into New World colonization. In 1509, to cement an alliance between Spain and England, the future Henry VIII married Catherine of Aragon. As a result of this marital arrangement, English merchants enjoyed limited rights to trade in Spain's American colonies, but any attempt by England at independent colonization would have threatened those rights and jeopardized the alliance.

By the end of the sixteenth century, however, conditions within England had changed dramatically, in part as a result of the **Protestant Reformation.** As they did, the English began to consider their former ally, Spain, to be the greatest threat to English aspirations. Tudor monarchs, especially Henry VIII (r. 1509–1547) and his daughter Elizabeth I (r. 1558–1603), developed a strong central administration, while England became more and more a Protestant society. The merger of English Protestantism and English nationalism affected all aspects of public life. It helped propel England into a central role in European affairs and was crucial in creating a powerful sense of an English identity among all classes of people.

Popular anticlericalism helped spark religious reformation in England. Although they observed traditional Catholic ritual, the English people had long resented paying monies to a pope who lived in far-off Rome. Early in the sixteenth century, criticism of the clergy grew increasingly vocal. Cardinal Thomas Wolsey, the most powerful prelate in England, flaunted his immense wealth and unwittingly became a symbol of spiritual corruption. Parish priests were objects of ridicule. Poorly educated men for the most part, they seemed theologically ignorant and perpetually grasping. Anticlericalism did not run as deep in England as it had in Martin Luther's Germany, but by the late 1520s, the Catholic Church could no longer take for granted the allegiance of the great mass of the population. The people's growing anger is central to an understanding of the English Reformation. Put simply, if ordinary men and women throughout the kingdom had not accepted separation from Rome, then Henry VIII could not have forced them to leave the church.

The catalyst for Protestant Reformation in England was the king's desire to rid himself of his wife, Catherine of Aragon, who happened to be the daughter of the former king of Spain. Their marriage had produced a daughter, Mary, but, as the years passed, no son. The need for a male heir obsessed Henry. He and his counselors assumed a female ruler could not maintain domestic peace and England would fall once again into civil war. The answer seemed to be remarriage. Henry petitioned Pope Clement VII for a divorce (technically, an annulment), but the Spanish had other ideas. Unwilling to tolerate the public humiliation of Catherine, they forced the pope to procrastinate. In 1527, time ran out. The passionate Henry fell in love with Anne Boleyn, who later bore him a daughter, Elizabeth. The king decided to divorce Catherine with or without papal consent.

The final break with Rome came swiftly. Between 1529 and 1536, the king, acting through Parliament, severed all ties with the pope, seized church lands, and dissolved many of the monasteries. In March 1534, the Act of Supremacy boldly announced, "The King's Majesty justly and rightfully is supreme head of the Church of England." The entire process, which one historian termed a "state reformation," was conducted with impressive efficiency. Land formerly owned by the Catholic Church passed quickly into private hands, and within a short period, property holders throughout England had acquired a vested interest in Protestantism. Beyond breaking with the papacy, Henry showed little enthusiasm for theological change. Many Catholic ceremonies survived.

The split with Rome, however, opened the door to increasingly radical religious ideas. The year 1539 saw the publication of the first Bible in English. Before then the Scripture had been available only in Latin, the language of an educated elite. For the first time in English history, ordinary people could read the word of God in the vernacular. It was a liberating experience that persuaded some men and women that Henry had not sufficiently reformed the English church.

With Henry's death in 1547, England entered a period of acute political and religious instability. Edward VI, Henry's young son by his third wife, Jane Seymour, came to the throne, but he was still a child and sickly besides. Militant Protestants took advantage of the political uncertainty, insisting the Church of England remove every trace of its Catholic origins. With the death of young Edward in 1553, these ambitious efforts came to a sudden halt. Henry's eldest daughter, Mary, next ascended the throne. Fiercely loyal to the Catholic faith of her mother, Catherine of Aragon, Mary I vowed to return England to the pope.

However misguided were the queen's plans, she possessed her father's iron will. Hundreds of Protestants were executed; others scurried off to the safety of Geneva and Frankfurt, where they absorbed the most radical Calvinist doctrines of the day. When Mary died in 1558 and was succeeded by Elizabeth, the "Marian exiles" flocked back to England, more eager than ever to rid the Tudor church of Catholicism. Mary had inadvertently advanced the cause of Calvinism by creating so many Protestant martyrs, reformers burned for their faith and now celebrated in the woodcuts of the most popular book of the period, John Foxe's *Acts and Monuments*, commonly known as the *Book of Martyrs* (1563). The Marian exiles served as the leaders of the Elizabethan church, an institution that remained fundamentally Calvinist until the end of the sixteenth century.

Militant Protestantism

By the time Mary Tudor came to the throne, the vast popular movement known as the Reformation had swept across northern and central Europe, and as much as any of the later great political revolutions, it had begun to transform the character of the modern world. The Reformation started in Germany when, in 1517, a relatively obscure German monk, Martin Luther, publicly challenged the central tenets of Roman Catholicism. Within a few years, the religious unity of Europe was permanently shattered. The Reformation divided kingdoms, sparked bloody wars, and unleashed an extraordinary flood of religious publication.

Luther's message was straightforward, one ordinary people could easily comprehend. God spoke through the Bible, Luther maintained, not through the pope or priests. Scripture taught that women and men were saved by faith alone. Pilgrimages, fasts, alms, indulgences—none of the traditional ritual

John Foxe's Book of Martyrs *(1563), depicting the sufferings of English dissenters executed under the Catholic queen Mary. It provided powerful propaganda for the advance of the Protestant faith.* ❖

observances could assure salvation. The institutional structure of Catholicism was challenged as Luther's radical ideas spread rapidly across northern Germany and Scandinavia.

After Luther, other Protestant theologians—religious thinkers who would determine the course of religious reform in England, Scotland, and the early American colonies—mounted an even more strident attack on Catholicism. The most influential of these was John Calvin, a lawyer turned theologian, who lived most of his adult life in the Swiss city of Geneva. Calvin stressed God's omnipotence over human affairs. The Lord, he maintained, chose some persons for "election," the gift of salvation, while condemning others to eternal damnation. A man or woman could do nothing to alter this decision.

Common sense suggests that such a bleak doctrine—known as predestination—might lead to fatalism or hedonism. After all, why not enjoy the world's pleasures to the fullest if such actions have no effect on God's judgment? But many sixteenth-century Europeans did not share modern notions of what constitutes common sense. Indeed, Calvinists were constantly "up and doing," searching for signs that they had received God's gift of grace. The uncertainty of their eternal state proved a powerful psychological spur, for as long as people did not know whether they were scheduled for heaven or hell, they worked diligently to demonstrate that they possessed at least the seeds of grace.

John Calvin's *Institutes of the Christian Religion* (1536) contained a powerful statement of the new faith, and his teachings spawned religious movements in most northern European countries. In France, the reformed Protestants were known as Huguenots. In Scotland, people of Calvinist persuasion founded the Presbyterian Church. And in seventeenth-century England and America, most of those who put Calvin's teachings into practice were called Puritans.

Woman in Power

Queen Elizabeth demonstrated that Henry and his advisers had been mistaken about the capabilities of female rulers. She was a woman of such talent that modern biographers find little to criticize in her decisions. She governed the English people from 1558 to 1603, an intellectually exciting period during which some of her subjects took the first halting steps toward colonizing the New World.

Elizabeth recognized her most urgent duty as queen was to end the religious turmoil that had divided the country for a generation. She had no desire to restore Catholicism. After all, the pope openly referred to her as a woman of illegitimate birth. Nor did she want to re-create the church exactly as it had been in the final years of her father's reign. Rather, Elizabeth established a unique institution, Catholic in much of its ceremony and government but clearly Protestant in doctrine. Under her so-called Elizabethan settlement, the queen assumed the title "Supreme Head of the Church." Some churchmen who had studied with Calvin in Geneva urged her to drop immediately all Catholic rituals, but she ignored these strident reformers. The young queen understood she could not rule effectively without the full support of her people, and as the examples of Edward and Mary before her demonstrated, neither radical change nor widespread persecution gained a monarch lasting popularity.

The state of England's religion was not simply a domestic concern. One scholar aptly termed this period of European history "the Age of Religious Wars." Catholicism and Protestantism influenced the way ordinary men and women across the continent interpreted the experiences of everyday life. Religion shaped political and economic activities. Protestant leaders, for example, purged the English calendar of the many saints' days that had punctuated the agricultural year in Catholic countries. The Reformation certainly had a profound impact on the economic development of Calvinist countries. Max Weber, a brilliant German sociologist of the early twentieth century, argued in his *Protestant Ethic and Spirit of Capitalism* that a gnawing sense of self-doubt created by the doctrine of "predestination" drove Calvinists to extraordinary diligence. They generated large profits not because they wanted to become rich, but because they wanted to be doing the Lord's work, to show they might be among God's "elect."

Indeed, it is helpful to view Protestantism and Catholicism as warring ideologies, bundles of deeply held beliefs that divided countries and families much as communism and capitalism did during the late twentieth century. The confrontations between the two faiths affected Elizabeth's entire reign. Soon after she became queen, Pope Pius V excommunicated her, and in his papal bull *Regnans in Exelsis* (1570), he stripped Elizabeth of her "pretended title to the kingdom." Spain, the most fervently Catholic state in Europe, vowed to restore England to the "true" faith, and Catholic militants constantly plotted to overthrow the Tudor monarchy.

Religion, War, and Nationalism

Slowly, but steadily, English Protestantism and English national identity merged. A loyal English subject in the late sixteenth century loved the queen, supported the Church of England, and hated Catholics, especially those who happened to live in Spain. Elizabeth herself came to symbolize this militant new chauvinism. Her subjects adored the Virgin Queen, and they applauded when her famed "Sea Dogs"—dashing figures such as Sir Francis Drake and Sir John Hawkins—seized Spanish treasure ships in American waters. The English sailors' raids were little more than piracy, but in this undeclared state of war, such instances of harassment passed for national victories. There seemed to be no reason patriotic Elizabethans should not share in the wealth of the New World. With each engagement, each threat, each plot, English nationalism took deeper root. By the 1570s, it had become obvious the English people were driven by powerful ideological forces similar to those that had moved the Spanish subjects of Isabella and Ferdinand almost a century earlier.

In the mid-1580s, Philip II, who had united the empires of Spain and Portugal in 1580, decided that England's arrogantly Protestant queen could be tolerated no longer. He ordered the construction of a mighty fleet, hundreds of transport vessels designed to carry Spain's finest infantry across the English channel. When one of Philip's lieutenants viewed the Armada at Lisbon in May 1588, he described it as *la felicissima armada,* the invincible fleet. The king believed that with the support of England's oppressed Catholics, Spanish troops would sweep Elizabeth from power.

It was a grand scheme; it was an even grander failure. In 1588, a smaller, more maneuverable English navy dispersed Philip's Armada, and severe storms finished it off. Spanish hopes for Catholic England lay wrecked along the rocky coasts of Scotland and Ireland. English Protestants interpreted victory in providential terms: "God breathed and they were scattered."

Irish Rehearsal for American Settlement

After the defeat of the Armada, it seemed as if England had fulfilled the prerequisites for American colonization. Before they crossed the Atlantic, however, English settlers moved to Ireland. Their experiences there powerfully shaped how later migrants would view the New World. It was on this island that enterprising Englishmen first learned to subdue a foreign population and to seize its lands. When Elizabeth assumed the throne, Ireland's one million inhabitants were scattered across the countryside. There were few villages, most of which were located along the coast. To the English eye, the Irish people seemed wild and barbaric. They were also fiercely independent and difficult to control. The English dominated a small region around Dublin by force of arms, but much of Ireland's territory remained in the hands of Gaelic-speaking Catholics who presumably lived beyond the reach of civilization.

English Conquest of Ireland

During the 1560s and 1570s, various enterprising English people decided that considerable fortunes could be made in Ireland. There were substantial risks, of course, not the least of which was the resistance of the Irish. Nevertheless, private "projectors" sponsored English settlements, and, in turn, these colonists forced the Irish either into tenancy or off the land altogether. It was during this period that semimilitary colonies were planted in Ulster and Munster.

As one might expect, colonization produced severe cultural strains. The English settlers, however humble their origins, felt superior to the Irish. After all, the English people had championed the Protestant religion. They had constructed a complex market economy and created a powerful nation-state. To the English settlers, the Irish appeared to be lazy, licentious, superstitious, even stupid. English settlers ridiculed unfamiliar local customs, and it is not surprising that even educated representatives of the two cultures found communication almost impossible. English colonists, for example, criticized the pastoral farming methods prevalent in sixteenth-century Ireland. It seemed perversely wasteful for the Irish to be forever moving about, since as any English person could see, such practices retarded the development of towns. Sir John Davies, a leading English colonizer, declared that if the Irish were left to themselves, they would "never (to the end of the world) build houses, make townships or villages or manure or improve the land *as it ought to be.*" Such stubborn inefficiency—surely (the English reasoned) the Irish must have known better—became the standard English justification for the seizure of large tracts of land.

English Brutality

English ethnocentrism was relatively benign so long as the Irish accepted the subservient roles the colonizers assigned them. But when they rebelled against the invaders, something they did with great frequency, English condescension turned to violence. Resistance smacked of disrespect and, moreover, to ensure the safety of the English, it had to be crushed. The brutality of Sir Humphrey Gilbert in Ireland would have made even the most insensitive Spanish conquistador uneasy. Gilbert was a talented man who wrote treatises on geography, explored the coast of North America, and entertained Queen Elizabeth with witty conversation. But as a colonizer in a strange land—in what some historians now call England's "permissive frontier"—he tolerated no opposition.

In 1569, he was appointed military governor of Munster, and when the Irish in his district rose up, he executed everyone he could catch, "mane, woman and childe." Gilbert's excesses would never have been permitted in England no matter how serious the rebellion. He cut off the heads of many enemy soldiers killed in battle, and in the words of one contemporary, Gilbert laid his macabre trophies "on the ground by each side of the way leading to his tent, so that none should come into his tent for any cause but commonly he must pass through a lane of heads." Such behavior was not only unprecedented, it was also calamitous. Instead of bringing peace and security, it helped generate a hatred so deep that Ireland remains divided to this day.

The Irish experiments served as models for later English colonies in the New World, just as the Canary Island plantations had done for Spain. Indeed, one modern Irish scholar argues that "English colonization in Virginia was a logical continuation of the Elizabethan conquest of Ireland." English adventurers in the New World commonly compared Native Americans with the "wild" Irish, a kind of ethnocentric shorthand that equated all alien races. This mental process was a central element in the transfer of English culture to America. The English, like the Spanish and the French, did not perceive America in objective terms. Instead, they saw an America they had already constructed in their imaginations, and the people and objects that greeted them on the other side of the Atlantic were forced into Old World categories, one of which was "Irish."

An Unpromising Beginning: Mystery at Roanoke

By the 1570s, English interest in the New World had revived. An increasing number of wealthy gentlemen were in an expansive mood, ready to challenge Spain and reap the profits of Asia and America. Yet the adventurers who directed Elizabethan expeditions were only dimly aware of Cabot's voyages, and their sole experience in settling distant outposts was in Ireland. Over the last three decades of the sixteenth century, English adventurers made almost every mistake one could possibly imagine. They did, however, acquire valuable information about winds and currents, supplies and finance.

Sir Walter Ralegh's experience provided all English colonizers with a sobering example of the difficulties that awaited them in America. In 1584, he dispatched two captains to the coast of present-day North Carolina to claim land granted to him by Elizabeth. The men returned with glowing reports, no doubt aimed in part at potential financial backers. "The soile," declared Captain Arthur Barlow, "is the most plentifull, sweete, fruitfull, and wholesome of all the world."

Ralegh diplomatically renamed this marvelous region Virginia, in honor of his patron, the Virgin Queen. Indeed, highly gendered vocabulary figured prominently in the European conquest of the New World. As historian Kathleen M. Brown explains,

John White depicted fishing techniques practiced by the Algonquian Indians of the present-day Carolinas. In the canoe, dip nets and multipronged spears are used. In the background, Indians stab at fish with long spears. At left, a weir traps fish by taking advantage of the river current's natural force. ❖

CHRONOLOGY

24,000–17,000 B.C.	Indians cross the Bering Strait into North America
2000–1500 B.C.	Agricultural Revolution transforms Native American life
A.D. 1001	Norsemen establish a small settlement in Vinland (Newfoundland)
1030	Death of War Jaabi (king of Takrur), first Muslim ruler in West Africa
1450	Gutenberg perfects movable type
1469	Marriage of Isabella and Ferdinand leads to the unification of Spain
1481	Portuguese build castle at Elmina on the Gold Coast of Africa
1492	Columbus lands at San Salvador
1497	Cabot leads first English exploration of North America
1498	Vasco da Gama of Portugal reaches India by sailing around Africa
1502	Montezuma becomes emperor of the Aztecs
1506	Columbus dies in Spain after four voyages to America
1517	Martin Luther's protest sparks Reformation in Germany
1521	Cortés defeats the Aztecs at Tenochtitlán
1529–1536	Henry VIII provokes English Reformation
1534	Cartier claims Canada for France
1536	Calvin's *Institutes* published
1540	Coronado explores the Southwest for Spain
1558	Elizabeth I becomes queen of England
1585	First Roanoke settlement established on coast of North Carolina
1588	Spanish Armada defeated by the English
1608	Champlain founds Quebec

"Associations of the land with virgin innocence reinforced the notion that Virginia had been saved from the Spaniard's lust to be conquered by the chaste English." Elizabeth encouraged Ralegh in private conversation but rejected his persistent requests for money. With rumors of war in the air, she did not want to alienate Philip II unnecessarily by sponsoring a colony on land long ago claimed by Spain.

Ralegh finally raised the funds for his adventure, but his enterprise seemed ill-fated from the start. Despite careful planning, everything went wrong. The settlement was poorly situated. Located inside the Outer Banks—perhaps to avoid detection by the Spanish—the Roanoke colony proved extremely difficult to reach. Even experienced navigators feared the treacherous currents and storms off Cape Hatteras. Sir Richard Grenville, the leader of the expedition, added to the colonists' troubles by destroying an entire Indian village in retaliation for the suspected theft of a silver cup.

Grenville hurried back to England in the autumn of 1585, leaving the colonists to fend for themselves. Although they coped quite well, a peculiar series of accidents transformed Ralegh's settlement into a ghost town. In the spring of 1586, Sir Francis Drake was returning from a Caribbean voyage and decided to visit Roanoke. Since an anticipated shipment of supplies was overdue, the colonists climbed aboard Drake's ships and went home.

In 1587, Ralegh launched a second colony. This time he placed in charge John White, a veteran administrator and talented artist, who a few years earlier had produced a magnificent sketchbook of the Algonquian Indians who lived near Roanoke. Once again, Ralegh's luck turned sour. The Spanish Armada severed communication between England and America. Every available English vessel was pressed into military service, and between 1587 and 1590, no ship visited the Roanoke colonists. When rescuers eventually reached the island, they found the village deserted. The fate of the "lost" colonists remains a mystery. The best guess is that they were absorbed by neighboring groups of natives, some from as far as the southern shore of the James River.

Conclusion: Campaign to Sell America

Had it not been for Richard Hakluyt, the Younger, who publicized explorers' accounts of the New World, the dream of American colonization might have died in England. Hakluyt, a supremely industrious man, never saw America. Nevertheless, his vision of the New World powerfully shaped English public opinion. He interviewed captains and sailors upon their return from distant voyages and carefully collected their stories in a massive book titled *The Principall Navigations, Voyages, and Discoveries of the English Nation* (1589).

The work appeared to be a straightforward description of what these sailors had seen across the sea. That was its strength. In reality, Hakluyt edited each piece so it would drive home the book's central point: England needed American colonies. Indeed, they were essential to the nation's prosperity and independence. In Hakluyt's America, there were no losers. "The earth bringeth fourth all things in aboundance, as in the first creations without toil or labour," he wrote of Virginia. His blend of piety, patriotism, and self-interest proved immensely popular, and his *Voyages* went through many editions.

As a salesperson for the New World, Hakluyt was as misleading as he was successful. He failed to appreciate, or purposely ignored, the rich cultural diversity of the Native Americans and the varied backgrounds of the Europeans. He said not a word about the sufferings of Africans in America. Instead, he and many other polemicists for colonization led the ordinary English men and women who traveled to America to expect nothing less than a paradise on earth. This European perspective on the resources of the New World invited continuous human suffering and ecological disaster.

Recommended Reading

The histories of three different peoples coming together for the first time in the New World has sparked innovative scholarship. Many interdisciplinary works explore diverse patterns of cultural adaptation. Some of the best titles bring fresh insights to the Native Americans' response to radical environmental and social change. Among these are Inga Clendinnen, *Aztecs: An Interpretation* (1991); James H. Merrell, *The Indians' New World: Catawbas and Their Neighbors From European Contact Through the Era of Removal* (1989); and James F. Brooks, *Captives and Cousins: Slavery, Kinship and Community in the Southwest Borderlands* (2002). Other broad-ranging volumes examine how early European invaders imagined the New World and how they translated what they thought they had seen into a familiar and unthreatening language: Stephen Greenblatt, *Marvelous Possessions: The Wonder of the New World* (1991), and Anthony Pagden, *European Encounters with the New World: From Renaissance to Romanticism* (1992). The impact of the environment—a major theme of this chapter—is the topic of three pioneering investigations: A. W. Crosby, *The Columbian Voyages, The Columbian Exchange, and Their Historians* (1987); William Cronon, *Changes in the Land: Indians, Colonists, and the Ecology of New England* (1983); and Shepard Krech III, *The Ecological Indian: Myth and History* (1999). The best overview of the European response to the Conquest is John H. Elliott, *The Old World and New, 1492–1650* (1970). For the Irish experience one should consult Nicholas Canny, *Making Ireland British 1580–1650* (2001). Two outstanding interpretations of the English Reformation are Ethan H. Shagan, *Popular Politics and the English Reformation* (2003) and Eamon Duffy, *The Stripping of the Altars: Traditional Religion in England 1400–1580* (1992). Books that offer boldly original interpretations of the Conquest are Kirkpatrick Sale, *The Conquest of Paradise: Christopher Columbus and the Columbian Legacy* (1990); and Kathleen M. Brown, *Good Wives, Nasty Wenches, and Anxious Patriarchs: Gender, Race, and Power in Colonial Virginia* (1996).

For a list of additional titles related to this chapter's topics, please see http://www.ablongman.com/divine.

Suggested Web Sites

Vikings in the New World

http://emuseum.mnsu.edu/prehistory/vikings/vikhome.html
This site explores the history of some of the earliest European visitors to America.

Sir Francis Drake

http://www.mcn.org/2/oseeler/drake.htm
This comprehensive site covers much of Drake's life and voyages.

Ancient Mesoamerican Civilizations

http://www.angelfire.com/ca/humanorigins/index.html
Kevin L. Callahan of the University of Minnesota Department of Anthropology maintains this page that supplies information regarding Mesoamerican civilizations with well-organized essays and photos.

National Museum of the American Indian

http://www.si.edu/nmai
The Smithsonian Institution maintains the site, providing information about the museum. The museum is dedicated to everything about Native Americans.

1492: An Ongoing Voyage

http://www.loc.gov/exhibits/1492
An exhibit of the Library of Congress, Washington, D.C. With brief essays and images about early civilizations and contact in the Americas.

Cahokia Mounds

http://medicine.wustl.edu/~mckinney/cahokia/cahokia.html
The Cahokia Mounds State Historical Site gives information about a fascinating pre-Columbian culture in North America.

The Computerized Information Retrieval System on Columbus and the Age of Discovery

http://muweb.millersv.edu/~columbus/
The History Department and Academic Computing Services of Millersville University, Pennsylvania, provide this text retrieval system containing more than 1000 text articles from various magazines, journals, newspapers, speeches, official calendars, and other sources relating to various encounter themes.

Mexico Pre-Columbian History

http://www.mexonline.com/precolum.htm
This site "provides information on the Aztecs, Maya, Mexica, Olmecs, Toltec, Zapotecs and other pre-European cultures, as well as information on museums, archeology, language, and education."

White Oak Fur Post

http://www.whiteoak.org/
This site documents an eighteenth-century fur trading post among the Indians in what would become Minnesota.

La Salle Shipwreck Project

http://www.thc.state.tx.us/belle/lasbelle.html
Texas Historical Commission site about the archaeological dig to recover the ship of one of America's famous early explorers.

The Discoverers' Web

http://www.win.tue.nl/cs/fm/engels/discovery/
Andre Engels maintains this complete collection of information on the various efforts at exploration.

Chapter 2

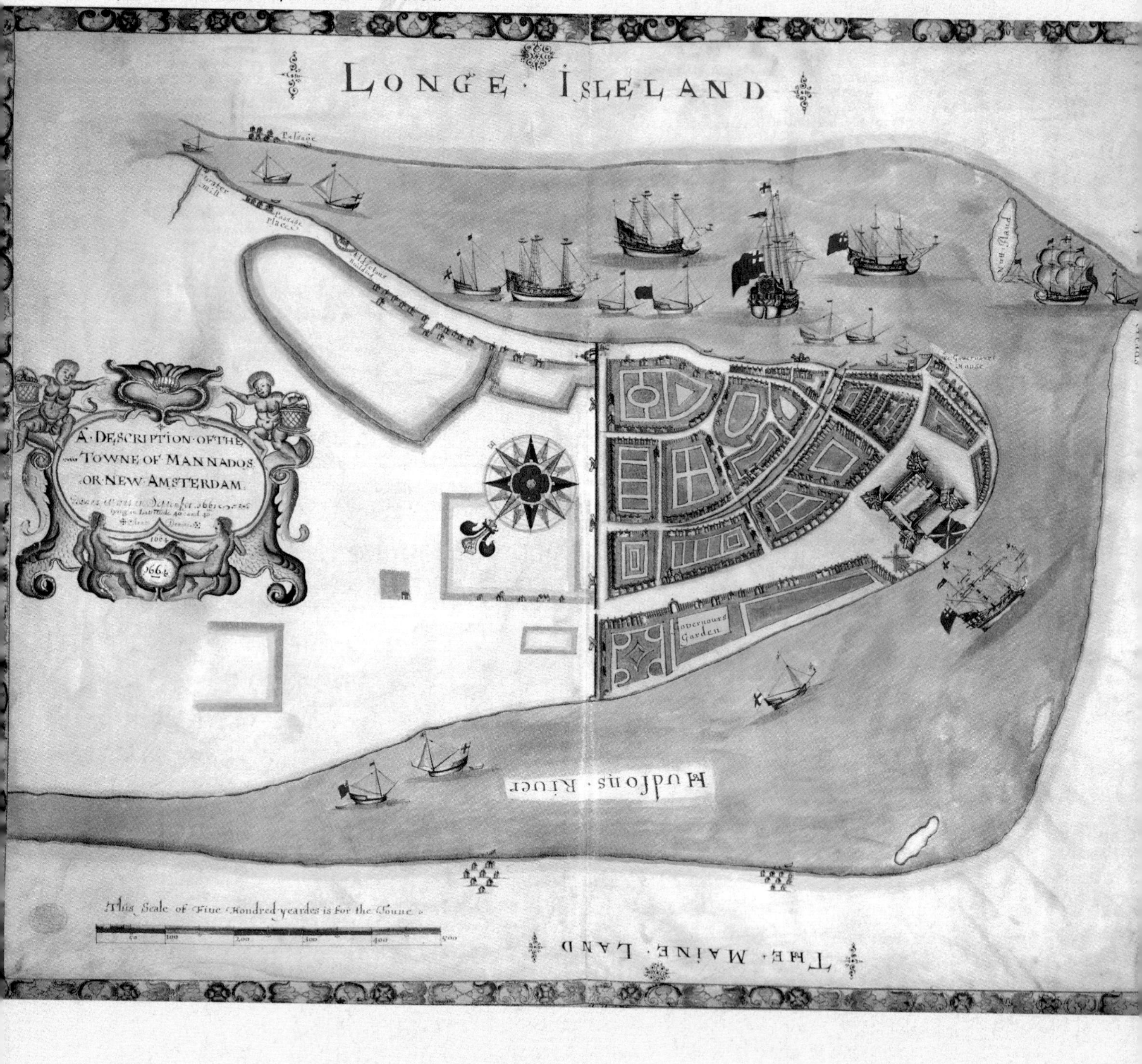

Map of New York City presented to James, Duke of York (the future James II), shortly after the English captured New Amsterdam from the Dutch in 1664. ❖

New World Experiments: England's Seventeenth-Century Colonies

Profit and Piety: Competing Visions for English Settlement

In the spring of 1644, John Winthrop, governor of Massachusetts Bay, learned that Native Americans had overrun the scattered tobacco plantations of Virginia, killing as many as five hundred colonists. Winthrop never thought much of the Chesapeake settlements. He regarded the people who had migrated to that part of America as grossly materialistic, and because Virginia had recently expelled several Puritan ministers, Winthrop decided the hostilities were God's way of punishing the tobacco planters for their worldliness. "It was observable," he related, "that this massacre came upon them soon after they had driven out the godly ministers we had sent to them." When Virginians appealed to Massachusetts for military supplies, they received a cool reception. "We were weakly provided ourselves," Winthrop explained, "and so could not afford them any help of that kind."

In 1675, the tables turned. Native Americans declared all-out war against the New Englanders, and soon reports of the destruction of Puritan communities were circulating in Virginia. "The Indians in New England have burned Considerable Villages," wrote one leading tobacco planter, "and have made them [the New Englanders] desert more than one hundred and fifty miles of those places they had formerly seated."

Sir William Berkeley, Virginia's royal governor, was not displeased by news of New England's adversity. He and his friends held the Puritans in contempt. Indeed, the New Englanders reminded them of the religious fanatics who had provoked civil war in England and who in 1649 had executed Charles I. During this particular crisis, Berkeley noted that he might have shown more pity for the beleaguered New Englanders "had they deserved it of the King." The governor, sounding like a Puritan himself, described the warring Indians as the "Instruments" with which God intended "to destroy the King's Enemies." For good measure, Virginia outlawed the export of foodstuffs to their embattled northern neighbors.

SUCH EXTRAORDINARY DISUNITY in the colonies—not to mention lack of compassion—comes as a surprise to anyone searching for the roots of modern nationalism in this early period. English colonization in the seventeenth century did not spring from a desire to build a centralized empire in the New World similar to that of Spain or France. Instead, the English crown awarded colonial charters to a wide variety of entrepreneurs, religious idealists, and aristocratic adventurers who established separate and profoundly different colonies. Not only did New Englanders have little in common with the earliest Virginians and Carolinians, but they were often divided among themselves.

Migration itself helps to explain this striking competition and diversity. At different times, different colonies appealed to different sorts of people. Men and women moved to the New World for various reasons, and as economic, political, and religious conditions changed on both sides of the Atlantic during the course of the seventeenth century, so too did patterns of English migration.

Outline

Feature Essay

Breaking Away

English people in the early decades of the seventeenth century experienced what seemed to them an accelerating pace of social change. What was most evident was the rapid growth of population. Between 1580 and 1650, a period during which many men and women elected to journey to the New World, the population of England expanded from about 3.5 million to more than 5 million. Among other things, the expansion strained the nation's agrarian economy. Competition for food and land drove up prices, and people desperate for work took to the roads. Those migrants, many of them drawn into the orbit of London by tales of opportunity, frightened the traditional leaders of English society. To the propertied class, the wandering poor represented a threat to good order, and, particularly during the early decades of the seventeenth century, landholders urged local magistrates throughout the kingdom to enforce the laws against vagrancy.

Even by modern standards, the English population of this period was quite mobile. To be sure, most men and women lived out their days rooted in the tiny country villages of their birth. A growing number of English people, however, were migrant laborers who took seasonal work. Many others relocated from the countryside to London, already a city of several hundred thousand inhabitants by the early seventeenth century. Because health conditions in London were poor, a large number of the new arrivals quickly died, and had their places not been taken by other migrants from the rural villages, the population of London would almost certainly have decreased.

Other, more exotic destinations also beckoned. A large number of English settlers migrated to Ireland, while lucrative employment and religious freedom attracted people to Holland. The Pilgrims, people who separated themselves from the established Church of England, initially hoped to make a new life in Leyden. The migrations within Europe serve as reminders that ordinary people had choices. A person who was upset about the state of the Church of England or who had lost a livelihood did not have to move to America. That some men and women consciously selected this much more dangerous and expensive journey set them apart from their contemporaries.

English colonists crossed the Atlantic for many reasons. Some wanted to institute a purer form of worship, more closely based on their interpretation of Scripture. Others dreamed of owning land and improving their social position. A few came to the New World to escape bad marriages, jail terms, or the dreary prospect of lifelong poverty. Since most seventeenth-century migrants, especially those who transferred to the Chesapeake colonies, left almost no records of their previous lives in England, it is futile to try to isolate a single cause or explanation for their decision to leave home.

In the absence of detailed personal information, historians usually have assumed that poverty, or the fear of soon falling into poverty, drove people across the Atlantic. No doubt economic considerations figured heavily in the final decision. But so too did religion, and it was not uncommon for the poor of early modern England to be among those demanding the most radical ecclesiastical reform. As a recent historian of seventeenth-century migration concluded, "Individuals left for a variety of motives, some idealistic, others practical, some simple, others complex, many perhaps contradictory and imperfectly understood by the migrants themselves."

Whatever their reasons for crossing the ocean, English migrants to America in this period left a nation wracked by recurrent, often violent political and religious controversy. During the 1620s, autocratic Stuart monarchs—James I (r. 1603–1625) and his son Charles I (r. 1625–1649)—who succeeded Queen Elizabeth on the English throne fought constantly with the elected members of Parliament. At stake were rival notions of constitutional and representative government.

Many royal policies—the granting of lucrative commercial monopolies to court favorites, for example—fueled popular discontent, but the crown's hostility to far-reaching religious reform sparked the most vocal protest. Throughout the kingdom, Puritans became adamant in their demand for radical purification of ritual.

Tensions grew so severe that in 1629, Charles attempted to rule the country without Parliament's assistance. The autocratic strategy backfired. When Charles finally was forced to recall Parliament in 1640 because he was running out of money, Parliament demanded major constitutional reforms. Militant Puritans, supported by many members of Parliament, insisted on restructuring the church—abolishing the office of bishop was high on their list. In this angry political atmosphere, Charles took up arms against the supporters of Parliament. The confrontation between Royalists and Parliamentarians set off a long and bloody conflict, known as the English Civil War. In 1649, the victorious Parliamentarians beheaded Charles, and for almost a decade, Oliver Cromwell, a skilled general and committed Puritan, governed England as Lord Protector.

In 1660, following Cromwell's death from natural causes, the Stuarts returned to the English throne. During a period known as the Restoration, neither Charles II (r. 1660–1685) nor James II (r. 1685–1688)—both sons of Charles I—was able to establish genuine political stability. When the authoritarian James lifted some of the restrictions governing Catholics, a Protestant nation rose up in what the

THE STUART MONARCHS

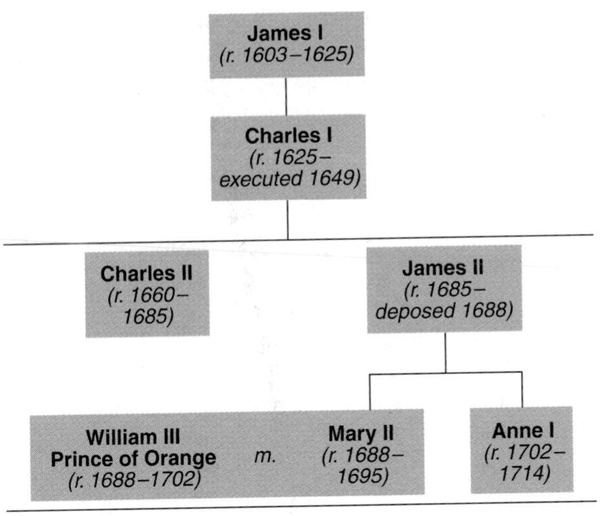

English people called the **Glorious Revolution** (1688) and sent James into permanent exile.

The Glorious Revolution altered the course of English political history and, therefore, that of the American colonies as well. The monarchs who followed James II surrendered some of the prerogative powers that had destabilized English politics for almost a century. The crown was still a potent force in the political life of the nation, but never again would an English king or queen attempt to govern without Parliament.

Such political events, coupled with periodic economic recession and religious repression, determined, in large measure, the direction and flow of migration to America. During times of political turmoil, religious persecution, and economic insecurity, men and women thought more seriously about transferring to the New World than they did during periods of peace and prosperity. Obviously, people who moved to America at different times came from different social and political environments. A person who emigrated to Pennsylvania in the 1680s, for example, left an England unlike the one that a Virginian in 1607 or a Bay Colonist in 1630 might have known. Moreover, the young men and women who migrated to London in search of work and who then, in their frustration and poverty, decided to move to the Chesapeake carried a very different set of memories from those people who moved directly to New England from the small rural villages of their homeland.

Regardless of the exact timing of departure, English settlers brought with them ideas and assumptions that helped them make sense of their everyday experiences in an unfamiliar environment. Their values were tested and sometimes transformed in the New World, but they were seldom destroyed. Settlement involved a complex process of adjustment. The colonists developed different subcultures in America, and in each it is possible to trace the interaction between the settlers' values and the physical elements, such as the climate, crops, and soil, of their new surroundings. The Chesapeake, the New England colonies, the Middle Colonies, and the Southern Colonies formed distinct regional identities that have survived to the present day.

The Chesapeake: Dreams of Wealth

After the Roanoke debacle in 1590, English interest in American settlement declined, and only a few aging visionaries such as Richard Hakluyt kept alive the dream of colonies in the New World. These advocates argued that the North American mainland contained resources of incalculable value. An innovative group, they insisted, might reap great profits and at the same time supply England with raw materials that it would otherwise be forced to purchase from European rivals: Holland, France, and Spain.

Moreover, any enterprise that annoyed Catholic Spain or revealed its weakness in America seemed a desirable end in itself to patriotic English Protestants. Anti-Catholicism and hatred of Spain became an integral part of English national identity during this period, and unless one appreciates just how deeply those sentiments ran in the popular mind, one cannot fully understand why ordinary people who had no direct financial stake in the New World so generously supported English efforts to colonize America. Soon after James I ascended to the throne, adventurers were given an opportunity to put their theories into practice in the colonies of Virginia and Maryland, an area known as the Chesapeake, or somewhat later, as the Tobacco Coast.

Entrepreneurs in Virginia

During Elizabeth's reign, the major obstacle to successful colonization of the New World had been raising money. No single person, no matter how rich or well connected, could underwrite the vast expenses a New World settlement required. The solution to this financial problem was the **joint-stock company,** a business organization in which scores of people could invest without fear of bankruptcy. A merchant or landowner could purchase a share of stock at a stated price, and at the end of several years the investor could anticipate recovering the initial amount plus a portion of whatever profits the company had made. Joint-stock ventures sprang up like mushrooms. Affluent English citizens, and even some of more modest fortunes, rushed to invest in the companies and, as a result, some projects were able to amass large amounts of capital, enough certainly to launch a new colony in Virginia.

On April 10, 1606, James issued the first Virginia charter. The document authorized the London Company to establish plantations in Virginia. The London Company was an ambitious business venture. Its leader, Sir Thomas Smith, was reputedly London's wealthiest merchant. Smith and his partners gained possession of the territory lying between present-day North Carolina and the Hudson River. These were generous but vague boundaries, to be sure, but the Virginia Company—as the London Company soon called itself—set out immediately to find the treasures Hakluyt had promised.

In December 1606, the *Susan Constant,* the *Godspeed,* and the *Discovery* sailed for America. The ships carried 104 men and boys who had been instructed to establish a fortified outpost some hundred miles up a large navigable river. The natural beauty and economic potential of the region was apparent to everyone. A voyager on the expedition reported seeing "faire meaddowes and goodly tall trees, with such fresh waters running through the woods, as almost ravished [us] at first sight."

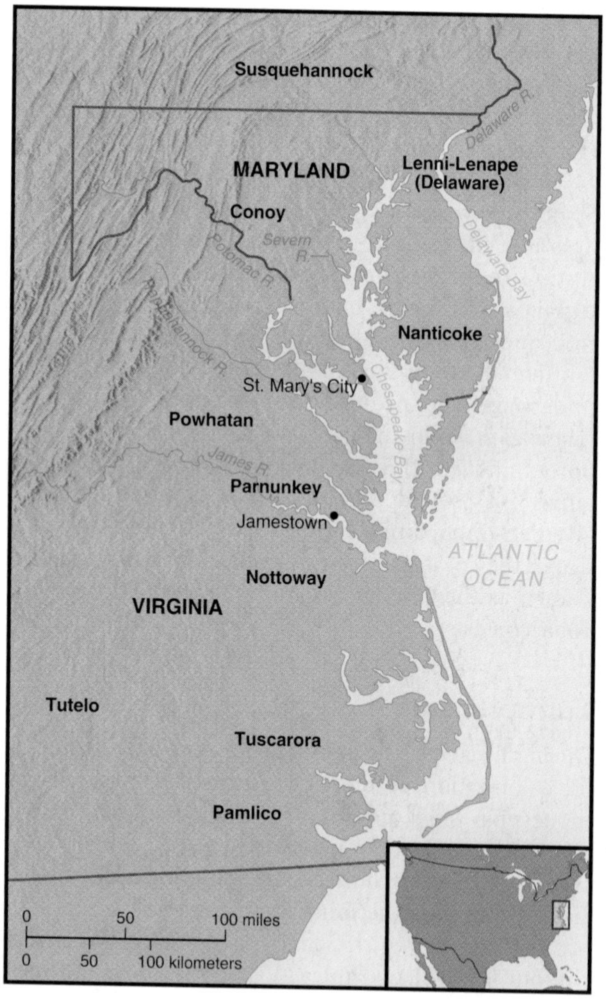

CHESAPEAKE COLONIES, 1640 *The many deep rivers flowing into the Chesapeake Bay provided scattered English planters with a convenient transportation system, linking them directly to European markets.*

The leaders of the colony selected—without consulting resident Native Americans—what the Europeans considered a promising location more than thirty miles from the mouth of the James River. A marshy peninsula jutting out into the river became the site for one of America's most unsuccessful villages, Jamestown. Modern historians have criticized the choice, for the low-lying ground proved to be a disease-ridden death trap; even the drinking water was contaminated with salt. But the first Virginians were neither stupid nor suicidal. Jamestown seemed the ideal place to build a fort, since surprise attack by Spaniards or Native Americans rather than sickness appeared the more serious threat in the early months of settlement.

Almost immediately, dispirited colonists began quarreling. The adventurers were not prepared for the challenges that confronted them in America. Part of the problem was cultural. Most of them had grown up in a depressed agricultural economy that could not provide full-time employment for all who wanted it. In England, laborers shared what little work was available. One man, for example, might perform a certain chore while others simply watched. Later, the men who had been idle were given an opportunity to work for an hour or two. This labor system may have been appropriate for England, but in Virginia it nearly destroyed the colony. Adventurers sat around Jamestown while other men performed crucial agricultural tasks. It made little sense, of course, to share work in an environment in which people were starving because too little labor was expended on the planting and harvesting of crops. Not surprisingly, some modern historians—those who assumed all workers should put in an eight-hour day—branded the early Virginians as lazy, irresponsible beings who preferred to play while others labored. In point of fact, however, the first settlers were merely attempting to replicate a traditional work experience.

Avarice exacerbated the problems. The adventurers had traveled to the New World in search of the sort of instant wealth they imagined the Spaniards to have found in Mexico and Peru. Published tales of rubies and diamonds lying on the beach probably inflamed their expectations. Even when it must have been apparent that such expectations were unfounded, the first settlers often behaved in Virginia as if they fully expected to become rich. Instead of cooperating for the common good—guarding or farming, for example—individuals pursued personal interests. They searched for gold when they might have helped plant corn. No one was willing to take orders, and those who were supposed to govern the colony looked after their private welfare while disease, war, and starvation ravaged the settlement.

Spinning Out of Control

Virginia might have gone the way of Roanoke had it not been for Captain John Smith. By any standard, he was a resourceful man. Before coming to Jamestown, he had traveled throughout Europe and fought with the Hungarian army against the Turks—and, if Smith is to be believed, he was saved from certain death by various beautiful women. Because of his reputation for boasting, historians have discounted Smith's account of life in early Virginia. Recent scholarship, however, has affirmed the truthfulness of his curious story. In Virginia, Smith brought order out of anarchy. While members of the council in Jamestown debated petty politics, he traded with the local Indians for food, mapped the Chesapeake Bay, and may even have been rescued from execution by a young Indian girl, Pocahontas. In the fall of 1608, he seized control of the ruling council and instituted a tough military discipline. Under Smith, no one enjoyed special privilege. Individuals whom he forced to work came to hate him. But he managed to keep them alive, no small achievement in such a deadly environment.

Leaders of the Virginia Company in London recognized the need to reform the entire enterprise. After all, they had spent considerable sums and had received nothing in return. In 1609, the company directors obtained a new charter from the king, which completely reorganized the Virginia government. Henceforth all commercial and political decisions affecting the colonists rested with the company, a fact that had not been made sufficiently clear in the 1606 charter. Moreover, in an effort to raise scarce capital, the original partners opened the joint-stock company to the

Chief Opechancanough, who succeeded his brother Powhatan as leader of the Chesapeake Algonquian Confederacy, is shown in a symbolic confrontation with Captain John Smith of Jamestown. Confrontations in 1622 and again in 1644 would lead to the destruction of Powhatan supremacy in the Chesapeake. ❖

❖ A Look at the Past ❖

Armor

The earliest English settlers to Virginia may have come with insufficient food and too few practical tools, but they did supply themselves with arms and armor. Armor like this breastplate recovered from James Fort reveals how carefully the settlers prepared in advance for military combat. Could the imagined enemy have been other Europeans such as the Spanish? If so, why might they have attacked Jamestown during its infancy? Would such heavy armor have offered much protection against the weapons of Powhatan's warriors?

general public. For a little more than £12—approximately one year's wages for an unskilled English laborer—a person or group of persons could purchase a stake in Virginia. It was anticipated that in 1616 the profits from the colony would be distributed among the shareholders. The company sponsored a publicity campaign; pamphlets and sermons extolled the colony's potential and exhorted patriotic English citizens to invest in the enterprise.

The burst of energy came to nothing. Bad luck and poor planning plagued the Virginia Company. A vessel carrying additional settlers and supplies went aground in Bermuda, and while this misadventure did little to help the people at Jamestown, it provided Shakespeare with the idea for *The Tempest.* The governor, Lord De La Warr, added to the confusion by postponing his departure for America. Even the indomitable Captain Smith suffered a gunpowder accident and was forced to return to England.

Between 1609 and 1611, the remaining Virginia settlers lacked capable leadership, and perhaps as a result, they lacked food. The terrible winter of 1609–1610 was termed the "starving time." A few desperate colonists were driven to cannibalism, an ironic situation since early explorers had assumed that only Native Americans would eat human flesh. In England, Smith heard that one colonist had killed his wife, powdered [salted] her, and "had eaten part of her before it was known; for which he was executed." The captain, who possessed a droll sense of humor, observed, "Now, whether she was better roasted, broiled, or carbonadoed [sliced], I know not, but such a dish as powdered wife I never heard of." Other people simply lost the will to live.

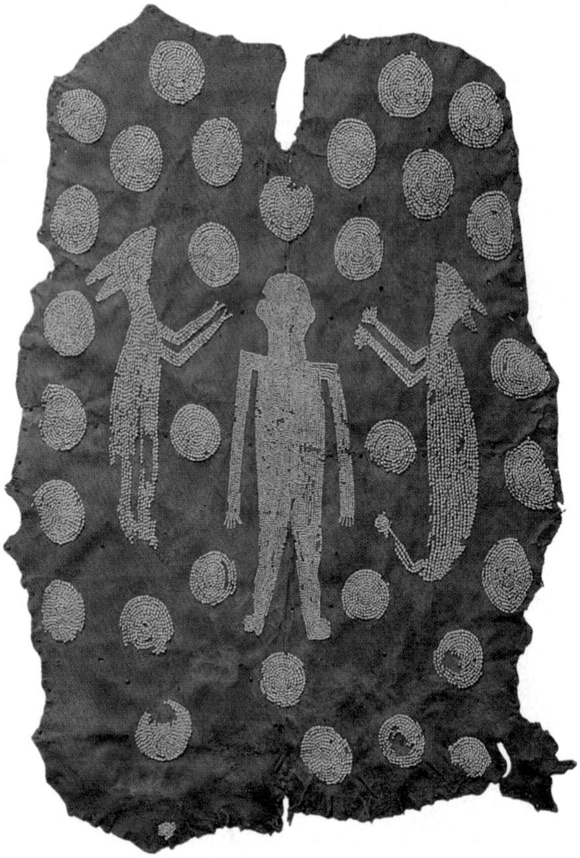

In 1608, Powhatan, the father of Pocahontas, gave this shell-decorated ceremonial cloak to Captain Christopher Newport. During the seventeenth century, this beautiful Native American artifact was given to Oxford University, where it can still be seen today. ❖

The presence of so many Native Americans heightened the danger. The first colonists found themselves living—or attempting to live—in territory controlled by what was probably the most powerful Indian confederation east of the Mississippi River. Under the leadership of their *werowance,* Powhatan, these Indians had by 1608 created a loose association of some thirty tribes, and when Captain John Smith arrived to lead several hundred adventurers, the Powhatans (named for their king) numbered some 14,000 people, of whom 3200 were warriors. These people hoped initially to enlist the Europeans as allies against native enemies. When it became clear that the two groups, holding such different notions about labor and property and about the exploitation of the natural environment, could not coexist in peace, the Powhatans tried to drive the invaders out of Virginia, once in 1622 and again in 1644. The failure of the second campaign ended in the complete destruction of the Powhatan empire.

In June 1610, the settlers who had survived despite starvation and conflicts with the Indians actually abandoned Virginia. Through a stroke of luck, however, they encountered De La Warr just as they commenced their voyage down the James River. The governor and the deputy governors who succeeded him, Sir Thomas Gates and Sir Thomas Dale, ruled by martial law. The new colonists, many of them male and female servants employed by the company, were marched to work by the beat of the drum. Such methods saved the colony but could not make it flourish. In 1616, company shareholders received no profits. Their only reward was the right to a piece of unsurveyed land located three thousand miles from London.

"Stinking Weed"

The economic solution to Virginia's problems grew in the vacant lots of Jamestown. Only Indians bothered to cultivate tobacco until John Rolfe, a settler who achieved notoriety by marrying Pocahontas, realized this local weed might be a valuable export. Rolfe experimented with the crop, eventually growing in Virginia a milder variety that had been developed in the West Indies and was more appealing to European smokers.

This tobacco label advertises Virginia's valuable export—tobacco. Despite King James's initial attitude toward the "stinking weed," once the government saw that tobacco made a profit, it dropped its moral criticism of the American crop. ❖

Virginians suddenly possessed a means to make money. Tobacco proved relatively easy to grow, and settlers who had avoided work now threw themselves into its production with single-minded diligence. In 1617, one observer found that Jamestown's "streets and all other spare places [are] planted with tobacco . . . the Colony dispersed all about planting tobacco." Although King James I originally considered smoking immoral and unhealthy, he changed his mind when the duties he collected on tobacco imports began to mount. He was neither the first nor the last ruler who decided a vice that generates revenue is not really so bad.

The company sponsored another ambitious effort to transform Virginia into a profitable enterprise. In 1618, Sir Edwin Sandys (pronounced Sands) led a faction of stockholders that began to pump life into the dying organization by instituting a series of sweeping reforms and eventually ousting Sir Thomas Smith and his friends. Sandys wanted private investors to develop their own estates in Virginia. Before 1618, there had been little incentive to do so, but by relaxing Dale's martial law and promising an elective representative assembly called the **House of Burgesses,** Sandys thought he could make the colony more attractive to wealthy speculators.

Even more important was Sandys's method for distributing land. Colonists who covered their own transportation cost to America were guaranteed a **headright,** a 50-acre lot for which they paid only a small annual rent. Adventurers were granted additional headrights for each servant they brought to the colony. This procedure allowed prosperous planters to build up huge estates while they also acquired dependent laborers. This land system persisted long after the company's collapse. So too did the notion that the wealth of a few justified the exploitation of many others.

Sandys had only just begun. He also urged the settlers to diversify their economy. Tobacco alone, he argued, was not a sufficient base. He envisioned colonists busily producing iron and tar, silk and glass, sugar and cotton. There was no end to his suggestions. He scoured Europe for skilled artisans and exotic plant cuttings. To finance such a huge project, Sandys relied on a lottery, a game of chance that promised a continuous flow of capital into the company's treasury. The final element in the grand scheme was people. Sandys sent new English settlers by the thousand to Jamestown, ordinary men and women swept up by the same hopes that had carried the colonists of 1607 to the New World.

Time of Reckoning

Between 1619 and 1622, colonists arrived in Virginia in record number. Company records reveal that during this short period, 3570 individuals were sent to the colony. People seldom moved to Virginia in families. Although the first women arrived in Jamestown in 1608, most emigrants were single males in their teens or early twenties who came to the New World as indentured servants. In exchange for transportation across the Atlantic, they agreed to serve a master for a stated number of years. The length of service depended in part on the age of the servant. The younger the servant, the longer he or she served. In return, the master promised to give the laborers proper care and, at the conclusion of their contracts, to provide them with tools and clothes according to "the custom of the country."

Powerful Virginians corrupted the system. Poor servants wanted to establish independent tobacco farms. As they discovered, however, headrights were awarded not to the newly freed servant, but to the great planter who had borne the cost of the servant's transportation to the New World and paid for food and clothing during the indenture. And even though **indentured servants** were promised land at the moment of freedom, they were most often cheated, becoming members of a growing, disaffected landless class in seventeenth-century Virginia.

Whenever possible, planters in Virginia purchased able-bodied workers, in other words, persons (preferably male) capable of performing hard agricultural labor. This preference dramatically skewed the colony's sex ratio. In the early decades, men outnumbered women by as much as six to one. As one historian, Edmund S. Morgan, observed, "Women were scarcer than corn or liquor in Virginia and fetched a higher price." Such gender imbalance meant that even if a male servant lived to the end of his indenture—an unlikely prospect—he could not realistically expect to start a family of his own. Moreover, despite apparent legal safeguards, masters could treat dependent workers as they pleased; after all, these people were legally considered property. Servants were sold, traded, even gambled away in games of chance. It does not require much imagination to see that a society that tolerated such an exploitative labor system might later embrace slavery.

Most Virginians then did not live long enough to worry about marriage. Death was omnipresent. Indeed, extraordinarily high mortality was a major reason the Chesapeake colonies developed so differently from those of New England. On the eve of the 1618 reforms, Virginia's population stood at approximately 700. The company sent at least 3000 more people, but by 1622 only 1240 were still alive. "It Consequentilie followes," declared one angry shareholder, "that we had then lost 3000 persons within those 3 yeares." The major killers were contagious diseases. Salt in the water supply also took a toll. And on Good Friday, March 22, 1622, the Powhatans slew 347 Europeans in a well-coordinated surprise attack.

No one knows for certain what effect such a horrendous mortality rate had on the men and women who survived. At the very least, it must have created a sense of impermanence, a desire to escape Virginia with a little money before sickness or violence ended the adventure. The settlers who drank to excess aboard the tavern ships anchored in the James River described the colony "not as a place of Habitacion but only of a short sojourninge."

Corruption and Reform

On both sides of the Atlantic, people wondered who should be blamed. Why had so many colonists died in a land so rich in potential? The burden of responsibility lay in large measure with the Virginia Company. Sandys and his supporters were in too great a hurry to make a profit. Settlers were shipped to America, but neither housing nor food awaited them in Jamestown. Weakened by the long sea voyage, they quickly succumbed to contagious disease.

Company officials in Virginia also bore a share of guilt. They were so eager to line their own pockets that they consistently failed to provide for the common good. Various governors and their councilors grabbed up the indentured servants and sent them to their own private plantations to cultivate tobacco, and, as the 1622 surprise attack demonstrated, officials ignored the colony's crumbling defenses. Jamestown took on all the most unattractive characteristics of a boomtown. There was no shared sense of purpose, no common ideology, except perhaps unrestrained self-advancement, to keep the society from splintering into highly individualistic, competitive fragments.

The company's scandalous mismanagement embarrassed the king, and in 1624, he dissolved the bankrupt enterprise and transformed Virginia into a royal colony. The crown appointed a governor and a council. No provision was made, however, for continuing the local representative assembly, an institution the Stuarts heartily opposed. The House of Burgesses had first convened in 1619. While elections to the Burgesses were hardly democratic, the assembly did provide wealthy planters with a voice in government. Even without the king's authorization, the representatives gathered annually after 1629, and in 1639, Charles recognized the body's existence.

He had no choice. The colonists who served on the council or in the assembly were strong-willed, ambitious men. They had no intention of surrendering control over local affairs. Since Charles was having political troubles of his own and lived three thousand

A reconstruction of a free white planter's house from the late seventeenth-century Chesapeake. Even well-to-do colonists lived in structures that seemed by English standards quite primitive. ❖

miles from Jamestown, he usually allowed the Virginians to have their own way. In 1634, the assembly divided the colony into eight counties. In each one, a group of appointed justices of the peace—the wealthy planters of the area—convened as a court of law as well as a governing body. The "county court" was the most important institution of local government in Virginia, and long after the American Revolution, it served as a center for social, political, and commercial activities.

Changes in government had little impact on the character of daily life in Virginia. The planters continued to grow tobacco, ignoring advice to diversify, and as the Indians were killed, made into tributaries, or pushed north and south, Virginians took up large tracts of land along the colony's many navigable rivers. The focus of their lives was the isolated plantation, a small cluster of buildings housing the planter's family and dependent workers. These were modest wooden structures. Not until the eighteenth century did the Chesapeake gentry build the great Georgian mansions that still attract tourists. The dispersed pattern of settlement retarded the development of institutions such as schools and churches. Besides Jamestown there were no population centers, and as late as 1705, Robert Beverley, a leading planter, reported that Virginia did not have a single place "that may reasonably bear the Name of a Town."

Maryland: A Troubled Refuge for Catholics

By the end of the seventeenth century, Maryland society looked remarkably like that of its Chesapeake neighbor, Virginia. At the time of first settlement in 1634, however, no one would have predicted that Maryland, a colony wholly owned by a Catholic nobleman, would have survived, much less become a flourishing tobacco colony.

The driving force behind the founding of Maryland was Sir George Calvert, later Lord Baltimore. Calvert, a talented and well-educated man, enjoyed the patronage of James I. He was awarded lucrative positions in the government, the most important being the king's secretary of state. In 1625, Calvert shocked almost everyone by publicly declaring his Catholicism; in this fiercely anti-Catholic society, persons who openly supported the Church of Rome were immediately stripped of civil office. Although forced to resign as secretary of state, Calvert retained the crown's favor.

Before resigning, Calvert sponsored a settlement on the coast of Newfoundland, but after visiting the place, the proprietor concluded that no English person, whatever his or her religion, would transfer to a place where the "ayre [is] so intolerably cold." He turned his attention to the Chesapeake, and on June 30, 1632, Charles I granted George Calvert's son, Cecilius, a charter for a colony to be located north of Virginia. The boundaries of the settlement, named Maryland in honor of Charles's queen, were so vaguely defined that they generated legal controversies not fully resolved until the mid-eighteenth century when Charles Mason and Jeremiah Dixon surveyed their famous line between Pennsylvania and Maryland.

Cecilius, the second Lord Baltimore, wanted to create a sanctuary for England's persecuted Catholics. He also intended to make money. Without Protestant settlers, it seemed unlikely Maryland would prosper, and Cecilius instructed his brother Leonard, the colony's governor, to do nothing that might frighten off hypersensitive Protestants. The governor was ordered to "cause all Acts of the Roman Catholic Religion to be done as privately as may be and . . . [to] instruct all Roman Catholics to be silent upon all occasions of discourse concerning matters of Religion." On March 25, 1634, the *Ark* and the *Dove*, carrying about 150 settlers, landed safely, and within days, the governor purchased from the Yaocomico Indians a village that became St. Mary's City, the capital of Maryland.

The colony's charter was an odd document, a throwback to an earlier feudal age. It transformed Baltimore into a "palatine lord," a proprietor with almost royal powers. Settlers swore an oath of allegiance not to the king of England but to Lord Baltimore. In England, such practices had long ago passed into obsolescence. As the proprietor, Lord Baltimore owned outright almost 6 million acres; he possessed absolute authority over anyone living in his domain.

On paper, at least, everyone in Maryland was assigned a place in an elaborate social hierarchy. Members of a colonial ruling class, persons who purchased 6000 acres from Baltimore, were called lords of the manor. These landed aristocrats were permitted to establish local courts of law. People holding less acreage enjoyed fewer privileges, particularly in government. Baltimore figured that land sales and rents would adequately finance the entire venture.

Baltimore's feudal system never took root in Chesapeake soil. People simply refused to play the social roles the lord proprietor had assigned. These tensions affected the operation of Maryland's government. Baltimore assumed that his brother, acting as his deputy in America, and a small appointed council of local aristocrats would pass necessary laws and carry out routine administration. When an elected assembly first convened in 1635, Baltimore allowed the delegates to discuss only those acts he had prepared. The members of the assembly bridled at such restrictions, insisting on exercising traditional parliamentary privileges. Neither side gained a clear victory in the assembly, and for almost twenty-five years, legislative squabbling contributed to the widespread political instability that almost destroyed Maryland.

Cecilius Calvert, the second Lord Baltimore, insisted that Maryland tolerate all Christian religions, including Catholicism, something no other colony was willing to do. The young slave in the background reminds us who did the hard labor in the Chesapeake Colonies. ❖

The colony drew both Protestants and Catholics, and the two groups might have lived in harmony had civil war not broken out in England. When Cromwell and the Puritan faction executed Charles, transforming England briefly into a republic, it seemed Baltimore might lose his colony. To head off such an event and to placate Maryland's restless Protestants, in 1649, the proprietor drafted the famous "Act concerning Religion," which extended toleration to all individuals who accepted the divinity of Christ. At a time when European rulers regularly persecuted people for their religious beliefs, Baltimore championed liberty of conscience.

However laudable the act may have been, it did not heal religious divisions in Maryland, and when local Puritans seized the colony's government, they promptly repealed the act. For almost two decades, vigilantes roamed the countryside, and during the "Plundering Time" (1644–1646), one armed group temporarily drove Leonard Calvert out of Maryland. In 1655, civil war flared again.

In this troubled sanctuary, ordinary planters and their workers cultivated tobacco on plantations dispersed along riverfronts. In 1678, Baltimore complained that he could not find fifty houses in a space of thirty miles. Tobacco affected almost every aspect of local culture. "In Virginia and Maryland," one Calvert explained, "Tobacco, as our Staple, is our all, and indeed leaves no room for anything Else." A steady stream of indentured servants supplied the plantations with dependent laborers—until they were replaced by African slaves at the end of the seventeenth century.

Europeans sacrificed much by coming to the Chesapeake. For most of the century, their standard of living was primitive when compared with that of people of the same social class who had remained in England. Two-thirds of the planters, for example, lived in houses of only two rooms and of a type associated with the poorest classes in contemporary English society.

Reforming England in America

The Pilgrims enjoy almost mythic status in American history. These brave refugees crossed the cold Atlantic in search of religious liberty, signed a democratic compact aboard the *Mayflower,* landed at Plymouth Rock, and gave us our Thanksgiving Day. As with most legends, this one contains only a core of truth.

The Pilgrims were not crusaders who set out to change the world. Rather, they were humble English farmers. Their story began in the early 1600s in Scrooby Manor, a small community located approximately 150 miles north of London. Many people living in this area believed the Church of England retained too many traces of its Catholic origin. To support such a corrupt institution was like winking at the devil. Its very rituals compromised God's true believers, and so, in the early years of the reign of James I, the Scrooby congregation formally left the established state church. Like others who followed this logic, they were called Separatists. Since English statute required citizens to attend Anglican services, the Scrooby Separatists moved to Holland in 1608–1609 rather than compromise.

The Netherlands provided the Separatists with a good home—too good. The members of the little church feared they were losing their distinct identity; their children were becoming Dutch. In 1617, therefore, a portion of the original Scrooby congregation vowed to sail to America. Included in this group was William Bradford, a wonderfully literate man who wrote *Of Plymouth Plantation,* one of the first and certainly most poignant accounts of an early American settlement.

Poverty presented the major obstacle to the Pilgrims' plans. They petitioned for a land patent from the Virginia Company of London. At the same time, they looked for someone willing to underwrite the staggering costs of colonization. The negotiations went well, or so it seemed. After stopping in England to take on supplies and laborers, the Pilgrims set off for America in 1620 aboard the *Mayflower,* armed with a patent to settle in Virginia and indebted to a group of English investors who were only marginally interested in religious reform.

Because of an error in navigation, the Pilgrims landed not in Virginia but in New England. The patent for which they had worked so diligently had no validity in the region. In fact, the crown had granted New England to another company. Without a patent, the colonists possessed no authorization to form a civil government, a serious matter since some sailors who were not Pilgrims threatened mutiny. To preserve the struggling community from anarchy, 41 men signed an agreement known as the **Mayflower Compact** to "covenant and combine our selves together into a civil body politick."

Although later praised for its democratic character, the Mayflower Compact could not ward off disease and hunger. During the first months in Plymouth, death claimed approximately half of the 102 people who had initially set out from England. Moreover, debts contracted in England severely burdened the new colony. To their credit, the Pilgrims honored their financial obligations, but it took almost twenty years to satisfy the English investors. Without Bradford, whom they elected as governor, the settlers might have allowed adversity to overwhelm them. Through strength of will and self-sacrifice, however, Bradford persuaded frightened men and women that they could survive in America.

Bradford had a lot of help. Almost anyone who has heard of the Plymouth Colony knows of Squanto, a Patuxt Indian who welcomed the first Pilgrims in excellent English. In 1614 unscrupulous adventurers kidnapped Squanto and sold him in Spain as a slave. Somehow this resourceful man escaped bondage, making his way to London, where a group of merchants who owned land in Newfoundland taught him to speak English. They apparently hoped that he would deliver moving public testimonials about the desirability of moving to the New World. In any case, Squanto returned to the Plymouth area just before the Pilgrims arrived. Squanto joined Massasoit, a local Native American leader, in teaching the Pilgrims much about hunting and agriculture, a debt that Bradford freely acknowledged. Although evidence for the so-called "First Thanksgiving" is extremely sketchy, it is certain that without Native American support the Europeans would have starved.

In time, the Pilgrims replicated the humble little farm communities they had once known in England. They formed Separatist congregations to their liking; the population slowly increased. The settlers experimented with commercial fishing and the fur trade, but the efforts never generated substantial income. Most families relied on mixed husbandry, grain, and livestock. Because Plymouth offered only limited economic prospects, it attracted only a trickle of new settlers. In 1691, the colony was absorbed into its larger and more prosperous neighbor, Massachusetts Bay.

"The Great Migration"

In the early decades of the seventeenth century, an extraordinary spirit of religious reform burst forth in England, and before it had burned itself out, Puritanism had transformed the face of England and America. Modern historians have difficulty comprehending this powerful spiritual movement. Some consider the **Puritans** rather neurotic individuals who condemned liquor and sex, dressed in drab clothes, and minded their neighbors' business.

The crude caricature is based on a profound misunderstanding of the actual nature of this broad popular movement. The seventeenth-century Puritans were more like today's radical political reformers, men and women committed to far-reaching institutional change, than like naive do-gooders or narrow fundamentalists. To their enemies, of course, the Puritans were irritants, always pointing out civil and ecclesiastical imperfections and urging everyone to try to fulfill the commands of Scripture. A great many people, however, shared their vision, and not only did they found several American colonies, but they also sparked the English Civil War, an event that generated bold new thinking about republican government and popular sovereignty.

The Puritans were products of the Protestant Reformation. They accepted a Calvinist notion that an omnipotent God predestined some people to salvation and damned others throughout eternity (see Chapter 1). But instead of waiting passively for Judgment Day, the Puritans examined themselves for signs of grace, for hints that God had in fact placed them among his "elect." A member of this select group, they argued, would try to live according to Scripture, to battle sin and eradicate corruption.

For the Puritans, the logic of everyday life was clear. If the Church of England contained unscriptural elements—clerical vestments, for example—then they must be eliminated. If the pope in Rome was in league with the Antichrist, then Protestant kings had better not form alliances with Catholic states. If God condemned licentiousness and intoxication, then local officials should punish whores and drunks. There was nothing improper about an occasional beer or passionate physical love within marriage, but when sex and drink became ends in themselves, the Puritans thought England's ministers and magistrates should speak out. Persons of this temperament were more combative than the Pilgrims had been. They wanted to purify the Church of England from within, and before the 1630s at least, separatism held little appeal for them.

From the Puritan perspective, the early Stuarts, James I and Charles I, seemed unconcerned about the spiritual state of the nation. James tolerated corruption within his own court; he condoned gross public extravagance. His foreign policy appeased European Catholic powers. At one time, he even tried to marry his son to a Catholic princess. Neither king showed interest in purifying the Anglican Church. In fact, Charles assisted the rapid advance of William Laud, a bishop who represented everything the Puritans detested. Laud defended church ceremonies that they found obnoxious. He persecuted Puritan ministers, forcing them either to conform to his theology or lose their licenses to preach. As long as Parliament met, Puritan voters in the various boroughs and countries throughout England elected men sympathetic to their point of view. These outspoken representatives criticized royal policies and hounded Laud. Because of their defiance, Charles decided in 1629 to rule England without Parliament and four years later named Laud archbishop of Canterbury. The last doors of reform slammed shut. The corruption remained.

John Winthrop, the future governor of Massachusetts Bay, was caught up in these events. Little about his background suggested such an auspicious future. He owned a small manor in Suffolk, one that never produced sufficient income to support his growing family. He dabbled in law. But the core of Winthrop's life was his faith in God, a faith so intense his contemporaries immediately identified him as a Puritan. The Lord, he concluded, was displeased with England. Time for reform was running out. In May 1629, he wrote to his wife, "I am verily perswaded God will bringe some heavye Affliction upon this lande, and that speedylye." He was, however, confident that the Lord would "provide a shelter and a hidinge place for us."

Other Puritans, some wealthier and politically better connected than Winthrop, reached similar conclusions about England's future. They turned their attention to the possibility of establishing a colony in America, and on March 4, 1629, their Massachusetts Bay Company obtained a charter directly from the king. Charles and his advisers apparently thought the Massachusetts Bay Company was a commercial venture no different from the dozens of other joint-stock companies that had recently sprung into existence.

Voters in Massachusetts who were called "freemen" reelected John Winthrop governor many times, an indication of his success in translating Puritan values into practical policy. ❖

Winthrop and his associates knew better. On August 26, 1629, twelve of them met secretly and signed the Cambridge Agreement. They pledged to be "ready in our persons and with such of our severall familyes as are to go with us . . . to embark for the said plantation by the first of March next." There was one loophole. The charters of most joint-stock companies designated a specific place where business meetings were to be held. For reasons not entirely clear—a timely bribe is a good guess—the charter of the Massachusetts Bay Company did not contain this standard clause. It could hold meetings anywhere the stockholders, called "freemen," desired, even America, and if they were in America, the king and his archbishop could not easily interfere in their affairs.

"A City on a Hill"

The Winthrop fleet departed England in March 1630. By the end of the first year, almost 2,000 people had arrived in Massachusetts Bay, and before the "Great Migration" concluded in the early 1640s, more than

16,000 men and women had arrived in the new Puritan colony.

A great deal is known about the background of these particular settlers. A large percentage of them originated in an area northeast of London called East Anglia, a region in which Puritan ideas had taken deep root. London, Kent, and the West Country also contributed to the stream of emigrants. In some instances, entire villages were reestablished across the Atlantic. Many Bay Colonists had worked as farmers in England, but a surprisingly large number came from industrial centers, such as Norwich, where cloth was manufactured for the export trade.

Whatever their backgrounds, they moved to Massachusetts as nuclear families, fathers, mothers, and their dependent children, a form of migration strikingly different from the one that peopled Virginia and Maryland. Moreover, because the settlers had already formed families in England, the colony's sex ratio was more balanced than that found in the Chesapeake colonies. Finally, and perhaps more significantly, once they had arrived in Massachusetts, these men and women survived. Indeed, their life expectancy compares favorably to that of modern Americans. Many factors help explain this phenomenon—clean drinking water and a healthy climate, for example. While the Puritans could not have planned to live longer than did colonists in other parts of the New World, this remarkable accident reduced the emotional shock of long-distance migration.

The first settlers possessed another source of strength and stability. They were bound together by a common sense of purpose. God, they insisted, had formed a special covenant with the people of Massachusetts Bay. On his part, the Lord expected them to live according to Scripture, to reform the church, in other words, to create an Old Testament "city on a hill" that would stand as a beacon of righteousness for the rest of the Christian world. If they fulfilled their side of the bargain, the settlers could anticipate peace and prosperity. No one, not even the lowliest servant, was excused from this divine covenant, for as Winthrop stated, "Wee must be knitt together in this worke as one man." Even as the first ships were leaving England, John Cotton, a popular Puritan minister, urged the emigrants to go forth "with a publicke spirit, looking not on your owne things only, but also on the things of others." Many people throughout the ages have espoused such communal rhetoric, but these particular men and women went about the business of forming a new colony as if they truly intended to transform a religious vision into social reality.

In ecclesiastical affairs, the colonists proceeded by what one founder called "experimental footsteps." They arrived in Massachusetts Bay without a precise plan for their church. Although the rituals and ceremonies enforced by Laud had no place in Massachusetts, the American Puritans refused to separate formally from the Church of England. In this matter, they thought the Pilgrims had made a serious mistake. After all, what was the point of reforming an institution if the reformers were no longer part of it?

The Bay Colonists gradually came to accept a highly innovative form of church government known as Congregationalism. Under the system, each village church was independent of outside interference. The American Puritans, of course, wanted nothing of bishops. The people (the "saints") were the church, and as a body, they pledged to uphold God's law. In the Salem Church, for example, the members

One early Puritan meetinghouse was called the Old Ship Meetinghouse in Hingham, Massachusetts. Its name derives from its interior design, which resembles the hull of a ship. The oldest wooden church in the United States, it could accommodate about seven hundred people, nearly the entire population of seventeenth-century Hingham. Members of the congregation would have sat on backless wooden benches in the unheated building, listening to the preacher address them, not from an altar but from an undecorated square speaking box. ❖

Built in 1668, the house at 54 Turner Street in Salem, Massachusetts, is the oldest surviving seventeenth-century wooden mansion in New England. It was later made famous by Nathaniel Hawthorne as the "House of the Seven Gables," so called for its steeply pitched gable roofs. ❖

covenanted "with the Lord and with one another and do bind ourselves in the presence of God to walk together in all his ways."

Simply because a person happened to live in a certain community did not mean he or she automatically belonged to the local church. The churches of Massachusetts were voluntary institutions, and in order to join one a man or woman had to provide testimony—a confession of faith—before neighbors who had already been admitted as full members. It was a demanding process. Whatever the personal strains, however, most men and women in early Massachusetts aspired to full membership, which entitled them to the sacraments, and gave some of them responsibility for choosing ministers, disciplining backsliders, and determining difficult questions of theology. Although women and blacks could not vote for ministers, they did become members of the Congregational churches. Over the course of the seventeenth century, women made up an increasingly large share of the membership.

There were limits on Congregational autonomy, to be sure, and colonial magistrates sometimes ferreted out heretical beliefs. Those who did not become church members were compelled to attend regular religious services. Perhaps because of the homogeneity of the colony's population, however, the loose polity of the Congregational churches held together for the entire colonial period.

Some aspects of community religiosity in early Massachusetts may, of course, strike modern Americans as morbid. Ministers expected people convicted of capital crimes to offer a full public confession of their sins just before their own execution. Such rituals reinforced everyday moral values by reminding ordinary men and women—those who listened to the confession—of the fatal consequences awaiting those who ignored the teachings of Scripture. (See the Feature Essay, "Capital Punishment in Early America," pp. 46–47.)

In creating a civil government, the Bay Colonists faced a particularly difficult challenge. Their charter allowed the investors in a joint-stock company to set up a business organization. When the settlers arrived in America, however, company leaders—men like Winthrop—moved quickly to transform the commercial structure into a colonial government. An early step in this direction took place on May 18, 1631, when the category of "freeman" was extended to all adult males who had become members of a Congregational church. This decision greatly expanded the franchise of Massachusetts Bay, and historians estimate that during the 1630s, at least 40 percent of the colony's adult males could vote in elections. While this percentage may seem low by modern or even Jacksonian standards, it was higher than anything the emigrants would have known in England. The freemen voted annually for a governor, a group of magistrates called the Court of Assistants, and after 1634, deputies who represented the interests of the individual towns. Even military officers were elected every year in Massachusetts Bay.

Two popular misconceptions about this government should be dispelled. It was neither a democracy nor a theocracy. The magistrates elected in Massachusetts did not believe they represented the voters, much less the whole populace. They ruled in the name of the electorate, but their responsibility as rulers was to God. In 1638, Winthrop warned against overly democratic forms, since "the best part [of the people] is always the least, and of that best part the wiser is always the lesser." And second, the Congregational ministers possessed no formal political authority in Massachusetts Bay. They could not

The Wages of Sin;

OR,

Robbery juſtly Rewarded:

A

POEM;

Occaſioned by the untimely Death of

Richard Wilſon,

Who was Executed on *Boſton* Neck, for Burglary,

On *Thurſday* the 19th of *October*, 1732.

THis Day from Goal muſt *Wilſon* be
conveyed in a Cart,
By Guards unto the Gallows-Tree,
to die as his Deſert.

Here we may ſee what Men for Stealth
and Robbing muſt endure;
And what the Gain of ill got Wealth
will in the End procure.

is excessively great. And such Children do usually die *before their Time.*" Lest the boys and girls missed his point, Mather added, "[It] is greatly to be observed that most of those that die upon the Gallows do confess that they have been guilty of disobedience to Parents."

In 1713, Cotton Mather, Increase's son, delivered an execution sermon specifically designed to strike terror in the hearts of the young. Look, he said, pointing to a felon about to die, "[Here] is a poor Young man before you, that is just *going to the Dead.* God this day is holding up a *Young man* in Chains, that all the *Young People* of New England, may . . . be withheld from Sinning."

The execution ritual reaffirmed the traditional moral order; rebellion against elders was rebellion against God. The ministers knew the adolescents before them would probably not end their days as murderers or rapists. But by making a spectacle of an extreme case, by transforming the execution into a public drama, they hoped to discourage lesser vices.

Without the cooperation of the condemned, the execution lost much of its social meaning. Most men and women—people about to be hanged and without hope of clemency—not only voluntarily confessed to a host of moral failings, but also admonished the crowds to avoid a life of sin. Esther Rodgers ended her life with these words: "I beg of all to have Care. Be Obedient to your Parents and Masters; Run not at Nights, especially on Sabbath Nights, Refrain bad Company for the Lord's Sake. . . . " Her moving performance made for a "good" execution. James Morgan, a convicted murderer, also fulfilled everyone's expectations. "Have a care of that Sin of Drunkenness," he warned the citizens of Boston in 1686, "for that is a sin that leads to all manner of sins and wickedness." And just before he died, Morgan cried out, "I am going out of this World; O take warning by me, and beg God to keep you from this Sin which hath been my ruine."

Although the ministers may have encouraged the public displays of penance—they may have even suggested the actual wording—there is no reason to doubt the criminals' sincerity. They too shared the religious values of the seventeenth century, and however far from the accepted norms they may have strayed, they desired in some small way to win favor in the sight of the Lord. As the Reverend William Cooper observed in 1733, "It may be [that] there is no Place in the World, where such Pains are taken with condemned Criminals to prepare them for their Death; that in *the Destruction of the Flesh, the Spirit may be saved in the Day of the Lord Jesus.*" Standing on the gallows, men and women rarely expressed even a hint of bitterness. In fact, they frequently praised their judges, noting that the magistrates had merely carried out God's will.

Soon after the execution, colonial printers issued pamphlets containing the execution sermon, the criminal's dying confession, and, in some cases, a lurid woodcut depicting an individual about to hang. These works sold quite well. The account of James Morgan's execution went through several editions. Others bore provocative titles such as *The Wicked Man's Portion* and *Death The Certain Wages of Sin.* The most ambitious production was Cotton Mather's *Pillars of Salt. An HISTORY OF SOME CRIMINALS Executed in this Land; for Capital Crimes. With some of their Dying Speeches; Collected and Published, For the WARNING of such as Live in Destructive Courses of Ungodliness* (1699). What effect the execution rituals had upon colonial Americans—spectators as well as readers—is impossible to judge. Some may have reformed their evil ways; for others, the theater of punishment may have involved no more than an "Entertaining DEATH."

Hutchinson; in this intense theological debate, she more than held her own. She knew as much about the Bible as did her inquisitors.

Hutchinson defied the ministers and magistrates to demonstrate exactly where she had gone wrong. Just when it appeared Hutchinson had outmaneuvered—indeed, thoroughly embarrassed—her opponents, she let down her guard, declaring forcefully that what she knew of God came "by an immediate revelation. . . . By the voice of his own spirit to my soul." Here was what her accusers had suspected all along but could not prove. She had confessed in open court that the Spirit can live without the Moral Law. This Antinomian statement fulfilled the worst fears of the Bay rulers, and they were relieved to exile Hutchinson and her followers to Rhode Island.

Mobility and Division

Massachusetts Bay spawned four new colonies, three of which survived to the American Revolution. New Hampshire became a separate colony in 1677. Its population grew very slowly, and for much of the colonial period, New Hampshire remained economically dependent on Massachusetts, its commercial neighbor to the south.

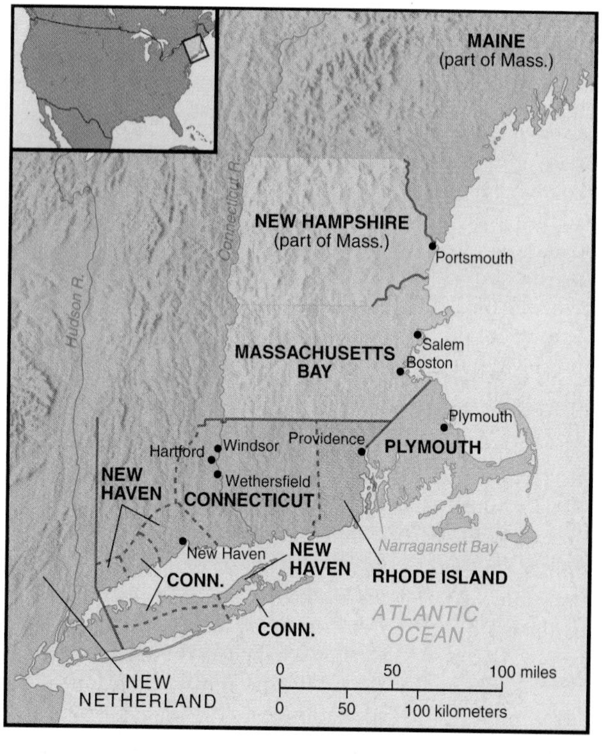

NEW ENGLAND COLONIES, 1650 *The early settlers quickly carved up New England. New Haven briefly flourished as a separate colony before being taken over by Connecticut in 1662. Long Island later became part of New York; Plymouth was absorbed into Massachusetts, and in 1677 New Hampshire became a separate colony.* ❖

Far more people were drawn to the fertile lands of the Connecticut River Valley. In 1636, settlers founded the villages of Hartford, Windsor, and Wethersfield. No one forced these men and women to leave Massachusetts, and in their new surroundings, they created a society that looked much like the one they had known in the Bay Colony. Through his writings, Thomas Hooker, Connecticut's most prominent minister, helped all New Englanders define Congregational church polity. Puritans on both sides of the Atlantic read Hooker's beautifully crafted works. In 1639, representatives from the Connecticut towns passed the Fundamental Orders, a blueprint for civil government, and in 1662, Charles II awarded the colony a charter of its own.

In 1638, another group, led by Theophilus Eaton and the Reverend John Davenport, settled New Haven and several adjoining towns along Long Island Sound. These emigrants, many of whom had come from London, lived briefly in Massachusetts Bay but then insisted on forming a Puritan commonwealth of their own, one that established a closer relationship between church and state than the Bay Colonists had allowed. The New Haven colony never prospered, and in 1662, it was absorbed into Connecticut.

Rhode Island experienced a wholly different history. From the beginning, it drew people of a highly independent turn of mind, and according to one Dutch visitor, Rhode Island was "the receptacle of all sorts of riff-raff people. . . . All the cranks of New-England retire thither." This description, of course, was an exaggeration. Roger Williams founded Providence in 1636; two years later, Anne Hutchinson took her followers to Portsmouth. Other groups settled around Narragansett Bay. Not surprisingly, these men and women appreciated the need for toleration. No one was persecuted in Rhode Island for his or her religious beliefs.

One might have thought the separate Rhode Island communities would cooperate for the common good. They did not. Villagers fought over land and schemed with outside speculators to divide the tiny colony into even smaller pieces. In 1644, Parliament issued a patent for the "Providence Plantations," and in 1663, the Rhode Islanders obtained a royal charter. These successes did not calm political turmoil. For most of the seventeenth century, colonywide government existed in name only. Despite their constant bickering, however, the settlers of Rhode Island built up a profitable commerce in agricultural goods.

Diversity in the Middle Colonies

New York, New Jersey, Pennsylvania, and Delaware were settled for quite different reasons. William Penn, for example, envisioned a Quaker sanctuary; the Duke of York worried chiefly about his own income. Despite the founders' intentions, however, some common characteristics emerged. Each colony developed a strikingly heterogeneous population, men and women of different ethnic and religious backgrounds. This cultural diversity became a major influence on the economic, political, and ecclesiastical institutions of the Middle Colonies. The raucous, partisan public life of the Middle Colonies foreshadowed later American society.

Anglo-Dutch Rivalry on the Hudson

By the early decades of the seventeenth century, the Dutch had established themselves as Europe's most aggressive traders. Holland—a small, loosely federated nation—possessed the world's largest merchant fleet. Its ships vied for the commerce of Asia, Africa, and America. Dutch rivalry with Spain, a fading though still formidable power, was in large measure responsible for the settlement of New Netherland. While searching for the elusive Northwest Passage in 1609, Henry Hudson, an English explorer employed by a Dutch company, sailed up the river that now bears his name. Further voyages led to the establishment of trading posts in New Netherland, although permanent settlement did not occur until 1624. The area also seemed an excellent base from which to attack Spain's colonies in the New World.

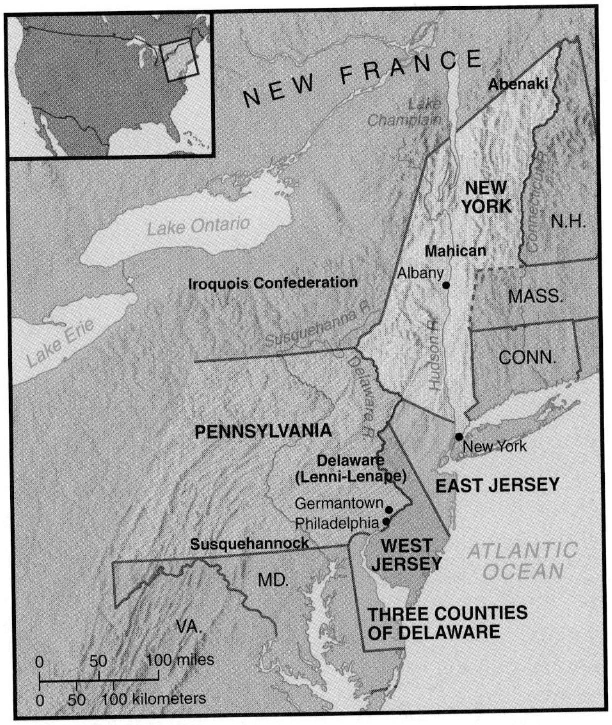

MIDDLE COLONIES, 1685 *Until the Revolution, the Iroquois blocked European expansion into Western New York. The Jerseys and Pennsylvania initially attracted English and Irish Quakers, who were soon joined by thousands of Protestant Irish and Germans.* ❖

The directors of the Dutch West India Company sponsored two small outposts, Fort Orange (Albany) located well up the Hudson River and New Amsterdam (New York City) on Manhattan Island. The first Dutch settlers were not actually colonists. Rather, they were salaried employees, and their superiors in Holland expected them to spend most of their time gathering animal furs. They did not receive land for their troubles. Needless to say, this arrangement attracted relatively few Dutch immigrants.

The colony's population may have been small, only 270 in 1628, but it contained an extraordinary ethnic mix. One visitor to New Amsterdam in 1644 maintained he had heard "eighteen different languages" spoken in the city. Even if this report was exaggerated, there is no doubt the Dutch colony drew English, Finns, Germans, and Swedes. By the 1640s, a sizable community of free blacks (probably former slaves who had gained their freedom through self-purchase) had developed in New Amsterdam, adding African tongues to the cacophony of languages. The colony's culture was further fragmented by New England Puritans who left Massachusetts and Connecticut to stake out farms on eastern Long Island.

New Netherland lacked capable leadership. The company sent a number of director-generals to oversee judicial and political affairs. Without exception, these men were temperamentally unsuited to govern an American colony. They adopted autocratic procedures, lined their own pockets, and, in one case, blundered into a war that needlessly killed scores of Indians and settlers. The company made no provision for an elected assembly. As much as they were able, the scattered inhabitants living along the Hudson River ignored company directives. They felt no loyalty to the trading company that had treated them so shabbily. Long Island Puritans complained bitterly about the absence of representative institutions. The Dutch system has aptly been described as "unstable pluralism."

In August 1664, the Dutch lost their tenuous hold on New Netherland. The English crown, eager to score an easy victory over a commercial rival, dispatched a

Dutch colonization in the first half of the seventeenth century extended from New Amsterdam (New York City) up the Hudson River to Fort Orange (Albany). Another important settlement was at Wiltwyck (Kingston), where traces of colonization are still evident in the architecture. This stone building, known as the Hoffman House, displays several characteristics of early American-Dutch housing, including rubble construction, a front porch, and shuttered windows. ❖

fleet of warships to New Amsterdam. The commander of this force, Colonel Richard Nicolls, ordered the colonists to surrender. The last director-general, a colorful character named Peter Stuyvesant (1647–1664), rushed wildly about the city urging the settlers to resist the English. But no one obeyed. Even the Dutch remained deaf to Stuyvesant's appeals. They accepted the Articles of Capitulation, a generous agreement that allowed Dutch nationals to remain in the province and to retain their property.

Charles II had already granted his brother, James, the Duke of York, a charter for the newly captured territory and much else besides. The duke became absolute proprietor over Maine, Martha's Vineyard, Nantucket, Long Island, and the rest of New York all the way to Delaware Bay. The king perhaps wanted to encircle New England's potentially disloyal Puritan population, but whatever his aims may have been, he created a bureaucratic nightmare.

During the English Civil War, the duke had acquired a thorough aversion to representative government. After all, Parliament had executed the duke's father, Charles I, and raised up Oliver Cromwell. The new proprietor had no intention of letting such a participatory system take root in New York. "I cannot *but* suspect," the duke announced, that an assembly "would be of dangerous consequence." The Long Islanders felt betrayed. In part to appease these outspoken critics, Governor Nicolls—one of the few competent administrators to serve in the Middle Colonies—drew up in March 1665 a legal code known as the Duke's Laws. It guaranteed religious toleration and created local governments.

There was no provision, however, for an elected assembly or, for that matter, for democratic town meetings. The legal code disappointed the Puritan migrants on Long Island, and when the duke's officers attempted to collect taxes, these people protested that they were "inslav'd under an Arbitrary Power."

The Dutch kept silent. For several decades they remained a large unassimilated ethnic group. They continued to speak their own language, worship in their own churches (Dutch Reformed Calvinist), and eye their English neighbors with suspicion. In fact, the colony seemed little different from what it had been under the Dutch West India Company: a loose collection of independent communities ruled by an ineffectual central government.

Confusion in New Jersey

Only three months after receiving a charter for New York, the Duke of York made a terrible mistake—something this stubborn, humorless man was prone to do. As a gift to two courtiers who had served Charles during the English Civil War, the duke awarded the land lying between the Hudson and Delaware rivers to John, Lord Berkeley, and Sir George Carteret. This colony was named New Jersey in honor of Carteret's birthplace, the Isle of Jersey in the English Channel. When Nicolls heard what the duke had done, he exploded. In his estimation, this fertile region contained the "most improveable" land in all New York, and to give it away so casually seemed the height of folly.

The duke's impulsive act bred confusion. Soon it was not clear who owned what in New Jersey. Before Nicolls had learned of James's decision, the governor had allowed migrants from New England to take up farms west of the Hudson River. He promised the settlers an opportunity to establish an elected assembly, a headright system, and liberty of conscience. In exchange for these privileges, Nicolls asked only that they pay a small annual quitrent to the duke. The new proprietors, Berkeley and Carteret, recruited colonists on similar terms. They assumed, of course, that they would receive the rent money.

The result was chaos. Some colonists insisted that Nicolls had authorized their assembly. Others, equally insistent, claimed that Berkeley and Carteret had done so. Both sides were wrong. Neither the proprietors nor Nicolls possessed any legal right whatsoever to set up a colonial government. James could transfer land to favorite courtiers, but no matter how many times the land changed hands, the government remained his personal responsibility. Knowledge of the law failed to quiet the controversy. Through it all, the duke showed not the slightest interest in the peace and welfare of the people of New Jersey.

Berkeley grew tired of the venture. It generated headaches rather than income, and in 1674, he sold his proprietary rights to a group of surprisingly quarrelsome Quakers. The sale necessitated the division of the colony into two separate governments known as East and West Jersey. Neither half prospered. Carteret and his heirs tried unsuccessfully to turn a profit in East Jersey. In 1677, the Quaker proprietors of West Jersey issued a remarkable democratic plan of government, the Laws, Concessions, and Agreements. But they fought among themselves with such intensity that not even William Penn could bring tranquility to their affairs. Penn wisely turned his attention to the unclaimed territory across the Delaware River. The West Jersey proprietors went bankrupt, and in 1702, the crown reunited the two Jerseys into a single royal colony.

In 1700, the population of New Jersey stood at approximately fourteen thousand. Largely because it lacked a good deepwater harbor, the colony never developed a commercial center to rival New York City or Philadelphia. Its residents lived on scattered, often isolated farms; villages of more than a few hundred people were rare. Visitors commented on the diversity of the settlers. There were colonists from almost every European nation. Congregationalists, Presbyterians, Quakers, Baptists, Anabaptists, and Anglicans somehow managed to live together peacefully in New Jersey.

QUAKERS IN AMERICA

The founding of Pennsylvania cannot be separated from the history of the Quaker movement. Believers in an extreme form of Antinomianism, the **Quakers** saw no need for a learned ministry, since one person's interpretation of Scripture was as valid as anyone else's. This radical religious sect, a product of the social upheaval in England during the Civil War, gained its name from the derogatory term that English authorities sometimes used to describe those who "tremble at the word of the Lord." The name persisted even though the Quakers preferred being called Professors of the Light or, more commonly, Friends.

Quaker Beliefs and Practice

By the time the Stuarts regained the throne in 1660, the Quakers had developed strong support throughout England. One person responsible for their remarkable success was George Fox (1624–1691), a poor shoemaker whose own spiritual anxieties sparked a powerful new religious message that pushed beyond traditional reformed Protestantism. According to Fox, he experienced despair "so that I had nothing outwardly to help me . . . [but] then, I heard a voice which said, 'There is one, even Christ Jesus, that can speak to thy condition.'" Throughout his life, Fox and his growing number of followers gave testimony to the working of the Holy Spirit. Indeed, they informed ordinary men and women that if only they would look, they too would discover they possessed an "Inner Light." This was a wonderfully liberating invitation, especially for persons of lower-class origin. With the Lord's personal assistance, they could attain greater spiritual perfection on earth. Gone was the stigma of original sin; discarded was the notion of eternal predestination. Everyone could be saved.

Quakers practiced humility in their daily lives. They wore simple clothes and employed old-fashioned forms of address that set them apart from their neighbors. Friends refused to honor worldly position and accomplishment or to swear oaths in courts of law. They were also pacifists. According to Fox, all persons were equal in the sight of the Lord, a belief that generally annoyed people of rank and achievement.

Moreover, the Quakers never kept their thoughts to themselves. They preached conversion constantly, spreading the "Truth" throughout England, Ireland, and America. The Friends played important roles in the early history of New Jersey, Rhode Island, and North Carolina, as well as Pennsylvania. In some places, the "publishers of Truth" wore out their welcome. English authorities harassed the Quakers. Thousands, including Fox himself, were jailed, and in Massachusetts Bay between 1659 and 1661, Puritan magistrates ordered several Friends put to death. Such measures proved counterproductive, for persecution only inspired the martyred Quakers to redouble their efforts.

Penn's "Holy Experiment"

William Penn lived according to the Inner Light, a commitment that led eventually to the founding of Pennsylvania. Penn possessed a curiously complex personality. He was an athletic person who threw himself into intellectual pursuits. He was a bold visionary capable of making pragmatic decisions. He came from an aristocratic family and yet spent his entire adult life involved with a religious movement associated with the lower class.

Penn's father had served with some distinction in the English navy. Through luck and skill, he acquired a considerable estate in Ireland, and as a wealthy landowner, he naturally hoped his son would be a favorite at the Stuart court. He befriended the king, the Duke of York, and several other powerful Restoration figures. But William disappointed his father. He was expelled from Oxford University for holding unorthodox religious views. Not even a grand tour through Europe could dissuade the young man from joining the Society of Friends. His political connections and driving intellect quickly propelled him to a position of prominence within the struggling sect. Penn wrote at least forty-two books testifying to his deep attachment to Quaker principles. Even two years in an English jail could not weaken his faith.

Precisely when Penn's thoughts turned to America is not known. He was briefly involved with the West Jersey proprietorship. This venture may have suggested the possibility of an even larger enterprise. In any case, Penn negotiated in 1681 one of the more impressive

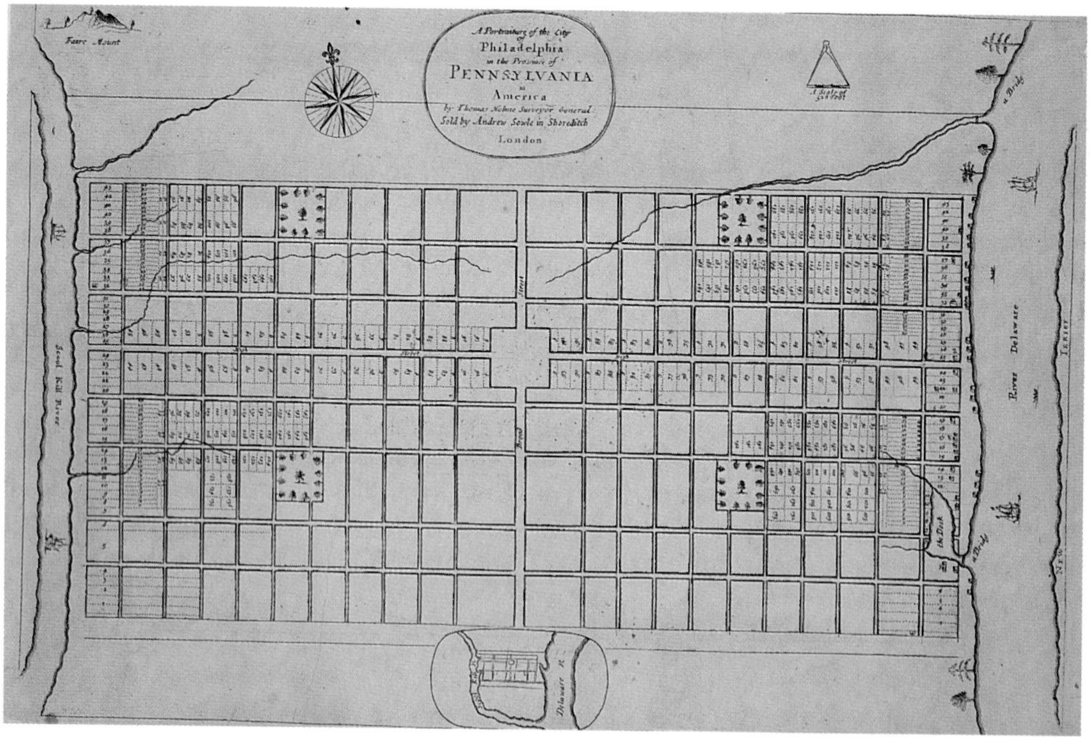

Penn's plan for Philadelphia shows the city laid out where the Scool Kill (Schuylkill) and Delaware rivers parallel each other. Four of the five public squares were intended to be parks while the fifth (at the center) was designated for public buildings. Today, it is the site of Philadelphia's city hall. ❖

land deals in the history of American real estate. Charles II awarded Penn a charter making him the sole proprietor of a vast area called Pennsylvania (literally, "Penn's woods"). The name embarrassed the modest Penn, but he knew better than to look the royal gift horse in the mouth.

Why the king bestowed such generosity on a leading Quaker who had recently been released from prison remains a mystery. Perhaps Charles wanted to repay an old debt to Penn's father. The monarch may have regarded the colony as a means of ridding England of its troublesome Quaker population, or, quite simply, he may have liked Penn. In 1682, the new proprietor purchased from the Duke of York the so-called Three Lower Counties that eventually became Delaware. This astute move guaranteed that Pennsylvania would have access to the Atlantic and determined even before Philadelphia had been established that it would become a commercial center.

Penn lost no time in launching his "Holy Experiment." In 1682, he set forth his ideas in an unusual document known as the Frame of Government. The charter gave Penn the right to create any form of government he desired, and his imagination ran wild. His plan blended traditional notions about the privileges of a landed aristocracy with quite daring concepts of personal liberty. Penn guaranteed that settlers would enjoy among other things liberty of conscience, freedom from persecution, no taxation without representation, and due process of law.

In designing his government, Penn drew heavily on the writings of James Harrington (1611–1677). This English political philosopher argued that no government could ever be stable unless it reflected the actual distribution of landed property within society. Both the rich and poor had to have a voice in political affairs; neither should be able to overrule the legitimate interests of the other class. The Frame of Government envisioned a governor appointed by the proprietor, a 72-member Provincial Council responsible for initiating legislation, and a 200-person Assembly that could accept or reject the bills presented to it. Penn apparently thought the Council would be filled by the colony's richest landholders, or in the words of the Frame, "persons of most note for their wisdom, virtue and ability." The governor and Council were charged with the routine administration of justice. Smaller landowners spoke through the Assembly. It was a clumsy structure, and in America the entire edifice crumbled under its own weight.

Settling Pennsylvania

Penn promoted his colony aggressively throughout England, Ireland, and Germany. He had no choice. His only source of revenue was the sale of land and the collection of quitrents. Penn commissioned pamphlets in several languages extolling the quality of Pennsylvania's rich farmland. The response was overwhelming. People poured into Philadelphia and the surrounding area. In 1685 alone, eight thousand immigrants arrived. Most of the settlers were Irish, Welsh, and English Quakers, and they generally moved to America as families. But Penn opened the door to men and women of all nations. He asserted that the people of Pennsylvania "are a collection of divers nations in Europe, as French, Dutch, Germans, Swedes, Danes, Finns, Scotch, Irish, and English."

The settlers were by no means all Quakers. The founder of Germantown, Francis Daniel Pastorius, called the vessel that brought him to the New World a "Noah's Ark" of religions, and within his own household, there were servants who subscribed "to the Roman [Catholic], to the Lutheran, to the Calvinistic, to the Anabaptist, and to the Anglican church, and only one Quaker." Ethnic and religious diversity were crucial in the development of Pennsylvania's public institutions, and its politics took on a quarrelsome quality absent in more homogeneous colonies such as Virginia and Massachusetts.

Penn himself emigrated to America in 1682. His stay, however, was unexpectedly short and unhappy. The Council and Assembly—reduced now to more manageable size—fought over the right to initiate legislation. Wealthy Quaker merchants, most of them residents of Philadelphia, dominated the Council. By contrast, the Assembly included men from rural settlements and the Three Lower Counties who showed no concern for the Holy Experiment.

Penn did not see his colony again until 1699. During his absence, much had changed. The settlement had prospered. Its agricultural products, especially its excellent wheat, were in demand throughout the Atlantic world. Despite this economic success, however, the population remained deeply divided. Even the Quakers had briefly split into hostile factions. Penn's handpicked governors had failed to win general support for the proprietor's policies, and one of them exclaimed in anger that each Quaker "prays for his neighbor on First Days and then preys on him the other six." As the seventeenth century closed, few colonists still shared the founder's desire to create a godly, paternalistic society.

In 1701, legal challenges in England again forced Penn to depart for the mother country. Just before he sailed, Penn signed the Charter of Liberties, a new frame of government that established a unicameral or one-house legislature (the only one in colonial America) and gave the representatives the right to initiate bills. Penn also allowed the Assembly to conduct its business without proprietary interference. The charter provided for the political separation of the Three Lower Counties (Delaware) from Pennsylvania, something people living in the area had demanded for years. This hastily drafted document served as Pennsylvania's constitution until the American Revolution.

His experience in America must have depressed Penn, now both old and sick. In England, Penn was imprisoned for debts incurred by dishonest colonial agents, and in 1718, Pennsylvania's founder died a broken man.

Planting the Carolinas

In some ways, Carolina society looked much like the one that had developed in Virginia and Maryland. In both areas, white planters forced African slaves to produce staple crops for a world market. But such superficial similarities masked substantial regional differences. In fact, "the South"—certainly the fabled solid South of the early nineteenth century—did not exist during the colonial period. The Carolinas, joined much later by Georgia, stood apart from their northern neighbors. As a historian of colonial Carolina explained, "the southern colonies were never a cohesive section in the same way that New England was. The great diversity of population groups . . . discouraged southern sectionalism."

Proprietors of the Carolinas

Carolina was a product of the Restoration of the Stuarts to the English throne. Court favorites who had followed the Stuarts into exile during the Civil War demanded tangible rewards for their loyalty. New York and New Jersey were obvious plums. So too was Carolina. Sir John Colleton, a successful English planter returned from Barbados, organized a group of eight powerful courtiers who styled themselves the True and Absolute Lords Proprietors of Carolina. On March 24, 1663, the king granted these proprietors a charter to the vast territory between Virginia and Florida and running west as far as the "South Seas."

The failure of similar ventures in the New World taught the Carolina proprietors valuable lessons. Unlike the first Virginians, for example, this group did not expect instant wealth. Rather, the proprietors reasoned that they would obtain a steady source of income from rents. What they needed, of course, were settlers to pay those rents. Recruitment turned out to be no easy task. Economic and social conditions in the mother country improved considerably after its civil war, and English people were no longer so willing to transfer to the New World. Even if they had shown interest, the cost of transporting settlers across the Atlantic seemed prohibitively expensive. The proprietors concluded, therefore, that with the proper incentives—a generous land policy, for example—they could attract men and women from established American colonies and thereby save themselves a great deal of money. Unfortunately for the men who owned Carolina, such people were not easily persuaded. They had begun to take for granted certain rights and privileges, and as the price of settlement, they demanded a representative assembly, liberty of conscience, and a liberal headright system.

The Carolina proprietors divided their grant into three distinct jurisdictions, anticipating no doubt that

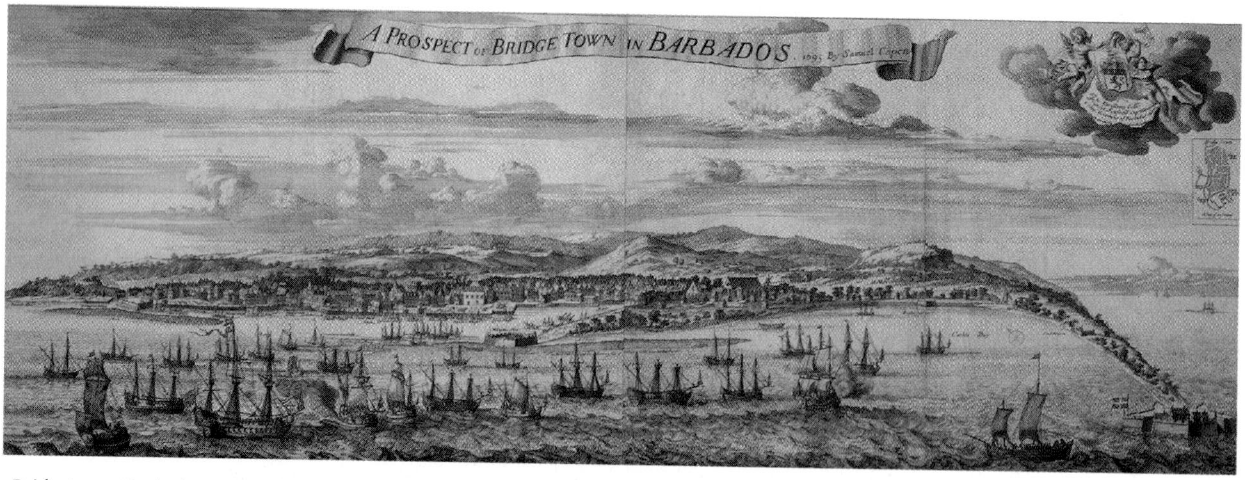

Bridgetown, Barbados, was a thriving Caribbean trading port in the seventeenth century, as depicted in this engraving from 1695. But overcrowding, tropical disease, and a series of natural disasters drove many merchants to emigrate. A popular destination for Barbadians was colonial Carolina, particularly the Port Royal area in present-day South Carolina. ❖

these areas would become the centers of settlement. The first region, called Albemarle, abutted Virginia. As the earlier ill-fated Roanoke colonists had discovered, the region lacked a good deepwater port. Nevertheless, it attracted a number of dissatisfied Virginians who drifted south in search of fresh land. Farther south, the mouth of the Cape Fear River seemed a second likely site for development. And third, within the present state of South Carolina, the Port Royal region contained a maze of fertile islands and meandering tidal streams.

Colleton and his associates waited for the money to roll in, but to their dismay, no one seemed particularly interested in moving to the Carolina frontier. A tiny settlement at Port Royal failed. One group of New Englanders briefly considered taking up land in the Cape Fear area, but these people were so disappointed by what they saw that they departed, leaving behind only a sign that "tended not only to the disparagement of the Land . . . but also to the great discouragement of all those that should hereafter come into these parts to settle." By this time, a majority of surviving proprietors had given up on Carolina.

The Barbadian Connection

Anthony Ashley Cooper, later Earl of Shaftesbury, was the exception. In 1669, he persuaded the remaining Carolinian proprietors to invest their own capital in the colony. Without such financial support, Ashley recognized, the project would surely fail. Once he received sufficient funds, this energetic organizer dispatched three hundred English colonists to Port Royal under the command of Joseph West. The fleet put in briefly at Barbados to pick up additional recruits, and in March 1670, after being punished by Atlantic gales that destroyed one ship, the expedition arrived at its destination. Only one hundred people were still alive. The unhappy settlers did not remain long at Port Royal, an unappealing, low-lying place badly exposed to Spanish attack. They moved northward, locating eventually along the more secure Ashley River. Later the colony's administrative center, Charles Town (it did not become Charleston until 1783) was established at the junction of the Ashley and Cooper rivers.

Ashley also wanted to bring order to the new society. With assistance from John Locke, the famous English philosopher (1632–1704), Ashley devised the Fundamental Constitutions of Carolina. Like Penn, Ashley had been influenced by the writings of Harrington. The constitutions created a local aristocracy consisting of proprietors and lesser nobles called *landgraves* and *cassiques,* terms as inappropriate to the realities of the New World as was the idea of creating a hereditary landed elite. Persons who purchased vast tracts of land automatically received a title and the right to sit in the Council of Nobles, a body designed to administer justice, oversee civil affairs, and initiate legislation. A parliament in which smaller landowners had a voice could accept or reject bills drafted by the council. The very poor were excluded from political life altogether. Ashley thought his scheme maintained the proper "Balance of Government" between aristocracy and democracy, a concept central to Harrington's philosophy. Not surprisingly, the constitutions had little impact on the actual structure of government.

Before 1680, almost half the men and women who settled in the Port Royal area came from Barbados. This small Caribbean island, which produced an annual fortune in sugar, depended on slave labor. By the third quarter of the seventeenth century, Barbados had become overpopulated. Wealthy families could not provide their sons and daughters with sufficient land to maintain social status, and as the crisis intensified, Barbadians looked to Carolina for relief.

These migrants, many of whom were quite rich, traveled to Carolina both as individuals and family groups. Some even brought gangs of slaves with them to the American mainland. The Barbadians carved out plantations on the tributaries of the Cooper River and established themselves immediately as the colony's most powerful political faction. "So it was," wrote historian Richard Dunn, "that these Caribbean pioneers helped to create on the North American coast a slave-based plantation society closer in temper to the islands they fled from than to any other mainland English settlement."

Much of the planters' time was taken up with the search for a profitable crop. The early settlers experimented with a number of plants: tobacco, cotton, silk, and grapes. The most successful items turned out to be beef, skins, and naval stores (especially tar used to maintain ocean vessels). By the 1680s, some Carolinians had built up great herds of cattle—seven or eight hundred head in some cases. Traders who dealt with Indians brought back thousands of deerskins from the interior, and they often returned with Indian slaves as well. These commercial resources together with tar and turpentine enjoyed a good market. It was not until the 1690s that the planters came to appreciate fully the value of rice, but once they had done so, it quickly became the colony's main staple.

Proprietary Carolina was in a constant political uproar. Factions vied for special privilege. The Barbadian settlers, known locally as the Goose Creek Men, resisted the proprietors' policies at every turn. A large community of French Huguenots located in Craven County distrusted the Barbadians. The proprietors—an ineffectual group following the death of Shaftesbury—appointed a series of utterly incompetent governors who only made things worse. One visitor observed that "the Inhabitants of Carolina should be as free from Oppression as any [people] in the Universe . . . if their own Differences amongst themselves do not occasion the contrary." By the end of the century, the Commons House of Assembly had assumed the right to initiate legislation. In 1719, the colonists overthrew the last proprietary governor, and in 1729, the king created separate royal governments for North and South Carolina.

The Founding of Georgia

The early history of Georgia was strikingly different from that of Britain's other mainland colonies. Its settlement was really an act of aggression against Spain, a country that had as good a claim to this area as did the English. During the eighteenth century, the two nations were often at war (see Chapter 4), and South Carolinians worried that the Spaniards moving up from bases in Florida would occupy the disputed territory between Florida and the Carolina grant.

The colony owed its existence primarily to James Oglethorpe, a British general and member of Parliament who believed that he could thwart Spanish designs on the area south of Charles Town while at the same time providing a fresh start for London's worthy poor, saving them from debtors' prison. Although Oglethorpe envisioned Georgia as an

England's Principal Mainland Colonies

Name	Original Purpose	Date of Founding	Principal Founder	Major Export	Estimated Population ca. 1700
Virginia	Commercial venture	1607	Captain John Smith	Tobacco	64,560
New Amsterdam (New York)	Commercial venture	1613 (made English colony, 1664)	Peter Stuyvesant, Duke of York	Furs, grain	19,107
Plymouth	Refuge for English Separatists	1620 (absorbed by Massachusetts, 1691)	William Bradford	Grain	Included with Massachusetts
New Hampshire	Commercial venture	1623	John Mason	Wood, naval stores	4,958
Massachusetts	Refuge for English Puritans	1628	John Winthrop	Grain, wood	55,941
Maryland	Refuge for English Catholics	1634	Lord Baltimore (George Calvert)	Tobacco	34,100
Connecticut	Expansion of Massachusetts	1635	Thomas Hooker	Grain	25,970
Rhode Island	Refuge for dissenters from Massachusetts	1636	Roger Williams	Grain	5,894
New Sweden (Delaware)	Commercial venture	1638 (included in Penn grant, 1681; given separate assembly, 1703)	Peter Minuit, William Penn	Grain	2,470
North Carolina	Commercial venture	1663	Anthony Ashley Cooper	Wood, naval stores, tobacco	10,720
South Carolina	Commercial venture	1663	Anthony Ashley Cooper	Naval stores, rice, indigo	5,720
New Jersey	Consolidation of new English territory, Quaker settlement	1664	Sir George Carteret	Grain	14,010
Pennsylvania	Refuge for English Quakers	1681	William Penn	Grain	18,950
Georgia	Discourage Spanish expansion; charity	1733	James Oglethorpe	Rice, wood, naval stores	5,200 (in 1750)

Sources: U.S. Bureau of the Census, *Historical Statistics of the United States: Colonial Times to 1970,* Washington, D.C., 1975; John J. McCusker and Russell R. Menard, *The Economy of British America, 1607–1789,* Chapel Hill, 1985.

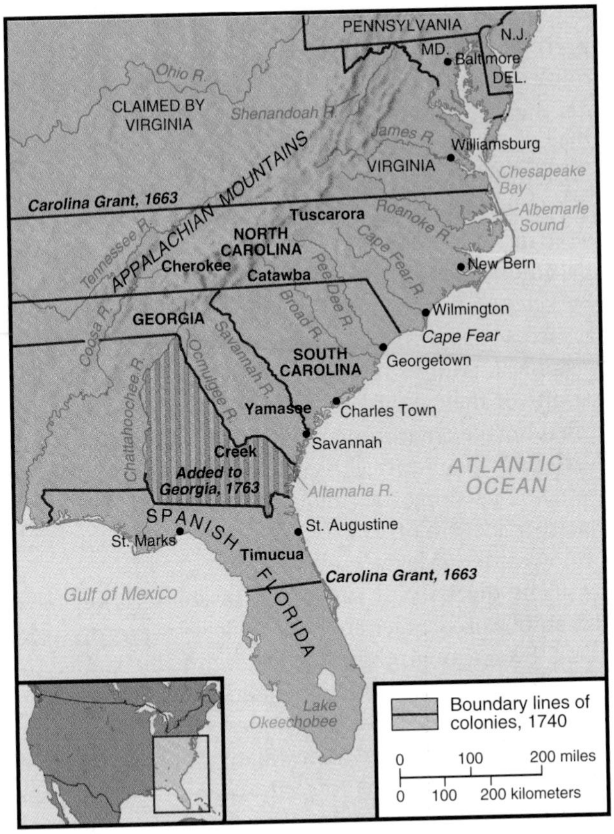

THE CAROLINAS AND GEORGIA *Caribbean sugar planters migrated to the Goose Creek area where, with knowledge supplied by African slaves, they eventually mastered rice cultivation. Poor harbors in North Carolina retarded the spread of European settlement in that region.* ✧

asylum as well as a garrison, the military aspects of his proposal were especially appealing to the leaders of the British government. In 1732, the king granted Oglethorpe and a board of trustees a charter for a new colony to be located between the Savannah and Altamaha rivers and from "sea to sea." The trustees living in the mother country were given complete control over Georgia politics, a condition the settlers soon found intolerable.

During the first years of colonization, Georgia fared no better than had earlier utopian experiments. The poor people of England showed little desire to move to an inclement frontier, and the trustees, in their turn, provided little incentive for emigration. Each colonist received only 50 acres. Another 50 acres could be added for each servant transported to Georgia, but in no case could a settler amass more than 500 acres. Moreover, land could be passed only to an eldest son, and if a planter had no sons at the time of his death, the holding reverted to the trustees. Slavery was prohibited. So too was rum.

Almost as soon as they arrived in Georgia, the settlers complained. The colonists demanded slaves, pointing out to the trustees that unless the new planters possessed an unfree labor force, they could not compete economically with their South Carolina neighbors. The settlers also wanted a voice in local government. In 1738, 121 people living in Savannah petitioned for fundamental reforms in the colony's constitution. Oglethorpe responded angrily, "The idle ones are indeed for Negroes. If the petition is countenanced, the province is ruined." The settlers did not

CHRONOLOGY

1607	First English settlers arrive at Jamestown
1608–1609	Scrooby congregation (Pilgrims) leaves England for Holland
1609–1611	"Starving time" in Virginia threatens survival of the colonists
1616–1618	Plague destroys Native American populations of coastal New England
1619	Virginia assembly, called House of Burgesses, meets for the first time ✧ First slaves sold at Jamestown
1620	Pilgrims sign the Mayflower Compact
1622	Surprise Indian attack devastates Virginia
1624	Dutch investors create permanent settlements along Hudson River ✧ James I, king of England, dissolves Virginia Company
1625	Charles I ascends English throne
1630	John Winthrop transfers Massachusetts Bay charter to New England
1634	Colony of Maryland is founded
1636	Harvard College is established ✧ Puritan settlers found Hartford and other Connecticut Valley towns
1638	Anne Hutchinson exiled to Rhode Island ✧ Theophilus Eaton and John Davenport lead settlers to New Haven Colony
1639	Connecticut towns accept Fundamental Orders
1644	Second major Indian attack in Virginia
1649	Charles I executed during English Civil War
1660	Stuarts restored to the English throne
1663	Rhode Island obtains royal charter ✧ Proprietors receive charter for Carolina
1664	English soldiers conquer New Netherland
1677	New Hampshire becomes a royal colony
1681	William Penn granted patent for his "Holy Experiment"
1702	East and West Jersey unite to form single colony
1732	James Oglethorpe receives charter for Georgia

give up. In 1741, they again petitioned Oglethorpe, this time addressing him as "our Perpetual Dictator."

While the colonists grumbled about various restrictions, Oglethorpe tried and failed to capture the Spanish fortress at Saint Augustine (1740). This personal disappointment coupled with the growing popular unrest destroyed his interest in Georgia. The trustees were forced to compromise their principles. In 1738, they eliminated all restrictions on the amount of land a man could own; they allowed women to inherit land. In 1750, they permitted the settlers to import slaves. Soon Georgians could drink rum. In 1751, the trustees returned Georgia to the king, undoubtedly relieved to be free of what had become a hard-drinking, slave-owning plantation society much like that in South Carolina. The king authorized an assembly in 1751, but even with these social and political changes, Georgia attracted very few new settlers.

Conclusion: Living with Diversity

Long after he had returned from his adventures in Virginia, Captain John Smith reflected on the difficulty of establishing colonies in the New World. It was a task for which most people were not temperamentally suited. "It requires," Smith counseled, "all the best parts of art, judgment, courage, honesty, constancy, diligence, and industry, [even] to do neere well." On another occasion, Charles I warned Lord Baltimore that new settlements "commonly have rugged and laborious beginnings."

Over the course of the seventeenth century, women and men had followed leaders such as Baltimore, Smith, Winthrop, Bradford, Penn, and Berkeley to the New World in anticipation of creating a successful new society. Some people were religious visionaries; others were hardheaded businessmen. The results of their efforts, their struggles to survive in an often hostile environment, and their interactions with various Native American groups yielded a spectrum of settlements along the Atlantic coast, ranging from the quasi-feudalism of South Carolina to the Puritan commonwealth of Massachusetts Bay.

The diversity of early English colonization must be emphasized precisely because it is so easy to overlook. Even though the colonists eventually banded together and fought for independence, persistent differences separated New Englanders from Virginians, Pennsylvanians from Carolinians. The interpretive challenge, of course, is to comprehend how European colonists managed over the course of the eighteenth century to overcome fragmentation and to develop the capacity to imagine themselves a nation.

Recommended Reading

The literature of seventeenth-century English settlement in North America is immense. To comprehend better the diversity of American colonial experience, it is wise to start with the society from which the settlers migrated. Two good introductions to England's participation in an Atlantic World are David Armitage and Michael J. Braddick, eds., *The British Atlantic World, 1500–1800* (2002) and Nicholas Canny, ed., *The Oxford History of the British Empire, vol. 1, The Origins of Empire: English Overseas Enterprise from the Beginning to the Close of the Seventeenth Century* (1998). The best single work on Puritanism remains Perry Miller, *The New England Mind: From Colony to Province* (1956). David D. Hall explores popular religious practice in New England in *Worlds of Wonder, Days of Judgment: Popular Religious Belief in Early New England* (1989). Also valuable is Michael P. Winship, *Making Heretics: Militant Protestantism and Free Grace in Massachusetts, 1636–1641* (2002). On the challenge of creating new social and political institutions in early Massachusetts, see Kenneth A. Lockridge, *A New England Town: The First Hundred Years* (1970). Two brilliantly original studies of the founding of Virginia are Edmund S. Morgan, *American Slavery, American Freedom: The Ordeal of Colonial Virginia* (1975) and Kathleen M. Brown, *Good Wives, Nasty Wenches, and Anxious Patriarchs: Gender, Race, and Power in Colonial Virginia* (1996). T. H. Breen compares the development of seventeenth-century New England and the Chesapeake in *Puritans and Adventurers: Change and Persistence in Early America* (1980). The forces that drove migration to the New World during this period are the subject of David Cressy's *Coming Over: Migration and Communication Between England and New England in the Seventeenth Century* (1987) and James Horn's, *Adapting to a New World: English Society in the Seventeenth-Century Chesapeake* (1994). On the rituals of public execution, see Daniel A. Cohen, *Pillars of Salt, Monuments of Grace: New England Crime Literature and the Origins of American Popular Culture, 1674–1860* (1993). Useful investigations of the founding of New York and Pennsylvania are Gary B. Nash, *Quakers and Politics: Pennsylvania 1681–1726* (1968); Richard S. Dunn and Mary Maples Dunn, eds., *The World of William Penn* (1986); and Joyce D. Goodfriend, *Before the Melting Pot: Society and Culture in Colonial New York City, 1664–1730* (1995).

For a list of additional titles related to this chapter's topics, please see http://www.ablongman.com/divine.

Suggested Web Sites

The Plymouth Colony Archive Project at the University of Virginia

http://etext.virginia.edu/users/deetz

This site contains comprehensive and fairly extensive information about late seventeenth-century Plymouth Colony.

Jamestown Rediscovery

http://www.apva.org

This site mounted by the Association for the Preservation of Virginia Antiquity has excellent material on archaeological excavations at Jamestown.

Georgia Before Oglethorpe

http://www.spanishflorida.net/gboindex.htm

This resources guide informs about Native American Georgia in the seventeenth century.

William Penn, Visionary Proprietor

http://xroads.virginia.edu/~CAP/PENN/pnhome.html

William Penn had an interesting life, and this site is a good introduction to the man and some of his achievements.

LVA Colonial Records Project—Index of digital facsimiles of documents on early Virginia.

http://eagle.vsla.edu/colonial/

This site contains numerous early documents, but it is unguided and a little difficult to use.

Chapter 3

The Mason Children: David, Joanna, and Abigail, *c.1670, an early portrait of three children from a wealthy Massachusetts Bay Colony family. The artist lavished attention on the details of the children's clothing and the objects they hold, marks of their social status and prosperity.* ❖

Putting Down Roots: Opportunity and Oppression in Colonial Society

Families in an Atlantic Empire

The Witherspoon family moved from Great Britain to the South Carolina backcountry early in the eighteenth century. Although otherwise indistinguishable from the thousands of other ordinary families that put down roots in English America, the Witherspoons were made historical figures by the candid account of pioneer life produced by their son, Robert, who was only a small child at the time of their arrival.

The Witherspoons' initial reaction to the New World—at least, that of the mother and children—was utter despondence. "My mother and us children were still in expectation that we were coming to an agreeable place," Robert confessed, "but when we arrived and saw nothing but a wilderness and instead of a fine timbered house, nothing but a very mean dirt house, our spirits quite sunk." For many years, the Witherspoons feared they would be killed by Indians, become lost in the woods, or be bitten by snakes.

The Witherspoons managed to survive the early difficult years on the Black River. To be sure, the Carolina backcountry did not look very much like the world they had left behind. The discrepancy, however, apparently did not greatly discourage Robert's father. He had a vision of what the Black River settlement might become. "My father," Robert recounted, "gave us all the comfort he [could] by telling us we would get all these trees cut down and in a short time [there] would be plenty of inhabitants, [and] that we could see from house to house."

ROBERT WITHERSPOON'S ACCOUNT REMINDS US just how much the early history of colonial America was an intimate story of families, and not, as some commentators would have us believe, of individuals. Neither the peopling of the Atlantic frontier, the cutting down of the forests, nor the creation of new communities where one could see from "house to house" was a process that involved what we would today recognize as state policy. Men and women made significant decisions about the character of their lives within families. It was within this primary social unit that most colonists earned their livelihoods, educated their children, defined gender, sustained religious tradition, and nursed each other in sickness. In short, the family was the source of their societal and cultural identities.

Early colonial families did not exist in isolation. They were part of larger societies. As we have already discovered, the character of the first English settlements in the New World varied substantially (see Chapter 2). During much of the seventeenth century, these initial differences grew stronger as each region responded to different environmental conditions and developed its own traditions. The various local societies in

OUTLINE

FEATURE ESSAY

LAW AND SOCIETY

which families like the Witherspoons put down roots reflected several critical elements: supply of labor, abundance of land, unusual demographic patterns, and commercial ties with European markets. In the Chesapeake, for example, an economy based almost entirely on a single staple—tobacco—created an insatiable demand for indentured servants and black slaves. In Massachusetts Bay, the extraordinary longevity of the founders generated a level of social and political stability that Virginians and Marylanders did not attain until the very end of the seventeenth century.

By 1660, it seemed regional differences had undermined the idea of a unified English empire in America. During the reign of Charles II, however, a trend toward cultural convergence began. Although subcultures had evolved in strikingly different directions, countervailing forces such as common language and religion gradually pulled English American settlers together. Parliament took advantage of this trend and began to establish a uniform set of rules for the expanding American empire. The process was slow and uneven, often sparking violent colonial resistance. By the end of the seventeenth century, however, England had made significant progress toward transforming New World provinces into an empire that produced needed raw materials and purchased manufactured goods. If a person was black and enslaved, however, he or she was more apt to experience oppression rather than opportunity in British America.

Sources of Stability: New England Colonies of the Seventeenth Century

Seventeenth-century New Englanders successfully replicated in America a traditional social order they had known in England. The transfer of a familiar way of life to the New World seemed less difficult for these Puritan migrants than it did for the many English men and women who settled in the Chesapeake colonies. Their contrasting experiences, fundamental to an understanding of the development of both cultures, can be explained, at least in part, by the extraordinary strength and resilience of New England families.

Immigrant Families and New Social Order

Early New Englanders believed God ordained the family for human benefit. It was essential to the maintenance of social order, since outside the family, men and women succumbed to carnal temptation. Such people had no one to sustain them or remind them of Scripture. "Without Family care," declared the Reverend Benjamin Wadsworth, "the labour of Magistrates and Ministers for Reformation and Propagating Religion, is likely to be in great measure unsuccessful."

The godly family, at least in theory, was ruled by a patriarch, father to his children, husband to his wife, the source of authority and object of unquestioned obedience. The wife shared responsibility for the raising of children, but in decisions of importance, especially those related to property, she was expected to defer to her spouse.

The New Englanders' concern about the character of the godly family is not surprising. This institution played a central role in shaping their society. In contrast to those who migrated to the colonies of Virginia and Maryland, New Englanders crossed the Atlantic within nuclear families. That is, they moved within established units consisting of a father, mother, and their dependent children rather than as single youths and adults. People who migrated to America within families preserved local English customs more fully than did the youths who traveled to other parts of the continent as single men and women. The comforting presence of immediate family members reduced the shock of adjusting to a strange environment three thousand miles from home. Even in the 1630s, the ratio of men to women in New England was fairly well balanced, about three males for every two females. Persons who had not already married in England before coming to the New World could expect to form nuclear families of their own.

The great migration of the 1630s and early 1640s brought approximately 20,000 persons to New England. After 1642, the English Civil War reduced the flood of people moving to Massachusetts Bay to a trickle. Nevertheless, by the end of the century, the population of New England had reached almost 120,000, an amazing increase considering the small number of original immigrants. Historians have been hard pressed to explain this striking rate of growth. Some have suggested that New Englanders married very young, thus giving couples extra years in which to produce large families. Other scholars have maintained that New England women must have been more fertile than their Old World counterparts.

Neither demographic theory adequately explains how so few migrants produced such a large population so rapidly. Early New England marriage patterns, for example, did not differ substantially from those recorded in seventeenth-century England. The average age for men at first marriage was the mid-twenties.

Wives were slightly younger than their husbands, the average age being about 22. There is no evidence that New Englanders favored child brides. Nor, for that matter, were Puritan families unusually large by European standards of the period.

The explanation for the region's impressive growth turned out to be survival rather than fertility. Put simply, people who, under normal conditions, would have died in contemporary Europe lived in New England. Indeed, the life expectancy of seventeenth-century settlers was not very different from our own. Males who survived infancy might have expected to see their seventieth birthday. Twenty percent of the men of the first generation reached the age of eighty. The figures for women were only slightly lower. Why the early settlers lived so long is not entirely clear. No doubt, pure drinking water, a cool climate that retarded the spread of fatal contagious disease, and a dispersed population promoted general good health.

Longer life altered family relations. New England males lived not only to see their own children reach adulthood but also to witness the birth of grandchildren. One historian, John Murrin, has suggested that New Englanders "invented" grandparents. In other words, this society produced real patriarchs, males of recognized seniority and standing. This may have been one of the first societies in recorded history in which a person could reasonably anticipate knowing his or her grandchildren, a demographic surprise that contributed to social stability. The traditions of particular families and communities literally remained alive in the memories of the colony's oldest citizens.

Commonwealth of Families

The life cycle of the seventeenth-century New England family began with marriage. Young men and women generally initiated courtships. If parents exercised a voice in such matters, it was to discourage union with a person of unsound moral character. Puritan ministers advised single people to choose godly partners, warning:

> The Wretch that is alone to Mannon Wed,
> May chance to find a Satan in the bed.

In this highly religious society, there was not much chance that young people would stray far from shared community values. The overwhelming majority of the region's population married, for in New England, the single life was not only morally suspect but also physically difficult.

A couple without land could not support an independent and growing family in these agrarian communities. While men generally brought farmland to the marriage, prospective brides were expected to provide a dowry worth approximately one-half what the bridegroom offered. Women often contributed money or household goods.

African Americans often appeared in the formal portraits of elite white families. This eighteenth-century overmantle (oil on wood) depicts the Potter family of Rhode Island with a black child. In the northern colonies, most slaves worked as house and body servants. ❖

T Time cuts down all
Both great and small.

U Uriah's beauteous Wife
Made David seek his
Life.

W Whales in the Sea
God's Voice obey.

X Xerxes the great did
die,
And so must you & I.

Y Youth forward slips
Death soonest nips.

Z Zacheus he
Did climb the Tree
His Lord to see.

Now the Child being entred in his Letters and Spelling, let him learn these and such like Sentences by Heart, whereby he will be both instructed in his Duty, and encouraged in his Learning.

The Dutiful Child's Promises,

I Will fear GOD, and honour the KING.
I will honour my Father & Mother.
I will Obey my Superiours.
I will Submit to my Elders.
I will Love my Friends.
I will hate no Man.
I will forgive my Enemies, and pray to God for them.
I will as much as in me lies keep all God's Holy Commandments.

New England parents took seriously their responsibility for the spiritual welfare of their children. To seek the word of God, young people had to learn to read. The New-England Primer, *shown here, was their primary vehicle.* ❖

The household was primarily a place of work—very demanding work. The primary goal, of course, was to clear enough land to feed the family. Additional cultivation allowed the farmer to produce a surplus that could then be sold or bartered, and since agrarian families required items that could not be manufactured at home—metal tools, for example—they usually grew more than they consumed. Early American farmers were not economically self-sufficient; the belief that they were is a popular misconception.

During the seventeenth century, men and women generally lived in the communities of their parents and grandparents. New Englanders usually managed to fall in love with a neighbor, and most marriages took place between men and women living less than 13 miles apart. Moving to a more fertile region might have increased their earnings, but such thoughts seldom occurred to early New Englanders. Religious values, a sense of common purpose, and the importance of family reinforced traditional communal ties.

Towns, in fact, were collections of families, not individuals. Over time, these families intermarried, so the community became an elaborate kinship network. Social historians have discovered that in many New England towns, the original founders dominated local politics and economic affairs for several generations. Not surprisingly, newcomers who were not absorbed into the family system tended to move away from the village with greater frequency than did the sons and daughters of the established lineage groups.

Congregational churches were also built on a family foundation. During the earliest years of settlement, the churches accepted persons who could demonstrate they were among God's "elect." Members were drawn from a broad social spectrum. Once the excitement of establishing a new society had passed, however, New Englanders began to focus more attention on the spiritual welfare of their own families. This quite normal parental concern precipitated a major ecclesiastical crisis. The problem was the status of the children within a gathered church. Sons and daughters of full church members regularly received baptism, usually as infants, but as these people grew to adulthood, they often failed to provide testimony of their own "election." Moreover, they wanted their own children to be baptized. A church synod—a gathering of Congregational ministers—responded to this generational crisis by adopting the so-called Half-Way Covenant (1662). The compromise allowed the grandchildren of persons in full communion to be baptized even though their parents could not demonstrate conversion. Congregational ministers assumed that "God cast the line of election in the loins of godly parents." Because of the New Englanders' growing obsession with family—termed *tribalism* by some historians—the Congregational churches by the end of the seventeenth century were increasingly turning inward, addressing the spiritual needs of particular lineage groups rather than reaching out to the larger Christian community.

Colonists regarded education as primarily a family responsibility. Parents were supposed to instruct children in the principles of Christianity, and so it was necessary to teach boys and girls how to read. In 1642, the Massachusetts General Court reminded the Bay Colonists of their obligation to catechize their families. Five years later, the legislature ordered towns containing at least fifteen families to open an elementary school supported by local taxes. Villages of a hundred or more families had to maintain more advanced grammar schools, which taught a basic knowledge of Latin. At least eleven schools were operating in 1647, and despite their expense, new schools were established throughout the century.

This family-based education system worked. A large majority of the region's adult males could read and write, an accomplishment not achieved in the Chesapeake colonies for another century. The literacy rate for women was somewhat lower, but by the standards of the period, it was still impressive. A printing press operated in Cambridge as early as 1639. *The New-England Primer,* first published in 1690 in Boston by Benjamin Harris, taught children the alphabet as well as the Lord's Prayer. This primer announced:

> He who ne'er learns his ABC,
> forever will a blockhead be.
> But he who to his book's inclined,
> will soon a golden treasure find.

The best-seller of seventeenth-century New England was Rev. Michael Wigglesworth's *The Day of Doom* (1662), a poem of 224 stanzas describing in terrifying detail the fate of sinners on Judgment Day. In words that even young readers could comprehend, Wigglesworth wrote of these unfortunate souls:

> They cry, no, no: Alas! and wo!
> Our Courage all is gone:
> Our hardiness (fool hardiness)
> Hath us undone, undone.

Many New Englanders memorized the entire poem.

After 1638, young men could attend Harvard College, the first institution of higher learning founded in England's mainland colonies. The school was originally intended to train ministers, and of the 465 students who graduated during the seventeenth century, more than half became Congregational divines. Harvard had a demanding curriculum. The boys read logic, rhetoric, divinity, and several ancient languages, including Hebrew. Yale College followed Harvard's lead, admitting its first students in 1702.

Women's Lives in Puritan New England

The role of women in the agrarian societies north of the Chesapeake is a controversial subject among colonial historians. Some scholars point out that common law as well as English custom treated women as inferior to men. Other historians, however, depict the colonial period as a "golden age" for women. According to this interpretation, wives worked alongside their husbands. They were not divorced from meaningful, productive labor. They certainly were not transformed into the frail, dependent beings allegedly much admired by middle-class males of the nineteenth century. Both views provide insights into the lives of early American women, but neither fully recaptures their community experiences.

To be sure, women worked on family farms. They did not, however, necessarily do the same jobs that men performed. Women usually handled separate tasks, including cooking, washing, clothes making, dairying, and gardening. Their production of food was absolutely essential to the survival of most households. Sometimes wives—and the overwhelming majority of adult seventeenth-century women were married—raised poultry, and by selling surplus birds they achieved some economic independence. When people in one New England community chided a man for allowing his wife to peddle her fowl, he responded, "I meddle not with the geese nor turkeys for they are hers." In fact, during this period women were often described as "deputy husbands," a label that drew attention to their dependence on family patriarchs as well as to their roles as decision makers.

Women also joined churches in greater number than men. Within a few years of founding, many New England congregations contained two female members for every male, a process historians describe as the "feminization of colonial religion." Contemporaries offered different explanations for the gender shift. Cotton Mather, the leading Congregational minister of Massachusetts Bay, argued that God had created "far more *godly Women*" than men. Others thought that the life-threatening experience of childbirth gave women a deeper appreciation of religion. The Quakers gave women an even larger role in religious affairs, which may help to explain the popularity of this sect among ordinary women.

In political and legal matters, society sharply curtailed the rights of colonial women. According to English common law, a wife exercised no control over property. She could not, for example, sell land, although if her husband decided to dispose of their holdings, he was free to do so without her permission. Divorce was extremely difficult to obtain in any colony before the American Revolution. Indeed, a person married to a cruel or irresponsible spouse had little recourse but to run away or accept the unhappy situation.

Yet most women were neither prosperous entrepreneurs nor abject slaves. Surviving letters indicate that men and women generally accommodated themselves to the gender roles they thought God had ordained. One of early America's most creative poets, Anne Bradstreet, wrote movingly of the fulfillment she had found with her husband. In a piece titled "To my Dear and loving Husband," Bradstreet declared:

> If ever two were one, then surely we.
> If ever man were lov'd by wife, then thee;
> If ever wife was happy in a man,
> Compare with me ye women if you can.

Although Puritan couples worried that the affection they felt for a husband or a wife might turn their thoughts away from God's perfect love, this was a danger they were willing to risk.

Social Hierarchy in New England

During the seventeenth century, the New England colonies attracted neither noblemen nor paupers. The absence of these social groups meant that the American social structure seemed incomplete by contemporary European standards. The settlers were not displeased that the poor remained in the Old World. The lack of very rich persons—and in this period great wealth frequently accompanied noble title—was quite another matter. According to the prevailing hierarchical view of the structure of society, well-placed individuals were natural rulers, people intended by God to exercise political authority over the rank and file. Migration forced the colonists, however, to choose their rulers from men of more modest status. One minister told a Plymouth congregation that since its members were "not furnished with any persons of *special eminency above the rest,* to be chosen by you into office of government," they would have to make due with neighbors, "not beholding in them the *ordinariness of their persons.*"

The colonists gradually sorted themselves out into distinct social groupings. Persons who would never have been "natural rulers" in England became provincial gentry in the various northern colonies. It helped, of course, if an individual possessed wealth and education, but these attributes alone could not guarantee a newcomer would be accepted into the local ruling elite, at least not during the early decades of settlement. In Massachusetts and Connecticut, Puritan voters expected their leaders to join Congregational churches and defend orthodox religion.

The Winthrops, Dudleys, and Pynchons—just to cite a few of the more prominent families—fulfilled these expectations, and in public affairs they assumed

❖ A Look at the Past ❖

Freake Portraits

Bright colors, lace, embroidery, and other lavish details on the clothing John and Elizabeth Freake wore for their portraits, painted by an anonymous artist in the 1670s, refute the notion that Puritans wore only somber clothes. The Freakes's attire also reveals attitudes about children and gender roles. Elizabeth is holding her son, dressed in a gown as both male and female babies were at the time. Note how similar their gowns are; her son's is nearly a miniature version of Elizabeth's. If babies wore miniaturized adult clothing, what does that suggest about the lives of children? Was childhood a distinctive developmental stage to be relished? Why are we surprised by the splendor of the Freake's dress?

dominant roles. They took their responsibilities quite seriously and certainly did not look kindly on anyone who spoke of their "ordinariness." A colonist who jokingly called a Puritan magistrate a "just ass" found himself in deep trouble with civil authorities.

The problem was that while most New Englanders accepted a hierarchical view of society, they disagreed over their assigned places. Both Massachusetts Bay and Connecticut passed sumptuary laws—statutes that limited the wearing of fine apparel to the wealthy and prominent—to curb the pretensions of those of lower status. Yet such restraints could not prevent some people from rising and others from falling within the social order.

Governor John Winthrop provided a marvelous description of the unplanned social mobility that occurred in early New England. During the 1640s, he recorded in his diary the story of a master who could not afford to pay a servant's wages. To meet this obligation, the master sold a pair of oxen, but the transaction barely covered the cost of keeping the servant. In desperation, the master asked the employee, a man of lower social status, "How shall I do . . . when all my cattle are gone?" The servant replied, "You shall then serve me, so you may have your cattle again." In the margin of his diary next to this account, Winthrop scribbled "insolent."

Most northern colonists were yeomen (independent farmers) who worked their own land. While few became rich in America, even fewer fell hopelessly into debt. Their daily lives, especially for those who settled New England, centered on scattered little communities where they participated in village meetings, church-related matters, and militia training. Possession of land gave agrarian families a sense of independence from external authority. As one man bragged to those who had stayed behind in England, "Here are no hard landlords to rack us with high rents or extorting fines. . . . Here every man may be master of his own labour and land . . . and if he have nothing but his hands he may set up his trade, and by industry grow rich."

❖ A Look at the Past ❖

Gravestones

Seventeenth-century Puritan carvers transformed the production of gravestones into a distinctive folk art form. Each symbolic element in the design has a spiritual significance. Examine closely the two early New England headstones shown here, noting the details of the carvings as well as the dates. What elements do they have in common? What differences do you see? What do the ornate sculpture and the images on these gravestones suggest about Puritans' attitudes toward death? Do the differences in the two stones suggest any shift in attitudes toward death?

During the seventeenth century, this independence was balanced by an equally strong feeling of local identity. Not until the late eighteenth century, when many New Englanders left their familial villages in search of new land, did many northern yeomen place personal material ambition above traditional community bonds.

It was not unusual for northern colonists to work as servants at some point in their lives. This system of labor differed greatly from the pattern of servitude that developed in seventeenth-century Virginia and Maryland. New Englanders seldom recruited servants from the Old World. The forms of agriculture practiced in this region, mixed cereal and dairy farming, made employment of large gangs of dependent workers uneconomic. Rather, New England families placed their adolescent children in nearby homes. These young persons contracted for four or five years and seemed more like apprentices than servants. Servitude was not simply a means by which one group exploited another. It was a form of vocational training program in which the children of the rich as well as the poor participated.

By the end of the seventeenth century, the New England Puritans had developed a compelling story about their own history in the New World. The founders had been extraordinarily godly men and women, and in a heroic effort to establish a purer form of religion, pious families had passed "over the vast ocean into this vast and howling wilderness." Although the children and grandchildren of the first generation sometimes questioned their own ability to please the Lord, they recognized the mission to the New World had been a success: they were "as Prosperous as ever, there is Peace & Plenty, & the Country flourisheth."

The Challenge of the Chesapeake Environment

An entirely different regional society developed in England's Chesapeake colonies, Virginia and Maryland. This contrast with New England seems puzzling. After all, the two areas were founded at roughly the same time by men and women from the same mother country. In both regions, settlers spoke English, accepted Protestantism, and gave allegiance to one crown. And yet, to cite an obvious example, seventeenth-century Virginia looked nothing like Massachusetts Bay. In an effort to explain the difference, colonial historians have studied environmental conditions, labor systems, and agrarian economies. The most important reason for the distinctiveness of these early southern plantation societies, however, turned out to be the Chesapeake's death rate, a frighteningly high mortality that tore at the very fabric of traditional family life.

Family Life at Risk

Unlike New England's settlers, the men and women who emigrated to the Chesapeake region did not move in family units. They traveled to the New World as young unmarried servants, youths cut off from the security of traditional kin relations. Although these immigrants came from a cross section of English society, most had been poor to middling farmers. It is now estimated that 70 to 85 percent of the white colonists who went to Virginia and Maryland during the seventeenth century were not free; that is, they owed four or five years' labor in exchange for the cost of passage to America. If the servant was under age 15, he or she had to serve a full seven years. The overwhelming majority of these laborers were males between the ages of 18 and 22. In fact, before 1640, the ratio of males to females stood at 6 to 1. This figure dropped to about 2½ to 1 by the end of the century, but the sex ratio in the Chesapeake was never as favorable as it had been in early Massachusetts.

Most immigrants to the Chesapeake region died soon after arriving. It is difficult to ascertain the exact cause of death in most cases, but malaria and other diseases took a frightful toll. Recent studies also indicate that drinking water contaminated with salt killed many colonists living in low-lying areas. Throughout the entire seventeenth century, high mortality rates had a profound effect on this society. Life expectancy for Chesapeake males was about 43, some ten to twenty years less than for men born in New England! For women, life was even shorter. A full 25 percent of all children died in infancy; another 25 percent did not see their twentieth birthdays. The survivors were often weak or ill, unable to perform hard physical labor.

These demographic conditions retarded normal population increase. Young women who might have become wives and mothers could not do so until they had completed their terms of servitude. They thus lost several reproductive years, and in a society in which so many children died in infancy, late marriage greatly restricted family size. Moreover, because of the unbalanced sex ratio, many adult males simply could not find wives. Migration not only cut them off from their English families but also deprived them of an opportunity to form new ones. Without a constant flow of immigrants, the population of Virginia and Maryland would have actually declined.

High mortality compressed the family life cycle into a few short years. One partner in a marriage usually died within seven years. Only one in three Chesapeake marriages survived as long as a decade.

Not only did children not meet grandparents—they often did not even know their own parents. Widows and widowers quickly remarried, bringing children by former unions into their new homes, and it was not uncommon for a child to grow up with persons to whom he or she bore no blood relation. The psychological effects of such experiences on Chesapeake settlers cannot be measured. People probably learned to cope with a high degree of personal insecurity. However they adjusted, it is clear family life in this region was vastly more impermanent than it was in the New England colonies during the same period.

Women were obviously in great demand in the early southern colonies. Some historians have argued that scarcity heightened the woman's bargaining power in the marriage market. If she was an immigrant, she did not have to worry about obtaining parental consent. She was on her own in the New World and free to select whomever she pleased. If a woman lacked beauty or strength, if she were a person of low moral standards, she could still be confident of finding an American husband. Such negotiations may have provided Chesapeake women with a means of improving their social status.

Nevertheless, liberation from some traditional restraints on seventeenth-century women must not be exaggerated. As servants, women were vulnerable to sexual exploitation by their masters. Moreover, in this unhealthy environment, childbearing was extremely dangerous, and women in the Chesapeake usually died twenty years earlier than their New England counterparts.

The Structure of Planter Society

Colonists who managed somehow to survive grew tobacco—as much tobacco as they possibly could. This crop became the Chesapeake staple, and since it was relatively easy to cultivate, anyone with a few acres of cleared land could harvest leaves for export. Cultivation of tobacco did not, however, produce a society roughly equal in wealth and status. To the contrary, tobacco generated inequality. Some planters amassed large fortunes; others barely subsisted. Labor made the difference, for to succeed in this staple economy, one had to control the labor of other men and women. More workers in the fields meant larger harvests, and, of course, larger profits. Since free persons showed no interest in growing another man's tobacco, not even for wages, wealthy planters relied on white laborers who were not free, as well as on slaves. The social structure that developed in the seventeenth-century Chesapeake reflected a wild, often unscrupulous scramble to bring men and women of three races—black, white, and Indian—into various degrees of dependence.

Great planters dominated Chesapeake society. The group was small, only a trifling portion of the population of Virginia and Maryland. During the early decades of the seventeenth century, the composition of Chesapeake gentry was continually in flux. Some gentlemen died before they could establish a secure claim to high social status; others returned to England, thankful to have survived. Not until the 1650s did the family names of those who would become famous eighteenth-century gentry appear in the records. The first gentlemen were not—as genealogists sometimes discover to their dismay—dashing cavaliers who had fought in the English Civil War for King Charles I. Rather, such Chesapeake gentry as the Burwells, Byrds, Carters, and Masons consisted originally of the younger sons of English merchants and artisans.

These ambitious men arrived in America with capital. They invested immediately in laborers, and one way or another, they obtained huge tracts of the best tobacco-growing land. The members of this gentry were not technically aristocrats, for they did not possess titles that could be passed from generation to generation. They gave themselves military titles, sat as justices of the peace on the county courts, and directed local (Anglican) church affairs as members of the vestry. Over time, these gentry families intermarried so frequently that they created a vast network of cousins. During the eighteenth century, it was not uncommon to find a half dozen men with the same surname sitting simultaneously in the Virginia House of Burgesses.

Freemen formed the largest class in Chesapeake society. Their origins were strikingly different from those of the gentry, or for that matter, from those of New England's yeomen farmers. Chesapeake freemen traveled to the New World as **indentured servants** and, by sheer good fortune, managed to remain alive to the end of their contracts. If they had dreamed of becoming great planters, they were gravely disappointed. Most seventeenth-century freemen lived on the edge of poverty. Some freemen, of course, did better in America than they would have in contemporary England, but in both Virginia and Maryland, historians have found a sharp economic division separating the gentry from the rest of white society.

Below the freemen came indentured servants. Membership in this group was not demeaning; after all, servitude was a temporary status. But servitude in the Chesapeake colonies was not the benign institution it was in New England. Great planters purchased servants to grow tobacco. No one seemed overly concerned whether these laborers received decent food and clothes, much less whether they acquired trade skills. Young people, thousands of them, cut off from family ties, sick often to the point of death, unable to obtain normal sexual release, regarded their servitude

This painting, Henry Darnall III as a Child *(ca. 1710), by the German émigré painter Justus Engelhardt Kuhn depicts the son of a wealthy planter family in Maryland armed with a bow and arrow. To the left, an African American slave holds a dead bird. This is the earliest known depiction of an African American in a colonial American painting. The formal architecture and gardens in the background suggest an idealized European landscape and a connection to European culture that some members of the colonial gentry imagined for themselves.* ❖

as a form of slavery. Not surprisingly, the gentry worried that unhappy servants and impoverished freemen, what the planters called the "giddy multitude," would rebel at the slightest provocation, a fear that turned out to be fully justified.

The character of social mobility—and this observation applies only to whites—changed considerably during the seventeenth century. Until the 1680s, it was relatively easy for a newcomer who possessed capital to become a member of the planter elite. No one paid much attention to the reputation or social standing of one's English family.

Sometime after the 1680s, however—the precise date is impossible to establish—a dramatic demographic shift occurred. Although infant mortality remained high, life expectancy rates for those who survived childhood in the Chesapeake improved significantly, and for the first time in the history of Virginia and Maryland, important leadership positions went to men who had actually been born in America. This transition has been described by one political historian as the "emergence of a creole majority," in other words, as the rise of an indigenous ruling elite. Before this time, immigrant leaders had died without heirs or had returned as quickly as possible to England. The members of the new creole class took a greater interest in local government. Their activities helped give the tobacco colonies the kind of political and cultural stability that had eluded earlier generations of planter adventurers. Not surprisingly, it was during this period of demographic transition that creole leaders founded the College of William and Mary (1693) and authorized the construction of an impressive new capital called Williamsburg. These were changes that, in the words of one creole Virginian, provided the colony "with a sense of permanence and legitimacy . . . it had never before possessed."

The key to success in this creole society was ownership of slaves. Those planters who held more blacks could grow more tobacco and thus could acquire fresh capital needed to purchase additional laborers. Over time, the rich not only became richer; they also formed a distinct ruling elite that newcomers found increasingly difficult to enter.

Opportunities for advancement also decreased for freemen in the region. Studies of mid-seventeenth-century Maryland reveal that some servants managed to become moderately prosperous farmers and small officeholders. But as the gentry consolidated its hold on political and economic institutions, ordinary people discovered it was much harder to rise in Chesapeake society. Those men and women with more ambitious dreams headed for Pennsylvania, North Carolina, or western Virginia.

Social institutions that figured importantly in the daily experience of New Englanders were either weak or nonexistent in the Chesapeake colonies. In part, the sluggish development resulted from the continuation of high infant mortality rates. There was little incentive to build elementary schools, for example, if half the children would die before reaching adulthood. The great planters sent their sons to England or Scotland for their education, and even after the founding of the College of William and Mary in Virginia, the gentry continued to patronize English schools. As a result of this practice, higher education in the South languished for much of the colonial period.

Tobacco influenced the spread of other institutions in the region. Planters were scattered along the rivers, often separated from their nearest neighbors by miles of poor roads. Since the major tobacco growers traded directly with English merchants, they had no need for towns. Whatever items they required were either made on the plantation or imported from Europe. Other than the centers of colonial government, Jamestown (and later Williamsburg) and St. Mary's City (and later Annapolis), there were no vil-

Undated, unsigned, and hidden on the back of another painting, the two-part painting Virginian Luxuries *depicts a white man kissing a black woman and a white man whipping a black man. Indeed, the brutal system of slavery afforded slave owners such "luxuries" as rape and torture.*

lages capable of sustaining a rich community life before the late eighteenth century. Seventeenth-century Virginia did not even possess a printing press. In fact, Governor Sir William Berkeley bragged in 1671, "There are no free schools, nor printing in Virginia, for learning has brought disobedience, and heresy . . . into the world, and printing had divulged them . . . God keep us from both!"

Race and Freedom in British America

Many people who landed in the colonies had no desire to come to the New World. They were Africans taken as slaves to cultivate rice, sugar, and tobacco. As the Native Americans were exterminated and the supply of white indentured servants dried up, European planters demanded ever more African laborers.

Roots of Slavery

A great deal is known about the transfer of African peoples across the Atlantic. During the entire history of this human commerce, between the sixteenth and nineteenth centuries, slave traders carried almost eleven million blacks to the Americas. Most of these men and women were sold in Brazil or in the Caribbean. A relatively small number of Africans reached British North America, and of this group, the majority arrived after 1700. Because slaves performed hard physical labor, planters preferred purchasing young males. In many early slave communities, men outnumbered women by a ratio of two to one.

English colonists did not hesitate to enslave black people or, for that matter, Native Americans. While the institution of slavery had long before died out in the mother country, New World settlers quickly discovered how well this particular labor system operated in the Spanish and Portuguese colonies. The decision to bring African slaves to the colonies, therefore, was based primarily on economic considerations.

English masters, however, seldom justified the practice purely in terms of planter profits. Indeed, they adopted a quite different pattern of rhetoric. English writers associated blacks in Africa with heathen religion, barbarous behavior, sexual promiscuity—in fact, with evil itself. From such a racist perspective, the enslavement of Africans seemed unobjectionable. The planters maintained that if black slaves converted to Christianity, shedding their supposedly savage ways, they would benefit from their loss of freedom.

Africans first landed in Virginia in 1619 as a cargo of slaves stolen by a Dutch trader from a Spanish merchant ship in the Caribbean. For the next fifty years, the status of the colony's black people remained unclear. English settlers classified some black laborers as slaves for life, as chattel to be bought and sold at the master's will. But other Africans became servants, presumably for stated periods of time, and it was even possible for a few blacks to purchase their freedom. Several seventeenth-century Africans became successful Virginia planters. These rare exceptions in a long history of oppression remind modern Americans that once, long ago, it was possible to imagine a more open, less racially defined society. (See the Feature Essay, "Anthony Johnson, A Free Black Planter on Pungoteague Creek," pp. 74–75.)

One reason Virginia lawmakers tolerated such confusion was that the black population remained very small. By 1660, fewer than fifteen hundred people

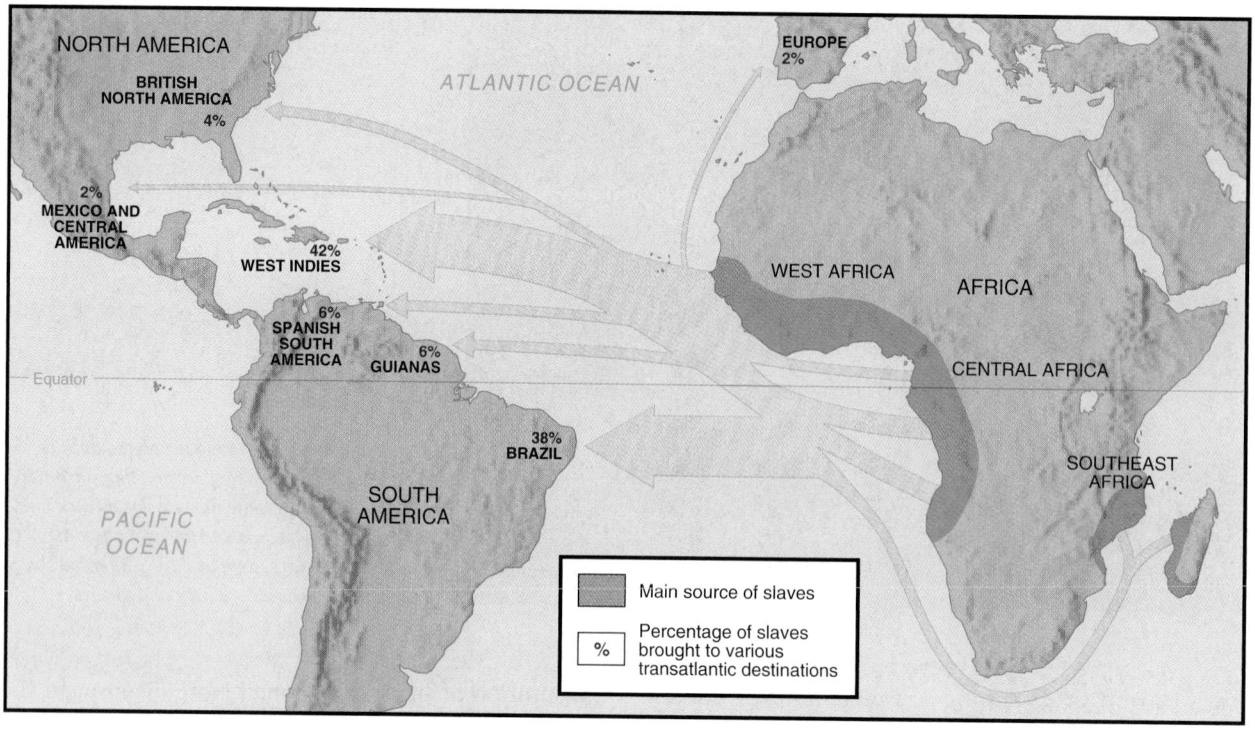

ORIGINS AND DESTINATIONS OF AFRICAN SLAVES, 1619–1760 *Although many African slaves were carried to Britain's North American colonies, far more slaves were sold in the Caribbean Sugar Colonies and Brazil, where because of horrific health conditions, the death rate far exceeded that of the British Mainland Colonies.* ❖

of African origin lived in the entire colony (compared to a white population of approximately twenty-six thousand), and it hardly seemed necessary for the legislature to draw up an elaborate slave code to control so few men and women. If the planters could have obtained more black laborers, they certainly would have done so. There is no evidence that the great planters preferred white indentured servants to black slaves. The problem was supply. During this period, slave traders sold their cargoes on Barbados or the other sugar islands of the West Indies, where they fetched higher prices than Virginians could afford. In fact, before 1680, most blacks who reached England's colonies on the North American mainland came from Barbados or through New Netherland rather than directly from Africa.

By the end of the seventeenth century, the legal status of Virginia's black people was no longer in doubt. They were slaves for life, and so were their children after them. This transformation reflected changes in the supply of Africans to British North America. After 1672, the Royal African Company was chartered to meet the colonial planters' demands for black laborers. Historian K. G. Davies terms this organization "the strongest and most effective of all European companies formed exclusively for the African trade." Between 1695 and 1709, more than eleven thousand Africans were sold in Virginia alone; many others went to Maryland and the Carolinas. Although American merchants—most of them based in Rhode Island—entered the trade during the eighteenth century, the British continued to supply the bulk of the slaves to the mainland market for the entire colonial period.

The expanding black population apparently frightened white colonists, for as the number of Africans increased, lawmakers drew up ever stricter slave codes. It was during this period that racism, always a latent element in New World societies, was fully revealed. By 1700, slavery was unequivocally based on the color of a person's skin. Blacks fell into this status simply because they were black. A vicious pattern of discrimination had been set in motion. Even conversion to Christianity did not free the African from bondage. The white planter could deal with his black property as he alone saw fit, and one revolting Virginia statute excused masters who killed slaves, on the grounds that no rational person would purposely "destroy his own estate." Black women constantly had to fear sexual violation by a master or his sons. Children born to a slave woman became slaves regardless of the father's race. Unlike the Spanish colonies, where persons of lighter color enjoyed greater privileges in society, the English

This watercolor, Slave Deck of the Albanoz *(1846), by naval officer Lieutenant Godfrey Meynell, shows slaves packed with cargo in the hold of a ship after being taken captive in West Africa. Because it was expected that many slaves would die en route, ship captains increased their profits by crowding even more slaves into the hold.* ❖

colonies tolerated no mixing of the races. Mulattoes and pure Africans received the same treatment.

Constructing African American Identities

The slave experience varied substantially from colony to colony. The daily life of a black person in South Carolina, for example, was quite different from that of an African American who happened to live in Pennsylvania or Massachusetts Bay. The size and density of the slave population determined in large measure how successfully blacks could maintain a separate cultural identity. In the lowlands of South Carolina during the eighteenth century, 60 percent of the population was black. The men and women were placed on large, isolated rice plantations, and their contact with whites was limited. In these areas blacks developed creole languages, which mixed the basic vocabulary of English with words borrowed from various African tongues. Until the end of the nineteenth century, one creole language, Gullah, was spoken on some of the Sea Islands along the Georgia–South Carolina coast. Slaves on the large rice plantations also were able to establish elaborate and enduring kinship networks that may have helped reduce the more dehumanizing aspects of bondage.

In the New England and Middle Colonies, and even in Virginia, African Americans made up a smaller percentage of the population: 40 percent in Virginia, 8 percent in Pennsylvania, and 3 percent in Massachusetts. In such environments, contact between blacks and whites was more frequent than in South Carolina and Georgia. These population patterns had a profound effect on northern and Chesapeake blacks, for while they escaped the physical drudgery of rice cultivation, they found the preservation of an independent African identity difficult. In northern cities, slaves working as domestics and living in the houses of their masters saw other blacks but had little opportunity to develop creole languages or reaffirm a common African past.

In eighteenth-century Virginia, native-born or creole blacks, people who had learned to cope with whites on a daily basis, looked with contempt on slaves who had just arrived from Africa. These "outlandish" Negroes, as they were called, were forced by blacks as well as whites to accept elements of English culture. It was especially important for newcomers to speak English. Consider, for example, the pain of young Olaudah Equiano, an African sold in Virginia in 1757. This 12-year-old slave declared, "I was now exceedingly miserable, and thought myself worse off than any . . . of my companions; for they could talk to each other [in English], but I had no person to speak to that I could understand. In this state I was constantly grieving and pining, and wishing for death."

Newly arrived men and women from Africa were far more likely to run away, assault their masters, and organize rebellion than were the creole slaves. The people described in colonial newspaper advertisements as "New Negroes" desperately tried to regain control over their lives. In 1770—just to cite one example—two young Africans, both recently sold in Virginia, "went off with several others, being persuaded that they could find their way back to their own Country."

Despite such wrenching experiences, black slaves creatively preserved elements of an African heritage. The process of establishing African American traditions involved an imaginative reshaping of African and European customs into something that was neither African nor European. It was African American. The

Feature Essay

Anthony Johnson

A Free Black Planter on Pungoteague Creek

During the first decades of settlement, a larger proportion of Virginia's black population achieved freedom than at any time until the Civil War ended slavery. Despite considerable obstacles, these free black men and women—their number in these early years was quite small—formed families, acquired property, earned community respect, and helped establish a distinctive African American culture. One member of this group was Anthony Johnson, an immigrant who rose from slavery to prominence on Virginia's Eastern Shore.

Johnson came to Virginia aboard the English vessel *James* in 1621, just two years after the first blacks had arrived in the colony. As a slave known simply as "Antonio a Negro," Johnson found life a constant struggle for survival. Working in the tobacco fields of the Bennett plantation located on the south side of the James River, he endured long hours, poor rations, fearful epidemics, and haunting loneliness—conditions that, more often than not, brought an early death to slaves as well as indentured servants. Johnson, however, was a tough, intelligent, and lucky man.

Exactly how Johnson achieved freedom is not known. Early records reveal that while still living at the Bennett plantation, he took a wife, "Mary a Negro woman." Anthony was fortunate to find her. Because of an exceedingly unequal sex ratio in early Virginia, few males—regardless of color—had an opportunity to form families. Anthony and Mary reared at least four children. Even more remarkable, in a society in which most unions were broken by death within a decade, their marriage lasted more than forty years.

Sometime during the 1630s, Anthony and Mary gained their freedom, perhaps with the help of someone named Johnson. Their bondage probably ended through self-purchase, an arrangement that allowed enterprising slaves to buy their liberty through labor. Later, again under unknown circumstances, the Johnsons migrated to Northampton County on the Eastern Shore of Virginia. During the 1640s, they acquired an estate of 250 acres on Pungoteague Creek, where they raised cattle, horses, and hogs and cultivated tobacco. To work these holdings, Anthony Johnson apparently relied on the labor of indentured servants and at least one black slave named Casor.

As the "patriarch of Pungoteague Creek," Johnson participated as fully as most whites in Northampton society. He traded with wealthy white landowners and apparently shared their assumptions about the sanctity of property and the legitimacy of slavery. When two white neighbors attempted to steal Casor, Johnson hauled them into court and forced them to return his laborer. On another occasion, Johnson appealed to the court for tax relief after an "unfortunate fire" destroyed much of his plantation.

The Johnsons also maintained close ties with other free blacks, such as Anthony Payne and Emmanuel Driggus, who had similarly attained freedom and prosperity through their own efforts. Johnson's strongest links were with his family. Although his children lived in separate homes after reaching adulthood, his two sons laid out holdings in the 1650s adjacent to their father's plantation, and in times of crisis, parents and children participated in family conferences. These close bonds persisted even after the Johnson clan moved to Somerset County, Maryland, in the 1660s, and Anthony Johnson's subsequent death. When he purchased land in Somerset in 1677, Johnson's grandson, a third-generation free black colonist, named his plantation Angola, perhaps in memory of his grandfather's African homeland.

Interpreting Johnson's remarkable life has proved surprisingly difficult. An earlier generation of historians considered Johnson a curiosity, a sort of black Englishman who did not fit neatly into familiar racial categories. Even some recent writers, concerned about tracing the roots of slavery and prejudice in the United States, have paid scant attention to Johnson and the other free blacks on the Eastern Shore.

Most historians would now agree that Johnson's life illustrated the complexity of race relations in early Virginia. His surprising progression from slave to slaveholder and his easy participation in the world of the white gentry and in a network of black friendships and family ties demonstrated that relations among blacks and whites conformed to no single pattern in the fluid society of mid-seventeenth-century Virginia. Rather, they took a variety of forms—conflict, cooperation, exploitation, accommodation—depending on the goals, status, experience, and environment of the participants. Race was only a single factor—and by no means the decisive one—shaping relations among colonists.

The opportunities that had been available to Anthony Johnson and other Virginia blacks, however, disappeared during the last quarter of the seventeenth century. A growing reliance on slave labor rather than white indentured servitude brought about a rapid increase in the black population of Virginia and an accompanying curtailment of civil liberties on racial grounds. The rise of a group of great planters who dominated the colonial economy soon drove free black farmers into poverty. No longer did they enjoy the security, as had one black farmer in the 1640s, of having "myne owne ground and I will work when I please and play when I please." It is not surprising that after 1706, a time when Virginia's experiment in a genuinely multiracial free society was all but over, the Johnson family disappeared from the colonial records. When modern Americans discuss the history of race relations in the United States, they might consider the factors that allowed some of the first blacks who settled in America to achieve economic and social success.

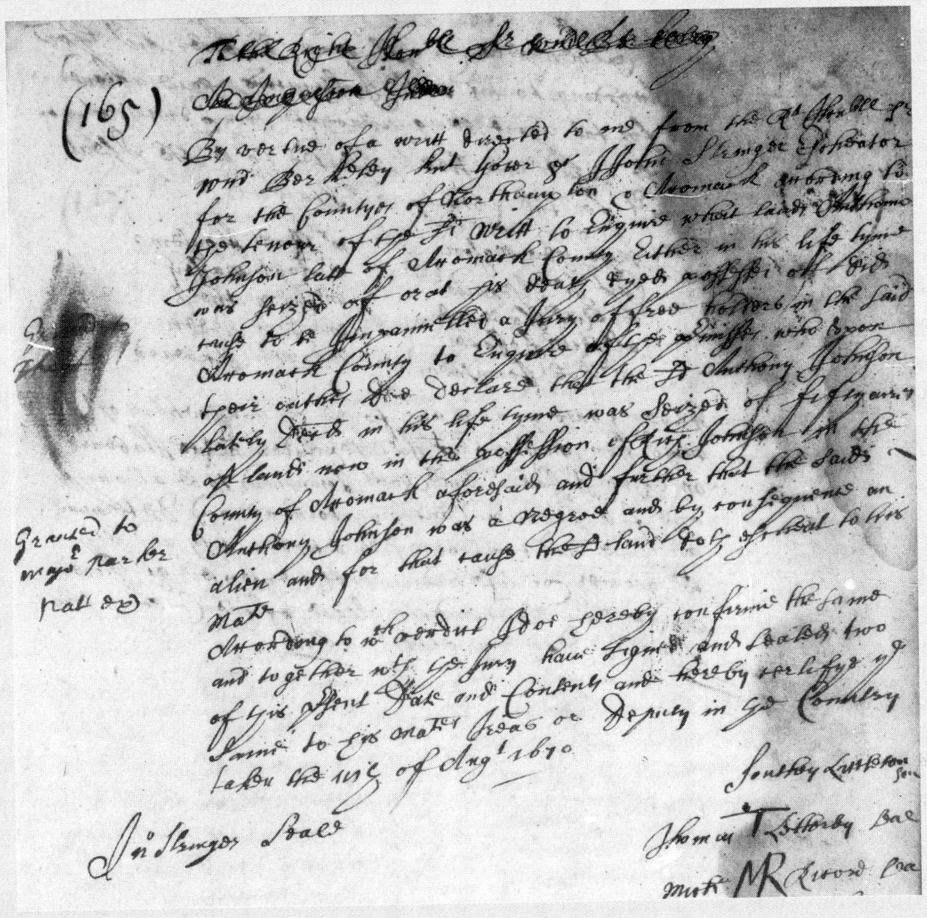

A few months after Anthony Johnson died in 1670, a Virginia court ruled that because "he was a Negro and by consequence an alien," the 250 acres of land that he had owned should revert to England. Shown here is a portion of the court document with that decree. ❖

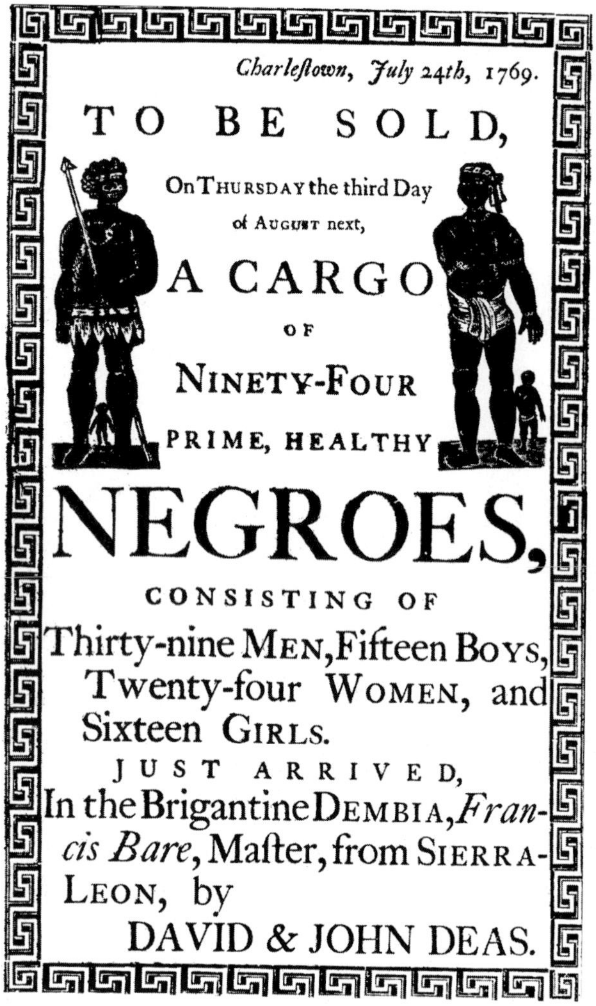

A public notice announces a slave auction to be held at the Charles Town wharf (1769). ❖

slaves accepted Christianity, but they did so on their own terms—terms their masters seldom fully understood. Blacks transformed Christianity into an expression of religious feeling in which an African element remained vibrant. In music and folk art, they gave voice to a cultural identity that even the most degrading conditions could not eradicate.

A major turning point in the history of African American people occurred during the early decades of the eighteenth century. At this time, blacks living in England's mainland colonies began to reproduce successfully. The number of live births exceeded deaths, and from that date, the expansion of the African American population owed more to natural increase than to the importation of new slaves. Even though thousands of new Africans arrived each year, the creole population was always much larger than that of the immigrant blacks. This demographic shift did not take place in the Caribbean or South American colonies until a much later date. Historians believe that North American blacks enjoyed a healthier climate and better diet than did other New World slaves.

Although mainland blacks lived longer than the blacks of Jamaica or Barbados, they were, after all, still slaves. They protested their debasement in many ways, some in individual acts of violence, others in organized revolt. The most serious slave rebellion of the colonial period was the Stono Uprising, which took place in September 1739. One hundred fifty South Carolina blacks rose up and, seizing guns and ammunition, murdered several white planters. "With Colours displayed, and two Drums beating," they marched toward Spanish Florida, where they had been promised freedom. The local militia soon overtook the rebellious slaves and killed most of them. Although the uprising was short-lived, such incidents helped persuade whites everywhere that their own blacks might secretly be planning bloody revolt. When a white servant woman in New York City announced in 1741 that blacks intended to burn the town, authorities executed 34 suspected arsonists (30 blacks and 4 whites) and dispatched 72 others either to the West Indies or to Madeira off the north coast of Africa. While the level of interracial violence in colonial society was quite low, everyone recognized that the blacks—in the words of one Virginia governor—longed "to Shake off the fetters of Slavery."

Even within the constraints of slavery, African Americans sometimes found opportunities that afforded a degree of personal freedom. Recent scholarship has discovered, for example, that during the eighteenth century a large number of black men became mariners. It is now estimated that by 1803, African Americans held at least 18 percent of all jobs open to American seamen, and although the number of positions may have been fewer before the Revolution, black colonial sailors—many of them slaves—sought work on sailing vessels to escape the drudgery of life on rice or tobacco plantations. These African American seamen connected black communities scattered throughout the Caribbean and along the mainland coast, bringing news about distant rebellions and spreading radical political ideologies to slaves who might otherwise not have known much about the transforming events of the eighteenth century.

Rise of a Commercial Empire

In 1661, John Norton, a respected Congregational minister, delivered a remarkable sermon before the assembled legislators of Massachusetts Bay. "It is not a Gospel-spirit to be against Kings," Norton lectured, "'tis neither Gospel nor English Spirit for any of us to be against the Government by Kings, Lords and Commons." It was as if after some thirty years of vir-

Old Plantation, *a watercolor by an unknown artist (about 1800), shows that African customs survived plantation slavery. The man and women in the center dance (possibly to celebrate a wedding) to the music of drum and banjo. Instruments, turbans, and scarves reflect a distinctive African American culture in the New World.* ❖

tual freedom, the American Puritans had to be reminded of the political ties that bound them to England. As Norton sensed, however, the times were changing. The newly restored Stuart monarchy was beginning to establish rules for the entire empire, and the planters of the Chesapeake as well as the Puritans of New England would soon discover they were not as independent as they had imagined.

Until the middle of the seventeenth century, English political leaders largely ignored the American colonists. Private companies and aristocratic proprietors had created these societies, some for profit, others for religious sanctuary, but in no case did the crown provide financial or military assistance. After the Restoration of Charles II in 1660, intervention replaced indifference. Englishmen of various sorts—courtiers, merchants, parliamentarians—concluded that the colonists should be brought more tightly under the control of the mother country. The regulatory policies that evolved during this period formed a framework for an empire that survived with only minor adjustment until 1765.

Response to Economic Competition

The famous eighteenth-century Scottish economist Adam Smith coined the term *mercantilist system* to describe Great Britain's commercial regulations, and ever since, his phrase has appeared in history books. An advocate of free trade, Smith argued that it made no sense for European states to exclude commercial competitors from their own colonial markets. More trade increased general prosperity. Smith's specific term, however, is misleading. **Mercantilism** suggests that English policymakers during the reign of Charles II had developed a well-integrated set of ideas about the nature of international commerce and a carefully planned set of mercantilist government policies to implement them.

They did nothing of the sort. Administrators responded to particular problems, usually on an individual basis. In 1668, Charles informed his sister, "The thing which is nearest the heart of the nation is trade and all that belongs to it." National interest alone, however, did not shape public policy. Instead, the needs of several powerful interest groups led to the rise of English commercial regulation.

Each group looked to colonial commerce to solve a different problem. For his part, the king wanted money. For their part, English merchants were eager to exclude Dutch rivals from lucrative American markets and needed government assistance to compete successfully with the Dutch, even in Virginia or Massachusetts Bay. From the perspective of the landed gentry who sat in Parliament, England needed a stronger navy, and that in turn meant expansion of the domestic shipbuilding industry. And almost everyone agreed England should establish a more favorable balance of trade, that is, increase exports, decrease imports, and grow richer at the expense of other European states. None of these ideas was particularly innovative, but taken together they provided a blueprint for England's first empire.

Regulating Colonial Trade

After some legislation in that direction during the Commonwealth, Parliament passed a Navigation Act in 1660. The statute was the most important piece of imperial legislation drafted before the American Revolution. Colonists from New Hampshire to the Carolinas paid close attention to the details of this statute, which stated (1) that no ship could trade in the colonies unless it had been constructed in either England or America and carried a crew that was at least 75 percent English (for these purposes, colonists counted as Englishmen), and (2) that certain **enumerated goods** of great value that were not produced in England—tobacco, sugar, cotton, indigo, dyewoods, ginger—could be transported from the colonies only to an English or another colonial port. In 1704, Parliament added rice and molasses to the enumerated list; in 1705, rosins, tars, and turpentines needed for shipbuilding were included.

The act of 1660 was masterfully conceived. It encouraged the development of domestic shipbuilding and prohibited European rivals from obtaining enumerated goods anywhere except in England. Since the Americans had to pay import duties in England (for this purpose colonists did not count as Englishmen) on such items as sugar and tobacco, the legislation also provided the crown with another source of income.

In 1663, Parliament passed a second Navigation Act known as the Staple Act, which stated that, with a few noted exceptions, nothing could be imported into America unless it had first been transshipped through England, a process that greatly added to the price ultimately paid by colonial consumers.

The **Navigation Acts** attempted to eliminate the Dutch, against whom the English fought three wars in this period (1652–1654, 1664–1667, and 1672–1674), as the intermediaries of American commerce. Just as English merchants were celebrating their victory, however, an unanticipated rival appeared on the scene: New England merchant ships sailed out of Boston, Salem, and Newport to become formidable world competitors in maritime commerce.

During the 1660s, the colonists showed little enthusiasm for the new imperial regulations. Reaction to the Navigation Acts varied from region to region. Virginians bitterly protested them. The collection of English customs on tobacco greatly reduced the colonial planters' profits. Moreover, the exclusion of the Dutch from the trade meant that growers often had to sell their crops at artificially low prices. The Navigation Acts hit the small planters especially hard, for they were least able to absorb increased production costs. Even though the governor of Virginia lobbied on the planters' behalf, the crown turned a deaf ear. By 1670, import duties on tobacco accounted for almost £100,000, a sum the king could scarcely do without.

At first, New Englanders simply ignored the commercial regulations. Indeed, one Massachusetts merchant reported in 1664 that Boston entertained "near one hundred sail of ships, this year, of ours and strangers." The strangers, of course, were the Dutch, who had no intention of obeying the Navigation Acts so long as they could reach colonial ports. Some New England merchants found clever ways to circumvent the Navigation Acts. These crafty traders picked up cargoes of enumerated goods such as sugar or tobacco, sailed to another colonial port (thereby technically fulfilling the letter of the law), and then made directly for Holland or France. Along the way they paid no customs.

To plug the loophole, Parliament passed the Navigation Act of 1673. This statute established a plantation duty, a sum of money equal to normal English customs duties to be collected on enumerated products at the various colonial ports. New Englanders could now sail wherever they pleased within the empire, but they could not escape paying customs. Parliament also extended the jurisdiction of the London Customs Commissioners to America. And in 1675, as part of the new imperial firmness, the Privy Council formed a powerful subcommittee, the Lords of Trade, whose members monitored colonial affairs.

Despite these legal reforms, serious obstacles impeded the execution of imperial policy. The customs service did not have enough effective agents in American ports to enforce the Navigation Acts fully, and some men sent from the mother country did more harm than good. Edward Randolph, head of the imperial customs service in New England, was such a person. He was dispatched to Boston in 1676 to gather information about the conduct of colonial trade. His behavior was so obnoxious, his reports about New Englanders so condescending, that he became the most hated man in late-seventeenth-century Massachusetts.

Parliament passed the last major piece of imperial legislation in 1696. Among other things, the statute tightened enforcement procedures, putting pressure specifically on the colonial governors to keep England's competitors out of American ports. The act of 1696 also expanded the American customs service and for the first time set up vice-admiralty courts in the colonies. This decision eventually rankled the colonists. Established to settle disputes that occurred at sea, vice-admiralty courts required neither juries nor oral cross-examination, both traditional elements of the common law. But they were effective and sometimes even popular for resolving maritime questions quickly enough to send the ships to sea again with little delay. The year 1696 witnessed one other significant change in the imperial system. William III replaced the ineffective Lords of Trade with a body of policy advisers that came to be known as the Board of Trade. This group was expected to monitor colonial affairs closely and to provide government officials with the best available advice on commercial and other problems. For several decades, at least, it energetically carried out its responsibilities.

The members of Parliament believed these reforms would belatedly compel the colonists to accept the Navigation Acts, and in large measure they were correct. By 1700, American goods transshipped through the mother country accounted for a quarter of all English exports, an indication the colonists found it profitable to obey the commercial regulations. In fact, during the eighteenth century, smuggling from Europe to America dried up almost completely.

Colonial Factions Spark Political Revolt, 1676–1691

The Navigation Acts created an illusion of unity. English administrators superimposed a system of commercial regulation on a number of different, often unstable American colonies and called it an empire. But these statutes did not remove long-standing differences. Within each society, men and women struggled to bring order out of disorder, to establish stable ruling elites, to diffuse ethnic and racial tensions, and to cope with population pressures that imperial planners only dimly understood. During the final decades of the seventeenth century, these efforts sometimes sparked revolt.

First, the Virginians rebelled, and then a few years later, political violence swept through Maryland, New York, and Massachusetts Bay, England's most populous mainland colonies. Historians once interpreted these events as rehearsals for the American Revolution, or even for Jacksonian democracy. They perceived the rebels as frontier democrats, rising in protest against an entrenched aristocracy.

Recent research suggests, however, that this view seriously misconstrued the character of these late-seventeenth-century rebellions. The uprisings certainly did not involve confrontations between ordinary people and their rulers. Indeed, the events were not in any modern sense of the word ideological. In each colony, the local gentry split into factions, usually the "outs" versus the "ins," and each side proclaimed its political legitimacy.

Civil War in Virginia: Bacon's Rebellion

After 1660, the Virginia economy suffered a prolonged depression. Returns from tobacco had not been good for some time, and the Navigation Acts reduced profits even further. Into this unhappy environment came thousands of indentured servants, people drawn to Virginia, as the governor explained, "in hope of bettering their condition in a Growing Country."

The reality bore little relation to their dreams. A hurricane destroyed one entire tobacco crop, and in 1667, Dutch warships captured the tobacco fleet just as it was about to sail for England. Indentured servants complained about lack of food and clothing. No wonder that Virginia's governor, Sir William Berkeley, despaired of ever ruling "a People where six parts of seven at least are Poor, Endebted, Discontented and Armed." In 1670, he and the House of Burgesses disfranchised all landless freemen, persons they regarded as troublemakers, but the threat of social violence remained.

Enter Nathaniel Bacon. This ambitious young man arrived in Virginia in 1674. He came from a respectable English family and set himself up immediately as a substantial planter. But he wanted more. Bacon envied the government patronage monopolized by Berkeley's cronies, a group known locally as the Green Spring faction. When Bacon attempted to obtain a license to engage in the fur trade, he was rebuffed. This lucrative commerce was reserved for the governor's friends. If Bacon had been willing to wait, he probably would have been accepted into the ruling clique, but as subsequent events would demonstrate, Bacon was not a man of patience.

Events beyond Bacon's control thrust him suddenly into the center of Virginia politics. In 1675, Indians reacting to white encroachment attacked several outlying plantations, killing a few colonists, and Virginians expected the governor to send an army to retaliate. Instead, early in 1676, Berkeley called for the construction of a line of defensive forts, a plan that seemed to the settlers both expensive and ineffective. Indeed, the strategy raised embarrassing questions. Was Berkeley protecting his own fur monopoly? Was he planning to reward his friends with contracts to build useless forts?

While people speculated about such matters, Bacon stepped forward. He boldly offered to lead a volunteer army against the Indians at no cost to the hard-pressed Virginia taxpayers. All he demanded was an official commission from Berkeley giving him military command and the right to attack other Indians, not just the hostile Susquehannocks. The governor steadfastly refused. With some justification, Berkeley regarded his upstart rival as a fanatic on the subject of Indians. The governor saw no reason to exterminate peaceful tribes simply to avenge the death of a few white settlers.

What followed would have been comic had not so many people died. Bacon thundered against the governor's treachery; Berkeley labeled Bacon a traitor. Both men appealed to the populace for support. On several occasions, Bacon marched his followers to the frontier, but they either failed to find the enemy or, worse, massacred friendly Indians. At one point, Bacon burned Jamestown to the ground, forcing the governor to flee to the colony's Eastern Shore. Bacon's bumbling lieutenants chased Berkeley across Chesapeake Bay only to be captured themselves. Thereupon, the governor mounted a new campaign.

As **Bacon's Rebellion** dragged on, it became increasingly apparent that Bacon and his gentry supporters had only the vaguest notion of what they were trying to achieve. The members of the planter elite never seemed fully to appreciate that the rank-and-file soldiers, often black slaves and poor white servants, had serious, legitimate grievances against Berkeley's corrupt government and were demanding substantial reforms, not just a share in the governor's fur monopoly.

Although women had not been allowed to vote in colony elections, they made their political views clear enough during the rebellion. Some were apparently more violent than others. Sarah Glendon, for example, agitated so aggressively in support of Bacon that Berkeley later refused to grant her a pardon. Another outspoken rebel, Lydia Chiesman, defended her husband before Governor Berkeley, noting that the man would not have joined Bacon's forces had she not persuaded him to do so. "Therefore," Lydia Chiesman concluded, ". . . since what her husband had done, was by her meanes, and so, by consequence, she most guilty, that she might be hanged and he pardoned."

When Charles II learned of the fighting in Virginia, he dispatched a thousand regular soldiers to Jamestown. By the time they arrived, Berkeley had regained full control over the colony's government. In October 1676, Bacon died after a brief illness, and within a few months, his band of rebel followers had dispersed.

Berkeley, now an old and embittered man, was recalled to England in 1677. His successors, especially Lord Culpeper (1680–1683) and Lord Howard of Effingham (1683–1689), seemed interested primarily in enriching themselves at the expense of the Virginia planters. Their self-serving policies, coupled with the memory of near anarchy, helped heal divisions within the Virginia ruling class. For almost a century, in fact, the local gentry formed a united front against greedy royal appointees.

The Glorious Revolution in the Bay Colony

During John Winthrop's lifetime, Massachusetts settlers developed an inflated sense of their independence from the mother country. After 1660, however, it became difficult even to pretend that the Puritan colony was a separate state. Royal officials such as Edward Randolph demanded full compliance with the Navigation Acts. Moreover, the growth of commerce attracted new merchants to the Bay Colony, men who were Anglicans rather than Congregationalists and who maintained close business contacts in London. These persons complained loudly of Puritan intolerance. The Anglican faction was never large, but its presence, coupled with Randolph's unceasing demands, divided Bay leaders. A few Puritan ministers and magistrates regarded compromise with England as treason, a breaking of the Lord's covenant. Other spokesmen, recognizing the changing political realities within the empire, urged a more moderate course.

In 1675, in the midst of this ongoing political crisis, the Indians dealt the New Englanders a terrible setback. Metacomet, a Wampanoag chief the whites called King Philip, declared war against the colonists. The powerful Narragansetts, whose lands the settlers had long coveted, joined Metacomet, and in little more than a year of fighting, the Indians destroyed scores of frontier villages, killed hundreds of colonists, and disrupted the entire regional economy. More than one thousand Indians and New Englanders died in the conflict. The war left the people of Massachusetts

Metacomet, the Wampanoag chief known to the English colonists as King Philip, led Native Americans in a major war designed to remove the Europeans from New England. ❖

deeply in debt and more than ever uncertain of their future. As in other parts of colonial America, the defeated Indians were forced off their lands, compelled by events to become either refugees or economically marginal figures in white society.

In 1684, the debate over the Bay Colony's relation to the mother country ended abruptly. The Court of Chancery, sitting in London and acting on a petition from the king, annulled the charter of the Massachusetts Bay Company. In one stroke of a pen, the patent that Winthrop had so lovingly carried to America in 1630, the foundation for a "city on a hill," was gone. The decision forced the most stubborn Puritans to recognize they were part of an empire run by people who did not share their particular religious vision.

James II, a monarch who disliked representative institutions—after all, Parliament, a representative assembly, had executed his father, Charles I—decided to restructure the government of the entire region in the Dominion of New England. In various stages from 1686 to 1689, the Dominion incorporated Massachusetts, Connecticut, Rhode Island, Plymouth, New York, New Jersey, and New Hampshire under a single appointed royal governor. For this demanding position, James selected Sir Edmund Andros (pronounced Andrews), a military veteran of tyrannical temperament. Andros arrived in Boston in 1686, and within a matter of months he had alienated everyone: Puritans, moderates, and even Anglican merchants. Not only did Andros abolish elective assemblies, but he also enforced the Navigation Acts with such rigor that he brought about commercial depression. Andros declared normal town meetings illegal, collected taxes the people never approved, and packed the courts with supporters who detested the local population. Eighteenth-century historian and royal governor Thomas Hutchinson compared Andros unfavorably with the Roman tyrant Nero.

Early in 1689, news of the Glorious Revolution reached Boston. The previous fall, the ruling class of England had deposed James II, an admitted Catholic, and placed his Protestant daughter Mary and her husband, William of Orange, on the throne as joint monarchs (see the chart of the Stuart monarchs on p. 33). As part of the settlement, William and Mary accepted a Bill of Rights, a document stipulating the constitutional rights of all Englishmen. Almost immediately, the Bay Colonists overthrew the hated Andros regime. The New England version of the Glorious Revolution (April 18, 1689) was so popular that no one came to the governor's defense. Andros was jailed without a single shot having been fired. According to Cotton Mather, a leading Congregational minister, the

William III and Mary II, joint monarchs of England after the Glorious Revolution of 1688. Mary ascended the throne when her father, James II, was deposed. Her husband William ruled Holland before accepting the English throne. ❖

colonists were united by the "most Unanimous Resolution perhaps that was ever known to have Inspir'd any people."

However united as they may have been, the Bay Colonists could not take the crown's support for granted. William III could have declared the New Englanders rebels and summarily reinstated Andros. But thanks largely to the tireless lobbying of Increase Mather, Cotton's father, who pleaded the colonists' case in London, William abandoned the Dominion of New England, and in 1691, Massachusetts received a new royal charter. This document differed substantially from the company patent of 1629. The freemen no longer selected their governor. The choice now belonged to the king. Membership in the General Court was determined by annual election, and these representatives in turn chose the men who sat in the council or upper house, subject always to the governor's veto. Moreover, the franchise, restricted here as in other colonies to adult males, was determined on the basis of personal property rather than church membership, a change that brought Massachusetts into conformity with general English practice. On the local level, town government remained much as it had been in Winthrop's time.

Of all seventeenth-century New England clergy, Cotton Mather (1663–1728) was the best known and most acknowledged theologian. Son and grandson of famous Puritan clergymen, Mather brought controversy to his reputation with the publication of Memorable Providences, Relating to Witchcrafts and Possessions *(1689), a pamphlet frequently cited as a contributing cause to the Salem witchcraft frenzy of the 1690s.* ❖

Contagion of Witchcraft

The instability of the Massachusetts government following Andros's arrest—what Reverend Samuel Willard described as "the short Anarchy accompanying our late Revolution"—allowed what under normal political conditions would have been an isolated, though ugly, local incident to expand into a major colonial crisis. Excessively fearful men and women living in Salem Village, a small, unprosperous farming community, nearly overwhelmed the new rulers of Massachusetts Bay.

Accusations of witchcraft were not uncommon in seventeenth-century New England. Puritans believed that an individual might make a compact with the devil, but during the first decades of settlement, authorities executed only about fifteen alleged witches. Sometimes villagers simply left suspected witches alone. Never before had fears of witchcraft plunged an entire community into panic.

The terror in Salem Village began in late 1691, when several adolescent girls began to behave in strange ways. They cried out for no apparent reason; they twitched on the ground. When concerned neighbors asked what caused their suffering, the girls announced they were victims of witches, seemingly innocent persons who lived in the community. The arrest of several alleged witches did not relieve the girls' "fits," nor did prayer solve the problem. Additional accusations were made, and at least one person confessed, providing a frightening description of the devil as "a thing all over hairy, all the face hairy, and a long nose." In June 1692, a special court convened and began to send men and women to the gallows. By the end of the summer, the court had hanged nineteen people; another was pressed to death. Many more suspects were in jail awaiting trial.

Then suddenly, the storm was over. Led by Increase Mather, a group of prominent Congregational ministers belatedly urged leniency and restraint. Especially troubling to the clergymen was the court's decision to accept **spectral evidence**, that is, reports of dreams and visions in which the accused appeared as the devil's agent. Worried about convicting people on such dubious testimony, Mather declared, "It were better that ten suspected witches should escape, than that one innocent person should be condemned." The colonial government accepted the ministers' advice and convened a new court, which promptly acquitted, pardoned, or released the remaining suspects. After the Salem nightmare, witchcraft ceased to be a capital offense.

No one knows exactly what sparked the terror in Salem Village. The community had a history of religious discord, and during the 1680s, the people split into angry factions over the choice of a minister. Economic tensions played a part as well. Poorer, more traditional farmers accused members of prosperous, commercially oriented families of being witches. The underlying misogyny of the entire culture meant the victims were more often women than men. Terror of attack by Native Americans may also have played a part in this ugly affair. Indians in league with the French in Canada had recently raided nearby communities, killing people related to the families of the bewitched Salem girls, and significantly, during the trials some victims described the Devil as a "tawny man."

Whatever the ultimate social and psychological sources of this event may have been, jealousy and bitterness apparently festered to the point that adolescent girls who normally would have been disciplined were allowed to incite judicial murder. As so often happens in incidents like this one—the McCarthy hearings of the 1950s, for example—the accusers later came to their senses and apologized to the survivors for the needless suffering they had inflicted on the community.

(For further discussion of the Salem witchcraft trials, see "Witches and the Law," pp. 86–90.)

The Glorious Revolution in New York and Maryland

The Glorious Revolution in New York was more violent than it had been in Massachusetts Bay. Divisions within New York's ruling class ran deep and involved ethnic as well as religious differences. English newcomers and powerful Anglo-Dutch families who had recently risen to commercial prominence in New York City opposed the older Dutch elite.

Much like Nathaniel Bacon, Jacob Leisler was a man entangled in events beyond his control. Leisler, the son of a German minister, emigrated to New York in 1660 and through marriage aligned himself with the Dutch elite. While he achieved moderate prosperity as a merchant, Leisler resented the success of the Anglo-Dutch.

When news of the Glorious Revolution reached New York City in May 1689, Leisler raised a group of militiamen and seized the local fort in the name of William and Mary. As leader of **Leisler's Rebellion**, he apparently expected an outpouring of popular support, but it was not forthcoming. His rivals waited, watching while Leisler desperately attempted to legitimize his actions. Through bluff and badgering, Leisler managed to hold the colony together, especially after French forces burned Schenectady (February 1690), but he never established a secure political base.

In March 1691, a new royal governor, Henry Sloughter, reached New York. He ordered Leisler to surrender his authority, but when Sloughter refused to prove he had been sent by William rather than by the deposed James, Leisler hesitated. The pause cost Leisler his life. Sloughter declared Leisler a rebel, and in a hasty trial, a court sentenced him and his chief lieutenant, Jacob Milbourne, to be hanged "by the Neck and being Alive their bodyes be Cutt downe to Earth and Their Bowells to be taken out and they being Alive, burnt before their faces. . . ." In 1695, Parliament officially pardoned Leisler, but he not being "Alive," the decision arrived a bit late. Long after his death, political factions calling themselves Leislerians and Anti-Leislerians struggled to dominate New York government. Indeed, in no other eighteenth-century colony was the level of bitter political rivalry so high.

During the last third of the seventeenth century, the colony of Maryland stumbled from one political crisis to another. Protestants in the colony's lower house resisted Lord Baltimore's Catholic friends in the upper house or council. When news of James's overthrow reached Maryland early in 1689, pent-up antiproprietary and anti-Catholic sentiment exploded. John Coode, a member of the assembly and an outspoken Protestant, formed a group called the Protestant Association, which in August forced Baltimore's governor, William Joseph, to resign.

Coode avoided Leisler's fatal mistakes. The Protestant Association, citing many wrongs suffered at the hands of local Catholics, petitioned the crown to transform Maryland into a royal colony. After reviewing the case, William accepted Coode's explanation, and in 1691, the king dispatched a royal governor to Maryland. A new assembly dominated by Protestants declared Anglicanism the established religion. Catholics were excluded from public office on the grounds that they might be in league with French Catholics in Canada. Lord Baltimore lost control of the colony's government, but he and his family did retain title to Maryland's undistributed lands. In 1715, the crown restored to full proprietorship the fourth Lord Baltimore, who had been raised a member of the Church of England, and Maryland remained in the hands of the Calvert family until 1776.

CHRONOLOGY

1619	First blacks arrive in Virginia
1660	Charles II is restored to the English throne ❖ First Navigation Act passed by Parliament
1663	Second Navigation (Staple) Act passed
1673	Plantation duty imposed to close loopholes in commercial regulations
1675	King Philip's (Metacomet's) War devastates New England
1676	Bacon's Rebellion threatens Governor Berkeley's government in Virginia
1681	William Penn receives charter for Pennsylvania
1684	Charter of the Massachusetts Bay Company revoked
1685	Duke of York becomes James II
1686	Dominion of New England established
1688	James II driven into exile during Glorious Revolution
1689	Rebellions break out in Massachusetts, New York, and Maryland
1691	Jacob Leisler executed
1692	Salem Village wracked by witch trials
1696	Parliament establishes Board of Trade
1739	Stono Uprising of South Carolina slaves terrifies white planters

Conclusion: Local Aspirations Within an Atlantic Empire

"It is no little Blessing of God," Cotton Mather announced proudly in 1700, "that we are part of the *English* nation." A half century earlier, John Winthrop would not have spoken these words, at least not with such enthusiasm. The two men were, of course, products of different political cultures. It was not so much that the character of Massachusetts society had changed. In fact, the Puritan families of 1700 were much like those of the founding generation. Rather, the difference was in England's attitude toward the colonies. Rulers living more than three thousand miles away now made political and economic demands that Mather's contemporaries could not ignore.

The creation of a new imperial system did not, however, erase profound sectional differences. By 1700, for example, the Chesapeake colonies were more, not less, committed to the cultivation of tobacco and slave labor. Although the separate regions were being pulled slowly into England's commercial orbit, they did not have much to do with each other. The elements that sparked a powerful sense of nationalism among colonists dispersed over a huge territory would not be evident for a very long time. It would be a mistake, therefore, to anticipate the coming of the American Revolution.

Recommended Reading

The most innovative research of chapters covered in this chapter explores the history of New World slavery during the period before the American Revolution. Much of this literature is boldly interdisciplinary, providing not only a fresh comparative interpretation of the creation and development of African American cultures in the New World, but also splendid insight into how imaginative scholars reconstruct the pasts of peoples who for a very long time have been denied a voice in mainstream histories. Among the more impressive contributions are Ira Berlin, *Many Thousands Gone: The First Two Centuries of Slavery in North America* (2000); Philip Morgan, *Slave Counterpoint: Black Culture in the Eighteenth-Century Chesapeaks and Lowcountry* (1998); and Robin Blackburn, *The Making of New World Slavery, 1492–1800* (1997). A pioneering work of high quality is Winthrop D. Jordan, *White Over Black: American Attitudes Toward the Negro, 1550–1812* (1968). Peter Wood provides an original interpretation of the evolution of race relations in *Black Majority: Negroes in Colonial South Carolina from 1670 Through the Stono Rebellion* (1974). The world of Anthony Johnson, the focus of the Feature Essay, is reconstructed in T. H. Breen and Stephen Innes, *"Myne Owne Ground": Race and Freedom on Virginia's Eastern Shore, 1640–1676* (1980). The most recent account of the Salem witch trials can be found in Mary Beth Norton, *In the Devil's Snare: The Salem Witchcraft Crisis of 1692* (2002). Richard Godbeer offers a solid account of the Puritans' intimate lives in *Sexual Revolution in Early America* (2002), but one should also consult Laurel T. Ulrich, *Good Wives: Image and Reality in the Lives of Women in Northern New England, 1650–1750* (1982), and a path-breaking essay by Lois G. Carr and Lorena Walsh, "The Planter's Wife: The Experience of White Women in Seventeenth-Century Maryland," *William and Mary Quarterly*, 3rd ser., 34 (1977): 542–571. A provocative discussion of cultural tensions within the British Empire can be found in Linda Colley, *Captives: The Story of Britain's Pursuit of Empire and How its Soldiers and Civilians Were Held Captive by the Dream of Global Supremacy, 1600–1850* (2002).

For a list of additional titles related to this chapter's topics, please see http://www.ablongman.com/divine.

Suggested Web Sites

DPLS Archive: Slave Movement During the 18th and 19th Centuries (Wisconsin)

http://dpls.dacc.wisc.edu/slavedata/index.html

This site explores the slave ships and the slave trade that carried thousands of Africans to the New World.

Excerpts from Slave Narratives

http://vi.uh.edu/pages/mintz/primary.htm

Accounts of slavery from the seventeenth through nineteenth centuries speak volumes about the many impacts of slavery.

Salem Witch Trials: Documentary Archive and Transcription Project

http://www.iath.virginia.edu/salem/home.html

Extensive archive of the 1692 trials and life in late seventeenth-century Massachusetts.

Colonial Documents

http://www.yale.edu/lawweb/avalon/18th.htm

The key documents of the Colonial Era are reproduced here, as are some important documents from earlier and later periods in American history.

LVA Colonial Records Project—Index of digital facsimiles of documents on early Virginia.

http://eagle.vsla.edu/colonial/

This site contains numerous early documents, but it is unguided and a little difficult to use.

Africans in America

http://www.pbs.org/wgbh/aia/home.html

This PBS site contains images and documents recounting slavery in America.

Law and Society

Witches and the Law

A Problem of Evidence in 1692

The events that occurred at Salem Village in 1692 haunt modern memory. In popular American culture, the incident has come to represent our worst nightmare—a community-sanctioned witch hunt that ferrets out deviants in the name of law. What seems most unsettling about the incident is the failure of allegedly good men and women to bear witness against judicial terror. The ordeal of Salem Village links a distant colonial past with the infamous McCarthy hearings of the 1950s as well as other, more recent witch hunts. The story of this deeply troubled town challenges us to confront the possibility that we, too, might allow law and authority to become instruments of injustice.

The challenge in exploring law and society is how best to interpret the Salem trials. It would be easy to insist that Puritan magistrates were gross hypocrites, figures who consciously manipulated the law for their own hateful purposes. But such conclusions are simplistic; they fail to place the Salem nightmare in proper historical context. The participants in this intense social drama acted on a complex set of seventeenth-century assumptions—legal, religious, and scientific—and if judges and jurors wronged innocent people, they did so by the standards of a society very different from our own.

Few New Englanders doubted the existence of witches. For centuries, European communities had identified certain persons as agents of the devil, and when the Puritans migrated to America, they carried these beliefs with them. They recognized no conflict between rational religion and the possible existence of a satanic world populated by witches. Ordinary farmers regarded unusual events—the strange death of a farm animal, for example—as evidence of witchcraft. New England's intellectual leaders sustained popular superstition in impressive scientific publications. In his *Memorable Providences, Relating to Witchcrafts and Possessions* (1689), the Reverend Cotton Mather declared, "I am resolv'd . . . never to use . . . one grain of patience with any man that shall . . . impose upon me a Denial of Devils, or of Witches. I shall . . . count him down-right Impudent if he Assert the Non-Existence of things which we have had such palpable Convictions of."

Colonial New Englanders did more than talk and write about witches; as early as 1647, they executed several. Before the Salem outbreak, ninety-one people had been tried for witchcraft in Massachusetts and Connecticut, and eighteen of them were hanged (not burned as some historians have claimed). In addition, hundreds of people had accused neighbors of witchcraft, but for many reasons—usually lack of convincing evidence—they stopped short of taking such disputes before the court. These were isolated incidents. Before 1692, fear of witches had not sparked mass hysteria.

Salem Village was different. In this instance, charges of witchcraft shattered a community already deeply divided against itself. The predominantly agricultural Salem Village lay a few miles up the Ipswich Road from the bustling commercial port of Salem Town. The farmers of the Village envied their neighbors' prosperity. Even more, they resented the control that Town authorities exerted over the Village church and government. This tension found expression in numerous personal and family rivalries. In 1689, the congregation at Salem Village ordained the Reverend Samuel Parris, a troubled figure who provoked "disquietness" and "restlessness" and who fanned the factionalism that had long plagued the community.

The witchcraft crisis began suddenly in mid-January 1692, when two girls in the Parris household experienced violent convulsions and frightening visions. A local physician examined the afflicted children but found no "natural" cause for their condition. Soon anxious families raised the possibility of witchcraft, a move which set off a storm of accusations that did not abate until October. By that time, 19 people had died and more than 150 prisoners still awaited trial.

Although the witch hysteria affected everyone—men and women, rich and poor, farmers and merchants—the accusers and their targets were not evenly distributed among the population of Salem Village. Twenty of the thirty-four persons who claimed to have been bewitched were girls between the ages of 11 and 20. Women a full generation older than the accusers were most likely to be identified as witches; more than 40 percent of the accused fell into this category. Although men and women from many different backgrounds were accused, one widely shared characteristic was a history of socially unacceptable behavior. Sarah Good, for example, smoked a pipe and was known for cursing her enemies. John Aldin's accusers described him as "a bold fellow . . . who lies with Indian squaws . . . [and stands] with his hat on before the judges." Bridget Bishop ran a scandalous tavern and dressed in a particularly flashy, immodest manner. Those who testified against the supposed witches came from all classes, both genders, and every age group. Indeed, virtually the entire community was drawn into the ugly business of charge and countercharge, fear and betrayal.

New England's intellectual leaders—most of them Harvard-educated clergymen—tried to make sense out of reports coming out of Salem. Since the colonies did not yet have a newspaper, the reflections of these prominent figures significantly shaped how the entire society interpreted the frightening events of 1692. During the spring of that year, accusations of witchcraft mounted while magistrates interrogated everyone touched by the contagion.

Arriving from England in mid-May at the height of the witch hunt, the new royal governor of Massachusetts Bay, William Phips, appointed a special court of law (a court of "oyer and terminer") to try the cases at Salem Village. The seven judges he appointed all had previous experience in the colony's law courts. Phips wanted the trials to be as fair as possible and procedurally correct. A proper jury was impaneled. Despite precautions, however, the court itself soon succumbed to the frenzy. Chief judge and deputy governor William Stoughton, for example, staunchly believed the girls had been bewitched, and he had little doubt that "real" witches were responsible for the trouble at Salem Village. By contrast, Nathaniel Saltonstall was highly skeptical of the witchcraft charges. After witnessing the first round of executions, Saltonstall resigned from the court and turned to alcohol to persuade himself the court had not made a terrible mistake. Although the judges and jury may have felt ambivalent about what was happening, the law stated that persons convicted as witches must die.

This elegantly gabled house, built about 1675, stands at 310-1/2 Essex Street in Salem, Massachusetts. The residence of Jonathan Corwin, a magistrate for the court of oyer and terminer that heard the witchcraft cases in 1692, the structure became known as the Witch House. ❖

Everything turned on evidence. Confession offered the most reliable proof of witchcraft, and it occurred surprisingly often. We will never know what compelled people to confess. Some may have actually believed they had cast spells on their neighbors or had foretold the future. Many women, though believing themselves innocent, may have confessed because of guilt for impure thoughts that they had privately entertained. Perhaps the psychological strain of imprisonment, coupled with intense social scrutiny, convinced them they might have unwittingly entered into a contract with the devil. Regardless, the stories they told undoubtedly mortified those who heard them and fueled the growing frenzy. Imagine the reaction to Ann Foster's July 18 confession:

> Ann Foster . . . confessed that the devill in the shape of a black man appeared to her with [Martha] Carrier about six yeare since when they made her a witch and that she promised to serve the devill two years: upon which the Devill promised her prosperity and many things but never performed it, that she and Martha Carrier did both ride on a stick or pole when they went to the witch meeting at Salem Village and that the stick broak: as they were carried in the air above the tops of the trees and they fell but she did hang fast about the neck of [Martha] Carrier and were presently at the village, . . . she further saith that she heard some of the witches say that there was three hundred and five in the whole Country and that they would ruin that place the Village . . .

Most of the accused did not confess, however, forcing the judges to produce tangible evidence of witchcraft. The charge was difficult because the crime of bewitchment was, by nature, an invisible act. Earthly laws and magistrates had difficulty dealing with crimes that occurred in the spiritual world. In this situation, the beleaguered judges used a few customary tests. All witches supposedly had a "witch's teat," usually a flap of skin located anywhere on the body, from which they gave suck to the devil. The judges subjected almost every defendant to a humiliating physical examination in order to find such biological abnormalities. Witches could also be discovered by having them touch a girl in the midst of her torments. If the girl's fits ceased, then the person who touched her was assumed responsible for her agony. Since this form of evidence was immediately observable, judges relied on it heavily, oftentimes parading accused witches before the possessed girls waiting to see whose touch would calm them.

Had the terrible ordeal turned solely on unsightly warts, the trials might have ended without further note. But that did not happen. The judges allowed the jury to entertain a different sort of evidence, "spectral evidence," and it was this material that hanged people at Salem Village. New Englanders believed that witches worked by dispatching a specter, a phantom spirit, to torment their victims. This meant that witches had power over great distances; they were invisible. They entered people's dreams, and dozens of good New Englanders complained of having been bitten, pinched, or even choked by specters that looked a lot like their neighbors. The judges regularly accepted spectral testimony of the sort offered by 18-year-old John Cook:

> . . . one morning about sun rising as I was in bed . . . I saw [Bridget] Bishop . . . Standing in the chamber by the window and she looked on me & . . . presently struck me on the Side of the head w'ch did very much hurt me & then I Saw her goe Out under the End window at a little Creviss about So bigg as I Could thrust my hand into. I Saw her again the Same day . . . walke & Cross the roome & having at the time an apple in my hand it flew Out of my hand into my mothers lapp who stood Six or Eight foot distance from me & then She disappeared & though my mother & Severall others were in the Same room yet they affirmed they Saw her not.

A view of Gallows Hill at Salem. On this site, condemned witches were hanged. ❖

As far as the witch hunters were concerned, Bridget Bishop had been caught in the act. To the modern observer, however, the problems with this kind of evidence seem obvious. First, how could one tell whether Cook was lying? The power of his story lay in its inability to be corroborated, for one could never check the authenticity of an intensely private dream or vision. The second problem was that persons accused of being witches had no defense against spectral testimony. When Captain John Aldin stood before his accusers, for example, they immediately fell to the ground, writhing in pain. When asked why he tormented the girls, Aldin firmly denied any wrongdoing, inquiring why the judges "suppose[d he had] no better things to do than to come to Salem to afflict these persons that I never knew or saw before." Aldin's defense did not carry much weight when set against the testimony of the suffering girls, and rather than conclude the accusers manifested a "lying spirit," the judges admitted all spectral evidence as incontestable proof of witchcraft.

Very early in the trials, a few people expressed doubts about the reliability of this particular form of evidence. Cotton Mather and other ministers, for example, issued a statement urging the judges to use spectral evidence with "a very critical and exquisite caution." Some feared the devil could assume the shape of innocent people. If this was the case, then the visions of the afflicted proved nothing but the devil's ability to deceive humans. In the absence of spectral evidence, the cases against most of the witches boiled down to little more than long-standing complaints against obnoxious neighbors. The fury of prosecution silenced the skeptical voices, however, and chief judge William Stoughton continued to accept dreams and visions as proof of witchcraft.

Fantastic testimony about flying witches and pinching specters lent an almost circuslike air to the proceedings at Salem. Before the judges and the members of the jury, the afflicted girls would fall to the ground, convulsing and screaming, claiming to see witches that remained invisible to the court. Hundreds of spectators sat horrified as Satan caused suffering before their own eyes. For seventeenth-century New Englanders who felt the presence of the spiritual world in their everyday lives, the courtroom at Salem offered the opportunity to witness the struggle between the forces of darkness and light. Because of the gravity of the situation, no one expected the judges to deal lightly with those who had sworn allegiance to the devil. Indeed, in the interest of obtaining a confession, the judges conducted harsh interrogations, usually assuming the guilt of the defendant. The intense psychological pressure inflicted on the defendants is revealed in the questioning of Sarah Good, a woman subsequently hanged as a witch:

Judge: Sarah Good, what evil spirit have you familiarity with?
Good: None.
Judge: Why do you hurt these children?
Good: I do not hurt them. I scorn it.
Judge: Who do you employ then to do it?
Good: I employ nobody.
Judge: Have you made a contract with the devil?
Good: No.
Judge: Sarah Good . . . why do you not tell us the truth? Why do you thus torment these poor children?
Good: I do not torment them.

Even the ministers who advised caution applauded the judges' "assiduous endeavors" and encouraged the "vigorous prosecution" of the witches. As the witch hysteria gained momentum, few people dared to defend the witches for fear of being accused themselves. The humble pleas of those who genuinely thought themselves innocent fell on the deaf ears of a community convinced of its own righteousness.

By late September, with twenty people already executed, the emotional intensity that had sustained the witch hunt in its early stages began to ebb. For one thing, the accusations spun wildly out of control as the afflicted girls began naming unlikely candidates as witches: prominent ministers, a judge's mother-in-law, and even the governor's wife! Such accusations discredited the entire procedure by which the witches had been discovered. Also, although the jails could barely hold the 150 people still awaiting trial, the accusations kept coming. The terror was feeding on itself.

In mid-October, Governor Phips dismissed the original court and appointed a new one, this time barring spectral evidence. All remaining defendants were quickly acquitted, although, curiously enough, three women still confessed to having practiced witchcraft. In a letter to the king, Phips explained his decision to end the trials, claiming that "the people" had become "dissatisfied and disturbed." Men and women who had been so eager to purify the community of evil, to murder neighbors in the name of a higher good, now spoke of their fear of divine retribution. Perhaps the dying words of Sarah Good, uttered in response to the assistant minister of Salem Town, echoed in their ears: "I am no more a witch than you are a wizard, and if you take away my life, God will give you blood to drink."

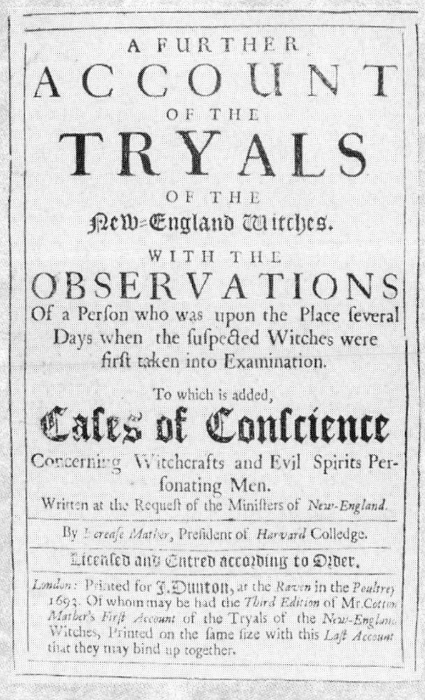
A FURTHER
ACCOUNT
OF THE
TRYALS
OF THE
New-England Witches.
WITH THE
OBSERVATIONS
Of a Perſon who was upon the Place ſeveral Days when the ſuſpected Witches were firſt taken into Examination.

To which is added,
Caſes of Conſcience
Concerning Witchcrafts and Evil Spirits Perſonating Men.
Written at the Requeſt of the Miniſters of *New-England.*

By *Increaſe Mather*, Preſident of *Harvard* Colledge.

Licenſed and Entred according to Order.

London: Printed for J. Dunton, at the *Raven* in the *Poultrey* 1693. Of whom may be had the *Third Edition* of Mr. *Cotton Mather's First Account* of the Tryals of the *New-England* Witches, Printed on the ſame ſize with this *Laſt Account* that they may bind up together.

Title page of *A Further Account of the Tryals of the New England Witches* (1693), Increase Mather's reflection on the incidents at Salem Village. Mather's *Cases of Conscience Concerning Witchcrafts and Evil Spirits* is credited with helping end the witchcraft executions in Salem. ❖

Soon after the trials ended, the witch hunters quickly turned confessors. In 1706, Ann Putnam, one of the most prolific accusers, publicly asked for forgiveness: "I desire to be humbled before God. . . . It was a great delusion of Satan that deceived me in that time." Nine years earlier, the Salem jurors had issued a similar statement, asking the community to understand the particular pressures that compelled them to convict so many people:

> We confess that we . . . were not capable to understand, nor able to withstand the mysterious delusions of the Powers of Darkness . . . ; but were for want of Knowledge in our selves, and better Information from others, prevailed with to take up with such

> Evidence against the Accused, as on further consideration, and better Information, we justly fear was insufficient for the touching the Lives of any . . . whereby we fear we have been instrumental with others, tho Ignorantly and unwittingly, to bring upon our selves, and this People of the Lord, the Guilt of Innocent Blood.

The state never again executed citizens for witchcraft. The experience at Salem had taught New Englanders that, although witches may have existed, no human court could identify a witch beyond a reasonable doubt. The Reverend Increase Mather summed up the attitude of a post-Salem New England: "It were better that ten suspected witches should escape than that one innocent person should be condemned."

What triggered the tragic events of 1692 remains a mystery. Some historians view the witch hunt as a manifestation of Salem Village's socioeconomic troubles. This interpretation helps explain why the primary accusers came from the agrarian village while the alleged witches either resided in or were somehow connected to the market-oriented town. Perhaps the charge of witchcraft masked a deep resentment for their neighbors' monetary success and the new set of values that accompanied the market economy. Other historians believe the witch hunt reflected a deep ambivalence about gender roles in New England society. Young girls lashed out at older nonconforming women because they symbolized a freedom that was achievable within New England society, yet vehemently criticized. Facing the choice between becoming their husbands' servants or being free, the accusers may have expressed this cultural frustration in lethal ways. Terror of Indian attack may have exacerbated community fear. Some accusers described the devil as a "tawney man," a clear reference to Native Americans. These and many other factors contributed to the witch phenomenon.

Regardless of which interpretation one favors, one must acknowledge that Salem Village had indeed been possessed. The blame rests on the community as a whole, not just on a few vindictive judges. In 1697, another repentant witch hunter, the Reverend John Hale, tried to explain how well-meaning people had caused such harm:

> I am abundantly satisfyed that those who were most concerned to act and judge in those matters, did not willingly depart from the rules of righteousness. But such was the darkness of that day, . . . that we walked in the clouds, and could not see our way.

Hale's words ring hollow. They came too late to do much good. As other communities have learned throughout the long history of this nation, it is easier to apologize after the fact than to stand up courageously against the first injustice.

Questions for Discussion

- Do the interpretations for the Salem witch hunt provided by modern historians seem adequate to explain what happened in 1692? Why or why not?
- What could the people of Massachusetts Bay have done to halt the legal proceedings at an early stage?
- Since science and theology seemed to be on their side, can we hold the leading ministers and magistrates of the colony responsible for not halting the trials before so many executions had taken place? Should we judge their record by modern standards of evidence?
- Should the magistrates who sat in judgment at Salem have been tried later for incompetence or malfeasance? Or forced publicly to apologize for their actions?
- What can modern Americans learn from the events of 1692?

Chapter 4

World commerce defined urban life in late colonial America. This engraving of a work originally done by William Burgis celebrates the impact of Anglo-American trade on mid-eighteenth-century Boston. ❖

Experience of Empire: Eighteenth-Century America

Constructing an Anglo-American Identity: The Journal of William Byrd

William Byrd II (1674–1744) was a type of British American one would not have encountered during the earliest years of settlement. This successful Tidewater planter was a product of a new, more cosmopolitan environment, and as an adult, Byrd seemed as much at home in London as in his native Virginia. In 1728, at the height of his political influence in Williamsburg, the capital of colonial Virginia, Byrd accepted a commission to help survey a disputed boundary between North Carolina and Virginia. During his long journey into the distant backcountry, Byrd kept a detailed journal, a satiric, often bawdy chronicle of daily events that is now regarded as a classic of early American literature.

On his trip into the wilderness, Byrd met many different people. No sooner had he departed a familiar world of tobacco plantations than he came across a self-styled "Hermit," an Englishman who apparently preferred the freedom of the woods to the constraints of society. "He has no other Habitation but a green Bower or Harbour," Byrd reported, "with a Female Domestick as wild & as dirty as himself."

As the boundary commissioners pushed farther into the backcountry, they encountered highly independent men and women of European descent, small frontier families that Byrd regarded as living no better than savages. He attributed their uncivilized behavior to a diet of too much pork. "The Truth of it is, these People live so much upon Swine's flesh . . . [that it] makes them . . . extremely hoggish in their Temper, & many of them seem to Grunt rather than Speak in their ordinary conversation." The wilderness journey also brought Byrd's party of surveyors into regular contact with Native Americans, whom he properly distinguished as Catawbas, Tuscaroras, Usherees, and Sapponis.

BYRD'S JOURNAL INVITES US TO VIEW the rapidly developing eighteenth-century backcountry from a fresh perspective. It was not a vast empty territory awaiting the arrival of European settlers. Maps often sustain this erroneous impression, depicting cities and towns, farms and plantations clustered along the Atlantic coast; they suggest a "line of settlement" steadily pushing outward into a huge blank area with no mark of civilization. The people Byrd met on his journey into the backcountry would not have understood such maps. After all, the empty space on the maps was their home. They experienced the frontier as populous zones of many cultures stretching from the English and French settlements in the north all the way to the Spanish borderlands in the far southwest.

The point is not to discount the significance of the older Atlantic settlements. During the eighteenth century, Britain's thirteen mainland colonies underwent a profound transformation. The population in the colonies grew at unprecedented rates.

OUTLINE

FEATURE ESSAY

William Byrd II. Byrd's History of the Dividing Line Run in the Year 1728 *contains a marvelously satirical account of the culture of poor country farmers in North Carolina.* ❖

German and Scots-Irish immigrants arrived in huge numbers. So too did African slaves.

Wherever they lived, colonial Americans of this period were less isolated from one another than colonists had been during most of the seventeenth century. Indeed, after 1690, men and women expanded their cultural horizons, becoming part of a larger Anglo-American empire. The change was striking. Colonists whose parents or grandparents had come to the New World to confront a "howling wilderness" now purchased imported European manufactures, read English journals, participated in imperial wars, and sought favors from a growing number of resident royal officials. No one—not even the inhabitants of the distant frontiers—could escape the influence of Britain. The cultural, economic, and political links connecting the colonists to the imperial center in London grew stronger with time.

This surprising development raises a difficult question for the modern historian. If the eighteenth-century colonists were so powerfully attracted to Great Britain, then why did they ever declare independence? The answer may well be that as the colonists became more British, they inevitably became more American as well. This was a development of major significance, for it helps to explain the appearance after midcentury of genuine nationalist sentiment. Political, commercial, and military links that brought the colonists into more frequent contact with Great Britain also made them more aware of other colonists. It was within an expanding, prosperous empire that they first began seriously to consider what it meant to be American.

Growth and Diversity

The phenomenal growth of British America during the eighteenth century amazed Benjamin Franklin, one of the first persons to bring mathematical rigor to the study of demography. The population of the English colonies doubled approximately every twenty-five years, and, according to calculations Franklin made in 1751, if the expansion continued at such an extraordinary rate for another century or so, "the greatest Number of Englishmen will be on this Side [of] the water."

Accurate population data from the colonial period are extremely difficult to find. The first national census did not occur until 1790. Still, various sources surviving from prerevolutionary times indicate that the total white population of Britain's thirteen mainland colonies rose from about 250,000 in 1700 to 2,150,000 in 1770, an annual growth rate of 3 percent.

Few societies in recorded history have expanded so rapidly, and if the growth rate had not dropped substantially during the nineteenth and twentieth centuries, the current population of the United States would stand at well more than one billion people. Natural reproduction was responsible for most of the growth. More families bore children who in turn lived long enough to have children of their own. Because of this sudden expansion, the population of the late colonial period was strikingly young; approximately one-half of the populace at any given time was under age 16.

Not only was the total population increasing at a very rapid rate; it also was becoming more dispersed and heterogeneous. Each year witnessed the arrival of thousands of non-English Europeans. Unlike those seventeenth-century English settlers in search of religious sanctuary or instant wealth (see Chapter 2), the newcomers generally transferred in the hope of obtaining their own land and setting up as independent farmers. These people often traveled to the **backcountry,** a region stretching approximately eight hundred miles from western Pennsylvania to Georgia.

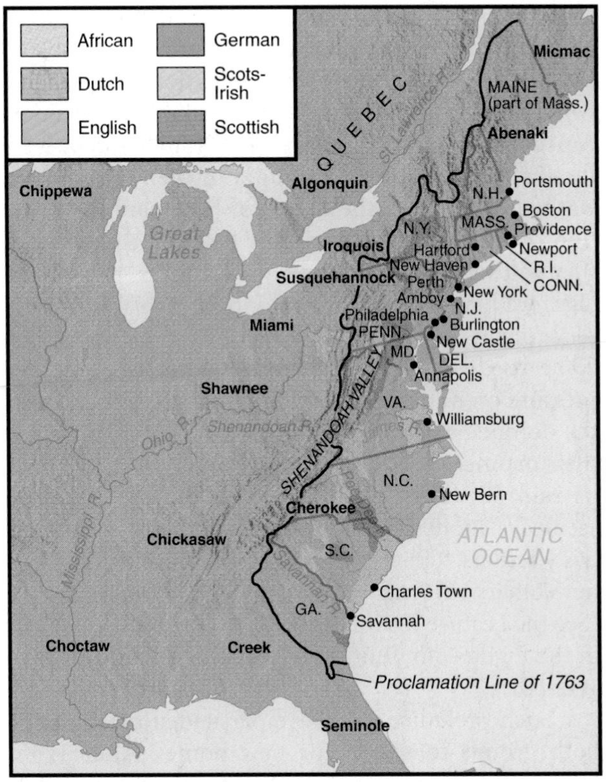

DISTRIBUTION OF EUROPEAN AND AFRICAN IMMIGRANTS IN THE THIRTEEN COLONIES

A flood of non-English immigrants swept the British colonies between 1700 and 1775.

Although they planned to follow customs they had known in Europe, they found the challenge of surviving on the British frontier far more demanding than they had anticipated. They plunged into a complex, fluid, often violent society that included large numbers of Native Americans and African Americans as well as other Europeans.

Scots-Irish Flee English Oppression

Non-English colonists poured into American ports throughout the eighteenth century, creating rich ethnic diversity in areas originally settled by Anglo-Saxons. The largest group of newcomers consisted of Scots-Irish. The experiences of these people in Great Britain influenced not only their decision to move to the New World but also their behavior once they arrived.

During the seventeenth century, English rulers thought they could thoroughly dominate Catholic Ireland by transporting thousands of lowland Scottish Presbyterians to the northern region of that war-torn country. The plan failed. English officials who were members of the Anglican Church discriminated against the Presbyterians. They passed laws that placed the Scots-Irish at a severe disadvantage when they traded in England; they taxed them at exorbitant rates.

After several poor harvests, many of the Scots-Irish elected to emigrate to America, where they hoped to find the freedom and prosperity that had been denied them in Ireland. "I have seen some of their letters to their friends here [Ireland]," one British agent reported in 1729, ". . . in which after they set forth and recommend the fruitfulness and commodities of the country [America], they tell them, that if they will but carry over a little money with them, they may for a small sum purchase considerable tracts of land." Often entire Presbyterian congregations followed charismatic ministers to the New World, intent on replicating a distinctive, fiercely independent culture on the frontier. It is estimated that 150,000 Scots-Irish migrated to the colonies before the Revolution.

Most Scots-Irish immigrants landed initially in Philadelphia, but instead of remaining in that city, they carved out farms on Pennsylvania's western frontier. The colony's proprietors welcomed the influx of new settlers, for it seemed they would form an ideal barrier between the Indians and the older, coastal communities. The Penn family soon had second thoughts, however. The Scots-Irish squatted on whatever land looked best, and when colony officials pointed out that large tracts had already been reserved, the immigrants retorted that "it was against the laws of God and nature that so much land should be idle when so many Christians wanted it to labour on and to raise their bread." Wherever they located, the Scots-Irish challenged established authority.

Germans Search for a Better Life

A second large body of non-English settlers, more than 100,000 people, came from the upper Rhine Valley, the German Palatinate. Some of the migrants, especially those who relocated to America around the turn of the century, belonged to small pietistic Protestant sects whose religious views were somewhat similar to those of the Quakers. These Germans moved to the New World primarily in the hope of finding religious toleration. Under the guidance of Francis Daniel Pastorius (1651–1720), a group of Mennonites established in Pennsylvania a prosperous community known as Germantown.

By midcentury, however, the characteristics of the German migration had begun to change. Large numbers of Lutherans transferred to the Middle Colonies. Unlike members of the pietistic sects, these men and women were not in search of religious freedom. Rather, they traveled to the New World looking to better their material lives. The Lutheran Church in Germany initially tried to maintain control over the distant congregations, but even though the migrants themselves fiercely preserved many aspects of traditional German culture, they were eventually forced to accommodate to new social conditions. Henry Melchior Mühlenberg (1711–1787), a tireless leader, helped German Lutherans through a difficult cultural adjustment, and in 1748, Mühlenberg organized a meeting of local pastors and lay delegates that ordained ministers of their own choosing, an act of spiritual independence that has been called "the most important single event in American Lutheran history."

The German migrants—mistakenly called Pennsylvania Dutch because the English confused *deutsch* (meaning "German") with *Dutch* ("a person from Holland")—began reaching Philadelphia in large numbers after 1717, and by 1766, persons of German stock accounted for more than one-third of Pennsylvania's total population. Even their most vocal detractors admitted the Germans were the best farmers in the colony.

Ethnic differences in Pennsylvania bred disputes. The Scots-Irish as well as the Germans preferred to live with people of their own background, and they sometimes fought to keep members of the other nationality out of their neighborhoods. The English were suspicious of both groups. They could not comprehend why the Germans insisted on speaking German in America. In 1753, for example, Franklin described these settlers as "the most stupid of their nation." He warned that "unless the stream of [German] importation could be turned from this to other colonies . . . they will soon outnumber us, . . . [and] all the advantages we have, will in my opinion, be not able to preserve our language, and even our government will become precarious." As Franklin's remarks suggest, the pressure on non-English colonists to accommodate to the dominant culture—in other words, to "Anglicize" their manners and behavior—was very great. In comparison to some of his contemporaries, Franklin seemed a moderate critic of the German and Scots-Irish settlers. Others threatened violence against the newcomers who refused to conform to English ways. (See the Feature Essay, "Learning to Live with Diversity in the Eighteenth Century: What Is an American?" pp. 100–101.)

This folk art painting from the cover of a clothes box depicts a well-dressed German-American farmer. The farmer's hat, his coat, and walking stick indicate that he enjoyed a middling to high status. ❖

Such prejudice may have persuaded members of both groups to search for new homes. After 1730, Germans and Scots-Irish pushed south from western Pennsylvania into the Shenandoah Valley, thousands of them settling in the backcountry of Virginia and the Carolinas. The Germans usually remained wherever they found unclaimed fertile land. By contrast, the Scots-Irish often moved two or three times, acquiring a reputation as a rootless people.

Wherever the newcomers settled, they often found themselves living beyond the effective authority of the various colonial governments. To be sure, backcountry residents petitioned for assistance during wars against the Indians, but most of the time they preferred to be left alone. These conditions heightened the importance of religious institutions within the small ethnic communities. Although the original stimulus for coming to America may have been a desire for economic independence and prosperity, backcountry families—especially the Scots-Irish—flocked to evangelical Protestant preachers, to Presbyterian, and later Baptist and Methodist ministers who not only fulfilled the settlers' spiritual needs but also gave scattered backcountry communities a pronounced moral character that survived long after the colonial period.

Convict Settlers

Since the story of European migration tends to be upbeat—men and women engaged in a largely successful quest for a better material life—it often is forgotten that British courts compelled many people to come to America. Indeed, the African slaves were not the only large group of people coerced into moving to the New World. In 1718, Parliament passed the Transportation Act, allowing judges in England, Scotland, and Ireland to send convicted felons to the American colonies. Between 1718 and 1775, the courts shipped approximately fifty thousand convicts across the Atlantic. Some of these men and women may actually have been dangerous criminals, but the majority seem to have committed minor crimes against property. Although transported convicts—almost 75 percent of whom were young males—escaped the hangman, they found life difficult in the colonies. Eighty percent of them were sold in the Chesapeake colonies as indentured servants. At best they faced an uncertain future, and it is probably not surprising that few former convicts prospered in America.

British authorities lavished praise on this system. According to one writer, transportation drained "the Nation of its offensive Rubbish, without taking away their Lives." Although Americans purchased the convict servants, they expressed fear that these men and women would create a dangerous criminal class. In one irate essay, Benjamin Franklin asked his readers to consider just how the colonists might repay the leaders of Great Britain for shipping so many felons to America. He suggested that rattlesnakes might be the appropriate gift. "I would propose to have them carefully distributed . . . ," Franklin wrote, "in the Gardens of all the Nobility and Gentry throughout the Nation; but particularly in the Gardens of the Prime Ministers, *the Lords of Trade* and *Members of Parliament.*" The Revolution forced the British courts to redirect the flow of convicts to another part of the world; an indirect result of American independence was the founding of Australia by transported felons.

Native Americans Stake Out a Middle Ground

In some histories of the colonial period, Native Americans make only a brief appearance, usually during the earliest years of conquest and settlement. After initial contact with the first European invaders, the Indians seem mysteriously to disappear from the central narrative of colonization, and it is not until the nineteenth century that they turn up again, this time to wage a last desperate battle against the encroachment of white society.

This obviously inadequate account slights one of the richer chapters of Native American history. During much of the seventeenth century, various Indian

Elizabeth Canning, convicted of perjury, stands at the bar to receive her sentence from the London court. For her crime, she was sentenced to one month's imprisonment and transport for seven years to the American colonies. ❖

groups who contested the English settlers for control of coastal lands suffered terribly, sometimes from war, but more often from the spread of contagious diseases such as smallpox. The two races found it very difficult to live in close proximity. As one Indian informed the members of the Maryland assembly in 1666, "Your hogs & Cattle injure Us, You come too near Us to live & drive Us from place to place. We can fly no farther; let us know where to live & how to be secured for the future from the Hogs & Cattle."

Against such odds the Indians managed to survive. By the eighteenth century, the site of the most intense and creative contact between the races had shifted to the cis-Mississippian west, that is, to the huge territory between the Appalachian Mountains and the Mississippi River, where several hundred thousand Native Americans made their homes.

Many Indians had only recently migrated to the area. The Delawares, for example, retreated to far western Pennsylvania and the Ohio Valley to escape almost continuous confrontation with advancing European invaders. Other Indians drifted west in less happy circumstances. They were refugees, the remnants of Native American groups who had lost so many people that they could no longer sustain an independent cultural identity. These survivors joined with other Indians to establish new multiethnic communities. In this respect, the Native American villages may not have seemed all that different from the mixed European settlements of the backcountry.

Stronger groups of Indians such as the Creek, Choctaw, Chickasaw, Cherokee, and Shawnee generally welcomed the refugees. Strangers were formally adopted to take the places of family members killed in battle or overcome by sickness, and it should be appreciated that many seemingly traditional Indian villages of the eighteenth century actually represented innovative responses to rapidly shifting external conditions. As historian Peter Wood explained, "Physically and linguistically diverse groups moved to form loosely organized confederacies, unions of mutual convenience, that effectively restrained interethnic hostilities."

The concept of a *middle ground*—a term that has only recently entered the interpretive vocabulary—helps us more fully to comprehend how eighteenth-century Indians held their own in the backcountry beyond the Appalachian Mountains. The Native Americans never intended to isolate themselves completely from European contact. They relied on white traders, French as well as English, to provide essential metal goods and weapons. The goal of the Indian confederacies was rather to maintain a strong independent voice in these commercial exchanges, whenever possible playing the French against the British, and so long as they had sufficient military strength—that is, large numbers of healthy armed warriors—they compelled everyone who came to negotiate in the "middle ground" to give them proper respect. It would be incorrect, therefore, to characterize their relations with the Europeans as a stark choice between resistance or accommodation, between total war or abject surrender. Native Americans took advantage of rivals when possible; they compromised when necessary. It is best to imagine the Indians' middle ground as an open, dynamic process of creative interaction.

The Susquehannocks understood the rules of the middle ground. Indeed, they mastered the eighteenth-century language of commercial negotiation. When backcountry traders charged the Indians seemingly exorbitant prices for European goods, the angry Susquehannocks took their complaint to James Hamilton, the lieutenant governor of Pennsylvania. In fact, they forced Hamilton to give them a short lecture on international economics, an event that shows the Indians were fully capable of grasping the essential elements of modern capitalism. "You know we dont make the Goods ourselves," Hamilton whined, "they are made in England, and the Transporting them over the Seas is dangerous in time of War and very expensive, so that . . . their prices change, as the risque and demand for them is greater or less."

However desirable they may have appeared, European goods subtly eroded traditional structures of Native American authority. During the period of earliest encounter with white men, Indian leaders reinforced their own power by controlling the character and flow of commercial exchange. If a trader wanted a rich supply of animal skins, for example, he soon learned that he had better negotiate directly with a chief or tribal elder. But as the number of European traders operating within the "middle ground" expanded, ordinary Indians began to bargain on their own account, obtaining colorful and durable manufactured items without first consulting a Native American leader. Independent commercial dealings of this sort tended further to weaken the Indians' ability to resist organized white aggression. As John Stuart, a superintendent of Indian affairs, explained in 1761, "A modern Indian cannot subsist without Europeans; And would handle a Flint Ax or any other rude utensil used by his ancestors very awkwardly; So that what was only convenience at first is now become Necessity."

The survival of the middle ground depended ultimately on factors over which the Native Americans had little control. Imperial competition between France and Great Britain enhanced the Indians' bargaining position, but after the British defeated the French in 1763, the Indians no longer received the same solicitous attention as they had in earlier times. Keeping old allies happy seemed to the British a need-

Tishcohan, chief of the Delaware tribe that lost much of its land in Thomas Penn's Walking Purchase of 1737, is shown here in a 1735 portrait by Gustavus Hesselius. Although treaties and agreements with European settlers were often detrimental to Native Americans, some alliances in the "middle ground" allowed the tribes to play off the French against the British. Alliances were often signified by tokens such as certificates, calumets (ceremonial pipes), wampum belts, and medals. ❖

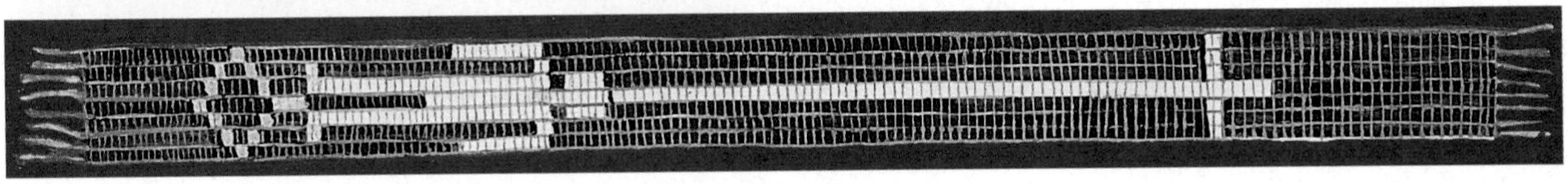

less expense. Moreover, contagious disease continued to take a fearful toll. In the southern backcountry between 1685 and 1790, the Indian population dropped an astounding 72 percent. In the Ohio Valley, the numbers suggest similar rates of decline. In fact, there is some evidence that British military officers practiced germ warfare against the Native Americans, giving them blankets contaminated by smallpox. Based on experience, the officers knew that personal belongings such as blankets taken from the sick were contaminated and, thus, that giving these items to the Indians would put them at risk. By the time the United States took control of this region, the middle ground itself had become a casualty of history.

Spanish Borderlands of the Eighteenth Century

In many traditional histories of North America, the Spanish make only a brief appearance, usually as fifteenth-century conquistadors. But as soon as they have conquered Mexico, they are dropped from the story as if they had no serious part to play in the ongoing development of the continent. This is, of course, a skewed perspective that masks the roots of ethnic diversity in the United States. The Spanish empire did not disappear. Indeed, it continued to shape the character of borderlands societies well into the eighteenth century. As anyone who visits the modern American Southwest quickly discovers, Spanish administrators and priests—not to mention ordinary settlers—left a lasting imprint on the cultural landscape of this country.

Until 1821, when Mexico declared independence from Madrid, Spanish authorities struggled to control a vast northern frontier. During the eighteenth century, the Spanish empire in North America included widely dispersed settlements such as San Francisco, San Diego, Santa Fe, San Antonio, and St. Augustine. In these borderland communities, European colonists mixed with peoples of other races and backgrounds, forming multicultural societies. According to historian Ramón A. Gutiérrez, the Spanish provinces present a story of "the complex web of interactions between men and women, young

Feature Essay

Learning to Live with Diversity in the Eighteenth Century

What Is an American?

Americans have had a hard time dealing with difference. It is only recently that some commentators have begun to describe social diversity as a positive good. For most of our history, attempts to define national identity have inevitably excluded members of minority groups or newcomers whose language and culture were not English. Over the past two centuries those in authority have devised various strategies for accommodating ethnic and racial diversity, some more successful than others, but all of them at any moment is likely to produce anger and violence as mutual understanding. These explosive issues first sparked public debate during the eighteenth century, long before Americans advocated independence.

The sudden arrival of thousands of men and women born in Ireland and Germany worried colonial leaders who assumed that being British meant that a person spoke English and accepted the basic traditions of English law and politics. Problems related to ethnic diversity seemed most pressing in the Middle Colonies such as Pennsylvania, for after the 1720s poor people from the German Palatinate and the area around Belfast flocked to America in search of economic opportunity. James Logan, the provincial secretary of Pennsylvania, sounded the alarm, warning those of English stock of the "foreigners" who threatened to transform the local culture. Because of the number of Germans entering the colony, Logan argued, "these colonies will in time be lost to the Crown." Although the Scots-Irish spoke English, they seemed even more menacing. These Protestant migrants who fled the north of Ireland to escape chronic poverty appeared intent on making "themselves Proprietors of the Province."

Painted floral motifs adorn this 1790 pine schrank (wardrobe) from Lancaster County, Pennsylvania. Closets were rare in German homes in Pennsylvania so families stored all their clothing in such schränke. ❖

It might have been predicted that English colonists would have welcomed so many able workers, people who could pay taxes and defend the frontiers. But such was not the case. Benjamin Franklin, often depicted as a voice of reason, almost panicked when he contemplated the growing diversity. Why, he demanded, should the Germans be allowed "to swarm into our Settlements, and by herding together establish their Language and Manners to the Exclusion of ours? Why should Pennsylvania, founded by the English, become a Colony of *Aliens?*" In fact, Franklin predicted that "Instead of their Learning our Language, we must learn their's, or live as in a foreign Country." As in so many cultural confrontations of this sort, the representatives of the dominant group defined difference as a contest in which one either won or lost. Accommodation had little appeal for those so anxious to preserve the purity of their own heritage.

The question for people such as Franklin was how best to make the Germans and the Scots-Irish more like the English. It was thought that education might save the day. After all, the "foreigners" could be taught to accept a common set of values that obviously served as the foundation for society. Pennsylvania leaders contended that the standards rested ultimately on "the noble Privilege or Birth-Right of an *English Subject.*" As anyone could see,

English identity meant developing a deep respect for the law, property, and institutions originally erected by migrants from England and their descendants. During the years of heaviest immigration, those who claimed to speak for the cultural mainstream, extolled the "sober and prudent conduct of the ancient Settlers and their Successors," in other words, those who understood that "the Rights and Privileges of this Colony, [rested] on the true basis of English *Liberty and Property.*" Some enthusiasts even encouraged the colonial legislature to pass laws for the encouragement of "Virtue, Sobriety, and Industry . . . [to] prevent an English Plantation from Being turned into a Colony of Aliens."

The key to preserving social order in face of growing diversity was Anglicization, a process of transforming Germans and Scots-Irish into people who at least seemed English. Success was just a matter of time. Strange languages, customs, and beliefs could be made to disappear under a veneer of Englishness. Thomas Penn, whose family actually owned Pennsylvania, predicted that the Germans would "certainly by degrees loose their attachment to their Language, and become English, and as they acquire property I dare prophecy will become good Subjects." Indeed, so confident was his brother John of the ability of the Germans to acculturate that he concluded "we ought by no Means to Debar their coming over," because "when settled these [people] will Esteem themselves Pennsylvanians." To accomplish this goal, "Foreigners imported, should not be allowed to settle in large separate Districts . . . because for many Generations they may continue, as it were, a separate People in Language, Modes of Religion, Customs and Manners." The newcomers, therefore, were best "intermixed with the *British* settlers." But one had to be on guard. By "distinguishing themselves" from the dominant culture the members of these groups showed contempt for English traditions. After all, asked a colonial official, "How far is it consistent with the Peace, Honour or Security of an English Government that they, who . . . have had the utmost Protection, should upon Occasions, be thus nationally distinguished?"

All the advice apparently fell on deaf ears. The migrants failed to measure up to English standards, and differences came to be seen as rejection and hostility. To the chagrin of fully Anglicized Pennsylvanians, the German settlers could not be "restrained" from forming tight-knit ethnic communities. They refused to abandon the culture they had known in Europe. Moreover, they did not intermarry with those from other groups, established newspapers in their own language, and set up German-speaking schools. The Scots-Irish raised even more hackles. Although they had demonstrated their loyalty to the British crown in the Old World, they seemed in the New to "have little Honesty and less Sense." An unruly people, they squatted on lands owned by the Penn family or the Native Americans. What is more, they showed no desire to mix with neighbors of different ethnicity. The Scots-Irish held that "no strangers should be admitted to settle within [their] Bounds," and instead of taking their legal disputes to the province's official courts—as any proper Englishman would do—they relied on church elders. To make matters worse for critics such as Franklin, they often reacted to minor insults with violence and were "generally rough" with the Indians. When some Scots-Irish murdered twenty Native Americans in 1763, Franklin called them "Christian white savages," while another colonial official dubbed them "the very scum of mankind."

As has been so often the case with cultural tensions of this sort, the various participants gradually reached an accommodation, often perhaps without even realizing how much they had adjusted to changing conditions. The "foreigners" did not in fact destroy Pennsylvania. Indeed, political leaders who identified themselves as English were soon soliciting the votes of the migrant population, and over time, it became clear that the colony's prosperity in the Atlantic World owed a lot to hard-working aliens. And on the eve of revolution, some Americans had come to realize that diversity was not all that objectionable. As one patriot who called himself "A Son of Liberty" observed in 1768, "It is true that the first emigrations were from *England;* but upon the whole, more settlers have come from *Ireland, Germany,* and other parts of *Europe,* than from *England.*"

The Donegal Presbyterian Church in Lancaster County, Pennsylvania, recalls the cultural heritage of the Scots-Irish settlers of the region. ❖

and old, rich and poor, slave and free, Spaniard and Indian, all of whom fundamentally depended on the other for their own self-definition."

Conquering the Northern Frontier

Not until late in the sixteenth century did Spanish settlers, led by Juan de Oñate, establish European communities north of the Rio Grande. The Pueblos resisted the invasion of colonists, soldiers, and missionaries, and in a major rebellion in 1680 led by El Popé, the native peoples drove the whites completely out of New Mexico. "The heathen have conceived a mortal hatred for our holy faith and enmity for the Spanish nation," concluded one imperial bureaucrat. Not until 1692 were the Spanish able to reconquer this fiercely contested area. By then, Native American hostility coupled with the settlers' failure to find precious metal had cooled Spain's enthusiasm for the northern frontier.

The Mission Nuestra Señora del Espiritu Santo de Zuniga was established in 1722 on the coast of Texas and moved inland in 1749. It was the first large cattle ranch in Texas and supplied the needs of Spanish settlements as far away as Louisiana. It would serve a prominent role in the Texas Revolution and fall into ruin by the twentieth century. Reconstructed by Civilian Conservation Corps in the 1930s, it has become a symbol of Spanish heritage in the American Southwest. This was part of a chain of Spanish missions that dotted the frontier of northern New Spain from Florida to California. ❖

Concern over French encroachment in the Southeast led Spain to colonize St. Augustine (Florida) in 1565. Although the enterprise never flourished, it claims attention as the first permanent European settlement established in what would become the United States, predating the founding of Jamestown and Plymouth by several decades. Pedro Menéndez de Avilés brought some fifteen hundred soldiers and settlers to St. Augustine, where they constructed an impressive fort, but the colony failed to attract additional Spanish migrants. "It is hard to get anyone to go to St. Augustine because of the horror with which Florida is painted," the governor of Cuba complained in 1673. "Only hoodlums and the mischievous go there from Cuba."

California never figured prominently in Spain's plans for the New World. Early explorers reported finding only impoverished Indians living along the Pacific coast. Adventurers saw no natural resources worth mentioning, and since the area proved extremely difficult to reach from Mexico City—the overland trip could take months—California received little attention. Fear that the Russians might seize the entire region belatedly sparked Spanish activity, however, and after 1769, two indomitable servants of empire, Fra Junípero Serra and Don Gaspar de Portolá, organized permanent missions and *presidios* (forts) at San Diego, Monterey, San Francisco, and Santa Barbara.

Peoples of the Spanish Borderlands

In sharp contrast to the English frontier settlements of the eighteenth century, the Spanish outposts in North America grew very slowly. A few Catholic priests and imperial administrators traveled to the northern provinces, but the danger of Indian attack as well as a harsh physical environment discouraged ordinary colonists. The European migrants were overwhelmingly male, most of them soldiers in the pay of the empire. Although some colonists came directly from Spain, most had been born in other Spanish colonies such as Minorca, the Canaries, or New Spain, and because European women rarely appeared on the frontier, Spanish males formed relationships with Indian women, fathering large numbers of mestizos, children of mixed race.

As in other European frontiers of the eighteenth century, encounters with Spanish soldiers, priests, and traders altered Native American cultures. The experience here was quite different from that of the whites and Indians in the British backcountry. The Spanish exploited Native American labor, reducing entire Indian villages to servitude. Many Indians moved to the Spanish towns, and although they lived in close

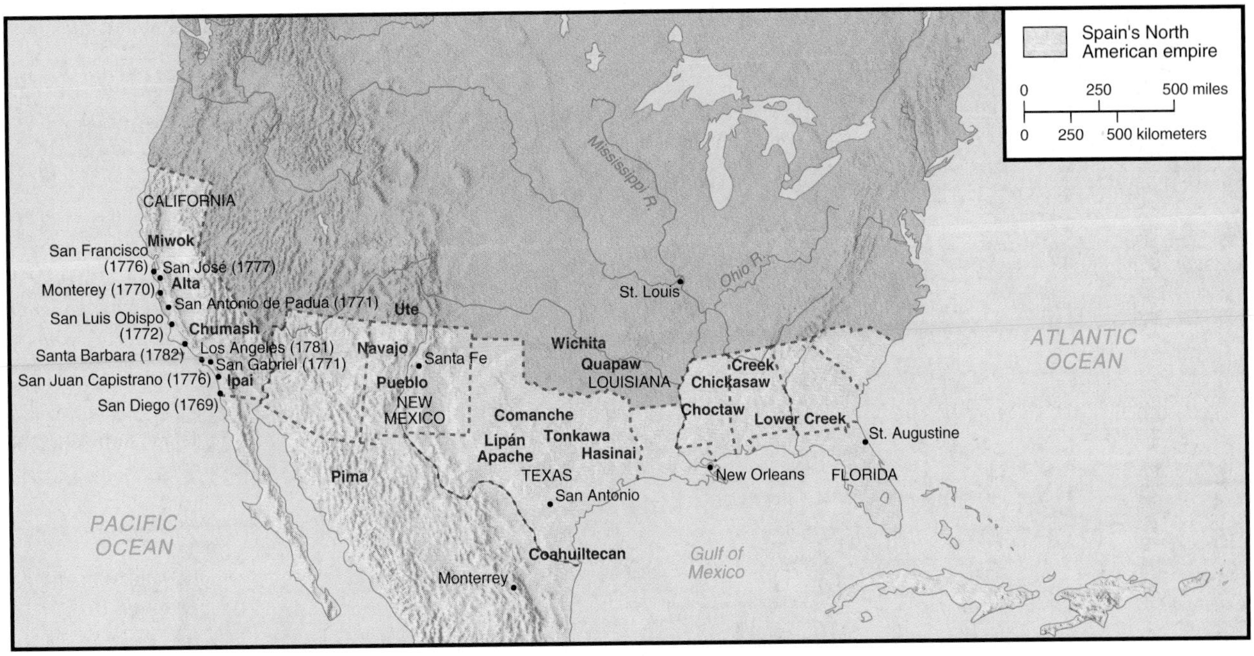

THE SPANISH BORDERLANDS, CA. 1770 *In the late eighteenth century, Spain's North American empire extended across what is now the southern United States from Florida through Texas and New Mexico to California.* ❖

proximity to the Europeans—something rare in British America—they were consigned to the lowest social class, objects of European contempt. However much their material conditions changed, the Indians of the Southwest resisted strenuous efforts to convert them to Catholicism. The Pueblos maintained their own religious forms—often at great personal risk—and they sometimes murdered priests who became too intrusive. Angry Pueblos at Taos reportedly fed the hated Spanish friars corn tortillas containing urine and mouse meat.

The Spanish empire never had the resources necessary to secure the northern frontier fully. The small military posts were intended primarily to discourage other European powers such as France, Great Britain, and Russia from taking possession of territory claimed by Spain. It would be misleading, however, to stress the fragility of Spanish colonization. The urban design and public architecture of many southwestern cities still reflect the vision of the early Spanish settlers, and to a large extent, the old borderlands remain Spanish speaking to this day.

The Impact of European Ideas on American Culture

The character of the older, more established British colonies changed almost as rapidly as that of the backcountry. The rapid growth of an urban cosmopolitan culture impressed eighteenth-century commentators, and even though most Americans still lived on scattered farms, they had begun to participate aggressively in an exciting consumer marketplace that expanded their imaginative horizons.

Provincial Cities

Considering the rate of population growth, it is surprising to discover how few eighteenth-century Americans lived in cities. Boston, Newport, New York, Philadelphia, and Charles Town—the five largest cities—contained only about 5 percent of the colonial population. In 1775, none had more than forty thousand persons. The explanation for the relatively slow development of colonial American cities lies in their highly specialized commercial character. Colonial port towns served as entrepôts, intermediary trade and shipping centers where bulk cargoes were broken up for inland distribution and where agricultural products were gathered for export. They did not support large-scale manufacturing. Indeed, the pool of free urban laborers was quite small, since the type of person who was forced to work for wages in Europe usually became a farmer in America.

Yet despite the limited urban population, cities profoundly influenced colonial culture. It was in the cities that Americans were exposed to and welcomed the latest English ideas. Wealthy colonists—merchants and lawyers—tried to emulate the culture of the mother country. They sponsored concerts and plays; they learned to dance. Women as well as men picked

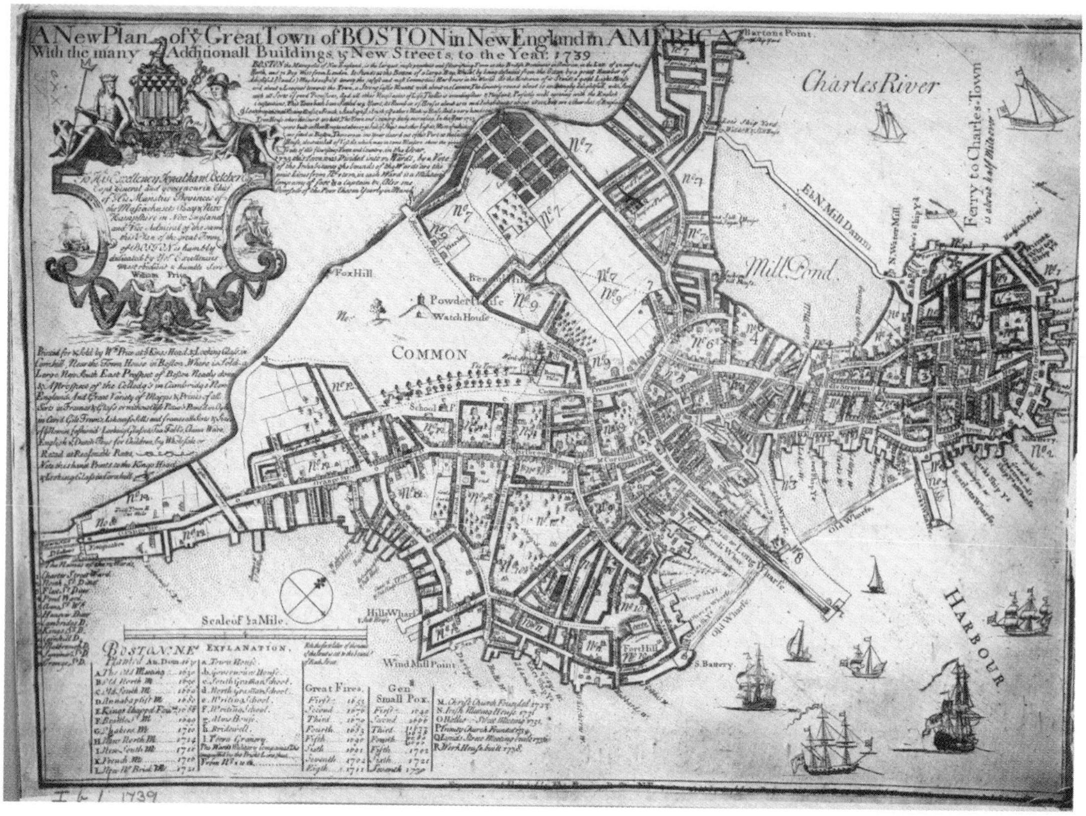

This 1743 map of Boston depicts the port city as an active commercial and cultural center, with many wharves, buildings, churches, and meeting halls. ❖

up the new fashions quickly, and even though most of them had never been outside the colony of their birth, they sometimes appeared to be the products of London's best families.

It was in the cities, also, that wealthy merchants transformed commercial profits into architectural splendor, for, in their desire to outdo one another, they built grand homes of enduring beauty. Most of these buildings are described as Georgian because they were constructed during the reign of Britain's early Hanoverian kings, who all happened to be named George. Actually these homes were provincial copies of grand country houses of Great Britain. They drew their inspiration from the great Italian Renaissance architect Andrea Palladio (1508–1580), who had incorporated classical themes into a rigidly symmetrical form. Palladio's ideas were popularized in the colonies by James Gibbs, an Englishman whose *Book of Architecture* (1728) provided blueprints for the most spectacular homes of mid-eighteenth-century America.

Their owners filled the houses with fine furniture. Each city patronized certain skilled craftsmen, but the artisans of Philadelphia were known for producing magnificent copies of the works of Thomas Chippendale, Great Britain's most famous furniture designer. These developments gave American cities an elegance they had not possessed in the previous century. One foreign visitor noted of Philadelphia in 1748 that "its natural advantages, trade, riches and power, are by no means inferior to any, even of the most ancient towns of Europe." As this traveler understood, the cultural impact of the cities went far beyond the number of people who actually lived there.

American Enlightenment

European historians often refer to the eighteenth century as an Age of Reason. During this period, a body of new, often radical, ideas swept through the salons and universities, altering the way that educated Europeans thought about God, nature, and society. This intellectual revolution, called the **Enlightenment,** involved the work of Europe's greatest minds, men such as Newton and Locke, Voltaire and Hume. The writings of these thinkers eventually reached the colonies, where they received a mixed reception. On the whole, the American Enlightenment was a rather tame affair compared to its European counterpart, for while the colonists welcomed experi-

❖ A Look at the Past ❖

Westover

By the mid-eighteenth century, a native-born elite took shape in Virginia and other colonies. Many wealthy Americans constructed estates to signify their status and power. Few were as grand as Westover in Virginia, probably built by William Byrd III, ca. 1750, but all "great houses" impressed visitors with their size and level of interior decoration. Such houses required vast sums of money as well as knowledge of the latest European styles to construct, maintain, and furnish. The funds needed to maintain these estates often came from the production of export crops such as tobacco and rice, crops cultivated by an unfree black labor force. What did the difference between great houses like Westover and the typical one-room dwellings suggest about eighteenth-century Virginia society? How did building large, elaborate, and fashionable houses contribute to cementing gentry power?

mental science, they defended the tenets of traditional Christianity.

Enlightenment thinkers shared basic assumptions. Philosophers of the Enlightenment replaced the concept of original sin with a much more optimistic view of human nature. A benevolent God, having set the universe in motion, gave human beings the power of reason to enable them to comprehend the orderly workings of his creation. Everything, even human society, operated according to these mechanical rules. The responsibility of right-thinking men and women, therefore, was to make certain that institutions such as church and state conformed to self-evident natural laws. It was possible—or so some of the *philosophes* claimed—to achieve perfection in this world. In fact, human suffering had come about only because people had lost touch with the fundamental insights of reason.

For many Americans, the appeal of the Enlightenment was its focus on a search for useful knowledge, ideas, and inventions that would improve the quality of human life. What mattered was practical experimentation. A speech delivered in 1767 before the members of the American Society in Philadelphia reflected the new utilitarian spirit: "Knowledge is of little Use when confined to mere Speculation," the colonist explained, "But when speculative Truths are reduced to Practice, when Theories grounded upon Experiments . . . and the Arts of Living made more easy and comfortable . . . Knowledge then becomes really useful." The Enlightenment spawned scores of earnest scientific tinkerers, people who dutifully recorded changes in temperature, the appearance of strange plants and animals, and the details of astronomic phenomena. While these eighteenth-century Americans made few earth-shattering discoveries, they did encourage their countrymen, especially those who attended college, to apply reason to the solution of social and political problems.

Benjamin Franklin

Benjamin Franklin (1706–1790) absorbed the new cosmopolitan culture. European thinkers regarded him as a genuine *philosophe,* a person of reason and science, a role that he self-consciously cultivated when he visited England and France in later life. Franklin had little formal education, but as a young man working in his brother's print shop, he managed to keep up with the latest intellectual currents. In his *Autobiography,* Franklin described the excitement of discovering a new British journal. It was like a breath of fresh air to a boy growing up in Puritan New England. "I met with an odd volume of *The Spectator,*" Franklin recounted; ". . . I had never before seen any of them. I bought it, read it over and over, and was much delighted with it. I thought the writing excellent, and wished if possible to imitate it."

Franklin's opportunity came in August 1721 when he and his brother founded the *New England Courant,* a weekly newspaper that satirized Boston's political and religious leaders in the manner of the contemporary British press. Writing under the name Silence Dogood, young Franklin asked his readers "Whether a Commonwealth suffers more by hypocritical Pretenders to Religion, or by the openly Profane?" Proper Bostonians were not prepared for a journal that one minister described as "full freighted with Nonesense, Unmannerliness, Railery, Prophaneness, Immorality, Arrogance, Calumnies, Lyes, Contradictions, and what not, all tending to Quarrels and Divisions and to Debauch and Corrupt the Minds and Manners of New England." Franklin got the point; he left Massachusetts in 1723 in search of a less hostile intellectual environment.

After he had moved to Philadelphia, leaving behind an irritable brother as well as New England Puritanism, Franklin devoted himself to the pursuit of useful knowledge, ideas that would increase the happiness of his fellow Americans. Franklin never denied the existence of God. Rather, he pushed the Lord aside, making room for the free exercise of human reason. Franklin tinkered, experimented, and reformed. Almost everything he encountered in his daily life aroused his curiosity. His investigation of electricity brought him world fame, but Franklin was never satisfied with his work in this field until it yielded practical application. In 1756, he invented the lightning rod. He also designed a marvelously efficient stove that is still used today. In modern America, Franklin has become exactly what he would

Benjamin Franklin (left) exemplified the scientific curiosity and search for practical knowledge characteristic of enlightenment thinkers of the eighteenth century. Franklin's experiments on electricity became world famous and inspired many others to study the effects of the strange force. The citizens shown above (right), eager to try out a new phenomenon, are rubbing metal rods together to produce static electricity. ❖

have wanted to be, a symbol of material progress through human ingenuity.

Franklin energetically promoted the spread of reason. In Philadelphia, he organized groups that discussed the latest European literature, philosophy, and science. In 1727, for example, he "form'd most of my ingenious Acquaintances into a Club for mutual Improvement, which we call'd the Junto." Four years later Franklin took a leading part in the formation of the Library Company, a voluntary association that for the first time allowed people like him to pursue "useful knowledge." The members of these societies communicated with Americans living in other colonies, providing them not only with new information but also with models for their own clubs and associations. Such efforts broadened the intellectual horizons of many colonists, especially those who lived in cities.

Economic Transformation

The colonial economy kept pace with the stunning growth in population. During the first three-quarters of the eighteenth century, the population increased at least tenfold, and yet even with so many additional people to feed and clothe, the per capita income did not decline. Indeed, with the exception of poor urban dwellers, such as sailors whose employment varied with the season, white Americans did quite well. An abundance of land and the extensive growth of agriculture accounted for their economic success. New farmers were able not only to provide for their families' well-being but also to sell their crops in European and West Indian markets. Each year, more Americans produced more tobacco, wheat, or rice—to cite just the major export crops—and by this means, they maintained a high level of individual prosperity without developing an industrial base.

At midcentury, colonial exports flowed along well-established routes. More than half of American goods produced for export went to Great Britain. The Navigation Acts (see Chapter 3) were still in effect, and "enumerated" items such as tobacco had to be landed first at a British port. Furs were added to the restricted list in 1722. The White Pines Acts passed in 1711, 1722, and 1729 forbade Americans from cutting white pine trees without a license. The purpose of this legislation was to reserve the best trees for the use of the Royal Navy. The Molasses Act of 1733—also called the Sugar Act—placed a heavy duty on molasses imported from foreign ports; the Hat and Felt Act of 1732 and the Iron Act of 1750 attempted to limit the production of colonial goods that competed with British exports.

These statutes might have created tensions between the colonists and the mother country had they been rigorously enforced. Crown officials, however, generally ignored the new laws. New England merchants imported molasses from French Caribbean islands without paying the full customs; ironmasters in the Middle Colonies continued to produce iron. Even without the Navigation Acts, however, a majority of colonial exports would have been sold on the English market. The emerging consumer society in Great Britain was beginning to create a new generation of buyers who possessed enough income to purchase American goods, especially sugar and tobacco. This rising demand was the major market force shaping the colonial economy.

Colonial merchants operating out of Boston, Newport, and Philadelphia also carried substantial tonnage to the West Indies. In 1768, this market accounted for 27 percent of all American exports. If there was a triangular trade that included the west coast of Africa, it does not seem to have been economically significant. Colonial ships carrying food sailed for the Caribbean and returned immediately to the Middle Colonies or New England with cargoes of molasses, sugar, and rum. In fact, recent research indicates that during the eighteenth century, trade with Africa involved less than 1 percent of all American exports. Slaves were transported directly to colonial ports where they were sold for cash or credit.

The West Indies played a vital role in preserving American credit in Europe. Without this source of income, colonists would not have been able to pay for the manufactured items they purchased in the mother country. To be sure, they exported American products in great quantity to Great Britain, but the value of the exports seldom equaled the cost of British goods shipped back to the colonists. To cover this small but recurrent deficit, colonial merchants relied on profits made in the West Indies.

Birth of a Consumer Society

After midcentury, however, the balance of trade turned dramatically against the colonists. The reasons for this change were complex, but, in simplest terms, Americans began buying more English goods than their parents or grandparents had done. Between 1740 and 1770, English exports to the American colonies increased by an astounding 360 percent.

In part, this shift reflected a fundamental transformation in the British economy. Although the Industrial Revolution was still far in the future, the pace of the British economy picked up dramatically after 1690. Small factories produced certain goods more efficiently and more cheaply than the colonists could. The availability of these products altered the lives of most Americans, even those with modest incomes. Staffordshire china replaced crude earthenware; imported cloth replaced homespun. Franklin noted in

❖ A Look at the Past ❖

Tea Set

A flood of British manufactured goods transformed the material culture of mid-eighteenth-century America. Some historians have called this dramatic change in the character of everyday life a "consumer revolution." Even ordinary men and women discovered that they could purchase colorful fabrics, fashionable ceramics, and other imported goods that they regarded as better made and more desirable than those produced in their own households. Decorative porcelain teapots, cups, and saucers, such as shown in this photograph of a 1770 English-made tea set, became part of a tea service, a domestic ritual that marked the arrival of a new cosmopolitan taste. Do you think that the mid-eighteenth-century flood of imported goods affected how the colonists felt about Great Britain? By copying English styles of dress, decoration, and behavior–drinking tea, for example–did the colonists strengthen their ties to the mother country? Do you think the availability of so many consumer items created class tensions between those Americans who could afford the latest imports and those who could not? How would colonists have known what items they were expected to purchase?

his *Autobiography* how changing consumer habits affected his life. For years, he had eaten his breakfast in an earthenware bowl with a pewter spoon, but one morning it was served "in a china bowl, with a spoon of silver." Franklin observed that "this was the first appearance of plate and china in our house which afterwards in the course of years, as our wealth increased, augmented gradually to several hundred pounds in value." In this manner, British industrialization undercut American handicraft and folk art.

To help Americans purchase manufactured goods, British merchants offered generous credit. Colonists deferred settlement by agreeing to pay interest on their debts. The temptation to acquire English finery blinded many people to hard economic realities. They gambled on the future, hoping bumper farm crops would reduce their dependence on the large merchant houses of London and Glasgow. Obviously, some persons lived within their means, but the aggregate American debt continued to grow. Colonial leaders tried various expedients to remain solvent—issuing paper money, for example—and while these efforts delayed a crisis, the balance-of-payments problem was clearly very serious.

The eighteenth century also saw a substantial increase in intercoastal trade. Southern planters sent tobacco and rice to New England and the Middle Colonies, where these staples were exchanged for meat and wheat as well as goods imported from Great Britain. By 1760, approximately 30 percent of the colonists' total tonnage capacity was involved in this extensive "coastwise" commerce. In addition, backcountry farmers in western Pennsylvania and the Shenandoah Valley carried their grain to market along an old Iroquois trail that became known as the Great Wagon Road, a rough, hilly highway that by the time of the Revolution stretched 735 miles along the Blue Ridge Mountains to Camden, South Carolina. Most of their produce was carried in long, gracefully designed Conestoga wagons. These vehicles—sometimes called the "wagons of empire"—had been invented by German immigrants living in the Conestoga River Valley in Lancaster County, Pennsylvania.

The shifting patterns of trade had immense effects on the development of an American culture. First, the flood of British imports eroded local and regional identities. Commerce helped to "Anglicize" American culture by exposing colonial consumers to a common range of British manufactured goods. Deep sectional differences remained, of course, but Americans from New Hampshire to Georgia were increasingly drawn into a sophisticated economic network centered in London. Second, the expanding coastal and overland trade brought colonists of different backgrounds into more frequent contact. Ships that sailed between New England and South Carolina, and between Virginia and Pennsylvania, provided dispersed Americans with a means to exchange ideas and experiences on a more regular basis. Mid-eighteenth-century printers, for example, established several dozen new journals; these were weekly newspapers that carried information not only about the mother country and world commerce but also about events in other colonies.

Religious Revivals in Provincial Societies

A sudden, spontaneous series of Protestant revivals known as the **Great Awakening** had a profound impact on the lives of ordinary people. This unprece-

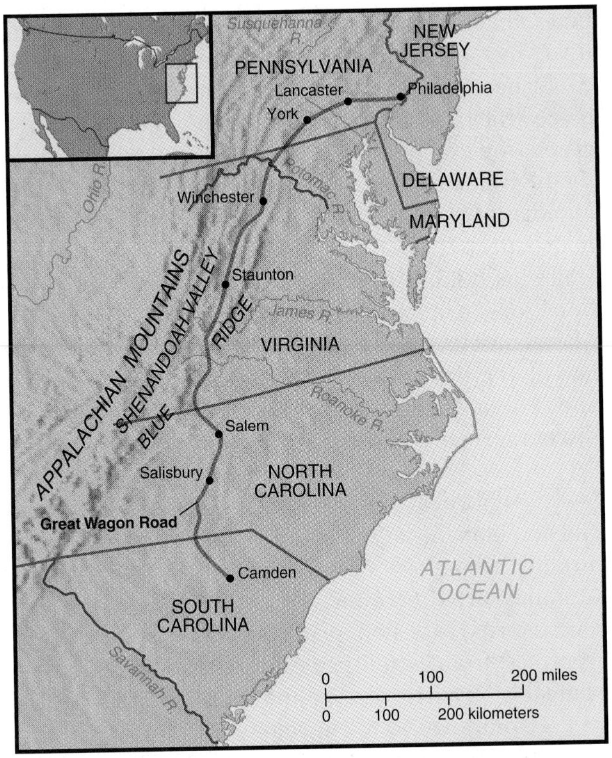

THE GREAT WAGON ROAD *By the mid-eighteenth century, the Great Wagon road had become the major highway for the settlers in the Virginia and Carolina backcountry.*

dented evangelical outpouring altered the course of American history. In our own time, of course, the force of religious revival has been witnessed in different regions throughout the world. It is no exaggeration to claim that a similar populist movement took place in mid-eighteenth-century America, and the new, highly personal appeal to a "new birth" in Christ caused men and women of all backgrounds to rethink basic assumptions about church and state, institutions and society.

The Great Awakening

Only with hindsight does the Great Awakening seem a unified religious movement. Revivals occurred in different places at different times; the intensity of the events varied from region to region. The first signs of a spiritual awakening appeared in New England during the 1730s, but within a decade the revivals in this area had burned themselves out. It was not until the 1750s and 1760s that the Awakening made more than a superficial impact on the people of Virginia. The revivals were most important in Massachusetts, Connecticut, Rhode Island, Pennsylvania, New Jersey, and Virginia. Their effect on religion in New York, Delaware, and the Carolinas was marginal. No single religious denomination or sect monopolized the Awakening. In New England, revivals shattered Congregational churches, and in the South, especially in Virginia, they had an impact on Presbyterians, Methodists, and Baptists. Moreover, there was nothing peculiarly American about the Great Awakening. Mid-eighteenth-century Europe experienced a similar burst of religious emotionalism.

Whatever their origins, the seeds of revival were generally sown on fertile ground. In the early decades of the century, many Americans—but especially New Englanders—complained that organized religion had lost vitality. They looked back at Winthrop's generation with nostalgia, assuming that common people at that time must have possessed greater piety than did later, more worldly colonists. Congregational ministers seemed obsessed with dull, scholastic matters; they no longer touched the heart. And in the Southern Colonies, there were simply not enough ordained ministers to tend to the religious needs of the population.

The Great Awakening arrived unexpectedly in Northampton, a small farm community in western Massachusetts, sparked by Jonathan Edwards, the local Congregational minister. Edwards accepted the traditional teachings of Calvinism (see Chapter 1), reminding his parishioners that their eternal fate had been determined by an omnipotent God, there was nothing they could do to save themselves, and they were totally dependent on the Lord's will. He thought his fellow ministers had grown soft. They left men and women with the mistaken impression that sinners might somehow avoid eternal damnation simply by performing good works. "How dismal will it be," Edwards told his complacent congregation, "when you are under these racking torments, to know assuredly that you never, never shall be delivered from them." Edwards was not exaggerating his message in an attempt to be dramatic. He spoke of God's omnipotence with such self-assurance that even people who had not thought deeply about religious matters were shaken by his words.

Why this uncompromising message set off several religious revivals during the mid-1730s is not known. Whatever the explanation for the popular response to Edwards's preaching, young people began flocking to the church. They experienced a searing conversion, a sense of "new birth" and utter dependence on God. "Surely," Edwards pronounced, "this is the Lord's doing, and it is marvelous in our eyes." The excitement spread, and evangelical ministers concluded that God must be preparing Americans, his chosen people, for the millennium. "What is now seen in America and especially in New England," Edwards explained, "may prove the dawn of that glorious day."

The Voice of Popular Religion

Edwards was a brilliant theologian, but he did not possess the dynamic personality required to sustain the revival. That responsibility fell to George Whitefield, a young, inspiring preacher from England who toured the colonies from New Hampshire to Georgia. While Whitefield was not an original thinker, he was an extraordinarily effective public speaker. And like his friend Benjamin Franklin, he came to symbolize the powerful cultural forces that were transforming the Atlantic world. According to Edwards's wife, Sarah, it was wonderful to witness what a spell Whitefield "casts over an audience . . . I have seen upwards of a thousand people hang on his words with breathless silence, broken only by an occasional half-suppressed sob."

Whitefield's audiences came from all groups of American society: rich and poor, young and old, rural and urban. While Whitefield described himself as a Calvinist, he welcomed all Protestants. He spoke from any pulpit that was available. "Don't tell me you are a Baptist, an Independent, a Presbyterian, a dissenter," he thundered, "tell me you are a Christian, that is all I want."

Whitefield was a brilliant entrepreneur. Like Franklin, with whom he published many popular volumes, the itinerant minister possessed an almost intuitive sense of how this burgeoning consumer society could be turned to his own advantage, and he embraced the latest merchandising techniques. He appreciated, for example, the power of the press in selling the revival, and he regularly promoted his own work in advertisements placed in British and American newspapers. The crowds flocked to hear Whitefield, while his critics grumbled about the commercialization of religion. One anonymous writer in Massachusetts noted that there was "a very wholesome law of the province to discourage Pedlars in Trade" and it seemed high time "to enact something for the discouragement of Pedlars in Divinity also."

Other American-born **itinerant preachers** followed Whitefield's example. The most famous was Gilbert Tennent, a Presbyterian of Scots-Irish background who had been educated in the Middle Colonies. His sermon "On the Danger of an Unconverted Ministry," printed in 1741, set off a storm of protest from established ministers who were understandably insulted. Lesser known revivalists traveled from town to town, colony to colony, challenging local clergymen who seemed hostile to evangelical religion. Men and women who thronged to hear the itinerants were called "New Lights," and during the 1740s and 1750s, many congregations split between defenders of the new emotional preaching and those who regarded the entire movement as dangerous nonsense.

The fervor of the Great Awakening was intensified by the eloquence of itinerant preachers such as George Whitefield, the most popular evangelical of the mid-eighteenth century. ❖

Despite Whitefield's successes, many ministers remained suspicious of the itinerants and their methods. Some complaints may have amounted to little more than sour grapes. One "Old Light" spokesman labeled Tennent "a monster! impudent and noisy." He claimed Tennent told anxious Christians that "they were damned! damned! damned! This charmed them; and, in the most dreadful winter I ever saw, people wallowed in snow, night and day, for the benefit of his beastly brayings; and many ended their days under these fatigues." Charles Chauncy, minister of the prestigious First Church of Boston, raised much more troubling issues. How could the revivalists be certain God had sparked the Great Awakening? Perhaps the itinerants had relied too much on emotion? "Let us esteem those as friends of religion," Chauncy advised, " . . . who warn us of the danger of enthusiasm, and would put us on our guard, that we may not be led aside by it."

While Tennent did not condone the excesses of the Great Awakening, his attacks on formal learning invited the crude anti-intellectualism of such fanatics as James Davenport. This deranged revivalist traveled along the Connecticut coast in 1742 playing upon popular emotion. At night, under the light of smoky torches, he danced and stripped, shrieked and laughed. He also urged people to burn books written by authors who had not experienced the New Light as defined by Davenport. Like so many fanatics throughout history who have claimed a special knowledge of the "truth," Davenport later recanted and begged pardon for his disruptive behavior.

To concentrate on the bizarre activities of Davenport—as many critics of the Great Awakening have done—is to obscure the positive ways in which this vast revival changed American society. First, despite occasional anti-intellectual outbursts, the New Lights founded several important centers of higher learning. They wanted to train young men who would carry on the good works of Edwards, Whitefield, and Tennent. In 1746, New Light Presbyterians established the College of New Jersey, which later became Princeton University. Just before his death, Edwards was appointed its president. The evangelical minister Eleazar Wheelock launched Dartmouth (1769); other revivalists founded Brown (1764) and Rutgers (1766).

The Great Awakening also encouraged men and women who had been taught to remain silent before traditional figures of authority to speak up, to take an active role in their salvation. They could no longer rely on ministers or institutions. The individual alone stood before God. Knowing this, New Lights made religious choices that shattered the old harmony among Protestant sects, and in its place, they introduced a noisy, often bitterly fought competition. As one New Jersey Presbyterian explained, "There are so many particular *sects* and *Parties* among professed Christians . . . that we know not . . . in which of these different *paths*, to steer our course for *Heaven*."

Expressive evangelicalism struck a particularly responsive chord among African Americans. Itinerant ministers frequently preached to large sympathetic audiences of slaves. Richard Allen (1760–1831), founder of the African Methodist Episcopal Church, reported he owed his freedom in part to a traveling Methodist minister who persuaded Allen's master of the sinfulness of slavery. Allen himself was converted, as were thousands of other black colonists. According to one historian, evangelical preaching "shared enough with traditional African styles and beliefs such as spirit possession and ecstatic expression . . . to allow for an interpenetration of African and Christian religious beliefs."

With religious contention came an awareness of a larger community, a union of fellow believers that extended beyond the boundaries of town and colony. In fact, evangelical religion was one of several forces at work during the mid-eighteenth century that brought scattered colonists into contact with one another for the first time. In this sense, the Great Awakening was a "national" event long before a nation actually existed.

People who had been touched by the Great Awakening shared an optimism about the future of America. With God's help, social and political progress was possible, and from this perspective, of course, the New Lights did not sound much different than the mildly rationalist American spokesmen of the Enlightenment. Both groups prepared the way for the development of a revolutionary mentality in colonial America.

Clash of Political Cultures

The political history of this period illuminates a growing tension within the empire. Americans of all regions repeatedly stated their desire to replicate British political institutions. Parliament, they claimed, provided a model for the American assemblies. They revered the English constitution. However, the more the colonists studied British political theory and practice—in other words, the more they attempted to become British—the more aware they became of major differences. By trying to copy Great Britain, they unwittingly discovered something about being American.

The English Constitution

During the eighteenth century, political discussion began with the British constitution. It was the object of universal admiration. Unlike the U.S. Constitution of 1788, the British constitution was not a formal written document. It was something much more elusive. The English constitution found expression in a growing body of law, court decisions, and statutes, a sense of traditional political arrangements that people of all classes believed had evolved from the past, preserving life, liberty, and property. Eighteenth-century political commentators reluctantly admitted that the constitution had in fact changed. Historic confrontations between king and Parliament had generated new understandings about what the constitution did or did not allow. Nevertheless, almost everyone regarded change as dangerous and destabilizing, a threat to the political tradition that seemed to explain Britain's greatness.

In theory, the English constitution contained three distinct parts. The monarch was at the top, advised by handpicked court favorites. Next came the House of Lords, a body of 180 aristocrats who served with 26 Anglican bishops as the upper house of Parliament. And third was the House of Commons, composed of 558 members elected by various constituencies scattered throughout the realm.

Political theorists waxed eloquent on workings of the British constitution. Each of the three parts of government, it seemed, represented a separate socioeconomic interest: king, nobility, and common people. Acting alone, each body would run to excess, even tyranny, but operating within a mixed system, they automatically checked each other's ambitions for the common good. "Herein consists the excellence of the English government," explained the famed eighteenth-century jurist Sir William Blackstone, "that all parts of it form a mutual check upon each other." Unlike the delegates who wrote the Constitution of the United States, eighteenth-century Englishmen did not perceive their constitution as a balance of executive, legislative, and judicial branches.

The Reality of British Politics

The reality of daily political life in Great Britain, however, bore little relation to theory. The three elements of the constitution did not, in fact, represent distinct socioeconomic groups. Men elected to the House of Commons often came from the same social background as those who served in the House of Lords. All represented the interests of Britain's landed elite. Moreover, there was no attempt to maintain strict constitutional separation. The king, for example, organized parliamentary associations, loose groups of political followers who sat in the House of Commons and who openly supported the monarch's policies in exchange for patronage or pension.

The claim that the members of the House of Commons represented all the people of England also seemed far-fetched. As of 1715, no more than 20 percent of Britain's adult males had the right to vote. Property qualifications or other restrictions often greatly reduced the number of eligible voters. In addition, the size of the electoral districts varied throughout the kingdom. In some boroughs, representatives to Parliament were chosen by several thousand voters. In many districts, however, a handful of electors controlled the result. These tiny, or "rotten," boroughs were an embarrassment. The Methodist leader John Wesley complained that Old Sarum, an almost uninhabited borough, "in spite of common sense, without house or inhabitant, still sends two members to the parliament." Since these districts were so small, a wealthy lord or ambitious politician could easily bribe or otherwise "influence" the entire constituency, something done regularly throughout the century.

Before 1760, few people spoke out against these constitutional abuses. The main exception was a group of radical publicists whom historians have labeled the Commonwealthmen. These writers decried the corruption of political life, noting that a nation that compromised civic virtue, that failed to stand vigilant against fawning courtiers and would-be despots, deserved to lose its liberty and property. The most famous Commonwealthmen were John Trenchard and Thomas Gordon, who penned a series of essays titled *Cato's Letters* between 1720 and 1723. If England's rulers were corrupt, they warned, then the people could not expect the balanced constitution to save them from tyranny. In one typical article, Trenchard and Gordon observed, "The Appitites . . . of Men, especially of Great Men, are carefully to be observed and stayed, or else they will never stay themselves. The Experience of every Age convinces us, that we must not judge of Men by what they ought to do, but by what they will do."

But however shrilly these writers protested, they won little support for political reforms. Most eighteenth-century Englishmen admitted there was more than a grain of truth in the commonwealth critique, but they were not willing to tamper with a system of government that had so recently survived a civil war and a Glorious Revolution. Americans, however, took Trenchard and Gordon to heart.

Governing the Colonies: The American Experience

The colonists assumed—perhaps naively—that their own governments were modeled on the balanced constitution of Great Britain. They argued that within their political systems, the governor corresponded to the king and the governor's council to the House of Lords. The colonial assemblies were perceived as American reproductions of the House of Commons and were expected to preserve the interests of the people against those of the monarch and aristocracy. As the colonists discovered, however, general theories about a mixed constitution were even less relevant in America than they were in Britain.

By midcentury a majority of the mainland colonies had royal governors appointed by the crown. Many were career army officers who through luck, charm, or family connection had gained the ear of someone close to the king. These patronage posts did not generate income sufficient to interest the most powerful or talented personalities of the period, but they did draw middle-level bureaucrats who were ambitious, desperate, or both. It is perhaps not surprising that most governors decided simply not to "consider any Thing further than how to sit easy."

George Clinton, who served as New York's governor from 1743 to 1753, was probably typical of the men who hoped to "sit easy." Before coming to the colonies, Clinton had compiled an extraordinary record of ineptitude as a naval officer. He gained the governorship more as a means to get him out of England than as a sign of respect. When he arrived in New York City, Clinton ignored the colonists. "In a province given to hospitality," wrote one critic, "he [Clinton] erred by immuring himself in the fort, or retiring to a grotto in the country, where his time was spent with his bottle and a little trifling circle."

Whatever their demerits, royal governors in America possessed enormous powers. In fact, royal governors could do certain things in America that a king could not do in eighteenth-century Britain. Among these were the right to veto legislation and dismiss judges. The governors also served as military commanders in each province.

Political practice in America differed from the British model in another crucial respect. Royal governors were advised by a council, usually a body of about twelve wealthy colonists selected by the Board of Trade in London upon the recommendation of the governor. During the seventeenth century, the council had played an important role in colonial government, but its ability to exercise independent authority declined steadily over the course of the eighteenth century. Its members certainly did not represent a distinct aristocracy within American society.

If royal governors did not look like kings, nor American councils like the House of Lords, colonial assemblies bore little resemblance to the eighteenth-century House of Commons. The major difference was the size of the American franchise. In most colonies, adult white males who owned a small amount of land could vote in colonywide elections. One historian estimates that 95 percent of this group in Massachusetts were eligible to participate in elections. The number in Virginia was about 85 percent. These figures were much higher than those in contemporary England and have led some scholars to view the colonies as "middle-class democracies." The term describes societies run by yeomen farmers who—in politics at least—exercised independent judgment. There were too many of them to bribe, no "rotten" boroughs, and when these people moved west, colonial assemblies usually created new electoral districts.

Colonial governments were not democracies in the modern sense of that term. Possessing the right to vote was one thing, exercising it quite another. Americans participated in elections when major issues were at stake—the formation of banks in mid-eighteenth-century Massachusetts, for example—but most of the time they were content to let members of the rural and urban gentry represent them in the assemblies. To be sure, unlike modern democracies, these colonial politics excluded women and nonwhites from voting. The point to remember, however, is that the power to expel legislative rascals was always present in America, and it was this political reality that kept autocratic gentlemen from straying too far from the will of the people.

Colonial Assemblies

Elected members of the colonial assemblies believed that they had a special obligation to preserve colonial liberties. They perceived any attack on the legislature as an assault on the rights of Americans. The elected representatives brooked no criticism, and several colonial printers landed in jail because they criticized actions taken by a lower house.

So aggressive were these bodies in seizing privileges, determining procedures, and controlling money bills that some historians have described the political development of eighteenth-century America as "the rise of the assemblies." The long series of imperial wars against the French, demanding large public expenditures, transformed the small, amateurish assemblies of the seventeenth century into the more professional legislatures of the eighteenth.

This political system seemed designed to generate hostility. There was simply no reason for the colonial legislators to cooperate with appointed royal governors. Alexander Spotswood, Virginia's governor from 1710 to 1722, for example, attempted to institute a bold new land program backed by the crown. He tried persuasion and gifts and, when these failed, chicanery. But the members of the House of Burgesses refused to support a plan that did not suit their own interests. Before leaving office, Spotswood gave up trying to carry out royal policy in America. Instead, he allied himself with the local Virginia gentry who controlled the House as well as the Council. Because they awarded their new friend with large tracts of land, he became a wealthy man.

A few governors managed briefly to re-create in America the political culture of patronage, the system that eighteenth-century Englishmen took for granted. Most successful in this endeavor was William Shirley, who held office in Massachusetts from 1741 to 1757. The secret to his political successes in America was connection to people who held high office in Great Britain. But Shirley's practices—and those of men like him—clashed with the colonists' perception of politics. They really believed in the purity of the balanced constitution. They insisted on complete separation of executive and legislative authority. Therefore, when Americans suspected a governor, or even some of their own representatives, of employing patronage to influence government decisions, their protests seem to have been lifted directly from the pages of *Cato's Letters.*

A major source of shared political information was the weekly journal, a new and vigorous institution in American life. In New York and Massachusetts especially, weekly newspapers urged readers to preserve civic virtue, to exercise extreme vigilance against the spread of privileged power. In the first issue of the *Independent Reflector,* published in New York (November 30, 1752), the editor announced defiantly that no discouragement shall "deter me from vindicating the *civil and religious RIGHTS* of my Fellow-Creatures: From exposing the peculiar Deformity of publick *Vice,* and *Corruption;* and displaying the amiable Charms of Liberty, with the detestable Nature of *Slavery* and *Oppression.*" Through such journals, a pattern of political rhetoric that in Britain had gained only marginal respectability became after 1765 America's normal form of political discourse.

The rise of the assemblies shaped American culture in other, subtler ways. Over the course of the century, the language of the law became increasingly Anglicized. The Board of Trade, the Privy Council, and Parliament scrutinized court decisions and legislative actions from all thirteen mainland colonies. As a result, varying local legal practices that had been widespread during the seventeenth century became standardized. Indeed, according to one historian, the colonial legal system by 1750 "was substantially that of the mother country." Not surprisingly, many men who served in colonial assemblies were either lawyers or persons who had received legal training. When Americans from different regions met—as they frequently did in the years before the Revolution—they discovered that they shared a commitment to the preservation of the English common law.

As eighteenth-century political developments drew the colonists closer to the mother country, they also brought Americans a greater awareness of each other. As their horizons widened, they learned they operated within the same general imperial system, and the problems confronting the Massachusetts House of Representatives were not too different from those facing Virginia's House of Burgesses or South Carolina's Commons House. Like the revivalists and merchants—people who crossed old boundaries—colonial legislators laid the foundation for a larger cultural identity.

THE Massachusetts Spy

A Weekly, Political, and Commercial PAPER; open to ALL Parties, but influenced by None.

VOL. I.] THURSDAY, March 7, 1771. [NUMB. 1.

Colonial newspapers were an important means of political participation. The masthead of this edition of The Massachusetts Spy *declares its journalistic objectivity: "A Weekly, Political, and Commercial Paper; open to ALL Parties, but influenced by None."* ❖

CENTURY OF IMPERIAL WAR

The scope and character of warfare in the colonies changed radically during the eighteenth century. The founders of England's mainland colonies had engaged in intense local conflicts with the Indians, such as King Philip's War (1675–1676) in New England. But after 1690, the colonists were increasingly involved in hostilities that originated on the other side of the Atlantic, in rivalries between Great Britain and France over political and commercial ambitions. The external threat to security forced people in different colonies to devise unprecedented measures of military and political cooperation.

On paper, at least, the British colonies enjoyed military superiority over the settlements of New France. Louis XIV (r. 1643–1715) possessed an impressive army of 100,000 well-armed troops, but he dispatched few of them to the New World. He left the defense of Canada and the Mississippi Valley to the companies engaged in the fur trade. Meeting this challenge seemed almost impossible for the French outposts strung out along the St. Lawrence River and the Great Lakes. In 1754, New France contained only 75,000 inhabitants as compared to 1.2 million people living in Britain's mainland colonies.

For most of the century, the theoretical advantages enjoyed by the English colonists did them little

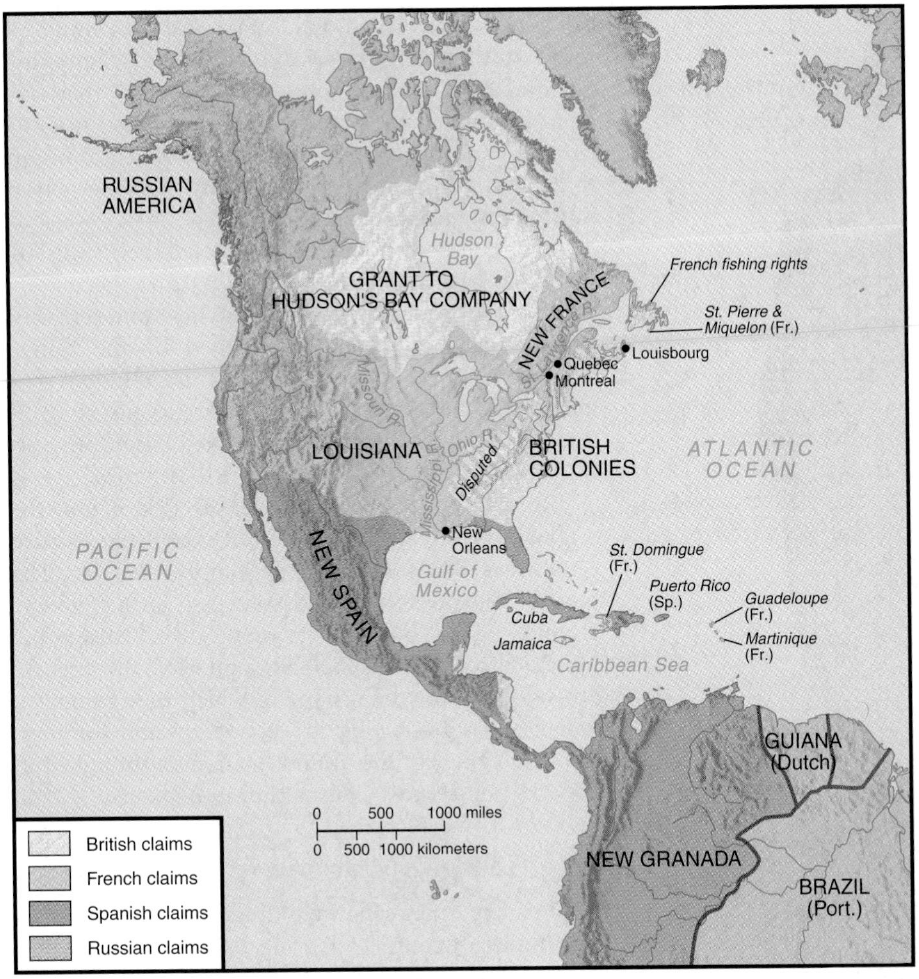

NORTH AMERICA, 1750
By 1750, the French had established a chain of settlements southward through the heart of the continent from Quebec to New Orleans. The British saw this development as a threat to their own seaboard colonies, which were expanding westward.

good. While the British settlements possessed a larger and more prosperous population, they were divided into separate governments that sometimes seemed more suspicious of each other than of the French. When war came, French officers and Indian allies exploited these jealousies with considerable skill. Moreover, although the population of New France was comparatively small, it was concentrated along the St. Lawrence, so that while the French found it difficult to mount effective offensive operations against the English, they could easily mass the forces needed to defend Montreal and Quebec.

King William's and Queen Anne's Wars

Colonial involvement in imperial war began in 1689, when England's new king, William III, declared war on Louis XIV. Europeans called this struggle the War of the League of Augsburg, but to the Americans, it was simply King William's War. Canadians commanded by the Comte de Frontenac raided the northern frontiers of New York and New England, and while they made no territorial gains, they caused considerable suffering among the civilian populations of Massachusetts and New York.

The war ended with the Treaty of Ryswick (1697), but the colonists were drawn almost immediately into a new conflict. Queen Anne's War, known in Europe as the War of the Spanish Succession (1702–1713), was fought across a large geographic area. The bloody combat along the American frontier ended in 1713 when Great Britain and France signed the Treaty of Utrecht. European negotiators showed little interest in the military situation in the New World. Their major concern was preserving a balance of power among the European states. More than two decades of intense fighting had taken a heavy toll in North America, but neither French nor English colonists had much to show for their sacrifice.

After George I replaced Anne on the throne in 1714, parliamentary leaders were determined to preserve peace—mainly because of the rising cost of war. Yet on the American frontier, the hostilities continued with raids and reprisals. As people on both sides of this conflict now realized, the stakes of war were very high;

Native Americans often depended on trade goods supplied by the British and sometimes adopted British dress. Here the Mohawk chief Theyanoguin, called King Hendrick by the British, wears a cloak he received from Queen Anne of England during a visit to London in 1710. During the Seven Years' War, Theyanoguin mobilized Mohawk support for the British. ❖

they were fighting for control over the entire West, including the Mississippi Valley.

Both sides viewed this great contest in conspiratorial terms. From South Carolina to Massachusetts Bay, colonists believed the French planned to "encircle" the English settlements, to confine the English to a narrow strip of land along the Atlantic coast. The English noted that in 1682, La Salle had claimed for the king of France a territory—Louisiana—that included all the people and resources located on "streams and Rivers" flowing into the Mississippi River. To make good on their claim, the French constructed forts on the Chicago and Illinois rivers. In 1717, they established a military post two hundred miles up the Alabama River, well within striking distance of the Carolina frontier, and in 1718, they settled New Orleans. One New Yorker declared in 1715 that "it is impossible that we and the French can both inhabit this Continent in peace but that one nation must at last give way to the other."

On their part, the French suspected their rivals intended to seize all of North America. Land speculators and frontier traders pushed aggressively into territory claimed by the French and owned by the Native Americans. In 1716, one Frenchman urged his government to hasten the development of Louisiana, since "it is not difficult to guess that their [the British] purpose is to drive us entirely out . . . of North America."

To their great sorrow and eventual destruction, the original inhabitants of the frontier, the Native Americans, were swept up in this undeclared war. The Indians maneuvered to hold their own in the "middle ground." The Iroquois favored the British; the Algonquian peoples generally supported the French. But regardless of the groups to which they belonged, Indian warriors—acting independently and for their own strategic reasons—found themselves enmeshed in imperial policies set by distant European kings.

King George's War and Its Aftermath

In 1743, the Americans were dragged once again into the imperial conflict. During King George's War (1743–1748), known in Europe as the War of the Austrian Succession, the colonists scored a magnificent victory over the French. Louisbourg, a gigantic fortress on Cape Breton Island, the easternmost promontory of Canada, guarded the approaches to the Gulf of St. Lawrence and Quebec. It was described as the Gibraltar of the New World. An army of New England troops under the command of William Pepperrell captured Louisbourg in June 1745, a feat that demonstrated the British colonists were able to fight and to mount effective joint operations.

The Americans, however, were in for a shock. When the war ended with the signing of the Treaty of Aix-la-Chapelle in 1748, the British government handed Louisbourg back to the French in exchange for concessions elsewhere. Such decisions exposed the deep and continuing ambivalence the colonists felt about participation in imperial wars. They were proud to support Great Britain, of course, but the Americans seldom fully understood why the wars were being fought, why certain tactics had been adopted, and why the British accepted treaty terms that so blatantly ignored colonial interests.

The French were not prepared to surrender an inch. But as they recognized, time was running against them. Not only were the English colonies growing more populous, but they also possessed a seemingly inexhaustible supply of manufactured goods to trade with the Indians. The French decided in the early 1750s, therefore, to seize the Ohio Valley before the Virginians could do so. They established forts throughout the region, the most formidable being Fort Duquesne, located at the strategic fork in the Ohio River and later renamed Pittsburgh.

Although France and England had not officially declared war, British officials advised the governor of Virginia to "repell force by force." The Virginians needed little encouragement. They were eager to make good their claim to the Ohio Valley, and in 1754, militia companies under the command of a promising young officer, George Washington, constructed Fort Necessity not far from Fort Duquesne. The plan failed. French and Indian troops overran the badly exposed outpost (July 3, 1754). Among other things, the humiliating setback revealed that a single colony could not defeat the French.

Albany Congress and Braddock's Defeat

Benjamin Franklin, for one, appreciated the need for intercolonial cooperation. When British officials invited representatives from the colonies to Albany (June 1754) to discuss relations with the Iroquois, Franklin used the occasion to present a bold blueprint for colonial union. His so-called **Albany Plan** envisioned the formation of a Grand Council, made up of elected delegates from the various colonies, to oversee matters of common defense, western expansion, and Indian affairs. A President General appointed by the king would preside. Franklin's most daring suggestion involved taxation. He insisted the council be authorized to collect taxes to cover military expenditures.

The first political cartoon to appear in an American newspaper was created by Benjamin Franklin in 1754 to emphasize the importance of the Albany Plan. ❖

First reaction to the Albany Plan was enthusiastic. To take effect, however, it required the support of the separate colonial assemblies as well as Parliament. It received neither. The assemblies were jealous of their fiscal authority, and the English thought the scheme undermined the crown's power over American affairs.

In 1755, the Ohio Valley again became the scene of fierce fighting. Even though there was still no formal declaration of war, the British resolved to destroy Fort Duquesne, and to that end, they dispatched units of the regular army to America. In command was Major General Edward Braddock, an obese, humorless veteran who inspired neither fear nor respect. One colonist described Braddock as "very indolent, Slave to his passions, women & wine, as great an Epicure as could be in his eating, tho a brave man."

On July 9, Braddock led a joint force of twenty-five hundred British redcoats and colonists to

This mid-eighteenth-century lithograph portrays colonial assault troops, under the command of William Pepperrell, establishing a beachhead at Freshwater Cove near Louisbourg. Pepperrell's troops went on to capture the French fortress at Louisbourg. ❖

A Century of Conflict: Major Wars, 1689–1763

Dates	European Name	American Name	Major Allies	Issues	Major American Battle	Treaty
1689–1697	War of the League of Augsburg	King William's War	Britain, Holland, Spain, their colonies, and Native American allies against France, its colonies, and Native American allies	Opposition to French bid for control of Europe	New England troops assault Quebec under Sir William Phips (1690)	Treaty of Ryswick (1697)
1702–1713	War of the Spanish Succession	Queen Anne's War	Britain, Holland, their colonies, and Native American allies against France, Spain, their colonies, and Native American allies	Austria and France hold rival claims to Spanish throne	Attack on Deerfield (1704)	Treaty of Utrecht (1713)
1743–1748	War of the Austrian Succession (War of Jenkin's Ear)	King George's War	Britain, its colonies, and Native American allies, and Austria against France, Spain, their Native American allies, and Prussia	Struggle among Britain, Spain, and France for control of New World territory; among France, Prussia, and Austria for control of central Europe	New England forces capture of Louisbourg under William Pepperrell (1745)	Treaty of Aix-la-Chapelle (1748)
1756–1763	Seven Years' War	French and Indian War	Britain, its colonies, and Native American allies against France, its colonies, and Native American allies	Struggle among Britain, Spain, and France for worldwide control of colonial markets and raw materials	British and Continental forces capture Quebec under Major General James Wolfe (1759)	Peace of Paris (1763)

humiliating defeat. The French and Indians opened fire as Braddock's army waded across the Monongahela River, about eight miles from Fort Duquesne. Along a narrow road already congested with heavy wagons and confused men, Braddock ordered a counterattack, described by one of his officers as "without any form or order but that of a parcell of school boys coming out of s[c]hool." Nearly 70 percent of Braddock's troops were killed or wounded in western Pennsylvania. The general himself died in battle. The French, who suffered only light casualties, remained in firm control of the Ohio Valley.

The entire affair profoundly angered Washington, who fumed, "We have been most scandalously beaten by a trifling body of men." The British thought their allies the Iroquois might desert them after the embarrassing defeat. The Indians, however, took the news in stride, observing that "they were not at all surprised to hear it, as they [Braddock's redcoats] were men who had crossed the Great Water and were unacquainted with the arts of war among the Americans."

Seven Years' War

Britain's imperial war effort had hit bottom. No one in England or America seemed to possess the leadership necessary to drive the French from the Mississippi Valley. The cabinet of George II (r. 1727–1760) lacked the will to organize and finance a sustained military campaign in the New World, and colonial assemblies balked every time Britain asked them to raise men and money. On May 18, 1756, the British officially declared war on the French, a conflict called the French and Indian War in America and the **Seven Years' War** in Europe.

Had it not been for William Pitt, the most powerful minister in George's cabinet, the military stalemate might have continued. This supremely self-confident Englishman believed he was the only person capable of saving the British empire, an opinion he publicly expressed. When he became effective head of the ministry in December 1756, Pitt had an opportunity to demonstrate his talents.

In the past, warfare on the European continent had worked mainly to France's advantage. Pitt saw no point in continuing to concentrate on Europe, and in 1757 he advanced a bold new imperial policy, one based on commercial assumptions. In Pitt's judgment, the critical confrontation would take place in North America, where Britain and France were struggling to control colonial markets and raw materials. Indeed, according to Pitt, America was "where England and Europe are to

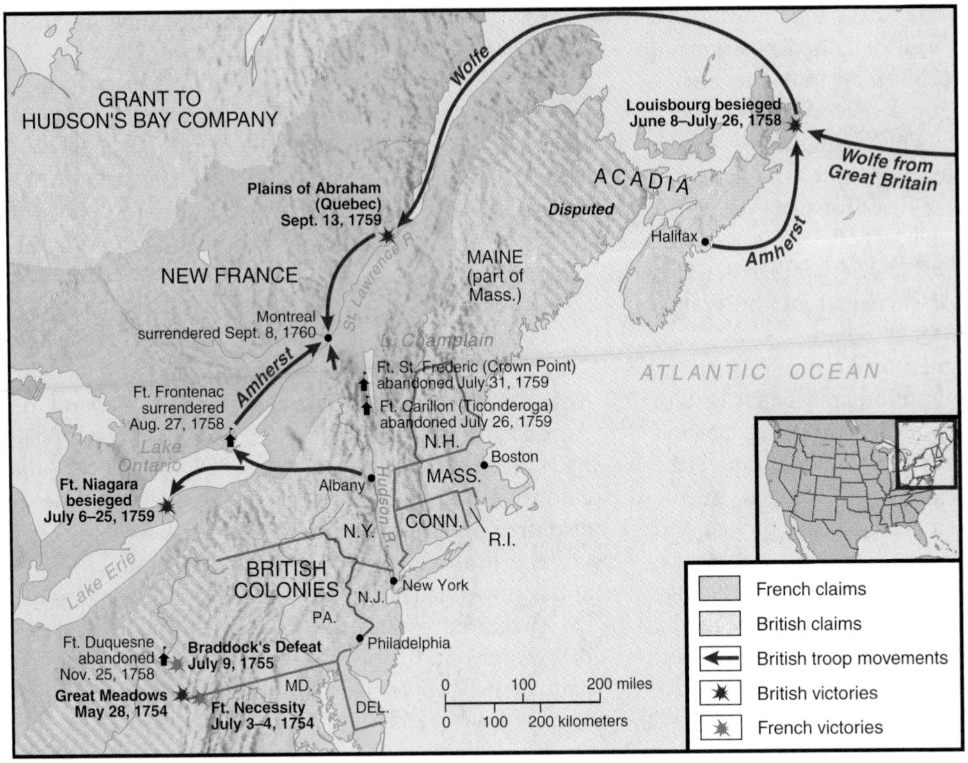

THE SEVEN YEARS' WAR, 1756–1763 *Major battle sites. The conflict ended with Great Britain driving the French from mainland North America.* ❖

be fought for." He was determined, therefore, to expel the French from the continent, however great the cost.

To effect this ambitious scheme, Pitt took personal command of the army and navy. He mapped strategy. He even promoted young promising officers over the heads of their superiors. He also recognized that the success of the war effort could not depend on the generosity of the colonial assemblies. Great Britain would have to foot most of the bill. Pitt's military expenditures, of course, created an enormous national debt that would soon haunt both Britain and its colonies, but at the time, no one foresaw the fiscal consequences of victory in America.

To direct the grand campaign, Pitt selected two relatively obscure officers, Jeffrey Amherst and James Wolfe. It was a masterful choice, one that a less self-assured man than Pitt would never have risked. Both officers were young, talented, and ambitious, and on July 26, 1758, forces under their direction captured Louisbourg, the same fortress the colonists had taken a decade earlier!

This victory cut the Canadians' main supply line with France. The small population of New France could no longer meet the military demands placed on it. As the situation became increasingly desperate, the French forts of the Ohio Valley and the Great Lakes began to fall. Duquesne was simply abandoned late in 1758 as French and Indian troops under the Marquis de Montcalm retreated toward Quebec and Montreal. During the summer of 1759, the French surrendered key forts at Ticonderoga, Crown Point, and Niagara.

The climax to a century of war came dramatically in September 1759. Wolfe, now a major general, assaulted Quebec with nine thousand men. But it was not simply force of arms that brought victory. Wolfe proceeded as if he were preparing to attack the city

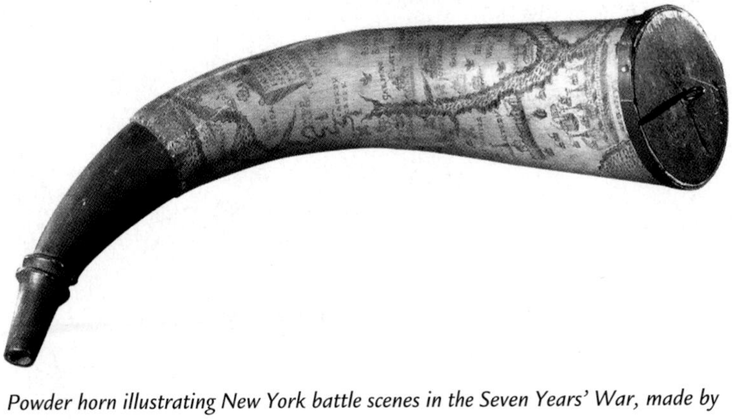

Powder horn illustrating New York battle scenes in the Seven Years' War, made by Samuel Davidson, May 27, 1765. ❖

directly, but under cover of darkness, his troops scaled a cliff to dominate a less well defended position. At dawn on September 13, 1759, they took the French from the rear by surprise. The decisive action occurred on the Plains of Abraham, a bluff high above the St. Lawrence River. Both Wolfe and Montcalm were mortally wounded. When an aide informed Wolfe the French had been routed, he sighed, "Now, God be praised, I will die in peace." On September 8, 1760, Amherst accepted the final surrender of the French army at Montreal.

The Peace of Paris signed on February 10, 1763, almost fulfilled Pitt's grandiose dreams. Great Britain took possession of an empire that stretched around the globe. Only Guadeloupe and Martinique, the Caribbean sugar islands, were given back to the French. After a centurylong struggle, the French had been driven from the mainland of North America. Even Louisiana passed out of France's control into Spanish hands. The treaty gave Britain title to Canada, Florida, and all the land east of the Mississippi River. Moreover, with the stroke of a diplomat's pen, eighty thousand French-speaking Canadians, most of them Catholics, became the subjects of George III.

The Americans were overjoyed. It was a time of good feelings and national pride. Together, the English and their colonial allies had thwarted the "Gallic peril." Samuel Davies, a Presbyterian who had brought the Great Awakening to Virginia, announced confidently that the long-awaited victory would inaugurate "a new heaven and a new earth."

Perceptions of War

The Seven Years' War made a deep impression on American society. Even though Franklin's Albany Plan had failed, the military struggle had forced the colonists to cooperate on an unprecedented scale. It also drew them into closer contact with Britain. They became aware of being part of a great empire, military and commercial, but in the very process of waging war, they acquired a more intimate sense of an America that lay beyond the plantation and the village. Conflict had carried thousands of young men across colonial

NORTH AMERICA AFTER 1763 *The Peace of Paris (1763) redrew the map of North America. Great Britain received all the French holdings except a few islands in the Atlantic and some sugar-producing islands in the Caribbean.*

boundaries, exposing them to a vast territory full of opportunities for a booming population. Moreover, the war trained a corps of American officers, people like George Washington, who learned from firsthand experience that the British were not invincible.

British officials later accused the Americans of ingratitude. England, they claimed, had sent troops and provided funds to liberate the colonists from the threat of French attack. The Americans, appreciative of the aid from England, cheered on the British but dragged their feet at every stage, refusing to pay the bills. These charges were later incorporated into a general argument justifying parliamentary taxation in America.

The British had a point. The colonists were, in fact, slow in providing the men and materials needed to fight the French. Nevertheless, they did make a significant contribution to the war effort, and it was perfectly reasonable for Americans to regard themselves at the very least as junior partners in the empire. After all, they had supplied almost twenty thousand soldiers and spent well over £2 million. In a single year, in fact, Massachusetts enlisted five thousand men out of an adult male population of about fifty thousand, a commitment that, in the words of one military historian, meant "the war was being waged on a scale comparable to the great wars of modern times."

After making such a sacrifice and demonstrating their loyalty to England, the colonists would surely have been disturbed to learn that General James Wolfe, the hero of Quebec, had stated, "The Americans are in general the dirtiest, the most contemptible, cowardly dogs that you can conceive. There is no depending upon them in action. They fall down in their own dirt and desert in battalions, officers and all."

Conclusion: Rule Britannia?

James Thomson, an Englishman, understood the hold of empire on the popular imagination of the eighteenth century. In 1740, he composed words that British patriots have proudly sung for more than two centuries:

> Rule Britannia, rule the waves,
> Britons never will be slaves.

Colonial Americans—at least, those of British background—joined the chorus. By midcentury they took their political and cultural cues from Great Britain. They fought its wars, purchased its consumer goods, flocked to hear its evangelical preachers, and read its many publications. Without question, the empire provided the colonists with a compelling source of identity.

CHRONOLOGY

1680	El Popé leads Pueblo revolt against the Spanish in New Mexico
1689	William and Mary accede to the English throne
1706	Birth of Benjamin Franklin
1714	George I of Hanover becomes monarch of Great Britain
1732	Colony of Georgia is established ❖ Birth of George Washington
1734–1736	First expression of the Great Awakening at Northampton, Massachusetts
1740	George Whitefield electrifies listeners at Boston
1745	Colonial troops capture Louisbourg
1748	American Lutheran ministers ordained in Philadelphia
1754	Albany Congress meets
1755	Braddock is defeated by the French and Indians in western Pennsylvania
1756	Seven Years' War is formally declared
1759	British are victorious at Quebec; Wolfe and Montcalm are killed in battle
1760	George III becomes king of Great Britain
1763	Peace of Paris ending French and Indian War is signed
1769	Junípero Serra begins to build missions in California
1821	Mexico declares independence from Spain

An editor justified the establishment of New Hampshire's first newspaper in precisely these terms. "By this Means," the publisher observed, "the spirited *Englishman*, the mountainous *Welshman*, the brave *Scotchman*, and *Irishman*, and the loyal *American*, may be firmly united and mutually RESOLVED to guard the glorious Throne of BRITANNIA . . . as *British Brothers*, in defending the Common Cause." Even new immigrants, the Germans, Scots-Irish, and Africans, who felt no political loyalty to Great Britain and no affinity to English culture, had to assimilate to some degree to the dominant English culture of the colonies.

Americans hailed Britannia. In 1763, they were the victors, the conquerors of the backcountry. In their moment of glory, the colonists assumed that Britain's rulers saw the Americans as "Brothers," as equal partners in the business of empire. Only slowly would they learn the British had a different perception. For them, "American" was a way of saying "not quite English."

Recommended Reading

The central theme of this chapter has been the re-integration of the American colonies into an increasingly powerful and prosperous British Empire. A good introduction to the imperial dimension of eighteenth-century experience is P. J. Marshall, ed., *The Oxford History of the British Empire, vol. 2, The Eighteenth Century* (1998). In *Britons: Forging the Nation, 1707–1837* (1992), Linda Colley provides an excellent discussion of the aggressive spirit of the British nationalism that the Americans came to celebrate. The arrival of new ethnic groups is examined in Eric Hinderaker and Peter C. Mancall, *At the Edge of Empire: The Backcountry in British North America* (2003); Patrick Griffin, *The People with No Name: Ulster's Presbyterians in a British Atlantic World, 1688–1763* (2001); Bernard Bailyn, *The Peopling of British North America: An Introduction* (1988); and Bernard Bailyn and Philip D. Morgan, eds., *Strangers Within the Realm: Cultural Margins of the First British Empire* (1991). Richard White has transformed how we think about Native American resistance during this period in *The Middle Ground: Indians, Empires, and Republics in the Great Lakes Region* (1991). Two other fine books explore the Indians' response to the expanding European empires: Timothy Shannon, *Indians and Colonists at the Crossroads of Empire: The Albany Congress of 1754* (2000) and Gregory Evans Dowd, *War Under Heaven: Pontiac, The Indian Nations and the British Empire* (2002). The complex story of Spanish colonization of the Southwest is told masterfully in David J. Weber, *The Spanish Frontier in North America* (1992). Fred Anderson offers the most complete treatment of war and empire in *Crucible of War: The Seven Years' War and the Fate of Empire in British North America, 1754–1766* (2000). A splendid examination of Benjamin Franklin as a colonial voice of the Enlightenment is Edmund S. Morgan, *Benjamin Franklin* (2002). The extraordinary impact of evangelical religion on colonial life is addressed in Mark A. Noll, *America's God: From Jonathan Edwards to Abraham Lincoln* (2002); Frank Lambert, *"Pedlar of Divinity": George Whitefield and the Transatlantic Revivals, 1734–1770* (1994); and Timothy D. Hall, *Contested Boundaries: Itinerancy and the Reshaping of the Colonial Religious World* (1994). The cultural concerns of a rising Anglicized colonial middle class are analyzed in David S. Shields, *Civil Tongues and Polite Letters in British America* (1997).

For a list of additional sites related to this chapter's topics, please see http://www.ablongman.com/divine.

Suggested Web Sites

History Buff—American History Library

http://www.historybuff.com/library

Brief journalistic essays on newspaper coverage of sixteenth- to eighteenth-century American history.

Benjamin Franklin Documentary History Web Site

http://www.english.udel.edu/lemay/franklin/

University of Delaware professor J. A. Leo Lemay tells the story of Franklin's varied life in seven parts on this intriguing site.

Jonathan Edwards

http://www.jonathanedwards.com/

Speeches by this famous preacher of the Great Awakening are on this site.

Religion and the Founding of the American Republic

http://lcweb.loc.gov/exhibits/religion/religion.html

This Library of Congress site is an on-line exhibit about religion and the creation of the United States.

The French and Indian War

http://web.syr.edu/~laroux/

This site is about French soldiers who came to New France between 1755 and 1760 to fight in the French and Indian War.

National Museum of the American Indian

http://www.si.edu/nmai

The Smithsonian Institution maintains this site, providing information about the museum. The museum is dedicated to everything about Native Americans.

Smithsonian Institution: You Be the Historian

http://www.americanhistory.si.edu/hohr/springer

Part of the Smithsonian's on-line museum, this exhibit enables students to examine artifacts from the home of New Castle, Delaware, residents Thomas and Elizabeth Springer and interpret the lives of a late eighteenth-century American family.

DoHistory, Harvard University Film Study Center

http://www.dohistory.org/

Focusing on the life of Martha Ballard, a late eighteenth-century New England woman, this site employs selections from her diary, excerpts from a book and film of her life, and other primary documents to enable students to conduct their own historical investigation.

Chapter 5

The Battle of Bunker Hill *by Winthrop Chandler, also shows the Burning of Charles Town.* ❖

The American Revolution: From Elite Protest to Popular Revolt, 1763–1783

Rethinking the Meaning of Social Equality

During the American Revolution, a captured British officer spent some time at the plantation of Colonel Thomas Mann Randolph, a leader of Virginia's gentry. The Englishman described the arrival of three ordinary farmers who were members of the local militia. He characterized the militiamen as "peasants," for without asking their host's permission, the Americans drew chairs up to the fire, pulled off their muddy boots, and began spitting.

The British officer was appalled; after the farmers departed, he observed they had not shown Randolph proper deference. The colonel responded that such behavior had come to be expected, for "the spirit of independency" had been transformed into "equality." Indeed, every American who "bore arms" during the Revolution considered himself as good as his neighbors. "No doubt," Randolph remarked to the officer, "each of these men conceives himself, in every respect, my equal."

This chance encounter illuminates the character of the American Revolution. The initial stimulus for rebellion came from the gentry, from the rich and wellborn, who resented Parliament's efforts to curtail their rights within the British empire. They voiced their unhappiness in carefully reasoned statements and in speeches before elected assemblies. Passionate rhetoric made them uneasy.

But as these influential planters, wealthy merchants, and prominent clergymen discovered, the revolutionary movement generated a momentum that they could not control. As relations with Britain deteriorated, particularly after 1765, the traditional leaders of colonial society encouraged the ordinary folk to join the protest—as rioters, as petitioners, and finally, as soldiers. Newspapers, sermons, and pamphlets helped transform what had begun as a squabble among the gentry into a mass movement, and as Randolph learned, once the people had become involved in shaping the nation's destiny, they could never again be excluded.

HAD IT NOT BEEN FOR those pushy "peasant" militiamen in the various colonies, the British would have easily crushed American resistance. Although some accounts of the Revolution downplay the military side of the story, leaving the impression that a few famous "Founding Fathers" effortlessly carried the nation to independence, a more persuasive explanation must recognize the centrality of armed violence in achieving nationhood.

The American Revolution involved a massive military commitment. If common American soldiers had not been willing to stand up to seasoned British troops, to face the terror of the bayonet charge, independence would have remained a dream of intellectuals.

OUTLINE

FEATURE ESSAY

The colonial American military forces were drawn from all social classes. Some soldiers were poorly equipped. Although the militiamen depicted in this engraving have rifles and warm clothing, one is without shoes.

Proportionate to the population, a greater percentage of Americans died in military service during the Revolution than in any war in American history, with the exception of the Civil War. The concept of liberty so magnificently expressed in revolutionary pamphlets was not, therefore, simply an abstraction, an exclusive concern of political theorists such as Thomas Jefferson and John Adams. It also motivated ordinary folk—mud-covered Virginia militiamen, for example—to take up weapons and risk death. Those who survived the ordeal were never quite the same, for the very experience of fighting, of assuming responsibility in battle and perhaps even of taking the lives of British officers, gave dramatic new meaning to the idea of social equality.

Structure of Colonial Society

Colonists who were alive during the 1760s did not anticipate the coming of national independence. It is only from a modern perspective that we see how the events of this period would lead to the formation of the United States. The colonists, of course, did not know what the future would bring. They would probably have characterized these years as "postwar," as a time of heightened economic and political expectation following the successful conclusion of the Seven Years' War (see Chapter 4).

For many Americans, the period generated optimism. The population continued to grow. Indeed, in 1776, approximately 2.5 million people, black and white, were living in Great Britain's thirteen mainland colonies. The striking ethnic and racial diversity of these men and women amazed European visitors who apparently rated homogeneity more highly than did the Americans. In 1775, for example, a traveler corrected the impression in London that the "colonists are the offspring of Englishmen." To be sure, many families traced their roots to Great Britain, but one also encountered "French, Dutch, Germans innumerable, Indians, Africans, and a multitude of felons." He then asked rhetorically, "Is it possible to tell which are the most turbulent amongst such a mixture of people?"

The American population on the eve of Independence was also extraordinarily young, a fact of great importance in understanding the development of effective political resistance. Nearly 60 percent of the American people were under age 21. This is a fact of considerable significance. At any given time, most people in this society were small children, and many of the young men who fought the British during the Revolution either had not been born or had been infants during the Stamp Act crisis. Any explanation for the coming of independence, therefore, must take into account the continuing political mobilization of so many young people.

Postwar Americans also experienced a high level of prosperity. To be sure, some major port cities went through a difficult period as colonists who had been employed during the fighting were thrown out of work. Sailors and ship workers, for example, were especially vulnerable to layoffs of this sort. In general, however, white Americans did very well. The quality of their material lives was not substantially lower than that of the English. In 1774, the per capita wealth of the Americans—this figure includes blacks as well as whites—was £37.4. This sum exceeds the per capita wealth of many developing countries today. On the eve of revolution, £37.4 would have purchased about 310 bushels of wheat, 1600 pounds of rice, 11 cows, or 6 horses. A typical white family of five—a father, mother, and three dependent children—not only would have been able to afford decent food, clothing, and housing but also would have had money left over with which to purchase consumer goods. Even the poorest colonists seem to have benefited from a rising standard of living, and although they may not have done as well as their wealthier neighbors, they too wanted to preserve gains they had made.

Wealth, however, was not evenly distributed in this society. Regional variations were striking. The Southern Colonies enjoyed the highest levels of personal wealth in America, which can be explained in part by the ownership of slaves. More than 90 percent of America's unfree workers lived in the South, and they represented a huge capital investment. Even without including the slaves in these wealth estimates, the South did quite well. In terms of aggregate wealth, the Middle Colonies also scored impressively. In fact, only New England lagged noticeably behind, a reflection of its relative inability to produce large amounts of exports for a growing world market.

Breakdown of Political Trust

Ultimate responsibility for preserving the empire fell to George III. When he became king of England in 1760, he was only 22 years of age. In public, contemporaries praised the new monarch. In private, however, they expressed grave reservations. The youth had led a sheltered, loveless life; his father, an irresponsible playboy, had died in 1751 before ascending the throne. Young George had not received a good education, and even though he demonstrated considerable mechanical ability, his grandfather, George II, thought his grandson dull-witted, an opinion widely shared. As one might expect, George grew up hating not only his grandfather but almost everyone associated with the reign of George II.

To hide his intellectual inadequacies, the new king adopted a pedantic habit of correcting people for small faults, a characteristic made all the more annoying by his obvious inability to grasp the larger implications of government policy. During a difficult period that demanded imagination, generosity, and wisdom, George muddled along as best he could.

The new monarch was determined to play an aggressive role in government. This decision caused considerable dismay among England's political leaders. For decades, a powerful, though loosely associated, group of men who called themselves **Whigs** had set policy and controlled patronage. George II had accepted this situation, and so long as the Whigs in Parliament did not meddle with his beloved army, the king had let them rule the nation.

In one stroke, George III destroyed this cozy relationship. He selected as his chief minister the Earl of Bute, a Scot whose chief qualification for office appeared to be his friendship with the young king. The Whigs who dominated Parliament were outraged. Bute had no ties with the members of the House of Commons; he owed them no favors. It seemed to the Whigs that with the appointment of Bute, George was trying to turn back the clock to the time before the Glorious Revolution, in other words, attempting to reestablish a personal Stuart monarchy free from traditional constitutional restraints. The Whigs blamed Bute for every wrong, real or imagined. George did not, in fact, harbor such arbitrary ambitions, but his actions threw customary political practices into doubt.

By 1763 Bute, despairing of public life, left office. His departure, however, neither restored the Whigs to

Coat of Arms of George III, c.1760-1770. The royal coat of arms was evident in the American colonies as a representation of the British empire. After the early 1770s many dissatisfied colonists viewed it as emblematic of a monarchy that did not understand or care about their problems. ❖

preeminence nor dampened the king's enthusiasm for domestic politics. Everyone agreed George had the right to select whomever he desired for cabinet posts, but until 1770, no one seemed able to please the monarch. Ministers came and went, often for no other reason than George's personal distaste. Because of this chronic instability, subministers (minor bureaucrats who directed routine colonial affairs) did not know what was expected of them. In the absence of clear long-range policy, some ministers made narrowly based decisions; others did nothing. Most devoted their energies to finding a political patron capable of satisfying the fickle king. Talent played little part in the scramble for office, and incompetent hacks were advanced as frequently as were men of vision. With such turbulence surrounding him, the king showed little interest in the American colonies.

The king, however, does not bear the sole responsibility for England's loss of empire. The members of Parliament who actually drafted the statutes that gradually drove a wedge between the colonies and Britain must share the blame, for they failed to provide innovative answers to the explosive constitutional issues of the day. The problem was not stupidity or even obstinacy, qualities found in equal measure among all peoples.

In part, the impasse resulted from sheer ignorance. Few Englishmen active in government had ever visited America. For those who attempted to follow colonial affairs, accurate information proved extremely difficult to obtain. Packet boats carrying passengers and mail sailed regularly between London and the various colonial ports, but the voyage across the Atlantic required at least four weeks. Furthermore, all correspondence was laboriously copied in longhand by overworked clerks serving in understaffed offices. One could not expect to receive from America an answer to a specific question in less than three months. As a result of the lag in communication between England and America, rumors sometimes passed for true accounts, and misunderstanding influenced the formulation of colonial policy.

Cartoons became a popular means of criticizing government during this period. Here, King George III watches as the kilted Lord Bute slaughters the goose America. A cabinet member holds a basket of golden eggs at rear. At front left, a dog relieves itself on a map of North America. ❖

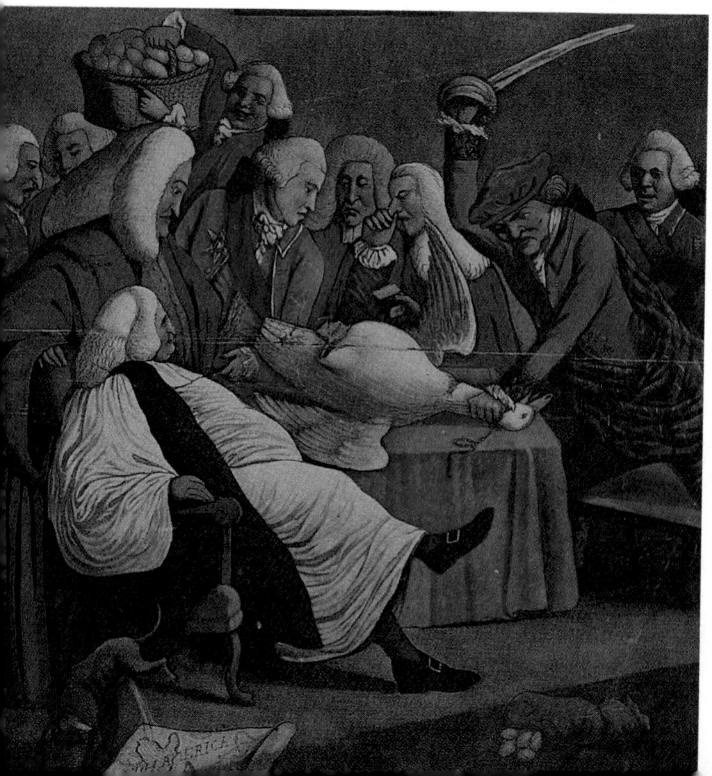

But failure of communication alone was not to blame for the widening gap between the colonies and England. Even when complete information was available, the two sides were often unable to understand each other's positions. The central element in this Anglo-American debate was a concept known as **parliamentary sovereignty.** The English ruling classes viewed the role of Parliament from a historical perspective that most colonists never shared. They insisted that Parliament was the dominant element within the constitution. Indeed, this elective body protected rights and property from an arbitrary monarch. During the reign of the Stuarts, especially under Charles I (r. 1625–1649), the authority of Parliament had been challenged, and it was not until the Glorious Revolution of 1688 that the English crown formally recognized Parliament's supreme authority in matters such as taxation. Almost no one, including George III, would have dissented from a speech made in 1766 before the House of Commons, in which a representative declared, "The parliament hath, and must have, from the nature and essence of the constitution, has had, and ever will have a sovereign supreme power and jurisdiction over every part of the dominions of the state, *to make laws in all cases whatsoever.*"

Such a constitutional position did not leave much room for compromise. Most members of Parliament took a hard line on this issue. The notion of dividing or sharing sovereignty simply made no sense to the English ruling class. As Thomas Hutchinson, royal governor of Massachusetts, explained, no middle ground existed "between the supreme authority of Parliament and the total dependence of the colonies: it is impossible there should be two independent legislatures in one and the same state."

The logic of this argument seemed self-evident to the British. In fact, parliamentary leaders could never quite understand why the colonists were so difficult to persuade. In frustration, Lord Hillsborough, the British secretary of state, admonished the colonial agent for Connecticut, "It is essential to the constitution to preserve the supremacy of Parliament inviolate; and tell your friends in America . . . that it is as much their interest to support the constitution and preserve the supremacy of Parliament as it is ours."

No Taxation Without Representation: The American Perspective

Americans most emphatically did not see it in their "interest" to maintain the "supremacy of Parliament." The crisis in imperial relations forced the colonists first to define and then to defend principles deeply rooted in their own political culture. For more than a century, their ideas about the colonies' role within the British empire had remained a vague, untested bundle of assumptions about personal liberties, property rights, and representative institutions.

By 1763, however, certain fundamental American beliefs had become clear. From Massachusetts to Georgia, colonists aggressively defended the powers of the provincial assemblies. They drew on a rich legislative history of their own. Over the course of the century, the American assemblies had steadily expanded their authority over taxation and expenditure. Since no one in Britain bothered to clip their legislative wings, these provincial bodies assumed a major role in policymaking and routine administration. In other words, by midcentury the assemblies looked like American copies of Parliament. It seemed unreasonable, therefore, for the British suddenly to insist on the supremacy of Parliament, for as the legislators of Massachusetts observed in 1770, "This house has the same inherent rights in this province as the house of commons in Great Britain."

The constitutional debate turned ultimately on the meaning of representation itself. In 1764, a British official informed the colonists that even though they had not elected members to Parliament—indeed, even though they had had no direct contact with the current members—they were nevertheless "virtually" represented by that august body. The members of Parliament, he declared, represented the political interests of everyone who lived in the British empire. It did not really matter whether everyone had cast a vote.

The colonists ridiculed this notion of **virtual representation.** The only representatives the Americans recognized as legitimate were those actually chosen by the people for whom they spoke. On this crucial point they would not compromise. As John Adams insisted, a representative assembly should actually mirror its constituents: "It should think, feel, reason, and act like them." Since the members of Parliament could not possibly "think" like Americans, it followed logically they could not represent them. And if they were not genuine representatives, the members of Parliament—pretensions to sovereignty notwithstanding—had no business taxing the American people. Thus, in 1764 the Connecticut Assembly declared in bold letters, "NO LAW CAN BE MADE OR ABROGATED WITHOUT THE CONSENT OF THE PEOPLE BY THEIR REPRESENTATIVES."

Ideas About Power and Virtue

The political ideology that had the greatest popular appeal among the colonists contained a strong moral component, one that British rulers and American **Loyalists** (people who sided with the king and Parliament during the Revolution) never fully understood. The origins of this highly religious perspective on civil government are difficult to locate with precision, but certainly, the Great Awakening created a general awareness of an obligation to conduct public as well as private affairs according to Scripture (see Chapter 4).

Americans expressed their political beliefs in a language they had borrowed from English writers. The person most frequently cited was John Locke, the influential seventeenth-century philosopher whose *Two Treatises of Government* (first published in 1690) seemed, to colonial readers at least, a brilliant description of what was in fact American political practice. Locke claimed that all people possessed natural and inalienable rights. In order to preserve these God-given rights—the rights of life, liberty, and property, for example—free men (the status of women in Locke's work was less clear) formed contracts. These agreements were the foundation of human society as well as civil government, and they required the consent of the people who were actually governed. There could be no coercion. Locke justified rebellion against arbitrary forms of government that were by their very nature unreasonable. Americans delighted in Locke's ability to unite traditional religious values with a spirited defense of popular government, and even when they did not fully understand his technical writings, they seldom missed a chance to quote from the works of "the Great Mr. Locke."

Colonial Americans also enthusiastically subscribed to the so-called Commonwealthman tradition, a body of political assumptions generally identified with two eighteenth-century English publicists, John Trenchard and Thomas Gordon (see Chapter 4). The writings of such figures—most of whom spent their lives in political opposition—helped persuade the colonists that *power* was extremely dangerous, a force that would surely destroy liberty unless it was countered by *virtue.* Persons who shared this highly charged moral outlook regarded bad policy as not simply the result of human error. Rather, it was an indication of sin and corruption.

Insistence on public virtue—sacrifice of self-interest to the public good—became the dominant theme of revolutionary political writing. American pamphleteers seldom took a dispassionate, legalistic approach to their analysis of power and liberty. More commonly, they exposed plots hatched by corrupt courtiers, such as the Earl of Bute. None of them—or their readers—had any doubt that Americans were more virtuous than were the people of England.

During the 1760s, however, popular writers were not certain how long the colonists could hold out against arbitrary taxation, standing armies, Anglican bishops—in other words, against a host of external threats designed to crush American liberty. In 1774, for example, the people of Farmington, Connecticut, declared that "the present ministry, being instigated by the devil and led by their wicked and corrupt hearts, have a design to take away our liberties and properties, and to enslave us forever." Indeed, these Connecticut farmers described Britain's leaders as "pimps and parasites." This highly emotional, conspiratorial rhetoric sometimes shocks modern readers who assume that America's revolutionary leaders were products of the Enlightenment, persons who relied solely on reason to solve social and political problems. Whatever the origins of their ideas may have been, the colonial pamphleteers successfully roused ordinary men and women to resist Britain with force of arms.

Colonial newspapers spread these ideas through a large dispersed population. A majority of adult white males—especially those in the Northern Colonies—were literate, and it is not surprising that the number of journals published in this country increased dramatically during the revolutionary period. For the first time in American history, persons living in various parts of the continent could closely follow events that occurred in distant American cities. Because of the availability of newspapers, the details of Bostonians' confrontations with British authorities were known throughout the colonies, and these shared political experiences drew Americans more closely together, making it possible—in the words of John Adams—for "Thirteen clocks . . . to strike together—a perfection of mechanism which no artist had ever before effected."

Eroding the Bonds of Empire

The Seven Years' War saddled Great Britain with a national debt so huge that more than half the annual national budget went to pay the interest on it. Almost everyone in government assumed that with the cessation of hostilities, the troops would be disbanded, thus saving a lot of money. George III had other plans. He insisted on keeping the largest peacetime army in British history on active duty, supposedly to protect Indians from predatory frontiersmen and to preserve order in the newly conquered territories of Florida and Quebec.

Maintaining such a force so far distant from the mother country fueled the budgetary crisis. The growing financial burden weighed heavily on restive English taxpayers and sent government leaders scurrying in search of new sources of revenue.

For their part, colonists doubted the value of this expensive army. Britain did not leave enough troops in America to maintain peace on the frontier effectively. The weakness of the army was dramatically demonstrated during the spring of 1763. The native peoples of the backcountry—the Senecas, Ottawas, Miamis, Creeks, and Cherokees—had begun discussing how they might turn back the tide of white settlement. The powerful spiritual leader Neolin, known as the Delaware Prophet and claiming vision from the "Master of Life," helped these Indians articulate their fear and anger. He urged them to restore their cultures to the "original state that they were in before the white people found out their country." If moral regeneration required violence, so be it. Neolin converted Pontiac, an Ottawa warrior, to the cause, and he, in turn, coordinated an uprising among the western Indians who had been French allies and who hated all British people—even those sent to protect them from land-grabbing colonists. The formidable Native American resistance was known as Pontiac's Rebellion. In May, Pontiac attacked Detroit; other Indians harassed the Pennsylvania and Virginia frontiers. At the end of the year, after his followers began deserting, Pontiac sued for peace. During even this brief outbreak, the British army proved unable to defend exposed colonial settlements, and several thousand people lost their lives.

From the perspective of the Native Americans who inhabited the Ohio Valley this was a period of almost unmitigated disaster. In fact, more than any other group, the Indians suffered as a direct result of imperial reorganization. The defeat of the French made it impossible for native peoples to play off one imperial power against European rivals (see Chapter 4), and the victorious British made it clear that they regarded their former Indian allies as little more than a nuisance. Diplomatic gifts stopped; humiliating restrictions were placed on trade. But even worse, Pontiac's rising unloosed vicious racism along the colonial frontier, and American colonists often used any excuse to attack local Indians, peaceful or not. Late in 1763 a group of vigilantes known as the Paxton Boys murdered a score of Christian Indians, women and children, living near Lancaster, Pennsylvania. White neighbors treated the killers as heroes, and the atrocity ended only after the Paxton Boys threatened

Chronicle of Colonial–British Tension

Legislation	Date	Provisions	Colonial Reaction
Sugar Act	April 5, 1764	Revised duties on sugar, coffee, tea, wine, other imports; expanded jurisdiction of vice-admiralty courts	Several assemblies protest taxation for revenue
Stamp Act	March 22, 1765; repealed March 18, 1766	Printed documents (deeds, newspapers, marriage licenses, etc.) issued only on special stamped paper purchased from stamp distributors	Riots in cities; collectors forced to resign; Stamp Act Congress (October 1765)
Quartering Act	May 1765	Colonists must supply British troops with housing, other items (candles, firewood, etc.)	Protest in assemblies; New York Assembly punished for failure to comply, 1767
Declaratory Act	March 18, 1766	Parliament declares its sovereignty over the colonies "in all cases whatsoever"	Ignored in celebration over repeal of the Stamp Act
Townshend Revenue Acts	June 26, 29, July 2, 1767; all repealed—except duty on tea, March 1770	New duties on glass, lead, paper, paints, tea; customs collections tightened in America	Nonimportation of British goods; assemblies protest; newspapers attack British policy
Tea Act	May 10, 1773	Parliament gives East India Company right to sell tea directly to Americans; some duties on tea reduced	Protests against favoritism shown to monopolistic company; tea destroyed in Boston (December 16, 1773)
Coercive Acts (Intolerable Acts)	March–June 1774	Closes port of Boston; restructures Massachusetts government; restricts town meetings; troops quartered in Boston; British officials accused of crimes sent to England or Canada for trial	Boycott of British goods; First Continental Congress convenes (September 1774)
Prohibitory Act	December 22, 1775	Declares British intention to coerce Americans into submission; embargo on American goods; American ships seized	Drives Continental Congress closer to decision for independence

When news of the Tea Party reached London in January 1774, the North ministry was stunned. The people of Boston had treated parliamentary supremacy with utter contempt, and British rulers saw no humor whatsoever in the destruction of private property by subjects of the Crown dressed in costume. To quell such rebelliousness, Parliament passed a series of laws called the **Coercive Acts.** (In America, they were referred to as the Intolerable Acts.) The legislation (1) closed the port of Boston until the city fully compensated the East India Company for the lost tea; (2) restructured the Massachusetts government by transforming the upper house from an elective to an appointed body and restricting the number of legal town meetings to one a year; (3) allowed the royal governor to transfer British officials arrested for offenses committed in the line of duty to England, where there was little likelihood they would be convicted; and (4) authorized the army to quarter troops wherever they were needed, even if this required the compulsory requisition of uninhabited private buildings. George III enthusiastically supported this tough policy; he appointed General Thomas Gage to serve as the colony's new royal governor. Gage apparently won the king's favor by announcing that in America, "Nothing can be done but by forcible means."

The sweeping denial of constitutional liberties confirmed the colonists' worst fears. To men like Samuel Adams, it seemed as if Britain really intended to enslave the American people. Colonial moderates found their position shaken by the vindictiveness of the Coercive Acts. Edmund Burke, one of America's last friends in Parliament, noted sadly on the floor of Commons, that "this is the day, then, that you wish to go to war with all America, in order to conciliate that country to this."

In the midst of the constitutional crisis, Parliament announced plans to establish a new civil government for the Canadian province of Quebec (Quebec Act, June 22, 1774). This territory had been ruled by military authority following the Seven Years' War. The Quebec Act not only failed to create an elective assembly—an institution the Americans regarded as essential for the protection of liberty—but also awarded French Roman

Catholics a large voice in local political affairs. Moreover, since Quebec extended all the way south to the Ohio River and west to the Mississippi River, Americans concluded that Parliament wanted to deny the American settlers and traders in this fast-developing region their constitutional rights, a threat that affected all colonists, not just those of Massachusetts Bay.

If in 1774 the House of Commons thought it could isolate Boston from the rest of America, it was in for a rude surprise. Colonists living in other parts of the continent recognized immediately that the principles at stake in Boston affected all Americans. As one Virginian explained, "there were no Heats and Troubles in Virginia till the Blockade of Boston." Few persons advocated independence, but they could not remain passive while Boston was destroyed. They sent food and money and, during the fall of 1774, reflected more deeply than ever on what it meant to be a colonist in the British empire.

The sticking point remained—as it had been in 1765—the sovereignty of Parliament. No one in Britain could think of a way around this constitutional impasse. In 1773, Benjamin Franklin had offered a suggestion. "The Parliament," he observed, "has no right to make any law whatever, binding on the colonies ... the king, and not the king, lords, and commons collectively, is their sovereign." But so long as it still seemed possible to coerce the Americans into obedience, to punish these errant children, Britain's rulers had little incentive to accept such a humiliating compromise.

Steps Toward Independence

During the summer of 1774, committees of correspondence analyzed the perilous situation in which the colonists found themselves. Something, of course, had to be done. But what? Would the Southern Colonies support resistance in New England? Would Pennsylvanians stand up to Parliament? Not surprisingly, the committees endorsed a call for a Continental Congress, a gathering of fifty-five elected delegates from twelve colonies (Georgia sent none but agreed to support the action taken). This **First Continental Congress** convened in Philadelphia on September 5. It included some of America's most articulate, respected leaders; among them were John Adams, Samuel Adams, Patrick Henry, Richard Henry Lee, Christopher Gadsden, and George Washington.

The delegates were strangers to one another. They knew little about the customs and values, the geography and economy of Britain's other provinces. As John Adams explained on September 18, "It has taken Us much Time to get acquainted with the Tempers, Views, Characters, and Designs of Persons and to let them into the Circumstances of our Province." During the early sessions of the Congress, the delegates eyed each other closely, trying to gain a sense of the strength and integrity of the men with whom they might commit treason.

Differences of opinion soon surfaced. Delegates from the Middle Colonies—Joseph Galloway of Pennsylvania, for example—wanted to proceed with caution, but Samuel Adams and other more radical members pushed the moderates toward confrontation. Boston's master politician engineered congressional commendation of the Suffolk Resolves, a bold statement drawn up in Suffolk County, Massachusetts, that encouraged forcible resistance of the Coercive Acts.

After this decision, the tone of the meeting was established. Moderate spokesmen introduced conciliatory measures, which received polite discussion but failed to win a majority vote. Just before returning to their homes (September 1774), the delegates created the "Association," an intercolonial agreement to halt all commerce with Britain until Parliament repealed the Intolerable Acts. This was a totally revolutionary decision. The Association authorized a vast network of local committees to enforce **nonimportation.** Violators were exposed, shamed, forced either to apologize publicly for their actions or to be shunned by all their patriot neighbors. In many of the communities, the committees *were* the government, distinguishing, in the words of James Madison, "Friends from Foes." George III sneered at these activities. "I am not sorry," he confided, "that the line of conduct seems now chalked out ... the New England Governments are in a state of Rebellion, blows must decide whether they are to be subject to this country or independent."

Shots Heard Around the World

The king was correct. Before Congress reconvened, "blows" fell at Lexington and Concord, two small farm villages in eastern Massachusetts. On the evening of April 18, 1775, General Gage dispatched troops from Boston to seize rebel supplies. Paul Revere, a renowned silversmith and active patriot, warned the colonists that the redcoats were coming. The militia of Lexington, a collection of ill-trained farmers, boys as well as old men, decided to stand on the village green on the following morning, April 19, as the British soldiers passed on the road to Concord. No one planned to fight, but in a moment of confusion, someone (probably a colonist) fired; the redcoats discharged a volley, and eight Americans lay dead.

Word of the incident spread rapidly, and by the time the British force reached its destination, the countryside swarmed with "minutemen," special com-

This 1775 engraving by Amos Doolittle, an eyewitness, shows the American attack on the British regulars as they marched from Concord back to Boston. The minutemen fired from cover, killing and wounding many redcoats who expected little armed resistance. ❖

panies of Massachusetts militia prepared to respond instantly to military emergencies. The redcoats found nothing of significance in Concord and so returned. The long march back to Boston turned into a rout. Lord Percy, a British officer who brought up reinforcements, remarked more in surprise than bitterness that "whoever looks upon them [the American soldiers] as an irregular mob, will find himself much mistaken." On June 17, colonial militiamen again held their own against seasoned troops at the battle of Bunker Hill (actually Breed's Hill). The British finally took the hill, but after this costly "victory" in which he suffered 40 percent casualties, Gage complained that the Americans had displayed "a conduct and spirit against us, they never showed against the French."

Beginning "The World Over Again"

Members of the **Second Continental Congress** gathered in Philadelphia in May 1775. They faced an awesome responsibility. British government in the mainland colonies had almost ceased to function, and with Americans fighting redcoats, the country desperately needed strong central leadership. Slowly, often reluctantly, Congress took control of the war. The delegates formed a Continental Army and appointed George Washington its commander, in part because he seemed to have greater military experience than anyone else available and in part because he looked like he should be commander in chief. The delegates were also eager to select someone who did not come from Massachusetts, a colony that seemed already to possess too much power in national councils. The members of Congress purchased military supplies and, to pay for them, issued paper money. But while they were assuming the powers of a sovereign government, the congressmen refused to declare independence. They debated and fretted, listened to the appeals of moderates who played on the colonists' remaining loyalty to Britain, and then did nothing.

Indecision drove men such as John Adams nearly mad. In one tirade against his timid colleagues, he exclaimed that they possessed "the vanity of the ape, the tameness of the ox, or the stupid servility of the ass." Haste, however, would have been a terrible mistake. While Adams and Richard Henry Lee of Virginia were willing to sever ties with Britain, many Americans were not convinced that such a step was either desirable or necessary. If Congress had moved too quickly, it might have become vulnerable to charges of extremism, in which case the rebellion would have seemed—and indeed, might have been—

more like an overthrow by a faction or clique than an expression of popular will.

The British government appeared intent on transforming colonial moderates into angry rebels. In December 1775, Parliament passed the Prohibitory Act, declaring war on American commerce. Until the colonists begged for pardon, they could not trade with the rest of the world. The British navy blockaded their ports and seized American ships on the high seas. Lord North also hired German mercenaries (the Russians drove too hard a bargain) to put down the rebellion. And in America, Virginia's royal governor Lord Dunmore further undermined the possibility of reconciliation by urging the colony's slaves to take up arms against their masters. Few did so, but the effort to stir up black rebellion infuriated the Virginia gentry.

Thomas Paine (1737–1809) pushed the colonists even closer to independence. Nothing in this man's background suggested he would write the most important pamphlet in American history. In England, Paine had tried and failed in a number of jobs, and exactly why he elected to move to America in 1774 is not clear. While still in England, Paine had the good fortune to meet Benjamin Franklin, who presented him with letters of introduction to the leading patriots of Pennsylvania. At the urging of his new American friends, Paine produced ***Common Sense,*** an essay that became an instant best-seller. In only three months, it sold more than 120,000 copies. Paine confirmed in forceful prose what the colonists had been thinking but had been unable to state in coherent form. "My motive and object in all my political works," he declared, " . . . have been to rescue man from tyranny and false systems of government, and enable him to be free."

Common Sense systematically stripped kingship of historical and theological justification. For centuries, the English had maintained the fiction that the monarch could do no wrong. When the government oppressed the people, the royal counselors received the blame. The crown was above suspicion. To this, Paine cried nonsense. Monarchs ruled by force. George III was simply a "royal brute," who by his arbitrary behavior had surrendered his claim to the colonists' obedience. The pamphlet also attacked the whole idea of a mixed and balanced constitution. Indeed, *Common Sense* was a powerful democratic manifesto.

Paine's greatest contribution to the revolutionary cause was persuading ordinary folk to sever their ties with Great Britain. It was not reasonable, he argued, to regard England as the mother country. "Europe, and not England," he explained, "is the parent country of America. This new world hath been the asylum for the persecuted lovers of civil and religious liberty from *every part* of Europe." No doubt that message made a deep impression on Pennsylvania's German population. The time had come for the colonists to form an independent republic. "We have it in our power," Paine wrote in one of his most moving statements, "to begin the world over again . . . the birthday of a new world is at hand."

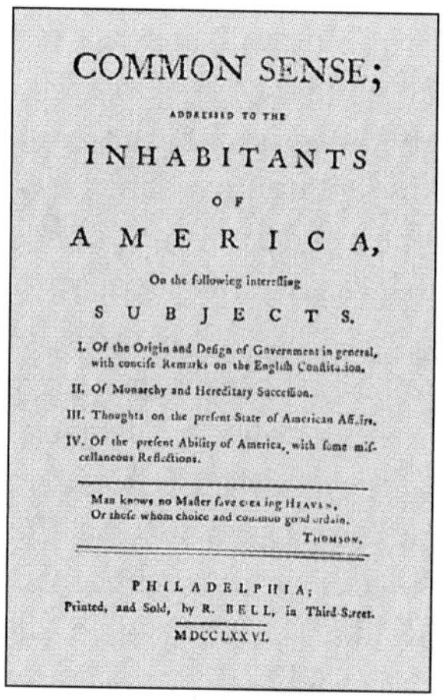
COMMON SENSE;
ADDRESSED TO THE
INHABITANTS
OF
AMERICA,
On the following interesting
SUBJECTS.
I. Of the Origin and Design of Government in general, with concise Remarks on the English Constitution.
II. Of Monarchy and Hereditary Succession.
III. Thoughts on the present State of American Affairs.
IV. Of the present Ability of America, with some miscellaneous Reflections.

Man knows no Master save creating HEAVEN,
Or those whom choice and common good ordain.
THOMSON.

PHILADELPHIA;
Printed, and Sold, by R. BELL, in Third Street.
MDCCLXXVI.

The message of Thomas Paine's pamphlet Common Sense *(title page shown) was clear and direct. Paine's powerful argument called for "The Free and Independent States of America." He assured ordinary Americans not only that they could live without a king, but also that they would win the war.* ❖

On July 2, 1776, after a long and tedious debate, Congress finally voted for independence. The motion passed: twelve states for, none against (with New York abstaining). Thomas Jefferson, a young Virginia lawyer and planter who enjoyed a reputation as a graceful writer, drafted a formal declaration that was accepted with alterations two days later. Much of the Declaration of Independence consisted of a list of specific grievances against George III and his government. Like the skilled lawyer he was, Jefferson presented the evidence for independence. The document did not become famous for those passages. Long after the establishment of the new republic, the Declaration challenged Americans to make good on the principle that "all men are created equal." John Adams nicely expressed the patriots' fervor when he wrote on July 3, "Yesterday the greatest question was decided, which ever was debated in America, and a greater perhaps, never was or will be decided among men."

Many revolutionary leaders throughout the modern world—in Europe as in Asia—have echoed Adams's assessment. Of all the documents written during this period, including the Constitution, the Declaration remains the most powerful and radical invitation to Americans of all backgrounds to demand their equality and full rights as human beings.

Congress Voting Independence, *oil painting by Robert Edge Pine and Edward Savage, 1785. The committee appointed by Congress to draft a declaration of independence included (center, standing) John Adams, Roger Sherman, Robert Livingston, Thomas Jefferson, and (center foreground, seated) Benjamin Franklin. The committee members are shown submitting Jefferson's draft to the speaker.* ❖

FIGHTING FOR INDEPENDENCE

Only fools and visionaries expressed optimism about America's prospects of winning independence in 1776. The Americans had taken on a formidable military power. The population of Britain was perhaps four times that of its former colonies. England also possessed a strong manufacturing base, a well-trained regular army supplemented by thousands of hired German troops (Hessians), and a navy that dominated the world's oceans. Many British officers had battlefield experience. They already knew what the Americans would slowly learn: Waging war requires discipline, money, and sacrifice.

The British government entered the conflict fully confident that it could beat the Americans. In 1776, Lord North and his colleagues regarded the war as a police action. They anticipated that a mere show of armed force would intimidate the upstart colonists. As soon as the rebels in Boston had been humbled, the British argued, people living in other colonies would desert the cause for independence. General Gage, for example, told the king that the colonists "will be Lions, whilst we are Lambs, . . . if we take a resolute part they will undoubtedly prove very weak." Since this advice confirmed George's views, he called Gage "an honest determined man."

As later events demonstrated, of course, Britain had become involved in an impossible military situation, in some ways analogous to that in which the United States would find itself in Vietnam some two hundred years later. Three separate elements neutralized advantages held by the larger power over its adversary. First, the British had to transport men and supplies across the Atlantic, a logistic challenge of unprecedented complexity. Unreliable lines of communication broke down under the strain of war.

Second, America was too vast to be conquered by conventional military methods. Redcoats might gain control over the major port cities, but as long as the Continental Army remained intact, the rebellion continued. As Washington explained, "the possession of our Towns, while we have an Army in the field, will avail them little . . . It is our Arms, not defenceless Towns, they have to subdue." Even if England had recruited enough soldiers to occupy the entire country, it would still have lost the war. As one Loyalist instructed the king, "if all America becomes a garrison, she is not worth your attention." Britain could only win by crushing the American will to resist.

And third, British strategists never appreciated the depth of the Americans' commitment to a political ideology. In the wars of eighteenth-century Europe, such beliefs had seldom mattered. European troops before the French Revolution served because they were paid or because the military was a vocation, but most certainly not because they hoped to advance a set of constitutional principles. Americans were different. To be sure, some young men were drawn to the military by bounty money or by the desire to escape unhappy families. A few were drafted. But taking such people into account, one still encounters among the American troops a remarkable commitment to republican ideals. One French officer reported from the United States, "It

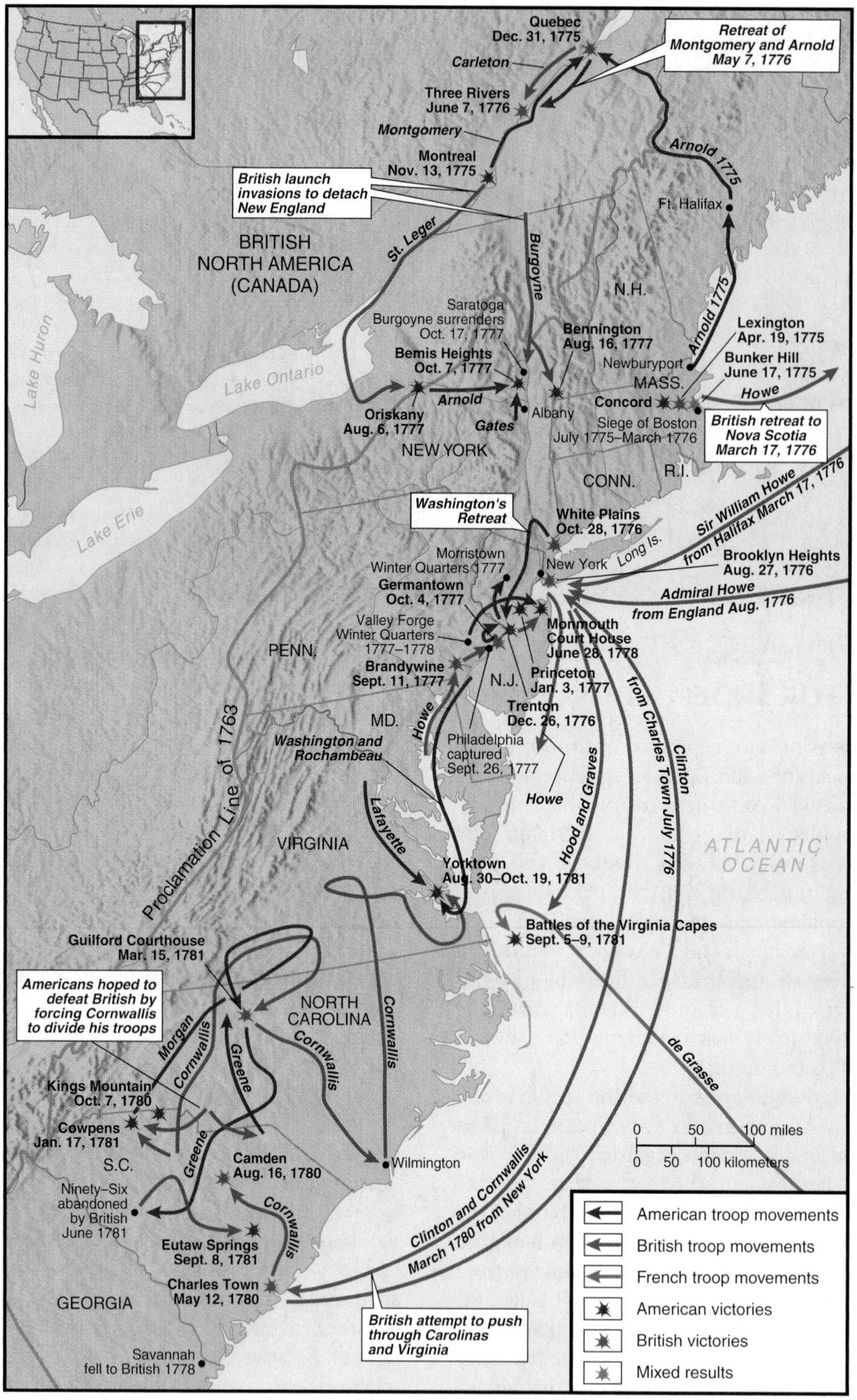

THE AMERICAN REVOLUTION, 1775–1781 *The War for Independence ranged over a huge area. Battles were fought in the colonies, on the western frontier, and along the Gulf of Mexico. The major engagements of the first years of the war, from the spontaneous rising at Concord in 1775 to Washington's well-coordinated attack on Trenton in December 1776, were fought in the northern colonies. In the middle theater of war, Burgoyne's attempt in 1777 to cut off New England from the rest of the colonies failed when his army was defeated at Saratoga. Action in the final years of the war, from the battles at Camden, Kings Mountain, Cowpens, and Guilford Courthouse to the final victory at Yorktown, occurred in the southern theater of war.* ❖

is incredible that soldiers composed of men of every age, even of children of fifteen, of whites and blacks, almost naked, unpaid, and rather poorly fed, can march so well and withstand fire so steadfastly."

Building a Professional Army

During the earliest months of rebellion, American soldiers—especially those of New England—suffered no lack of confidence. Indeed, they interpreted their courageous stands at Concord and Bunker Hill as evidence that brave yeomen farmers could lick British regulars on any battlefield. George Washington spent the first years of the war disabusing the colonists of this foolishness, for as he had learned during the French and Indian War, military success depended on endless drill, careful planning, and tough discipline—rigorous preparation that did not characterize the minutemen's methods.

Washington insisted on organizing a regular well-trained field army. Some advisers urged the commander in chief to wage a guerrilla war, one in which small partisan bands would sap Britain's will to rule Americans. But Washington rejected that course. He recognized that the Continental Army served not only as a fighting force but also as a symbol of the republican cause. Its very existence would sustain American hopes, and so long as the army survived, American agents could plausibly solicit foreign aid. This thinking shaped Washington's wartime strategy; he studiously avoided "general actions" in which the Continental Army might be destroyed. Critics complained about Washington's caution, but as they soon discovered, he understood better than they what independence required.

If the commander in chief was correct about the army, however, he failed to comprehend the political importance of the militia. These scattered, almost amateur, military units seldom altered the outcome of battle, but they did maintain control over large areas of the country not directly affected by the British army. Throughout the war, they compelled men and women who would rather have remained neutral to actively support the American effort. In 1777, for example, the militia of Farmington, Connecticut, visited a group of suspected Tories, as Loyalists were called, and after "educating" these people in the fundamentals of republican ideology, a militia spokesman announced, "They were indeed grossly ignorant of the true grounds of the present war with Great Britain . . . [but] They appeared to be penitent of their former conduct, [and] professed themselves convinced . . . that there was no such thing as remaining neuters." Without local political coercion, Washington's task would have been considerably more difficult.

For the half million African American colonists, most of them slaves, the fight for independence took on special poignancy. After all, they wanted to achieve personal as well as political freedom, and many African Americans supported those who seemed most likely to deliver them from bondage. As one historian explained, "the black soldier was likely to join the side that made him the quickest and best offer in terms of those 'unalienable rights' of which Mr. Jefferson had spoken." It is estimated that some five thousand African Americans took up arms to fight against the British. The Continental Army included two all-black units, one from Massachusetts and the other from Rhode Island. In 1778, the legislature of Rhode Island voted to free any slave who volunteered to serve, since, according to the lawmakers, history taught that "the wisest, the freest, and bravest nations . . . liberated their slaves, and enlisted them as soldiers to fight in defence of their country." In the South, especially in Georgia and South Carolina, more than ten thousand African Americans supported the British, and after the patriots had won the war, these men and women left the United States, relocating to Nova Scotia, Florida, and Jamaica, with some eventually resettling in Africa.

Testing the American Will

After the embarrassing defeats in Massachusetts, the king appointed General Sir William Howe to replace the ill-fated Gage. British rulers now understood that a simple police action would not be sufficient to crush the American rebellion. Parliament authorized sending more than fifty thousand troops to the mainland colonies, and after evacuating Boston—an untenable strategic position—the British forces stormed ashore at Staten Island in New York Harbor on July 3, 1776. From this more central location, Howe believed he could cut the New Englanders off from the rest of America. He enjoyed the powerful support of the British navy under the command of his brother, Admiral Lord Richard Howe.

When Washington learned the British were planning to occupy New York City, he transferred many of his inexperienced soldiers to Long Island, where they suffered a major defeat (August 27, 1776). In a series of engagements disastrous for the Americans, Howe drove the Continental Army across the Hudson River into New Jersey. Because of his failure to take full advantage of the situation, however, General Howe lost what seemed in retrospect an excellent opportunity to annihilate Washington's entire army. Nevertheless, the Americans were on the run, and in the fall of 1776, contemporaries predicted the rebels would soon capitulate.

"Times That Try Men's Souls"

Swift victories in New York and New Jersey persuaded General Howe that few Americans enthusiastically supported independence. He issued a general pardon, therefore, to anyone who would swear allegiance to George III. The results were encouraging. More than three thousand men and women who lived in areas occupied by the British army took the oath. This group included one intimidated signer of the Declaration of Independence. Howe perceived that a lasting peace in America would require his troops to treat "our enemies as if they might one day become our friends." A member of Lord North's cabinet grumbled that this was "a sentimental manner of making war," a shortsighted view considering England's experience in attempting to pacify the Irish. The pardon plan eventually failed not because Howe lacked toughness but because his soldiers and officers regarded loyal Americans as inferior provincials, an attitude that did little to promote good relations. In any case, as soon as the redcoats left a pardoned region, the rebel militia retaliated against those who had deserted the patriot cause.

In December 1776, Washington's bedraggled army retreated across the Delaware River into Pennsylvania. American prospects appeared bleaker than at any other time during the war. The Continental Army lacked basic supplies, and many men who had signed up for short-term enlistments prepared to go home. "These are the times that try men's souls," Paine wrote in a pamphlet titled *American Crisis.* "The summer soldier and the sunshine patriot will, in this crisis, shrink from the service of their country, but he that stands it *now* deserves . . . love and thanks . . . " Before winter, Washington determined to attempt one last desperate stroke.

Howe played into Washington's hands. The British forces were dispersed in small garrisons across the state of New Jersey, and while the Americans could not possibly have defeated the combined British army, they did possess the capacity—with luck—to capture an exposed post. On the night of December 25, Continental soldiers slipped over the ice-filled Delaware River and at Trenton took nine hundred sleeping Hessian mercenaries by complete surprise.

Cheered by success, Washington returned a second time to Trenton, but on this occasion the Continental Army was not so fortunate. A large British force under Lord Cornwallis trapped the Americans. Instead of standing and fighting—really an impossible challenge—Washington secretly, by night, marched his little army around Cornwallis's left flank. On January 3, 1777, the Americans surprised a British garrison at Princeton. Washington then went into winter quarters. The British, fearful of losing more outposts, consolidated their troops, thus leaving much of the state in the hands of the patriot militia.

Victory in a Year of Defeat

In 1777, England's chief military strategist, Lord George Germain, still perceived the war in conventional European terms. A large field army would somehow maneuver Washington's Continental troops into a decisive battle in which the British would enjoy a clear advantage. Complete victory over the Americans cer-

British defeat at the Battle of Princeton, *oil painting by William Mercer, ca. 1786–1790. The painting shows George Washington (left, on horseback) directing cannon fire with his sword. Often risking his own life, Washington led the American troops into battle. The artist's father was mortally wounded in the battle.* ❖

tainly seemed within England's grasp. Unfortunately for the men who advocated this plan, the Continental forces proved extremely elusive, and while one British army vainly tried to corner Washington in Pennsylvania, another was forced to surrender in the forests of upstate New York.

In the summer of 1777, General John Burgoyne, a dashing though overbearing officer, descended from Canada with a force of more than seven thousand troops. They intended to clear the Hudson Valley of rebel resistance; join Howe's army, which was to come up to Albany; and thereby cut New England off from the other states. Burgoyne fought in a grand style. Accompanied by a German band, thirty carts filled with the general's liquor and belongings, and two thousand dependents and camp followers, the British set out to thrash the Americans. The campaign was a disaster. Military units, mostly from New England, cut the enemy force apart in the deep woods north of Albany. At the battle of Bennington (August 16), the New Hampshire militia under Brigadier General John Stark overwhelmed a thousand German mercenaries. After this setback, Burgoyne's forces struggled forward, desperately hoping that Howe would rush to their rescue, but when it became clear that their situation at Saratoga was hopeless, the haughty Burgoyne was forced to surrender fifty-eight hundred men to the American General Horatio Gates (October 17).

Soon after Burgoyne left Canada, General Howe unexpectedly decided to move his main army from New York City to Philadelphia. Exactly what he hoped to achieve was not clear, even to Britain's rulers, and of course, when Burgoyne called for assistance, Howe was sitting in the new nation's capital still trying to devise a way to destroy the Continental Army. Howe's campaign began in late July. The British forces sailed to the head of the Chesapeake Bay and then marched north to Philadelphia. Washington's troops obstructed the enemy's progress, first at Brandywine Creek (September 11) and then at Paoli (September 20), but the outnumbered Americans could not stop the British from entering Philadelphia.

Anxious lest these defeats discourage Congress and the American people, Washington attempted one last battle before the onset of winter. In an engagement at Germantown (October 4), the Americans launched a major counterattack on a fog-covered battlefield, but just at the moment when success seemed assured, they broke off the fight. "When every thing gave the most flattering hopes of victory," Washington complained, "the troops began suddenly to retreat." Bad luck, confusion, and incompetence contributed to the failure. A discouraged Continental Army dug in at Valley Forge, twenty miles outside of Philadelphia, where camp diseases took twenty-five hundred American lives. In their misery, few American soldiers realized their situation was not nearly as desperate as it had been in 1776.

The French Alliance

Even before the Americans declared their independence, agents of the government of Louis XVI began to explore ways to aid the colonists, not so much because the French monarchy favored the republican cause but because it hoped to embarrass the English. The French deeply resented the defeat they had sustained during the Seven Years' War. During the early months of the Revolution, the French covertly sent tons of essential military supplies to the Americans. The negotiations for these arms involved secret agents and fictitious trading companies, the type of clandestine operation more typical of modern times than of the eighteenth century. But when American representatives, Benjamin Franklin for one, pleaded for official recognition of American independence or for outright military alliance, the French advised patience. The international stakes were too great for the king openly to back a cause that had little chance of success.

The American victory at Saratoga convinced the French that the rebels had formidable forces and were serious in their resolve. Indeed, Lord North drew the same conclusion. When news of Saratoga reached London, North muttered, "This damned war." In private conversation, he expressed doubts about England's ability to win the contest, knowing the French would soon enter the fray.

In April 1778, North tried to avert a greatly expanded war by sending a peace commission to America. He instructed this group, headed by the Earl of Carlisle, to bargain with the Continental Congress "as if it were a legal body." If the colonists would agree to drop their demand for independence, they could turn the imperial calendar back to 1763. Parliament belatedly conceded the right of Americans to tax themselves, even to elect their own governors. It also promised to remove all British troops in times of peace. The proposal might have gained substantial support back in 1776. The war, however, had hardened American resolve; the Congress refused to deal with Carlisle.

In Paris, Franklin performed brilliantly. In meetings with French officials, he hinted that the Americans might accept a British peace initiative. If the French wanted the war to continue, if they really wanted to embarrass their old rival, then they had to do what the English refused: formally recognize the independence of the United States.

The stratagem paid off handsomely. On February 6, 1778, the French presented American representatives with two separate treaties. The first, called the Treaty of Amity and Commerce, established commercial relations between France and the United States. It tacitly accepted the existence of a new, independent republic. The Treaty of Alliance was even more generous, considering America's obvious military and economic weaknesses. In the event that France and England went to war (they did so on June 14, as everyone expected), the French agreed to reject "either Truce or Peace with Great Britain . . . until the independence of the United States shall have been formally or tacitly assured by the Treaty or Treaties that shall terminate the War." Even more amazing, France surrendered its claim to all territories formerly owned by Great Britain east of the Mississippi River. The Americans pledged they would not sign a separate peace with Britain without first informing their new ally. And in return, France made no claim to Canada, asking only for the right to take possession of certain British islands in the Caribbean. Never had Franklin worked his magic to greater effect.

French intervention instantly transformed British military strategy. What had been a colonial rebellion suddenly became a world conflict, a continuation of the great wars for empire of the late seventeenth century (see Chapter 4). Scarce military resources, especially newer fighting ships, had to be diverted from the American theater to guard the English Channel. In fact, there was talk in London of a possible French invasion. Although the threat of such an assault was not very great until 1779, the British did have cause for concern. The French navy posed a serious challenge to the overextended British fleet. By concentrating their warships in a specific area, the French could hold off or even defeat British squadrons, an advantage that would figure significantly in the American victory at Yorktown.

The Final Campaign

British General Henry Clinton replaced Howe, who resigned after the battle of Saratoga. Clinton was a strangely complex individual. As a subordinate officer, he had impressed his superiors as imaginative but easily provoked to anger. When he took command of the British army, his resolute self-confidence suddenly dissolved. Perhaps he feared failure. Whatever the explanation for his vacillation, Clinton's record in America was little better than Howe's or Gage's.

Military strategists calculated that Britain's last chance of winning the war lay in the Southern Colonies, a region largely untouched in the early years of fighting. Intelligence reports reaching London indicated that Georgia and South Carolina contained a sizable body of Loyalists, men who would take up arms for the crown if only they received support and encouragement from the regular army. The southern strategy devised by Germain and Clinton in 1779 turned the war into a bitter guerrilla conflict, and during the last months of battle, British officers worried that their search for an easy victory had inadvertently opened a Pandora's box of uncontrollable partisan furies.

The southern campaign opened in the spring of 1780. Savannah had already fallen, and Clinton reckoned that if the British could take Charles Town, they would be able to control the entire South. A large fleet carrying nearly eight thousand redcoats reached South Carolina in February. Complacent Americans had allowed the city's fortifications to decay, and in a desper-

French assistance on land and sea helped the Americans defeat the British in the American Revolution. In this French print of the battle at Yorktown, French ships block the entrance of Chesapeake Bay, preventing British vessels from resupplying their troops on land. Yorktown, which was unknown to the French artist who made this print, is depicted as a European walled city. ❖

Battle of Cowpens *by William Ranny (1813–1857). On January 17, 1781, Daniel Morgan led an American army of Continental regulars and South Carolina militia against Cornwallis's forces under Banastre Tarleton. Cowpens would begin a chain of American victories that led directly to Yorktown and Cornwallis's surrender.* ❖

ate, last-minute effort to preserve Charles Town, General Benjamin Lincoln's forces dug trenches and reinforced walls, but to no avail. Clinton and his second in command, General Cornwallis, gradually encircled the city, and on May 12, Lincoln surrendered an American army of almost six thousand men.

The defeat took Congress by surprise, and without making proper preparations, it dispatched a second army to South Carolina under Horatio Gates, the hero of Saratoga. He too failed. At Camden, Cornwallis outmaneuvered the raw American recruits, capturing or killing 750 during the course of battle (August 16). Poor Gates galloped from the scene and did not stop until he reached Hillsboro, North Carolina, two hundred miles away.

Even at this early stage of the southern campaign, the dangers of partisan warfare had become evident. Tory raiders showed little interest in serving as regular soldiers in Cornwallis's army. They preferred night riding, indiscriminate plundering or murdering of neighbors against whom they harbored ancient grudges. The British had unleashed a horde of banditti across South Carolina. Men who genuinely supported independence or who had merely fallen victim to Loyalist guerrillas bided their time. They retreated westward, waiting for their enemies to make a mistake. Their chance came on October 7 at King's Mountain, North Carolina. In the most vicious fighting of the Revolution, the backwoodsmen decimated a force of British regulars and Tory raiders who had strayed too far from base. One witness reported that when a British officer tried to surrender, he was summarily shot down by at least seven American soldiers.

Cornwallis, badly confused and poorly supplied, squandered his strength chasing American forces across the Carolinas. Whatever military strategy had compelled him to leave Charles Town had long since been abandoned, and in early 1781, Cornwallis informed Clinton, "Events alone can decide the future Steps." Events, however, did not run in the British favor. Congress sent General Nathanael Greene to the South with a new army. This young Rhode Islander was the most capable general on Washington's staff. Greene joined Daniel Morgan, leader of the famed Virginia Riflemen, and in a series of tactically brilliant engagements, they sapped the strength of Cornwallis's army, first at Cowpens, South Carolina (January 17, 1781), and later at Guilford Courthouse, North Carolina (March 15). Clinton fumed in New York City. In his estimation, the inept Cornwallis had left "two valuable colonies behind him to be overrun and conquered by the very army which he boasts to have completely routed but a week or two before."

Cornwallis pushed north into Virginia, planning apparently to establish a base of operations on the coast. He selected Yorktown, a sleepy tobacco market located on a peninsula bounded by the York and James rivers. Washington watched these maneuvers closely. The canny Virginia planter knew this territory intimately, and he sensed that Cornwallis had made a serious blunder. When Washington learned the French fleet could gain temporary dominance in the

Chesapeake Bay, he rushed south from New Jersey. With him marched thousands of well-trained French troops under the Comte de Rochambeau. All the pieces fell into place. The French admiral, the Comte de Grasse, cut Cornwallis off from the sea, while Washington and his lieutenants encircled the British on land. On October 19, 1781, Cornwallis surrendered his entire army of six thousand men. When Lord North heard of the defeat at Yorktown, he moaned, "Oh God! It is all over." The British still controlled New York City and Charles Town, but except for a few skirmishes, the fighting ended. The task of securing the independence of the United States was now in the hands of the diplomats.

The Loyalist Dilemma

The war lasted longer than anyone had predicted in 1776. While the nation won its independence, many Americans paid a terrible price. Indeed, a large number of men and women decided that however much they loved living in America, they could not accept the new government.

No one knows for certain how many Americans actually supported the crown during the Revolution. Some Loyalists undoubtedly kept silent and avoided making a public commitment that might have led to banishment or loss of property. But for many persons, neutrality proved impossible. Almost 100,000 men and women permanently left America. While a number of these exiles had served as imperial officeholders—Thomas Hutchinson, for example—in the main, they came from all ranks and backgrounds. A large number of humble farmers, more than 30,000, resettled in Canada. Others relocated to England, the West Indies, or Africa.

The political ideology of the Loyalists was not substantially different from that of their opponents. Like other Americans, they believed that men and women were entitled to life, liberty, and the pursuit of happiness. The Loyalists were also convinced that independence would destroy those values by promoting disorder. By turning their backs on Britain, a source of tradition and stability, the rebels seemed to have encouraged licentiousness, even anarchy in the streets. The Loyalists suspected that Patriot demands

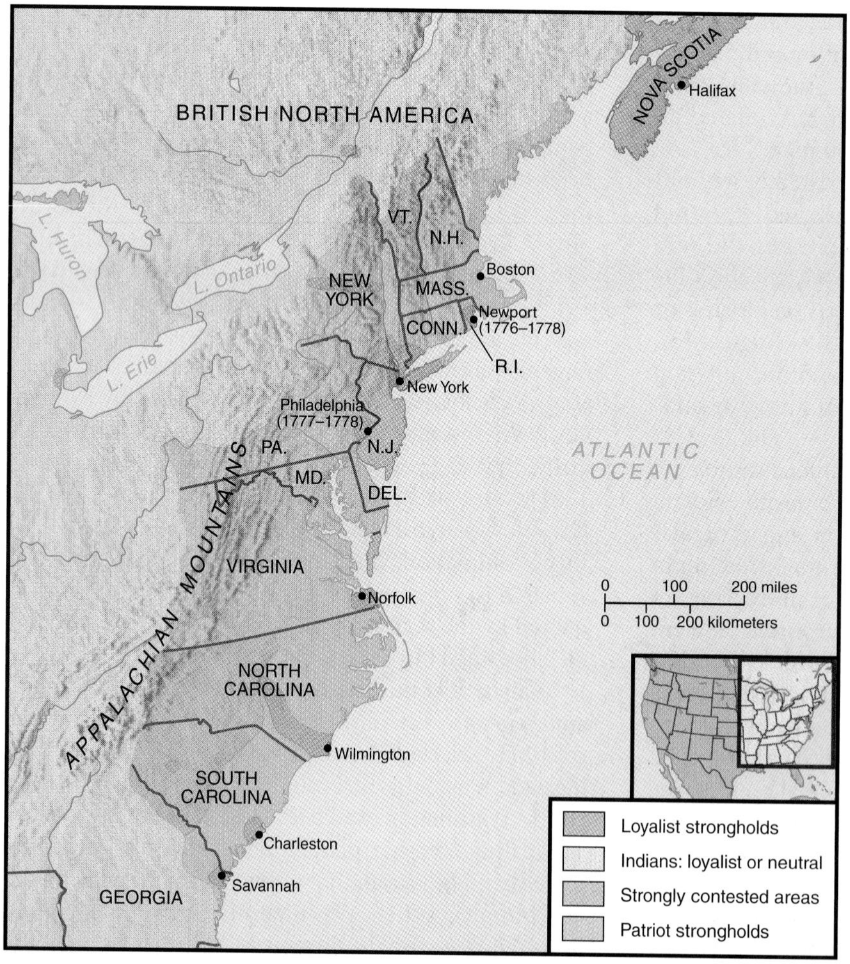

LOYALIST STRONGHOLDS *The highest concentration of Loyalists were in the colonies of New York, North Carolina, South Carolina, and Georgia, especially in the areas around port cities such as New York City, Wilmington, Charleston, and Savannah.*

for freedom were self-serving, even hypocritical, for as Perserved Smith, a Loyalist from Ashfield, Massachusetts, observed, "Sons of liberty . . . did not deserve the name, for it was evident all they wanted was liberty from oppression that they might have liberty to oppress!"

The Loyalists were caught in a difficult squeeze. The British never quite trusted them. After all, they were Americans. During the early stages of the war, Loyalists organized militia companies and hoped to pacify large areas of the countryside with the support of the regular army. The British generals were unreliable partners, however, for no sooner had they called on loyal Americans to come forward than the redcoats marched away, leaving the Tories exposed to rebel retaliation. And in England, the exiles found themselves treated as second-class citizens. While many of them received monetary compensation for their sacrifice, they were never regarded as the equals of native-born English citizens. Not surprisingly, the Loyalist community in London was gradually transformed into a collection of bitter men and women who felt unwelcome on both sides of the Atlantic.

Americans who actively supported independence saw these people as traitors who deserved their fate of constant, often violent, harassment. In many states—but especially in New York—revolutionary governments confiscated Loyalist property. Other friends of the king received beatings, or as the rebels called them, "grand Toory [sic] rides." A few were even executed. According to one patriot, "A Tory is a thing whose head is in England, and its body in America, and its neck ought to be stretched."

Long after the victorious Americans turned their attentions to the business of building a new republic, Loyalists remembered a receding colonial past, a comfortable, ordered world that had been lost forever at Yorktown. Although many Loyalists eventually returned to their homes, a sizable number could not do so. For them, the sense of loss remained a heavy emotional burden. Perhaps the most poignant testimony came from a young mother living in exile in Nova Scotia. "I climbed to the top of Chipman's Hill and watched the sails disappear in the distance," she recounted, "and such a feeling of loneliness came over me that though I had not shed a tear through all the war I sat down on the damp moss with my baby on my lap and cried bitterly."

CHRONOLOGY

1763	Peace of Paris ends the Seven Years' War
1764	Parliament passes Sugar Act to collect American revenue
1765	Stamp Act receives support of House of Commons (March) ❖ Stamp Act Congress meets in New York City (October)
1766	Stamp Act repealed the same day that Declaratory Act becomes law (March 18)
1767	Townshend Revenue Acts stir American anger (June–July)
1768	Massachusetts assembly refuses to rescind circular letter (February)
1770	Parliament repeals all Townshend duties except one on tea (March) ❖ British troops "massacre" Boston civilians (March)
1772	Samuel Adams forms committee of correspondence
1773	Lord North's government passes Tea Act (May) ❖ Bostonians hold Tea Party (December)
1774	Parliament punishes Boston with Coercive Acts (March–June) ❖ First Continental Congress convenes (September)
1775	Patriots take stand at Lexington and Concord (April) ❖ Second Continental Congress gathers (May) ❖ Americans hold their own at Bunker Hill (June)
1776	Congress votes for independence; Declaration of Independence is signed ❖ British defeat Washington at Long Island (August) ❖ Americans score victory at Trenton (December)
1777	General Burgoyne surrenders at Saratoga (October)
1778	French treaties recognize independence of the United States (February)
1780	British take Charles Town (May)
1781	Washington forces Cornwallis to surrender at Yorktown (October)
1783	Peace treaty signed (September) ❖ British evacuate New York City (November)

Winning the Peace

Congress appointed a skilled delegation to negotiate a peace treaty: Benjamin Franklin, John Adams, and John Jay. According to their official instructions, they were to insist only on the recognition of the independence of the United States. On other issues, Congress ordered its delegates to defer to the counsel of the French government.

But the political environment in Paris was much different from what the diplomats had been led to expect. The French had formed a military alliance with

Spain, and French officials announced that they could not consider the details of an American settlement until after the Spanish had recaptured Gibraltar from the British. The prospects for a Spanish victory were not good, and in any case, it was well known that Spain coveted the lands lying between the Appalachian Mountains and the Mississippi River. Indeed, there were even rumors afloat in Paris that the great European powers might intrigue to deny the United States its independence.

While the three American delegates publicly paid their respects to French officials, they secretly entered into negotiations with an English agent. The peacemakers drove a remarkable bargain, a much better one than Congress could have expected. The preliminary agreement signed on September 3, 1783, not only guaranteed the independence of the United States; it also transferred all the territory east of the Mississippi River, except Spanish Florida, to the new republic. The treaty established generous boundaries on the north and south and gave the Americans important fishing rights in the North Atlantic. In exchange, Congress promised to help British merchants collect debts contracted before the Revolution and compensate Loyalists whose lands had been confiscated by the various state governments. Even though the Americans negotiated separately with the British, they did not sign a separate peace. The preliminary treaty did not become effective until France reached its own agreement with Great Britain. Thus did the Americans honor the French alliance. It is difficult to imagine how Franklin, Adams, and Jay could have negotiated a more favorable conclusion to the war. In the fall of 1783, the last redcoats sailed from New York City, ending 176 years of colonial rule.

Conclusion: Preserving Independence

The American people had waged war against the most powerful nation in Europe and emerged victorious. The treaty marked the conclusion of a colonial rebellion, but it remained for the men and women who had resisted taxation without representation to work out the full implications of republicanism. What would be the shape of the new government? What powers would be delegated to the people, the states, the federal authorities? How far would the wealthy, well-born leaders of the rebellion be willing to extend political, social, and economic rights?

For many Americans the challenge of nation building appeared even more formidable than waging war against Great Britain. As Philadelphia physician Dr. Benjamin Rush explained, "There is nothing more common than to confound the terms of American Revolution with those of the late American war. The American war is over, but this is far from being the case with the American Revolution. On the contrary, nothing but the first act of the great drama is closed."

Recommended Reading

Several books have had a profound impact on how historians think about the ideas that energized the Revolution. In a moving narrative account, Edmund S. Morgan and Helen M. Morgan explore how Americans interpreted the first great imperial controversy: *The Stamp Act Crisis: Prologue to Revolution* (1953). In his classic study, *The Ideological Origins of the American Revolution* (1967), Bernard Bailyn maps an ideology of power that informed colonial protest. Gordon Wood extends this argument in *The Radicalism of the American Revolution* (1992). In *Marketplace of Revolution: How Consumer Politics Shaped American Independence* (2004), T. H. Breen attempts to integrate more fully the experiences of ordinary men and women into the analysis of popular mobilization. Alfred F. Young demonstrates that it is possible to write about revolution from the perspective of working class colonists in *The Shoemaker and the Tea Party: Memory and the American Revolution* (2000). Works that focus productively on popular mobilization in specific colonies include Rhys Isaac, *The Transformation of Virginia, 1740–1790* (1983); Robert A. Gross, *The Minutemen and Their World* (1976); Woody Holton, *Forced Founders: Indians, Debtors, Slaves and the Making of the American Revolution in Virginia* (1999); and T. H. Breen, *Tobacco Culture: The Mentality of the Great Tidewater Planters on the Eve of Revolution* (1985). The tragedy that visited the Native Americans is examined in Colin C. Calloway, *American Revolution in Indian Country: Crisis and Diversity in Native American Communities* (1995) and Gregory Evans Dowd, *War Under Heaven: Pontiac, The Indian Nations and the British Empire* (2002). A useful study of the aspirations and disappointments of American women during this period is Linda Kerber, *Women of the Republic: Intellect and Ideology in Revolutionary America* (1980). Charles Royster investigates the changing attitudes of the American people about the Continental Army in *A Revolutionary People at War: The Continental Army and American Character, 1775–1783* (1979). Also valuable is John W. Shy, *A People Numerous and Armed: Reflections on the Military Struggle for American Independence*, rev. ed. (1990). Sidney Kaplan, *The Black Presence in the Era of the American Revolution* (1973), documents the hopes of African Americans during a period of radical political change.

For a list of additional titles related to this chapter's topics, please see http://www.ablongman.com/divine.

Suggested Web Sites

Canada History

http://www.civilization.ca/indexe.asp
Canada and the United States shared a colonial past but developed differently in the long run. This site is a part of the virtual museum of the Canadian Museum of Civilization Corporation.

Georgia's Rare Map Collection

http://scarlett.libs.uga.edu/darchive/hargrett/maps/colamer.html
http://scarlett.libs.uga.edu/darchive/hargrett/maps/revamer.html
These two sites contain maps for Colonial and Revolutionary America.

Maryland Loyalism and the American Revolution

http://users.erols.com/candidus/index.htm
This look at Maryland's loyalists promotes the author's book, but the site has good information about an underappreciated phenomenon, including loyalist songs and poems.

The American Revolution

http://revolution.h-net.msu.edu/
This site accompanies the PBS series *Revolution* with essays and resource links.

Chapter 6

Francis Guy, Tontine Coffee House, *1797. The Tontine is the large building at left, on the corner of Wall and Water Streets in New York City, where merchants and traders met daily to transact business.* ❖

The Republican Experiment

A New Political Morality

In 1788, Lewis Hallam and John Henry petitioned the General Assembly of Pennsylvania to open a theater. Although a 1786 state law banned the performance of stage plays and other "disorderly sports," many Philadelphia leaders favored the request to hold "dramatic representations" in their city. A committee appointed to study the issue concluded that a theater would contribute to "the general refinement of manners and the polish of society." Some supporters even argued that the sooner the United States had a professional theater the sooner the young republic would escape the "foreign yoke" of British culture.

The Quakers of Philadelphia dismissed such claims out of hand. They warned that such "seminaries of lewdness and irreligion" would quickly undermine "the virtue of the people." They pointed out that "no sooner is a playhouse opened than it becomes surrounded with . . . brothels." Since Pennsylvania was already suffering from a "stagnation of commerce [and] a scarcity of money"—unmistakable signs of God's displeasure—it seemed unwise to risk divine punishment by encouraging new "hot-beds of vice."

Such rhetoric did not sit well with other citizens who interpreted the revolutionary experience from an entirely different perspective. At issue, they insisted, was not popular morality, but state censorship. If the government silenced the stage, then "the same authority . . . may, with equal justice, dictate the shape and texture of our dress, or the modes and ceremonies of our worship." Depriving those who wanted to see plays of an opportunity to do so, they argued, "will abridge the natural right of every freeman, to dispose of his time and money, according to his own tastes and dispositions."

THROUGHOUT POST–REVOLUTIONARY AMERICA everyday matters such as the opening of a new playhouse provoked passionate public debate. These divisions were symptomatic of a new, uncertain political culture struggling to find the proper balance between public morality and private freedom. During the long fight against Great Britain, Americans had defended individual rights. The problem was that the same people also believed that a republic that compromised its virtue could not long preserve liberty and independence.

In 1776, Thomas Paine had reminded ordinary men and women that "the sun never shined on a cause of greater worth. . . . 'Tis not the concern of a day, a year, or an age; posterity are virtually involved in the contest, and will be more or less affected, even to the end of time, by the proceedings now." During the 1780s Americans understood their responsibility not only to each other, but also to history. They worried, however, that they might not successfully meet the challenge. The dangers were manifest. Individual states seemed intent on looking out for local interests rather than the national welfare. Revolutionary leaders such as George Washington and James Madison concluded that the United States needed a strong central government to protect rights and property. Their creative quest for solutions brought forth a new and enduring constitution.

OUTLINE

FEATURE ESSAY

LAW AND SOCIETY

Defining Republican Culture

Today, the term *republican* no longer possesses the evocative power it did for most eighteenth-century Americans. For them, it defined an entire political culture. After all, they had done something that no other people had achieved for a very long time. They founded a national government without a monarch or aristocracy; in other words, a genuine republic. Making the new system work was a daunting task. Those Americans who read deeply in ancient and renaissance history knew that most republics had failed, often within a few years, only to be replaced by tyrants who cared not at all what ordinary people thought about the public good. To preserve their republic from such a fate, victorious revolutionaries such as Samuel Adams recast fundamental political values. For them, **republicanism** represented more than a particular form of government. It was a way of life, a core ideology, an uncompromising commitment to liberty and equality.

Adams and his contemporaries certainly believed that creating a new nation-state involved more than simply winning independence from Great Britain. More than did any other form of government, they insisted, a republic demanded an exceptionally high degree of public morality. If American citizens substituted "luxury, prodigality, and profligacy" for "prudence, virtue, and economy," then their revolution surely would have been in vain. Maintaining popular virtue was crucial to success. An innocent stage play, therefore, set off alarm bells. Such "foolish gratifications" seemed to compromise republican goals. It is not surprising that confronted by such temptations Adams thundered, "Rome, Athens, and all the cities of renown, whence came your fall?"

White Americans came out of the Revolution with an almost euphoric sense of the nation's special destiny. This expansive outlook, encountered among so many ordinary men and women, owed much to the spread of Protestant evangelicalism. However skeptical Jefferson and Franklin may have been about revealed religion, the great mass of American people subscribed to an almost utopian vision of the country's future. To this new republic, God had promised progress and prosperity. The signs were visible for everyone. "There is not upon the face of the earth a body of people more happy or rising into consequence with more rapid stride," one man announced in 1786, "than the Inhabitants of the United States of America. Population is increasing, new houses building, new lands clearing, new settlements forming, and new manufactures establishing with a rapidity beyond conception."

Such experience did not translate easily or smoothly into the creation of a strong central government. Modern Americans tend to take for granted the acceptance of the Constitution. Its merits seem self-evident largely because it has survived for two centuries. But in the early 1780s, no one could have predicted that the Constitution as we know it would have been written, much less ratified. It was equally possible that the Americans would have supported a weak confederation or perhaps allowed the various states and regions to go their separate ways.

In this uncertain political atmosphere, Americans divided sharply over the relative importance of *liberty* and *order.* The revolutionary experience had called into question the legitimacy of any form of special privilege. As one republican informed an aristocratic colleague in the South Carolina assembly, "the day is Arrived when *goodness,* and not *Wealth,* are the only *Criterions of greatness.*" A legislative leader in Pennsylvania put the point even more bluntly: "No man has a greater claim of special privilege for his $100,000 than I have for my $5." The man who passionately defended social equality for those of varying economic status, however, may still have resisted the extension of civil rights to women or blacks. Nevertheless, liberty was contagious, and Americans of all backgrounds began to make new demands on society and government. For them, the Revolution had suggested radical alternatives, and in many forums throughout the nation—especially in the elected state assemblies—they insisted on being heard.

In certain quarters, the celebration of liberty met with mixed response. Some Americans—often the very men who had resisted British tyranny—worried that the citizens of the new nation were caught up in a wild, destructive scramble for material wealth. Democratic excesses seemed to threaten order, to endanger the rights of property. Surely a republic could not long survive unless its citizens showed greater self-control. For people concerned about the loss of order, the state assemblies appeared to be the greatest source of instability. Popularly elected representatives lacked what men of property defined as real civic virtue, an ability to work for the common good rather than their private interests.

Working out the tensions between order and liberty, between property and equality, generated an outpouring of political genius. At other times in American history, persons of extraordinary talent have been drawn to theology, commerce, or science, but during the 1780s, the country's intellectual leaders—Thomas Jefferson, James Madison, Alexander Hamilton, and John Adams, among others—focused their creative energies on the problem of how republicans ought to govern themselves.

Living in the Shadow of Revolution

Revolution changed American society, often in ways no one had planned. This phenomenon is not surprising. The great revolutions of modern times produced radical transformations in French, Russian, and Chinese societies. By comparison, the immediate results of the American Revolution appear much tamer, less wrenching. Nevertheless, national independence compelled people to reevaluate hierarchical social relations that they had taken for granted during the colonial period. The faltering first steps of independence raised fundamental questions about the meaning of equality in American society, some of which remain as pressing today as during the 1780s.

Social and Political Reform

Following the war, Americans aggressively ferreted out and, with republican fervor, denounced any traces of aristocratic pretense. As colonists, they had long resented the claims that certain Englishmen made to special privilege simply because of noble birth. Even so committed a republican as George Washington had to be reminded that artificial status was contrary to republican principles. In 1783, he and the officers who had served during the Revolution formed the Society of the Cincinnati, a hereditary organization in which membership passed from father to eldest son. The soldiers meant no harm; they simply wanted to maintain old friendships. But anxious republicans throughout America let out a howl of protest, and one South Carolina legislator, Aedanus Burke, warned that the Society intended to create "an hereditary peerage . . . [which would] undermine the Constitution and destroy civil liberty." After an embarrassed Washington called for appropriate reforms of the Society's bylaws, the Cincinnati crisis receded. The fear of privilege remained, however, and wealthy Americans dropped honorific titles such as "esquire." Lawyers of republican persuasion chided judges who had adopted the English custom of wearing great flowing wigs to court.

The appearance of equality was as important as its actual achievement. In fact, the distribution of wealth in postwar America was more uneven than it had been in the mid-eighteenth century. The sudden accumulation of large fortunes by new families made other Americans particularly sensitive to aristocratic display, for it seemed intolerable that a revolution waged against a monarchy should produce a class of persons legally, or even visibly, distinguished from their fellow citizens.

In an effort to root out the notion of a privileged class, states abolished laws of primogeniture and entail. In colonial times, these laws allowed a landholder either to pass his entire estate to his eldest son or to declare that his property could never be divided, sold, or given away. Jefferson claimed that the repeal of these practices would eradicate "antient [sic] and future aristocracy; a foundation [has been] laid for a government truly republican." Jefferson may have exaggerated the social impact of this reform. But however many planters actually suffered from entail or primogeniture, the symbolism of the law counted as much as real social practice. Republican legislators wanted to cleanse traces of the former feudal order from the statute books.

Republican ferment also encouraged many states to lower property requirements for voting. After the

Questions of equality in the new republic extended to the rights of women. In this illustration, which appeared as the frontispiece in the 1792 issue of The Lady's Magazine and Repository of Entertaining Knowledge, *the "Genius of the Ladies Magazine" and the "Genius of Emulation" (holding in her hand a laurel crown) present to Liberty a petition for the rights of woman.* ❖

break with Great Britain, such a step seemed logical. As one group of farmers declared, no man can be "free & independent" unless he possesses "a voice . . . in the choice of the most important Officers in the Legislature." Pennsylvania and Georgia allowed all white male taxpayers to participate in elections. Other states were less democratic, but with the exception of Massachusetts, they reduced property qualifications. The reforms, however, did not significantly expand the American electorate. Long before the Revolution, an overwhelming percentage of free white males had owned enough land to vote. In any case, during the 1780s, republican lawmakers were not prepared to experiment with universal manhood suffrage; John Adams observed that if the states pushed the reforms too far, "New claims will arise, women will demand a vote . . . and every man who has not a farthing, will demand an equal vote with any other."

The most important changes in voting patterns were the result of western migration. As Americans moved to the frontier, they received full political representation in their state legislatures, and because new districts tended to be poorer than established coastal settlements, their representatives seemed less cultured, less well trained than those sent by eastern voters. Moreover, western delegates resented traveling so far to attend legislative meetings, and they lobbied successfully to transfer state capitals to more convenient locations. During this period, Georgia moved the seat of its government from Savannah to Augusta, South Carolina from Charles Town to Columbia, North Carolina from New Bern to Raleigh, Virginia from Williamsburg to Richmond, New York from New York City to Albany, and New Hampshire from Portsmouth to Concord.

After gaining independence, Americans also reexamined the relation between church and state. Republican spokespersons such as Thomas Jefferson insisted that rulers had no right to interfere with the free expression of an individual's religious beliefs. As governor of Virginia, he strenuously advocated the disestablishment of the Anglican Church, an institution that had received tax monies and other benefits during the colonial period. Jefferson and his allies regarded such special privilege not only as a denial of religious freedom—after all, rival denominations did not receive tax money—but also as a vestige of aristocratic society.

In 1786, Virginia cut the last ties between church and state. Other southern states disestablished the Anglican Church, but in Massachusetts and New Hampshire, Congregational churches continued to enjoy special status. Moreover, while Americans championed toleration, they seldom favored philosophies that radically challenged Christian values.

African Americans in the New Republic

Revolutionary fervor forced Americans to confront the most appalling contradiction to republican principles—slavery. The Quaker leader John Woolman (1720–1772) probably did more than any other white person of the era to remind people of the evils of this institution. A trip he took through the Southern Colonies as a young man forever impressed upon Woolman "the dark gloominess" of slavery. In a sermon, the outspoken humanitarian declared "that Men having Power too often misapplied it; that though we made Slaves of the Negroes, and the Turks made Slaves of the Christians, I believed that Liberty was the natural Right of all Men equally."

A 1797 sketch by architect and engineer Benjamin Henry Latrobe depicting African Americans in Norfolk, Virginia, shaving and dressing in preparation for a Sunday afternoon. Latrobe's drawings of blacks in the American South offer valuable glimpses of daily life in the region. ❖

This engraving of Phillis Wheatley appeared in her volume of verse, Poems on Various Subjects, Religious and Moral *(1773), the first book published by an African American.*

During the revolutionary period, abolitionist sentiment spread. Both in private and in public, people began to criticize slavery in other than religious language. No doubt, the double standard of their own political rhetoric embarrassed many white Americans. They hotly demanded liberation from parliamentary enslavement at the same time that they held several hundred thousand blacks in permanent bondage.

By keeping the issue of slavery before the public through writing and petitioning, African Americans powerfully undermined arguments advanced in favor of human bondage. They demanded freedom, reminding white lawmakers that African American men and women had the same natural right to liberty as did other Americans. In 1779, for example, a group of African Americans living in Connecticut pointedly asked the members of the state assembly "whether it is consistent with the present Claims, of the United States, to hold so many Thousands, of the Race of Adam, our Common Father, in perpetual Slavery." In New Hampshire, nineteen persons who called themselves "natives of Africa" reminded local legislators that "private or public tyranny and slavery are alike detestable to minds conscious of the equal dignity of human nature."

The scientific accomplishments of Benjamin Banneker (1731–1806), Maryland's African American astronomer and mathematician, and the international fame of Phillis Wheatley (1753–1784), Boston's celebrated "African muse," made it increasingly difficult for white Americans to maintain credibly that African Americans could not hold their own in a free society. Wheatley's poems went through many editions, and after reading her work, the great French philosopher Voltaire rebuked a friend who had claimed "there never would be Negro poets." As Voltaire discovered, Wheatley "writes excellent verse in English." Banneker, like Wheatley, enjoyed a well-deserved reputation, in his case for contributions as a scientist. After receiving a copy of an almanac that Banneker had published in Philadelphia, Thomas Jefferson concluded "that nature has given to our black brethren, talents equal to those of the other colors of men."

In the northern states, there was no real economic justification for slavery, and white laborers, often recent European immigrants, resented having to compete in the workplace against slaves. This economic situation, combined with the acknowledgment of the double standard represented by slavery, contributed to the establishment of antislavery societies. In 1775, Franklin helped organize a group in Philadelphia called the Society for the Relief of Free Negroes, Unlawfully Held. John Jay, Alexander Hamilton, and other prominent New Yorkers founded a Manumission Society in 1785. By 1792, antislavery societies were meeting from Virginia to Massachusetts, and in the northern states at least, these groups, working for the same ends as various Christian evangelicals, put slaveholders on the intellectual defensive for the first time in American history.

In several states north of Virginia, the abolition of slavery took a number of different forms. Even before achieving statehood, Vermont drafted a constitution (1777) that specifically prohibited slavery. In 1780, the Pennsylvania legislature passed a law effecting the gradual emancipation of slaves. Although the Massachusetts assembly refused to address the issue directly, the state courts took up the challenge and liberated the African Americans. (For further discussion of the end of slavery in Massachusetts, see "The Strange Ordeal of Quok Walker," pp. 186–189.) A judge ruled slavery unconstitutional in Massachusetts because it conflicted with a clause in the state bill of rights declaring "all men . . . free and equal." According to one enthusiast, this decision freed "a Grate number of Blacks . . . who . . . are held in a state of slavery within the bowels of a free and christian Country." By 1800, slavery was well on the road to extinction in the northern states.

These positive developments did not mean that white people accepted blacks as equals. In fact, in the very states that outlawed slavery, African Americans faced systematic discrimination. Free blacks were generally excluded from voting, juries, and militia duty—they were denied rights and responsibilities usually associated with full citizenship. They rarely enjoyed access to education, and in cities such as Philadelphia and New York, where African Americans went to look for work, they ended up living in segregated wards or neighborhoods. Even in the churches—institutions that had often spoken out against slavery—free African Americans were denied equal standing with white worshipers. Humiliations of this sort persuaded African Americans to form their own churches. In Philadelphia, Richard Allen, a former slave, founded the Bethel Church for Negro Methodists (1793) and later organized the African Methodist Episcopal Church (1814), an institution of great cultural as well as religious significance for nineteenth-century American blacks.

Even in the South, where African Americans made up a large percentage of the population, slavery disturbed thoughtful white republicans. Some planters simply freed their slaves, and by 1790, the number of free blacks living in Virginia was 12,766. By 1800, the figure had reached 30,750. There is no question that this trend reflected the uneasiness among white masters. Richard Randolph, one of Virginia's wealthier planters, explained that he freed his slaves "to make restitution, as far as I am able, to an unfortunate race of bond-men, over whom my ancestors have usurped and exercised the most lawless and monstrous tyranny." George Washington also manumitted his slaves. To be sure, most southern slaveholders, especially those living in South Carolina and Georgia, rejected this course of action. Their economic well-being depended on slave labor. Perhaps more significant, however, is the fact that no southern leader during the era of republican experimentation defended slavery as a positive good. Such overtly racist rhetoric did not become part of the public discourse until the nineteenth century.

Born to slaves, Richard Allen became a zealous evangelical minister. Allen organized the African Methodist Episcopal Church in 1814. ❖

Despite promising starts in that direction, the southern states did not abolish slavery. The economic incentives to maintain a servile labor force, especially after the invention of the cotton gin in 1793 and the opening up of the Alabama and Mississippi frontier, overwhelmed the initial abolitionist impulse. An opportunity to translate the principles of the American Revolution into social practice had been lost, at least temporarily. Jefferson reported in 1805, "I have long since given up the expectation of any early provision for the extinction of slavery among us." Unlike some contemporary Virginians, the man who wrote the Declaration of Independence condoned slavery on his own plantation, even fathering several children by a woman who, since she was his slave, had little choice in the matter of her pregnancy.

The Challenge of Women's Rights

The revolutionary experience accelerated changes in the way ordinary people viewed the family. At the beginning of the eighteenth century, fathers claimed authority over other members of their families simply on the grounds that they were fathers. As patriarchs, they demanded obedience. If they behaved like brutal despots, so be it; fathers could treat wives and children however they pleased. The English philosopher John Locke (1632–1704) powerfully undermined arguments of this sort. In his extremely popular treatise *Some Thoughts Concerning Education* (1693), Locke insisted that the mind was not formed at birth. The child learned from experience, and if the infant witnessed violent, arbitrary behavior, then the baby would become an abusive adult. As Locke warned parents, "If you punish him [the child] for what he sees you practice yourself, he will not think that Severity to proceed from Kindness in you careful to amend a Fault in him; but will be apt to interpret it, as Peevishness and Arbitrary Imperiousness of a Father."

Good eighteenth-century mothers and fathers—especially, fathers—condemned tyranny in the home.

At the time of the American Revolution few seriously accepted the notion that fathers—be they tyrannical kings or heads of ordinary families—enjoyed unlimited powers over women and children. Indeed, people in England as well as America increasingly described the family in terms of love and companionship. Instead of duties, they spoke of affection. This transformation in the way men and women viewed relations of power within the family was most evident in the popular novels of the period. Americans devoured *Pamela* and *Clarissa,* stories by the English writer Samuel Richardson about women who were the innocent victims of unreformed males, usually deceitful lovers and unforgiving fathers.

It was in this changing intellectual environment that American women began making new demands not only on their husbands but also on republican institutions. Abigail Adams, one of the generation's most articulate women, instructed her husband, John, as he set off for the opening of the Continental Congress: "I desire you would Remember the Ladies, and be more generous and favourable to them than your ancestors. Do not put such unlimited power into the hands of the Husbands." John responded in a condescending manner. The "Ladies" would have to wait until the country achieved independence. In 1777, Lucy Knox took an even stronger line with her husband, General Henry Knox. When he was about to return home from the army, she warned him, "I hope you will not consider yourself as commander in chief in your own house—but be convinced . . . that there is such a thing as equal command."

If Knox accepted Lucy's argument, he did so because she was a good republican wife and mother. In fact, women justified their assertiveness largely on the basis of political ideology. If survival of republics really depended on the virtue of their citizens, they argued, then it was the special responsibility of women as mothers to nurture the right values in their children and as wives to instruct their husbands in proper behavior. Contemporaries claimed that the woman who possessed "virtue and prudence" could easily "mold the taste, the manners, and the conduct of her admirers, according to her pleasure." In fact, "nothing short of a general reformation of manners would take place, were the ladies to use their power in discouraging our licentious manners."

Ill-educated women could not possibly fulfill these high expectations. Women required education that was at least comparable to what men received. Scores of female academies were established during this period to meet what many Americans, men as well as women, now regarded as a pressing social need. The schools may have received widespread encouragement

Abigail Adams, wife of President John Adams, was a brilliant woman whose plea to limit the power of husbands gained little sympathetic attention. This portrait of her by Benjamin Blyth is from c. 1766. ❖

precisely because they did not radically alter traditional gender roles. After all, the educated republican woman of the late eighteenth century did not pursue a career; she returned to the home, where she followed a familiar routine as wife and mother. The frustration of not being allowed to develop her talents may explain the bitterness of a graduation oration delivered by an otherwise obscure woman in 1793: "Our high and mighty Lords . . . have denied us the means of knowledge, and then reproached us for want of it. . . . They doom'd the sex to servile or frivolous employments, on purpose to degrade their minds, that they themselves might hold unrivall'd, the power and pre-eminence they had usurped."

During this period, women began to petition for divorce on new grounds. One case is particularly instructive concerning changing attitudes toward women and the family. In 1784, John Backus, an undistinguished Massachusetts silversmith, was hauled before a local court and asked why he beat his wife. He responded that "it was Partly owing to his Education for his father treated his mother in the same manner." The difference between Backus's case and his father's was that Backus's wife refused to tolerate such abuse, and she sued successfully for divorce. Studies of divorce patterns in Connecticut and Pennsylvania

This needlepoint sampler extolling virtue and the value of an education was created in 1786 by Nabby Martin, a student at the Mary Balch School, an Academy for girls established in 1785 in Providence, Rhode Island. Many fine examples of needlework, an important part of girls' school curriculum in addition to academic subjects, came out of the Balch School. ❖

show that after 1773, women divorced on about the same terms as men.

The war itself presented some women with fresh opportunities. In 1780, Ester DeBerdt Reed founded a large volunteer women's organization in Philadelphia—the first of its kind in the United States—that raised more than $300,000 for Washington's army. Other women ran family farms and businesses while their husbands fought the British. And in 1790, the New Jersey legislature explicitly allowed women who owned property to vote.

Despite these scattered gains, republican society still defined women's roles exclusively in terms of mother, wife, and homemaker. Other pursuits seemed unnatural, even threatening, and it is perhaps not surprising, therefore, that in 1807, New Jersey lawmakers—angry over a close election in which women voters apparently determined the result—repealed female suffrage in the interests of "safety, quiet, and good order and dignity of the state." Even an allegedly progressive thinker such as Jefferson could not imagine allowing women to participate in serious politics. When in 1807 his secretary of the treasury, Albert Gallatin, called attention to the shortage of educated people to serve in government jobs and suggested recruiting women, Jefferson responded sharply: "The appointment of a woman to office is an innovation for which the public is not prepared, nor am I."

Postponing Full Liberty

The Revolution did not bring about a massive restructuring of American society, at least not in the short term. Nevertheless, republicans such as Samuel Adams and Thomas Jefferson raised issues of immense significance for the later history of the United States. They insisted that equality, however narrowly defined, was an essential element of republican government. Even though they failed to abolish slavery, institute universal manhood suffrage, or apply equality to women, they vigorously articulated a set of assumptions about people's rights and liberties that challenged future generations of Americans to make good on the promise of the Revolution.

The States: Experiments in Republicanism

In May 1776, the Second Continental Congress invited the states to adopt constitutions. The old colonial charters filled with references to king and Parliament were clearly no longer adequate, and within a few years, most states had taken action. Rhode Island and Connecticut already enjoyed republican government by virtue of their unique seventeenth-century charters that allowed the voters to select both governors and legislators. Eleven other states plus Vermont created new political structures, and their deliberations reveal how Americans living in different regions and reacting to different social pressures defined fundamental republican principles.

Several constitutions were boldly experimental, and some states later rewrote documents that had been drafted in the first flush of independence. These early constitutions were provisional, but they nevertheless provided the framers of the federal Constitution of 1787 with invaluable insights into the strengths and weaknesses of government based on the will of the people.

Blueprints for State Government

Despite disagreements over details, Americans who wrote the various state constitutions shared certain political assumptions. First, they insisted on preparing *written* documents. For many of them, of course, this seemed a natural step. As colonists, they had lived under royal charters, documents that described the workings of local government in detail. The Massachusetts Bay charter of 1629, for example (see Chapter 2), guaranteed that the Puritans would enjoy the rights of Englishmen even after they had moved to the New World. And in New England, Congregationalists drew up church covenants stating in clear contractual language the rights and responsibilities of the entire congregation.

However logical the decision to produce written documents may have seemed to the Americans, it represented a major break with English practice. Political philosophers in the mother country had long boasted of Britain's unwritten constitution, a collection of judicial reports and parliamentary statutes. But this highly vaunted system had not protected the colonists from oppression; hence, after declaring independence, Americans demanded that their state constitutions explicitly define the rights of the people as well as the power of their rulers.

Natural Rights and the State Constitutions

The authors of the state constitutions believed men and women possessed certain **natural rights** over which government exercised no control whatsoever. So that future rulers—potential tyrants—would know the exact limits of authority, these fundamental rights were carefully spelled out. Indeed, the people of Massachusetts rejected the proposed state constitution of 1778 largely because it lacked a full statement of their basic rights. They demanded a guarantee of "rights of conscience, and . . . security of persons and property, which every member in the State hath a right to expect from the supreme power."

Eight state constitutions contained specific declarations of rights. The length and character of these lists varied, but, in general, they affirmed three fundamental freedoms: religion, speech, and press. They protected citizens from unlawful searches and seizures; they upheld trial by jury. George Mason, a shrewd political thinker who had written important revolutionary pamphlets, penned the most influential declaration of rights. It was appended to the Virginia Constitution of 1776, and the words were incorporated into other state constitutions as well as the famed Bill of Rights of the federal Constitution.

In almost every state, delegates to constitutional conventions drastically reduced the power of the governor. The constitutions of Pennsylvania and Georgia abolished the governor's office. In four other states, terms such as *president* were substituted for *governor.* Even when those who designed the new state governments provided for a governor, they severely circumscribed his authority. He was allowed to make almost no political appointments, and while the state legislators closely monitored his activities, he possessed no veto over their decisions (Massachusetts being the lone exception). Most early constitutions lodged nearly all effective power in the legislature. This decision made good sense to men who had served under powerful royal governors during the late colonial period. These ambitious crown appointees had used executive patronage to influence members of the colonial assemblies, and as the Americans drafted their new republican constitutions, they were determined to bring their governors under tight control. In fact, the writers of the state constitutions were so fearful of the concentration of power in the hands of a single person, they failed to appreciate that elected governors—like the representatives themselves—were now the servants of a free people.

The legislature dominated early state government. The constitutions of Pennsylvania and Georgia provided for a unicameral, or one-house, system, and since any male taxpayer could cast a ballot in these states, their legislatures became the nation's most democratic. Other states authorized the creation of two houses, but even as they did so, some of the more demanding republicans wondered why America needed a senate or upper house at all. What social and economic interests, they asked, did that body represent that could not be more fully and directly voiced in the lower house? After all, America had just freed itself of an aristocracy. The two-house form survived the Revolution largely because it was familiar and because some persons had already begun to suspect that certain checks on the popular will, however arbitrary they might have appeared, were necessary to preserve minority rights.

Power to the People

Massachusetts did not adopt a constitution until 1780, several years after the other states had done so. The experience of the people of Massachusetts is particularly significant because in their efforts to establish a workable system of republican government, they hit on a remarkable political innovation. After the rejection of two constitutions drafted by the state legislature, the responsibility fell to a specially elected convention of delegates whose sole purpose was the "formation of a new Constitution."

John Adams took a position of leadership at this convention and served as the chief architect of the governmental framework of Massachusetts. This framework included a house and senate, a popularly elected governor—who, unlike the chief executives of other states, possessed a veto over legislative bills—and property qualifications for officeholders as well as voters. The most striking aspect of the 1780 constitution, however, was the wording of its opening sentence: "We . . . the people of Massachusetts . . . agree upon, ordain, and establish." This powerful statement would be echoed in the federal Constitution. The Massachusetts experiment reminded Americans that ordinary officeholders could not be trusted to define fundamental rights. That important task required a convention of delegates who could legitimately claim to speak for the people.

In 1780, no one knew whether the state experiments would succeed. There was no question that a different type of person had begun to appear in public office, one who seemed, to the local gentry at least, a little poorer and less polished than they would have liked. When one Virginian surveyed the newly elected House of Burgesses in 1776, he discovered it was "composed of men not quite so well dressed, nor so politely educated, nor so highly born as some Assemblies I have formerly seen." This particular Virginian approved of such change, for he believed that "the People's men," however plain they might appear, possessed honesty and sincerity. They were, in fact, representative republicans, people who insisted they were anyone's equal in this burgeoning society.

John Dickinson, a highly respected lawyer, conceived a bold plan in 1776 for a strong central government, but the members of Congress saw it as a dangerous threat to the sovereignty of the states. ❖

Other Americans were less optimistic about the nation's immediate prospects. The health of a small republic depended entirely on the virtue of its people. If they or their elected officials succumbed to material temptation, if they failed to comprehend the moral dimensions of political power, or if personal liberty threatened the rights of property, then the state constitutions were no more than worthless pieces of paper. The risk of excess seemed great. In 1778, a group of New Englanders, fearful that unbridled freedom would create political anarchy, observed, "The idea of liberty has been held up in so dazzling colours that some of us may not be willing to submit to that subordination necessary in the freest states."

Stumbling Toward a New National Government

When the Second Continental Congress convened in 1775, the delegates found themselves waging war in the name of a country that did not yet exist. As the military crisis deepened, Congress gradually—often reluctantly—assumed greater authority over national affairs, but everyone agreed such narrowly conceived measures were a poor substitute for a legally constituted government. The separate states could not possibly deal with the range of issues that now confronted the American people. Indeed, if independence meant anything in a world of sovereign nations, it implied the creation of a central authority capable of conducting war, borrowing money, regulating trade, and negotiating treaties.

Articles of Confederation

The challenge of creating a viable central government proved more difficult than anyone anticipated. Congress appointed a committee to draw up a plan for confederation. John Dickinson, the lawyer who had written an important revolutionary pamphlet titled *Letters from a Farmer in Pennsylvania,* headed the committee. Dickinson envisioned the creation of a strong central government, and the report his committee presented on July 12, 1776, shocked delegates who assumed that the constitution would authorize a loose confederation of states. Dickinson's plan placed the western territories, land claimed by the separate states, under congressional control. In addition, Dickinson's committee called for equal state representation in Congress.

Since some states, such as Virginia and Massachusetts, were more populous than others, the plan fueled tensions between large and small states. Also unsettling was Dickinson's recommendation that taxes be paid to Congress on the basis of a state's total population, black as well as white. Angered Southerners argued that slaves should not be counted at all. Indeed, even before the British evacuated Boston, Dickinson's committee raised many difficult political questions that would divide Americans for several decades.

Not surprisingly, the draft of the plan—the **Articles of Confederation**—that Congress finally approved in November 1777 bore little resemblance to Dickinson's original plan. The Articles jealously guarded the sovereignty of the states. The delegates who drafted the framework shared a general republican conviction that power—especially power so far removed from the people—was inherently dangerous. They believed that the only way to preserve liberty was to place as many constraints as possible on federal authority.

The result was a government that many people regarded as powerless. The Articles provided for a single legislative body consisting of representatives selected annually by the state legislatures. Each state possessed a single vote in Congress. It could send as many as seven delegates, as few as two, but if they divided evenly on a certain issue, the state lost its vote. There was no independent executive and no veto over legislative decisions. The Articles also denied Congress the power of taxation, a serious oversight in time of war. The national government could obtain funds only by asking the states for contributions, called requisitions, but if a state failed to cooperate—and many did—Congress limped along without financial support. Amendments to this constitution required assent by all thirteen states. The authors of the new system expected the weak national government to handle foreign relations, military matters, Indian affairs, and interstate disputes. They most emphatically did not award Congress ownership of the lands west of the Appalachian Mountains.

The new constitution sent to the states for ratification encountered apathy and hostility. Most Americans were far more interested in local affairs than in the actions of Congress. When a British army marched through a state, creating a need for immediate military aid, people spoke positively about central government. As soon as the threat had passed, they sang a different tune. During this period, even the slightest encroachment on state sovereignty rankled republicans who feared centralization would inevitably promote corruption.

Western Land: Key to the First Constitution

The major bone of contention with the Articles, however, was the disposition of the vast, unsurveyed territory west of the Appalachians that everyone hoped the British would soon surrender. Although the region was claimed by the various states, most of it actually belonged to the Native Americans. In a series of land grabs that federal negotiators called treaties, the United States government took the land comprising much of modern Ohio, Indiana, Illinois, and Kentucky. Since the Indians had put their faith in the British during the war, they could do little to resist the humiliating treaty agreements at Fort McIntosh (1785), Fort Stanwix (1784), and Fort Finney (1786). As John Dickinson, then serving as the president of the Supreme Executive Council of Pennsylvania, told the Indians that since Great Britain has surrendered "the back country with all the forts . . . that they [the Indians] must now depend upon us for the preservation." If they dared to resist, "we will instantly turn upon them our armies . . . and extirpate them from the land where they were born and now live."

Some states, such as Virginia and Georgia, claimed land all the way from the Atlantic Ocean to the elusive "South Seas," in effect extending their boundaries to the Pacific coast by virtue of royal charters. State

NORTHWEST TERRITORY *The U.S. government auctioned off the land in the Northwest Territory, the region defined by the Ohio River, the Great Lakes, and the Mississippi River. Proceeds from the sale of one section in each township were set aside for the creation and support of public schools.*

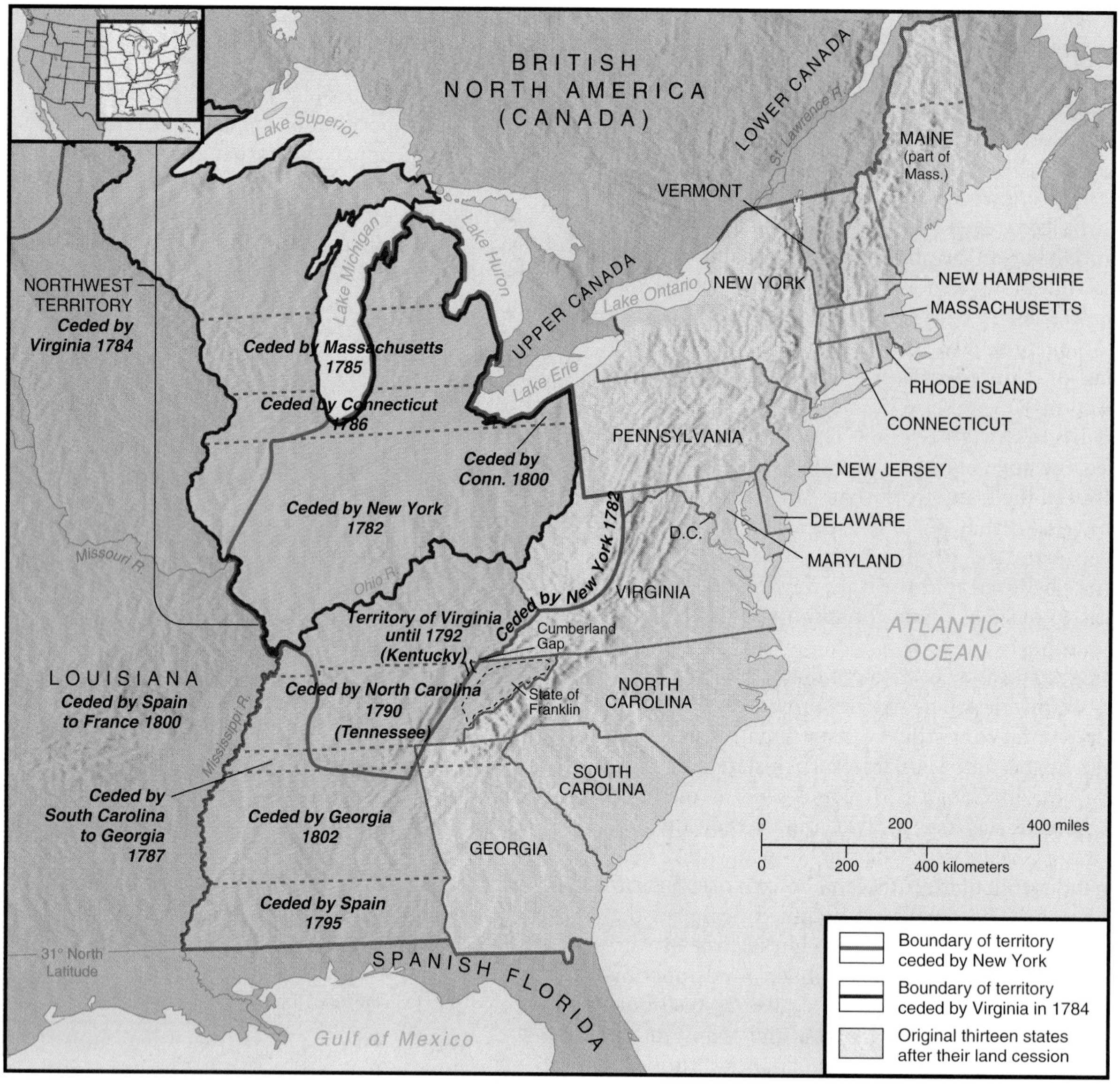

WESTERN LAND CLAIMS CEDED BY THE STATES *After winning the war, the major issue facing the Continental Congress under the Articles of Confederation was mediating conflicting states' claims to rich western land. By 1802, the states had ceded all rights to the federal government.*

legislators—their appetites whetted by aggressive land speculators—anticipated generating large revenues through land sales. Connecticut, New York, Pennsylvania, and North Carolina also announced intentions to seize blocks of western land.

Other states were not blessed with vague or ambiguous royal charters. The boundaries of Maryland, Delaware, and New Jersey had been established many years earlier, and it seemed as if people living in these states would be permanently cut off from the anticipated bounty. In protest, these "landless" states stubbornly refused to ratify the Articles of Confederation. Marylanders were particularly vociferous. All the states had made sacrifices for the common good during the Revolution, they complained, and it appeared only fair that all states should profit from the fruits of victory, in this case, from the sale of western lands. Maryland's spokesmen feared that if Congress did not void Virginia's excessive claims to all of the Northwest Territory (the land west of Pennsylvania and north of the Ohio River) as well as to a large area south of the Ohio, beyond the Cumberland Gap, known as Kentucky, then Marylanders would desert their home state in search of cheap Virginia farms, leaving Maryland an underpopulated wasteland.

Virginians scoffed at the pleas for equity. They suspected that behind the Marylanders' statements of high purpose lay the greed of speculators. Private land companies had sprung up before the Revolution and purchased large tracts from the Indians in areas claimed by Virginia. Their agents petitioned Parliament to legitimize these questionable transactions. Their efforts failed. After the Declaration of Independence, however, the companies shifted the focus of their lobbying to Congress, particularly to the representatives of landless states like Maryland. By liberally distributing shares of stock, officials of the Indiana, Illinois, and Wabash companies gained powerful supporters such as Benjamin Franklin, Robert Morris, and Thomas Johnson, governor of Maryland. These activities encouraged Delaware and New Jersey to modify their demands and join the Confederation, while Maryland held out for five years. The leaders of Virginia, though, remained firm. Why, they asked, should Virginia surrender its historic claims to western lands to enrich a handful of selfish speculators?

The states resolved the bitter controversy in 1781 as much by accident as by design. Virginia agreed to cede its holdings north of the Ohio River to the Confederation on condition that Congress nullify the land companies' earlier purchases from the Indians. A practical consideration had softened Virginia's resolve. Republicans such as Jefferson worried about expanding their state beyond the mountains; with poor transportation links, it seemed impossible to govern such a large territory effectively from Richmond. The western settlers might even come to regard Virginia as a colonial power insensitive to their needs. Marylanders who dreamed of making fortunes on the land market grumbled, but when a British army appeared on their border, they prudently accepted the Articles (March 1, 1781). Congress required another three years to work out the details of the Virginia cession. Other landed states followed Virginia's example. These transfers established an important principle, for after 1781, it was agreed that the West belonged not to the separate states but to the United States. In this matter, at least, the national government now exercised full sovereignty.

No one greeted ratification of the Articles with much enthusiasm. When they thought about national politics at all, Americans concerned themselves primarily with winning independence. The new government gradually developed an administrative bureaucracy, and in 1781, it formally created the Departments of War, Foreign Affairs, and Finance. By far the most influential figure in the Confederation was Robert Morris (1734–1806), a freewheeling Philadelphia merchant who was appointed the first superintendent of finance. Although he was a brilliant manager, Morris's decisions as superintendent provoked controversy, indeed, deep suspicion. He hardly seemed a model republican. Morris mixed public funds under his control with personal accounts, and he never lost an opportunity to make a profit. While such practices were not illegal, his apparent improprieties undermined his own political agenda. He desperately wanted to strengthen the central government, but highly vocal critics resisted, labeling Morris a "pecuniary dictator."

Northwest Ordinance: The Confederation's Major Achievement

Whatever the weaknesses of Congress may have been, it did score one impressive triumph. Congressional action brought order to western settlement, especially in the Northwest Territory, and incorporated frontier Americans into an expanding federal system. In 1781, the prospects for success did not seem promising. For years, colonial authorities had ignored people who migrated far inland, sending neither money nor soldiers to protect them from Indian attack. Tensions between the seaboard colonies and the frontier regions had sometimes flared into violence. Disorders occurred in South Carolina in 1767, in North Carolina in 1769, and in Vermont in 1777. With thousands of men and women, most of them squatters, pouring across the Appalachian Mountains, Congress had to act quickly to avoid the past errors of royal and colonial authorities.

The initial attempt to deal with this explosive problem came in 1784. Jefferson, then serving as a member of Congress, drafted an ordinance that became the basis for later, more enduring legislation. Jefferson recommended carving ten new states out of the western lands located north of the Ohio River and recently ceded to the United States by Virginia. He specified that each new state establish a republican form of government. When the population of a territory equaled that of the smallest state already in the Confederation, the region could apply for full statehood. In the meantime, free white males could participate in local government, a democratic guarantee that frightened some of Jefferson's more conservative colleagues.

The impoverished Congress was eager to sell off the western territory as quickly as possible. After all, the frontier represented a source of income that did not depend on the unreliable generosity of the states. A second ordinance, passed in 1785 and called the Land Ordinance, established an orderly process for laying out new townships and marketing public lands.

The 1785 scheme possessed geometric elegance. Surveyors marked off townships, each running directly from east to west. These units, 6 miles square, were subdivided into 36 separate sections of 640 acres (1 square mile) each. (Roads and property boundaries established according to this grid pattern survived long

LAND ORDINANCE OF 1785

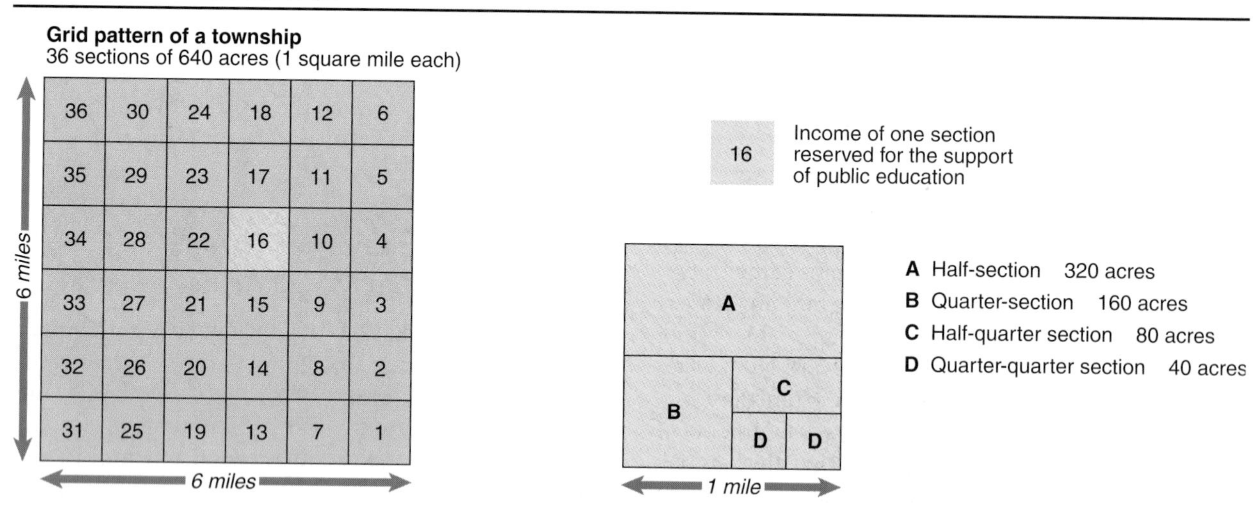

after the Confederation had passed into history.) The government planned to auction off its holdings at prices of not less than $1 an acre. Congress set the minimum purchase at 640 acres, and near-worthless paper money was not accepted as payment. Section 16 was set aside for public education; the federal government reserved four other sections for its own use.

Public response disappointed Congress. Surveying the lands took far longer than anticipated, and few persons possessed enough hard currency to make even the minimum purchase. Finally, a solution to the problem came from Manasseh Cutler, a New England minister turned land speculator and congressional lobbyist, and his associates, who included several former officers of the Continental Army.

Cutler and his associates, representing the Ohio and Scioto companies, offered to purchase more than 6 million unsurveyed acres of land located in present-day southeastern Ohio by persuading Congress to accept, at full face value, government loan certificates that had been issued to soldiers during the Revolution. On the open market, the Ohio company could pick up the certificates for as little as 10 percent of their face value; thus, the company stood to make a fortune. Like so many other get-rich-quick schemes, however, this one failed to produce the anticipated millions. Unfortunately for Cutler and his friends, small homesteaders settled wherever they pleased, refusing to pay either government or speculators for the land.

Congress worried about the excess liberty on the frontier. In the 1780s, the West seemed to be filling up with people who by eastern standards were uncultured. Timothy Pickering, a New Englander, declared that "the emigrants to the frontier lands are the least worthy subjects in the United States. They are little less savage than the Indians; and when possessed of the most fertile spots, for want of industry, live miserably." The charge was as old as the frontier itself. Indeed, seventeenth-century Englishmen had said the same things of the earliest Virginians. The lawless image stuck, however, and even a sober observer such as Washington insisted that the West crawled with "banditti." The Ordinance of 1784 placed the government of the territories in the hands of people about whom congressmen and speculators had second thoughts.

These various currents shaped the Ordinance of 1787, one of the final acts passed under the Confederation. The bill, also called the **Northwest Ordinance,** provided a new structure for government of the Northwest Territory. The plan authorized the creation of between three and five territories, each to be ruled by a governor, a secretary, and three judges appointed by Congress. When the population reached five thousand, voters who owned property could elect an assembly, but its decisions were subject to the governor's absolute veto. Once sixty thousand persons resided in a territory, they could write a constitution and petition for full statehood. While these procedures represented a retreat from Jefferson's original proposal, the Ordinance of 1787 contained several significant features. A bill of rights guaranteed the settlers the right to trial by jury, freedom of religion, and due process of law. In addition, the act outlawed slavery, a prohibition that freed the future states of Ohio, Indiana, Illinois, Michigan, and Wisconsin from the curse of human bondage.

By contrast, settlement south of the Ohio River received far less attention from Congress. Long before the end of the war, thousands of Americans streamed through the Cumberland Gap into a part of Virginia known as Kentucky. The most famous of these settlers was Daniel Boone. In 1775, the population of Kentucky was approximately one hundred; by 1784, it had jumped to thirty thousand. Speculators purchased large tracts from the Indians, planning to resell this acreage to settlers at handsome profits. In 1776, one land company asked Congress to reorganize the company's holdings into a new state called Transylvania. While nothing came of this self-serving request, another, even more aggressive group of speculators in 1784 carved the State of Franklin out of a section of present-day Tennessee, then claimed by North Carolina. Rival speculators prevented formal recognition of Franklin's government. By 1790, the entire region south of the Ohio River had been transformed into a crazy quilt of claims and counterclaims that generated lawsuits for many years to come.

Strengthening Federal Authority

Despite its success in bringing order to the Northwest Territory, the Confederation increasingly came under heavy fire from critics who wanted a stronger central government. Complaints varied from region to region, from person to person, but most disappointment reflected economic frustration. Americans had assumed that peace would restore economic growth, but recovery following the Revolution was slow.

The Nationalist Critique

Even before England signed a treaty with America, its merchants flooded American ports with consumer items and offered easy credit. Families that had postponed purchases of imported goods—either because of British blockade or personal hardship—now rushed to buy European finery.

This sudden renewal of trade with Great Britain on such a large scale strained the American economy. Gold and silver flowed back across the Atlantic, leaving the United States desperately short of hard currency. When large merchant houses called in their debts, ordinary American consumers often found themselves on the brink of bankruptcy. "The disagreeable state of our commerce," observed James Wilson, an advocate of strong national government, has been the result "of extravagant and injudicious importation. . . . We seemed to have forgot that to pay was as necessary in trade as to purchase."

To blame the Confederation alone for the economic depression would be unfair. Nevertheless, during the 1780s, many people agreed that a stronger central government could somehow have brought greater stability to the struggling economy. In their rush to acquire imported luxuries, Americans seemed to have deserted republican principles, and a weak Congress was helpless to restore national virtue.

Critics pointed to the government's inability to regulate trade. Whenever a northern congressman suggested restricting British access to American markets, southern representatives, who feared any controls on the export of tobacco or rice, bellowed in protest. Southerners anticipated that navigation acts written by the Confederation would put planters under the yoke of northern shipping interests.

The country's chronic fiscal instability increased public anxiety. While the war was still in progress, Congress printed well over $200 million in paper money, but because of extraordinarily high inflation, the rate of exchange for Continental bills soon declined to a fraction of their face value. In 1781, Congress, facing insolvency, turned to the states for help. They were asked to retire the depreciated currency. The situation was spinning out of control. Several states—pressed to pay their own war-related debts—not only recirculated the Continental bills but also issued nearly worthless money of their own.

A heavy burden of state and national debt compounded the general sense of economic crisis. Revolutionary soldiers had yet to be paid. Women and men who had loaned money and goods to the government clamored for reimbursement. Foreign creditors demanded interest on funds advanced during the Revolution. These pressures grew, but Congress was unable to respond. The Articles specifically prohibited Congress from taxing the American people. It required little imagination to see that the Confederation would soon default on its legal obligations unless something was done quickly.

In response, an aggressive group of men announced that they knew how to save the Confederation. The **nationalists**—persons such as Alexander Hamilton, James Madison, and Robert Morris—called for major constitutional reforms, the chief of which was an amendment allowing Congress to collect a 5 percent tax on imported goods sold in the states. Revenues generated by the proposed Impost of 1781 would be used by the Confederation to reduce the national debt. On this point the nationalists were adamant. They recognized that whoever paid the public debt would gain the public trust. If the states assumed the responsibility, then the country could easily fragment into separate republics. "A national debt," Hamilton explained in 1781, "if it is not excessive, will be to us a national blessing. It will be a powerful cement to our union." Twelve states accepted the Impost amendment, but Rhode Island—where local interests argued that the tax would make Congress "independent of their constituents"—resolutely refused to co-

❖ A Look at the Past ❖

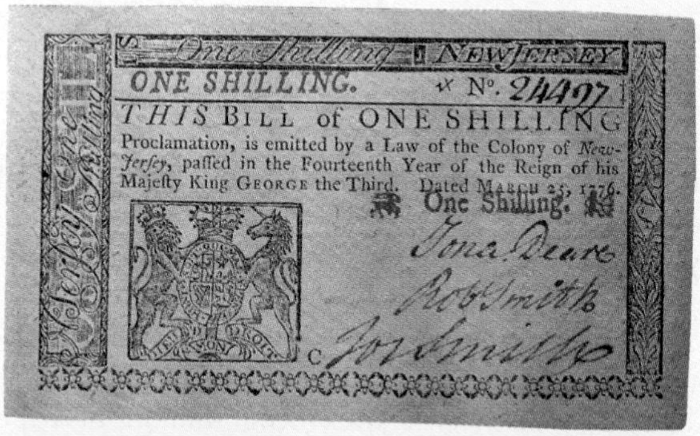

Paper Currency

Fighting the American Revolution cost a lot of money. The new government of the United States simply did not have sufficient gold and silver—called specie—to pay the troops and buy weapons. Pressed on all sides by creditors, the fledgling government issued huge quantities of paper money. The flood of Continental currency sparked massive inflation, as nearly worthless money chased a finite supply of consumer goods. Considering the threat of economic instability, should the Continental Congress have printed so much paper money? Did it have other realistic alternatives? What sorts of people in this society were most harmed by hyperinflation?

operate. One negative vote on this proposed constitutional change, and the taxing scheme was dead.

State leaders frankly thought the nationalists were up to no good. The "localists" were especially apprehensive of fiscal plans advanced by Robert Morris. His profiteering as superintendent of finance appeared a threat to the moral fiber of the young republic. Richard Henry Lee and Samuel Adams, men of impeccable patriotic credentials, decried Morris's efforts to create a national bank. Such an institution would bring forth a flock of social parasites, the kind of people that Americans associated with corrupt monarchical government. One person declared that if an impost ever passed, Morris "will have all [the money] in his Pocket."

The nationalists regarded their opponents as economically naive. A country with the potential of the United States required a complex, centralized fiscal system. But for all their pretensions to realism, the nationalists of the early 1780s were politically inept. They underestimated the depth of republican fears, and in their rush to strengthen the Articles, they overplayed their hand.

A group of extreme nationalists even appealed to the army for support. To this day, no one knows the full story of the Newburgh Conspiracy of 1783. Officers of the Continental Army stationed at Newburgh, New York, worried that Congress would disband them without funding their pensions, began to lobby intensively for relief. In March, they scheduled general meetings to protest the weakness and duplicity of Congress. The officers' initial efforts were harmless enough, but frustrated nationalists such as Morris and Hamilton hoped that if the army exerted sufficient pressure on the government, perhaps even threatened a military takeover, then stubborn Americans might be compelled to amend the Articles.

The conspirators failed to take George Washington's integrity into account. No matter how much he wanted a strong central government, he would not tolerate insubordination by the military. Washington confronted the officers directly at Newburgh, intending to read a prepared statement. Fumbling with his glasses before his men, he commented, "Gentlemen, you must pardon me. I have grown gray in your service and now find myself growing blind." The unexpected vulnerability of this great soldier reduced the troops to tears, and in an instant, the rebellion was broken. Washington deserves credit for preserving civilian rule in this country.

In April 1783, Congress proposed a second impost, but it too failed to win unanimous ratification. Even a personal appeal by Washington could not save the amendment. As one opponent explained, if "permanent Funds are given to Congress, the aristocratic Influence, which predominates in more than a major part of the United States, will fully establish an arbitrary Government." With this defeat, nationalists gave up on the Confederation. Morris retired from government, and Madison returned to Virginia utterly depressed by what he had witnessed.

Diplomatic Humiliation

In foreign affairs, Congress endured further embarrassment. It could not even enforce the provisions of its own peace treaty. American negotiators had promised Great Britain that its citizens could collect debts contracted before the Revolution. The states, however, dragged their heels, and several even passed laws obstructing the settlement of legitimate prewar claims. Congress was powerless to force compliance. The British responded to this apparent provocation by refusing to evacuate troops from posts located in the Northwest Territory. A strong national government would have driven the redcoats out, but without adequate funds, the weak Congress could not provide soldiers for such a mission.

Congress's postrevolutionary dealings with Spain were equally humiliating. That nation refused to accept the southern boundary of the United States established by the Treaty of Paris. Spain claimed sovereignty over much of the land located between Georgia and the Mississippi River, and its agents schemed with Indian tribes in this region to resist American expansion. On July 21, 1784, Spain fueled the controversy by closing the lower Mississippi River to citizens of the United States.

This unexpected decision devastated western farmers. Free use of the Mississippi was essential to the economic development of the entire Ohio Valley. Because of the prohibitively high cost of transporting freight for long distances over land, western settlers—and southern planters eyeing future opportunities in this area—demanded a secure water link with the world's markets. Their spokesmen in Congress denounced anyone who claimed that navigation of the Mississippi was a negotiable issue.

In 1786, a Spanish official, Don Diego de Gardoqui, opened talks with John Jay, a New Yorker appointed by Congress to obtain rights to navigation of the Mississippi. Jay soon discovered that Gardoqui would not compromise. After making little progress, Jay seized the initiative. If Gardoqui would allow American merchants to trade directly with Spain, thus opening up an important new market to ships from New England and the middle states, then the United States might forgo navigation of the Mississippi for twenty-five years. When southern delegates heard of Jay's concessions, they were outraged. It appeared to them as if representatives of northern commerce were ready to abandon the southern frontier. Angry congressmen accused New Englanders of attempting to divide the United States into separate confederations, for as one Virginian exclaimed, the proposed Spanish treaty "would weaken if not destroy the union by disaffecting the Southern States . . . to obtain a trivial commercial advantage." Congress wisely terminated the negotiations with Spain.

By the mid-1780s, the Confederation could claim several notable achievements. It designed an administrative system that lasted far longer than did the Articles. It also brought order out of the chaos of conflicting western land claims. Still, as anyone could see, the government was struggling. Congress met irregularly. Some states did not even bother to send delegates, and pressing issues often had to be postponed for lack of a quorum. The nation even lacked a permanent capital, and Congress drifted from Philadelphia to Princeton to Annapolis to New York City, prompting one humorist to suggest that the government purchase an air balloon. This newly invented device, he explained, would allow the members of Congress to "float along from one end of the continent to the other" and "suddenly pop down into any of the states they please."

"Have We Fought for This?"

By 1785, the country seemed to have lost direction. The buoyant optimism that sustained revolutionary patriots had dissolved into pessimism and doubt. Many Americans, especially those who had provided leadership during the Revolution, agreed something had to be done. In 1786, Washington bitterly observed, "What astonishing changes a few years are capable of producing. Have we fought for this? Was it with these expectations that we launched into a sea of trouble, and have bravely struggled through the most threatening dangers?"

The Genius of James Madison

The conviction of people such as Washington that the nation was indeed in a state of crisis reflected tensions within republican thought. To be sure, they supported open elections and the right of individuals to advance their own economic well-being, but when these elements seemed to undermine social and political order, they expressed the fear that perhaps liberty had been carried too far. The situation had changed quite rapidly. As recently as the 1770s, men of republican persuasion had insisted that the greatest threat to the American people was concentration of power in the hands of unscrupulous rulers. With this principle in mind, they transformed state governors into mere figureheads and weakened the Confederation in the name of popular liberties.

By the mid-1780s, persons of property and standing saw the problem in a different light. Recent experience suggested to them that ordinary citizens did not in fact possess sufficient virtue to sustain a republic. The states had been plagued not by executive tyranny but by an excess of democracy, by a failure of the majority to preserve the property rights of the minority, by an unrestrained individualism that promoted anarchy rather than good order.

Many state leaders did not seem particularly concerned about the fiscal health of the national government. Local presses churned out worthless currency, and in some states, assemblies passed laws impeding the collection of debt. In Rhode Island, the situation became absurd. State legislators made it illegal for merchants to reject Rhode Island money even though everyone knew it had no value. No wonder Governor William Livingston of New Jersey declared in 1787, "We do not exhibit the virtue that is necessary to support a republican government."

As Americans tried to interpret these experiences within a republican framework, they were checked by the most widely accepted political wisdom of the age. Baron de Montesquieu (1689–1755), a French political philosopher of immense international reputation and author of *The Spirit of the Laws* (1748), declared flatly that a republican government could not flourish in a large territory. The reasons were clear. If the people lost direct control over their representatives, they would fall prey to tyrants. Large distances allowed rulers to hide their corruption; physical separation presented aristocrats with opportunities to seize power.

In the United States, most learned men treated Montesquieu's theories as self-evident truths. His writings seemed to demonstrate the importance of preserving the sovereignty of the states, for however much these small republics abused the rights of property and ignored minority interests, it was plainly unscientific to maintain that a republic consisting of thirteen states, several million people, and thousands of acres of territory could long survive.

James Madison rejected Montesquieu's argument, and in so doing, he helped Americans to think of republican government in radical new ways. This soft-spoken, rather unprepossessing Virginian was the most brilliant American political thinker of his generation. One French official described Madison as "a man one must study a long time in order to make a fair appraisal." Those who listened carefully to what Madison had to say, however, soon recognized his genius for translating theory into practice.

Madison delved into the writings of a group of Scottish philosophers, the most prominent being David Hume (1711–1776), and from their works he concluded that Americans need not fear a greatly expanded republic. Madison perceived that "inconveniences of popular States contrary to prevailing Theory, are in proportion not to the extent, but to the narrowness of their limits." Indeed, it was in small states such as Rhode Island that legislative majorities tyrannized the propertied minority. In a large territory, Madison explained, "the Society becomes broken into a greater variety of interest, of pursuits, of passions, which check each other, whilst those who may feel a common sentiment have less opportunity of communication and contact."

Madison did not, however, advocate a modern "interest-group" model of political behavior. The contending parties were incapable of working for the common good. They were too mired in their own local, selfish concerns. Rather, Madison thought competing factions would neutralize each other, leaving the business of running the central government to the ablest, most virtuous persons the nation could produce. In other words, Madison's federal system was not a small state writ large; it was something entirely different, a government based on the will of the people and yet detached from their narrowly based demands. This thinking formed the foundation of Madison's most famous political essay, *The Federalist* No. 10.

Constitutional Reform

A concerted movement to overhaul the Articles of Confederation began in 1786, when Madison and his friends persuaded the Virginia assembly to recommend a convention to explore the creation of a unified system of "commercial regulations." Congress supported the idea. In September, delegates from five states arrived in Annapolis, Maryland, to discuss issues that extended far beyond commerce. The small turnout was disappointing, but the occasion provided strong nationalists with an opportunity to hatch an even bolder plan. The Annapolis delegates advised Congress to hold a second meeting in Philadelphia "to take into consideration the situation of the United States, to devise such further provisions as shall appear to them necessary to render the constitution of the Federal Government adequate to the exigencies of the Union." Whether staunch states' rights advocates in Congress knew what was afoot is not clear. In any case, Congress authorized a grand convention to gather in May 1787.

Events played into Madison's hands. Soon after the Annapolis meeting, an uprising known as **Shays's Rebellion,** involving several thousand impoverished farmers, shattered the peace of western Massachusetts. No matter how hard these men worked the soil, they always found themselves in debt to eastern creditors. They complained of high taxes, of high interest rates, and, most of all, of a state government insensitive to their problems. In 1786, Daniel Shays, a veteran of the battle of Bunker Hill, and his armed neighbors closed a county courthouse where creditors were suing to foreclose farm mortgages. At one point, the rural insurgents threatened to seize the federal arsenal located at Springfield. Congress did not have funds sufficient to support an army, and the arsenal might have fallen had not a group of wealthy Bostonians raised an army

This 1787 woodcut portrays Daniel Shays with one of his chief officers, Jacob Shattucks. Shays led farmers in western Massachusetts in revolt against a state government that seemed insensitive to the needs of poor debtors. Their rebellion strengthened the demand for a strong new federal government. ❖

of four thousand troops to put down the insurrection. The victors were in for a surprise. At the next general election, Massachusetts voters selected representatives sympathetic to Shays's demands, and a new liberal assembly reformed debtor law.

Nationalists throughout the United States were not so forgiving. From their perspective, Shays's Rebellion symbolized the breakdown of law and order that they had long predicted. "Great commotions are prevailing in Massachusetts," Madison wrote. "An appeal to the sword is exceedingly dreaded." The time had come for sensible people to speak up for a strong national government. The unrest in Massachusetts persuaded persons who might otherwise have ignored the Philadelphia meeting to participate in drafting a new constitution.

The Philadelphia Convention

In the spring of 1787, fifty-five men representing twelve states traveled to Philadelphia. Rhode Island refused to take part in the proceedings, a decision that Madison attributed to its "wickedness and folly." Thomas Jefferson described the convention as an "assembly of demi-Gods," but this flattering depiction is misleading. However much modern Americans revere the Constitution, they should remember that the individuals who wrote it did not possess divine insight into the nature of government. They were practical people—lawyers, merchants, and planters—many of whom had fought in the Revolution and served in the Congress of the Confederation. The majority were in their thirties or forties. The gathering included George Washington, James Madison, George Mason, Robert Morris, James Wilson, John Dickinson, Benjamin Franklin, and Alexander Hamilton, just to name some of the more prominent participants. Absent were John Adams and Thomas Jefferson, who were conducting diplomacy in Europe; Patrick Henry, a localist suspicious of strong central government, remained in Virginia, announcing he "smelled a rat."

As soon as the Constitutional Convention opened on May 25, the delegates made several procedural decisions of the utmost importance. First, they voted "that nothing spoken in the House be printed, or communicated without leave." The rule was stringently enforced. Sentries guarded the doorways to keep out uninvited visitors, windows stayed shut in the sweltering heat to prevent sound from either entering or leaving the chamber, and members were forbidden to copy the daily journal without official permission. As Madison explained, the secrecy rule saved "both the convention and the community from a thousand erroneous and perhaps mischievous reports." It also has made it extremely difficult for modern lawyers and judges to determine exactly what the delegates had in mind when they wrote the Constitution (see the Feature Essay "The Elusive Constitution: Search for Original Intent," pp. 178–179).

In a second procedural move, the delegates decided to vote by state, but, in order to avoid the kinds of problems that had plagued the Confederation, they ruled that key proposals needed the support of only a majority instead of the nine states required under the Articles.

Inventing a Federal Republic

Madison understood that whoever sets the agenda controls the meeting. Even before all the delegates had arrived, he drew up a framework for a new federal system known as the **Virginia Plan.** Madison wisely persuaded Edmund Randolph, Virginia's popular governor, to present this scheme to the convention on May 29. Randolph claimed that the Virginia Plan merely revised sections of the Articles, but everyone, including Madison, knew better. "My ideas," Madison confessed, "strike . . . deeply at the old Confederation." He was determined to restrain the state assemblies, and in the original Virginia Plan, Madison gave the federal government power to veto state laws.

The Virginia Plan envisioned a national legislature consisting of two houses, one elected *directly* by the people, the other chosen by the first house from nominations made by the state assemblies. Representation in both houses was proportional to the state's population. The Virginia Plan also provided for an executive elected by Congress. Since most delegates at the Philadelphia convention sympathized with the nationalist position, Madison's blueprint for a strong federal government initially received broad support, and the Virginia Plan was referred to further study and debate. A group of men who allegedly had come together to reform the Confederation found themselves discussing the details of "a *national* Government . . . consisting of a *supreme* Legislature, Executive, and Judiciary."

The Virginia Plan had been pushed through the convention so fast that opponents hardly had an opportunity to present their objections. On June 15, they spoke up. William Paterson, a New Jersey lawyer, advanced the so-called **New Jersey Plan,** a scheme that retained the unicameral legislature in which each state possessed one vote and that at the same time gave Congress extensive new powers to tax and regulate trade. Paterson argued that these revisions, while more modest than Madison's plan, would have greater appeal for the American people. "I believe," he said, "that a little practical virtue is to be preferred to the finest theoretical principles, which cannot be carried into effect." The delegates listened politely and then soundly rejected the New Jersey Plan on June 19. Indeed, only New Jersey, New York, and Delaware voted in favor of Paterson's scheme.

Rejection of this framework did not resolve the most controversial issue before the convention. Paterson and others feared that under the Virginia Plan, small states would lose their separate identities. These delegates maintained that unless each state possessed an equal vote in Congress, the small states would find themselves at the mercy of their larger neighbors.

This argument outraged the delegates who favored a strong federal government. It awarded too much power to the states. "For whom [are we] forming a Government?" Wilson cried. "Is it for men, or for the imaginary beings called States?" It seemed absurd to claim that the 68,000 people of Rhode Island should have the same voice in Congress as Virginia's 747,000 inhabitants.

Compromise Saves the Convention

The mood of the convention was tense. Hard work and frustration, coupled with Philadelphia's sweltering summer heat, frayed nerves, prompting some members to predict that the meeting would accomplish nothing of significance. But despite the growing pessimism, the gathering did not break up. The delegates desperately wanted to produce a constitution, and they refused to give up until they had explored every avenue of reconciliation. Perhaps cooler heads agreed with Washington: "To please all is impossible, and to attempt it would be vain. The only way, therefore, is . . . to form such a government as will bear the scrutinizing eye of criticism, and trust it to the good sense and patriotism of the people."

Mediation clearly offered the only way to overcome what Roger Sherman, a Connecticut delegate, called "a full stop." On July 2, a "grand committee" of one person from each state was elected by the convention to resolve persistent differences between the large and small states. Franklin, at age 81 the oldest delegate, served as chair. The two fiercest supporters of proportional representation based on population, Madison and Wilson, were left off the grand committee, a sure sign that the small states would salvage something from the compromise.

The committee recommended that the states be equally represented in the upper house of Congress, while representation was to be proportionate in the lower house. Only the lower house could initiate money bills. Franklin's committee also decided that one member of the lower house should be selected for every thirty thousand inhabitants of a state. Southern delegates insisted that this number include slaves. In the so-called three-fifths rule, the committee agreed that for the purpose of determining representation in the lower house, slaves would be counted, but not as much as free persons. For every five slaves, a congressional district received credit for three free voters, a deal that gave the South much greater power in the new government than it would have otherwise received. As with most compromise solutions, the one negotiated by Franklin's committee fully satisfied no one. It did, however, overcome a major impasse, and after the small states gained an assured voice in the upper house, the Senate, they cooperated enthusiastically in creating a strong central government.

Compromising with Slavery

During the final days of August, a deeply disturbing issue came before the convention. It was an omen of the great sectional crisis to come in the nineteenth century. Many northern representatives detested the slave trade and wanted it to end immediately. They despised the three-fifths ruling that seemed to award slaveholders

Revolution or Reform?
The Articles of Confederation and the Constitution Compared

Political Challenge	Articles of Confederation	Constitution
Mode of ratification or amendment	Require confirmation by every state legislature	Requires confirmation by three-fourths of state conventions or legislatures
Number of houses in legislature	One	Two
Mode of representation	Two to seven delegates represent each state; each state holds only one vote in Congress	Two senators represent each state in upper house; each senator holds one vote. One representative to lower house represents every 30,000 people (in 1788) in a state; each representative holds one vote
Mode of election and term of office	Delegates appointed annually by state legislatures	Senators chosen by state legislatures for six-year term (direct election after 1913); representatives chosen by vote of citizens for two-year term
Executive	No separate executive: delegates annually elect one of their number as president, who possesses no veto, no power to appoint officers or to conduct policy. Administrative functions of government theoretically carried out by Committee of States, practically by various single-headed departments	Separate executive branch: president elected by electoral college to four-year term; granted veto, power to conduct policy and to appoint ambassadors, judges, and officers of executive departments established by legislation
Judiciary	Most adjudication left to state and local courts; Congress is final court of appeal in disputes between states	Separate branch consisting of Supreme Court and inferior courts established by Congress to enforce federal law
Taxation	States alone can levy taxes; Congress funds the Common Treasury by making requisitions for state contributions	Federal government granted powers of taxation
Regulation of commerce	Congress regulates foreign commerce by treaty but holds no check on conflicting state regulations	Congress regulates foreign commerce by treaty; all state regulations must obtain congressional consent

extra power in government simply because they owned slaves. "It seemed now to be pretty well understood," Madison jotted in his private notes, "that the real difference of interest lay, not between the large and small but between the N. and Southn. States. The institution of slavery and its consequences formed a line of discrimination."

Whenever northern delegates—and on this point they were by no means united—pushed too aggressively, Southerners threatened to bolt the convention, thereby destroying any hope of establishing a strong national government. Curiously, even recalcitrant Southerners avoided using the word *slavery*. They seemed embarrassed to call the institution by its true name, and in the Constitution itself, slaves were described as "other persons," "such persons," "persons held to Service or Labour," in other words, as everything but slaves.

A few northern delegates such as Roger Sherman of Connecticut sought at every turn to mollify the Southerners, especially the South Carolinians who spoke so passionately about preserving slavery. Gouverneur Morris, a Pennsylvania representative, would have none of it. He regularly reminded the convention that "the inhabitant of Georgia and S.C. who goes to the Coast of Africa, and in defiance of the most sacred laws of humanity tears away his fellow creatures from their dearest connections and damns them to the most cruel bondage, shall have more votes in a Government instituted for the protection of the rights of mankind, than the Citizen of Pa. or N. Jersey."

Largely ignoring Morris's stinging attacks, the delegates reached an uneasy compromise on the continuation of the slave trade. Southerners feared that the new Congress would pass commercial regulations adversely affecting the planters—taxes on the export of rice and tobacco, for example. They demanded, therefore, that no trade laws be passed without a two-thirds majority of the federal legislature. They backed down on this point, however, in exchange for guarantees that Congress would not interfere with the slave trade until 1808 (see Chapter 8). The South even came away with

Feature Essay

THE ELUSIVE CONSTITUTION

Search for Original Intent

Many prominent national leaders, alarmed at a perceived "judicial imperialism" in recent activist courts, have urged that judges interpret the Constitution strictly according to the "intent of the Framers." Arguing that a "jurisprudence of original intent" is the "only legitimate basis for constitutional decision making," *intentionalists* demand that judges measure decisions against a "demonstrable consensus among the Framers and ratifiers as to principles stated or implied in the Constitution."

Yet when one considers circumstances surrounding the Constitution's framing, demonstration of the Founders' intent proves elusive indeed. Delegates to the Constitutional Convention in Philadelphia in 1787 deliberately veiled the purpose of the convention in secrecy to avoid pressure by local constituencies who harbored deep suspicions concerning strong central government. Newspapers, barred from access to the convention, printed only occasional rumors. Delegates refused to speak or correspond with outsiders concerning the proceedings.

The strictness with which delegates observed the rule of secrecy not only restricted contemporary knowledge of what transpired but has also limited the number of sources in which subsequent generations may search for original intent. Only three members preserved complete accounts of convention debates. These records remained unpublished for more than thirty years, forcing the first generation of lawyers and federal judges to rely on the words of the Constitution alone for clues to the Framers' intent.

The publication of the three accounts did not necessarily make the delegates' intent more accessible. The *Journal, Acts and Proceedings of the Convention Assemblies in Philadelphia,* recorded by the convention secretary, William Jackson, provided only a chronological listing of motions, resolutions, and vote tallies. His unpublished manuscript of convention debates, which could have fleshed out the published *Journal's* "mere skeleton" of the proceedings, was lost.

The notes of New York delegate Robert Yates appeared in 1821 as *Secret Proceedings and Debates of the Convention Assembled at Philadelphia,* but the circumstances of their publication rendered them thoroughly unreliable. Their editor, the former French minister Citizen Edmond Genêt, attained notoriety in the 1790s when he violated American neutrality in the Anglo-French war by commissioning American privateers against British shipping. Genêt supported states' rights and popular government and manipulated Yates's notes to support his views. A comparison of *Secret Proceedings* with the two surviving pages of Yates's manuscript reveals that Genêt altered or deleted more than half the original text.

If the intent of the delegates survives anywhere, Madison's *Notes of Debates in the Federal Convention of 1787* provides its likeliest repository. The "father of the Constitution," as contemporaries called him, carefully preserved notes on convention proceedings and took every measure to ensure their accuracy. Recognizing his own limitations as a stenographer, Madison did not try to record everything said but sought manuscript copies of delegates' speeches that he incorporated into his notes at the end of each day. Madison also waited until the end of each day to record his own speeches, every one of which was extemporaneous, from memory. At the convention's end, he obtained a manuscript copy of secretary Jackson's notes, which he used to supplement and correct his own. Though Madison tinkered at times with his notes over the next thirty years, recent analysis has demonstrated that none of these minor corrections impaired the faithfulness of the text.

Yet in spite of the meticulous care that Madison lavished on his notes, they remain, at best, incomplete repositories of the Framers' original intent. Each day's notes contain only a few minutes of oral discourse, whereas actual delivery occupied between five and seven hours. Furthermore, written manuscripts of speeches may have approximated only roughly what the debaters actually said. Madison's speech on the benefits of a large republic, for example, occupies two closely reasoned pages in his notes. Yet others who took notes seem to have recorded a much shorter and far less impressive oral version. Such discrepancies raise important questions. How did the Framers understand the actual speeches on the convention floor? How did their understanding shape their intentions? How much of their intent is lost in the vast omissions?

These questions take on even greater significance when one considers that the Constitution was forged through a series of compromises among representatives whose interests and intentions differed widely. No delegate was completely satisfied, and the finished document permitted some functions none had intended. Madison himself complained, for example, that the principle of judicial review "was never intended and can never be proper."

Moreover, he thought it would be a mistake to search for the original intent of convention delegates. The delegates' intent could never possibly determine constitutional interpretation, he argued, for "the only authoritative intentions were those of the people of the States, as expressed thro' the Conventions which ratified the Constitution."

Yet the works most commonly cited from the time of state ratification raise problems with the application of this principle as well. Stenographers who recorded the *Debates of the Several State Conventions on the Adoption of the Federal Constitution* did not possess skills adequate to their task, and Federalist partisans edited the speeches with abandon in order to promote their own views. Evidence also suggests that Jonathan Eliot, the journalist who published the debates in 1836, altered them further.

Given the limitations of sources most often cited by modern judges and lawyers, the original intent of most Framers remains as elusive today as it was for the first generation who had no access to those documents. The Constitution's often ambiguous wording, which furnished the sole guide to the Framers' intent in their day, remains the best recourse in our own.

James Madison, by Charles Willson Peale. Among the framers of the Constitution, Madison was the most effective advocate of a strong central government. ❖

The State House of Philadelphia in an engraving of 1776 by John McRae. After the Revolution and the drafting of the Constitution, the building became known as Independence Hall. During the hot summer of 1787, delegates kept the windows closed so that no one on the street could hear the debates. ❖

Although the words slave *and* slavery *do not appear in the U.S. Constitution, debate over slavery and the slave trade resulted in a compromise in which both institutions persisted in the new Republic. Not everyone was pleased with the compromise. The Library Company of Philadelphia commissioned this painting* Liberty Displaying the Arts and Sciences *(1792) by Samuel Jennings. The broken chain at the feet of the goddess Liberty is meant to demonstrate her opposition to slavery.* ❖

a clause assuring the return of fugitive slaves. "We have obtained," Charles Cotesworth Pinckney told the planters of South Carolina, "a right to recover our slaves in whatever part of America they may take refuge, which is a right we had not before."

Although these deals disappointed many Northerners, they conceded that establishing a strong national government was of greater immediate importance than ending the slave trade. "Great as the evil is," Madison wrote, "a dismemberment of the union would be worse."

The Last Details

On July 26, the convention formed a Committee of Detail, a group that prepared a rough draft of the Constitution. After the committee completed its work—writing a document that still, after so many hours of debate, preserved the fundamental points of the Virginia Plan—the delegates reconsidered each article. The task required the better part of a month.

During these sessions, the members of the convention concluded that the president, as they now called the executive, should be selected by an electoral college, a body of prominent men in each state chosen by local voters. The number of "electoral" votes held by each state equaled its number of representatives and senators. This awkward device guaranteed that the president would not be indebted to the Congress for his office. Whoever received the second largest number of votes in the electoral college automatically became vice president. In the event that no person received a majority of the votes, the election would be decided by the lower house—the House of Representatives—with each state casting a single vote. Delegates also armed the chief executive with veto power over legislation as well as the right to nominate judges. Both privileges, of course, would have been unthinkable a decade earlier, but the state experiments revealed the importance of having an independent executive to maintain a balanced system of republican government.

As the meeting was concluding, some delegates expressed concern about the absence in the Constitution of a bill of rights. Such declarations had been included in most state constitutions, and Virginians such as George Mason insisted that the states and their citizens needed explicit protection from possible excesses by the federal government. While many delegates sympathized with Mason's appeal, they noted that the hour was late and, in any case, that the proposed Constitution provided sufficient security for individual rights. During the hard battles over ratification, the delegates to the convention may have regretted passing over the issue so lightly.

We, the People

The delegates adopted an ingenious procedure for ratification. Instead of submitting the Constitution to the various state legislatures, all of which had a vested interest in maintaining the status quo and most of which had two houses, either of which could block approval, they called for the election of thirteen state conventions especially chosen to review the new federal government. The delegates may have picked up this idea from the Massachusetts experiment of 1780. Moreover, the Constitution would take effect after the assent of only nine states. There was no danger, therefore, that the proposed system would fail simply because a single state like Rhode Island withheld approval.

The convention asked Gouverneur Morris of Pennsylvania, a delegate noted for his urbanity, to make final stylistic changes in the wording of the Constitution. When Morris examined the working draft, he discovered that it spoke of the collection of states forming a new government. This wording presented problems. Ratification required only nine states. No one knew whether all the states would accept the Constitution, and if not, which nine would. A strong possibility existed that several New England states would reject the document. Morris's brilliant phrase "We the People of the United States" eliminated this difficulty. The new nation was a republic of the people, not of the states.

On September 17, thirty-nine men signed the Constitution. A few members of the convention, like Mason, could not support the document. Others had already gone home. For more than three months, Madison had served as the convention's driving intellectual force. He now generously summarized the experience: "There never was an assembly of men, charged with a great and arduous trust, who were more pure in their motives, or more exclusively or anxiously devoted to the object committed to them."

Whose Constitution? Struggle for Ratification

Supporters of the Constitution recognized that ratification would not be easy. After all, the convention had been authorized only to revise the Articles, but instead it produced a new plan that fundamentally altered relations between the states and the central government. The delegates dutifully dispatched copies of the Constitution to the Congress of Confederation, then meeting in New York City, and that powerless body referred the document to the separate states without any specific recommendation. The fight for ratification had begun.

Federalists and Antifederalists

Proponents of the Constitution enjoyed great advantages over the unorganized opposition. In the contest for ratification, they took no chances. Their most astute move was the adoption of the label **Federalist.** The term cleverly suggested that they stood for a confederation of states rather than for the creation of a supreme national authority. Critics of the Constitution, who tended to be somewhat poorer, less urban, and less well educated than their opponents, cried foul, but there was little they could do. They were stuck with the name **Antifederalist,** a misleading term that made their cause seem far more obstructionist than it actually was.

The Federalists recruited the most prominent public figures of the day. In every state convention, speakers favoring the Constitution were more polished and more fully prepared than were their opponents. In New York, the campaign to win ratification sparked publication of ***The Federalist,*** a brilliant series of essays written by Madison, Hamilton, and Jay during the fall and winter of 1787 and 1788. The nation's newspapers threw themselves overwhelmingly behind the new government. In fact, few journals even bothered to carry Antifederalist writings. In some states, the Federalists adopted tactics of questionable propriety in order to gain ratification. In Pennsylvania, for example, they achieved a legal quorum for a crucial vote by dragging several opposition delegates into the meeting from the streets. In New York, Hamilton intimidated upstate Antifederalists with threats that New York City would secede from the state unless the state ratified the Constitution.

In these battles, the Antifederalists articulated a political philosophy that had broad popular appeal. They spoke the language of the Commonwealthmen (see Chapter 4). Like the extreme republicans who drafted the first state constitutions, the Antifederalists were deeply suspicious of political power. During the debates over ratification, they warned that public officials, however selected, would be constantly scheming to expand their authority.

The preservation of individual liberty required constant vigilance. It seemed obvious that the larger the republic, the greater the opportunity for political corruption. Local voters could not possibly know what their representatives in a distant national capital were doing. The government outlined in the Constitution invited precisely the kinds of problems that Montesquieu had described in his famous essay, *The Spirit of the Laws.* "In so extensive a republic," one Antifederalist declared, "the great officers of government would soon become above the control of the people, and abuse their power."

Antifederalists demanded direct, personal contact with their representatives. They argued that elected officials should reflect the character of their constituents as closely as possible. It seemed unlikely that in large congressional districts, the people would be able to preserve such close ties with their representatives. According to the Antifederalists, the Constitution favored persons wealthy enough to have forged a reputation that extended beyond a single community. Samuel Chase told the members of the Maryland ratifying convention that under the new system, "the distance between the people and their representatives will be so great that there is no probability of a farmer or planter being chosen . . . only the *gentry,* the *rich,* and the well-born will be elected."

Federalist speakers mocked their opponents' localist perspective. The Constitution deserved general support precisely because it ensured that future Americans would be represented by "natural aristocrats," individuals possessing greater insights, skills, and training than did the ordinary citizen. These talented leaders, the Federalists insisted, could discern the interests of the entire population. They were not tied to the selfish needs of local communities. "The little demagogue of a petty parish or county will find his importance annihilated [under the Constitution] and his intrigues useless," predicted Charles Cotesworth Pinckney, a South Carolina Federalist.

Historians have generally accepted the Federalist critique. It would be a mistake, however, to see the Antifederalists as "losers" or as persons who could not comprehend social and economic change. Although their rhetoric echoed an older moral view of political culture, they accepted more easily than did many Federalists a liberal marketplace in which ordinary citizens competed as equals with the rich and well-born. They believed the public good was best served by allowing individuals like themselves to pursue their own private interests. That is what they had been doing on the local level during the 1780s, and they resented the imposition of elite controls over their affairs. Although the Antifederalists lost the battle over ratification, their ideas about political economy later found many champions in the age of Andrew Jackson.

The Constitution drew support from many different types of people. In fact, historians have been unable to discover sharp correlations between wealth

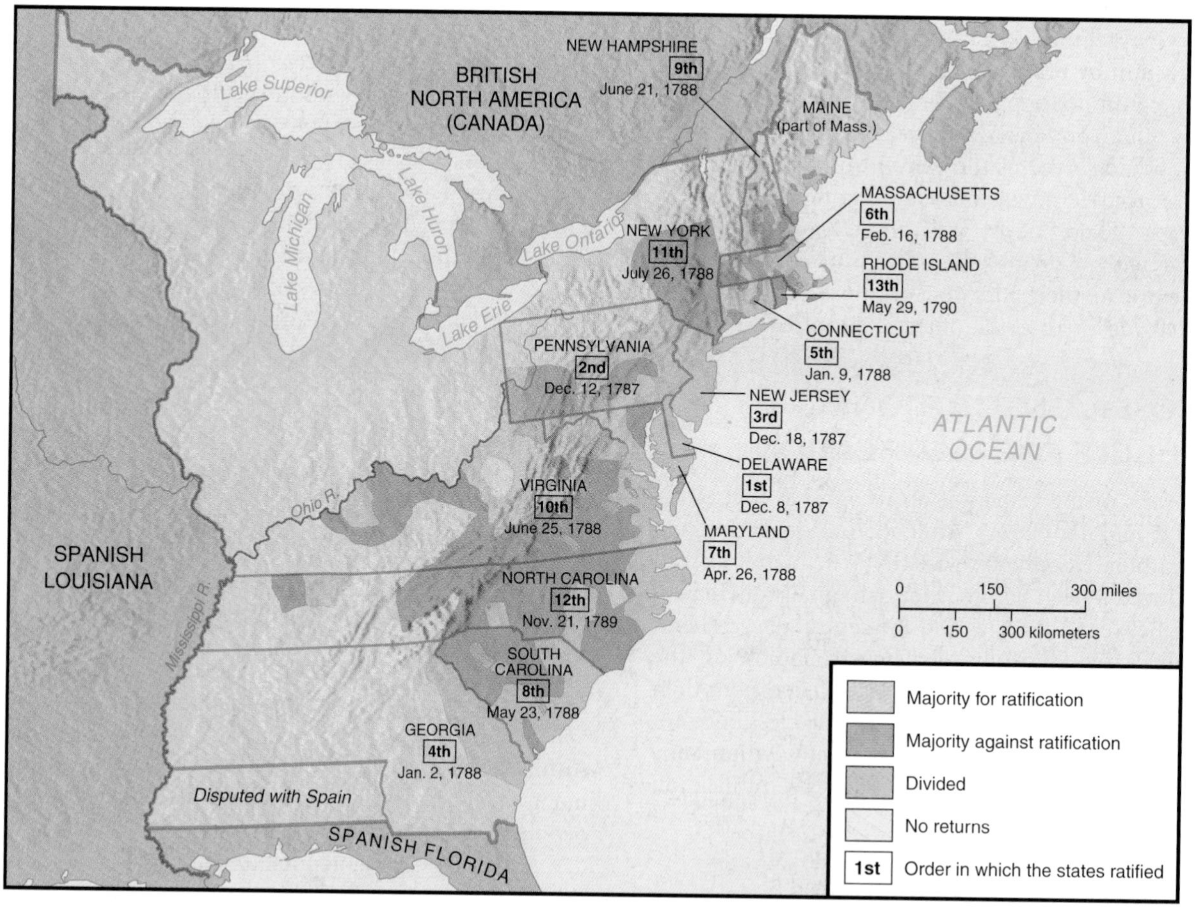

RATIFICATION OF THE CONSTITUTION *Advocates of the new Constitution called themselves Federalists, and those who opposed its ratification were known as Antifederalists.*

and occupation on the one hand and attitudes toward the proposed system of central government on the other. In general, Federalists lived in more commercialized areas than did their opponents. In the cities, artisans as well as merchants called for ratification, while those farmers who were only marginally involved in commercial agriculture frequently voted Antifederalist.

Despite passionate pleas from Patrick Henry and other Antifederalists, most state conventions quickly adopted the Constitution. Delaware acted first (December 7, 1787), and within eight months of the Philadelphia meeting, eight of the nine states required to launch the government had ratified the document. The contests in Virginia (June 1788) and New York (July 1788) generated bitter debate, but they too joined the union, leaving only North Carolina and Rhode Island outside the United States. Eventually (November 21, 1789, and May 29, 1790), even these states ratified the Constitution. Still, the vote had been very close. The Constitution was ratified in New York by a tally of 30 to 27, in Massachusetts by 187 to 168, and in Virginia by 89 to 79. A swing of a few votes in several key states could have defeated the new government.

While the state conventions sparked angry rhetoric, Americans soon closed ranks behind the Constitution. An Antifederalist who represented one Massachusetts village explained that "he had opposed the adoption of this Constitution; but that he had been overruled . . . by a majority of wise and understanding men [and that now] he should endeavor to sow the seeds of union and peace among the people he represented."

CHRONOLOGY

1776	Second Continental Congress authorizes colonies to create republican government (May) ❖ Eight states draft new constitutions; two others already enjoy republican government by virtue of former colonial charters
1777	Congress accepts Articles of Confederation after long debate (November)
1780	Massachusetts finally ratifies state constitution
1781	States ratify Articles of Confederation following settlement of Virginia's western land claims ❖ British army surrenders at Yorktown (October)
1782	States fail to ratify proposed Impost tax
1783	Newburgh Conspiracy thwarted (March) ❖ Society of the Cincinnati raises a storm of criticism ❖ Treaty of peace signed with Great Britain (September)
1785	Land Ordinance for Northwest Territory passed by Congress
1786	Jay-Gardoqui negotiations over Mississippi navigation anger southern states ❖ Annapolis Convention suggests second meeting to revise the Articles of Confederation (September) ❖ Shays's Rebellion frightens American leaders
1787–1788	The federal Constitution is ratified by all states except North Carolina and Rhode Island
1791	Bill of Rights (first ten amendments to the Constitution) ratified by states

Adding the Bill of Rights

The first ten amendments to the Constitution are the major legacy of the Antifederalist argument. In almost every state convention, opponents of the Constitution pointed to the need for greater protection of individual liberties, rights that people presumably had possessed in a state of nature. "It is necessary," wrote one Antifederalist, "that the sober and industrious part of the community should be defended from the rapacity and violence of the vicious and idle. A bill of rights, therefore, ought to set forth the purposes for which the compact is made, and serves to secure the minority against the usurpation and tyranny of the majority." The list of fundamental rights varied from state to state, but most Antifederalists demanded specific guarantees for jury trial and freedom of religion. They wanted prohibitions against cruel and unusual punishments. There was also considerable, though not universal, support for freedom of speech and freedom of the press.

Madison and others regarded the proposals with little enthusiasm. In *The Federalist* No. 84, Hamilton bluntly reminded the American people that "the constitution is itself . . . a BILL OF RIGHTS." But after the adoption of the Constitution had been assured, Madison moderated his stand. If nothing else, passage of a bill of rights would appease able men such as George Mason and Edmund Randolph, who might otherwise remain alienated from the new federal system. "We have in this way something to gain," Madison concluded, "and if we proceed with caution, nothing to lose."

The crucial consideration was caution. A number of people throughout the nation advocated calling a second constitutional convention, one that would take Antifederalist criticism into account. Madison wanted

Patrick Henry and George Mason tirelessly pressed for a bill of rights to be added to the Constitution. They feared that without specific protections, the language of the document might be twisted to tyrannical ends. The Bill of Rights, composed of the first ten amendments to the Constitution, was added in 1789 after long and contentious debate. ❖

to avoid such a meeting, and he feared that some members of the first Congress might use a bill of rights as an excuse to revise the entire Constitution or to promote a second convention.

Madison carefully reviewed these recommendations as well as the various declarations of rights that had appeared in the early state constitutions, and on June 8, 1789, he placed before the House of Representatives a set of amendments designed to protect individual rights from government interference. Madison told the members of Congress that the greatest dangers to popular liberties came from "the majority [operating] against the minority." A committee compressed and revised his original ideas into ten amendments that were ratified and became known collectively as the **Bill of Rights**. For many modern Americans these amendments are the most important section of the Constitution. Madison had hoped that additions would be inserted into the text of the Constitution at the appropriate places, not tacked onto the end, but he was overruled.

The Bill of Rights protected the freedoms of assembly, speech, religion, and the press; guaranteed speedy trial by an impartial jury; preserved the people's right to bear arms; and prohibited unreasonable searches. Other amendments dealt with legal procedure. Some opponents of the Constitution urged Congress to provide greater safeguards for states' rights, but Madison had no intention of backing away from a strong central government. Only the Tenth Amendment addressed the states' relation to the federal system. This crucial article, designed to calm Antifederalist fears, specified that those "powers not delegated to the United States by the Constitution, nor prohibited by it to the States, are reserved to the States respectively, or to the people."

On September 25, 1789, the Bill of Rights passed both houses of Congress, and by December 15, 1791, the amendments had been ratified by three-fourths of the states. Madison was justly proud of his achievement. He had effectively secured individual rights without undermining the Constitution. When he asked his friend Jefferson for his opinion of the Bill of Rights, Jefferson responded with typical republican candor: "I like [it] . . . as far as it goes; but I should have been for going further."

Conclusion: Success Depends on the People

By 1789, one phase of American political experimentation had come to an end. During these years, the people gradually, often haltingly, learned that in a republican society, they themselves were sovereign. They could no longer blame the failure of government on inept monarchs or greedy aristocrats. They bore a great responsibility. Americans had demanded a government of the people only to discover during the 1780s that in some situations, the people could not be trusted with power, majorities could tyrannize minorities, and the best of governments could abuse individual rights.

Contemporaries had difficulty deciding just what had been accomplished. A writer in the *Pennsylvania Packet* thought the American people had preserved order. "The year 1776 is celebrated," the newspaper observed, "for a revolution in favor of liberty. The year 1787 . . . will be celebrated with equal joy, for a revolution in favor of Government." But some aging patriots grumbled that perhaps order had been achieved at too high a price. In 1788, Richard Henry Lee remarked, "Tis really astonishing that the same people, who have just emerged from a long and cruel war in defense of liberty, should now agree to fix an elective despotism upon themselves and their posterity."

But most Americans probably would have accepted Franklin's optimistic assessment. As he watched the delegates to the Philadelphia convention come forward to sign the Constitution, he noted that there was a sun carved on the back of George Washington's chair. "I have," the aged philosopher noted, " . . . often in the course of the session . . . looked at [the sun] behind the President without being able to tell whether it was rising or setting; but now at length I have the happiness to know that it is a rising and not a setting sun."

Recommended Reading

The best way to comprehend the major issues debated at the Philadelphia Convention and then later at the separate state ratifying conventions is to examine the key documents of the period. One could do no better than reading James Madison, *Journal of the Federal Constitution* (reprinted in many modern editions), our only detailed account of what actually occurred during the closed debates in Philadelphia. A good introduction to the contest between the Federalists and Antifederalists over ratification is Bernard Bailyn, ed., *The Debate on the Constitution: Federalist and Antifederalist Speeches, Articles, and Letters During the Struggle Over Ratification* (1993). Gordon S. Wood analyzes late-eighteenth-century republican political thought in *The Creation of the American Republic, 1776–1787* (1969). Three recent titles interpret the complex political experience of the 1780s: Jack N. Rakove, *The Beginnings of National Politics: An Interpretive History of the Continental Congress* (1979) and *Original Meanings: Politics and Ideas in the Making of the Constitution* (1996); and Peter Onuf, *Statehood and Union: A History of the Northwest Ordinance* (1987). For a thoughtful investigation of the many different meanings of "republicanism," see Richard Beeman et al., eds., *Beyond Confederation: Origins of the Constitution and American National Identity* (1987) and Daniel T. Rodgers, "Republicanism: The Career of a Concept," *Journal of American History*, Vol. 79 (June 1992), 1–38. On the expectations of African Americans and women during this period, see the final sections of Winthrop Jordan, *White Over Black: American Attitudes Toward the Negro, 1550–1812* (1968); T. H. Breen, "Making History: The Force of Public Opinion and the Last Years of Slavery in Revolutionary Massachusetts," in Ronald Hoffman, et al., eds., *Through a Glass Darkly: Reflections on Personal Identity in Early America* (1997), 67–95; and Ronald Hoffman and Peter J. Albert, eds., *Women in the Age of the American Revolution* (1990). The Newburgh Conspiracy is explored in Richard H. Kohn, *Eagle and Sword: The Federalists and the Creation of the Military Establishment in America, 1783–1802* (1975). On Shays's Rebellion, see Robert A. Gross, ed., *In Debt to Shays: The Bicentennial of an Agrarian Rebellion* (1993).

For a list of additional titles related to this chapter's topics, please see http://www.ablongman.com/divine.

Suggested Web Sites

The Leslie Brock Center for the Study of Colonial Currency

http://etext.lib.virginia.edu/users/brock

This site includes both useful primary and secondary documents on early American currency.

Northwest Territory Alliance

http://www.nwta.com/main.html

This Revolutionary Era reenactment organization site contains several links and is an interesting look at historical reenactment.

Independence Hall National Historical Park

http://www.nps.gov/inde/visit.html

This site includes images and historical accounts of Independence Hall and other Philadelphia buildings closely associated with the nation's founding.

Biographies of the Founding Fathers

http://www.colonialhall.com/

This site provides interesting information about the men who signed the Declaration of Independence and includes a trivia section.

The Federalist Papers

http://www.law.emory.edu/FEDERAL/federalist/

This site is a collection of the most important Federalist Papers, a series of documents designed to convince people to support the new Constitution and the Federalist party.

The Constitution and the Amendments

http://www.law.emory.edu/FEDERAL/usconst.html

A searchable site to the Constitution, especially useful for its information about the Bill of Rights and other constitutional amendments.

Documents from the Continental Congress and the Constitutional Convention, 1774–1789

http://memory.loc.gov/ammem/bdsds/bdsdhome.html

The Continental Congress Broadside Collection (253 titles) and the Constitutional Convention Broadside Collection (21 titles) contain 274 documents relating to the work of Congress and the drafting and ratification of the Constitution. Items include extracts of the journals of Congress, resolutions, proclamations, committee reports, treaties, and early printed versions of the United States Constitution and the Declaration of Independence. Most broadsides are one page long; others range from one to twenty-eight pages.

The Strange Ordeal of Quok Walker

Slavery on Trial in Revolutionary Massachusetts

Revolutionary Americans bitterly denounced what they saw as Britain's plan to enslave a free people. If the conspiracy succeeded, ordinary men and women would be stripped of fundamental human rights. Throughout the colonies, gifted political thinkers such as John Adams, John Dickinson, and Thomas Jefferson condemned the plot against liberty, and in the words of the Declaration of Independence, the members of the Continental Congress dismissed George III as "unfit to be the ruler of a free people."

Such strident rhetoric raised an embarrassing problem, one that contemporary Americans, black as well as white, fully appreciated. The cause of freedom that mobilized so many patriots obviously excluded the hundreds of thousands of African Americans who had endured real slavery in every colony from Georgia to New Hampshire. Did they not, contemporaries asked, possess the same human rights as did white citizens? Was it not profoundly hypocritical to demand political freedom—"life, liberty, and the pursuit of happiness"—while every state in the new republic sanctioned racial slavery? As Abigail Adams observed to her husband, John, in 1774, "It always appeared a most iniquitous scheme to me to fight ourselves for what we are daily robbing and plundering from those who have as good a right to freedom as we have."

African Americans shared Abigail Adams's concern. During this period, they responded to the call of freedom in various ways. Some circulated petitions advocating the abolition of slavery. Others refused to wait for lawmakers and, at considerable personal risk, proclaimed their own independence from bondage. One such person was Quok Walker, a Massachusetts slave who accepted the egalitarian rhetoric of the Revolution at face value. By demanding that he be paid a fair wage for his labor, he announced that he now regarded himself as a free man. Had Walker served a less obstinate master, a person who might perhaps have acceded to the force of ideological change, this black man might have slipped unnoticed from the pages of history. Had Walker shown less courage, he might have compromised his own freedom. But that is not what occurred. The obstinate master fought to preserve his investment in a human being. When Walker courageously resisted, the entire matter came before the courts of Massachusetts Bay.

Quok Walker was born in 1753, probably in Africa soon after slave traders had captured his mother. At the age of 9 months, he was sold at public auction to a man who lived in Worcester, Massachusetts. The bill of sale listed "a certain negro man named Mingo, about twenty Years of Age, and also one negro wench named Dinah, about nineteen years of age, with child Quako." Presumably Mingo and Dinah were Quok's parents. The slave trader described the baby as "All sound & well." Following the death of his original owner a decade later, Quok Walker became the property of the man's widow. When she remarried, Walker found himself included in the new husband's estate. This man, Nathaniel Jennison, had a reputation as a harsh master. Walker spent the next fifteen years working on Jennison's farm in a small central Massachusetts village known today as Barre. In an isolated rural community that always had a very small black population, Jennison seems to have owned twelve other slaves.

Walker took control of his own life one spring day in 1781. Claiming that his "old master said [he] should be free at twenty-one," the 28-year-old Walker deserted Jennison's farm. Instead of leaving Barre—after all, other members of his family still lived in the town—

Walker offered his services for a reasonable wage to a pair of neighboring farmers, John and Seth Caldwell. Short of help during the planting season, they hired Walker, treating him like any other free laborer. Why Walker chose this precise moment to desert Jennison is not clear. Perhaps brutality was involved. An unexpected opportunity to escape may suddenly have presented itself. And surely the radical political ideas that were transforming the character of Massachusetts society played a part in Walker's decision. Somehow he had learned of a recently drafted state constitution which boldly announced that "all men are born free and equal." Walker probably interpreted these words as an invitation to judge for himself who would purchase his labor and at what rate, a right of free contract that white men in New England had long taken for granted.

Jennison rejected this line of reasoning. After searching for several weeks, he finally tracked Walker down. Jennison severely punished the fugitive. He beat Walker "about his head" and then dragged him back to his own farm, where he bound Walker and locked him in a shed. A writ presented in a later civil suit captured the horror of the event. Jennison, the court paper observed, "with force & arms . . . did make an assault, and then and there with force & arms aforesaid, seized the said Quok and threw him down and struck him several violent blows upon his back and arms with the handle of a whip."

By refusing to accept Walker's self-proclaimed emancipation and confining him, Jennison apparently believed he was acting like any slave owner who had been challenged by an insolent bondsman. Intent on forcing Walker to work on the same terms as he had before, Jennison probably thought that he had successfully concluded the matter. The next move, however, belonged to Walker.

Walker asked for and received the assistance of two young antislavery lawyers, Levi Lincoln and Caleb Strong. These recent Harvard graduates would later enjoy distinguished careers in politics and the law. On Walker's behalf, they filed civil suit against Jennison in the Worcester Inferior Court of Common Pleas, claiming damages for the assault and confinement their client had endured. Jennison could not believe what was happening. He testified in court that his actions represented the "necessary corrections" that any unruly slave could expect. Lincoln and Strong responded that no man had the right to impose such cruel treatment upon another, even if that man or woman was a slave. And although the lawyers attempted to introduce arguments concerning the legitimacy of slavery in Massachusetts, the local judges did not give Lincoln and Strong the latitude to do so. As a result, the initial case turned more on the facts of the assault itself than on the constitutional question of slavery.

Slave owners considered slaves property and marked them as such. This branding iron was used to mark a slave with the owner's initials. ❖

Jennison was a tenacious adversary. Even as the original assault case made its way through the Worcester court, he filed suit against John and Seth Caldwell, the farmers in whose fields Walker had found employment as a free laborer. The very wording of Jennison's complaint suggests the possibility that he suspected—perhaps through the currents he detected in legal and popular opinion—that his and other slave owners' human property might soon become free men and women. Jennison claimed that the Caldwells had "unlawfully solicited & seduced [his] *servant*," not that they had stolen or absconded with his slave. Using the term servant redefined Jennison's relationship in regard to Walker from that of owner to employer. In this way, Jennison attempted to exclude the issue of constitutionality of slavery from the legal proceedings.

At this moment, the various moves and countermoves in the state courts became extremely complex. But whatever legal strategies came into play, the heart of the contest remained an African's right to freedom. Through it all, Walker repeatedly swore that he was "a free man, and not the proper slave of the said Nathaniel [Jennison]." Although the issues were clear enough to Walker, he learned a hard lesson about the workings of the law. It follows its own logic, however strange that may seem to outsiders. The Inferior Court of Common Pleas ruled for Walker in his complaint against Jennison, agreeing that he "was not the proper

Negro slave of the defendant" and therefore the assault represented a clear violation of Walker's civil rights. Damages against Jennison amounted to £50, a sizable sum in revolutionary Massachusetts. But Jennison also won a victory. In his case against the Caldwells, the judges ruled in favor of Jennison, awarding him £25 to compensate for the difficulty of "reclaiming and reducing his servant to his business and services, [the Caldwells] knowing [the] said Negro to be the plaintiff's servant."

Whether the judges reached their verdicts with the larger question of the constitutionality of slavery in mind remains unclear. The members of the inferior court did not explain their decisions. The judges in Walker's suit, headed by the respected Justice Moses Gill, may have been persuaded by Walker's claim to previous manumission and may have ruled solely on the issue of assault and battery. The very fact that a slave had won such a verdict, however, clipped away at the moral and legal standing of slavery in Massachusetts. The losing defendants in each case, Jennison and the Caldwells, appealed to the Supreme Judicial Court of Massachusetts, and in those arguments the matter of slavery clearly dominated the proceedings. And it was in this forum that one man's protest against injustice acquired larger significance in the great story of human emancipation.

Even before Walker's case reached final resolution, it raised difficult questions concerning relations between the law and society in revolutionary Massachusetts. To describe Walker as a passive figure in this legal narrative would be a serious mistake. To be sure, the creation of a new republican government transformed how everyone in this state defined concepts such as freedom and equality. The explosive ideological climate shaped the character of public opinion, and this in turn affected how judges and lawyers applied the law on specific controversies. But if Walker had not declared himself a free man and resisted Jennison's tyrannical designs, the case of *Walker* v. *Jennison* would never have come before the state courts. By bearing witness against bondage, Walker became an agent for constitutional change. Timing was critical. Walker's ordeal would surely have ended in tragedy had his lawsuit not coincided with a profound shift in popular thinking about slavery.

Walker was not alone. Other slaves seized on the doctrine of natural rights and human equality. Felix Cuff of Waltham, Massachusetts, for example, fled his master along with several other slaves in 1781. When the master gathered a posse to track the fugitives down, Cuff sued the entire group for rioting. The white community refused to support the slave owner, and Cuff won. Still another Massachusetts slave, Elizabeth Freeman, known as Mumbet, put her case before the state courts at about the same time as Quok Walker. Her master's wife had wounded the black woman during a domestic argument, and Freeman cited the "insult and outrage" as the major reason she deserted the household. Claiming her liberty under the Massachusetts Declaration of Rights, she enlisted the assistance of a local lawyer to sue for manumission. When asked how she had arrived at her conviction that the law had already declared her free, she answered, "While waiting table, [she] heard gentlemen talking . . . that all people were born free and equal." And after "thinking about it," Freeman announced that she belonged "among them." A white jury concluded that the wording of the state constitution sustained her claim to equal humanity, and Mumbet spent the rest of her days working for wages in a household that treated her with respect.

However significant these cases may have been, it was Walker who made constitutional history. In the review of *Walker* v. *Jennison,* the Supreme Judicial Court allowed Levi Lincoln, who still represented Walker, to argue far beyond the specific evidence of Jennison's assault upon his client. Lincoln mounted a comprehensive attack on the intellectual and legal structures that had so long bolstered the institution of chattel slavery. Lincoln insisted upon Walker's human right as a man naturally and inalienably "free and equal," a phrase taken directly from the state's Declaration of Rights. Walker had "common origins, was descended from a common parent, clothed in the same kind of flesh, breathed the same breath of life," as did Jennison or any other man. Discounting Jennison's claim that slavery was an accepted local custom, Lincoln argued that "customs . . . against reason and right, are void." Lincoln challenged the judges to choose between possible interpretations of a flawed statute and "a higher law, the law of God."

Jennison's defense stubbornly resisted the argument of human equality. His attorneys contended that the sense of "free and equal" as Walker and Lincoln had construed it was "very different from what the people apprehended at the time the [state constitution] was established." They declared that the document would never have been ratified had the people understood that it would abolish slavery. Jennison's lawyer also implied that such a liberal reading would not be well received in the southern states and that the unity of the new republic would be seriously damaged if the Massachusetts court ruled in favor of Walker. In one last desperate attempt to hold on to his human property, Jennison maintained that slaveholders fed and cared for their aged slaves and that without such paternalism, African Americans would soon perish. At an earlier time, such self-serving arguments might have swayed the judges. But the Revolution had radi-

A portrait of Elizabeth Freeman at about age 70, painted in 1811 by Susan Sedgwick, a member of the family who helped her win her freedom. Freeman worked as a housekeeper for the Sedgwick family for many years. She is buried in the Sedgwick family plot in Stockbridge, Massachusetts. ❖

cally transformed how the law defined equality, at least in Massachusetts, and it was Walker, not Jennison, who better understood the character of the new republican society.

The court of appeals upheld the verdict against Jennison in Walker's civil suit. Jennison's lawyers failed to file proper documents with the court in his action against the Caldwells, and that verdict was overturned. Perhaps Jennison's attorneys sensed a losing battle and decided to cut their losses. Jennison later sought through legislative petition to reenter his appeal in his case against the Caldwells, but the state senate refused his request. Later that year, a criminal court at Worcester indicted Jennison on charges of "assault, battery, and false imprisonment." A jury of white men found him guilty of those offenses, and the local judges sentenced him to pay a stiff fine plus court costs. In all three actions Jennison lost, and in the words of a contemporary observer, the Reverend Jeremy Belknap, these decisions dealt "a mortal wound to slavery in Massachusetts."

After the disposition of *Walker* v. *Jennison*, slaveholders throughout the state dropped other suits and appeals that were pending, concluding wisely that no court was prepared any longer to define human beings as property. Although they endured discrimination, African Americans had broken the chains of slavery and now received wages for their work. Defiant to the end, Jennison went to court once again, this time demanding to be relieved of "his obligation to support" his "remaining slaves." The judges did not even bother to comment on the merits of the request. Walker lived out his remaining days in rural Barre, an African slave who had successfully fought for freedom in the New World.

Quok Walker's courage did not bring down the institution of slavery in the American South. In that region for a very long time, many whites mouthed similar arguments to those that Jennison had advanced before a Massachusetts court. Even the United States Constitution compromised on the issue of slavery, making a mockery of the declaration that "all men are created equal." But Walker's story should not be dismissed as an insignificant chapter in the history of resistance to racial injustice. He demonstrated that a determined individual can stand up for civil rights. Although the nation's courts have often turned a deaf ear to appeals for social equality, they have sometimes—especially in the late twentieth century—done more to protect civil rights than have the other branches of government. Occasionally, all that it takes to gain a hearing is the righteousness of a person like Quok Walker.

Questions for Discussion

- Why do you think Quok Walker equated a wage-paying job with freedom?
- Why did it take a brutal beating before the white people of Walker's community bore witness against the institution of slavery?
- Although the leaders of the Revolution protested against their own "slavery" to the British Parliament, they were slow to appreciate the need to liberate African Americans from bondage in the new republic. How can we explain the Founding Fathers' seeming hypocrasy?
- Why have modern Americans so often assumed that whites "gave" freedom to the African Americans?
- What arguments did Jennison use to persuade the judges? If he had employed different arguments do you think he would have won the case?
- Do you think that Quok Walker saw himself as a heroic figure in the fight for civil rights?

Chapter 7

Well-wishers spread flowers in front of George Washington as he rides through Trenton on his way from Virginia to New York for his inauguration as the first president of the United States in 1789. ❖

Democracy in Distress: The Violence of Party Politics, 1788–1800

Force of Public Opinion

While presiding over the first meeting of the U.S. Senate in 1789, Vice President John Adams called the senators' attention to a pressing procedural question: How would they address George Washington, the newly elected president? Adams insisted that Washington deserved an impressive title, a designation lending dignity and weight to his office. The vice president warned the senators that if they called Washington simply "president of the United States," the "common people of foreign countries [as well as] the sailors and soldiers [would] despise him to all eternity." Adams recommended "His Highness, the President of the United States, and Protector of their Liberties," but some senators favored "His Elective Majesty" or "His Excellency."

Adams's initiative caught many persons, including Washington, completely by surprise. They regarded the entire debate as ridiculous. James Madison, a member of the House of Representatives, announced that pretentious European titles were ill suited to the "genius of the people" and "the nature of our Government." Thomas Jefferson, who was then residing in Paris, could not comprehend what motivated the vice president, and in private correspondence, he repeated Benjamin Franklin's judgment that Adams "means well for his Country, is always an honest Man, often a wise one, but sometimes, and in some things, absolutely out of his senses." When the senators learned that their efforts embarrassed Washington, they dropped the topic. The leader of the new republic would be called president of the United States. One wag, however, dubbed the portly Adams "His Rotundity."

THE COMIC-OPERA QUALITY of the debate about how to address Washington should not obscure the participants' serious concern about setting government policy. The members of the first Congress could not take the survival of republican government for granted. All of them, of course, wanted to secure the Revolution. The recently ratified Constitution transferred sovereignty from the states to the people, a bold and unprecedented decision that many Americans feared would generate chronic instability. Translating constitutional abstractions into practical legislation would have been difficult, even under the most favorable conditions. But these were especially trying times. Great Britain and France, rivals in a century of war, put nearly unbearable pressures on the leaders of the new republic and, in the process, made foreign policy a bitterly divisive issue.

Although no one welcomed them, political parties gradually took shape during this period. Neither the Jeffersonians (also called the Republicans) nor the Federalists—as the two major groups were called—doubted that the United States would one day become a great commercial power. They differed, however, on how best to manage the transition from an agrarian household economy to an international system of trade and

Outline

Feature Essay

industry. The Federalists encouraged rapid integration of the United States into a world economy, but however enthusiastic they were about capitalism, they did not trust the people or local government to do the job effectively. A modern economy, they insisted, required strong national institutions that would be directed by a social elite who understood the financial challenge and who would work in the best interests of the people.

Such claims frightened persons who came to identify themselves as Jeffersonians. Strong financial institutions, they thought, had corrupted the government of Great Britain from which they had just separated themselves. They searched for alternative ways to accommodate the needs of commerce and industry. Unlike the Federalists, the Jeffersonians put their faith in the people, defined for the most part politically as white yeoman farmers. The Jeffersonians insisted that ordinary entrepreneurs, if they could be freed from intrusive government regulations, could be trusted to resist greed and crass materialism and to sustain the virtue of the republic.

During the 1790s, former allies were surprised to discover themselves at odds over such basic political issues. One person—Hamilton, for example—would stake out a position. Another, such as Jefferson or Madison, would respond, perhaps speaking a little more extravagantly than a specific issue demanded, goaded by the rhetorical nature of public debate. The first in turn would rebut passionately the new position. By the middle of the decade, this dialectic had almost spun out of control, taking the young republic to the brink of political violence.

Leaders of every persuasion had to learn to live with "public opinion." The revolutionary elite had invited the people to participate in government, but the gentlemen assumed that ordinary voters would automatically defer to their social betters. Instead, the Founders discovered they had created a rough-and-tumble political culture, a robust public sphere of cheap newspapers and street demonstrations. The newly empowered "public" followed the great debates of the period through articles they read in hundreds of highly partisan journals and magazines.

Just as television did in the twentieth century, print journalism opened politics to a large audience that previously might have been indifferent to the activities of elected officials. By the time John Adams left the presidency in 1800, he had learned this lesson well. The ordinary workers and farmers of the United States, feisty individuals who thought they were as good as anyone else and who were not afraid to let their political opinions be known, were not likely to let their president become an "Elective Majesty."

Principle and Pragmatism: Establishing a New Government

In 1788, George Washington enjoyed great popularity throughout the nation. The people remembered him as the selfless leader of the Continental Army, and even before the states had ratified the Constitution, everyone assumed he would be chosen president of the United States. He received the unanimous support of the electoral college, an achievement that no subsequent president has duplicated. Adams, a respected Massachusetts lawyer who championed national independence in 1776, was selected vice president. As Washington left his beloved Virginia plantation, Mount Vernon, for New York City, he recognized that the people—now so vocal in their support—could be fickle. "I fear," he explained with mature insight, "if the issue of public measures should not correspond with their sanguine expectations, they will turn the extravagant . . . praise . . . into equally extravagant . . . censures."

Washington bore great responsibility. The political stability of the young republic depended in large measure on how he handled himself in office. In the eyes of his compatriots, he had been transformed into a living symbol of the new government, and during his presidency (1789–1797), he carried himself with studied dignity and reserve—never ostentatious, he was the embodiment of classical republican values. Contemporaries persuaded themselves that although Washington put himself forward for elective office, he somehow stood above the hurly-burly of routine politics. A French diplomat who witnessed Washington's first inauguration in New York City reported in awe: "He has the soul, look, and figure of a hero united in him." But the adulation of Washington—however well meant—seriously affected the conduct of public affairs, for criticism of his administration was regarded as an attack on the president and, by extension, on the republic itself. During the earliest years of Washington's presidency, therefore, American public opinion discouraged partisan politics.

Washington created a strong, independent presidency. He had long advocated a strong federal government. Indeed, unlike some of his contemporaries, Washington rejected shrill states' rights claims, fearing that local political loyalties might compromise the integrity of the struggling republic, leaving it vulnerable to the predatory ambitions of European empires. While he discussed pressing issues with the members of his cabinet, he left no doubt that he alone made policy. Moreover, the first president resisted congressional efforts to restrict executive authority, especially in foreign affairs.

The first Congress quickly established executive departments. Some congressmen wanted to prohibit presidents from dismissing cabinet-level appointees without Senate approval, but James Madison—still a voice for a strong, independent executive—led a successful fight against this restriction on presidential authority. Madison recognized that the chief executive could not function unless he had personal confidence in the people with whom he worked. In 1789, Congress created the Departments of War, State, and the Treasury, and as secretaries, Washington nominated Henry Knox, Thomas Jefferson, and Alexander Hamilton, respectively. Edmund Randolph served as part-time attorney general, a position that ranked slightly lower in prestige than the head of a department. Since the secretary of the treasury oversaw the collection of customs and other future federal taxes, Hamilton could anticipate having several thousand jobs to dispense, an obvious source of political patronage.

To modern Americans accustomed to a huge federal bureaucracy, the size of Washington's government seems amazingly small. When Jefferson arrived in New York to take over the State Department, for example, he found two chief clerks, two assistants, and a part-time translator. With this tiny staff, he not only maintained contacts with the representatives of foreign governments, collected information about world affairs, and communicated with U.S. officials living overseas, but also organized the entire federal census! Since the Constitution tied congressional representation to state population, it was extremely important to count the number of inhabitants fairly and efficiently, a task that strained the resources of the new administration. In 1790, at a cost of only $44,377.28, hundreds of federal enumerators were dispatched to obtain an accurate tally of the nation's inhabitants. Anxious to impress predatory European monarchies with the rapid growth of the United States, Washington hoped the number would be large. The final figure of 3,929,214 people, of which some 700,000 were African American slaves, disappointed the president.

Jefferson immediately recognized that his new job would allow him little leisure for personal interests. The situation in other departments was similar. Overworked clerks scribbled madly just to keep up with the press of correspondence. John Adams, reviewing a bundle of letters and memos, grumbled that "often the handwriting is almost illegible." Considering these working conditions, it is not surprising that the president had difficulty persuading able people to accept positions in the new government. It is even more astonishing that Hamilton and Jefferson were able to accomplish as much as they did with so little assistance.

This unfinished portrait of George Washington was done by the portrait painter Gilbert Stuart in 1796. Because of the large popular demand for images of the first president, Stuart developed a good business copying his original painting. The image of Washington that appears on the U.S. dollar bill is based on this "Athenaeum" portrait. ❖

Congress also provided for a federal court system. The Judiciary Act of 1789, the work primarily of Connecticut Congressman Oliver Ellsworth, created a Supreme Court staffed by a chief justice and five associate justices. In addition, the statute set up thirteen district courts authorized to review the decisions of the state courts. John Jay, a leading figure in New York politics, agreed to serve as chief justice, but since federal judges in the 1790s were expected to travel hundreds of miles over terrible roads to attend sessions of the inferior courts, few persons of outstanding talent and training joined Jay on the federal bench. One who did, Judge James Iredell, complained that service on the Supreme Court had transformed him into a "travelling postboy."

Remembering the financial insecurity of the old Confederation government, the newly elected congressmen passed the tariff of 1789, a tax of approximately 5 percent on imports. The new levy generated considerable revenue for the young republic. Even before it went into effect, however, the act sparked controversy. Southern planters, who relied heavily on European imports and the northern shippers who could control the flow of imports into the South,

A view of the west front of George Washington's Virginia mansion, Mount Vernon, here depicted by an unknown artist in the 1790s. The house was the site of the first cabinet meetings of the new government of the United States. ❖

claimed that the tariff discriminated against southern interests in favor of those of northern merchants.

Conflicting Visions: Jefferson and Hamilton

Washington's first cabinet included two extraordinary personalities, Alexander Hamilton and Thomas Jefferson. Both had served the country with distinction during the Revolution, were recognized by contemporaries as men of special genius as well as high ambition, and brought to public office a powerful vision of how the American people could achieve greatness. The story of their opposing views during the decade of the 1790s provides insight into the birth and development of political parties. It also reveals how a common political ideology, republicanism, (see Chapter 6) could be interpreted in such vastly different ways that decisions about government policy turned friends into adversaries. Indeed, the falling out of Hamilton and Jefferson reflected deep, potentially explosive political divisions within American society.

Hamilton was a brilliant, dynamic young lawyer who had distinguished himself as Washington's aide-de-camp during the Revolution. Born in the West Indies, the child of an adulterous relationship, Hamilton employed charm, courage, and intellect to fulfill his inexhaustible ambition. He strove not for wealth but for reputation. Men and women who fell under his spell found him almost irresistible, but to enemies, Hamilton appeared a dark, calculating, even evil, genius. He advocated a strong central government and refused to be bound by the strict wording of the Constitution, a document Hamilton once called "a shilly shally thing." While he had fought for American independence, he admired British culture, and during the 1790s, he advocated closer commercial and diplomatic ties with the former mother country, with whom, he said, "we have a similarity of tastes, language, and general manners."

Jefferson possessed a profoundly different temperament. This tall Virginian was more reflective and shone less brightly in society than Hamilton. Contemporaries sometimes interpreted his retiring manner as lack of ambition. They misread Jefferson. He thirsted not for power or wealth but for an opportunity to advance the democratic principles that he had stated so eloquently in the Declaration of Independence. When Jefferson became secretary of state in January 1790, he had just returned from Paris where he witnessed the first exhilarating moments of the French Revolution. These earthshaking events, he believed, marked the beginning of a worldwide republican assault on absolute monarchy and aristocratic privilege. His European experiences biased Jefferson in favor of France over Great Britain when the two nations clashed.

The contrast between these two powerful figures during the early years of Washington's administration should not be exaggerated. They shared many fundamental beliefs. Indeed, both Hamilton and Jefferson insisted they were working for the creation of a strong, prosperous republic, one in which commerce would play an important role. Hamilton was publicly accused of being a secret monarchist, but he never repudiated the ideals of the American Revolution. Rather than being spokespersons for competing ideologies, Hamilton and Jefferson were different kinds of republicans who, during the 1790s, attempted as best they could to cope with unprecedented political challenges.

However much these two men had in common, serious differences emerged. Washington's secretaries disagreed on precisely how the United States should fulfill its destiny. As head of the Treasury Department, Hamilton urged his fellow citizens to think in terms of bold commercial development, of farms and factories embedded within a complex financial network that would reduce the nation's reliance on foreign trade. Because Great Britain had already established an elaborate system of banking and credit, the secretary looked to that country for economic models that might be reproduced on this side of the Atlantic.

Hamilton also voiced concerns about the role of the people in shaping public policy. His view of human nature caused him to fear democratic excess. He assumed that in a republican society, the gravest threat to political stability was anarchy rather than monarchy. "The truth," he claimed, "unquestionably is, that the only path to a subversion of the republican system of the Country is, by flattering the prejudices of the people, and exciting their jealousies and apprehensions, to throw affairs into confusion and bring on civil commotion." The best hope for the survival of the republic, Hamilton believed, lay with the country's monied classes. If the wealthiest people could be persuaded their economic self-interest could be advanced—or at least made less insecure—by the central government, then they would work to strengthen it, and by so doing, bring a greater measure of prosperity to the common people. From Hamilton's perspective, there was no conflict between private greed and public good; one was the source of the other.

On almost every detail, Jefferson challenged Hamilton's analysis. The secretary of state assumed that the strength of the American economy lay not in its industrial potential but in its agricultural productivity. The "immensity of land" represented the country's major economic resource. Contrary to the claims of some critics, Jefferson did not advocate agrarian self-sufficiency or look back nostalgically to a golden age dominated by simple yeomen. He recognized the necessity of change, and while he thought that persons who worked the soil were more responsible citizens than were those who labored in factories for wages, he encouraged the nation's farmers to participate in an expanding international market. Americans could exchange raw materials "for finer manufactures than they are able to execute themselves."

Unlike Hamilton, Jefferson expressed faith in the ability of the American people to shape policy. Throughout this troubled decade, even when the very survival of constitutional government seemed in doubt, Jefferson maintained a boundless optimism in the judgment of the common folk. He instinctively trusted the people, feared that uncontrolled government power might destroy their liberties, and insisted public officials follow the letter of the Constitution, a frame of government he described as "the wisest ever presented to men." The greatest threat to the young

During the first years of Washington's administration, neither Hamilton (left) nor Jefferson (right) recognized the full extent of their differences. But as events forced the federal government to make decisions on economic and foreign affairs, the two secretaries increasingly came into open conflict. ❖

republic, he argued, came from the corrupt activities of pseudoaristocrats, persons who placed the protection of "property" and "civil order" above the preservation of "liberty." To tie the nation's future to the selfish interests of a privileged class—bankers, manufacturers, and speculators—seemed cynical as well as dangerous. He despised speculators who encouraged "the rage of getting rich in a day," since such "gaming" activities inevitably promoted the kinds of public vice that threatened republican government. To mortgage the future of the common people by creating a large national debt struck Jefferson as particularly insane. But the responsibility for shaping the economy of the new nation fell mainly to Alexander Hamilton as the first secretary of the treasury.

Hamilton's Plan for Prosperity and Security

The unsettled state of the nation's finances presented the new government with a staggering challenge. In August 1789, the House of Representatives announced that "adequate provision for the support of public credit [is] a matter of high importance to the national honor and prosperity." However pressing the problem appeared, no one was prepared to advance a solution, and the House asked the secretary of the treasury to make suggestions.

Congress may have received more than it bargained for. Hamilton threw himself into the task. He read deeply in abstruse economic literature. He even developed a questionnaire designed to find out how the U.S. economy really worked and sent it to scores of commercial and political leaders throughout the country. But when Hamilton's three major reports—on public credit, on banking, and on manufacturers—were complete, they bore the unmistakable stamp of his own creative genius. The secretary synthesized a vast amount of information into an economic blueprint so complex, so innovative that even his allies were slightly baffled. Theodore Sedgwick, a congressman who supported Hamilton's program, explained weakly that the secretary's ideas were "difficult to understand . . . while we are in our infancy in the knowledge of Finance." Certainly, Washington never fully grasped the subtleties of Hamilton's plan.

The secretary presented his *Report on the Public Credit* to Congress on January 14, 1790. His research revealed that the nation's outstanding debt stood at approximately $54 million. This sum represented various obligations that the U.S. government had incurred during the Revolutionary War. In addition to foreign loans, the figure included loan certificates the government had issued to its own citizens and soldiers. But that was not all. The states still owed creditors approximately $25 million. During the 1780s, Americans desperate for cash had been forced to sell government certificates to speculators at greatly discounted prices, and it was estimated that approximately $40 million of the nation's debt was owed to twenty thousand people, only 20 percent of whom were the original creditors.

Funding and Assumption

Hamilton's *Report on the Public Credit* contained two major recommendations covering the areas of funding and assumption. First, under his plan, the United States promised to fund its foreign and domestic obligations at full face value. Current holders of loan certificates, whoever they were and no matter how they obtained them, could exchange the old certificates for new government bonds bearing a moderate rate of interest. Second, the secretary urged the federal government to assume responsibility for paying the remaining state debts.

Hamilton reasoned that his credit system would accomplish several desirable goals. It would significantly reduce the power of the individual states in shaping national economic policy, something Hamilton regarded as essential in maintaining a strong federal government. Moreover, the creation of a fully funded national debt signaled to investors throughout the world that the United States was now solvent, that its bonds represented a good risk. Hamilton argued that investment capital, which might otherwise flow to Europe, would remain in this country, providing a source of money for commercial and industrial investment. In short, Hamilton invited the country's wealthiest citizens to invest in the future of the United States. Critics claimed that the only people who stood to profit from the scheme were Hamilton's friends—some of whom sat in Congress and who had purchased great numbers of public securities at very low prices.

To Hamilton's great surprise, Madison—his friend and collaborator in writing *The Federalist*—attacked the funding scheme in the House of Representatives. The Virginia congressman agreed that the United States should honor its debts. He worried, however, about the citizens and soldiers who, because of personal financial hardship, had been compelled to sell their certificates at prices far below face value. Why should wealthy speculators now profit from their hardship? If the government treated the current holders of certificates less generously, Madison declared, then there might be sufficient funds to provide equitable treatment for the distressed patriots. Whatever the moral justification for Madison's plan may have been, it proved unworkable on the national level. Far too many records had been lost since the Revolution for the Treasury Department to be able to identify all the original holders. In February 1790, Congress soundly defeated Madison's proposal.

The assumption portion of Hamilton's plan unleashed even greater criticism. Some states had already paid their revolutionary debts, and Hamilton's program seemed designed to reward certain states—Massachusetts and South Carolina, for example—simply because they had failed to put their finances in order. In addition, the secretary's opponents in Congress became suspicious that assumption was merely a ploy to increase the power and wealth of Hamilton's immediate friends. "The Secretary's people scarce disguise their design," observed William Maclay, a crusty Scots-Irish senator from Pennsylvania, "which is to create a mass of debts which will justify them in seizing all the sources of government."

No doubt, Maclay and others expressed genuine fears. Some of those who protested, however, were simply looking after their own speculative schemes. These men had contracted to purchase huge tracts of vacant western lands from the state and federal governments. They anticipated that when settlers finally arrived in these areas, the price of land would skyrocket. In the meantime, the speculators had paid for the land with revolutionary certificates, often purchased on the open market at fifteen cents on the dollar. This meant that one could obtain 1000 acres for only $150. Hamilton's assumption proposal threatened to destroy these lucrative transactions by cutting off the supply of cut-rate securities. On April 12, a rebellious House led by Madison defeated assumption.

The victory was short-lived. Hamilton and congressional supporters resorted to legislative horse trading to revive his foundering program. In exchange for locating the new federal capital on the Potomac River, a move that would stimulate the depressed economy of northern Virginia, several key congressmen who shared Madison's political philosophy changed their votes on assumption. Hamilton may also have offered to give the state of Virginia more federal money than it actually deserved. Whatever the details of these negotiations may have been, in August, Washington signed assumption and funding into law. The first element of Hamilton's design was now securely in place.

❖ A Look at the Past ❖

Eagle Decoration

Following the American Revolution, patriotic symbols and themes became common in decorative arts. Eagles, a traditional symbol of strength, enjoyed especial popularity. English manufacturers printed eagles on ceramics and textiles. Women embroidered eagles and appliquéd them onto quilts and coverlets like the one pictured here. Even fine furniture displayed eagles. Such objects reflected pride in a new, untested republic. Why would consumers want patriotic emblems on their fine fabric and furniture? Were all Americans encouraged to celebrate the spirit of nationalism?

Interpreting the Constitution: The Bank Controversy

The persistent Hamilton submitted his second report to Congress in January 1791. He proposed that the U.S. government charter a national bank. This privately owned institution would be funded in part by the federal government. Indeed, since the **Bank of the United States** would own millions of dollars of new U.S. bonds, its financial stability would be tied directly to the strength of the federal government and, of course, to the success of Hamilton's program. The secretary of the treasury argued that a growing financial community required a central bank to facilitate increasingly complex commercial transactions. The institution not only would serve as the main depository of the U.S. government but also would issue currency acceptable in payment of federal taxes. Because of that guarantee, the money would maintain its value while in circulation.

Madison and others in Congress immediately raised a howl of protest. While they were not oblivious to the many important services a national bank might provide for a growing country, they suspected that banks—especially those modeled on British institutions—might "perpetuate a large monied interest" in the United States. And how was one to interpret the Constitution? That document said nothing specifically about chartering financial corporations, and critics warned that if Hamilton and his supporters were allowed to stretch fundamental law on this occasion, they could not be held back in the future. Popular liberties would be at the mercy of whoever happened to be in office. "To take a single step," Jefferson warned, "beyond the boundaries thus specifically drawn around the powers of Congress is to take possession of a boundless field of power, no longer susceptible to definition." On this issue, Hamilton stubbornly refused to compromise, announcing angrily, "This is the first symptom of a spirit which must either be killed or will kill the constitution of the United States."

This intense controversy involving his closest advisers worried the president. Even though the bank bill passed Congress (February 8), Washington seriously considered vetoing the legislation on constitutional grounds. Before doing so, however, he requested written opinions from the members of his cabinet. Jefferson's rambling, wholly predictable attack on the Bank of the United States was not one of his more persuasive performances. By contrast, in only a few days, Hamilton prepared a masterful essay titled "Defense of the Constitutionality of the Bank." He assured the president that Article I, Section 8 of the Constitution—"The Congress shall have Power . . . To make all Laws which shall be necessary and proper for carrying into Execution the foregoing Powers"—justified issuing charters to national banks. The "foregoing Powers" on which Hamilton placed so much weight were taxation, regulation of commerce, and making war. He boldly articulated a doctrine of *implied powers,* an interpretation of the Constitution that neither Madison nor Jefferson had anticipated. Hamilton's "loose construction" carried the day, and on February 25, 1791, Washington signed the bank act into law.

Hamilton triumphed in Congress, but the general public looked on his actions with growing fear and hostility. Many persons associated huge national debts and privileged banks with the decay of public virtue. Men of Jefferson's temperament believed that Great Britain—a country Hamilton held in high regard—had compromised the purity of its ancient constitution by allowing speculators to worm their way into positions of political power.

Hamilton seemed intent on reproducing this corrupt system in the United States. When news of his proposal to fund the national debt at full face value leaked out, for example, urban speculators rushed to rural areas, where they purchased loan certificates from unsuspecting citizens at bargain prices. To backcountry farmers, making money without actually engaging in physical labor appeared immoral, unrepublican, and, certainly, un-American. When the greed of a former Treasury Department official led to several serious bankruptcies in 1792, ordinary citizens began to listen more closely to what Madison, Jefferson, and their associates were saying about growing corruption in high places.

Setback for Hamilton

In his third major report, *Report on Manufactures,* submitted to Congress in December 1791, Hamilton revealed the final details of his grand design for the economic future of the United States. This lengthy document suggested ways by which the federal government might stimulate manufacturing. If the country wanted to free itself from dependence on European imports, Hamilton observed, then it had to develop its own industry, textile mills for example. Without direct government intervention, however, the process would take decades. Americans would continue to invest in agriculture. But, according to the secretary of the treasury, protective tariffs and special industrial bounties would greatly accelerate the growth of a balanced economy, and with proper planning, the United States would soon hold its own with England and France.

In Congress, the battle lines were clearly drawn. Hamilton's opponents—not yet a disciplined party but a loose coalition of men who shared Madison's and Jefferson's misgivings about the secretary's program—ignored his economic arguments. Instead, they engaged him on moral and political grounds. Madison railed against the dangers of "consolidation," a process that threatened to concentrate all power in the federal government, leaving the states defenseless. Under the Confederation, of course, Madison had stood with the nationalists against the advocates of extreme states' rights. His disagreements with Hamilton over economic policy, coupled with the necessity of pleasing the voters of his Virginia congressional district every two years, transformed Madison into a spokesman for the states, echoing the substance of Antifederalist arguments he had once hotly rejected (see Chapter 6).

Jefferson attacked the *Report on Manufactures* from a different angle. He assumed—largely because he had been horrified by Europe's urban poverty—that cities breed vice. The government, Jefferson argued, should do nothing to promote their development. He believed that Hamilton's proposal guaranteed that American workers would leave the countryside and crowd into urban centers. "I think our government will remain virtuous for many centuries," Jefferson explained, "as long as they [the people] are chiefly agricultural. . . . When they get piled upon one another in large cities, as in Europe, they will become corrupt as in Europe." And southern congressmen saw tariffs and bounties as vehicles for enriching Hamilton's northern friends at the planters' expense. The recommendations in the *Report on Manufactures* were soundly defeated in the House of Representatives.

Washington detested political squabbling. The president, of course, could see that the members of his cabinet disagreed on many issues, but in 1792, he still believed that Hamilton and Jefferson—and the people who looked to them for advice—could be reconciled. In August, he personally begged them to rise above the "internal dissensions [that are] . . . harrowing and tearing at our vitals." The appeal came too late. By the conclusion of Washington's first term, neither secretary trusted the other's judgment. Their sparring had produced congressional factions, but as yet no real political parties with permanent organizations that engaged in campaigning had come into existence. At this point, Hamilton and Jefferson only dimly appreciated the force of public opinion in shaping federal policy.

Charges of Treason: The Battle over Foreign Affairs

During Washington's second term (1793–1797), war in Europe dramatically thrust foreign affairs into the forefront of American life. The impact of this development on the conduct of domestic politics was devastating. Officials who had formerly disagreed on economic policy now began to identify their interests with either Britain or France, Europe's most powerful nations. Differences of political opinion, however trivial, were suddenly cited as evidence that one group or the other had entered into treasonous correspondence with external enemies eager to compromise the independence and prosperity of the United States. As Jefferson observed during the troubled summer of 1793, European conflict "kindled and brought forward the two parties with an ardour which our own interests merely, could never excite." The spirit of nationalism even spilled over into scientific debate. The normally dispassionate Jefferson reacted very badly when a French writer claimed, among other things, that North American animals were smaller than those found in Europe. (See the Feature Essay, "Defense of Superiority: Science in the Service of Nationalism in the Early Republic," pp. 200–201.)

Formal political organizations—the Federalists and Republicans—were born in this poisonous atmosphere. The clash between the groups developed over how best to preserve the new republic. The Republicans (Jeffersonians) advocated states' rights, strict interpretation of the Constitution, friendship with France, and vigilance against "the avaricious, monopolizing Spirit of Commerce and Commercial Men." The Federalists urged a strong national government, central economic planning, closer ties with Great Britain, and maintenance of public order, even if that meant calling out federal troops.

The Peril of Neutrality

Great Britain treated the United States with arrogance. The colonists had defeated the redcoats on land, but on the high seas, the Americans were no match for the British navy, the strongest in the world. Indeed, the young republic could not even compel its old adversary to comply with the Treaty of 1783, in which the British had agreed to vacate military posts in the Northwest Territory. In 1794, approximately a thousand British soldiers still occupied American land, an obstruction that Governor George Clinton of New York claimed had excluded U.S. citizens "from a very valuable trade to which their situation would naturally have invited them." Moreover, even though 75 percent of American imports came from Great Britain, that country refused to grant the United States full commercial reciprocity. Among other provocations, it barred American shipping from the lucrative West Indian trade.

France presented a very different challenge. In May 1789, Louis XVI, desperate for revenue, authorized a meeting of a representative assembly known as the Estates General. By so doing, the king unleashed explosive revolutionary forces that toppled the monarchy and cost him his life (January 1793). The men who seized power—and they came and went rapidly—were militant republicans, ideologues eager to liberate all Europe from feudal institutions. In the early years of the **French Revolution,** France drew on the American experience, and Thomas Paine and the Marquis de Lafayette enjoyed great popularity. But the French found they could not stop the violence of revolution. Constitutional reform turned into bloody purges, and one radical group, the Jacobins, guillotined thousands of people who were suspected of monarchist sympathies during the so-called Reign of Terror (October 1793–July 1794). These horrific events left Americans confused. While those who shared Jefferson's views cheered the spread of republicanism, others who sided with Hamilton condemned French expansionism and political excess.

In the face of growing international tension, neutrality seemed the most prudent course for the United States. But that policy was easier for a weak country to proclaim than to defend. In February 1793, France declared war on Great Britain—what the leaders of revolutionary France called the "war of all peoples against all kings"—and these powerful European rivals immediately challenged the official American position on

Feature Essay

DEFENSE OF SUPERIORITY

Science in the Service of Nationalism in the Early Republic

Nationalism promotes patriotism. Sometimes, however, expressions of pride turn malicious, belittling outsiders as inferior. When claims of superiority seem to have scientific justification, the rhetoric of nationalism can become dangerous, often outright racist. Such a situation developed during the earliest years of the American republic.

Even before the Revolution, respected scientists such as Benjamin Franklin resented disparaging remarks about American inferiority. Europeans accepted as fact the notion that New World animals and humans were smaller, slower, and less clever than those found in the Old World. Franklin dismissed the theory as nonsense, and at a dinner party in Paris he took the opportunity to demonstrate that if size really mattered, then the Americans were bigger. When the abbe Raynal, a French naturalist, announced that everything American was substandard compared to European experience, Franklin challenged his host to a test. All the Americans at the table stood; so did the French. Franklin noted with satisfaction that the Americans had the "finest stature and form." Raynal, he observed, was a "mere shrimp."

Although Franklin may have won the battle of the dinner table, other Americans still worried that New World creatures fell short of Europe standards. The seeds of doubt could be traced to a widely read scientific treatise entitled *Histoire naturelle*, the first volumes of which appeared in 1749. The author, French philosopher Comte de Buffon, argued that the climate of North America produced animals of smaller size than those encountered in the Old World. As evidence, Buffon cited the absence of elephants, lions, and other large beasts in the New World. He scoffed that the Brazilian tapir was no bigger than "the six month-old calf" of an African elephant. The only New World creatures that exceeded their Old World counterparts in size, he declared, were the toads and snakes that thrived in North America's abundant swamps. Worse yet, Buffon asserted that America's climate caused animals found in Europe to "shrink and diminish" when transported to the New World.

For Buffon, Native Americans were a case in point. On the basis of superficial reports of Indian weakness, Buffon announced that conditions in the New World were "pernicious to men, who are degenerated, debilitated, and vitiated in a surprising manner in all parts of their organization." The implications of this idea were not lost on people such as Franklin. If the American environment sapped the Indians of vitality, it was only a matter of time until European settlers who breathed the same air, drank the same water, and cultivated the same land succumbed to sloth. One of Buffon's followers counseled those colonists condemned to live in such an unpromising environment "to know how to make themselves happy . . . with mediocrity," leaving intellectual greatness to those who had wisely remained in the Old World.

After simmering for thirty years, American anger over Buffon's theory came to a boil following the American Revolution. The new nation had its honor to defend. If, as the French scientist had maintained, the North American climate caused the physical, mental, and moral abilities of humans to decline, then the republican experiment of the young United States seemed destined to fail. Having already asserted that "all men are created equal" in the Declaration of Independence, Thomas Jefferson set out to prove American equality through science. An uncompromising patriot, he devoted himself almost entirely to the defense of the fledgling republic, spending much of the 1780s poring over accounts of American animals in search of holes in Buffon's theory.

Jefferson published his results in 1785. In *Notes on the State of Virginia* he countered Buffon with a lengthy series of tables comparing the weight of European and American animals. Not surprisingly, Jefferson always tipped the scale in favor of the New World. While

A Comparative View of the Quadrupeds of Europe and America

	Europe lb.	America lb.
Bear	153.7	410.0
Red deer	288.8	273.0
Beaver	18.5	45.0
Otter	8.9	12.0
Cow	763.0	2500.0

Source: Adapted from Thomas Jefferson, *Notes on the State of Virginia* (1787).

Europe's puny flying squirrels weighed only 2.2 pounds, America could boast of impressive 4-pound squirrels. American bears were three times fatter than Old World bears. And most telling, America had once been the home of huge Ice Age animals called woolly mammoths. They looked a lot like elephants, and one recently unearthed in Kentucky matched the best Old World elephants in terms of size. In terms of size, Americans apparently had nothing to fear.

Jefferson did not stop there. Determined to use science to improve the international reputation of the United States, Jefferson commissioned the governor of New Hampshire to kill a giant moose, which was then shipped to Paris as a present for Buffon. The plan miscarried. While hunters managed to shoot the moose and drag it from the forest, the unrefrigerated voyage to France made for an extremely foul-smelling gift. For Jefferson, the unlucky moose's decay was a minor problem, since by his own reasoning, he had put to rest misguided European ideas about animal deficiency in the new American republic.

Turning from moose to men, Jefferson took a step that transformed a harmless squabble over the weight of squirrels into something much more alarming. Using the latest scientific research, Jefferson claimed that climate had almost no effect on human beings. Instead, a person's race determined his or her size, vitality, and intelligence. In this scheme, European Americans and Native Americans were equal. And, according to Jefferson, both were vastly superior to Africans. A celebration of national pride had now become a defense of racism.

To make his case, Jefferson first defended Native Americans against Buffon's assertions of climate-induced inferiority. Buffon had suggested that Indians' beardless faces and "lack of ardour for their female" demonstrated their physical inadequacy in comparison to manly Europeans. In response, Jefferson outlined the practice of face plucking. "With them it is disgraceful to be hairy," he claimed of Native Americans, because many believed "it likens them to hogs." Moreover, the Indians did not value French-style womanizing. Jefferson explained that "Their soul is wholly bent upon war," a trait that "procures them glory among men, and makes them the admiration of women." Differences between whites and Indians could be attributed not to the environment, but to culture. Indeed, he saw the two groups as a single race, so closely related that he recommended letting them "intermix, and become one people."

Jefferson rejected completely any notion that Africans in America could be part of this "one people." An unbridgeable biological gulf separated whites and Indians—groups that Jefferson lumped together as "Homo Sapiens Europaeus"—from blacks. Jefferson argued that while Europeans and Native Americans produced fine arts and engaged in brilliant oratory, African slaves exhibited no skill in painting or sculpture, and never "uttered a thought above the level of plain narration." With only anecdotal evidence to support his claims, Jefferson concluded that blacks were "inferior to the whites in the endowments of both body and mind." According to Jefferson, the harsh truth was that whether found in Africa, on Carolina rice plantations, or on the streets of Boston, Africans were a "different species of the same genus." They were a separate race, unworthy of genuine political and social equality.

Illustration of frogs from Comte de Buffon's *Histoire Naturelle*, 1749. Buffon declared that in the damp American climate only cold-blooded animals such as snakes and frogs flourished and grew larger than their European counterparts. ❖

During the late eighteenth and early nineteenth centuries, American nationalists seized upon Jefferson's ideas, seeing *Notes on the State of Virginia* as a blueprint for a republican society, grounded in rational science and dedicated to racial inequality. In a world still dominated by powerful monarchies and Old World cultures, Americans of all European backgrounds took comfort in being equal to each other and superior to African Americans. In an atmosphere of strident nationalism, few were willing to explain differences between whites and blacks as cultural or environmental. There existed, in Jefferson's words, a "real distinction which nature has made." White Americans were destined to be free, while enslaved blacks, whose labor formed the backbone of the whites' economy, must accept their lesser place in the nation's future. Jefferson's scientific thinking about race—inspired by national insecurity and a Frenchman's musing on New World toads—promoted a divisiveness in American society that continues to trouble the nation.

The execution of Louis XVI by French revolutionaries served to deepen the growing political division in America. Although they deplored the excesses of the Reign of Terror, Jeffersonian Republicans continued to support the French people. Federalists feared that the violence and lawlessness would spread to the United States. ❖

shipping: "free ships make free goods," meaning that belligerents should not interfere with the shipping of neutral carriers. To make matters worse, no one was certain whether the Franco-American treaties of 1778 (see Chapter 5) legally bound the United States to support its old ally against Great Britain.

Both Hamilton and Jefferson wanted to avoid war. The secretary of state, however, believed that nations desiring American goods should be forced to honor American neutrality and, therefore, that if Britain treated the United States as a colonial possession, if the Royal Navy stopped American ships on the high seas and forced seamen to serve the king—in other words, if it impressed American sailors—then the United States should award France special commercial advantages. Hamilton thought Jefferson's scheme insane. He pointed out that Britain possessed the largest navy in the world and was not likely to be coerced by American threats. The United States, he counseled, should appease the former mother country even if that meant swallowing national pride.

A newly appointed French minister to the United States, Edmond Genêt, precipitated the first major diplomatic crisis. This incompetent young man arrived in Charleston, South Carolina, in April 1793. He found considerable popular enthusiasm for the French Revolution, and, buoyed by this reception, he authorized privately owned American vessels to seize British ships in the name of France. Such actions clearly violated U.S. neutrality and invited British retaliation. When U.S. government officials warned Genêt to desist, he threatened to take his appeal directly to the American people, who presumably loved France more than did members of Washington's administration.

This confrontation particularly embarrassed Jefferson, the most outspoken pro-French member of the cabinet. He described Genêt as "hot headed, all imagination, no judgment, passionate, disrespectful and even indecent towards the President." Washington did not wait to discover whether the treaties of 1778 were still in force. Before he had formally received the impudent French minister, the president issued a Proclamation of Neutrality (April 22). Ironically, after Genêt learned that the Jacobins intended to cut off his head if he returned to France, he requested asylum, married into an extremely wealthy family, and spent the remainder of his life in New York.

Jay's Treaty Sparks Domestic Unrest

Great Britain failed to take advantage of Genêt's insolence. Instead, it pushed the United States to the brink of war. British forts in the Northwest Territory remained a constant source of tension. In June 1793, a new element was added. The London government blockaded French ports to neutral shipping, and in November, its navy captured several hundred American vessels trading in the French West Indies. The British had not even bothered to give the United States advance warning of a change in policy. Outraged members of Congress, especially those who identified with Jefferson and Madison, demanded retaliation, an embargo, a stoppage of debt payment, even war.

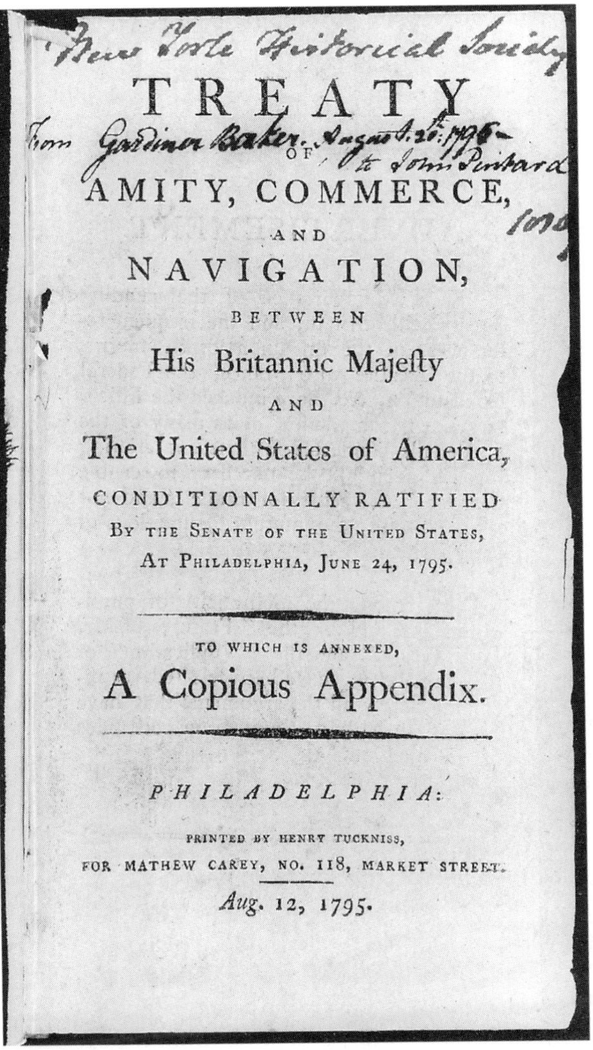
TREATY
OF
AMITY, COMMERCE,
AND
NAVIGATION,
BETWEEN
His Britannic Majefty
AND
The United States of America,
CONDITIONALLY RATIFIED
BY THE SENATE OF THE UNITED STATES,
AT PHILADELPHIA, JUNE 24, 1795.

TO WHICH IS ANNEXED,
A Copious Appendix.

PHILADELPHIA:
PRINTED BY HENRY TUCKNISS,
FOR MATHEW CAREY, NO. 118, MARKET STREET.
Aug. 12, 1795.

Printer Matthew Carey helped fire the protest over Jay's Treaty by printing the terms of the agreement and adding a series of partisan comments to the appendix. ❖

Before this rhetoric produced armed struggle, Washington made one final effort to preserve peace. In May 1794, he sent Chief Justice John Jay to London to negotiate a formidable list of grievances. The effort resulted in a political humiliation known simply as **Jay's Treaty.** Jay's main objectives were removal of the British forts on U.S. territory, payment for ships taken in the West Indies, improved commercial relations, and acceptance of the American definition of neutral rights.

Jefferson's supporters—by now openly called the Republican interest—anticipated a treaty favorable to the United States. After all, they explained, the war with France had not gone well for Great Britain, and the British people were surely desperate for American foodstuffs. Even before Jay departed, however, his mission stood little chance of success. Hamilton, anxious as ever to placate the British, had already secretly informed British officials that the United States would compromise on most issues.

Not surprisingly, when Jay reached London, he encountered polite but firm resistance. The chief justice did persuade the British to abandon their frontier posts and to allow small American ships to trade in the British West Indies, but they rejected out of hand the U.S. position on neutral rights. The Royal Navy would continue to search American vessels on the high seas for contraband and to impress sailors suspected of being British citizens. Moreover, there would be no compensation for the ships seized in 1793 until the Americans paid British merchants for debts contracted before the Revolution. And to the particular annoyance of Southerners, not a word was said about the slaves the British army had carried off at the conclusion of the war. While Jay salvaged the peace, he appeared to have betrayed the national interest.

News of Jay's Treaty—perhaps more correctly called Hamilton's Treaty—produced an angry outcry in the nation's capital. Even Washington was apprehensive. He submitted the document to the Senate without recommending ratification, a sign that the president was not entirely happy with the results of Jay's mission. After an extremely bitter debate, the upper house, controlled by Federalists, accepted a revised version of the treaty (June 1795). The vote was 20 to 10, a bare two-thirds majority.

The details of the Jay agreement soon leaked to the press. This was an important moment in American political history. The popular journals sparked a firestorm of objection. Throughout the country, people who had generally been apathetic about national politics were swept up in a wave of protest. Urban mobs condemned Jay's alleged sellout; rural settlers burned him in effigy. Jay jokingly told friends he could find his way across the country simply by following the light of those fires. Southerners announced they would not pay prerevolutionary debts to British merchants. The Virginia legislature proposed a constitutional amendment reducing the Senate's role in the treaty-making process. As Fisher Ames, a Federalist congressman, noted darkly, "These little whirlwinds of dry leaves and dirt portend a hurricane."

His prediction proved accurate. The storm broke in the House of Representatives. Republican congressmen, led by Madison, thought they could stop Jay's Treaty by refusing to appropriate funds for its implementation. As part of their plan, they demanded that Washington show the House state papers relating to Jay's mission. The challenge raised complex issues of constitutional law. The House, for example, was claiming a voice in treaty ratification, a power explicitly reserved to the Senate. Second, there was the question of executive secrecy in the interest of national security. Could the president withhold information from the public? According to Washington—as well as all subsequent presidents—the answer was yes. He took the occasion to lecture the rebellious representatives that "the nature of foreign negotiations requires caution; and their success must often depend on secrecy."

The president still had a trump card to play. He raised the possibility that the House was really contemplating his impeachment. Such an action was, of course, unthinkable. Even criticizing Washington in public was politically dangerous, and as soon as he redefined the issue before Congress, petitions supporting the president flooded into the nation's capital. The Maryland legislature, for example, declared its "unabated reliance on the integrity, judgment, and patriotism of the President of the United States," a statement that clearly called into question the patriotism of certain Republican congressmen. The Federalists won a stunning tactical victory over the opposition. Had a less popular man than Washington occupied the presidency, however, they would not have fared so well. The division between the two parties was beyond repair. The Republicans labeled the Federalists "the British party"; the Federalists believed that the Republicans were in league with the French.

By the time Jay's Treaty became law (June 14, 1795), the two giants of Washington's first cabinet had retired. Late in 1793, Jefferson returned to his Virginia plantation, Monticello, where, despite his separation from day-to-day political affairs, he remained the chief spokesman for the Republican party. His rival, Hamilton, left the Treasury in January 1795 to practice law in New York City. He maintained close ties with important Federalist officials, and even more than Jefferson, Hamilton concerned himself with the details of party organization.

Pushing the Native Americans Aside

Before Great Britain finally withdrew its troops from the Great Lakes and Northwest Territory, its military officers encouraged local Indian groups—the Shawnees, Chippewas, and Miamis—to attack settlers and traders from the United States. The Indians, who even without British encouragement fully appreciated that the newcomers intended to seize their land, won several impressive victories over federal troops in the area that would become western Ohio and Indiana. In 1790, General Josiah Harmar led his soldiers into an ambush. The following year, an army under General Arthur St. Clair suffered more than nine hundred casualties near the Wabash River. But the Indians were militarily more vulnerable than they realized, for when confronted with a major U.S. army under the command of General Anthony Wayne, they received no support from their former British allies. At the battle of Fallen Timbers (August 20, 1794), Wayne's forces crushed Indian resistance in the Northwest Territory, and the native peoples were compelled to sign the Treaty of Greenville, formally ceding to the U.S. government the land that became Ohio. In 1796, the last British soldiers departed for Canada.

Shrewd negotiations mixed with pure luck helped secure the nation's southwestern frontier. For complex

At the Treaty of Greenville in 1795, negotiators shared this calumet, or peace pipe, a spiritually symbolic act for Native Americans. This superficial recognition of the legitimacy of Native American cultures barely disguised the Indians' crushing loss of sovereignty. ❖

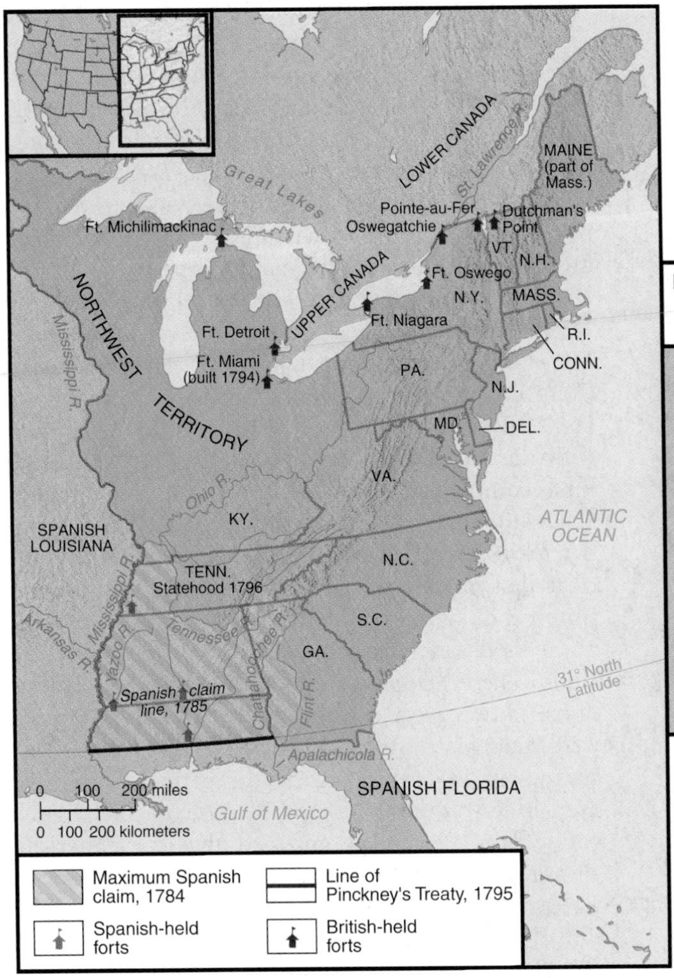

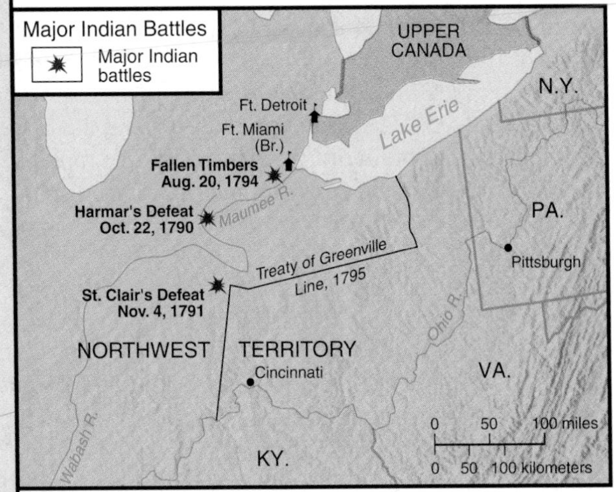

CONQUEST OF THE WEST *Withdrawal of the British, defeat of Native Americans, and negotiations with Spain secured the nation's frontiers.* ❖

reasons having to do with the state of European diplomacy, Spanish officials in 1795 encouraged the U.S. representative in Madrid to discuss the navigation of the Mississippi River. Before this initiative, the Spanish government not only had closed the river to American commerce but also had incited the Indians of the region to harass settlers from the United States (see Chapter 6). Relations between the two countries probably would have deteriorated further had the United States not signed Jay's Treaty. The Spanish assumed—quite erroneously—that Great Britain and the United States had formed an alliance to strip Spain of its North American possessions.

To avoid this imagined disaster, officials in Madrid offered the American envoy, Thomas Pinckney, extraordinary concessions: the opening of the Mississippi, the right to deposit goods in New Orleans without paying duties, a secure southern boundary on the 31st parallel (a line roughly parallel to the northern boundary of Florida and running west to the Mississippi), and a promise to stay out of Indian affairs. An amazed Pinckney signed the Treaty of San Lorenzo (also called Pinckney's Treaty) on October 27, 1795, and in March the Senate ratified the document without a single dissenting vote. Pinckney, who came from a prominent South Carolina family, instantly became the hero of the Federalist party.

Popular Political Culture

More than any other event during Washington's administration, ratification of Jay's Treaty generated intense political strife. Even as members of Congress voted as Republicans or Federalists, they condemned the rising partisan spirit as a grave threat to the stability of the United States. Popular writers equated "party" with "faction" and "faction" with "conspiracy to overthrow legitimate authority." Party conflict also suggested that Americans had lost the sense of common purpose that had united them during the Revolution. Contemporaries did not appreciate the beneficial role that parties could play by presenting alternative solutions to foreign and domestic problems. Organized opposition smacked of disloyalty and therefore had to be eliminated by any means—fair or foul. These intellectual currents coupled with the existence of two parties created an atmosphere that bred suspicion. In the name of national unity, Federalists as well as Republicans advocated the destruction of political adversaries.

Informing the Public: News and Politics

More than any other single element, newspapers transformed the political culture of the United States. Americans were voracious readers. In 1789, a foreign visitor observed, "The common people [here] are on a footing, in point of literature, with the middle ranks of Europe. They all read and write, and understand arithmetic; almost every little town now furnishes a circulating library."

A rapidly expanding number of newspapers appealed to this large literate audience. John Fenno established the *Gazette of the United States* (1789), a journal that supported Hamilton's political philosophy. The Republicans responded in October 1790 with Philip Freneau's influential *National Gazette.* While the format of the publications was similar to that of the colonial papers, their tone was quite different. These fiercely partisan journals presented rumor and opinion as fact. Public officials were regularly dragged through the rhetorical mud. Jefferson, for example, was accused of cowardice; Hamilton, vilified as an adulterer. As party competition became more bitter, editors showed less restraint. One Republican paper even suggested that George Washington had been a British agent during the Revolution. No wonder Fisher

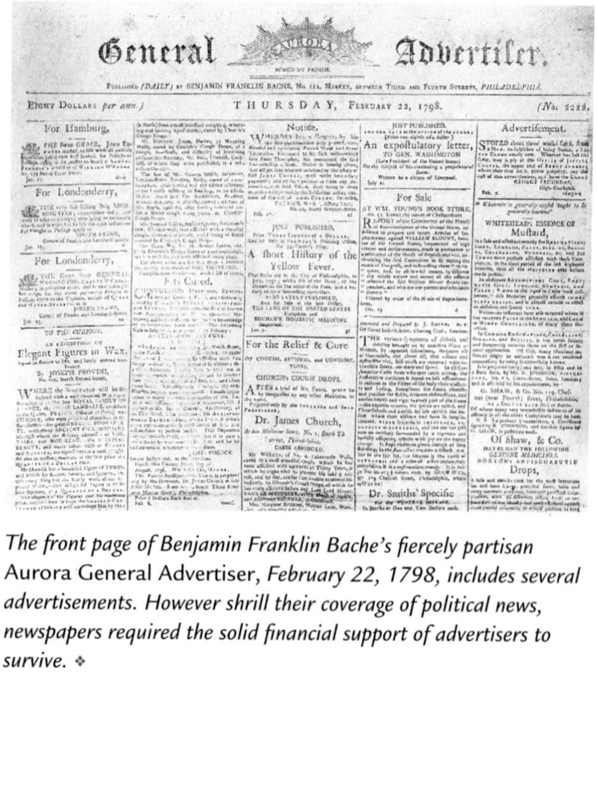
General AURORA Advertiser.
Published (DAILY) by BENJAMIN FRANKLIN BACHE, No. 112, Market, between Third and Fourth Streets, PHILADELPHIA.
Eight Dollars per ann.) THURSDAY, February 22, 1798. (No. 2222.
For Hamburg,
For Londonderry,
For Londonderry,
Notice.
JUST PUBLISHED.
An expostulatory letter,
TO GEN. WASHINGTON
For Sale
AT WM. YOUNG'S BOOK STORE,
A short History of the Yellow Fever.
For the Relief & Cure
Dr. James Church,
Dr. Smith's Specific
Advertisement.
WHITEHEAD'S ESSENCE OF Mustard,
Of Shaw, & Co.
Drops,
Elegant Figures in Wax.

The front page of Benjamin Franklin Bache's fiercely partisan Aurora General Advertiser, *February 22, 1798, includes several advertisements. However shrill their coverage of political news, newspapers required the solid financial support of advertisers to survive.* ❖

Ames announced in 1801, "The newspapers are an overmatch for any government."

Even poets and essayists were caught up in the political fray. The better writers—and this was not a period of outstanding artistic achievement in the United States—often produced party propaganda. However much Freneau aspired to fame as a poet, he is remembered today chiefly as a champion of the Republican cause. Noah Webster, who later published *An American Dictionary of the English Language* (1828), spent the 1790s editing a strident Federalist journal, *American Minerva,* in New York City. And Joel Barlow, a Connecticut poet of modest talent, celebrated the French Revolution in verse, thus identifying himself with the party of Jefferson. American writers sometimes complained that the culture of the young republic was too materialistic, too unappreciative of the subtler forms of art then popular in Europe. But it was clear that poets who ignored patriotism and politics simply did not sell well in the United States.

This decade also witnessed the birth of political clubs. These "Democratic" or "Republican" associations, as they were called, first appeared in 1793 and were modeled on the political debating societies that sprang up in France during the early years of the French Revolution. Perhaps because of the French connection, Federalists assumed that the American clubs represented the interests of the Republican party. Their purpose was clearly political indoctrination. The Philadelphia Society announced it would "cultivate a just knowledge of rational liberty." A Democratic club in New York City asked each member to declare himself a "firm and steadfast friend of the EQUAL RIGHTS OF MAN."

By 1794, at least twenty-four clubs were holding regular meetings. How many Americans actually attended their debates is not known, but regardless of the number, the clubs obviously complemented the newspapers in providing the common people with highly partisan political information.

Whiskey Rebellion: Charges of Republican Conspiracy

Political tensions became explosive in 1794. The Federalists convinced themselves that the Republicans were actually prepared to employ violence against the U.S. government. Although the charge was without foundation, it took on plausibility in the context of growing party strife.

The crisis developed when a group of farmers living in western Pennsylvania protested a federal excise tax on distilled whiskey that Congress had originally passed in 1791. These men did not relish paying any taxes, but this tax struck them as particularly unfair.

Frontier farmers in western Pennsylvania regarded Hamilton's excise tax on whiskey as a direct threat to their survival. Crops of rye and corn could not be economically transported to eastern markets from the frontier because of bulk and poor roads, so distilled whiskey, more easily transported, became the currency of the frontier. Crying "Liberty and No Excise" these frontier rebels tarred and feathered federal revenue agents and brought tax collection to a halt. Washington ended their activities with an army of 15,000 militia in 1794 (he is shown here reviewing the army) and minimum violence. Victory brought the federal government renewed respect, but created new powerful popular opposition to the Hamiltonian Federalists and figured prominently in the evolution of the two-party system. ❖

They made a good deal of money distilling their grain into whiskey, and the excise threatened to put them out of business.

Largely because the Republican governor of Pennsylvania refused to suppress the angry farmers, Washington and other leading Federalists assumed that the insurrection represented a direct political challenge. The president called out fifteen thousand militiamen, and, accompanied by Hamilton, he marched against the rebels. The expedition was an embarrassing fiasco. The distillers disappeared, and predictably enough, no one living in the Pittsburgh region seemed to know where the troublemakers had gone. Two supposed rebels were convicted of high crimes against the United States; one was reportedly a "simpleton" and the other insane. Washington eventually pardoned both men. As peace returned to the frontier, Republicans gained much electoral support from voters the Federalists had alienated.

In the national political forum, however, the **Whiskey Rebellion** had just begun. Spokesmen for both parties offered sinister explanations for the seemingly innocuous affair. Washington blamed the Republican clubs for promoting civil unrest. He apparently believed that the opposition party had dispatched French agents to western Pennsylvania to undermine the authority of the federal government. In November 1794, Washington informed Congress that these "self-created societies"—in other words, the Republican political clubs—had inspired "a spirit inimical to all order." Indeed, the Whiskey Rebellion had been "fomented by combinations of men who . . . have disseminated, from an ignorance or perversion of facts, suspicions, jealousies, and accusations of the whole Government."

The president's interpretation of this rural tax revolt was no less charitable than the conspiratorial explanation offered by the Republicans. Jefferson labeled the entire episode a Hamiltonian device to create an army for the purpose of intimidating Republicans. How else could one explain the administration's gross overreaction to a few disgruntled farmers? "An insurrection was announced and proclaimed and armed against," Jefferson noted, "but could never be found." The response of both parties reveals a pervasive fear of some secret evil design to destroy the republic. The clubs and newspapers—as yet unfamiliar tools for mobilizing public opinion—fanned these anxieties, convincing many government officials that the First Amendment should not be interpreted as protecting political dissent.

Washington's Farewell

In September 1796, Washington published his famed **Farewell Address,** formally declaring his intention to retire from the presidency. In the address, which was printed in newspapers throughout the country, Washington warned against all political factions. Written in large part by Hamilton, who drew on a draft prepared several years earlier by Madison, the address served narrowly partisan ends. The product of growing political strife, it sought to advance the Federalist cause in the forthcoming election. By waiting until September to announce his retirement, Washington denied the Republicans valuable time to organize an effective campaign. There was an element of irony in this initiative. Washington had always maintained he stood above party. While he may have done so in the early years of his presidency, events such as the signing of Jay's Treaty and the suppression of the Whiskey Rebellion transformed him in the eyes of many Americans into a spokesman solely for Hamilton's Federalist party.

Washington also spoke to foreign policy matters in the address. He counseled the United States to avoid making any permanent alliances with distant nations that had no real interest in promoting American security. This statement guided foreign relations for many years and became the credo of later American isolationists, who argued that the United States should steer clear of foreign entanglements.

John Adams in the suit and sword he wore for his 1797 inauguration. The portrait is by English artist William Winstanley, 1798. Throughout his presidency, Adams was plagued by political extremists, Federalist as well as Republican. ❖

The Adams Presidency

The election of 1796 took place in an atmosphere of mutual distrust. Jefferson, soon to be the vice president, informed a friend that "an Anglican and aristocratic party has sprung up, whose avowed object is to draw over us the substance, as they have already done the forms, of British government." On their part, the Federalists were convinced their Republican opponents wanted to hand the government over to French radicals. By modern standards, the structures of both political parties were primitive. Leaders of national stature, such as Madison and Hamilton, wrote letters encouraging local gentlemen around the country to support a certain candidate, but no one attempted to canvass the voters in advance of the election.

During the campaign, the Federalists sowed the seeds of their eventual destruction. Party stalwarts agreed that John Adams should stand against the Republican candidate, Thomas Jefferson. Hamilton, however, could not leave well enough alone. From his law office in New York City, he schemed to deprive Adams of the presidency. His motives were obscure. He apparently feared that an independent-minded Adams would be difficult to manipulate. He was correct.

Hamilton exploited an awkward feature of the electoral college. In accordance with the Constitution, each elector cast two ballots, and the person who gained the most votes became president. The runner-up, regardless of party affiliation, served as vice president. Ordinarily the Federalist electors would have cast one vote for Adams and one for Thomas Pinckney, the hero of the negotiations with Spain and the party's choice for vice president. Everyone hoped, of course, there would be no tie. Hamilton secretly urged southern Federalists to support only Pinckney, even if that meant throwing away an elector's second vote. If everything had gone according to plan, Pinckney would have received more votes than Adams, but when New Englanders loyal to Adams heard of Hamilton's

The Election of 1796

Candidate	Party	Electoral Vote
J. Adams	Federalist	71
Jefferson	Republican	68
T. Pinckney	Federalist	59
Burr	Republican	30

maneuvering, they dropped Pinckney. When the votes were counted, Adams had 71, Jefferson 68, and Pinckney 59. Hamilton's treachery not only angered the new president but also heightened tensions within the Federalist party.

Adams assumed the presidency under intolerable conditions. He found himself saddled with the members of Washington's old cabinet, a group of second-raters who regularly consulted with Hamilton behind Adams's back. The two most offensive were Timothy Pickering, secretary of state, and James McHenry, secretary of war. But to have dismissed them summarily would have called Washington's judgment into question, and Adams was not prepared to take that risk publicly.

Adams also had to work with a Republican vice president. Adams hoped that he and Jefferson could cooperate as they had during the Revolution—they had served together on the committee that drafted the Declaration of Independence—but partisan pressures soon overwhelmed the president's good intentions. Jefferson recorded their final attempt at reconciliation. Strolling home one night after dinner, Jefferson and Adams reached a place "where our road separated, his being down Market Street, mine along Fifth, and we took leave; and he [Adams] never after that . . . consulted me as to any measure of the government."

The XYZ Affair and Domestic Politics

Foreign affairs immediately occupied Adams's full attention. The French government regarded Jay's Treaty as an affront. By allowing Great Britain to define the conditions for neutrality, the United States had in effect sided with that nation against the interests of France.

Relations between the two countries had steadily deteriorated. The French refused to receive Charles Cotesworth Pinckney, the U.S. representative in Paris. Pierre Adet, the French minister in Philadelphia, openly tried to influence the 1796 election in favor of the Republicans. His meddling in domestic politics not only embarrassed Jefferson, it also offended the American people. The situation then took a violent turn. In 1797, French privateers began seizing American ships. Since neither the United States nor France officially declared war, the hostilities came to be known as the Quasi-War.

Hamilton and his friends welcomed a popular outpouring of anti-French sentiment. The High Federalists—as members of Hamilton's wing of the party were called—counseled the president to prepare for all-out war, hoping that war would purge the United States of French influence. Adams was not persuaded to escalate the conflict. He dispatched a special commission in a final attempt to remove the sources of antagonism. This famous negotiating team consisted of Charles Pinckney, John Marshall, and Elbridge Gerry. They were instructed to obtain compensation for the ships seized by French privateers as well as release from the treaties of 1778. Federalists still worried that this old agreement might oblige the United States to defend French colonies in the Caribbean against British attack, something they were extremely reluctant to do. In exchange, the commission offered France the same commercial privileges granted to Great Britain in Jay's Treaty. While the diplomats negotiated for peace, Adams talked of strengthening American defenses, rhetoric that pleased the militant members of his own party.

The commission was shocked by the outrageous treatment it received in France. Instead of dealing directly with Talleyrand, the minister of foreign relations, they met with obscure intermediaries who demanded a huge bribe. The commission reported that Talleyrand would not open negotiations unless he was given \$250,000. In addition, the French government expected a "loan" of millions of dollars. The Americans refused to play this insulting game. Pinckney angrily sputtered,

This cartoon, Property Protected, à la Françoise *(1798), captures the anti-French sentiment many Americans felt after President Adams disclosed the papers of the XYZ Affair. America—depicted as a young maiden—is being plundered by five Frenchmen, who represent the five directors of the French government.* ❖

"No, no, not a sixpence," and with Marshall he returned to the United States. When they arrived home, Marshall offered his much-quoted toast: "Millions for defense, but not one cent for tribute."

Diplomatic humiliation set off a domestic political explosion. When Adams presented the commission's official correspondence before Congress—the names of Talleyrand's lackeys were labeled X, Y, and Z—the Federalists burst out with a war cry. At last, they would be able to even old scores with the Republicans. In April 1798, a Federalist newspaper in New York City announced ominously that any American who refused to censure France "must have a soul black enough to be *fit for treasons, strategems,* and *spoils.*" Rumors of conspiracy, referred to as the **XYZ Affair,** spread throughout the country. Personal friendships between Republicans and Federalists were shattered. Jefferson described the tense political atmosphere in a letter to an old colleague: "You and I have formerly seen warm debates and high political passions. But gentlemen of different politics would then speak to each other, and separate the business of the Senate from that of society. It is not so now. Men who have been intimate all their lives, cross the streets to avoid meeting, and turn their heads another way, lest they should be obliged to touch their hats."

Crushing Political Dissent

In the spring of 1798, High Federalists assumed that it was just a matter of time until Adams asked Congress for a formal declaration of war. In the meantime, they pushed for a general rearmament, new fighting ships, additional harbor fortifications, and most important, a greatly expanded U.S. Army. About the need for land forces, Adams remained understandably skeptical. He saw no likelihood of French invasion.

The president missed the political point. The army the Federalists wanted was intended not to thwart French aggression but to stifle internal opposition. Indeed, militant Federalists used the XYZ Affair as the occasion to institute what Jefferson termed the "reign of witches." The threat to the Republicans was not simply a figment of the vice president's overwrought imagination. When Theodore Sedgwick, now a Federalist senator from Massachusetts, first learned of the commission's failure, he observed in words that capture the High Federalists' vindictiveness, "It will afford a glorious opportunity to destroy faction. Improve it."

During the summer of 1798, a provisional army gradually came into existence. George Washington agreed to lead the troops, but he would do so only on condition that Adams appoint Hamilton as second in command. This demand placed the president in a terrible dilemma. Several revolutionary veterans—Henry Knox, for example—outranked Hamilton. Moreover, the former secretary of the treasury had consistently undermined Adams's authority, and to give Hamilton a position of real power in the government seemed awkward at best. When Washington insisted, however, Adams was forced to support Hamilton.

The chief of the High Federalists threw himself into the task of recruiting and supplying the troops. No detail escaped his attention. He and Secretary of War McHenry made certain that in this political army, only loyal Federalists received commissions. They even denied Adams's son-in-law a post. The entire enterprise took on an air of unreality. Hamilton longed for military glory, and he may have contemplated attacking Spain's Latin American colonies. His driving obsession, however, was the restoration of political order. No doubt, he agreed with a Federalist senator from Connecticut who predicted that the Republicans "never will yield till violence is introduced; we must have a partial civil war . . . and the bayonet must convince some, who are beyond the reach of other arguments."

Hamilton should not have treated Adams with such open contempt. After all, the Massachusetts statesman was still the president, and without presidential cooperation, Hamilton could not fulfill his grand military ambitions. Yet whenever pressing questions concerning the army arose, Adams was nowhere to be found. He let commissions lie on his desk unsigned; he took overlong vacations to New England. He made it quite clear his first love was the navy. In May 1798, the president persuaded Congress to establish the Navy Department. For this new cabinet position, he selected Benjamin Stoddert, a person who did not take orders from Hamilton. Moreover, Adams further infuriated the High Federalists by refusing to ask Congress for a formal declaration of war. When they pressed him, Adams threatened to resign, making Jefferson president. As the weeks passed, the American people increasingly regarded the idle army as an expensive extravagance.

Silencing Political Opposition: The Alien and Sedition Acts

The Federalists did not rely solely on the army to crush political dissent. During the summer of 1798, the party's majority in Congress passed a group of bills known collectively as the **Alien and Sedition Acts.** This legislation authorized the use of federal courts and the powers of the presidency to silence the Republicans. The acts were born of fear and vindictiveness, and in their efforts to punish the followers of Jefferson, the Federalists created the nation's first major crisis over civil liberties.

Congress drew up three separate Alien Acts. The first, the Alien Enemies Law, vested the president with extraordinary wartime powers. On his own authority, he could detain or deport citizens of nations with which the United States was at war and who behaved in a manner he thought suspicious. Since Adams refused to ask for a declaration of war, this legislation never went into effect. A second act, the Alien Law, empowered the president to expel any foreigner from the United States simply by executive decree. Congress limited the acts to two years, and while Adams did not attempt to enforce them, the mere threat of arrest caused some Frenchmen to flee the country. The third act, the Naturalization Law, was the most flagrantly political of the group. The act established a fourteen-year probationary period before foreigners could apply for full U.S. citizenship. Federalists recognized that recent immigrants, especially the Irish, tended to vote Republican. The Naturalization Law, therefore, was designed to keep "hordes of wild Irishmen" away from the polls for as long as possible.

The Sedition Law struck at the heart of free political exchange. It defined criticism of the U.S. government as criminal libel; citizens found guilty by a jury were subject to fines and imprisonment. Congress entrusted enforcement of the act to the federal courts. Republicans were justly worried that the Sedition Law undermined rights guaranteed by the First Amendment. When they protested, however, the High Federalists dismissed their complaints. The Constitution, they declared, did not condone "the most groundless and malignant lies, striking at the safety and existence of the nation." They were determined to shut down the opposition press and were willing to give the government what seemed almost dictatorial powers to achieve that end. The Jeffersonians also expressed concern over the federal judiciary's expanded role in punishing sedition. They believed such matters were best left to state officials.

Americans living in widely scattered regions of the country soon witnessed political repression firsthand. District courts staffed by Federalist appointees indicted seventeen people for criticizing the government. Several cases were absurd. In Newark, New Jersey, for example, a drunkard staggered out of a tavern to watch a sixteen-gun salute fired in honor of President Adams. When the man expressed the hope a cannonball might lodge in Adams's ample posterior, he was arrested. No wonder a New York City journal declared that "joking may be very dangerous even to a free country."

The most celebrated trial occurred in Vermont. A Republican congressman, Matthew Lyon, who was running for reelection, publicly accused the Adams administration of mishandling the Quasi-War. This was not the first time this Irish immigrant had angered the Federalists. On the floor of the House of Representatives, Lyon once spit in the eye of a Federalist congressman from Connecticut. Lyon was immediately labeled the "Spitting Lyon," and one Bostonian declared, "I feel grieved that the saliva of an Irishman should be felt upon the face of an American & he, a New Englandman." A Federalist court was pleased to have the opportunity to convict him of libel. But Lyon enjoyed the last laugh. While he sat in jail, his constituents reelected him to Congress.

As this and other cases demonstrated, the federal courts had become political tools. While the fumbling efforts at enforcement of the Sedition Law did not

In the early years of the republic, political dissent sometimes escalated to physical violence. This fistfight took place on the floor of Congress, February 15, 1798. The combatants are Republican Matthew Lyon and Federalist Roger Griswold. ❖

silence opposition—indeed, they sparked even greater criticism and created martyrs—the actions of the administration persuaded Republicans that the survival of free government was at stake. Time was running out. "There is no event," Jefferson warned, " . . . however atrocious, which may not be expected."

Kentucky and Virginia Resolutions

By the fall of 1798, Jefferson and Madison were convinced that the Federalists envisioned the creation of a police state. According to Madison, the Sedition Law "ought to produce universal alarm." It threatened the free communication of ideas that he "deemed the only effectual guardian of every other right." Some extreme Republicans such as John Taylor of Virginia recommended secession from the Union; others advocated armed resistance. But Jefferson wisely counseled against such extreme strategies. "This is not the kind of opposition the American people will permit," he reminded his desperate supporters. The last best hope for American freedom lay in the state legislatures.

As the crisis deepened, Jefferson and Madison drafted separate protests known as the **Kentucky and Virginia Resolutions.** Both statements vigorously defended the right of individual state assemblies to interpret the constitutionality of federal law. Jefferson wrote the Kentucky Resolutions in November 1798, and in an outburst of partisan anger, he flirted with a doctrine of nullification as dangerous to the survival of the United States as anything advanced by Hamilton and his High Federalist friends.

In the Kentucky Resolutions, Jefferson described the federal union as a compact. The states transferred certain explicit powers to the national government, but, in his opinion, they retained full authority over all matters not specifically mentioned in the Constitution. Jefferson rejected Hamilton's broad interpretation of the "general welfare" clause. "Every state," Jefferson argued, "has a natural right in cases not within the compact . . . to nullify of their own authority all assumptions of power by others within their limits." Carried to an extreme, this logic could have led to the breakup of the federal government, and in 1798, Kentucky legislators were not prepared to take such a radical stance. While they diluted Jefferson's prose, they fully accepted his belief that the Alien and Sedition Acts were unconstitutional and ought to be repealed.

When Madison drafted the Virginia Resolutions in December, he took a stand more temperate than Jefferson's. Madison urged the states to defend the rights of the American people, but he resisted the notion that a single state legislature could or should have the authority to overthrow federal law.

The Virginia and Kentucky Resolutions must be viewed in proper historical context. They were not intended as statements of abstract principles and most certainly not as a justification for southern secession. They were pure political party propaganda. Jefferson and Madison dramatically reminded American voters during a period of severe domestic tension that the Republicans offered a clear alternative to Federalist rule. No other state legislatures passed the Resolutions, and even in Virginia, where the Republicans enjoyed broad support, several important figures such as John Marshall and George Washington censured the states' rights argument.

Adams's Finest Hour

In February 1799, President Adams belatedly declared his independence from the Hamiltonian wing of the Federalist party. Throughout the confrontation with France, Adams had shown little enthusiasm for war. Following the XYZ debacle, he began to receive informal reports that Talleyrand had changed his tune. The French foreign minister told Elbridge Gerry and other Americans that the bribery episode had been an unfortunate misunderstanding and that if the United States sent new representatives, he was prepared to negotiate in good faith. The High Federalists ridiculed this report. But Adams, still brooding over Hamilton's appointment to the army, decided to throw his own waning prestige behind peace. In February, he suddenly asked the Senate to confirm William Vans Murray as U.S. representative to France.

The move caught the High Federalists totally by surprise. They sputtered with outrage. "It is solely the President's act," Pickering cried, "and we were all thunderstruck when we heard of it." Adams was just warming to the task. In May, he fired Pickering and McHenry, an action he should have taken months earlier. With peace in the offing, American taxpayers complained more and more about the cost of maintaining an unnecessary army. The president was only too happy to dismantle Hamilton's dream.

When the new negotiators—Oliver Ellsworth and William Davie joined Murray—finally arrived in France in November 1799, they discovered that yet another group had come to power there. This government, headed by Napoleon Bonaparte, cooperated in drawing up an agreement known as the Convention of Mortefontaine. The French refused to compensate the Americans for vessels taken during the Quasi-War, but they did declare the treaties of 1778 null and void. Moreover, the convention removed annoying French restrictions on U.S. commerce. Not only had Adams avoided war, but he had also created an atmosphere of mutual trust that paved the way for the purchase of the Louisiana Territory. The president declared with considerable justification that the second French mission was "the most disinterested, the most determined and the most successful [act] of my whole life." It also cost him reelection.

The Election of 1800

Candidate	Party	Electoral Vote
Jefferson	Republican	73
Burr	Republican	73
J. Adams	Federalist	65
C. Pinckney	Federalist	64

The Peaceful Revolution: The Election of 1800

On the eve of the election of 1800, the Federalists were fatally divided. Adams enjoyed wide popularity among the Federalist rank and file, especially in New England, but articulate party leaders such as Hamilton vowed to punish the president for his betrayal of their militant policies. Hamilton even composed a scathing pamphlet titled *Letter Concerning the Public Conduct and Character of John Adams,* an essay that questioned Adams's ability to hold high office.

Once again the former secretary of the treasury attempted to rig the voting in the electoral college so that the party's vice presidential candidate, Charles Cotesworth Pinckney, would receive more ballots than Adams and America would be saved from "the fangs of Jefferson." As in 1796, the conspiracy backfired. The Republicans gained 73 votes while the Federalists trailed with 65.

To everyone's surprise, however, the election was not resolved in the electoral college. When the ballots were counted, Jefferson and his running mate, Aaron Burr, had tied. This accident—a Republican elector should have thrown away his second vote—sent the selection of the next president to the House of Representatives, a lame-duck body still controlled by members of the Federalist party.

As the House began its work on February 27, 1801, excitement ran high. Each state delegation cast a single vote, with nine votes needed for election. On the first ballot, Jefferson received the support of eight states, Burr six, and two states divided evenly. People predicted a quick victory for Jefferson, but after dozens of ballots, the House had still not selected a president. "The scene was now ludicrous," observed one witness. "Many had sent home for night-caps and pillows, and wrapped in shawls and great-coats, lay about the floor of the committee-rooms, or sat sleeping in their seats."

The cast of ballots by presidential electors in December 1800 resulted in a tie between Thomas Jefferson and Aaron Burr, who each received 73 votes. The election was finally decided in February 1801 when the House of Representatives, on the thirty-sixth ballot, chose Jefferson by a vote of 10 to 4. This flag commemorates Jefferson's victory in the election. ❖

The drama dragged on for days. To add to the confusion, Burr unaccountably refused to withdraw. Contemporaries thought his ambition had overcome his good sense.

The logjam finally broke when leading Federalists decided that Jefferson, whatever his faults, would make a more responsible president than would the shifty Burr. Even Hamilton labeled Burr "the most dangerous man of the community." On the thirty-sixth ballot, Representative James A. Bayard of Delaware announced he no longer supported Burr. This decision, coupled with Burr's inaction, gave Jefferson the presidency, ten states to four.

The Twelfth Amendment, ratified in 1804, saved the American people from repeating this potentially dangerous turn of events. Henceforth, the electoral college cast separate ballots for president and vice president.

During the final days of his presidency, Adams appointed as many Federalists as possible to the federal bench. Jefferson protested the hasty manner in which these "midnight judges" were selected. One of them, John Marshall, became chief justice of the United States, a post he held with distinction for thirty-four years. But behind the last-minute flurry of activity lay bitterness and disappointment. Adams never forgave Hamilton. "No party," the Federalist president wrote, "that ever existed knew itself so little or so vainly overrated its own influence and popularity as ours. None ever understood so ill the causes of its own power, or so wantonly destroyed them." On the morning of Jefferson's inauguration, Adams slipped away from the capital—now located in Washington, D.C.—unnoticed and unappreciated.

In the address that Adams missed, Jefferson attempted to quiet partisan fears. "We are all republicans; we are all federalists," the new president declared. By this statement, he did not mean to suggest that party differences were no longer important. Jefferson reminded his audience that whatever the politicians might say, the people shared a deep commitment to a federal union based on republican ideals set forth during the American Revolution. Indeed, the president interpreted the election of 1800 as a revolutionary episode, as the fulfillment of the principles of 1776.

Recent battles, of course, colored Jefferson's judgment. The contests of the 1790s had been hard fought, the outcome often in doubt. Jefferson looked back at this period as a confrontation between the "advocates of republican and those of kingly government," and he believed that only the vigilance of his own party had saved the country from Federalist "liberticide."

The Federalists were thoroughly dispirited by the entire experience. In the end, it had not been Hamilton's foolish electoral schemes that destroyed the party's chances in 1800. Rather, the Federalists had lost touch with a majority of the American people. In office, Adams and Hamilton—whatever their own differences may have been—betrayed their doubts about

CHRONOLOGY

1787	Constitution of the United States signed (September)
1789	George Washington inaugurated (April) ❖ Louis XVI of France calls meeting of the Estates General (May)
1790	Congress approves Hamilton's plan for funding and assumption (July)
1791	Bank of the United States is chartered (February) ❖ Hamilton's *Report on Manufactures* rejected by Congress (December)
1793	France's revolutionary government announces a "war of all people against all kings" (February) ❖ Genêt affair strains relations with France (April) ❖ Washington issues Proclamation of Neutrality (April) ❖ Spread of "Democratic" clubs alarms Federalists ❖ Jefferson resigns as secretary of state (December)
1794	Whiskey Rebellion put down by U.S. Army (July–November) ❖ General Anthony Wayne defeats Indians at battle of Fallen Timbers (August)
1795	Hamilton resigns as secretary of the treasury (January) ❖ Jay's Treaty divides the nation (June) ❖ Pinckney's Treaty with Spain is a welcome surprise (October)
1796	Washington publishes Farewell Address (September) ❖ John Adams elected president (December)
1797	XYZ Affair poisons U.S. relations with France (October)
1798–1800	Quasi-War with France
1798	Congress passes the Alien and Sedition Acts (June and July) ❖ Provisional army is formed ❖ Virginia and Kentucky Resolutions protest the Alien and Sedition Acts (November and December)
1799	George Washington dies (December)
1800	Convention of Mortefontaine is signed with France, ending Quasi-War (September)
1801	House of Representatives elects Thomas Jefferson president (February)

popular sovereignty too often, and when it came time to marshal broad support, to mobilize public opinion in favor of the party of wealth and privilege, few responded. As Secretary of War Oliver Wolcott observed on hearing of Jefferson's victory, "Have our party shown that they possess the necessary skill and courage to deserve . . . to govern? What have they done? . . . They write private letters. To whom? To each other, but they do nothing to give a proper direction to the public mind."

Conclusion: Danger of Political Extremism

From a broader historical perspective, the election of 1800 seems noteworthy for what did not occur. There were no riots in the streets, no attempted coup by military officers, no secession from the Union, nothing except the peaceful transfer of government from the leaders of one political party to those of the opposition.

Americans had weathered the Alien and Sedition Acts, the meddling by predatory foreign powers in domestic affairs, the shrilly partisan rhetoric of hack journalists, and now, at the start of a new century, they were impressed with their own achievement. As one woman who attended Jefferson's inauguration noted, "The changes of administration which in every government and in every age have most generally been epochs of confusion, villainy and bloodshed, in this our happy country take place without any species of distraction, or disorder." But as she well understood—indeed, as modern Americans must constantly relearn—extremism in the name of partisan political truth can easily unravel the delicate fabric of representative democracy and leave the republic at the mercy of those who would manipulate the public for private benefit.

Recommended Reading

The sudden development of deeply partisan politics on the national level dominated public life during the 1790s. Several recent accounts capture the sense of anger and disappointment that informed the political culture: Joanne B. Freeman, *Affairs of Honor: National Politics in the New Republic* (2001) and Joseph J. Ellis, *Founding Brothers: The Revolutionary Generation* (2000). Joyce Appleby provides useful insights into the ideological tensions that divided former allies in *Liberalism and Republicanism in the Historical Imagination* (1992). Jack N. Rakove offers a fine short introduction to James Madison's political thought in *James Madison and the Creation of the American Republic* (1990). An excellent discussion of the conflicting economic visions put forward by Hamilton and Jefferson can be found in Drew McCoy, *The Elusive Republic: The Political Economy in Jeffersonian America* (1980). Anyone curious about the controversial rise of political parties should consult Richard Hofstadter, *The Idea of a Party System: The Rise of Legitimate Opposition in the United States, 1780–1840* (1997) and Stanley Elkins and Eric McKitrick, *The Age of Federalism: The Early Republic* (1993). One can obtain many useful and readable biographies of the dominant leaders of the period. Two more analytic studies are Peter Onuf, ed., *Jeffersonian Legacies* (1993) and Paul K. Longmore, *The Invention of George Washington* (1999). How Americans constructed a convincing sense of national identity is examined in David Waldstreicher, *In the Midst of Perpetual Fetes: The Making of American Nationalism, 1776–1820* (1997). Two regional studies suggest how republican values worked themselves out among ordinary people: Alan Taylor, *Liberty Men and Great Proprietors: The Revolutionary Settlement of the Maine Frontier, 1760–1820* (1990) and Andrew Cayton, *Frontier Republic: Ideology and Politics in Ohio Country, 1780–1825* (1986). Conor Cruise O'Brien helps explain why foreign affairs, especially with the leaders of the French Revolution, disrupted domestic politics: *The Long Affair: Thomas Jefferson and the French Revolution, 1785–1800* (1996). A scientific debate driven by nationalism is the subject of Gordon S. Wood, "The Bigger the Beast the Better," *American History Illustrated,* Vol. 17 (1982), 30–37.

For a list of additional titles related to this chapter's topics, please see http://www.ablongman.com/divine.

Suggested Web Sites

Temple of Liberty—Building the Capitol for a New Nation

http://www.lcweb.loc.gov/exhibits/us.capitol/s0.html

Compiled from holdings in the Library of Congress, this site contains detailed information on the design and early construction of the Capitol building in Washington, D.C.

U.S. Electoral College

http://www.nara.gov/fedreg/elctcoll/index.html

This National Archives and Records Administration site explains how the electoral college works.

George Washington Papers

http://www.virginia.edu/gwpapers/

Information on the publishing project, with selected documents, essays, and an index of the published volumes.

George Washington's Mount Vernon

http://www.mountvernon.org/

Pictures and documents of Mount Vernon, the home of the first president, George Washington.

George Washington Papers at the Library of Congress, 1741–1799

http://memory.loc.gov/ammem/gwhtml/gwhome.html

This site is "the complete George Washington Papers from the Manuscript Division at the Library of Congress and consists of approximately 65,000 documents. This is the largest collection of original Washington documents in the world."

Archiving Early America

http://earlyamerica.com/

Old newspapers are excellent windows into the issues of the past. This site includes the Keigwin and Matthews collection of historic newspapers.

John Adams

http://www.ipl.org/div/potus/jadams.html

This Internet Public Library page contains biographical information about the second president, his inaugural address, and links to more information.

Chapter 8

William Birch's illustration of the partially-constructed United States capitol building in Washington, D.C, in 1800. When Jefferson first took office, the nation's new capital was little more than a swampy and isolated village. ❖

Republican Ascendancy: The Jeffersonian Vision

Limits of Equality

British visitors often expressed contempt for Jeffersonian society. Wherever they traveled in the young republic, they met ill-mannered people inspired with a ruling passion for liberty and equality. Charles William Janson, an Englishman who lived in the United States for thirteen years, recounted an exchange he found particularly unsettling that had occurred at the home of an American acquaintance. "On knocking at the door," he reported, "it was opened by a servant maid, whom I had never before seen." The woman's behavior astonished Janson. "The following is the dialogue, word for word, which took place on this occasion:—'Is your master at home?'—'I have no master.'—'Don't you live here?'—'I stay here.'—'And who are you then?'—'Why, I am Mr. ———'s *help.* I'd have you know, *man,* that I am no *sarvant* [sic]; none but *negers* [sic] are *sarvants.*'"

Standing on his friend's doorstep, Janson encountered the authentic voice of Jeffersonian republicanism—self-confident, assertive, blatantly racist, and having no intention of being relegated to low social status. The maid who answered the door believed she was her employer's equal, perhaps not in wealth but surely in character. She may have even dreamed of someday owning a house staffed with "*help.*" American society fostered such ambition. In the early nineteenth century, thousands of settlers poured across the Appalachian Mountains or moved to cities in search of opportunity. Thomas Jefferson and individuals who stood for public office under the banner of the Republican party claimed to speak for these people.

The limits of the Jeffersonian vision were obvious even to contemporaries. The people who spoke most eloquently about equal opportunity often owned slaves. As early as the 1770s, the famed English essayist Samuel Johnson had chided Americans for their hypocrisy. "How is it," he asked the indignant rebels, "that we hear the loudest yelps for liberty from the drivers of Negroes?" Little had changed since the Revolution. African Americans, who represented one-fifth of the population of the United States, were totally excluded from the new opportunities opening up in the cities and the West. Indeed, the maid in the incident just described insisted—with no apparent sense of inconsistency—that her position was superior to that of blacks, who were brought involuntarily to lifelong servitude.

IT IS NOT SURPRISING THAT in this highly charged racial climate leaders of the Federalist party accused the Republicans, especially those who lived in the South, of disingenuousness, and in 1804, one Massachusetts Federalist sarcastically defined "Jeffersonian" as "an Indian word, signifying '*a great tobacco planter, who had herds of black slaves.*'" The race issue was always just beneath the surface of political maneuvering. Indeed, the acquisition of the Louisiana Territory and the War of 1812 fanned fundamental disagreement about the spread of slavery to the western territories.

Outline

Feature Essay

In other areas, the Jeffersonians did not fulfill even their own high expectations. As members of an opposition party during the presidency of John Adams, they insisted on a strict interpretation of the Constitution, peaceful foreign relations, and a reduction of the role of the federal government in the lives of the average citizens. But following the election of 1800, Jefferson and his supporters discovered that unanticipated pressures, foreign and domestic, forced them to moderate these goals. Before he retired from public office, Jefferson interpreted the Constitution in a way that permitted the government to purchase the Louisiana Territory when the opportunity arose; he regulated the national economy with a rigor that would have surprised Alexander Hamilton; and he led the country to the brink of war. Some Americans praised the president's pragmatism; others felt betrayed. For a man who played a leading role in the revolt against George III, it must have been shocking in 1807 to find himself labeled a "despot" in a popular New England newspaper. "Give ear no longer to the siren voice of democracy and Jeffersonian liberty," the editor shrieked. "It is a cursed delusion, adopted by traitors, and recommended by sycophants."

Regional Identities in a New Republic

During the early decades of the nineteenth century, the population of the United States experienced substantial growth. The 1810 census counted 7,240,000 Americans, a jump of almost 2 million in just ten years. Of this total, approximately 20 percent were black slaves, the majority of whom lived in the South. The large population increase in the nation was the result primarily of natural reproduction, since during Jefferson's presidency few immigrants moved to the New World. The largest single group in this society was children under the age of sixteen, boys and girls who were born after Washington's election and who defined their own futures at a time when the nation's boundaries were rapidly expanding. For white Americans, it was a time of heightened optimism, and many people possessing entrepreneurial skills or engineering capabilities aggressively made their way in a society that seemed to rate personal merit higher than family background.

Even as Americans defended the rights of individual states, they were forming strong regional identifi-

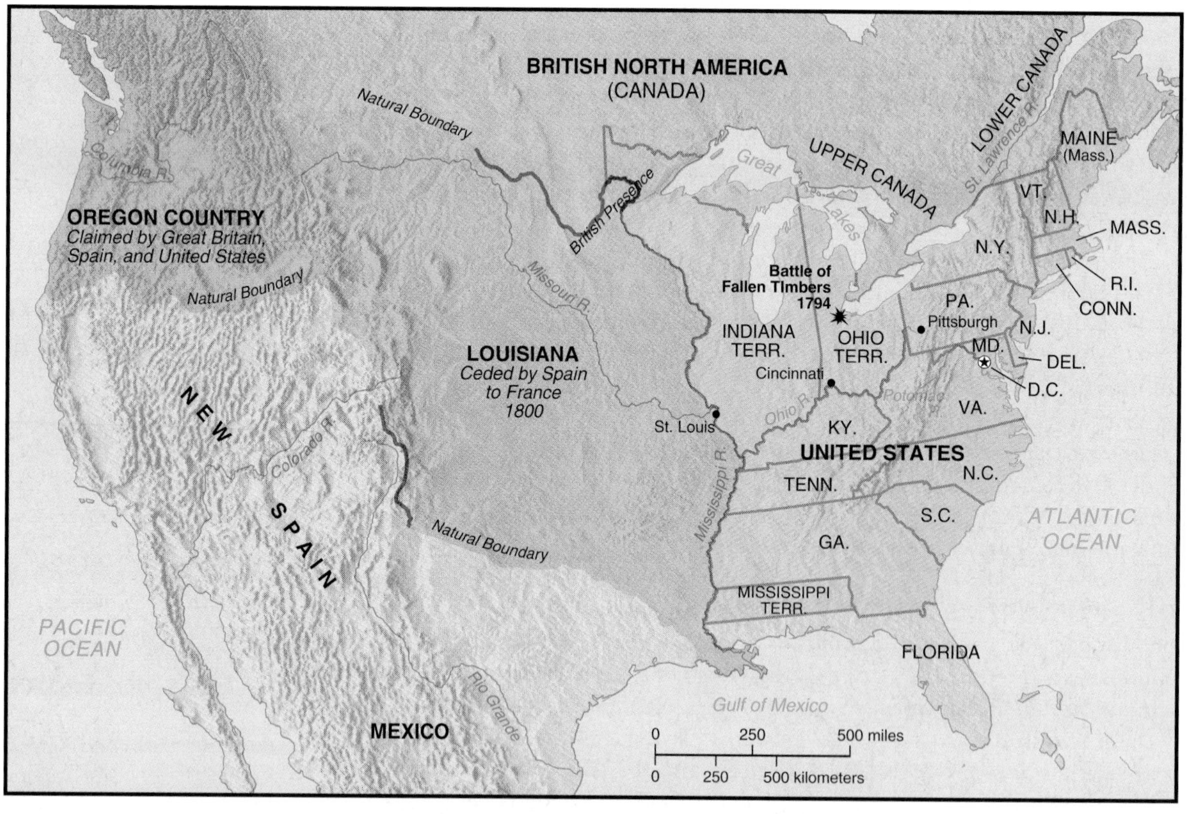

NORTH AMERICA IN 1800 *In the 1790s, diplomatic agreements with Britain and Spain and defeat of the Native Americans at the battle of Fallen Timbers opened the way to U.S. settlement of the land beyond the Appalachian Mountains.* ❖

cations. In commerce and politics, they perceived themselves as representatives of distinct subcultures—as Southerners, New Englanders, or Westerners. No doubt, the broadening geographic horizons reflected improved transportation links that enabled people to travel more easily within the various sections. But the growing regional mentality was also the product of defensiveness. While local writers celebrated New England's cultural distinctiveness, for example, they were clearly uneasy about the region's rejection of the democratic values that were sweeping the rest of the nation. Moreover, during this period people living south of the Potomac River began describing themselves as Southerners, not as citizens of the Chesapeake or the Carolinas as they had done in colonial times.

This shifting focus of attention resulted not only from an awareness of shared economic interests but also from a sensitivity to outside attacks on slavery. Several times during the first fifteen years of the nineteenth century, conspirators actually advocated secession, and though the schemes failed, they revealed the powerful sectional loyalties that threatened national unity.

Westward the Course of Empire

The most striking changes occurred in the West. Before the end of the American Revolution, only Indian traders and a few hardy settlers had ventured across the Appalachians. After 1790, however, a flood of people rushed west to stake out farms on the rich soil. Many settlers followed the so-called northern route across Pennsylvania or New York into the old Northwest Territory. Pittsburgh and Cincinnati, both strategically located on the Ohio River, became important commercial ports. In 1803, Ohio joined the Union, and territorial governments were formed in Indiana (1800), Louisiana (1805), Michigan (1805), Illinois (1809), and Missouri (1812). Southerners poured into the new states of Kentucky (1792) and Tennessee (1796). Wherever they located, Westerners depended on water transportation. Because of the extraordinarily high cost of hauling goods overland, riverboats represented the only economical means of carrying agricultural products to distant markets. The Mississippi River was the crucial commercial link for the entire region, and Westerners did not feel secure so long as New Orleans, the southern gate to the Mississippi, remained under Spanish control.

Families that moved west attempted to transplant familiar eastern customs to the frontier. In some areas such as the Western Reserve, a narrow strip of land along Lake Erie in northern Ohio, the influence of New England remained strong. In general, however, a creative mixing of peoples of different backgrounds in a strange environment generated distinctive folkways. Westerners developed their own heroes, such as Mike

View of the City of Pittsburgh in 1817, *painted by a Mrs. Gibson while on her honeymoon. As the frontier moved west, Pittsburgh became an important trade and manufacturing center.* ❖

Fink, the legendary keelboatman of the Mississippi River; Daniel Boone, the famed trapper and Indian fighter; and the eye-gouging "alligatormen" of Kentucky and Tennessee. Americans who crossed the mountains were ambitious and self-confident, excited by the challenge of almost unlimited geographic mobility. A French traveler observed in 1802 that throughout the region he visited, there was not a single farm "where one cannot with confidence ask the owner from whence he had emigrated, or, according to the light manners of the Americans, 'What part of the world do you come from?'" These rootless people, he explained, "incline perpetually toward the most distant fringes of American settlement."

Native American Resistance

At the beginning of the nineteenth century, a substantial number of Native Americans lived in the greater Ohio Valley; the land belonged to them. The tragedy was that the Indians, many dependent on trade with the white people and ravaged by disease, lacked unity. Small groups of Native Americans, allegedly representing the interests of an entire tribe, sold off huge pieces of land, often for whiskey and trinkets.

Such fraudulent transactions disgusted the Shawnee leaders Tenskwatawa (known as the Prophet) and his brother Tecumseh. Tecumseh rejected classification as a Shawnee and may have been the first native leader to identify himself self-consciously as "Indian." These men desperately attempted to revitalize native cultures, and against overwhelming odds, they briefly persuaded Native Americans living in the Indiana Territory to avoid contact with whites, to resist alcohol, and, most important, to hold on to their land. White intruders saw Tecumseh as a threat to progress, and during the War of 1812, they shattered the Indians' dream of cultural renaissance. The populous Creek nation, located in the modern states of Alabama and Mississippi, also resisted the settlers' advance, but its warriors were crushed by Andrew Jackson's Tennessee militia at the battle of Horseshoe Bend (March 1814).

Well-meaning Jeffersonians disclaimed any intention to destroy the Indians. The president talked of creating a vast reservation beyond the Mississippi River, just as the British had talked before the Revolution of a sanctuary beyond the Appalachian Mountains. He sent federal agents to "civilize" the Indians, to transform them into yeoman farmers. But even the most enlightened white thinkers of the day did not believe the Indians possessed cultures worth preserving. In fact, in 1835, the Democratic national convention selected a vice presidential candidate whose major qualification for high office seemed to be that he had killed Tecumseh. And as early as 1780, Jefferson himself—then serving as the governor of Virginia—instructed a military leader on the frontier, "If we are to wage a campaign against these Indians the end proposed should be their extermination, or their removal beyond the lakes of the Illinois river. The same world will scarcely do for them and us."

Tenskwatawa, known as the Prophet, provided spiritual leadership for the union of the native peoples he and his brother Tecumseh organized to resist white encroachment on Native American lands. ❖

Commercial Life in the Cities

Before 1820, the prosperity of the United States depended primarily on its agriculture and trade. Jeffersonian America was by no stretch of the imagination an industrial economy. The overwhelming majority of the population—84 percent in 1810—was directly involved in agriculture. Southerners concentrated on the staple crops of tobacco, rice, and cotton, which they sold on the European market. In the North, people generally produced livestock and cereal crops. Regardless of location, however, the nation's farmers followed a backbreaking work routine that did not differ substantially from that of their parents and grandparents. Except for the cotton gin, important chemical and mechanical inventions did not appear in the fields for another generation. Probably the major innovation of this period was the agricultural fair, an idea first advanced in 1809 by a Massachusetts farmer, Elkanah Watson. In hopes of improving animal breeding, he offered prizes for the best livestock in the country. The experiment was a great success, for as Watson reported, "Many farmers, and even women, were excited by curiosity to attend this first novel, and humble exhibition."

The merchant marine represented an equally important element in America's preindustrial economy. At the turn of the century, ships flying the Stars and Stripes transported a large share of the world's trade. Merchants in Boston, New York, and Philadelphia received handsome profits from such commerce. Their vessels provided essential links between European countries and their Caribbean colonies. France, for example, relied heavily on American transport for its sugar. These lucrative transactions, coupled with the export of domestic staples, especially cotton, generated impressive fortunes. Between 1793 and 1807, the year Jefferson imposed the embargo against Britain and France, American commerce enjoyed a more than 300 percent increase in the value of exports and in net earnings. Unfortunately, the boom did not last. The success of the "carrying trade" depended in large measure on friendly relations between the United States and the major European powers. When England and France began seizing American ships—as they both did after 1805—national prosperity suffered.

The cities of Jeffersonian America functioned chiefly as depots for international trade. Only about 7 percent of the nation's population lived in urban centers, and most of these people owed their livelihoods either directly or indirectly to the carrying trade. Recent studies revealed that several major port cities of the early republic—New York, Philadelphia, and Baltimore, for example—had some of the highest population densities ever recorded in this country's history. In 1800, more than 40,000 New Yorkers crowded into an area of only 1.5 square miles; in Philadelphia, some 46,000 people were packed into less than one square mile. As one historian explained, "The cities contained disproportionate numbers of young white males, free black men and women, and white widows. These people had below-average incomes and also an increasing propensity to live on their own rather than as dependents." As is common today, many city dwellers rented living space, and since the demand for housing exceeded the supply, the rents were high.

Within these densely crowded urban centers, artisans maintained the fleet; skilled workers produced new ships; laborers loaded cargoes. And as some merchant families became wealthy, they demanded luxury items such as fine furniture. This specialized market drew a small, but highly visible, group of master craftspeople, and their extraordinarily beautiful and intricate pieces—New England tall clocks, for example—were perhaps the highest artistic achievement of the period.

Despite these accomplishments, American cities exercised only a marginal influence on the nation's vast hinterland. Because of the high cost of land transportation, urban merchants seldom purchased goods

Before the Industrial Revolution, national prosperity depended on commercial capitalism. Jonathan Budington's painting of Cannon House and Wharf *(1792), the busy dock area of lower Manhattan, reflects the robust maritime trade of the new republic.* ❖

Although cotton was an important trade item in the early nineteenth century, technological advances in textile production were slow to take hold. Some spinning mills, such as the one pictured here, were built in New England, but what historians call the "Industrial Revolution" did not begin for several more decades. ❖

for export—flour, for example—from a distance of more than 150 miles. The separation between rural and urban Americans was far more pronounced during Jefferson's presidency than it was after the development of canals and railroads a few decades later.

The booming carrying trade may actually have retarded the industrialization of the United States. The lure of large profits drew investment capital—a scarce resource in a developing society—into commerce. By contrast, manufacturing seemed too risky. One contemporary complained, "The brilliant prospects held out by commerce, caused our citizens to neglect the mechanical and manufacturing branches of industry."

This man may have exaggerated slightly to make his point. Samuel Slater, an English-born designer of textile machinery, did establish several cotton-spinning mills in New England, but until the 1820s these plants employed only a small number of workers. In fact, during this period far more cloth was produced in individual households than in factories. Another farsighted inventor, Robert Fulton, sailed the first American steamship up the Hudson River in 1807. In time, this marvelous innovation opened new markets for domestic manufacturers, especially in the West. At the end of the War of 1812, however, few people anticipated how greatly power generated by fossil fuel would eventually transform the character of the American economy.

Ordinary workers often felt threatened by the new machines. Skilled artisans who had spent years mastering a trade and who took pride in producing an object that expressed their own personalities found the industrial workplace alienating. Moreover, they rightly feared that innovative technology designed to achieve greater efficiency might throw traditional craftspeople out of work or, if not that, transform independent entrepreneurs into dependent wage laborers. One New Yorker, for example, writing in the *Gazette and General Advertiser* in 1801, warned tradespeople to be on guard against those who "will screw down the wages to the last thread . . . [and destroy] the independent spirit, so distinguished at present in our mechanics, and so useful in republics."

Jefferson as President

The District of Columbia seemed an appropriate capital for a Republican president. At the time of Jefferson's first inauguration, Washington was still an isolated rural village, a far cry from the crowded centers of Philadelphia and New York. Jefferson fit comfortably into Washington society. He despised formal ceremony and sometimes shocked foreign dignitaries by meeting them in his slippers or a threadbare jacket. He spent as much time as his official duties allowed in reading and reflection. Isaac, one of Jefferson's slaves, recounted, "Old master had abundance of books: sometimes would have twenty of 'em down on the floor at once; read fust one then tother."

The president was a poor public speaker. He wisely refused to deliver annual addresses before Congress. In personal conversation, however, Jefferson exuded considerable charm. His dinner parties were major intellectual as well as social events, and in this forum, the president regaled politicians with his knowledge of literature, philosophy, and science.

According to Margaret Bayard Smith, the wife of a congressman, the president "has more ease than grace—all the winning softness of politeness, without the artificial polish of courts."

Notwithstanding his commitment to the life of the mind, Jefferson was a politician to the core. He ran for the presidency in order to achieve specific goals: the reduction of the size and cost of federal government, the repeal of obnoxious Federalist legislation such as the Alien Acts, and the maintenance of international peace. To accomplish his program, Jefferson realized he needed the full cooperation of congressional Republicans, some of whom were fiercely independent men. Over such figures Jefferson exercised political mastery. He established close ties with the leaders of both houses of Congress, and while he seldom announced his plans in public, he made certain his legislative lieutenants knew exactly what he desired. Contemporaries who described Jefferson as a weak president—and some Federalists did just that—did not read the scores of memoranda he sent to political friends or witness the informal meetings he held at the executive mansion with important Republicans. In two terms as president, Jefferson never had to veto a single act of Congress.

Jefferson carefully selected the members of his cabinet. During Washington's administration, he had witnessed—even provoked—severe infighting; as president, he nominated only those who enthusiastically supported his programs. James Madison, the leading figure at the Constitutional Convention, became secretary of state. For the Treasury, Jefferson chose Albert Gallatin, a Swiss-born financier who understood the complexities of the federal budget. "If I had the universe to choose from," the president announced, "I could not change one of my associates to my better satisfaction."

Jeffersonian Reforms

A top priority of the new government was cutting the national debt. Throughout American history, presidents have advocated such reductions, but such rhetoric has seldom yielded tangible results. Jefferson succeeded. He and Gallatin regarded a large federal deficit as dangerous to the health of republican institutions. In fact, both men associated debt with Alexander Hamilton's Federalist financial programs, measures they considered harmful to republicanism. Jefferson claimed that legislators elected by the current generation did not have the right to mortgage the future of unborn Americans.

Jefferson also wanted to diminish the activities of the federal government. He urged Congress to repeal all direct taxes, including the tax that had sparked the Whiskey Rebellion in 1794. Secretary Gallatin linked federal income to the carrying trade. He calculated that the entire cost of national government could be borne by customs receipts. As long as commerce flourished, revenues provided sufficient sums. When international war closed foreign markets, however, the flow of funds dried up.

To help pay the debt inherited from the Adams administration, Jefferson ordered substantial cuts in the national budget. The president closed several American embassies in Europe. He also slashed military spending. In his first term, Jefferson reduced the size of the U.S. Army by 50 percent. This decision left only three thousand soldiers to guard the entire frontier. In addition, he retired a majority of the navy's warships. When New Englanders claimed the cuts left the country defenseless, Jefferson countered with a glib argument. As ships of the U.S. Navy sailed the world's oceans, he claimed, they were liable to provoke hostilities, perhaps even war; hence, by reducing the size of the fleet, he promoted peace.

More than budgetary considerations prompted Jefferson's military reductions. He was deeply suspicious of standing armies. In the event of foreign attack, he reasoned, the militia would rise in defense of the republic. No doubt, his experiences during the Revolution influenced his thinking on military affairs, for in 1776, an aroused populace had taken up arms against the British. To ensure that the citizen soldiers would receive professional leadership in battle, Jefferson created the Army Corps of Engineers and the military academy at West Point in 1802.

Political patronage was a great burden to the new president. Loyal Republicans throughout the United States had worked hard for Jefferson's victory, and as soon as he took office, they stormed the executive mansion seeking federal employment. While the president controlled several hundred jobs, he refused to dismiss all the Federalists. To be sure, he acted quickly to remove the so-called midnight appointees, highly partisan selections that Adams had made after learning of Jefferson's election. But to transform federal hiring into an undisciplined spoils system, especially at the highest levels of the federal bureaucracy, seemed to Jefferson to be shortsighted. Moderate Federalists might be converted to the Republican party, and, in any case, there was a good chance they possessed the expertise needed to run the government. At the end of his first term, half of the people holding office were appointees of Washington and Adams.

Jefferson's political moderation helped hasten the demise of the Federalist party. This loose organization had nearly destroyed itself during the election of 1800, and following Adams's defeat, prominent Federalist spokesmen such as Fisher Ames and John Jay withdrew from national affairs. They refused to adopt the popular forms of campaigning that the Republicans had developed so successfully during the late 1790s. The mere prospect of flattering the common people was odious enough to drive some Federalists into political retirement.

Many of them also sensed that national expansion worked against their interests. The creation of new states and congressional reapportionment inevitably seemed to increase the number of Republican representatives in Washington. By 1805, the Federalists retained only a few seats in New England and Delaware. "The power of the [Jefferson] Administration," confessed John Quincy Adams in 1802, "rests upon the support of a much stronger majority of the people throughout the Union than the former administrations ever possessed since the first establishment of the Constitution."

After 1804, a group of younger Federalists belatedly attempted to pump life into the dying party. They experimented with popular election techniques. In some states, they tightened party organization, held nominating conventions, and campaigned energetically for office. These were essential reforms, but with the exception of a brief Federalist revival in the Northeast between 1807 and 1814, the results of these activities were disappointing. Even the younger Federalists thought it demeaning to appeal for votes. Diehards such as Timothy Pickering promoted wild secessionist schemes in New England, while the most promising moderates—John Quincy Adams, for example—joined the Republicans.

The Louisiana Purchase

When Jefferson first took office, he was confident that Louisiana as well as Florida would eventually become part of the United States. After all, Spain owned the territory, and Jefferson assumed he could persuade the rulers of that notoriously weak nation to sell their colonies. If that peaceful strategy failed, the president was prepared to threaten forcible occupation.

In May 1801, however, prospects for the easy or inevitable acquisition of Louisiana suddenly darkened. Jefferson learned that Spain had secretly transferred title to the entire region to France, its powerful northern neighbor. To make matters worse, the French leader Napoleon seemed intent on reestablishing an empire in North America. Even as Jefferson sought additional information concerning the details of the transfer, Napoleon was dispatching a large army to put down a rebellion in France's sugar-rich Caribbean colony, Haiti. From that island stronghold in the West Indies, French troops could occupy New Orleans and close the Mississippi River to American trade.

A sense of crisis enveloped Washington. Some congressmen urged Jefferson to prepare for war against France. Tensions increased when the Spanish officials who still governed New Orleans announced the closing of that port to American commerce (October 1802). Jefferson and his advisers assumed that the Spanish had acted on orders from France, but despite this serious provocation, the president preferred negotiations to war. In January 1803, he asked James Monroe, a loyal Republican from Virginia, to join the American minister, Robert Livingston, in Paris. The president instructed the two men to explore the possibility of purchasing the city of New Orleans. Lest they underestimate the importance of their diplomatic mission, Jefferson reminded them, "There is on the globe one single spot, the possessor of which is our natural and habitual enemy. It is New Orleans." If Livingston and Monroe failed, Jefferson realized he would be forced to turn to Great Britain for military assistance. Dependence on that country seemed repellent, but he recognized that as soon as French troops moved into Louisiana, "we must marry ourselves to the British fleet and nation."

By the time Monroe joined Livingston in France, Napoleon had lost interest in establishing an American empire. The army he sent to Haiti succumbed to tropical diseases. By the end of 1802, more than thirty thousand veteran troops had died. In a fit of disgust, Napoleon announced, "Damn sugar, damn coffee, damn colonies . . . I renounce Louisiana." The diplomats from the United States knew nothing of these developments. They were taken by complete surprise, therefore, when they learned that Talleyrand, the French minister for foreign relations, had offered to sell the entire Louisiana Territory in April 1803. For only $15 million, the Americans doubled the size of the United States with the **Louisiana Purchase.** In fact, Livingston and Monroe were not certain how much land they had actually purchased. When they asked Talleyrand whether the deal included Florida, he responded ambiguously, "You have made a noble bargain for yourselves, and I suppose you will make the most of it." Even at that moment, Livingston realized that the transaction would alter the course of American history. "From this day," he wrote, "the United States take their place among the powers of first rank."

The American people responded enthusiastically to news of the Louisiana Purchase. The only criticism came from a few disgruntled Federalists in New England who thought the United States was already too large. Jefferson, of course, was immensely relieved. The nation had avoided war with France. Nevertheless, he worried that the purchase might be unconstitutional. The president pointed out that the Constitution did

President Jefferson recognized the strategic location of New Orleans and determined to buy it from the French. By 1803, when this view was painted, New Orleans was already a thriving port and an important outlet for exports produced by new communities along the Ohio and Mississippi Valleys. ❖

not specifically authorize the acquisition of vast new territories and the incorporation of thousands of foreign citizens. To escape this apparent legal dilemma, Jefferson proposed an amendment to the Constitution. Few persons, even his closest advisers, shared the president's scruples. Events in France soon forced Jefferson to adopt a more pragmatic course. When he heard that Napoleon had become impatient for his money, Jefferson rushed the papers to a Senate eager to ratify the agreement, and nothing more was said about amending the Constitution.

Jefferson's fears about the incorporation of this new territory were not unwarranted. The area that eventually became the state of Louisiana (1812) contained many people of French and Spanish background who possessed no familiarity with representative institutions. Their laws had been autocratic, their local government corrupt. To allow such persons to elect a representative assembly struck the president as dangerous. He did not even know whether the population of Louisiana would remain loyal to the United States. Jefferson, therefore, recommended to Congress a transitional government consisting entirely of appointed officials. In March 1804, the Louisiana Government Bill narrowly passed the House of Representatives. Members of the president's own party attacked the plan. After all, it imposed taxes on the citizens of Louisiana without their consent. According to one outspoken Tennessee congressman, the bill "establishes a complete despotism." Most troubling perhaps was the fact that the legislation ran counter to Jefferson's well-known republican principles.

The Lewis and Clark Expedition

In the midst of the Louisiana controversy, Jefferson dispatched a secret message to Congress requesting $2500 for the exploration of the Far West (January 1803). How closely this decision was connected to the Paris negotiations is not clear. Whatever the case may have been, the president asked his talented private secretary, Meriwether Lewis, to discover whether the Missouri River "may offer the most direct & practicable water communication across this continent for the purposes of commerce." The president also regarded the expedition as a wonderful opportunity to collect precise data about flora and fauna. He personally instructed Lewis in the latest techniques of scientific observation. While preparing for this great adventure, Lewis's second in command, William Clark, assumed such a prominent role that the effort became known as the **Lewis and Clark Expedition.** The effort owed much of its success to a young Shoshoni woman known as Sacagawea. She served as a translator and helped persuade suspicious Native Americans that the explorers meant no harm. As Clark explained, "A woman with a party of men is a token of peace."

The exploring party set out from St. Louis in May 1804, and after barely surviving crossing the snow-covered Rocky Mountains, with their food supply running dangerously low, the Americans reached the Pacific

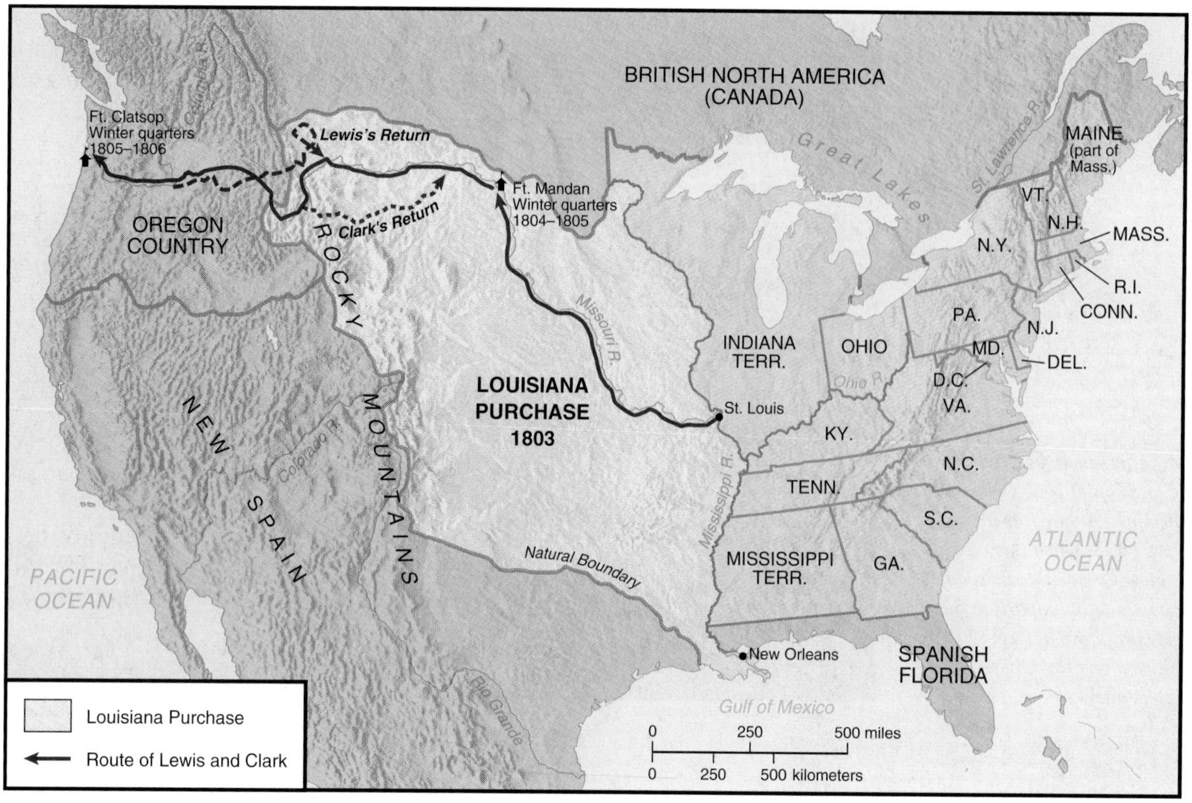

THE LOUISIANA PURCHASE AND THE ROUTE OF LEWIS AND CLARK *Not until Lewis and Clark had explored the Far West did citizens of the United States realize just how much territory Jefferson had acquired through the Louisiana Purchase.* ❖

Ocean in November 1805. The group returned safely the following September. The results of the expedition not only fulfilled Jefferson's scientific expectations but also reaffirmed his faith in the future economic prosperity of the United States.

Conflict with the Barbary States

During this period, Jefferson dealt with another problem. For several decades, the North African states of Tangier, Algiers, Tripoli, and Tunis—the Barbary States—had preyed on commercial shipping. (See the Feature Essay, "Barbary Pirates and American Captives: The Nation's First Hostage Crisis," pp. 230–231.) Most European nations paid the pirates tribute, hoping thereby to protect merchants trading in the Mediterranean. In 1801, Jefferson, responding to Tripoli's increased demand for tribute, decided the extortion had become intolerable and dispatched a small fleet to the Barbary Coast, where, according to one commander, the Americans intended to negotiate "through the mouth of a cannon." Tripoli put up stiff resistance, however, and in one mismanaged engagement it captured the U.S. frigate *Philadelphia*. Ransoming the crew cost Jefferson's government another $60,000. An American land assault across the Libyan desert provided inspiration for the words of the "Marines' Hymn"—"to the shores of Tripoli"—but no smashing victory.

Despite a generally unimpressive American military record, a vigorous naval blockade brought hostilities to a conclusion. In 1805, the president signed a treaty formally ending the **Barbary War.** One diplomat crowed, "It must be mortifying to some of the neighboring European powers to see that the Barbary States have been taught their first lessons of humiliation from the Western World."

Jefferson concluded his first term on a wave of popularity. He had maintained the peace, reduced taxes, and expanded the boundaries of the United

THE ELECTION OF 1804

Candidate	Party	Electoral Vote
Jefferson	Republican	162
C. Pinckney	Federalist	14

States. Not surprisingly, he overwhelmed his Federalist opponent in the presidential election of 1804. In the electoral college, Jefferson received 162 votes to Charles Cotesworth Pinckney's 14. Republicans controlled Congress. John Randolph, the most articulate member of the House of Representatives, exclaimed, "Never was there an administration more brilliant than that of Mr. Jefferson up to this period. We were indeed in 'the full tide of successful experiment!'"

Jefferson's Critics

At the moment of Jefferson's greatest electoral victory, a perceptive person might have seen signs of serious division within the Republican party and within the country. The president's heavy-handed attempts to reform the federal courts stirred deep animosities. Republicans had begun sniping at other Republicans, and one leading member of the party, Aaron Burr, became involved in a bizarre plot to separate the West from the rest of the nation. Congressional debates over the future of the slave trade revealed the existence of powerful sectional loyalties and profound disagreement on the issue.

Attack on the Judges

Jefferson's controversy with the federal bench commenced the moment he became president. The Federalists, realizing they would soon lose control over the executive branch, had passed the Judiciary Act of 1801. This bill created several circuit courts

❖ A Look at the Past ❖

Buffalo Robe

Lewis and Clark collected Native American artifacts, including this Mandan buffalo robe. They sent the robe to Jefferson following a winter spent with the Mandans. Why would the Mandans give Lewis and Clark a robe that depicted a recent battle with their traditional enemies, the Sioux? Why would Lewis and Clark send the robe to Jefferson?

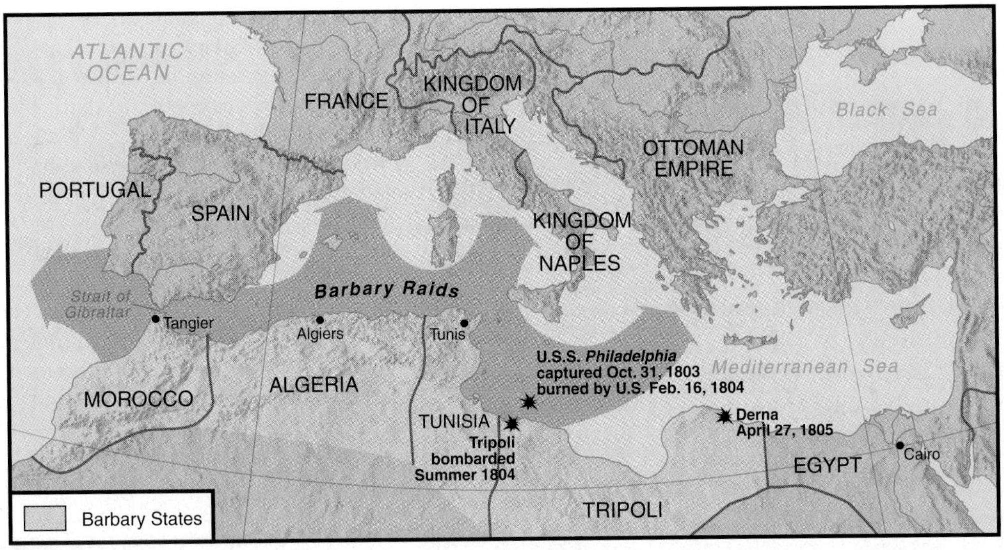

THE BARBARY STATES *In 1801, President Jefferson refused to continue paying the tribute that pirates of the Barbary States had received for decades.* ❖

Feature Essay

Barbary Pirates and American Captives

The Nation's First Hostage Crisis

For more than a quarter-century after Independence, terror haunted American sailors and challenged the new republic's influence throughout the world. Pirates from North Africa preyed on commercial vessels in the Mediterranean Sea and along the European Coast. Those unlucky enough to be captured faced enslavement or death. Although such piracy had been going on for a very long time, American entrepreneurs were always willing to risk the dangers to make a profit. The crew of one ship, the *Polly,* left a record of the horrors awaiting those who encountered the Barbary pirates, North African Muslims based in Algiers, Morocco, Tunis, and Tripoli.

Sailing out of Baltimore in autumn 1793, the *Polly* was on its way to a Spanish port when a sailor on watch reported a "strange sail". No one seems to have anticipated trouble.

They were in for a dreadful surprise. When the strange vessel drew alongside the *Polly,* someone "dressed in the Christian habit" hailed the Americans from the deck. Then, without warning, "a great number" of men "dressed in the Turkish habit" poured over the railings brandishing "scimitars and pistols . . . pikes, spears, lances, and knives." The Americans had no defense. The pirates plundered the ship then stripped the Americans of all clothing except "a shirt and a pair of drawers" and chained them in preparation for the voyage to Algiers, reputed to be the cruelest "of any state in all Barbary."

Print depicting the bombardment of Tripoli by U.S. naval vessels in 1804. ❖

The *Polly's* crew had become casualties of the young republic's first prolonged hostage crisis involving Muslim states. By the end of the year, Barbary pirates had seized the crews of at least ten other vessels. The captives were thrown into prisons, where they labored in terrible conditions alongside sailors who had been in Algiers for as long as a decade. Algerian guards beat their captives. The enslaved Americans were driven in chains each day to a quarry outside the city of Algiers. Their masters forced them to drag twenty-ton rocks to construction sites. Anyone who attempted escape faced execution. Overcrowded prisons invited epidemic disease.

News of the captives' ordeal offended American pride. Outraged American citizens organized charitable societies pledged to oppose the pirates, send relief to the captives, and lobby Congress to take effective action for their release. In Baltimore, sailors resolved "not to proceed to sea, until they can do so without apprehension of insult and robbery." Some Americans advocated paying ransom to liberate the prisoners, but others pointed out that such a policy would only encourage more attacks on the nation's merchant marine.

The outpouring of private action and nationalist sentiment forced the U. S. government, which had championed a policy of free trade throughout the world, to adjust to the changing realities of international relations. If

Images of American captives enduring various forms of torture at the hands of their Barbary captors. ❖

the United States allowed itself to be humiliated by the Barbary states—places where "bribery, treachery, rapine, murder, and all the hideous offspring of accursed tyranny, have often drenched the streets with blood"—then it could not expect other, more powerful states to respect its hard-won independence.

U.S. military power frightened no one, especially the rulers of Barbary states. Neither the French nor the British showed interest in helping the Americans. After all, they viewed them as commercial competitors in the region. In 1795, the federal government finally recognized the seriousness of the problem. President Washington ordered U.S. envoy Joseph Donaldson, Jr., to negotiate release of the captives and to sign treaties ensuring that Algiers would no longer molest American shipping. For these alleged favors, the United States had to promise a humiliating sum totaling nearly $1 million. The combination of debt payments and annual tribute represented about one-sixth of each year's federal budget. Treaties with Tripoli and Tunis also included yearly payments for peace, raising the total even higher.

A policy that essentially condoned blackmail continued until Thomas Jefferson won election as president in 1800. Hoping to extort a larger share of the annual ransom monies, the Pasha of Tripoli forced Jefferson's hand by declaring war on the United States. This preemptive move confirmed belief that attempts to buy off extortionists only generated further greed. It also compelled the United States to back up its world commerce with military might, a decision congressional budget-cutters had tried to avoid.

Vowing not to pay "one penny in tribute," Jefferson dispatched U.S. naval vessels to blockade Tripoli's harbor. Despite brave talk, American intervention proved a failure, at least initially. One battleship went aground and had to be destroyed by marines. Eventually, Commodore Edward Preble and Captain Stephen Decatur showed fighting spirit sufficient to turn defeat into a draw. The American consul at Tunis, William Eaton, even attempted an early form of "regime change," leading a company of Mediterranean mercenaries in an unauthorized effort to depose the Pasha and install his brother. Eaton's mission "to the shores of Tripoli" failed. In 1805 the Pasha, whose power was unshaken, decided that war was becoming too expensive, and he negotiated a peace with the United States that included a payment of $60,000 to ransom the last prisoners.

During the long ordeal with the Barbary pirates, American nationalists portrayed North African states as the opposite of their free republic. Survivors of captivity published narratives containing lurid descriptions of the despotism and cruelty they had endured under their Muslim masters. The popular press castigated Muslims as enemies of civilized society and devoid of human compassion. Several so-called Algerian plays became audience favorites by creating innocent, but heroic American characters who embodied liberty and courage against a backdrop of Islamic tyranny.

Propaganda against Muslim pirates generated its own embarrassing backlash. Shrill nationalist rhetoric reminded many Americans of the uncomfortable similarities between the white slavery of the Barbary states and the African slavery that flourished throughout the southern United States. The African American abolitionist Absalom Jones could discern no real difference between "the unconstitutional bondage in which multitudes of our fellows in complexion are held" and "the deplorable . . . situation of citizens of the United States captured and enslaved . . . in Algiers."

America's first hostage crisis produced a complex legacy. It forced ordinary citizens of the new republic to take stock of themselves within a larger international framework. The war in Tripoli encouraged Jefferson, who had always disfavored a permanent military establishment, to accept a professional navy. Preparedness, he concluded, was the price of maintaining free trade throughout the world. War provided a stark contrast between liberty and tyranny and stimulated the loud celebration of American freedom. In doing so, it also intensified debate over the republic's most glaring domestic contradiction, the persistence of slavery within a nation that was prepared to fight in distant places in the name of liberty.

and sixteen new judgeships. Through his "midnight" appointments, Adams had quickly filled these positions with stalwarts of the Federalist party. Such blatantly partisan behavior angered Jefferson. In the courts, he explained, the Federalists hoped to preserve their political influence, and "from that battery all the works of Republicanism are to be beaten down and erased." Even more infuriating was Adams's appointment of John Marshall as the new chief justice. This shrewd, largely self-educated Virginian of Federalist background, whose training in the law consisted of a series of lectures he attended at the College of William and Mary in 1780, was clearly a man who could hold his own against the new president.

In January 1802, Jefferson's congressional allies called for repeal of the Judiciary Act. In public debate, they studiously avoided the obvious political issue. The new circuit courts should be closed not only because they were staffed by Federalists but also, as they argued, because they were needlessly expensive. The judges did not hear enough cases to warrant continuance. The Federalists mounted an able defense. The Constitution, they observed, provided for the removal of federal judges only when they were found guilty of high crimes and misdemeanors. By repealing the Judiciary Act, the legislative branch would in effect be dismissing judges without a trial, a clear violation of their constitutional rights. This argument made little impression on the Republican party. In March, the House, following the Senate, voted for repeal.

While Congress debated the Judiciary Act, another battle erupted. One of Adams's "midnight" appointees, William Marbury, complained that the new administration would not give him his commission for the office of justice of the peace for the District of Columbia. He sought redress before the Supreme Court, demanding that the federal justices compel James Madison, the secretary of state, to deliver the necessary papers. When they learned that Marshall had agreed to hear this case, the Republicans were furious. Apparently the chief justice wanted to provoke a confrontation with the executive branch.

Marshall was too clever to jeopardize the independence of the Supreme Court over such a relatively minor issue. In his celebrated ***Marbury* v. *Madison*** decision (February 1803), Marshall berated the secretary of state for withholding Marbury's commission. Nevertheless, he concluded that the Supreme Court did not possess jurisdiction over such matters. Poor Marbury was out of luck. The Republicans proclaimed victory. In fact, they were so pleased with the outcome that they failed to examine the logic of Marshall's decision. He had ruled that part of the earlier act of Congress, the one on which Marbury based his appeal, was unconstitutional. This was the first time the Supreme Court asserted its right to judge the constitutionality of congressional acts, and while contemporaries did not fully appreciate the significance of Marshall's doctrine, *Marbury* v. *Madison* later served as an important precedent for judicial review of federal statutes.

Neither Marbury's defeat nor repeal of the Judiciary Act placated extreme Republicans. They insisted that federal judges should be made more responsive to the will of the people. One solution, short of electing federal judges, was impeachment. This clumsy device provided the legislature with a way of removing particularly offensive individuals. Early in 1803, John Pickering, an incompetent judge from New Hampshire, presented the Republicans with a curious test case. This Federalist appointee suffered from alcoholism as well as insanity. While his outrageous behavior on the bench embarrassed everyone, Pickering had not committed any high crimes against the U.S. government. Ignoring such legal niceties, Jefferson's congressional allies pushed for impeachment. Although the Senate convicted Pickering (March 1804), many senators refused to compromise the letter of the Constitution and were conspicuously absent on the day of the final vote.

Jefferson was apparently so eager to purge the courts of Federalists that he failed to heed these warnings. By the spring of 1803, he had set his sights on a target far more important than John Pickering. In a Baltimore newspaper, the president stumbled on the transcript of a speech allegedly delivered before a federal grand jury. The words seemed almost treasonous. The person responsible was Samuel Chase, a justice of the Supreme Court, who had frequently attacked Republican policies. Jefferson leapt at the chance to remove Chase from office. Indeed, the moment he learned of Chase's actions, the president wrote to a leading Republican congressman, asking, "Ought the seditious and official attack on the principles of our Constitution . . . go unpunished?" The congressman took the hint. In a matter of weeks, the Republican-controlled House of Representatives indicted Chase.

Even at this early stage of the impeachment, some members of Congress expressed uneasiness. The charges drawn up against the judge were purely political. There was no doubt that the judge's speech had been indiscreet. He had told the Baltimore jurors that "our late reformers"—in other words, the Republicans—threatened "peace and order, freedom and property." But while Chase lacked good judgment, his attack on the Jefferson administration hardly seemed criminal. Nathaniel Macon, a powerful Republican congressman from North Carolina, wondered aloud, "Is error of opinion to be dreaded where enquiry is free?" This was the sort of question that Jefferson himself had asked the Federalists following passage of the Alien and Sedition Acts, but in 1804, Macon went unanswered. It

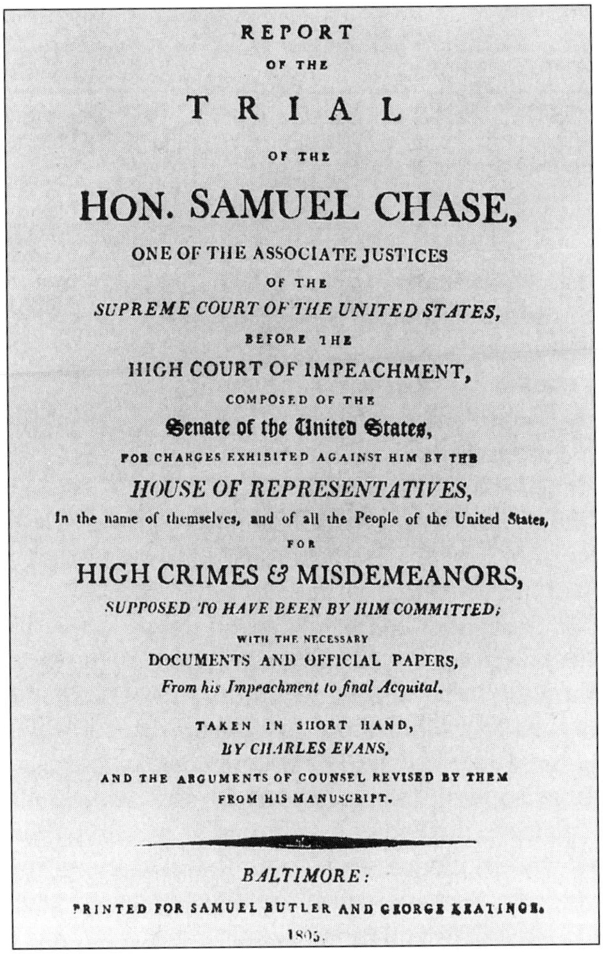
REPORT
OF THE
TRIAL
OF THE
HON. SAMUEL CHASE,
ONE OF THE ASSOCIATE JUSTICES
OF THE
SUPREME COURT OF THE UNITED STATES,
BEFORE THE
HIGH COURT OF IMPEACHMENT,
COMPOSED OF THE
Senate of the United States,
FOR CHARGES EXHIBITED AGAINST HIM BY THE
HOUSE OF REPRESENTATIVES,
In the name of themselves, and of all the People of the United States,
FOR
HIGH CRIMES & MISDEMEANORS,
SUPPOSED TO HAVE BEEN BY HIM COMMITTED;
WITH THE NECESSARY
DOCUMENTS AND OFFICIAL PAPERS,
From his Impeachment to final Acquital.
TAKEN IN SHORT HAND,
BY CHARLES EVANS,
AND THE ARGUMENTS OF COUNSEL REVISED BY THEM
FROM HIS MANUSCRIPT.
BALTIMORE:
PRINTED FOR SAMUEL BUTLER AND GEORGE KEATINGE.
1805.

Presiding officer Aaron Burr ordered extra seating installed in the Senate chamber to accommodate the spectators who attended Justice Chase's impeachment trial. ❖

was clear that if the Senate convicted Chase, every member of the Supreme Court, including Marshall, might also be dismissed.

Chase's trial before the U.S. Senate was one of the most dramatic events in American legal history. Aaron Burr, the vice president, organized the proceedings. For reasons known only to himself, Burr redecorated the Senate chamber so that it looked more like the British House of Lords than the meeting place of a republican legislature. In this luxurious setting, Chase and his lawyers conducted a masterful defense. By contrast, John Randolph, the congressman who served as chief prosecutor, behaved in an erratic manner, betraying repeatedly his ignorance of relevant points of law. While most Republican senators personally disliked the arrogant Chase, they refused to expand the constitutional definition of impeachable offenses to suit Randolph's argument, and on March 1, 1805, the Senate acquitted the justice of all charges. The experience apparently convinced Chase of the need for greater moderation. After returning to the federal bench, he refrained from attacking Republican policies. His Jeffersonian opponents also learned something important. American politicians did not like tampering with the Constitution in order to get rid of specific judges, even an imprudent one like Chase.

Politics of Desperation

The collapse of the Federalists on the national level encouraged dissension within the Republican party. Extremists in Congress insisted on monopolizing the president's ear, and when he listened to political moderates, they rebelled. The members of the most vociferous faction called themselves "the *good old* republicans"; the newspapers labeled them the "Tertium Quids," loosely translated as "nothings" or "no accounts." During Jefferson's second term, the Quids argued that the president's policies, foreign and domestic, sacrificed virtue for pragmatism. Their chief spokesmen were two members from Virginia, John Randolph and John Taylor of Caroline (the name of his plantation), both of whom were convinced that Jefferson had betrayed the republican purity of the Founders. They both despised commercial capitalism. Taylor urged Americans to return to a simple agrarian way of life. Randolph's attacks were particularly shrill. He saved his sharpest barbs for Gallatin and Madison, Republican moderates who failed to appreciate the congressman's self-righteous posturing.

The Yazoo controversy raised the Quids from political obscurity. This complex legal battle began in 1795 when a thoroughly corrupt Georgia assembly sold 35 million acres of western land, known as the Yazoo claims, to private companies at bargain prices. It soon became apparent that every member of the legislature had been bribed, and in 1796, state lawmakers rescinded the entire agreement. Unfortunately, some land had already changed hands. When Jefferson became president, a specially appointed federal commission attempted to clean up the mess. It recommended that Congress set aside 5 million acres for buyers who had unwittingly purchased land from the discredited companies.

Randolph immediately cried foul. Such a compromise, however well-meaning, condoned fraud. Republican virtue hung in the balance. For months, the Quids harangued Congress about the Yazoo business, but in the end, their impassioned oratory accomplished nothing. The Marshall Supreme Court upheld the rights of the original purchasers in *Fletcher* v. *Peck* (1810). The justices unanimously declared that legislative fraud did not impair private contracts and that the Georgia assembly of 1796 did not have authority to take away lands already sold to innocent buyers. This important case upheld the Supreme Court's authority to rule on the constitutionality of state laws.

Murder and Conspiracy: The Curious Career of Aaron Burr

Vice President Aaron Burr created far more serious difficulties for the president. The two men had never been close. Burr's strange behavior during the election of 1800 raised suspicions that he had conspired to deprive Jefferson of the presidency. Whatever the truth may have been, the vice president entered the new administration under a cloud. He played only a marginal role in shaping policy, a situation extremely frustrating for a person as ambitious as Burr.

In the spring of 1804, Burr decided to run for the governorship of New York. Although he was a Republican, he entered into political negotiations with High Federalists who were plotting the secession of New England and New York from the Union. In a particularly scurrilous contest—and New York politics were always abusive—Alexander Hamilton described Burr as " . . . a dangerous man . . . who ought not to be trusted with the reins of government" and urged Federalists in the state to vote for another candidate.

Whether Hamilton's appeals influenced the voters is not clear. Burr, however, blamed Hamilton for his subsequent defeat and challenged him to a duel. Even though Hamilton condemned this form of violence—his own son had recently been killed in a duel—he accepted Burr's "invitation," describing the foolishness as a matter of personal honor. On July 11, 1804, at Weehawken, New Jersey, the vice president shot and killed the former secretary of the treasury. Both New York and New Jersey indicted Burr for murder. If he returned to either state, he would immediately be arrested. His political career lay in shambles.

Large caliber, smoothbore flintlock pistols used in the duel between Aaron Burr and Alexander Hamilton on July 11, 1804. Burr was not hit, but Hamilton was mortally wounded and died the next day. Though many condemned the practice of dueling, it was a fairly common means of resolving grievances in America until the time of the Civil War. ❖

In his final weeks as vice president, Burr hatched a scheme so audacious that the people with whom he dealt could not decide whether he was a genius or a madman. On a trip down the Ohio River in April 1805, after his term as vice president was over, he hinted broadly that he was planning a private military adventure against a Spanish colony, perhaps Mexico. Burr also suggested that he envisioned separating the western states and territories from the Union. The region certainly seemed ripe for secession. The citizens of New Orleans acted as if they wanted no part of the United States. Burr covered his tracks well. No two contacts ever heard the same story. Wherever Burr traveled, he recruited adventurers; he mingled with the leading politicians of Kentucky, Ohio, and Tennessee. James Wilkinson, commander of the U.S. Army in the Mississippi Valley, accepted an important role in this vaguely defined conspiracy. The general was a thoroughly corrupt opportunist. Randolph described him as "the only man that I ever saw who was from bark to the very core a villain."

In the late summer of 1806, Burr put his ill-defined plan into action. A small group of volunteers constructed riverboats on a small island in the Ohio River owned by Harman Blennerhassett, an Irish immigrant who, like so many contemporaries, found Burr's charm irresistible. By the time this armed band set out to join Wilkinson's forces, however, the general had experienced a change of heart. He frantically dispatched letters to Jefferson denouncing Burr. Wilkinson's betrayal destroyed any chance of success, and conspirators throughout the West rushed pell-mell to save their own skins. Facing certain defeat, Burr tried to escape to Spanish Florida. It was already too late. Federal authorities arrested Burr in February 1807 and took him to Richmond to stand trial for treason. The prospect of humiliating his old rival was hardly displeasing to the president. Even before a jury had been called, Jefferson announced publicly that Burr's guilt "is placed beyond all question."

Jefferson spoke prematurely. John Adams wisely observed, if Burr's "guilt is as clear as the Noon day Sun, the first Magistrate ought not to have pronounced it so before a Jury had tryed him." The trial judge was John Marshall, a strong Federalist not likely to do the Republican administration any favors. During the entire proceedings, Marshall insisted on a narrow constitutional definition of treason. He refused to hear testimony regarding Burr's supposed intentions. "Troops must be embodied," Marshall thundered, "men must be actually assembled." He demanded two witnesses to each overt act of treason.

Burr, of course, had been too clever to leave this sort of evidence. While Jefferson complained bitterly about the miscarriage of justice, the jurors declared on September 1, 1807, that the defendant was "not proved guilty by any evidence submitted to us." The public was outraged, and Burr prudently went into exile in Europe. The president threatened to introduce an amendment to the Constitution calling for the election of federal judges. Nothing came of his proposal. And Marshall, who behaved in an undeniably partisan manner, inadvertently helped protect the civil rights of all Americans. If the chief justice had allowed circumstantial evidence into the Richmond courtroom, if he had listened to rumor and hearsay, he would have made it much easier for later presidents to use trumped-up conspiracy charges to silence legitimate political opposition.

The Slave Trade

Slavery sparked angry debate at the Constitutional Convention of 1787 (see Chapter 6). If delegates from the northern states had refused to compromise on this issue, Southerners would not have supported the new government. The slave states demanded a great deal in return for cooperation. According to an agreement that determined the size of a state's congressional delegation, a slave counted as three-fifths of a free white male. This political formula meant that while blacks did not vote, they helped increase the number of southern representatives. The South in turn gave up very little, agreeing only that after 1808 Congress *might consider* banning the importation of slaves into the United States. Slaves even influenced the outcome of national elections. Had the three-fifths rule not been in effect in 1800, for example, Adams would surely have had the votes to defeat Jefferson in the electoral college.

In an annual message sent to Congress in December 1806, Jefferson urged the representatives to prepare legislation outlawing the slave trade. During the early months of 1807, congressmen debated various ways of ending the embarrassing commerce. It was clear that the issue cut across party lines. Northern representatives generally favored a strong bill; some even wanted to make smuggling slaves into the country a capital offense. But there was a serious problem. The northern congressmen could not figure out what to do with black people captured by the customs agents who would enforce the legislation. To sell these Africans would involve the federal government in slavery, which many Northerners found morally repugnant. Nor was there much sympathy for freeing them. Ignorant of the English language and lacking personal possessions, these blacks seemed unlikely to long survive free in the American South.

Southern congressmen responded with threats and ridicule. They explained to their northern colleagues that no one in the South regarded slavery as evil. It appeared naive, therefore, to expect local planters to enforce a ban on the slave trade or to inform federal agents when they spotted a smuggler. The notion that these culprits deserved capital punishment seemed viciously inappropriate. At one point in the debate, Peter Early, a congressman from Georgia, announced that the South wanted "no civil wars, no rebellions, no insurrections, no resistance to

Although the external slave trade was officially outlawed in 1808, the commerce in humans persisted. An estimated 250,000 African slaves were brought illicitly to the United States between 1808 and 1860. The internal slave trade continued as well. Folk artist Lewis Miller sketched this slave coffle marching from Virginia to new owners in Tennessee under the watchful eyes of mounted white overseers. ❖

the authority of government." All he demanded, in fact, was to let the states regulate slavery. To this, a Republican congressman from western Pennsylvania retorted that Americans who hated slavery would not be "terrified by the threat of civil war."

The bill that Jefferson finally signed in March 1807 probably pleased no one. The law prohibited the importation of slaves into the United States after the new year. Whenever customs officials captured a smuggler, the slaves were to be turned over to state authorities and disposed of according to local custom. Southerners did not cooperate, and for many years African slaves continued to pour into southern ports. Even more blacks would have been imported had Great Britain not outlawed the slave trade in 1807. As part of their ban of the slave trade, ships of the Royal Navy captured American slave smugglers off the coast of Africa, and when anyone complained, the British explained that they were merely enforcing the laws of the United States.

Embarrassments Overseas

During Jefferson's second term (1805–1809), the United States found itself in the midst of a world at war. A brief peace in Europe ended abruptly in 1803, and the two military giants of the age, France and Great Britain, fought for supremacy on land and sea. This was a kind of total war unknown in the eighteenth century. Napoleon's armies carried the ideology of the French Revolution across the Continent. The emperor—as Napoleon Bonaparte called himself after December 1804—transformed conquered nations into French satellites. Only Britain offered effective resistance. On October 21, 1805, Admiral Horatio Nelson destroyed the main French fleet at the battle of Trafalgar, demonstrating decisively the absolute supremacy of the Royal Navy. But only a few weeks later (December 2, 1805), Napoleon crushed Britain's allies, Austria and Russia, at the battle of Austerlitz and confirmed his clear superiority on land.

During the early stages of the war, the United States profited from European adversity. As "neutral carriers," American ships transported goods to any port in the world where they could find a buyer, and American merchants grew wealthy serving Britain and France. Since the Royal Navy did not allow direct trade between France and its colonies, American captains conducted "broken voyages." American vessels sailing out of French ports in the Caribbean would put in briefly in the United States, pay nominal customs, and then leave for France. For several years, the British did little to halt this obvious subterfuge.

Napoleon's successes on the battlefield, however, quickly strained Britain's economic resources. In July 1805, a British admiralty court announced in the *Essex* decision that henceforth "broken voyages" were illegal. The Royal Navy began seizing American ships in record number. Moreover, as the war continued, the British stepped up the impressment of sailors on ships flying the U.S. flag. Estimates of the number of men impressed ranged as high as nine thousand.

Beginning in 1806, the British government issued a series of trade regulations known as the Orders in Council. These proclamations forbade neutral commerce with the Continent and threatened seizure of any ship that violated these orders. The declarations created what were in effect "paper blockades," for even the powerful British navy could not monitor the activities of every Continental port.

Napoleon responded to Britain's commercial regulations with his own paper blockade called the Continental System. In the Berlin Decree of November 1806 and the Milan Decree of December 1807, he announced the closing of all continental ports to British trade. Since French armies occupied most of the territory between Spain and Germany, the decrees obviously cut the British out of a large market. The French emperor also declared that neutral vessels carrying British goods were liable to seizure. For the Americans there was no escape. They were caught between two conflicting systems. The British ordered American ships to stop off to pay duties and secure clearances in England on the way to the Continent; Napoleon was determined to seize any vessel that obeyed the British.

This unhappy turn of international events baffled Jefferson. He had assumed that civilized countries would respect neutral rights; justice obliged them to do so. Appeals to reason, however, made little impression on states at war. "As for France and England," the president growled, "... the one is a den of robbers, the other of pirates." In a desperate attempt to avoid hostilities for which the United States was ill prepared, Jefferson ordered James Monroe and William Pinckney to negotiate a commercial treaty with Great Britain. The document they signed on December 31, 1806, said nothing about impressment, and an angry president refused to submit the treaty to the Senate for ratification.

The United States soon suffered an even greater humiliation. A ship of the Royal Navy, the *Leopard,* sailing off the coast of Virginia, commanded an American warship to submit to a search for deserters (June 22, 1807). When the captain of the *Chesapeake* refused to cooperate, the *Leopard* opened fire, killing three men and wounding eighteen. The attack clearly violated the sovereignty of the United States. Official protests received only a perfunctory apology from the British government, and the American people demanded revenge.

Despite the pressure of public opinion, however, Jefferson played for time. He recognized that the

United States was unprepared for war against a powerful nation such as Great Britain. The president worried that an expensive conflict with Great Britain would quickly undo the fiscal reforms of his first term. As Gallatin explained, in the event of war, the United States "will be poorer, both as a nation and as a government, our debt and taxes will increase, and our progress in every respect be interrupted."

Embargo Divides the Nation

Jefferson found what he regarded as a satisfactory way to deal with European predators with a policy he called "peaceable coercion." If Britain and France refused to respect the rights of neutral carriers, then the United States would keep its ships at home. Not only would this action protect them from seizure, but it would also deprive the European powers of much needed American goods, especially food. The president predicted that a total embargo of American commerce would soon force Britain and France to negotiate with the United States in good faith. "Our commerce is so valuable to them," he declared, "that they will be glad to purchase it when the only price we ask is to do us justice." Congress passed the **Embargo Act** by large majorities, and it became law on December 22, 1807.

"Peaceable coercion" turned into a Jeffersonian nightmare. The president apparently believed the American people would enthusiastically support the embargo. That was a naive assumption. Compliance required a series of enforcement acts that over fourteen months became increasingly harsh.

By the middle of 1808, Jefferson and Gallatin were involved in the regulation of the smallest details of American economic life. Indeed, in the words of one of Jefferson's biographers, the president assumed the role of "commissar of the nation's economy." The federal government supervised the coastal trade, lest a ship sailing between two states slip away to Europe or the West Indies. Overland trade with Canada was proscribed. When violations still occurred, Congress gave customs collectors the right to seize a vessel merely on suspicion of wrongdoing. A final desperate act, passed in January 1809, prohibited the loading of any U.S. vessel, regardless of size, without authorization from a customs officer who was supported by the army, navy, and local militia. Jefferson's eagerness to pursue a reasonable foreign policy blinded him to the fact that he and a Republican Congress would have had to establish a police state to make it work.

Northerners hated the embargo. Persons living near Lake Champlain in upper New York State simply ignored the regulations, and they roughed up collectors who interfered with the Canadian trade. The administration was determined to stop the smugglers. Jefferson

*The Ograbme (*embargo *spelled backward) snapping turtle, created by cartoonist Alexander Anderson, is shown here biting an American tobacco smuggler who is breaking the embargo.* ❖

urged the governor of New York to call out the militia. "I think it so important," the president explained in August 1808, " . . . to crush these audacious proceedings, and to make the offenders feel the consequences of individuals daring to oppose a law by force, that no effort should be spared to compass the object." In a decision that Hamilton might have applauded, Jefferson dispatched federal troops—led by the conspiratorial General Wilkinson—to overawe the citizens of New York.

New Englanders regarded the embargo as lunacy. Merchants of the region were willing to take their chances on the high seas, but for reasons that few people understood, the president insisted that it was better to preserve ships from possible seizure than to make profits. Sailors and artisans were thrown out of work. The popular press maintained a constant howl of protest. One writer observed that embargo in reverse spelled "O grab me!" A poem published in July 1808 captured the growing frustration:

> Our ships, all in motion,
> Once whitened the ocean,
> They sail'd and returned with a cargo;
> Now doom'd to decay
> They have fallen a prey
> To Jefferson, worms, and Embargo.

Not surprisingly, the Federalist party experienced a brief revival in New England, and a few extremists suggested the possibility of state assemblies nullifying federal law.

By 1809, the bankruptcy of Jefferson's foreign policy was obvious. The embargo never seriously damaged the British economy. In fact, British merchants rushed to take over the lucrative markets that the Americans had been forced to abandon. Napoleon liked the embargo, since it seemed to harm Great Britain more than it did France. Faced with growing popular opposition, the Republicans in Congress panicked. One newly elected representative declared that "peaceful coercion" was a "miserable and mischievous failure" and joined his colleagues in repealing the embargo a few days before James Madison's inauguration. Relations between the United States and the great European powers were much worse in 1809 than they had been in 1805. During his second term, the pressures of office weighed heavily on Jefferson, and after so many years of public service, he welcomed retirement to Monticello.

A New Administration Goes to War

As president, James Madison suffered from several personal and political handicaps. Although his intellectual abilities were great, he lacked the qualities necessary for effective leadership. In public gatherings, he impressed people as being "exceedingly modest," and one foreign visitor claimed that the new president "... always seems to grant that the one with whom he talks is his superior in mind and training." Critics argued that Madison's humility revealed a weak, vacillating character.

During the election of 1808, Randolph and the Quids tried unsuccessfully to persuade James Monroe to challenge Madison's candidacy. Jefferson favored his old friend Madison. In the end, a caucus of Republican congressmen gave the official nod to Madison, the first time in American history that such a congressional group controlled a presidential nomination. The former secretary of state defeated his Federalist rival, Charles Cotesworth Pinckney, in the electoral college by a vote of 122 to 47, with New Yorker George Clinton receiving 6 ballots. The margin of victory was substantially lower than Jefferson's had been in 1804, a warning of political troubles ahead. The Federalists also made impressive gains in the House of Representatives, raising their delegation from 24 to 48.

The new president confronted the same foreign policy problems that had occupied his predecessor. Neither Britain nor France showed the slightest interest in respecting American neutral rights. Threats against either nation rang hollow so long as the United States failed to develop its military strength. Out of weakness, therefore, Madison was compelled to put the Non-Intercourse Act into effect. Congress passed this clumsy piece of legislation at the same time as it repealed the embargo (March 1, 1809). The new bill authorized the resumption of trade between the United States and all nations of the world *except* Britain and France. Either of these countries could restore full commercial relations simply by promising to observe the rights of neutral carriers.

The British immediately took advantage of this offer. Their minister to the United States, David M. Erskine, informed Madison that the British government had modified its position on a number of sensitive commercial issues. The president was so encouraged by these talks that he publicly announced that trade with Great Britain could resume in June 1809. Unfortunately, Erskine had not conferred with his superiors on the details of these negotiations. George Canning, the British foreign secretary, rejected the agreement out of hand, and while an embarrassed Madison fumed in Washington, the Royal Navy seized the American ships that had already put to sea.

The Election of 1808

Candidate	Party	Electoral Vote
Madison	Republican	122
C. Pinckney	Federalist	47

Canning's apparent betrayal led the artless Madison straight into a French trap. In May 1810, Congress passed Macon's Bill Number Two, an act sponsored by Nathaniel Macon of North Carolina. In a complete reversal of strategy, this poorly drafted legislation reestablished trade with *both* England and France. It also contained a curious carrot-and-stick provision. As soon as either of these European states repealed restrictions upon neutral shipping, the U.S. government promised to halt all commerce with the other.

Napoleon spotted a rare opportunity. He informed the U.S. minister in Paris that France would no longer enforce the hated Berlin and Milan Decrees. Again, Madison acted impulsively. Without waiting for further information from Paris, he announced that unless Britain repealed the Orders in Council by November, the United States would cut off commercial relations. Only later did the president learn that Napoleon had no intention of living up to his side of the bargain; his agents continued to seize American ships. Madison, who had been humiliated by the Erskine experience, decided to ignore the French provocations, to pretend the emperor was behaving in an honest manner. The British could not explain why the United States tolerated such obvious deception. No one in London would have suspected that the president really had no other options left.

Events unrelated to international commerce fueled anti-British sentiment in the newly conquered parts of the United States. Westerners believed—incorrectly, as it turned out—that British agents operating out of Canada had persuaded Tecumseh's warriors to resist the spread of American settlement. According to the rumors that ran through the region, the British dreamed of monopolizing the fur trade. In any case, General William Henry Harrison, governor of the Indiana Territory, marched an army to the edge of a large Shawnee village at the mouth of Tippecanoe Creek near

Dolley Madison, in a portrait by Gilbert Stuart, 1804, hosted popular informal entertainments at the White House. ❖

the banks of the Wabash River. On the morning of November 7, 1811, the American troops routed the Indians at the battle of Tippecanoe. Harrison immediately became a national hero, and several decades later the American people rewarded "Tippecanoe" by electing him president. This incident forced Tecumseh—a brilliant leader who was trying to restore the confidence and revitalize tribal cultures of the Indians of the Indiana Territory—to seek British military assistance in battling the Americans, something he probably would not have done had Harrison left him alone.

Fumbling Toward Conflict

In 1811, the anti-British mood of Congress intensified. A group of militant representatives, some of them elected to Congress for the first time in the election of 1810, announced they would no longer tolerate national humiliation. They called for action, for resistance to Great Britain, for any course that promised to achieve respect for the United States and security for its republican institutions. These aggressive nationalists, many of them elected in the South and West, have sometimes been labeled the **War Hawks.** The group included Henry Clay, an earthy Kentucky congressman who served as speaker of the House, and John C. Calhoun, a brilliant South Carolinian. These fiery orators spoke of honor and pride, as if foreign relations were a sort of duel between gentlemen. While the War Hawks were Republicans, they repudiated Jefferson's policy of peaceful coercion.

Madison surrendered to the War Hawks. On June 1, 1812, he sent Congress a declaration of war against Great Britain. The timing of his action was peculiar. Over the preceding months, tensions between the two nations had relaxed. No new attacks had occurred. Indeed, at the very moment Madison called for war, the British government was suspending the Orders in Council, a conciliatory gesture that in all likelihood would have preserved the peace.

However inadequately Madison communicated his goals, he did seem to have had a plan. His major aim was to force the British to respect American maritime rights, especially in Caribbean waters. The president's problem was to figure out how a small, militarily weak nation like the United States could bring effective pressure on Great Britain. Madison's answer seemed to be Canada. This colony supplied Britain's Caribbean possessions with much needed foodstuffs. The president reasoned, therefore, that by threatening to seize Canada, the Americans might compel the British to make concessions on maritime issues. It was this logic that Secretary of State James Monroe had in mind when he explained in June 1812 that "it might be necessary to invade Canada, not as an object of the war but as a means to bring it to a satisfactory conclusion."

Congressional War Hawks, of course, may have had other goals in mind. Some expansionists were probably more concerned about conquering Canada than they were about the impressment of American seamen. For others, the whole affair may have truly been a matter of national pride. Andrew Jackson wrote, "*For what are we going to fight?* . . . we are going to fight for the reestablishment of our national character, misunderstood and vilified at home and abroad." New Englanders in whose commercial interests the war would supposedly be waged ridiculed such chauvinism. The vote in Congress was close, 79 to 49 in the House, 19 to 13 in the Senate. With this doubtful mandate, the country marched to war against the most powerful maritime nation in Europe. Division over the war question was reflected in the election of 1812. A faction of antiwar Republicans nominated De Witt Clinton of New York, who was endorsed by the Federalists. Nevertheless Madison, the Republican, won narrowly, gaining 128 electoral votes to Clinton's 89.

The Election of 1812

Candidate	Party	Electoral Vote
Madison	Republican	128
Clinton	Republican* (antiwar faction)	89

*Clinton was nominated by a convention of antiwar Republicans and endorsed by the Federalists.

The Strange War of 1812

Optimism for the **War of 1812** ran high. The War Hawks apparently believed that even though the United States possessed only a small army and navy, it could easily sweep the British out of Canada. Such predictions flew in the face of political and military realities. Not only did the Republicans fail to appreciate how unprepared the country was for war, but they also refused to mobilize needed resources. The House rejected proposals for direct taxes and authorized naval appropriations only with the greatest reluctance. Indeed, even as they planned for battle, the Republican members of Congress were haunted by the consequences of their political and economic convictions. They did not seem to understand that a weak, highly decentralized government—the one that Jeffersonians championed—was incapable of waging an expensive war against the world's greatest sea power.

❖ A Look at the Past ❖

"We Owe Allegiance to No Crown"

Patriotic symbols abound in this print by John Archibald Woodside, Jr. Miss Liberty, carrying a liberty cap on a pole, crowns an American sailor with a laurel wreath, signifying that American liberty is victorious. The sentiment expressed visually and emphatically, "We Owe Allegiance to No Crown," seems appropriate for the revolutionary era, but in fact this print dates much later, to the early nineteenth century, when the War of 1812 sparked nationalism. What does this print suggest about American confidence at that time? Does it raise questions about United States–British relations following the American Revolution?

New Englanders refused to cooperate with the war effort. In July 1812, one clergyman in Massachusetts urged the people of the region to "proclaim an honourable neutrality." Many persons did just that. New Englanders carried on a lucrative, though illegal, commerce with the enemy. When the U.S. Treasury appealed for loans to finance the war, wealthy northern merchants failed to respond. The British government apparently believed the New England states might negotiate a separate peace, and during the first year of war, the Royal Navy did not bother to blockade the major northern ports.

American military operations focused initially on the western forts. The results were discouraging. On August 16, 1812, Major General William Hull surrendered an entire army to a smaller British force at Detroit. Michilimackinac was lost. Poorly coordinated marches against the enemy at Niagara and Montreal achieved nothing. These experiences demonstrated that the militia, led by aging officers with little military aptitude, no matter how enthusiastic, was no match for well-trained European veterans. On the sea, the United States did much better. In August, Captain Isaac Hull's *Constitution* defeated the HMS *Guerrière* in a fierce battle, and American privateers destroyed or captured a number of British merchant ships. These successes were somewhat deceptive, however. So long as Napoleon threatened the Continent, Great Britain could spare few warships for service in America. As soon as peace returned to Europe in the spring of 1814, Britain redeployed its fleet and easily blockaded the tiny U.S. Navy.

The campaigns of 1813 revealed that conquering Canada would be more difficult than the War Hawks ever imagined. Both sides in this war recognized that whoever controlled the Great Lakes controlled the West. On Lake Erie, the Americans won the race for naval superiority. On September 10, 1813, Oliver Hazard Perry destroyed a British fleet at Put-in-Bay, and in a much quoted letter written immediately after the battle, Perry exclaimed, "We have met the enemy; and they are ours." On October 5, General Harrison overran an army of British troops and Indian warriors at the battle of Thames River. During this engagement, Tecumseh was killed. On the other fronts, however, the war went badly for the Americans. General Wilkinson suffered an embarrassing defeat near Montreal (battle of Chrysler's Farm, November 11), and the British navy held its own on Lake Ontario.

In 1814, the British took the offensive. Following their victory over Napoleon, British strategists planned to increase pressure on three separate American fronts: the Canadian frontier, Chesapeake coastal settlements, and New Orleans. Sir George Prevost, commander of the British forces in Canada,

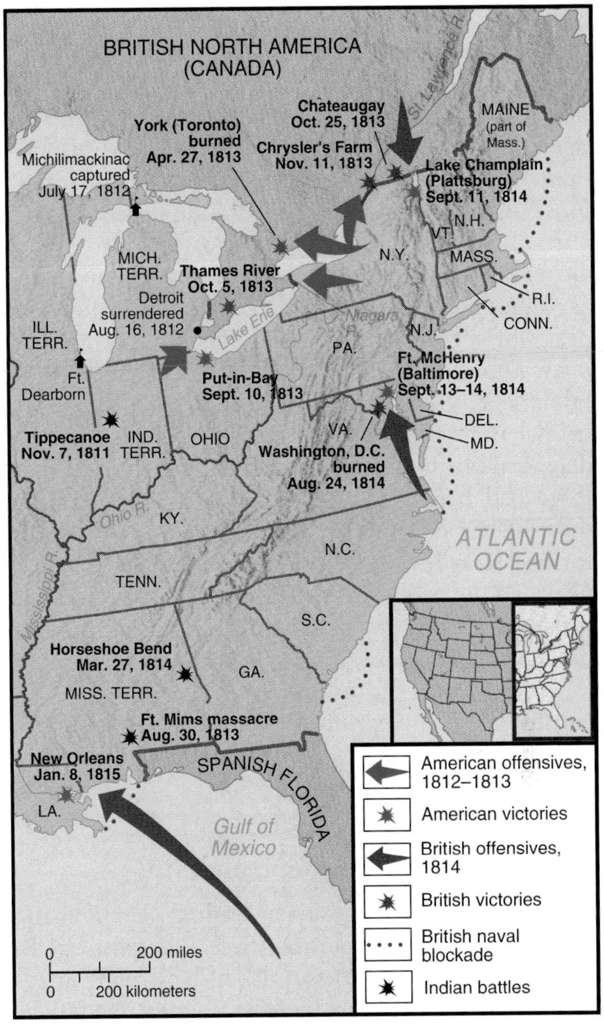

THE WAR OF 1812 *Major battles of the War of 1812 brought few lasting gains to either the British or the Americans.*

marched his army south into upper New York State. A hastily assembled American fleet led by Captain Thomas Macdonough turned back a British flotilla off Plattsburg on Lake Champlain (September 11, 1814). When Prevost learned of this setback, he retreated quickly into Canada. Although the Americans did not realize the full significance of this battle, the triumph accelerated peace negotiations, for after news of Plattsburg reached London, the British government concluded that major land operations along the Canadian border were futile.

Throughout the year, British warships harassed the Chesapeake coast. To their surprise, the British found the region almost totally undefended, and on August 24, 1814, in retaliation for the Americans' destruction of the capital of Upper Canada (York, Ontario), a small force of British marines burned the American capital, a victory more symbolic than strategic. Encouraged by their easy success and contemptuous of America's ragtag soldiers, the British launched a full-scale attack on Baltimore (September 13–14). To everyone's surprise, the fort guarding the harbor held out against a heavy naval bombardment, and the British gave up the operation. The survival of Fort McHenry inspired Francis Scott Key to write "The Star-Spangled Banner."

The battle of New Orleans should never have occurred. The British landed a large assault force under General Edward Pakenham at precisely the same time as diplomats in Europe were preparing the final drafts of a peace treaty. The combatants, of course, knew nothing of these distant developments, and on January 8, 1815, Pakenham foolishly ordered a frontal attack against General Andrew Jackson's well-defended positions. In a short time, the entire British force had been destroyed. The Americans suffered only light casualties. The victory not only transformed Jackson into a national folk hero, but it also provided the people of the United States with a much needed source of pride. Even in military terms, the battle was significant, for if the British had managed to occupy New Orleans, they would have been difficult to dislodge regardless of the specific provisions of the peace treaty.

Hartford Convention: The Demise of the Federalists

In the fall of 1814, a group of leading New England politicians, most of them moderate Federalists, gathered in Hartford to discuss relations between the people of their region and the federal government. The **Hartford Convention** delegates were angry and hurt by the Madison administration's seeming insensitivity to the economic interests of the New England states. The embargo had soured New Englanders on Republican foreign policy, but the events of the War of 1812 added insult to injury. When British troops occupied the coastal villages of Maine, then part of Massachusetts, the president did nothing to drive out the enemy. Of course, the self-righteous complaints of convention organizers overlooked New England's tepid support for the war effort.

The men who met at Hartford on December 15 did not advocate secession from the Union. Although people living in other sections of the country cried treason, the convention delegates only recommended changes in the Constitution. They drafted a number of amendments that reflected the New Englanders' growing frustration. One proposal suggested that congressional representation be calculated on the basis of the number of white males living in a state. New England congressmen were tired of the three-fifths rule that gave southern slaveholders a disproportionately large voice in the House. The convention also wanted to limit each president to a single term in office, a reform that New Englanders hoped might end Virginia's monopoly of the executive mansion. And finally, the delegates insisted that a two-thirds majority was necessary before Congress could declare war, pass commercial regulations, or admit new states to the Union. The moderate Federalists of New England were confident these changes would protect their region from the tyranny of southern Republicans.

The convention dispatched its resolutions to Washington, but soon after an official delegation reached the federal capital, the situation became ex-

CHRONOLOGY

1800	Thomas Jefferson elected president
1801	Adams makes "midnight" appointments of federal judges
1802	Judiciary Act is repealed (March)
1803	Chief Justice John Marshall rules on *Marbury v. Madison* (February); sets precedent for judicial review ❖ Louisiana Purchase concluded with France (May)
1803–1806	Lewis and Clark explore the Northwest
1804	Aaron Burr kills Alexander Hamilton in a duel (July) ❖ Jefferson elected to second term
1805	Justice Samuel Chase acquitted by Senate (March)
1807	Burr is tried for conspiracy (August–September) ❖ Embargo Act passed (December)
1808	Slave trade is ended (January) ❖ Madison elected president
1809	Embargo is repealed; Non-Intercourse Act passed (March)
1811	Harrison defeats Indians at Tippecanoe (November)
1812	Declaration of war against Great Britain (June) ❖ Madison elected to second term, defeating De Witt Clinton of New York
1813	Perry destroys British fleet at battle of Put-in-Bay (September)
1814	Jackson crushes Creek Indians at Horseshoe Bend (March) ❖ British marines burn Washington, D.C. (August) ❖ Hartford Convention meets to recommend constitutional changes (December) ❖ Treaty of Ghent ends War of 1812 (December)
1815	Jackson routs British at battle of New Orleans (January)

tremely awkward. Everyone was celebrating the victory of New Orleans and the announcement of peace. Republican leaders in Congress accused the hapless New Englanders of disloyalty, and people throughout the country were persuaded that a group of wild secessionists had attempted to destroy the Union. The Hartford Convention accelerated the final demise of the Federalist party.

Treaty of Ghent Ends the War

In August 1814, the United States dispatched a distinguished negotiating team to Ghent, a Belgian city where the Americans opened talks with their British counterparts. During the early weeks of discussion, the British made impossible demands. They insisted on territorial concessions from the United States, the right to navigate the Mississippi River, and the creation of a large Indian buffer state in the Northwest Territory. The Americans listened to this presentation, more or less politely, and then rejected the entire package. In turn, they lectured their British counterparts about maritime rights and impressment.

Fatigue finally broke the diplomatic deadlock. The British government realized that no amount of military force could significantly alter the outcome of hostilities in the United States. Weary negotiators signed the Treaty of Ghent on Christmas Eve 1814. The document dealt with virtually none of the topics contained in Madison's original war message. Neither side surrendered territory; Great Britain refused even to discuss the topic of impressment. In fact, after more than two years of hostilities, the adversaries merely agreed to end the fighting, postponing the vexing issues of neutral rights until a later date. The Senate apparently concluded that stalemate was preferable to continued conflict and ratified the treaty 35 to 0.

Most Americans—except perhaps the diehard Federalists of New England—viewed the War of 1812 as an important success. Even though the country's military accomplishments had been unimpressive, the people of the United States had been swept up in a contagion of nationalism. The Hartford debacle served to discredit secessionist fantasies for several decades. Americans had waged a "second war of independence" and in the process transformed the Union into a symbol

This engraving by Joseph Yeager (ca. 1815) depicts the Battle of New Orleans and the death of British Major General Edward Packenham. The death of the British commander was a turning point in the battle in which over 2,000 British soldiers died at the hands of General Andrew Jackson and the American army. ❖

of national destiny. "The war," reflected Gallatin, had made Americans "feel and act more as a nation; and I hope that the permanency of the Union is thereby better secured." That nationalism had flourished in times of war was an irony that Gallatin's contemporaries did not fully appreciate. After the Treaty of Ghent, however, Americans came gradually to realize they had nothing further to fear from Europe, and in an era of peace, the process of sectional divergence began to quicken, threatening to destroy the republic that Jefferson and Madison had worked so hard to preserve.

Conclusion: Republican Legacy

During the 1820s, it became fashionable to visit retired presidents. These were not, of course, ordinary leaders. Jefferson, Adams, and Madison linked a generation of younger men and women to the heroic moments of the early republic. When they spoke about the Declaration of Independence or the Constitution of the United States, their opinions carried symbolic weight for a burgeoning society anxious about its political future.

A remarkable coincidence occurred on July 4, 1826, the fiftieth anniversary of the Declaration of Independence. On that day, Thomas Jefferson died at Monticello. His last words were, "Is it the Fourth?" On the same day, several hundred miles to the north, John Adams also passed his last day on earth. His mind was on his old friend and sometimes adversary, and during his final moments, Adams found comfort in the assurance that "Thomas Jefferson still survives."

James Madison lived on at his Virginia plantation, the last of the Founders. Throughout a long and productive career, he had fought for republican values. He championed a Jeffersonian vision of a prosperous nation in which virtuous, independent citizens pursued their own economic interests. He tolerated no aristocratic pretensions. Leaders of a Jeffersonian persuasion—and during his last years, that probably included John Adams—brought forth a democratic, egalitarian society. Although they sometimes worried that the obsessive grubbing for wealth might destroy public virtue, they were justly proud of the republic they had helped to create.

But many visitors who journeyed to Madison's home at Montpelier before he died in 1836 were worried about another legacy of the founding generation. Why, they asked the aging president, had the early leaders of this nation allowed slavery to endure? How did African Americans fit into the republican scheme? Try as they would, neither Madison nor the politicians who claimed the Jeffersonian mantle could provide satisfactory answers. In an open, egalitarian society, there seemed no place for slaves, and a few months before Madison died, a visitor reported sadly, "With regard to slavery, he owned himself almost to be in despair."

Recommended Reading

A challenge for historians of this period is explaining how Thomas Jefferson and his followers managed to reconcile Republican theories of government with the practical responsibilities of the presidency. The fullest account of his administration can be found in Merrill D. Peterson, *Thomas Jefferson and the New Nation: A Biography* (1970). Three more recent books examine Jefferson's complex character as well as the impact of Republican policies on the larger society: Peter S. Onuf, *Jeffersonian America* (2001); Joseph J. Ellis, *American Sphinx: The Character of Thomas Jefferson* (1997); and James Horn, et al., eds., *The Revolution of 1800: Democracy, Race, and the New Republic* (2002). The tensions that made this political culture so explosive are treated in Roger Sharp, *American Politics in the Early Republic: The New Nation in Crisis* (1993) and Bernard A. Weisberger, *America Afire: Jefferson, Adams, and the Revolutionary Election of 1800* (2000). The controversies over how best to interpret the Constitution and the politics of the Supreme Court are explored in Jean Edward Smith, *John Marshall: Definer of a Nation* (1996). Also valuable for understanding difficult legal issues are Richard E. Ellis, *The Jeffersonian Crisis: Courts and Politics in the Young Republic* (1971); Leonard W. Levy, *Emergence of a Free Press* (1985); and Morton J. Horowitz, *The Transformation of American Law, 1780–1860* (1977). The Louisiana Purchase is the subject of Alexander DeConde, *The Affair of Louisiana* (1976). On the Lewis and Clark Expedition, see James P. Ronda, *Lewis and Clark Among the Indians* (1984) and Donald Jackson, *Thomas Jefferson and the Stony Mountains: Exploring the West from Monticello* (1981). Several fine studies chronicle the politics of slavery and Jefferson's own problems with freeing African Americans; Henry Wiencek tells how Washington confronted the problem in *An Imperfect God: George Washington, His Slaves, and the Creation of America* (2003). On foreign relations, see Peter S. Onuf, ed., *America and the World: Diplomacy, Politics, and War* (1991); J. C. A. Stagg, *Mr. Madison's War: Politics, Diplomacy, and Warfare in the Early American Republic* (1983); James E. Lewis, Jr., *The American Union and the Problem of Neighborhood: The United States and the Collapse of the Spanish Empire, 1783–1829* (1998); and Paul Baepler, ed., *White Slaves, African Masters: An Anthology of American Barbary Captivity Narratives* (1999). Two splendid works demonstrate how Evangelical Protestantism shaped early nineteenth-century public culture: Nathan O. Hatch, *The Democratization of American Christianity* (1989) and Mark A. Noll, *America's God: From Jonathan Edwards to Abraham Lincoln* (2002).

For a list of additional titles related to this chapter's topics, please see http://www.ablongman.com/divine.

Suggested Web Sites

Thomas Jefferson

http://www.pbs.org/jefferson/

A companion site to the Public Broadcasting Service series on Jefferson, especially important because it contains a fine collection of other people's view of Jefferson.

White House Historical Association

http://www.whitehousehistory.org/

This site contains a timeline of the history of the White House and several interesting photos and links.

Thomas Jefferson Digital Archive at the University of Virginia

http://etext.virginia.edu/jefferson/

Mr. Jefferson's University—the University of Virginia—houses this site with numerous on-line resources about Jefferson and his times, including electronic versions of texts by Jefferson, a page of selected quotations, and a comprehensive annotated bibliography of works on Jefferson from 1826 to 1997.

Lewis and Clark: The Maps of Exploration 1507–1814

http://www.lib.virginia.edu/speccol/exhibits/lewis_clark/home.html

Maps and charts reveal knowledge and conceptions about the known and the unknown. This site includes a number of eighteenth-century maps.

PBS Online—Lewis and Clark

http://www.pbs.org/lewisandclark/

This is a companion site to Ken Burns's documentary on Lewis and Clark containing a timeline of the expedition, a collection of related links, a bibliography, and more than 800 minutes of unedited, full-length RealPlayer interviews with seven experts featured in the film.

The War of 1812

http://members.tripod.com/~war1812/index.html

In-depth and varied information about the War of 1812.

Chapter 9

An exuberant crowd celebrates in the square outside Independence Hall in this painting Election Day in Philadelphia *(1815) by German American artist John Lewis Krimmel.* ❖

Nation Building and Nationalism

A Revolutionary War Hero Revisits America in 1824

When the Marquis de Lafayette returned to the United States in 1824 he found a peaceful and prosperous nation. For more than a year, the great French hero of the American Revolution toured the country that he had helped to bring into being, and he marveled at how much had changed since he had fought beside George Washington more than forty years before. He was greeted by adoring crowds in places that had been unsettled or beyond the nation's borders four decades earlier. Besides covering the eastern seaboard, Lafayette went west to New Orleans, then up the Mississippi and the Ohio by steamboat. He thus sampled a new mode of transportation that was helping to bring the far-flung outposts and settlements of a much enlarged nation into regular contact with each other. Such travel was still hazardous. Lafayette had to be rescued from a sinking steamboat on the Ohio before he could complete his journey to Cincinnati, hub city of the newly settled trans-Appalachian West.

Everywhere Lafayette was greeted with patriotic oratory celebrating the liberty, prosperity, and progress of the new nation. Speaking before a joint session of both houses of Congress, the old hero responded in kind, telling his hosts exactly what they wanted to hear. He hailed "the immense improvements" and "admirable communications" that he had witnessed and declared himself deeply moved by "all the grandeur and prosperity of these happy United States, which . . . reflect on every part of the world the light of a far superior political civilization."

Americans had good reasons to make Lafayette's return the occasion for patriotic celebration and reaffirmation. Since the War of 1812, the nation had been free from serious foreign threats to its independence and way of life. It was growing rapidly in population, size, and wealth. Its republican form of government, which many had considered a risky experiment at the time of its origin, was apparently working well. James Monroe, the current president, had proclaimed in his first inaugural address that "the United States have flourished beyond example. Their citizens individually have been happy and the nation prosperous." Expansion "to the Great Lakes and beyond the sources of the great rivers which communicate through our whole interior" meant that "no country was ever happier with respect to its domain." As for the government, it was so near to perfection that "in respect to it we have no essential improvement to make."

BENEATH THE OPTIMISM AND SELF-CONFIDENCE, however, lay undercurrents of doubt and anxiety about the future. The visit of the aged Lafayette signified the passing of the Founders. Less than a year after his departure, Jefferson and Adams, except for Madison the last of the great Founders, died within hours of each other on the fiftieth anniversary of the Declaration of Independence. Most Americans

OUTLINE

FEATURE ESSAY

saw the coincidence as a good omen for the nation. But, some asked, could their example of republican virtue and self-sacrifice be maintained in an increasingly prosperous and materialistic society? Many in fact believed public virtue had declined since the heroic age of the Revolution. And what about the place of black slavery in a "perfect" democratic republic? Lafayette himself noted with disappointment that the United States had not yet extended freedom to southern slaves.

But the peace following the War of 1812 did open the way for a great surge of nation building. As new lands were acquired or opened up for settlement, hordes of pioneers often rushed in. Improvements in transportation soon gave many of them access to distant markets, and advances in the processing of raw materials led to the first stirrings of industrialization. Politicians looked for ways to encourage the process of growth and expansion, and an active judiciary handed down decisions that served to promote economic development and assert the priority of national over state and local interests. To guarantee the peace and security essential for internal progress, statesmen proclaimed a foreign policy designed to insulate America from external involvements. A new nation of great potential wealth and power was emerging.

Sheet music of a "grand march and quick step" to welcome the Marquis de Lafayette to the United States in 1824. ❖

Expansion and Migration

The peace concluded with Great Britain in 1815 allowed Americans to shift their attention from Europe and the Atlantic to the vast lands of North America. Two treaties negotiated with Great Britain dealt with northern borders. The Rush-Bagot Agreement (1817) limited U.S. and British naval forces on the Great Lakes and Lake Champlain and guaranteed that the British would never try to invade the United States from Canada and that the United States would never try to take Canada from the British. The Anglo-American Convention of 1818 set the border between the lands of the Louisiana Purchase and Canada at the 49th parallel and provided for joint U.S. and British occupation of Oregon.

Between the Appalachians and the Mississippi, settlement had already begun, especially in the new states of Ohio, Kentucky, and Tennessee. In the lower Mississippi Valley, the former French colony of Louisiana had been admitted as a state in 1812, and a thriving settlement existed around Natchez in the Mississippi Territory. Elsewhere in the trans-Appalachian west white settlement was sparse and much land remained in Indian hands. Diplomacy, military action (or at least the threat of it) and massive westward migration and settlement were needed before the continent would yield up its wealth to its white inhabitants.

Extending the Boundaries

Postwar expansionists turned their attention first to Spanish holdings, which included Florida and much of the present-day American West. The first goal of postwar expansionists was to obtain Florida from Spain. In the eyes of the Spanish, their possession extended along the Gulf Coast to the Mississippi. Between 1810 and 1812, however, the United States had annexed the area between the Mississippi and the Perdido River in what became Alabama, claiming that it was part of the Louisiana Purchase. The remainder, known as East Florida, became a prime object of territorial ambition for President James Monroe and his energetic secretary of state, John Quincy Adams. Adams had a grand design for continental expansion that required nullifying or reducing Spanish claims west of the Mississippi as well as east of it; he eagerly awaited an opportunity to apply pressure for that purpose.

General Andrew Jackson provided such an opportunity. In 1816, U.S. troops first crossed into East Florida in pursuit of hostile Seminole Indians. This

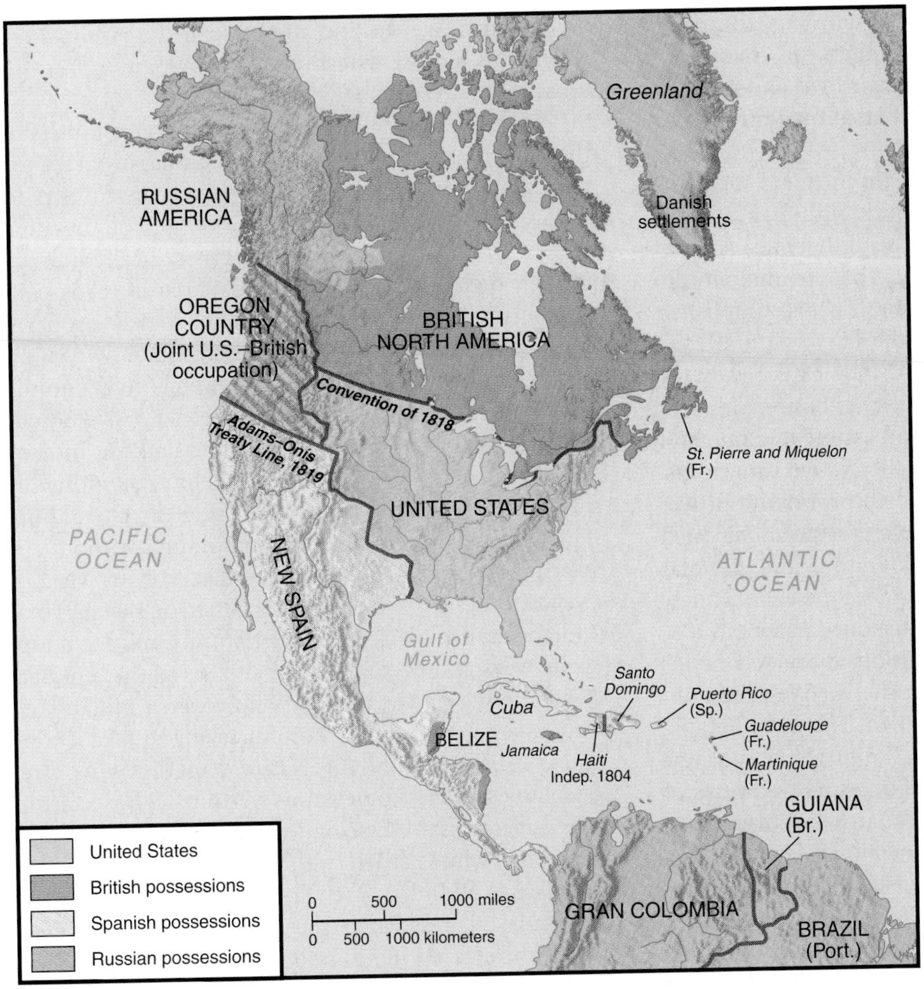

NORTH AMERICA, 1819
Treaties with Britain following the War of 1812 setting the border between the United States and Canada (British North America) made this border the longest unfortified boundary line in the world. ❖

raid touched off a wider conflict, and after taking command in late 1817, Jackson went beyond his official orders and occupied East Florida in April and May of 1818. Except for Adams, all the members of Monroe's cabinet privately condemned this aggressive action; so did a report of the House of Representatives. But no disciplinary action was taken, mainly because public opinion rallied behind the hero of New Orleans.

In November 1818, Secretary Adams informed the Spanish government that the United States had acted in self-defense and that further conflict would be avoided only if East Florida was ceded to the United States. The Madrid government, weakened by Latin American revolutions and the breaking up of its empire, was in no position to resist American bullying. As part of the **Adams-Onís Treaty,** signed on February 22, 1819, Spain relinquished Florida to the United States. In return, the United States assumed $5 million of the financial claims of American citizens against Spain.

A strong believer that the United States had a continental destiny, Adams also used the confrontation over Florida to make Spain give up its claim to the Pacific Coast north of California, thus opening a path for future American expansion. Taking advantage of Spain's desire to keep its title to Texas—a portion of which the United States had previously claimed as part of the Louisiana Purchase—Adams induced the Spanish minister Luis de Onís to agree to the creation of a new boundary between American and Spanish territory that ran north of Texas but extended all the way to the Pacific. Great Britain and Russia still had competing claims to the Pacific Northwest, but the United States was now in a better position to acquire frontage on a second ocean.

Interest in exploitation of the Far West continued to grow during the second and third decades of the nineteenth century. In 1811, a New York merchant, John Jacob Astor, founded the fur-trading post of Astoria at the mouth of the Columbia River in the Oregon Country. Astor's American Fur Company operated out of St. Louis in the 1820s and 1830s, with fur traders working their way up the Missouri to the northern Rockies and beyond. First they limited themselves to trading for furs with the Indians, but later, businesses such as the Rocky Mountain Fur Company, founded in 1822, relied on trappers or "mountain men" who went after game on their own and sold the furs to agents of the company at an annual meeting or "rendezvous."

These colorful characters, who included such legendary figures as Jedediah Smith, Jim Bridger, Kit Carson, and Jim Beckwourth (one of the many African Americans who contributed to the opening of the West as fur traders, scouts, or settlers), accomplished prodigious feats of survival under harsh natural conditions. Following Indian trails, they explored many parts of the Rockies and the Great Basin. Many of them married Indian women and assimilated much of the culture and technology of the Native Americans. Although they actually depleted the animal resources on which the Indians depended, the mountain men were portrayed in American literature and popular mythology as exemplars of a romantic ideal of lonely self-reliance in harmony with unspoiled nature.

Reports of military expeditions provided better documented information about the Far West than did the tales of illiterate mountain men. The most notable of the postwar expeditions was mounted by Major Stephen S. Long in 1819–1820. Long surveyed parts of the Great Plains and Rocky Mountains, but his reports encouraged the misleading view that the Plains were a "great American desert" unfit for cultivation or settlement. For the time being, the Far West remained beyond American dreams of agrarian expansion. The real focus of attention between 1815 and the 1840s was the nearer West, the rich agricultural lands between the Appalachians and the Mississippi that were being opened up for settlement.

Settlement to the Mississippi

To completely occupy and exploit the trans-Appalachian interior, white Americans generally believed they had to displace the Indian communities still inhabiting that region in 1815. In the Ohio Valley and the Northwest Territory, military defeat had already made Native Americans only a minor obstacle to the ambitions of white settlers and land speculators. When the British withdrew from the Old Northwest in 1815, they left their former Indian allies virtually defenseless before the tide of whites who rushed into the region. Consigned by treaty to reservations outside the main lines of white advance, most of the tribes were eventually forced west of the Mississippi. The last stand of the Indians in this region occurred in 1831–1832, when a faction of the confederated Sac and Fox Indians under Chief Black Hawk refused to abandon their lands east of the Mississippi. Federal troops and Illinois state militia pursued Black Hawk's band and drove the Indians back to the river, where they were almost exterminated while attempting to cross to the western bank.

Uprooting once populous Indian communities of the Old Northwest was part of a national program for removing Indians of the eastern part of the country to an area beyond the Mississippi. Whites of the time viewed Indian society and culture as radically inferior to their own and doomed by the march of "progress." Furthermore, the fact that Indians based property rights to land on use rather than absolute ownership was regarded as an insuperable obstacle to economic development. As originally conceived by Thomas Jefferson, removal would have allowed those Indians who became "civilized" to remain behind on individually owned farms and qualify for American citizenship. This policy would reduce Indian holdings without appearing to violate American standards of justice. Not everyone agreed with Thomas Jefferson's belief that Indians, unlike blacks, had the natural ability to adopt white ways and become useful citizens of the republic. People living on the frontier who coveted Indian land and risked violent retaliation for trying to take it were more likely to think of Native Americans as irredeemable savages, or even as vermin to be exterminated if necessary. During the Monroe era, it became clear that white settlers wanted nothing less than the removal of all Indians, "civilized" or not. The issue was particularly pressing in the South. Greed combined with racism as land-grabbing state governments pressed for the total extinction of Indian land titles within their borders.

In the South, as in the Old Northwest, a series of treaties negotiated between 1815 and 1830 reduced tribal holdings and provided for the eventual removal of most Indians to the trans-Mississippi West. But some southern tribes held on tenaciously to their homelands. Many members of the so-called five civilized tribes—the Cherokee, Creek, Seminole, Choctaw, and Chickasaw—had become settled agriculturists. It was no easy task to induce the civilized tribes to give up the substantial and relatively prosperous enclaves in Georgia, Florida, Alabama, and Mississippi that they still held in the 1820s. But the pressure continued to mount. The federal government used a combination of deception, bribery, and threats to induce land cessions. When federal action did not yield results fast enough to suit southern whites who coveted Indian land for mining, speculation, and cotton production, state governments began to act on their own, proclaiming state jurisdiction over lands still allotted by federal treaty to Indians within the state's borders. The stage was thus set for the forced removal of the five civilized tribes to Oklahoma during the administration of Andrew Jackson. (See the Feature Essay,

Mountain men such as Jim Beckwourth (left) and Native Americans met at a rendezvous to trade their furs to company agents in exchange for food, ammunition, and other goods. Feasting, drinking, gambling, and sharing exploits were also part of the annual event. Moccasins trimmed with trade beads (right), worn by both Native Americans and trappers, show how trade influenced both cultures. (Bottom) The painting Rendezvous *(ca. 1837) by Alfred Jacob Miller.* ❖

"Confronting New Land," pp. 252–253. Jackson's Indian Removal policy is discussed in further detail in Chapter 10).

While Indians were being hustled or driven beyond the Mississippi, settlers poured across the Appalachians and filled the agricultural heartland of the United States. In 1810, only about one-seventh of the American population lived beyond the Appalachians; by 1840, more than one-third did. During that period, Illinois grew from a territory with 12,282 inhabitants to a state with 476,183; Mississippi's population of about 40,000 increased tenfold; and Michigan grew from a remote frontier area with fewer than 5,000 people into a state with more than 200,000. Eight new western states were added to the Union during this period. Because of the government's removal policies, few settlers actually had to fight Indians. But they did have to obtain possession of land and derive a livelihood from it. For many, this was no easy task.

Much of the vast acreage opened up by the westward movement passed through the hands of land speculators before it reached farmers and planters. Government lands in the western territories were first surveyed and then sold at auction. In the prosperous period following the War of 1812, and again during the boom of the early to mid-1830s, speculation in public lands proceeded at a massive and feverish rate. After a financial panic in 1819 brought ruin to many who had purchased tracts on credit, the minimum price was lowered from $2.00 to $1.25 an acre, but full payment was required in cash. Since few settlers could

Feature Essay

Confronting New Land

Relocating Indians to make room for white settlers was U.S. government policy from the presidency of Thomas Jefferson until the end of the nineteenth century when Indians were last placed on reservations. Persuasion and the promise of compensation were the preferred methods for inducing Indians to move. But if these methods failed, force could be applied. In his address to Congress on December 6, 1830, President Andrew Jackson celebrated the progress of his vigorous Indian removal policy, and chided those being removed for their ingratitude:

> Our [white] children by thousands yearly leave the land of their birth to seek new homes in distant regions. Does Humanity weep at these painful separations from every thing, animate and inanimate, with which the young heart has become entwined? Far from it. It is rather a source of joy that our country affords scope where our young population may range unconstrained. . . .

Indeed there were two westward migrations in the antebellum era—one by European American settlers, one by Native Americans. During the same decades that hundreds of thousands of white farmers moved to Illinois and Missouri, tens of thousands of Indians were removed to present-day Kansas and Oklahoma. Despite obvious differences, these two streams of migration had something in common. Both groups of migrants had to adapt to the same unfamiliar prairie environment.

A pioneer family's sod house on the Kansas plains. Unlike the eastern woodlands, the prairie offered little timber for building log cabins and settlers there often built houses of sod bricks. ❖

European Americans and Eastern Indians were woodland people. They lived at the tail end of the "Age of Wood" when forests provided the primary material for building, fencing, and heating, not to mention habitat for game that supplemented their diets. The ideal landscape was a clearing for a farm or small village surrounded by thick forest. In the prairie, emigrants confronted an opposite landscape: huge openings—"barrens"—fringed by trees. "To one unaccustomed to it, there is something inexpressibly lonely in the solitude of a prairie," wrote Washington Irving. "The loneliness of the forest seems nothing to it." Settlers clustered at the prairie's edge, and only partly for the timber. The grassland had a reputation for fire, dryness, and infertility. James Madison, writing to Thomas Jefferson, expressed the conviction that Illinois was a "miserably poor" country that would never bear "a single bush." Unsurprisingly, therefore, most of the early setters to the prairie states gravitated to the relatively rare hilly and wooded areas that reminded them from where they had come.

At the time, most Americans believed that vegetation revealed its soil's fertility: the bigger the greenery, the richer the earth. Soil that produced no trees seemed mighty poor indeed. People eventually tried farming the prairie, of course, and discovered the truth: The soil was, in fact, so immensely fertile it supported a thick shield of tangled roots. "Sod-busting" required oxen, tools, and muscle; before the John Deere iron plow became readily available in the mid-nineteenth century, most early settlers were not up to the difficult task.

If Illinois initially seemed barren, the lands of present-day Kansas-Oklahoma seemed positively sterile. In 1820, a government surveyor gave an exaggerated but well-publicized name to this swath of the continent: "The Great American Desert." It was here that a diverse assemblage of Indian refugees tried their best to set up new homes in the removal era. In addition to the well-known Five Civilized Tribes from the South, the newcomers included groups from the Northeast

This 1839 satire on western emigration depicts a battered wagon of half-starved pioneers returning to New England after suffering hardships in Illinois, while an optimistic traveler is on his way there. ❖

and Old Northwest, including the Chippewa, Kickapoo, Miami, Ottawa, Potawatomi, Sac-Fox, Seneca, and Winnebago, among others.

For these woodland peoples, the sea of grass came as a shock. No wonder that many of the relocated Indians complained to the "Great Father"—the federal government. Writing to Indian agent William Clark (of Lewis and Clark fame), Shawnee leaders related that they "traveled three days through prairies and thought we were in the land of the great spirit, for we could see nothing but what was above us and the earth we walked upon." The Wyandot Nation of Ohio decided to send an "unbiased, unprejudiced" exploring expedition to see their promised land on the Missouri-Kansas border. The report was discouraging: "[T]here is but little timber and what there is, is of a low scrubby, knotty and twisted kind and fit for nothing but firewood. . . . [T]here is not good timber sufficient for the purposes of a people that wish to pursue agriculture."

From its inception, federal Indian policy meant to turn natives into sedentary farmers, as European-style agriculture was assumed to be the mark of "civilization." In fact, Eastern Indians like the Wyandot had extensive experience with various forms of agriculture. But old methods could not be easily replicated on the prairie, where the soil was too hard to be easily cultivated, and water was scarce. A few Indian groups, such as the Cherokees, had learned to grow marketable crops in their traditional homelands and continued to do so in the new lands after removal. Nonetheless, some Cherokees chose to become seasonal bison hunters on the Southern Plains. Even with changes in their farming and hunting methods, it took decades for the Cherokee to recover from the dispossession of their towns and farms in Georgia. Adaptation was made more difficult by the staggering human losses they suffered on their forced march to the West.

The sickness and death on the Cherokee Trail of Tears—nearly a third of the migrants died on the way—was an extreme form of an experience that European American settlers also faced. For whites and natives alike, moving west meant growing ill; the body became unsettled in its new environment. A spokesperson for tribes removed from upstate New York to Kansas called it "a poor barren unhealthy country where many families have lost all their children in a course of a few years." For both races, catching the "ague" was an inevitable part of "seasoning" in this new country, which had a reputation for sickliness. Now understood as malaria, the ague commonly presented itself in cycles of shaking. Indeed, the experience was so common that there were essentially two types of settlers: veterans of the "pioneer shakes" and greenhorns. Likewise, it was impossible to completely avoid "the chills" because it could arrive on the very air that permeated wooden cabins.

Antebellum settlers attributed many of their maladies to "miasma." Noah Webster defined it as "infecting substances floating in the air; the effluvia of any putrefying bodies, rising and floating in the atmosphere." According to popular belief, miasma came from rot in humus-rich forests, fertile bottomlands, and well-watered prairie. When settlers broke the prairie in order to "improve" the land, they released foul airs. People attempted to fight miasma by purging the air with coal smoke or wearing strong-smelling bags of herbs around the neck. But the land got sicker before it got healthier. The irony was not lost on settlers. Timothy Flint, who published an influential western guidebook in 1831, wrote that "there appears to be in the great plan of Providence a scale, in which the advantages and disadvantages of human condition are balanced. Where the lands are extremely fertile, it seems to be appended to them, as a drawback to that advantage, that they are generally sickly."

In the antebellum period, many Americans believed that land, like bodies, had intrinsic constitutions or states of health. Ideally, individuals and races could be matched to their "proper" environment (an idea used to defend slavery). Many Northerners and Indians from the North feared for their health when migrating to the hot, humid Mississippi basin. Billy Caldwell, a half-Irish, half-Indian chief from the Great Lakes region declared that Kansas was "unhealthy for people from a cold climate." There was always the hope that the new Indian homelands would prove unsuitable to white settlers. In 1836, en route to their new home, the Sac and Fox Indians said with bitter sarcasm that "the south side of the Missouri River is intended by the great spirit for the Red skins and for this reason he made so much prairie, that it would not suit . . . the white man, and if this had not been the case the red man would in short time have been without a home." In a matter of time, though, the "white man" would find the prairie suitable and would claim this homeland, too.

View of the Great Treaty Held at Prairie du Chien *(1825). Representatives of eight Native American tribes met with government agents at Prairie du Chien, Wisconsin, in 1825 to define the boundaries of their respective land claims. The United States claimed the right to make "an amicable and final adjustment" of the claims. Within twenty-five years, most of the tribes present at Prairie du Chien had ceded their land to the government.* ❖

afford the necessary outlays, wealthy speculators continued to acquire most good land.

Eventually, most of the land did find its way into the hands of actual cultivators. In some areas, squatters arrived before the official survey and formed claims associations that policed land auctions to prevent "outsiders" from bidding up the price and buying their farms out from under them. Squatters also agitated for formal right of first purchase or **preemption** from the government. Between 1799 and 1830, Congress passed a number of special acts that granted squatters in specific areas the right to purchase at the minimum price the land that they had already improved. In 1841, Congress formally acknowledged the right to farm on public lands with the assurance of a *future* preemption right.

Settlers who arrived after speculators had secured title had to deal with land barons. Fortunately for the settlers, most speculators operated on credit and needed a quick return on their investment. They did this by selling land at a profit to settlers who had some capital, by renting out farms until tenants had earned enough to buy them, or by loaning money to squatters who would later pay for the land in installments. As a result, the family farm or owner-operated plantation became the characteristic unit of western agriculture.

Since the pioneer family was likely to be saddled with debt of one kind or another, it was often forced from the beginning to do more than simply raise enough food to subsist. Farmers also had to produce something for market. Not surprisingly, most of the earliest settlement was along rivers that provided a natural means of transportation for flatboats loaded with corn, wheat, cotton, or cured meat. From more remote areas, farmers drove livestock over primitive trails and roads to eastern markets. To turn bulky grain, especially corn, into a more easily transportable commodity, farmers in remote regions often distilled grain into whiskey. To meet the needs of farmers, local marketing centers quickly sprang up, usually at river junctions. Some of these grew into small cities virtually overnight. In the Midwest especially, the rapid rise of towns and cities serving surrounding farming areas greatly accelerated regional development.

Most frontier people welcomed the opportunity to sell some of their crops in order to acquire the consumer goods they could not produce for themselves. Women especially benefited from the chance to buy some household necessities that they had previously made at home, such as soap, candles, and some articles of clothing. But many of them also valued self-sufficiency and tried to produce enough of the necessities of life to survive when cash crops failed or prices were low.

The People and Culture of the Frontier

Most of the settlers who populated the West were farmers from the seaboard states. Rising land prices and declining fertility of the soil in the older regions often motivated their migration. Few sought to escape or repudiate the "civilized" and settled way of life they had known in the East. Most moved in family units and tried to re-create their former ways of life as soon as possible. Women were often reluctant to migrate in the first place, and when they arrived in new areas, they strove valiantly to recapture the comfort and stability they had left behind.

New Englanders moving to western New York or northern Ohio, Indiana, and Illinois brought with them their churches, schools, notions of community uplift, Puritan ideals of hard work and self-denial, and respect for law and government. The Southerners who emigrated from Virginia, the Carolinas, and Georgia to Kentucky, Tennessee, Alabama, and Mississippi, as well as the lower part of the Midwest, were more devoted to the defense of personal or family honor and independence. They therefore tended to be less committed to the development of public authority and institutions.

In general, pioneers sought out the kind of terrain and soil with which they were already familiar. People from eastern uplands favored western hill country. Piedmont and Tidewater farmers or planters usually made for the lower and flatter areas. Early settlers avoided the fertile prairies of the Midwest preferring instead river bottoms or wooded sections because they were more like home and could be farmed by tried-and-true methods. Rather than being the bold and deliberate innovators pictured in American mythology, typical agricultural pioneers were deeply averse to changing their habits.

Yet adjustments were necessary simply to survive under frontier conditions. Initially, at least, isolated homesteads required a high degree of self-sufficiency. Men usually cut down trees, built cabins, broke the soil, and put in crops. Besides cooking, keeping house, and caring for children, women made clothes, manufactured soap and other household necessities, churned butter, preserved food for the winter, and worked in the fields at busy times; at one time or another, women performed virtually all the tasks required by frontier farming. Crops had to be planted, harvested, and readied for home consumption with simple tools brought in wagons from the East—often little more than an axe, a plow, and a spinning wheel.

But this picture of frontier self-reliance is not the whole story. Most settlers in fact found it extremely difficult to accomplish all the tasks using only family labor. A more common practice was the sharing of work by a number of pioneer families. Except in parts of the South, where frontier planters had taken slaves with them, the normal way to get heavy labor done in newly settled regions was through mutual aid. Assembling the neighbors to raise a house, burn the woods, roll logs, harvest wheat, husk corn, pull flax, or make quilts helped turn collective work into a festive social occasion. Passing the jug was a normal feature of these "bees," and an uproarious good time often resulted from the various contests or competitions that speeded the work along. These communal events represented a creative response to the shortage of labor and at the same time provided a source for community solidarity. They probably tell us more about the "spirit of the frontier" than the conventional image of the pioneer as a lonely individualist.

While some settlers remained in one place and "grew up with the country," many others moved on after a relatively short time. The wandering of young Abraham Lincoln's family from Kentucky to Indiana and finally to Illinois between 1816 and 1830 was fairly typical. The physical mobility characteristic of nineteenth-century Americans in general was particularly pronounced in frontier regions. Improved land could be sold at a profit and the proceeds used to buy new acreage beyond the horizon where the soil was reportedly richer. The temptations of small-scale land speculation and the lure of new land farther west induced a large proportion of new settlers to pull up stakes and move on after only a few years. Few early nineteenth-century American farmers developed the kind of attachment to the land that often characterized rural populations in other parts of the world.

Americans who remained in the East often ignored the frontier farmers and imagined the West as an

This rude log cabin in Tennessee served as General Andrew Jackson's home from 1804 to 1819 and was the original Hermitage, later rebuilt as a grand plantation house. Frontier dwellings were often rough and unfinished until the owner could afford better accommodations. The guesthouse in the background would entertain famous visitors like Aaron Burr and James Madison. ❖

untamed American wilderness. They believed the West to be inhabited by Indians and solitary white "pathfinders" who learned to live in harmony with nature. James Fenimore Cooper, the first great American novelist, fostered this mythic view of the West in his stories of the frontier. He began in 1823 to publish a series of novels featuring Natty Bumppo, or "Leatherstocking"—a character who became the prototype for the western hero of popular fiction. Natty Bumppo was a hunter and scout who preferred the freedom of living in the forest to the constraints of civilization. Through Natty Bumppo, Cooper engendered a main theme of American romanticism—the superiority of a solitary life in the wilderness. Most real pioneers, however, aspired to a more settled kind of existence surrounded by families, schools, and churches.

A Revolution in Transportation

It took more than the spread of settlements to bring prosperity to new areas and ensure that they would identify with older regions or with the country as a whole. Along the eastern seaboard, land transportation was so primitive that in 1813 it took seventy-five days for one wagon of goods drawn by four horses to make a trip of about a thousand miles from Worcester, Massachusetts, to Charleston, South Carolina. Coastal shipping eased the problem to some extent in the East and stimulated the growth of port cities. Traveling west over the mountains, however, meant months on the trail.

After the War of 1812, political leaders realized that national security, economic progress, and political unity were all more or less dependent on a greatly improved transportation network. Accordingly, President Madison called for a federally supported program of "internal improvements" in 1815. Recommending such a program in Congress, Representative John C. Calhoun described it as a great nationalizing enterprise: "Let us, then, bind the nation together with a perfect system of roads and canals. Let us conquer space." In ensuing decades, Calhoun's vision of a transportation revolution was realized to a considerable extent, although the direct role of the federal government proved to be less important than anticipated.

Roads and Steamboats

Americans who wanted to get from place to place rapidly and cheaply needed, at a bare minimum, new and improved roads. The first great federal transportation project was the building of the National Road between Cumberland, Maryland, on the Potomac and Wheeling, Virginia, on the Ohio (1811–1818). This impressive toll road had a crushed stone surface and immense stone bridges. It was subsequently extended to reach Vandalia, Illinois, in 1838. Another thoroughfare to the West completed during this period was the Lancaster Turnpike connecting Philadelphia and Pittsburgh. Other major cities were also linked by turnpikes—privately owned toll roads chartered by the states. By about 1825, thousands of miles of turnpikes crisscrossed southern New England, upstate New York, much of Pennsylvania, and northern New Jersey.

By themselves, however, the toll roads failed to meet the demand for low-cost transportation over long distances. For the most part, travelers benefited more than transporters of bulky freight. The latter usually found that total expenses—toll plus the cost and maintenance of heavy wagons and great teams of horses—were too high to guarantee a satisfactory profit from haulage. Hence traffic was less than anticipated, and the tolls collected were often insufficient to provide an adequate return to investors.

Even the National Road itself had severe limitations. Although it was able to carry a substantial east-west traffic of settler parties and wagonloads of manufactured goods, as well as a reverse flow of livestock being driven to market, it could not offer the low freight costs required for the long-distance hauling of wheat, flour, and the other bulky agricultural products of the Ohio Valley. For these commodities, water transportation of some sort was required.

The United States' natural system of river transportation was one of the most significant reasons for its rapid economic development. The Ohio-Mississippi system in particular provided ready access to the rich agricultural areas of the interior and a natural outlet for their products. By 1815, large numbers of flatboats loaded with wheat, flour, and salt pork were making a part of the 2000-mile trip from Pittsburgh to New Orleans. On the lower Mississippi and its main tributaries, cotton could be loaded from plantation or town wharves onto rivercraft or small seagoing vessels and carried to the same destination. Even after the coming of the steamboat, flatboats continued to carry a major share of the downriver trade.

The flatboat trade, however, was necessarily one-way. A farmer from Ohio or Illinois, or someone hired to do the job, could float down to New Orleans easily enough, but there was generally no way to get back except by walking overland through rough country. Until the problem of upriver navigation was solved, the Ohio-Mississippi could not carry the manufactured goods that farmers desired in exchange for their crops.

Fortunately, a solution was readily at hand: the use of steam power. Late in the eighteenth century, a num-

The Clermont on the Hudson *(1830–1835) by Charles Pensee. Although some called his* Clermont *"Fulton's Folly," Robert Fulton immediately turned a profit from his fleet of steamboats, which reduced the cost and increased the speed of river transport.* ❖

ber of American inventors had experimented with steam-driven riverboats. John Fitch even exhibited an early model to delegates at the Constitutional Convention. But making a commercially successful craft required further refinement. In 1807, inventor Robert Fulton, backed by Robert R. Livingston—a New Yorker of great wealth and political prominence—demonstrated the full potential of the steamboat by successfully propelling the *Clermont* 150 miles up the Hudson River. The first steamboat launched in the West was the *New Orleans,* which made the long trip from Pittsburgh to New Orleans in 1811–1812. Besides becoming a principal means of passenger travel on the inland waterways of the East, the river steamboat revolutionized western commerce. In 1815, the *Enterprise* made the first return trip from New Orleans to Pittsburgh. Within five years, sixty-nine steamboats with a total capacity of 13,890 tons were plying western waters.

Steam transport was a great boon for farmers and merchants. It reduced costs, increased the speed of moving goods and people, and allowed a two-way commerce on the Mississippi and Ohio. Eastern manufacturers and merchants now had a better way to reach interior markets than the old method of hauling everything over the Appalachians by road.

The steamboat quickly captured the American imagination. Great paddle wheelers became luxurious floating hotels, the natural habitats of gamblers, confidence men, and mysterious women. For the pleasure of passengers and onlookers, steamboats sometimes raced against each other, and their more skillful pilots became folk heroes. But the boats also had a lamentable safety record, frequently running aground, colliding, or blowing up. The most publicized disasters of antebellum America were spectacular boiler explosions that claimed the lives of hundreds of passengers. As a result of such accidents, the federal government began in 1838 to attempt to regulate steamboats and monitor their construction and operation. The legislation, which failed to create an agency capable of enforcing minimum safety standards, stands as virtually the only federal effort in the pre–Civil War period to regulate domestic transportation.

The Canal Boom

A transportation system based solely on rivers and roads had one enormous gap—it did not provide an economical way to ship western farm produce directly east to ports engaged in transatlantic trade or to the growing urban market of the seaboard states. The solution offered by the politicians and merchants of the Middle Atlantic and midwestern states was to build a system of canals that linked seaboard cities directly to the Great Lakes, the Ohio, and ultimately the Mississippi.

The best natural location for a canal connecting a river flowing into the Atlantic with one of the Great Lakes was between Albany and Buffalo, a relatively flat stretch of 364 miles. The potential value of such a project had long been recognized, but when it was actually approved by the New York legislature in 1817, it was justly hailed as an enterprise of breathtaking boldness. At that time, no more than about 100 miles of canal existed in the entire United States, and the longest single canal extended only 26 miles. Credit for the project belongs mainly to New York's vigorous and farsighted governor, De Witt Clinton. He persuaded the New York state legislature to underwrite the project by issuing bonds, and construction began in 1818. In less than two years, 75 miles were already finished and the first tolls were being collected. In 1825, the entire canal was opened with great public acclaim and celebration.

At 364 miles long, 40 feet wide, and 4 feet deep, and containing 84 locks, the Erie Canal was the most spectacular engineering achievement of the young republic. Furthermore, it was a great economic success. It reduced the cost of moving goods from Buffalo to Albany to one-twelfth the previous rate. It not only lowered the cost of western products in the East but caused an even sharper decline in the price of goods imported from the East by Westerners. It also helped to make New York City the commercial capital of the nation.

The great success of the Erie Canal inspired other states to extend public credit for canal building. Between 1826 and 1834, Pennsylvania constructed an even longer and more elaborate canal, covering the 395 miles from Philadelphia to Pittsburgh and requiring twice as many locks as its New York competitor. But the Pennsylvania Main Line Canal did not do as well as the Erie, partly because of a bottleneck at the crest of the Alleghenies where an inclined-plane railroad had to haul canalboats over a high ridge. Ohio also embarked on an ambitious program of canal construction, completing an artificial waterway from the Ohio River to Cleveland on Lake Erie in 1833. Shorter canals were built in many other states, connecting navigable rivers with sea or lake ports. The last of these was the Illinois and Michigan Canal, completed in 1848. It linked Chicago and the Great Lakes with the Illinois River and the Mississippi.

The canal boom ended when it became apparent in the 1830s and 1840s that most of the waterways were unprofitable. State credit had been overextended, and the panic and depression of the late 1830s and early 1840s forced retrenchment. Moreover, by this time railroads were beginning to compete successfully for the same traffic, and a new phase in the transportation revolution was beginning.

But canals should not be written off as economic failures that contributed little to the improvement of transportation. Some of them continued to be important arteries up to the time of the Civil War and well beyond. Furthermore, the "failure" of many of the canals was due solely to their inability to yield an adequate return on the money invested in them. Concerning one failing canal, a contemporary argued

Illustration of a lock on the Erie Canal at Lockport, New York, 1838. The successful canal facilitated trade by linking the Great Lakes regions to the eastern seaports. ❖

that it "has been more useful to the public, than to the owners." Had the canals been thought of as providing a service rather than yielding a profit—in the manner, for example, of modern interstate highways—their vital contribution to the nation's economic development would have been better appreciated.

Emergence of a Market Economy

The desire to reduce the costs and increase the speed of shipping heavy freight over great distances laid the groundwork for a new economic system. Canals made it less expensive and more profitable for western farmers to ship wheat and flour to New York and Philadelphia and also gave manufacturers in the East ready access to an interior market. Steamboats reduced shipping costs on the Ohio and Mississippi and put farmers in the enviable position of receiving more for their crops and paying less for the goods they needed to import. Hence improved transport increased farm income and stimulated commercial agriculture.

The Beginning of Commercial Agriculture

At the beginning of the nineteenth century, the typical farming household consumed most of what it produced and sold only a small surplus in nearby markets. Most manufactured articles were produced at home. Easier and cheaper access to distant markets caused a decisive change in this pattern. Between 1800 and 1840, agricultural output increased at an annual rate of approximately 3 percent, and a rapidly growing portion of this production consisted of commodities grown for sale rather than consumed at home. The rise in productivity was partly due to technological advances. Iron or steel plows proved better than wooden ones, the grain cradle displaced the scythe for harvesting, and better varieties or strains of crops, grasses, and livestock were introduced. But the availability of good land and the revolution in marketing were the most important spurs to profitable commercial farming. Good land made for high yields, at least for a time, and when excessive planting wore out the soil, a farmer could migrate to more fertile lands farther west. The existence or extension of transportation facilities made distant markets available and plugged farmers into a commercial network that provided credit and relieved them of the need to do their own selling.

The emerging exchange network encouraged movement away from diversified farming and toward regional concentration on staple crops. Wheat was the main cash crop of the North, and the center of its cultivation moved westward as soil depletion, pests, and plant diseases lowered yields in older regions. In 1815, the heart of the wheat belt was New York and Pennsylvania. By 1839, Ohio was the leading producer and Indiana and Illinois were beginning to come into their own. On the rocky hillsides of New England, sheep raising was displacing the mixed farming of an earlier era. But the prime examples of successful staple production in this era were in the South. Tobacco continued to be a major cash crop of the upper South (despite declining fertility and a shift to wheat in some areas), rice was important in coastal South Carolina, and sugar was a staple of southern Louisiana. Cotton, however, was the "king" crop in the lower South as a whole. In the course of becoming the nation's principal

✦ A Look at the Past ✦

Merino Sheep

Increasing commercialism and industrialism affected both urban and rural dwellers during the early nineteenth century. Farmers could choose to participate in the changing economy in several ways. Supplying factories with raw materials and workers with food numbered among their options. Successful agriculture required farmers to alter their strategies. Some farmers intensified production, experimented with scientific methods, increased their herd sizes, and imported improved livestock breeds such as these very woolly merino sheep. Importing livestock, breeding improved varieties, and increasing production required money. What kind of a risk did a farmer take by enthusiastically producing for factories? What do the changes farmers made reveal about economic attitudes?

export commodity, it brought wealth and prosperity to a belt of states running from South Carolina to Louisiana.

A number of factors made the Deep South the world's greatest producer of cotton. First was the great demand generated by the rise of textile manufacturing in England and, to a lesser extent, in New England. Second was the effect of the cotton gin on processing. Invented by Eli Whitney in 1793, this simple device cut the labor costs involved in cleaning short-staple cotton, thus making it an easily marketable commodity.

A third reason for the rise of cotton was the availability of good land in the Southwest. As yields fell in original areas of cultivation—mainly South Carolina and Georgia—the opening of the rich and fertile plantation areas or "black belts" of Alabama, Mississippi, and Louisiana shifted the Cotton Kingdom westward and resulted in a vast increase in total production. In 1816, New Orleans, the great marketing center for western crops, received 37,000 bales; in 1830, 428,000 arrived; in 1840, the annual number had reached 923,000. Between 1817 and 1840, the amount of cotton produced in the South tripled from 461,000 to 1,350,000 bales.

A fourth factor—the existence of slavery, which provided a flexible system of forced labor—permitted operations on a scale impossible for the family labor system of the agricultural North. Finally, the cotton economy benefited from the South's splendid natural transportation system—its great network of navigable rivers extending deep into the interior from the cotton ports of Charleston, Savannah, Mobile, and, of course, New Orleans. The South had less need than other agricultural regions for artificial internal improvements such as canals and good roads. Planters could simply establish themselves on or near a river and ship their crops to market via natural waterways.

Commerce and Banking

As regions specialized in growing commercial crops, a new system of marketing emerged. During the early stages in many areas, farmers did their marketing personally, even when it required long journeys overland or by flatboat. With the growth of country towns, local merchants took charge of the crops near their sources, bartering clothing and other manufactured goods for produce. These intermediaries shipped the farmers' crops to larger local markets such as Pittsburgh, Cincinnati, and St. Louis. From there the commodities could be sent on to Philadelphia, New York, or New Orleans. Cotton growers in the South were more likely to deal directly with factors or agents in the port cities from which their crop was exported. But even in the South, commission merchants in such inland towns as Macon, Atlanta, Montgomery, Shreveport, and Nashville became increasingly important as intermediaries.

Credit was a crucial element in the whole system. Farmers borrowed from local merchants, who received an advance of their own when they consigned crops to a commission house or factor. The commission agents relied on credit from merchants or manufacturers at the ultimate destination, which might be Liverpool or New York City. The intermediaries all charged fees and interest, but the net cost to the farmers was less than when they had handled their own marketing. The need for credit encouraged the growth of money and banking.

Before the revolutions in transportation and marketing, small-scale local economies could survive to a considerable extent on barter. Farmers could give grain to blacksmiths who could in turn exchange grain for iron from a local forge. But long-distance transactions involving credit and deferred payment required money and lots of it. Under the Constitution, the U.S. government is the only agency authorized to coin money and regulate its value. But in the early to mid-nineteenth century, the government printed no paper money and produced gold and silver coins in such small quantities that it utterly failed to meet the expanding economy's need for a circulating currency.

Private or state banking institutions filled the void by issuing banknotes, promises to redeem their paper in specie—gold or silver—on the bearer's demand. After Congress failed to recharter the Bank of the United States in 1811, existing state-chartered banks took up the slack. Many of them, however, lacked adequate reserves and were forced to suspend specie payments during the War of 1812. The demand for money and credit during the immediate postwar boom led to a vast increase in the number of state banks—from 88 to 208 within two years. The resulting flood of state banknotes caused this form of currency to depreciate well below its face value and threatened a runaway inflation. In an effort to stabilize the currency, Congress established a second Bank of the United States in 1816. The Bank was expected to serve as a check on the state banks by forcing them to resume specie payments.

But it did not perform this task well in its early years. In fact, its own free lending policies contributed to the overextension of credit that led to financial panic and depression in 1819. When the economy collapsed, as it would do again in 1837, many Americans questioned whether the new system of banking and credit was as desirable as it had seemed to be in times of prosperity. As a result, hostility to banks became a prominent feature of American politics.

Early Industrialism

The growth of a market economy also created new opportunities for industrialists. In 1815, most manufacturing in the United States was carried on in households, in the workshops of skilled artisans, or in small mills, which used waterpower to turn wheat into flour or timber into boards. The factory form of production, in which supervised workers tended or operated machines under one roof, was rare. It was found mainly in southern New England, where a number of small spinning mills, relying heavily on the labor of women and children, accomplished one step in the manufacture of cotton textiles. But most spinning of thread, as well as the weaving, cutting, and sewing of cloth, was still done by women working at home.

As late as 1820, about two-thirds of the clothing worn by Americans was made entirely in households by female family members—wives and daughters. A growing proportion, however, was produced for market rather than direct home consumption. Under the "putting-out" system of manufacturing, merchant capitalists provided raw material to people in their own homes, picked up finished or semifinished products, paid the workers, and took charge of distribution. Items such as simple shoes and hats were also made under the putting-out system. Home manufacturing of this type was centered in the Northeast and often involved farm families making profitable use of their slack seasons. It did not usually present a direct challenge to the economic preeminence of agriculture, nor did it seriously disrupt the rural pattern of life.

The making of articles that required greater skill—such as high-quality shoes and boots, carriages or wagons, mill wheels, and barrels or kegs—was mostly carried on by artisans working in small shops in towns. But in the decades after 1815, shops expanded in size, masters tended to become entrepreneurs rather than working artisans, and journeymen often became wage earners rather than aspiring masters. At the same time, the growing market for low-priced goods led to a stress on speed, quantity, and standardization in the methods of production. Even where no substantial mechanization was involved, shops dealing in handmade goods for a local clientele tended to become small factories turning out cheaper items for a wider public.

A fully developed factory system emerged first in textile manufacturing. The establishment of the first cotton mills utilizing the power loom as well as spinning

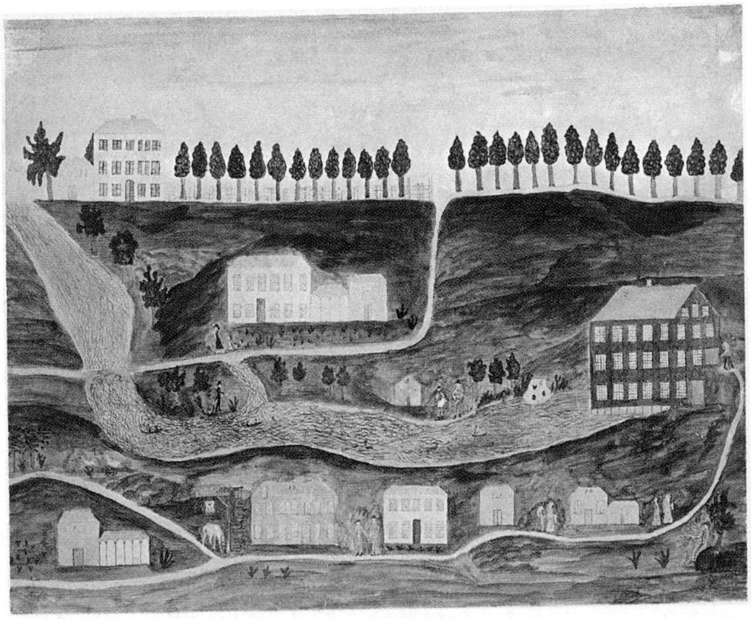

Lowell, Massachusetts, became America's model industrial town in the first half of the nineteenth century. In this painting of the town in 1814, (when it was still called East Chelmsford), a multi-story brick mill is prominent on the river. Textile mills sprang up throughout Lowell in the 1820s and 1830s, employing thousands of workers, mostly women. At right, Lowell mill workers are shown working at the looms. ❖

machinery—thus making it possible to turn fiber into cloth in a single factory—resulted from the efforts of a trio of Boston merchants: Francis Cabot Lowell, Nathan Appleton, and Patrick Tracy Jackson. On a visit to England in 1810–1811, Lowell succeeded in memorizing the closely guarded industrial secret of how a power loom was constructed. Returning to Boston, he joined with Appleton and Jackson to acquire a water site at nearby Waltham and to obtain a corporate charter for textile manufacturing on a new and expanded scale.

Under the name of the Boston Manufacturing Company, the associates began their Waltham operation in 1813. Its phenomenal success led to the erection of a larger and even more profitable mill at Lowell, Massachusetts, in 1822 and another at Chicopee in 1823. Lowell became the great showplace for early American industrialization. Its large and seemingly contented workforce of unmarried young women residing in supervised dormitories, its unprecedented scale of operation, its successful mechanization of almost every stage of the production process—all captured the American middle-class imagination in the 1820s and 1830s. But in the late 1830s and 1840s conditions in the mills changed for the worse as the owners began to require more work for lower pay, and some of the mill girls became militant labor activists. One of these was Sarah Bagley, who helped found the Lowell Female Labor Reform Association in 1844. She subsequently led a series of protests against long hours and changes in the work routine that required more work from each operative. Other mills using similar labor systems sprang up throughout New England, and the region became the first important manufacturing area in the United States.

The shift in textile manufacture from domestic to factory production shifted the locus of women's economic activity. As the New England textile industry grew, the putting-out system rapidly declined. Between 1824 and 1832, household production of textiles dropped from 90 to 50 percent in most parts of New England. The shift to factory production changed the course of capitalist activity in the region. Before the 1820s, New England merchants concentrated mainly on international trade, and Boston mercantile houses made great profits. A major source of capital was the lucrative China trade carried on by fast, well-built New England vessels. When the success of Waltham and Lowell became clear, many merchants shifted their capital away from oceanic trade and into manufacturing. This change had important political consequences, as leading politicians such as Daniel Webster no longer advocated a low tariff that favored importers over exporters. They now became leading proponents of a high duty designed to protect manufacturers from foreign competition.

The development of other "infant industries" of the postwar period was less dramatic and would not come to fruition until the 1840s and 1850s. Technology to improve the rolling and refining of iron was imported from England; it gradually encouraged a domestic iron industry centered in Pennsylvania. The use of interchangeable parts in the manufacture of small arms, pioneered by Eli Whitney and Simeon North, helped to modernize the weapons industry while also contributing to the growth of new forms of mass production.

Although most manufacturing was centered in the Northeast, the West also experienced modest industrial progress. Increasing rapidly in number and size were facilities for processing farm products, such as gristmills, slaughterhouses, and tanneries. Distilleries in Kentucky and Ohio began during the 1820s to produce vast quantities of corn whiskey for a seemingly insatiable public.

One should not assume, however, that America had already experienced an industrial revolution by 1840. In that year, 63.4 percent of the nation's labor force was still employed in agriculture. Only 8.8 percent of workers were directly involved in factory production (others were employed in trade, transportation, and the professions). Although this represented a significant shift since 1810, when the figures were 83.7 and 3.2 percent, the numbers would have to change a good deal more before it could be said that industrialization had really arrived. The revolution that did occur during these years was essentially one of distribution rather than production. The growth of a market economy of national scope—still based mainly on agriculture but involving a rapid flow of capital, commodities, and services from region to region—was the major economic development of this period. And it was one that had vast repercussions for all aspects of American life.

For those who benefited from it most directly, the market economy provided firm evidence of progress and improvement. But many of those who suffered from its periodic panics and depressions regretted the loss of the individual independence and security that had existed in a localized economy of small producers. These victims of boom and bust were receptive to politicians and reformers who attacked corporations and "the money power."

The Politics of Nation Building After the War of 1812

Geographic expansion, economic growth, and the changes in American life that accompanied them were bound to generate political controversy. Farmers, merchants, manufacturers, and laborers were affected by the changes in different ways. So were Northerners, Southerners, and Westerners. Federal and state policies that were meant to encourage or control growth and expansion did not benefit all these groups or sections equally, and unavoidable conflicts of interest and ideology occurred.

But, for a time, these conflicts were not prominently reflected in the national political arena. During the period following the War of 1812, a single party dominated politics. Without a party system in place, politicians did not have to band together to offer the voters a choice of programs and ideologies. A myth of national harmony prevailed, culminating in the **"era of good feeling"** during James Monroe's two terms as president. Behind this facade, individuals and groups fought for advantage, as always, but without the public accountability and need for broad popular approval that a party system would have required. As a result, popular interest in national politics fell.

The absence of party discipline and programs did not completely immobilize the federal government. Congress did manage to legislate on some matters of national concern. Although the president had little control over congressional action, he could still take important initiatives in foreign policy. The third branch of government—the Supreme Court—was in a position to make far-reaching decisions affecting the relationship between the federal government and the states. The common theme of the public policies that emerged between the War of 1812 and the age of Andrew Jackson, which began in the late 1820s, was an awakening nationalism—a sense of American pride and purpose that reflected the expansionism and material progress of the period.

The Republicans in Power

By the end of the War of 1812, the Federalist party was no longer capable of winning a national election. The party of Jefferson, now known simply as the Republicans, was so completely dominant that it no longer had to distinguish itself from its opponents. Retreating from their original philosophy of states' rights and limited government, party leaders now openly embraced some of the programs of their former Federalist rivals—policies that seemed dictated by postwar conditions. In December 1815, President Madison proposed to Congress that it consider such measures as the reestablishment of a national bank, a mildly protective tariff for industry, and a program of federally financed internal improvements to bind "more closely together the various parts of our extended confederacy." Thus did Jefferson's successor endorse parts of a program enunciated by Alexander Hamilton.

In Congress, Henry Clay of Kentucky took the lead in advocating that the government take action to promote economic development. The keystone of what Clay called the **American System** was a high protective tariff to stimulate industrial growth and provide a "home market" for the farmers of the West, making the nation economically self-sufficient and free from a dangerous dependence on Europe.

In 1816, Congress took the first step toward establishing a neo-Federalist American System. It enacted a tariff raising import duties an average of 25 percent. The legislation was deemed necessary because a flood of British manufactured goods was beginning to threaten the infant industries that had sprung up during the period when imports had been shut off by the embargo and the war. The tariff had substantial support in all parts of the country, both from a large majority of congressmen from New England and the Middle Atlantic states and from a respectable minority of the southern delegation. In 1816, manufacturing was not so much a powerful interest as a patriotic concern. Many Americans believed the preservation of political independence and victory in future wars required industrial independence for the nation. Furthermore, important sectors of the agricultural economy also felt the need of protection—especially hemp growers of Kentucky, sugar planters of Louisiana, and wool producers of New England.

Later the same year, Congress voted to establish the second Bank of the United States. The new national bank had a twenty-year charter, an authorized capital of $35 million, and the right to establish branches throughout the country as needed. Organized much like the first bank, it was a mixed public-private institution, with the federal government owning one-fifth of its stock and appointing five of its twenty-five directors. The Bank served the government by providing a depository for its funds, an outlet for marketing its securities, and a source of redeemable banknotes that could be used to pay taxes or purchase public lands. State banking interests and strict constructionists opposed the bank bill, but the majority of Congress found it a necessary and proper means for promoting financial stability and meeting the federal government's constitutional responsibility to raise money from taxation and loans.

Legislation dealing with internal improvements made less headway in Congress because it aroused stronger constitutional objections and invited disagreements among sectional groups over who would benefit from specific projects. Except for the National Road, the federal government undertook no major transportation projects during the Madison and Monroe administrations. Both presidents believed that internal improvements were desirable but that a constitutional amendment was required before federal monies could legally be used for the building of roads and canals within individual states. In 1817, just before leaving office, Madison vetoed a bill that would have distributed $1.5 million among the states for local transportation projects.

The following year, the House of Representatives held a lengthy debate on the question of whether Congress had the authority to make appropriations for internal improvements. Although a preliminary vote approved the principle, further discussion led to its rejection. In 1822, Monroe vetoed legislation for the repair and administration of the National Road, arguing that even this modest activity was beyond the constitutional powers of Congress. Consequently, public aid for the building of roads and canals continued to come mainly from state and local governments.

Monroe as President

As did Jefferson before him, President Madison chose his own successor in 1816. James Monroe thus became the third successive Virginian to occupy the White House. He served two full terms and was virtually uncontested in his election to each. Monroe was well qualified in terms of experience, having been an officer in the Revolution, governor of Virginia, a special emissary to France, and secretary of state. He was reliable, dignified, and high principled, as well as stolid and unimaginative, lacking the intellectual depth and agility of his predecessors. He projected an image of a disinterested statesman in the tradition of the Founders. (He even dressed in the outmoded fashions of the revolutionary era.) Nominated, as was the custom of the time, by a caucus of Republicans in the House of Representatives, Monroe faced only nominal Federalist opposition in the general election.

Monroe avoided controversy in his effort to maintain the national harmony that was the keynote of his presidency. His first inaugural address expressed the complacency and optimism of the time, and he followed it up with a goodwill tour of the country, the first made by a president since Washington. A local newspaper was so impressed with Monroe's warm reception in Federalist Boston that it announced that party strife was a thing of the past and that an "era of good feeling" had begun.

A principal aim of Monroe's administrations was to encourage the good feelings. He hoped to accommodate or conciliate all the sectional or economic interests of the country and devote his main attention to the task of asserting American power and influence on the world stage.

The first challenge to Monroe's hopes for domestic peace and prosperity was the Panic of 1819, which brought an abrupt end to the postwar boom. After a period of rampant inflation, easy credit, and massive land speculation, the Bank of the United States pricked the bubble by calling in loans and demanding the immediate redemption in specie of the state banknotes in its possession. This retrenchment brought a drastic downturn in the economy, as prices fell sharply, businesses failed, and land bought on credit was foreclosed.

The Election of 1816

Candidate	Party	Electoral Vote
Monroe	Republican	183
King	Federalist	34

In 1821, Congress responded weakly to the resulting depression by passing a relief act that eased the terms for paying debts owed on public land. Monroe himself had no program to relieve the economic crisis because he did not feel called on to exert that kind of leadership, and the voters did not seem to have expected it of him. The one-party system then prevailing left the president without the ability to work through an organized majority party in Congress; one-party rule had in fact degenerated into a chaotic "no-party" system. Unlike later presidents, Monroe could retain his popularity during a depression that began during his watch.

Monroe prized national harmony even more than economic prosperity. But during his first administration, a bitter controversy developed between the North and the South over the admission of Missouri to the Union. Once again Monroe remained above the battle and suffered little damage to his own prestige. It was left entirely to the legislative branch of the government to deal with the nation's most serious domestic political crisis between the War of 1812 and the late 1840s.

The Missouri Compromise

In 1817, the Missouri territorial assembly applied for statehood. Since there were two to three thousand slaves already in the territory and the petition made no provision for their emancipation or for curbing further introduction of slaves, it was clear that Missouri would enter the Union as a slave state unless Congress took special action. Missouri was slated to be the first state, other than Louisiana, to be carved out of the Louisiana Purchase, and resolution of the status of slavery there would have implications for the rest of the trans-Mississippi West.

When the question came before Congress in early 1819, sectional fears and anxieties bubbled to the surface. Many Northerners resented southern control of the presidency and the fact that the three-fifths clause

THE ELECTION OF 1820

Candidate	Party	Electoral Vote
Monroe	Republican	231
J. Q. Adams	No party designation	1

of the Constitution, by which every five slaves were counted as three persons in figuring the state's population, gave the South's free population added weight in the House of Representatives and the electoral college. The South, on the other hand, feared for the future of what it regarded as a necessary balance of power between the sections. Up until 1819, a strict equality had been maintained by alternately admitting slave and free states; in that year, there were eleven of each. But northern population was growing more rapidly than southern, and the North had built up a decisive majority in the House of Representatives. Hence the South saw its equal vote in the Senate as essential for preservation of the balance.

In February 1819, Congressman James Tallmadge of New York introduced an amendment to the statehood bill, banning further introduction of slaves into Missouri and requiring steps toward the gradual elimination of slavery within the state. After a heated debate, the House approved the Tallmadge amendment by a narrow margin. The Senate, however, voted it down. The issue remained unresolved until a new Congress convened in December 1819. In the great debate that ensued in the Senate, Federalist leader Rufus King of New York argued that Congress was within its rights to require restriction of slavery before Missouri could become a state. Southern senators protested that denying Missouri's freedom in this matter was an attack on the principle of equality among the states and showed that Northerners were conspiring to upset the balance of power between the sections. They were also concerned about the future of African American slavery and the white racial privilege that went with it.

A statehood petition from the people of Maine, who were seeking to be separated from Massachusetts, suggested a way out of the impasse. In February 1820, the Senate passed the **Missouri Compromise,** voting to couple the admission of Missouri as a slave state with the admission of Maine as a free state. A further amendment was also passed prohibiting slavery in the rest of the Louisiana Purchase north of the southern border of Missouri, or above the latitude of 36°30', and allowing it below that line. The Senate's compromise then went to the House, where it was initially rejected. Through the adroit maneuvering of Henry Clay—who broke the proposal into three separate bills—it eventually won House approval. The measure authorizing

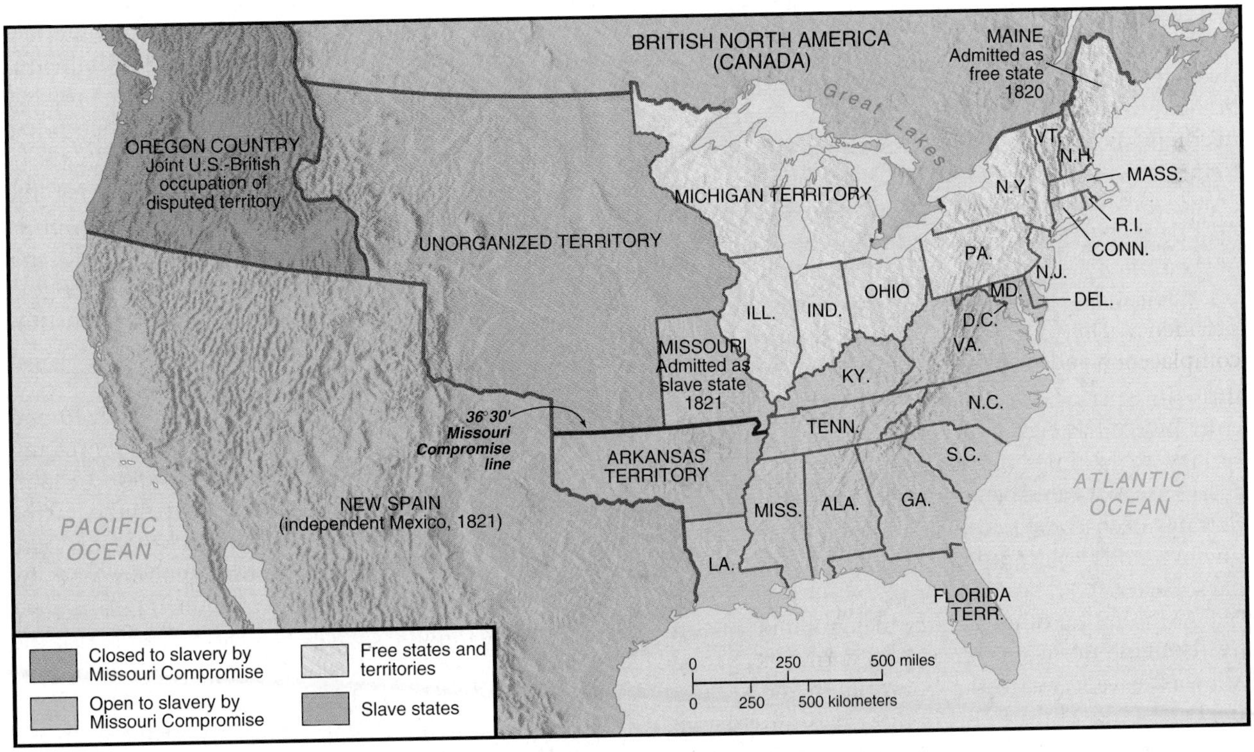

THE MISSOURI COMPROMISE, 1820–1821 *The Missouri Compromise kept the balance of power in the Senate by admitting Missouri as a slave state and Maine as a free state. The agreement temporarily settled the argument over slavery in the territories.* ❖

Missouri to frame a constitution and apply for admission as a slave state passed by a razor-thin margin of 90 to 87, with most northern representatives remaining opposed.

A major sectional crisis had been resolved. But the Missouri affair had ominous overtones for the future of North-South relations. Thomas Jefferson described the controversy as "a fire bell in the night," threatening the peace of the Union. In 1821, he wrote prophetically of future dangers: "All, I fear, do not see the speck on our horizon which is to burst on us as a tornado, sooner or later. The line of division lately marked out between the different portions of our confederacy is such as will never, I fear, be obliterated." The congressional furor had shown that when the issue of slavery or its extension came directly before the people's representatives, regional loyalties took precedence over party or other considerations. An emotional rhetoric of morality and fundamental rights issued from both sides, and votes followed sectional lines much more closely than on any other issue. If the United States were to acquire any new territories in which the status of slavery had to be determined by Congress, renewed sectional strife would be unavoidable.

Postwar Nationalism and the Supreme Court

While the Monroe administration was proclaiming national harmony and congressional leaders were struggling to reconcile sectional differences, the third branch of government—the Supreme Court—was making a more substantial and enduring contribution to the growth of nationalism and a strong federal government. Much of this achievement was due to the firm leadership and fine legal mind of the chief justice of the United States, John Marshall.

A Virginian, a Federalist, and the devoted disciple and biographer of George Washington, Marshall served as chief justice from 1801 to 1835, and during that entire period he dominated the Court as no other chief justice has ever done. Discouraging dissent and seeking to hammer out a single opinion on almost every case that came before the Court, he played a role that has been compared to that of a symphony conductor who is also composer of the music and principal soloist.

As the author of most of the major opinions issued by the Supreme Court during its formative period, Marshall gave shape to the Constitution and clarified the crucial role of the Court in the American system of government. He placed the protection of individual liberty, especially the right to acquire property, above the attainment of political, social, or economic equality. Ultimately he was a nationalist, believing that the strength, security, and happiness of the American people depended mainly on economic growth and the creation of new wealth.

Chief Justice John Marshall affirmed the Supreme Court's authority to overrule state laws and congressional legislation that it held to be in conflict with the Constitution. The portrait is by Chester Harding, ca. 1829. ❖

The role of the Supreme Court, in Marshall's view, was to interpret and enforce the Constitution in a way that encouraged economic development, especially against efforts of state legislatures to interfere with the constitutionally protected rights of individuals or combinations of individuals to acquire property through productive activity. To limit state action, he cited the contract clause of the Constitution that prohibited a state from passing a law "impairing the obligation of contracts." As the legal watchdog of an enterprising, capitalist society, the Court could also approve a liberal grant of power for the federal government so that the latter could fulfill its constitutional responsibility to promote the general welfare by encouraging economic growth and prosperity.

In a series of major decisions between 1819 and 1824, the Marshall Court enhanced judicial power and used the contract clause of the Constitution to limit the power of state legislatures. It also strengthened the federal government by sanctioning a broad or loose construction of its constitutional powers and by clearly affirming its supremacy over the states.

In ***Dartmouth College* v. *Woodward*** (1819), the Court was asked to rule whether the legislature of New Hampshire had the right to convert Dartmouth from a private college into a state university. Daniel Webster, arguing for the college and against the state, contended that Dartmouth's original charter of 1769 was a valid and irrevocable contract. The Court accepted his argument. Speaking for all the justices, Marshall made the far-reaching determination that any charter granted by a state to a private corporation was fully protected by the contract clause.

In practical terms, the Court's ruling in the Dartmouth case meant that the kinds of business enterprises then being incorporated by state governments—such as turnpike or canal companies and textile manufacturing firms—could hold on indefinitely to any privileges or favors that had been granted in their original charters. The decision therefore increased the power and independence of business corporations by weakening the ability of the states to regulate them or withdraw their privileges. The ruling helped foster the growth of the modern corporation as a profit-making enterprise with only limited public responsibilities.

About a month after the Dartmouth ruling, in March 1819, the Marshall Court handed down its most important decision. The case of ***McCulloch* v. *Maryland*** arose because the state of Maryland had levied a tax on the Baltimore branch of the Bank of the United States. The unanimous opinion of the Court, delivered by Marshall, was that the Maryland tax was unconstitutional. The two main issues were whether Congress had the right to establish a national bank and whether a state had the power to tax or regulate an agency or institution created by Congress.

In response to the first question, Marshall set forth his doctrine of "implied powers." Conceding that no specific authorization to charter a bank could be found in the Constitution, the chief justice argued that such a right could be deduced from more general powers and from an understanding of the "great objects" for which the federal government had been founded. Marshall thus struck a blow for loose construction of the Constitution and a broad grant of power to the federal government to encourage economic growth and stability.

In answer to the second question—the right of a state to tax or regulate a federal agency—Marshall held that the Bank was indeed such an agency and that giving a state the power to tax it would also give the state the power to destroy it. In an important assertion of the supremacy of the national government, Marshall argued that the American people "did not design to make their government dependent on the states." This opinion ran counter to the view of many Americans, particularly in the South, that the Constitution did not take away sovereignty from the states. The debate over federal-state relations was not resolved until the northern victory in the Civil War decisively affirmed the dominance of federal authority. But Marshall's decision gave great new weight to a nationalist constitutional philosophy.

The ***Gibbons* v. *Ogden*** decision of 1824 bolstered the power of Congress to regulate interstate commerce. A steamboat monopoly granted by the state of New York was challenged by a competing ferry service operating between New York and New Jersey. The Court declared the New York grant unconstitutional because it amounted to state interference with Congress's exclusive right to regulate interstate commerce. The Court's ruling went a long way toward freeing private interests engaged in furthering the transportation revolution from state interference.

This case clearly showed the dual effect of Marshall's decision making. It broadened the power of the federal government at the expense of the states while at the same time encouraging the growth of a national market economy. The actions of the Supreme Court provide the clearest and most consistent example of the main nationalistic trends of the postwar period—the acknowledgment of the federal government's major role in promoting the growth of a powerful and prosperous America and the rise of a nationwide capitalist economy.

Nationalism in Foreign Policy: The Monroe Doctrine

The new spirit of nationalism was also reflected in foreign affairs. The main diplomatic challenge facing Monroe after his reelection in 1820 was how to respond to the successful revolt of most of Spain's Latin American colonies after the Napoleonic wars. In Congress, Henry Clay called for immediate recognition of the new republics. In doing so, he expressed the belief of many Americans that their neighbors to the south were simply following the example of the United States in its own struggle for independence.

Before 1822, the administration stuck to a policy of neutrality. Monroe and Secretary of State Adams feared that recognizing the revolutionary governments would antagonize Spain and impede negotiations to acquire Florida. But pressure for recognition grew in Congress; in 1821, the House of Representatives, responding to Clay's impassioned oratory, passed a resolution of sympathy for Latin American revolutionaries and made it clear to the president that he would have the support of Congress if and when he decided to accord recognition. After the Adams-Onís treaty ceding Florida to the United States had been formally ratified in 1821, Monroe agreed to recognition and the establishment of diplomatic ties with the Latin American republics. Mexico and Colombia were recognized in 1822, Chile and Argentina in 1823, Brazil (which had separated from Portugal) and the Federation of Central American States in 1824, and Peru in 1826.

Recognizing the republics put the United States on a possible collision course with the major European powers. Austria, Russia, and Prussia were committed to rolling back the tides of liberalism, self-government, and national self-determination that had arisen during the French Revolution and its Napoleonic aftermath. After Napoleon's first defeat in 1814, the monarchs of Europe had joined in a "Grand Alliance" to protect "legitimate" authoritarian governments from democratic challenges. Great Britain was originally a member of this concert of nations but withdrew when it found that its own interests conflicted with those of the other members. In 1822, the remaining alliance members, joined now by the restored French monarchy, gave France the green light to invade Spain and restore a Bourbon regime that might be disposed to reconquer the empire. Both Great Britain and the United States were alarmed by this prospect.

Particularly troubling to American policymakers was the role of Czar Alexander I of Russia in the maneuverings. An outspoken opponent of Latin American independence, the czar wanted to extend Russian claims on the Pacific Coast of North America south to the 51st parallel—into the Oregon Country the United States wanted for itself.

The threat from the Grand Alliance pointed to a need for American cooperation with Great Britain, which had its own reasons for wanting to prevent a restoration of Spanish or French power in the New World. Independent nations offered better and more open markets for British manufactured goods than the colonies of other nations, and the spokesmen for burgeoning British industrial capitalism anticipated a profitable economic dominance over Latin America. In early 1823, the British foreign secretary, George Canning, tried to exact from the French a pledge that they would make no attempt to acquire territories in Spanish America. When that venture failed, he sought to involve the United States in a joint policy to prevent the Grand Alliance from intervening in Latin America.

In August 1823, Canning broached the possibility of joint Anglo-American action against the designs of the Alliance to Richard Rush. Rush, U.S. minister to Great Britain, referred the suggestion to the president. Monroe welcomed the British initiative. He believed the United States should take an active role in transatlantic affairs by playing one European power against another. When Monroe presented the question to his cabinet, however, he encountered the opposition of Secretary of State Adams, who favored a different approach. Adams distrusted the British and differed from the president in his general view of proper relations between the United States and Europe. Adams believed the national interest would best be served by avoiding all entanglements in European politics while at the same time discouraging European intervention in the Americas.

Political ambition also predisposed Adams against joint action with Great Britain; he hoped to be the next president and did not want to give his rivals the chance to label him as pro-British. He therefore advocated unilateral action by the United States rather than a joint declaration with the British. As he told the cabinet in November, "It would be more candid, as well as more dignified, to avow our principles explicitly to Russia and France, than to come in as a cock-boat of the British man-of-war."

In the end, Adams managed to swing Monroe and the cabinet around to his viewpoint. In his annual message to Congress on December 2, 1823, Monroe included a far-reaching statement on foreign policy that was actually written mainly by Adams. What came to be known as the **Monroe Doctrine** solemnly declared that the United States opposed any further colonization in the Americas or any effort by European nations to extend their political systems outside their own hemisphere. In return, the United States pledged not to involve itself in the internal affairs of Europe or to take part in European wars. The statement envisioned a North and South America composed entirely of independent republics—with the United States preeminent among them.

Although the Monroe Doctrine made little impression on the great powers of Europe at the time it was proclaimed, it signified the rise of a new sense of independence and self-confidence in American attitudes toward the Old World. The United States would now go its own way free of involvement in European conflicts and would energetically protect its own sphere of influence from European interference.

The Troubled Presidency of John Quincy Adams

Monroe endorsed John Quincy Adams to succeed him as president. An intelligent and high-minded New Englander and the son of the second president, Adams seemed remarkably well qualified for the highest office in the land. More than anyone else, except perhaps Monroe himself, he seemed to stand for a nonpartisan nationalism that put the public good above special interests. Early in his career, Adams lost a seat in the Senate for supporting the foreign policies of Thomas Jefferson in defiance of the Federalist majority of his home state of Massachusetts. After becoming a National Republican, he served mainly in diplomatic posts, culminating in his tenure as secre-

John Quincy Adams in an 1828 portrait by Gilbert Stuart, the outstanding American portrait painter. As secretary of state under James Monroe, Adams advocated a policy of national self-interest and freedom from entanglement in European affairs. Elected president in 1824, he served one term. ❖

tary of state. In this office, he did more than negotiate treaties. Believing that the rising greatness of America should be reflected not only in economic development and territorial expansion but also in scientific and intellectual achievement, he single-handedly produced a monumental report prescribing a uniform system of weights and measures for the United States. For three years, he rose early every morning in order to put in several hours of research on the project before doing a full day's work conducting the nation's foreign policy. Uniformity of weights and measures, he argued, was essential to scientific and technological progress. Showing that his nationalism was not of a narrow and selfish kind, he called for an agreement with Great Britain and France to promote a single universal system.

Adams represented a type of leadership that could not survive the growth of the sectional and economic divisions foreshadowed by the Missouri controversy and the fallout from the Panic of 1819. Adams did become president, but only after a hotly contested election that led to the revival of partisan political conflict. As the nation's chief executive, he tried to gain support for government-sponsored scientific research and higher education, only to find the nation was in no mood for public expenditures that offered nothing immediate and tangible to most voters. As a highly educated "gentleman," he projected an image that was out of harmony with a rising spirit of democracy and veneration of "the common man."

CHRONOLOGY

1813	Boston Manufacturing Company founds cotton mill at Waltham, Massachusetts
1815	War of 1812 ends
1816	James Monroe elected president
1818	Andrew Jackson invades Florida
1819	Supreme Court hands down far-reaching decision in Dartmouth College case and in *McCulloch v. Maryland* ❖ Adams-Onís treaty cedes Spanish territory to the United States ❖ Financial panic is followed by a depression lasting until 1823
1820	Missouri Compromise resolves nation's first sectional crisis ❖ Monroe reelected president almost unanimously
1823	Monroe Doctrine proclaimed
1824	Lafayette revisits the United States ❖ Supreme Court decides *Gibbons v. Ogden*
1825	Erie Canal completed; canal era begins

Conclusion: The End of the "Era of Good Feeling"

The consensus on national goals and leadership that Monroe had represented could not sustain itself. The "era of good feeling" turned out to be a passing phase and something of an illusion. Although the pursuit of national greatness would continue, there would be sharp divisions over how it should be achieved. A general commitment to settlement of the West and the development of agriculture, commerce, and industry would endure despite serious differences over what role government should play in the process. However, the concept of leadership that Monroe and Adams had advanced—that an elite of nonpartisan statesmen could define common purposes and reconcile differences—would no longer be viable in the more democratic America of the Jacksonian era.

Recommended Reading

The standard surveys of the period between the War of 1812 and the age of Jackson are two works by George Dangerfield: *The Era of Good Feelings* (1952) and *Awakening of American Nationalism, 1815–1828* (1965); but see also the early chapters of Charles Sellers, *The Market Revolution: Jacksonian America, 1815–1846* (1991). For a positive account of the venturesome, entrepreneurial spirit of the age, see Joyce Appleby, *Inheriting the Revolution: The First Generations of Americans* (2000). On westward expansion, see Richard White, *It's Your Misfortune and None of My Own* (1992) and Malcolm J. Rohrbough, *The Trans-Appalachian Frontier* (1978).

Outstanding studies of economic transformation and the rise of a market economy are George R. Taylor, *The Transportation Revolution, 1815–1860* (1951); Paul W. Gates, *The Farmer's Age: Agriculture, 1815–1860* (1960); Stuart Bruchey, *Growth of the Modern American Economy* (1975); and Douglas C. North, *The Economic Growth of the United States, 1790–1860* (1961). Early manufacturing is described in David J. Jeremy, *Transatlantic Industrial Revolution* (1981) and Robert F. Dalzell, *The Boston Associates and the World They Made* (1987). On early mill workers, see Thomas Dublin, *Women at Work: The Transformation of Work and Community in Lowell, Massachusetts, 1826–1860* (1979).

On the Marshall Court's decisions see Robert K. Faulkner, *The Jurisprudence of John Marshall* (1968) and G. Edward White, *The Marshall Court and Cultural Change, 1815–1835* (1991). Samuel F. Bemis, *John Quincy Adams and the Foundations of American Policy* (1949) provides the classic account of the statesmanship that led to the Monroe Doctrine. But see also Ernest May, *The Making of the Monroe Doctrine* (1976), for a persuasive newer interpretation of how the doctrine originated.

For a list of additional titles related to this chapter's topics, please see http://www.ablongman.com/divine.

Suggested Web Sites

The Era of the Mountain Men

http://www.xmission.com/~drudy/amm.html

Private letters can speak volumes about the concerns and environment of the writers and recipients. Letters from early settlers west of the Mississippi River are offered on this site.

Prairietown, Indiana

http://www.connerprairie.org/explore/prairietown.html

This fictional model of a town and its inhabitants on the early frontier says much about America's movement westward and the everyday lives of Americans.

The Seminole Tribe of Florida

http://www.seminoletribe.com/

Before he was president, Andrew Jackson began a war against the Seminole Indians. This site presents information on their history and culture.

Erie Canal On-line

http://www.syracuse.com/features/eriecanal

This site, built around the diary of a 14-year-old girl who traveled from Amsterdam to Syracuse, New York, in the early nineteenth century, explores the construction and importance of the Erie Canal.

Whole Cloth: Discovering Science and Technology Through American Textile History

http://www.si.edu/lemelson/centerpieces/whole_cloth/

The Jerome and Dorothy Lemelson Center for the Study of Invention and Innovation/Society for the History of Technology put together this site which includes excellent activities and sources concerning early American manufacturing and industry.

Road Through the Wilderness: The Making of the National Road

http://www.connerprairie.org/historyonline/ntlroad.html

The National Road was a hot political topic in the Early Republic and was part of the beginning of the development of America's infrastructure. This on-line essay by historian Timothy Crumrin discusses the making of the National Road.

Chapter 10

In Richard Cruikshank's engraving, "All Creation Going to the White House," crowds of supporters pour into the White House to celebrate the victory of "common man" Andrew Jackson in the presidential election of 1828. ❖

The Triumph of White Men's Democracy

Democratic Space: The New Hotels

During the 1820s and 1830s the United States became a more democratic country for at least some of its population. The emerging spirit of popular democracy found expression in a new institution—the large hotel with several stories and hundreds of rooms. President-elect Andrew Jackson, the political figure who best represented the spirit of the age, stayed in the recently opened National Hotel when he arrived in Washington in 1829 to prepare for his administration. After a horde of well-wishers made a shambles of the White House during his inaugural reception, Jackson retreated to the hotel for a little peace and a chance to consult with his advisers. The National was only one of several large "first class" hotels that opened immediately before or during Jackson's presidency. Among the others were the Tremont House in Boston, the Baltimore City Hotel, and New York's Astor House.

The hotel boom responded to the increasing tendency of Americans in the 1820s and 1830s to move about the country. It was to service the rising tides of travelers, transients, and new arrivals that entrepreneurs erected these large places of accommodation. There they provided lodging, food, and drink on an unprecedented scale. These establishments were as different from the inns of the eighteenth century as the steamboat was from the flatboat.

According to historian Doris Elizabeth King, "the new hotels were so obviously 'public' and 'democratic' in their character that foreigners were often to describe them as a true reflection of American society." Their very existence showed that many people, white males in particular, were on the move geographically and socially. Among the hotels' patrons were traveling salesmen, ambitious young men seeking to establish themselves in a new city, and restless pursuers of "the main chance" (unexpected economic opportunities) who were not yet ready to put down roots.

Hotel managers shocked European visitors by failing to enforce traditional social distinctions among their clientele. Under the "American plan," guests were required to pay for their meals and to eat at a common "table d'hôte" with anyone who happened to be there, including servants traveling with their employers. Ability to pay was the only requirement for admission (unless one happened to be an unescorted woman or dark-skinned), and every white male patron, regardless of social background and occupation, enjoyed the kind of personal service previously available only to a privileged class. Many patrons experienced such amenities as gaslight, indoor plumbing, and steam heat for the first time in their lives. Because a large proportion of the American population stayed in hotels at one time or another—a privilege that was, in Europe, reserved for the elite—foreigners inferred that there was widespread prosperity and a much greater "equality of condition" than existed in Europe.

Outline

Feature Essay

New York's Astor House, completed in 1836, was one of the grandest of the new American hotels, offering fine accommodations to travelers who could afford to pay for them. ❖

THE HOTEL CULTURE REVEALED some of the limitations of the new era of democratic ideals and aspirations. African Americans, Native Americans, and women were excluded or discriminated against, just as they were denied suffrage at a time when it was being extended to all white males. The genuinely poor—of whom there were more than met the eye of most European visitors—simply could not afford to patronize the hotels and were consigned to squalid rooming houses. If the social equality *within* the hotel reflected a decline in traditional status distinctions, the broad gulf between potential patrons and those who could not pay the rates signaled the growth of inequality based squarely on wealth rather than inherited status.

The hotel life also reflected the emergence of democratic politics. Professional politicians of a new breed, pursuing the votes of a mass electorate, spent much of their time in hotels as they traveled about. Those elected to Congress or a state legislature often stayed in hotels during the session, and the political deals and bargains required for effective party organization or legislative success were sometimes concluded in these establishments.

The hotel can thus be seen as a fitting symbol for the democratic spirit of the age, one that shows its limitations as well as its strengths. The new democracy was first of all political, involving the extension of suffrage to virtually all white males and the rise of modern political parties appealing to a mass electorate. It was also social in that it undermined the habit of deferring to people because of their birth or ancestry and offered a greater expectation that individuals born in relatively humble circumstances could climb the ladder of success. But the ideals of equal citizenship and opportunity did not extend across the lines of race and gender, which actually hardened to some degree during this period.

Democracy in Theory and Practice

During the 1820s and 1830s, the term *democracy* first became a generally accepted term to describe how American institutions were supposed to work. The Founders had defined democracy as direct rule by the people; most of them rejected this concept of a democratic approach to government because it was at odds with their conception of a well-balanced republic led by a "natural aristocracy." For champions of popular government in the Jacksonian period, however, the people were truly sovereign and could do no wrong. "The voice of the people is the voice of God" was their clearest expression of this principle. Others were less certain of the wisdom of the common folk. But even they were coming to recognize that public opinion had to be won over before major policy decisions could be made.

Besides evoking a heightened sense of "popular sovereignty," the democratic impulse seemed to stimulate a process of social leveling. Earlier Americans had usually assumed that the rich and wellborn should be treated with special respect and recognized as natural leaders of the community and guardians of its culture and values. By the 1830s, the disappearance of inherited social ranks and clearly defined aristocracies or privileged groups struck European visitors such as Alexis de Tocqueville as the most radical feature of democracy in America. Historians have described this development as a decline of the spirit of "deference."

The decline of deference meant that "self-made men" of lowly origins could now rise more readily to positions of power and influence and that exclusiveness and aristocratic pretensions were likely to provoke popular hostility or scorn. But economic equality, in the sense of an equitable sharing of wealth, was not part of the mainstream agenda of the Jacksonian period. This was, after all, a competitive capitalist society. The watchword was equality of *opportunity*, not equality of *reward*. Life was a race, and so long as white males appeared to have an equal start, there could be no reason for complaint if some were winners and some were losers. Historians now generally agree that economic inequality—the gap between rich and poor Americans—was actually increasing during this period of political and social democratization.

Democracy and Society

Although some types of inequality persisted or even grew during the age of democracy, they did so in the face of a growing belief that equality was the governing principle of American society. What this meant in practice was that no one could expect special privileges because of family connections. The plain folk, who in an earlier period would have known their place and deferred to their betters, were now likely to greet claims for special treatment with indifference or scorn. High-status Europeans who traveled in America were constantly affronted by democratic attitudes and manners. One aristocrat was rudely rebuffed when he tried to hire an entire stagecoach for himself and his valet. On other occasions, such blue-blooded tourists were forced to eat at the same table as teamsters and stagecoach drivers or share rooms in country inns with rough characters of all kinds. Another irritation to European visitors was the absence of special first-class accommodations on steamboats and railroads.

With the exception of slaveholders, wealthy Americans could not depend on a distinctive social class for domestic service. Instead of keeping "servants," they hired "help"—household workers who refused to wear livery, agreed to work for only short periods of time, and sometimes insisted on eating at the same table as their employers. As noted in the maid's comments quoted at the beginning of Chapter 8, no true American was willing to be considered a member of a servant class, and those who engaged in domestic work regarded it as a temporary stopgap. Except as a euphemistic substitute for the word *slave*, the term *servant* virtually disappeared from the American vocabulary.

The decline of distinctive modes of dress for upper and lower classes conveyed the principle of equality in yet another way. The elaborate periwigs and knee breeches worn by eighteenth-century gentlemen gave way to short hair and pantaloons, a style that was adopted by men of all social classes. Fashionable dress among women also ceased to be a sure index of gentility; serving girls on their day off wore the same kind of finery as the wives and daughters of the wealthy. Those with a good eye for detail might detect subtle differences in taste or in quality of materials, but the casual observer of crowds in a large city could easily conclude that all Americans belonged to a single social class.

Of course Americans were not all of one social class. In fact, inequality based on control of productive resources was increasing during the Jacksonian period. A growing percentage of the population, especially in urban areas, possessed no real estate and little other property. The rise of industrialization was creating a permanent class of low-paid, unorganized wage earners. In rural areas, there was a significant division between successful commercial farmers and smallholders, or tenants who subsisted on marginal land, as well as

Village Tavern *(1814) by John Lewis Krimmel. In the early republic, people gathered in taverns to catch up on news—both the local news exchanged with their neighbors and the national news printed in newspapers and often read aloud to the patrons.* ❖

enormous inequality of status between southern planters and their black slaves. But most foreign observers overlooked the widening gap between the propertied middle class and the laboring population; their attention was riveted on the fact that all white males were equal before the law and at the polls, a situation that was genuinely radical by European standards.

Traditional forms of privilege and elitism were also under strong attack, as evidenced by changes in the organization and status of the learned professions. Under Jacksonian pressure, state legislatures abolished the licensing requirements for physicians, previously administered by local medical societies. As a result, practitioners of unorthodox modes of healing were permitted to compete freely with established medical doctors. One popular therapy was Thomsonianism, a form of treatment based entirely on the use of common herbs and roots. Thomsonians argued that their own form of medicine would "make every man his own physician." The democratic tide also struck the legal profession. Local bar associations continued to set the qualifications for practicing attorneys, but in many places they lowered standards and admitted persons with little or no formal training and only the most rudimentary knowledge of the law.

For the clergy, "popular sovereignty" meant being increasingly under the thumb of the laity. The growing dependence of ministers on the support and approval of their congregations forced them to develop a more popular and emotional style of preaching. Ministers had ceased to command respect merely because of their office. To succeed in their calling, they had to please their public, in much the same way as a politician had to satisfy the electorate.

In this atmosphere of democratic leveling, the popular press came to play an increasingly important role as a source of information and opinion. Written and read by common folk, hundreds of newspapers and magazines ushered the mass of white Americans into the political arena. New political views—which in a previous generation might have been silenced by those in power—could now find an audience. Reformers of all kinds could easily publicize their causes, and the press became the venue for the great national debates on issues such as the government's role in banking and the status of slavery in new states and territories. As a profession, journalism was open to those who were literate and thought they had something to say. The editors of newspapers with a large circulation were the most influential opinion makers of the age.

Democratic Culture

The democratic spirit also found expression in the rise of new forms of literature and art directed at a mass audience. The intentions of individual artists and writers varied considerably. Some sought success by pandering to popular taste in defiance of traditional standards of high culture. Others tried to capture the spirit of the age by portraying the everyday life of ordinary Americans rather than the traditional subjects of "aristocratic" art. A notable few hoped to use literature and art as a way of improving popular taste and instilling deeper moral and spiritual values. But all of them were aware that their audience was the broad citizenry of a democratic nation rather than a refined elite.

The romantic movement in literature, which came to the fore in the early nineteenth century in both Europe and America, valued strong feeling and mystical intuition over the calm rationality and appeal to common experience that had prevailed in the writing of the eighteenth century. Romanticism was not necessarily connected with democracy; in Europe, it sometimes went along with a reaffirmation of feudalism and the right of a superior few to rule over the masses. In the American setting, however, romanticism often appealed to the feelings that all people were thought to possess: the innate love of goodness, truth, and beauty. Writers in search of popularity and economic success, however, often deserted the high plane of romantic art for crass sentimentalism. They were willing to pull out all emotional stops to thrill readers or bring them to tears.

A mass market for popular literature was made possible by a rise in literacy and a revolution in the technology of printing. An increase in the number of potential readers and a decrease in publishing costs led to a flood of lurid and sentimental novels, some of which became the first American best-sellers. By the 1840s and 1850s, writers such as George Lippard, Mrs. E. D. E. N. Southworth, and Augusta Jane Evans had perfected the formulas that led to commercial success. Gothic horror and the perils of virtuous heroines threatened by dastardly villains were among the ingredients that readers came to expect from popular fiction. Lippard's *Quaker City* (1844) is a sensational tale of vice and corruption in Philadelphia. Southworth's *Hidden Hand* (1859) features an heiress who must go to extraordinary lengths to fend off villainous suitors. In one scene, which was extremely popular in the stage version, she disposes of the villain by springing a trap door conveniently located in her bedroom. Many of the new sentimental novels were written by and for women. Some women writers implicitly protested against their situation by portraying men in general as tyrannical, unreliable, or vicious and the women they abandoned or failed to support as resourceful individualists capable of making their own way in a man's world. But the standard happy endings sustained the convention that a woman's place was in the home, for a virtuous and protective man usually turned up and saved the heroine from independence.

In the theater, melodrama became the dominant genre. Despite religious objections, theater-going was a popular recreation in the cities during the Jacksonian era. The standard fare involved the inevitable trio of beleaguered heroine, mustachioed villain, and a hero who asserted himself in the nick of time. Patriotic comedies extolling the common sense of the rustic Yankee who foiled the foppish European aristocrat were also popular and served to arouse the democratic sympathies of the audience. Men and women of all classes went to the theater, and those in the cheap seats often behaved raucously and even violently when they did not like what they saw. Unpopular actors or plays could even provoke serious riots. In an 1849 incident in New York, 23 people were killed in disorders stemming from hostility toward an English actor who was the rival of Edwin Forrest, the most popular American thespian of the time.

The spirit of "popular sovereignty" expressed itself less dramatically in the visual arts, but its influence was felt nonetheless. Beginning in the 1830s, painters turned from portraying great events and famous people to depicting scenes from everyday life. Democratic genre painters such as William Sidney Mount and George Caleb Bingham captured the lives of plain folk with great skill and understanding. Mount, who painted lively rural scenes, expressed the credo of the democratic artist: "Paint pictures that will take with the public—never paint for the few but the many." Bingham was noted for his graphic images of Americans voting, carrying goods on riverboats, and engaging in other everyday activities.

Architecture and sculpture reflected the democratic spirit in a different way; they were viewed as civic art forms meant to glorify the achievements of the republic. In the 1820s and 1830s, the Greek style with its columned facades not only predominated in the architecture of public buildings but was also favored for banks, hotels, and private dwellings. Besides symbolizing an identification of the United States with the democracy of ancient Greece, it achieved monumental impressiveness at a fairly low cost. Even in newly settled frontier communities, it was relatively easy and inexpensive to put up a functional square building and then add a classical facade. Not everyone could live in structures that looked like Greek temples, but almost everyone could admire them from the outside or conduct business within their walls.

Sculpture was intended strictly for public admiration or inspiration, and its principal subjects were the heroes of the republic. The sculptors who accepted public commissions had to make sure their work met the expectations of politicians and taxpayers, who favored stately, idealized images. Horatio Greenough, the greatest sculptor of the pre–Civil War era, got into trouble when he unveiled a seated George Washington, dressed in classical garb and nude from the waist up. Much more acceptable was the equestrian figure of Andrew Jackson executed for the federal government by Clark Mills and unveiled in 1853.

William Sidney Mount, Rustic Dance After a Sleigh Ride, *1830. Mount's portrayals of country people folk dancing, gambling, playing music, or horse trading were pieces that appealed strongly to contemporaries. Art historians have found much to praise in his use of architecture, particularly that of the common barn, to achieve striking compositional effects.* ❖

Kindred Spirits *(1849) by Asher Durand, depicting William Cullen Bryant and Thomas Cole in Kaaterskill Clove. Durand was an artist of the Hudson River School, a group of landscape painters who worked mainly in the area of the Hudson River and Catskill Mountains. Although the artists were not a formally organized group, they did share a sense of wonder at the grandeur of the American landscape, and they devoted painstaking attention to the details of nature in their works.* ❖

What most impressed the public was that Mills had succeeded in balancing the horse on two legs.

Serious exponents of a higher culture and a more refined sensibility sought to reach the new public in the hope of enlightening or uplifting it. The "Brahmin poets" of New England—Henry Wadsworth Longfellow, James Russell Lowell, and Oliver Wendell Holmes—offered lofty sentiments and moral messages to a receptive middle class; Ralph Waldo Emerson carried his philosophy of spiritual self-reliance to lyceums and lecture halls across the country; and great novelists such as Nathaniel Hawthorne and Herman Melville experimented with the popular romantic genres. But Hawthorne and Melville failed to gain a large readership. The ironic and pessimistic view of life that pervaded their work clashed with the optimism of the age. For later generations of American critics, however, the works of Melville and Hawthorne became centerpieces of the American literary "renaissance" of the mid-nineteenth century. Hawthorne's *The Scarlet Letter* (1850) and Melville's *Moby-Dick* (1851) are now regarded as masterworks of American fiction.

The great landscape painters of the period—Thomas Cole, Asher Durand, and Frederic Edwin Church—believed their representations of untamed nature would elevate popular taste and convey moral truths. The modern ideal of art for art's sake was utterly alien to the instructional spirit of mid-nineteenth-century American culture. The responsibility of the artist in a democratic society, it was generally assumed, was to contribute to the general welfare by encouraging virtue and proper sentiments. Only Edgar Allan Poe seemed to fit the European image of romantic genius, rebelling against middle-class pieties. But in his own way, Poe exploited the popular fascination with death in his verse and used the conventions of Gothic horror in his tales. The most original of the antebellum poets, Walt Whitman, sought to be a direct mouthpiece for the rising democratic spirit, but his abandonment of traditional verse forms and his freedom in dealing with the sexual side of human nature left him relatively isolated and unappreciated during his most creative years.

Democratic Political Institutions

The supremacy of democracy was most obvious in the new politics of universal white manhood suffrage and mass political parties. By the 1820s, most states had removed the last remaining barriers to voting participation by all white males. This change was not as radical or controversial as it would be later in nineteenth-century Europe; ownership of land was so common in the United States that a general suffrage did not mean men without property became a voting majority.

Accompanying this broadening of the electorate was a rise in the proportion of public officials who were elected rather than appointed. More and more judges, as well as legislative and executive officeholders, were chosen by "the people." A new style of politicking developed. Politicians had to get out and campaign, demonstrating in their speeches on the stump that they could mirror the fears and concerns of the voters. Electoral politics began to assume a more festive and dramatic quality.

Skillful and farsighted politicians—such as Martin Van Buren in New York—began in the 1820s to build stable statewide political organizations out of what had been loosely organized factions. Before the rise of effective national parties, politicians created true party organizations on the state level by dispensing government jobs to friends and supporters, and by attacking rivals as enemies of popular aspirations. Earlier politicians had regarded parties as a threat to republican virtue and had embraced them only as a temporary expedient, but Van Buren regarded a permanent two-party system as essential to democratic government. In his opinion, parties were an effective check on the temptation to abuse power, a tendency deeply planted in the human heart. The major breakthrough in American political thought during the 1820s and 1830s was the idea of a "loyal opposition," ready to capitalize politically on the mistakes or excesses of the "ins" without denying the right of the "ins" to act the same way when they became the "outs."

Changes in the method of nominating and electing a president fostered the growth of a two-party system on the national level. By 1828, presidential electors were chosen by popular vote rather than by state legislatures in all but two of the twenty-four states. The new need to mobilize grassroots voters behind particular candidates required national organization. Coalitions of state parties that could agree on a single standard-bearer gradually evolved into the great national parties of the Jacksonian era—the Democrats and the Whigs. When national nominating conventions made their appearance in 1831, candidate selection became a matter to be taken up by representative party assemblies, not congressional caucuses or ad hoc political alliances.

New political institutions and practices encouraged a great upsurge of popular interest and participation. In the presidential election of 1824, the proportion of adult white males voting was less than 27 percent. In 1828, it rose sharply to 55 percent; it held at that level for the elections of 1832 and 1836 and then shot up to 78 percent in 1840—the first election in which two fully organized national parties each nominated a single candidate and campaigned for their choices in every state in the Union.

Economic Issues

Economic questions dominated the political controversies of the 1820s and 1830s. The Panic of 1819 and the subsequent depression heightened popular interest in government economic policy, first on the state and then on the national level. No one really knew how to solve the problems of a market economy that went through cycles of boom and bust, but many people thought they had the answer. Some, especially small farmers, favored a return to a simpler and more "honest" economy without banks, paper money, and the easy credit that encouraged speculation. Others, particularly emerging entrepreneurs, saw salvation in government aid and protection for venture capital. Entrepreneurs appealed to state governments for charters that granted special privileges to banks, transportation enterprises, and manufacturing corporations. Politicians attempted to respond to the conflicting views about the best way to restore and maintain prosperity. Out of the economic distress of the early 1820s came a rapid growth of state-level political activity and organization that foreshadowed the rise of national parties, which would be organized around economic programs.

The party disputes that arose over corporations, tariffs, banks, and internal improvements involved more than the direct economic concerns of particular interest groups. The republican ideology of the revolutionary period survived in the form of widespread fears of conspiracy against American liberty and equality. Whenever any group appeared to be exerting decisive influence over public policy, people who did not identify with that group's aspirations were quick to charge its members with corruption and the unscrupulous pursuit of power.

The notion that the American experiment was a fragile one, constantly threatened by power-hungry conspirators, eventually took two principal forms. Jacksonians believed that "the money power" endangered the survival of republicanism; their opponents feared that populist politicians like Jackson himself—alleged "rabble-rousers"—would gull the electorate into ratifying high-handed and tyrannical actions contrary to the true interests of the nation.

An object of increasing concern for both sides was the role of the federal government. Should it take positive steps to foster economic growth, as the National Republicans and later the Whigs contended, or should it simply attempt to destroy what Jacksonians decried as "special privilege" or "corporate monopoly"? Almost everyone favored equality of opportunity, but there was serious disagreement over whether this goal could best be achieved by active government support of commerce and industry or by divorcing the government from the economy in the name of laissez-faire and free competition.

Labor Radicalism and Equal Rights

For one group of dissenters, democracy took on a more radical meaning. Working men's parties and trade unions emerged in eastern cities during the late 1820s and early 1830s. Their leaders condemned the growing gap between the rich and the poor resulting from early industrialization and the growth of a market economy. They argued that an expansion of low-paying labor was putting working people under the dominance of their employers to such an extent that the American tradition of "equal rights" was in grave danger. Society, in their view, was divided between "producers"—laborers, artisans, farmers, and small-business owners who ran their own enterprises—and nonproducing "parasites"—bankers, speculators, and merchant capitalists. Working men's parties aimed to give the producers greater control over the fruits of their labor.

These radicals called for a number of reforms to achieve their goal of equal rights. Thomas Skidmore,

Working men's parties of the late 1820s and 1830s sought to protect and defend workers and to improve working conditions. This poster called for workers to unite in protest over the conviction of union shoemakers for conspiracy. ❖

a founder of the New York Working Men's party, advocated the abolition of inheritance and a redistribution of property. Champions of the rights of labor also demanded greatly extended and improved systems of public education. But education reform, however radical or extensive, could provide equal opportunities only to future generations. To relieve the plight of adult artisans and craftspeople at a time when their economic and social status was deteriorating, labor reformers and trade unionists experimented with cooperative production and called for a ten-hour workday, abolition of imprisonment for debt, and a currency system based exclusively on hard money so workers could no longer be paid in depreciated banknotes.

Philadelphia was an especially active center of labor politics and trade union activity. In 1827, the city's skilled artisans formed the Mechanics Union of Trade Associations, the nation's first metropolitan labor movement, and shortly thereafter launched the Working Men's party to compete in local elections. In 1834, fifty craft associations incorporated into the General Trades' Union of the City and County of Philadelphia, and within a year the union took the leading role in the first general strike in American history. The strike was successful in getting the ten-hour day accepted in most Philadelphia industries, but the depression that began in 1837 destroyed the General Trades' Union and nullified most of its gains. The same pattern of temporary success and ultimate defeat was repeated in other major cities. Nevertheless, American labor had set a precedent for the use of mass action aimed at the achievement of better working conditions.

In the 1830s and 1840s, northern abolitionists and early proponents of women's rights made other efforts to extend the meaning and scope of democracy. But Jacksonian America was too permeated with racism and male chauvinism to give much heed to claims that the equal rights prescribed by the Declaration of Independence should be extended to blacks and women. Most of those who advocated democratization explicitly limited its application to white males, and in some ways, the civil and political status of blacks and women actually deteriorated during "the age of the common *man*." (See Chapter 12 for a discussion of these movements.)

Jackson and the Politics of Democracy

The public figure who came to symbolize the triumph of democracy was Andrew Jackson, who came out a loser in the presidential election of 1824. His victory four years later, his actions as president, and the great political party that formed around him refashioned national politics in a more democratic mold. No wonder historians have called the spirit of the age **Jacksonian Democracy.**

The Election of 1824 and J. Q. Adams's Administration

As Monroe's second term ended, the ruling Republican party was in disarray and could not agree on who should succeed to the presidency. The party's congressional caucus chose William Crawford of Georgia, an old-line Jeffersonian. But a majority of congressmen showed their disapproval of this outmoded method of nominating candidates by refusing to attend the caucus. Monroe himself favored John Quincy Adams of Massachusetts. This gave the New England statesman an important boost but did not discourage others from entering the contest. Supporters of Henry Clay and John C. Calhoun mounted campaigns for their favorites, and a group of local leaders in his home state of Tennessee tossed Jackson's hat into the ring.

Initially, Jackson was not given much of a chance. Unlike other aspirants, he had not played a conspicuous role in national politics; his sole claim to fame was as a military hero, and not even his original supporters believed this would be sufficient to catapult him into the White House. But after testing the waters, Calhoun withdrew and chose instead to run for vice president. Then Crawford suffered a debilitating stroke that weakened his chances. With one Southerner out of the race and another disabled, Jackson began to pick up support in slaveholding states. He also found favor among those in the North and West who were disenchanted with the economic nationalism of Clay and Adams.

In the election, Jackson won a plurality of the electoral votes, but he lacked the necessary majority. The contest was thrown into the House of Representatives, where the legislators were to choose from among the three top candidates. There Adams emerged victorious over Jackson and Crawford. Clay, who had just missed making the final three, provided the winning margin by persuading his supporters to vote for Adams. When Adams proceeded to appoint Clay as his secretary of state, the Jacksonians charged that a "corrupt bargain" had deprived their favorite of the presidency. Although there was no evidence that Clay had bartered votes for the promise of a high office, the charge was widely believed. As a result, Adams assumed office under a cloud of suspicion.

Adams had a difficult and frustrating presidency. The political winds were blowing against nationalistic programs, partly because the country was just recovering from a depression that many thought had been caused or exacerbated by federal banking and tariff policies. Adams refused to bow to public opinion and called for an expansion of federal activity.

When it was clear that he would not win the presidency in 1824, Henry Clay, shown here in an 1822 portrait by Charles Bird King, threw his support to John Quincy Adams. ❖

The Election of 1824

Candidate	Party	Popular Vote	Electoral Vote*
J. Q. Adams	No party designations	108,740	84
Jackson		153,544	99
Clay		47,136	37
Crawford		46,618	41

*No candidate received a majority of the electoral votes. Adams was elected by the House of Representatives.

Advocates of states' rights and a strict construction of the Constitution were aghast, and the opposition that developed in Congress turned the administration's domestic program into a pipe dream.

The new Congress elected in 1826 was clearly under the control of men hostile to the administration and favorable to the presidential aspirations of Andrew Jackson. The tariff issue was the main business on their agenda. Pressure for greater protection came not only from manufacturers but also from many farmers, especially wool and hemp growers, who would supply critical votes in the upcoming presidential election. The cotton-growing South—the only section where tariffs of all kinds were unpopular—was assumed to be safely in the general's camp regardless of his stand on the tariff. Therefore, promoters of Jackson's candidacy felt safe in supporting a high tariff to swing critical votes in Jackson's direction. Jackson himself had never categorically opposed protective tariffs so long as they were "judicious."

As it turned out, the resulting tariff law was anything but judicious. Congress had operated on a give-and-take principle, trying to provide something for everybody. Those favoring protection for farmers agreed to protection for manufacturers and vice versa. The substantial across-the-board increase in duties that resulted, however, angered southern free traders and became known as the **tariff of abominations.** Historians long erred in explaining the 1828 tariff as a complex Jacksonian plot that backfired; it was in fact an early example of how special-interest groups can achieve their goals in democratic politics by trading votes in the legislative bargaining process known as logrolling.

Jackson Comes to Power

The campaign of 1828 actually began with Adams's election in 1824. Rallying around the charge of a corrupt bargain between Adams and Clay, Jackson's supporters began to organize on the state and local level with an eye to reversing the outcome of the election. By late 1827, a Jackson committee was functioning in virtually every county and important town or city in the

❖ A Look at the Past ❖

Portrait of Andrew Jackson

Andrew Jackson's presidency ushered in a more democratic era and his fashionable clothing reflects that spirit. By the early nineteenth century, plain, dark fabrics had become common for men's suits. No longer did wealthy men flaunt their financial success by wearing sumptuous, richly colored fabrics trimmed with gold and lace. As decent-quality, manufactured textiles and cheaper, ready-made clothing started to become available, fabric quality and fit became less likely to indicate expense. In short, distinctions in men's clothing lessened. The change from the elaborate and body-conscious fashions of the eighteenth century to the modest and somber styles of the nineteenth century suggests that other changes were underway in the culture as well. How do Jackson's clothes suggest an egalitarian society? Why did American men abandon elaborate, body-conscious fashions and adopt somber, concealing suits? In addition to becoming more democratic, in what other ways was the United States changing in the early nineteenth century, and how did changes in men's fashion reflect those changes?

nation. Influential state or regional leaders who had supported other candidates in 1824 now rallied behind the Tennessean to create a formidable coalition.

The most significant of these were Vice President Calhoun, who now spoke for the militant states' rights sentiment of the South; Senator Martin Van Buren, who dominated New York politics through the political machine known as the Albany Regency; and two Kentucky editors, Francis P. Blair and Amos Kendall, who worked in the West to mobilize opposition to Henry Clay and his "American System," which advocated government encouragement of economic development through such measures as protective tariffs and federally funded internal improvements. As they prepared themselves for the canvass of 1828, these leaders and their many local followers laid the foundations for the first modern American political party—the Democrats. The fact that the Democratic party was founded to promote the cause of a particular presidential candidate revealed a central characteristic of the emerging two-party system. From this time on, according to historian Richard P. McCormick, national parties existed primarily "to engage in a contest for the presidency." Without this great prize, there would have been less incentive to create national organizations out of the parties and factions developing in the several states.

The election of 1828 saw the birth of a new era of mass democracy. The mighty effort on behalf of Jackson featured the widespread use of such electioneering techniques as huge public rallies, torchlight parades, and lavish barbecues or picnics paid for by the candidate's supporters. Many historians believe that the massive turnout at such events during much of the rest of the nineteenth century revealed a deeper popular engagement with politics than at other times in American history. But it is also possible, as others have argued, that it merely showed that politicians had learned that providing entertainment and treats could lure people to the polls. Personalities and mudslinging dominated the campaign of 1828. The Democratic party press and a legion of pamphleteers bombarded the public with vicious personal attacks on Adams and praise of "Old Hickory," as Jackson was called. The supporters of Adams responded in kind; they even sank to the level of accusing Jackson's wife, Rachel, of bigamy and adultery because she had unwittingly married Jackson before being officially divorced from her first husband. The Democrats then came up with the utterly false charge that Adams's wife was born out of wedlock!

What gave Jacksonians the edge was their success in portraying their candidate as an authentic man of the people, despite his substantial fortune in land and slaves. His backwoods upbringing, his record as a popular military hero and Indian fighter, and even his lack of education were touted as evidence that he was a true representative of the common people, especially the plain folk of the South and the West. In the words of one of his supporters, Jackson had "a judgment unclouded by the visionary speculations of the academician." Adams, according to Democratic propagandists, was the exact opposite—an overeducated aristocrat, more at home in the salon and the study than among plain people. Nature's nobleman was pitted against the aloof New England intellectual, and Adams never really had a chance.

Jackson won by a popular vote margin of 150,000 and by more than 2 to 1 in the electoral college. Clearly, Jackson's organization had been more effective and his popular appeal substantially greater. He had piled up massive majorities in the Deep South, but the voters elsewhere divided fairly evenly. Adams, in fact, won a majority of the electoral vote in the northern

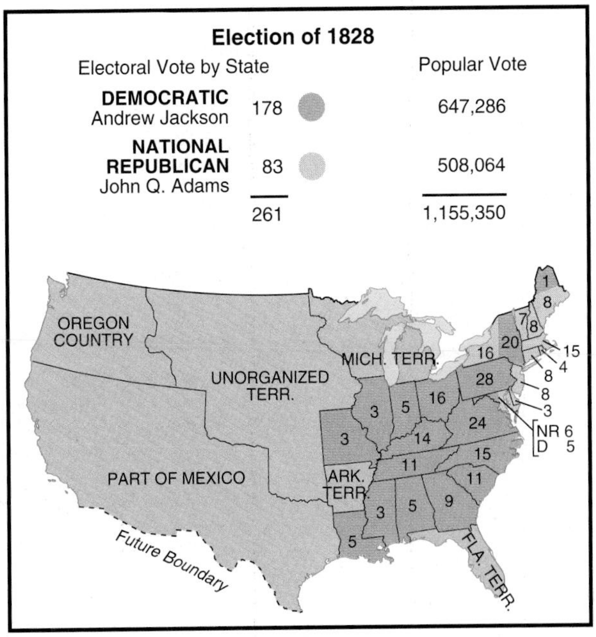

states. Furthermore, it was not clear what kind of mandate Jackson had won. Most of the politicians in his camp favored states' rights and limited government as against the nationalism of Adams and Clay, but the general himself had never taken a clear public stand on such issues as banks, tariffs, and internal improvements. He did, however, stand for the removal of Indians from the Gulf states, and this was a key to his immense popularity in that region.

Jackson turned out to be one of the most forceful and domineering of American presidents. His most striking character traits were an indomitable will, an intolerance of opposition, and a prickly pride that would not permit him to forgive or forget an insult or supposed act of betrayal. It is sometimes hard to determine whether his political actions were motivated by principle or personal spite. As a young man on his own in a frontier environment, he had learned to fight his own battles. Somewhat violent in temper and action, he fought a number of duels and served in wars against the British, the Spanish, and the Indians with a zeal his critics found excessive. His experiences had made him tough and resourceful but had also deprived him of the flexibility normally associated with successful politicians. Yet he generally got what he wanted.

Jackson's presidency commenced with his open endorsement of rotation of officeholders or what his critics called "the spoils system." Although he did not actually depart radically from his predecessors in the extent to which he removed federal officeholders and replaced them with his supporters, he was the first president to defend this practice as a legitimate application of democratic doctrine. He proclaimed in his

Jackson's resigning cabinet members were, according to this cartoon, rats deserting a crumbling house as Jackson tries to sweep them away with a broom. Vice President John Calhoun is depicted as a terrier menacing the Secretary of State Van Buren rat, who is kept from climbing the "Ladder of Political Preferment" by an eagle. ❖

first annual message that "the duties of all public officers are . . . so plain and simple that men of intelligence may readily qualify themselves for their performance" and that "no man has any more intrinsic claim to office than another."

Midway through his first administration, Jackson completely reorganized his cabinet, replacing almost all of his original appointees. At the root of this upheaval was a growing feud between Jackson and Vice President Calhoun, but the incident that brought it to a head was the Peggy Eaton affair. Peggy O'Neale Eaton, the daughter of a Washington tavern owner, married Secretary of War John Eaton in 1829. Because of gossip about her moral character, the wives of other cabinet members refused to receive her socially. Jackson became her fervent champion, partly because he found the charges against her reminiscent of the slanders against his late wife, who had died in 1828. When he raised the issue of Mrs. Eaton's social status at a cabinet meeting, only Secretary of State Van Buren, a widower, supported his stand. This seemingly trivial incident led to the resignation of all but one of the cabinet members, and the president was able to begin again with a fresh slate. Although Van Buren resigned with the rest to promote a thorough reorganization, his loyalty was rewarded by his appointment as minister to England and strong prospects of future favor.

Indian Removal

The first major policy question facing the Jackson administration concerned the fate of Native Americans. Jackson had long favored removing eastern Indians to lands beyond the Mississippi. In his military service on the southern frontier, he had been directly involved in persuading and coercing tribal groups to emigrate. Jackson's support of removal was no different from the policy of previous administrations. The only real issues to be determined were how rapidly and thoroughly the process should be carried out and by what means. At the time of Jackson's election, the states of Georgia, Alabama, and Mississippi, distressed by the federal government's failure to eliminate the substantial Indian enclaves remaining within their boundaries, were clamoring for quick action. Since Adams seemed to have dragged his feet on the issue, voters in these states turned overwhelmingly to Jackson, who promised to expel the Indians without delay.

The greatest obstacle to voluntary relocation was the Cherokee nation, which held lands in Georgia, Alabama, North Carolina, and Tennessee. The Cherokees refused to move. They had instituted a republican form of government for themselves, achieved literacy in their own language, and made considerable progress toward adopting a settled agrarian way of life similar to that of southern whites. The professed aim of the government's Indian policy was the "civilization" of the Indians, and the official reason given for removal was that this aim could not be accomplished in areas surrounded by white settlements, subject to demoralizing frontier influences. Missionaries and northeastern philanthropists argued that the Cherokees were a major exception and should be allowed to remain where they were.

The southern states disagreed. Immediately after Jackson's election, Georgia extended its state laws over the Cherokees. Before his inauguration, Alabama and Mississippi took similar action by asserting state authority over the tribes in their own states. This legislation defied provisions of the Constitution giving the federal government exclusive jurisdiction over Indian affairs and also violated specific treaties. As anticipated, Jackson quickly gave his endorsement to the state actions. His own attitude toward Indians was that they were children when they did the white man's bidding and savage beasts when they resisted. He was also keenly aware of his political debt to the land-hungry states of the South. Consequently, in his December 1829 message to Congress, he advocated a new and more coercive removal policy. He denied Cherokee autonomy, asserted the primacy of states' rights over Indian rights, and called for the speedy and thorough removal of all eastern Indians to designated areas beyond the Mississippi.

Sequoyah's invention of the Cherokee alphabet enabled thousands of Cherokees to read and write primers and newspapers published in their own language. ❖

Early in 1830, the president's congressional supporters introduced a bill to implement this policy. The ensuing debate was vigorous and heated. Opponents took up the cause of the Cherokees in particular and charged that the president had defied the Constitution by removing federal protection from the southeastern tribes. But Jackson and his supporters were determined to ride roughshod over humanitarian or constitutional objections to Indian dispossession. With strong support from the South and the western border states, the removal bill passed the Senate by a vote of 28 to 19 and the House by the narrow margin of 102 to 97.

Jackson then moved quickly to conclude the necessary treaties, using the threat of unilateral state action to bludgeon the tribes into submission. In 1832, he condoned Georgia's defiance of a Supreme Court decision (*Worcester* v. *Georgia*) that denied the right of a state to extend its jurisdiction over tribal lands. By 1833, all the southeastern tribes except the Cherokees had agreed to evacuate their ancestral homes. A stubbornly resisting majority faction of the Cherokees held out until 1838 when military pressure forced them to march to Oklahoma. This trek—known as the **Trail of Tears**—was made under such harsh conditions that almost four thousand of approximately sixteen thousand marchers died on the

Robert Lindneux, The Trail of Tears *(1942). Cherokees, carrying their few possessions, are prodded along by U.S. soldiers on the Trail of Tears. Several thousand Native Americans died on the ruthless forced march from their homelands in the East to the newly established Indian Territory in Oklahoma.* ❖

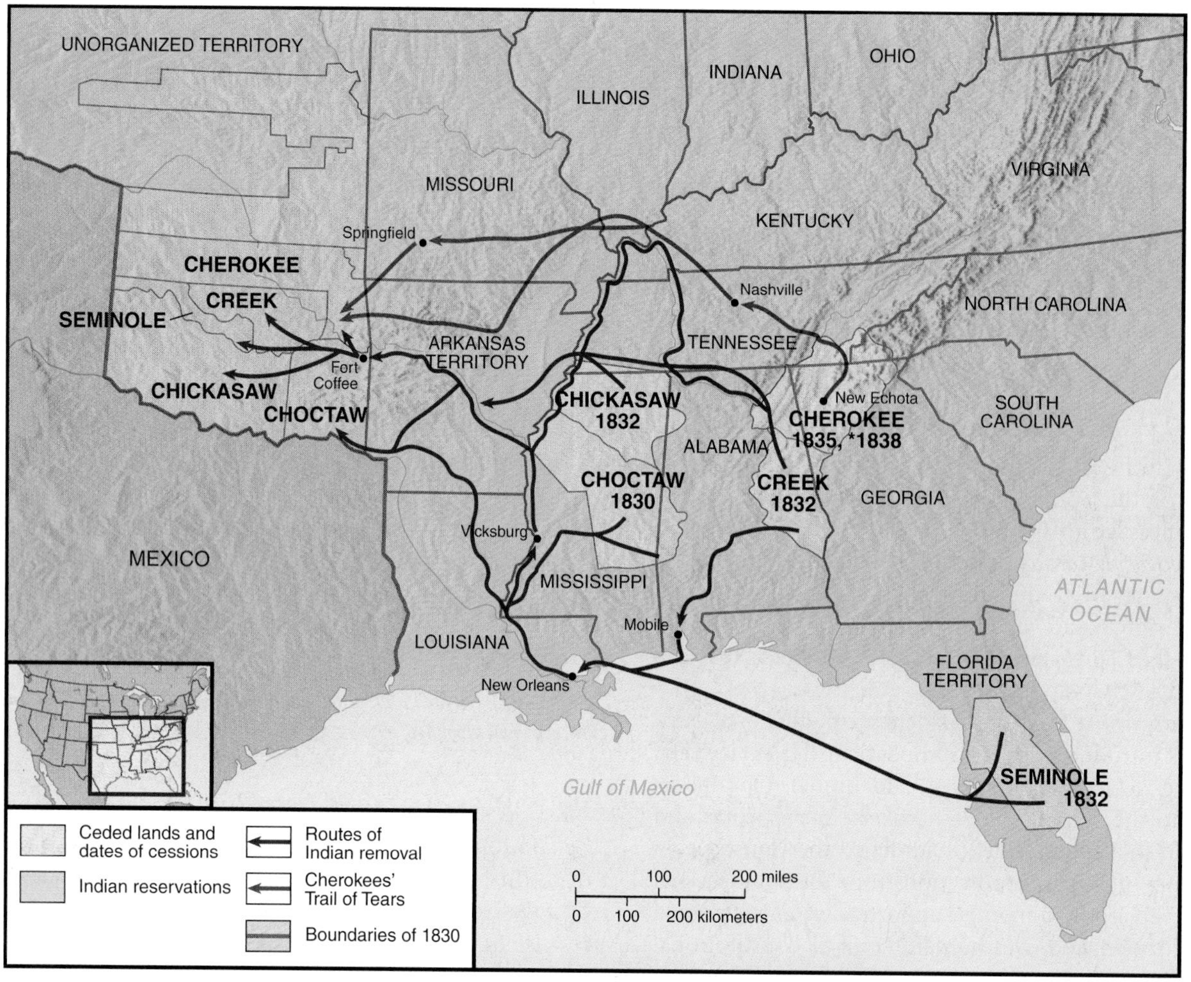

INDIAN REMOVAL *Because so many Native Americans, uprooted from their lands in the East, died on the forced march to Oklahoma, the route they followed became known as the Trail of Tears.* ❖
*Treaty signed in 1835 by a minority faction was met with defiance from the majority, but removal was forced in 1838.

way. The Cherokee removal exposed the prejudiced and greedy side of Jacksonian democracy.

The Nullification Crisis

During the 1820s, Southerners became increasingly fearful of federal encroachment on the rights of the states. Behind this concern, in South Carolina at least, was a strengthened commitment to the preservation of slavery and a resulting anxiety about possible uses of federal power to strike at the "peculiar institution." Hoping to keep the explosive slavery issue out of the political limelight, South Carolinians seized on another genuine grievance—the protective tariff—as the issue on which to take their stand in favor of a state veto power over federal actions they viewed as contrary to their interests. As a staple-producing and exporting region, the South had sound economic reasons for favoring free trade. Tariffs increased the prices that southern agriculturists paid for manufactured goods and threatened to undermine their foreign markets by inciting counterprotection. An economic crisis in the South Carolina upcountry during the 1820s made that state particularly receptive to extreme positions on the tariff and states' rights.

Vice President John C. Calhoun emerged as the leader of the states' rights insurgency in South Carolina, abandoning his earlier support of nationalism and the American system. After the passage of the tariff of abominations in 1828, the state legislature declared the new duties unconstitutional and endorsed a lengthy statement—written anonymously by Calhoun—that affirmed **nullification,** or the right of an individual state to set aside federal law. Calhoun supported Jackson in 1828 and planned to serve amicably as his vice president, expecting Jackson to support his native

Vice President John C. Calhoun emerged as a champion of states' rights during the nullification crisis, when cartoons such as this example depicted the emaciated South burdened by tariffs while the North grew fat at the southerners' expense. ❖

region on questions involving the tariff and states' rights. He also entertained hopes of succeeding Jackson as president.

Early in his administration, Jackson appeared well attuned to the southern slaveholding position on state versus federal authority. Besides acquiescing in Georgia's de facto nullification of federal treaties upholding Indian tribal rights, he vetoed a major internal improvements bill in 1830, invoking a strict construction of the Constitution to deny federal funds for the building of the Maysville Road in Kentucky.

In the meantime, however, a bitter personal feud developed between Jackson and Calhoun. The vice president and his wife were viewed by Jackson as prime movers in the ostracism of Peggy Eaton. Furthermore, evidence came to light that Calhoun, as secretary of war in Monroe's cabinet in 1818, had privately advocated punishing Jackson for his incursion into Florida. As Calhoun lost favor with Jackson, it became clear that Van Buren rather than the vice president would be Jackson's designated successor. The personal breach between Jackson and Calhoun colored and intensified their confrontation over nullification and the tariff.

The two men differed on matters of principle as well. Although generally a defender of states' rights and strict construction of the Constitution, Jackson opposed the theory of nullification as a threat to the survival of the Union. In his view, federal power should be held in check, but this did not mean the states were truly sovereign. His nationalism was that of a military man who had fought for the United States against foreign enemies, and he was not about to permit the nation's disintegration at the hands of domestic dissidents. The differences between Jackson and Calhoun came into the open at the Jefferson Day dinner in 1830, when Jackson offered the toast "Our Union: It must be preserved," to which Calhoun responded, "The Union. Next to Liberty, the most dear. May we always remember that it can only be preserved by distributing equally the benefits and the burdens of the Union."

In 1830 and 1831, the movement against the tariff gained strength in South Carolina. Calhoun openly took the lead, elaborating further on his view that states had the right to set aside federal laws. In 1832, Congress passed a new tariff that lowered the rates slightly but retained the principle of protection. Supporters of nullification argued that the new law simply demonstrated that no genuine relief could be expected from Washington. They then succeeded in persuading the South Carolina state legislature to call a special convention. When the convention met in November 1832, the members voted overwhelmingly to nullify the tariffs of 1828 and 1832 and to forbid the collection of customs duties within the state.

Jackson reacted with characteristic decisiveness. He alerted the secretary of war to prepare for possible military action, issued a proclamation denouncing nullification as a treasonous attack on the Union, and asked Congress to vote him the authority to use the army to enforce the tariff. At the same time, he sought to pacify the nullifiers somewhat by recommending a lower tariff. Congress responded by enacting the Force Bill—which gave the president the military powers he sought—and the compromise tariff of 1833. The latter was primarily the work of Jackson's political enemy Henry Clay, but the president signed it anyway. Faced with Jackson's clear intention to use force if necessary and somewhat appeased by the prospect of a lower tariff, South Carolina suspended the nullification ordinance in late January 1833 and formally rescinded it in March, after the new tariff had been enacted. To demonstrate that they had not conceded their constitutional position, the convention delegates concluded their deliberations by nullifying the Force Bill.

The nullification crisis revealed that South Carolinians would not tolerate any federal action that seemed contrary to their interests or raised doubts about the institution of slavery. The nullifiers' philosophy implied the right of secession as well as the right to declare laws of Congress null and void. As subsequent events would show, a fear of northern meddling with slavery was the main spur to the growth of a militant doctrine of state sovereignty in the South. At the time of the nullification crisis, the other slave states had not yet developed such strong anxieties about the future of the "peculiar institution" and had not embraced South Carolina's radical conception of state sovereignty. Jackson was himself a Southerner and a slaveholder, a man who detested abolitionists and everything they stood for. In general, he was a proslavery president; later he would use his executive power to stop antislavery literature from being carried by the U.S. mails.

Some farsighted southern loyalists, however, were alarmed by the Unionist doctrines that Jackson propounded in his proclamation against nullification. More strongly than any previous president, he had asserted that the federal government was supreme over the states and that the Union was indivisible. What was more, he had justified the use of force against states that denied federal authority.

THE BANK WAR AND THE SECOND PARTY SYSTEM

Jackson's most important and controversial use of executive power was his successful attack on the Bank of the United States. The **Bank war** revealed some of the deepest concerns of Jackson and his supporters and dramatically expressed their concept of democracy. It also aroused intense opposition to the president and his policies, an opposition that crystallized in a new national party—the Whigs. The destruction of the Bank and the economic disruption that followed brought to the forefront the issue of the government's relationship to the nation's financial system. Differences on this question helped to sustain and strengthen the new two-party system.

Mr. Biddle's Bank

The Bank of the United States had long been embroiled in public controversy. Its role in precipitating the Panic of 1819 by first extending credit freely and then suddenly calling in its loans had led many, especially in the South and the West, to blame the Bank for the subsequent depression. But after Nicholas Biddle took over the Bank's presidency in 1823, the institution regained public confidence. Biddle was an able manager who probably understood the mysteries of banking and currency better than any other American of his generation. A Philadelphia gentleman of broad culture, extensive education, and some political experience, his major faults were his arrogance and his vanity. He was inclined to rely too much on his own judgment and refused to admit his mistakes until it was too late to correct them. But his record prior to the confrontation with Jackson was a good one. In 1825 and again in 1828, he acted decisively to curb an overextension of credit by state banks and helped avert a recurrence of the boom-and-bust cycle.

The actual performance of the Bank was not the only target of criticism about it. Old-line Jeffersonians had always opposed it on principle, both because they viewed its establishment as unconstitutional and because it placed too much power in the hands of a small, privileged group. The Bank was a chartered monopoly, an essentially private corporation that performed public services in return for exclusive economic rights. "In 1828," according to historian Robert Remini, "the Bank was a financial colossus, entrenched in the nation's economy, possessing the means of draining specie from state banks at will and regulating the currency according to its own estimate of the nation's needs."

Because of its great influence, the Bank tended to be blamed for anything that went wrong with the economy. For those who had misgivings about the rise of the national market, the Bank represented the forces threatening the independence and prosperity of small producers. In an era of rising white men's democracy, an obvious and telling objection to the Bank was simply that it possessed great power and privilege without being under popular control.

The Bank Veto and the Election of 1832

Jackson came into office with strong reservations about banking and paper money in general—in part as a result of his own brushes with bankruptcy after accepting promissory notes that depreciated in value. He also harbored suspicions that branches of the Bank of the United States had illicitly used their influence on behalf of his opponent in the presidential election. In his annual messages in 1829 and 1830, Jackson called on Congress to begin discussing "possible modification of a system which cannot continue to exist in its present form without . . . perpetual apprehensions and discontent on the part of the States and the People."

Biddle began to worry about the fate of the Bank's charter when it came up for renewal in 1836. At the same time, Jackson was listening to the advice of close friends and unofficial advisers—members of his "Kitchen Cabinet"—especially Amos Kendall and Francis P. Blair, who thought an attack on the Bank would provide a good party issue for the election of 1832. Biddle then made a fateful blunder. Panicked by the presidential messages and the anti-Bank oratory of congressional Jacksonians such as Senator Thomas Hart Benton of Missouri, he determined to seek recharter by Congress in 1832, four years ahead of schedule. Senator Henry Clay, leader of the antiadministration forces on Capitol Hill, encouraged this move because he was convinced that Jackson had chosen the unpopular side of the issue and would be embarrassed or even discredited by a congressional endorsement of the Bank.

The bill to recharter, which was introduced in the House and Senate in early 1832, aroused Jackson and unified his administration and party against renewal. The bill found many supporters in Congress, however. A number of legislators had received loans from the Bank, and the economy seemed to be prospering under the Bank's guidance. As a result, the bill to recharter passed Congress with ease.

The next move was Jackson's, and he made the most of the opportunity. He vetoed the bill and defended his action with ringing statements of principle. After repeating his opinion that the Bank was unconstitutional, notwithstanding the Supreme Court's ruling on the issue, he went on to argue that it violated the fundamental rights of the people in a democratic society: "In the full enjoyment of the gifts of Heaven and the fruits of superior industry, economy, and virtue, every man is equally entitled to protection by law; but when the laws undertake to add to those natural and just advantages artificial distinctions, to grant . . . exclusive privileges, the humble members of society—the farmers, mechanics, and laborers—who have neither the time nor the means of securing like favors to themselves, have a right to complain of the injustice of their government." Government, he added, should "confine itself to equal protection."

Jackson thus called on the common people to join him in fighting the "monster" corporation. His veto message was the first ever to use more than strictly constitutional arguments and to deal directly with social and economic issues. Congressional attempts to override the veto failed, and Jackson resolved to take the entire issue to the people in the upcoming presidential election.

The 1832 election, the first in which candidates were chosen by national nominating conventions, pitted Jackson against Henry Clay, standard-bearer of the National Republicans. Although the Democrats did not adopt a formal platform, the party stood firmly behind Jackson in his opposition to rechartering the Bank. Clay and the National Republicans attempted to marshal the pro-Bank sentiment that was strong in many parts of the country. But Jackson won a great personal triumph, garnering 219 electoral votes to 49 for Clay. His share of the popular vote was not quite as high as it had been in 1828, but it was substantial enough to be interpreted as a mandate for continuing the war against the Bank.

The Election of 1832

Candidate	Party	Popular Vote	Electoral Vote
Jackson	Democratic	688,242	219
Clay	National Republican	473,462	49
Wirt	Anti-Masonic	101,051	7
Floyd	Independent Democratic	*	11

*Delegates chosen by South Carolina legislature

Killing the Bank

Not content with preventing the Bank from getting a new charter, the victorious Jackson now resolved to attack it directly by removing federal deposits from Biddle's vaults. Jackson told Van Buren, "The bank . . . is trying to kill me, but I will kill it." The Bank had indeed used all the political influence it could muster in an attempt to prevent Jackson's reelection, in an act of self-defense. Old Hickory regarded Biddle's actions as a personal attack, part of a devious plot to destroy the president's reputation and deny him the popular approval he deserved. Although he presided over the first modern American political party, Jackson did not really share Van Buren's belief in the

Aided by Van Buren (center), Jackson wields his veto rod against the Bank of the United States, whose heads represent the directors of the state branches. Bank president Nicholas Biddle is wearing the top hat. ❖

legitimacy of a competitive party system. In his view, his opponents were not merely wrong; they were evil and deserved to be destroyed. Furthermore, the election results convinced him that he was the people's chosen instrument in the struggle against corruption and privilege, the only man who could save the pure republicanism of Jefferson and the Founders from the "monster bank."

In order to remove the deposits from the Bank, Jackson had to overcome strong resistance in his own cabinet. When one secretary of the treasury refused to support the policy, he was shifted to another cabinet post. When a second balked at carrying out removal, he was replaced by Roger B. Taney, a Jackson loyalist and dedicated opponent of the Bank. Beginning in late September 1833, Taney ceased depositing government money in the Bank of the United States and began to withdraw the funds already there. Although Jackson had earlier suggested that the government keep its money in some kind of public bank, he had never worked out the details or made a specific proposal to Congress. The problem of how to dispose of the funds was therefore resolved by an ill-advised decision to place them in selected state banks. By the end of 1833, twenty-three state banks had been chosen as depositories. Opponents charged that the banks had been selected for political rather than fiscal reasons and dubbed them Jackson's "pet banks." Since Congress refused to approve administration proposals to regulate the credit policies of these banks, Jackson's effort to shift to a hard-money economy was quickly nullified by the use the state banks made of the new deposits. They extended credit more recklessly than before and increased the amount of paper money in circulation.

The Bank of the United States counterattacked by calling in outstanding loans and instituting a policy of credit contraction that helped bring on an economic recession. Biddle hoped to win support for recharter by demonstrating that weakening the Bank's position would be disastrous for the economy. With some justification, the president's supporters accused Biddle of deliberately and unnecessarily causing economic distress out of personal resentment and a desire to maintain his unchecked powers and privileges. The Bank never regained its charter.

Strong opposition to Jackson's fiscal policies developed in Congress. Henry Clay and his supporters contended that the president had violated the Bank's charter and exceeded his constitutional authority when he removed the deposits. They eventually persuaded the Senate to approve a motion of censure. Jacksonians in the House were able to block such action, but the president was further humiliated when the Senate refused to confirm Taney as secretary of the treasury. Not all of the criticism and obstructionism can be attributed to sour grapes on the part of pro-Bank politicians. Some congressmen who originally defended Jackson's veto now became disenchanted with the president because they thought he had gone too far in asserting the powers of his office.

The Emergence of the Whigs

The coalition that passed the censure resolution in the Senate provided the nucleus for a new national party—the **Whigs.** The leadership of the new party and a majority of its support came from National Republicans associated with Clay and New England ex-Federalists led by Senator Daniel Webster of Massachusetts. The Whigs also picked up critical support from southern proponents of states' rights who had been upset by Jackson's stand on nullification and then saw an unconstitutional abuse of power in his withdrawal of federal deposits from the Bank of the United States. Even Calhoun and his nullifiers occasionally cooperated with the Whig camp. The initial rallying cry for this diverse anti-Jackson coalition was "executive usurpation." The Whig label was chosen because of its associations with both English and American revolutionary opposition to royal power and prerogatives. In their propaganda, the Whigs portrayed the tyrannical designs of "King Andrew" and his court.

The Whigs also gradually absorbed the Anti-Masonic party, a surprisingly strong political movement that had arisen in the northeastern states in the late 1820s and early 1830s. Capitalizing on the hysteria aroused by the 1826 disappearance and apparent murder of a New Yorker who had threatened to reveal the secrets of the Masonic order, the Anti-Masons exploited traditional American fears of secret societies and conspiracies. They also appealed successfully to the moral concerns of the northern middle class under the sway of an emerging evangelical Protestantism. Anti-Masons detested Jacksonianism mainly because it stood for a toleration of diverse lifestyles. Democrats did not think government should be concerned about people who drank, gambled, or found better things to do than go to church on Sundays. Their opponents from the Anti-Masonic tradition believed government should restrict such "sinful" behavior. This desire for moral and religious uniformity contributed an important cultural dimension to northern Whiggery.

As the election of 1836 approached, the government's fiscal policies also provoked a localized rebellion among the urban working-class elements of the Democratic coalition. In New York City, a dissident faction broke with the regular Democratic organization mainly over issues involving banking and currency. These radicals—called Loco-Focos after the matches they used for illumination when their opponents turned off the gaslights at a party meeting—favored a strict hard-money policy and condemned Jackson's transfer of federal deposits to the state banks as inflationary. Because they wanted working people to be paid in specie rather than banknotes, the Loco-Focos went beyond opposition to the Bank of the United States and attacked state banks as well. Seeing no basis for cooperation with the Whigs, they established the independent Equal Rights party and nominated a separate state ticket for 1836.

Jackson himself had hard-money sentiments and regarded the "pet bank" solution as a stopgap measure rather than a final solution to the money problem. Somewhat reluctantly, he surrendered to congressional pressure in early 1836 and signed legislation allocating surplus federal revenues to the deposit banks, increasing their numbers, and weakening federal controls over them. The result was runaway inflation. State banks in the South and West responded to demands from land-speculating interests by issuing a new flood of paper money. Reacting somewhat belatedly to the speculative mania he had inadvertently helped to create, Jackson pricked the bubble on July 11, 1836. He issued his **specie circular,** requiring that after August 15 only gold and silver would be accepted in payment for public lands. The action served to curb inflation and land speculation but did so in such a sudden and drastic way that it helped precipitate the financial panic of 1837.

The Rise and Fall of Van Buren

As his successor, Jackson chose Martin Van Buren, who had served him loyally as vice president during his second term. Van Buren was the greatest master of practical politics in the Democratic party, and the Democratic national convention of 1835 unanimously confirmed Jackson's choice. In accepting the nomination, Van Buren promised to "tread generally in the footsteps of General Jackson."

The newly created Whig party, reflecting the diversity of its constituency, did not try to decide on a single standard-bearer. Instead, each region chose candidates—Daniel Webster in the East, William Henry Harrison of Ohio (also the Anti-Masonic nominee) in the Old Northwest, and Hugh Lawson White of Tennessee (a former Jackson supporter) in the South. Whigs hoped to deprive Van Buren of enough electoral votes to throw the election into the House of Representatives where one of the Whigs might stand a chance.

The stratagem proved unsuccessful. Van Buren carried fifteen of the twenty-six states and won a clear majority in the electoral college. But the election foreshadowed future trouble for the Democrats, particularly in the South. There the Whigs ran virtually even, erasing the enormous majorities that Jackson had run up in 1828 and 1832. The emergence of a two-party system in the previously solid Deep South resulted

THE ELECTION OF 1836

Candidate	Party	Popular Vote	Electoral Vote
Van Buren	Democratic	764,198	170
Harrison	Whig	549,508	73
White	Whig	145,342	26
Webster	Whig	41,287	14
Mangum	Independent Democratic	*	11

*Delegates chosen by South Carolina legislature

from two factors—opposition to some of Jackson's policies and the image of Van Buren as an unreliable Yankee politician. The division did not reflect basic disagreement on the slavery issue. Southern Whigs and Democrats shared a commitment to protecting slavery, and each tried to persuade the electorate they could do the job better than the opposition.

As he took office, Van Buren was immediately faced with a catastrophic depression. The price of cotton fell by almost 50 percent, banks all over the nation suspended specie payments, many businesses went bankrupt, and unemployed persons demonstrated in several cities. The sale of public lands fell off so drastically that the federal surplus, earmarked in 1836 for distribution to the states, became a deficit.

The **Panic of 1837**, economic historians have concluded, was not exclusively, or even primarily, the result of government policies. It was in fact international in scope and reflected some complex changes in the world economy that were beyond the control of American policymakers. But the Whigs were quick to blame the state of the economy on Jacksonian finance, and the administration had to make a politically effective response. Since Van Buren and his party were committed to a policy of laissez-faire on the federal level, there was little or nothing they could do to relieve economic distress through subsidies or relief measures. But Van Buren could at least try to salvage the federal funds deposited in shaky state banks and devise a new system of public finance that would not contribute to future panics by fueling speculation and credit expansion.

Van Buren's solution was to establish a public depository for government funds with no connections whatsoever to commercial banking. His proposal for such an "independent subtreasury" aroused intense opposition from the congressional Whigs, who strongly favored the reestablishment of a national bank as the only way to restore economic stability. Whig resistance stalled the Independent Subtreasury Bill for three years; it was not until 1840 that it was enacted into law. In the meantime, the economy had temporarily revived in 1838, only to sink again into a deeper depression the following year.

Cartoon depicting the plight of tradesmen during the Panic of 1837, whose financial hardship the artist ascribes to Loco Foco politics supporting Van Buren's anti-federal bank policies and the effects of the specie circular, or "specie clause." The hungry children ask their unemployed and penniless father for some "specie claws" to eat. ❖

❖ A Look at the Past ❖

Columbian Star Dishes

The election of 1840 set a new standard for political campaigns: exuberant and energetic. Rallies and parades awakened interest while a vast array of campaign paraphernalia maintained that interest. Whigs used log cabins to suggest that wealthy William Henry Harrison actually possessed a humble origin. Fabric, bandannas, sheet music, and ceramics came decorated with Whig campaign emblems. Dishes in the Columbian Star pattern, made in England, were available for purchase as individual pieces, entire sets, and even in miniature sizes. Why would consumers willingly, and sometimes eagerly, set their tables with pro-Whig dishes? What does that willingness reveal about the political culture of the time?

Van Buren's chances for reelection in 1840 were undoubtedly hurt by the state of the economy. The Whigs had the chance to offer alternative policies that promised to restore prosperity. In 1836, the Whigs had been disorganized and had not fully mastered the new democratic politics. But in 1840, they settled on a single nominee and matched the Democrats in grassroots organization and popular electioneering. The Whigs passed over the true leader of their party, Henry Clay. Instead they found their own Jackson in William Henry Harrison, a military hero of advanced age who was associated in the public mind with the battle of Tippecanoe and the winning of the West. To balance the ticket and increase its appeal in the South, they chose John Tyler of Virginia, a converted states' rights Democrat, to be Harrison's running mate.

Using the slogan "Tippecanoe and Tyler, too," the Whigs pulled out all stops in their bid for the White House. Rallies and parades were organized in every locality, complete with posters, placards, campaign hats and emblems, special songs, and even movable log cabins filled with coonskin caps and barrels of cider for the faithful. Imitating the Jacksonian propaganda against Adams in 1828, they portrayed Van Buren as a luxury-loving aristocrat and compared him with their own homespun candidate. There was an enormous turnout on election day—78 percent of those eligible to vote. When it was over, Harrison had parlayed a narrow edge in the popular vote into a landslide in the electoral college. He carried 19 of the 26 states and won 234 electoral votes to 60 for Van Buren. Buoyed by the electorate's belief that their policies might revive the economy, the Whigs also won control of both houses of Congress.

Contrary to what most historians used to believe, personalities and hoopla did not decide the election of 1840. (See the Feature Essay, "Grassroots Democracy in Michigan," pp. 294–295.) The economy was in dire straits, and the Whigs, unlike the Democrats, had a program that seemed to offer hope for a solution—the latest version of Henry Clay's American System. Whigs proposed to revive the Bank of the United States in order to restore fiscal stability, raise tariffs to protect manufacturers and manufacturing jobs, and distribute federal revenues to the states for internal improvements that would stimulate

Feature Essay

Grassroots Democracy in Michigan

The new popular politics of the Jacksonian era thrived on the local level. The electioneering and party competition found in Michigan was typical of the breadth and intensity of the democratic impulse. Democrats and Whigs alike could be deadly serious about their party affiliations, which rivaled their religious commitments as sources of identity and self-esteem.

In 1838, a Whig in western Michigan was invited to join the Democrats. "Sooner than vote the Democratic ticket," he reportedly replied, "I would crawl on my hands and knees from Battle Creek to Detroit, and be struck by lightning every other mile." A Democrat who confessed to having once voted the Whig ticket recalled that on the next day, goaded by his sins, he bought half a dozen candles and took them home "to light them and sit up and hate himself by them." Politics was very serious business for the common voter in the age of Jackson, full of important ritual; it was also the best show in town.

Political candidates of the Jacksonian era traveled from town to town giving stump speeches. The political gatherings at which they spoke provided entertainment as well as an excellent source of political news. The sketch is by George Caleb Bingham, one of the most prolific of the democratic genre painters. ❖

As did revivalist "camp meetings," political gatherings brought crowds and speakers into direct contact with the speakers working to entertain, inform, and convert the crowd. Between the first of July and the autumn election day, wandering political orators and local candidates would go from village to township, speaking to ready audiences on the topics of the day. An old tree stump or "husting" would often be the only stage, leading citizens to call all small-town political orators "stump" speakers. These **hustings** visits would inform the voters of each party's stance on the issues of the day; before the era of the telegraph, stump speakers were the best source of political news.

Party workers organized parades and barbecues to boost the size and enthusiasm of the crowds. The parades would begin in the morning, at first informally as people arrived in groups from surrounding areas, and then with great pageantry, with brass bands and wagons full of farmers and artisans joining in. A Michigan college student in 1851 recalled a time eleven years earlier, in "those glorious days of Tippecanoe and Tyler, too," when a 9-year-old from Troy, Michigan, a boy who had earnestly declared himself a Whig, was seen "on the fourth of July of that eventful year, seated upon the reach of a double wagon 45 feet long, in company with some fifty others of his party, on his way to assist in the ceremonies of the day." The informant added that "our youthful politician, in his zeal, inflicted a severe castigation upon a young gentleman of about his age because he had the audacity to mar the solemnity of the occasion, by shouting for 'Young Hickory.'" The youthful Whig, it seems, had become "gloriously fuddled" by a combination of partisan spirit and hard cider.

Such festivities would lead into the speeches. Candidates for office would either speak on their own or debate their opponents. Before and after speaking, the politicians would mix with the crowd. A Michigan schoolteacher described a favorite politician "familiarly mingling among the

Democrats at their meetings, taking seat with them before the speaking began, and as one of them, talking freely on the subjects incident to the occasion. I used to think that here was where [he] got his power with the masses." That practice of elbow rubbing closed the distance between audience and speaker, between the leader and the led.

The audiences did their part to fill the gap, typically responding generously during the stump speech and filling the air with political songs between addresses. A conservative observer from Michigan noted in 1845 that prior to a typical political speech, the "miserable rabble" would greet the prospective speaker with "unmeaning and bacchanalian cries." The hurrahs of the audience (and songs with lyrics such as "Van, Van, he's a used-up man" and "The mustang colt has a killing pace / he's bound to win in the White House race") would inspire the orator. "It is well known that unless heartily cheered the 'stump orator' can do nothing," the sanctimonious onlooker continued. "It has therefore been supposed that in this kind of oratory the elements of eloquence are latently contained in cheers and are then conveyed through some unknown medium, perhaps animal magnetism, to the speaker."

Good stump speakers possessed a dramatic ability to communicate to the audience its own fears and concerns. The nearly mystic communication between speaker and hearer comes through in the following depiction of a Michigan Whig's eloquence and sincerity on the stump: "In whatever crowd or assembly he might be his mind would catch with marvelous facility the general tendency of the mind of the audience, and a chemical process, as it were, would take place within his mind. How could he fail then to force attention of those to whom he returned their own thoughts strengthened, broadened, and adorned with superb flights of eloquence."

In retrospect, these spectacular stump-speaking trips to where the voters lived helped to affirm the democratic nature of Jacksonian politics. Politicians in the era were typically far more educated and wealthy than their constituents, but they were supposed to represent faithfully the concerns of the common citizens. Mutual participation in the ritual of the hustings celebrated the people's significance in a manner that no faraway convention or latter-day press release could.

In a later era, popular politics would be less critical to a politician's election. The post–Civil War period was an era of stenography and the telegraph, of industrialism and class strife. Political speeches would be widely reported, and constituencies were more economically heterogeneous. Those conditions forced politicians to become far more cautious about what they would say, when, and to whom. To a large degree, the technology of the industrial age put an end to the stump speeches of Jacksonian America, and to a certain extent that same technology severed—for better or worse—the intimate bond between America's politicians and the rural electorate.

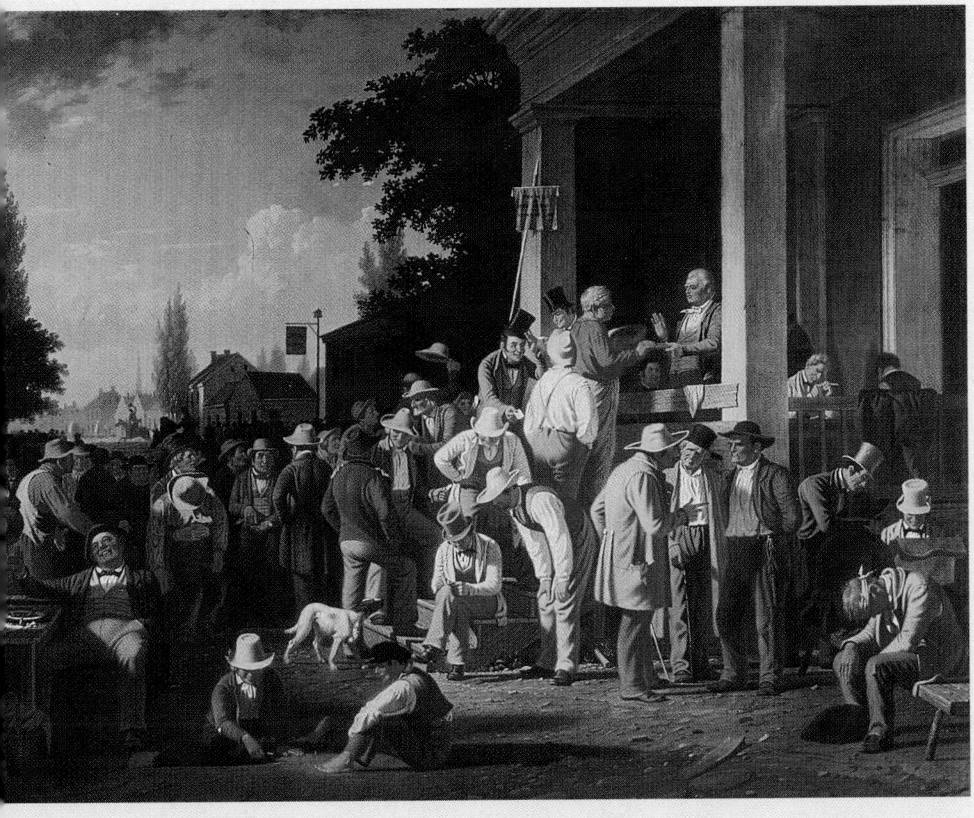

County Election by George Caleb Bingham portrays the variety of activities that occurred on election day. Some men cast their ballots, while others exchange their views or enjoy refreshments. Note the absence of women in the scene. ❖

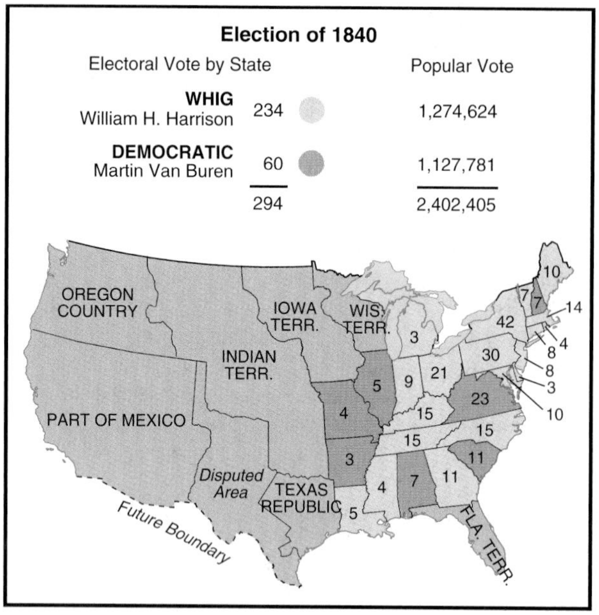

commerce and employment. Whig victories in the state and local elections of 1840, many of which preceded the presidential vote, strongly suggest that voters were responding to the party and its program, not merely to the man who headed the ticket and to the Whigs' newfound skill at entertaining the electorate.

Heyday of the Second Party System

America's **second party system** came of age in the election of 1840. Unlike the earlier competition between Federalists and Jeffersonian Republicans, the rivalry of Democrats and Whigs made the two-party pattern a normal feature of electoral politics in the United States. During the 1840s, the two national parties competed on fairly equal terms for the support of the electorate. Allegiance to one party or the other became an important source of personal identity for many Americans and increased their interest and participation in politics.

In addition to drama and entertainment, the parties offered the voters a real choice of programs and ideologies. Whigs stood for a "positive liberal state"—which meant government had the right and duty to subsidize or protect enterprises that could contribute to general prosperity and economic growth. Democrats normally advocated a "negative liberal state." According to them, government should keep its hands off the economy; only by doing nothing could it avoid favoring special interests and interfering with free competition. They charged that granting subsidies or special charters to any group would create pockets of privilege or monopoly and put ordinary citizens under the thumb of the rich and powerful.

Conflict over economic issues helped determine each party's base of support. In the Whig camp were industrialists who wanted tariff protection, merchants who favored internal improvements as a stimulus to commerce, and farmers and planters who had adapted successfully to a market economy. Democrats appealed mainly to smaller farmers, workers, declining gentry, and emerging entrepreneurs who were excluded from the established commercial groups that stood to benefit most from Whig programs. Democratic rhetoric about monopoly and privilege appealed to those who had mixed or negative feelings about the rise of a national market economy. To some extent, this division pitted richer, more privileged Americans against those who were poorer and less economically or socially secure. But it did not follow class lines in any simple or direct way. Many businessmen were Democrats, and large numbers of wage earners voted Whig. Merchants engaged in the import trade had no use for Whiggish high tariffs, whereas workers in industries clamoring for protection often concluded that their jobs depended on such duties.

Economic interest and ideology was not the only factor behind the choice of parties. Lifestyles and ethnic or religious identities strongly affected party loyalties during this period. In the northern states, one way to tell the typical Whig from the typical Democrat was to see what each did on Sunday. A person who went to one of the evangelical Protestant churches was very likely to be a Whig. On the other hand, the person who attended a ritualized service—Catholic, Lutheran, or Episcopalian—or did not go to church at all was most probably a Democrat.

The Democrats were the favored party of immigrants, Catholics, freethinkers, backwoods farmers, and those of all classes who enjoyed traditional amusements condemned by the new breed of moral reformers. One thing all these groups had in common was a desire to be left alone, free of restrictions on their freedom to think and behave as they liked. The Whigs enjoyed particularly strong support among Protestants of old stock living in smaller cities, towns, and prosperous rural areas devoted to market farming. In general, the Whigs welcomed a market economy but wanted to restrain the individualism and disorder it created by enforcing cultural and moral values derived from the Puritan tradition. Most of those who sought to be "their brothers' keepers" were Whigs. Some of the roots of party allegiance can be found in local divisions between old-stock Americans and immigrants over such matters as temperance, keeping the Sabbath, and reading the Protestant Bible in public schools.

CHRONOLOGY

1824	House of Representatives elects John Quincy Adams president
1828	Congress passes "tariff of abominations" ❖ Jackson elected president over J. Q. Adams
1830	Jackson vetoes the Maysville Road bill ❖ Congress passes Indian Removal Act
1831	Jackson reorganizes his cabinet ❖ First national nominating conventions meet
1832	Jackson vetoes the bill rechartering the Bank of the United States ❖ Jackson reelected, defeating Henry Clay (National Republican candidate)
1832–1833	Crisis erupts over South Carolina's attempt to nullify the tariff of 1832
1833	Jackson removes federal deposits from the Bank of the United States
1834	Whig party comes into existence
1836	Jackson issues "specie circular" ❖ Martin Van Buren elected president
1837	Financial panic occurs, followed by depression lasting until 1843
1840	Congress passes the Independent Sub-treasury Bill ❖ Harrison (Whig) defeats Van Buren (Democrat) for the presidency

Nevertheless, party conflict in Congress continued to center on national economic policy. Whigs stood firm for a loose construction of the Constitution and federal support for business and economic development. The Democrats persisted in their defense of strict construction, states' rights, and laissez-faire. Debates over tariffs, banking, and internal improvements remained vital and vigorous during the 1840s.

True believers in both parties saw a deep ideological or moral meaning in the clash over economic issues. Whigs and Democrats had conflicting views of the good society, and their policy positions reflected these differences. The Democrats were the party of white male equality and personal liberty. They perceived the American people as a collection of independent and self-sufficient white men. The role of government was to see to it that the individual was not interfered with—in his economic activity, in his personal habits, and in his religion (or lack of it). Democrats were ambivalent about the rise of the market economy because of the ways it threatened individual independence. The Whigs, on the other hand, were the party of orderly progress under the guidance of an enlightened elite. They believed that the propertied, the well-educated, and the pious were responsible for guiding the masses toward the common good. Believing sincerely that a market economy would benefit everyone in the long run, they had no qualms about the rise of a commercial and industrial capitalism.

Conclusion: Tocqueville's Wisdom

The French traveler Alexis de Tocqueville, author of the most influential account ever written of the emergence of American democracy, visited the United States in 1831 and 1832. He departed well before the presidential election and had relatively little to say about national politics and the formation of political parties. For him, the essence of American democracy was local self-government, such as he observed in the town meetings of New England. The participation of ordinary citizens in the affairs of their communities impressed him greatly, and he praised Americans for not conceding their liberties to a centralized state, as he believed the French had done.

Despite his generally favorable view of the American experiment, Tocqueville was acutely aware of the limitations of American democracy. He knew that the kind of democracy men were practicing was not meant for women. Observing how women were strictly assigned to a separate domestic sphere, he concluded that Americans had never supposed "that democratic principles should undermine the husband's authority and make it doubtful who is in charge of the family." He also believed the nullification crisis foreshadowed destruction of the Union and predicted the problem of slavery would lead eventually to civil war and racial conflict. He noted the power of white supremacy, providing an unforgettable firsthand description of the sufferings of an Indian community in the course of forced migration to the West, as well as a graphic account of the way free blacks were segregated and driven from the polls in northern cities such as Philadelphia. White Americans, he believed, were deeply prejudiced against people of color, and he doubted it was possible "for a whole people to rise . . . above itself." Perhaps a despot could force the equality and mingling of the races, but "while American democracy remains at the head of affairs, no one would dare attempt any such thing, and it is possible to forsee that the freer the whites in America are, the more they will seek to isolate themselves." His observations have value because of their clear-sighted insistence that the democracy and equality of the Jacksonian era were meant for only some of the people. His belief that problems associated with slavery would endanger the union was keenly prophetic.

Recommended Reading

Arthur M. Schlesinger, Jr., *The Age of Jackson* (1945), sees Jacksonian democracy as a progressive protest against big business and stresses the participation of urban workers. Marvin Meyers, *The Jacksonian Persuasion: Politics and Belief* (1960), argues that Jacksonians appealed to nostalgia for an older America—"an idealized ancestral way" they believed was threatened by commercialization. Lee Benson, *The Concept of Jacksonian Democracy: New York as a Test Case* (1964), finds an ethnocultural basis for democratic allegiance. A sharply critical view of Jacksonian leadership—one that stresses opportunism, greed, and demagoguery—can be found in Edward Pessen, *Jacksonian America: Society, Personality, and Politics*, rev. ed. (1979). An excellent survey of Jacksonian politics is Harry L. Watson, *Liberty and Power* (1990), which stresses the crisis of "republicanism" at a time of "market revolution." Daniel Feller, *Jacksonian Promise: America, 1815–1840* (1995), focuses on the optimism that marked all sides of the political conflict and points to the similarities between the political parties. Development of the view that Jacksonianism was a negative reaction to the rise of market capitalism can be found in Charles Sellers, *The Market Revolution* (1991).

The classic study of the new party system is Richard P. McCormick, *The Second Party System: Party Formation in the Jacksonian Era* (1966). On who the anti-Jacksonians were, what they stood for, and what they accomplished, see Michael Holt's magisterial, *The Rise and Fall of the American Whig Party* (1999). James C. Curtis, *Andrew Jackson and the Search for Vindication* (1976), provides a good introduction to Jackson's career and personality. On Jackson's popular image, see John William Ward, *Andrew Jackson: Symbol for an Age* (1955). His Indian removal policy is the subject of Anthony F. C. Wallace, *The Long Bitter Trail: Andrew Jackson and the Indians* (1993). On the other towering political figures of the period, see Merrill D. Peterson, *The Great Triumvirate: Webster, Clay, and Calhoun* (1987). The culture of the period is well surveyed in Russel B. Nye, *Society and Culture in America, 1830–1860* (1960). Alexis de Tocqueville, *Democracy in America*, 2 vols. (1945), is a foreign visitor's wise and insightful analysis of American life in the 1830s.

On nullification, see William Freehling, *Prelude to Civil War: The Nullification Controversy in South Carolina, 1816–1836* (1966) and Richard B. Ellis, *The Union at Risk: Jacksonian Democracy, States' Rights, and the Nullification Crisis* (1987).

On the role of race in the formation of political parties and social divisions during this period, see David Roediger, *The Wages of Whiteness: Race and the Making of the American Working Class* (1991); Jean H. Baker, *Affairs of Party: The Political Culture of Northern Democrats in the Mid-Nineteenth Century* (1983); and Alexander Saxton, *The Rise and Fall of the White Republic: Class, Politics, and Mass Culture in Nineteenth-Century America* (1990).

For a list of additional titles related to this chapter's topics, please see http://www.ablongman.com/divine.

Suggested Web Sites

Indian Affairs: Laws and Treaties, compiled and edited by Charles J. Kappler (1904)

http://digital.library.okstate.edu/kappler

This digitized text at Oklahoma State University includes pre-removal treaties with the Five Civilized Tribes and other tribes.

Medicine of Jacksonian America

http://www.connerprairie.org/historyonline/jmed.html

Survival was far from certain in the Jacksonian Era. This site discusses some of the reasons and some of the possible cures of the times.

The University of Pennsylvania in 1830

http://www.archives.upenn.edu/histy/features/1830/

This "virtual tour" shows what a fairly typical campus looked like and what student life was like at one of the larger universities in the Antebellum Era.

19th Century Scientific American On-line

http://www.history.rochester.edu/Scientific_American/

Magazines and journals are windows through which we can view society. This site provides on-line editions of one of the more interesting nineteenth-century journals.

National Museum of the American Indian

http://www.si.edu/nmai

The Smithsonian Institution maintains this site, providing information about the museum, which is dedicated to the history and culture of Native Americans.

The Alexis de Tocqueville Tour: Exploring Democracy in America

http://www.tocqueville.org/

Text, images, and teaching suggestions are a part of this companion site to C-SPAN's programming on de Tocqueville.

Chapter 11

A Ride for Liberty—The Fugitive Slaves *by Eastman Johnson depicts a slave family in flight to the North.* ❖

Slaves and Masters

Nat Turner's Rebellion: A Turning Point in the Slave South

On August 22, 1831, the worst nightmare of southern slaveholders became reality. A group of slaves in Southampton County, Virginia, rose in open and bloody rebellion. Their leader was Nat Turner, a preacher and prophet who believed God had given him a sign that the time was ripe to strike for freedom; a vision of black and white angels wrestling in the sky had convinced him that divine wrath was about to be visited upon the white oppressor.

Beginning with a few followers and rallying others as he went along, Turner led his band from plantation to plantation and oversaw the killing of nearly sixty whites. The rebellion was short-lived; after only forty-eight hours, white forces dispersed the rampaging slaves. The rebels were then rounded up and executed, along with dozens of other slaves who were vaguely suspected of complicity. Nat Turner was the last to be captured, and he went to the gallows unrepentant, convinced he had acted in accordance with God's will.

After the initial panic and rumors of a wider insurrection had passed, white Southerners went about the grim business of making sure such an incident would never happen again. Their anxiety and determination were strengthened by the fact that 1831 also saw the emergence of a more militant northern abolitionism. Just two years after African American abolitionist David Walker published his *Appeal to the Colored Citizens of the World,* calling for blacks to take up arms against slavery, William Lloyd Garrison put out the first issue of his newspaper, *The Liberator,* the first publication by a white author to demand immediate abolition of slavery rather than gradual emancipation. Nat Turner and William Lloyd Garrison were viewed as two prongs of a revolutionary attack on the southern way of life. Although no evidence came to light that Turner was directly influenced by abolitionist propaganda, many whites believed that he must have been or that future rebels might be. Consequently, they launched a massive campaign to quarantine the slaves from possible exposure to antislavery ideas and attitudes.

A series of new laws severely restricted the rights of slaves to move about, assemble without white supervision, or learn to read and write. The wave of repression did not stop at the color line; laws and the threat of mob action prevented white dissenters from publicly criticizing or even questioning the institution of slavery. For the most part, the South became a closed society with a closed mind. Loyalty to the region was firmly identified with defense of it, and proslavery agitators sought to create a mood of crisis and danger requiring absolute unity and single-mindedness among the white population. This embattled attitude lay behind the growth of a more militant sectionalism and inspired threats to secede from the Union unless the South's peculiar institution could be made safe from northern or abolitionist attack.

THE CAMPAIGN FOR REPRESSION after the Nat Turner rebellion apparently achieved its original aim. Between 1831 and the Civil War, there were no further uprisings resulting in the mass killing of whites. This fact once led some historians to conclude that African American slaves were brainwashed into a state of docility. But

Outline

Feature Essay

This woodcut from 1831 titled Horrid Massacre in Virginia *depicts scenes of Nat Turner's rebellion in Southampton County in which slaves who murdered white owners were driven by troops into hiding places in the woods. The slave revolt sparked a wave of repression against blacks in the South.* ❖

resistance to slavery simply took less dangerous forms than open revolt. The brute force employed in response to the Turner rebellion and the elaborate precautions taken against its recurrence provided slaves with a more realistic sense of the odds against direct confrontation with white power. As a result, they sought and perfected other methods of asserting their humanity and maintaining their self-esteem. The heroic effort to endure slavery without surrendering to it gave rise to an African American culture of lasting value.

This culture combined unique family arrangements, religious ideas of liberation, and creative responses to the oppression of servitude. Among white Southerners, the need to police and control the huge population of enslaved people influenced every aspect of daily life and produced an increasingly isolated, divided, and insecure society. While long-standing racial prejudice contributed to the divided society, the determination of whites to preserve the institution of slavery derived in large part from the important role slavery played in the southern economy.

The Divided Society of the Old South

Slavery would not have lasted as long as it did—and Southerners would not have reacted so strongly to real or imagined threats to its survival—if an influential class of whites had not had a vital and growing economic interest in this form of human exploitation. Since the early colonial period, forced labor had been considered essential to the South's plantation economy. In the period between the 1790s and the Civil War, plantation agriculture expanded enormously, and so did dependence on slave labor; unfree blacks were the only workers readily available to landowners who sought to profit from expanding market opportunities by raising staple crops on a large scale. As slavery increased in its importance to the Southern economy and society, the divisions within that society grew increasingly apparent.

Most fundamentally, the fact that all whites were free and most blacks were slaves created a sharp cleavage between the races in Southern society.

Indeed, during the last decades before the Civil War, the racial divide grew ever more congruent with the split between free and unfree. Yet the overwhelming importance of race gives an impression of a basic equality within the "master race" that some would say is an illusion. The truth may lie somewhere in between. In the language of sociologists, inequality in the **Old South** was determined in two ways: by class (differences in status resulting from unequal access to wealth and productive resources) and by caste (inherited advantages or disadvantages associated with racial ancestry). Awareness of both systems of social ranking is necessary for an understanding of southern society.

White society was divided by class and by region; both were important for determining a white Southerner's relationship to the institution of slavery. More than any other factor, the ownership of slaves determined gradations of social prestige and influence among whites. The large planters were the dominant class, and nonslaveholders were of lower social rank. Planters (defined as those who owned twenty or more slaves) tended to live in the plantation areas of the "Cotton Belt" stretching from Georgia across Alabama, Mississippi, Louisiana, and Texas, as well as the low country of South Carolina. In upcountry and frontier areas lived yeoman farmers who owned few or no slaves.

In 1860, only one-quarter of all white Southerners belonged to families owning slaves. Even in the Cotton Belt, slaveholders were a minority of whites on the eve of the Civil War—about 40 percent. Planters were the minority of a minority, just 4 percent of the total white population of the South in 1860. Twenty percent of whites owned twenty slaves or less, and the remaining majority, three-fourths of all whites, owned no slaves at all. Thus, Southern society was dominated by a planter class that was a numerical and geographically isolated minority; inequalities of class became divisions of region as well.

There were also divisions within black society. Most African Americans in the South were slaves, but a small number, about 6 percent, were free. Even free blacks faced increasing restrictions on their rights during the antebellum era. Among slaves, the great majority lived on plantations and worked in agriculture, but a small number worked either in industrial jobs or in a variety of tasks in urban settings. Even on plantations, there were some differences in status and experience between field hands and servants who worked in the house or in skilled jobs such as carpentry or blacksmithing. Yet because all blacks, even those who were free, suffered under the yoke of racial prejudice and legal inequality, these diverse experiences did not translate into the kind of class divisions that caused rifts within white Southern society. Rather, most blacks shared the goal of ending slavery.

The World of Southern Blacks

Most African Americans of the early to mid-nineteenth century experienced slavery on plantations; the majority of slaves lived on units owned by planters who had twenty or more slaves. On the other hand, only 2.4 percent lived on very large plantations of more than two-hundred slaves. Few slaves lived in all-black worlds like those of some Caribbean plantations, where it was possible to create autonomous black communities with little white intervention in daily life. In the South, most slaves lived in close contact with their masters and suffered their masters' strenuous efforts to maintain control over all aspects of their lives.

The masters of these agrarian communities sought to ensure their personal safety and the profitability of their enterprises by using all the means—physical and psychological—at their command to make slaves docile and obedient. By word and deed, they tried to convince the slaves that whites were superior and had a right to rule over blacks. Masters also drew constant attention to their awesome power and ability to deal harshly with rebels and malcontents. As increasing numbers of slaves were converted to Christianity and attended white-supervised services, they were forced to hear, over and over again, that God had commanded slaves to serve and obey their masters.

Despite these pressures, most African Americans managed to retain an inner sense of their own worth and dignity. When conditions were right, they openly asserted their desire for freedom and equality and showed their disdain for white claims that slavery was a positive good.

Some historians have argued that a stress on the strength of slave culture obscures the harshness and cruelty of the system and its damaging effect on the African American personality. Slavery was often a demoralizing and even brutalizing experience, and it provided little opportunity for learning about the world outside the plantation, developing mental skills, and exercising individual initiative. Compared with serfs in Russia or even with slaves on some of the large sugar plantations of the Caribbean, slaves on the relatively small southern plantations or farms, with their high turnover of personnel, had less chance to develop communal ties of the kind associated with peasant villages. Nevertheless, their sense of being part of a distinctive group with its own beliefs and ways of doing things, fragile and precarious though it may have been, made *psychic survival* possible and helped engender an

African American ethnicity that would be a source of strength in future struggles.

Although slave culture did not normally provoke violent resistance to the slaveholders' regime, the inner world that slaves made for themselves gave them the spiritual strength to thwart the masters' efforts to take over their hearts and minds. After emancipation, this resilient cultural heritage would combine with the tradition of open protest created by rebellious slaves and free black abolitionists to inspire and sustain new struggles for equality.

Slaves' Daily Life and Labor

Slaves' daily life varied enormously depending on the region in which they lived and the type of plantation or farm on which they worked. By the time of the Civil War, 90 percent of the South's four million slaves worked on plantations or farms, with the remainder working in industry or in cities. Slaves were close to half of the total population in the "Black Belt" or "Cotton Belt" of the lower South—South Carolina, Georgia, Alabama, Mississippi, Louisiana, Arkansas, and Texas—and many lived in plantation regions with a slave majority. In the upper South—North Carolina, Virginia, Maryland, Delaware, Kentucky, Tennessee, and Missouri—whites outnumbered slaves by more than three to one, and slaves were far more likely to live on farms where they worked side by side with an owner.

On large plantations in the Cotton Belt, most slaves worked in "gangs" under an overseer. White overseers, sometimes helped by black "drivers," enforced a workday from sundown to sunup, six days a week. Cotton cultivation required year-round labor, so there was never a slack season under "King Cotton." Enslaved women and children were expected to work in the fields as well, often bringing babies and young children to the fields where they could be cared for by older children, and nursed by their mothers during brief breaks. Some older children worked in "trash gangs," doing lighter tasks such as weeding and yard cleaning. Life on the sugar plantations was even more harsh, sometimes entailing work well into the night during the harvest season. Mortality rates in some parts of sugar-growing Louisiana were very high.

Although cotton cultivation required constant attention, many of the tasks involved were relatively simple. Thus on a plantation the majority of slaves, including women and children, were field hands who performed the same tasks. Here a slave family stands behind baskets of picked cotton in a Georgia cotton field. ❖

Not all slaves in agriculture worked in gangs. In the low country of South Carolina and Georgia, slaves who cultivated rice worked under a "task system" that gave them more control over the pace of labor. With less supervision, many were able to complete their tasks within an eight-hour day. Likewise, slaves who lived on small farms often worked side by side with their masters rather than in large groups of slaves, although such intimacy did not necessarily mean a leveling of power relationships. Yet despite masters' efforts to control the pace of work, even under the gang system, slaves resisted working on "clock" time, enforcing customary rights to take breaks and especially to take Sunday off completely.

While about three-quarters of slaves were field workers, slaves performed many other kinds of labor. They dug ditches, built houses, worked on boats and in mills (often hired out by their masters for a year at a time), and labored as house servants, cooking, cleaning, and gardening. Some slaves also worked within the slave community as preachers, caretakers of children, and healers, especially women. While white masters sometimes treated domestic workers or other personal servants as having a special status, it would be a mistake to assume that their ranking system was shared by slaves. What evidence we have suggests that those with the highest status within slave communities were preachers and healers, people whose special skills and knowledge directly benefited their communities.

A small number of slaves, about 5 percent, worked in industry in the South. The closest thing to a factory in the Old South was the Tredegar Iron Works in Richmond, Virginia, staffed almost entirely by slaves. Slaves also built most of the railroads that existed in the Southern states, but these were few relative to the North before the Civil War. Overall, the South remained predominantly agricultural throughout the antebellum era, and most slaves worked in the fields.

Slaves in cities took on a wider range of jobs than plantation slaves, and in general enjoyed more autonomy. Some urban slaves even lived apart from their masters and hired out their own time, returning a por-

The small number of slaves who were not employed in agriculture worked mainly in textile mills, ironworks, tobacco factories, and saltworks. In port cities, slaves might be dockworkers or longshoremen. The Tredegar Iron Works in Richmond, Virginia, was one of the South's largest industrial users of slave labor. ❖

tion of their wages to their owners. They also worked in eating and drinking establishments, hotels, and as skilled laborers in tradesmen's shops.

In addition to the work they did for their masters in the fields or in other jobs, most slaves kept gardens or small farm plots for themselves to supplement their daily food rations. They also fished, hunted, and trapped animals. Many slaves also worked "overtime" for their own masters on Sundays or holidays in exchange for money or goods, or hired out their overtime hours to others. This "underground economy" suggests slaves' overpowering desire to provide for their families, sometimes even raising enough funds to purchase their freedom.

Slave Families, Kinship, and Community

More than any other, the African American family was the institution that prevented slavery from becoming utterly demoralizing. Contrary to what historians and sociologists used to believe, slaves had a strong and abiding sense of family and kinship. But the nature of the families or households that predominated on particular plantations or farms varied according to local circumstances. On large plantations with relatively stable slave populations, a substantial majority of slave children lived in two-parent households, and many marriages lasted for as long as twenty to thirty years. They were more often broken up by the death or sale of one of the partners than by voluntary dissolution of the union. Here mothers, fathers, and children were closely bonded, and parents shared child-rearing responsibilities (within the limits allowed by the masters). Marital fidelity was encouraged by masters who believed that stable unions produced more offspring and by Christian churches that viewed adultery and divorce as sinful.

But in areas where most slaves lived on farms or small plantations, and especially in areas of the upper South where the trading and hiring out of slaves was frequent, a different pattern seems to have prevailed. Under these circumstances, slaves frequently had spouses who resided on other plantations or farms, often some distance away, and ties between husbands and wives were looser and more fragile. The result was that female-headed families were the norm, and responsibility for child rearing was vested in mothers, assisted in most cases by female relatives and friends. Mother-centered families with weak conjugal ties were a natural response to the infrequent presence of fathers and to the prospect of their being moved or sold beyond visiting distance. Where the breakup of unions by sale or relocation could be expected at any time, it did not pay to invest all of one's emotions in a conjugal relationship. But whether the basic family form was nuclear or matrifocal (female-headed), the ties that it created were infinitely precious to its members. Masters acquired great leverage over the behavior of slaves by invoking the threat of family breakup through sale to enforce discipline.

The terrible anguish that usually accompanied the breakup of families through sale showed the depth of

On large plantations, slave men and women formed stable monogamous unions that often lasted until the couple was broken up by the death or sale of one of the partners. This painting by Christian Mayr portrays a slave wedding celebrated in White Sulphur Springs, Virginia, in 1838. The wedding couple wears white attire. ❖

kinship feelings. Masters knew that the first place to look for a fugitive was in the neighborhood of a family member who had been sold away. Indeed, many slaves tried to shape their own sales in order to be sold with family members or to the same neighborhood. These efforts were fraught with danger. As one ex-slave recalled, "The mistress asked her which she loved the best her mammy or her daddy and she thought it would please her daddy to say that she loved him the best so she said 'my daddy' but she regretted it very much when she found this caused her to be sold [along with her father] the next day."

After emancipation, thousands of freed slaves wandered about looking for spouses, children, or parents from whom they had been forcibly separated years before. Harriet Jacobs, an escaped slave famous for her published autobiography, hid in her grandmother's attic for seven years while attempting to secure her children's freedom. (For more on Harriet Jacobs, see the Feature Essay, "Harriet Jacobs and Maria Norcom: Women of Southern Households," pp. 314–315.) The famous spiritual "Sometimes I Feel Like a Motherless Child" was far more than an expression of religious need; it also reflected the family anxieties and personal tragedies of many slaves.

Feelings of kinship and mutual obligation extended beyond the primary family. Grandparents, uncles, aunts, and even cousins were often known to slaves through direct contact or family lore. A sense of family continuity over three or more generations was revealed in the names that slaves gave to their children or took for themselves. Infants were frequently named after grandparents, and those slaves who assumed surnames often chose that of an ancestor's owner rather than the family name of a current master.

Kinship ties were not limited to blood relations. When families were broken up by sale, individual members who found themselves on plantations far from home were likely to be "adopted" into new kinship networks. Orphans or children without responsible parents were quickly absorbed without prejudice into new families. Soon after the Civil War, one Reconstruction official faced an elderly ex-slave named Roger, who demanded land "to raise crop on" for his "family of sixty 'parents,' that is, relations, children included." A family with sixty parents made no sense to this official, but it made sense in a community in which families were defined by ties of affection and cooperation rather than "blood" relation.

What becomes apparent from studies of the slave family is that kinship provided a model for personal relationships and the basis for a sense of community. For some purposes, all the slaves on a plantation were in reality members of a single extended family, as their forms of address clearly reveal. Elderly slaves were addressed by everyone else as "uncle" and "aunty," and younger unrelated slaves commonly called each other "brother" or "sister." Slave culture was a family culture, and this was one of its greatest sources of strength and cohesion. Strong kinship ties, whether real or fictive, meant slaves

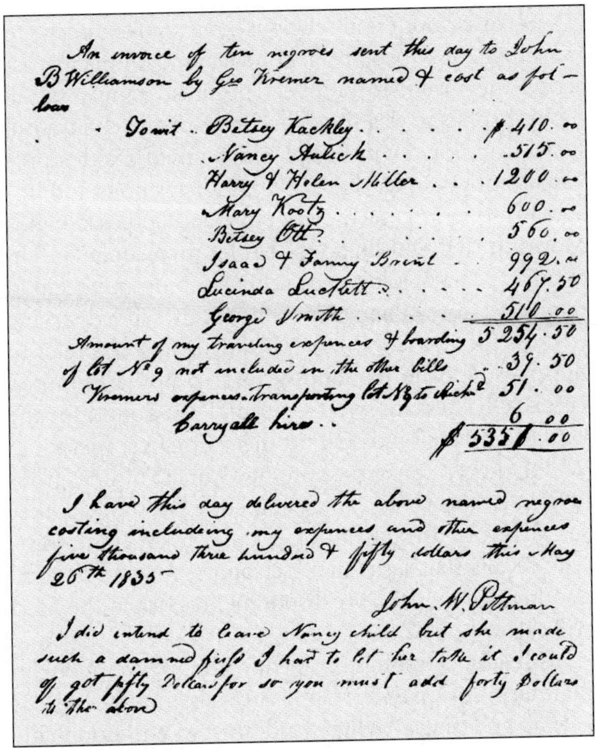

An invoice of ten negroes sent this day to John B Williamson by Geo Kremer named & cost as follows

To wit	Betsey Kackley	$410.00
	Nancy Aulick	515.00
	Harry & Helen Miller	1200.00
	Mary Kootz	600.00
	Betsey Ott	560.00
	Isaac & Fanny Brent	992.00
	Lucinda Luckett	467.50
	George Smith	510.00
		5254.50
Amount of my traveling expences & boarding of lot No 9 not included in the other bills		39.50
Kremers expences. Transporting lot No 9 to Richd		51.00
Carryall hire		6.00
		$5351.00

I have this day delivered the above named negroes costing including my expences and other expences five thousand three hundred & fifty dollars this May 26th 1835

John W. Pittman

I did intend to leave Nancy child but she made such a damned fuss I had to let her take it I could of got fifty Dollars for so you must add forty Dollars to the above

Some slave families managed to stay together, as shown by the footnote to this 1835 bill of sale: "I did intend to leave Nancy['s] child but she made such a damned fuss I had to let her take it. . . . " ❖

could depend on one another in times of trouble. The kinship network also provided a vehicle for the transmission of African American folk traditions from one generation to the next. Together with slave religion, kinship gave African Americans some sense that they were members of a community, not just a collection of individuals victimized by oppression.

African American Religion

From the realm of culture and fundamental beliefs, African Americans drew the strength to hold their heads high and look beyond their immediate condition. Religion was the cornerstone of this emerging African American culture. Black Christianity may have owed its original existence to the efforts of white missionaries, but it was far from a mere imitation of white religious forms and beliefs. This distinctive variant of evangelical Protestantism incorporated elements of African religion and stressed those portions of the Bible that spoke to the aspirations of an enslaved people thirsting for freedom.

Most slaves did not encounter Christianity in a church setting. There were a few independent black churches in the antebellum South, which mainly served free blacks and urban slaves with indulgent masters. Free blacks who seceded from white congregations that discriminated against them formed a variety of

Though many slave families were broken up by death or sale of members, some families, especially those on large, stable plantations, managed to stay together. This 1862 photograph by Timothy H. O'Sullivan shows five generations of a slave family, all born on the plantation of J. J. Smith in Beaufort, South Carolina. ❖

autonomous Baptist groups as well as Southern branches of the highly successful **African Methodist Episcopal (AME) Church,** organized as a national denomination under the leadership of the Reverend Richard Allen of Philadelphia in 1816. But the mass of blacks did not have access to the independent churches.

Plantation slaves who were exposed to Christianity either attended the neighboring white churches or worshiped at home. On large estates, masters or white missionaries often conducted Sunday services. But the narratives and recollections of ex-slaves reveal that white-sanctioned religious activity was only a superficial part of the slaves' spiritual life. The true slave religion was practiced at night, often secretly, and was led by black preachers. Historian Albert J. Raboteau has described this underground black Christianity as "the invisible institution."

This covert slave religion was a highly emotional affair that featured singing, shouting, and dancing. In some ways, the atmosphere resembled a backwoods revival meeting. But much of what went on was actually an adaptation of African religious beliefs and customs. The chanting mode of preaching—with the congregation responding at regular intervals—and the expression of religious feelings through rhythmic movements, especially the counterclockwise movement known as the ring shout, were clearly African in origin. The black conversion experience was normally a state of ecstasy more akin to possession by spirits—a major form of African religious expression—than to the agony of those "struck down" at white revivals. The emphasis on sinfulness and fear of damnation that were core themes of white evangelicalism played a lesser role among blacks. For them, religion was more an affirmation of the joy of life than a rejection of worldly pleasures and temptations.

Slave sermons and religious songs spoke directly to the plight of a people in bondage and implicitly asserted their right to be free. The most popular of all biblical subjects was the deliverance of the children of Israel from slavery in Egypt. The book of Exodus provided more than its share of texts for sermons and images for songs. In one moving spiritual, God commands Moses to "tell Old Pharaoh" to "let my people Go." In another, Mary is told she can stop weeping and begin to rejoice because "Pharaoh's army got drownded" trying to cross the Red Sea. Many sermons and songs refer to the crossing of Jordan and the arrival in the Promised Land. "Oh Canaan, sweet Canaan, I am bound for the land of Canaan" and "Oh brothers, don't get weary. . . . We'll land on Canaan's shore" are typical of lines from spirituals known to have been sung by slaves. Other songs invoke the liberation theme in different ways. One recalls that Jesus had "set poor sinners free," and another prophesies, "We'll soon be free, when the Lord will call us home."

Most of the songs of freedom and deliverance can be interpreted as referring exclusively to religious salvation and the afterlife—and this was undoubtedly how slaves hoped their masters would understand them. But the slaves did not forget that God had once freed a people from slavery in this life and punished their masters. The Bible thus gave African Americans the hope that they, as a people, would repeat the experience of the Israelites and be delivered from bondage. During the Civil War, observers noted that freed slaves seemed to regard their emancipation as something that had been preordained, and some were inclined to view Lincoln as the reincarnation of Moses.

Besides being the basis for a deep-rooted hope for eventual freedom, religion helped the slaves endure bondage without losing their sense of inner

John Antrobus, Plantation Burial, *ca. 1860. The painting depicts slaves gathering in a forest to bury a fellow slave. Many spirituals sung by the slaves on such occasions portrayed death as a welcome release from bondage and created an image of an afterlife in which the trials and cares of this life were unknown.* ❖

worth. Unless their masters were unusually pious, religious slaves could regard themselves as superior to their owners. Some slaves even believed that all whites were damned because of their unjust treatment of blacks, while all slaves would be saved because any sins they committed were the involuntary result of their condition.

More important, the "invisible institution" of the church gave African Americans a chance to create and control a world of their own. Preachers, elders, and other leaders of slave congregations could acquire a sense of status within their own community that had not been conferred by whites; the singers who improvised the spirituals found an outlet for independent artistic expression. Although religion seldom inspired slaves to open rebellion, it must be regarded as a prime source of resistance to the dehumanizing effects of enslavement. It helped create a sense of community, solidarity, and self-esteem among slaves by giving them something of their own that they found infinitely precious.

Resistance and Rebellion

Open rebellion, the bearing of arms against the oppressors by organized groups of slaves, was the most dramatic and clear-cut form of slave resistance. In the period between 1800 and 1831, a number of slaves participated in revolts that showed their willingness to risk their lives in a desperate bid for liberation. In 1800, a Virginia slave named Gabriel Prosser mobilized a large band of his fellows to march on Richmond. But a violent storm dispersed "Gabriel's army" and enabled whites to suppress the uprising without any loss of white life.

In 1811, several hundred Louisiana slaves marched on New Orleans brandishing guns, waving flags, and beating drums. It took three hundred soldiers of the U.S. Army, aided by armed planters and militiamen, to stop the advance and to end the rebellion. In 1822, whites in Charleston, South Carolina, uncovered an extensive and well-planned conspiracy, organized by a free black man named Denmark Vesey, to seize local armories, arm the slave population, and take possession of the city. Although the **Vesey conspiracy** was nipped in the bud, it convinced South Carolinians that blacks were "the Jacobins of the country [a reference to the militants of the French Revolution] against whom we should always be on guard."

Only a year after the Vesey affair, whites in Norfolk County, Virginia, complained of the activities of a marauding band of runaway slaves that had killed several whites. The militia was sent out and captured the alleged leader—a fugitive of several years' standing named Bob Ferebee. Groups of runaways, who hid for years in places such as the Great Dismal Swamp of Virginia, continued to raid plantations throughout the antebellum period and were inclined to fight to the death rather than be recaptured.

As we have already seen, the most bloody and terrifying of all slave revolts was the Nat Turner insurrection of 1831. Although it was the last slave rebellion of this kind during the pre–Civil War period, armed resistance had not ended. Indeed, the most sustained and successful effort of slaves to win their freedom by force of arms took place in Florida between 1835 and 1842, when hundreds of black fugitives fought in the Second Seminole War alongside the Indians who had given them a haven. The Seminoles were resisting removal to Oklahoma, but for the blacks who took part, the war was a struggle for their own freedom, and when it ended, most of them were allowed to accompany their Indian allies to the trans-Mississippi West.

Only a tiny fraction of all slaves ever took part in organized acts of violent resistance against white power. Most realized that the odds against a successful revolt were very high, and bitter experience had shown them that the usual outcome was death to the rebels. As a consequence, they characteristically devised safer or more ingenious ways to resist white dominance.

One way of protesting against slavery was to run away, and thousands of slaves showed their discontent and desire for freedom in this fashion. Most fugitives never got beyond the neighborhood of the plantation; after "lying out" for a time, they would return, often after negotiating immunity from punishment. But many escapees remained free for years by hiding in swamps or other remote areas, and a fraction made it to freedom in the North or Mexico. Some fugitives stowed away aboard ships heading to northern ports; others traveled overland for hundreds of miles, avoiding patrols and inquisitive whites by staying off the roads and moving only at night. Some were able to escape with the help of the **Underground Railroad,** an informal network of sympathetic free blacks (and a few whites) who helped fugitives make their way North. Light-skinned blacks sometimes made it to freedom by passing for white, and one resourceful slave even had himself packed in a box and shipped to the North.

The typical fugitive was a young, unmarried male from the upper South. For the majority of slaves, however, flight was not a real option. Either they lived too deep in the South to have any chance of reaching free soil, or they were reluctant to leave family and friends behind. Slaves who did not or could not leave the plantation had to register their opposition to the masters' regime while remaining under the yoke of bondage.

The normal way of expressing discontent was engaging in a kind of indirect or passive resistance. Many

SLAVE REBELLIONS AND UPRISINGS, 1800–1831 *Although slave uprisings were infrequent, the fear that their slaves would rise up in rebellion was a constant worry for white slaveholders.*

slaves worked slowly and inefficiently, not because they were naturally lazy (as whites supposed) but as a gesture of protest or alienation as conveyed in the words of a popular slave song, "You may think I'm working / But I ain't." Others withheld labor by feigning illness or injury. Stealing provisions—a very common activity on most plantations—was another way to show contempt for authority. According to the code of ethics prevailing in the slave quarters, theft from the master was no sin; it was simply a way for slaves to get a larger share of the fruits of their own labors.

Substantial numbers of slaves committed acts of sabotage. Tools and agricultural implements were deliberately broken, animals were willfully neglected or mistreated, and barns or other outbuildings were set afire. Often masters could not identify the culprits because slaves did not readily inform on one another. The ultimate act of clandestine resistance was poisoning the master's food. Some slaves, especially the "conjure" men and women who practiced a combination of folk medicine and witchcraft, knew how to mix rare, virtually untraceable poisons; and a suspiciously large number of plantation whites became suddenly and mysteriously ill. Sometimes whole families died from obscure "diseases" that did not infect the slave quarters.

The basic attitude behind such actions was revealed in the folktales that slaves passed down from generation to generation. The famous Brer Rabbit stories showed how a small, apparently defenseless animal could overcome a bigger and stronger one through cunning and deceit. Although these tales often had an African origin, they also served as an allegory for the black view of the master-slave relationship. Other stories—which were not told in front of whites—openly portrayed the slave as a clever trickster outwitting the master. In one such tale, a slave reports to his master that seven hogs have died of "malitis." Thinking this is a dread disease, the master agrees to let the slaves have all the meat. What really happened, so the story goes, was this: "One of the strongest Negroes got up early in the morning" and "skitted to the hog pen with a heavy mallet in his hand. When he tapped Mister Hog 'tween the eyes with that mallet, 'malitis' set in mighty quick."

Henry "Box" Brown emerges from the crate in which he escaped from slavery in Richmond, Virginia, to freedom in Philadelphia. ❖

Free Blacks in the Old South

Southern society was shaped by the need to protect slavery. The attacks of abolitionists and the constant fear of slave revolt hardened the line that divided free whites from enslaved blacks. This intensification of the South into an even more sharply defined "slave society" threatened the status of all blacks who tried to live freely in the South.

Free blacks in the South were subject to a set of direct controls that tended to make them semi-slaves. Beginning in the 1830s, all of the Southern states passed a series of laws cracking down on free blacks, in part as a reaction to Nat Turner's rebellion. These laws forced free people of color to register or have white guardians who were responsible for their behavior. Invariably, free blacks were required to carry papers proving their free status, and in some states, they had to obtain official permission to move from one county to another. Licensing laws were invoked to exclude blacks from several occupations, and attempts by blacks to hold meetings or form organizations were frequently blocked by the authorities. Sometimes vagrancy and apprenticeship laws were used to force free blacks into a state of economic dependency barely distinguishable from outright slavery. Although beset by special problems of their own, most free blacks identified with the suffering of the slaves; when circumstances allowed, they protested against the peculiar institution and worked for its abolition. Many of them had once been slaves themselves or were the children of slaves; often they had close relatives who were still in bondage. Furthermore, they knew that the discrimination from which they suffered was rooted in slavery and the racial attitudes that accompanied it. So long as slavery existed, their own rights were likely to be denied, and even their freedom was at risk; former slaves who could not prove they had been legally freed were subject to reenslavement. This threat existed even in the North: Under federal fugitive slave laws, escaped slaves could be returned to bondage. Even blacks who were born free were not perfectly safe. Kidnapping or fraudulent seizure by slave-catchers was always a possibility.

Because of the elaborate system of control and surveillance, free blacks in the South were in a relatively weak position to work against slavery. The case of Denmark Vesey showed that a prosperous and well-situated free black might make a stand in the struggle for freedom, but it also revealed the dangers of revolutionary activity and the odds against success. The wave of repression against the free black population that followed the Vesey conspiracy heightened the dangers and increased the odds. Consequently, most free blacks found that survival depended on creating the impression of loyalty to the planter regime. In some parts of the lower South, groups of relatively privileged free Negroes, mostly of racially mixed origin, were sometimes persuaded that it was to their advantage to preserve the status quo. As skilled artisans and small-business owners dependent on white favors and patronage, they had little incentive to risk everything by taking the side of the slaves. In southern Louisiana, there was even a small group of mulatto planters who lived in luxury, supported by the labor of other African Americans.

However, although some free blacks were able to create niches of relative freedom, their position in southern society became increasingly precarious in the late antebellum period. Beginning in the 1830s, Southern whites sought to draw the line between free and unfree more firmly as a line between black and white. Free blacks were an anomaly in this system; increasingly, the Southern answer was to exclude, degrade, and even enslave those free people of color who remained within their borders. Just before the outbreak of the Civil War, a campaign developed in some southern states to carry the pattern of repression and discrimination to its logical conclusion: Several state legislatures proposed laws giving free Negroes the choice of emigrating from the state or being enslaved.

White Society in the Antebellum South

Those who know the Old South only from modern novels, films, and television programs are likely to envision a land filled with majestic plantations. Pillared mansions behind oak-lined carriageways are portrayed as scenes of aristocratic splendor, where courtly gentlemen and elegant ladies, attended by hordes of uniformed black servants, lived in refined luxury. It is easy to conclude from such images that the typical white Southerner was an aristocrat who belonged to a family that owned large numbers of slaves.

The great houses existed—many of them can still be seen in places such as the low country of South Carolina and the lower Mississippi Valley—and some wealthy slaveholders did maintain as aristocratic a lifestyle as was ever seen in the United States. But census returns indicate that this was the world of only a small percentage of slaveowners and a minuscule portion of the total white population. The number of large planters who had the means to build great houses and entertain lavishly, those who owned at least fifty slaves, comprised fewer than 1 percent of all whites.

Most Southern whites were nonslaveholding yeoman farmers. Yet even those who owned no slaves grew to depend on slavery in other ways, whether economically, because they hired slaves, or psychologically, because having a degraded class of blacks below them made them feel better about their own place in society. However, the class divisions between slaveholders and nonslaveholders did contribute to the political rifts that became increasingly apparent on the eve of the Civil War.

The Planters' World

The great planters, although few in number, had a weighty influence on southern life. They set the tone and values for much of the rest of society, especially for the less wealthy slaveowners who sought to imitate the planters' style of living to the extent that resources allowed. Although many of them were too busy tending to their plantations to become openly involved in politics, wealthy planters held more than their share of high offices and often exerted a decisive influence on public policy. Within those regions of the South in which plantation agriculture predominated, they were a ruling class in every sense of the term. Contrary to legend, a majority of the great planters of the pre–Civil War period were self-made rather than descendants of the old colonial gentry. Some were ambitious young men who married planters' daughters. Others started as lawyers and used their fees and connections to acquire plantations.

As the Cotton Kingdom spread westward from South Carolina and Georgia to Alabama, Mississippi, and Louisiana, the men who became the largest slave-

Painting by Adrien Persac depicting the back of a plantation house in Louisiana as seen from the bayou. Persac was commissioned to paint some of the great houses in the region, and in 1858 he published a map showing the plantations along the Mississippi River from Natchez to New Orleans. ❖

holders were less and less likely to have come from old and well-established planter families. A large proportion of them began as hard-driving businessmen who built up capital from commerce, land speculation, banking, and even slave trading. They then used their profits to buy plantations. The highly competitive, boom-or-bust economy of the western Gulf states put a greater premium on sharp dealing and business skills than on genealogy. Stephen Duncan of Mississippi, probably the most prosperous cotton planter in the South during the 1850s (he owned eight plantations and 1018 slaves), had invested the profits from his banking operations. Among the largest sugar planters of southern Louisiana at this time were Maunsel White and John Burnside, Irish immigrants who had prospered as New Orleans merchants, and Isaac Franklin, former king of the slave traders.

To be successful, a planter had to be a shrewd entrepreneur who kept a careful eye on the market, the prices of slaves and land, and the extent of his indebtedness. Reliable "factors"—the agents who marketed the crop and provided advances against future sales—could assist him in making decisions, but a planter who failed to spend a good deal of time with his account books could end up in serious trouble. Managing the slaves and plantation production was also difficult and time-consuming, even when overseers were available to supervise day-to-day activities. Hence few planters could be the men of leisure featured in the popular image of the Old South.

Likewise, the responsibility of running an extended household that produced much of its own food and clothing kept plantation mistresses from being the idle ladies of legend. Despite typical images of women in the Old South—full hoop skirts and wide front porches, elaborate parties in plantation houses dripping with Spanish moss, elegant ladies gossiping over tea—few women fit the stereotype of the southern belle. Not only were plantation mistresses a tiny minority of the women who lived and worked in the slave states before the Civil War, but even those who were part of the planter elite rarely lived lives of leisure. (See the Feature Essay, "Harriet Jacobs and Maria Norcom: Women of Southern Households," pp. 314–315.) Some of the richest and most secure plantation families did aspire to live in the manner of a traditional landed aristocracy. A few were so successful that they were accepted as equals by visiting English nobility. Big houses, elegant carriages, fancy-dress balls, and excessive numbers of house servants all reflected aristocratic aspirations. The romantic cult of chivalry, described in the popular novels of Sir Walter Scott, was in vogue in some circles and even led to the nonviolent reenactment of medieval tournaments. Dueling, despite efforts to repress it, remained the standard way to settle "affairs of honor" among gentlemen. Another sign of gentility was the tendency of planters' sons to avoid "trade" as a primary or secondary career in favor of law or the military. Planters' daughters were trained from girlhood to play the piano, speak French, dress in the latest fashions, and sparkle in the drawing room or on the dance floor. The aristocratic style originated among the older gentry of the seaboard slave states, but by the 1840s and 1850s it had spread southwest as a second generation of wealthy planters began to displace the rough-hewn pioneers of the Cotton Kingdom.

Planters and Paternalism

No assessment of the planters' outlook or "worldview" can be made without considering their relations with their slaves. Planters, by the census definition, owned more than half of all the slaves in the South and set standards for treatment and management. It is clear from their private letters and journals, as well as from proslavery propaganda, that most planters liked to think of themselves as benevolent masters. Rather than seeing slavery as a brutal form of economic exploitation, they argued that blacks needed the slave system to ensure that they were cared for and protected. Often they referred to their slaves as if they were members of an extended patriarchal family—a favorite phrase was "our people." According to this ideology of paternalism, blacks were a race of perpetual children requiring constant care and supervision by superior whites. Paternalistic rhetoric increased greatly after abolitionists began to charge that most slaveholders were sadistic monsters.

While some historians have argued that paternalism was part of a social system that was organized like a family hierarchy rather than a brutal, profit-making arrangement, there was no inconsistency between planters' paternalism and capitalism. Slaves were themselves a form of capital; that is, they were both the main tools of production for a booming economy as well as an asset in themselves valuable for their rising prices, like shares in the stock market today. The ban on the transatlantic slave trade in 1808 was effective enough to make it economically necessary to the continuation of slavery for the slave population to reproduce itself. Rising slave prices also inhibited extreme physical abuse and deprivation. It was in the interest of masters to see that their slave property remained in good enough condition to work hard and produce large numbers of children. Furthermore, a good return on their investment enabled southern planters to spend more on slave maintenance than could masters in less prosperous plantation economies.

Much of the slaveholders' "paternalist" writing discussed "the coincidence of humanity and interest,"

Feature Essay

Harriet Jacobs and Maria Norcom

Women of Southern Households

Harriet Jacobs, born enslaved in North Carolina in 1813, became a slave in James and Maria Norcom's household in 1825. James began to "whisper foul words" in Harriet's ears when she was a young teenager. Harriet had no one to whom she could turn, except for her free black grandmother, who lived in the town. Although her grandmother had been a slave, Harriet's master "dreaded her scorching rebukes" and furthermore "he did not wish to have his villainy made public." For a time, this wish to "keep up some outward show of decency" protected Harriet.

Harriet Jacobs's grandmother was an unusual woman, who had worked after hours for years to buy her children's freedom, only to be cheated out of her earnings at the end. Like most free black women, Harriet's grandmother was the unmarried head of her own household, separated long ago from the father of her children. Running their own households gave some free black women a measure of autonomy, but also left them with little support in the daily struggle against poverty and racism.

Maria Norcom, as the wife of a prominent doctor and large plantation owner, lived a life very different from Harriet's or her grandmother's. Yet it was not the life of carefree luxury sometimes portrayed in the magnolia-scented stereotypes of movies and books about the Old South. Compared to poorer women in the South, Maria had more access to education and periods of recreation and relaxation. But as a lady of the upper class, she was expected to master strict rules of womanhood that demanded moral purity and virtue. She also had to learn the personal and managerial skills necessary to oversee a household staffed by slaves.

Most southern white women worked hard to keep households and families together, and they all lived within a social system that denied them legal rights by placing them under the domination of husbands and fathers. James Norcom's behavior, while it certainly violated his vows of marriage, was not egregious enough to have won Maria a divorce under the laws of North Carolina.

Whether they were rich or poor, free or enslaved, women were, to a large degree, defined by their relationship to the head of the household, nearly always a white man. Although there were expectations that husbands would protect and care for their wives, women had little recourse against husbands who departed from those expectations. For example, Marion S.D. Converse, a woman from a prominent South Carolina family, dreaded her abusive second husband, Augustus. Through years of vicious beatings and jealous tirades, Marion was unable to escape the bonds of marriage because Augustus's deplorable conduct fell short of legal grounds for divorce in South Carolina (divorce was available only for abandonment or impotence). Yet Marion Converse was able to gain aid and protection from her prominent family, who shielded her from the worst consequences of an abusive marriage.

When Maria Norcom discovered her husband's overtures toward Harriet, she was distraught and took Harriet to sleep in her own room. Yet, as Harriet later described it, Maria "pitied herself as a martyr; but she was incapable of feeling for the condition of shame and misery in which her unfortunate, helpless slave was placed." Harriet often woke to find Maria bending over her, and came to fear for her safety around this "jealous mistress." Harriet Jacobs's and Maria Norcom's story illustrates that planters ruled their wives as well as their slaves. All southern women were embedded in a social system that gave authority over their lives and choices to men. Despite this commonality, few women were able to reach across the

$100 REWARD

WILL be given for the approhension and delivery of my Servant Girl HARRIET. She is a light mulatto, 21 years of age, about 5 feet 4 inches high, of a thick and corpulent habit, having on her head a thick covering of black hair that curls naturally, but which can be easily combed

Portion of a reward notice posted by James Norcom offering a reward for the return of runaway slave Harriet Jacobs. ❖

This 1836 engraving from an anti-slavery novel depicts a plantation mistress scolding a slave woman while the master looks on. Though white women were also subjugated to the authority of white men in southern society, the divide of race prevented plantation ladies and slaves from finding potential solidarity as women. ❖

divides of race and class to recognize these similarities. Tormented by jealousy and humiliation, Maria came to blame the slave rather than her husband for their intimacy, imagining that Harriet herself had seduced him.

Harriet managed to elude her master's advances, in part due to Maria's vigilance. Enslaved women such as Harriet Jacobs were the most vulnerable of Southern women. They were subject to a level of violence and sexual assault that was unknown to other women in the South; and when they were victims of violence they lacked even the limited legal defenses that were open to poor white women. Because black women were considered unable to give or withhold consent, it was not a crime to rape a black woman. And had Harriet fought back physically against her master's advances, she risked criminal prosecution and even death. For example, when the slave Celia killed the master who had been raping her for years, her court-appointed lawyer argued that she should not be criminally liable, based on a Georgia statute allowing women to use force to defend their "honor" against a rapist. The court, however, decreed that black women were not "women" within the meaning of the statute. Celia had no honor that the law recognized. She was thus convicted of murder, sentenced to death, and hanged.

Excluding black women from the laws of rape also reinforced common images of black women as either sexually aggressive "Jezebels" or sexless, nurturing "Mammies." The first stereotype justified the sexual exploitation of slave women and the second fed the slaveowners' fantasy that their slaves loved and cared for them. Of course, neither of these images corresponded to the realities and hardships of slave life. Enslaved women were often assigned backbreaking labor that paid little attention to common distinctions about "women's work." They were expected to do all of the normal tasks assigned to women—sewing, washing, child care—as well as working a full day in the fields. Despite these brutal conditions, slave women organized communities and households, and tried to protect them against the worst excesses of the slave system. Harriet and her grandmother were involved in a complicated network of extended kin, and invested a great deal of energy in protecting brothers and sons from sale "up the river."

Harriet eventually escaped from the Norcoms in 1835, hiding in her grandmother's attic for seven years. Escaped from the bonds of slavery, Harriet eventually joined the battle to abolish it. Harriet's book, *Incidents in The Life of A Slave Girl, The Autobiography of Linda Brent,* was published in 1861, with the help of abolitionist novelist Lydia Maria Child. For many years, critics dismissed the narrative as either a work of fiction or the product of Child's own pen; but historians today have laid those charges to rest, recognizing Harriet Jacobs's important contribution to the struggle against slavery and to American literature.

We know much less about what happened to Maria Norcom, who neither kept a diary nor wrote her own story. All that we know is that she continued in her unhappy marriage to James Norcom. Her daughter Mary Matilda, when she came of age, pursued and attempted to reclaim Harriet as her slave under the Fugitive Slave Act. In order to thwart this effort, Harriet allowed an abolitionist friend to buy her and set her free.

In slaveholding households like that of the Norcoms, all the women, whether white or black, free or enslaved, were subject to the will of the master of the household. Most Southern women depended on white men legally and socially, giving them little recourse against men like James Norcom, who burst the bounds of "decency." Despite their shared submission to James, an impassable gulf separated Harriet and Maria, and its name was race. After the Civil War Southern women, white and black, reorganized their households in a changed society, but it would still be another century before they began to bridge that gulf.

❖ A Look at the Past ❖

Slave Clothing

Slaves typically received a yearly clothing allotment of one complete outfit and a pair of shoes. Slaves sometimes received cast-off clothing or lengths of decent fabric to make the year's new outfit, but generally they were given the cheapest fabric on the market, osnaburg, a coarse factory-woven cloth. While northern factories spun cotton and wove it into osnaburg for the southern market, men and women throughout New England earned extra money making brogans for slaves. Coarsely put together with soles pegged on rather than sewn, brogans were cheap and quick to make. How did slaves' clothing reinforce their position? What do northern fabric and shoes made especially for the slave market suggest about connections between slavery and the northern economy?

by which they meant that treating slaves well (including firm discipline) was in their best economic interest. Thus, there was a grain of truth in the planters' claim that their slaves were relatively well provided for. Recent comparative studies have suggested that North American slaves of the pre–Civil War period enjoyed a somewhat higher standard of living than those in other New World slave societies, such as Brazil and the West Indian sugar islands. Their food, clothing, and shelter were normally sufficient to sustain life and labor at slightly above a bare subsistence level, and the rapid increase of the slave population in the Old South stands in sharp contrast to the usual failure of slave populations to reproduce themselves.

But some planters did not behave rationally. They failed to control their tempers or tried to work more slaves than they could afford to maintain. Consequently, there were more cases of physical abuse and undernourishment than a purely economic calculation would lead us to expect.

The testimony of slaves themselves and of some independent white observers suggests that masters of large plantations generally did not have close and intimate relationships with the mass of field slaves. The kind of affection and concern associated with a father figure appears to have been limited mainly to relationships with a few favored house servants or other elite slaves, such as drivers and highly skilled artisans. The field hands on large estates dealt mostly with overseers who were hired or fired because of their ability to meet production quotas.

The limits of paternalism were revealed in the slave market. Planters who looked down on slave traders as less than respectable gentlemen nevertheless broke apart families by selling slaves "down river" when they found themselves in need of money. Even slaveholders who claimed not to participate in the slave market themselves often mortgaged slaves to secure debts; as many as one-third of all slave sales in the South were court-ordered sheriff's auctions when such masters defaulted on their debts.

While paternalism may have moderated planters' behavior to some extent, especially when economic self-interest reinforced "humanity," it is important to remember that most departures from unremitting labor and harsh conditions were concessions wrested from owners through slaves' defiance and resistance, at great personal risk.

Furthermore, when they were being most realistic, planters conceded that the ultimate basis of their authority was the slaves' fear of force and intimidation, rather than the natural obedience resulting from a loving parent-child relationship. Scattered among their statements are admissions that they re-

Not all slaves and masters had the benevolent relationship cited in defense of slavery. In fact, some masters devised various instruments of torture and punishment to control their slaves. For example, a slave fitted with this belled slave collar could not make a move without alerting the master. ❖

lied on the "principle of fear," "more and more on the power of fear," or—most graphically—that it was necessary "to make them stand in fear." Devices for inspiring fear included whipping—a common practice on most plantations—and the threat of sale away from family and friends. Planters' manuals and instructions to overseers reveal that certain and swift punishment for any infraction of the rules or even for a surly attitude was the preferred method for maintaining order and productivity.

When some masters inevitably yielded to the temptations of power or to their bad tempers and tortured or killed their slaves or raped slave women, the slaves had little recourse. Slaves lacked legal protection against such abuse because their testimony was not accepted in court. Abolitionists were correct in condemning slavery on principle because it gave one human being nearly absolute power over another. This system was bound to result in atrocities and violence. Even Harriet Beecher Stowe acknowledged in *Uncle Tom's Cabin,* her celebrated antislavery novel of 1852, that most slaveholders were not as sadistic and brutish as Simon Legree. But—and this was her real point—there was something terribly wrong with an institution that made a Simon Legree possible.

Small Slaveholders

As we have seen, 88 percent of all slaveholders in 1860 owned fewer than twenty slaves and thus were not planters in the usual sense of the term. Of these, the great majority had fewer than ten. Some of the small slaveholders were urban merchants or professional men who needed slaves only for domestic service, but more typical were farmers who used one or two slave families to ease the burden of their own labor. Relatively little is known about life on these small slaveholding farms; unlike the planters, the owners left few records behind. We do know that life was relatively spartan. Masters lived in log cabins or small frame cottages, and slaves lived in lofts or sheds that were not usually up to plantation housing standards.

For better or worse, relations between owners and their slaves were more intimate than on larger estates. Unlike planters, these farmers often worked in the fields alongside their slaves and sometimes ate at the same table or slept under the same roof. But such closeness did not necessarily result in better treatment. Slave testimony reveals that both the best and the worst of slavery could be found on these farms, depending on the character and disposition of the master. Given a choice, most slaves preferred to live on plantations because they offered the sociability, culture, and kinship of the slave quarters, as well as better prospects for adequate food, clothing, and shelter. Marginal slaveholders often sank into poverty and were forced either to sell their slaves or give them short rations.

Yeoman Farmers

Just below the small slaveholders on the social scale was a substantial class of **yeoman** farmers who owned land they worked themselves. Contrary to another myth about the Old South, most of these people did not fit the image of the degraded, shiftless poor white. Poor whites did exist, mainly as squatters on stretches of barren or sandy soil that no one else wanted. In parts of the South, a significant proportion of those working the land were tenants; some of these were "shiftless poor whites," but others were ambitious young men seeking to accumulate the capital to become landowners. The majority of the nonslaveholding rural population were proud, self-reliant farmers whose way of life did not differ markedly from that of family farmers in the Midwest during the early stages of settlement. If they were disadvantaged in comparison with farmers elsewhere in the United States, it was because the lack of economic development and urban growth perpetuated frontier conditions and denied them the opportunity to produce a substantial surplus for market.

The yeomen were mostly concentrated in the backcountry where slaves and plantations were rarely seen. In every southern state, there were hilly sections unsuitable for plantation agriculture. The foothills or interior valleys of the Appalachians and the Ozarks offered reasonably good soils for mixed farming, and long stretches of piney barrens along the Gulf Coast were suitable for raising livestock. In such regions slaveless farmers concentrated, giving rise to the "white counties" that complicated southern politics. A somewhat distinct group were the genuine mountaineers, who lived too high up to succeed at farming and relied heavily on hunting, lumbering, and distilling whiskey.

Yeoman women, much more than their wealthy counterparts, participated in every dimension of household labor. They worked in the garden, made handicrafts and clothing, and even labored in the fields when it was necessary. Women in the most dire economic circumstances even worked for wages in small businesses or on nearby farms. They also raised much larger families than their wealthier neighbors because having many children supplied a valuable labor pool for the family farm. Although yeoman farmers often recognized that their success was due to the help of their wives and daughters, they did not abandon the legal and cultural power they held as the heads of households.

Carl G. Von Iwonski, Block House, New Braunfels. *The majority of slaveholders in the South were not large plantation owners but small farmers of modest means who lived not in pillared mansions but in small, rough log cabins. Another substantial portion of Southerners were yeoman farmers who owned no slaves. Yet pervasive racism convinced most white Southerners they were entitled to own blacks, even if they had not yet acquired enough capital to afford slaves.* ❖

There were also a greater number of lower-class women who lived outside of male-headed households. Despite the pressures of respectability, there was a greater acceptance and sympathy in less affluent communities for women who bore illegitimate children or were abandoned by their husbands. Working women created a broader definition of "proper households" and navigated the challenges of holding families together in precarious economic conditions. The lack of transportation facilities, more than some failure of energy or character, limited the prosperity of the yeomen. A large part of their effort was devoted to growing subsistence crops, mainly corn. They raised a small percentage of the South's cotton and tobacco, but production was severely limited by the difficulty of marketing. Their main source of cash was livestock, especially hogs. Hogs could be walked to market over long distances, and massive droves from the backcountry to urban markets were commonplace. But southern livestock, which was generally allowed to forage in the woods rather than being fattened on grain, was of poor quality and did not bring high prices or big profits to raisers.

Although they did not benefit directly from the peculiar institution, most yeomen and other nonslaveholders tolerated slavery and were fiercely opposed to abolitionism in any form. A few antislavery Southerners, most notably Hinton R. Helper of North Carolina, tried to convince the yeomen that they were victimized by planter dominance and should work for its overthrow. These dissenters presented a plausible set of arguments, emphasizing that slavery and the plantation system created a privileged class and severely limited the economic opportunities of the nonslaveholding white majority.

Most yeomen were staunch Jacksonians who resented aristocratic pretensions and feared concentrations of power and wealth in the hands of the few. When asked about the gentry, they commonly voiced their disdain of "cotton snobs" and rich planters generally. In state and local politics, they sometimes expressed such feelings by voting against planter interests on issues involving representation, banking, and internal improvements. Why, then, did they fail to respond to antislavery appeals that called on them to strike at the real source of planter power and privilege?

One reason was that some nonslaveholders hoped to get ahead in the world, and in the South this meant acquiring slaves of their own. Just enough of the more prosperous yeomen broke into the slaveholding classes to make this dream seem believable. Planters, anxious to ensure the loyalty of nonslaveholders, strenuously encouraged the notion that every white man was a potential master.

Even if they did not aspire to own slaves, white farmers often viewed black servitude as providing a guarantee of their own liberty and independence. A society that gave them the right to vote and the chance to be self-sufficient on land of their own encouraged the feeling they were fundamentally equal to the largest slaveholders. Although they had no natural love of planters and slavery, they believed—or could be induced to believe—that abolition would threaten their liberty and independence. In part, their anxieties were economic; freed slaves would compete with them for land or jobs. But an intense racism deepened their fears and made their opposition to black freedom implacable. "Now suppose they was free," a nonslaveholder told a northern traveler, "you see they'd think themselves just as good as we . . . just suppose you had a family of children, how would [you] like to hev a niggar feeling just as good as a white man? how'd you like to hev a niggar steppin' up to your darter?" Emancipation was unthinkable because it would remove the pride and status that automatically went along with a white skin in this acutely race-conscious society. Slavery, despite its drawbacks, served to keep blacks "in their place" and to make all whites, however poor and uneducated they might be, feel they were free and equal members of a master race.

A Closed Mind and a Closed Society

Despite the tacit assent of most nonslaveholders, the dominant planters never lost their fear that lower-class whites would turn against slavery. They felt threatened from two sides: from the slave quarters where a new Nat Turner might be gathering his forces, and from the backcountry where yeomen and poor whites might heed the call of abolitionists and rise up against planter domination. Beginning in the 1830s, the ruling element tightened the screws of slavery and used their control of government and communications to create a mood of impending catastrophe designed to ensure that all southern whites were of a single mind on the slavery issue.

Before the 1830s, open discussion of the rights or wrongs of slavery had been possible in many parts of the South. Apologists commonly described the institution as "a necessary evil." In the upper South, as late as the 1820s, there had been significant support for the **American Colonization Society,** with its program of gradual voluntary emancipation accompanied by deportation of the freedmen. In 1831 and 1832—in the wake of the Nat Turner uprising—the Virginia state legislature debated a gradual emancipation plan. Major support for ensuring white safety by getting rid of both slavery and blacks came from representatives of the yeoman farmers living west of the Blue Ridge Mountains. But the defeat of the proposal effectively ended the discussion. The argument that slavery was "a positive good"—rather than an evil slated for gradual elimination—won the day.

The "positive good" defense of slavery was an answer to the abolitionist charge that the institution was inherently sinful. The message was carried in a host of books, pamphlets, and newspaper editorials published between the 1830s and the Civil War. Who, historians have asked, was it meant to persuade? Partly, the argument was aimed at the North, as a way of bolstering the strong current of antiabolitionist sentiment. But Southerners themselves were a prime target; the message was clearly calculated to resolve the kind of doubts and misgivings that had been freely expressed before the 1830s. Much of the message may have been over the heads of nonslaveholders, many of whom were semiliterate, but some of the arguments, in popularized form, were used to arouse racial anxieties that tended to neutralize antislavery sentiment among the lower classes.

The proslavery argument was based on three main propositions. The first and foremost was that enslavement was the natural and proper status for people of African descent. Blacks, it was alleged, were innately inferior to whites and suited only for slavery. Biased scientific and historical evidence was presented to support this claim. Second, slavery was held to be sanctioned by the Bible and Christianity—a position made necessary by the abolitionist appeal to Christian ethics. Ancient Hebrew slavery was held up as a divinely sanctioned model, and Saint Paul was quoted endlessly on the duty of servants to obey their masters. Southern churchmen took the lead in reconciling slavery with religion and also made renewed efforts to convert the slaves as a way of showing that enslavement could be a means for spreading the gospel.

Finally, efforts were made to show that slavery was consistent with the humanitarian spirit of the nineteenth century. The premise that blacks were naturally dependent led to the notion that they needed some kind of "family government" or special regime equivalent to the asylums that existed for the small numbers of whites who were also incapable of caring for themselves. The plantation allegedly provided such an environment, as benevolent masters guided and ruled this race of "perpetual children."

By the 1850s, the proslavery argument had gone beyond mere apology for the South and its peculiar institution and featured an ingenious attack on the free-labor system of the North. According to Virginian George Fitzhugh, the master-slave relationship was more humane than the one prevailing between employers and wage laborers in the North. Slaves had security against unemployment and a guarantee of care in old age, whereas free workers might face destitution and even starvation at any time. Worker insecurity in free societies led inevitably to strikes, bitter class conflicts, and the rise of socialism; slave societies, on the other hand, could more effectively protect property rights and maintain other traditional values because its laboring class was better treated and, at the same time, more firmly controlled.

In addition to arguing against the abolitionists, proslavery Southerners attempted to seal off their region from antislavery ideas and influences. Whites who were bold enough to criticize slavery publicly were mobbed or persecuted. One of the last and bravest of the southern abolitionists, Cassius M. Clay of Kentucky, armed himself with a brace of pistols when he gave speeches, until the threat of mob violence finally forced him across the Ohio River. In 1856, a University of North Carolina professor was fired because he admitted he would vote for the moderately antislavery Republican party if he had a chance. Clergymen who questioned the morality of slavery were driven from their pulpits, and northern travelers suspected of being abolitionist agents were tarred and feathered. When abolitionists tried to send their literature through the mails during the 1830s, it was seized in southern post offices and publicly burned.

Such flagrant denials of free speech and civil liberties were inspired in part by fears that nonslaveholding whites and slaves would get subversive ideas about slavery. Hinton R. Helper's book *The Impending Crisis of the South,* an 1857 appeal to nonslaveholders to resist the planter regime, was suppressed with particular vigor; those found with copies were beaten up or even lynched. But the deepest fear was that slaves would hear the abolitionist talk or read antislavery literature and be inspired to rebel. Such anxieties rose to panic pitch after the Nat Turner rebellion. Consequently, new laws were passed making it a crime to teach slaves to read and write. Other repressive legislation aimed at slaves banned meetings unless a white man was present, severely restricted the activities of black preachers, and suppressed independent black churches. Free blacks, thought to be possible instigators of slave revolt, were denied basic civil liberties and were the object of growing surveillance and harassment.

All these efforts at thought control and internal security did not allay planters' fears of abolitionist subversion, lower-class white dissent, and, above all, slave revolt. The persistent barrage of proslavery propaganda and the course of national events in the 1850s created a mood of panic and desperation. By this time, an increasing number of Southerners had become

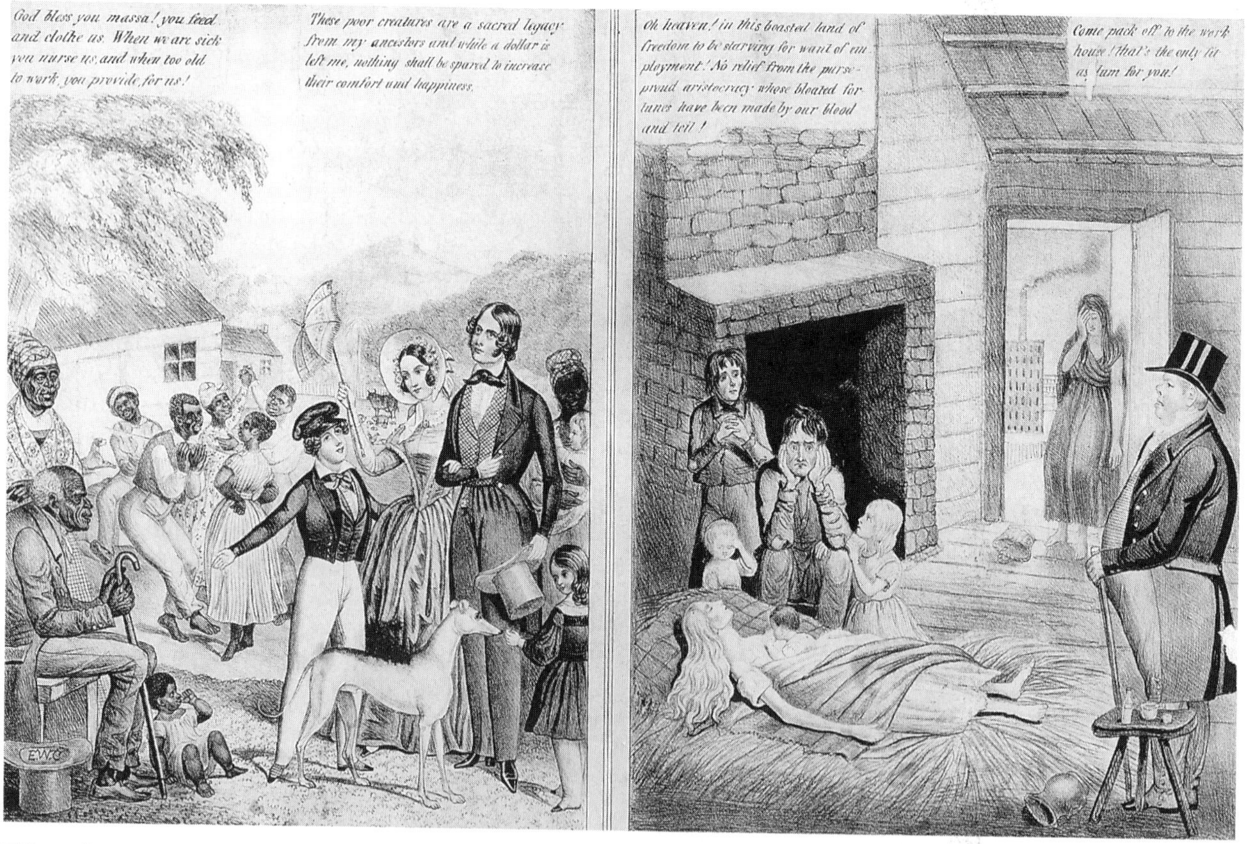

This proslavery cartoon of 1841 contends that the slave in America had a better life than did the working-class white in England. Supposedly, the grateful slaves were clothed, fed, and cared for in their old age by kindly and sympathetic masters, while starving English workers were mercilessly exploited by factory owners. ❖

convinced that safety from abolitionism and its associated terrors required a formal withdrawal from the Union—secession.

Slavery and the Southern Economy

Southern society transformed itself according to the needs of the slave system because slavery played such a crucial role in the economic life of the South. Despite the internal divisions of Southern society, white Southerners from all regions and classes came to perceive their interests tied up with slavery, whether because they owned slaves themselves or because they believed in slavery as essential to the "Southern way of life" or "white men's democracy." And because slavery was the cornerstone of the Southern economy, it affected white Southerners' attitudes toward landholding and toward industrialization.

For the most part, the expansion of slavery—the number of slaves in the South more than tripled between 1810 and 1860 to nearly 4 million—can be attributed to the rise of "King Cotton." The cotton-growing areas of the South were becoming more and more dependent on slavery, at the same time that agriculture in the upper South was actually moving away from the institution. Yet slavery continued to remain important to the economy of the upper South in a different way, through the slave trade. To understand Southern thought and behavior, it is necessary to bear in mind this major regional difference between a slave plantation society and a farming and slave-trading region.

The Internal Slave Trade

Tobacco, the original plantation crop of the colonial period, continued to be the principal slave-cultivated commodity of the upper tier of southern states during the pre–Civil War era. But markets were often depressed, and profitable tobacco cultivation was hard to sustain for very long in one place because the crop rapidly depleted the soil. During the lengthy depression of the tobacco market that lasted from the 1820s to the 1850s, tobacco farmers in Virginia and Maryland experimented with fertilizer use, crop rotation, and diversified farming, all of which increased the need for capital but reduced the demand for labor.

As slave prices rose (because of high demand in the lower South) and demand for slaves in the upper South fell, the "internal" slave trade took off. Increasingly, the most profitable business for slaveholders in Virginia, Kentucky, Maryland, and the Carolinas was selling "surplus" slaves from the upper South to regions of the lower South, where staple crop production was more profitable. This interstate slave trade sent an estimated six- to seven-hundred-thousand slaves in a southwesterly direction between 1815 and 1860. Historian Michael Tadman estimates that the chances of a slave child in the Upper South in the 1820s to be "sold South" by 1860 was as high as 30 percent. Such sales were wrenching, not only splitting families, but making it especially unlikely that the slaves sold would ever see friends or family again.

Some economic historians have concluded that the most important crop produced in the tobacco kingdom was not the "stinking weed" but human beings cultivated for the auction block. Respectable planters did not like to think of themselves as raising slaves for market, but few would refuse to sell some of their "people" if they needed money to get out of debt or make expensive improvements. For the region as a whole, the slave trade provided a crucial source of capital in a period of transition and innovation.

Lewis Miller, Slave Sale, Virginia, *probably 1853. Slave auctions, such as the one depicted in this sketch from Lewis Miller's sketchbook, were an abomination and embarrassment to many Americans. To southern plantation owners dependent on slave labor, however, such activities were essential.* ❖

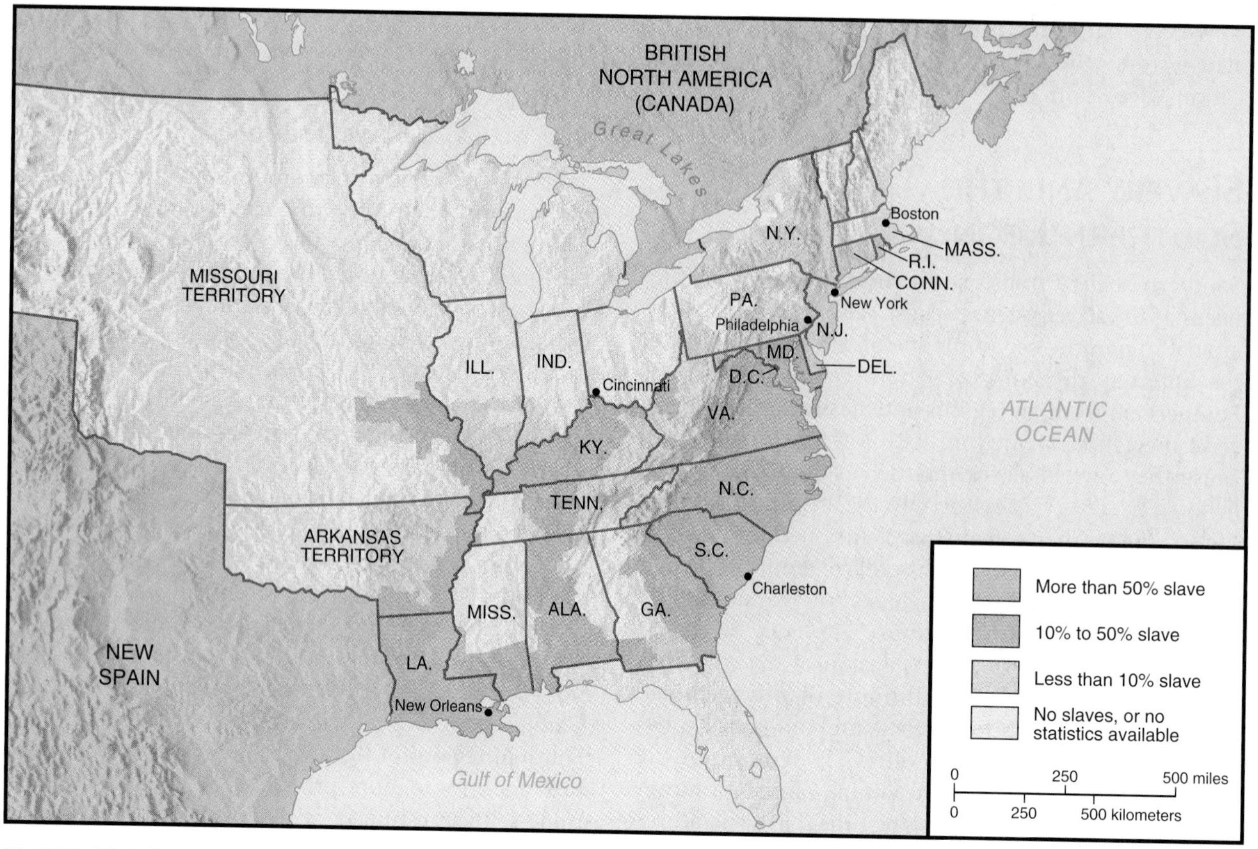

SLAVE CONCENTRATION, 1820 *In 1820, most slaves lived in the eastern seaboard states of Virginia and South Carolina and in Louisiana on the Gulf of Mexico.* ❖

Nevertheless, the fact that slave labor was declining in importance in the upper South meant the peculiar institution had a weaker hold on public loyalty there than in the cotton states. Diversification of agriculture was accompanied by a more rapid rate of urban and industrial development than was occurring elsewhere in the South. As a result, Virginians, Marylanders, and Kentuckians were seriously divided on whether their ultimate future lay with the Deep South's plantation economy or with the industrializing free-labor system that was flourishing just north of their borders.

The Rise of the Cotton Kingdom

The warmer climate and good soils of the lower tier of southern states made it possible to raise crops more naturally suited than tobacco or cereals to the plantation form of agriculture and the heavy use of slave labor. Since the colonial or revolutionary periods, rice and a special long-staple variety of fine cotton had been grown profitably on vast estates along the coast of South Carolina and Georgia. In lower Louisiana, between New Orleans and Baton Rouge, sugar was the cash crop. As in the West Indies, sugar production required a large investment and a great deal of backbreaking labor: in other words, large, well-financed plantations and small armies of slave laborers. Cultivation of rice, long-staple cotton, and sugar was limited by natural conditions to peripheral, semitropical areas. It was the rise of short-staple cotton as the South's major crop that strengthened the hold of slavery and the plantation on the southern economy.

Short-staple cotton differed from the long-staple variety in two important ways: Its bolls contained seeds that were much more difficult to extract by hand, and it could be grown almost anywhere south of Virginia and Kentucky—the main requirement was a guarantee of two hundred frost-free days. Before the 1790s, the seed extraction problem had prevented short-staple cotton from becoming a major market crop. The invention of the **cotton gin** in 1793 resolved that difficulty, however, and the subsequent westward expansion opened vast areas for cotton cultivation. Unlike rice and sugar, cotton could be grown on small farms as well as on plantations. But large planters enjoyed certain advantages that

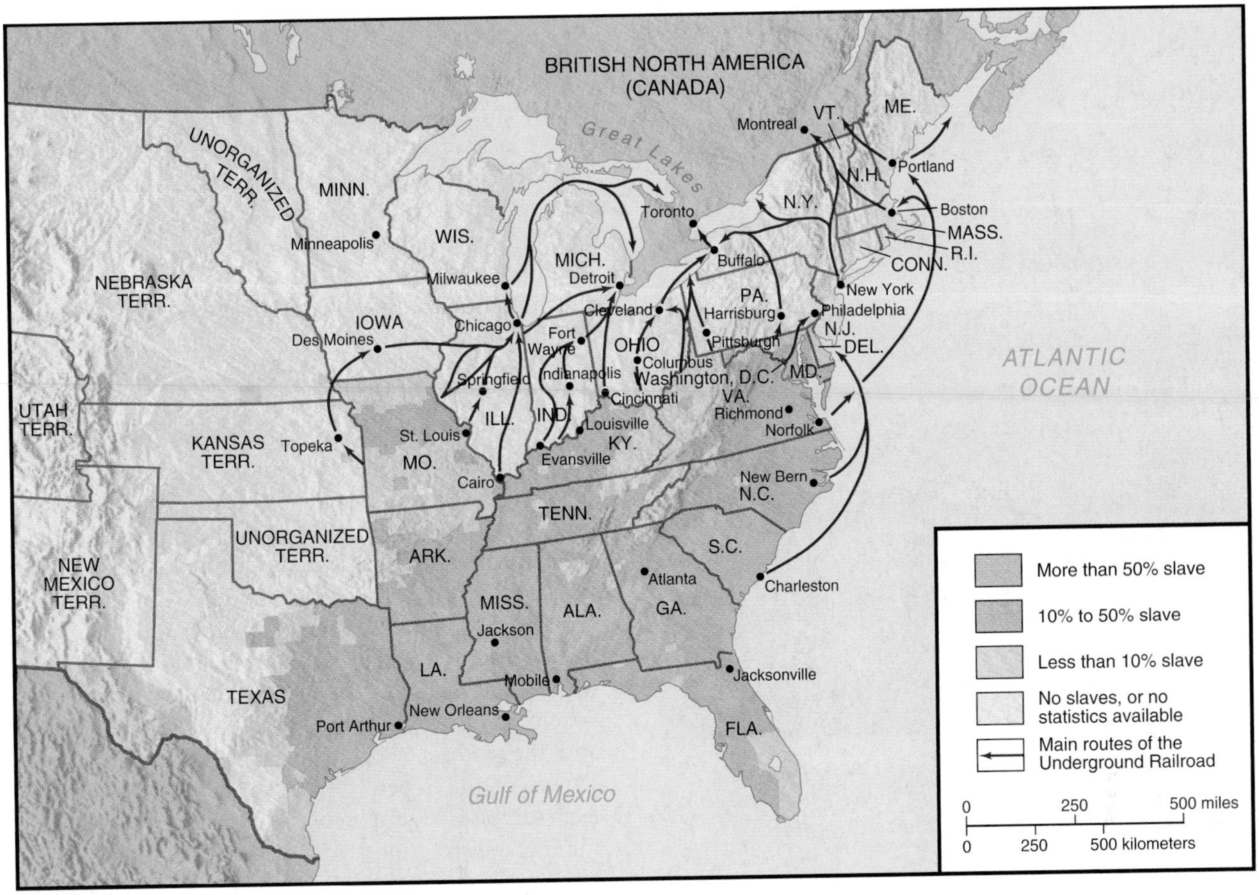

SLAVE CONCENTRATION, 1860 *In 1860, slavery had extended throughout the southern states, with the greatest concentrations of slaves in the states of the Deep South. There were also sizable slave populations in the new states of Missouri, Arkansas, Texas, and Florida.* ❖

made them the main producers. Only relatively large operators could afford their own gins or possessed the capital to acquire the fertile bottomlands that brought the highest yields. They also had lower transportation costs because they were able to monopolize land along rivers and streams that were the South's natural arteries of transportation.

The first major cotton-producing regions were inland areas of Georgia and South Carolina but the center of production shifted rapidly westward during the nineteenth century. By the 1830s, Alabama and Mississippi had surpassed Georgia and South Carolina as cotton-growing states. By the 1850s, Arkansas, northwest Louisiana, and east Texas were the most prosperous and rapidly growing plantation regions. The rise in total production that accompanied this geographic expansion was phenomenal. Between 1792 and 1817, the South's output of cotton rose from about 13,000 bales to 461,000; by 1840, it was 1.35 million; and in 1860, production peaked at the colossal figure of 4.8 million bales. Most of the cotton went to supply the booming textile industry of Great Britain. Lesser proportions went to the manufacturers of continental Europe and the northeastern United States.

"Cotton is king!" proclaimed a southern orator in the 1850s, and he was right. By that time, three-quarters of the world's supply of cotton came from the American South, and this single commodity accounted for more than half the total dollar value of American exports. Cotton growing and the network of commercial and industrial enterprises that marketed and processed the crop constituted the most important economic interest in the United States on the eve of the Civil War. Since slavery and cotton seemed inextricably linked, it appeared obvious to many Southerners that their peculiar institution was the keystone of national wealth and economic progress.

Despite its overall success, however, the rise of the Cotton Kingdom did not bring a uniform or steady prosperity to the lower South. Many planters worked the land until it was exhausted and then took their slaves westward to richer soils, leaving depressed and ravaged areas in their wake.

Planters were also beset and sometimes ruined by fluctuations in markets and prices. Boom periods and

A row of steamboats in New Orleans await bales of cotton for shipment. By 1860 production of "king" cotton in the south peaked at 4.8 million bales. ❖

flush times were followed by falling prices and waves of bankruptcies. The great periods of expansion and bonanza profits were 1815–1819, 1832–1837, and 1849–1860. The first two booms were deflated by a fall in cotton prices resulting from overproduction and depressed market conditions. During the eleven years of rising output and high prices preceding the Civil War, however, the planters gradually forgot their earlier troubles and began to imagine they were immune to future economic disasters.

Despite the insecurities associated with cotton production, most of the time the crop represented the Old South's best chance for profitable investment. Prudent planters who had not borrowed too heavily during flush times could survive periods of depression by cutting costs, making their plantations self-sufficient by shifting acreage away from cotton and planting subsistence crops. For those with worn-out land, two options existed: They could sell their land and move west, or they could sell their slaves to raise capital for fertilization, crop rotation, and other improvements that could help them survive where they were. Hence planters had little incentive to seek alternatives to slavery, the plantation, and dependence on a single cash crop. From a purely economic point of view, they had every reason to defend slavery and to insist on their right to expand it.

Slavery and Industrialization

As the sectional quarrel with the North intensified, Southerners became increasingly alarmed by their region's lack of economic self-sufficiency. Dependence on the North for capital, marketing facilities, and manufactured goods was seen as evidence of a dangerous subservience to "external" economic interests. Southern nationalists such as J. D. B. DeBow, editor of the influential *DeBow's Review,* called during the 1850s for the South to develop its own industries, commerce, and shipping. As a fervent defender of slavery, DeBow did not believe such diversification would require a massive shift to free wage labor. He saw no reason for slaves not to be used as the main workforce in an industrial revolution. But his call for a diversified economy went unanswered. Men with capital were doing too well in plantation agriculture to risk their money in other ventures.

It is difficult to determine whether the main factor that kept most slaves working on plantations and farms was some inherent characteristic of slavery as a labor system or simply the strong market demand for cotton and the South's capacity to meet it. A minority of slaves—about 5 percent during the 1850s—were, in fact, successfully employed in industrial tasks such as mining, construction, and mill work. In the 1840s and 1850s, a debate raged among white capitalists over whether the South should use free whites or enslaved blacks as the labor supply for industry. William Gregg of South Carolina, the foremost promoter of cotton mills in the Old South, defended a white labor policy, arguing that factory work would provide new economic opportunities for a degraded class of poor whites. But other advocates of industrialization feared that the growth of a free working class would lead to social conflict among whites and preferred using slaves for all supervised manual labor. In practice, some factories employed slaves, others white workers, and a few even experimented with integrated workforces. It is clear, however, that the union of slavery and cotton that was central to the South's prosperity impeded industrialization and left the region dependent on a one-crop agriculture and on the North for capital and marketing.

The "Profitability" Issue

Some Southerners were making money, and a great deal of it, using slave labor to raise cotton. The great mansions of the Alabama "black belt" and the lower Mississippi could not have been built if their owners had not been successful. But did slavery yield a good return for the great majority of slaveholders who were not large planters? Did it provide the basis for general prosperity and a relatively high standard of living for the southern population in general, or at least for the two-thirds of it who were white and free? These questions have been hotly debated by economic historians. Some knowledge of the main arguments regarding its "profitability" is helpful to an understanding of the South's attachment to slavery.

For many years, historians believed that slave-based agriculture was, on the average, not very lucrative. Planters' account books seemed to show at best a modest return on investment. In the 1850s, the price of slaves rose at a faster rate than the price of cotton, allegedly squeezing many operators. Some historians even concluded that slavery was a dying institution by the time of the Civil War. Profitability, they argued, depended on access to new and fertile land suitable for plantation agriculture, and virtually all such land within the limits of the United States had already been taken up by 1860. Hence slavery had allegedly reached its natural limits of expansion and was on the verge of becoming so unprofitable that it would fall of its own weight in the near future.

A more recent interpretation, based on modern economic theory, holds that slavery was in fact still an economically sound institution in 1860 and showed no signs of imminent decline. A reexamination of planters' records using modern accounting methods shows that during the 1850s, planters could normally expect an annual return of 8 to 10 percent on capital invested. This yield was roughly equivalent to the best that could then be obtained from the most lucrative sectors of northern industry and commerce.

Furthermore, it is no longer clear that plantation agriculture had reached its natural limits of expansion by 1860. Production in Texas had not yet peaked, and construction of railroads and levees was opening up new areas for cotton growing elsewhere in the South. With the advantage of hindsight, economic historians have pointed out that improvements in transportation and flood control would enable the post–Civil War South to double its cotton acreage. Those who now argue that slavery was profitable and had an expansive future have made a strong and convincing case.

But the larger question remains: What sort of economic development did a slave plantation system foster? The system may have made slaveholders wealthy, but did the benefits trickle down to the rest of the population—to the majority of whites who owned no slaves and to the slaves themselves? Did it promote efficiency and progressive change? Economists Robert Fogel and Stanley Engerman have argued that the plantation's success was due to an internally efficient enterprise with good managers and industrious, well-motivated workers. Other economic historians have attributed the profitability almost exclusively to favorable market conditions.

Large plantation owners were the only segment of the population to enjoy the full benefits of the slave economy. Small slaveholders and nonslaveholders shared only to a very limited extent in the bonanza profits of the cotton economy. Because of various insecurities—lack of credit, high transportation costs, and a greater vulnerability to market fluctuations—they had to devote a larger share of their acreage to subsistence crops, especially corn and hogs, than did the planters. They were thus able to survive, but their standard of living was lower than that of most northern farmers. Slaves received sufficient food, clothing, and

CHRONOLOGY

1793	Eli Whitney invents the cotton gin
1800	Gabriel Prosser leads abortive slave rebellion in Virginia
1811	Slaves revolt in Point Coupée section of Louisiana
1822	Denmark Vesey conspiracy uncovered in Charleston, South Carolina
1829	David Walker publishes *Appeal* calling for slave insurrection
1830	First National Negro Convention meets
1831	Slaves under Nat Turner rebel in Virginia, killing almost sixty whites
1832	Virginia legislature votes against gradual emancipation
1835–1842	Blacks fight alongside Indians in the Second Seminole War
1837	Panic of 1837 is followed by major depression of the cotton market
1847	Frederick Douglass publishes the *North Star,* a black antislavery newspaper
1849	Cotton prices rise, and a sustained boom commences
1851	Group of free blacks rescues escaped slave Shadrack from federal authorities in Boston
1852	Harriet Beecher Stowe's antislavery novel *Uncle Tom's Cabin* is published and becomes a best-seller
1857	Hinton R. Helper attacks slavery on economic grounds in *The Impending Crisis of the South;* the book is suppressed in the southern states
1860	Cotton prices and production reach all-time peak

shelter for their subsistence and to make them capable of working well enough to keep the plantation afloat economically, but their living standard was below that of the poorest free people in the United States. It was proslavery propaganda rather than documented fact, to maintain that slaves were better off than northern wage laborers.

The South's economic development was skewed in favor of a single route to wealth, open only to the minority possessing both a white skin and access to capital. The concentration of capital and business energies on cotton production foreclosed the kind of diversified industrial and commercial growth that would have provided wider opportunities. Thus, in comparison to the industrializing North, the South was an underdeveloped region in which much of the population had little incentive to work hard. A lack of public education for whites and the denial of even minimal literacy to slaves represented a critical failure to develop human resources. The South's economy was probably condemned so long as it was based on slavery.

Conclusion: Worlds in Conflict

If slaves lived to some extent in a separate and distinctive world of their own, so did planters, less affluent whites, and even free blacks. The Old South was thus a deeply divided society. The northern traveler Frederick Law Olmsted, who made three journeys through the slave states in the 1850s, provided a vivid sense of how diverse in outlook and circumstances southern people could be. Visiting a great plantation, he watched the slaves stop working as soon as the overseer turned away; on a small farm, he saw a slave and his owner working in the fields together. Treatment of slaves, he found, ranged from humane paternalism to flagrant cruelty. Olmsted heard nonslaveholding whites damn the planters as "cotton snobs" but also talk about blacks as "niggars" and express fear of interracial marriages if slaves were freed. He received hospitality from poor whites living in crowded one-room cabins as well as from fabulously wealthy planters in pillared mansions, and he found life in the backcountry radically different from that in the plantation belts.

In short, he showed that the South was a kaleidoscope of groups divided by class, race, culture, and geography. What held it together and provided some measure of unity were a booming plantation economy and a web of customary relationships and loyalties that could obscure the underlying cleavages and antagonisms. The fractured and fragile nature of this society would soon become apparent when it was subjected to the pressures of civil war.

Recommended Reading

Major works that take a broad view of slavery are Kenneth M. Stampp, *The Peculiar Institution: Slavery in the Antebellum South* (1956), which stresses its coercive features; John W. Blassingame, *The Slave Community: Plantation Life in the Antebellum South* (1972), which focuses on slave culture and psychology; and Eugene D. Genovese, *Roll, Jordan, Roll: The World the Slaves Made* (1974), which probes the paternalistic character of the institution and the way in which slaves made a world for themselves within its bounds. An insightful interpretation of antebellum southern society is James Oakes, *Slavery and Freedom: An Interpretation of the Old South* (1990). For an overview of the history of slavery, see Peter Kolchin, *American Slavery, 1619–1877* (1993).

On the economics of slavery, see Gavin Wright, *The Political Economy of the Cotton South: Households, Markets, and Wealth in the Nineteenth Century* (1978). On women in the Old South, see Laura F. Edwards, *Scarlett Doesn't Live Here Anymore: Southern Women in the Civil War Era* (2000) and Deborah Gray White, *Ar'n't I a Woman: Female Slaves in the Plantation South* (1985). On the slave trade, see two excellent studies: Michael Tadman, *Speculators and Slaves: Masters, Traders, and Slaves in the Old South* (1989) and Walter Johnson, *Soul by Soul: Life Inside the Antebellum Slave Market* (1999). For the history of the slave family, see Herbert Gutman, *The Black Family in Slavery and Freedom, 1750-1925* (1976); Brenda Stevenson, *Life in Black and White: Family and Community in the Slave South* (1996); and Marie Jenkins Schwartz, *Born in Bondage: Growing Up Enslaved in the Antebellum South* (2000). For Southern law and slavery, see Thomas D. Morris, *Southern Slavery and the Law, 1619-1860* (1996) and Ariela J. Gross, *Double Character: Slavery and Mastery in the Antebellum Southern Courtroom* (2000).

Black resistance to slavery is described in Vincent Harding, *There Is a River: The Black Struggle for Freedom in America* (1981). Slave culture is examined in Albert J. Raboteau, *Slave Religion: The "Invisible Institution" in the Antebellum South* (1978); Lawrence W. Levine, *Black Culture and Consciousness: Afro-American Folk Thought from Slavery to Freedom* (1977); Sterling Stuckey, *Slave Culture: Nationalist Theory and the Foundations of Black America* (1987); and Sharla M. Fett, *Healing, Health, and Power on Southern Slave Plantations* (2002).

For a list of additional titles related to this chapter's topics, please see http://www.ablongman.com/divine.

Suggested Web Sites

"Been Here So Long": Selections from the WPA American Slave Narratives

http://newdeal.feri.org/asn/index.htm
Slave narratives are some of the more interesting primary sources about slavery.

Exploring Amistad

http://amistad.mysticseaport.org/main/welcome.html
Mystic Seaport runs this site that includes extensive collections of historical resources relating to the revolt and subsequent trial of enslaved Africans.

Africans in America: America's Journey Through Slavery

http://www.pbs.org/wgbh/aia/home.html
This PBS site contains images and documents recounting slavery in America.

Amistad Trials (1839–1840)

http://www.law.umkc.edu/faculty/projects/ftrials/amistad/AMISTD.HTM
Images, chronology, court and official documents comprise this site by Dr. Doug Linder at University of Missouri–Kansas City Law School.

Slave Narratives

http://docsouth.unc.edu/neh/neh.html
This site presents the telling narratives of several slaves housed at the Documents of the American South collection and the University of North Carolina.

The Settlement of African Americans in Liberia

http://www.loc.gov/exhibits/african/perstor.html
This site contains images and text relating to the colonization movement to return African Americans to Africa.

Images of African Americans from the Nineteenth Century

http://digital.nypl.org/schomburg/images_aa19/
The New York Public Library–Schomburg Center for Research in Black Culture site contains numerous visuals.

Images of African American Slavery and Freedom

http://lcweb.loc.gov/rr/print/082_slave.html
This site contains numerous photographs and other images of slaves and free blacks from the Library of Congress.

St. Louis Circuit Court Historical Records Project

http://stlcourtrecords.wustl.edu/resources.cfm
This site contains links to full-text reproductions of slaves' freedom suits in Missouri, including Dred Scott's case, and many other African American history links.

Chapter 12

Jeremiah Paul, Revival Meeting ❖

The Pursuit of Perfection

Redeeming the Middle Class

In the winter of 1830 to 1831, a wave of religious revivals swept the northern states. The most dramatic and successful took place in Rochester, New York. Large audiences, composed mostly of respectable and prosperous citizens, heard Presbyterian evangelist Charles G. Finney preach that every man or woman had the power to choose Christ and a godly life. Finney broke with his church's traditional belief that it was God's inscrutable will that decided who would be saved when he preached that "sinners ought to be made to feel that they have something to do, and that something is to repent. That is something that no other being can do for them, neither God nor man, and something they can do and do now."

For six months, Finney held prayer meetings almost daily, putting intense pressure on those who had not experienced salvation. Hundreds came forth to declare their faith, and church membership doubled during his stay. The newly awakened Christians of Rochester were urged to convert relatives, neighbors, and employees. If enough people enlisted in the evangelical crusade, Finney proclaimed, the millennium would be achieved within months.

Finney's call for religious and moral renewal fell on fertile ground in Rochester. The bustling boomtown on the Erie Canal was suffering from severe growing pains and tensions arising from rapid economic development. Leading families were divided into quarreling factions, and workers were threatening to break free from the control their employers had previously exerted over their daily lives. Most of the early converts were from the middle class. Businessmen who had been heavy drinkers and irregular churchgoers now abstained from alcohol and went to church at least twice a week. They also pressured the employees in their workshops, mills, and stores to do likewise. More rigorous standards of proper behavior and religious conformity unified Rochester's elite and increased its ability to control the rest of the community. As in other cities swept by the revival, evangelical Protestantism provided the middle class with a stronger sense of identity and purpose.

BUT THE WAR ON SIN was not always so unifying. Among those converted in Rochester and elsewhere were some who could not rest easy until the nation as a whole conformed to the pure Christianity of the Sermon on the Mount. Finney expressed such a hope himself, but he concentrated on religious conversion and moral uplift of the individual, trusting that the purification of American society and politics would automatically follow. Other religious and moral reformers were inspired to crusade against those social and political institutions that failed to measure up to the standards of Christian perfection. They proceeded to attack such collective "sins" as the liquor traffic, war, slavery, and even government.

Religiously inspired reformism cut two ways. On the one hand, it imposed a new order and cultural unity to previously divided and troubled communities like Rochester. But it also inspired a variety of more radical movements or experiments that threatened

Outline

Feature Essay

Law and Society

to undermine established institutions that failed to live up to the principles of the more idealistic reformers. One of these movements—abolitionism—challenged the central social and economic institution of the southern states and helped trigger political upheaval and civil war.

THE RISE OF EVANGELICALISM

American Protestantism was in a state of constant ferment during the early nineteenth century. The separation of church and state, a process that began during the Revolution, was now complete. Government sponsorship and funding had ended, or would soon end, for the established churches of the colonial era, such as the Congregationalists of New England and the Episcopalians of the South. Dissenting groups, such as Baptists and Methodists, welcomed full religious freedom because it offered a better chance to win new converts. All pious Protestants, however, were concerned about the spread of "infidelity"—a term they applied to Catholics, freethinkers, Unitarians, Mormons, and anyone else who was not an evangelical Christian. But they faced opposition to their effort to make the nation officially Protestant. Some of the Founders of the nation had set a troubling example by their casual or even unfriendly attitude toward religious orthodoxy. Secular ideas drawn from the Enlightenment of the late eighteenth century had achieved wide acceptance as a basis for the establishment of a democratic republic, and opposition to mixing religion with public life remained strong during the age of Jackson. As deism—the belief in a God who expressed himself through natural laws accessible to human reason—declined in popularity in the early to mid-nineteenth century, Catholic immigration increased, and the spread of "Popery" became the main focus of evangelical concern. Both Catholics and Unitarians (who quietly carried forward the rationalistic traditions of the eighteenth century) resented and resisted the evangelicals' efforts to convert them to "the Christianity of the heart." Most of those who accepted Christ as their personal savior in revival meetings previously had been indifferent to religion rather than adhering to an alternative set of beliefs.

Revivalism proved to be a very effective means to extend religious values and build up church membership. The Great Awakening of the mid-eighteenth century had shown the wonders that evangelists could accomplish, and new revivalists repeated this success by greatly increasing the proportion of the population that belonged to Protestant churches. They also capitalized on the growing willingness of Americans to form voluntary organizations. Spiritual renewals were often followed by mobilization of the faithful into associations to spread the gospel and reform American morals.

According to some historians, evangelical revival and the reform movements it inspired reflected the same spirit as the new democratic politics. In a sense this is true: Jacksonian politicians and evangelists both sought popular favor and assumed that individuals were free agents capable of self-direction and self-improvement. But leaders of the two types of movements made different kinds of demands on ordinary people. Jacksonians idealized common folk pretty much as they found them and saw no danger to the community if individuals pursued their worldly interests. Evangelical reformers, who tended to support the Whigs or to reject both parties, believed that the common people, and not just the elite, needed to be redeemed and uplifted—committed to a higher goal than self-interest. They did not trust a democracy of unbelievers and sinners. The republic would be safe, they insisted, only if a right-minded minority preached, taught, and agitated until the mass of ordinary citizens was reborn into a higher life.

The Second Great Awakening: The Frontier Phase

The **Second Great Awakening** began in earnest on the southern frontier around the turn of the century. In 1801, a crowd estimated at nearly fifty thousand gathered at Cane Ridge, Kentucky. According to a contemporary observer:

> The noise was like the roar of Niagara. The vast sea of human beings seemed to be agitated as if by a storm. I counted seven ministers all preaching at once. . . . Some of the people were singing, others praying, some crying for mercy . . . while others were shouting most vociferously. . . . At one time I saw at least five hundred swept down in a moment, as if a battery of a thousand guns had been opened upon them, and then followed immediately shrieks and shouts that rent the heavens.

Highly emotional camp meetings, organized usually by Methodists or Baptists but sometimes by Presbyterians, became a regular feature of religious life in the South and the lower Midwest. On the frontier, the camp meeting met social as well as religious needs. In the sparsely settled southern backcountry, it was difficult to sustain local churches with regular ministers. Methodists solved part of the problem by sending out circuit riders. Baptists licensed uneducated farmers to preach to their neighbors. But for many people, the only way to get baptized or married or to have a communal religious experience was to attend a camp meeting.

Rowdies and scoffers also attended, drinking whiskey, carousing, and fornicating on the fringes of the small city of tents and wagons. Sometimes they were "struck down" by a mighty blast from the pulpit. Evangelists loved to tell stories of such conversions or near conversions. According to Methodist preacher Peter Cartwright, one scoffer was seized by the "jerks"—a set of involuntary bodily movements often observed at camp meetings. Normally such an exercise would lead to conversion, but this particular sinner was so hardhearted that he refused to surrender to God. The result was that he kept jerking until his neck was broken.

Lithograph depicting a camp meeting. Religious revival meetings on the frontier attracted hundreds of people who camped for days to listen to the preacher and to share with their neighbors in a communal religious experience. Notice that the men and women are seated in separate sections. ❖

Camp meetings obviously provided an emotional outlet for rural people whose everyday lives were often lonely and tedious. They could also promote a sense of community and social discipline. Conversion at a camp meeting could be a rite of passage, signifying that a young man or woman had outgrown wild or antisocial behavior and was now ready to become a respectable member of the community.

In the southern states, Baptists and Presbyterians eventually deemphasized camp meetings in favor of "protracted meetings" in local churches, which featured guest preachers holding forth day after day for up to two weeks. Southern evangelical churches, especially Baptist and Methodist, grew rapidly in membership and influence during the first half of the nineteenth century and became the focus of community life in rural areas. Although they fostered societies to improve morals—to encourage temperance and discourage dueling, for example—they generally shied away from social reform. The conservatism of a slaveholding society discouraged radical efforts to change the world.

The Second Great Awakening in the North

Reformist tendencies were more evident in the distinctive kind of revivalism that originated in New England and western New York. Northern evangelists were mostly Congregationalists and Presbyterians, strongly influenced by New England Puritan traditions. Their greatest successes were not in rural or frontier areas but in small- to medium-sized towns and cities. Their revivals could be stirring affairs but were less extravagantly emotional than the camp meetings of the South. The northern brand of evangelism resulted in formation of societies devoted to the redemption of the human race in general and American society in particular.

The reform movement in New England began as an effort to defend Calvinism against the liberal views of religion fostered by the Enlightenment. The Reverend Timothy Dwight, who became president of Yale College in 1795, was alarmed by the younger generation's growing acceptance of the belief that the Deity was the benevolent master architect of a rational universe rather than an all-powerful, mysterious God. Dwight was particularly disturbed by those religious liberals whose rationalism reached the point of denying the doctrine of the Trinity and who proclaimed themselves to be "Unitarians."

To Dwight's horror, Unitarians captured some fashionable and sophisticated New England congregations and even won control of the Harvard Divinity School. He fought back by preaching to Yale undergraduates that they were "dead in sin" and succeeded in provoking a series of campus revivals. But the harshness and pessimism of orthodox Calvinist doctrine, with its stress on original sin and predestination, had limited appeal in a republic committed to human freedom and progress.

A younger generation of Congregational ministers reshaped New England Puritanism to increase its appeal to people who shared the prevailing optimism about human capabilities. The main theologian of early-nineteenth-century neo-Calvinism was Nathaniel Taylor, a disciple of Dwight, who also held forth at Yale. Taylor softened the doctrine of predestination almost out of existence by contending that every individual was a free agent who had the ability to overcome a natural inclination to sin.

The first great practitioner of the new evangelical Calvinism was Lyman Beecher, another of Dwight's pupils. In the period just before and after the War of 1812, Beecher helped promote a series of revivals in the Congregational churches of New England. Using his own homespun version of Taylor's doctrine of free agency, Beecher induced thousands—in his home church in Litchfield, Connecticut, and in other churches that offered him their pulpits—to acknowledge their sinfulness and surrender to God.

During the late 1820s, Beecher was forced to confront the new and more radical form of revivalism being practiced in western New York by Charles G. Finney. Upstate New York was a seedbed for religious enthusiasms of various kinds. A majority of its population were transplanted New Englanders who had left behind their close-knit village communities and ancestral churches but not their Puritan consciences. Troubled by rapid economic changes and the social dislocations that went with them, they were ripe for a new faith and a fresh moral direction.

Although he worked within Congregational and Presbyterian churches (which were then cooperating under a plan of union established in 1804), Finney departed radically from Calvinist doctrines. In his hands, free agency became unqualified free will. One of his sermons was titled "Sinners Bound to Change Their Own Hearts." Finney was relatively indifferent to theological issues. His appeal was to emotion or to the heart rather than to doctrine or reason. He wanted converts to feel the power of Christ and become new men and women. He eventually adopted the extreme view that redeemed Christians could be totally free of sin—as perfect as their Father in Heaven.

Beginning in 1823, Finney conducted a series of highly successful revivals in towns and cities of western New York, culminating in the aforementioned triumph in Rochester in 1830–1831. Even more controversial than his freewheeling approach to theology were the means he used to win converts. Finney sought instantaneous conversions through a variety of new methods. These included holding protracted meetings that lasted all night or several days in a row, placing an "anxious bench" in front of the congregation where those in the process of repentance could receive special attention, and encouraging women to pray publicly for the souls of male relatives.

The results could be dramatic. Sometimes listeners fell to the floor in fits of excitement. "If I had had a sword in my hand," Finney recalled, "I could not have cut them off as fast as they fell." Although he appealed to emotion, Finney had a practical, almost manipulative, attitude toward the conversion process: it "is not a miracle or dependent on a miracle in any sense. . . . It is purely a philosophical result of the right use of constituted means."

Lyman Beecher and eastern evangelicals were disturbed by Finney's new methods and by the emotionalism that accompanied them. They were also upset

The Beecher family, shown here in a photograph by Mathew Brady, contributed four influential members to the reform movement. Lyman Beecher (seated center) was a successful preacher and a master strategist in the organized campaign against sin and "infidelity." His eldest daughter, Catharine (on his right), was a leader in the movement supporting higher education for women. Another daughter, Harriet (seated far right), wrote the novel Uncle Tom's Cabin. *Lyman's son, Henry Ward Beecher (standing far right), was an ardent antislavery advocate and later became one of the most celebrated preachers of the post–Civil War era. He also became involved in a notorious scandal and trial.* ❖

because he violated long-standing Christian tradition by allowing women to pray aloud in church. An evangelical summit meeting between Beecher and Finney, held at New Lebanon, New York, in 1827, failed to reach agreement on this and other issues. Beecher even threatened to stand on the state line if Finney attempted to bring his crusade into Connecticut. But it soon became clear that Finney was not merely stirring people to temporary peaks of excitement; he also was leaving strong and active churches behind him, and eastern opposition gradually weakened. Finney eventually founded a tabernacle in New York City that became a rallying point for evangelical efforts to reach the urban masses.

From Revivalism to Reform

The northern wing of the Second Great Awakening, unlike the southern, inspired a great movement for social reform. Converts were organized into voluntary associations that sought to stamp out sin and social evil and win the world for Christ. An activist and outgoing Christianity was being advanced, not one that called for withdrawal from a sinful world. Most of the converts of northern revivalism were middle-class citizens already active in the lives of their communities. They were seeking to adjust to the bustling world of the market revolution in ways that would not violate their traditional moral and social values. Their generally optimistic and forward-looking attitudes led to hopes that a wave of conversions would save the nation and the world.

In New England, Beecher and his evangelical associates were behind the establishment of a great network of missionary and benevolent societies. In 1810, Presbyterians and Congregationalists founded a Board of Commissioners for Foreign Missions and soon dispatched two missionaries to India. In 1816, the Reverend Samuel John Mills took the leading role in organizing the American Bible Society. By 1821, the society had distributed 140,000 Bibles, mostly in parts of the West where churches and clergymen were scarce.

Another major effort went into publication and distribution of religious tracts, mainly by the American Tract Society, founded in 1825. Special societies targeted groups beyond the reach of regular churches, such as seamen, Native Americans, and the urban poor. In 1816 to 1817, middle-class women in New York, Philadelphia, Charleston, and Boston formed societies to spread the gospel in lower-class wards—where, as one of their missionaries put it, there was "a great mass of people beyond the restraints of religion."

Evangelicals founded moral reform societies as well as missions. Some of these aimed at curbing irreligious activity on the Sabbath; others sought to stamp out dueling, gambling, and prostitution. In New York in 1831, a zealous young clergyman published a sensational report claiming there were ten

Temperance propaganda warned that the drinker who began with "a glass with a friend" would inevitably follow the direct path to poverty, despair, and death. ❖

thousand prostitutes in the city laying their snares for innocent young men. As a result of this exposé, an asylum was established for the redemption of "abandoned women." When middle-class women became involved in this crusade, they shifted its focus to the men who patronized prostitutes, and they proposed that teams of observers record and publish the names of men seen entering brothels. The plan was abandoned because it offended those who thought the cause of virtue would be better served by suppressing public discussion and investigation of sexual vices.

Beecher was especially influential in the **temperance movement,** the most successful of the reform crusades; his published sermons against drink were the most important and widely distributed of the early tracts calling for total abstinence from "demon rum." The temperance movement was directed at a real social evil. Since the Revolution, whiskey had become the most popular American beverage. Made from corn by individual farmers or, by the 1820s, in commercial distilleries, it was cheaper than milk or beer and safer than water (which was often contaminated). In some parts of the country, rum and brandy were also popular. Hard liquor was frequently consumed with food as a table beverage, even at breakfast, and children sometimes imbibed along with adults. Per capita annual consumption of distilled beverages in the 1820s was almost triple what it is today, and alcoholism had reached epidemic proportions.

The temperance reformers viewed indulgence in alcohol as a threat to public morality. Drunkenness was seen as a loss of self-control and moral responsibility that spawned crime, vice, and disorder. Above all, it threatened the family. Drinking was mainly a male vice, and the main target of temperance propaganda was the husband and father who abused, neglected, or abandoned his wife and children because he was a slave to the bottle. Women played a vital role in the movement and were instrumental in making it a crusade for the protection of the home. The drinking habits of the poor or laboring classes also aroused great concern. Particularly in urban areas, the "respectable" and propertied elements lived in fear that lower-class mobs, crazed with drink, would attack private property and create social chaos.

Many evangelical reformers regarded intemperance as the greatest single obstacle to a republic of God-fearing, self-disciplined citizens. In 1826, a group of clergymen previously active in mission work organized the American Temperance Society to coordinate and extend the work already begun by local churches and moral reform societies. The original aim was to encourage abstinence from "ardent spirits" or hard liquor; there was no agreement on the evils of beer and wine. The society sent out lecturers, issued a flood of literature, and sponsored essay contests. Its agents organized revival meetings and called on those in attendance to sign a pledge promising abstinence from spirits.

The campaign was enormously effective. By 1834, there were five thousand local branches with more than a million members, a large proportion of them women. Although it may be doubted whether huge numbers of confirmed drunkards were cured, the movement did succeed in altering the drinking habits of middle-class American males by making temperance a mark of respectability. Per capita consumption of hard liquor declined more than 50 percent during the 1830s.

Cooperating missionary and reform societies—collectively known as "the benevolent empire"—were a major force in American culture by the early 1830s. Efforts to modify American attitudes and institutions seemed to be bearing fruit. The middle class was embracing a new ethic of self-control and self-discipline, equipping individuals to confront a new world of economic growth and social mobility without losing their cultural and moral bearings.

Domesticity and Changes in the American Family

The evangelical culture of the 1820s and 1830s influenced the family as an institution and inspired new conceptions of its role in American society. Many parents viewed children's rearing as essential preparation for self-disciplined Christian life and performed their nurturing duties with great seriousness and self-consciousness. Women—regarded as particularly susceptible to religious and moral influences—were increasingly confined to the domestic circle, but they assumed a greater importance within it.

Marriage for Love

The white middle-class American family underwent major changes in the decades between the Revolution and the mid-nineteenth century. One was the triumph of marriage for love. Parents now exercised even less control over their children's selection of mates than they had in the colonial period. The desire to protect family property and maintain social status remained strong, but mutual affection was now considered absolutely essential to a proper union. Beginning in the late eighteenth century, romantic novels popularized the idea that marriage should be based exclusively on the promptings of the heart. It became easier for sons to marry while their fathers were still alive and for younger daughters to wed before their oldest sisters—trends that reflected a weakening of the traditional parental role.

Wives now began to behave more like the companions of their husbands and less like their servants or children. In the main, eighteenth-century correspondence between spouses had been formal and distant in tone. The husband often assumed a patriarchal role, even using such salutations as "my dear child" and rarely confessing that he missed his wife or craved her company. Letters from women to their husbands were highly deferential and did not usually give advice or express disapproval.

By the early nineteenth century, first names, pet names, and terms of endearment such as "honey" or "darling" were increasingly used by both sexes, and absent husbands frequently confessed they felt lost without their mates. In their replies, wives responded to their husbands as equals and offered counsel on a wide range of subjects. One wrote to a husband who had admitted to flirting with pretty women that she was more than "a little jealous." She asked him angrily how he would feel if she made a similar confession: "Would it be more immoral in me than in you?"

The change in middle- and upper-class marriage should not be exaggerated or romanticized. In law, and in cases of conflict between spouses, the husband remained the unchallenged head of the household. True independence or equality for women was impossible at a time when men held exclusive legal authority over a couple's property and children. Divorce was difficult for everyone, but the double standard made it easier for husbands than wives to dissolve a marriage on grounds of adultery.

The Cult of Domesticity

Such power as women exerted within the home came from their ability to affect the decisions of men who had learned to respect their moral qualities and good sense. The evangelical movement encouraged this quiet expression of feminine influence. The revivals not only gave women a role in converting men but presented as the main object of worship a Christ with stereotypical feminine characteristics. A nurturing, loving, merciful savior, mediating between a stern father and his erring children, provided the model for woman's new role as spiritual head of the home. Membership in evangelical church–based associations inspired and prepared women for new roles as civilizers of men and guardians of domestic culture and morality. Female reform societies taught women the strict ethical code they were to instill in other family members; organized mothers' groups gave instruction in how to build character and encourage piety in children.

Historians have described the new conception of woman's role as the **Cult of Domesticity** or the "Cult of True Womanhood." In the view of most men, a woman's place was in the home and on a pedestal. The ideal wife and mother was "an angel in the house," a model of piety and virtue who exerted a wholesome moral and religious influence over members of the coarser sex. A poem published in 1846 expressed a masculine view of the true woman:

> I would have her as pure as the snow on the mount—
> As true as the smile that to infancy's given—
> As pure as the wave of the crystalline fount,
> Yet as warm in the heart as the sunlight of heaven.

The sociological reality behind the Cult of True Womanhood was an increasing division between the working lives of men and women. In the eighteenth century and earlier, most economic activity had been centered in and near the home, and husbands and wives often worked together in a common enterprise. By the early to mid-nineteenth century this way of life was declining, especially in the Northeast. In towns and cities, the rise of factories and countinghouses severed the home from the workplace. Men went forth every morning to their places of labor, leaving their wives at home to tend the house and the children. Married women were therefore increasingly deprived of a productive economic role. The cult of domesticity made a virtue of the fact that men were solely responsible for running the affairs of the world and building up the economy.

A new conception of gender roles justified and glorified this pattern. The "doctrine of two spheres"—as set forth in novels, advice literature, and the new women's magazines—sentimentalized the woman who kept a spotless house, nurtured her children, and offered her husband a refuge from the heartless world of commerce and industry. From a modern point of view, it is easy to condemn the cult of domesticity as a rationalization for male dominance; to a considerable extent, it was. But many women of the early to mid-nineteenth century do not seem to have felt oppressed or degraded by the new arrangement. The earlier pattern of cooperation had not implied sexual equality—normally, men had been very much in charge of farms or home industries and had often treated their wives more like servants than partners. The new norm of confinement to the home did not necessarily imply that women were inferior. By the standards of evangelical culture, women in the domestic sphere could be viewed as superior to men, since women were in a good position to cultivate the "feminine" virtues of love and self-sacrifice and thus act as official guardians of religious and moral values.

The domestic ideology had real meaning only for relatively affluent women. Working-class wives were not usually employed outside the home during this period, but they labored long and hard within the household.

The sentiment on this sampler, stitched in 1820 by Ruth Titus, typifies beliefs about woman's proper role, according to the Cult of True Womanhood.

Besides cleaning, cooking, and taking care of large numbers of children, they often took in washing or piecework to supplement a meager family income. Their endless domestic drudgery made a sham of the notion that women had the time and energy for the "higher things of life." Life was especially hard for African American women. Most of those who were "free Negroes" rather than slaves did not have husbands who made enough to support them, and they were obliged to serve in white households or work long hours at home doing other people's washing and sewing.

In urban areas, unmarried working-class women often lived on their own and toiled as household servants, in the sweatshops of the garment industry, and in factories. Barely able to support themselves and at the mercy of male sexual predators, they were in no position to identify with the middle-class ideal of elevated, protected womanhood. For some of them, the relatively well-paid and gregarious life of the successful prostitute seemed to offer an attractive alternative to a life of loneliness and privation.

For middle-class women whose husbands or fathers earned a good income, freedom from industrial or farm labor offered some tangible benefits. They now had the leisure to read extensively the new literature directed primarily at housewives, to participate in female-dominated charitable activities, and to cultivate deep and lasting friendships with other women. The result was a distinctively feminine subculture emphasizing "sisterhood" or "sorority." This growing sense of solidarity with other women and of the importance of sexual identity could transcend the private home and even the barriers of social class. Beginning in the 1820s, urban women of the middle and upper classes organized societies for the relief and rehabilitation of poor or "fallen" women. The aim of the organizations was not economic and political equality with men but the elevation of all women to true womanhood.

For some women, the domestic ideal even sanctioned efforts to extend their sphere until it conquered the masculine world outside the home. This domestic feminism was reflected in women's involvement in crusades to stamp out such masculine sins as intemperance, gambling, and sexual vice.

In the benevolent societies and reform movements of the Jacksonian era, especially those designated as women's organizations, women handled money, organized meetings and public appeals, made contracts, and sometimes even gave orders to male subordinates—activities they could not usually perform in their own households. The desire to extend the feminine sphere was the motivating force behind Catharine Beecher's campaign to make schoolteaching a woman's occupation. A prolific and influential writer on the theory and practice of domesticity, this unmarried daughter of Lyman Beecher saw the spinster-teacher as equivalent to a mother. By instilling in young males the virtues that only women could teach, the schoolmarm could help liberate America from corruption and materialism.

But Beecher and other domestic feminists continued to emphasize the role of married women who stayed home and did their part simply by being wives and mothers. Reforming husbands was difficult: They were away much of the time and tended to be preoccupied with business. But this very fact gave women primary responsibility for the rearing of children—an activity to which nineteenth-century Americans attached almost cosmic significance. Since women were considered particularly well qualified to transmit piety and morality to future citizens of the republic, the cult of domesticity exalted motherhood and encouraged a new concern with childhood as the time of life when "character" was formed.

❖ A Look at the Past ❖

Gothic Revival Cottage

Sentimentality and romanticism strengthened their hold on American culture after 1820. At the same time, a cult of domesticity arose, which promoted family life as critical to a person's moral regeneration. Evangelism and a wide variety of reform movements swept the nation as well. Middle-class Americans engaged enthusiastically in these social and cultural developments, spending money or hours buying or making materials that revealed their participation. New houses provided clean, neat spaces—and more of them—for family members to pursue their interests together. Styles such as the Gothic Revival embodied the romantic and spiritual sentiments of the age. Gothic Revival presented home as more than a haven; home became a spiritual sanctuary. What does this house remind you of? If homes became sanctuaries, what role did women play in creating and maintaining that sanctuary?

The Discovery of Childhood

The nineteenth century has been called "the century of the child." More than before, childhood was seen as a distinct stage of life requiring the special and sustained attention of adults. The family now became "child-centered," which meant that the care, nurture, and rearing of children was viewed as the family's main function. In earlier times, adults treated children in a more casual way, often sending them away from home for education or apprenticeship at a very early age. Among the well-to-do, children spent more time with servants or tutors than with their parents.

By the early decades of the nineteenth century, however, children were staying at home longer and receiving much more attention from parents, especially mothers. Much less common was the colonial custom—nearly inconceivable today—of naming a child after a sibling who had died in infancy. Each child was now looked on as a unique and irreplaceable individual.

New customs and fashions heralded the "discovery" of childhood. Books aimed specifically at juveniles began to roll off the presses. Parents became more self-conscious about their responsibilities and sought help from a new literature providing expert advice on child rearing. One early-nineteenth-century mother wrote, "There is scarcely any subject concerning which I feel more anxiety than the proper education of my children. It is a difficult and delicate subject, the more I feel how much is to be learnt by myself."

The new concern for children resulted in more intimate relations between parents and children. The ideal family described in the advice manuals and sentimental literature was bound together by affection rather than authority. Firm discipline remained at the core of "family government," but there was a change in the preferred method of enforcing good behavior. Corporal punishment declined, partially displaced by shaming or withholding of affection. Disobedient middle-class children were now more likely to be confined to their rooms to reflect on their sins than to receive a good thrashing. Discipline could no longer be justified as the constant application of physical force over naturally wayward beings. In an age of moral perfectionism, the role of discipline was to induce repentance and change basic attitudes. The intended result was often described as "self-government"; to achieve it, parents used guilt, rather than fear, as their main source of leverage. A mother's sorrow or a father's stern and prolonged silence was deemed more effective in forming character than were blows or angry words.

Child-centered families also meant smaller families. If nineteenth-century families had remained as large as those of earlier times, it would have been impossible to lavish so much care and attention on individual offspring. For reasons that are still not completely understood, the average number of children born to each woman during her fertile years dropped from 7.04 in 1800 to 5.42 in 1850. As a result, the average number of children per family declined about 25 percent, beginning a long-range trend lasting to the present day.

A Look at the Past

Manufactured Toy

Manufactured toys, such as this pull toy, became common during the early nineteenth century and suggest dramatic changes in family life and consumer behavior. Before toys were manufactured in the United States, most parents or children themselves had to make toys or games from available materials, or if they were wealthy enough, they might purchase wood, tin, or cast iron toys imported from Europe. The availability of cheap manufactured goods gave mothers the opportunity to lavish attention on their children, without the toil. What does the emergence of a toy manufacturing industry reveal about attitudes toward children?

The practice of various forms of birth control undoubtedly contributed to this demographic revolution. Ancestors of the modern condom and diaphragm were openly advertised and sold during the pre–Civil War period, but it is likely that most couples controlled family size by practicing the withdrawal method or limiting the frequency of intercourse. Abortion was also surprisingly common and was on the rise. One historian has estimated that by 1850 there was one abortion for every five or six live births.

Parents seemed to understand that having fewer children meant they could provide their offspring with a better start in life. Such attitudes were appropriate in a society that was beginning to shift from agriculture to commerce and industry. For rural households short of labor, large families were an economic asset. For urban couples who hoped to send their children into a competitive world that demanded special talents and training, they were a financial liability.

Institutional Reform

The family could not carry the whole burden of socializing and reforming individuals. Children needed schooling as well as parental nurturing, and many were thought to lack a proper home environment. Some adults, too, seemed to require special kinds of attention and treatment. Seeking to extend the advantages of "family government" beyond the domestic circle, reformers worked to establish or improve public institutions that were designed to shape individual character and instill a capacity for self-discipline.

The Extension of Education

The period from 1820 to 1850 saw an enormous expansion of free public schools. The new resolve to put more children in school for longer periods reflected many of the same values that exalted the child-centered family. Up to a certain age, children could be effectively nurtured and educated in the home. But after that they needed formal training at a character-molding institution that would prepare them to make a living and bear the burdens of republican citizenship. Intellectual training at school was regarded as less important than moral indoctrination.

Sometimes more than just an extension of the family, the school served as a substitute for it. Educational reformers were alarmed at the masses of poor and immigrant children who allegedly failed to get proper nurturing at home. It was up to schools to make up for this disadvantage. Otherwise, the republic would be in danger from masses of people "incapable of self-government."

Before the 1820s, schooling in the United States was a haphazard affair. The wealthy sent their children to private schools, and some of the poor sent their children to charity or "pauper" schools that were usually financed in part by local governments. Public education was most highly developed in the New England states, where towns were required by law to support elementary schools. It was weakest in the South, where almost all education was private.

Agitation for expanded public education began in the 1820s and early 1830s as a central demand of the workingmen's movements in eastern cities. These hard-pressed artisans viewed free schools open to all as a way of countering the growing gap between rich and poor. Initially, strong opposition came from more affluent taxpayers who did not see why they should pay for the education of other people's children. But middle-class reformers soon seized the initiative, shaped educational reform to their own end of social discipline, and provided the momentum needed for legislative success.

The most influential supporter of the common school movement was Horace Mann of Massachusetts. As a lawyer and member of the state legislature, Mann worked tirelessly to establish a state board of education and adequate tax support for local schools. In 1837, he persuaded the legislature to enact his proposals, and he subsequently resigned his seat to become the first secretary of the new board, an office he held with great distinction until 1848. He believed children were clay in the hands of teachers and school officials and could be molded to a state of perfection. Like advocates of child rearing through moral influence rather than physical force, he discouraged corporal punishment except as a last resort. His position on this issue led to a bitter controversy with Boston schoolmasters who retained a Calvinist sense of original sin and favored a freer use of the rod.

Against those who argued that school taxes violated property rights, Mann contended that private property was actually held in trust for the good of the community. "The property of this commonwealth," he wrote, "is pledged for the education of all its youth up to such a point as will save them from poverty and vice, and prepare them for the adequate performance of their social and civil duties." Mann's conception of public education as a means of social discipline converted the middle and upper classes to the cause. By teaching middle-class morality and respect for order, the schools could turn potential rowdies and revolutionaries into law-abiding citizens. They could also encourage social mobility by opening doors for lower-class children who were determined to do better than their parents.

In practice, new or improved public schools often alienated working-class pupils and their families rather than reforming them. Compulsory attendance laws in Massachusetts and other states deprived poor families of needed wage earners without guaranteeing new occupational opportunities for those with an elementary education. As the laboring class became increasingly immigrant and Catholic in the 1840s and 1850s, dissatisfaction arose over the evangelical Protestant tone of "moral instruction" in the schools. Quite consciously, Mann and his disciples were trying to impose a uniform culture on people who valued differing traditions.

In addition to the "three Rs" ("reading, 'riting, and 'rithmetic"), the public schools of the mid-nineteenth century taught the "Protestant ethic"—industry, punctuality, sobriety, and frugality. These were the virtues stressed in the famous *McGuffey's Eclectic Readers*, which first appeared in 1836. Millions of children

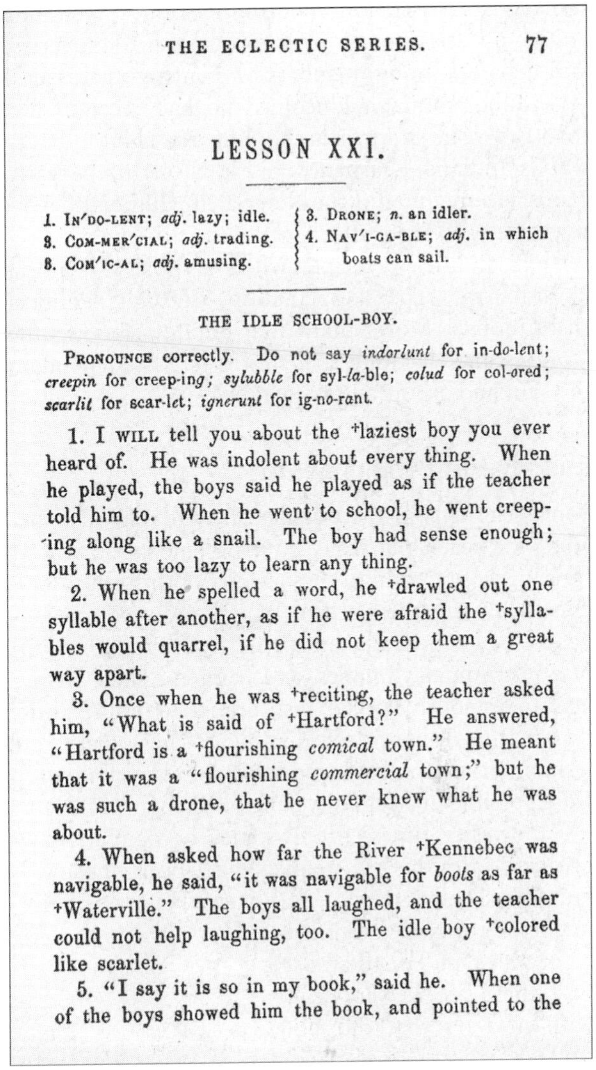

THE ECLECTIC SERIES. 77

LESSON XXI.

1. IN'DO-LENT; *adj.* lazy; idle.
8. COM-MER'CIAL; *adj.* trading.
8. COM'IC-AL; *adj.* amusing.
3. DRONE; *n.* an idler.
4. NAV'I-GA-BLE; *adj.* in which boats can sail.

THE IDLE SCHOOL-BOY.

PRONOUNCE correctly. Do not say *indorlunt* for in-do-lent; *creepin* for creep-ing; *sylubble* for syl-*la*-ble; *colud* for col-ored; *scarlit* for scar-let; *ignerunt* for ig-no-rant.

1. I WILL tell you about the +laziest boy you ever heard of. He was indolent about every thing. When he played, the boys said he played as if the teacher told him to. When he went to school, he went creep-ing along like a snail. The boy had sense enough; but he was too lazy to learn any thing.

2. When he spelled a word, he +drawled out one syllable after another, as if he were afraid the +syllables would quarrel, if he did not keep them a great way apart.

3. Once when he was +reciting, the teacher asked him, "What is said of +Hartford?" He answered, "Hartford is a +flourishing *comical* town." He meant that it was a "flourishing *commercial* town;" but he was such a drone, that he never knew what he was about.

4. When asked how far the River +Kennebec was navigable, he said, "it was navigable for *boots* as far as +Waterville." The boys all laughed, and the teacher could not help laughing, too. The idle boy +colored like scarlet.

5. "I say it is so in my book," said he. When one of the boys showed him the book, and pointed to the

The lessons and examples in McGuffey's Eclectic Readers *upheld the basic virtues of thrift, honesty, and charity, and taught that evil deeds never went unpunished.* ❖

learned to read by digesting McGuffey's parables about the terrible fate of those who gave in to sloth, drunkenness, or wastefulness. Such moral indoctrination helped produce generations of Americans with personalities and beliefs adapted to the needs of an industrializing society—people who could be depended on to adjust to the precise and regular routines of the factory or the office. But as an education for self-government—in the sense of learning to think for oneself—it left much to be desired.

Fortunately, however, education was not limited to the schools nor devoted solely to children. Every city and almost every town or village had a lyceum, debating society, or mechanics' institute where adults of all social classes could broaden their intellectual horizons. Lyceums featured discourses on such subjects as "self-reliance" or "the conduct of life" by creative thinkers such as Ralph Waldo Emerson, explanations and demonstrations of the latest scientific discoveries, and debates among members on controversial issues.

Young Abraham Lincoln, who had received less than two years of formal schooling as a child in backwoods Indiana, sharpened his intellect in the early 1830s as a member of the New Salem (Illinois) debating society. In 1838, after moving to Springfield, he set forth his political principles when he spoke at the local lyceum on "The Perpetuation of Our Political Institutions." More than the public schools, the lyceums and debating societies fostered independent thought and encouraged new ideas.

Discovering the Asylum

Some segments of the population were obviously beyond the reach of family government and character training provided in homes and schools. In the 1820s and 1830s, reformers became acutely aware of the danger to society posed by an apparently increasing number of criminals, lunatics, and paupers. Their answer was to establish special institutions to house those deemed incapable of self-discipline. Their goals were humanitarian; they believed reform and rehabilitation were possible in a carefully controlled environment.

In earlier times, the existence of paupers, lawbreakers, and insane persons had been taken for granted. Their presence was viewed as the consequence of divine judgment or original sin. For the most part, these people were dealt with in ways that did not isolate them from local communities. The insane were allowed to wander about if harmless and were confined at home if they were dangerous; the poor were supported by private charity or the dole provided by towns or counties; convicted criminals were whipped, held for limited periods in local jails, or—in the case of very serious offenses—executed.

By the early nineteenth century, these traditional methods had come to seem both inadequate and inhumane. Dealing with deviants in a neighborly way broke down as economic development and urbanization made communities less cohesive. At the same time, reformers were concluding that all defects of mind and character were correctable—the insane could be cured, criminals reformed, and paupers taught to pull themselves out of destitution. The result was what historian David Rothman termed "the discovery of the asylum"—the invention and establishment of special institutions for the confinement and reformation of deviants.

The 1820s and 1830s saw the emergence of state-supported prisons, insane asylums, and poorhouses. New York and Pennsylvania led the way in prison reform. Institutions at Auburn, New York, and Philadelphia attracted international attention as model penitentiaries, mainly because of their experiments in isolating inmates from one another. Solitary confinement was viewed as a humanitarian and therapeutic policy because it gave inmates a chance to reflect on their sins, free from the corrupting influence of other convicts. In theory, prisons and asylums substituted for the family. Custodians were meant to act as parents, providing moral advice and training.

In practice, the institutions were far different from the affectionate families idealized by the cult of domesticity. Most accommodated only a single sex or maintained a strict segregation of male and female inmates. Their most prominent feature was the imposition of a rigid daily routine. The early superintendents and wardens believed the enforcement of a rigorous set of rules and procedures would encour-

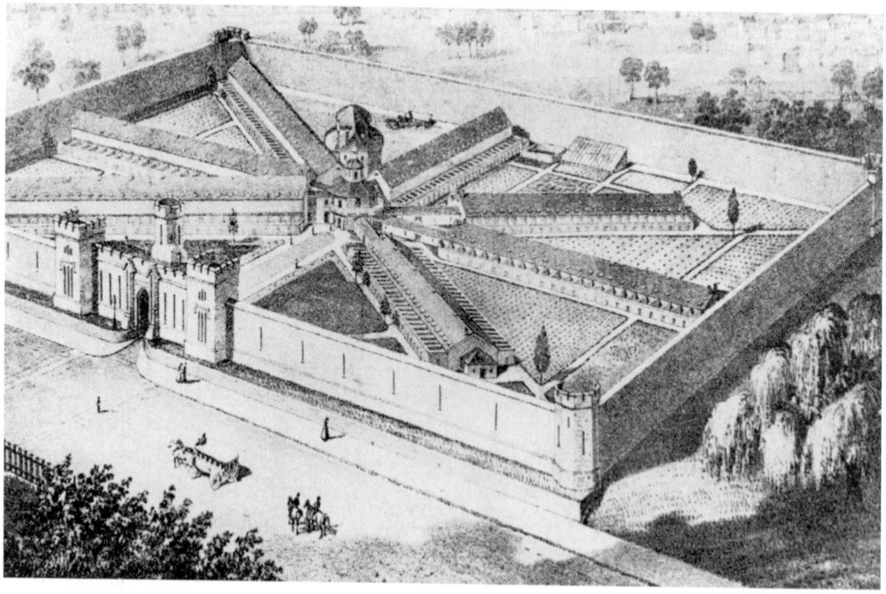

The Eastern State Penitentiary in Philadelphia followed the Pennsylvania system of prison design. Prisoners were kept in solitary confinement in individual cells, and seven long cellblocks radiated out from a central rotunda. Each cell had two front doors—one of wood and the other of metal equipped with a trap through which meals were passed to the inmate. The cell also had a back door that opened to a small exercise yard. A strict regimen of silence was meant to encourage prisoners to reflect on their crimes. ❖

Dorothea Dix (1802–1887). Her efforts on behalf of the mentally ill led to the building of more than thirty institutions in the United States and the reform and restaffing—with well-trained personnel—of existing hospitals. She died in Trenton, New Jersey, in 1887, in a hospital that she had founded. ❖

age self-discipline. The French observers Alexis de Tocqueville and Gustave de Beaumont summed up these practical expectations after a tour of American prisons in 1831 and 1832: "The habits or order to which the prisoner is subjected for several years . . . the obedience of every moment to inflexible rules, the regularity of a uniform life . . . are calculated to produce a deep impression upon his mind. Perhaps, leaving the prison he is not an honest man, but he has contracted honest habits."

Prisons, asylums, and poorhouses did not achieve the aims of their founders. Public support was inadequate to meet the needs of a growing inmate population, and the personnel of the institutions often lacked the training needed to help the incarcerated. The results were overcrowding and the use of brutality to keep order. For the most part, prisons failed to reform hardened criminals, and the primitive psychotherapy known as "moral treatment" failed to cure most asylum patients. Poorhouses rapidly degenerated into sinkholes of despair. A combination of naive theories and poor performance doomed the institutions to a custodial rather than a reformatory role.

Conditions would have been even worse had it not been for Dorothea Dix. Between 1838 and the Civil War, this remarkable woman devoted her energies and skills to publicizing the inhumane treatment prevailing in prisons, almshouses, and insane asylums and to lobbying for corrective action. As a direct result of her activities, fifteen states opened new hospitals for the insane and others improved their supervision of penitentiaries, asylums, and poorhouses. Dix ranks as one of the most practical and effective of all the reformers of the pre–Civil War era.

Reform Turns Radical

During the 1830s, internal dissension split the great reform movement spawned by the Second Great Awakening. Efforts to promote evangelical piety, improve personal and public morality, and shape character through familial or institutional discipline continued and even flourished. But bolder spirits went beyond such goals and set their sights on the total liberation and perfection of the individual.

Divisions in the Benevolent Empire

Early-nineteenth-century reformers were, for the most part, committed to changing existing attitudes and practices gradually and in ways that would not invite conflict or disrupt society. But by the mid-1830s, a new mood of impatience and perfectionism surfaced within the benevolent societies. In 1836, for example, the Temperance Society split over two issues—whether the abstinence pledge should be extended to include beer and wine and whether pressure should be applied to producers and sellers of alcoholic beverages as well as to consumers. Radicals insisted on a total commitment to "cold water" and were prepared to clash head-on with an important economic interest. Moderates held back from such goals and tactics because they wanted to avoid hostility from prominent citizens who drank wine or had money invested in the liquor industry.

A similar rift occurred in the American Peace Society, an antiwar organization founded in 1828 by clergymen seeking to promote Christian concern for world peace. Most of the founders admitted the propriety of "defensive wars" and were shocked when some members of the society began to denounce all use of force as a violation of the Sermon on the Mount. Dissidents, who called themselves "nonresistants," withdrew from the organization in 1838. Led by Henry C. Wright, they formed the New England Non-Resistance Society to promote an absolute pacifism, which denied the right of self-defense to nations or individuals and repudiated all forms of government coercion.

The new perfectionism realized its most dramatic and important success within the antislavery movement. Before the 1830s, most people who expressed religious and moral concern over slavery were affiliated with the **American Colonization Society,** a benevolent organization founded in 1817. Most colonizationists admitted that slavery was an evil, but they also viewed it as a deeply rooted social and economic institution that could be eliminated only very gradually and with the cooperation of slaveholders. Reflecting the power of racial prejudice, they proposed to provide transportation to Africa for free blacks who chose to go, or were emancipated for the purpose, as a way of relieving southern fears that a race war would erupt if slaves were simply released from bondage and allowed to remain in America. In 1821, the society established the colony of Liberia in West Africa, and during the next decade a few thousand African Americans were settled there.

Colonization proved to be grossly inadequate as a step toward the elimination of slavery. Many of the blacks transported to Africa were already free, and those liberated by masters influenced by the movement represented only a tiny percentage of the natural increase of the southern slave population. Northern blacks denounced the enterprise because it denied the prospect of racial equality in America. Black opposition to colonizationism helped persuade William Lloyd Garrison and other white abolitionists to repudiate the Colonization Society and support immediate emancipation without emigration.

Garrison launched a new and more radical antislavery movement in 1831 in Boston, when he began to publish a journal called the *Liberator.* Besides calling for immediate and unconditional emancipation, Garrison denounced colonization as a slaveholder's plot to remove troublesome free blacks and as an ignoble surrender to un-Christian prejudices. His rhetoric was as severe as his proposals were radical. As he wrote

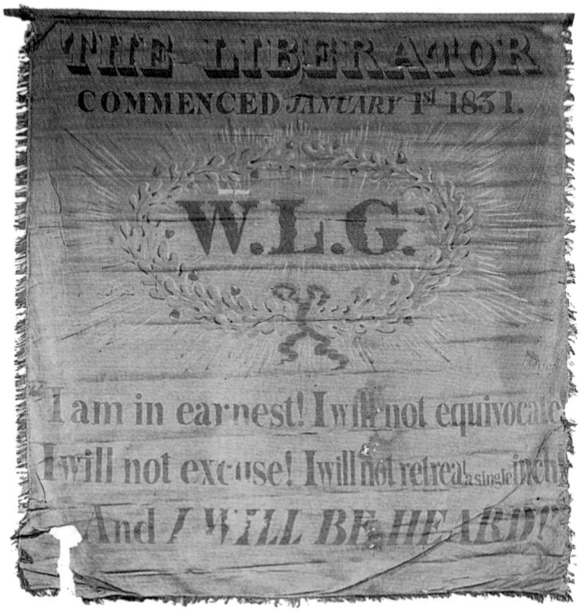

In the inaugural issue of his antislavery weekly, the Liberator, *William Lloyd Garrison announced that he was launching a militant battle against the evil and sin of slavery. The stirring words that appeared in that first issue are repeated on the* Liberator's *banner.* ❖

in the first issue of the *Liberator,* "I will be as harsh as truth and as uncompromising as justice. . . . I am in earnest—I will not equivocate—I will not excuse—I will not retreat a single inch—And I WILL BE HEARD!" Heard he was. In 1833, Garrison and other abolitionists founded the American Anti-Slavery Society. "We shall send forth agents to lift up the voice of remonstrance, of warning, of entreaty, and of rebuke," its Declaration of Sentiments proclaimed. The colonization movement was placed on the defensive, and during the 1830s, many of its most active northern supporters became abolitionists.

The Abolitionist Enterprise

The abolitionist movement, like the temperance crusade, was a direct outgrowth of the Second Great Awakening. Many leading abolitionists had undergone conversion experiences in the 1820s and were already committed to a life of Christian activism before they dedicated themselves to freeing the slaves. Several were ministers or divinity students seeking a mission in life that would fulfill spiritual and professional ambitions.

The career of Theodore Dwight Weld exemplified the connection between revivalism and abolitionism. Weld came from a long line of New England ministers. After dropping out of divinity school because of a combination of physical and spiritual ailments, he migrated to western New York. There he fell under the influence of Charles G. Finney and, after a long struggle, underwent a conversion experience in 1826. He then became an itinerant lecturer for various reform causes. By the early 1830s, he focused his attention on the moral issues raised by the institution of slavery. After a brief flirtation with the colonization movement, Weld was converted to abolitionism in 1832, recognizing that colonizationists did not really accept blacks as equals or "brothers-in-Christ." In 1834, he instigated what amounted to a series of abolitionist revivals at Lane Theological Seminary in Cincinnati. When the trustees of the seminary attempted to suppress further discussion of the case for immediate emancipation, Weld led a mass walkout of most students. The "Lane rebels" then relocated to Oberlin, Ohio, bringing new students and faculty to Oberlin College.

In 1835 and 1836, Weld toured Ohio and western New York preaching abolitionism. He also supervised and trained other agents and orators as part of a campaign to convert the entire region to immediate emancipation. The tried-and-true methods of the revival—fervent preaching, protracted meetings, and the call for individuals to come forth and announce their redemption—were put at the service of the antislavery movement. Weld and his associates often had to face movement. Weld and his associates often had to face angry mobs, but they left behind them tens of thousands of new abolitionists and hundreds of local antislavery societies. As a result of their efforts, northern Ohio and western New York became hotbeds of abolitionist sentiment.

Antislavery orators and organizers tended to have their greatest successes in the small- to medium-sized towns of the upper North. The typical convert came from an upwardly mobile family engaged in small business, the skilled trades, or market farming. In larger towns and cities, or when they ventured close to the Mason-Dixon line, abolitionists were more likely to encounter fierce and effective opposition. In 1835, Garrison was mobbed in the streets of Boston and almost lynched. In New York City, the Tappan brothers—Lewis and Arthur—were frequent objects of threats and violence. These two successful merchants were key figures in the movement because they used their substantial wealth to finance antislavery activities. In 1835–1836, they supported a massive effort to print antislavery pamphlets and distribute them through the U.S. mails. But they made relatively few converts in their own city; most New Yorkers regarded them as dangerous radicals.

Abolitionists who thought of taking their message to the fringes of the South had reason to pause, given the fate of the antislavery editor Elijah Lovejoy. In 1837, while attempting to defend himself and his printing press from a mob in Alton, Illinois, just across the Mississippi River from slaveholding Missouri, Lovejoy was shot and killed.

Racism was a major cause of antiabolitionist violence in the North. Rumors that abolitionists advocated or practiced interracial marriage could easily incite an urban crowd. If it could not find white abolitionists, the mob was likely to turn on local blacks. Working-class whites tended to fear that economic and social competition with blacks would increase if abolitionists succeeded in freeing slaves and making them citizens. But a striking feature of many of the mobs was that they were dominated by "gentlemen of property and standing." Solid citizens resorted to violence, it would appear, because abolitionism threatened their conservative notions of social order and hierarchy.

By the end of the 1830s, the abolitionist movement was under great stress. Besides the burden of external repression, there was dissension within the movement. Becoming an abolitionist required an exacting conscience and an unwillingness to compromise on matters of principle. These character traits also made it difficult for abolitionists to work together and maintain a united front. During the late 1830s, Garrison, the most visible proponent of the cause, began to adopt positions that some other abolitionists found extreme and divisive. He embraced the nonresistant or "no-government" philosophy of Henry C. Wright and urged abolitionists to abstain from voting or otherwise participating in a corrupt political system. He also attacked the clergy and the churches for refusing to take a strong antislavery stand and encouraged his followers to "come out" of the established denominations rather than continuing to work within them.

These positions alienated those members of the Anti-Slavery Society who continued to hope that organized religion and the existing political system could be influenced or even taken over by abolitionists. But it was Garrison's stand on women's rights that led to an open break at the national convention of the American Anti-Slavery Society in 1840. Following their leader's principle that women should be equal partners in the crusade, a Garrison-led majority elected a woman abolitionist to the society's executive committee. A minority, led by Lewis Tappan, then withdrew to form a competing organization—the American and Foreign Anti-Slavery Society.

The new organization never amounted to much, but the schism did weaken Garrison's influence within the movement. When he later repudiated the U.S. Constitution as a proslavery document and called for northern secession from the Union, few antislavery people in the Middle Atlantic or midwestern states went along. Outside New England, most abolitionists worked within the churches and avoided controversial side issues such as women's rights and nonresistant pacifism. Some antislavery advocates chose the path of political action. The **Liberty party,** organized in 1840, was their first attempt to enter the electoral arena under their own banner; it signaled a new effort to turn antislavery sentiment into political power.

Black Abolitionists

From the beginning the abolitionist movement depended heavily on the support of the northern free black community. Most of the early subscribers to Garrison's *Liberator* were African Americans. Black orators, especially escaped slaves such as Frederick Douglass, made northern audiences aware of the realities of bondage. But relations between white and black abolitionists were often tense and uneasy. Blacks protested that they did not have their fair share of leadership positions or influence over policy. Eventually a black antislavery movement emerged that was largely independent of the white-led crusade. In addition to Douglass, prominent black male abolitionists were Charles Remond, William Wells Brown, Robert Purvis, and Henry Highland Garnet. Outspoken women such as Sojourner Truth, Maria Stewart, and Frances Harper also played a significant role in black antislavery activity. The Negro Convention movement, which sponsored national meetings of black leaders beginning in 1830, provided an important forum for independent black expression. Their most eloquent statement came in 1854, when black leaders met in Cleveland to declare their faith in a separate identity, proclaiming, "We pledge our integrity to use all honorable means, to unite us, as one people, on this continent."

African American leaders in the abolitionist movement included Frederick Douglass (right) and William Whipper (left). Douglass, who escaped from slavery in 1838, became one of the most effective voices in the crusade against slavery. In 1837, twelve years before Thoreau's essay "Civil Disobedience," Whipper published an article titled "An Address on Non-Resistance to Offensive Aggression." Whipper was also one of the founders of the American Moral Reform Society, an African American abolitionist organization. ❖

Black newspapers, such as *Freedom's Journal,* first published in 1827, and the *North Star,* founded by Douglass in 1847, gave black writers a chance to preach their gospel of liberation to black readers. African American authors also produced a stream of books and pamphlets attacking slavery, refuting racism, and advocating various forms of resistance. One of the most influential publications was David Walker's *Appeal . . . to the Colored Citizens of the World,* which appeared in 1829. Walker denounced slavery in the most vigorous language possible and called for a black revolt against white tyranny.

Free blacks in the North did more than make verbal protests against racial injustice. They were also the main conductors on the fabled Underground Railroad that opened a path for fugitives from slavery. It has been supposed that benevolent whites were primarily responsible for organized efforts to guide and assist fugitive slaves, but modern research has shown that the Underground Railroad was largely a black-operated enterprise. Courageous ex-slaves such as Harriet Tubman and Josiah Henson made regular forays into the slave states to lead other blacks to freedom, and many of the "stations" along the way were run by free blacks. In northern towns and cities, free blacks organized "vigilance committees" to protect fugitives and thwart the slave-catchers. Groups of blacks even used force to rescue recaptured fugitives from the authorities. In Boston in 1851, one such group seized a slave named Shadrack from a U.S. marshal who was in the process of returning him to bondage. In deeds as well as words, free blacks showed their unyielding hostility to slavery and racism.

Historians have debated the question of whether the abolitionist movement of the 1830s and early 1840s was a success or a failure. It obviously failed to convert a majority of Americans to its position that slavery was a sinful institution that should be abolished immediately. This position implied that blacks should be granted equality as American citizens, so it ran up against the powerful commitment to white supremacy prevailing in all parts of the country. In the South, abolitionism caused a strong counteraction and helped inspire a more militant and uncompromising defense of slavery. The belief that peaceful agitation, or what abolitionists called "moral suasion," would convert slaveholders and their northern sympathizers to abolition was obviously unrealistic.

But in another sense the crusade was successful. It brought the slavery issue to the forefront of public consciousness and convinced a substantial and growing segment of the northern population that the South's peculiar institution was morally wrong and potentially dangerous to the American way of life. The South helped the antislavery cause in the North by responding hysterically and repressively to abolitionist agitation. In 1836, Southerners in Congress forced

Harriet Tubman, far left, is shown here with some of the slaves she helped escape on the Underground Railroad. Born a slave in Maryland, she escaped to Philadelphia in 1849. She is said to have helped as many as three-hundred African Americans flee slavery. She led many of them all the way to Canada, where they would be beyond the reach of the Fugitive Slave Law. ❖

adoption of a "gag rule" requiring that abolitionist petitions be tabled without being read; at about the same time, the post office refused to carry antislavery literature into the slave states. Prominent Northerners who had not been moved to action by abolitionist depictions of slave suffering became more responsive to the movement when it appeared their own civil liberties might be threatened. The politicians who later mobilized the North against the expansion of slavery into the territories drew strength from the antislavery and antisouthern sentiments that abolitionists had already called forth.

From Abolitionism to Women's Rights

Abolitionism also served as a catalyst for the women's rights movement. From the beginning, women were active participants in the abolitionist crusade. Between 1835 and 1838, the American Anti-Slavery Society bombarded Congress with petitions, mostly calling for abolition of slavery in the District of Columbia. More than half of the thousands of antislavery petitions sent to Washington had women's signatures on them.

Some antislavery women went further and defied conventional ideas of their proper sphere by becoming public speakers and demanding an equal role in the leadership of antislavery societies. The most famous of these were the Grimké sisters, Sarah and Angelina, who attracted enormous attention being the rebellious daughters of a South Carolina slaveholder. When some male abolitionists objected to their speaking in public to mixed audiences of men and women, Garrison came to their defense and helped forge a link between blacks' and women's struggles for equality.

The battle to participate equally in the antislavery crusade made a number of women abolitionists acutely aware of male dominance and oppression. For them, the same principles that justified the liberation of the slaves also applied to the emancipation of women from all restrictions on their rights as citizens. In 1840, Garrison's American followers withdrew from the first World's Anti-Slavery Convention in London because the sponsors refused to seat the women in their delegation. Among the women thus excluded were Lucretia Mott and Elizabeth Cady Stanton.

Wounded by men's reluctance to extend the cause of emancipation to include women, Stanton and Mott began discussing plans for a women's rights convention. They returned to New York, where a campaign was already underway to reform the state's laws limiting the rights of married women, spearheaded by a young Jewish activist, Ernestine Rose, and Judge Thomas Herttell, the political radical and freethinker who had introduced the first bill to reform the state's marriage laws to the New York state legislature. (See the Law and Society essay, "The Legal Rights of Married Women: Reforming the Law of Coverture, pp. 354–357.) The campaign for women's rights came to a head at the famous **Seneca Falls Convention** Stanton and Mott organized in upstate New York in 1848. The Declaration of Sentiments issued by this first national gathering of feminists charged that "the history of mankind is a history of repeated injuries and usurpations on the part of man toward woman, having in direct object the establishment of an absolute tyranny over her." It went on to demand that all women be given the right to vote and that married women be freed from unjust laws giving husbands control of their property, persons, and children. Rejecting the cult of domesticity with its doctrine of separate spheres, these women and their male supporters launched the modern movement for gender equality.

Radical Ideas and Experiments

Hopes for individual or social perfection were not limited to reformers inspired by evangelicalism. Between the 1820s and 1850s, a great variety of schemes for human redemption came from those who had rejected orthodox Protestantism. Some were secular humanists carrying on the freethinking tradition of the Enlightenment, but most were seekers of new paths to spiritual or religious fulfillment. A movement that achieved remarkable success or notoriety was spiritualism—the belief that one could communicate with the dead. (See the Feature Essay, "Spiritualism: Religion or Entertainment?" pp. 348–349.) These philosophical and religious radicals attacked established institutions, prescribed new modes of living, and founded utopian communities to put their ideas into practice.

Elizabeth Cady Stanton, a leader of the women's rights movement, reared seven children. In addition to her pioneering work, especially for woman suffrage, she also lectured frequently on family life and child care. ❖

A radical movement of foreign origin that gained a toehold in Jacksonian America was utopian socialism. In 1825–1826, the British manufacturer and reformer Robert Owen visited the United States and founded a community based on common and equal ownership of property at New Harmony, Indiana. About the same time, Owen's associate Frances Wright gathered a group of slaves at Nashoba, Tennessee, and set them to work earning their freedom in an atmosphere of "rational cooperation." The rapid demise of both of these model communities suggested that utopian socialism did not easily take root in American soil.

But the impulse survived. In the 1840s, a number of Americans, including the prominent editor Horace Greeley, became interested in the ideas of the French utopian theorist Charles Fourier. Fourier called for cooperative communities in which everyone did a fair share of the work and tasks were allotted to make use of the natural abilities and instincts of the members. Between 1842 and 1852, about thirty Fourierist "phalanxes" were established in the northeastern and midwestern states, and approximately a hundred thousand people lived for a time in these communities or otherwise supported the movement. The phalanxes were not purely socialistic; in fact, they were organized as joint-stock companies. But they did give the members an opportunity to live and work in a communal atmosphere. Like the Owenite communities, they were short-lived, surviving for an average of only two years. The common complaint of the founders was that Americans were too individualistic to cooperate in the ways that Fourier's theories required.

Two of the most successful and long-lived manifestations of pre–Civil War **utopianism** were the Shakers and the Oneida community. The **Shakers**—officially known as the Millennial Church or the United Society of Believers—began as a religious movement in England. In 1774, a Shaker leader, Mother Ann Lee, brought their radical beliefs to the United States. Lee believed herself to be the feminine incarnation of Christ and advocated a new theology based squarely on the principle of sexual equality. The Shakers, named for their expressions of religious fervor through vigorous dancelike movements, believed in communal ownership and strict celibacy. They lived simply and minimized their contact with the outside world because they expected Christ's Second Coming to occur momentar-

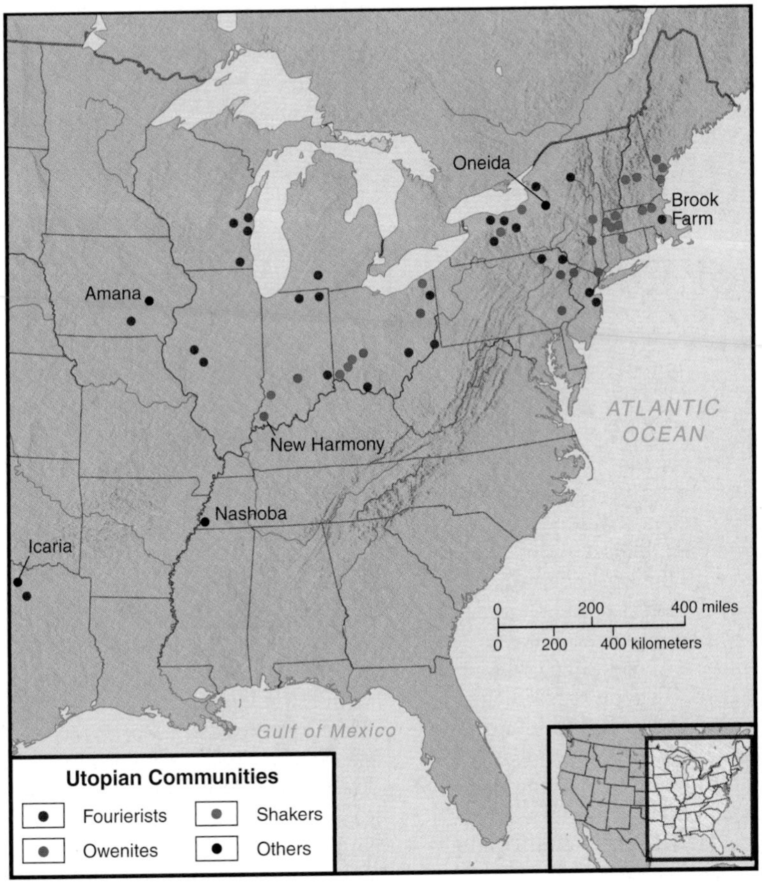

UTOPIAN COMMUNITIES BEFORE THE CIVIL WAR *The search for new paths to spiritual or religious fulfillment attracted many to utopian communitarian societies. By far the largest of these societies during the period before the Civil War was the Shakers, who by the 1830s had established twenty settlements in seven states with a combined membership of approximately six thousand. Their rule of celibacy meant that Shaker communities gained members through adoption and conversion, rather than by natural reproduction.* ❖

ily. The **Oneida community** was established in 1848 at Oneida, New York, and was inspired by an unorthodox brand of Christian perfectionism. Its founder, John Humphrey Noyes, believed the Second Coming of Christ had already occurred; hence human beings were no longer obliged to follow the moral rules that their previously fallen state had required. At Oneida, traditional marriage was outlawed, and a carefully regulated form of "free love" was put into practice.

It was a literary and philosophical movement known as **transcendentalism** that inspired the era's most memorable experiments in thinking and living on a higher plane. The main idea was that the individual could transcend material reality and ordinary understanding, attaining through a higher form of reason—or intuition—a oneness with the universe as a whole and with the spiritual forces that lay behind it. Transcendentalism was the major American version of the romantic and idealist thought that emerged in the early nineteenth century. Throughout the Western world, and especially in Germany, romanticism was challenging the rationalism and materialism of the Enlightenment in the name of exalted feeling and cosmic spirituality. Most American transcendentalists were Unitarians or ex-Unitarians who were dissatisfied with the sober rationalism of their denomination and sought a more intense kind of spiritual experience. Unable to embrace evangelical Christianity because of intellectual resistance to its doctrines, they sought inspiration from a philosophical and literary idealism of German origin.

Their prophet was Ralph Waldo Emerson, a brilliant essayist and lecturer who preached that each individual could commune directly with a benign spiritual force that animated nature and the universe, which he called the "oversoul." Emerson was a radical individualist committed to "self-culture" and "the sufficiency of the private man." He carefully avoided all involvement in organized movements or associations because he believed they limited the freedom of the individual to develop inner resources and find a personal path to spiritual illumination. In the vicinity of Emerson's home in Concord, Massachusetts, a group of like-minded seekers of truth and spiritual fulfillment gathered during the 1830s and 1840s. Among them for a time was Margaret Fuller, the leading woman intellectual of the age. In *Woman in*

Feature Essay

SPIRITUALISM

Religion or Entertainment?

On November 26, 1855, George Templeton Strong, a prominent New York attorney, returned home from an elegant dinner. That night, he sat down to record in his diary the day's events, including a long conversation about how many of his friends and neighbors had embraced spiritualism—the belief that it was possible to communicate with the spirits of the dead. He asked his diary,

> What would I have said six years ago to anybody who predicted that before the enlightened nineteenth century was ended hundreds of thousands of people in this country would believe themselves able to communicate daily with the ghosts of their grandfathers? It is surely one of the most startling events that have occurred for centuries and one of the most significant. A New Revelation, hostile to that of Church and the Bible, finding acceptance on the authority of knocking ghosts . . . is a momentous fact in history, throwing light on the intellectual caliber and moral tone of the age in which multitudes adopt it.

Indeed, by the mid-1850s it seemed as if everyone in the country was talking about spirits. Most scholars have agreed that during the decade at least a million Americans were active believers in spiritualism. Many more were exposed to the belief through articles and editorials in popular magazines such as *Harper's* and *Atlantic Monthly*. Stories about hauntings and seances also appeared on the front pages of newspapers such as the *New York Times* and the *New York Tribune*. Hundreds of books and pamphlets described encounters with the world beyond and spiritualism was featured in popular plays, poems, and songs. Some notable Americans, including governors, clergymen, and scientists, publicly declared their belief in the ability to make contact with the spirit world. Spiritualist themes even found their way into the work of authors such as Nathaniel Hawthorne, Ralph Waldo Emerson, and Henry James.

Many Americans were shocked by the sudden popularity of talking to the dead. Some critics saw the passion for spiritualism as foolish or dangerous; they accused spiritualists of perpetrating a "humbug," a fraud that was less credible than the exhibits found at P. T. Barnum's American Museum. Others, however, thought that the belief in the spirits was a kind of witchcraft or even a sign of widespread insanity. Because of this opposition, some people who claimed that they talked to the spirits were thrown in jail or taken to insane asylums. Given these tensions, respected scientists investigated spiritualism in the hopes of explaining what caused the manifestations. In 1857, one committee, led by several professors from Harvard University, offered $500 to anyone who could provide proof of spiritualism. After a number of mediums failed to provide convincing evidence of their powers, the committee announced that spiritualism was a "contaminating influence."

Even spiritualists argued over what the manifestations meant. For some, contacting the spirits was mainly a form of entertainment. Others argued that the spirits provided the basis for a new philosophy—or even a new religion. The view of spiritualism as entertainment grew out of the experiences of two girls in Hydesville, a small village in upstate New York. On March 28, 1848, Kate and Margaret Fox reported hearing loud raps and poundings on the walls and floorboards of their bedroom. The girls assumed that the noises were spirits who were attempting to communicate and asked questions of the spirits, who allegedly rapped their answers in a code. Soon, curious onlookers filled the Fox house, and the girls' parents sent them to live with their sister Leah in Rochester, New York. The rapping spirits followed the girls, and their fame spread. Before long, the three girls were performing in New York City, where their demonstrations created a sensation. By the time the sisters left the city, hundreds of mediums were operating to the accompaniment of raps, spirit voices, and ghostly music. Many people gathered in parlors to hold séances or attended public displays of "spirit rapping" in hope of receiving proof of the existence of spirits. For many of the observers, spiritualism offered the thrill of a magic show or the solace of talking to a departed loved one.

The view of spiritualism as a philosophical system began in 1847 with the publication of Andrew Jackson Davis's book, *The Principles of*

The three Fox sisters, Margaret, Kate, and Leah, shown here in solemn pose, became professional mediums who thrilled audiences at their performances with loud rappings, tilting tables, and visions and materialization of spirits. ❖

Nature. In this long work, Davis described the world of spirits he visited while in a hypnotic trance. He argued that the spirits were trying to teach people a better way of life and interpreted his experiences with the spirit world as a call for a new philosophy, which he called Harmonialism. Davis, and spiritualists who shared his reforming dreams, saw spiritualism as an agent of universal reform—a way to use the knowledge of the spirit realm to revolutionize religion, medicine, and society and to make the human world more closely resemble the "summer land" of the spirits.

One crucial issue was the relationship between spiritualism and Christianity. Many people believed that it was possible to be a Christian and a spiritualist; after all, spiritualism proved the Bible's claim that spirits lived past death. Others believed that talking to spirits was evil and a form of heresy condemned by Christ. For the latter, spiritualism was not a religion—it was a sin. Yet spiritualism definitely resembled a religion in some of the answers it provided believers. For example, it offered guidance about the best way to live and information about the world beyond death. Unlike most religions, however, it had no dogma that defined spiritualist beliefs, no special places to worship, and no established religious leaders. Individual spiritualists were left to determine for themselves what it meant to be talking to the spirits of the dead.

Although spiritualism answered some of the same questions as more mainstream religions, in some ways spiritualism operated in a very nonreligious fashion. Most religions required that certain beliefs, such as the existence of God, be taken on faith—people accepted those beliefs without proof. Spiritualists, however, could see and hear the spirits of the dead, which eliminated the need to trust in faith alone. For some believers, spiritualism was a "scientific" religion that offered evidence of the existence of life after death. The séance parlor became a kind of religious laboratory where spiritualists sought scientific proof for religious hypotheses.

Spiritualism continued to be popular through the Civil War. Séances even were conducted in the Lincoln White House. Immediately following the war, spiritualism experienced a revival as a generation of Americans grappled with the death of more than 600,000 soldiers. As the memory of the war waned, the popularity of spiritualism declined, although its notoriety rose and fell throughout the rest of the nineteenth century. The interest in the spirit world spread into other pursuits, such as the scientific exploration of the paranormal by Harvard professor William James (brother of the novelist Henry James) and the founding of the American Society for Psychical Research in 1885.

Ritualized dances were part of the Shakers' spiritual preparation for the Second Coming. The dancers in this nineteenth-century etching exemplify the mixed heritage of the Shaker community. ❖

the Nineteenth Century (1845), she made a strong claim for the spiritual and artistic equality of women.

One group of transcendentalists, led by the Reverend George Ripley, rejected Emerson's radical individualism and founded a cooperative community at **Brook Farm,** near Roxbury, Massachusetts, in 1841. For the next four years, group members worked the land in common, conducted an excellent school on the principle that spontaneity rather than discipline was the key to education, and allowed ample time for conversation, meditation, communion with nature, and artistic activity of all kinds. Visitors and guest lecturers included such luminaries as Emerson, Margaret Fuller, and Theodore Parker, the Unitarian theologian and radical reformer. In 1845, Brook Farm was reconstituted as a Fourierist phalanx, but some of the original spirit persisted until its dissolution in 1849.

Another experiment in transcendental living adhered more closely to the individualistic spirit of the movement. Between 1845 and 1847, Henry David Thoreau, a young disciple of Emerson, lived by himself in the woods along the shore of Walden Pond and carefully recorded his thoughts and impressions. In a sense, he pushed the ideal of self-culture to its logical outcome—a utopia of one. The result was *Walden* (published in 1854), one of the greatest achievements in American literature.

Henry David Thoreau explained that he went to live in solitude in the woods because he wanted to "front only the essential facts of life." The sketch at right appeared on the title page of the first edition of Walden *(1854), the remarkable record of his experiment in living.* ❖

CHRONOLOGY

1801	Massive revival held at Cane Ridge, Kentucky
1826	American Temperance Society organized
1830–1831	Charles G. Finney evangelizes Rochester, New York
1831	William Lloyd Garrison publishes first issue of the *Liberator*
1833	Abolitionists found American Anti-Slavery Society
1835–1836	Theodore Weld advocates abolition in Ohio and upstate New York
1836	American Temperance Society splits into factions
1837	Massachusetts establishes a state board of education ❖ Abolitionist editor Elijah Lovejoy killed by a proslavery mob
1840	American Anti-Slavery Society splits over women's rights and other issues
1841	Transcendentalists organize a model community at Brook Farm
1848	Feminists gather at Seneca Falls, New York, and found the women's rights movement
1854	Henry David Thoreau's *Walden* published

Conclusion: Counterpoint on Reform

One great American writer observed at close quarters the perfectionist ferment of the age but held himself aloof, suggesting in his novels and tales that pursuit of the ideal led to a distorted view of human nature and possibilities. Nathaniel Hawthorne lived in Concord, knew Emerson and Margaret Fuller, and even spent time at Brook Farm. But his sense of human frailty made him skeptical about the claims of transcendentalism and utopianism. He satirized transcendentalism as unworldly and overoptimistic in his allegorical tale "The Celestial Railroad" and gently lampooned the denizens of Brook Farm in his novel *The Blithedale Romance* (1852). His view of the dangers of pursuing perfection too avidly came out in his tale of a father who kills his beautiful daughter by trying to remove her one blemish, a birthmark. His greatest novels, *The Scarlet Letter* (1850) and *The House of the Seven Gables* (1851), imaginatively probed New England's Puritan past and the shadows it cast on the present. By dwelling on original sin as a psychological reality, Hawthorne told his contemporaries that their efforts to escape from guilt and evil were futile. One simply had to accept the world as an imperfect place. Although he did not engage in polemics against humanitarian reformers and cosmic optimists, Hawthorne wrote parables and allegories that implicitly questioned the fundamental assumptions of pre–Civil War reform.

One does not have to agree with Hawthorne's antiprogressive view of the human condition to acknowledge that the dreams of perfectionist reformers promised more than they could possibly deliver. Revivals could not make all men like Christ; temperance could not solve all social problems; abolitionist agitation could not bring a peaceful end to slavery; and transcendentalism (as Emerson himself sometimes conceded) could not fully emancipate people from the limitations and frustrations of daily life. The consequences of perfectionist efforts were often far different from what their proponents expected. In defense of the reformers, however, one could argue that Hawthorne's skepticism and

Hester Prynne and her daughter Pearl in an illustration from The Scarlet Letter *by Nathaniel Hawthorne. In the novel, which stands as one of the masterpieces of American literature, Hawthorne probes the dark side of human nature as he explores the effect of sin—actual and symbolic—on the characters.* ❖

fatalism were a prescription for doing nothing in the face of intolerable evils. If the reform impulse was long on inspirational rhetoric but somewhat short on durable, practical achievements, it did at least disturb the complacent and opportunistic surface of American life and open the way to necessary changes. Nothing could possibly change for the better unless people were willing to dream of improvement.

Recommended Reading

Alice Felt Tyler, *Freedom's Ferment: Phases of American Social History from the Colonial Period to the Outbreak of the Civil War* (1944), gives a lively overview of the varieties of pre–Civil War reform activity. Ronald G. Walters, *American Reformers, 1815–1860, rev. ed.* (1997), provides a modern interpretation of these movements. Steven Mintz, *Moralists and Modernizers: America's Pre–Civil War Reformers* (1995), provides another good overview of the reform activities during this period. A particularly useful collection of documents on reform movements and other aspects of antebellum culture is David Brion Davis, *Antebellum American Culture: An Interpretive Anthology* (1979).

The best general work on the revivalism of the Second Great Awakening is William G. McLoughlin, *Modern Revivalism* (1959). A general survey of the religious ferment of this period is Nathan O. Hatch, *The Democratization of American Christianity* (1989). Paul E. Johnson, *A Shopkeeper's Millennium: Society and Revivals in Rochester, New York, 1815–1837* (1978), incisively describes the impact of the revival on a single community. The connection between religion and reform is described in Robert H. Abzug, *Cosmos Crumbling: American Reform and the Religious Imagination* (1994).

A good introduction to the changing roles of women and the family in nineteenth-century America is Carl N. Degler, *At Odds: Women and the Family in America from the Revolution to the Present* (1980). On the rise of the domestic ideology, see Nancy F. Cott, *The Bonds of Womanhood: "Woman's Sphere" in New England, 1780–1835* (1977). The condition of working-class women is incisively treated in Christine Stansell, *City of Women: Sex and Class in New York, 1789–1860* (1986). For an extended history of the *Cruger* case and an excellent legal history of marriage and divorce, see Hendrick Hartog, *Man and Wife in America: A History* (2000).

David J. Rothman, *The Discovery of the Asylum: Social Order and Disorder in the New Republic* (1971), provides a penetrating analysis of the movement for institutional reform. For good surveys of abolitionism, see James Brewer Stewart, *Holy Warriors: The Abolitionists and American Slavery* (1976) and Paul Goodman, *Of One Blood: Abolitionism and Racial Equality* (1998). On transcendentalism, see Charles Capper and Conrad E. Wright, *Transient and Permanent: The Transcendentalist Movement and Its Contexts* (1999).

For a list of additional titles related to this chapter's topics, please see http://www.ablongman.com/divine.

Suggested Web Sites

America's First Look into the Camera: Daguerreotype Portraits and Views, 1839–1862

http://memory.loc.gov/ammem/daghtml/daghome.html

The Library of Congress's daguerreotype collection consists of more than 650 photographs dating from 1839 to 1864. Portraits, architectural views, and some street scenes make up most of the collection.

1830s Clothing

http://www.connerprairie.org/historyonline/clothing.html

See how clothing worn in the Early Republic was quite different from what people wear today.

Votes for Women: Selections from the National American Woman Suffrage Association Collection, 1848–1921

http://memory.loc.gov/ammem/naw/nawshome.html

This Library of Congress site contains 167 books, pamphlets, and other artifacts documenting the suffrage campaign.

History of Women's Suffrage

http://www.rochester.edu/SBA/history.html

This site includes a chronology, important texts relating to women's suffrage, and biographical information about Susan B. Anthony and Elizabeth Cady Stanton.

By Popular Demand: "Votes for Women" Suffrage Pictures, 1850–1920

http://memory.loc.gov/ammem/vfwhtml/vfwhome.html
Portraits, suffrage parades, picketing suffragists, an antisuffrage display, and cartoons commenting on the movement make up this Library of Congress site.

Women in America, 1820 to 1842

http://xroads.virginia.edu/~HYPER/DETOC/FEM/home.htm
This University of Virginia site takes a look at women in antebellum America.

Godey's Lady's Book On-line

http://www.history.rochester.edu/godeys/
Here is on-line text of this interesting nineteenth-century journal.

Influence of Prominent Abolitionists

http://www.loc.gov/exhibits/african/afam006.html
An exhibit site from the Library of Congress, with pictures and text, which discusses some key African American abolitionists and their efforts to end slavery.

Law and Society

The Legal Rights of Married Women

Reforming the Law of Coverture

By the common law in effect in the United States in the early nineteenth century, women lost their legal personality when they married. The system of *coverture* governed the union of husband and wife; married women were under the "wing, protection, or *cover*" of their husbands.

Coverture was based on the English medieval feudal system in which lords and vassals owed allegiance to the king, and commoners to lords and vassals. Under the common law of England, husband and wife were referred to as "baron" and "feme." William Blackstone, the English jurist, professor of common law, and author of *Commentaries on the Law of England,* explained, "the word baron, or lord, attributes to the husband not a very courteous superiority . . . if the baron kills his feme, it is the same as if he had killed a stranger, or any other person; but if the feme kills her baron, it is regarded by the laws as a much more atrocious crime; as she not only breaks through the restraints of humanity and conjugal affection, but throws off all subjection to the authority of her husband. And therefore the law denominates her crime, a species of treason, and condemns her to the same punishment as if she had killed the king." As Blackstone explained, "By marriage, the husband and wife are one person in the law."

Coverture denied married women their rights to own and manage property, to form contracts, to sue and be sued, and to exercise legal control over children. Upon marriage, all of a wife's personal property became her husband's, which he could give or will to someone else if he chose. The husband could not sell his wife's real estate, but he could control and manage it, and any profits derived from the property belonged to him.

Coverture had a few benefits for women. Husbands took legal responsibility for any crimes their wives committed, and sometimes wives could avoid responsibility for unwise financial transactions because they had had no legal right to enter into them. A widow had a right to one-third of her husband's property (her "dower"), if he died without a will. And a husband had a limited obligation to provide for his wife's "necessaries." Blackstone concluded his chapter on husband and wife with the observation that "even the disabilities, which the wife lies under, are for the most part intended for her protection and benefit. So great a favourite is the female sex of the laws of England."

In practice, some women, especially wealthy women, were able to get around some of the laws of coverture by taking advantage of loopholes in the law. First of all, women could go to courts of "equity" or "chancery," in which a chancellor, rather than a jury, could decide the fair or just outcome based on the facts of the individual case, rather than applying rules of law. (These two court systems of law and equity are merged into one in most states today.) An equity court had the power not only to assign money damages but to require a contract to be carried out. For example, a couple might specify in a prenuptial contract—made before the marriage was entered into—that the wife could keep her own property from before the marriage in a "separate estate." It was also possible for a husband to assign some of his property to his wife after the marriage in a "marriage settlement." And often they arranged for the wife's separate estate to be held in "trust" and managed by a third-party trustee, usually a man.

It was the legal arrangement of coverture into which Harriet Douglas, a rich New York heiress, resisted entering. Harriet Douglas had very definite ideas about what she wanted in a husband. If she married, she intended to keep control over all of her property, "in obedience to, and conformity with the opinions and precepts of her parents," and she wanted her husband to renounce his own name, his home, and his profession, to devote himself to her and her family property. As historian Hendrik Hartog observed, according to the norms of early America, Harriet Douglas effectively wanted "her husband [to] become her wife." Henry Cruger, a young lawyer who came to New York from South Carolina and who courted Harriet Douglas, at first chafed at the restrictions she proposed for a marriage arrangement. Henry argued that "the husband ought always to possess an absolute control over the wife's property." But a few years later, Henry rethought his position, writing to Harriet in 1829 that he would accept her terms, "however derogatory to proper pride . . . and self-respect." After extensive negotiations, they finally married in 1833. Henry took "D" for his middle initial without changing his last name, and Harriet was to be known as "Mrs. Douglas Cruger." Harriet agreed to sign a property settlement agreement after rather than before the marriage ceremony, because Henry claimed that a premarital contract would become part of an embarrassing public record.

Harriet's and Henry's marriage fell almost immediately on hard times, largely over money matters. Henry repeatedly threatened to return to legal practice if Harriet did not give him more freedom to control their property, urging her, "Take away this poignard of ice from between us . . . I desire no interests separate from yours, for I love you, and we are married." On several occasions, Harriet drew up new "agency" agreements, giving Henry more control of her estate as her "agent." Her friends all urged her to "relieve" Henry "from a state of dependence" that could only be galling to a "man of honor." After years of Henry's ranting and lobbying, in 1841 Harriet signed an order guaranteeing him one-half of her income for life. That same year, their marriage fell apart completely.

It took eight more years in New York courts to work out Henry's and Harriet's rights to her property. Henry argued that their marriage settlement was invalid because it came after rather than before the marriage. Harriet claimed the original settlement should be enforced, but the 1841 gift was invalid because Henry and his friends had coerced her into signing it. In 1848, the case ended up in the New York Supreme Court, where Judge Selah Strong decreed that the original marriage settlement was valid, giving Harriet control over her own property, but that the 1841 order was enforceable as well, giving control over half of it to Henry. Years later, Strong wrote, "She was mad and he was bad, and the legal muddle they brought about between them was very deep and formidable."

At the end of their legal muddle, Henry emerged victorious with control over half of Harriet's separate estate. Despite her strenuous efforts to be an independent married woman, she had failed. In disgust, she "had her marriage bed cut in two, transforming it into two 'slightly peculiar' sofas."

The New York Supreme Court made its final decision in *Cruger v. Cruger*, just one year after the New York Legislature passed its first Married Women's Property Act, allowing women for the first time to maintain ownership and control over property they had inherited before they married. Over the course of the middle decades of the nineteenth century, an increasingly vocal minority of women chafed against the laws of husband and wife that restricted the independence of women like Harriet Cruger. They demanded the reform of the laws of coverture, first through Married Women's Property Acts, and then through Earnings Laws. Nowhere were they more vocal and successful than in New York.

At first, women's rights reformers concentrated on changing people's hearts and minds, as had temperance reformers, abolitionists, and others who were part of the great wave of reform in the United States in the early nineteenth century. In their private writings, women's rights reformers were often more frank than in public discussion, about how marriage kept women subjugated to their husbands. They often compared the married woman to a slave—with no right to own property, sign a contract, sue another, or even keep her own name.

After 1840, as in so many of the reform movements sparked by the religious fervor of the Second Great Awakening, women's rights reformers began to turn to legal solutions. The first group of advocates for women's rights took particular aim at the laws of marriage and divorce. They also organized women's rights activity on a large scale for the first time. On July 19–20, 1848, the first women's rights convention in the world took place at Seneca Falls, New York. Elizabeth Cady Stanton, a women's rights activist and an organizer of the convention, delivered the "Declaration of Sentiments," modeled on the Declaration of Independence: "We hold these truths to be self-evident: that all men and women are created equal . . . " Stanton declared further that "The history of mankind is a history of repeated injuries and usurpations on the part of man toward woman, having in direct object the establishment of an absolute tyranny over her."

The declaration listed a series of wrongs, followed by twelve resolutions. While winning the right to vote was part of the women's aim, their chief focus was reforming the laws of marriage. Eleven resolutions passed unanimously; the twelfth, calling for the extension of the vote to women, passed narrowly only after abolitionist and former slave Frederick Douglass made a rousing speech in its favor. The Declaration of Sentiments quickly became famous around the world, sparking women's rights reform movements in England and across Europe.

New York's first Married Women's Property Act, passed in 1848, the same year as the Seneca Falls convention, was the product of a number of factors. The persistent petition campaigns of feminist reformers had some influence on the legislators, but several other forces were at work as well. There was a strong movement in New York to "codify" the common law into written codes, accessible to everyone, thereby minimizing the power of judges and lawyers to shape decisions as they pleased. The leaders of that movement especially took aim at equity courts, which they saw as undemocratic institutions whose individually tailored settlements benefited only the propertied elite. For these politicians, reform of the laws governing married women's property was a way to democratize property law, making available to everyone the "separate estates" that wealthy families had been able to arrange through equity courts. Finally, wealthy Dutch landowners in the Hudson Valley saw the acts as a way to protect family property. Thus, the Married Women's Property Acts, in New York and elsewhere, were a good example of the way that legal reform comes about as a result of reformers' efforts coming together with other circumstances and constituencies.

The 1848 act pronounced that "the real and personal property of any female who may hereafter marry, and which she shall own at the time of the marriage, and the rents issues and profits thereof, shall not be subject to the disposal of her husband, nor be liable for his debts, and shall continue her sole and separate property, as if she were a single female." It also provided that gifts to married women could remain their separate property, and that marriage settlements and prenuptial agreements would be enforced. The second act, in 1849, made it possible for women to sell or transfer their separate property under certain conditions, and for the trustees of their separate estates to deed property to them if a judge found them capable of managing it.

Despite the Married Women's Property Acts, women who did not have substantial property to inherit from their families still suffered severe legal constraints, most importantly because they still did not control their earnings. New Yorker Ernestine Rose, an early activist for women's rights, observed, "Here is some provision for the favored few; but for the laboring many, there is none. The mass of people commence life with no other capital than the union of heads, hearts and hands. To the benefit of this best of capital, the wife has no right. If they are unsuccessful in married life, who suffers more the bitter consequences of poverty than the wife? But if successful, she can not call a dollar her own."

In the summer of 1854, Elizabeth Cady Stanton rose to address the Joint Judiciary Committee of the New York State Legislature, the first time a woman had ever spoken before that body. She began: "The thinking minds of all nations call for change. There is a deep-lying struggle in the whole fabric of society; a boundless grinding collision of the New with the Old." Stanton asked the legislators to consider the "legal disabilities under which [women] labor."

On behalf of women, Stanton demanded the right to vote, the right to sit on juries, and the reform of the law of coverture. "Look at the position of woman as wife," she demanded. "The wife who inherits no property holds about the same legal position that does the slave on the Southern plantation. She can own nothing, sell nothing. She has no right even to the wages she earns; her person, her time, her services are the property of another. . . . But the wife who is so fortunate as to have inherited property, has, by the new law in this State, been redeemed from her lost condition." Stanton told the legislators that she spoke on behalf of the "daughters of the revolution-

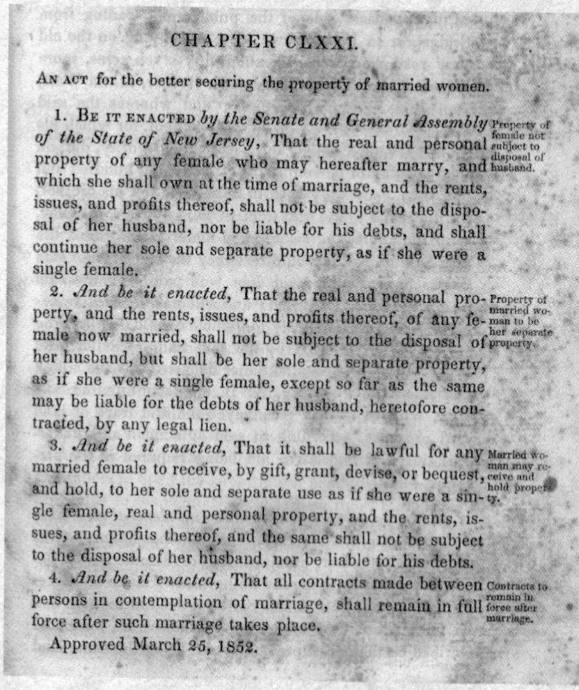

CHAPTER CLXXI.

AN ACT for the better securing the property of married women.

1. BE IT ENACTED *by the Senate and General Assembly of the State of New Jersey*, That the real and personal property of any female who may hereafter marry, and which she shall own at the time of marriage, and the rents, issues, and profits thereof, shall not be subject to the disposal of her husband, nor be liable for his debts, and shall continue her sole and separate property, as if she were a single female. — Property of female not subject to disposal of husband.

2. *And be it enacted*, That the real and personal property, and the rents, issues, and profits thereof, of any female now married, shall not be subject to the disposal of her husband, but shall be her sole and separate property, as if she were a single female, except so far as the same may be liable for the debts of her husband, heretofore contracted, by any legal lien. — Property of married woman to be her separate property.

3. *And be it enacted*, That it shall be lawful for any married female to receive, by gift, grant, devise, or bequest, and hold, to her sole and separate use as if she were a single female, real and personal property, and the rents, issues, and profits thereof, and the same shall not be subject to the disposal of her husband, nor be liable for his debts. — Married woman may receive and hold property.

4. *And be it enacted*, That all contracts made between persons in contemplation of marriage, shall remain in full force after such marriage takes place. — Contracts to remain in force after marriage.

Approved March 25, 1852.

New Jersey's 1852 Married Women's Property Act. Several states introduced married women's property acts in the years following New York's successful 1848 legislation. ❖

Women's rights activist Ernestine Rose began petitioning for married women's property rights in New York in 1836. ❖

ary heroes of '76," and exhorted them to be true to the goals of the Revolution, mocking their claims to republicanism: "How like feudal barons you freemen hold your women." At the same time that Stanton spoke before the legislature, she presented more than six thousand petitions from women across the state.

Six years later, in 1860, New York passed the first Earnings Act in the nation, providing that a married woman could "carry on any trade or business, and perform any labor or services on her sole and separate account, and the earnings of any married woman, from her trade, business, labor or services, shall be her sole and separate property, and may be used or invested by her in her own name." By the 1870s, most states had passed some version of married women's property acts, and many Northern states passed Earning Acts as well.

By and large, courts interpreted the Earnings Act narrowly. For example, in one 1876 case, the New York Supreme Court ruled that a wife who kept a boardinghouse and nursed a very ill man for several years could not control her earnings because work done in the home was considered to be on the "family account," rather than her "sole and separate account," and was therefore the property of the husband. Repeatedly, courts held that women's labor in the household belonged to the husband, so that only wages earned outside the home—although a minor part of most women's earnings—were covered by the act.

In the Iowa case of *Miller* v. *Miller,* a husband and wife attempted to create their own marriage contract, in which both spouses promised to "refrain from scolding, fault-finding and anger." Mr. Miller promised to provide for family necessaries as well as a sum of $16.66 per month for Mrs. Miller's individual use, and she promised to "keep her home and family in a comfortable and reasonably good condition." When Mrs. Miller sued her husband to enforce this contract, she was turned away by the court because she had promised to do only what she was already obligated to do, but he had promised far more than marriage required from a husband, which was only to provide "necessaries."

⚖

New York's 1860 Earnings Act was a limited victory for reformers—they won a change in the law, but courts limited its reach through narrow interpretation. Had courts interpreted the act more broadly to cover all forms of women's earnings, it would have gone a long way to making women independent legally and economically.

Although the 1860 Earnings Act gained some legal rights for women, it failed to resolve completely the inequities that women faced. In the later nineteenth century, women's rights advocates became convinced that political power was the way to secure civil rights, and they began to focus more specifically on winning the right to vote. Achieving that goal would take another sixty years.

Discussion Questions

- What was the system of "coverture"? How could couples avoid some of the legal disabilities of coverture? Could they avoid all of them?
- What were the chief concerns of women's rights advocates in the mid-nineteenth century? How did their aims and tactics resemble those of other reform movements during this period?
- How did the Married Women's Property Acts and Earnings Act improve the legal status of married women, and in what ways did they fall short of reformers' aims? Why do you think these acts were passed?

Chapter 13

St. Louis, Missouri, in the 1850s. Steamboat traffic on the Mississippi River helped develop this busy inland port. By 1850, St. Louis was one of the nation's largest cities. ❖

An Age of Expansionism

The Spirit of Young America

In the 1840s and early 1850s, politicians, writers, and entrepreneurs frequently proclaimed themselves champions of **Young America.** One of the first to use the phrase was Ralph Waldo Emerson, who told an audience of merchants and manufacturers in 1844 that the nation was entering a new era of commercial development, technological progress, and territorial expansion. Emerson suggested that a progressive new generation—the Young Americans—would lead this surge of physical development. More than a slogan and less than an organized movement, Young America stood for a positive attitude toward the market economy and industrial growth, a more aggressive and belligerent foreign policy, and a celebration of America's unique strengths and virtues.

Young Americans favored enlarging the national market by acquiring new territory. They called for the annexation of Texas, asserted an American claim to all of Oregon, and urged the appropriation of vast new territories from Mexico. They also celebrated the technological advances that would knit this new empire together, especially the telegraph and the railroad. Telegraphs, according to one writer, would "flash sensation and volition . . . to and from towns and provinces as if they were organs and limbs of a single organism"; railroads would provide "a vast system of iron muscles which, as it were, move the limbs of the mighty organism."

Young America was a cultural and intellectual movement as well as an economic and political one. In 1845, a Washington journal hailed the election of the 49-year-old James K. Polk, at that time the youngest man to have been elected president, as a sign that youth will "dare to take antiquity by the beard, and tear the cloak from hoary-headed hypocrisy. Too young to be corrupt . . . it is Young America, awakened to a sense of her own intellectual greatness by her soaring spirit. It stands in strength, the voice of the majority." During the Polk administration, Young American writers and critics—mostly based in New York City—called for a new and distinctive national literature, free of subservience to European themes or models and expressive of the democratic spirit. Their organ was the *Literary World,* founded in 1847, and its ideals influenced two of the greatest writers America has produced: Walt Whitman and Herman Melville.

Whitman captured much of the exuberance and expansionism of Young America in his "Song of the Open Road":

> From this hour I ordain myself loos'd of limits and imaginary lines,
> Going where I list, my own master total and absolute,
> . . . .
> I inhale great draughts of space,
> The east and the west are mine, and the north and the south are mine.
> I am larger, better than I thought.

In *Moby-Dick,* Herman Melville produced a novel sufficiently original in form and conception to more than fulfill the demand of Young Americans for "a New Literature to fit the New Man in the New Age." But Melville was too deep a thinker not to see the perils that underlay the soaring ambition and aggressiveness of the new

Outline

Feature Essay

Walt Whitman in the "carpenter portrait" that appeared in the first edition of his great work, Leaves of Grass, *in 1855. The poet's rough clothes and slouch hat signify his identification with the common people.* ❖

New York native Herman Melville, shown here in an 1870 portrait by Joseph Oriel Eaton, shaped the knowledge he gained as a merchant sailor into Moby-Dick, *a cautionary saga about the dark side of human ambition.* ❖

age. The whaling captain Ahab, who brings destruction to himself and his ship by his relentless pursuit of the white whale, symbolized—among other things—the dangers facing a nation that was overreaching itself by indulging its pride and exalted sense of destiny with too little concern for the moral and practical consequences.

THE YOUNG AMERICAN IDEAL—the idea of a young country led by young men into new paths of prosperity and greatness—appealed to many people and found support across political party lines. But the attitude came to be identified primarily with young Democrats who wanted to move their party away from its traditional fear of the expansion of commerce and industry. Unlike old-line Jeffersonians and Jacksonians, Young Americans had no qualms about the market economy and the speculative, materialistic spirit it called forth.

Before 1848 the Young American impulse focused mainly on the great expanse of western lands that lay just beyond the nation's borders. After the Mexican-American War, when territorial gains extended the nation's boundaries from the Atlantic to the Pacific, attention shifted to internal development. New discoveries of gold in the nation's western territories fostered economic growth, technological advances spurred industrialization, and increased immigration brought more people to populate the lands newly acquired—by agreement or by force.

Movement to the Far West

In the 1830s and 1840s, the westward movement of population left the valley of the Mississippi behind and penetrated the Far West all the way to the Pacific. Pioneers pursued fertile land and economic opportunity beyond the existing boundaries of the United States and thus helped set the stage for the annexations and international crises of the 1840s. Some went for material gain, others went for adventure, and a significant minority sought freedom from religious persecution. Whatever their reasons, they brought American attitudes into regions that were already occupied or claimed by Mexico or Great Britain.

Borderlands of the 1830s

U.S. expansionists directed their ambitions to the north, west, and southwest. For a time, it seemed that both Canada and Mexico might be frontiers for expansionism. Conflicts over the border between the United States and British North America led periodically to calls for diplomatic or military action to wrest the northern half of the continent from the British; similar conflicts in Mexican territory led ultimately to the United States' capture and acquisition of much of northern Mexico.

Since the birth of the republic, there had been a major dispute over the boundary between Maine and the Canadian province of New Brunswick. In 1839, fighting broke out between Canadian lumberjacks and the Maine militia. This long-festering controversy poisoned Anglo-American relations until 1842, when Secretary of State Daniel Webster concluded an agreement with the British government, represented by Lord Ashburton. The **Webster-Ashburton Treaty** gave over half of the disputed territory to the United States and established a definite northeastern boundary with Canada.

On the other side of the continent, the United States and Britain both laid claim to Oregon, a vast area that lay between the Rockies and the Pacific from the 42nd parallel (the northern boundary of California) to the latitude of 54°0' (the southern boundary of Alaska). In 1818, the two nations agreed to joint occupation for ten years, an agreement that was renewed indefinitely in 1827. Meanwhile, the Americans had strengthened their claim by acquiring Spain's rights to the Pacific Northwest in the Adams-Onís Treaty (see Chapter 9), and the British had gained effective control of the northern portion of the Oregon Country through the activities of the Hudson's Bay Company, a well-financed fur-trading concern. Blocking an equitable division was the reluctance on both sides to surrender access to the Columbia River basin and the adjacent territory extending north to the 49th parallel (which later became the northern border of the state of Washington).

The Oregon Country was scarcely populated before 1840. The same could not be said of the Mexican borderlands that lay directly west of Jacksonian America. Spanish settlements in present-day New Mexico date from the late sixteenth century. By 1820, about forty thousand people of Spanish descent populated this province, engaging mainly in sheep raising and mining. In 1821, Spain granted independence to Mexico, which then embraced areas that currently make up the states of Texas, New Mexico, Arizona, California, Nevada, Utah, and much of Colorado. Spain's mercantilist policies had closed the region to outside traders, but the Republic of Mexico opted for a free-trade policy. Mexico in 1821 informed its northern neighbors of the changed laws encouraging trade. This action succeeded in stimulating commercial prosperity but also whetted expansionist appetites on the Anglo side of the border.

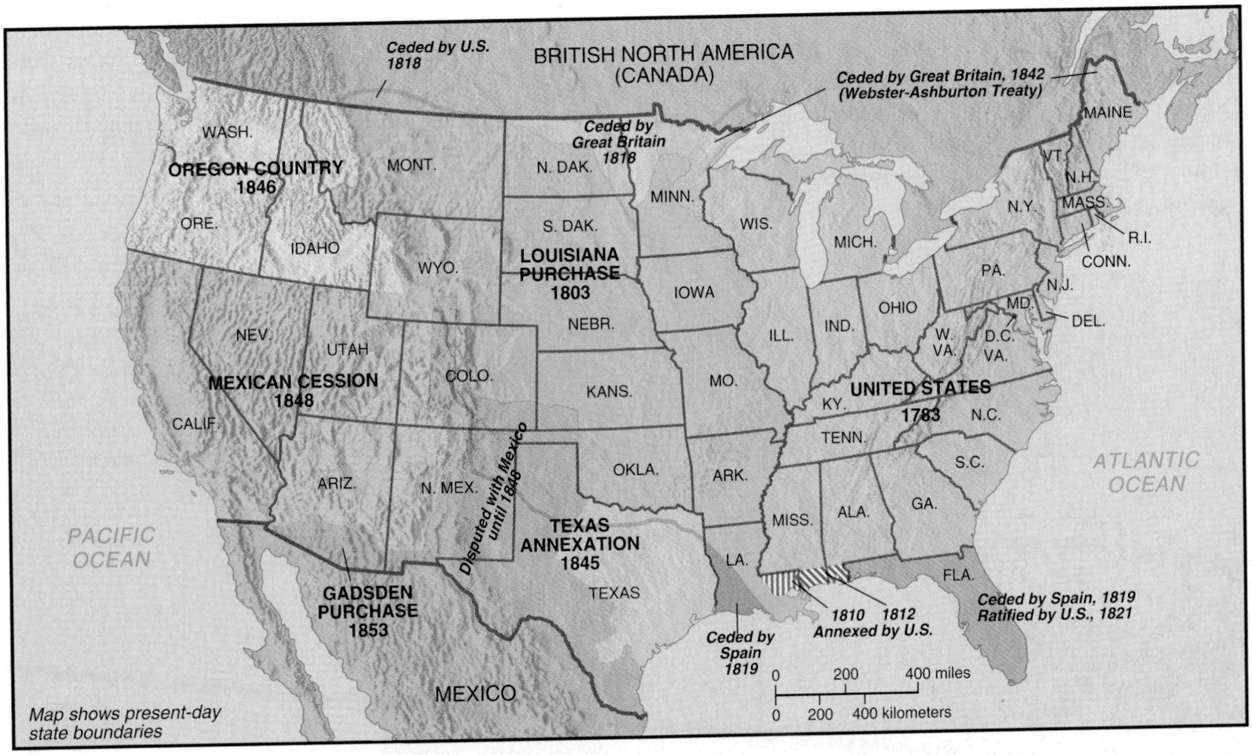

TERRITORIAL EXPANSION BY THE MID-NINETEENTH CENTURY *Fervent nationalists identified the growth of America through territorial expansion as the divinely ordained "Manifest Destiny" of a chosen people.* ◆

California was the other major northward extension of Mexico. Spanish missionaries and soldiers had taken control of the region in the late eighteenth century. In the 1820s and 1830s, this land of huge estates and enormous cattle herds was far less populous than New Mexico—only about four thousand Mexicans of Spanish origin lived in California in 1827. The region's other inhabitants were the thirty thousand Indians, many of whom were forced to work on vast land tracts owned by Spanish missions. At the beginning of the 1830s, a chain of twenty-one mission stations, stretching from San Diego to north of San Francisco, controlled most of the province's land and wealth. Great as the Indian population may seem, the number represented only a small fraction of the original indigenous population; there had been a catastrophic decline in Indian population during the previous sixty years of Spanish rule. The stresses and strains of forced labor and exposure to European diseases had taken an enormous toll.

In 1833, the Mexican Congress's "secularization act" emancipated the Indians from church control and opened the mission lands to settlement. The government awarded immense tracts of the mission land to Mexican citizens and left the Indians landless. A new class of large landowners, or *rancheros,* replaced the *padres* as rulers of Old California and masters of the province's indigenous population. Seven hundred grantees took possession of *ranchos* ranging up to nearly 50,000 acres and proceeded to subject the Indians to a new and even harsher form of servitude. During the fifteen years they held sway, the rancheros created an American legend through their lavish hospitality, extravagant dress, superb horsemanship, and taste for violent and dangerous sports. Their flamboyant lifestyle and devotion to the pursuit of pleasure captured the fancy and aroused the secret envy of many American visitors and traders.

The Americans who saw California in the 1830s were mostly merchants and sailors involved in the oceanic trade between Boston and California ports. New England clipper ships sailed around Cape Horn at the southern tip of South America to barter manufactured goods for cowhides. One Boston firm came away with more than 500,000 hides in a twenty-year period. By the mid-1830s, several Yankee merchants had taken up permanent residence in towns such as Monterey and San Diego in order to conduct the California end of the business. The reports they sent back about the Golden West sparked interest in eastern business circles.

The Texas Revolution

At the same time as some Americans were trading with California, others were taking possession of Texas. In the early 1820s, Mexican officials encouraged settlers from the United States to settle in Texas. Newly independent Mexico granted Stephen F. Austin, son of a onetime Spanish citizen, a huge piece of land in hopes he would help attract and settle new colonists from the United States. Some fifteen other Anglo-American *empresarios* received land grants in the 1820s. In 1823, three hundred families from the United States were settled on the Austin grant, and within a year, the colony's population had swelled to 2021. The offer of fertile and inexpensive land attracted many American immigrants.

This painting by James Walker depicts ornately dressed rancheros rounding up a cattle herd. With their thrilling lifestyles and exotic costumes, the hacienda owners contributed to the vivid images associated with California in the 1830s. ❖

Friction soon developed between the Mexican government and the Anglo-American colonists over the status of slavery and the authority of the Catholic Church. At its core, the dispute centered on the unwillingness of Anglo-American settlers to become Mexicans. Under the terms of settlement, all people living in Texas had to become Mexican citizens and adopt the Roman Catholic faith. Slavery presented another problem, for in 1829 Mexico freed all slaves under its jurisdiction. Slaveholders in Texas were given a special exemption that allowed them to emancipate their slaves and then sign them to lifelong contracts as indentured servants, but many refused to limit their ownership rights in any way. Settlers either converted to Catholicism only superficially or ignored the requirement entirely.

A Mexican government commission reported in 1829 that Americans were the great majority of the Texas population and were flagrantly violating Mexican law—refusing to emancipate their slaves, evading import duties on goods from the United States, and failing to convert to Catholicism. The following year, the Mexican Congress prohibited further American immigration and importation of slaves to Texas.

Enforcement of the new law was feeble, and the flow of settlers, slaves, and smuggled goods continued virtually unabated. A long-standing complaint of the Texans was the failure of the Mexican constitution to grant them local self-government. Under the Mexican federal system, Texas was joined to the state of Coahuila, and Texan representatives were outnumbered three to one in the state legislature. In 1832, the colonists showed their displeasure with Mexican rule by rioting in protest against the arrest of several Anglo-Americans by a Mexican commander.

Austin went to Mexico City in 1833 to present the Texans' grievances and seek concessions from the central government. He succeeded in having the ban against American immigration lifted, but he got only vague promises about tariff relief and failed to win agreement to the separation of Texas from Coahuila. As he was about to return to Texas, Austin was arrested and imprisoned for writing a letter recommending that Texans set up a state government without Mexico City's consent.

In 1835, some Texans revolted against Mexico's central government. The insurrectionists claimed they were fighting for freedom against a long experience of oppression. Actually, Mexican rule had not been harsh; the worst that can be said was that it was inefficient, inconsistent, and sometimes corrupt. Furthermore, the Texans' devotion to "liberty" did not prevent them from defending slavery against Mexico's attempt to abolish it. Texans had done pretty much what they pleased, despite laws to the contrary and angry rumblings from south of the Rio Grande.

Developments in 1834 had threatened their status as "tolerated guests." In that year, General Antonio López de Santa Anna made himself dictator of Mexico and abolished the federal system of government. News of these developments reached Texas late in the year, accompanied by rumors of the impending disfranchisement and even expulsion of American immigrants. The rebels, already aroused by earlier restrictive policies, were influenced by the rumors and prepared to resist Santa Anna's effort to enforce tariff regulations by military force.

When he learned that Texans were resisting customs collections, Santa Anna sent reinforcements. On June 30, 1835, before any additional troops could arrive, a band of settlers led by William B. Travis captured the Mexican garrison at Anahuac without firing a shot. The settlers first engaged Mexican troops at Gonzales in October and forced the retreat of a cavalry detachment. Shortly thereafter, Austin laid siege to San Antonio with a force of five hundred men and after six weeks forced its surrender, thereby capturing most of the Mexican troops then in Texas.

The Republic of Texas

While this early fighting was going on, delegates from the American communities in Texas convened and after

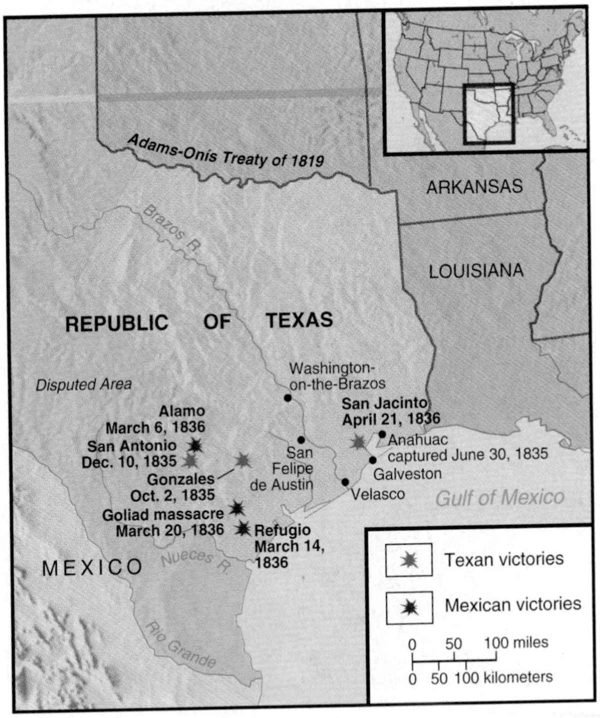

TEXAS REVOLUTION *Major battles of the Texas Revolution. The Texans suffered severe losses at the Alamo and Goliad, but they scored a stunning victory at San Jacinto.*

some hesitation voted overwhelmingly to declare their independence on March 2, 1836. A constitution, based closely on that of the United States, was adopted for the new Republic of Texas, and a temporary government was installed to carry on the military struggle. Although the ensuing conflict was largely one of Americans against Mexicans, some Texas Mexicans, or *Tejanos,* joined the fray on the side of the Anglo rebels. They too wanted to be free of Santa Anna's heavy-handed rule. (Most of the Tejanos would become victims of the same anti-Mexican prejudice that spurred the revolt. Tejano leader Juan Seguin, who served as a captain in the Texas army and became a hero of the independence struggle, was driven off his land by Anglo-Texans in 1841.)

Within days after Texas declared itself a republic, rebels and Mexican troops in San Antonio fought the famous battle of the **Alamo.** Myths about that battle have magnified the Anglo rebels' valor at the Mexicans' expense. The folklore is based on fact—only 187 rebels fought off a far larger number of Mexican soldiers for more than a week before eventually capitulating—but it is not true that all rebels, including the folk hero Davy Crockett, fought to the death. Crockett and seven other survivors were captured and then executed. Moreover, the rebels fought from inside a strong fortress with superior weapons against march-weary Mexican conscripts. Nevertheless, a tale that combined actual and mythical bravery inside the Alamo gave the insurrection new inspiration, moral sanction, outside support, and the rallying cry "Remember the Alamo."

The revolt ended with an exchange of slaughters. A few days after the Alamo battle, another Texas detachment was surrounded and captured in an open plain near the San Antonio River and was marched to the town of Goliad, where most of its 350 members were executed. The next month, on April 21, 1836, the main Texas army, under General Sam Houston, assaulted Santa Anna's troops at an encampment near the San Jacinto River during the siesta hour. The final count showed that 630 Mexicans and only a handful of Texans had been killed. Santa Anna was captured and marched to Velasco, the meeting place of the Texas government, where he was forced to sign treaties recognizing the independence of Texas and its claim to territory all the way to the Rio Grande. The Mexican Congress immediately repudiated the treaty, but their argument was in vain; although a strip of land between the Nueces River and the Rio Grande would be disputed during the next decade, Mexico failed to impose its authority on the victorious Texas rebels.

Sam Houston, the hero of San Jacinto, became the first president of Texas. His platform sought annexation to the United States, and one of his first acts in of-

Battle of San Jacinto *by H.A. McArdle. In this panorama of the Texas Revolution's decisive battle at San Jacinto, Sam Houston leads the charge against Santa Anna's forces.* ❖

fice was to send an emissary to Washington to test the waters. Houston's agent found much sympathy for Texas independence but was told by Andrew Jackson and others that domestic politics and fear of a war with Mexico made immediate annexation impossible. The most that he could win from Congress and the Jackson administration was formal recognition of Texas sovereignty.

In its ten-year existence as the Lone Star Republic, Texas drew settlers from the United States at an accelerating rate. The Panic of 1837 impelled many debt-ridden and land-hungry farmers to take advantage of the free grants of 1280 acres that Texas offered to immigrating heads of white families. In the decade after independence, the population of Texas soared from 30,000 to 142,000. Most of the newcomers assumed, as did the old settlers, that they would soon be annexed and restored to American citizenship.

Trails of Trade and Settlement

After New Mexico opened its trade to American merchants, a thriving commerce developed along the trail that ran from Missouri to Santa Fe. The first of these merchants to reach the New Mexican capital was William Becknell, who arrived with his train of goods late in 1821. Others followed rapidly. To protect themselves from the hostile Indians whose territory they had to cross, the traders traveled in large caravans, one or two of which would arrive in Santa Fe every summer. The federal government assisted them by providing troops when necessary and by appropriating money to purchase rights of passage from various tribes. Even so, the trip across the Cimarron desert and the southern Rockies was often difficult and hazardous. But profits from the exchange of textiles and other manufactured goods for furs, mules, and precious metals were substantial enough to make the risk worth taking.

Relations between the United States and Mexico soured following the Texas revolution, and this had a devastating effect on the Santa Fe trade. Much of the ill feeling was caused by further Anglo-American aggressions. An expedition of Texas businessmen and soldiers to Santa Fe in 1841 alarmed the Mexican authorities, who arrested its members. In retaliation, a volunteer force of Texas avengers attacked Mexican troops along the Santa Fe Trail. The Mexican government then moved to curtail the Santa Fe trade. In April 1842, it passed a new tariff banning the importation of many of the goods sold by American merchants and prohibiting the export of gold and silver. Further restrictions in 1843 denied American traders full access to the Santa Fe market.

The famous Oregon Trail was the great overland route that brought the wagon trains of American migrants to the West Coast during the 1840s. Extending for two thousand miles, across the northern Great Plains and the mountains beyond, it crossed the Rockies at South Pass and then forked; the main northern route led to the Willamette Valley of Oregon, but alternative trails were opened during the decade for overlanders heading for California. The journey from Missouri to the West Coast took about six months; most parties departed in May, hoping to arrive in November before the great snows hit the last mountain barriers.

After small groups had made their way to both Oregon and California in 1841 and 1842, a mass migration—mostly to Oregon—began in 1843. Within two years, five thousand Americans, living in the Willamette Valley south of the Columbia River, were demanding the extension of full American sovereignty over the Oregon Country.

The Mormon Trek

An important and distinctive group of pioneers followed the Oregon Trail as far as South Pass and then veered southwestward to establish a thriving colony in the region of the Great Salt Lake. These were Mormons, members of the largest religious denomination founded on American soil—the Church of Jesus Christ of Latter-day Saints.

The background of the Mormon trek was a history of persecution in the eastern states. Joseph Smith of Palmyra, New York, the founder of Mormonism, revealed in 1830 that he had received over many years a series of revelations that called upon him to establish Christ's pure church on earth. As the prophet of this faith, he published the *Book of Mormon,* a new scripture that he claimed to have discovered and translated with the aid of an angel. It was the record of a community of pious Jews who left the Holy Land six centuries before the birth of Christ and sailed to the American continent. After his crucifixion and resurrection, Christ appeared to this community and proclaimed the Gospel. Four hundred years later, a fratricidal war annihilated the believing Christians but not all of the descendents of the original Jewish migrants. Mormons held that the survivors had contributed to the ancestry of the American Indians. Smith and those he converted to his new faith were committed to restoring the pure religion that had once thrived on American soil by founding a western Zion where they could practice their faith unmolested and carry out their special mission to convert the Native Americans.

In the 1830s, the Mormons established communities in Ohio and Missouri, but the former went

Carl Christian Anton Christensen, Handcart, *ca. 1840. Instead of buying wagons and oxen, some groups of Mormon colonists made their trek to Deseret on foot, hauling their possessions in handcarts and working together as families to move their heavy loads.* ❖

bankrupt in the Panic of 1837 and the latter was the target of angry mobs and vigilante violence. After the Mormons lost the "war" they fought against the Missourians in 1839, Smith led his followers back across the Mississippi to Illinois, where he received a liberal charter from the state legislature to found a town at Nauvoo. Here the Mormons had a temporary measure of security and self-government, but Smith soon reported new revelations that engendered dissension among his followers and hostility from neighbor-

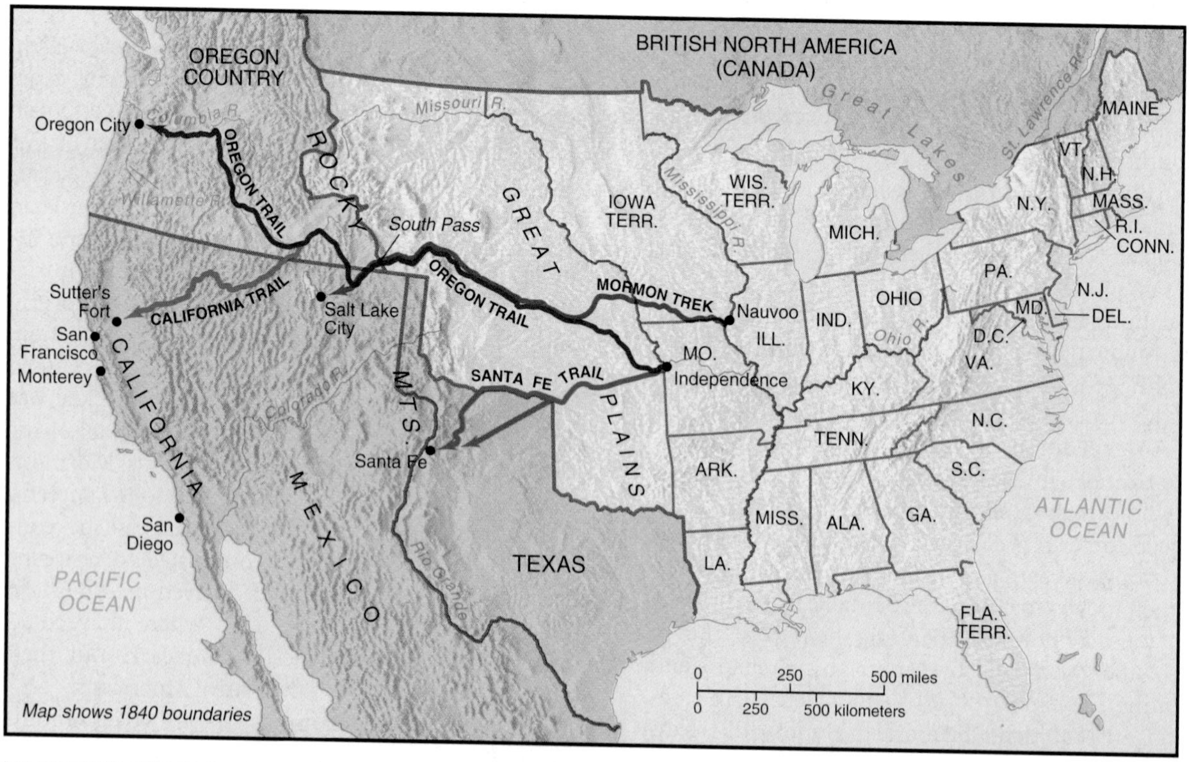

WESTERN TRAILS *Among the greatest hazards faced by those migrating to the West was the rough and unfamiliar terrain over which their wagon trains traveled.* ❖

ing "gentiles." Most controversial was his authorization of polygamy, or plural marriage. In 1844, Smith was killed by a mob while being held in jail in Carthage, Illinois, on a charge stemming from his quarrels with dissident Mormons who objected to his new policies.

The death of Smith confirmed the growing conviction of the Mormon leadership that they needed to move beyond the borders of the United States to establish their Zion in the wilderness. In late 1845, Smith's successor, Brigham Young, decided to send a party of fifteen hundred men to assess the chances of a colony in the vicinity of the Great Salt Lake (then part of Mexico). Nauvoo was quickly depopulated as twelve thousand Mormons took to the trail in 1846. The following year, Young himself arrived in Utah and sent back word to the thousands encamped along the trail that he had found the promised land.

The Mormon community that Young established in Utah is one of the great success stories of western settlement. In contrast to the rugged individualism and disorder that often characterized mining camps and other new communities, "the state of Deseret" (the name the Mormons originally applied to Utah) was a model of discipline and cooperation. Because of its communitarian form of social organization, its centralized government, and the religious dedication of its inhabitants, this frontier society was able to expand settlement in a planned and efficient way and develop a system of irrigation that "made the desert bloom."

Utah's main problem was the determination of its political status. When the Mormons first arrived, they were encroaching illegally into Mexican territory. After Utah came under American sovereignty in 1848, the state of Deseret fought to maintain its autonomy and its custom of polygamy against the efforts of the federal government to extend American law and set up the usual type of territorial administration. In 1857, President Buchanan sent a military force to bring Utah to heel, and the Mormons prepared to repel this "invasion." But after a heavy snow prevented the army from crossing the Rockies, Buchanan offered an olive branch in the form of a general pardon for Mormons who had violated federal law but agreed to cooperate with U.S. authorities in the future. The Mormons accepted, and in return, Brigham Young called off his plan to resist the army by force and accepted the nominal authority of an appointed territorial governor.

Manifest Destiny and the Mexican-American War

The rush of settlers beyond the nation's borders in the 1830s and 1840s inspired politicians and propagandists to call for annexation of those areas occupied by migrants. Some went further and proclaimed it was the **Manifest Destiny** of the United States to expand until it had absorbed all of North America, including Canada and Mexico. Such ambitions—and the policies they inspired—led to a major diplomatic confrontation with Great Britain and a war with Mexico.

Tyler and Texas

President John Tyler initiated the politics of Manifest Destiny. He was vice president when William Henry Harrison died in office in 1841 after serving scarcely a month. The first of America's "accidental presidents," Tyler was a states' rights, proslavery Virginian who had been picked as Harrison's running mate to broaden the appeal of the Whig ticket. Profoundly out of sympathy with the mainstream of his own party, he soon broke with the Whigs in Congress, who had united behind the latest version of Henry Clay's "American System." Although he lacked a base in either of the major parties, Tyler hoped to be elected president in his own right in 1844. To accomplish this difficult feat, he needed a new issue around which he could build a following that would cut across established party lines.

In 1843, Tyler decided to put the full weight of his administration behind the annexation of Texas. He anticipated that incorporation of the Lone Star Republic would be a popular move, especially in the South where it would feed the appetite for additional slave states. With the South solidly behind him, Tyler expected to have a good chance in the election of 1844.

To achieve his objective, Tyler enlisted the support of John C. Calhoun, the leading political defender of slavery and state sovereignty. Calhoun saw the annexation issue as a way of uniting the South and taking the offensive against the abolitionists. Success or failure in this effort would constitute a decisive test of whether the North was willing to give the southern states a fair share of national power and adequate assurances for the future of their way of life. If antislavery sentiment succeeded in blocking the acquisition of Texas, the Southerners would at least know where they stood and could begin to "calculate the value of the union."

To prepare the public for annexation, the Tyler administration launched a propaganda campaign in the summer of 1843 based on reports of British designs on Texas. According to information supplied by Duff Green, an unofficial American agent in England, the British were preparing to guarantee Texas independence and make a loan to the financially troubled republic in return for the abolition of slavery. It is doubtful the British had such intentions, but the stories were believed and used to give urgency to the annexation cause.

Secretary of State Abel Upshur, a proslavery Virginian and protégé of Calhoun, began negotiating an annexation treaty. After Upshur was killed in an accident, Calhoun replaced him and carried the negotiations to a successful conclusion. When the treaty was brought before the Senate in 1844, Calhoun denounced the British for attempting to subvert the South's essential system of labor and racial control by using Texas as a base for abolitionist operations. According to the supporters of Tyler and Calhoun, the South's security and well-being—and by extension that of the nation—required the immediate incorporation of Texas into the Union.

The strategy of linking annexation explicitly to the interests of the South and slavery led northern antislavery Whigs to charge that the whole scheme was a proslavery plot meant to advance the interest of one section of the nation against the other. Consequently, the Senate rejected the treaty by a decisive vote of 35 to 16 in June 1844. Tyler then attempted to bring Texas into the Union through an alternative means—a joint resolution of both houses of Congress admitting it as a state—but Congress adjourned before the issue came to a vote, and the whole question hung fire in anticipation of the election of 1844.

The Triumph of Polk and Annexation

Tyler's initiative made the future of Texas the central issue in the 1844 campaign. But party lines held firm, and the president himself was unable to capitalize on the issue because his stand was not in line with the views of either party. Tyler tried to run as an independent, but his failure to gain significant support eventually forced him to withdraw from the race.

If the Democratic party convention had been held in 1843—as it was originally scheduled—ex-President Martin Van Buren would have won the nomination. But postponement of the Democratic conclave until May 1844 weakened his chances. In the meantime, the annexation question came to the fore, and Van Buren was forced to take a stand on it. He persisted in the view he had held as president—that incorporation of Texas would risk war with Mexico, arouse sectional strife, and destroy the unity of the Democratic party. Fears of sectional and party division seemed confirmed in 1844 when the dominant party faction in Van Buren's home state of New York came out against Tyler's Texas policy. In an effort to keep the issue out of the campaign, Van Buren struck a gentleman's agreement with Henry Clay, the overwhelming favorite for the Whig nomination. Van Buren and Clay agreed they would both publicly oppose immediate annexation.

Van Buren's letter opposing annexation appeared shortly before the Democratic convention, and it cost him the nomination. Angry southern delegates, who secured a rule requiring approval by a two-thirds vote, blocked Van Buren's nomination. After several ballots, a dark horse candidate—James K. Polk of Tennessee—emerged triumphant. Polk, a protégé of Andrew Jackson, had been speaker of the House of Representatives and governor of Tennessee.

An avowed expansionist, Polk ran on a platform calling for the simultaneous annexation of Texas and assertion of American claims to all of Oregon. He identified himself and his party with the popular cause of turning the United States into a continental nation, an aspiration that attracted support from all parts of the country. His was a much more astute political strategy than the overtly prosouthern expansionism advocated by Tyler and Calhoun. The Whig nominee, Henry Clay, was basically antiexpansionist, but his sense of the growing popularity of Texas annexation among southern Whigs caused him to waffle on the issue during the campaign. This vacillation in turn cost Clay the support of a small but crucial group of northern antislavery Whigs, who defected to the abolitionist Liberty party.

Polk won the fall election by a relatively narrow popular margin. His triumph in the electoral college—170 votes to 105—was secured by victories in New York and Michigan, where the Liberty party candidate, James G. Birney, had taken away enough votes from Clay to affect the outcome. The closeness of the election meant the Democrats had something less than a clear mandate to implement their expansionist policies, but this did not prevent them from claiming that the people had backed an aggressive campaign to extend the borders of the United States.

The Liberty Party Swings an Election

Candidate	Party	Actual Vote in New York	National Electoral Vote	If Liberty Voters had Voted Whig	Projected Electoral Vote
Polk	Democratic	237,588	170	237,588	134
Clay	Whig	232,482	105	248,294	141
Birney	Liberty	15,812	0	—	—

The Election of 1844

Candidate	Party	Popular Vote	Electoral Vote
Polk	Democratic	1,338,464	170
Clay	Whig	1,300,097	105
Birney	Liberty	62,300	—

After the election, Congress reconvened to consider the annexation of Texas. The mood had changed as a result of Polk's victory, and some leading senators from both parties who had initially opposed Tyler's scheme for annexation by joint resolution of Congress now changed their position. As a result, annexation was approved a few days before Polk took office.

The Doctrine of Manifest Destiny

The expansionist mood that accompanied Polk's election and the annexation of Texas was given a name and a rationale in the summer of 1845. John L. O'Sullivan, a proponent of the Young America movement and editor of the influential *United States Magazine and Democratic Review,* charged that foreign governments were conspiring to block the annexation of Texas in an effort to thwart "the fulfillment of our manifest destiny to overspread the continent allotted by providence for the free development of our yearly multiplying millions."

Besides coining the phrase Manifest Destiny, O'Sullivan pointed to the three main ideas that lay behind it. One was that God was on the side of American expansionism. This notion came naturally out of the long tradition, going back to the New England Puritans, that identified the growth of America with the divinely ordained success of a chosen people. A second idea, implied in the phrase *free development,* was that the spread of American rule meant what other propagandists for expansion described as "extending the area of freedom." Democratic institutions and local self-government would follow the flag if areas claimed by autocratic foreign governments were annexed to the United States. O'Sullivan's third premise was that population growth required the outlet that territorial acquisitions would provide. Behind this notion lurked a fear that growing numbers would lead to diminished opportunity and a European-type polarization of social classes if the restless and the ambitious were not given new lands to settle and exploit.

In its most extreme form, the doctrine of Manifest Destiny meant that the United States would someday occupy the entire North American continent, that nothing less would appease its land-hungry population. "Make way, I say, for the young American Buffalo," bellowed a Democratic orator in 1844, "—he has not yet got land enough. . . . I tell you we will give him Oregon for his summer shade, and the region of Texas as his winter pasture. (Applause) Like all of his race, he wants salt, too. Well, he shall have the use of two oceans—the mighty Pacific and the turbulent Atlantic. . . . He shall not stop his career until he slakes his thirst in the frozen ocean. (Cheers)"

Polk and the Oregon Question

In 1845 and 1846, the United States came closer to armed conflict with Great Britain than at any time since the War of 1812. The willingness of some Americans to go to war over Oregon was expressed in the rallying cry "Fifty-four forty or fight" (referring to the latitude of the northern boundary of the desired territory). This slogan was actually coined by Whigs seeking to ridicule Democratic expansionists, but Democrats later took it over as a vivid expression of their demand for what is now British Columbia. Polk fed this expansionist fever by laying claim in his inaugural address to all of the Oregon Country, then jointly occupied by Britain and the United States. Privately, however, he was willing to accept the 49th parallel as a dividing line. What made the situation so tense was that Polk was dedicated to an aggressive diplomacy of bluff and bluster. As historian David M. Pletcher has put it, Polk "set forth on a foreign policy of strong stands, over-stated arguments, and menacing

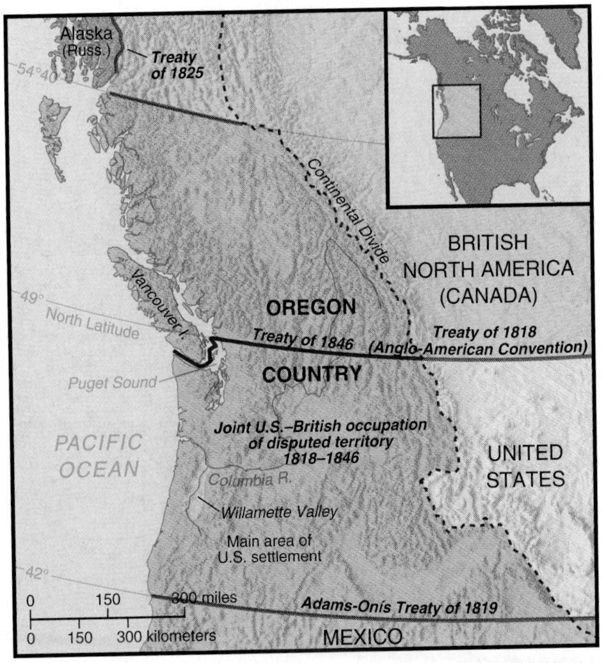

NORTHWEST BOUNDARY DISPUTE *President Polk's policy of bluff and bluster nearly involved the United States in a war with Great Britain over the disputed boundary in Oregon.*

public announcements, not because he wanted war but because he felt that this was the only policy which his foreign adversaries would understand."

In July 1845, Polk authorized Secretary of State James Buchanan to reply to the latest British request for terms by offering a boundary along the 49th parallel. The offer did not meet the British demand for all of Vancouver Island and free navigation of the Columbia River, and the British ambassador rejected the proposal out of hand. This rebuff infuriated Polk who saw his offer as a generous and conciliatory retreat from his public position. He subsequently withdrew it and refused a British request of December 1845 that he renew the offer and submit the dispute to international arbitration. Instead he called on Congress to terminate the agreement for joint occupation of the Pacific Northwest. Congress complied in April 1846, and Polk submitted the required year's notice to the British on May 21.

Since cancelling the joint agreement implied that the United States would attempt to extend its jurisdiction north to 54°40', the British government decided to take the diplomatic initiative in an effort to avert war, while at the same time dispatching warships to the Western Hemisphere in case conciliation failed. Their new proposal accepted the 49th parallel as the border to a point where the boundary would veer south so that Britain could retain Vancouver Island. It also provided for British navigation rights on the Columbia River. When the draft treaty was received in June, Polk refused either to endorse or reject it and took the unusual step of submitting it directly to the Senate for advice. The Senate recommended the treaty be accepted with the single change that British rights to navigate the Columbia be made temporary. It was ratified in that form on June 15.

This 1846 cartoon titled "This Is the House That Polk Built" shows President Polk sitting forlornly in a house of cards, which represents the delicately balanced issues facing him. ❖

Polk was prompted to settle the Oregon question because he now had a war with Mexico on his hands. His reckless and aggressive diplomacy had brought the nation within an eyelash of being involved in two wars at the same time. American policymakers got what they wanted from the Oregon treaty, namely Puget Sound and the strait that led into it south of Vancouver Island. Acquisition of this splendid natural harbor gave the United States its first deepwater port on the Pacific. Polk's initial demand for all of Oregon was made partly for domestic political consumption and partly to bluff the British into making more concessions. It was a dangerous game on both fronts. When Polk finally agreed to the solution, he alienated expansionist advocates in the Old Northwest who had supported his call for "all of Oregon."

For many Northerners, the promise of new acquisitions in the Pacific Northwest was the only thing that made annexation of Texas palatable. They hoped new free states could be created to counterbalance the admission of slaveholding Texas to the Union. As this prospect receded, the charge of antislavery advocates that Texas annexation was a southern plot became more believable; to Northerners, Polk began to look more and more like a president concerned mainly with furthering the interests of his native region.

War with Mexico

While the United States was avoiding a war with Great Britain, it was getting into one with Mexico. Although they had recognized Texas independence in 1845, the Mexicans rejected the Lone Star Republic's dubious claim to the unsettled territory between the Nueces River and the Rio Grande. When the United States annexed Texas and assumed its claim to the disputed area, Mexico broke off diplomatic relations and prepared for armed conflict.

Polk responded by placing troops in Louisiana on the alert and by dispatching John Slidell as an emissary to Mexico City in the hope he could resolve the boundary dispute and also persuade the Mexicans to sell New Mexico and California to the United States. The Mexican government refused to receive Slidell

Handkerchief depicting Major General Zachary Taylor in battle scenes from the Mexican War. When the popular hero displeased President Polk with his actions in the capture of Monterrey, he was replaced by Winfield Scott. Scott carried out Polk's plan for the attack on the port city of Veracruz, which led to the capture of Mexico City. ❖

because the nature of his appointment ignored the fact that regular diplomatic relations were suspended. While Slidell was cooling his heels in Mexico City in January 1846, Polk ordered General Zachary Taylor, commander of American forces in the Southwest, to advance well beyond the Nueces and proceed toward the Rio Grande, thus invading territory claimed by both sides.

By April, Taylor had taken up a position near Matamoros on the Rio Grande. On the opposite bank of the river, Mexican forces had assembled and erected a fort. On April 24, sixteen hundred Mexican soldiers crossed the river and the following day met and attacked a small American detachment, killing eleven and capturing the rest. After learning of the incident, Taylor sent word to the president: "Hostilities," he reported, "may now be considered as commenced."

The news was neither unexpected nor unwelcome. Polk in fact was already preparing his war message to Congress when he learned of the fighting on the Rio Grande. A short and decisive war, he had concluded, would force the cession of California and New Mexico to the United States. When Congress declared war on May 13, American agents and an "exploring expedition" under John C. Frémont were already in California stirring up dissension against Mexican rule, and ships of the U.S. Navy lay waiting expectantly off the shore. Two days later, Polk ordered a force under Colonel Stephen Kearny to march to Santa Fe and take possession of New Mexico.

The **Mexican-American War** lasted much longer than expected because the Mexicans refused to make peace despite a succession of military defeats. In the first major campaign of the conflict, Taylor followed up his victory in two battles fought north of the Rio Grande by crossing the river, taking Matamoros, and marching on Monterrey. In September, his forces assaulted and captured this major city of northern Mexico after overcoming fierce resistance.

Taylor's controversial decision to allow the Mexican garrison to go free and his unwillingness or inability to advance farther into Mexico angered Polk and led him to adopt a new strategy for winning the war and a new commander to implement it. General Winfield Scott was ordered to prepare an amphibious attack on Veracruz with the aim of placing an American army within striking distance of Mexico City itself. With half his forces detached for the new invasion, Taylor was left to hold his position in northern Mexico. But this did not deprive him of a final moment of glory. At Buena Vista, in February 1847, he claimed victory over a sizable Mexican army sent northward to dislodge him. Despite his unpopularity with the administration, Taylor was hailed as a national hero and a possible candidate for president.

Meanwhile, the Kearny expedition captured Santa Fe, proclaimed the annexation of New Mexico by the United States, and set off for California. There they found that American settlers, in cooperation with John C. Frémont's exploring expedition, had revolted against Mexican authorities and declared their independence as the Bear Flag Republic. The navy had also captured the port of Monterey. With the addition of Kearny's troops, a relatively small number of Americans were able to take possession of California against scattered and disorganized Mexican opposition, a process that was completed by the beginning of 1847.

The decisive Veracruz campaign was slow to develop because of the massive and careful preparations required. But in March 1847, the main American army under General Scott finally landed near that crucial port city and laid siege to it. Veracruz fell after eighteen days, and then Scott began his advance on Mexico City. In the most important single battle of the war, Scott met forces under General Santa Anna at Cerro Gordo on April 17 and 18. The Mexicans occupied an apparently impregnable position on high ground blocking the way to Mexico City. A daring flanking maneuver that required soldiers to scramble up the mountainsides enabled Scott to win the decisive victory that opened the road to the Mexican capital. By August, American troops were drawn up in front of Mexico City. After a temporary armistice, a brief respite that the Mexicans used to regroup and improve their defenses, Scott ordered the massive assault that captured the city on September 14.

Settlement of the Mexican-American War

Accompanying Scott's army was a diplomat, Nicholas P. Trist, who was authorized to negotiate a peace treaty whenever the Mexicans decided they had had enough. Despite a sequence of American victories and the imminent fall of Mexico City, Trist made little progress. No Mexican leader was willing to invite the wrath of an intensely proud and patriotic citizenry by agreeing to the kind of terms that Polk wanted to impose. Even after the United States had achieved an overwhelming military victory, Trist found it difficult to exact an acceptable treaty from the Mexican government. In November, Polk ordered Trist to return to Washington. Radical adherents of Manifest Destiny were now clamoring for the annexation of all Mexico, and Polk himself may have been momentarily tempted by the chance to move from military occupation to outright annexation.

Trist ignored Polk's instructions and lingered in Mexico City. On February 2, 1848, he signed a treaty that gained all the concessions he had been commissioned to obtain. The **Treaty of Guadalupe Hidalgo** ceded New Mexico and California to the United States for $15 million, established the Rio Grande as the border between Texas and Mexico, and promised that the U.S. government would assume the substantial claims of American citizens against Mexico. The treaty also provided that the Mexican residents of the new territories would become U.S. citizens. When the agreement reached Washington, Polk censured Trist for disobeying orders but approved most of his treaty, which he sent to the Senate for ratification. Senate approval by a vote of 38 to 14 came on March 10.

As a result of the Mexican-American War, the United States gained 500,000 square miles of territory. The treaty of 1848 enlarged the size of the nation by about 20 percent, adding to its domain the present states of California, Utah, New Mexico, Nevada, and Arizona and parts of Colorado and Wyoming. Soon those interested in a southern route for a transcontinental railroad pressed for even more territory along the southern border of the cession. That pressure led in 1853 to the Gadsden Purchase, through which the United States acquired the southernmost parts of present-day Arizona and New

Richard Caton Woodville's, War News from Mexico, *suggests the role of the newspaper in keeping the public informed of developments in the expanding nation's quest for new territory.* ✣

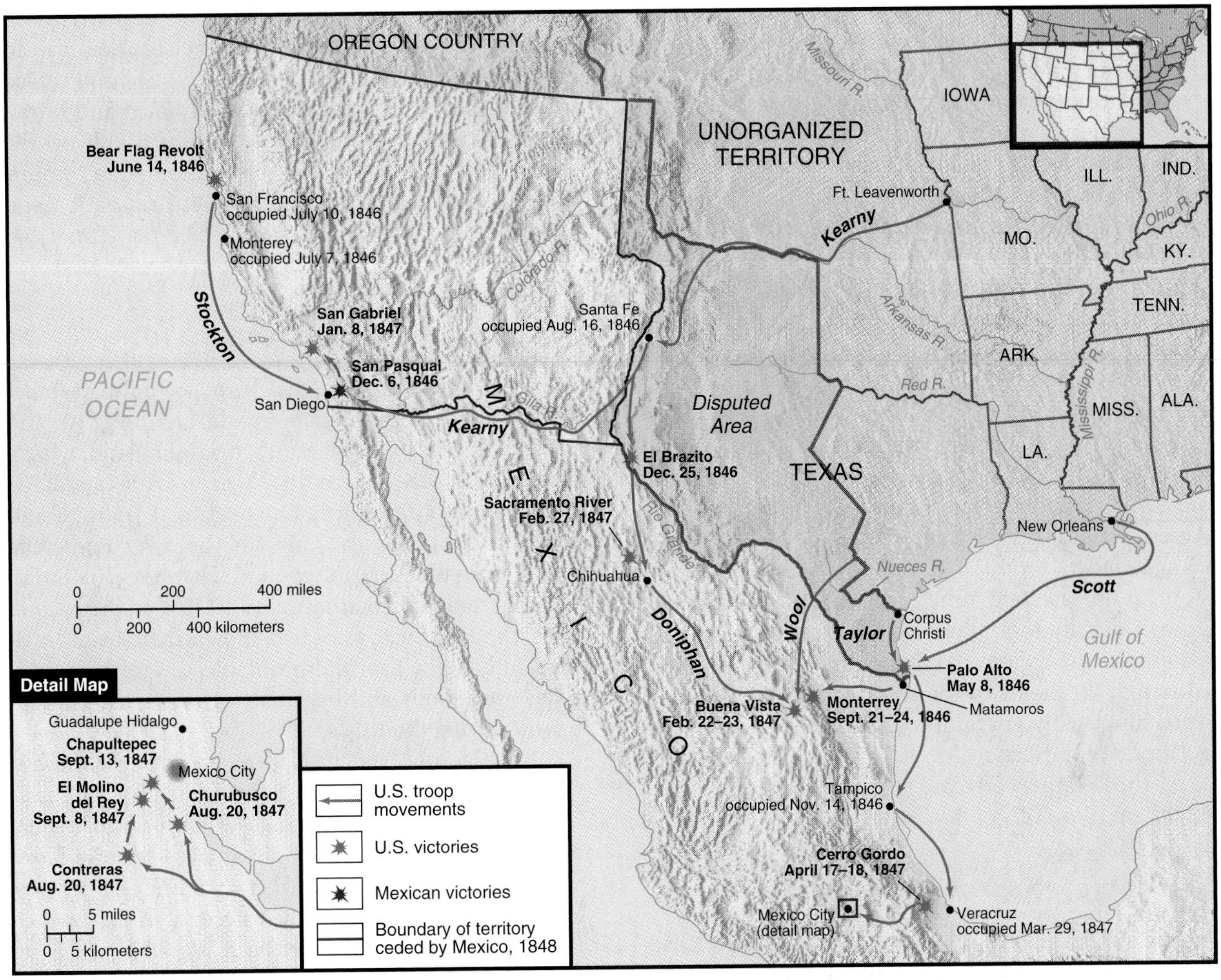

THE MEXICAN-AMERICAN WAR *The Mexican-American War added half a million square miles of territory to the United States, but the cost was high: $100 million and 13,000 lives.* ❖

Mexico. But one intriguing question remains. Why, given the expansionist spirit of the age, did the campaign to acquire *all* of Mexico fail?

According to historian Frederick Merk, a major factor was the peculiar combination of racism and anticolonialism that dominated American opinion. It was one thing to acquire thinly populated areas that could be settled by "Anglo-Saxon" pioneers. It was something else again to incorporate a large population that was mainly of mixed Spanish and Indian origin. These "mongrels," charged racist opponents of the "All Mexico" movement, could never be fit citizens of a self-governing republic. They would have to be ruled in the way the British governed India, and the possession of colonial dependencies was contrary to American ideals and traditions.

Merk's thesis sheds light on why the general public had little appetite for swallowing all of Mexico, but those actually making policy had more mundane and practical reasons for being satisfied with what was obtained at Guadalupe Hidalgo. What they had really wanted all along, historian Norman Graebner contended, were the great California harbors of San Francisco and San Diego. From these ports, Americans could trade directly with the Orient and dominate the commerce of the Pacific. Once acquisition of California had been assured, policymakers had little incentive to press for more Mexican territory.

The war with Mexico divided the American public and provoked political dissension. A majority of the Whig party opposed the war in principle, arguing that the United States had no valid claims to the area south of the Nueces. Whig congressmen voted for military appropriations while the conflict was going on, but they constantly criticized the president for starting it. More ominous was the charge of some Northerners from both parties that the real purpose of the war was to spread the institution of slavery and increase the political power of the southern states. While battles were being fought in Mexico, Congress was debating the Wilmot Proviso, a proposal to prohibit slavery in any territories that might be acquired from Mexico. A bitter sectional quarrel over the status of slavery in new areas was a major legacy of the Mexican-American War (see Chapter 14).

The domestic controversies aroused by the war and the propaganda of Manifest Destiny revealed the limits of mid-nineteenth-century American expansionism and put a damper on additional efforts to extend the nation's boundaries. Concerns about slavery and race impeded acquisition of new territory in Latin America and the Caribbean. Resolution of the Oregon dispute clearly indicated that the United States was not willing to go to war with a powerful adversary to obtain large chunks of British North America, and the old ambition of incorporating Canada faded. From 1848 until the revival of expansionism in the late nineteenth century, American growth usually took the form of populating and developing the vast territory already acquired. Although the rights of former inhabitants of Mexico were supposedly guaranteed by treaty, they in effect became second-class citizens of the United States. (See the Feature Essay, "Hispanic America After 1848," pp. 376–377.)

Internal Expansionism

Young American expansionists saw a clear link between acquisition of new territory and other forms of material growth and development. In 1844, Samuel F. B. Morse perfected and demonstrated his electric telegraph, a device that would make it possible to communicate rapidly over the expanse of a continental nation. Simultaneously, the railroad was becoming increasingly important as a means of moving people and goods over the same great distances. Improvements in manufacturing and agricultural methods led to an upsurge in the volume and range of internal trade, and the beginnings of mass immigration were providing human resources for the exploitation of new areas and economic opportunities.

After gold was discovered in newly acquired California in 1848, a flood of emigrants from the East and several foreign nations arrived by ship or wagon train, their appetites whetted by the thought of striking it rich. The gold they unearthed spurred the national economy, and the rapid growth of population centers on the Pacific Coast inspired projects for transcontinental telegraph lines and railroad tracks.

Despite the best efforts of the Young Americans, the spirit of Manifest Destiny and the thirst for acquiring new territory waned after the Mexican-American War. The expansionist impulse was channeled instead into internal development. Although the nation ceased to grow in size, the technological advances and population increase of the 1840s continued during the 1850s. The result was an acceleration of economic growth, a substantial increase in industrialization and urbanization, and the emergence of a new American working class.

The Triumph of the Railroad

More than anything else, the rise of the railroad transformed the American economy during the 1840s and 1850s. The technology came from England, where steam locomotives were first used to haul cars along tracks at the beginning of the century. In 1830 and 1831, two American railroads began commercial operation—the Charleston and Hamburg in South Carolina and the Baltimore and Ohio in Maryland. After these pioneer lines had shown that steam locomotion was practical and profitable, several other railroads were built and began to carry passengers and freight during the 1830s.

Canals, however, proved to be strong competitors, especially for the freight business. By 1840, railroads had 2818 miles of track—a figure almost equal to the combined length of all canals—but the latter still carried a much larger volume of goods. Passengers might prefer the speed of trains, which reached astonishing velocities of 20 to 30 miles an hour, but the lower unit cost of transporting freight on the canalboats prevented most shippers from changing their habits. Furthermore, states such as New York and Pennsylvania had invested heavily in canals and resisted chartering a competitive form of transportation. Most of the early railroads reached out from port cities, such as Boston and Baltimore, that did not have good canal routes to the interior. Steam locomotion provided them a chance to cut into the enormous commerce that flowed along the Erie Canal and gave New York an advantage in the scramble for western trade.

During the 1840s, rails extended beyond the northeastern and Middle Atlantic states, and mileage increased more than threefold, reaching a total of more than 9000 miles by 1850. Expansion, fueled by massive European investment, was even greater in the following decade, when about 20,000 miles of additional track were laid. By 1860, all the states east of the Mississippi had rail service, and a traveler could go by train from New York to Chicago and return by way of Memphis. Throughout the 1840s and 1850s, railroads cut deeply into the freight business of the canals and

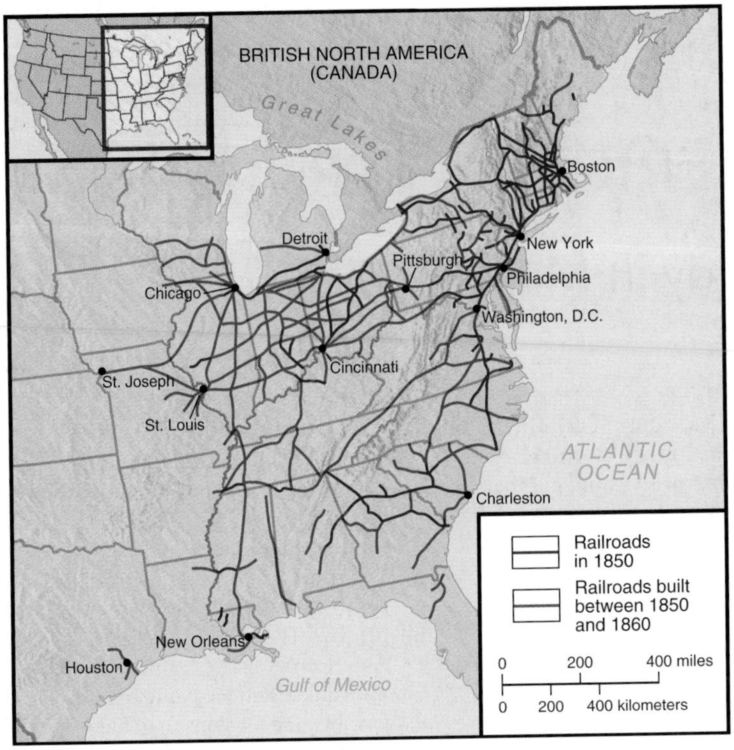

RAILROADS, 1850 AND 1860 *During the 1840s and 1850s, railroad lines moved rapidly westward. By 1860, more than 30,000 miles of track had been laid.* ❖

succeeded in driving many of them out of business. The cost of hauling goods by rail decreased dramatically because of improved track construction and the introduction of powerful locomotives that could haul more cars. New York and Pennsylvania were slow to encourage rail transportation because of their early commitment to canals, but by the 1850s, both states had accepted the inevitable and were promoting massive railroad building.

The development of railroads had an enormous effect on the economy as a whole. Although the burgeoning demand for iron rails was initially met mainly by importation from England, it eventually spurred development of the domestic iron industry. Since railroads required an enormous outlay of capital, their promoters pioneered new methods for financing business enterprise. At a time when most manufacturing and mercantile concerns were still owned by families or partnerships, the railroad companies sold stock to the general public and helped to set the pattern for the separation of ownership and control that characterizes the modern corporation. They also developed new types of securities, such as "preferred stock" (with no voting rights but the assurance of a fixed rate of return) and long-term bonds at a set rate of interest.

The gathering and control of private capital did not fully meet the desires of the early railroad barons. State and local governments, convinced that railroads were the key to their future prosperity, loaned the railroads money, bought their stock, and guaranteed their bonds. Despite the dominant philosophy of laissez-faire (which meant that the government should keep its hands off the economy), the federal government became involved by surveying the routes of projected lines and providing land grants. In 1850, for example, several million acres of public land were granted to the Illinois Central. In all, forty companies received such aid before 1860, setting a precedent for the massive land grants of the post-Civil War era.

The Industrial Revolution Takes Off

While railroads were initiating a revolution in transportation, American industry was entering a new phase of rapid and sustained growth. The factory mode of production, which had originated before 1840 in the cotton mills of New England, was extended to a variety of other products (see Chapter 9). The weaving and processing of wool, instead of being carried on in different locations, was concentrated in single production units beginning in the 1830s, and by 1860 some of the largest textile mills in the country were producing wool cloth. In the coal and iron regions of eastern Pennsylvania, iron was being forged and rolled in factories by 1850. Among the other

Feature Essay

HISPANIC AMERICA AFTER 1848

A Case Study in Majority Rule

With the discovery of gold in 1848, more than one thousand Californians of Mexican ancestry joined the frenetic rush to the Sierras. Among them was Don Antonio Franco Coronel, a Los Angeles school teacher, who led a group of fellow *Californios* into the rich goldfields. Just months before the expedition, the United States and Mexico had concluded the Treaty of Guadalupe Hidalgo, which transformed Coronel and his companions from Mexicans to Americans. At the insistence of the Mexican government, the treaty stipulated that Mexicans living in the newly acquired territories would be granted "all the rights of citizens of the United States . . . according to the principles of the Constitution." Coronel's gold-seeking enterprise would put that promise to the test. While panning rivers and staking claims, Coronel's company came into competitive contact with large numbers of Yankee miners. The interactions between the two ethnic communities suggested that a rough road lay ahead for Hispanic Americans.

Upon arriving in gold country, Coronel and his men immediately hit pay dirt. In the first day alone, Coronel pulled 45 ounces of gold from the ground; within eight days, one of his associates had amassed a pile of gold weighing a staggering 52 pounds. The *Californios* seemed to have a head start in the race for gold. They understood the terrain, cooperated among themselves, and were familiar with the best mining techniques. Not surprisingly, their dramatic successes stirred the envy of their Anglo-American competitors. Though the Mexican-American War had technically made the Yankee and Hispanic miners compatriots, the tensions of gold fever exposed the shallowness of that new relationship.

Blessing of the Enrequita Mine, 1860, by Alexander Edouart. Spaniards and Mexicans, men and women, surround the makeshift altar where the priest is saying the blessing to dedicate the Enrequita Mine in northern California. The idyllic scene does not hint at the violent and rough treatment Hispanic miners experienced during the California gold rush days. ❖

After a year of relatively peaceful competition, Anglo miners began to express their resentments. Lumping *Californios* with all other "foreigners," they unleashed a barrage of physical and political attacks against their competitors. Lynch mobs, camp riots, and legal harassment were common forms of Yankee intimidation. Despite their entitlements to the rights of citizenship, the *Californios* were badgered and bullied into retreat. Fearing for his life, Coronel returned to Southern California, where Hispanics still outnumbered the newcomers. Earning prestige and prosperity in Los Angeles, Coronel went on to become mayor and state treasurer. But to the end of his life, he still painfully remembered his experiences in Northern California, where his rights as a U.S. citizen were so easily disregarded by his fellow Americans.

Coronel's experiences exemplify two truths about the effect U.S. expansion had on the lives of Mexicans who suddenly found themselves in American territory. First, in areas where Anglo-American settlement grew rapidly—such as Northern California—the Hispanic community typically faced discrimination, intimidation, and a denial of the very civil rights that Guadalupe Hidalgo had supposedly guaranteed. Second, in areas where the Hispanic population remained a majority—such as Southern California—Spanish-speaking Americans were able to exercise the rights of republican citizenship, often wielding considerable political influence. Coronel had a taste of both experiences, going from intimidated miner to powerful politician. However, as Anglo settlers began to stream into Southern California, even that region ceased to be a safe haven for Hispanic rights.

West Side Main Plaza, San Antonio, Texas by W. G. M. Samuel. San Antonio's religious and political history is reflected in this 1849 painting of the city's main plaza. The building at the center is San Fernando Cathedral; behind the cathedral an American flag flies over the nearby Military Plaza. The large house at the far right is the home of José Cassiano, a Mexican who sided with the Texans in the revolution against Mexico. ❖

By the mid-1840s Hispanics living in Texas, known as *Tejanos,* were outnumbered by Anglos at a ratio of twenty-to-one. True to the pattern described above, this decided minority faced intense prejudice. Among the most notable victims of this prejudice was Juan Sequin, a hero of the Texas war for independence (see p. 363). Perhaps no *Tejano* family fell further or faster than the posterity of Don Martin de Leon. The scion of an aristocratic family, de Leon had spearheaded Spanish efforts to colonize Texas and continued to organize settlements after Mexican independence. Establishing extensive cattle ranches, the de Leons enjoyed prominence and wealth on their holdings. As with most *Tejanos,* they fervently supported the struggle for Texan independence, fighting shoulder to shoulder with their Anglo neighbors. But when the war ended, the de Leon estate fell under siege from the surging wave of new settlers. Relying on the intricacies of Anglo-American law and the power of an electoral majority, the newcomers quickly encroached on de Leon's lands. With frightening rapidity, the de Leon family was reduced from its preeminent position to abject poverty.

The de Leons were not alone. A contemporary observed that many Anglo settlers worked "dark intrigues against the native families, whose only crime was that they owned large tracts of land and desirable property." Even after U.S. annexation of the Lone Star Republic, Hispanics continued to be pushed off their land. In 1856 a Texas newspaper reported that "The people of Matagorda county have held a meeting and ordered every Mexican to leave the county. To strangers this may seem wrong, but we hold it to be perfectly right and highly necessary." For many Mexican Americans, life on U.S. soil taught the cruelest lesson in white man's democracy.

Yet majority rule actually worked to the favor of Hispanics living in New Mexico, where they enjoyed numerical dominance. When U.S. troops entered Santa Fe in 1846, Albino Chacón, a prominent city judge, controlled his own future. Although he had been loyal to the Mexican government throughout the war, the U.S. Army offered him the opportunity to retain his judgeship. Given similar offers, other New Mexicans who had initially opposed the U.S. invasion accepted positions of prominence, such as Donanciano Vigil, who served as interim governor of the territory. But Chacón lived by a strict code of honor and could not switch loyalties so easily. Opting for exile, Chacón moved out of Santa Fe, left the practice of law, and took up farming. Aside from such self-imposed changes, however, American rule actually had little impact on most New Mexicans' lives. Hispanics still formed the demographic and political backbone of the territory and often served their new nation with distinction. Chacón's own son, Rafael, served as a Union officer during the Civil War, winning acclaim in defending New Mexico against a Confederate invasion from Texas, and was eventually elected as territorial senator. Rafael's son studied law at Notre Dame and held several important positions in the Department of Justice. Majority status afforded New Mexican Hispanics opportunities in the American system that were denied their compatriots living in Anglo-dominated regions.

As settlement increased throughout the century, such Hispanic-controlled communities dwindled. The rise of the railroad acted as a funnel through which Anglo-Americans poured into western territories, and remaining pockets of Hispanic dominance rapidly disappeared. American majoritarianism and racism combined to place Hispanics in positions subordinate to those of the Anglo newcomers. Throughout the region the story was sadly similar; as Hispanic Americans lost their majority status, they also lost many of their basic rights.

industries that adopted the factory system during this period were those producing firearms, clocks, and sewing machines.

The essential features of the emerging mode of production were the gathering of a supervised workforce in a single place, the payment of cash wages to workers, the use of interchangeable parts, and manufacture by "continuous process." Within a factory setting, standardized parts, manufactured separately and in bulk, could be efficiently and rapidly assembled into a final product by an ordered sequence of continuously repeated operations. Mass production, which involved the division of labor into a series of relatively simple and repetitive tasks, contrasted sharply with the traditional craft mode of production, in which a single worker produced the entire product out of raw materials.

The bulk of American manufacturing of the 1840s and 1850s, however, was still carried on by traditional methods. Small workshops continued to predominate in most industries, and some relatively large factories were not yet mechanized. But mass production was clearly the wave of the future. The transformation of a craft into a modern industry is well illustrated by the evolution of shoemaking. The independent cobbler producing shoes for order was first challenged by a putting-out system involving the assignment of various tasks to physically separated workers and then was virtually displaced by the great shoe factories that by the 1860s were operating in cities such as Lynn, Massachusetts.

New technology often played an important role in the transition to mass production. Just as power looms and spinning machinery had made textile mills possible, the development of new and more reliable machines or industrial techniques revolutionized other industries. Elias Howe's invention of the sewing machine in 1846 laid the basis for the ready-to-wear clothing industry and also contributed to the mechanization of shoemaking. During the 1840s, iron manufacturers adopted the British practice of using coal rather than charcoal for smelting and thus produced a metal better suited to industrial needs. Charles Goodyear's discovery in 1839 of the process for the vulcanization of rubber made a new range of manufactured items available to the American consumer, most notably the overshoe.

Perhaps the greatest triumph of American technology during the mid-nineteenth century was the development of the world's most sophisticated and

❖ A Look at the Past ❖

Steel Plow

In 1837, John Deere invented a plow with a smooth steel blade and successfully tested it on a farm in Illinois. Earlier plows had a blade made of cast iron. Deere's plow quickly became popular with pioneer farmers in the Midwest as an essential tool in cultivating the land. Why do you think Deere's new plow was necessary in the midwestern prairie? Why wouldn't a cast iron plow used in the East work equally well?

A revolution in farming followed the introduction of new farm implements such as Cyrus McCormick's reaper, which could do ten times the work of a single person. The lithograph, by an anonymous artist, is titled The Testing of the First Reaping Machine near Steele's Tavern, Virginia, 1831. ❖

CHRONOLOGY

1822	Santa Fe opened to American traders
1823	Earliest American settlers arrive in Texas
1830	Mexico attempts to halt American migration to Texas
1831	American railroads begin commercial operation
1834	Cyrus McCormick patents mechanical reaper
1835	Revolution breaks out in Texas
1836	Texas becomes independent republic
1837	John Deere invents steel plow
1841	President John Tyler inaugurated
1842	Webster-Ashburton Treaty fixes border between Maine and New Brunswick
1843	Mass migration to Oregon begins ❖ Mexico closes Santa Fe trade to Americans
1844	Samuel F. B. Morse demonstrates electric telegraph ❖ James K. Polk elected president on platform of expansionism
1845	Mass immigration from Europe begins ❖ United States annexes Texas ❖ John L. O'Sullivan coins slogan "Manifest Destiny"
1846	War with Mexico breaks out ❖ United States and Great Britain resolve diplomatic crisis over Oregon
1847	American conquest of California completed ❖ Mormons settle Utah ❖ American forces under Zachary Taylor defeat Mexicans at Buena Vista ❖ Winfield Scott's army captures Veracruz and defeats Mexicans at Cerro Gordo ❖ Mexico City falls to American invaders
1848	Treaty of Guadalupe Hidalgo consigns California and New Mexico to United States ❖ Gold discovered in California
1849	"Forty-niners" rush to California to dig for gold
1858	War between Utah Mormons and U.S. forces averted

CONCLUSION: THE COSTS OF EXPANSION

By 1860, industrial expansion and immigration had created a working class of men and women who seemed destined for a life of low-paid wage labor. This reality stood in contrast to America's self-image as a land of opportunity and upward mobility. Wage labor was popularly viewed as a temporary condition from which workers were supposed to extricate themselves by hard work and frugality. According to Abraham Lincoln, speaking in 1859 of the North's "free-labor" society, "there is no such thing as a freeman being fatally fixed for life, in the condition of a hired laborer." This ideal still had some validity in rapidly developing regions of the western states, but it was mostly myth when applied to the increasingly foreign-born industrial workers of the Northeast.

Both internal and external expansion had come at a heavy cost. Tensions associated with class and ethnic rivalries were only one part of the price of rapid economic development. The acquisition of new territories became politically divisive and would soon lead to a catastrophic sectional controversy. The Young America wing of the Democratic party fought vainly to prevent this from happening. Its leader in the late 1840s and early 1850s was Senator Stephen A. Douglas of Illinois, called the Little Giant because of his small stature and large public presence. More than anyone else of this period, he sought political power for himself and his party by combining an expansionist foreign policy with the encouragement of economic development within the territories already acquired. His youthful dynamism made him seem the very embodiment of the Young America ideal. Recognizing that the slavery question was the main obstacle to his program, he sought to neutralize it through compromise and evasion (see Chapter 14). His failure to win the presidency or even the Democratic nomination before 1860 showed that the Young Americans' dream of a patriotic consensus supporting headlong expansion and economic development could not withstand the tensions and divisions that expansionist policies created or brought to light.

RECOMMENDED READING

An overview of expansion to the Pacific is Ray A. Billington, *The Far Western Frontier, 1830–1860* (1956). The impulse behind Manifest Destiny has been variously interpreted. Albert K. Weinberg's classic *Manifest Destiny: A Study of National Expansionism in American History* (1935) describes and stresses the ideological rationale as does Anders Stephenson, *Manifest Destiny: American Expansion and the Empire of Right* (1995). Frederick Merk, *Manifest Destiny and Mission in American History* (1963), analyzes public opinion and shows how divided it was on the question of territorial acquisitions. Norman A. Graebner, *Empire on the Pacific: A Study in American Continental Expansionism*

(1956), highlights the desire for Pacific harbors as a motive for adding new territory. The most complete and authoritative account of the diplomatic side of expansionism in this period is David M. Pletcher, *The Diplomacy of Annexation: Texas, Oregon, and the Mexican War* (1973). Charles G. Sellers, *James K. Polk: Continentalist, 1843–1846* (1966), is the definitive work on Polk's election and the expansionist policies of his administration. A very good account of the Mexican-American War is John S. D. Eisenhower, *So Far from God: The U.S. War with Mexico* (1989). On gold rushes, see Malcolm J. Rohrbough, *Days of Gold: The California Gold Rush and the American Nation* (1997) and Elliott West, *The Contested Plains: Indians, Goldseekers, and the Rush to Colorado* (1998).

Economic developments of the 1840s and 1850s are well covered in George R. Taylor, *The Transportation Revolution, 1815–1960* (1952) and Albert Fishlow, *American Railroads and the Transformation of the Ante-Bellum Economy* (1965). For an overview of immigration in this period, see the early chapters of Roger Daniels, *Coming to America: Immigration and Ethnicity in American Life* (1990). On the Irish, see Kerby A. Miller, *Emigrants and Exiles: Ireland and the Irish Exodus to America* (1985). Oscar Handlin, *Boston Immigrants: A Study in Acculturation*, rev. ed. (1959), is a classic study of immigration to one city. A standard work on the antebellum working class is Sean Wilentz, *Chants Democratic: New York City and the Rise of the American Working Class, 1788–1850* (1984); for the new approach to labor history that emphasizes working-class culture, see Herbert G. Gutman, *Work, Culture, and Society in Industrializing America* (1976). For the rich public life of antebellum cities, see Mary P. Ryan, *Civic Wars: Democracy and Public Life in the American City During the Nineteenth Century* (1997). A pathbreaking and insightful study of workers in the textile industry is Thomas Dublin, *Women at Work: The Transformation of Work and Community in Lowell, Massachusetts, 1826–1860* (1979).

For a list of additional titles related to this chapter's topics, please see http://www.ablongman.com/divine.

Suggested Web Sites

Pioneering the Upper Midwest: Books from Michigan, Minnesota, and Wisconsin, ca. 1820–1910

http://memory.loc.gov/ammem/umhtml/umhome.html

This Library of Congress site looks at first-person accounts, biographies, promotional literature, local histories, ethnographic and antiquarian texts, colonial archival documents, and other works from the seventeenth to the early twentieth century. It covers many topics and issues that affected Americans in the settlement and development of the Upper Midwest.

The Mexican-American War Memorial Homepage

http://sunsite.dcaa.unam.mx/revistas/1847/

Images and text explain the causes, courses, and outcomes of the Mexican-American War.

On the Trail in Kansas

http://www.kancoll.org/galtrl.htm

This Kansas Collection site holds several good primary sources with images concerning the Oregon trail and America's early movement westward.

Mountain Men and the Fur Trade

http://www.xmission.com/~drudy/amm.html

Private letters can speak volumes about the concerns and environment of the writers and recipients. Letters from early settlers west of the Mississippi River are offered on this site, along with other resources relating to explorers, trappers, and traders.

Chapter 14

Henry Clay, shown here addressing the Senate, helped negotiate the Compromise of 1850 to settle the dispute over the extension of slavery in territories acquired as a result of the Mexican-American War. Daniel Webster, seated at left resting his head on his hand, supported Clay's proposed compromise. Ardent states' rightist John C. Calhoun, standing third from right, led the opposition. ❖

The Sectional Crisis

Brooks Assaults Sumner in Congress

On May 22, 1856, Representative Preston Brooks of South Carolina erupted onto the floor of the Senate with a cane in his hand. He approached Charles Sumner, the antislavery senator from Massachusetts who had recently given a fiery oration condemning the South for plotting to extend slavery to the Kansas Territory. What was worse, the speech had included insulting references to Senator Andrew Butler of South Carolina, a kinsman of Brooks. When he found Sumner seated at his desk, Brooks proceeded to batter him over the head. Amazed and stunned, Sumner made a desperate effort to rise and ripped his bolted desk from the floor. He then collapsed under a continued torrent of blows.

Sumner was so badly injured by the assault that he did not return to the Senate for three years. But his home state reelected him in 1857 and kept his seat vacant as testimony against southern brutality and "barbarism." In parts of the North that were up in arms against the expansion of slavery, Sumner was hailed as a martyr to the cause of "free soil." Brooks, denounced in the North as a bully, was lionized by his fellow Southerners. When he resigned from the House after a vote of censure had narrowly failed because of solid southern opposition, his constituents reelected him unanimously.

These contrasting reactions show how bitter sectional antagonism had become by 1856. Sumner spoke for the radical wing of the new Republican party, which was making a bid for national power by mobilizing the North against the alleged aggressions of "the slave power." Southerners viewed the very existence of this party as an insult to their section of the country and a threat to its vital interests. Sumner came closer to being an abolitionist than any other member of Congress, and nothing created greater fear and anxiety among Southerners than their belief that antislavery forces were plotting against their way of life. To many Northerners, "bully Brooks" stood for all the arrogant and violent slaveholders who were allegedly conspiring to extend their barbaric labor system. By 1856, therefore, the sectional cleavage that would lead to the Civil War had already undermined the foundations of national unity.

THE CRISIS OF THE MID-1850S came only a few years after the elaborate compromise of 1850 had seemingly resolved the dispute over the future of slavery in the territories acquired as a result of the Mexican War. The renewed agitation over the extension of slavery that led to Brooks's attack on Sumner was set in motion by the Kansas-Nebraska Act of 1854. This legislation revived the sectional conflict and led to the emergence of the Republican party. From that point on, a dramatic series of events increased sectional confrontation and destroyed the prospects for a new compromise. The caning of Charles Sumner was one of these events, and violence on the Senate floor foreshadowed violence on the battlefield.

Outline

Feature Essay

Law and Society

After his constituents learned of Preston Brooks's caning of Senator Sumner, they sent Brooks a gold-handled cowhide whip to use on other antislavery advocates. ❖

THE COMPROMISE OF 1850

The "irrepressible conflict" over slavery in the territories began in the late 1840s. The positions taken on this issue between 1846 and 1850 established the range of options that would reemerge after 1854. But during this earlier phase of the sectional controversy, the leaders of two strong national parties, each with substantial followings in both the North and the South, had a vested interest in resolving the crisis. Efforts to create uncompromising sectional parties failed to disrupt what historians call the second party system—the vigorous competition between Whigs and Democrats that had characterized elections since the 1830s. Furthermore, the less tangible features of sectionalism—emotion and ideology—were not as divisive as they would later become. Hence a fragile compromise was achieved through a kind of give-and-take that would not be possible in the changed environment of the mid-1850s.

The Problem of Slavery in the Mexican Cession

As the price of union between states committed to slavery and those in the process of abolishing it, the Founders had attempted to limit the role of the slavery issue in national politics. The Constitution gave the federal government the right to abolish the international slave trade but no definite authority to regulate or destroy the institution where it existed under state law. Although many of the Founders hoped for the eventual demise of slavery, they provided no direct means to achieve this end except voluntary state action. These ground rules limited the effect of northern attacks on the South's peculiar institution. It was easy to condemn slavery in principle but very difficult to develop a practical program to eliminate it without defying the Constitution.

Radical abolitionists saw this problem clearly and resolved it by rejecting the law of the land in favor of a "higher law" prohibiting human bondage. In 1844, William Lloyd Garrison publicly burned the Constitution, condemning it as "a Covenant with Death, an Agreement with Hell." But Garrison spoke for a small minority dedicated to freeing the North, at whatever cost, from the sin of condoning slavery.

During the 1840s, the majority of Northerners showed that while they disliked slavery, they also detested abolitionism. They were inclined to view slavery as a backward and unwholesome institution, much inferior to their own free-labor system, and could be persuaded that slaveholders were power-hungry aristocrats seeking more than their share of national political influence. But they regarded the Constitution as a binding contract between slave and free states and were likely to be prejudiced against blacks and reluctant to accept large numbers of them as free citizens. Consequently, they saw no legal or desirable way to bring about emancipation within the southern states.

But the Constitution had not predetermined the status of slavery in *future* states. Since Congress had the power to admit new states to the Union under any conditions it wished to impose, a majority arguably could require the abolition of slavery as the price of admission. An effort to use this power had led to the Missouri crisis of 1819–1820 (see Chapter 9). The resulting compromise was designed to decide future cases by drawing a line between slave and free states and extending it westward through the unsettled portions of what was then American soil. When specific territories were settled, organized, and prepared for statehood, slavery would be permitted south of the line and prohibited north of it.

The tradition of providing both the free North and the slave South with opportunities for expansion and the creation of new states broke down when new territories were wrested from Mexico in the 1840s. When Texas was admitted as a slave state, northern expansionists could still look forward to the admission of Oregon as a counterbalancing free state. But the Mexican War raised the prospect that California and New Mexico, both south of the Missouri Compromise line, would also be acquired. Since it was generally assumed in the North that Congress had the power to prohibit slavery in new territories, a movement developed in Congress to do just that.

The Wilmot Proviso Launches the Free-Soil Movement

The Free-Soil crusade began in August 1846, only three months after the start of the Mexican-American War, when Congressman David Wilmot, a Pennsylvania

Democrat, proposed an amendment to the military appropriations bill that would ban slavery in any territory that might be acquired from Mexico.

Wilmot spoke for the large number of northern Democrats who felt neglected and betrayed by the party's choice of Polk over Van Buren in 1844 and by the "prosouthern" policies of the Polk administration. Pennsylvanians like Wilmot were upset because the tariff of 1846 reduced duties to a level unacceptable to the manufacturing interests of their state. Others, especially Midwesterners, were annoyed that Polk had vetoed a bill to provide federal funds for the improvement of rivers and harbors. Democratic expansionists also felt betrayed because Polk had gone back on his pledge to obtain "all of Oregon" up to 54°40' and then had proceeded to wage war to win all of Texas and the Southwest. This twist in the course of Manifest Destiny convinced them that the South and its interests were dominating the party and the administration. David Wilmot spoke for many when he wrote that he was "jealous of the power of the South."

The pioneer Free-Soilers had a genuine interest in the issue actually at hand—the question of who would control and settle the new territories. Combining an appeal to racial prejudice with opposition to slavery as an institution, Wilmot defined his cause as involving the "rights of white freemen" to go to areas where they could live "without the disgrace which association with negro slavery brings on white labor." Wilmot proposed that slavery as well as settlement by free African Americans be prohibited in the territory obtained in the Mexican cession, thus giving the common folk of the North a fair chance by preventing job competition from slaves and free blacks. By linking racism with resistance to the spread of slavery, Wilmot appealed to a broad spectrum of northern opinion.

Northern Whigs backed the Proviso because they shared Wilmot's concern about the outcome of an unregulated competition between slave and free labor in the territories. Furthermore, voting for the measure provided a good outlet for their frustration at being unable to halt the annexation of Texas and the Mexican-American War. The preferred position of some Whig leaders was no expansion at all, but when expansion could not be avoided, the northern wing of the party endorsed the view that acquisition of Mexican territory should not be used to increase the power of the slave states.

In the first House vote on the **Wilmot Proviso,** party lines crumbled and were replaced by a sharp sectional cleavage. Every northern congressman with the exception of two Democrats voted for the amendment, and every Southerner except two Whigs went on record against it. After passing the House, the Proviso was blocked in the Senate by a combination of southern influence and Democratic loyalty to the administration. When the appropriations bill went back to the House without the Proviso, the administration's arm-twisting succeeded in changing enough northern Democratic votes to pass the bill and thus send the Proviso down to defeat.

Reactions to the Proviso on the state and local level provided further evidence of the polarizing effect of the territorial issue. Northern state legislatures, with one exception, endorsed the Proviso, while southern orators proclaimed that its passage would insult their section and violate the principle of equality among the states by denying slaveholding citizens access to federal territories.

The end of the Mexican-American War, the formal acquisition of New Mexico and California, and the approaching election of 1848 gave new urgency to a search for politically feasible solutions to the crisis. The extreme alternatives—the Proviso policy of free soil and the radical southern response that slavery could be extended to any territory—threatened to destroy the national parties because there was no bisectional support for either of them.

Squatter Sovereignty and the Election of 1848

After a futile attempt was made to extend the Missouri Compromise line to the Pacific—a proposal that was unacceptable to Northerners because most of the Mexican cession lay south of the line—a new approach was devised that appealed especially to Democrats. Its main proponent was Senator Lewis Cass of Michigan, an aspirant for the party's presidential nomination. Cass, who described his formula as "squatter sovereignty," would leave the determination of the status of slavery in a territory to the actual settlers. From the beginning, this proposal contained an ambiguity that allowed it to be interpreted differently in the North and the South. For northern Democrats, squatter sovereignty—or **popular sovereignty** as it was later called—meant the settlers could vote slavery up or down at the first meeting of a territorial legislature. For the southern wing of the party, it meant a decision would be made only at the time a convention drew up a constitution and applied for statehood. It was in the interest of national Democratic leaders to leave this ambiguity unresolved for as long as possible.

Congress failed to resolve the future of slavery in the Mexican cession in time for the election of 1848, and the issue entered the arena of presidential politics. The Democrats nominated Cass on a platform of squatter sovereignty. The Whigs evaded the question by running General Zachary Taylor—the hero of the battle of Buena Vista—without a platform. Taylor

The Election of 1848

Candidate	Party	Popular Vote	Electoral Vote
Taylor	Whig	1,360,967	163
Cass	Democratic	1,222,342	127
Van Buren	Free-Soil	291,263	—

refused to commit himself on the status of slavery in the territories, but northern Whigs favoring restriction took heart from the general's promise not to veto any territorial legislation passed by Congress. Southern Whigs went along with Taylor mainly because he was a Southerner who owned slaves and would presumably defend the interests of his native region.

Northerners who strongly supported the Wilmot Proviso—and felt betrayed that neither the Whigs nor the Democrats were supporting it—were attracted by a third-party movement. In August, a tumultuous convention in Buffalo nominated former president Van Buren to carry the banner of the **Free-Soil party.** Support for the Free-Soilers came from antislavery Whigs dismayed by their party's nomination of a slaveholder and its evasiveness on the territorial issue, disgruntled Democrats who had backed the Proviso and resented southern influence in their party, and some of the former adherents of the abolitionist Liberty party. Van Buren himself was motivated less by antislavery zeal than by bitterness at being denied the Democratic nomination in 1844 because of southern obstructionism. The founding of the Free-Soil party was the first significant effort to create a broadly based sectional party addressing itself to voters' concerns about the extension of slavery.

After a noisy and confusing campaign, Taylor came out on top, winning a majority of the electoral votes in both the North and the South and a total of 1,360,967 popular votes to 1,222,342 for Cass and 291,263 for Van Buren. The Free-Soilers failed to carry a single state but did quite well in the North, coming in second behind Taylor in New York, Massachusetts, and Vermont.

Taylor Takes Charge

Once in office, Taylor devised a bold plan to decide the fate of slavery in the Mexican cession. A brusque military man who disdained political give-and-take, he tried to engineer the immediate admission of California and New Mexico to the Union as states, thus bypassing the territorial stage entirely and avoiding a congressional debate on the status of slavery in the federal domain. Under the administration's urging, California, which was filling up rapidly with settlers drawn by the lust for gold, convened a constitutional convention and applied for admission to the Union as a free state.

Instead of resolving the crisis, President Taylor's initiative only worsened it. Once it was clear that California was going to be a free state, the administration's plan aroused intense opposition in the South. Fearing that New Mexico would also be free because Mexican law had prohibited slavery there, Southerners of both parties accused the president of trying to impose the Wilmot Proviso in a new form. The prospect that only free states would emerge from the entire Mexican cession inspired serious talk of secession.

In Congress, Senator John C. Calhoun of South Carolina saw a chance to achieve his long-standing

In this cartoon, Democrats Lewis Cass and John C. Calhoun and antislavery radicals Horace Greeley, William Lloyd Garrison, and Abby Folsom look on as Martin Van Buren, the Free-Soil party candidate in the election of 1848, attempts to bridge the chasm between the Democratic platform and that of the antislavery Whigs. The Free-Soil influence was decisive in the election; it split the New York Democratic vote, thus allowing Whig candidate Zachary Taylor to win New York and the presidency. ❖

goal of creating a southern voting bloc that would cut across regular party lines. State legislatures and conventions throughout the South denounced "northern aggression" against the rights of the slave states. As signs of southern fury increased, Calhoun rejoiced that the South had never been so "united . . . bold, and decided." In the fall and winter of 1849–1850, several southern states agreed to participate in a convention, to be held in Nashville in June, where grievances could be aired and demands made. For an increasing number of southern political leaders, the survival of the Union would depend on the North's response to the demands of the southern rights movement.

Forging a Compromise

When it became clear that the president would not abandon or modify his plan in order to appease the South, independent efforts began in Congress to arrange a compromise. Hoping that he could again play the role of "great pacificator" as he had in the Missouri Compromise of 1820, Senator Henry Clay of Kentucky offered a series of resolutions meant to restore sectional harmony. He hoped to reduce tension by providing mutual concessions on a range of divisive issues. On the critical territorial question, his solution was to admit California as a free state and organize the rest of the Mexican cession with no explicit prohibition of slavery—in other words, without the Wilmot Proviso. Noting that Mexican law had already abolished slavery there, he also pointed to the arid climate of the New Mexico region, which made it unsuitable for cotton culture and slavery. He also sought to resolve a major boundary dispute between New Mexico and Texas by granting the disputed region to New Mexico while compensating Texas through federal assumption of its state debt. As a concession to the North on another issue—the existence of slavery in the District of Columbia—he recommended prohibiting the buying and selling of slaves at auction and permitting the abolition of slavery itself with the consent of the District's white inhabitants. He also called for a more effective Fugitive Slave Law.

These proposals provided the basis for the **Compromise of 1850.** Proposed in February 1850, it took several months for the Compromise to get through Congress. One obstacle was President Taylor's firm resistance to the proposal; another was the difficulty of getting congressmen to vote for it in the form of a single package or "omnibus bill." Few politicians from either section were willing to go on record as

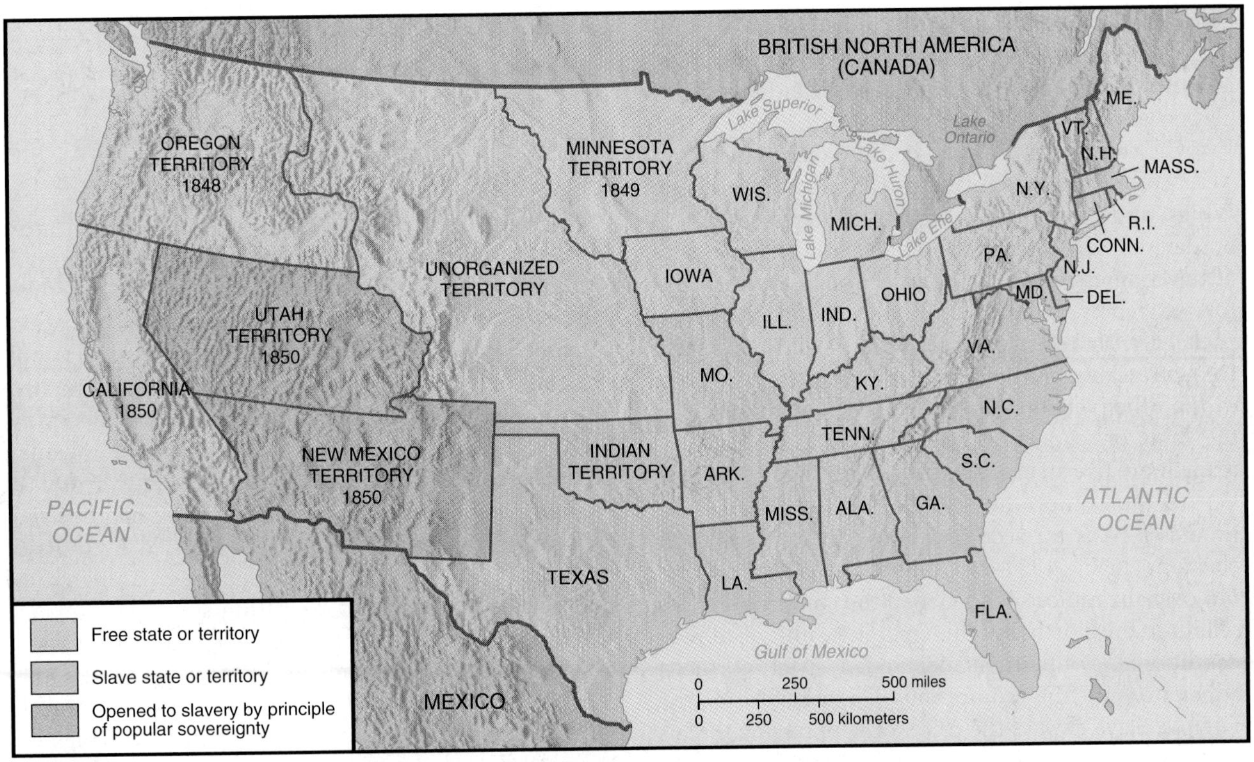

THE COMPROMISE OF 1850 *The "compromise" was actually a series of resolutions granting some concessions to the North—especially admission of California as a free state—and some to the South, such as a stricter Fugitive Slave Law.*

supporting the key concessions to the *other* section. The logjam was broken in July by two crucial developments: President Taylor died and was succeeded by Millard Fillmore, who favored the compromise; and a decision was made to abandon the omnibus strategy in favor of a series of measures that could be voted on separately. After the breakup of the omnibus bill, Democrats replaced the original Whig sponsors as leaders of the compromise movement, and some of Clay's proposals were modified to make them more acceptable to the South and the Democrats. Senator Stephen A. Douglas, a Democrat from Illinois, was particularly influential in maneuvering the separate provisions of the plan through Congress.

As the price of Democratic support, the popular sovereignty principle was included in the bills organizing New Mexico and Utah. Territorial legislatures in the Mexican cession were explicitly granted power over "all rightful subjects of legislation," which might include slavery. Half of the compensation to Texas for giving up its claims to New Mexico was paid directly to holders of Texas bonds, a decision that reflected intense lobbying by interested parties.

Abolition of slave auctions and depots in the District of Columbia and a new **Fugitive Slave Law** were also enacted. The latter was a particularly outrageous piece of legislation. As the result of southern pressures and amendments, suspected fugitives were now denied a jury trial, the right to testify in their own behalf, and other basic constitutional rights. As a result, there were no effective safeguards against false identification by accusers or against the kidnapping of blacks who were legally free.

The compromise passed because its key measures were supported by northern Democrats, southern Whigs, and representatives of both parties from the border states. No single bill was backed by a majority of the congressmen from both sections, and few senators or representatives actually voted for the entire package. Many northern Whigs and southern Democrats thought the end result conceded too much to the other section. Doubts therefore persisted over the value of workability of a "compromise" that was really more like an armistice or a cease-fire.

Yet the Compromise of 1850 did serve for a short time as a basis for sectional peace. In southern state elections during 1850–1851, moderate coalitions won out over the radicals who viewed the compromise as a sellout to the North. But this emerging "unionism" was conditional. Southerners demanded strict northern adherence to the compromise, especially to the Fugitive Slave Law, as the price for suppressing threats of secession. In the North, the compromise was backed by virtually the entire Democratic party and by one faction of the Whigs.

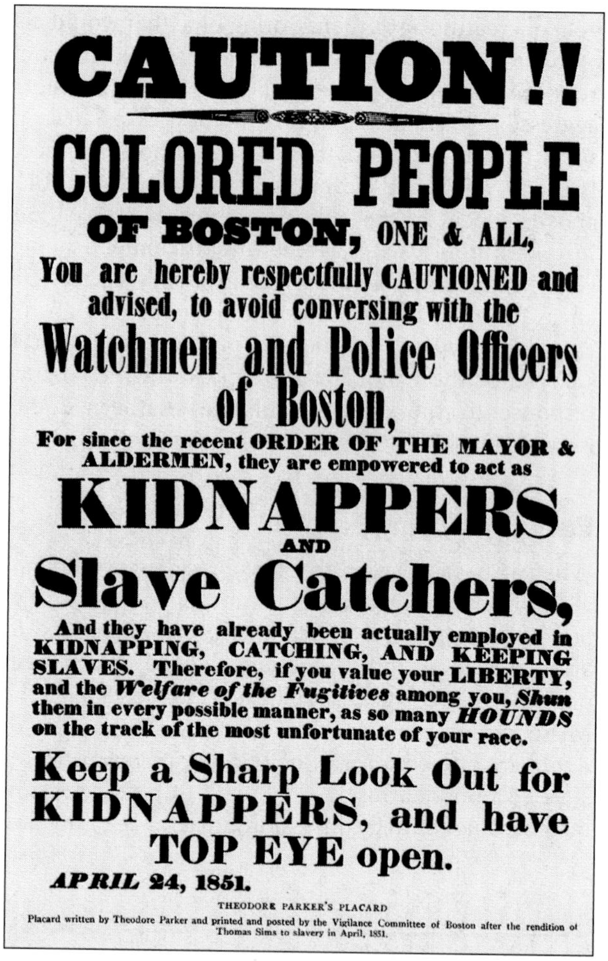

CAUTION!!

COLORED PEOPLE

OF BOSTON, ONE & ALL,

You are hereby respectfully CAUTIONED and advised, to avoid conversing with the

Watchmen and Police Officers of Boston,

For since the recent ORDER OF THE MAYOR & ALDERMEN, they are empowered to act as

KIDNAPPERS

AND

Slave Catchers,

And they have already been actually employed in KIDNAPPING, CATCHING, AND KEEPING SLAVES. Therefore, if you value your LIBERTY, and the *Welfare of the Fugitives* among you, *Shun* them in every possible manner, as so many *HOUNDS* on the track of the most unfortunate of your race.

Keep a Sharp Look Out for KIDNAPPERS, and have TOP EYE open.

APRIL 24, 1851.

THEODORE PARKER'S PLACARD

Placard written by Theodore Parker and printed and posted by the Vigilance Committee of Boston after the rendition of Thomas Sims to slavery in April, 1851.

This abolitionist broadside was printed in response to a ruling that fugitive slave Thomas Sims must be returned to his master in Georgia. ❖

The Fugitive Slave Law was unpopular in areas where abolitionism was particularly strong because it required Northerners to enforce slavery, and there were a few sensational rescues or attempted rescues of escaped slaves. In Boston in 1854, an antislavery mob led by armed abolitionists tried to free fugitive Anthony Burns from the courthouse where his extradition hearing was to take place. One of the men guarding Burns was killed, but the fugitive himself could not be reached. After the hearing had declared Burns an escaped slave, he was escorted by units of the U.S. Army through a hissing and groaning crowd of twenty thousand to a waiting ship. Despite such abolitionist resistance, the Fugitive Slave Law was enforced fairly successfully in the early 1850s. Other parts of the compromise were less troublesome. In 1852, when both the Democrats and the Whigs endorsed the compromise in their platforms, it seemed that sharp differences on the slavery issue had once again been banished from national politics.

POLITICAL UPHEAVAL, 1852–1856

The second party system—Democrats versus Whigs—survived the crisis over slavery in the Mexican cession, but in the long run the Compromise of 1850 may have weakened it. Although both national parties had been careful during the 1840s not to take stands on the slavery issue that would alienate their supporters in either section of the country, they had in fact offered voters alternative ways of dealing with the question. Democrats had endorsed headlong territorial expansion with the promise of a fair division of the spoils between slave and free states. Whigs had generally opposed annexations or acquisitions, because they were likely to bring the slavery question to the fore and threaten sectional harmony. With some shifts of emphasis and interpretation, each strategy could be presented to southern voters as a good way to protect slavery and to Northerners as a good way to contain it.

The consensus of 1852 meant the parties had to find other issues on which to base their distinctive appeals. Their failure to do so encouraged voter apathy and a disenchantment with the major parties. When the Democrats sought to revive the Manifest Destiny issue in 1854, they reopened the explosive issue of slavery in the territories. By this time, the Whigs were too weak and divided to respond with a policy of their own, and a purely sectional Free-Soil party—the Republicans—gained prominence. The collapse of the second party system released sectional agitation from the earlier constraints imposed by the competition of strong national parties.

The Party System in Crisis

The presidential campaign of 1852 was singularly devoid of major issues. With the slavery question under wraps, some Whigs tried to revive interest in the nationalistic economic policies that were the traditional hallmarks of their party. But convincing arguments in favor of a protective tariff, a national bank, and internal improvements were hard to make in a period of sustained prosperity. Business was thriving under the Democratic program of virtual laissez-faire.

Another tempting issue was immigration. Many Whigs were upset by the massive influx from Europe, partly because most of the new arrivals were Catholics, and the Whig following was largely evangelical Protestant. For office-seeking Whig politicians, a more urgent problem was the fact that immigrants voted overwhelmingly for their Democratic opponents. The Whig leadership was divided on whether to compete with the Democrats for the immigrant vote or respond to the prejudices of the party rank and file by calling for restrictions on immigrant voting rights.

THE ELECTION OF 1852

Candidate	Party	Popular Vote	Electoral Vote
Pierce	Democratic	1,601,117	254
Scott	Whig	1,385,453	42
Hale	Free-Soil	155,825	—

The Whigs nominated General Winfield Scott of Mexican-American War fame, who supported the faction that resisted nativism and sought to broaden the appeal of the party. The fact that Scott's daughters were being raised as Catholics was publicized to demonstrate his good intentions toward immigrant communities. This strategy backfired and contributed to disaster at the polls. For the most part, Catholic immigrants retained their Democratic allegiance, and some nativist Whigs apparently sat out the election to protest their party's disregard of their cultural prejudices.

But the main cause for Scott's crushing defeat was the support he lost in the South when he allied himself with the dominant northern antislavery wing of the party, led by Senator William Seward of New York. The Democratic candidate, Franklin Pierce of New Hampshire, was a colorless nonentity compared to his rival, but he ran up huge majorities in the Deep South, where Whigs stayed home in massive numbers. He also edged out Scott in most of the free states. In the most one-sided election since 1820, Pierce received 254 electoral votes from 27 states while Scott carried only 4 states with 42 electoral votes. This outcome revealed that the Whig party was in deep trouble because it lacked a program that would distinguish it from the Democrats and would appeal to voters in both sections of the country.

Despite their overwhelming victory in 1852, the Democrats had reasons for anxiety about the loyalty of their supporters. Because the major parties had ceased to offer clear-cut alternatives to the electorate, voter apathy or alienation was a growing trend in the early 1850s. The Democrats won majorities in both North and South in 1852 primarily because the public viewed them as the most reliable supporters of the Compromise of 1850, not because of firm party allegiance.

The Kansas-Nebraska Act Raises a Storm

In January 1854, Senator Stephen A. Douglas proposed a bill to organize the territory west of Missouri and Iowa. Since this region fell within the area where slavery had been banned by the Missouri Compromise,

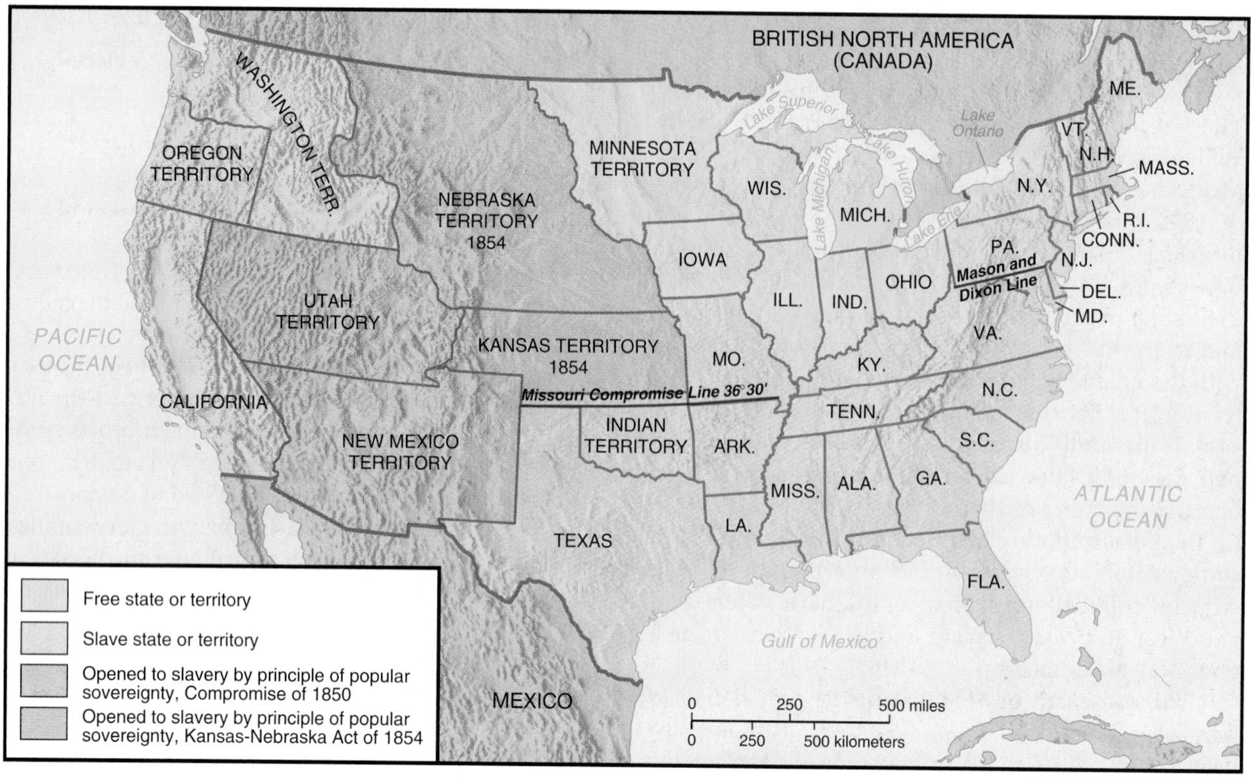

THE KANSAS-NEBRASKA ACT OF 1854 *The Kansas-Nebraska Act applied the principle of popular sovereignty to voters in the Kansas and Nebraska territories, allowing them to decide for themselves whether to permit slavery in their territories. The act repudiated the Missouri Compromise of 1820, which had prohibited slavery in the territory of the Louisiana Purchase north of 36°30' latitude.*

Douglas anticipated objections from Southerners concerned about the creation of more free states. To head off this opposition and keep the Democratic party united, Douglas disregarded the compromise line and sought to set up the territorial government in Kansas and Nebraska on the basis of popular sovereignty, relying on the alleged precedent set in the Compromise of 1850.

Douglas wanted to organize the Kansas-Nebraska area quickly because he was a strong supporter of the expansion of settlement and commerce. Along with other midwestern promoters of the economic development of the frontier, he hoped a railroad would soon be built to the Pacific with Chicago (or another midwestern city) as its eastern terminus. A long controversy over the status of slavery in the new territory would slow down the process of organization and settlement and might hinder the building of the railroad. As a leader of the Democratic party, Douglas also hoped his Kansas-Nebraska bill would revive the spirit of Manifest Destiny that had given the party cohesion and electoral success in the mid-1840s (see Chapter 13). As the main advocate for a new expansionism, he expected to win the Democratic nomination and the presidency.

The price of southern support, Douglas soon discovered, was the addition of an amendment explicitly repealing the Missouri Compromise. Although he realized this would "raise a hell of a storm," he reluctantly agreed. In this more provocative form, the bill made its way through Congress, passing the Senate by a large margin and the House by a narrow one. The vote in the House showed that Douglas had split his party rather than uniting it; exactly half of the northern Democrats voted against the legislation.

The Democrats who broke ranks created the storm that Douglas had predicted but underestimated. A manifesto of "independent Democrats" denounced the bill as "a gross violation of a sacred pledge." A memorial from three thousand New England ministers described it as a craven and sinful surrender to the slave power. For many Northerners, probably a majority, the **Kansas-Nebraska Act** was an abomination because it permitted the possibility of slavery in an area where it had previously been prohibited. Except for an aggressive minority, Southerners had not pushed for such legislation or even shown much interest in it, but now they felt obligated to support it. Their support provided deadly ammunition to those who were seeking to convince the northern public that there was a conspiracy to extend slavery.

Douglas's bill had a catastrophic effect on sectional harmony. It repudiated a compromise that many in the North regarded as a binding sectional compact, almost as sacred and necessary to the survival of the Union as the Constitution itself. In defiance of the whole compromise tradition, it made a concession to the South on the issue of slavery extension without providing an equivalent concession to the North. It also shattered the fragile sectional accommodation of 1850 and made future compromises less likely. From then on, northern sectionalists would be fighting to regain what they had lost, while Southerners would battle to maintain rights already conceded.

The act also destroyed what was left of the second party system. The already weakened and tottering Whig party totally disintegrated when its congressional representation split cleanly along sectional lines on the Kansas-Nebraska issue. The Democratic party survived, but its ability to act as a unifying national force was seriously impaired. Northern desertions and southern gains (resulting from the recruitment of proslavery Whigs) combined to destroy the sectional balance within the party and place it under firm southern control.

The congressional elections of 1854 revealed the political chaos Douglas had created. In the North, "anti-Nebraska" coalitions of Whigs, dissident Democrats, and Free-Soilers swept regular Democrats out of office. Most congressmen who had voted for the act were decisively defeated, and sixty-six of the ninety-one House seats held by northern Democrats were lost to opponents running under various labels. In some states, these anti-Democratic coalitions would evolve directly into a new and stronger Free-Soil party—the **Republicans.** In the Deep South, however, the Democrats routed the remaining Whigs and came close to ending two-party competition on the state level.

The furor over Kansas-Nebraska also doomed the efforts of the Pierce administration to revive an expansionist foreign policy. Pierce and Secretary of State William Marcy were committed to acquiring Cuba from Spain. In October 1854, the American ministers to England, France, and Spain met in Ostend, Belgium, and drew up a memorandum for the administration urging acquisition of Cuba by any means necessary—including force—if Spain refused to sell the island. The **Ostend Manifesto** became public in the midst of the controversy resulting from the Kansas-Nebraska Act. Those Northerners who were convinced that the administration was trying to extend slavery to the Great Plains were enraged to discover it was also scheming to fulfill the southern expansionist dream of a "Caribbean slave empire." The resulting storm of protest forced Pierce and his cohorts to abandon their scheme.

An Appeal to Nativism: The Know-Nothing Episode

The collapse of the Whigs created the opening for a new political party. The anti-Nebraska coalitions of 1854 suggested that such a party might be organized on the basis of northern opposition to the extension of slavery to the territories. Before such a prospect could be realized, however, an alternative emerged in the form of a major political movement based on hostility to immigrants. For a time, it appeared that the Whigs would be replaced by a nativist party rather than an antislavery one.

Massive immigration of Irish and Germans (see Chapter 13), most of whom were Catholic, led to increasing tension between ethnic groups during the 1840s and early 1850s. The fact that most of the new arrivals clustered in their own separate communities or neighborhoods helped arouse the suspicion and distrust of older-stock Americans. Native-born and even immigrant Protestants viewed the newcomers as bearers of alien cultures. They expressed their fears in bloody anti-Catholic riots, in church and convent burnings, and in a barrage of propaganda and lurid literature trumpeting the menace of "popery" to the American way of life. Nativist agitators charged that immigrants were agents of a foreign despotism, based in Rome, that was bent on overthrowing the American republic.

Political nativism first emerged during the 1840s in the form of local "American" parties protesting immigrant influence in cities such as New York and Philadelphia. In 1849, a secret fraternal organization, the Order of the Star-Spangled Banner, was founded in New York as a vehicle for anti-immigrant attitudes. When members were asked about the organization, they were instructed to reply, "I know nothing." The order grew rapidly in size, by 1854 reaching a membership of between 800,000 and 1,500,000. The political objective of the **Know-Nothing party** was to extend the period of naturalization in order to undercut immigrant voting strength and to keep aliens in their place.

From 1854 to 1855, the nativist movement surfaced as a major political force, the American party. Much of the party's backing came from Whigs looking for a new home, but the party also attracted some ex-Democrats. In addition, Know-Nothingism appealed to native-born workers who feared competition from low-paid immigrants. Many others supported the American party simply because it was an alternative for those who wanted to vote against the Democrats. In the North, Know-Nothing candidates

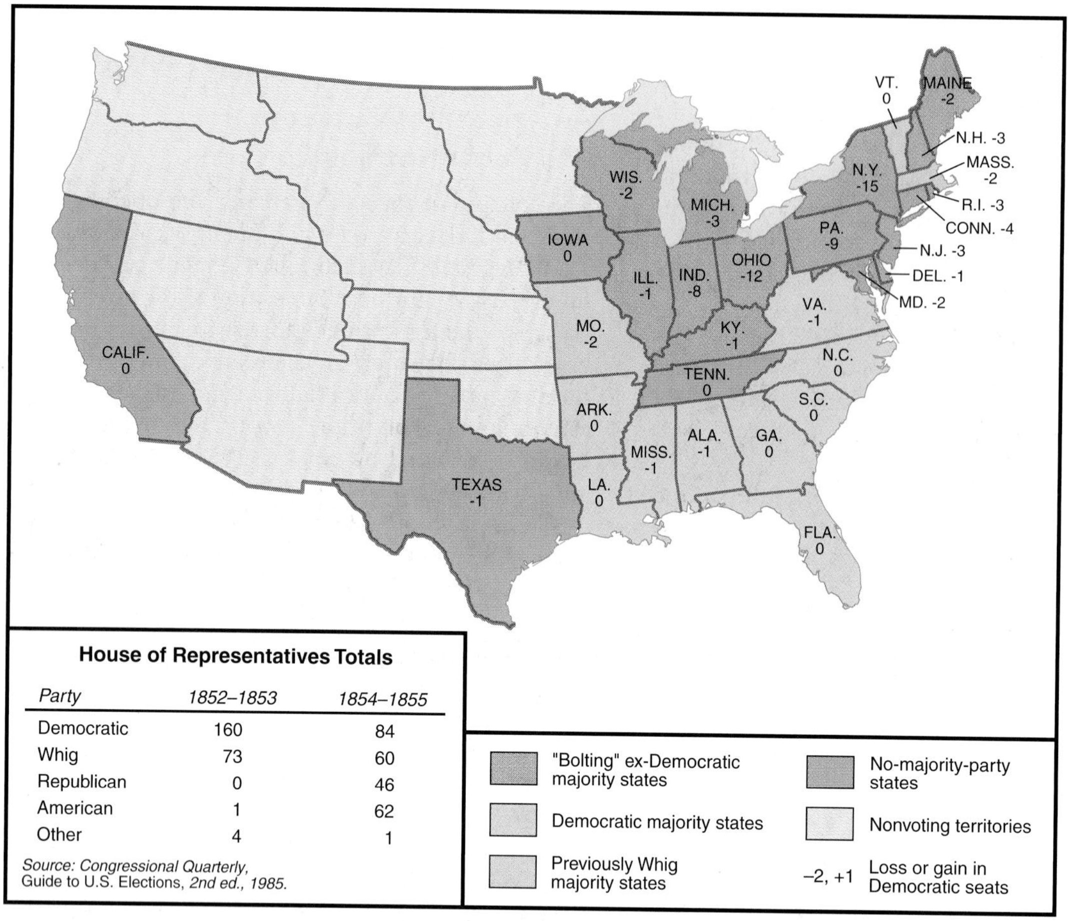

House of Representatives Totals

Party	*1852–1853*	*1854–1855*
Democratic	160	84
Whig	73	60
Republican	0	46
American	1	62
Other	4	1

Source: Congressional Quarterly, Guide to U.S. Elections, 2nd ed., 1985.

CONGRESSIONAL ELECTION OF 1854 *The impact of the Kansas-Nebraska Act was immediately felt in the election of 1854. "Anti-Nebraska" coalitions and the fledgling Republican party made gains in the North; the Democrats remained dominant in the South.*

generally opposed the Kansas-Nebraska Act, and some of their support came from voters who were more anxious about the expansion of slavery than about the evils of immigration.

The success of the new party was so dramatic that it was compared to a hurricane. In 1854, it won complete control in Massachusetts, capturing the governorship, most of the seats in the legislature, and the entire congressional delegation. In 1855, the Know-Nothings took power in three more New England states; swept Maryland, Kentucky, and Texas; and emerged as the principal opposition to the Democrats everywhere else except in the Midwest. By late 1855, the Know-Nothings showed every sign of displacing the Whigs as the nation's second party.

Yet, almost as rapidly as it had risen, the Know-Nothing movement collapsed. Its demise in 1856 is one of the great mysteries of American political history. As an intersectional party, its failure is understandable enough. When the Know-Nothings attempted to hold a national convention in 1856, northern and southern delegates split on the question of slavery in the territories, showing that former Whigs were still at odds over the same issue that had destroyed their old party.

Less clear is why the Know-Nothings failed to become the major opposition party to the Democrats in the North. The most persuasive explanation is that their Free-Soil Republican rivals, who were seeking to build a party committed to the containment of slavery, had an issue with wider appeal. In 1855 and 1856, the rate of immigration declined noticeably, and the conflict in Kansas heightened the concern about slavery. Consequently, voters who opposed both the expansion of slavery and unrestricted immigration were inclined to give priority to the former threat.

But the movement's peculiar "antipolitical" character also contributed to its rapid disintegration. Besides being a manifestation of real ethnic tensions, Know-Nothingism was a grassroots protest against the professional politicians who had led the Whig and Democratic parties. Concern about the effects of immigration on American culture and society would not have generated a mass political movement with the

Know-Nothings often charged that immigrant voters were stealing American elections. In the cartoon above, German and Irish immigrants, represented by German beer and Irish whiskey, steal a ballot box. An anti–Know-Nothing cartoon (right) portrays the Know-Nothings as gun-wielding ruffians. ❖

initial appeal of the Know-Nothings had it not been for the belief that political bosses were recruiting immigrant voters for their own corrupt purposes. As a result of the Know-Nothing party's distrust of conventional politics, most of its spokesmen and elected officials were neither professional politicians nor established community leaders. The very inexperience that was a major source of voter attraction to the party may have impeded development of organizational discipline. With inexperienced leaders and a lack of cohesion, the Know-Nothings were unable to make effective use of power once they had it. When voters discovered that the Know-Nothings also *did* nothing, or at least failed to do anything that a more conventional party could not do better, they looked for more competent and experienced leadership.

Kansas and the Rise of the Republicans

The new Republican party was an outgrowth of the anti-Nebraska coalition of 1854. The Republican name was first used in midwestern states such as Wisconsin and Michigan where Know-Nothingism failed to win a mass following. A new political label was required because Free-Soil Democrats—who were an especially important element in the midwestern coalitions—refused to march under the Whig banner or even support any candidate for high office who called himself a Whig.

When the Know-Nothing party split over the Kansas-Nebraska issue in 1856, most of the northern nativists went over to the Republicans. The Republican argument that the "slave-power conspiracy" was a greater threat to American liberty and equality than an alleged "popish plot" proved to be persuasive. But nativists did not have to abandon their ethnic and religious prejudices to become Republicans. Although Republican leaders generally avoided taking anti-immigrant positions—some out of strong principle and others with an eye to the votes of the foreign born—the party showed a clear commitment to the values of native-born evangelical Protestants. On the local level, Republicans generally supported causes that reflected an anti-immigrant or anti-Catholic bias—such as prohibition of the sale of alcoholic beverages, observance of the Sabbath, defense of Protestant Bible-reading in schools, and opposition to state aid for parochial education.

Unlike the Know-Nothings, the Republican party was led by seasoned professional politicians, men who had earlier been prominent Whigs or Democrats. Adept at organizing the grass roots, building coalitions, and employing all the techniques of popular campaigning, they built up an effective party apparatus in an amazingly short time. By late 1855, the party had won more than two-thirds of the anti-Nebraska congressmen elected in 1854. One of these, Nathaniel Banks of Massachusetts, was elected speaker of the House after a lengthy struggle. By early 1856, the new party was well established throughout the North and was preparing to make a serious bid for the presidency.

Underlying the rapid growth of the Republican party was the strong and growing appeal of its position on slavery in the territories. Republicans viewed the unsettled West as a land of opportunities, a place

The bitter contest over popular sovereignty in Kansas erupted into violence between proslavery and antislavery groups. The skirmishes, including the one at Hickory Point, near Leavenworth, depicted here, resulted in two hundred deaths and heavy property destruction before federal troops were brought in to restore order. ❖

to which the ambitious and hardworking could migrate in the hope of improving their social and economic position. Free soil would serve as a guarantee of free competition or "the right to rise." But if slavery was permitted to expand, the rights of "free labor" would be denied. Slaveholders would monopolize the best land, use their slaves to compete unfairly with free white workers, and block efforts at commercial and industrial development. They could also use their political control of new western states to dominate the federal government in the interest of the "slave power." Some Republicans also pandered to racial prejudice: They presented their policy as a way to keep African Americans out of the territories, thus preserving the new lands for exclusive white occupancy.

Although passage of the Kansas-Nebraska Act raised the territorial issue and gave birth to the Republican party, it was the turmoil associated with attempts to implement popular sovereignty in Kansas that kept the issue alive and enabled the Republicans to increase their following throughout the North. When Kansas was organized in the fall of 1854, a bitter contest began for control of the territorial government. New Englanders founded an Immigrant Aid Society to encourage antislavery settlement in Kansas, but the earliest arrivals came from slaveholding Missouri. In the first territorial elections, proslavery settlers were joined at the polls by thousands of Missouri residents who crossed the border to vote illegally. The result was a decisive victory for the slave-state forces. The legislature then proceeded to pass laws that not only legalized slavery but made it a crime to speak or act against it.

Settlers favoring free soil, most of whom came from the Midwest, were already a majority of the actual residents of the territory when the fraudulently elected legislature denied them the right to agitate against slavery. To defend themselves and their convictions, they took up arms and established a rival territorial government under a constitution that outlawed slavery. The Pierce administration and its appointed local agents refused to recognize this "free-state" initiative, but Republicans in Congress defended it.

A small-scale civil war then broke out between the rival regimes, culminating in May 1856 when proslavery adherents raided the free-state capital at Lawrence. Portrayed in Republican propaganda as

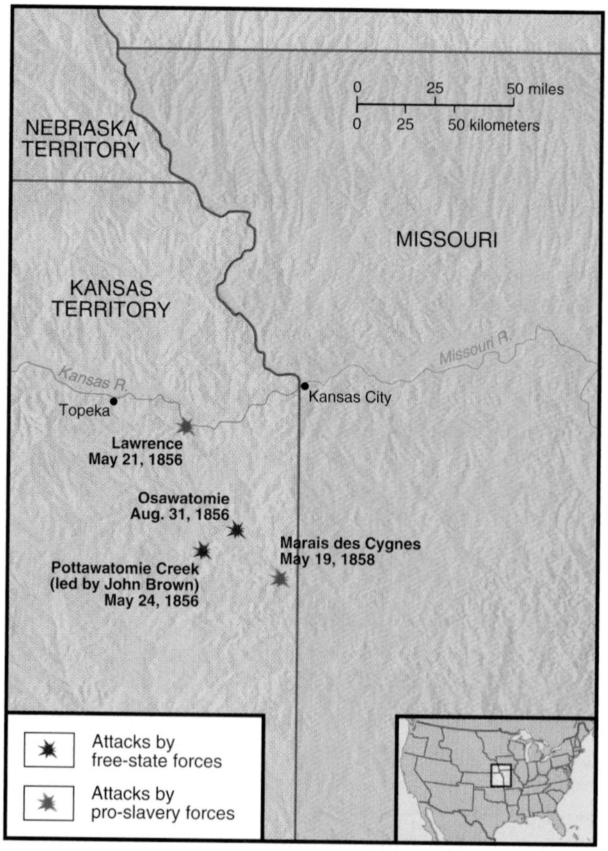

"BLEEDING KANSAS" *One result of the Kansas-Nebraska Act of 1854 was the border war that erupted between proslavery and antislavery forces in "bleeding" Kansas.* ❖

"the sack of Lawrence," this incursion resulted in substantial property damage but no loss of life. More bloody was the reprisal carried out by the antislavery zealot John Brown. Upon hearing of the attack on Lawrence, Brown and a few followers murdered five proslavery settlers in cold blood. During the next few months—until a truce was arranged by an effective territorial governor in the fall of 1856—a hit-and-run guerrilla war raged between free-state and slave-state factions. The national Republican press had a field day with the events in Kansas, exaggerating the extent of the violence but correctly pointing out that the federal government was favoring rule by a proslavery minority over a Free-Soil majority. Since the "sack of Lawrence" occurred at about the same time that Preston Brooks assaulted Charles Sumner on the Senate floor (see pp. 387–388), the Republicans launched their 1856 campaign under twin slogans "Bleeding Kansas" and "Bleeding Sumner." The image of an evil and aggressive "slave power," using violence to deny constitutional rights to its opponents, was a potent device for arousing northern sympathies and winning votes.

Sectional Division in the Election of 1856

The Republican nominating convention revealed the strictly sectional nature of the new party. Only a handful of the delegates from the slave states attended, and all of these were from the upper South. The platform called for liberation of Kansas from the slave power and for congressional prohibition of slavery in all territories. The nominee was John C. Frémont, explorer of the West and participant in the conquest of California during the Mexican-American War.

The Democratic convention dumped the ineffectual Pierce, passed over Stephen A. Douglas, and nominated James Buchanan of Pennsylvania, who had a long career in public service. The Democrats' platform endorsed popular sovereignty in the territories. The American party, a Know-Nothing remnant that survived mainly as the rallying point for anti-Democratic conservatives in the border states and parts of the South, chose ex-President Millard Fillmore as its standard-bearer and received the backing of those northern Whigs who resisted the Republicans and hoped to revive the tradition of sectional compromise.

The election was really two separate races—one in the North, where the main contest was between Frémont and Buchanan, and the other in the South, which pitted Fillmore against Buchanan. The Pennsylvania Democrat emerged victorious because he outpolled Fillmore in all but one of the slave states (Maryland) and edged out Frémont in four crucial

The Election of 1856

Candidate	Party	Popular Vote	Electoral Vote
Buchanan	Democratic	1,832,955	174
Frémont	Republican	1,339,932	114
Fillmore	American (Know-Nothing)	871,731	8

The Republican Party's presidential nominee in 1856 was John C. Frémont, explorer and Mexican-American War hero. Opposing the spread of slavery to the West, the Republican's call for "Free Speech! Free Men! Free Kansas," as shown on this campaign ribbon, stirred sectional tensions and revived talk of secession in the South. ❖

northern states—Pennsylvania, New Jersey, Indiana, and Illinois. But the Republicans did remarkably well for a party that was scarcely more than a year old. Frémont won eleven of the sixteen free states, sweeping the upper North with substantial majorities and winning a larger proportion of the northern popular vote than either of his opponents. Since the free states had a substantial majority in the electoral college, a future Republican candidate could win the presidency simply by overcoming a slim Democratic edge in the lower North.

In the South, where the possibility of a Frémont victory had revived talk of secession, the results of the election brought a momentary sense of relief tinged with deep anxiety about the future. The very existence of a sectional party committed to restricting the expansion of slavery constituted an insult to the Southerners' way of life. That such a party was genuinely popular in the North was profoundly alarming and raised grave doubts about the security of slavery within the Union. The continued success of a unified Democratic party under southern control was widely viewed as the last hope for the maintenance of sectional balance and "southern rights."

The House Divided, 1857–1860

The sectional quarrel deepened and became virtually "irreconcilable" in the years between Buchanan's election in 1856 and Lincoln's victory in 1860. A series of incidents provoked one side or the other, heightened the tension, and ultimately brought the crisis to a head. Behind the panicky reaction to public events lay a growing sense that the North and South were so different in culture and so opposed in basic interests that they could no longer coexist in the same nation.

Cultural Sectionalism

Signs of cultural and intellectual cleavage had appeared well before the triumph of sectional politics. In the mid-1840s, the Methodist and Baptist churches split into northern and southern denominations because of differing attitudes toward slaveholding. Presbyterians remained formally united but had informal northern and southern factions that went their separate ways on the slavery issue. Instead of unifying Americans around a common Protestant faith, the churches became nurseries of sectional discord. Increasingly, northern preachers and congregations denounced slaveholding as a sin, while most southern church leaders rallied to a biblical defense of the peculiar institution and became influential apologists for the southern way of life. Prominent religious leaders—such as Henry Ward Beecher, George B. Cheever, and Theodore Parker in the North and James H. Thornwell, Leonidas Polk, and Bishop Stephen Elliott in the South—were in the forefront of sectional mobilization. As men of God, they helped to turn political questions into moral issues and reduced the prospects for a compromise.

American literature also became sectionalized during the 1840s and 1850s. Southern men of letters, including such notable figures as novelist William Gilmore Simms and Edgar Allan Poe, wrote proslavery polemics. Popular novelists produced a flood of "plantation romances" that seemed to glorify southern civilization and sneer at that of the North. The notion that planter "cavaliers" were superior to money-grubbing Yankees was the message that most Southerners derived from the homegrown literature they read. In the North, prominent men of letters—Emerson, Thoreau, James Russell Lowell, and Herman Melville—expressed strong antislavery sentiments in prose and poetry, particularly after the outbreak of the Mexican-American War.

Literary abolitionism reached a climax in 1852 when Harriet Beecher Stowe published *Uncle Tom's Cabin,* an enormously successful novel (it sold more than 300,000 copies in a single year) that fixed in the

Abolitionist writer Harriet Beecher Stowe is best known for her hugely successful antislavery novel Uncle Tom's Cabin. ❖

❖ A Look at the Past ❖

Poster for *Uncle Tom's Cabin*

Three hundred thousand Americans purchased Harriet Beecher Stowe's *Uncle Tom's Cabin* in 1852, the year this poster appeared. While the poster might not have caused those sales, its design certainly appealed to middle-class readers. How does the scene depicted on the poster capture the ideal of domesticity? How does that ideal compare to the reality of slave life? Why would the scene have appealed to middle-class Americans?

northern mind the image of the slaveholder as a brutal Simon Legree. Much of its emotional impact came from the book's portrayal of slavery as a threat to the family and the cult of domesticity. When the saintly Uncle Tom was sold away from his adoring wife and children, Northerners shuddered with horror and some Southerners felt a painful twinge of conscience.

Southern defensiveness gradually hardened into cultural and economic nationalism. Northern textbooks were banished from southern schools in favor of those with a prosouthern slant; young men of the planter class were induced to stay in the South for higher education rather than going North (as had been the custom); and a movement developed to encourage southern industry and commerce as a way of reducing dependence on the North. Almost without exception, prominent southern educators and intellectuals of the late 1850s rallied behind southern sectionalism, and many even endorsed the idea of a southern nation.

The Dred Scott Case

When James Buchanan was inaugurated on March 4, 1857, the dispute over the legal status of slavery in the territories was an open door through which sectional fears and hatreds could enter the political arena. Buchanan hoped to close that door by encouraging the Supreme Court to resolve the constitutional issue once and for all.

The Court was then about to render its decision in the case of *Dred Scott* v. *Sandford.* (See the Law and Society essay, "The Case of Dred and Harriet Scott," pp. 412–416.) The plaintiff in the case was a Missouri slave who sued for his freedom on the grounds that he had lived for many years in an area where slavery had been outlawed by the Missouri Compromise. The Supreme Court could have decided the issue on the narrow ground that a slave was not a citizen and therefore had no right to sue in federal courts. But President-elect Buchanan, in the days just before the inauguration, encouraged the Court to render a broader decision that would settle the slavery issue.

On March 6, Chief Justice Roger B. Taney announced that the majority had ruled against Scott. Taney argued that no African American—slave or free—could be a citizen of the United States. But the real bombshell in the decision was the ruling that Dred Scott would not have won his case even if he had been a legal plaintiff. His residence in the Wisconsin Territory established no right to freedom because Congress had no power to prohibit slavery there. The Missouri Compromise was thus declared unconstitutional and so, implicitly, was the main plank in the Republican platform.

If Buchanan expected the decision to reduce sectional tension, he was quickly proved wrong. In the North, and especially among Republicans, the Court's verdict was viewed as the latest diabolical act of the "slave-power conspiracy." The charge that the decision was a political maneuver rather than a disinterested interpretation of the Constitution was supported by strong circumstantial evidence. Five of the six judges who voted in the majority were proslavery Southerners, and their resolution of the territorial issue was close to the extreme southern rights position long advocated by John C. Calhoun.

Republicans denounced the decision as "a wicked and false judgment" and as "the greatest crime in the annals of the republic"; but they stopped short of openly defying the Court's authority. Instead, they argued on narrow technical grounds that the decision as written was not binding on Congress and that a ban on slavery in the territories could still be enacted. The decision actually helped the Republicans build support; it lent credence to their claim that an aggressive slave power was dominating all branches of the federal government and attempting to use the Constitution to achieve its own ends.

The Lecompton Controversy

While the Dred Scott case was being decided, leaders of the proslavery faction in Kansas concluded that the time was ripe to draft a constitution and seek admission to the Union as a slave state. Since settlers with free-state views were now an overwhelming majority in the territory, the success of the plan required a rigged, gerrymandered election for convention delegates. When it became clear the election was fixed, the free-staters boycotted it, and the proslavery forces won complete control. The resulting constitution, drawn up at Lecompton, was certain to be voted down if submitted to the voters in a fair election and sure to be rejected by Congress if no referendum of any kind was held.

Stephen Douglas, the "Little Giant" from Illinois, won election to Congress when he was just 30 years old. Four years later, he was elected to the Senate. ❖

To resolve the dilemma, supporters of the **Lecompton constitution** decided to permit a vote on the slavery provision alone, giving the electorate the narrow choice of allowing or forbidding the future importation of slaves. Since there was no way to vote for total abolition, the free-state majority again resorted to a boycott, thus allowing ratification of a constitution that protected existing slave property and placed no restriction on importations. Meanwhile, however, the free-staters had finally gained control of the territorial legislature, and they authorized a second referendum on the constitution as a whole. This time, the proslavery party boycotted the election, and the Lecompton constitution was overwhelmingly rejected.

The Lecompton constitution was such an obvious perversion of popular sovereignty that Stephen A. Douglas spoke out against it. But the Buchanan administration, bowing to southern pressure, tried to push it through Congress in early 1858, despite overwhelming evidence that the people of Kansas did not want to enter the Union as a slave state. The resulting debate in Congress became so bitter and impassioned that it provoked fistfights between northern and southern members. Buchanan, using all the political muscle he could command, scored a victory in the Senate, which voted to admit Kansas under the Lecompton constitution on March 23. But on April 1, a coalition of Republicans and Douglas Democrats defeated the bill in the House. A face-saving compromise was then devised. It allowed resubmission of the constitution to the Kansas voters on the pretext that a change in the provisions for a federal land grant was required. Finally, in August 1858, the people of Kansas killed the Lecompton constitution when they voted it down by a margin of 6 to 1.

The Lecompton controversy aggravated the sectional quarrel and made it truly "irreconcilable," if it had not been before. For Republicans, the administration's frantic efforts to admit Kansas as a slave state exposed southern dominance of the Democratic party and the lengths to which proslavery conspirators would go to achieve their ends. Among Democrats, the affair opened a deep rift between the followers of Douglas and the backers of the Buchanan administration. Because of his anti-Lecompton stand, Douglas gained popularity in the North, and some Republicans even flirted with the idea of joining forces with him against the "doughfaces"—prosouthern Democrats—who stood with Buchanan.

For Douglas himself, however, the affair was a disaster; it destroyed his hopes of uniting the Democratic party and defusing the slavery issue through the application of popular sovereignty. What had happened in Kansas suggested that popular sovereignty in practice was an invitation to civil war. Furthermore, the Dred Scott decision implied that the voters of a territory could not legally decide the fate of slavery at any time before the constitution-making stage. Hence, the interpretation of popular sovereignty favored in the North was undermined, and Southerners could insist on full protection of their right to own human property in all federal territories. For his stand against Lecompton, Douglas was denounced as a traitor in the South, and his hopes of being elected president were seriously diminished.

Debating the Morality of Slavery

Douglas's more immediate problem was to win reelection to the Senate from Illinois in 1858. Here he faced surprisingly tough opposition from a Republican candidate who, in defiance of precedent, was nominated by a party convention. (At this time, senators were elected by state legislatures.) Douglas's rival, former Whig Congressman Abraham Lincoln, set out to convince the voters that Douglas could not be relied on to oppose the extension of slavery, even though he had opposed the admission of Kansas under a proslavery constitution.

In the famous speech that opened his campaign, Lincoln tried to distance himself from his opponent by taking a more radical position. He argued that the nation had reached the crisis point in the struggle between slavery and freedom: "'A house divided against itself cannot stand.' I believe this government cannot endure, permanently half *slave* and half *free.*" Lincoln then described the chain of events between the Kansas-Nebraska Act and the Dred Scott decision as evidence of a plot to extend and nationalize slavery and called for defensive actions to stop the spread of slavery and place it "where the public mind shall rest in the belief that it is in the course of ultimate extinction." He tried to link Douglas to this proslavery conspiracy by pointing to his rival's unwillingness to take a stand on the morality of slavery, to his professed indifference about whether slavery was voted up or down in the territories. For Lincoln, the only security against the triumph of slavery and the slave power was moral opposition to human bondage. Neutrality on the moral issue would lull the public into accepting the expansion of slavery until it was legal everywhere.

In the subsequent series of debates that focused national attention on the Illinois senatorial contest, Lincoln hammered away at the theme that Douglas was a covert defender of slavery because he was not a principled opponent of it. Douglas responded by accusing Lincoln of endangering the Union by his talk of putting slavery on the path to extinction. Denying that he was an abolitionist, Lincoln made a distinction between tolerating slavery in the South, where it was protected by the Constitution, and allowing it to expand to places where it could legally be prohibited. Restriction of slavery, he argued, had been the policy of the Founders, and it was Douglas and the Democrats who had departed from the great tradition of containing an evil that could not be immediately eliminated.

Abraham Lincoln, shown here in his first full-length portrait. Although Lincoln lost the contest for the Senate seat in 1858, the Lincoln-Douglas debates established his reputation as a rising star of the Republican party. ❖

In the debate at Freeport, Illinois, Lincoln questioned Douglas on how he could reconcile popular sovereignty with the Dred Scott decision. The Little Giant, as Douglas was called by his admirers, responded that slavery could not exist without supportive legislation to sustain it and that territorial legislatures could simply refrain from passing a slave code if they wanted to keep it out. Historians formerly believed that Douglas's "Freeport doctrine" suddenly alienated his southern supporters. In truth, Douglas's anti-Lecompton stand had already undermined his popularity in the slave states. But the Freeport speech undoubtedly hardened southern opposition to his presidential ambitions.

Douglas's most effective debating point was to charge that Lincoln's moral opposition to slavery implied a belief in racial equality. Lincoln, facing an intensely racist electorate, vigorously denied this charge and affirmed his commitment to white supremacy. He would grant blacks the right to the fruits of their own labor while denying them the "privileges" of citizenship. This was an inherently contradictory position, and Douglas made the most of it.

Although Republican candidates for the state legislature won a majority of the popular votes, the Democrats carried more counties and thus were able to send Douglas back to the Senate. Lincoln lost an office, but he won respect in Republican circles throughout the country. By stressing the moral dimension of the slavery question and undercutting any possibility of fusion between Republicans and Douglas Democrats, he had sharpened his party's ideological focus and had stiffened its backbone against any temptation to compromise its Free-Soil position.

The South's Crisis of Fear

After Kansas became a free territory instead of a slave state in August 1858, the issue of slavery in the territories lost some of its immediacy, although it continued to carry great emotional and symbolic meaning. The remaining unorganized areas, which were in the Rockies and northern Great Plains, were unlikely to attract slaveholding settlers. Southern expansionists still dreamed of annexations in the Caribbean and Central America but had little hope of winning congressional approval. Nevertheless, Southerners continued to demand the "right" to take their slaves into the territories, and Republicans persisted in denying it to them. Although the Republicans repeatedly promised they would not interfere with slavery where it already existed, Southerners refused to believe them and interpreted their unyielding stand against the extension of slavery as a threat to southern rights and security.

A chain of events in late 1859 and early 1860 turned southern anxiety about northern attitudes and policies into a "crisis of fear." The events alarmed slaveholders because they appeared to threaten their safety and dominance in a new and direct way.

The first of these incidents was John Brown's raid on Harpers Ferry, Virginia, in October 1859. (See the Feature Essay, "The Enigma of John Brown," pp. 406–407.) Brown, who had the appearance and manner of an Old Testament prophet, thought of himself as God's chosen instrument "to purge this land with blood" and eradicate the sin of slaveholding. On October 16, he led eighteen men from his band of twenty-two (which included five free blacks) across the Potomac River from his base in Maryland and seized the federal arsenal and armory in Harpers Ferry.

Brown's aim was to commence from havens in the Appalachians a guerrilla war that would eventually extend to the plantation regions of the lower South. But the neighboring slaves did not rise up to join him, and Brown's raiders were driven out of the armory and arsenal by the local militia and forced to take refuge in a fire-engine house. There they held out until their bastion was stormed by a force of U.S. Marines commanded by Colonel Robert E. Lee. In the course of the fighting, ten of Brown's men were killed or mortally wounded, along with seven of the townspeople and soldiers who opposed them.

The wounded Brown and his remaining followers were put on trial for treason against the state of Virginia. The subsequent investigation produced evidence that several prominent northern abolitionists had approved of Brown's plan—to the extent they understood it—and had raised money for his preparations. This seemed to confirm southern fears that abolitionists were actively engaged in fomenting slave insurrection.

After Brown was sentenced to be hanged, Southerners were further stunned by the outpouring of sympathy and admiration that his impending fate aroused in the North. As Ralph Waldo Emerson expressed it, Brown "would make the gallows as glorious as the cross." His actual execution on December 2 completed Brown's elevation to the status of a martyred saint of the antislavery cause. The day of his death was marked in parts of the North by the tolling of bells, the firing of cannons, and the holding of memorial services.

Although Republican politicians were quick to denounce John Brown for his violent methods, Southerners interpreted the wave of northern sympathy as an expression of the majority opinion and the Republicans' "real" attitude. According to historian James McPherson, "They identified Brown with the abolitionists, the abolitionists with Republicans, and Republicans with the whole North." Within the South, the raid and its aftermath touched off a frenzy of fear, repression, and mobilization. Witch-hunts searched for the agents of a vast imagined conspiracy to stir up slave rebellion; vigilance committees were organized in many localities to resist subversion and ensure control of slaves; and orators pointed increasingly to secession as the only way to protect southern interests.

This painting, The Last Moments of John Brown, *celebrates the passionate abolitionist as a hero and martyr to the antislavery cause. On his way to the gallows, he pauses to greet a slave mother and her child.* ❖

Brown was scarcely in his grave when another set of events put southern nerves on edge once more. Next to abolitionist-abetted rebellions, the slaveholding South's greatest fear was that the nonslaveholding majority would turn against the master class and the solidarity of southern whites behind the peculiar institution would crumble. When Congress met to elect a speaker of the House on December 5, Southerners bitterly denounced the Republican candidate—John Sherman of Ohio—because he had endorsed as a campaign document a condensed version of Hinton R. Helper's *Impending Crisis of the South.* Helper's book, which called on lower-class whites to resist planter dominance and abolish slavery in their own interest, was regarded by slaveholders as even more seditious than *Uncle Tom's Cabin,* and they feared the spread of "Helperism" among poor whites almost as much as they feared the effect of "John Brownism" on the slaves.

The ensuing contest over the speaker's office lasted almost two months. As the balloting went on, southern congressmen threatened secession if Sherman was elected, and feelings became so heated that some representatives began to carry weapons on the floor of the House. Since the Republicans did not have an absolute majority and needed the votes of a few members of the American party, it eventually became clear that Sherman could not be elected, and his name was withdrawn in favor of a moderate Republican who had refrained from endorsing Helper's book. The impasse over the speakership was thus resolved, but the contest helped persuade Southerners that the Republicans were committed to stirring up class conflict among southern whites.

Republicans' identification with Helper's ideas may have been decisive in convincing many conservative planters that a Republican victory in the presidential election of 1860 would be intolerable. Anxiety about the future allegiance of nonslaveholding whites had been growing during the 1850s because of changes in the pattern of slave ownership. A dramatic rise in the price of slaves was undermining the ambition of slaveless farmers to join the slaveholding ranks. During the decade, the proportion of white heads of families owning slaves had shrunk from 30 to 25 percent in all the slave states and from 50 to 40 percent in the cotton belt of the lower South. Perceiving in this trend the seeds of class conflict, proslavery extremists had called for the reopening of the Atlantic slave trade as a way to reduce the price of slaves and make them more widely available. Although the interest of large owners in preserving the appreciated value of their human property had helped prevent the "proslavery crusade" from gaining broad support, many slaveholders were concerned about the social and political consequences of their status as a shrinking minority. Even those most strongly committed to the Union were terrified by the prospect that a Republican party in control of the federal government would use its power to foster "Helperism" among the South's nonslaveholding majority.

Feature Essay

THE ENIGMA OF JOHN BROWN

On December 2, 1859, an old man with a thick white beard, who might have stepped out of the pages of the Old Testament, stood on a scaffold in Virginia awaiting execution for attempting to start a slave insurrection. He was unrepentant and without fear. Defiantly facing the assembled militiamen and other onlookers, he handed one of his attendants a prophetic message claiming that he had acted under divine inspiration and that it was God's will that "the crimes of this *guilty,* land: *will* never be purged *away;* but with Blood." His abortive raid on the federal arsenal at Harpers Ferry, Virginia, had sent a wave of fear through the slaveholding South, but the manner of his death and his strong antislavery sentiments made him a hero to many in the North. No single man did more to heighten the sectional crisis of the late 1850s and increase the probability of civil war.

But who was this man and how did he come to play such an important role in the sectional drama? Controversy surrounded him during his lifetime and has continued to do so ever since. Many African Americans have revered him as the rare example of a white man willing to give his life for black freedom. Unlike most white Americans, he seems to have been totally free of racial prejudice and at times identified with blacks so completely that he—and they—could almost forget that he was not one of them. But the means that he used to pursue his ends—his willingness to resort to violence, even to terrorism—has troubled many of those who find his objectives praiseworthy. The obvious impracticality of the plan for a massive slave uprising that he tried to put into effect at Harpers Ferry also has raised questions about his soundness of mind.

This is the earliest known photograph of John Brown, probably taken around 1846 in Springfield, Massachusetts. He pledges allegiance to an unknown flag, possibly an abolitionist banner. ❖

John Brown was born in Connecticut in 1800, the descendent of an old New England family that may have been represented on the Mayflower. He received little formal education and followed in his father's occupation as a tanner of leather. Lured westward like so many New Englanders of the time, he pursued the tanning business first in western Pennsylvania and then in Ohio. But unsuccessful land speculations and the hard times following the Panic of 1837 drove him into bankruptcy in 1842. He then became a wool dealer but faced ruin again in 1849 when his attempt to cut out the usual middlemen and make a direct sale of 200,000 pounds of American wool to buyers in England resulted in a huge loss. Such risk taking and the resulting ups and downs were normal experiences for the businessmen of the time. Brown may have been unluckier than some others, but the notion that his antislavery zeal was somehow a compensation for business failure makes little sense.

As early as 1834, at a time when his tannery was doing well, Brown proposed to raise a black boy in his own family as an experiment to show slaveholders that race was no obstacle to the building of character. He also considered opening a school for black children. By 1847, however, Brown had given up on the idea that education and example could end slavery. While still a successful wool merchant in Springfield, Massachusetts, he confided to the black abolitionist Frederick Douglass the germ of the plan he later tried to put into effect at Harpers Ferry: instigation of guerrilla war against slavery based in the mountains of the South. In 1851, Brown organized Springfield's blacks into a secret militia to resist enforcement of the Fugitive Slave Act of 1850. In 1854, he retired from the wool business with the intention of devoting the rest of his life to the cause of black freedom and equality. From a farm in North Elba, New York, he acted as patron of a struggling black agricultural colony

John Brown, shown here barricaded at Harpers Ferry with his followers and hostages, looked on his fight against slavery as a holy campaign ordained by God. In his last speech to the court before his execution for conviction of murder, promoting slave insurrection, and treason, Brown proclaimed, "Now, if it is deemed necessary that I should forfeit my life for the furtherance of the ends of justice and mingle my blood further with the blood of my children and with the blood of millions in this slave country whose rights are disregarded by wicked, cruel, and unjust enactments—I say, let it be done!" ❖

and also served as a conductor on the Underground Railroad when fugitives heading for Canada came his way.

By the fall of 1855 the frontline of the struggle against slavery was in Kansas (see p. 398). Following in the wake of his five sons, Brown went west to join the fray in September. After proslavery ruffians sacked the Free State capital of Lawrence in the spring of 1856, Brown led a retaliatory raid on proslavery settlers living along Pottawatamie Creek. In what can only be described as an act of terrorism, Brown and his men executed five defenseless men who had been rousted from their beds. His apparent objective was to instill fear and panic among the proslavery forces, possibly driving them to commit outrages of their own and thus further polarize the nation on the slavery question. Perhaps Brown already had concluded that a civil war, or something like it, was the only way to end slavery, and he appeared committed to bringing it about by any means necessary. For the next two years Brown operated as a guerrilla fighter in Kansas, raising money from eastern supporters who were unaware of his role in the Pottawatamie massacre.

In May 1858, when the threat of the admission of Kansas to the Union as a slave state had been averted, Brown started organizing his raid on Harpers Ferry. He began by assembling a convention of black fugitives and abolitionists in Canada to draw up the constitution for the independent black state that he hoped to establish in the southern mountains as the base for a guerrilla war against the slaveholders. He then sought financial support from northern abolitionists and gathered a racially integrated force of twenty-two volunteers, eighteen of whom raided the federal arsenal. The plan was to seize the arms and distribute them to rebellious slaves. The raid turned into a debacle when the local militia trapped Brown and his men in a fire-engine house. Ten of Brown's men, including two of his sons, died as a result of the shooting that ensued. The survivors, including Brown himself, were captured by a force of U. S. Marines sent from Washington and commanded by Colonel Robert E. Lee. Local slaves did not, as Brown had hoped, rise up spontaneously in rebellion once the violence had commenced.

If Brown was certain that his attempt to ignite a slave uprising and a guerrilla war would succeed, he was clearly deluded and possibly deranged. Frederick Douglass, whom Brown had invited to join the raiders, decided that the plan had no reasonable chance of success and refused to participate. But the fact that Brown seemed to welcome his martyrdom, almost rejoicing in it, raises another intriguing possibility. Brown may have realized that the odds were against him and that he would probably fail. But he may also have calculated, quite correctly as it turned out, that the panic that even an abortive raid would evoke from the South and the sympathy that the punishment of its perpetrators might arouse in the North would push the nation closer to the civil war that he had come to believe was the only way to end slavery. If the voice he heard in his head was indeed that of an angry God ready to punish the nation for the sin of slavery, his logic was irrefutable.

The Election of 1860

The Republicans, sniffing victory and generally insensitive to the depth of southern feeling against them, met in Chicago on May 16 to nominate a presidential candidate. The initial front-runner, Senator William H. Seward of New York, had two strikes against him: He had a reputation for radicalism and a record of strong opposition to the nativist movement. What a majority of the delegates wanted was a less controversial nominee who could win two or three of the northern states that had been in the Democratic column in 1856. Abraham Lincoln met their specifications: He was from Illinois, a state the Republicans needed to win; he had a more moderate image than Seward; and he had kept his personal distaste for Know-Nothingism to himself. In addition, he was a self-made man, whose rise from frontier poverty to legal and political prominence embodied the Republican ideal of equal opportunity for all. After trailing Seward by a large margin on the first ballot, Lincoln picked up enough strength on the second to pull virtually even and was nominated on the third.

The platform, like the nominee, was meant to broaden the party's appeal in the North. Although a commitment to halt the expansion of slavery remained, economic matters received more attention than they had in 1856. With an eye on Pennsylvania, the delegates called for a high protective tariff; other planks included endorsement of free homesteads, which was popular in the Midwest and among working people, and federal aid for internal improvements, especially a transcontinental railroad. The platform was cleverly designed to bring most ex-Whigs into the Republican camp while also accommodating enough renegade Democrats to give the party a solid majority in the northern states.

Election of 1860

Electoral Vote by State		Popular Vote
REPUBLICAN Abraham Lincoln	180	1,865,593
DEMOCRATIC, SOUTHERN John C. Breckinridge	72	848,356
DEMOCRATIC, NORTHERN Stephen A. Douglas	12	1,382,713
CONSTITUTIONAL UNION John Bell	39	592,906
	303	4,689,568

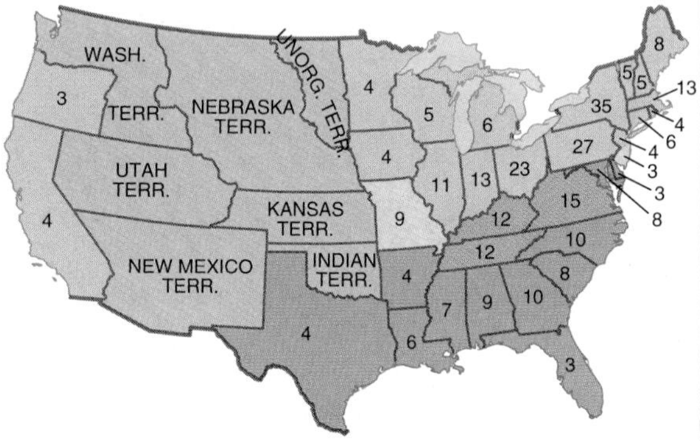

The Democrats failed to present a united front against this formidable challenge. When the party first met in the sweltering heat of Charleston in late April, Douglas commanded a majority of the delegates but was unable to win the two-thirds required for nomination because of unyielding southern opposition. He did succeed in getting the convention to endorse popular sovereignty as its slavery platform, but the price was a walkout by Deep South delegates who favored a federal slave code for the territories.

Unable to agree on a nominee, the convention adjourned to reconvene in Baltimore in June. The next time around, a fight developed over whether to seat newly selected pro-Douglas delegations from some Deep South states in place of the bolters from the first convention. When the Douglas forces won most of the contested seats, another and more massive southern walkout took place. The result was a fracture of the Democratic party. The delegates who remained nominated Douglas and reaffirmed the party's commitment to popular sovereignty, while the bolters convened elsewhere to nominate John Breckinridge of Kentucky on a platform of federal protection for slavery in the territories.

In this cartoon from the 1860 election, candidates Lincoln and Douglas struggle for control of the country, while Breckinridge tears away the South. John Bell of the Constitutional Union party futilely attempts to repair the damage to the torn nation. ❖

CHRONOLOGY

1846	David Wilmot introduces Proviso banning slavery in the Mexican cession
1848	Free-Soil party is founded ❖ Zachary Taylor (Whig) elected president, defeating Lewis Cass (Democrat) and Martin Van Buren (Free-Soil)
1849	California seeks admission to the Union as a free state
1850	Congress debates sectional issues and enacts Compromise of 1850
1852	Harriet Beecher Stowe publishes *Uncle Tom's Cabin* ❖ Franklin Pierce (Democrat) elected president by a large majority over Winfield Scott (Whig)
1854	Congress passes Kansas-Nebraska Act, repealing Missouri Compromise ❖ Republican party founded in several northern states ❖ Anti-Nebraska coalitions score victories in congressional elections in the North
1854–1855	Know-Nothing party achieves stunning successes in state politics
1854–1856	Free-state and slave-state forces struggle for control of Kansas Territory
1856	Preston Brooks assaults Charles Sumner on Senate floor ❖ James Buchanan wins presidency despite strong challenge in the North from John C. Frémont
1857	Supreme Court decides Dred Scott case and legalizes slavery in all territories
1858	Congress refuses to admit Kansas to Union under the proslavery Lecompton constitution ❖ Lincoln and Douglas debate slavery issue in Illinois
1859	John Brown raids Harpers Ferry, is captured and executed
1859–1860	Fierce struggle takes place over election of a Republican as speaker of the House (December–February)
1860	Republicans nominate Abraham Lincoln for presidency (May) ❖ Democratic party splits into northern and southern factions with separate candidates and platforms (June) ❖ Lincoln wins the presidency over Douglas, Breckinridge, and Bell

By the time the campaign was under way, four parties were running presidential candidates. In addition to the Republicans, the Douglas Democrats, and the "Southern Rights" Democrats, a remnant of conservative Whigs and Know-Nothings nominated John Bell of Tennessee under the banner of the Constitutional Union party. Taking no explicit stand on the issue of slavery in the territories, the Constitutional Unionists tried to represent the spirit of sectional accommodation that had led to compromise in 1820 and 1850. In effect, the race became a separate two-party contest in each section: In the North, the real choice was between Lincoln and Douglas; in the South, the only candidates with a fighting chance were Breckinridge and Bell. Douglas alone tried to carry on a national campaign, gaining some support in every state, but actually winning only in Missouri.

When the results came in, the Republicans had achieved a stunning victory. By gaining the electoral votes of all the free states except those from three districts of New Jersey that voted for Douglas Lincoln won a decisive majority—180 to 123 over his combined opponents. In the North, his 54 percent of the popular vote annihilated Douglas. In the South, where Lincoln was not even on the ballot, Breckinridge triumphed everywhere except in Virginia, Kentucky, and Tennessee, which went for Bell and the Constitutional Unionists. The Republican strategy of seeking power by trying to win decisively in the majority section was brilliantly successful. Although fewer than 40 percent of those who went to the polls throughout the nation actually voted for Lincoln, his support in the North was so solid that he would have won in the electoral college even if his opponents had been unified behind a single candidate.

Most Southerners saw the result of the election as a catastrophe. A candidate and a party with no support in their own section had won the presidency on a platform viewed as insulting to southern honor and hostile to vital southern interests. Since the birth of the republic, Southerners had either sat in the White House or exerted considerable influence over those who did. Those days might now be gone forever. Rather than accepting permanent minority status in American politics and facing the resulting dangers to black slavery and white "liberty," the political leaders of the lower South launched a movement for immediate secession from the Union.

Conclusion: Explaining the Crisis

Generations of historians have searched for the underlying causes of the crisis leading to disruption of the Union but have failed to agree on exactly what they were. Some have stressed the clash of economic interests between agrarian and industrializing regions. But this interpretation does not reflect the way people at the time expressed their concerns. The main issues in the sectional debates of the 1850s were whether slavery was right or wrong and whether it should be extended or contained. Disagreements over protective tariffs and other economic measures benefiting one section or the other were clearly secondary. Furthermore, it has never been clear why the interests of northern industry and those of the South's commercial agriculture were irreconcilable. From a purely economic point of view, there was no necessity for producers of raw materials to go to war with those who marketed or processed those raw materials.

Another group of historians blame the crisis on "irresponsible" politicians and agitators on both sides of the Mason-Dixon line. Public opinion, they argue, was whipped into a frenzy over issues that competent statesmen could have resolved. But this viewpoint has been sharply criticized for failing to acknowledge the depths of feeling that could be aroused by the slavery question and for underestimating the obstacles to a peaceful solution.

The dominant modern view is that the crisis was rooted in profound ideological differences over the morality and utility of slavery as an institution. Most interpreters are now agreed that the roots of the conflict lay in the fact that the South was a slave society and determined to stay that way, while the North was equally committed to a free-labor system. In the words of historian David Potter, "slavery really had a polarizing effect, for the North had no slaveholders—at least not of resident slaves—and the South had virtually no abolitionists." No other differences divided the regions in this decisive way, and it is hard to imagine that secessionism would have developed if the South had followed the North's example and abolished slavery in the postrevolutionary period.

Nevertheless, the existence or nonexistence of slavery will not explain why the crisis came when it did and in the way that it did. Why did the conflict become "irreconcilable" in the 1850s and not earlier or later? Why did it take the form of a political struggle over the future of slavery in the territories? Adequate answers to both questions require an understanding of political developments that were not directly caused by tensions over slavery.

By the 1850s, the established Whig and Democratic parties were in trouble partly because they no longer offered the voters clear-cut alternatives on economic issues that had been the bread and butter of politics during the heyday of the second party system. This situation created an opening for new parties and issues. After the Know-Nothings failed to make attitudes toward immigrants the basis for a political realignment, the Republicans used the issue of slavery in the territories to build the first successful sectional party in American history. They called for "free soil" rather than freedom for blacks because abolitionism conflicted with the northern majority's commitment to white supremacy and its respect for the original constitutional compromise that established a hands-off policy toward slavery in the southern states. For Southerners, the Republican party now became the main issue, and they fought against it from within the Democratic party until it ceased to function as a national organization in 1860.

If politicians seeking new ways to mobilize an apathetic electorate are seen as the main instigators of sectional crisis, the reasons that certain appeals were more effective than others must still be uncovered. Why did the slavery extension issue arouse such strong feelings in the two sections during the 1850s? The same issue had arisen earlier and had proved adjustable, even in 1820 when the second party system—with its vested interest in compromise—had not yet emerged. If the expansion of slavery had been as vital and emotional a question in 1820 as it was in the 1850s, the declining Federalist party presumably would have revived in the form of a northern sectional party adamantly opposed to the admission of slave states to the Union.

Ultimately, therefore, the crisis of the 1850s must be understood as having a deep social and cultural dimension as well as a purely political one. In *Uncle Tom's Cabin,* Harriet Beecher Stowe personified the cultural conflict in her depiction of two brothers with similar personalities, one of whom settled in Vermont "to rule over rocks and stones" and the other in Louisiana "to rule over men and women." The first became a deacon in the church, a member of the local abolition society, and, despite his natural authoritarianism, the adherent of "a democratic theory." The second became indifferent to religion, openly aristocratic, a staunch defender of slavery, and an extreme racist—"he considered the negro, through all possible gradations of color, as the intermediate link between man and animals." Stowe's comparison may have been biased, but she showed a good understanding of how the contrasting environments of slavery and freedom could lead very similar men to have sharply conflicting views of the world.

This divergence in basic beliefs and values had widened and become less manageable between the 1820s and the 1850s. Both sections continued to profess allegiance to the traditional "republican" ideals of individual liberty and independence, and both were strongly influenced by evangelical religion. But differences in the economic and social development of each region transformed a common culture into two conflicting cultures. In the North, a rising middle class adapted to the new market economy with the help of an evangelical Christianity that sanctioned self-discipline and social reform (see Chapter 12). The South, on the other hand, embraced slavery as a foundation for the liberty and independence of whites. Its evangelicalism encouraged personal piety but not social reform and gave only limited attention to building the kind of personal character that made for commercial success. The notion endured that white liberty and equality depended on resistance to social and economic change. The belief that continuing to have enslaved blacks to do menial labor became even more deeply entrenched.

When politicians appealed to sectionalism during the 1850s, therefore, they could evoke conflicting views of what constituted the good society. The South—with its allegedly idle masters, degraded unfree workers, and shiftless poor whites—seemed to a majority of Northerners to be in flagrant violation of the Protestant work ethic. From the dominant southern point of view, the North was a land of hypocritical money-grubbers who denied the obvious fact that the virtue, independence, and liberty of free citizens could be guaranteed only by keeping dependent laboring classes and racially inferior persons under the rigid control provided by slavery. According to the ideology of northern Republicans, the freedom of the individual depended on equality of opportunity for everyone. In the minds of southern sectionalists, it required that part of the population be enslaved. Once these contrary views of the world had become the main themes of political discourse, sectional compromise was no longer possible.

Recommended Reading

The best general account of the politics of the sectional crisis is David M. Potter, *The Impending Crisis, 1848–1861* (1976). This well-written and authoritative work combines a vivid and detailed narrative of events with a shrewd and detailed interpretation of them. For a shorter overview, see Bruce C. Levine, *Half Slave and Half Free: The Roots of the Civil War* (1991). On the demise of the Whigs, see Michael F. Holt, *The Rise and Fall of the American Whig Party* (1999). The best treatment of the Know-Nothing movement is Tyler Anbinder, *Nativism and Slavery: The Northern Know-Nothings and the Politics of the 1850s* (1992). The most important studies of northern political sectionalism are Eric Foner, *Free Soil, Free Labor, Free Men: The Ideology of the Republican Party Before the Civil War* (1970), and William E. Gienapp, *The Origins of the Republican Party, 1852–1856* (1987), on the Republican party generally; and Don E. Fehrenbacher, *Prelude to Greatness: Lincoln in the 1850s* (1962), on Lincoln's rise to prominence. On the climactic events of 1857, see Don E. Fehrenbacher, *The Dred Scott Case: Its Significance in American Law and Politics* (1978) and Kenneth M. Stampp, *America in 1857: A Nation on the Brink* (1990). On the background of southern separatism, see William W. Freehling, *The Road to Disunion: Secessionists at Bay, 1776–1854* (1990) and William L. Barney, *The Road to Secession: A New Perspective on the Old South* (1972).

For a list of additional titles related to this chapter's topics, please see http://www.ablongman.com/divine.

Suggested Web Sites

Secession Era Editorials Project

http://history.furman.edu/~benson/docs/
Furman University is digitizing editorials about the secession crisis and already includes scores of them on this site.

John Brown Trial Links

http://www.law.umkc.edu/faculty/projects/ftrials/Brown.html
For information about the trial of John Brown, this site provides a list of excellent links.

Abraham Lincoln and Slavery

http://odur.let.rug.nl/~usa/H/1990/ch5_p6.htm
This site discusses Lincoln's views and actions concerning slavery, especially the Lincoln-Douglas debate.

Bleeding Kansas

http://www.kancoll.org/galbks.htm
Contemporary and later accounts of America's rehearsal for the Civil War comprise this University of Kansas site.

The Compromise of 1850 and the Fugitive Slave Act

http://www.pbs.org/wgbh/aia/part4
From the series on Africans in America, an analysis of the Compromise of 1850 and of the effects of the Fugitive Slave Act on black Americans.

The 1850s: An Increasingly Divided Union

http://www.thoughtfultech.com/MMTS/50essay.html
A tutorial skills development site focusing on the events in the 1850s leading to the Civil War; from MMTS, the Multi-Media Thinking Skills project.

Words and Deeds in American History

http://lcweb2.loc.gov/ammem/mcchtml/corhome.html
A Library of Congress site containing links to Frederick Douglass; the Compromise of 1850; speeches by John C. Calhoun, Daniel Webster, and Henry Clay; and other topics from the Civil War era.

Law and Society

The Case of Dred and Harriet Scott

Blurring the Borders of Politics and Justice

The Missouri Compromise of 1820, which kept an even balance between the Union's slave states and free states by admitting Missouri as a slave state and Maine as a free state, was intended in part to answer the question of whether Congress had the authority to ban slavery in federal territories. That compromise, however, turned out to be only a temporary solution. Questions about the extension of slavery into new territories, the rights of slaveowners, and the status of slaves continued to plague Northerners and Southerners alike. Both the North and the South wanted to find a way to resolve these issues, but neither could agree on a compromise that would satisfy both sides. Finally, in 1857, a case came before the Supreme Court that seemed to address all these issues. To understand the Supreme Court's ruling in *Dred Scott* v. *Sandford*, it is necessary to go back to the year 1832, twenty-five years before the case reached the Court.

In the fall of 1832, with the Black Hawk War raging, a young physician named John Emerson accepted a temporary assignment as surgeon at Jefferson Barracks, an army post in Missouri. At this safe distance from any actual fighting, Dr. Emerson quickly became enamored of the life of a medical officer. As the war drew to a close, he sought and secured a full-time commission at Fort Armstrong, Illinois. Relieved to have obtained a permanent appointment, he headed north, setting the stage for the most controversial court decision in American history.

Emerson was accompanied on his journey by his sole slave, a pleasant looking man in his mid-thirties, known as Dred Scott. After arriving in Illinois, Scott continued to attend to Emerson's personal needs and performed most of the work on Emerson's land claims. For two years, Scott functioned as a contradiction in terms—a slave laboring in a free state. Scott's status grew even more complicated with Emerson's next transfer, which took the two men farther north. The pair traveled to Fort Snelling, in what was then Wisconsin Territory—an area where the Missouri Compromise explicitly forbade the practice of slavery. While in Wisconsin Territory, Scott met and married another transported slave, Harriet Robinson. Their union would last for the remainder of Dred Scott's life and produce four children, two of whom died in infancy. The surviving pair, Eliza and Lizzie, would join their parents in their famous fight for freedom.

When John Emerson died in December 1843, Dred and Harriet Scott found themselves back in Missouri and under the authority of Emerson's wife, Irene Sanford Emerson. Dred Scott attempted to purchase his family's freedom, but Mrs. Emerson refused his offer. Then, in the spring of 1846, the Scotts took Mrs. Emerson to court, claiming Dr. Emerson had forfeited all rights of ownership a decade earlier when he transported them into free territory. This relatively common maneuver by the Scotts initiated a series of legal struggles that would eventually wend all the way to the Supreme Court of the United States.

To avoid any direct challenge to the logic or legality of slavery, legal doctrine in Missouri required Dred and Harriet Scott to file a convoluted claim, which accused Mrs. Emerson of assault and false imprisonment. Such a claim did not directly argue the case for freedom, but in fact forced the court to decide on that very issue. If the Scotts were rightfully the slaves of Mrs. Emerson, her abusive behavior toward them would have been perfectly legitimate. If they were not her slaves, the claim of assault and false imprisonment would have been valid. Therefore, in order to consider the petitions of the Scotts, the court would first have to determine whether the Scotts were still slaves or whether their lengthy sojourn into free territory had automatically set them free. Such were the legal mazes made necessary by a slave regime.

One of the many myths that has developed about the Scott case claims that either the Scotts or their attorneys—who were paid for by white friends—had conceived of the suit as a test case, a chance to settle definitively some of the most perplexing questions posed by slavery. By all reliable accounts, however, Dred and Harriet Scott sought nothing more than freedom for themselves and their daughters. In fact, no one involved seems to have thought much about the possible political or legal implications of the particular case. Suits such as that filed by the Scotts were actually quite commonplace in the 1840s, and the typical outcome was freedom for the slave. Missouri courts had repeatedly held that slaves transported into free territory were thereby emancipated. A full decade before the Scotts' suit came to trial, a Missouri court had ruled in the slaves' favor in a case involving the specific issue of an army transfer. Given such precedents, the Scotts seemed to have a very strong case.

FRANK LESLIE'S ILLUSTRATED NEWSPAPER

No. 82.—VOL. IV.] NEW YORK, SATURDAY, JUNE 27, 1857. [PRICE 6 CENTS.

TO TOURISTS AND TRAVELLERS.

VISIT TO DRED SCOTT—HIS FAMILY—INCIDENTS OF HIS LIFE—DECISION OF THE SUPREME COURT.

The case of Dred and Harriet Scott resulted in a Supreme Court ruling that has been called the "most overturned decision in history." ❖

The Scotts also had the misfortune, however, of bringing their case to court at a time when public opinion in Missouri was experiencing a profound shift. As slavery came under increasing attack from the North and slaveholding became a fundamental element of Missourians' identity, judicial decisions grew steadily more hostile to the petitions of slaves. Missouri's precarious position as a border state intensified its preoccupation with any threat to the institution of slavery. As the premier student of the Scotts' case has commented, "the Scotts as suitors for freedom would become casualties of the sectional conflict."

When the trial finally began in June 1846, the Scotts' attorney brought a series of witnesses before the jury, all of whom testified that Dred Scott had indeed been at Forts Armstrong and Snelling. All that remained to secure the Scotts' freedom was the relatively simple task of proving what everyone already knew, that they were held as slaves by Mrs. Emerson. In a surprising legal move, Mrs. Emerson's lawyers raised doubts as to whether Mrs. Emerson, her brother, or her father actually claimed ownership of the Scotts. With bizarre logic, the jury returned the Scotts to Mrs. Emerson because the trial had failed to establish her as their rightful owner. The peculiar institution required a peculiar brand of law.

Undeterred, the Scotts moved for a retrial. After a series of complicated moves by both legal teams, the case came before the Missouri Supreme Court. The court handed down its decision in 1852, six years after the Scotts originally filed their petitions. During those six years, the slavery issue had reached a boiling point and no state felt its effects more than Missouri. Disputes over slavery had divided the state into two hostile factions.

Two of the Missouri supreme court justices stood squarely in the proslavery camp, and the third, a moderate, had neither the personality nor the inclination to oppose his colleagues on the Scott case. Relying heavily on a doctrine of states' rights, the court held that laws prohibiting slavery in Wisconsin Territory had no binding effect on the State of Missouri. Therefore, the court determined, the Scotts remained slaves. The decision explicitly referred to the deteriorating political climate, arguing that, "Times are not now as they were when the former decisions on this subject were made. Since then . . . States have been possessed with a dark and fell spirit in relation to slavery. . . . Under such circumstances it does not behoove the state of Missouri to show the least countenance to any measure which might gratify this spirit. . . ." Always closely related, law and politics had become indistinguishable in the Scott case.

Despite the ruling, neither the Scotts nor their supporters were prepared to give up the fight. The next step was to appeal to the nation's highest court, but such a move did not seem very promising. Not only did the United States Supreme Court have a majority of justices from slaves states, but one year earlier it had refused to hear a similar suit. In dismissing that case, Chief Justice Roger Taney followed the same logic that the Missouri Supreme Court had used in rejecting the Scotts' claims. Laws of federal territories, he reasoned, could have no effect on the policies of any state. Fearful of appealing to the court that had so recently issued an unfavorable ruling, the Scotts stalled.

Looking for a solution to the dilemma, the Scotts dropped the case of *Scott* v. *Emerson* and filed a new suit, *Scott* v. *Sandford.* (Somewhere along the way, Mrs. Emerson seems to have transferred her claim on the Scotts to her brother, John Sanford. In a misprint, the official court docket rendered his name as *Sandford.*) The terms of the new case would transform the Scotts' initially modest petition for freedom into a test case on the citizenship status of free African Americans and on the extent of federal prerogative in limiting the expansion of slavery. *Scott* v. *Sandford* thrust the Scotts immediately into a federal court and eventually into a national maelstrom. At this point, the two sides of the conflict seem to have lost sight of Dred and Harriet Scott, whose freedom could have easily been purchased by the resources that were devoted to the ensuing legal battle. They were being transformed from humble but determined slave petitioners into the icons of a national struggle.

Scott v. *Sandford* was tried in the small back room of a St. Louis store which served as the site of the United States Circuit Court for the District of Missouri. Neither side introduced new evidence or called witnesses; the case would be decided on the basis of evidence that had already been well established. The one new wrinkle was that by appealing to a federal court, the Scotts were making a claim for national citizenship, raising a controversial question that had yet to be resolved in American law: To what extent were free blacks entitled to the rights of citizens? The judge of the circuit court sidestepped this momentous issue to focus more narrowly on the specifics of the case. In May 1854, with the debate over the Kansas-Nebraska bill reaching a fevered pitch, a Missouri jury again refused to grant the Scotts their freedom. With no other recourse, the Scotts' attorney promptly made preparations to take their case to the U.S. Supreme Court.

Both sides pulled out the big guns for this final battle. Friends of the Scotts hired Montgomery Blair, a former U.S. solicitor general and a prominent figure in Washington society. Yet even a character as illustrious as Blair was outshone by Sanford's attorneys, among whom was Reverdy Johnson, a former U.S. attorney general, perhaps "the most respected constitutional lawyer in the country," and—even more importantly—the close personal friend of Chief Justice Taney. Dred and Harriet Scott were not in the courtroom as these eminent attorneys battled over their case; they remained in servitude in St. Louis. John Sanford also became a mere observer of the events. Battling mental illness throughout the period and finally seeking refuge in an asylum at the end of the year, Sanford grew increasingly irrelevant in a struggle that now overshadowed its original participants. Both legal teams pursued arguments that promoted their larger political objectives at the expense of their clients. Blair focused on the question of citizenship, which had already been *de facto* decided in Scott's favor by the lower court and could have been left alone. Instead of employing the proven strategy of claiming that territorial laws could not affect the policies of a given state, Sanford's attorneys used the more controversial but more consequential argument that federal antislavery laws were fundamentally unconstitutional.

After four days of such arguments, the Court surprisingly postponed the remainder of the trial until the next term, seven months away. During the lengthy recess, tensions in the country continued to rise at a frightening rate. In November, James Buchanan won a tight and acrimonious presidential race in which the extension of slavery had emerged as the preeminent political issue. The following month, with the nation still reeling from the bitter campaign, the trial resumed. The case was now more politicized than ever and the lawyers did not try to hide their respective agendas. Sanford's attorneys, in particular, frequently indulged in extensive defenses of the southern way of life. Not surprisingly, the debate grew hot and hostile. The Supreme Court had become the showcase for a nation coming apart at the seams.

Following the closing arguments, the justices gathered in early February to consider the Scott case. In addition to the specific question of the Scotts' freedom, the court debated the two weighty questions that had arisen from the trial: Were free African Americans citizens? Did Congress have the authority to prohibit slavery in the federal territories? The justices considered options that would have allowed them to decide on the Scotts' fate and still avoid the controversial issues, but there was immense public and political pressure for the Court to answer the broader questions once and for all. Chief Justice Taney was determined to do just that.

Roger Taney's presence on the bench loomed as the greatest single obstacle to the Scotts' freedom. In

Roger B. Taney, 1859 portrait by Emanuel Leutize. Taney's decision in the Dred Scott case evoked a variety of responses. Southern apologists for slavery applauded the ruling but abolitionists and opponents of slavery called the day of the decision one of the darkest in the history of the Republic. ❖

his late seventies when the Scott case was heard, Taney was a sickly man described by a colleague as "exceedingly feeble and broken." He had a stark courtroom demeanor and, despite his age and ill health, presided over the court with firmness. Taney spent most of his life in Maryland, and his views on slavery—and on just about everything else—were shaped by his experiences in that border state. A staunch Democrat and an unapologetic southerner, Taney doggedly defended states' rights against all federal encroachments. As the friction between North and South grew, the aged chief justice had become personally and emotionally embroiled in the issue. By the time the Scott case came before the Court, Taney was a "bitter sectionalist," anxious to put an end to "Northern insult and aggression."

On March 6, 1857, Taney addressed the packed courtroom and read the Court's official opinion, which he himself had composed. From start to Finish, Taney read for two full hours. As his tired voice concluded, the Scotts had lost their fight for freedom.

In rejecting the Scotts' claims, Taney tackled the issue of citizenship head on. The chief justice argued that the Constitution failed to afford blacks, slave or free, the rights of citizenship. Taney insisted that the framers of the Constitution considered people of African descent as a "subordinate and inferior class of beings, who had been subjugated by the dominant race, and, whether emancipated or not, yet remained subject to their authority, and had no rights or privileges but such as those who held the power . . . might chose to grant them." Emancipation, therefore, did not confer the rights of citizenship on blacks. Their race constituted a permanent mark of civil inferiority. In making the claim, Taney conspicuously failed to note that four New England states had already offered African Americans basic citizenship rights. Yet, despite this omission, the chief justice had actually been fairly accurate in gauging the era's prevailing mood. While Taney's racial doctrine seems extreme and even obscene by today's standards, it was representative of social attitudes of the time, even among many who opposed the institution of slavery. "Judge Taney's decision, infamous as it is," said Susan B. Anthony, "is but the reflection of the spirit and practice of the American people, North and South." It would take a war of unprecedented carnage before the nation was prepared to accept the citizenship of black Americans.

Having established that free blacks did not hold the rights of U.S. citizenship, Taney should have stopped. If Dred Scott was not entitled to bring a suit in federal court, the case was closed. But Taney was determined to issue an opinion on the second major question of the case, Congressional authority to prohibit slavery in the territories. The second half of Taney's ruling denied such Congressional authority and declared the Missouri Compromise unconstitutional. Taney relied on two highly questionable arguments to support this position: first, that the Constitution allowed Congress to legislate only on issues relating to the disposal of land, not on those affecting the legal status of the people living on that land, and second, that Congress only held such authority for land already claimed when the Constitution was drafted, excluding all territory acquired after 1787. Such arguments contradicted years of policy and precedent, including some of Taney's own rulings.

The Supreme Court's decision had four immediate effects. It outraged committed abolitionists, delighted apprehensive southerners, invalidated the principal plank of the new Republican party, and relieved worried moderates who believed the decision would lay the national controversy to rest. But despite the tremendous emotion the ruling evoked, many of its predicted effects proved illusory. It invited slavery to expand into the territories, but that never actually happened. It denied the Scotts their freedom, but they were shortly emancipated by new owners. And it claimed to answer fundamental questions of national importance, but those same questions continued to be debated until ultimately resolved by powder and shot.

The ruling's actual effects were quite different from those Taney expected. The emerging Republican Party, for instance, used the decision as a rallying point, decrying the slave power conspiracy that clearly controlled the highest court in the land. The party realized that it could overturn the decision only by changing the composition of the court and set its sights even more firmly on winning the presidency of 1860. By sparking intense political reactions and giving the Republican party a needed boost, the decision catalyzed sectional tensions, speeding the nation along the path to war.

Long after the Civil War had faded into history, *Scott* v. *Sandford* continued to leave its imprint on American law. The decision marked the first time the Supreme Court had actually struck down a major piece of federal legislation, paving the way for more aggressive judicial review in the future. It also signaled the development of a defining characteristic of American governance, a reliance on the courts to settle controversies that the normal processes of democracy cannot resolve. Ironically, *Scott* v. *Sandford* may have served as precedent for *Brown* v. *Board of Education.*

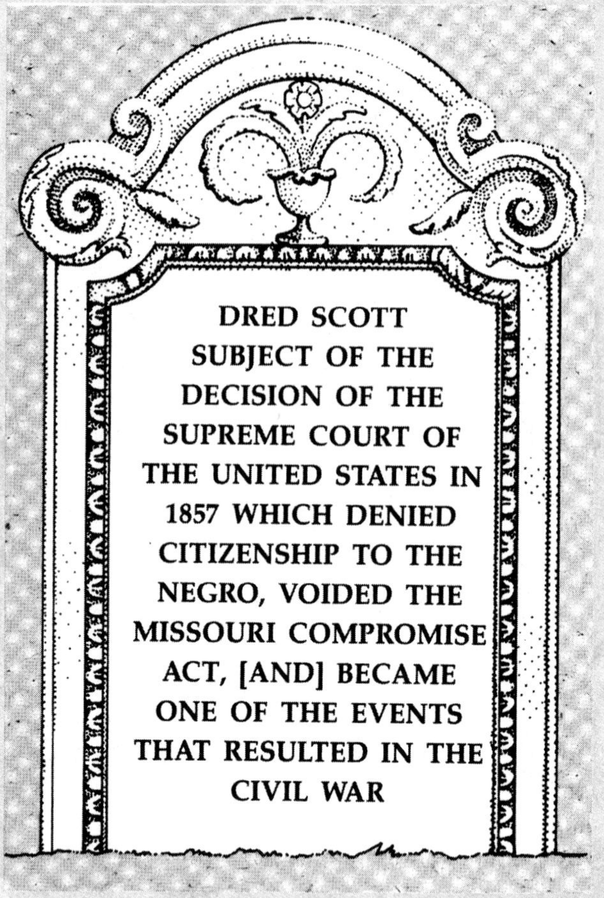

Although the legacy of the decision lives to this day, the major figures of this story did not long survive the momentous events. John Sanford died in an asylum two months after the Court handed down its decision. Dred and Harriet Scott remained in St. Louis after their emancipation where they worked as a hotel porter and a laundress; both died shortly before the onset of the Civil War. Roger Taney continued to serve as chief justice during the war. The southern octogenarian faced bitter animosity from the northern public, who considered him a traitor to the very government he claimed to serve. Taney died in 1864, not living to see the conclusion of the conflict he had helped start. As one sardonic contemporary noted, "The Hon. Old Roger B. Taney has earned the gratitude of his country by dying at last. Better late than never."

Questions for Discussion

- What made the Dred Scott decision so important in American history?
- What does the decision tell us about the status of African Americans in the United States on the eve of the Civil War?

Chapter 15

Off to the Front, painted by an unknown artist ca. 1861. This scene of wartime departure captures the grief of loved ones as families were forced to separate. As a husband and wife embrace, a tiny child holding a flag sits alone on the floor. ❖

Secession and the Civil War

The Emergence of Lincoln

The man elected to the White House in 1860 was striking in appearance—he was 6 feet 4 inches in height and seemed even taller because of his disproportionately long legs and his habit of wearing a high silk "stovepipe" hat. But Abraham Lincoln's previous career provided no guarantee he would tower over most of the other presidents in more than physical height. When Lincoln sketched the main events of his life for a campaign biographer in June 1860, he was modest almost to the point of self-deprecation. Especially regretting his "want of education," he assured the biographer that "he does what he can to supply the want."

Born to poor and illiterate parents on the Kentucky frontier in 1809, Lincoln received a few months of formal schooling in Indiana after the family moved there in 1816. But mostly he educated himself, reading and rereading a few treasured books by firelight. In 1831, when the family migrated to Illinois, he left home to make a living for himself in the struggling settlement of New Salem, where he worked as a surveyor, shopkeeper, and local postmaster. His brief career as a merchant was disastrous: He went bankrupt and was saddled with debt for years to come. But he eventually found a path to success in law and politics. While studying law on his own in New Salem, he managed to get elected to the state legislature. In 1837, he moved to Springfield, a growing town that offered bright prospects for a young lawyer-politician. Lincoln combined exceptional political and legal skills with a down-to-earth, humorous way of addressing jurors and voters. Consequently, he became a leader of the Whig party in Illinois and one of the most sought after of the lawyers who rode the central Illinois judicial circuit.

The high point of his political career as a Whig was one term in Congress (1847–1849). Lincoln did not seek reelection, but he would have faced certain defeat had he done so. His strong stand against the Mexican-American War alienated much of his constituency, and the voters expressed their disaffection in 1848 by electing a Democrat over the Whig who tried to succeed Lincoln. In 1849, President Zachary Taylor, for whom Lincoln had campaigned vigorously and effectively, failed to appoint him to a patronage job he coveted. Having been repudiated by the electorate and ignored by the national leadership of a party he had served loyally and well, Lincoln concentrated on building his law practice.

The Kansas-Nebraska Act of 1854, with its advocacy of popular sovereignty, provided Lincoln with a heaven-sent opportunity to return to politics with a stronger base of support. For the first time, his driving ambition for political success and his personal convictions about what was best for the country were easy to reconcile. Lincoln had long believed slavery was an unjust institution that should be tolerated only to the extent the Constitution and the tradition of sectional compromise required. He attacked Douglas's plan of popular sovereignty because it broke with precedents for federal containment or control of the growth of slavery. After trying in vain to rally Free-Soilers around the Whig standard, Lincoln threw in his lot with the Republicans, assumed leadership of the

Outline

Feature Essay

This campaign ribbon from the 1860 presidential election campaign depicts Republican candidate Abraham Lincoln as "the rail splitter of the West," a theme of the campaign intended to portray Lincoln as a figure with whom ordinary Americans could identify. ❖

new party in Illinois, attracted national attention in his bid for Douglas's Senate seat in 1858, and turned out to have the right qualifications when the Republicans chose a presidential nominee in 1860. The fact that he had split rails as a young man was used in the campaign to show that he was a man of the people.

After Lincoln's election provoked southern secession and plunged the nation into the greatest crisis in its history, there was understandable skepticism about him in many quarters: Was the former rail-splitter from Illinois up to the responsibilities he faced? Lincoln had less experience relevant to a wartime presidency than any previous chief executive; he had never been a governor, senator, cabinet officer, vice president, or high-ranking military officer. But some of his training as a prairie politician would prove extremely useful in the years ahead.

Another reason for Lincoln's effectiveness as a war leader was that he identified wholeheartedly with the northern cause and could inspire others to make sacrifices for it. In his view, the issue in the conflict was nothing less than the survival of the kind of political system that gave men like himself a chance for high office. In addressing a special session of Congress in 1861, Lincoln provided a powerful statement of what the war was all about:

> And this issue embraces more than the fate of these United States. It presents to the whole family of man, the question of whether a constitutional republic, or a democracy—a government of the people by the same people—can, or cannot, maintain its territorial integrity against its own domestic foes.

THE CIVIL WAR PUT ON TRIAL the very principle of democracy at a time when most European nations had rejected political liberalism and accepted the conservative view that popular government would inevitably collapse into anarchy. It also showed the shortcomings of a purely white man's democracy and brought the first hesitant steps toward black citizenship. As Lincoln put it in the Gettysburg Address, the only cause great enough to justify the enormous sacrifice of life on the battlefields was the struggle to preserve and extend the democratic ideal, or to ensure that "government of the people, by the people, for the people, shall not perish from the earth."

As he prepared to take office in 1861, Abraham Lincoln could scarcely anticipate the challenges he would face. The immediate problem was how to respond to the secession of the Deep South. But secession was just an expression of the larger question: Did the authority of the federal government outweigh the power of the individual states? No less important were questions about slavery: Was it morally acceptable for one person to "own" another? Could the Union continue to exist half-slave and half-free?

The sectionalism that had already led to a number of violent incidents—bloody fighting in Kansas, the assault on Charles Sumner, John Brown's raid on Harpers Ferry, his conviction on charges of treason against Virginia, and his eventual execution—continued to mount. Finally irreconcilable differences erupted into "total war" that left no part of society—North or South—untouched.

The Storm Gathers

Lincoln's election provoked the secession of seven states of the Deep South but did not lead immediately to armed conflict. Before the sectional quarrel would turn from a cold war into a hot one, two things had to happen: A final effort to defuse the conflict by compromise and conciliation had to fail, and the North needed to develop a firm resolve to maintain the Union by military action. Both of these developments may seem inevitable in retrospect, but for most of those living at the time, it was not clear until the guns blazed at Fort Sumter that the sectional crisis would have to be resolved on the battlefield.

The Deep South Secedes

South Carolina, which had long been in the forefront of southern rights and proslavery agitation, was the first state to secede. On December 20, 1860, a convention meeting in Charleston declared unanimously that "the union now subsisting between South Carolina and other states, under the name of the 'United States of America,' is hereby dissolved." The constitutional theory behind secession was that the Union was a "compact" among sovereign states, each of which could withdraw from the Union by the vote of a convention similar to the one that had ratified the Constitution in the first place. The South Carolinians justified seceding at that time by charging that "a sectional party" had elected a president "whose opinions and purposes are hostile to slavery."

In other states of the Cotton Kingdom, there was similar outrage at Lincoln's election but less certainty about how to respond to it. Those who advocated immediate secession by each state individually were opposed by the **cooperationists,** who believed the slave states should act as a unit. If the cooperationists had triumphed, secession would have been delayed until a southern convention had agreed on it. Some of these moderates hoped a delay would provide time to extort major concessions from the North and thus remove the need for dissolving the Union. But South Carolina's unilateral action set a precedent that weakened the cooperationists' cause.

Elections for delegates to secession conventions in six other Deep South states were hotly contested. Cooperationists did especially well in Georgia, Louisiana, and Texas. But nowhere did they stop secessionists from winning a majority. By February 1, seven states had removed themselves from the Union—South Carolina, Alabama, Mississippi, Florida, Georgia, Louisiana, and Texas. In the upper South, however, calls for immediate secession were unsuccessful; majority opinion in Virginia, North Carolina, Tennessee, and Arkansas did not subscribe to the view that Lincoln's election was a sufficient reason for breaking up the Union. In these states, a moderate Unionist element, deriving mainly from the old Whig party, had maintained its strength and cohesion despite the sectional crisis. Economic diversification had increased the importance of free labor and ties to the northern economy. Consequently, leaders in the border slave states were more willing than those in the lower South to seek a sectional compromise.

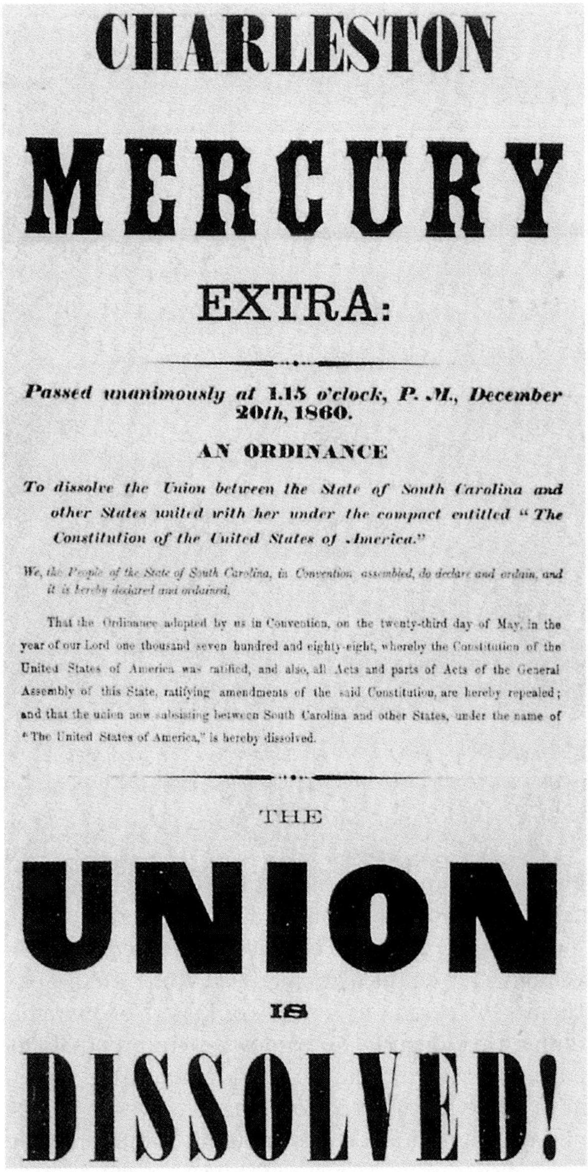
CHARLESTON

MERCURY

EXTRA:

Passed unanimously at 1.15 o'clock, P. M., December 20th, 1860.

AN ORDINANCE

To dissolve the Union between the State of South Carolina and other States united with her under the compact entitled "The Constitution of the United States of America."

We, the People of the State of South Carolina, in Convention assembled, do declare and ordain, and it is hereby declared and ordained,

That the Ordinance adopted by us in Convention, on the twenty-third day of May, in the year of our Lord one thousand seven hundred and eighty-eight, whereby the Constitution of the United States of America was ratified, and also, all Acts and parts of Acts of the General Assembly of this State, ratifying amendments of the said Constitution, are hereby repealed; and that the union now subsisting between South Carolina and other States, under the name of "The United States of America," is hereby dissolved.

THE

UNION

IS

DISSOLVED!

A South Carolina newspaper announces the dissolution of the Union. South Carolina's secession was celebrated in the South with bonfires, parades, and fireworks. ❖

Without waiting for their sister slave states to the north, delegates from the Deep South met in Montgomery, Alabama, on February 4 to establish the Confederate States of America. The convention acted as a provisional government while at the same time

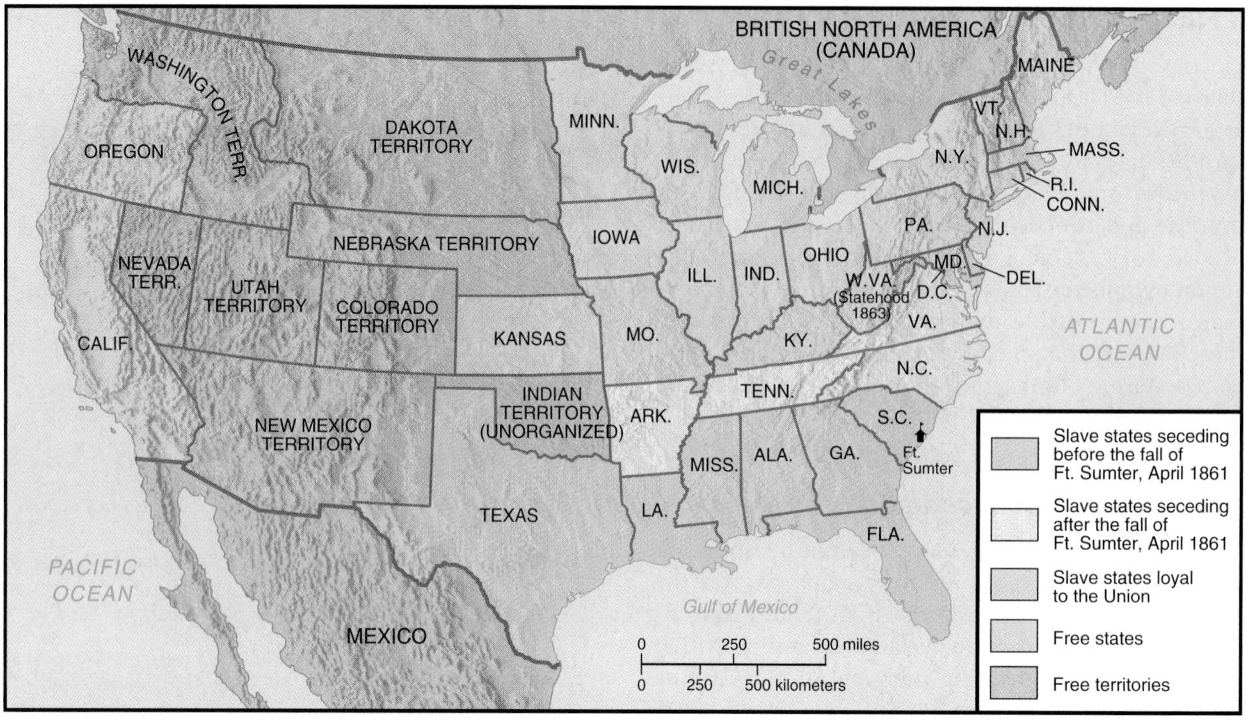

SECESSION *The fall of Fort Sumter was a watershed for the secessionist movement. With no room left for compromise, slave states of the upper South chose to join the Confederacy.*

drafting a permanent constitution. Relatively moderate leaders, most of whom had not supported secession until *after* Lincoln's election, dominated the proceedings and defeated or modified some of the pet schemes of a radical faction composed of extreme southern nationalists. Voted down were proposals to reopen the Atlantic slave trade, to abolish the three-fifths clause (in favor of counting all slaves in determining congressional representation), and to prohibit the admission of free states to the new Confederacy.

The resulting constitution was surprisingly similar to that of the United States. Most of the differences merely spelled out traditional southern interpretations of the federal charter: The central government was denied the authority to impose protective tariffs, subsidize internal improvements, or interfere with slavery in the states and was required to pass laws protecting slavery in the territories. As provisional president and vice president, the convention chose Jefferson Davis of Mississippi and Alexander Stephens of Georgia, men who had resisted secessionist agitation. Stephens, in fact, had led the cooperationist forces in his home state. Radical "fire eaters" such as William Yancey of Alabama and Robert Barnwell Rhett of South Carolina were denied positions of authority in the new government.

The moderation shown in Montgomery resulted in part from a desire to win support for the cause of secessionism in the reluctant states of the upper South, where such radical measures as reopening the slave trade were unpopular. But it also revealed something important about the nature of the separatist impulse even in the lower South. Proslavery reactionaries, who were totally lacking in reverence for the Union and wanted to found an aristocratic nation very different from the democratic United States, had never succeeded in getting a majority behind them. Most Southerners had been opposed to dissolving the Union and repudiating their traditional patriotic loyalties so long as there had been good reasons to believe slavery was safe from northern interference.

Lincoln's election and the panic that ensued gave Southerners cause to fear that Northerners would no longer keep their "hands off" southern slavery; but it was clear from the actions of the Montgomery convention that the goal of the new converts to secessionism was not to establish a slaveholder's reactionary utopia. What they really wanted was to re-create the Union as it had been before the rise of the new Republican party, and they opted for secession only when it seemed clear that separation was the only way to achieve their aim. The decision to allow free states to join the Confederacy reflected a hope that much of the old Union could be reconstituted under southern direction. Some optimists even predicted that all of the North except New England would eventually transfer its loyalty to the new government.

Jefferson Davis, inaugurated as president of the Confederacy on February 18, 1861, was a West Point graduate and had served as secretary of war under President Franklin Pierce. ❖

Secession and the formation of the Confederacy thus amounted to a very conservative and defensive kind of "revolution." The only justification for southern independence on which a majority could agree was the need for greater security for the "peculiar institution." Vice President Stephens spoke for all the founders of the Confederacy when he described the cornerstone of the new government as "the great truth that the negro is not equal to the white man—that slavery—subordination to the superior race—is his natural condition."

The Failure of Compromise

While the Deep South was opting for independence, moderates in the North and border slave states were trying to devise a compromise that would stem the secessionist tide before it could engulf the entire South. When the lame-duck Congress reconvened in December 1860, strong sentiment existed, even among some Republicans, to seek an adjustment of sectional differences. Senator John Crittenden of Kentucky presented a plan that served as the focus for discussion. The proposed **Crittenden compromise,** which resembled Henry Clay's earlier compromises, advocated extending the Missouri Compromise line to the Pacific to guarantee the protection of slavery in the southwestern territories and in any territories south of the line that might be acquired in the future. It also recommended federal compensation to the owners of escaped slaves and a constitutional amendment that would forever prohibit the federal government from abolishing or regulating slavery in the states.

Initially, congressional Republicans showed some willingness to give ground and take the proposals seriously. At one point, William Seward of New York, the leading Republican in the Senate, leaned toward supporting a version of the Crittenden plan. Somewhat confused about how firmly they should support the party position that slavery must be banned in all territories, Republicans in Congress turned for guidance to the president-elect, who had remained in Springfield and was refusing to make public statements on the secession crisis. An emissary brought back word that Lincoln was adamantly opposed to the extension of the compromise line. In the words of one of his fellow Republicans, he stood "firm as an oak."

The resounding no to the central provision of the Crittenden plan and other similar compromise proposals stiffened the backbone of congressional Republicans, and they voted against compromise in committee. Also voting against it, and thereby ensuring its defeat, were the remaining senators and congressmen of the seceding states, who had vowed in advance to support no compromise unless the majority of Republicans also endorsed it. Their purpose in taking this stand was to obtain guarantees that the northern sectional party would end its attacks on "southern rights." The Republicans did in the end agree to support Crittenden's "un-amendable" amendment guaranteeing that slavery would be immune from future federal action. This action was not really a concession to the South, because Republicans had always acknowledged that the federal government had no constitutional authority to meddle with slavery in the states.

Some historians have blamed Lincoln and the Republicans for causing an unnecessary war by rejecting a compromise that would have appeased southern pride without providing any immediate practical opportunities for the expansion of slavery. But it is questionable whether approval of the compromise would have halted secession of the Deep South. If the secessionists are taken at their word, they would have been satisfied with nothing less than federal protection of slavery in all territories and the active suppression of antislavery agitation in the North.

Furthermore, Lincoln and those who took his advice had what they considered to be very good reasons for not making territorial concessions. One of these derived from the mistaken northern notion that the secession movement was a conspiracy that reflected the will of only a minority of white Southerners.

Concessions would allegedly demoralize southern Unionists and moderates by showing that the "rule-or-ruin" attitude of the radical sectionalists paid dividends. It is doubtful, however, that Lincoln and the dedicated Free-Soilers for whom he spoke would have given ground even if they had realized the secession movement was genuinely popular in the Deep South. In their view, extending the Missouri Compromise line of 36°30' to the Pacific would not halt agitation for extending slavery to new areas. South of the line were Cuba and Central America, long the target of southern expansionists who dreamed of a Caribbean slave empire. The only way to resolve the crisis over the future of slavery and to reunite "the house divided" was to remove any chance that slaveholders could enlarge their domain.

Lincoln was also convinced that backing down in the face of secessionist threats would fatally undermine the democratic principle of majority rule. In his inaugural address of March 4, 1861, he recalled that during the winter, many "patriotic men" had urged him to accept a compromise that would "shift the ground" on which he had been elected. But to do so would have signified that a victorious presidential candidate "cannot be inaugurated till he betrays those who elected him by breaking his pledges, and surrendering to those who tried and failed to defeat him at the polls." Making such a concession would mean that "this government and all popular government is already at an end."

And the War Came

By the time of Lincoln's inauguration, seven states had seceded, formed an independent confederacy, and seized most federal forts and other installations in the Deep South without firing a shot. Lincoln's predecessor, James Buchanan, had denied the right of secession but had also refused to use "coercion" to maintain federal authority. In January, he sent an unarmed merchant ship, the *Star of the West,* to reinforce the federal garrison in Charleston Harbor, but the vessel turned back after being fired on. Buchanan's doubts about whether a Union held together by force was worth keeping were, for a time, widely shared in the North. Besides the business community, which was fearful of breaking commercial links with the cotton-producing South, some antislavery Republicans and abolitionists opposed coercive action because they thought the nation might be better off if "the erring sisters" of the Deep South were allowed "to depart in peace."

The collapse of compromise efforts eliminated the option of peaceful maintenance of the Union and narrowed the choices to peaceful separation or war between the sections. By early March, the tide of public opinion was beginning to shift in favor of strong action to preserve the Union. Once the business community realized conciliation would not keep the cotton states in the Union, it put most of its weight behind coercive measures, reasoning that a temporary disruption of commerce was better than the permanent loss of the South as a market and source of raw materials.

In his inaugural address, Lincoln called for a cautious and limited use of force. He would defend federal forts and installations not yet in Confederate hands but would not attempt to recapture the ones already taken. He thus tried to shift the burden for beginning hostilities to the Confederacy, which would have to attack before it would be attacked.

As Lincoln spoke, only four military installations within the seceded states were still held by U.S. forces. Two were in the remote Florida Keys and thus attracted

This contemporary Currier and Ives lithograph depicts the bombardment of Fort Sumter on April 12–13, 1861. The soldiers are firing from Fort Moultrie in Charleston Harbor, which the Union garrison had evacuated the previous December in order to strengthen Fort Sumter. ❖

little attention. The others were Fort Pickens in northern Florida, which was located in a defensible position on an island outside of the port of Pensacola, and Fort Sumter inside Charleston Harbor. Attention focused on Sumter because the Confederacy, egged on by South Carolina, was demanding the surrender of a garrison that was within easy reach of shore batteries and running low on supplies. Shortly after taking office, Lincoln was informed that Sumter could not hold out much longer and that he would have to decide whether to reinforce it or let it fall.

Initially, the majority of Lincoln's cabinet opposed efforts to reinforce or provision Sumter, on the grounds that it was indefensible anyway. Secretary of State Seward was so certain this would be the ultimate decision that he so advised representatives of the Confederacy. Lincoln kept his options open in regard to Sumter. On April 4, he ordered that an expedition be prepared to bring food and other provisions to the beleaguered troops in Charleston Harbor. Two days later, he discovered that his orders to reinforce Fort Pickens had not been carried out. Later that same day, he sent word to the governor of South Carolina that the relief expedition was being sent.

The expedition sailed on April 8 and 9, but before it arrived, Confederate authorities decided the sending of provisions was a hostile act and proceeded to attack the fort. Early on the morning of April 12, shore batteries opened fire; the bombardment continued for forty hours without loss of life but with heavy damage to the walls of the fort. Finally, on April 13, the Union forces under Major Robert Anderson surrendered, and the Confederate flag was raised over Fort Sumter. The South had won a victory but had also assumed responsibility for firing the first shot. Lincoln had taken pains to ensure that if the South was really determined to fight for its independence, it would have to begin by taking an aggressive action.

On April 15, Lincoln proclaimed that an insurrection against federal authority existed in the Deep South and called on the militia of the loyal states to provide 75,000 troops for short-term service to put it down. Two days later, a sitting Virginia convention, which had earlier rejected secession, reversed itself and voted to join the Confederacy. Within the next five weeks, Arkansas, Tennessee, and North Carolina followed suit. These slave states of the upper South had been unwilling to secede just because Lincoln was elected, but when he called on them to provide troops to "coerce" other southern states, they had to choose sides. Believing that secession was a constitutional right, they were quick to cut their ties with a government that opted for the use of force to maintain the Union and called on them to join in the effort.

In the North, the firing on Sumter evoked strong feelings of patriotism and dedication to the Union. "It seems as if we were never alive till now; never had a country till now," wrote a New Yorker; and a Bostonian noted, "I never before knew what a popular excitement can be." Stephen A. Douglas, Lincoln's former political rival, pledged his full support for the crusade against secession and literally worked himself to death rallying midwestern Democrats behind the government. By firing on the flag, the Confederacy united the North. Everyone assumed the war would be short and not very bloody. It remained to be seen whether Unionist fervor could be sustained through a long and costly struggle.

The entire Confederacy, which now moved its capital from Montgomery to Richmond, Virginia, contained only eleven of the fifteen states in which slavery was lawful. In the border slave states of Maryland, Delaware, Kentucky, and Missouri, a combination of local Unionism and federal intervention thwarted secession. Kentucky, the most crucial of these states, greeted the outbreak of war by proclaiming its neutrality. Kentucky eventually sided with the Union, mainly because Lincoln, who was careful to respect this tenuous neutrality, provoked the South into violating neutrality first by sending regular troops into the state. Maryland, which surrounded the nation's capital and provided it with access to the free states, was kept in the Union by more ruthless methods, which included the use of martial law to suppress Confederate sympathizers. In Missouri, the presence of regular troops, aided significantly by a staunchly pro-Union German immigrant population, stymied the secession movement. But pro-Union forces failed to establish order in this deeply divided frontier state. Brutal guerrilla fighting made wartime Missouri an unsafe and bloody place.

Hence the Civil War was not, strictly speaking, a struggle between slave and free states. Nor did it simply pit states that could not tolerate Lincoln's election against those that could. More than anything else, conflicting views on the right of secession determined the ultimate division of states and the choices of individuals in areas where sentiment was divided. General Robert E. Lee, for example, was neither a defender of slavery nor a southern nationalist. But he followed Virginia out of the Union because he was the loyal son of a "sovereign state." General George Thomas, another Virginian, chose the Union because he believed it was indissoluble. Although concern about the future of slavery had driven the Deep South to secede in the first place, the actual lineup of states and supporters meant the two sides would initially define the war less as a struggle over slavery than as a contest to determine whether the Union was indivisible.

Adjusting to Total War

The Civil War was a "total war" involving every aspect of society because the North could achieve its aim of restoring the Union only by defeating the South so thoroughly that its separatist government would be overthrown. It was a long war because the Confederacy put up "a hell of a fight" before it would agree to be put to death. Total war is a test of societies, economies, and political systems, as well as a battle of wits between generals and military strategists—and the Civil War was no exception.

Prospects, Plans, and Expectations

If the war was to be decided by sheer physical strength, then the North had an enormous edge in population, industrial capacity, and railroad mileage. Nevertheless, the South had some advantages that went a long way toward counterbalancing the North's demographic and industrial superiority. The South could do more with less, because its armies faced an easier task. To achieve its aim of independence, the Confederacy needed only to defend its own territory successfully. The North, on the other hand, had to invade and conquer the South. Consequently, the Confederacy faced a less serious supply problem, had a greater capacity to choose the time and place of combat, and could take advantage of familiar terrain and a friendly civilian population.

The nature of the war meant southern leaders could define their cause as defense of their homeland against an alien invader and thus appeal to the fervid patriotism of a white population that viewed Yankee domination as a form of slavery. The northern cause, however, was not nearly as clear-cut as that of the South. It seemed doubtful in 1861 that Northerners would be willing to give equally fervent support to a war fought for the seemingly abstract principle that the Union was sacred and perpetual.

Confederate optimism on the eve of the war was also fed by other—and more dubious—calculations. It was widely assumed that Southerners would make better fighting men than Yankees. Farm boys used to riding and shooting could allegedly whip several times their number among the clerks and factory workers (many of them immigrants) who, it was anticipated, would make up a large part of the Union army. (Actually, a majority of northern soldiers would also be farm boys.) When most of the large proportion of high-ranking officers in the U.S. Army who were of southern origin resigned to accept Confederate commands, Southerners confidently expected that their armies would be better led. If external help was needed, major foreign powers such as England and France might come to the aid of the Confederacy because the industrial economies of those European nations depended on southern cotton.

As they thought about strategy in the weeks and months after Fort Sumter, the leaders of both sides

RESOURCES OF THE UNION AND THE CONFEDERACY, 1861

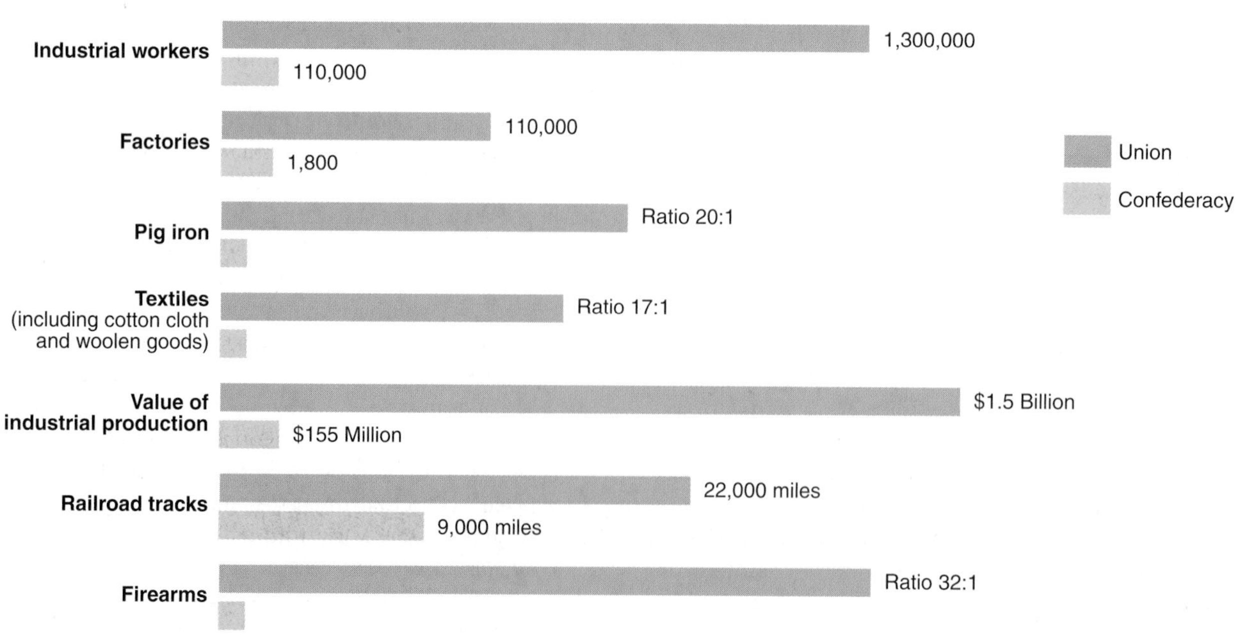

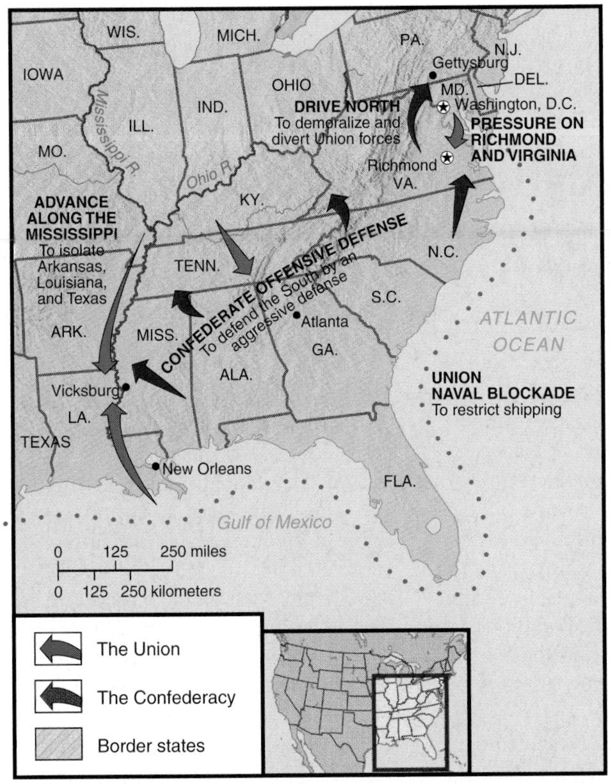

OVERVIEW OF CIVIL WAR STRATEGY *Confederate military leaders were convinced the South could not be defended unless they took the initiative to determine where critical battles would be fought.* ❖

tried to find the best way to capitalize on their advantages and compensate for their limitations. The choice before President Davis, who assumed personal direction of the Confederate military effort, was whether to stay on the defensive or seek a sudden and dramatic victory by invading the North. He chose to wage a mainly defensive war in the hope he could make the Union pay so dearly for its incursions into the South that the northern populace would soon tire of the effort. But this plan did not preclude invading the North for psychological or military effect when good opportunities presented themselves. Nor did it inhibit Confederate aggressiveness against exposed northern forces within the South. Although their primary strategic orientation was defensive, it was an "offensive defense" that southern commanders put into effect.

Northern military planners had greater difficulty in working out a basic strategy, and it took a good deal of trial and error (mostly error) before there was a clear sense of what had to be done. Some optimists believed the war could be won quickly and easily by sending an army to capture the Confederate capital of Richmond, scarcely a hundred miles from Washington. The "On to Richmond" solution died on the battlefields of Virginia when it soon became clear that difficult terrain and an ably led, hard-fighting Confederate army blocked the way. Aware of the costs of invading the South at points where its forces were concentrated, the aged General Winfield Scott—who commanded the Union army during the early months of the war—recommended an **anaconda policy.** Like a great boa constrictor, the North would squeeze the South into submission by blockading the southern coasts, seizing control of the Mississippi, and cutting off supplies of food and other essential commodities. This plan pointed to the West as the main locus of military operations.

Eventually Lincoln decided on a two-front war. He would keep the pressure on Virginia in the hope a breakthrough would occur there, while at the same time, he would authorize an advance down the Mississippi Valley with the aim of isolating Texas, Arkansas, and Louisiana. Lincoln also attached great importance to the coastal blockade and expected naval operations to seize the ports through which goods entered and left the Confederacy. His basic plan of applying pressure and probing for weaknesses at several points simultaneously was a good one because it took maximum advantage of the North's superiority in manpower and matériel. But it required better military leadership than the North possessed at the beginning of the war and took a painfully long time to put into effect.

Mobilizing the Home Fronts

The North and South faced similar problems in trying to create the vast support systems needed by armies in the field. At the beginning of the conflict, both sides had more volunteers than could be armed and outfitted. The South was forced to reject about 200,000 men in the first year of the war, and the North could commit only a fraction of its forces to battle. Further confusion resulted from the fact that recruiting was done primarily by the states, which were reluctant to surrender control of the forces they had raised. Both Lincoln and Davis had to deal with governors who resisted centralized direction of the military effort.

As it became clear that hopes for a short and easy war were false, the pool of volunteers began to dry up. Many of the early recruits, who had been enrolled for short terms, showed a reluctance to reenlist. To resolve this problem, the Confederacy passed a conscription law in April 1862, and the Union edged toward a draft in July when Congress gave Lincoln the power to assign manpower quotas to each state and resort to conscription if they were not met. (See the Feature Essay, "Soldiering in the Civil War," pp. 428–429.)

To produce the materials of war, both governments relied mainly on private industry. In the North, especially, the system of contracting with private firms and individuals to supply the army resulted in much corruption and inefficiency. The government at times

Feature Essay

SOLDIERING IN THE CIVIL WAR

Early in the Civil War, William Tecumseh Sherman told an audience of fresh-faced recruits, "There's many a boy here today who looks on war as all glory, but, boys, it is all hell." Letters from Civil War soldiers reveal that Sherman's lesson was painfully learned by young men in both armies over the four years of conflict. At the outset, the firing on Fort Sumter infected both North and South with war fever. What later became a national nightmare began as a glorious defense of home and country. Young men rushed to join up in great numbers, taxing the ability of the authorities to process enlistments.

In contrast to the typical soldier of modern warfare, many of the early Civil War volunteers had well developed ideas of what the war was about. On both sides, such troops formed a core of stalwart soldiers who were committed to the ideological and political implications of the struggle. In the democratic atmosphere of the nineteenth century, when governments had little power to coerce citizen-soldiers, neither army could have sustained four years of brutal fighting if significant numbers of their troops did not genuinely believe in their side's cause. The ideologically motivated troops may have accounted for about half of the fighting force.

The other half was another matter. As with any large military force, the Union and Confederate armies struggled to motivate and discipline men who cared little for the principles at the root of the conflict. Such soldiers, who were typically drafted, cajoled, or bribed into service, found numerous ways to avoid the dangers of combat. Known as skulkers and sneaks, these reluctant troops could avoid combat by feigning sickness, hiding, hanging back, asking for "bomb-proof" assignments, or simply deserting in droves. The bad blood between such soldiers and those who fervently believed in the war effort could be intense.

But the skulker and the ideologue shared one thing in common: Neither was fully prepared for the rigors of war.

Early Union defeats and a strategic stalemate not only ended talk in both the North and the South of a "short engagement filled with glory" but also revealed how undisciplined the troops were. Of the more than three million Civil War servicemen, two-thirds were younger than 23 years of age and came from rural areas. They were not accustomed to the regimentation necessary to military life; as a young recruit from Illinois put it, "It comes rather hard at first to be deprived of liberty." Inadequate leadership, as well as the beginnings of war weariness and the arrival of letters from home pleading for help with the harvest, led to a degree of military anarchy. The early battles were contests between armed mobs that might break and run with little provocation. Moreover, the long casualty lists from the early battles discouraged new waves of enlistments.

Both governments hit on similar methods of recruiting and disciplining troops. Enlistment and reenlistment bounties were instituted, and the nation's first conscription laws were passed. The dual aim was to maintain the ranks of the original volunteers while at the same time stimulating more enlistments. Terms of service were lengthened, in most cases to three years, and all nonenlisted men of military age were registered and called on to either volunteer or be faced with the disgrace of being drafted. Although some Southerners were exempted to oversee their large numbers of slaves, and Northerners could escape military duty by paying a $300 fee, the laws did spur enlistments. Between 1861 and 1865, more than half of the nation's 5.5 million men of military age were mustered into service.

The solution to the problem of training the troops was the army training camp. With its "50,000 pup tents and wigwams," the camp was the volunteer's way station between home and battlefield. It was the place the raw recruit received his first bitter taste of the tedium, hardship, and deprivation of soldiering. "A soldier is not his own man," a Louisiana recruit wrote, astonished at how markedly camp routines differed from civilian life. "He has given up all claim on himself. . . . I will give you a little information concerning every day business. consider yourself a private soldier and in camp . . . the drum beats for drill. you fall in and start. you here feel youre inferirority. even the Sargeants is hollering at you close up; Ketch step. dress to the right, and sutch like."

Youthful idealism is still evident on the faces of these young Civil War soldiers who have not yet learned General Sherman's message that "war is hell." ❖

Professional noncommissioned officers from the peacetime army were used, more effectively by the Union, to turn men into soldiers who could fire a rifle and understand simple commands. The liberal use of the court-martial and the board of review enabled the professional soldiers to rid the army of its most incompetent officer-politicians and instill discipline in the ranks. Many recruits spent their entire terms of service within the tent cities, forming a reserve on which field commanders could call to replace casualties.

The camps were themselves the sites of hundreds of thousands of Civil War casualties. Fewer men died of battle wounds than of dysentery, typhoid fever, and other waterborne diseases contracted in the camps, which were often located on swampy land without adequate fresh water. The army food was always the butt of soldier humor—one soldier complained the beef issued to him must have been carved from a bull "too old for the conscript law"—but it was also the source of its own set of diseases, particularly scurvy. Men in the field were condemned to a diet of "hardtack and half-cooked beans," and no soldier could expect to receive fresh fruit or vegetables. But food became steadily more plentiful in the Union camps, and doctors, officers, and agents of the U.S. Sanitary Commission teamed up to improve camp cleanliness. "Johnny Reb," however, had to survive under steadily worsening conditions. The Confederate supply system did not improve significantly during the course of the war and grew worse wherever the North invaded or blockaded. Nevertheless, the battlefield performance of fighting men on the two sides remained roughly on a par throughout the war.

Camp lessons were often forgotten in the heat of battle, particularly by green troops who "saw the elephant" (went into battle for the first time) and ran from it. Like the youth in Stephen Crane's *The Red Badge of Courage,* a Mississippian anxiously admitted after his first fight that "though i did not run i mite have if i had thought of it in time." The Union's ability to call more new men into service may have guaranteed ultimate victory, but it meant that battle-hardened Confederate veterans faced large numbers of raw northern recruits in every major battle. Since experience often counted for more than basic training and equipment, southern troops could expect to engage the enemy on fairly equal terms.

The Civil War was the most costly and brutal struggle in which American soldiers have ever been engaged. More American servicemen died in that war (618,000) than in the two world wars and Vietnam combined. Contests were decided by deadly charges in which muskets were exploded at such close range as to sear the faces of the contestants. The survivors, in their letters home, attempted to describe the inhuman events, but, as a Maine soldier wrote to his parents after the battle of Gettysburg: "You can form no idea of a battlefield. . . . no pen can describe it. No tongue can tell its horror[.] I hope none of my brothers will ever have to go into a fight."

bought shoddy uniforms that disintegrated in a heavy rain, defective rifles, and broken-down horses unfit for service. But the North's economy was strong at the core, and by 1863 its factories and farms were producing more than enough to provision the troops without significantly lowering the living standards of the civilian population.

The southern economy was much less adaptable to the needs of a total war. Because of the weakness of its industrial base, the South of 1861 depended on the outside world for most of its manufactured goods. As the Union blockade became more effective, the Confederacy had to rely increasingly on a government-sponsored crash program to produce war materials. In addition to encouraging and promoting private initiative, the government built its own munitions plants, including a gigantic powder factory at Augusta, Georgia. Astonishingly, the Confederate Ordnance Bureau, under the able direction of General Josiah Gorgas, succeeded in producing or procuring sufficient armaments to keep southern armies well supplied throughout the conflict.

Southern agriculture, however, failed to meet the challenge. Planters were reluctant to shift from staples that could no longer be readily exported to foodstuffs that were urgently needed. But more significant was the inadequacy of the South's internal transportation system. Its limited rail network was designed to link plantation regions to port cities rather than to connect food-producing areas with centers of population, as was the pattern in the North. New railroad construction during the war did not resolve the problem; most of the new lines were aimed at facilitating the movement of troops rather than the distribution of food.

When northern forces penetrated parts of the South, they created new gaps in the system. As a result, much of the corn or livestock that was raised could not reach the people who needed it. Although well armed, Confederate soldiers were increasingly undernourished, and by 1863 civilians in urban areas were rioting to protest shortages of food. To supply the troops, the Confederate commissary resorted to the impressment of available agricultural produce at below the market price, a policy resisted so vigorously by farmers and local politicians that it eventually had to be abandoned.

Another challenge faced by both sides was how to finance an enormously costly struggle. Although special war taxes were imposed, neither side was willing to resort to the heavy taxation that was needed to maintain fiscal integrity. Americans, it seems, were more willing to die for their government than to pay for it. Besides floating loans and selling bonds, both treasuries deliberately inflated the currency by printing large quantities of paper money that could not be redeemed in gold and silver. In August 1861, the Confederacy issued $100 million of such currency. In early 1862, the Union followed suit by printing $150 million in Treasury notes, known as **greenbacks** because of their color. The presses rolled throughout the war, and runaway inflation was the inevitable result. The problem was much less severe in the North because of the overall strength of its economy.

❖ A Look At the Past ❖

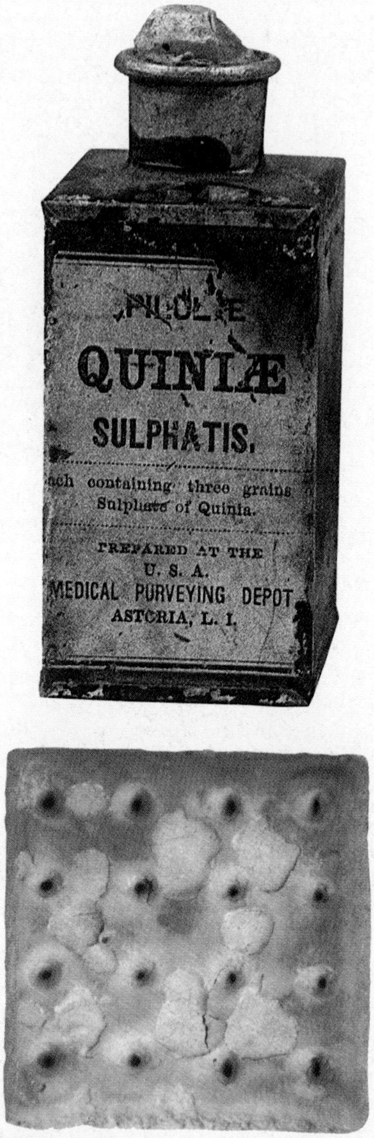

Civil War Rations

Civil War soldiers depended upon hardtack, a saltless hard biscuit, as a food staple. Quinine, a remedy for malaria, also represented an essential supply for soldiers. Together the items testify to the hardships soldiers endured. If these were essential supplies, how common do you suppose were disease, hunger, and malnutrition?

War taxes on income were more readily collectable than in the South, and bond issues were more successful.

The Confederacy was hampered from the outset by a severe shortage of readily disposable wealth that could be tapped for public purposes. Land and cotton could not easily be turned into rifles and cannons, and the southern treasury had to accept payments "in kind." As a result, Confederate "assets" eventually consisted mainly of bales of cotton that were unexportable because of the blockade. As the Confederate government fell deeper and deeper into debt and printed more and more paper money, its rate of inflation soared out of sight. By August 1863, a Confederate dollar was worth only eight cents in gold. Late in the war, it could be said with little exaggeration that it took a wheelbarrow full of money to buy a purse full of goods.

Political Leadership: Northern Success and Southern Failure

Total war also forced political adjustments, and both the Union and the Confederacy had to face the question of how much democracy and individual freedom could be permitted when military success required an unprecedented exercise of government authority. Since both constitutions made the president commander in chief of the army and navy, Lincoln and Davis took actions that would have been regarded as arbitrary or even tyrannical in peacetime. Nevertheless, "politics as usual"—in the form of free elections, public political controversy, and the maneuverings of parties, factions, and interest groups—persisted to a surprising degree.

Lincoln was especially bold in assuming new executive powers. After the fighting started at Fort Sumter, he expanded the regular army and advanced public money to private individuals without authorization by Congress. On April 27, 1861, he declared martial law, which enabled the military to arrest civilians suspected of aiding the enemy, and suspended the writ of habeas corpus in the area between Philadelphia and Washington, an action deemed necessary because of mob attacks on Union troops passing through Baltimore. Suspension of the writ enabled the government to arrest Confederate sympathizers and hold them without trial, and in September 1862 Lincoln extended this authority to all parts of the United States where "disloyal" elements were active. Such willingness to interfere with civil liberties was unprecedented and possibly unconstitutional, but Lincoln argued that "necessity" justified a flexible interpretation of his war powers. For critics of suspension, he had a question: "Are all the laws, *but one,* to go unexecuted, and the government itself to go to pieces, lest that one be violated?" In fact, however, most of the thousands of civilians arrested by military authorities were not exercising their right to criticize the government but were suspected deserters and draft dodgers, refugees, smugglers, or people who were simply found wandering in areas under military control.

For the most part, the Lincoln administration showed restraint and tolerated a broad spectrum of political dissent. Although the government closed down a few newspapers for brief periods when they allegedly published false information or military secrets, anti-administration journals were allowed to criticize the president and his party at will. A few politicians, including an Ohio Congressman, were arrested for pro-Confederate activity, but a large number of "Peace Democrats"—who called for restoration of the Union by negotiation rather than force—ran for office and sat in Congress and in state legislatures, and they thus had ample opportunity to present their views to the public. In fact, the persistence of vigorous two-party competition in the North during the Civil War strengthened Lincoln's hand. Since his war policies were also the platform of his party, he could usually rely on unified partisan backing for the most controversial of his decisions.

Lincoln was singularly adept at the art of party leadership; he was able to accommodate various factions and define party issues and principles in a way that would encourage unity and dedication to the cause. Since the Republican party served during the war as the main vehicle for mobilizing and maintaining devotion to the Union effort, these political skills assumed crucial importance. When a majority of the party came around to the view that freeing the slaves was necessary to the war effort, Lincoln found a way to comply with their wishes while minimizing the disenchantment of the conservative minority. Lincoln held the party together by persuasion, patronage, and flexible policymaking; this cohesiveness was essential to Lincoln's success in unifying the nation by force.

Jefferson Davis, most historians agree, was a less effective war leader than Lincoln. He defined his powers as commander in chief narrowly and literally, which meant he assumed personal direction of the armed forces but left policymaking for the mobilization and control of the civilian population primarily to the Confederate Congress. Unfortunately, he overestimated his capacities as a strategist and lacked the tact to handle field commanders who were as proud and testy as he was. Two of the South's best generals—Joseph E. Johnston and Pierre G. T. Beauregard—were denied the commands they deserved because they could not get along with Davis. One of the worst—Braxton E. Bragg—happened to be a personal favorite of the president and was allowed to keep a major

Gaunt southern citizens stare unbelievingly at a poster announcing a day of fasting proclaimed by a horned Jefferson Davis. Davis's insistent demands for his army aroused the hard-pressed Southerners' anger. ❖

command even after he had clearly demonstrated his incompetence.

Davis's greatest failing, however, was his lack of initiative and leadership in dealing with the problems of the home front. He devoted little attention to a deteriorating economic situation that caused great hardship and sapped Confederate morale. Although the South had a much more serious problem of internal division and disloyalty than the North, he refrained from declaring martial law on his own authority. The Confederate Congress grudgingly voted him such power when he asked for it but allowed it to be applied only in limited areas and for short periods.

As the war dragged on, Davis's political and popular support eroded. He was opposed and obstructed by state governors—such as Joseph E. Brown of Georgia and Zebulon Vance of North Carolina—who resisted conscription and other Confederate policies that violated the tradition of states' rights. The Confederate Congress served as a forum for bitter attacks on the administration's conduct of the war, and by 1863 a majority of southern newspapers were taking an anti-Davis stand. Even if he had been a more able and inspiring leader, Davis would have had difficulty maintaining his authority and credibility. Unlike Lincoln, he did not have an organized party behind him, for the Confederacy never developed a two-party system. As a result, it was difficult to mobilize the support required for hard decisions and controversial policies.

Early Campaigns and Battles

The war's first major battle was a disaster for northern arms. Against his better judgment, General Winfield Scott responded to the "On to Richmond" clamor and ordered poorly trained Union troops under General Irvin McDowell to advance against the Confederate forces gathered at Manassas Junction, Virginia. They attacked the enemy position near Bull Run Creek on July 21, 1861, and seemed on their way to victory until Confederate reinforcements arrived from the Shenandoah Valley. After Confederate General Thomas J. Jackson had earned the nickname "Stonewall" for holding the line against the northern assault, the augmented southern army counterattacked and routed the invading force. As they retreated toward Washington, the raw Union troops gave in to panic and broke ranks in their stampede to safety.

The humiliating defeat at Bull Run led to a shake-up of the northern high command. The man of the hour was George McClellan, who first replaced McDowell as commander of troops in the Washington area and then became general in chief when Scott was eased into retirement. A cautious disciplinarian, McClellan spent the fall and winter drilling his troops and whipping them into shape. President Lincoln, who could not understand why McClellan was taking so long to go into the field, became increasingly impatient and finally tried to order the army into action.

Before McClellan made his move, Union forces in the West won some important victories. In February 1862, a joint military-naval operation, commanded by General Ulysses S. Grant, captured Fort Henry on the Tennessee River and Fort Donelson on the Cumberland. Fourteen thousand prisoners were taken at Donelson, and the Confederate army was forced to withdraw from Kentucky and middle Tennessee. Southern forces in the West then massed at Corinth, Mississippi, just across the border from Tennessee. When a slow-moving Union army arrived just north of the Mississippi state line, the South launched a surprise attack on April 6. In the battle of Shiloh, one of the bloodiest of the war, only the timely arrival of reinforcements prevented the annihilation of Union troops backed up against the Tennessee River. After a second day of fierce fighting, the Confederates retreated to Corinth, leaving the enemy forces battered and exhausted.

Although the Union's military effort to seize control of the Mississippi Valley was temporarily halted at Shiloh, the Union navy soon contributed dramatically to the pursuit of that objective. On April 26, a fleet under Flag Officer David Farragut, coming up from the Gulf, captured the port of New Orleans after boldly running past the forts below the city. The occupation of New Orleans, besides securing the mouth of the Mississippi, climaxed a series of naval and amphibious operations around the edges of the Confederacy that had already succeeded in capturing South Carolina's Sea Islands and North Carolina's

Roanoke Island. Strategically located bases were thus available to enforce a blockade of the southern coast. The last serious challenge to the North's naval supremacy ended on March 9, 1862, when the Confederate ironclad vessel *Virginia* (originally the USS *Merrimac*)—which had demolished wooden-hulled northern ships in the vicinity of Hampton Roads, Virginia—was repulsed by the *Monitor,* an armored and turreted Union gunship.

Successes around the edges of the Confederacy did not relieve northern frustration at the inactivity or failure of Union forces on the eastern front. Only after Lincoln had relieved him of supreme command and ordered him to take the offensive at the head of the Army of the Potomac did McClellan start campaigning. Spurning the treacherous overland route to Richmond, he moved his forces by water to the peninsula southeast of the Confederate capital. After landing at Fortress Monroe, which had remained in Union hands, McClellan began moving up the peninsula in early April 1862. For a month he was bogged down before Yorktown, which he chose to besiege rather than assault directly. After Yorktown fell on May 4, he pushed ahead to a point twenty miles from Richmond, where he awaited the additional troops that he expected Lincoln to send.

The reinforcements were not forthcoming. While McClellan was inching his way up the peninsula, a relatively small southern force under Stonewall Jackson was on the rampage in the Shenandoah Valley, where it succeeded in pinning down a much larger Union army and defeating its detached units in a series of lightning moves. When it appeared by late May that Jackson might be poised to march east and attack the Union capital, Lincoln decided to withhold troops from McClellan so they would be available to defend Washington.

If McClellan had moved more boldly and decisively, he probably could have captured Richmond with the forces he had. But a combination of faulty intelligence reports and his own natural caution led him to falter in the face of what he wrongly believed to be superior numbers. At the end of May, the Confederates under Joseph E. Johnston took the offensive when they discovered McClellan's army was divided into two segments by the Chickahominy River. In the battle of Seven Pines, McClellan was barely able to hold his ground on the side of the river under attack until a corps from the other side crossed over just in time to save the day. During the battle, General Johnston was severely wounded; succeeding him in command of the Confederate Army of Northern Virginia was native Virginian and West Point graduate Robert E. Lee.

Toward the end of June, Lee began an all-out effort to expel McClellan from the outskirts of Richmond. In a series of battles that lasted for seven days, the two armies clawed at each other indecisively. Although McClellan repulsed Lee's final assaults at Malvern Hill, the Union general decided to retreat down the peninsula to a more secure base. This backward step convinced Lincoln that the peninsula campaign was an exercise in futility.

On July 11, Lincoln appointed General Henry W. Halleck, who had been in overall command in the

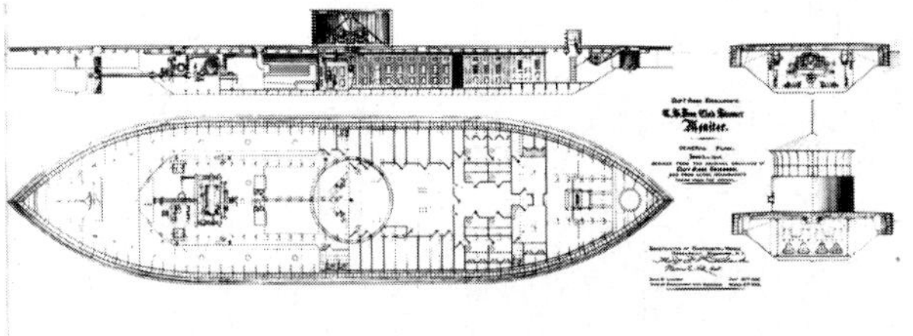

The Civil War would spur a leap in military technology, especially with the introduction of the steam-powered USS Monitor *(1862), designed by John Ericsson of iron armor with two 11-inch guns in a rotating turret, and called a cheesebox on a raft by its detractors. It would be the technological predecessor of the twentieth-century battleships of World Wars I and II.* ❖

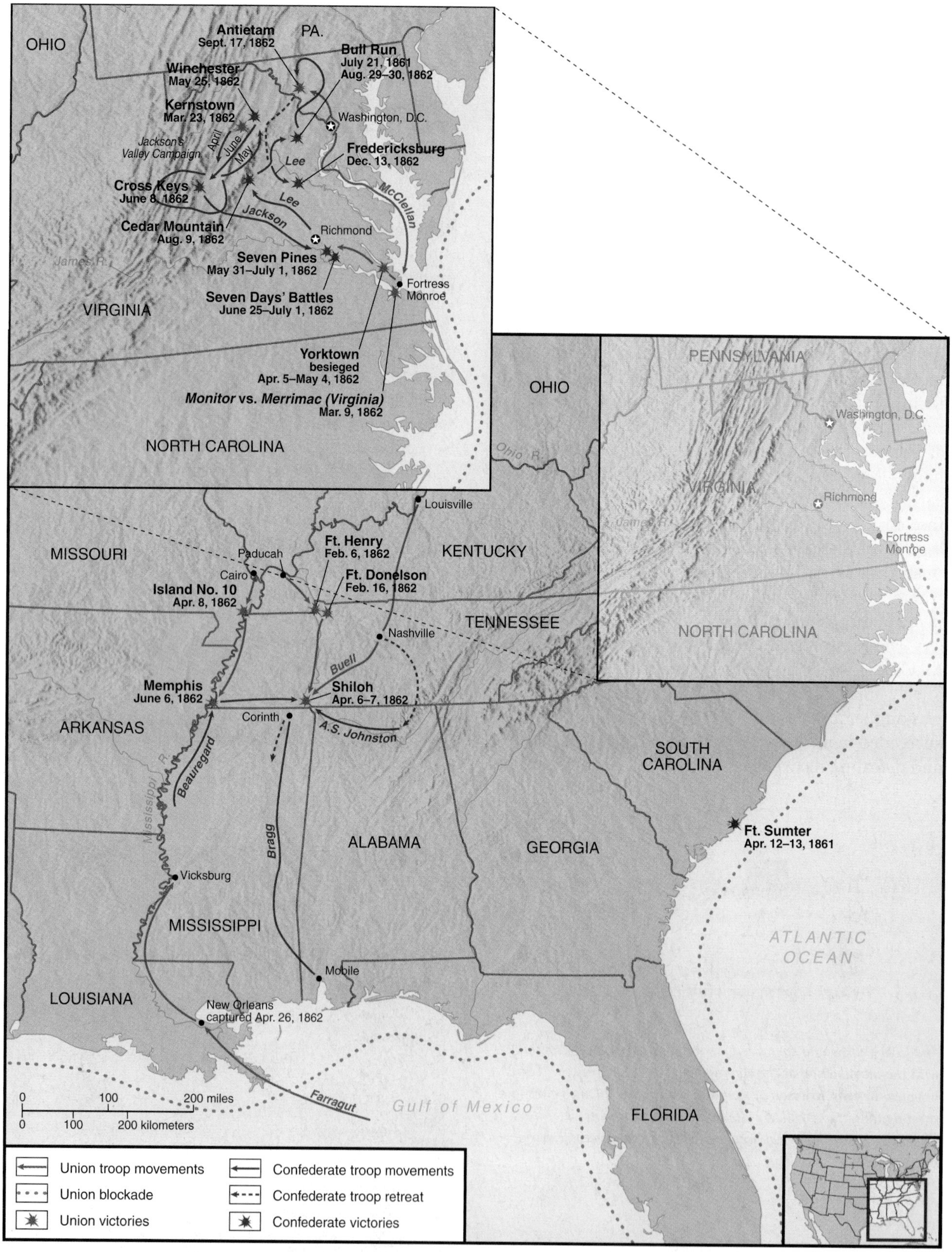

CIVIL WAR, 1861–1862 *Defeats on the battlefield forced a change in the Union's initial military campaign of capturing Richmond, the Confederate capital. The Union's targets in the West were the key cities of Vicksburg and New Orleans.* ❖

After Antietam, Lincoln visited McClellan's headquarters to urge the general to take action. McClellan is on the left facing the president. ❖

western theater, to be the new general in chief and through Halleck ordered McClellan to withdraw his army from the peninsula to join a force under General John Pope that was preparing to move on Richmond by the overland route. As usual, McClellan was slow in responding, and the Confederates got to Pope before he did. At the end of August, in the second battle fought near Bull Run, Lee established his reputation for brilliant generalship; he sent Stonewall Jackson to Pope's rear, provoked the rash Union general to attack Jackson with full force, and then threw the main Confederate army against the Union's flank. Badly beaten, Pope retreated to the defenses of Washington, where he was stripped of command. Out of sheer desperation, Lincoln reappointed McClellan to head the Army of the Potomac.

Lee proceeded to lead his exuberant troops on an invasion of Maryland, in the hope of isolating Washington from the rest of the North. McClellan caught up with him near Sharpsburg, and the bloodiest one-day battle of the war ensued. When the smoke cleared at Antietam on September 17, almost five thousand men had been killed on the two sides and more than eighteen thousand were wounded. The result was a draw, but Lee was forced to fall back south of the Potomac to protect his dangerously extended supply lines. McClellan was slow in pursuit, and Lincoln blamed him for letting the enemy escape.

Convinced that McClellan was fatally infected with "the slows," Lincoln once again sought a more aggressive general and put

Fresh recruits cannot avoid seeing battle casualties and field amputations as they wait to join the battle of Fredericksburg in this 1862 painting, The Battle of Fredericksburg *by John Richards, based on an engraving that appeared in* Harper's *shortly after the battle.* ❖

Ambrose E. Burnside in command of the Army of the Potomac. Burnside was aggressive enough, but he was also rather dense. His limitations were disastrously revealed at the battle of Fredericksburg, Virginia, on December 13, 1862, when he launched a direct assault to try to capture an entrenched and elevated position. Throughout the Civil War such uphill charges almost invariably failed because of the range and deadly accuracy of small-arms fire when concentrated on exposed troops. The debacle at Fredericksburg, where Union forces suffered more than twice as many casualties as their opponents, ended a year of bitter failure for the North on the eastern front.

The Diplomatic Struggle

The critical period of Civil War diplomacy was 1861 to 1862, when the South was making every effort to induce major foreign powers to recognize its independence and break the Union blockade. The hope that England and France could be persuaded to intervene on the Confederate side stemmed from the fact that these nations depended on the South for three-quarters of their cotton supply. In the case of Britain, the uninterrupted production of cotton textiles appeared essential to economic prosperity; an estimated 20 to 25 percent of its entire population was supported either directly or indirectly by this single industry.

The Confederate commissioners sent to England and France in May 1861 succeeded in gaining recognition of southern "belligerency," which meant the new government could claim some international rights of a nation at war. The North protested vigorously, but by declaring a blockade of southern ports, it had undermined its official position that the rebellion was merely a domestic insurrection. The main advantage of belligerent status was that it permitted the South to purchase and outfit privateers in neutral ports. As a result, Confederate raiders built and armed in British shipyards devastated northern shipping. One such vessel was the *Alabama,* which alone sank sixty-two ships. Rising insurance costs resulting from the danger of loss eventually forced most of the American merchant marine off the high seas for the duration of the war.

In the fall of 1861, the Confederate government dispatched James M. Mason and John Slidell to be its permanent envoys to England and France, respectively, and instructed them to push for full recognition of the Confederacy. They took passage on the British steamer *Trent,* which was stopped and boarded in international waters by a U.S. warship. Mason and Slidell were taken into custody by the Union captain, causing a diplomatic crisis that nearly led to war between England and the United States. Refusing to tolerate this flagrant violation of its maritime rights, Britain threatened war if the Confederate emissaries were not released. After a few weeks of ferocious posturing by both sides, Lincoln and Secretary of State Seward made the prudent decision to allow Mason and Slidell to proceed to their destinations.

These envoys may as well have stayed at home; they failed in their mission to obtain full recognition of the Confederacy from either England or France. The anticipated cotton shortage was slow to develop, for the bumper crop of 1860 had created a large surplus in British and French warehouses. Recognition did seem likely for a brief period in the fall of 1862. Napoleon III, the emperor of France, personally favored the southern cause, mainly because he was trying to set up a puppet government in Mexico and saw the chance to trade French support of the Confederacy for an acceptance of his regime south of the border. But he was unwilling to risk war with the United States unless the British would cosponsor his plan to mediate the American conflict and then recognize the Confederacy if—as expected—the North rejected the plan.

British opinion, both official and public, was seriously divided on how to respond to the American conflict. In 1861 and 1862, Lord Palmerston, the prime minister, and Lord Russell, the foreign secretary, played a cautious waiting game. Their government was sympathetic to the South but wary of the danger of war with the United States if they acted in support of their preference. Northern diplomats knew how to play on these fears: Secretary of State Seward and Charles Francis Adams, the American minister to Great Britain, could be relied on to threaten war at any hint of British recognition or support of the Confederacy.

In September 1862, the British cabinet debated mediation and recognition as serious possibilities. Lord Russell pressed for a pro-Confederate policy because he was convinced the South was now strong enough to secure its independence. But when word arrived that Lee had failed to win a clear victory at Antietam and was retreating, Lord Palmerston overruled the foreign secretary and decided to maintain a hands-off policy. The British would intervene, his decision suggested, only if the South won decisively on the battlefield.

The cotton famine finally hit in late 1862, causing massive unemployment in the British textile industry. But, contrary to southern hopes, public opinion did not compel the government to abandon its neutrality and use force to break the Union blockade. Historians used to believe that the suffering mill workers sympathy for the Union was a main cause of restraint. However, the British working class still lacked the right to vote and thus had relatively little influence over policy.

Influential interest groups that actually benefited from the famine provided the crucial support for continuing a policy of nonintervention. Among these groups were owners of large cotton mills, who had made bonanza profits on their existing stocks and were happy to see weaker competitors go under while they awaited new sources of supply. By early 1863, cotton from Egypt and India put the industry back on the track toward full production. Manufacturers of wool and linen textiles benefited from nonintervention, as did munitions makers who supplied both sides. The decline of American competition on the world's sea-lanes resulted in increased profits for British shipping interests. Since the British economy as a whole gained more than it lost from neutrality, it is not surprising that there was little effective pressure for a change in policy.

By early 1863, when it was clear that "King Cotton diplomacy" had failed, the Confederacy broke off formal relations with Great Britain. Its hopes for foreign intervention came to nothing because the European powers decided that the advantages of getting involved were not worth the risk of a long and costly war with the United States. Only a decisive military victory would have gained recognition for southern independence, and if the Confederacy had actually won such a victory, it would not have needed foreign backing.

Fight to the Finish

The last two and a half years of the struggle saw the implementation of more radical war measures. The most dramatic and important of these was the North's effort to follow through on Lincoln's decision to free the slaves and bring the black population into the war on the Union side. The tide of battle turned in the summer of 1863, but the South continued to resist valiantly for two more years, until it was finally overcome by the sheer weight of the North's advantages in manpower and resources.

The Coming of Emancipation

At the beginning of the war, when the North still hoped for a quick and easy victory, only dedicated abolitionists favored turning the struggle for the Union into a crusade against slavery. In the summer of 1861, Congress voted almost unanimously for a resolution affirming that the war was being fought only to preserve the Union and not to change the domestic institutions of any state. But as it became clear how hard it was going to be to subdue the "rebels," sentiment developed for striking a blow at the South's economic and social system by freeing its slaves. In a tentative move toward emancipation, Congress in July 1862 authorized the government to confiscate the slaves of masters who supported the Confederacy. By this time, the actions of the slaves themselves were influencing policymaking. They were voting for freedom with their feet by deserting their plantations in areas where the Union forces were close enough to offer a haven. In this way, they put pressure on the government to determine their status and, in effect, offered themselves as a source of manpower to the Union on the condition that they be made free.

Although Lincoln favored freedom for blacks as an ultimate goal, he was reluctant to commit his administration to a policy of immediate emancipation. In the fall of 1861 and again in the spring of 1862, he had disallowed the orders of field commanders who sought to free slaves in areas occupied by their forces, thus angering abolitionists and the strongly antislavery Republicans known as Radicals. Lincoln's caution stemmed from a fear of alienating Unionist elements in the border slave states and from his own preference for a gradual, compensated form of emancipation. He hoped that such a plan could be put into effect in loyal slaveholding areas and then extended to the rebellious states as the basis for a voluntary restoration of the Union.

Lincoln was also aware that one of the main obstacles to any program leading to emancipation was the strong racial prejudice of most whites in both the North and the South. Although personally more tolerant than most white Americans, Lincoln was pessimistic about prospects of equality for blacks in the United States. He therefore coupled moderate proposals with a plea for government subsidies to support the voluntary "colonization" of freed blacks outside of the United States, and he actively sought places that would accept them.

But the slaveholding states that remained loyal to the Union refused to endorse Lincoln's gradual plan, and the failure of Union arms in the spring and summer of 1862 increased the public clamor for striking directly at the South's peculiar institution. The Lincoln administration also realized that emancipation would win sympathy for the Union cause in England and France and thus might counter the growing threat that these nations would come to the aid of the Confederacy. In July, Lincoln drafted an emancipation proclamation and read it to his cabinet, but he was persuaded by Secretary of State Seward not to issue it until the North had won a victory and could not be accused of acting out of desperation. Later in the summer, Lincoln responded publicly to critics of his cautious policy, indicating that he would take any action in regard to slavery that would further the Union cause.

Finally, on September 22, 1862, Lincoln issued his preliminary **Emancipation Proclamation.** McClellan's

In this allegorical painting, President Lincoln extends a copy of his Proclamation to the goddess of liberty who is driving her chariot, Emancipation. ❖

success in stopping Lee at Antietam provided the occasion, but the president was also responding to growing political pressures. Most Republican politicians were now firmly committed to an emancipation policy, and many were on the verge of repudiating the administration for its inaction. Had Lincoln failed to act, his party would have been badly split, and he would have been in the minority faction. The proclamation gave the Confederate states one hundred days to give up the struggle without losing their slaves. There was little chance they would do so, but in offering them the chance, Lincoln left the door open for a more conservative and peaceful way of ending slavery than sudden emancipation at the point of a gun. In December, Lincoln proposed to Congress that it approve a series of constitutional amendments providing for gradual, compensated emancipation and subsidized colonization.

Since there was no response from the South and little enthusiasm in Congress for Lincoln's gradual plan, the president went ahead on January 1, 1863, and declared that all slaves in those areas under Confederate control "shall be . . . thenceforward, and forever free." He justified the final proclamation as an act of "military necessity" sanctioned by the war powers of the president, and he authorized the enlistment of freed slaves in the Union army. The language and tone of the document—one historian has described it as having "all the moral grandeur of a bill of lading"—made it clear that blacks were being freed for reasons of state and not out of humanitarian conviction.

Despite its uninspiring origin and limited application—it did not extend to slave states loyal to the Union or to occupied areas and thus did not immediately free a single slave—the proclamation did commit the Union to the abolition of slavery as a war aim. It also accelerated the breakdown of slavery as a labor system, a process that was already well under way by early 1863. The blacks who had remained in captured areas or deserted their masters to cross Union lines before 1863 had been kept in a kind of way station between slavery and freedom, in accordance with the theory that they were "contraband of war." As word spread among the slaves that emancipation was now official policy, larger numbers of them were inspired to run off and seek the protection of approaching northern armies. One slave who crossed the Union lines summed up their motives: "I wants to be free. I came in from the plantation and don't want to go back; . . . I don't want to be a slave again." Approximately one-quarter of the slave population gained freedom during the war under the terms of the Emancipation Proclamation and thus deprived the South of an important part of its agricultural workforce.

African Americans and the War

Almost 200,000 African Americans, most of them newly freed slaves, eventually served in the Union armed forces and made a vital contribution to the North's victory. Although they were enrolled in segregated units under white officers, were initially paid less than their white counterparts, and were used disproportionately for garrison duty or heavy labor behind the lines, "blacks in blue" fought heroically in several major battles during the last two years of the war. The assistant secretary of war observed them in action at Millikin's Bend on the Mississippi in June 1863 and reported that "the bravery of blacks in the battle . . . completely revolutionized the sentiment of the army with regard to the employment of Negro troops."

Those freed during the war who did not serve in the military were often conscripted to serve as contract wage laborers on cotton plantations owned or leased by "loyal" white planters within the occupied areas of the Deep South. Abolitionists protested that the coercion used by military authorities to get blacks back into the cotton fields amounted to slavery in a

This 1890 lithograph by Kurz and Allison commemorates the 54th Massachusetts Colored Regiment charging Fort Wagner, South Carolina, in July 1863. The 54th was the first African American unit recruited during the war. Charles and Lewis Douglass, sons of Frederick Douglass, served with this regiment. ❖

new form, but those in power argued that the necessities of war and the northern economy required such "temporary" arrangements. To some extent, regimentation of the freedmen within the South was a way of assuring racially prejudiced Northerners, especially in the Midwest, that emancipation would not result in a massive migration of black refugees to their region of the country.

The heroic performance of African American troops and the easing of northern fears of being swamped by black migrants led to a deepening commitment to emancipation as a permanent and comprehensive policy. Realizing that his proclamation had a shaky constitutional foundation and might apply only to slaves actually freed while the war was going on, Lincoln sought to organize and recognize loyal state governments in southern areas under Union control on condition that they abolish slavery in their constitutions. He also encouraged local campaigns to emancipate the slaves in the border states and saw these programs triumph in Maryland and Missouri in 1864.

Finally, Lincoln pressed for an amendment to the federal constitution outlawing involuntary servitude. After supporting its inclusion as a central plank in the Republican platform of 1864, Lincoln used all his influence to win congressional approval for the new Thirteenth Amendment. On January 31, 1865, the House approved the amendment by a narrow margin. There was an explosion of joy on the floor and in the galleries, and then the House voted to adjourn for the rest of the day "in honor of this immortal and sublime event." The cause of freedom for blacks and the cause of the Union had at last become one and the same. Lincoln, despite his earlier hesitations and misgivings, had earned the right to go down in history as the Great Emancipator.

The Tide Turns

By early 1863, the Confederate economy was in shambles and its diplomacy had collapsed. The social order of the South was also showing signs of severe strain. Masters were losing control of their slaves, and nonslaveholding whites were becoming disillusioned with the hardships of a war that some of them described as "a rich man's war and a poor man's fight." As slaves fled from the plantations, increasing numbers of lower-class whites deserted the army or refused to be drafted in the first place. Whole counties in the southern backcountry became "deserter havens," which Confederate officials could enter only at the risk of their lives. Appalachian mountaineers, who had remained loyal to the Union, resisted the Confederacy more directly by enlisting in the Union army or joining guerrilla units operating behind southern lines.

Yet the North was slow to capitalize on the South's internal weaknesses because it had its own serious morale problems. The long series of defeats on the eastern front had engendered war weariness, and the new policies that "military necessity" forced the government to adopt encountered fierce opposition.

Although popular with Republicans, emancipation was viewed by most Democrats as a betrayal of northern war aims. Racism was a main ingredient in their opposition to freeing blacks. According to one Democratic senator, "We mean that the United States . . . shall be the white man's home . . . and the nigger shall never be his equal." Riding a backlash against the preliminary proclamation, Democrats made significant gains in the congressional elections of 1862, especially in the Midwest, where they also captured several state legislatures.

The Enrollment Act of March 1863, which provided for outright conscription of white males but permitted men of wealth to hire substitutes or pay a fee to avoid military service, provoked a violent response from those unable to buy their way out of service and unwilling to "fight for the niggers." A series of antidraft riots broke out, culminating in one of the bloodiest domestic disorders in American history—the New York Riot of July 1863. The New York mob, composed mainly of Irish-American laborers, burned the draft offices, the homes of leading Republicans, and an orphanage for black children. They also lynched more than a dozen defenseless blacks who fell into their hands. At least 120 people died before federal troops restored order. Besides racial prejudice, the draft riots also reflected working-class anger at the wartime privileges and prosperity of the middle and upper classes; they showed how divided the North really was on the administration's conduct of the war.

To fight dissension and "disloyalty," the government used its martial law authority to arrest a few alleged ringleaders, including one prominent Democratic congressman—Clement Vallandigham of Ohio. Private patriotic organizations also issued a barrage of propaganda aimed at what they believed was a vast secret conspiracy to undermine the northern war effort. Historians disagree about the real extent of covert and illegal antiwar activity. No vast conspiracy existed, but militant advocates of "peace at any price"—popularly known as **Copperheads**—were certainly active in some areas, especially among the immigrant working classes of large cities and in southern Ohio, Indiana, and Illinois. Many Copperheads presented themselves as Jeffersonian believers in limited government who feared a war-induced growth of federal power. But it was opposition to emancipation on racial grounds rather than anxiety about big government that gave the movement most of its emotional force.

The only effective way to overcome the disillusionment that fed the peace movement was to start winning battles and thus convince the northern public that victory was assured. Before this could happen, the North suffered one more humiliating defeat on the eastern

An 1863 draft call in New York provoked violence against African Americans, viewed by the rioters as the cause of an unnecessary war, and rage against the rich men who had been able to buy exemptions from the draft. This 1863 illustration from Harper's Weekly *depicts a mob lynching a black man on Clarkson Street in New York City.* ❖

front. In early May 1863, Union forces under General Joseph Hooker were routed at Chancellorsville, Virginia, by a Confederate army less than half its size. Once again, Robert E. Lee demonstrated his superior generalship, this time by dividing his forces and sending Stonewall Jackson to make a devastating surprise attack on the Union right. The Confederacy prevailed, but it did suffer one major loss: Jackson himself died as a result of wounds he received in the battle.

In the West, however, a major Union triumph was taking shape. For more than a year, General Ulysses S. Grant had been trying to put his forces in position to capture Vicksburg, Mississippi, the almost inaccessible Confederate bastion that stood between the North and control of the Mississippi River. Finally, in late March 1863, he crossed to the west bank north of the city and moved his forces to a point south of it, where he joined up with naval forces that had run the Confederate batteries mounted on Vicksburg's high bluffs. In one of the boldest campaigns of the war, Grant crossed the river, deliberately cutting himself off from his sources of supply, and marched into the interior of Mississippi. Living off the land and out of communication with an anxious and perplexed Lincoln, his troops won a series of victories over two separate Confederate armies and advanced on Vicksburg from the east. After unsuccessfully assaulting the city's defenses, Grant settled down for a siege on May 22.

The Confederate government considered and rejected proposals to mount a major offensive into Tennessee and Kentucky in the hope of drawing Grant away from Vicksburg. Instead, President Davis approved Robert E. Lee's plan for an all-out invasion of the Northeast. Although this option provided no hope for relieving Vicksburg, it might lead to a dramatic victory that would more than compensate for the probable loss of the Mississippi stronghold. Lee's army crossed the Potomac in June and kept going until it reached Gettysburg, Pennsylvania. There Lee confronted a Union army that had taken up strong defensive positions on Cemetery Ridge and Culp's Hill. This was one of the few occasions in the war when the North could capitalize on the tactical advantage of choosing its ground and then defending it against an enemy whose supply lines were extended.

On July 2, a series of Confederate attacks failed to dislodge General George Meade's troops from the high ground they occupied. The following day, Lee faced the choice of retreating to protect his lines of communication or launching a final, desperate assault. With more boldness than wisdom, he chose to make a direct attack on the strongest part of the Union line. The resulting charge on Cemetery Ridge was disastrous; advancing Confederate soldiers dropped like flies under the barrage of Union artillery and rifle fire. Only a few made it to the top of the ridge, and they were killed or captured.

Retreat was now inevitable, and Lee withdrew his battered troops to the Potomac, only to find that the river was at flood stage and could not be crossed for several days. But Meade failed to follow up his victory with a vigorous pursuit, and Lee was allowed to escape a predicament that could have resulted in his annihilation. Vicksburg fell to Grant on July 4, the same day Lee began his withdrawal, and Northerners rejoiced at the simultaneous Independence Day victories that turned the tide of the war. The Union had secured control of the Mississippi and had at last won a major battle in the East. But Lincoln's joy turned to frustration when he learned his generals had missed the chance to capture Lee's army and bring a quick end to the war.

Last Stages of the Conflict

Later in 1863, the North finally gained control of the middle South, an area where indecisive fighting had been going on since the beginning of the conflict. The main Union target was Chattanooga, "the gateway to the Southeast." In September, troops under General William Rosecrans managed to maneuver the Confederates out of the city, only to be outfought and driven back at Chickamauga. The Union army then retreated into Chattanooga, where it was surrounded and besieged by southern forces. After Grant arrived from Vicksburg to take command, the encirclement was broken by daring assaults on the Confederate positions on Lookout Mountain and Missionary Ridge. As a result of its success in the battle of Chattanooga, the North was poised for an invasion of Georgia.

Grant's victories in the West earned him promotion to general in chief of all the Union armies. After assuming that position in March 1864, he ordered a multipronged offensive to finish off the Confederacy. The offensive's main movements were a march on Richmond under Grant's personal command and a thrust by the western armies, now led by General William Tecumseh Sherman, to Atlanta and the heart of Georgia.

In May and early June, Grant and Lee fought a series of bloody battles in northern Virginia that tended to follow a set pattern. Lee would take up an entrenched position in the path of the invading force, and Grant would attack it, sustaining heavy losses but also inflicting casualties the shrinking Confederate army could ill afford. When his direct assault had failed, Grant would move to his left, hoping in vain to maneuver Lee into a less defensible position. In the battles of the Wilderness, Spotsylvania, and Cold Harbor, the Union lost about sixty thousand men—

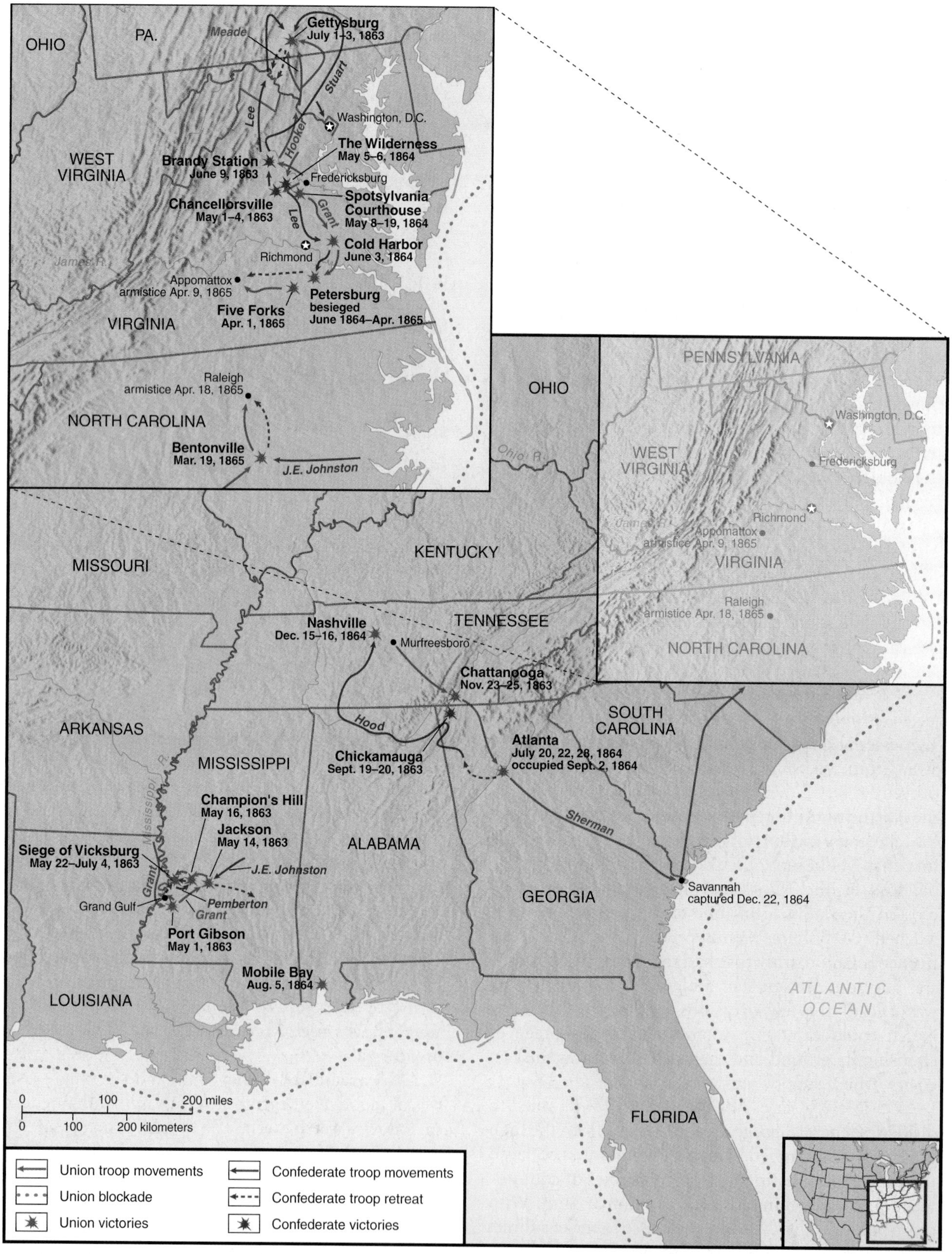

CIVIL WAR, 1863–1865 *In the western theater of war, Grant's victories at Port Gibson, Jackson, and Champion's Hill cleared the way for his siege of Vicksburg. In the east, after the hard-won Union victory at Gettysburg, the South never again invaded the North. In 1864 and 1865, Union armies gradually closed in on Lee's Confederate forces in Virginia. Leaving Atlanta in flames, Sherman marched to the Georgia coast, took Savannah, then moved his troops north through the Carolinas. Grant's army, though suffering enormous losses, moved on toward Richmond, marching into the Confederate capital on April 3, 1865, and forcing surrender.*

Destruction of churches, schools, and factories in the South during the Civil War was a massive problem after the war. These details come from Charleston, South Carolina, and include the destroyed Mills House (right) and the ruins of the pillars of the Circular Church (left). Notice the African American children who along with other freedmen had become refugees and a human issue that Reconstruction era governments would have to face. ❖

more than twice the number of Confederate casualties—without defeating Lee or opening the road to Richmond. After losing twelve thousand men in a single day at Cold Harbor, Grant decided to change his tactics and moved his army to the south of Richmond. There he drew up before Petersburg, a rail center that linked Richmond to the rest of the Confederacy; after failing to take it by assault, he settled down for a siege.

The siege of Petersburg was a long, drawn-out affair, and the resulting stalemate in the East caused northern morale to plummet during the summer of 1864. Lincoln was facing reelection, and his failure to end the war dimmed his prospects. Although nominated with ease in June—with Andrew Johnson, a proadministration Democrat from Tennessee, as his running mate—Lincoln confronted growing opposition within his own party, especially from Radicals who disagreed with his apparently lenient approach to the future restoration of seceded states to the Union. After Lincoln vetoed a Radical-supported congressional reconstruction plan in July, some Radicals began to call for a new convention to nominate another candidate.

The Democrats seemed to be in a good position to capitalize on Republican divisions and make a strong bid for the White House. Their platform appealed to war weariness by calling for a cease-fire followed by negotiations to reestablish the Union. The party's nominee, General George McClellan, announced he would not be bound by the peace plank and would pursue the war. But he promised to end the conflict sooner than Lincoln could because he would not insist on emancipation as a condition for reconstruction. By late summer, Lincoln confessed privately that he would probably be defeated.

But northern military successes changed the political outlook. Sherman's invasion of Georgia went well; between May and September, he employed a series of skillful flanking movements to force the Confederates to retreat to the outskirts of Atlanta. On September 2, the city fell, and northern forces occupied the hub of the Deep South. The news unified the Republican party behind Lincoln and improved his chances for defeating McClellan in November. The election itself was almost an anticlimax: Lincoln won 212 of a possible 233 electoral votes and 55 percent of the popular vote. The Republican cause of "liberty and Union" was secure.

The concluding military operations revealed the futility of further southern resistance. Cutting himself off from his supply lines and living off the land, Sherman marched unopposed through Georgia to the sea, destroying almost everything of possible military or economic value in a corridor three hundred miles long and sixty miles wide. The Confederate army that had opposed him at Atlanta, now under the command of General John B. Hood, moved northward into

The Election of 1864

Candidate	Party	Popular Vote	Electoral Vote*
Lincoln	Republican	2,213,655	212
McClellan	Democratic	1,805,237	21

*Out of a total of 233 electoral votes. The eleven secessionist states—Alabama, Arkansas, Florida, Georgia, Louisiana, Mississippi, North Carolina, South Carolina, Tennessee, Texas, and Virginia—did not vote.

Tennessee, where it was defeated and almost destroyed by Union forces under General George Thomas at Nashville in mid-December. Sherman captured Savannah on December 22 and presented the city to Lincoln as a Christmas present. He then turned north and carried his scorched-earth policy into South Carolina with the aim of continuing through North Carolina and eventually joining up with Grant at Petersburg near Richmond.

While Sherman was bringing the war to the Carolinas, Grant finally ended the stalemate at Petersburg. When Lee's starving and exhausted army tried to break through the Union lines, Grant renewed his attack and forced the Confederates to abandon Petersburg and Richmond on April 2, 1865. He then pursued them westward for a hundred miles, placing his forces in position to cut off their line of retreat to the south. Recognizing the hopelessness of further resistance, Lee surrendered his army at Appomattox Courthouse on April 9.

But the joy of the victorious North turned to sorrow and anger when John Wilkes Booth, a pro-Confederate actor, assassinated Abraham Lincoln as the president watched a play at Ford's Theater in Washington on April 14. Although Booth had a few accomplices—one of whom attempted to murder Secretary of State Seward—popular theories that the assassination was the result of a vast conspiracy involving Confederate leaders or (according to another version) Radical Republicans have never been substantiated.

The man who had spoken of the need to sacrifice for the Union cause at Gettysburg had himself given "the last full measure of devotion" to the cause of "government of the people, by the people, for the people." Four days after Lincoln's death, the only remaining Confederate force of any significance (the troops under Joseph E. Johnston, who had been opposing Sherman in North Carolina) laid down its arms. The Union was saved.

Effects of the War

The nation that emerged from four years of total war was not the same America that had split apart in 1861. The 618,000 young men who were in their graves, victims of enemy fire or the diseases that spread rapidly in military encampments in this era before modern medicine and sanitation, would otherwise have married, raised families, and contributed their talents to building up the country. The widows and sweethearts they left behind temporarily increased the proportion of unmarried women in the population, and some members of this generation of involuntary "spinsters" sought new opportunities for making a living or serving the community that went beyond the purely domestic roles previously prescribed for women.

During the war, northern women pushed the boundaries of their traditional roles by participating on the home front as fund-raisers and in the rear lines as army nurses and members of the **Sanitary Commission.** The Sanitary Commission promoted health in the northern army's camps through attention to cleanliness, nutrition, and medical care. However,

CASUALTIES OF WAR

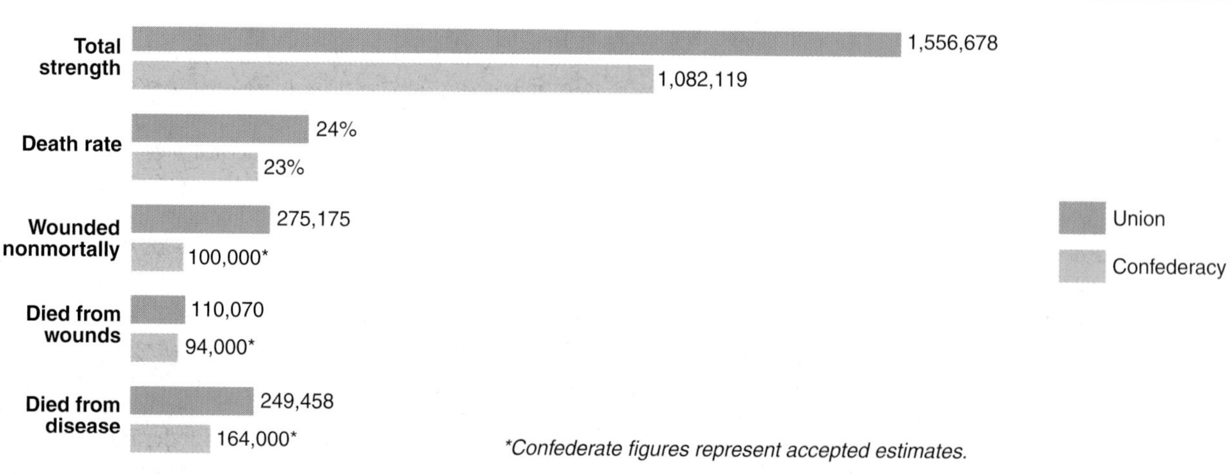

women were not limited to playing roles as nurses and "angels of mercy." Throughout the war, they also filled key positions in the administration and organization of patriotic organizations. Women in the North simultaneously utilized their traditional position as nurturers to participate in the war effort while they advanced new ideas about their role in society. The large number who had served as nurses or volunteer workers during the war were especially responsive to calls for broadening "the woman's sphere." Some of the northern women who were prominent in wartime service organizations—such as Louise Lee Schuyler, Josephine Shaw Lowell, and Mary Livermore—became leaders of postwar philanthropic and reform movements. The war did not destroy the barriers to sexual equality that had long existed in American society, but the efforts of women during the Civil War broadened beliefs about what women could accomplish outside of the home.

The effect on white women in the Confederacy was different from the effect of the war on women in the victorious North. Southern women had always been intimately involved in the administration of the farms and plantations of the South, but the coming of the war forced them to shoulder even greater burdens at home. This was true for wealthy plantation mistresses, who had to take over the administration and maintenance of huge plantations without the benefit of extensive training or the assistance of male relatives. The wives of small farmers found it hard to survive at all, especially at harvest time when they often had to do all the work themselves. The loss of fathers and brothers, the constant advance of Union troops, and the difficulty of controlling a slave labor force destroyed many southern women's allegiance to the Confederate cause. At the close of the conflict, southern women faced the challenge of rebuilding a society that had been permanently transformed by the experience of war. As in the North, the Civil War changed the situation of women in society. The devastation of the southern economy forced many women to play a more conspicuous public and economic role. These women responded by forming associations to assist returning soldiers, entering the workforce as educators, and establishing numerous benevolent and reform societies or temperance organizations. Although these changes created a more visible presence of southern women in public, the South remained more conservative in its views about women's "proper place" than did the North.

At enormous human and economic cost, the nation had emancipated four million African Americans from slavery, but it had not yet resolved that they would be equal citizens. At the time of Lincoln's assassination, most northern states still denied blacks equality under the law and the right to vote. Whether the North would extend more rights to southern freedmen than it had granted to "free Negroes" was an open question.

The impact of the war on white working people was also unclear. Those in the industrializing parts of the North had suffered and lost ground economically because prices had risen much faster than wages during the conflict. But Republican rhetoric stressing "equal opportunity" and the "dignity of labor" raised hopes that the crusade against slavery could be broadened into a movement to improve the lot of working people in general. Foreign-born workers had additional reason to be optimistic; the fact that so many

CHRONOLOGY

1860	South Carolina secedes from the Union (December)
1861	Rest of Deep South secedes: Confederacy is founded (January–February) ❖ Fort Sumter is fired upon and surrenders to Confederate forces (April) ❖ Upper South secedes (April–May) ❖ South wins first battle of Bull Run (July)
1862	Grant captures forts Henry and Donelson (February) ❖ Farragut captures New Orleans for the Union (April) ❖ McClellan leads unsuccessful campaign on the peninsula southeast of Richmond (March–July) ❖ South wins second battle of Bull Run (August) ❖ McClellan stops Lee at battle of Antietam (September) ❖ Lincoln issues preliminary Emancipation Proclamation (September) ❖ Lee defeats Union army at Fredericksburg (December)
1863	Lincoln issues final Emancipation Proclamation (January) ❖ Lee is victorious at Chancellorsville (May) ❖ North gains major victories at Gettysburg and Vicksburg (July) ❖ Grant defeats Confederate forces at Chattanooga (November)
1864	Grant and Lee battle in northern Virginia (May–June) ❖ Atlanta falls to Sherman (September) ❖ Lincoln is reelected president, defeating McClellan (November) ❖ Sherman marches through Georgia (November–December)
1865	Congress passes Thirteenth Amendment abolishing slavery (January) ❖ Grant captures Petersburg and Richmond; Lee surrenders at Appomattox (April) ❖ Lincoln assassinated by John Wilkes Booth (April) ❖ Remaining Confederate forces surrender (April–May)

During the war, many northern women replaced skilled male workers in the manufacturing force. At left, women are shown filling cartridges in the U.S. Arsenal at Watertown, New York. In the South, women contributed to the war effort by producing materials such as bandages and performing services such as mending military clothing. They also worked to keep plantations and farms running, a task made even more difficult by the advance of Union troops and the proximity of battlefronts. This 1862 photograph by Timothy H. O'Sullivan shows a family on their property near Cedar Mountain, Virginia, in front of the house where Confederate General Charles S. Winder died of wounds suffered in a major battle nearby. ❖

immigrants had fought and died for the Union cause had—for the moment—weakened nativist sentiment and encouraged ethnic tolerance.

What the war definitely decided was that the federal government was supreme over the states and had a broad grant of constitutional authority to act on matters affecting "the general welfare." The southern principle of state sovereignty and strict construction died at Appomattox, and the United States was on its way to becoming a true nation-state with an effective central government. But it retained a federal structure; although states could no longer claim the right to secede or nullify federal law, they still had primary responsibility for most functions of government. Everyone agreed that the Constitution placed limits on what the national government could do, and questions would continue to arise about where federal authority ended and states' rights began.

A broadened definition of federal powers had its greatest impact in the realm of economic policy. During the war, the Republican-dominated Congresses passed a rash of legislation designed to give stimulus and direction to the nation's economic development. Taking advantage of the absence of southern opposition, Republicans rejected the pre–Civil War tradition of virtual laissez-faire and enacted a Whiggish program of active support for business and agriculture. In 1862, Congress passed a high protective tariff, approved a homestead act intended to encourage settlement of the West by providing free land to settlers, granted huge tracts of public land to railroad companies to support the building of a transcontinental railroad, and gave the states land for the establishment of agricultural colleges. The following year, Congress set up a national banking system that required member banks to keep adequate reserves and invest one-third of their capital in government securities. The notes the national banks issued became the country's first standardized and reliable circulating currency.

These wartime achievements added up to a decisive shift in the relationship between the federal government and private enterprise. The Republicans took a limited government that did little more than seek to protect the marketplace from the threat of monopoly and changed it into an activist state that promoted and subsidized the efforts of the economically ambitious and industrious.

Conclusion: An Organizational Revolution

The most pervasive effect of the war on northern society was to encourage an "organizational revolution." Aided by government policies, venturesome businessmen took advantage of the new national market created by military procurement to build larger firms that could operate across state lines; some of the huge corporate enterprises of the postwar era began to take shape. Philanthropists also developed more effective national associations; the most notable of these were the Sanitary and Christian Commissions that ministered to the physical and spiritual needs of the troops. Efforts to care for the wounded influenced the development of the modern hospital and the rise of nursing as a female profession. Both the men who served in the army and those men and women who supported them on the home front or behind the lines became accustomed to working in large, bureaucratic organizations of a kind that had scarcely existed before the war.

Ralph Waldo Emerson, the era's most prominent man of letters, revealed in his Civil War writings that the conflict encouraged a dramatic shift in American thought about the relationship between the individual and society. Before the war, Emerson had generally championed "the transcendent individual," who stood apart from institutions and organizations and sought fulfillment in an inner world of imagination and cosmic intuition. During the conflict, he began to exalt the claims of organization, government, and "civilization" over the endeavors of "the private man" to find fulfillment through "self-culture." He even extolled military discipline and became an official visitor to West Point. In 1837, he had said of young men who aspired to political office: "Wake them up and they shall quit the false good and leap to the true, and leave governments to clerks and desks." Now he affirmed almost the opposite: "Government must not be a parish clerk, a justice of the peace. It has, of necessity, in any crisis of the state, the absolute powers of a dictator." In purging his thoughts of extreme individualism and hailing the need to accept social discipline and participate in organized, cooperative activity, Emerson epitomized the way the war affected American thought and patterns of behavior.

The North won the war mainly because it had shown a greater capacity than the South to organize, innovate, and "modernize." Its victory meant the nation as a whole would now be ready to embrace the conception of progress that the North had affirmed in its war effort—not only its advances in science and technology, but also its success in bringing together and managing large numbers of men and women for economic and social goals. The Civil War was thus a catalyst for the great transformation of American society from an individualistic society of small producers into the more highly organized and "incorporated" America of the late nineteenth century.

Recommended Reading

The best one-volume history of the Civil War is James M. McPherson, *Battle Cry of Freedom: The Civil War Era* (1988). Other valuable surveys of the war and its aftermath are J. G. Randall and David Herbert Donald, *The Civil War and Reconstruction*, 2nd ed. (1969), and James M. McPherson, *Ordeal by Fire: The Civil War and Reconstruction* (1981). An excellent shorter account is David Herbert Donald, *Liberty and Union* (1978). The Confederate experience is covered in Clement Eaton, *A History of the Southern Confederacy* (1954), and Emory M. Thomas, *The Confederate Nation, 1861–1865* (1979). Eaton stresses internal problems and weaknesses; Thomas highlights achievements under adversity. Gary W. Gallagher, *The Confederate War* (1997) argues, contrary to a common view, that the South lost the war simply because it was overpowered and not because of low morale or lack of a will to win. On the North's war effort, see Phillip Paludan, *A People's Contest: The Union and the Civil War, 1861–1865* (1988). The best one-volume introduction to the military side of the conflict is still Bruce Catton, *This Hallowed Ground: The Story of the Union Side of the Civil War* (1956).

Lincoln's career and wartime leadership are well treated in David Herbert Donald, *Lincoln* (1995). Another competent biography is Stephen B. Oates, *With Malice Toward None: The Life of Abraham Lincoln* (1977). A penetrating analysis of events immediately preceding the fighting is Kenneth M. Stampp, *And the War Came: The North and the Sectional Crisis* (1950). John Hope Franklin, *The Emancipation Proclamation* (1963), is a good short account of the North's decision to free the slaves. An incisive account of the transition from slavery to freedom is Barbara Jeanne Fields, *Slavery and Freedom on the Middle Ground: Maryland in the Nineteenth Century* (1985). The circumstances and activities of southern women during the war are covered in Drew Faust, *Mothers of Invention: Women of the Slaveholding States in the American Civil War* (1996) and in Laura F. Edwards, *Scarlett Doesn't Live Here Anymore: Southern Women in the Civil War Era* (2002). The experiences of northern women are described in Elizabeth D. Leonard, *Yankee Women: Gender Battles in the Civil War* (1994). Five leading historians offer conflicting interpretations in their attempts to explain the South's defeat in *Why the North Won the Civil War*, edited by David Donald (1960). A brilliant study of the writings of those who experienced the war is Edmund Wilson, *Patriotic Gore: Studies in the Literature of the American Civil War* (1962). On the intellectual impact of the war, see George M. Fredrickson, *The Inner Civil War: Northern Intellectuals and the Crisis of the Union*, 2nd ed. (1993).

For a list of additional titles related to this chapter's topics, please see http://www.ablongman.com/divine.

Suggested Web Sites

The American Civil War Homepage

http://sunsite.utk.edu/civil-war/warweb.html

This site has a great collection of hypertext links to the most useful identified electronic files about the American Civil War.

The Valley of the Shadow: Living the Civil War in Pennsylvania and Virginia

http://jefferson.village.virginia.edu/vshadow/vshadow.html

This project tells the histories of two communities on either side of the Mason-Dixon line during the Civil War. It includes narrative and an electronic archive of sources.

Civil War @ Charleston

http://www.awod.com/gallery/probono/cwchas/cwlayout.html

This site covers the history of the Civil War in and around Charleston, South Carolina.

Abraham Lincoln Association

http://www.alincolnassoc.com/

This site allows the search of digital versions of Lincoln's papers.

Crisis at Fort Sumter

http://www.tulane.edu/~latner/CrisisMain.html

This well-crafted use of hypermedia with assignments or problems explains and explores the events in and around the start of the Civil War.

U.S. Civil War Center

http://www.cwc.lsu.edu/

This is a site whose mission is to "locate, index, and/or make available all appropriate private and public data regarding the Civil War and to promote the study of the Civil War from the perspectives of all professions, occupations, and academic disciplines."

The Papers of Jefferson Davis Home Page

http://jeffersondavis.rice.edu

This site tells about the collection of Jefferson Davis papers and includes a chronology of his life, a family genealogy, some key Davis documents on-line, and a collection of related links.

History of African Americans in the Civil War

http://www.itd.nps.gov/cwss/history/aa_history.htm

This National Park Service site explores the history of the United States Colored Troops.

Civil War Women

http://scriptorium.lib.duke.edu/collections/civil-war-women.html

This site includes original documents, links, and biographical information about several women and their lives during the Civil War.

Assassination of President Abraham Lincoln

http://memory.loc.gov/ammem/alhtml/alrintr.html

Part of the American Memory series with introduction, timeline, and gallery.

Selected Civil War Photographs

http://memory.loc.gov/ammem/cwphtml/cwphome.html

Library of Congress site with more than one thousand photographs, many from Matthew Brady.

A Timeline of the Civil War

http://www.historyplace.com/civilwar/index.html

A complete timeline of the Civil War, well illustrated with photographs.

National Civil War Association

http://www.ncwa.org/info.html

One of the many Civil War reenactment organizations in the United States.

Chapter 16

The First Vote, *drawn by A. H. Ward for* Harper's Weekly, *November 16, 1867.* ❖

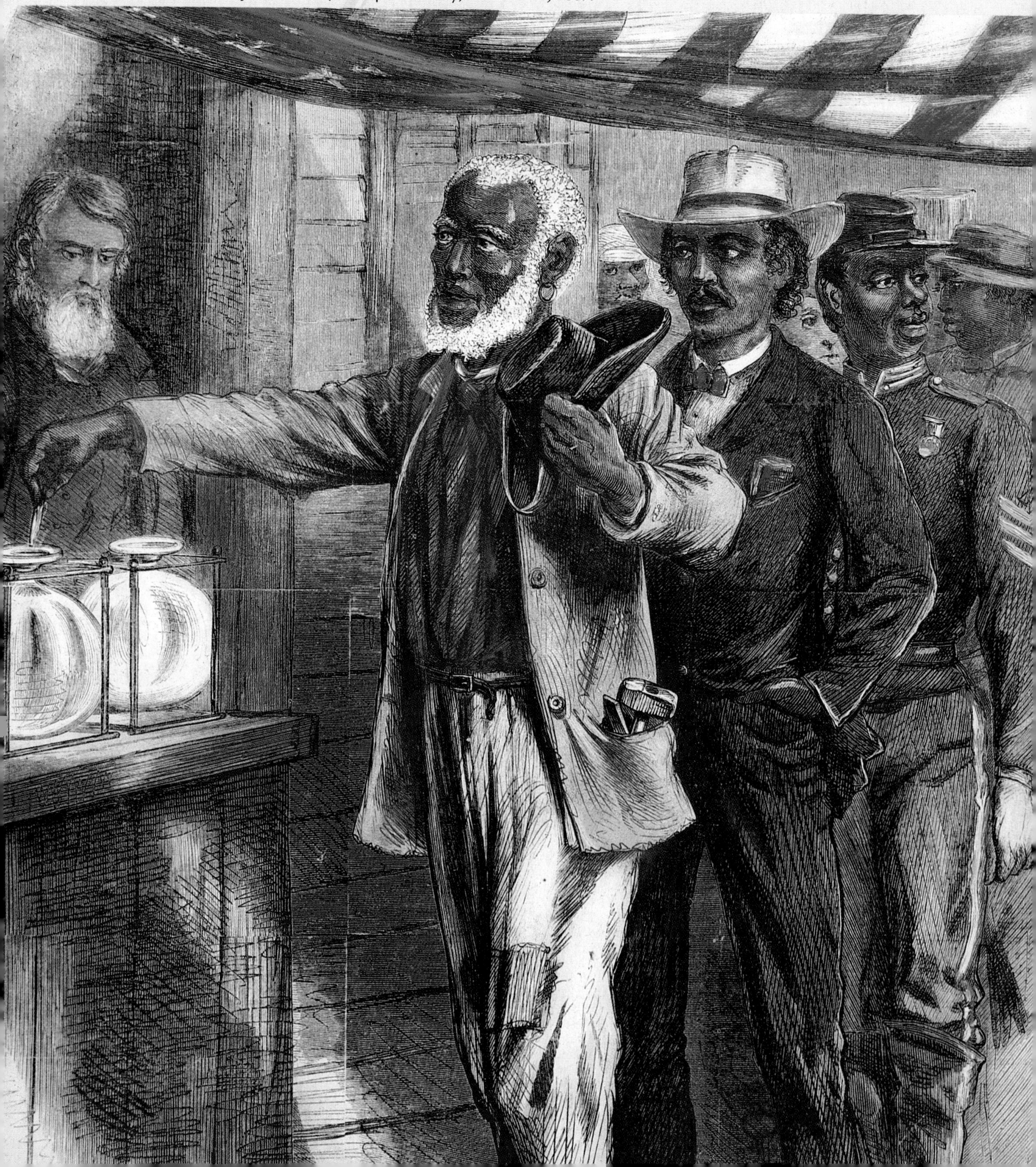

The Agony of Reconstruction

Robert Smalls and Black Politicians During Reconstruction

During the Reconstruction period immediately following the Civil War, African Americans struggled to become equal citizens of a democratic republic. They produced a number of remarkable leaders who showed that blacks were as capable as other Americans of voting, holding office, and legislating for a complex and rapidly changing society. Among these leaders was Robert Smalls of South Carolina. Although virtually forgotten by the time of his death in 1915, Smalls was perhaps the most famous and widely respected southern black leader of the Civil War and Reconstruction era. His career reveals some of the main features of the African American experience during that crucial period.

Born a slave in 1839, Smalls had a white father whose identity has never been clearly established. But his white ancestry apparently gained him some advantages, and as a young man he was allowed to live and work independently, hiring his own time from a master who may have been his half brother. Smalls worked as a sailor and trained himself to be a pilot in Charleston Harbor.

When the Union navy blockaded Charleston in 1862, Smalls, who was then working on a Confederate steamship called the *Planter,* saw a chance to win his freedom in a particularly dramatic way. At three o'clock in the morning on May 13, 1862, when the white officers of the *Planter* were ashore, he took command of the vessel and its slave crew, sailed it out of the heavily fortified harbor, and surrendered it to the Union navy. Smalls immediately became a hero to those antislavery Northerners who were seeking evidence that the slaves were willing and able to serve the Union. The *Planter* was turned into a Union army transport, and Smalls was made its captain after being commissioned as an officer. During the remainder of the war, he rendered conspicuous and gallant service as captain and pilot of Union vessels off the coast of South Carolina.

Like a number of other African Americans who had fought valiantly for the Union, Smalls went on to a distinguished political career during Reconstruction, serving in the South Carolina constitutional convention, in the state legislature, and for several terms in the U.S. Congress. He was also a shrewd businessman and became the owner of extensive properties in Beaufort, South Carolina, and its vicinity. (His first purchase was the house of his former master, where he had spent his early years as a slave.) As the leading citizen of Beaufort during Reconstruction and for some years thereafter, he acted like many successful white Americans, combining the acquisition of wealth with the exercise of political power.

The electoral organization Smalls established resembled in some ways the well-oiled "machines" being established in northern towns and cities. It was so effective that he was able to control local government and get himself elected to Congress even after the election of 1876 had placed the state under the control of white conservatives bent on depriving blacks of political power. Organized mob violence defeated him in 1878, but he bounced back to win by decision of Congress a contested congressional election in 1880. He did not leave the House of Representatives for good until 1886, when he lost another contested election that had to be decided by Congress. It revealed the

Outline

Feature Essay

With the help of several black crewmen, Robert Smalls—then twenty-three years old—commandeered the Planter, *a Confederate steamship used to transport guns and ammunition, and surrendered it to the Union vessel, U.S.S.* Onward. *Smalls provided distinguished service to the Union during the Civil War and after the war went on to become a successful politician and businessman.* ❖

changing mood of the country that his white challenger was seated despite evidence of violence and intimidation against black voters.

In their efforts to defeat him, Smalls's white opponents frequently charged that he had a hand in the corruption that was allegedly rampant in South Carolina during Reconstruction. But careful historical investigation shows that he was, by the standards of the time, an honest and responsible public servant. In the South Carolina convention of 1868 and later in the state legislature, he was a conspicuous champion of free and compulsory public education. In Congress, he fought for the enactment and enforcement of federal civil rights laws. Not especially radical on social questions, he sometimes bent over backward to accommodate what he regarded as the legitimate interests and sensibilities of South Carolina whites. Like other middle-class black political leaders in Reconstruction-era South Carolina, he can perhaps be faulted in hindsight for not doing more to help poor blacks gain access to land of their own. But in 1875, he sponsored congressional legislation that opened for purchase at low prices the land in his own district that had been confiscated by the federal government during the war. As a result, blacks were able to buy most of it, and they soon owned three-fourths of the land in Beaufort and its vicinity.

Robert Smalls spent the later years of his life as U.S. collector of customs for the port of Beaufort, a beneficiary of the patronage that the Republican party continued to provide for a few loyal southern blacks. But the loss of real political clout for Smalls and men like him was one of the tragic consequences of the fall of Reconstruction.

FOR A BRIEF PERIOD OF YEARS, black politicians such as Robert Smalls exercised more power in the South than they would for another century. A series of political developments on the national and regional stage made Reconstruction "an unfinished revolution," promising but not delivering true equality for newly freed African Americans. National party politics, shifting priorities among Northern Republicans, white Southerners' commitment to white supremacy, backed by legal restrictions, as well as massive extra-legal violence against blacks, all combined to stifle the promise of Reconstruction.

Yet the Reconstruction Era also saw major transformations in American society in the wake of the Civil War—new ways of organizing labor and family life, new institutions within and outside of the government, and new ideologies regarding the role of institutions and government in social and economic life. Many of the changes begun during Reconstruction laid the groundwork for later revolutions in American life.

The President versus Congress

The problem of how to reconstruct the Union in the wake of the South's military defeat was one of the most difficult and perplexing challenges ever faced by American policymakers. The Constitution provided no firm guidelines, for the framers had not anticipated a division of the country into warring sections. After emancipation became a northern war aim, the problem was compounded by a new issue: How far should the federal government go to secure freedom and civil rights for four million former slaves?

The debate that evolved led to a major political crisis. Advocates of a minimal Reconstruction policy favored quick restoration of the Union with no protection for the freed slaves beyond the prohibition of slavery. Proponents of a more radical policy wanted readmission of the southern states to be dependent on guarantees that "loyal" men would displace the Confederate elite in positions of power and that blacks would acquire basic rights of American citizenship. The White House favored the minimal approach, whereas Congress came to endorse the more radical and thoroughgoing form of Reconstruction. The resulting struggle between Congress and the chief executive was the most serious clash between two branches of government in the nation's history.

Wartime Reconstruction

Tension between the president and Congress over how to reconstruct the Union began during the war. Occupied mainly with achieving victory, Lincoln never set forth a final and comprehensive plan for bringing rebellious states back into the fold. But he did take initiatives that indicated he favored a lenient and conciliatory policy toward Southerners who would give up the struggle and repudiate slavery. In December 1863, he issued a Proclamation of Amnesty and Reconstruction, which offered a full pardon to all Southerners (with the exception of certain classes of Confederate leaders) who would take an oath of allegiance to the Union and acknowledge the legality of emancipation. This **Ten Percent Plan** provided that once 10 percent or more of the voting population of any occupied state had taken the oath, they were authorized to set up a loyal government. By 1864, Louisiana and Arkansas, states that were wholly or partially occupied by Union troops, had established Unionist governments. Lincoln's policy was meant to shorten the war. First, he hoped to weaken the southern cause by making it easy for disillusioned or lukewarm Confederates to switch sides. Second, he hoped to further his emancipation policy by insisting that the new governments abolish slavery

Congress was unhappy with the president's Reconstruction experiments and in 1864 refused to seat the Unionists elected to the House and Senate from Louisiana and Arkansas. A minority of congressional Republicans—the strongly antislavery **Radical Republicans**—favored protection for black rights (especially black male suffrage) as a precondition for the readmission of southern states. But a larger group of Congressional moderates opposed Lincoln's plan, not on the basis of black rights but because they did not trust the repentant Confederates who would play a major role in the new governments. They feared that the old ruling class would return to power and cheat the North of the full fruits of its impending victory.

Congress also believed the president was exceeding his authority by using executive powers to restore the Union. Lincoln operated on the theory that secession, being illegal, did not place the Confederate states outside the Union in a constitutional sense. Since individuals and not states had defied federal authority, the president could use his pardoning power to certify a loyal electorate, which could then function as the legitimate state government.

The dominant view in Congress, on the other hand, was that the southern states had forfeited their place in the Union and that it was up to Congress to decide when and how they would be readmitted. The most popular justification for congressional responsibility was based on the clause of the Constitution providing that "the United States shall guarantee to every State in this Union a Republican Form of Government." By seceding, Radicals argued, the Confederate states had ceased to be republican, and Congress had to set the conditions to be met before they could be readmitted.

After refusing to recognize Lincoln's 10 percent governments, Congress passed a Reconstruction bill of its own in July 1864. Known as the **Wade-Davis Bill,** this legislation required that 50 percent of the voters take an oath of future loyalty before the restoration process could begin. Once this had occurred, those who could swear they had never willingly supported the Confederacy could vote in an election for delegates to a constitutional convention. The bill in its final form did not require black suffrage, but it did give federal courts the power to enforce emancipation. Faced with this attempt to nullify his own program, Lincoln exercised a pocket veto by refusing to sign the bill before Congress adjourned. He justified his action by announcing that he did not want to be committed to any single Reconstruction plan. The sponsors of the bill responded with an angry manifesto, and Lincoln's relations with Congress reached their low.

Congress and the president remained stalemated on the Reconstruction issue for the rest of the war. During his last months in office, however, Lincoln showed some willingness to compromise. He persisted in his efforts to obtain full recognition for the governments he had nurtured in Louisiana and Arkansas but seemed receptive to the setting of other conditions—perhaps including black suffrage—for readmission of those states where wartime conditions had prevented execution of his plan. However, he died without clarifying his intentions, leaving historians to speculate whether his quarrel with Congress would have worsened or been resolved. Given Lincoln's past record of political flexibility, the best bet is that he would have come to terms with the majority of his party.

Andrew Johnson at the Helm

Andrew Johnson, the man suddenly made president by an assassin's bullet, attempted to put the Union back together on his own authority in 1865. But his policies eventually set him at odds with Congress and the Republican party and provoked the most serious crisis in the history of relations between the executive and legislative branches of the federal government.

Johnson's background shaped his approach to Reconstruction. Born in dire poverty in North Carolina, he migrated as a young man to eastern Tennessee, where he made his living as a tailor. Lacking

In this cartoon, President Andrew Johnson (left) and Thaddeus Stevens, the Radical Republican Congressman from Pennsylvania, are depicted as train engineers in a deadlock on the tracks. Indeed, neither Johnson nor Stevens would give way on his plans for Reconstruction. ❖

formal schooling, he did not learn to read and write until adult life. Entering politics as a Jacksonian Democrat, he became known as an effective stump speaker. His railing against the planter aristocracy made him the spokesman for Tennessee's nonslaveholding whites and the most successful politician in the state. He advanced from state legislator to congressman to governor and in 1857 was elected to the U.S. Senate.

When Tennessee seceded in 1861, Johnson was the only senator from a Confederate state who remained loyal to the Union and continued to serve in Washington. But his Unionism and defense of the common people did not include antislavery sentiments. Nor was he friendly to blacks. While campaigning in Tennessee, he had objected only to the fact that slaveholding was the privilege of a wealthy minority. He revealed his attitude when he wished that "every head of family in the United States had one slave to take the drudgery and menial service off his family."

During the war, while acting as military governor of Tennessee, Johnson endorsed Lincoln's emancipation policy and carried it into effect. But he viewed it primarily as a means of destroying the power of the hated planter class rather than as a recognition of black humanity. He was chosen as Lincoln's running mate in 1864 because it was thought that a pro-administration Democrat, who was a southern Unionist in the bargain, would strengthen the ticket. No one expected Johnson to succeed to the presidency; it is one of the strange accidents of American history that a southern Democrat, a fervent white supremacist, came to preside over a Republican administration immediately after the Civil War.

Some Radical Republicans initially welcomed Johnson's ascent to the nation's highest office. Their hopes make sense in the light of Johnson's record of fierce loyalty to the Union and his apparent agreement with the Radicals that ex-Confederates should be severely treated. More than Lincoln, who had spoken of "malice toward none and charity for all," Johnson seemed likely to punish southern "traitors" and prevent them from regaining political influence. Only gradually did the deep disagreement between the president and the Republican Congressional majority become evident.

The Reconstruction policy that Johnson initiated on May 29, 1865, created some uneasiness among the Radicals, but most Republicans were willing to give it a chance. Johnson placed North Carolina and eventually other states under appointed provisional governors chosen mostly from among prominent southern politicians who had opposed the secession movement and had rendered no conspicuous service to the Confederacy. The governors were responsible for calling constitutional conventions and ensuring that only "loyal" whites were permitted to vote for delegates. Participation required taking the oath of allegiance that Lincoln had prescribed earlier. Once again, Confederate leaders and former officeholders who had participated in the rebellion were excluded. To regain their political and property rights, those in the exempted categories had to apply for individual presidential pardons. Johnson made one significant addition to the list of the excluded: all those possessing taxable property exceeding $20,000 in value. In this fashion, he sought to prevent his longtime adversaries—the wealthy planters—from participating in the Reconstruction of southern state governments.

Once the conventions met, Johnson urged them to do three things: Declare the ordinances of secession illegal, repudiate the Confederate debt, and ratify the **Thirteenth Amendment** abolishing slavery. After governments had been reestablished under constitutions meeting these conditions, the president assumed that the Reconstruction process would be complete and that the ex-Confederate states could regain their full rights under the Constitution.

The results of the conventions, which were dominated by prewar Unionists and representatives of backcountry yeoman farmers, were satisfactory to the president but troubling to many congressional Republicans. Rather than quickly accepting Johnson's recommendations, delegates in several states approved them begrudgingly or with qualifications. Furthermore, all the resulting constitutions limited suffrage to whites, disappointing the large number of Northerners who hoped, as Lincoln had, that at least some African Americans—perhaps those who were educated or had served in the Union army—would be given the vote. Johnson on the whole seemed eager to give southern white majorities a free hand in determining the civil and political status of the freed slaves.

Republican uneasiness turned to disillusionment and anger when the state legislatures elected under the new constitutions proceeded to pass **Black Codes** subjecting former slaves to a variety of special regulations and restrictions on their freedom. Especially troubling were vagrancy and apprenticeship laws that forced African Americans to work and denied them a free choice of employers. Blacks in some states were also prevented from testifying in court on the same basis as whites and were subject to a separate penal code. To Radicals, the Black Codes looked suspiciously like slavery under a new guise. More upsetting to northern public opinion in general, a number of prominent ex-Confederate leaders were elected to Congress in the fall of 1865.

Johnson himself was partly responsible for this turn of events. Despite his lifelong feud with the planter class, he was generous in granting pardons to members of the old elite who came to him, hat in hand, and asked for them. When former Confederate Vice President Alexander Stephens and other proscribed ex-rebels were elected to Congress although they had not been pardoned, Johnson granted them special amnesty so they could serve.

The growing rift between the president and Congress came into the open in December, when the House and Senate refused to seat the recently elected southern delegation. Instead of endorsing Johnson's work and recognizing the state governments he had called into being, Congress established a joint committee, chaired by Senator William Pitt Fessenden of

"Slavery Is Dead?" asks this 1866 cartoon by Thomas Nast. To the cartoonist, the Emancipation Proclamation of 1863 and the North's victory in the Civil War meant little difference to the treatment of the freed slaves in the South. Freed slaves convicted of crimes often endured the same punishments as had slaves—sale, as depicted in the left panel of the cartoon, or beatings, as shown on the right. ❖

Maine, to review Reconstruction policy and set further conditions for readmission of the seceded states.

Congress Takes the Initiative

The struggle over how to reconstruct the Union ended with Congress doing the job of setting policy all over again. The clash between Johnson and Congress was a matter of principle and could not be reconciled. President Johnson, an heir of the Democratic states' rights tradition, wanted to restore the prewar federal system as quickly as possible and without change except that states would not have the right to legalize slavery or to secede.

Most Republicans wanted firm guarantees that the old southern ruling class would not regain regional power and national influence by devising new ways to subjugate blacks. They favored a Reconstruction policy that would give the federal government authority to limit the political role of ex-Confederates and provide some protection for black citizenship.

Republican leaders—with the exception of a few extreme Radicals such as Charles Sumner—lacked any firm conviction that blacks were inherently equal to whites. They did believe, however, that in a modern democratic state, all citizens must have the same basic rights and opportunities, regardless of natural abilities. Principle coincided easily with political expediency; southern blacks, whatever their alleged shortcomings, were likely to be loyal to the Republican party that had emancipated them. They could be used, if necessary, to counteract the influence of resurgent ex-Confederates, thus preventing the Democrats from returning to national dominance through control of the South.

The disagreement between the president and Congress became irreconcilable in early 1866, when Johnson vetoed two bills that had passed with overwhelming Republican support. The first extended the life of the **Freedmen's Bureau**—a temporary agency set up to aid the former slaves by providing relief, education, legal help, and assistance in obtaining land or employment. The second was a civil rights bill meant to nullify the Black Codes and guarantee to freedmen "full and equal benefit of all laws and proceedings for the security of person and property as is enjoyed by white citizens."

Johnson's vetoes shocked moderate Republicans who had expected the president to accept the relatively modest measures as a way of heading off more radical proposals, such as black suffrage and a prolonged denial of political rights to ex-Confederates. Presidential opposition to policies that represented the bare minimum of Republican demands on the South alienated moderates in the party and ensured a wide opposition to Johnson's plan of Reconstruction. Johnson succeeded in blocking the Freedmen's Bureau bill, although a modified version later passed. But the Civil Rights Act won the two-thirds majority necessary to override his veto, signifying that the president was now hopelessly at odds with most of the congressmen from what was supposed to be his own party. Never before had Congress overridden a presidential veto.

Johnson soon revealed that he intended to abandon the Republicans and place himself at the head of a new conservative party uniting the small minority of Republicans who supported him with a reviving Democratic party that was rallying behind his Reconstruction policy. In preparation for the elections of 1866, Johnson helped found the National Union movement to promote his plan to readmit the southern states to the Union without further qualifications. A National Union convention meeting in Philadelphia in August 1866 called for the election to Congress of men who endorsed the presidential plan for Reconstruction.

Meanwhile, the Republican majority on Capitol Hill, fearing that Johnson would not enforce civil rights legislation or that the courts would declare such federal laws unconstitutional, passed the **Fourteenth Amendment.** This, perhaps the most important of all the constitutional amendments, gave the federal government responsibility for guaranteeing equal rights under the law to all Americans. Section 1 defined national citizenship for the first time as extending to "all persons born or naturalized in the United States." The states were prohibited from abridging the rights of American citizens and could not "deprive any person of life, liberty, or property, without due process of law; nor deny to any person . . . equal protection of the laws."

The other sections of the amendment were important in the context of the time but had fewer long-term implications. Section 2 sought to penalize the South for denying voting rights to black men by reducing the congressional representation of any state that formally deprived a portion of its male citizens of the right to vote. Section 3 denied federal office to those who had taken an oath of office to support the U.S. Constitution and then had supported the Confederacy, and Section 4 repudiated the Confederate debt. The amendment was sent to the states with the understanding that Southerners would have no chance of being readmitted to Congress unless their states ratified it.

The congressional elections of 1866 served as a referendum on the Fourteenth Amendment. Johnson opposed the amendment on the grounds that it created a "centralized" government and denied states the right to manage their own affairs; he also counseled southern state legislatures to reject it, and all except Tennessee followed his advice. But the president's case for state autonomy was weakened by the publicity resulting from bloody race riots in New Orleans and Memphis. These and other reported atrocities against blacks made it clear that the existing southern state governments were failing abysmally to protect the "life, liberty, or property" of the ex-slaves.

Johnson further weakened his cause by taking the stump on behalf of candidates who supported his policies. In his notorious "swing around the circle," he toured the nation, slandering his opponents in crude language and engaging in undignified exchanges with hecklers. Enraged by southern inflexibility and the antics of a president who acted as if he were still campaigning in the backwoods of Tennessee, northern voters repudiated the administration. The Republican majority in Congress increased to a solid two-thirds in both houses, and the Radical wing of the party gained strength at the expense of moderates and conservatives.

Among the most influential of the Radical Republicans was Congressman Thaddeus Stevens of Pennsylvania. He advocated seizing land from southern planters and distributing it among the freed slaves. ❖

Congressional Reconstruction Plan Enacted

Congress was now in a position to implement its own plan of Reconstruction. In 1867 and 1868, it passed a series of acts that nullified the president's initiatives and reorganized the South on a new basis. Generally referred to as **Radical Reconstruction,** the measures actually represented a compromise between genuine Radicals and more moderate elements within the party.

Consistent Radicals such as Senator Charles Sumner of Massachusetts and Congressmen Thaddeus Stevens of Pennsylvania and George Julian of Indiana wanted to reshape southern society before readmitting ex-Confederates to the Union. Their program of "regeneration before Reconstruction" required an extended period of military rule, confiscation and redistribution of large landholdings among the freedmen, and federal aid for schools to educate blacks and whites for citizenship. But the majority of Republican congressmen found such a program unacceptable because it broke too sharply with American traditions of federalism and regard for property rights and might mean that decades would pass before the Union was back in working order.

The First Reconstruction Act, passed over Johnson's veto on March 2, 1867, did place the South under the rule of the army by reorganizing the region into five military districts. But military rule would last for only a short time. Subsequent acts of 1867 and 1868 opened the way for the quick readmission of any state that framed and ratified a new constitution providing for black suffrage. Ex-Confederates

Reconstruction Amendments, 1865–1870

Amendment	Main Provisions	Congressional Passage (2/3 majority in each house required)	Ratification Process (3/4 of all states required, including ex-Confederate states)
13	Slavery prohibited in United States	January 1865	December 1865 (27 states, including 8 southern states)
14	National citizenship; State representation in Congress reduced proportionally to number of voters disfranchised; Former Confederates denied right to hold office; Confederate debt repudiated	June 1866	Rejected by 12 southern and border states, February 1867; Radicals make readmission of southern states hinge on ratification; ratified July 1868
15	Denial of franchise because of race, color, or past servitude explicitly prohibited	February 1869	Ratification required for readmission of Virginia, Texas, Mississippi, Georgia; ratified March 1870

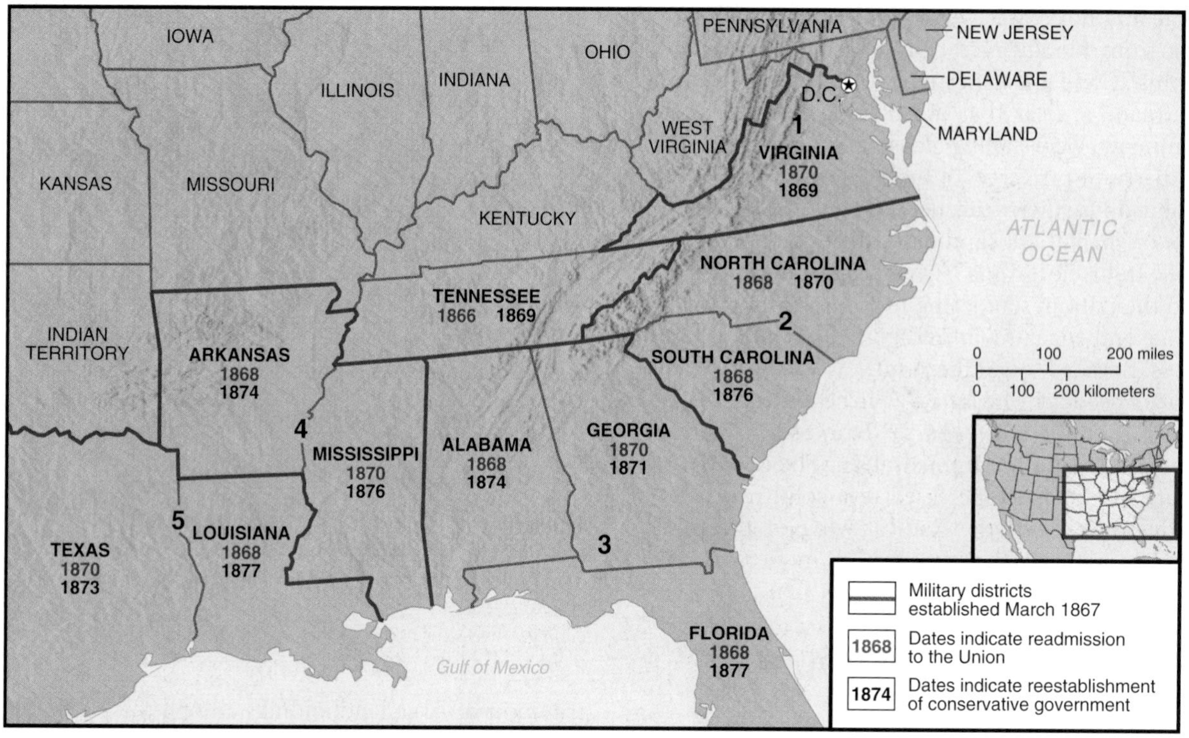

RECONSTRUCTION *During the Reconstruction era, the southern state governments passed through three phases: control by white ex-Confederates; domination by Republican legislators, both white and black; and, finally, the regain of control by conservative white Democrats.*

disqualified from holding federal office under the Fourteenth Amendment were prohibited from voting for delegates to the constitutional conventions or in the elections to ratify the conventions' work. Since blacks were allowed to participate in this process, Republicans thought they had found a way to ensure that "loyal" men would dominate the new governments. Radical Reconstruction was based on the dubious assumption that once blacks had the vote, they would have the power to protect themselves against white supremacists' efforts to deny them their rights. The Reconstruction Acts thus signaled a retreat from the true Radical position that a sustained use of federal authority was needed to complete the transition from slavery to freedom and prevent the resurgence of the South's old ruling class. (Troops were used in the South after 1868, but only in a very limited and sporadic way.) The majority of Republicans were unwilling to embrace centralized government and an extended period of military rule over civilians, and even Radicals such as Thaddeus Stevens supported the compromise as the best that could be achieved. Yet a genuine spirit of democratic idealism did give legitimacy and fervor to the cause of black male suffrage. Enabling people who were so poor and downtrodden to have access to the ballot box was a bold and innovative application of the principle of government by the consent of the governed. The problem was finding a way to enforce equal suffrage under conditions then existing in the postwar South.

The Impeachment Crisis

The first obstacle to enforcement of congressional Reconstruction was resistance from the White House. Johnson thoroughly disapproved of the new policy and sought to thwart the will of Congress by administering the plan in his own obstructive fashion. He immediately began to dismiss officeholders who sympathized with Radical Reconstruction, and he countermanded the orders of generals in charge of southern military districts who were zealous in their enforcement of the new legislation. Some Radical generals were transferred and replaced by conservative Democrats. Congress responded by passing laws designed to limit presidential authority over Reconstruction matters. One of the measures was the Tenure of Office Act, requiring Senate approval for the removal of cabinet officers and other officials whose appointment had needed the consent of the Senate. Another measure—a rider to an army appropriations bill—sought to limit Johnson's authority to issue orders to military commanders.

Johnson objected vigorously to the restrictions on the grounds that they violated the constitutional doctrine of the separation of powers. When it became clear that the president was resolute in fighting for his powers and using them to resist the establishment of Radical regimes in the southern states, some congressmen began to call for his impeachment. A preliminary effort foundered in 1867, but when Johnson tried to discharge Secretary of War Edwin Stanton—the only Radical in the cabinet—and persisted in his efforts despite the disapproval of the Senate, the pro-impeachment forces gained in strength.

In January 1868, Johnson ordered General Grant, who already commanded the army, to replace Stanton as head of the War Department. But Grant had his eye on the Republican presidential nomination and refused to defy Congress. Johnson subsequently appointed General Lorenzo Thomas, who agreed to serve. Faced with this apparent violation of the Tenure of Office Act, the House voted overwhelmingly to impeach the president on February 24, and he was placed on trial before the Senate.

Because seven Republican senators broke with the party leadership and voted for acquittal, the effort to convict Johnson and remove him from office fell one vote short of the necessary two-thirds. This outcome resulted in part from a skillful defense. Attorneys for the president argued for a narrow interpretation of the constitutional provision that a president could be impeached only for "high crimes and misdemeanors," asserting that this referred only to indictable offenses. Responding to the charge that Johnson had deliberately violated the Tenure of Office Act, the defense contended that the law did not apply to the removal of Stanton because he had been appointed by Lincoln, not Johnson.

The prosecution countered with a different interpretation of the Tenure of Office Act, but the core of their case was that Johnson had abused the powers of his office in an effort to sabotage the congressional Reconstruction policy. Obstructing the will of the legislative branch, they claimed, was sufficient grounds for conviction even if no crime had been committed. The Republicans who broke ranks to vote for acquittal could not endorse such a broad view of the impeachment power. They feared that removal of a president for essentially political reasons would threaten the constitutional balance of powers and open the way to legislative supremacy over the executive. In addition, the man who would have succeeded Johnson—Senator Benjamin Wade of Ohio, the president pro tem of the Senate—was unpopular with conservative Republicans because of his radical position on labor and currency questions.

Andrew Johnson's successful defense against conviction in his impeachment case centered on his invocation of the Constitution to defend his presidential rights and powers. Impeached in 1868, Johnson escaped conviction by a single vote. ❖

Although Johnson's acquittal by the narrowest of margins protected the American presidency from congressional domination, the impeachment episode helped create an impression in the public mind that the Radicals were ready to turn the Constitution to their own use to gain their objectives. Conservatives were again alarmed when Congress took action in 1868 to deny the Supreme Court's appellate jurisdiction in cases involving the military arrest and imprisonment of anti-Reconstruction activists in the South. But the evidence of congressional ruthlessness and illegality is not as strong as most historians used to think. Modern legal scholars have found merit in the Radicals' claim that their actions did not violate the Constitution.

Failure to remove Johnson from office was an embarrassment to congressional Republicans, but the episode did ensure that Reconstruction in the South would proceed as the majority in Congress intended. During the trial, Johnson helped influence the verdict by pledging to enforce the Reconstruction Acts, and he held to this promise during his remaining months in office. Unable to depose the president, the Radicals had at least succeeded in neutralizing his opposition to their program.

Reconstructing Southern Society

The Civil War left the South devastated, demoralized, and destitute. Slavery was dead, but what this meant for future relationships between whites and blacks was still in doubt. The overwhelming majority of southern whites wanted to keep blacks adrift between slavery and freedom—without rights, in a status resembling that of the "free Negroes" of the Old South. Blacks sought to be independent of their former masters and viewed the acquisition of land, education, and the vote as the best means of achieving this goal. The thousands of Northerners who went south after the war for materialistic or humanitarian reasons hoped to extend Yankee "civilization" to what they viewed as an unenlightened and barbarous region. For most of them, this reformation required the aid of the freedmen; not enough southern whites were willing to accept the new order and embrace northern middle-class values.

The struggle of these groups to achieve their conflicting goals bred chaos, violence, and instability. Unsettled conditions created many opportunities for corruption, crime, and terrorism. This was scarcely an ideal setting for an experiment in interracial democracy, but one was attempted nonetheless. Its success depended on massive and sustained support from the federal government. To the extent that this was forthcoming, progressive reform could be achieved. When it faltered, the forces of reaction and white supremacy were unleashed.

Reorganizing Land and Labor

The Civil War scarred the southern landscape and wrecked its economy. One devastated area—central South Carolina—looked to an 1865 observer "like a broad black streak of ruin and desolation—the fences are gone; lonesome smokestacks, surrounded by dark heaps of ashes and cinders, marking the spots where human habitations had stood; the fields all along the roads widely overgrown with weeds, with here and there a sickly patch of cotton or corn cultivated by negro squatters." Other areas through which the armies had passed were similarly ravaged. Several major cities—including Atlanta, Columbia, and Richmond—were gutted by fire. Most factories were dismantled or destroyed, and long stretches of railroad were torn up.

Physical ruin would not have been so disastrous if investment capital had been available for rebuilding. But the substantial wealth represented by Confederate currency and bonds had melted away, and emancipation of the slaves had divested the propertied classes of their most valuable and productive assets. According to some estimates, the South's per capita wealth in 1865 was only about half what it had been in 1860.

Recovery could not even begin until a new labor system replaced slavery. It was widely assumed in both the North and the South that southern prosperity would continue to depend on cotton and that the plantation was the most efficient unit for producing the crop. Hindering efforts to rebuild the plantation economy were lack of capital, the deep-rooted belief of southern whites that blacks would work only under compulsion, and the freedmen's resistance to labor conditions that recalled slavery.

Blacks strongly preferred to determine their own economic relationships, and for a time they had reason to hope the federal government would support their ambitions. The freed slaves were placed in a precarious position and were, in effect, fighting a two-front war. Although they were grateful for the federal aid in ending slavery, freed slaves often had ideas about freedom that contradicted the plans of their northern allies. Many ex-slaves wanted to hold on to the family-based communal work methods that they utilized during slavery. Freed slaves in areas of South Carolina, for example, attempted to maintain the family task system rather than adopting the individual piecework system pushed by northern capitalists. Many ex-slaves opposed plans to turn them into wage laborers who produced exclusively for a market. Finally, freed slaves often wanted to stay on the land their families had spent generations farming rather than move elsewhere to assume plots of land as individual farmers.

While not guaranteeing all of the freed slaves' hopes for economic self-determination, the northern military attempted to establish a new economic base for the freed men and women. General Sherman, hampered by the huge numbers of black fugitives that followed his army on its famous march, issued an order in January 1865 that set aside the islands and coastal areas of Georgia and South Carolina for exclusive black occupancy on 40-acre plots. Furthermore, the Freedmen's Bureau, as one of its many responsibilities, was given control of hundreds of thousands of acres of abandoned or confiscated land and was authorized to make 40-acre grants to black settlers for three-year periods, after which they would have the option to buy at low prices. By June 1865, forty thousand black farmers were at work on 300,000 acres of what they thought would be their own land.

But for most of them the dream of "forty acres and a mule," or some other arrangement that would give them control of their land and labor, was not to be realized. President Johnson pardoned the owners of most of the land consigned to the ex-slaves by Sherman and the Freedmen's Bureau, and proposals for an effective program of land confiscation and redistribution failed to get through Congress. Among the considerations prompting most congressmen to oppose land reform were a tenderness for property rights, fear of sapping the freedmen's initiative by giving them something they allegedly had not earned, and the desire to restore cotton production as quickly as possible to increase agricultural exports and stabilize the economy. Consequently, most blacks in physical possession of small farms failed to acquire title, and the mass of freedmen were left with little or no prospect of becoming landowners. Recalling the plight of southern blacks in 1865, an ex-slave later wrote that "they were set free without a dollar, without a foot of land, and without the wherewithal to get the next meal even."

Despite their poverty and landlessness, ex-slaves were reluctant to settle down and commit themselves to wage labor for their former masters. Many took to the road, hoping to find something better. Some were still expecting grants of land, but others were simply trying to increase their bargaining power. One freedman later recalled that an important part of being free was that, "we could move around [and] change bosses." As the end of 1865 approached, many freedmen had still not signed up for the coming season; anxious planters feared that blacks were plotting to seize land by force. Within a few weeks, however, most holdouts signed for the best terms they could get.

One common form of agricultural employment in 1866 was a contract labor system. Under this system, workers committed themselves for a year in return for fixed wages, a substantial portion of which was withheld until after the harvest. Since many planters were inclined to drive hard bargains, abuse their workers, or cheat them at the end of the year, the Freedmen's Bureau assumed the role of reviewing the contracts and enforcing them. But bureau officials had differing notions of what it meant to protect African Americans from exploitation. Some stood up strongly for the rights of the freedmen; others served as allies of the planters, rounding up available workers, coercing them to sign contracts for low wages, and then helping keep them in line.

The bureau's influence waned after 1867 (it was phased out completely by 1869), and the experiment with contract wage labor was abandoned. Growing up alongside the contract system and eventually displacing it was an alternative capital-labor relationship—**sharecropping.** First in small groups known as "squads" and later as individual families, blacks worked a piece of land independently for a fixed share of the crop, usually one-half. The advantage of this arrangement for credit-starved landlords was that it did not require much expenditure in advance of the harvest. The system also forced the tenant to share the risks of crop failure or a fall in cotton prices. These considerations loomed larger after disastrous harvests in 1866 and 1867.

African Americans initially viewed sharecropping as a step up from wage labor in the direction of landownership. But during the 1870s, this form of tenancy evolved into a new kind of servitude. Croppers had to live on credit until their cotton was sold, and planters or merchants seized the chance to "provision" them at high prices and exorbitant rates of interest. Creditors were entitled to deduct what was owed to them out of the tenant's share of the crop, and this left most sharecroppers with no net profit at the end of the year—more often than not with a debt that had to be worked off in subsequent years. Various methods, legal

The Civil War brought emancipation to slaves, but the sharecropping system kept many of them economically bound to their employers. At the end of a year the sharecropper tenants might owe most—or all—of what they had made to their landlord. Here a sharecropping family poses in front of their cabin. Ex-slaves often built their living quarters near woods in order to have a ready supply of fuel for heating and cooking. The cabin's chimney lists away from the house so that it can be easily pushed away from the living quarters should it catch fire. ❖

and extralegal, were eventually devised in an effort to bind indebted tenants to a single landlord for extended periods, but considerable movement was still possible.

Black Codes: A New Name for Slavery?

While landless African Americans in the countryside were being reduced to economic dependence, those in towns and cities found themselves living in an increasingly segregated society. The Black Codes of 1865 attempted to require separation of the races in public places and facilities; when most of the codes were overturned by federal authorities as violations of the Civil Rights Act of 1866, the same end was often achieved through private initiative and community pressure. In some cities, blacks successfully resisted being consigned to separate streetcars by appealing to the military during the period when it exercised authority or by organizing boycotts. But they found it almost impossible to gain admittance to most hotels, restaurants, and other privately owned establishments catering to whites. Although separate black, or "Jim Crow," cars were not yet the rule on railroads, African Americans were often denied first-class accommodations. After 1868, black-supported Republican governments passed civil rights acts requiring equal access to public facilities, but little effort was made to enforce the legislation.

The Black Codes had other onerous provisions meant to control African Americans and return them to quasi-slavery. Most codes even made black unemployment a crime, which meant blacks had to make long-term contracts with white employers or be arrested for vagrancy. Others limited the rights of African Americans to own property or engage in occupations other than those of servant or laborer. The codes were set aside by the actions of Congress, the military, and the Freedmen's Bureau, but vagrancy laws remained in force across the South.

Furthermore, private violence and discrimination against blacks continued on a massive scale unchecked by state authorities. Hundreds, perhaps thousands, of blacks were murdered by whites in 1865–1866, and few of the perpetrators were brought to justice. The imposition of military rule in 1867 was designed in part to protect former slaves from such violence and intimidation, but the task was beyond the capacity of the few thousand troops stationed in the South. When new constitutions were approved and states readmitted to the Union under the congressional plan in 1868, the problem became more severe. White opponents of Radical Reconstruction adopted systematic terrorism and organized mob violence to keep blacks away from the polls.

The freed slaves, in the face of opposition from both their Democratic enemies and some of their Republican allies, tried to defend themselves by organizing their own militia groups for protection and to assert their political rights. However, the militia groups were not powerful enough to overcome the growing power of the anti-Republican forces. Also, the military presence was progressively reduced, leaving the new Republican regimes to fight a losing battle against armed white supremacists. In the words of historian William Gillette, "there was simply no federal force large enough to give heart to black Republicans or to bridle southern white violence."

Republican Rule in the South

Hastily organized in 1867, the southern Republican party dominated the constitution making of 1868 and the regimes that came out of it. The party was an attempted coalition of three social groups (which varied in their relative strength from state to state). One was the same class that was becoming the backbone of the Republican party in the North—businessmen with an interest in enlisting government aid for private enterprise. Many Republicans of this stripe were recent arrivals from the North—the so-called **carpetbaggers**—but some were scalawags, former Whig planters or merchants who were born in the South or had immigrated to the region before the war and now saw a chance to realize their dreams for commercial and industrial development.

Poor white farmers, especially those from upland areas where Unionist sentiment had been strong during the Civil War, were a second element in the original coalition. These owners of small farms expected the Republican party to favor their interests over those wealthy landowners. They also expected that the party would assist them by enacting special legislation when they faced the loss of their homesteads to creditors. Newly enfranchised blacks were the third group to which the Republicans appealed. Blacks formed the vast majority of the Republican rank and file in most states and were concerned mainly with education, civil rights, and landownership.

Under the best of conditions, these coalitions would have been difficult to maintain. Each group had its own distinct goals and did not fully support the aims of the other segments. White yeomen, for example, had a deeply rooted resistance to black equality. And for how long could one expect essentially conservative businessmen to support costly measures for the elevation or relief of the lower classes of either race? In some states, astute Democratic politicians exploited these divisions by appealing to disaffected white Republicans.

But during the relatively brief period when they were in power in the South—varying from one to nine years depending on the state—the Republicans chalked up some notable achievements. They established (on paper at least) the South's first adequate systems of public education, democratized state and local government, and appropriated funds for an enormous expansion of public services and responsibilities.

As important as these social and political reforms were, they took second place to the Republicans' major effort—to foster economic development and restore southern prosperity by subsidizing the construction of railroads and other internal improvements. But the policy of aiding railroads turned out to be disastrous, even though it addressed the region's real economic needs and was initially very popular. Extravagance, corruption, and routes laid out in response to local political pressure rather than on sound economic grounds made for an increasing burden of public debt and taxation.

The policy did not produce the promised payoff of efficient, cheap transportation. Subsidized railroads frequently went bankrupt, leaving the taxpayers holding the bag. When the Panic of 1873 brought many southern state governments to the verge of bankruptcy, and railroad building came to an end, it was clear the Republicans' "gospel of prosperity" through state aid to private enterprise had failed miserably. Their political opponents, many of whom had originally favored such policies, now saw an opportunity to take advantage of the situation by charging that Republicans had ruined the southern economy.

In general, the Radical regimes failed to conduct public business honestly and efficiently. Embezzlement of public funds and bribery of state lawmakers or officials were common occurrences. State debts and tax burdens rose enormously, mainly because governments had undertaken heavy new responsibilities, but partly because of waste and graft. The situation varied from state to state; ruling cliques in Louisiana and South Carolina were guilty of much wrongdoing, yet Mississippi had a relatively honest and frugal regime.

Furthermore, southern corruption was not exceptional, nor was it a special result of the extension of suffrage to uneducated African Americans, as critics of Radical Reconstruction have claimed. It was part of a national pattern during an era when private interests considered buying government favors to be a part of the cost of doing business, and many politicians expected to profit by obliging them.

Blacks bore only a limited responsibility for the dishonesty of the Radical governments. Although sixteen African Americans served in Congress—two in the Senate—between 1869 and 1880, only in South Carolina did blacks constitute a majority of even one house of the state legislature. Furthermore, no black governors were elected during Reconstruction (although Pinkney B. S. Pinchback served for a time as acting governor of Louisiana). The biggest grafters were opportunistic whites. Some of the most notorious were carpetbaggers, but others were native Southerners. Businessmen offering bribes included members of the prewar gentry who were staunch opponents of Radical programs. Some black legislators went with the tide and accepted "loans" from those

On either side of Frederick Douglass on this poster are two African American heroes of the Reconstruction era. Senator Blanche K. Bruce of Mississippi, on the left, was the first African American to be elected to a full term in the U.S. Senate. Senator Hiram R. Revels, also representing Mississippi, was elected to the U.S. Senate in 1870 to fill the seat previously occupied by Confederate President Jefferson Davis. ❖

railroad lobbyists who would pay most for their votes, but the same men could usually be depended on to vote the will of their constituents on civil rights or educational issues.

If blacks served or supported corrupt and wasteful regimes, it was because the alternative was dire. Although the Democrats, or Conservatives as they called themselves in some states, made sporadic efforts to attract African American voters, it was clear that if they won control, they would attempt to strip blacks of their civil and political rights. But opponents of Radical Reconstruction were able to capitalize on racial prejudice and persuade many Americans that "good government" was synonymous with white supremacy.

Contrary to myth, the small number of African Americans elected to state or national office during Reconstruction demonstrated on the average more integrity and competence than their white counterparts. Most were fairly well educated, having been free Negroes or unusually privileged slaves before the war. Among the most capable were Robert Smalls (whose career was described earlier); Blanche K. Bruce of Mississippi, elected to the U.S. Senate in 1874 after rising to deserved prominence in the Republican party of his home state; Congressman Robert Brown Elliott of South Carolina, an adroit politician who was also a consistent champion of civil rights; and Congressman James T. Rapier of Alabama, who stirred Congress and the nation in 1873 with his eloquent appeals for federal aid to southern education and new laws to enforce equal rights for African Americans.

Claiming Public and Private Rights

As important as party politics to the changing political culture of the Reconstruction South were the ways that freed slaves claimed rights for themselves. They did so not only in negotiations with employers and in public meetings and convention halls, but also through the institutions they created, and perhaps most important, the households they formed.

As one black corporal in the Union Army told an audience of ex-slaves, "The Marriage covenant is at the foundation of all our rights. In slavery we could not have *legalized* marriage: *now* we have it . . . and we shall be established as a people." Through marriage, historian Laura Edwards tells us, African Americans claimed citizenship. Freedmen hoped that marriage would allow them to take on the rights that accrued to the independent head of a household, not only political rights, but the right to control the labor of wives and children for the first time.

Many states' Black Codes included apprenticeship provisions, providing for freed children to be apprenticed by courts to some white person (with preference given to former masters) if their parents were paupers, unemployed, of "bad character," or even simply if it were found to be "better for the habits and comfort of a child." Ex-slaves struggled to win their children back from what often amounted to re-enslavement for arbitrary reasons. Freedpeople challenged the apprenticeship system in county courts, and through the Freedmen's Bureau. As one group of petitioners from Maryland asserted, "Our homes are invaded and our little ones seized at the family fireside."

While many former slaves lined up eagerly to formalize their marriages, many also retained their own definitions of marriage and defied the efforts of the Freedmen's Bureau to use the marriage relation as a disciplinary tool. Perhaps as many as 50 percent of ex-slaves chose not to marry legally, and whites criticized them heavily for it. African American leaders worried about this refusal to follow white norms. The Army cor-

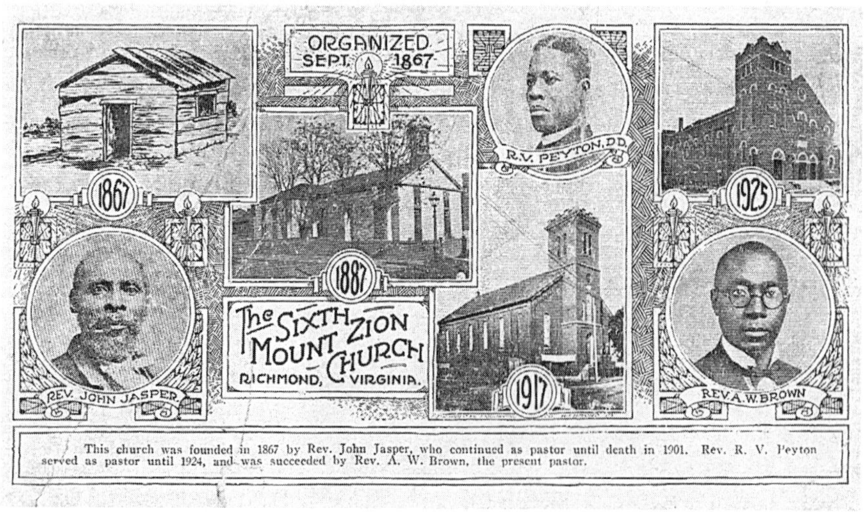

As slaves, many blacks attended white churches and listened to sermons preached by white ministers. After the Civil War and the end of slavery, African Americans joined or founded black churches, such as the Sixth Mount Zion Baptist Church of Richmond, Virginia. This postcard of the church's history includes a photograph of its founding pastor, John Jasper. ❖

A Freedmen's school, one of the more successful endeavors supported by the Freedmen's Bureau. The bureau, working with teachers from northern abolitionist and missionary societies, founded thousands of schools for freed slaves and poor whites. ❖

poral who had described marriage as "the foundation of all our rights" urged his audience: "Let us conduct ourselves worthy of such a blessing—and all the people will respect us." Yet many poor blacks continued to recognize as husband and wife people who cared for and supported one another without benefit of legal sanction. The new legal system punished couples who deviated from the legal norm through laws against bastardy, adultery, and fornication. Furthermore, the Freedmen's Bureau made the marriage of freedpeople a priority because, as historian Noralee Frankel explained, "The agency's overriding concern was keeping blacks from depending on the federal government for economic assistance." Once married, the husband became legally responsible for his family's support.

Some ex-slaves used institutions formerly closed to them like the courts to assert rights against white people as well as other blacks, suing over domestic violence, child support, assault, and debt. Freed women sued their husbands for desertion and alimony in order to enlist the Freedman's Bureau to help them claim property from men. Other ex-slaves mobilized kin networks and other community resources to make claims on property and family.

Immediately after the war, freedpeople flocked to create institutions that had been denied to them under slavery: churches, fraternal and benevolent associations, political organizations, and schools. Many joined all-black denominations such as the African Methodist Episcopal church, which provided freedom from white dominance and a more congenial style of worship. Black women formed all-black chapters of organizations such as the Women's Christian Temperance Union, and their own women's clubs to oppose lynching and work for "uplift" in the black community.

A top priority for most ex-slaves was the opportunity to educate their children; the first schools for freedpeople were all-black institutions established by the Freedmen's Bureau and various northern missionary societies. At the time, having been denied all education during the antebellum period, most blacks viewed separate schooling as an opportunity rather than as a form of discrimination. However, these schools were precursors to the segregated public school systems first instituted by Republican governments. Only in city schools of New Orleans and at the University of South Carolina were there serious attempts during Reconstruction to bring white and black students together in the same classrooms.

In a variety of ways, African American men and women during Reconstruction claimed freedom in the "private" realm as well as the public sphere, by claiming rights to their own families and building their own institutions. They did so in the face of the vigorous efforts of their former masters as well as the new government agencies to control their private lives and shape their new identities as husbands, wives, and citizens.

Retreat from Reconstruction

The era of Reconstruction began coming to an end almost before it got started. Although it was only a scant three years from the end of the Civil War, the impeachment crisis of 1868 represented the high point of popular interest in Reconstruction issues. That year, Ulysses S. Grant was elected president. Many historians blame Grant for the corruption of his administration and for the inconsistency and failure of his southern policy. He had neither the vision nor the sense of duty to tackle the difficult challenges the nation faced. From 1868 on, political issues other than southern Reconstruction moved to the forefront of national politics, and the plight of African Americans in the South receded in white consciousness.

Rise of the Money Question

In the years immediately following the Civil War, another issue already competing for public attention was the money question: whether to allow "greenbacks"—paper money issued during the war—to continue to circulate or to return to "sound" or "hard" money, meaning gold or silver. Supporters of paper money, known as **greenbackers,** were strongest in the credit-hungry West and among expansion-minded manufacturers. Defenders of hard money were mostly the commercial and financial interests in the East; they received crucial support from intellectuals who regarded government-sponsored inflation as immoral or contrary to the natural laws of classical economics.

In 1868, the money question surged briefly to the forefront of national politics. Faced with a business recession blamed on the Johnson administration's policy of contracting the currency, Congress voted to stop the retirement of greenbacks. The Democratic party, responding to Midwestern pressure, included in its platform for the 1868 national election a plan calling for the redemption of much of the Civil War debt in greenbacks rather than gold. Yet they nominated for president a sound-money supporter, so that the greenback question never became an issue in the 1868 presidential campaign. Grant, already a popular general, won the election handily with the help of the Republican-dominated Southern states.

In 1869 and 1870, a Republican-controlled Congress passed laws that assured payment in gold to most bondholders but eased the burden of the huge Civil War debt by exchanging bonds that were soon coming due for those that would not be payable for ten, fifteen, or thirty years. In this way, the public credit was protected.

Still unresolved, however, was the problem of what to do about the $356 million in greenbacks that remained in circulation. Hard-money proponents wanted to retire them quickly; inflationists thought more should be issued to stimulate the economy. The Grant administration followed the middle course of allowing the greenbacks to float until economic expansion would bring them to a par with gold, thus permitting a painless return to specie payments. But the Panic of 1873, which brought much of the economy to its knees, led to a revival of agitation to inflate the currency. Debt-ridden farmers, who would be the backbone of the greenback movement for years to come, now joined the soft-money clamor for the first time.

The Election of 1868

Candidate	Party	Popular Vote	Electoral Vote*
Grant	Republican	3,012,833	214
Seymour	Democratic	2,703,249	80
Not voted*			23

*Unreconstructed states did not participate in the election.

Responding to the money and credit crunch, Congress moved in 1874 to authorize a modest issue of new greenbacks. But Grant, influenced by the opinions of hard-money financiers, vetoed the bill. In 1875, Congress, led by Senator John Sherman of Ohio, enacted the Specie Resumption Act, which provided for a limited reduction of greenbacks leading to full resumption of specie payments by January 1, 1879. Its action was widely interpreted as deflation in the midst of depression. Farmers and workers, who were already suffering acutely from deflation, reacted with dismay and anger.

The Democratic Party could not capitalize adequately on these sentiments because of the influence of its own hard-money faction, and in 1876 an independent Greenback party entered the national political arena. The party's nominee for president, Peter Cooper, received an insignificant number of votes, but in 1878 the Greenback Labor party polled more than a million votes and elected fourteen congressmen. The Greenbackers were able to keep the money issue alive into the following decade.

Final Efforts of Reconstruction

The Republican effort to make equal rights for blacks the law of the land culminated in the **Fifteenth Amendment.** Passed by Congress in 1869 and ratified by the states in 1870, the amendment prohibited any state from denying a male citizen the right to vote because of race, color, or previous condition of servitude. A more radical version, requiring universal manhood suffrage, was rejected partly because it departed too sharply from traditional views of federal-state rela-

Shown seated at the table are feminist leaders Elizabeth Cady Stanton and Susan B. Anthony. They and their adherents split with Lucy Stone (right) and her followers over the Fifteenth Amendment and its failure to extend the vote to women. ❖

tions. States therefore could still limit the suffrage by imposing literacy tests, property qualifications, or poll taxes allegedly applying to all racial groups; such devices would eventually be used to strip southern blacks of the right to vote. But the makers of the amendment did not foresee this result. They believed their action would prevent future Congresses or southern constitutional conventions from repealing or nullifying the provisions for black male suffrage included in the Reconstruction Acts. A secondary aim was to enfranchise African Americans in those northern states that still denied them the vote.

Many feminists were bitterly disappointed that the amendment did not extend the vote to women as well as freedmen. A militant wing of the women's rights movement, led by Elizabeth Cady Stanton and Susan B. Anthony, was so angered that the Constitution was being amended in a way that, in effect, made gender a qualification for voting that they campaigned against ratification of the Fifteenth Amendment. Another group of feminists led by Lucy Stone supported the amendment on the grounds that this was "the Negro's hour" and that women could afford to wait a few years for the vote. This disagreement divided the woman suffrage movement for a generation to come.

The Grant administration was charged with enforcing the amendment and protecting black men's voting rights in the reconstructed states. Since survival of the Republican regimes depended on African American support, political partisanship dictated federal action, even though the North's emotional and ideological commitment to black citizenship was waning.

A Reign of Terror Against Blacks

Between 1868 and 1872, the main threat to southern Republican regimes came from the **Ku Klux Klan** and other secret societies bent on restoring white supremacy by intimidating blacks who sought to exercise their political rights. First organized in Tennessee in 1866, the Klan spread rapidly to other states, adopting increasingly lawless and brutal tactics. A grassroots vigilante movement and not a centralized conspiracy, the Klan thrived on local initiative and gained support from whites of all social classes. Its secrecy, decentralization, popular support, and utter ruthlessness made it very difficult to suppress. As soon as blacks had been granted the right to vote, hooded "night riders" began to visit the cabins of those who were known to be active Republicans; some victims were only threatened, but others were whipped or even murdered. One black Georgian related a typical incident: "They broke my door open, took me out of bed, took me to the woods and whipped me three hours or more and left me for dead. They said to me, 'Do you think you will vote for another damned radical ticket?'"

Such methods were first used effectively in the presidential election of 1868. Grant lost in Louisiana and Georgia mainly because the Klan—or the Knights of the White Camellia, as the Louisiana variant was called—launched a reign of terror to prevent prospective black voters from exercising their rights. In Louisiana, political violence claimed more than a thousand lives, and in Arkansas, which Grant managed to carry, more than two hundred Republicans, including a congressman, were assassinated.

Thereafter, Klan terrorism was directed mainly at Republican state governments. Virtual insurrections broke out in Arkansas, Tennessee, North Carolina, and parts of South Carolina. Republican governors called out the state militia to fight the Klan, but only the Arkansas militia succeeded in bringing it to heel. In Tennessee, North Carolina, and Georgia, Klan activities helped undermine Republican control, thus allowing the Democrats to come to power in all of these states by 1870.

This 1868 photograph shows typical regalia of members of the Ku Klux Klan, a secret white supremacist organization. Before elections, hooded Klansmen terrorized African Americans to discourage them from voting. ❖

Faced with the violent overthrow of the southern Republican Party, Congress and the Grant administration were forced to act. A series of laws passed in 1870–1871 sought to enforce the Fifteenth Amendment by providing federal protection for black suffrage and authorizing use of the army against the Klan. The **Force acts,** also known as the Ku Klux Klan acts, made interference with voting rights a federal crime and established provisions for government supervision of elections. In addition, the legislation empowered the president to call out troops and suspend the writ of habeas corpus to quell insurrection. In 1871–1872, thousands of suspected Klansmen were arrested by the military or U.S. marshals, and the writ was suspended in nine counties of South Carolina that had been virtually taken over by the secret order. Although most of the accused Klansmen were never brought to trial, were acquitted, or received suspended sentences, the enforcement effort was vigorous enough to put a damper on hooded terrorism and ensure relatively fair and peaceful elections in 1872.

A heavy black turnout in these elections enabled the Republicans to hold on to power in most states of the Deep South, despite efforts of the Democratic-Conservative opposition to cut into the Republican vote by taking moderate positions on racial and economic issues. This setback prompted the Democratic-Conservatives to make a significant change in their strategy and ideology. No longer did they try to take votes away from the Republicans by proclaiming support for black suffrage and government aid to business. Instead they began to appeal openly to white supremacy and to the traditional Democratic and agrarian hostility to government promotion of economic development. Consequently, they were able to bring back to the polls a portion of the white electorate, mostly small farmers, who had not been turning out because they were alienated by the leadership's apparent concessions to Yankee ideas.

This new and more effective electoral strategy dovetailed with a resurgence of violence meant to reduce Republican, especially black Republican, voting. The new reign of terror differed from the previously discussed Klan episode; its agents no longer wore masks but acted quite openly. They were effective because the northern public was increasingly disenchanted with federal intervention on behalf of what were widely viewed as corrupt and tottering Republican regimes. Grant used force in the South for the last time in 1874 when an overt paramilitary organization in Louisiana, known as the White League, tried to overthrow a Republican government accused of stealing an election. When another unofficial militia in Mississippi instigated a series of bloody race riots prior to the state elections of 1875, Grant refused the governor's request for federal troops. As a result, black

❖ A Look at the Past ❖

Cartoon "Worse Than Slavery"

Political cartoonist Thomas Nast offered his commentary on and critique of contemporary events through his cartoons in *Harper's Weekly,* a popular magazine that had a circulation of over 100,000 readers. This Nast cartoon, "Worse Than Slavery," appeared in the magazine on October 24, 1874. Carefully examine the individuals and items depicted in the cartoon. Note that the phrase near the top of the drawing, "This is a white man's government," is a quotation from the 1868 Democratic Party platform. According to the cartoon, what conditions or events are "worse than slavery"? What view of Reconstruction policy does the cartoonist appear to be expressing?

voters were successfully intimidated—one county registered only seven Republican votes where there had been a black majority of two thousand—and Mississippi fell to the Democratic-Conservatives. According to one account, Grant decided to withhold troops because he had been warned that intervention might cost the Republicans the crucial state of Ohio in the same off-year elections.

By 1876, Republicans held on to only three southern states: South Carolina, Louisiana, and Florida. Partly because of Grant's hesitant and inconsistent use of presidential power, but mainly because the northern electorate would no longer tolerate military action to sustain Republican governments and black voting rights, Radical Reconstruction was falling into total eclipse.

Spoilsmen Versus Reformers

One reason Grant found it increasingly difficult to take strong action to protect southern Republicans was the bad odor surrounding his stewardship of the federal government and the Republican Party. Reformers charged that a corrupt national administration was propping up bad governments in the South for personal and partisan advantage. An apparent case in point was Grant's intervention in Louisiana in 1872 on behalf of an ill-reputed Republican faction headed by his wife's brother-in-law, who controlled federal patronage as collector of customs in New Orleans.

The Republican party in the Grant era was losing the idealism and high purpose associated with the crusade against slavery. By the beginning of the 1870s, the men who had been the conscience of the party—old-line radicals such as Thaddeus Stevens, Charles Sumner, and Benjamin Wade—were either dead, out of office, or at odds with the administration. New leaders of a different stamp, whom historians have dubbed "spoilsmen" or "politicos," were taking their place. When he made common cause with hard-boiled manipulators such as senators Roscoe Conkling of New York and James G. Blaine of Maine, Grant lost credibility with reform-minded Republicans.

During Grant's first administration, an aura of scandal surrounded the White House but did not directly implicate the president. In 1869, the financial buccaneer Jay Gould enlisted the aid of a brother-in-law of Grant to further his fantastic scheme to corner the gold market. Gould failed in the attempt, but he did manage to save himself and come away with a huge profit.

Grant's first-term vice president, Schuyler Colfax of Indiana, was directly involved in the notorious Crédit Mobilier scandal. Crédit Mobilier was a construction company that actually served as a fraudulent device for siphoning off profits that should have gone to the stockholders of the Union Pacific Railroad, which was the beneficiary of massive federal land grants. In order to forestall government inquiry into this arrangement, Crédit Mobilier stock was distributed to influential congressmen, including Colfax (who was speaker of the House before he was elected vice president). The whole business came to light just before the campaign of 1872.

Republicans who could not tolerate such corruption or had other grievances against the administration broke with Grant in 1872 and formed a third party committed to "honest government" and "reconciliation" between the North and the South. Led initially by high-minded reformers such as Senator Carl Schurz of Missouri, the Liberal Republicans endorsed reform of the civil service to curb the corruption-breeding patronage system and advocated laissez-faire economic policies—which meant low tariffs, an end to government subsidies for railroads, and hard money. Despite their rhetoric of idealism and reform, the Liberal Republicans were extremely conservative in their notions of what government should do to assure justice for blacks and other underprivileged Americans.

The Election of 1872

Candidate	Party	Popular Vote	Electoral Vote*
Grant	Republican	3,597,132	286
Greeley	Democratic and Liberal Republican	2,834,125	Greeley died before the electoral college voted.

*Out of a total of 366 electoral votes. Greeley's votes were divided among the four minor candidates.

The Liberal Republicans' national convention nominated Horace Greeley, editor of the respected New York *Tribune*. This was a curious and divisive choice, since Greeley was at odds with the founders of the movement on the tariff question and was indifferent to civil service reform. The Democrats also nominated Greeley, mainly because he promised to end Radical Reconstruction by restoring "self-government" to the South.

But the journalist turned out to be a poor campaigner who failed to inspire enthusiasm from lifelong supporters of either party. Most Republicans stuck with Grant, despite the corruption issue, because they still could not stomach the idea of ex-rebels returning to power in the South. Many Democrats, recalling Greeley's previous record as a staunch Republican, simply stayed away from the polls. The result was a decisive victory for Grant, whose 56 percent of the popular vote was the highest percentage won by any candidate between Andrew Jackson and Theodore Roosevelt.

Grant's second administration seemed to bear out the reformers' worst suspicions about corruption in high places. In 1875, the public learned that federal revenue officials had conspired with distillers to defraud the government of millions of dollars in liquor taxes. Grant's private secretary, Orville E. Babcock, was indicted as a member of the "Whiskey Ring" and was saved from conviction only by the president's personal intercession. The next year, Grant's secretary of war, William W. Belknap, was impeached by the House after an investigation revealed he had taken bribes for the sale of Indian trading posts. He avoided conviction in the Senate only by resigning from office before his trial. Grant fought hard to protect Belknap, to the point of participating in what a later generation might call a cover-up.

There is no evidence that Grant profited personally from any of the misdeeds of his subordinates. Yet

In this Puck *cartoon, U. S. Grant clutches the Whiskey and Navy rings and supports an assortment of bosses, profiteers, and scandals associated with the Grant administration.* ❖

he is not entirely without blame for the corruption in his administration. He failed to take firm action against the malefactors, and, even after their guilt had been clearly established, he sometimes tried to shield them from justice. Ulysses S. Grant was the only president between Jackson and Wilson to serve two full and consecutive terms. But unlike other chief executives so favored by the electorate, Grant is commonly regarded as a failure. Although the problems he faced would have challenged any president, the shame of Grant's administration was that he made loyalty to old friends a higher priority than civil rights or sound economic principles.

Reunion and the New South

Congressional Reconstruction prolonged the sense of sectional division and conflict for a dozen years after the guns had fallen silent. Its final liquidation in 1877 opened the way to a reconciliation of North and South. But the costs of reunion were high for less privileged groups in the South. The civil and political rights of African Americans, left unprotected, were progressively and relentlessly stripped away by white supremacist regimes. Lower-class whites saw their interests sacrificed to those of capitalists and landlords. Despite the rhetoric hailing a prosperous "New South," the region remained poor and open to exploitation by northern business interests.

The Compromise of 1877

The election of 1876 pitted Rutherford B. Hayes of Ohio, a Republican governor untainted by the scandals of the Grant era, against Governor Samuel J. Tilden of New York, a Democratic reformer who had battled against Tammany Hall and the Tweed Ring. Honest government was apparently the electorate's highest priority. When the returns came in, Tilden had clearly won the popular vote and seemed likely to win a narrow victory in the electoral college. But the result was placed in doubt when the returns from the three southern states still controlled by the Republicans—South Carolina, Florida, and Louisiana—were contested. If Hayes were to be awarded these three states, plus one contested electoral vote in Oregon, Republican strategists realized, he would triumph in the electoral college by a single vote.

The outcome of the election remained undecided for months, plunging the nation into a major political crisis. To resolve the impasse, Congress appointed a special electoral commission of fifteen members to determine who would receive the votes of the disputed states. Originally composed of seven Democrats, seven Republicans, and an independent, the commission fell under Republican control when the independent member resigned to run for the Senate and a Republican was appointed to take his place. The commission split along party lines and voted eight to seven to award Hayes all of the disputed votes. But this decision still had to be ratified by both houses of Congress. The Republican-dominated Senate readily approved it, but the Democrats in the House planned a filibuster to delay the final counting of the electoral votes until after inauguration day. If the filibuster succeeded, neither candidate would have a majority and, as provided in the Constitution, the election would be decided by the House, where the Democrats controlled enough states to elect Tilden.

To ensure Hayes's election, Republican leaders negotiated secretly with conservative southern Democrats, some of whom seemed willing to abandon the filibuster if the last troops were withdrawn and home rule restored to the South. Eventually an informal bargain was struck, which historians have dubbed the **Compromise of 1877.** What precisely was agreed to and by whom remains a matter of dispute; but one

Election of 1876

	Uncontested Electoral Vote	Electoral Total	Popular Vote
REPUBLICAN Rutherford B. Hayes	165	185	4,036,298
DEMOCRATIC Samuel J. Tilden	184	184	4,300,590
GREENBACK Peter Cooper	—	—	81,737
	349		8,418,625

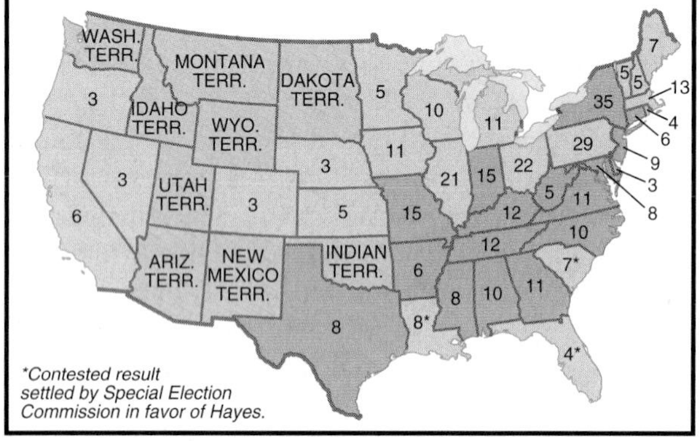

*Contested result settled by Special Election Commission in favor of Hayes.

thing at least was understood by both sides: Hayes would be president and southern blacks would be abandoned to their fate. In a sense, Hayes did not concede anything, because he had already decided to end federal support for the crumbling Radical regimes. But southern negotiators were heartened by firm assurances that this would indeed be the policy. Some also were influenced by vaguer promises involving federal support for southern railroads and internal improvements.

With southern Democratic acquiescence, the filibuster was broken, and Hayes took the oath of office. He immediately ordered the army not to resist a Democratic takeover of state governments in South Carolina and Louisiana. Thus fell the last of the Radical governments, and the entire South was firmly under the control of white Democrats. The trauma of the war and Reconstruction had destroyed the chances for a renewal of two-party competition among white Southerners.

Northern Republicans soon reverted to denouncing the South for its suppression of black suffrage. But this "waving of the bloody shirt," which also served as a reminder of the war and northern casualties, quickly degenerated into a campaign ritual aimed at northern voters who could still be moved by sectional antagonism.

"Redeeming" a New South

The men who came to power after Radical Reconstruction fell in one southern state after another are usually referred to as the **Redeemers.** They had differing backgrounds and previous loyalties. Some were members of the Old South's ruling planter class who had warmly supported secession and now sought to reestablish the old order with as few changes as possible. Others, of middle-class origin or outlook, favored commercial and industrial interests over agrarian groups and called for a New South committed to diversified economic development. A third group were professional politicians bending with the prevailing winds, such as Joseph E. Brown of Georgia, who had been a secessionist, a wartime governor, and a leading scalawag Republican before becoming a Democratic Redeemer.

Although historians have tried to assign the Redeemers a single coherent ideology or view of the world and have debated whether it was Old South agrarianism or New South industrialism they endorsed, these leaders can perhaps best be understood as power brokers mediating among the dominant interest groups of the South in ways that served their own political advantage. In many ways, the "rings" that they established on the state and county level were analogous to the political machines developing at the same time in northern cities. (See the Feature Essay, "Changing Views of Reconstruction," pp. 476–477.)

Redeemers did, however, agree on and endorse two basic principles: laissez-faire and white supremacy. Laissez-faire—the notion that government should be limited and should not intervene openly and directly in the economy—could unite planters, frustrated at seeing direct state support going to businessmen, and capitalist promoters who had come to realize that low taxes and freedom from government regulation were even more advantageous than state subsidies. It soon became clear that the Redeemers responded only to privileged and entrenched interest groups, especially landlords, merchants, and industrialists, and offered little or nothing to tenants, small farmers, and working people. As industrialization began to gather steam in the 1880s, Democratic regimes became increasingly accommodating to manufacturing interests and hospitable to agents of northern capital who were gaining control of the South's transportation system and its extractive industries.

White supremacy was the principal rallying cry that brought the Redeemers to power in the first place. Once in office, they found they could stay there by charging that opponents of ruling Democratic cliques were trying to divide "the white man's party" and open the way for a return to "black domination." Appeals to racism could also deflect attention from the economic grievances of groups without political clout.

The new governments were more economical than those of Reconstruction, mainly because they cut back

The growing industrialization that was characteristic of the New South is evident in this photograph of a South Carolina cotton mill. Steam power and the abundance of cheap coal in the Appalachians helped shift the textile industry from the North to the South. ❖

drastically on appropriations for schools and other needed public services. But they were scarcely more honest—embezzlement of funds and bribery of officials continued to occur to an alarming extent. Louisiana, for example, suffered for decades from the flagrant corruption associated with a state-chartered lottery.

The Redeemer regimes of the late 1870s and 1880s badly neglected the interests of small white farmers. Whites, as well as blacks, were suffering from the notorious crop lien system, which gave local merchants who advanced credit at high rates of interest during the growing season the right to take possession of the harvested crop on terms that buried farmers deeper and deeper in debt. As a result, increasing numbers of whites lost title to their homesteads and were reduced to tenancy. When a depression of world cotton prices added to the burden of a ruinous credit system, agrarian protesters began to challenge the ruling elite, first through the Southern Farmers' Alliance of the late 1880s and then by supporting its political descendant—the Populist party of the 1890s (see Chapter 20).

The Rise of Jim Crow

African Americans bore the greatest hardships imposed by the new order. From 1876 through the first decade of the twentieth century, Southern states imposed a series of restrictions on black civil rights known as **Jim Crow laws.** While segregation and disfranchisement began as informal arrangements, they culminated in a legal regime of separation and exclusion that took firm hold in the 1890s.

The rise of Jim Crow in the political arena was especially bitter for Southern blacks who realized that only political power could ensure other rights. The Redeemers promised, as part of the understanding that led to the end of federal intervention in 1877, that they would respect the rights of blacks as set forth in the Fourteenth and Fifteenth Amendments. Governor Wade Hampton of South Carolina was especially vocal in pledging that African Americans would not be reduced to second-class citizenship by the new regimes. But when blacks tried to vote Republican in the "redeemed" states, they encountered renewed violence and intimidation. "Bulldozing" African American voters remained common practice in state elections during the late 1870s and early 1880s; those blacks who withstood the threat of losing their jobs or being evicted from tenant farms if they voted for the party of Lincoln were visited at night and literally whipped into line. The message was clear: Vote Democratic, or vote not at all.

Furthermore, white Democrats now controlled the electoral machinery and were able to manipulate the black vote by stuffing ballot boxes, discarding unwanted votes, or reporting fraudulent totals. Some states also imposed complicated new voting requirements to discourage black participation. Full-scale disfranchisement did not occur until literacy tests and other legalized obstacles to voting were imposed in the period from 1890 to 1910, but by that time, less formal and comprehensive methods had already made a mockery of the Fifteenth Amendment.

Nevertheless, blacks continued to vote freely in some localities until the 1890s; a few districts, like the one Robert Smalls represented, even elected black Republicans to Congress during the immediate post-Reconstruction period. The last of these, Representative George H. White of North Carolina, served until 1901. His farewell address eloquently conveyed the agony of southern blacks in the era of Jim Crow (strict segregation):

> These parting words are in behalf of an outraged, heart-broken, bruised, and bleeding but God-fearing people, faithful, industrious, loyal people—rising people, full of potential force. . . . The only apology that I have to make for the earnestness with which I have spoken is that I am pleading for the life, the liberty, the future happiness, and manhood suffrage of one-eighth of the entire population of the United States.

The dark night of racism that fell on the South after Reconstruction seemed to unleash all the baser impulses of human nature. Between 1889 and 1899, an average of 187 blacks were lynched every year for alleged offenses against white supremacy. The protection of Southern white womanhood became the rallying cry for many lynch mobs, as African American men were accused, often with little or no evidence, of raping white women.

Those convicted of petty crimes against property were often little better off; many were condemned to be leased out to private contractors whose brutality rivaled that of the most sadistic slaveholders. The convict-lease system enabled entrepreneurs, such as mine owners and extractors of forest products, to rent prisoners from the state and treat them as they saw fit. Unlike slaveowners, they suffered no loss when a

Perhaps no event better expresses the cruel and barbaric nature of the racism and white supremacy that swept the South after Reconstruction than lynching. Although lynchings were not confined to the South, most occurred there and African American men were the most frequent victims. Here two men lean out of a barn window above a black man who is about to be hanged. Others below prepare to set on fire the pile of hay at the victim's feet. Lynchings were often public events, drawing huge crowds to watch the victim's agonizing death. ❖

CHRONOLOGY

1863	Lincoln sets forth 10 percent Reconstruction plan
1864	Wade-Davis Bill passes Congress but is pocket vetoed by Lincoln
1865	Johnson moves to reconstruct the South on his own initiative ❖ Congress refuses to seat representatives and senators elected from states reestablished under presidential plan (December)
1866	Johnson vetoes Freedmen's Bureau Bill (February) ❖ Johnson vetoes Civil Rights Act; it passes over his veto (April) ❖ Congress passes Fourteenth Amendment (June) ❖ Republicans increase their congressional majority in the fall elections
1867	First Reconstruction Act is passed over Johnson's veto (March)
1868	Johnson is impeached; he avoids conviction by one vote (February–May) ❖ Southern blacks vote and serve in constitutional conventions ❖ Grant wins presidential election, defeating Horatio Seymour
1869	Congress passes Fifteenth Amendment, granting African Americans the right to vote
1870–1871	Congress passes Ku Klux Klan Acts to protect black voting rights in the South
1872	Grant reelected president, defeating Horace Greeley, candidate of Liberal Republicans and Democrats
1873	Financial panic plunges nation into depression
1875	Congress passes Specie Resumption Act ❖ "Whiskey Ring" scandal exposed
1876–1877	Disputed presidential election resolved in favor of Republican Hayes over Democrat Tilden
1877	Compromise of 1877 ends military intervention in the South and causes fall of the last Radical governments

Supreme Court Decisions Affecting Black Civil Rights, 1875–1900

Case	Effects of Court's Decisions
Hall v. *DeCuir* (1878)	Struck down Louisiana law prohibiting racial discrimination by "common carriers" (railroads, steamboats, buses). Declared the law a "burden" on interstate commerce, over which states had no authority.
United States v. *Harris* (1882)	Declared federal laws to punish crimes such as murder and assault unconstitutional. Declared such crimes to be the sole concern of local government. Ignored the frequent racial motivation behind such crimes in the South.
Civil Rights Cases (1883)	Struck down Civil Rights Act of 1875. Declared that Congress may not legislate on civil rights unless a state passes a discriminatory law. Declared the Fourteenth Amendment silent on racial discrimination by private citizens.
Plessy v. *Ferguson* (1896)	Upheld Louisiana statute requiring "separate but equal" accommodations on railroads. Declared that segregation is *not* necessarily discrimination.
Williams v. *Mississippi* (1898)	Upheld state law requiring a literacy test to qualify for voting. Refused to find any implication of racial discrimination in the law, although it permitted illiterate whites to vote if they "understood" the Constitution. Using such laws, southern states rapidly disfranchised blacks.

forced laborer died from overwork. (Annual mortality rates in the convict camps ranged as high as 25 percent.) Even after convict leasing was banned in some states, blacks continued into the twentieth century to work on chain gangs and prison plantations such as the notorious Parchman Farm in Mississippi. Parchman Farm resembled a slave plantation more than a prison: Chained men picked cotton from sunup to sundown, constantly under the threat of being shot or whipped by "a leather strap, three feet long and six inches wide, known as 'Black Annie,' which hung from the driver's belt."

Finally, the dignity of blacks was cruelly affronted by the wave of segregation laws passed around the turn of the century, which served to remind them constantly that they were deemed unfit to associate with whites on any basis that implied equality. To some extent, the segregation laws were a white reaction to the refusal of many blacks to submit to voluntary segregation of railroads, streetcars, and other public facilities. On railroads, for example, elite free women of color had been accustomed to riding in the first-class ladies car; being relegated to the "smoking car" with men who were often drinking and gambling put them in physical danger of molestation.

The North and the federal government did little or nothing to stem the tide of racial oppression in the South. The high point of legislation came in 1875, when Congress passed a Civil Rights Act with far-reaching provisions to protect public and private discrimination on the basis of race. The Supreme Court invalidated the 1875 Act just eight years later, in an opinion that scolded the former slaves that "there must be some stage" when they "cease to be the special favorite of the laws." A series of Supreme Court decisions between 1878 and 1898 gutted the Reconstruction amendments and the legislation passed to enforce them, leaving blacks virtually defenseless against political and social discrimination.

Conclusion: Henry McNeal Turner and the "Unfinished Revolution"

The career of Henry McNeal Turner sums up the bitter side of the black experience in the South during and after Reconstruction. Born free in South Carolina in 1834, Turner became a minister of the African Methodist Episcopal (AME) Church just before the outbreak of the Civil War. During the war, he recruited African Americans for the Union army and later served as chaplain for black troops. After the fighting was over, he went to Georgia to work for the Freedmen's Bureau but encountered racial discrimination from white Bureau officers and left government service for church work and Reconstruction politics. Elected to the 1867 Georgia constitutional convention and to the state legislature in 1868, he was one of a number of black clergymen who assumed leadership roles among the freedmen. But whites won control of the Georgia legislature and expelled all the black members. Turner's reaction was an angry speech in which he proclaimed that white men were never to be trusted. As the inhabitant of a state in which blacks never gained the degree of power that they achieved in some other parts of the South, Turner was one of the first black leaders to see the failure of Reconstruction as the betrayal of African American hopes for citizenship.

Becoming a bishop of the AME Church in 1880, Turner emerged as the late nineteenth century's

Feature Essay

CHANGING VIEWS OF RECONSTRUCTION

A central issue of Reconstruction was the place of blacks in American life after slavery. Changing attitudes on this question strongly influenced later representations of the Reconstruction era, whether in historical writing or in the popular media. Indeed, what later generations imagined had happened in the South in the years immediately after the Civil War is a fairly reliable index of how they viewed black-white relations in their own time.

In the early twentieth century, when white supremacists were in control in the South and northern public opinion was learning to tolerate southern policies of rigid segregation and disfranchisement of blacks, historians played a major role in rationalizing the new order in southern race relations. According to historians such as Professor John W. Burgess of Columbia University, writing in 1902, Reconstruction governments represented an unholy alliance of corrupt northern carpetbaggers seeking to profit at the expense of the "prostrate South"; southern white opportunists of mean origins, known as "scalawags"; and black demagogues who sought power by putting false and dangerous aspirations for equality into the heads of newly freed slaves. What made this orgy of misrule possible, said Burgess, was the colossal blunder that Congress made when it extended the vote to "ignorant and vicious" blacks. In the eyes of Burgess and a whole school of historians, Reconstruction was "the most soul-sickening spectacle that Americans have ever been called upon to behold . . . here was government by the most ignorant and vicious part of the population for the vulgar, materialistic, brutal benefit of the governing set."

In 1915, the most ambitious film yet made by the fledgling American movie industry—D. W. Griffith's *Birth of a Nation*—popularized this image of Reconstruction and made its racism more lurid and explicit. To underscore the message of this technically brilliant film, words flashed on the screen describing Reconstruction as a callous attempt to "put the white South under the heel of the black South." In the film, leering blacks carry signs advocating interracial marriage. Mainly responsible for this state of affairs is a vengeful Congressman meant to represent Thaddeus Stevens, who hatches a devilish plot to oppress and humiliate the white South. One famous scene portrays the South Carolina state legislature as a mob of grinning barefoot blacks, carousing at the taxpayers' expense. The film's melodramatic plot features the suicide of one southern white maiden to escape the embraces of a black pursuer and the Ku Klux Klan's epic rescue of another damsel from a forced marriage to a mulatto politician.

Birth of a Nation's depiction of the Klan as saving white civilization from bestial blacks inspired vigorous protests from the recently founded National Association for the Advancement of Colored People (NAACP), and censors in a few northern cities deleted some of the more blatantly racist scenes. But President Woodrow Wilson endorsed the film. "My only regret is that it is all so terribly true," he is reported to have said. Most white moviegoers seemed to agree with the president rather than with the NAACP. Millions of Americans saw and applauded this cinematic triumph.

During the period between 1915 and the 1940s, most historians echoed the judgment of *Birth of a Nation* that efforts to enforce equal rights for blacks after the Civil War had been a grave mistake. One popular work of that era was *The Tragic Era,* and another summed up Reconstruction as "the blackout of honest government." The biases of mainstream historiography served to justify the Jim Crow system of the South by portraying blacks as unqualified for citizenship.

A few black historians of the 1920s and 1930s advanced the contrary view that Reconstruction was a noble effort to achieve a color-blind democracy, which failed because of the strength of white racism and conservative economic interests. The most powerful example of this early revisionism was W. E. B. DuBois's *Black Reconstruction in America* (1935).

During the 1950s and 1960s, another image of Reconstruction emerged. The majority of historians writing about the era finally rejected the exaggerations, distortions, and racist assumptions of the traditional view. The triumph of "revisionism" was evident in 1965 when Kenneth M. Stampp published his *Era of Reconstruction.* As influential northern opinion shifted from tolerance of segregation to support for the black struggle for equality in the South, a more favorable view of earlier efforts on behalf of civil rights became acceptable. White liberal historians like Stampp concentrated on rehabilitating the Radical Republicans by stressing their idealism, while black scholars like John Hope Franklin highlighted the constructive policies and positive achievements of the much maligned black leaders of the Reconstruction South. Previous moral judgments thus tended to be

reversed; white and black Republicans became the heroes, and the southern whites who resisted and eventually overthrew Reconstruction became the villains. The analogy between these earlier adversaries and the civil rights activists and southern segregationists of the 1960s was clear.

During the 1970s and early 1980s, a "postrevisionism" began to develop. As it became apparent that the dream of equality for blacks was still unrealized, historians responded to the changing perceptions and complex crosscurrents of black-white relations in their own time by taking another look at Reconstruction. They found, among other things, that those in charge of efforts to make blacks equal citizens in the late 1860s had views that were quite moderate by the standards of the post–civil rights era of the 1970s and early 1980s. Radical Reconstruction no longer seemed very radical. The reputations of carpetbaggers and upper-class scalawags went down again as historians emphasized their opportunism and probusiness economic policies at the expense of social justice. Black politicians, too, came in for critical reassessment. It was argued that many worked more for their own interests as members of a black middle class than for the kinds of policies—such as land reform—that would have met the vital needs of their impoverished constituents.

Eric Foner's widely acclaimed *Reconstruction: America's Unfinished Revolution, 1863–1877* (1998) reemphasized some of the achievements of Radical rule in the South. Reflecting the new trend toward "history from the bottom up," its heroes were local black activists rather than white Radicals or even the black elite. But Foner and W. E. B. DuBois, historians who have argued that Reconstruction was a noble and inspiring effort to achieve racial democracy, have had to acknowledge that it failed to prevent the restoration of a brutally oppressive form of white supremacy after the "Redemption" of the 1870s. Was that failure due primarily to the deep-seated racism that drove the white South to carry on a guerrilla war against black participation in politics and also prevented many white Republicans from identifying fully with the cause of black equality? Or did it result from the gulf between the economic interests of those in charge of implementing and managing Reconstruction and the poor people of the South who were supposed to be its beneficiaries? As historians debate this unresolved issue, they should be aware that policymakers and sociologists are currently engaged in similar debates about the relative significance of "race" and "class" as explanations for the persistence of black disadvantage in the United States.

leading proponent of black emigration to Africa. Because he believed that white Americans were so deeply prejudiced against blacks that they would never grant them equal rights, Turner became an early advocate of black nationalism and a total separation of the races. Emigration became a popular movement among southern blacks, who were especially hard hit by terror and oppression just after the end of Reconstruction. Still, a majority of blacks in the nation as a whole and even in Turner's own church refused to give up on the hope of eventual equality on American soil. But Bishop Turner's anger and despair were the understandable responses of a proud man to the way that he and his fellow African Americans had been treated in the post–Civil War period.

Henry McNeal Turner, who was born in freedom, became a bishop of the African Methodist Episcopal Church and was elected to the Georgia legislature. ❖

By the late 1880s, the wounds of the Civil War were healing, and white Americans were seized by the spirit of sectional reconciliation. Union and Confederate veterans were tenting together and celebrating their common Americanism. "Reunion" was becoming a cultural as well as political reality. But whites could come back together only because Northerners had tacitly agreed to give Southerners a free hand in their efforts to reduce blacks to a new form of servitude. The "outraged, heart-broken, bruised, and bleeding" African Americans of the South paid the heaviest price for sectional reunion. Reconstruction remained, in the words of historian Eric Foner, an "unfinished revolution." It would be another century before African Americans rose up once more to demand full civil and political rights.

Recommended Reading

The best one-volume account of Reconstruction is Eric Foner, *Reconstruction: America's Unfinished Revolution* (1988). Two excellent short surveys are Kenneth M. Stampp, *The Era of Reconstruction, 1865–1877* (1965), and John Hope Franklin, *Reconstruction: After the Civil War* (1961). Both were early efforts to synthesize modern "revisionist" interpretations. W. E. B. DuBois, *Black Reconstruction in America, 1860–1880* (1935), remains brilliant and provocative. On the politics of Reconstruction, see Stephen David Kantrowitz, *Ben Tillman and the Reconstruction of White Supremacy* (2001), Laura F. Edwards, *Gendered Strife and Confusion: The Political Culture of Reconstruction* (1997), J. Morgan Kousser and James M. McPherson, eds., *Region, Race, and Reconstruction: Essays in Honor of C. Vann Woodward* (1982), and Eric Foner, *Nothing But Freedom: Emancipation and Its Legacy* (1983).

Leon F. Litwack, *Been in the Storm So Long: The Aftermath of Slavery* (1979), provides a moving portrayal of the black experience of emancipation. On changing society and family life during Reconstruction, see Noralee Frankel, *Freedom's Women: Black Women and Families in Reconstruction Era Mississippi* (1999), Dylan Penningroth, *Claiming Kin and Property: African American Life Before and After Emancipation* (2003), and Amy Dru Stanley, *From Bondage to Contract: Wage Labor, Marriage, and the Market in the Age of Slave Emancipation* (1998). On what freedom meant in economic terms, see Gerald David Jaynes, *Branches Without Roots: Genesis of the Black Working Class in the American South, 1862–1882* (1986). A work that focuses on ex-slaves' attempts to create their own economic order is Julie Saville, *The Work of Reconstruction: Free Slave to Wage Laborer in South Carolina, 1860–1870* (1994). The best overview of the postwar southern economy is Gavin Wright, *Old South, New South* (1986). On the end of Reconstruction, see David W. Blight, *Race and Reunion: The Civil War in American Memory* (2000). On the character of the post-Reconstruction South, see the classic work by C. Vann Woodward, *Origins of the New South, 1877–1913* (1951) and Edward Ayers, *The Promise of the New South* (1992).

For a list of additional titles related to this chapter's topics, please see http://www.ablongman.com/divine.

Suggested Web Sites

Diary and Letters of Rutherford B. Hayes

http://www.ohiohistory.org/onlinedoc/hayes/index.cfm
The Rutherford B. Hayes Presidential Center in Fremont, Ohio, maintains this searchable database of Hayes's writings.

Images of African Americans from the Nineteenth Century

http://digital.nypl.org/schomburg/images_aa19/
The New York Public Library-Schomburg Center for Research in Black Culture site contains numerous visuals.

Freedmen and Southern Society Project (University of Maryland-College Park)

http://www.inform.umd.edu/ARHU/Depts/History/Freedman/home.html
This site contains a chronology and sample documents from several print collections or primary sources about emancipation and freedom in the 1860s.

Andrew Johnson

http://www.whitehouse.gov/WH/glimpse/presidents/html/aj17.html
White House history of Johnson.

Ulysses S. Grant

http://www.whitehouse.gov/WH/glimpse/presidents/html/ug18.html
White House history of Grant.

History of the Suffrage Movement

http://www.rochester.edu/SBA
This site includes a chronology, important texts relating to women's suffrage, and biographical information about Susan B. Anthony and Elizabeth Cady Stanton.

Chapter 17

Charles M. Russell, Cowboy Camp During Roundup, *ca. 1885–1887. Artist Charles Russell here documents the cowboys' activities during the annual spring roundup. Before setting off on the long trek to drive cattle to market, the cowboys had to rope and break in horses that might have gone a little wild over the winter.* ❖

The West: Exploiting an Empire

Lean Bear's Changing West

In 1863, federal Indian agents took a delegation of Cheyenne, Arapaho, Comanche, Kiowa, and Plains Apache to visit the eastern United States, hoping to impress them with the power of the white man. The visitors were, in fact, impressed. In New York City, they stared at the tall buildings and crowded streets, so different from the wide-open plains with which they were accustomed. They visited the museum of the great showman Phineas T. Barnum, who in turn put them on display; they even saw a hippopotamus.

In Washington, they met with President Abraham Lincoln. Lean Bear, a Cheyenne chief, assured Lincoln that Indians wanted peace but worried about the numbers of white people who were pouring into their country. Lincoln swore friendship, said the Indians would be better off if they began to farm, and promised he would do his best to keep the peace. But, he said, smiling at Lean Bear, "You know it is not always possible for any father to have his children do precisely as he wishes them to do."

Lean Bear, who had children of his own, understood what Lincoln had had to say in Washington, at least in a way. Just a year later, back on his own lands, he watched as federal troops, Lincoln's "children," approached his camp. Wearing a peace medal that Lincoln had given him, Lean Bear rode slowly toward the troops to once again offer his friendship. When he was twenty yards away, they opened fire, then rode closer and fired again and again into his fallen body.

AS LEAN BEAR HAD FEARED, in the last three decades of the nineteenth century, a flood of settlers ventured into the vast lands across the Mississippi River. Prospectors searched for "pay dirt," railroads crisscrossed the continent, eastern and foreign capitalists invested in cattle and land bonanzas, and farmers took up the promise of free western lands. In 1867, Horace Greeley, editor of the New York *Tribune,* told New York City's unemployed: "If you strike off into the broad, free West, and make yourself a farm from Uncle Sam's generous domain, you will crowd nobody, starve nobody, and neither you nor your children need evermore beg for something to do."

With the end of the Civil War, white Americans again claimed a special destiny to expand across the continent. In the process, they crushed the culture of the Native Americans and ignored the contributions of people of other races, such as the Chinese miners and laborers and the Mexican herdsmen. As millions moved west, the states of Colorado, Washington, Montana, the Dakotas, Idaho, Wyoming, and Utah were carved out of the lands across the Mississippi. At the turn of the century, only Arizona, New Mexico, and Oklahoma remained as territories.

The West became a great colonial empire, harnessed to eastern capital and tied increasingly to national and international markets. Its raw materials, sent east by wagon, train, and ship, helped fuel eastern factories. Western economies relied heavily on the federal government, which subsidized their railroads, distributed their land, and spent

OUTLINE

FEATURE ESSAY

millions of dollars for the upkeep of soldiers and Indians.

By the 1890s, the West of the lands beyond the Mississippi had undergone substantial change. In place of buffalo and unfenced vistas, there were cities and towns, health resorts, homesteads, sheep ranches, and, in the arid regions, the beginnings of the irrigated agriculture that would reshape the West in the twentieth century. Ghost towns, abandoned farms, and the scars in the earth left by miners and farmers spoke to the less favorable side of settlement. As the new century dawned, the West had become a place of conquest and exploitation, as well as a mythic land of cowboys and quick fortunes.

Beyond the Frontier

The line of white settlement had reached the edge of the Missouri timber country by 1840. Beyond lay an enormous land of rolling prairies, parched deserts, and rugged, majestic mountains. Emerging from the timber country, travelers first encountered the Great Plains—treeless, nearly flat, an endless "sea of grassy hillocks" extending from the Mississippi River to the Rocky Mountains. The Prairie Plains, the eastern part of the region, enjoyed rich soil and good rainfall; it included parts of present-day Wisconsin, Minnesota, the Dakotas, Nebraska, Kansas, Oklahoma, and Texas. To the west—covering Montana, Wyoming, Colorado, New Mexico, and Arizona—were the High Plains, rough, semiarid, rising gently to the foothills of the Rocky Mountains.

Running from Alaska to central New Mexico, the Rockies presented a formidable barrier. There were valuable beaver in the streams and gold near Pikes Peak. But most travelers hurried through the northern passes, emerging in the desolate basin of present-day southern Idaho and Utah. Native Americans lived there—the Ute, Paiute, Bannock, and Shoshone tribes—surviving in the harsh environment by digging for roots and gathering seeds and berries. On the west, the lofty Coast Ranges—the Cascades and Sierra Nevada—held back rainfall; beyond were the temperate lands of the Pacific Coast.

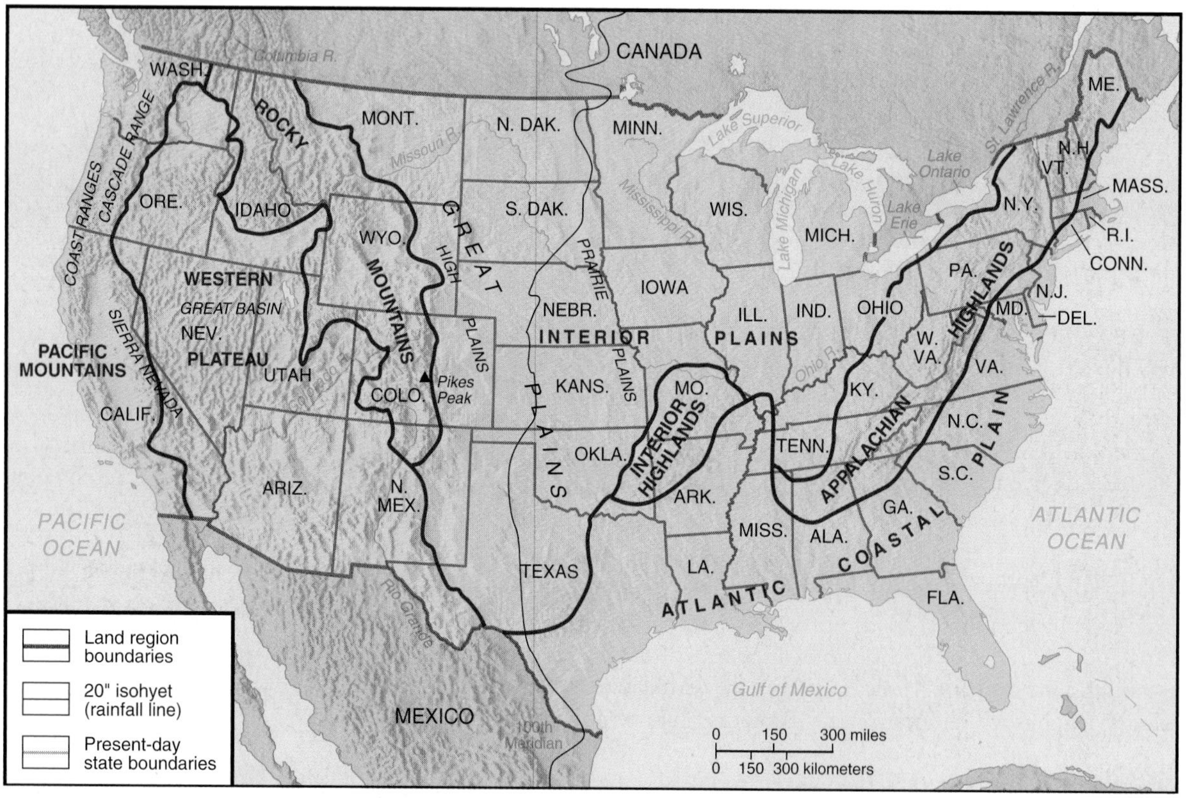

PHYSIOGRAPHIC MAP OF THE UNITED STATES *In the Great Plains and Rocky Mountains, the topography, altitudes, crops, and climate—especially the lack of rain west of the rainfall line shown here—led to changes in a mode of settlement that had been essentially uniform from the Atlantic Coast through Kentucky, Ohio, and Missouri. The rectangular land surveys and quarter-section lots that were traditional before could not accommodate Great Plains conditions.* ❖

Early explorers like Zebulon Pike thought the country beyond the Mississippi was uninhabitable, fit only, Pike said, for "wandering and uncivilized aborigines." Mapmakers agreed; between 1825 and 1860, American maps showed this land as "The Great American Desert." As a result, settlement paused on the edge of the Plains, and most early settlers headed directly for California and Oregon.

Few rivers cut through the Plains; those that did raged in the winter and trickled in the summer. Rainfall usually did not reach 15 inches a year, not enough to support extensive agriculture. There was little lumber for homes and fences, and the tools of eastern settlement—the cast-iron plow, the boat, and the ax—were virtually useless on the tough and treeless Plains soil. "East of the Mississippi," historian Walter Prescott Webb noted, "civilization stood on three legs—land, water, and timber; west of the Mississippi not one but two of these legs were withdrawn—water and timber—and civilization was left on one leg—land."

Hot winds seared the Plains in summer, and northers, blizzards, and hailstorms froze them in winter. Wildlife roamed in profusion. Antelope shared the open prairies with wolves, coyote, and millions of jackrabbits and prairie dogs. The American bison, better known as the buffalo, grazed in enormous herds from Mexico to Canada. In 1865, perhaps fifteen million buffalo lived on the Plains, so many they seemed like "leaves in a forest" to an early observer. A single herd sighted in 1871 had four million head.

Crushing the Native Americans

When Greeley urged New Yorkers to move West and "crowd nobody," he—like almost all white Americans—ignored the fact that large numbers of people already lived there. At the close of the Civil War, Native Americans inhabited nearly half the United States. By 1880, they had been driven onto smaller and smaller reservations and were no longer an independent people. A decade later, even their culture had crumbled under the impact of white domination.

In 1865, nearly a quarter million Native Americans lived in the western half of the country. Tribes such as the Winnebago, Menominee, Cherokee, and Chippewa were resettled there, forced out of their eastern lands by advancing white settlement. Other tribes were native to the region. In the Southwest there were the Pueblo groups, including the Hopi, Zuni, and Rio Grande Pueblos. Peaceful farmers and herders, they had built up complex traditions around a settled way of life.

The Pueblo groups were cultivators of corn. They lived on the subdesert plateau of present-day western New Mexico and eastern Arizona. Harassed by powerful neighboring tribes, they built communal houses of adobe brick on high mesas or in cracks in the cliffs. More nomadic were the Camp Dwellers, the Jicarilla Apache and Navajo who roamed eastern New Mexico and western Texas. Blending elements of the Plains and Plateau environments, they lived in tepees or mud huts, grew some crops to supplement their hunting, and moved readily from place to place. The Navajo herded sheep and produced beautiful ornamental silver, baskets, and blankets. Fierce fighters, Apache horsemen were feared by whites and fellow Indians across the southwestern Plains.

Farther west were the tribes that inhabited present-day California. Divided into many small bands, they eked out a difficult existence living on roots, grubs, berries, acorns, and small game. In the Pacific Northwest, where fish and forest animals made life easier, the Klamath, Chinook, Yurok, and Shasta tribes developed a rich civilization. They built plank houses and canoes, worked extensively in wood, and evolved a complex social and political organization. Settled and determined, they resisted the invasion of the whites.

By the 1870s, most of these tribes had been destroyed or beaten into submission. The powerful Ute, crushed in 1855, ceded most of their Utah lands to the United States and settled on a small reservation near Great Salt Lake. The Navajo and Apache fought back fiercely, but between 1865 and 1873 they too were confined to reservations. The Native Americans of California succumbed to the contagious diseases carried by whites during the Gold Rush of 1849. Miners burned their villages, and by 1880, fewer than twenty thousand Indians lived in California.

Life of the Plains Indians

In the mid-nineteenth century, nearly two-thirds of the Native Americans lived on the Great Plains. The Plains tribes included the Sioux of present-day Minnesota and the Dakotas; the Blackfoot of Idaho and Montana; the Cheyenne, Crow, and Arapaho of the central Plains; the Pawnee of western Nebraska; and the Kiowa, Apache, and Comanche of present-day Texas and New Mexico.

Nomadic and warlike, the Plains Indians depended on the buffalo and horse. The modern horse, first brought by Spanish explorers in the 1500s, spread north from Mexico onto the Plains, and by the 1700s the Plains Indians' way of life had changed. The Plains tribes gave up farming almost entirely and hunted the buffalo, ranging widely over the rolling plains. The men became superb warriors and horsemen, among the best light cavalry in the world.

After the buffalo was killed, women skinned the hide, cut up the meat, and then cured the hide, as shown in the painting Halcyon Days *by George Catlin. Women also decorated the tepees and preserved the meat by drying it in the sun.* ✤

Equipped with stout wooden bows 3 feet or less in length, Plains Indians were fierce warriors. Hiding their bodies behind their racing ponies, they drove deadly arrows clear through buffalo. Against white troops or settlers, the skillful Comanche rode three hundred yards and shot twenty arrows in the time it took a soldier to load his firearm once. The introduction of the new Colt six-shooters during the 1850s gave government troops a rapid-fire weapon but did not entirely offset the Indians' advantage.

Migratory in culture, the Plains Indians formed tribes of several thousand people but lived in smaller bands of three to five hundred. The Comanche, who numbered perhaps seven thousand, had thirteen bands with such names as Burnt Meat, Making Bags While Moving, and Those Who Move Often. Each band was governed by a chief and a council of elder men, and Indians of the same tribe transferred freely from band to band. Bands acted independently, making it difficult for the U.S. government to deal with the fragmented tribes.

The bands followed and lived off the buffalo. Buffalo provided food, clothing, and shelter; the Indians, unlike later white hunters, used every part of the animal. The meat was dried or "jerked" in the hot Plains air. The skins made tepees, blankets, and robes. Buffalo bones became knives; tendons were made into bowstrings; horns and hooves were boiled into glue. Buffalo "chips"—dried manure—were burned as fuel. All in all, the buffalo was "a galloping department store."

Warfare between tribes usually took the form of brief raids and skirmishes. Plains Indians fought few prolonged wars and rarely coveted territory. Most conflicts involved only a few warriors intent on stealing horses or "counting coup"—touching an enemy's body with the hand or a special stick. Tribes developed a fierce and trained warrior class, recognized for achievements in battle. Speaking different languages, Native Americans of various tribes were nevertheless able to communicate with one another through a highly developed sign language.

The Plains tribes divided labor tasks according to gender. Men hunted, traded, supervised ceremonial activities, and cleared ground for planting. They usually held the positions of authority, such as chief or medicine man. Women were responsible for child rearing and artistic activity. They also performed the camp work, grew vegetables, prepared buffalo meat and hides, and gathered berries and roots. In most tribes, women played an important role in political, economic, and religious activities. Among the Navajo and Zuni, kinship descended from the mother's side, and Navajo women were in charge of most of the family's property. In tribes such as the Sioux, there was little difference in status. Men were respected for hunting and war, women for their artistic skills with quill and paint.

"As Long as Waters Run": Searching for an Indian Policy

Before the Civil War, Americans used the land west of the Mississippi as "one big reservation." The government named the area "Indian Country," moved eastern tribes there with firm treaty guarantees, and in 1834 passed the Indian Intercourse Act, which prohibited any white person from entering Indian country without a license.

The situation changed in the 1850s. Wagon trains wound their way to California and Oregon, miners pushed into western goldfields, and there was talk of a transcontinental railroad. To clear the way for settlement, the federal government in 1851 abandoned "One Big Reservation" in favor of a new policy of concentration. For the first time, it assigned definite boundaries to each tribe. The Sioux, for example, were given the Dakota country north of the Platte River, the Crow a large area near the Powder River, and the Cheyenne and Arapaho the Colorado foothills between the North Platte and Arkansas rivers for "as long as waters run and the grass shall grow."

The concentration policy lasted only a few years. Accustomed to hunting widely for buffalo, many Native Americans refused to stay within their assigned areas. White settlers poured into Indian lands, then called on the government to protect them. Indians were pushed out of Kansas and Nebraska in the 1850s, even as white reformers fought to hold those territories open for free blacks. In 1859, gold miners moved into the Pikes Peak country, touching off warfare with the Cheyenne and Arapaho.

In 1864, tired of the fighting, the two tribes asked for peace. Certain that the war was over, Chief Black Kettle led his seven hundred followers to camp on Sand Creek in southeastern Colorado. Early on the morning of November 29, 1864, a group of Colorado militia led by Colonel John M. Chivington attacked the sleeping group. "Kill and scalp all, big and little," Chivington told his men. "Nits make lice." Black Kettle tried to stop the ambush, raising first an American flag and then a white flag. Neither worked. The Native

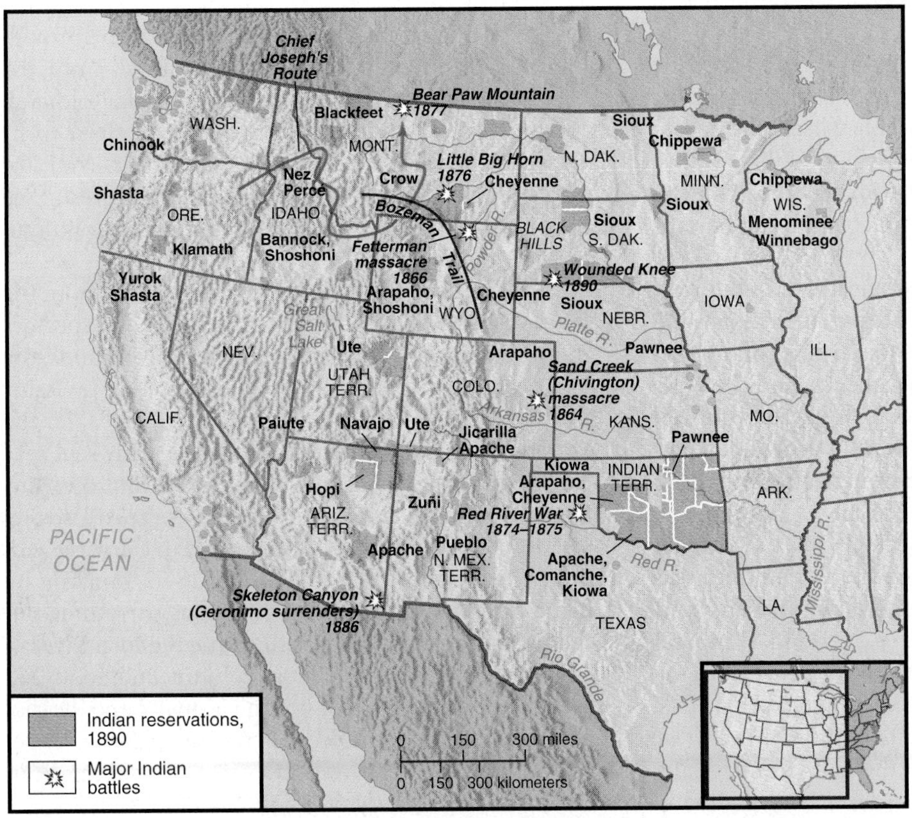

NATIVE AMERICANS IN THE WEST: MAJOR BATTLES AND RESERVATIONS
"They made us many promises, more than I remember, but they never kept but one; they promised to take our land, and they took it." So said Red Cloud of the Oglala Sioux, summarizing Native American–white relations in the 1870s. ❖

American men, women, and children were clubbed, stabbed, and scalped.

The Chivington massacre set off angry protests in Colorado and the East. Congress appointed an investigating committee, and the government concluded a treaty with the Cheyenne and Arapaho, condemning "the gross and wanton outrages." Still, the two tribes were forced to surrender their Sand Creek reservation in exchange for lands elsewhere. The Kiowa and Comanche were also ousted from areas they had been granted "forever" only a few years before. As the Sioux chief Spotted Tail said, "Why does not the Great Father put his red children on wheels so that he can move them as he will?"

Before long, the powerful Sioux were on the warpath in the great Sioux War of 1865–1867. Once again, an invasion of gold miners touched off the war, which flared even more intensely when the federal government announced plans to connect the various mining towns by building the Bozeman Trail through the heart of the Sioux hunting grounds in Montana. Red Cloud, the Sioux chief, determined to stop the trail. In December 1866, pursued by an army column under Captain William J. Fetterman, he lured the incautious Fetterman deep into the wilderness, ambushed him, and wiped out all eighty-two soldiers in his command.

The Fetterman massacre, coming so soon after the Chivington massacre, sparked a public debate over the nation's Indian policy. Like the policy itself, the debate reflected differing white views of the Native Americans. In the East, some reform, humanitarian, and church groups wanted a humane peace policy, directed toward educating and "civilizing" the tribes. Many white people, in the East and West, questioned this approach, convinced that Native Americans were savages unfit for civilization. Westerners, of course, had some reason to fear Indian attacks, and the fears often fed on wild rumors of scalped settlers and besieged forts. As a result, Westerners in general favored firm control over the Native Americans, including swift punishment of any who rebelled.

In 1867, the peace advocates won the debate. Halting construction on the Bozeman Trail, Congress created a Peace Commission of four civilians and three generals to end the Sioux War and eliminate permanently the causes of Indian wars. Setting out for the West, the Peace Commissioners agreed that only one policy offered a permanent solution: a policy of "small reservations" to isolate the Native Americans on distant lands, teach them to farm, and gradually "civilize" them.

The commissioners chose two areas to hold all the Plains Indians. Fifty-four thousand Native Americans on the northern Plains would be moved north of the Black Hills in Dakota Territory, far from prospective white settlement. On the southern Plains, eighty-six thousand Native Americans would be moved into present-day Oklahoma, a region also considered difficult to farm and unattractive to whites. In both areas, tribes would be assigned specific reservations where government agents could supervise them.

The Kiowa, Comanche, Cheyenne, and Arapaho agreed to the plan in 1867, the Sioux in 1868. The policy was extended beyond the Plains, and the Ute, Shoshone, Bannock, Navajo, and Apache tribes also accepted small reservations. "We have now selected and provided reservations for all, off the great road," an army commander wrote. "All who cling to their old hunting-grounds are hostile and will remain so till killed off."

Final Battles on the Plains

Few Native Americans settled peacefully into life on the new reservations. The reservation system not only changed their age-old customs; it chained them in a situation of poverty and isolation. Soon, young warriors and minor chiefs denounced the treaties and drifted back to the open countryside. In late 1868, warfare broke out again, and it took more than a decade of violence to beat the Indians into submission. The Kiowa and Comanche rampaged through the Texas Panhandle, looting and killing, until the U.S. Army—including the feared "buffalo soldiers," African American cavalrymen on the western frontier—crushed them in the Red River War of 1874–1875 and ended warfare in the Southwest. (See the Feature Essay, "Blacks in Blue: The Buffalo Soldiers in the West," pp. 488–489.)

On the northern Plains, fighting resulted from the Black Hills Gold Rush of 1875. As prospectors tramped across Native American hunting grounds, the Sioux gathered to stop them. They were led by Rain-in-the-Face, the great war chief Crazy Horse, and the famous medicine man Sitting Bull. The army sent several columns of troops after the Indians, but one, under flamboyant Lieutenant Colonel George Armstrong Custer, pushed recklessly ahead, eager to claim the victory. On the morning of June 25, 1876, thinking he had a small band of Native Americans surrounded in their village on the banks of the Little Bighorn River in Montana, Custer divided his column and took 265 men toward it. Instead of finding a small band, he discovered he had stumbled on the main Sioux camp with 2500 warriors. It was the largest Native American army ever assembled in the United States.

By midafternoon it was over; Custer and his men were dead. Custer was largely responsible for the loss, but "Custer's Last Stand," set in blazing headlines across the country, set off a nationwide demand for revenge. Within a few months, the Sioux were surrounded and

This pictogram by Oglala Sioux Amos Bad Heart Bull is a Native American version of the battle of the Little Bighorn, also known as Custer's Last Stand. ❖

beaten, three thousand of them surrendering in October 1876. Sitting Bull and a few followers who had fled to Canada gave up in 1881.

The Sioux War ended the major Indian warfare in the West, but occasional outbreaks occurred for several years thereafter. In 1877, the Nez Percé tribe of Oregon, a people who had warmly welcomed Lewis and Clark in 1805, rebelled against government policy. Hoping to reach Canada, Chief Joseph led the tribe on a courageous flight lasting 75 days and covering 1321 miles. They defeated the pursuing army at every turn but then ran out of food, horses, and ammunition. Surrendering, they were sent to barren lands in the Indian Country of Oklahoma, and there, most of them died from disease.

In 1890, the Teton Sioux of South Dakota, bitter and starving, became restless. Many of them turned to the **Ghost Dances,** a set of dances and rites that grew from a vision of a Paiute messiah named Wovoka. Performance of the dances, Wovoka said, would bring back Native American lands and would cause the whites to disappear. All Native Americans would reunite, the earth would be covered with dust, and a new earth would come upon the old. The vanished buffalo would return in great herds.

The army intervened to stop the dancing, touching off violence that killed Sitting Bull and a number of other warriors. Frightened Native Americans fled southwest to join other Ghost Dancers under the aging chief Big Foot. Moving quickly, troops of the Seventh Cavalry, Custer's old regiment, caught up with Big Foot's band and took them to the army camp on Wounded Knee Creek in South Dakota. A Native American, it is thought, fired the first shot, returned by the army's new machine guns. Firing a shell a second, they shredded tepees and people. In the infamous **Wounded Knee Massacre,** about two hundred men, women, and children were killed in the snow.

The End of Tribal Life

The final step in Indian policy came in the 1870s and 1880s. Some reformers had long argued against segregating the Native Americans on reservations, urging instead that the nation assimilate them individually into white culture. These "assimilationists" wanted to use education, land policy, and federal law to eradicate tribal society.

Congress began to adopt the policy in 1871 when it ended the practice of treaty making with Native American tribes. Since tribes were no longer separate nations, they lost many of their political and judicial functions, and the power of the chiefs was weakened. In 1882, Congress created a Court of Indian Offenses

Feature Essay

BLACKS IN BLUE

The Buffalo Soldiers in the West

On Saturday afternoons, youngsters used to sit in darkened movie theaters and cheer the victories of the U.S. Cavalry over the Indians. Typically, the Indians were about to capture a wagon train when army bugles suddenly sounded. Then the blue-coated cavalry charged over the hill. Few in the theaters cheered for the Indians; fewer still noticed the absence of black faces among the charging cavalry. But in fact, more than two thousand African American cavalrymen served on the western frontier between 1867 and 1890. Known as the buffalo soldiers, they made up one-fifth of the U.S. Cavalry.

Black troops were first used on a large scale during the Civil War. Organized in segregated units, with white officers, they fought with distinction. Nearly 180,000 blacks served in the Union army; 34,000 of them died. When the war ended in 1865, Congress for the first time authorized black troops to serve in the regular peacetime army. In addition to infantry, it created two cavalry regiments—the Ninth and Tenth, which became known as the famous buffalo soldiers.

Like other black regiments, the Ninth and Tenth Cavalry had white officers who took special examinations before they could serve. The chaplains were assigned not only to preach but to teach reading, writing, and arithmetic. The food was poor; racism was widespread. The army stocked the first black units with worn-out horses, a serious matter to men whose lives depended on the speed and stamina of their mounts. "Since our first mount in 1867 this regiment has received nothing but broken down horses and repaired equipment," an officer said in 1870.

Many white officers refused to serve with black troops. George Armstrong Custer, the handsome "boy general," turned down a position in the Ninth and joined the new Seventh Cavalry, headed for disaster at Little Bighorn. The *Army and Navy Journal* carried ads that told a similar story:

A FIRST LIEUTENANT
OF INFANTRY
(white)
Stationed at a
very desirable post
in the Department of the South
desires a transfer with
an officer of the same grade
on equal terms
if in a white regiment
but if in a colored regiment
a reasonable bonus
would be expected.

Although they were not, in fact, treated as well as the white soldiers in their regiments, many African American cavalrymen such as those pictured here were probably drawn into service by hard-sell recruitment posters such as the one shown on the facing page. ❖

The heritage and honor of the buffalo soldier were honored in 1992 by General Colin Powell, chairman of the Joint Chiefs of Staff, in dedication of a memorial at Fort Leavenworth, Kansas, home base to many of the buffalo soldiers of the nineteenth century. The monument was crafted by Eddie Dixon and shows a mounted African American cavalry soldier. ❖

There was no shortage of black troops for the officers to lead. Blacks enlisted because the army offered some advancement in a closed society. It also paid $13 a month, plus room and board.

In 1867, the Ninth and Tenth Cavalry were posted to the West, where they remained for two decades. Under Colonel Benjamin H. Grierson, a Civil War hero, the Tenth went to Fort Riley, Kansas; the regiment arrived in the midst of a great Indian war. The Kiowa, Comanche, Cheyenne, Arapaho, and Sioux were on the warpath. Troopers of the Tenth defended farms, stages, trains, and work crews building railroad tracks to the West. Cornered by a band of Cheyenne, they beat back the attack and won a new name. They had been known as the "brunettes" or "Africans," but the Cheyenne now called them the buffalo soldiers, a name that soon applied to all African American soldiers in the West.

From 1868 to 1874, the Tenth served on the Kansas frontier. The dull winter days were filled with drills and scouting parties outside the post. In spring and summer, the good weather brought forth new forays. Indian bands raided farms and ranches and stampeded cattle herds on the way north from Texas. They struck and then melted back into the reservations.

The Ninth Cavalry also had a difficult job. Commanded by Colonel Edward Hatch, who had served with Grierson in the Civil War, it was stationed in West Texas and along the Rio Grande. The summers were so hot that men collapsed with sunstroke, the winters so cold that water froze in canteens. Native Americans from outside the area frequently raided it. From the north, Kiowa and Comanche warriors rode down the Great Comanche War Trail; Kickapoos crossed the Rio Grande from Mexico. Gangs of Mexican bandits and restless Civil War veterans roamed and plundered at will.

From 1874 to 1875, the Ninth fought in the great Red River War, in which the Kiowa and Comanche, fed up with conditions on the reservations, revolted against Grant's peace policy. Marching, fighting, then marching again, the soldiers harried and wore out the Indians, who finally surrendered in the spring of 1875. Herded into a new and desolate reservation, the Mescalero Apache of New Mexico took to the warpath in 1877 and again in 1879. Each time, it took a year of grueling warfare to effect their surrender. In 1886, black cavalrymen surrounded and captured the famous Apache chief Geronimo. In that and other campaigns, several buffalo soldiers won the Congressional Medal of Honor.

Black troops hunted Big Foot and his band before the slaughter at Wounded Knee in 1890 (see p. 487), and they served in many of the West's most famous Indian battles. While one-third of all army recruits deserted between 1865 and 1890, the Ninth and Tenth Cavalry had few desertions. In 1880, the Tenth had the fewest desertions of any regiment in the country.

It was ironic that in the West, black men fought red men to benefit white men. Once the Indian wars ended, the buffalo soldiers worked to keep illegal settlers out of Indian or government land; much of the land was later opened to settlement. Both regiments saw action in the Spanish-American War, the Ninth at San Juan Hill, the Tenth in the fighting around Santiago. Unlike white veterans of the same campaigns, the old buffalo soldiers were forgotten in retirement, although some of them had the satisfaction of settling on the western lands they had done so much to pacify.

Tom Torlino, a Navajo Indian, photographed before and after his "assimilation." Torlino attended the Carlisle Indian School in Pennsylvania. ❖

to try Native Americans who broke government rules, and soon thereafter it made them answerable in regular courts for certain crimes.

While Congress worked to break down the tribes, educators trained young Native Americans to adjust to white culture. In 1879, fifty Pawnee, Kiowa, and Cheyenne youths were brought east to the new Carlisle Indian School in Carlisle, Pennsylvania. Other Native American schools soon opened, including the Haskell Institute in Kansas and numerous day schools on the western reservations. The schools taught students to fix machines and farm; they forced young Indians to trim their long hair and made them speak English, banned the wearing of tribal paint or clothes, and forbade tribal ceremonies and dances. "Kill the Indian and save the man," said Richard H. Pratt, the army officer who founded the Carlisle School.

Land ownership was the final and most important link in the new policy. Native Americans who owned land, it was thought, would become responsible, self-reliant citizens. Deciding to give each Native American a farm, Congress in 1887 passed the **Dawes Severalty Act,** the most important legal development in Indian-white relations in more than three centuries.

Aiming to end tribal life, the Dawes Act divided tribal lands into small plots for distribution among members of the tribe. Each family head received 160 acres, single adults 80 acres, and children 40 acres. Once the land was distributed, any surplus was sold to white settlers, with the profits going to Native American schools. To keep the Indians' land from falling into the hands of speculators, the federal government held it in trust for twenty-five years. Finally, American citizenship was granted to Native Americans who accepted their land, lived apart from the tribe, and "adopted the habits of civilized life."

Through the Dawes Act, 47 million acres of land were distributed to Native Americans and their families. There were another 90 million acres in the reservations, and these lands, often the most fertile, were sold to white settlers. Speculators evaded the twenty-five-year rule, leasing rather than purchasing the land from the Native Americans. Many Native Americans knew little about farming. Their tools were rudimentary, and in the culture of the Plains Indians, men had not ordinarily participated in farming. In 1934, the government returned to the idea of tribal land ownership, but by then 138 million acres of Indian land had shrunk to 48 million acres, half of which was barren.

The final blow to tribal life came not in the Dawes Act but in the virtual extermination of the buffalo, the Plains Indians' chief resource and the basis for their unique way of life. The killing began in the 1860s as the transcontinental railroads pushed west, and it stepped up as settlers found they could harm the Indians by harming the buffalo. "Kill every buffalo you can," an army officer said. "Every buffalo dead is an Indian gone." Then, in 1871, a Pennsylvania tannery discovered that buffalo hides made valuable leather. Professional hunters such as William F. "Buffalo Bill" Cody swarmed across the Plains, killing millions of the beasts.

Between 1872 and 1874, professional hunters slaughtered three million buffalo a year. In a frontier form of a factory system, riflemen, skinners, and transport wagons pushed through the vast herds, which shrank steadily behind them. A good hunter killed a hundred buffalo a day. Skinners took off the hides, removed the tongue, hump, and tallow, and left the rest. "I have seen their bodies so thick after being skinned," a hunter said, "that they would look like logs where a hurricane had passed through a forest."

By 1883, the buffalo were almost gone. When the government set out to produce the famous "buffalo nickel," the designer had to go to the Bronx Zoo in New York City to find a buffalo.

By 1900, there were only 250,000 Native Americans in the country. (There were 600,000 within the limits of the present-day United States in 1800, and more than 5 million in 1492, when Columbus first set foot in the New World.) Most of the Indians lived on reservations. Many lived in poverty. Alcoholism and unemployment were growing problems, and Native Americans, no longer able to live off the buffalo, became wards of the state. They lost their cultural distinctiveness. Once possessors of the entire continent, they had been crowded into smaller and smaller areas, overwhelmed by the demand to become settled, literate, and English-speaking. "Except for the internment of the West Coast Japanese during World War II," said historian Roger L. Nichols, "Indian removal is the only example of large-scale government-enforced migration in American history. For the Japanese, the move was temporary; for the Indians it was not."

Even as the Native Americans lost their identity, they entered the romantic folklore of the West. Dime novels, snapped up by readers young and old, told tales of Indian fighting on the Plains. "Buffalo Bill" Cody turned it all into a profitable business. Beginning in 1883, his Wild West Show ran for more than three decades, playing to millions of viewers in the United States, Canada, and Europe. It featured Plains Indians chasing buffalo, performing a war dance, and attacking a settler's cabin. In 1885, Sitting Bull himself, victor over Custer at the battle of Little Bighorn, performed in the show.

Settlement of the West

Between 1870 and 1900, white—and some African, Hispanic, and Asian—Americans settled the enormous total of 430 million acres west of the Mississippi; they took over more land than had been occupied by Americans in all the years before 1870.

People moved West for many reasons. Some sought adventure; others wanted to escape the drab routine of factory or city life. Many moved to California for their health. The Mormons settled Utah to escape religious persecution. Others followed the mining camps, the advancing railroads, and the farming and cattle frontier.

Whatever the specific reason, most people moved West to better their lot. On the whole, their timing was good, for as the nation's population grew, so did demand for the livestock and the agricultural, mineral, and lumber products of the expanding West. Contrary to older historical views, the West did not act as a major "safety valve," an outlet for social and economic tensions. The poor and unemployed did not have the means to move there and establish farms. "Moreover," as Douglass C. North, an economic historian, said, "most people moved West in good times . . . in periods of rising prices, of expanding demand,

Huge buffalo herds grazing along railroads in the West frequently blocked the path of passing trains. Passengers often killed for sport, shooting at the beasts with no intention of using or removing the animal carcasses, glad to know that they were harming the Native Americans by destroying their most important reserve. ❖

when the prospects for making money from this new land looked brightest; and this aspect characterized the whole pattern of settlement."

Men and Women on the Overland Trail

The first movement west aimed not for the nearby Plains but for California and Oregon on the continent's far shore. It started in the **Gold Rush of 1849** to California, and in the next three decades perhaps as many as half a million individuals made the long journey over the **Overland Trail** leading west. Some walked; others rode horses alone or in small groups. About half joined great caravans, numbering 150 wagons or more, that inched across the two thousand miles between the Missouri River and the Pacific Coast.

More often than not, men made the decision to make the crossing, but, except for the stampedes to the mines, migration usually turned out to be a family affair. Wives were consulted, though in some cases they had little real choice. They could either go along or live alone at home. While many women regretted leaving family and friends, they agreed to the trip, sometimes as eagerly as the men. "With good courage and not one sigh of regret I mounted my pony," Lydia Rudd said. "I would not be left behind," said Luzena Wilson, whose husband ached to join the Gold Rush to California. "I thought where he could go I could, and where I went I could take my two little toddling babies." Like the Wilsons, the majority of people traveled in family groups, including in-laws, grandchildren, aunts, and uncles. As one historian said, "The quest for something new would take place in the context of the very familiar."

Individuals and wagon trains set out from various points along the Missouri River. Leaving in the spring and traveling through the summer, they hoped to reach their destination before the first snowfall. During April, travelers gradually assembled in spring camp just across the Missouri River, waiting for the new grass to ripen into forage. They packed and repacked the wagons and elected the trains' leaders, who would set the line of march, look for water and campsites, and impose discipline. Some trains adopted detailed rules, fearing a lapse into savagery in the wild lands across the Missouri. "Every man to carry with him a Bible and other religious books, as we hope not to degenerate into a state of barbarism," one agreement said.

Setting out in early May, travelers divided the enormous route into manageable portions. The first leg of the journey followed the Platte River west to Fort Kearney in central Nebraska Territory, a distance of about three hundred miles. The land was even, with good supplies of wood, grass, and water. From a distance, the white-topped wagons seemed driven by a common force, but, in fact, internal discipline broke down almost immediately. Arguments erupted over the pace of the march, the choice of campsites, the number of guards to post, whether to rest or push on. Elected leaders quit; new ones were chosen. Every train was filled with individualists, and as the son of one train captain said, "If you think it's any snap to run a wagon train of 66 wagons with every man in the train having a different idea of what is the best thing to do, all I can say is that some day you ought to try it."

Men, women, and children had different tasks on the trail. Men concerned themselves almost entirely with hunting buffalo and antelope, guard duty, and transportation. They rose at 4 A.M. to hitch the wagons, and after breakfast began the day's march. At noon, they stopped and set the teams to graze. After the midday meal, the march continued until sunset. Then, while the men relaxed, the women fixed dinner and the next day's lunch, and the children kindled the fires, brought water to camp, and searched for wood or other fuel. Walking fifteen miles a day, in searing heat and mountain cold, travelers were exhausted by late afternoon. "We can all, as soon as we stop, lie down on the grass or anywhere and be asleep in less than no time almost," Rebecca Ketcham, an Oregon-bound emigrant, reported.

For women, the trail was lonely, and they worked to exhaustion. Before long, some adjusted their clothing to the harsh conditions, adopting the new bloomer pants, shortening their skirts, or wearing regular "wash dresses"—so called because they had shorter hemlines that did not drag on the wet ground on washday. Other women continued to wear their long dresses, thinking bloomers "indecent." Both men and women carried firearms in case of Indian attacks, but most emigrants saw few Indians en route.

What they often did see was trash, miles of it, for the wagon trains were an early example of the impact of migration and settlement on the western environment. On the Oregon and other trails, travelers sidestepped mounds of garbage, tin cans, furniture, cooking stoves, kegs, tools, and clothing, all discarded by people who had passed through before. Along a forty-mile trail in the Nevada desert, a migrant tallied two thousand abandoned wagons. On some trails, animals and people stirred up so much dust that drivers wore goggles to protect their eyes.

The first stage of the journey was deceptively easy, and travelers usually reached Fort Kearney by late May. The second leg led another 300 miles up the Platte River to Fort Laramie on the eastern edge of Wyoming Territory. The heat of June had dried the grass, and there was no wood. Anxious to beat the

The migration westward on the overland trail was long and difficult. In this photograph from the 1870s, a caravan of covered wagons stretches as far as the eye can see. Emigrants often chose oxen to pull the wagons because oxen were strong, less expensive than horses, and they could survive on a diet of prairie grasses. ❖

early snowfalls, travelers rested a day or two at the fort, then hurried on to South Pass, 280 miles to the west, the best route through the forbidding Rockies. The land was barren. It was now mid-July, but the mountain nights were so cold that ice formed in the water buckets.

Beyond South Pass, some emigrants turned south to the Mormon settlements on the Great Salt Lake, but most headed 340 miles north to Fort Hall on the Snake River in Idaho. It took another three months to cover the remaining 800 miles. California-bound travelers followed the Humboldt River through the summer heat of Nevada. Well into September, they began the final arduous push: first, a 55-mile stretch of desert; then 70 difficult miles up the eastern slopes of the Sierra Nevada, laboriously hoisting wagons over massive outcrops of rock; and finally the last 100 miles down the western slopes to the welcome sight of California's Central Valley in October.

Under the best of conditions the trip took six months, sixteen hours a day, dawn to dusk, of hard, grueling labor. Walking halfway across the continent was no easy task, and it provided a never-to-be-forgotten experience for those who did it. The wagon trains, carrying the dreams of thousands of individuals, reproduced society in small focus: individualistic, hopeful, mobile, divided by age and gender roles, apprehensive, yet willing to strike out for the distant and new.

Land for the Taking

As railroads pushed west in the 1870s and 1880s, locomotive trains replaced wagon trains, but the shift was gradual, and until the end of the century, emigrants often combined both modes of travel. Into the 1890s, travelers could be seen making their way across the West by any available means. Early railroad transportation was expensive, and the average farm family could not afford to buy tickets and ship supplies. Many Europeans traveled by rail to designated outfitting places and then proceeded West with wagons and oxen.

Traffic flowed in all directions, belying the image of a simple "westward" movement. Many people did go west, of course, but others, such as migrants from Mexico, became westerners by moving north, and Asian Americans moved eastward from the Pacific Coast. Whatever their route, they all ended up in the meeting ground of cultures that formed the modern West.

Why did they come? "The motive that induced us to part with the pleasant associations and the dear friends of our childhood days," explained Phoebe Judson, an early emigrant, "was to obtain from the government of the United States a grant of land that 'Uncle Sam' had promised to give to the head of each family who settled in this new country." A popular camp song reflected the same motive:

> Come along, come along—don't be alarmed,
> Uncle Sam is rich enough to give us all a farm.

Uncle Sam owned about one billion acres of land in the 1860s, much of it mountain and desert land unsuited for agriculture. By 1900, the various land laws had distributed half of it. Between 1862 and 1890, the government gave away 48 million acres under the **Homestead Act of 1862,** sold about 100 million acres to private citizens and corporations, granted 128 million acres to railroad companies to tempt them to build across the unsettled West, and sold huge tracts to the states.

The Homestead Act of 1862, a law of great significance, gave 160 acres of land to anyone who would pay a $10 registration fee and pledge to live on it and cultivate it for five years. The offer set off a mass migration of land-hungry Europeans, dazzled by a country that gave its land away. Americans also seized on the act's provisions, and between 1862 and 1900, nearly 600,000 families claimed free homesteads under it.

Railroad companies distributed elaborately illustrated brochures and broadsides to lure people to the West, where they could settle on land owned by the railroads, such as the 3 million acres in Nebraska advertised in this Union Pacific poster. ❖

Yet the Homestead Act did not work as Congress had hoped. Few farmers and laborers had the cash to move to the frontier, buy farm equipment, and wait out the year or two before the farm became self-supporting. Tailored to the timber and water conditions of the East, the act did not work as well in the semiarid West. In the fertile valleys of the Mississippi, 160 acres provided a generous farm. A farmer on the Great Plains needed either a larger farm for dry farming or a smaller one for irrigation.

The Timber Culture Act of 1873 attempted to adjust the Homestead Act to western conditions. It allowed homesteaders to claim an additional 160 acres if they planted trees on a quarter of it within four years. A successful act, it distributed 10 million acres of land, encouraged needed forestation, and enabled homesteaders to expand their farms to a workable size. Cattle ranchers lobbied for another law, the Desert Land Act of 1877, which allowed individuals to obtain 640 acres in the arid states for $1.25 an acre, provided they irrigated part of it within three years. The act invited fraud. Irrigation sometimes meant a bucket of water dumped on the ground, and ranchers used their hired hands to claim large tracts. More than 2.6 million acres of land were distributed, much of it fraudulently.

The Timber and Stone Act of 1878 applied only to lands "unfit for cultivation" and valuable chiefly for timber or stone. It permitted anyone in California, Nevada, Oregon, and Washington to buy up to 160 acres of forest land for $2.50 an acre. Like ranchers, lumber companies used employees to file false claims. Company agents rounded up seamen on the waterfront, marched them to the land office to file their claims, took them to a notary public to sign over the claims to the company, and then marched them back to the waterfront for payment in beer or cash. By 1900, 3.6 million acres of rich forest land had been claimed under the measure.

Speculators made ingenious use of the land laws. Sending agents in advance of settlement, they moved along choice river bottoms or irrigable areas, accumulating large holdings to be held for high prices. In the arid West, where control of water meant control of the surrounding land, shrewd ranchers plotted their holdings accordingly. In Colorado, one cattleman, John F. Iliff, owned only 105 small parcels of land, but by placing them around the few water holes, he effectively dominated an empire stretching over 6000 square miles.

Water, in fact, became a dominant western issue, since aside from the Pacific Northwest, northern California, parts of the Rocky Mountain West, and the eastern half of the Great Plains, much of the trans-Mississippi West was arid, receiving less than 20 inches of rainfall annually. People speculated in water as if it were gold and planned great irrigation systems in Utah, eastern Colorado, and California's Central Valley to "make the desert bloom." A sign in Modesto, California, read "Water, Wealth, Contentment, Health."

Irrigators received a major boost in 1902 when the **National Reclamation Act (Newlands Act)** set aside most of the proceeds from the sale of public lands in sixteen western states to finance irrigation projects in the arid states. Over the next decades, dams, canals, and irrigation systems channeled water into dry areas, creating a "hydraulic" society that was rich in crops and cities (such as Los Angeles and Phoenix), but ever thirstier and in danger of outrunning the precious water on which it all depended.

As beneficiaries of the government's policy of land grants for railway construction, the railroad companies were the West's largest landowners. Eager to have immigrants settle on the land they owned near the railroad right-of-way, and eager to boost their freight and passenger business, the companies sent agents to the East and Europe. Attractive brochures touted life in the West. The Union Pacific called the rocky Platte Valley in Nebraska "a flowery meadow of great fertility, clothed in nutritious grasses."

Railroad lines set up land departments and bureaus of immigration. The land departments priced the land, arranged credit terms, and even gave free farming courses to immigrants. The bureaus of immigration employed agents in Europe, met immigrants at eastern seaports, and ran special cars for land seekers heading west.

Half a billion acres of western land were given or sold to speculators and corporations. At the same time, only 600,000 homestead patents were issued, covering 80 million acres. Thus, only one acre in every nine initially went to individual pioneers, the intended beneficiaries of the nation's largesse. Two-thirds of all homestead claimants before 1890 failed in their efforts to farm their new land.

Territorial Government

As new areas of the West opened, they were organized as territories under the control of Congress and the president. The territorial system started with the famous Northwest Ordinance of 1787, which established the rules by which territories became states. Washington ran the territories like "a passive group of colonial mandates." The president appointed the governor and judges in each territory; Congress detailed their duties, set their budgets, and oversaw their activities. Territorial officials had almost absolute power over the territories.

Until they obtained statehood, then, the territories depended on the federal government for their existence. They became an important part of the patronage system, as sources of jobs for deserving politicians.

The national political parties, especially the Republicans, funneled government funds into the territorial economies, and in areas such as Wyoming and the Dakotas, where resources were scarce, economic growth depended on this money. Many early settlers held patronage jobs or hoped for them, traded with government-supported Native Americans, sold supplies to army troops, and speculated in government lands.

In a large portion of the trans-Mississippi West, a generation grew up under territorial rule. Inevitably, these citizens developed distinct ideas about politics, government, and the economy.

The Spanish-Speaking Southwest

In the nineteenth century, almost all Spanish-speaking people in the United States lived in California, Arizona, New Mexico, Texas, and Colorado. Their numbers were small—California had only 8,086 Mexican residents in 1900—but the influence of their culture and institutions was large. In some respects,

In Invitation to the Dance *by Theodore Gentilz, a young woman stands in the doorway of her San Antonio home to greet the group of* caballeros *riding up on their horses and making music on the violin and guitar. The caballeros' flared trousers, known as* calzoneras, *were well suited for riding and dancing. Note the distinctive architectural style of the white building at the left where a couple is dancing.* ❖

the southwestern frontier was more Spanish American than Anglo-American.

Pushing northward from Mexico, the Spanish gradually established the present-day economic structure of the Southwest. They brought with them techniques of mining, stock raising, and irrigated farming. After winning independence in the 1820s, the Mexicans brought new laws and ranching methods as well as chaps and the burro. Both Spanish and Mexicans created the legal framework for distributing land and water, a precious resource in the Southwest. They gave large grants of land to communities for grazing, to individuals as rewards for service, and to the various Native American pueblos.

In Southern California, the Californios, descendants of the original colonizers, began after the 1860s to lose their once vast landholdings to drought and mortgages. Some turned to crime and became feared bandidos; others, such as José María Amador, lived in poverty and remembered better days:

> When I was but a little boy I drained the
> chocolate pot,
> But now I am a poor man and am condemned
> to slop.

In 1875, Romualdo Pacheco, an aristocratic native son, served as governor of California and then went on to Congress. But as the Californios died out, Mexican Americans continued the Spanish-Mexican influence. In 1880, one-fourth of the residents of Los Angeles County were Spanish speaking.

In New Mexico, Spanish-speaking citizens remained the majority ethnic group until the 1940s, and the Spanish Mexican culture dominated the territory. Contests over land grants became New Mexico's largest industry; lawyers who dealt in them amassed huge holdings. After 1888, *Las Gorras Blancas* ("The White Caps"), a secret organization of Spanish Americans, attacked the movement of Anglo ranchers into the Las Vegas community land grant. Armed and hooded, they cut down fences and scattered the stock of those they viewed as intruders.

Throughout the Southwest, the Spanish Mexican heritage gave a distinctive shape to society. Men headed the families and dominated economic life. Women had substantial economic rights (though few political ones), and they enjoyed a status their English American counterparts did not have. Wives kept full control of property acquired before their marriage; they also held half title to all property in a marriage, which later caused many southwestern states to pass community property laws.

In addition, the Spanish Mexican heritage fostered a modified economic caste system, a strong Roman Catholic influence, and the primary use of the Spanish language. Continuous immigration from Mexico kept language and cultural ties strong. Spanish names and customs spread, even among Anglos. David Starr Jordan, arriving from Indiana to become the first president of Stanford University in California, bestowed Spanish names on streets, houses, and a Stanford dormitory. Spanish was the region's first or second language. Confronted by Sheriff Pat Garrett in a darkened room, New Mexico's famous outlaw Billy the Kid died asking, "Quién es? Quién es?" ("Who is it? Who is it?").

The Bonanza West

Between 1850 and 1900, wave after wave of newcomers swept across the trans-Mississippi West. There were riches for the taking, hidden in gold-washed streams, spread lushly over grass-covered prairies, or available in the gullible minds of greedy newcomers. The nineteenth-century West took shape in the search for mining, cattle, and land bonanzas that drew eager settlers from the East and around the world.

As with all bonanzas, the consequences in the West were uneven growth, boom-and-bust economic cycles, and wasted resources. Society seemed constantly in the making. People moved here and there, following river bottoms, gold strikes, railroad tracks, and other opportunities. "Instant cities" arose. San Francisco, Salt Lake City, and Denver were the most spectacular examples, but every cow town and mining camp witnessed similar phenomena of growth. Boston needed more than two centuries to attract one-third of a million people; San Francisco did the same in a little more than twenty years.

Many Westerners had left home to get rich quickly, and they adopted institutions that reflected that goal. As a contemporary poem said:

> Love to see the stir an' bustle
> In the busy town,
> Everybody on the hustle
> Saltin' profits down.
> Everybody got a wad a'
> Ready cash laid by;
> Ain't no flies on Colorado—
> Not a cussed fly.

In their lives, the West was an idea as well as a region, and the idea molded them as much as they molded it.

The Mining Bonanza

Mining was the first important magnet to attract people to the West. Many hoped to "strike it rich" in gold and silver, but at least half the newcomers had no intention of working in the mines. Instead, they pro-

Before the California Gold Rush of 1849, San Francisco was a sleepy little Spanish-Mexican village called Yerba Buena. Gold seekers turned it into a boomtown with an international population. Here, Spanish Mexican rancheros, white prospectors, Chinese laborers, and a top-hatted professional gambler mingle in a San Francisco saloon. ❖

vided food, clothing, and services to the thousands of miners. Leland Stanford and Collis P. Huntington, who later built the Central Pacific Railroad, set up a general store in Sacramento where they sold shovels and supplies. Stephen J. Field, later a prominent justice of the U.S. Supreme Court, followed the Gold Rush to California to practice law.

The California Gold Rush of 1849 began the mining boom and set the pattern for subsequent strikes in other regions. Individual prospectors made the first strikes, discovering pockets of gold along streams flowing westward from the Sierra Nevada. To get the gold, they used a simple process called **placer mining,** which required little skill, technology, or capital. A placer miner needed only a shovel, a washing pan, and a good claim. As the placers gave out, a great deal of gold remained, but it was locked in quartz or buried deep in the earth. Mining became an expensive business, far beyond the reach of the average miner.

Large corporations moved in to dig the deep shafts and finance costly equipment. Quartz mining required heavy rock crushers, mercury vats to dissolve the gold, and large retorts to recapture it. Eastern and European financiers assumed control, labor became unionized, and mining towns took on some of the characteristics of the industrial city. Individual prospectors meanwhile dashed on to the next find. Unlike other frontiers, the mining frontier moved from west to east, as the original California miners—the "yonder-siders," they were called—hurried eastward in search of the big strike.

In 1859, fresh strikes were made near Pikes Peak in Colorado and in the Carson River Valley of Nevada. News of both discoveries set off wild migrations—100,000 miners were in Pikes Peak country by June 1859. The gold there quickly played out, but the Nevada find uncovered a thick bluish black ore that was almost pure silver and gold. A quick-witted drifter named Henry T. P. Comstock talked his way into partnership in the claim, and word of the **Comstock Lode**—with ore worth $3,876 a ton—flashed over the mountains.

Thousands of miners climbed the Sierra Nevada that summer. On the rough slopes of Davidson Mountain, they created Virginia City, the prototype of the tumultuous western mining town. Mark Twain was there and described the scene in *Roughing It* (1872): "The sidewalks swarmed with people. . . . Joy sat on every countenance, and there was a glad, almost fierce, intensity in every eye, that told of the money-getting schemes that were seething in every brain and the high hope that held sway in every heart."

The biggest strike was yet to come. In 1873, John W. Mackay and three partners formed a company to dig deep into the mountain, and at 1,167 feet they hit the Big Bonanza, a seam of gold and silver more than 54 feet wide. It was the richest discovery in the history of mining. Between 1859 and 1879, the Comstock Lode produced gold and silver worth $306 million. Most of it went to financiers and corporations. Mackay himself became the richest person in the world, earning (according to a European newspaper) $25 a minute, $5 a minute more than Czar Alexander II of Russia.

In the 1860s and 1870s, important strikes were made in Washington, Idaho, Nevada, Colorado, Montana, Arizona, and Dakota. Extremely mobile, miners flocked from strike to strike, and new camps

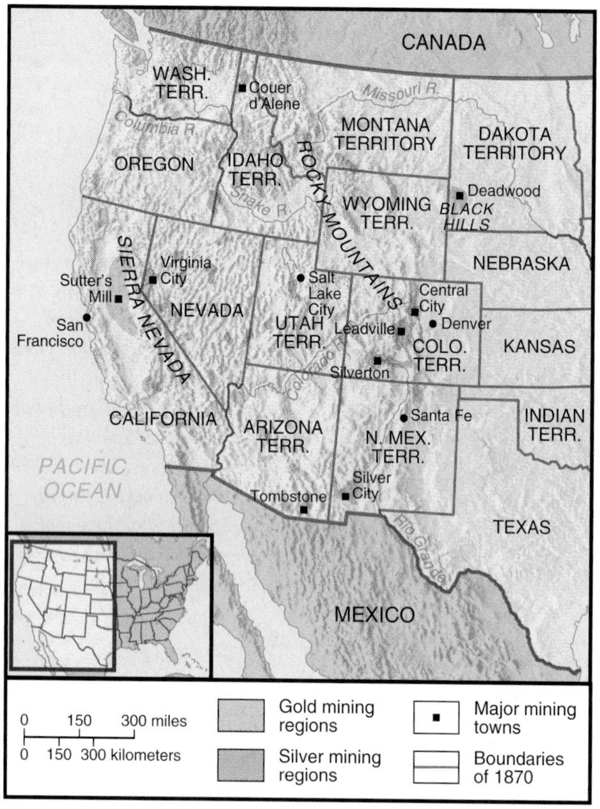

MINING REGIONS OF THE WEST *Gold and silver mines dotted the West, drawing settlers and encouraging political organization in many areas.* ❖

and mining towns sprang up overnight. "The miners of Idaho were like quicksilver," said Hubert Howe Bancroft, an early historian. "A mass of them dropped in any locality, broke up into individual globules, and ran off after any atom of gold in their vicinity. They stayed nowhere longer than the gold attracted them."

The final fling came in the Black Hills rush of 1874 to 1876. The army had tried to keep miners out of the area, the heart of the Sioux hunting grounds, and even sent a scientific party under Colonel George Armstrong Custer to disprove the rumors of gold and stop the miners' invasion. Instead, Custer found gold all over the hills, and the rush was on. Miners, gamblers, desperadoes, and prostitutes flocked to Deadwood, the most lawless of all the mining camps. There, Martha Jane Canary—a crack shot who, as Calamity Jane, won fame as a scout and teamster—fell in love with "Wild Bill" Hickok. Hickok himself—a western legend who had tamed Kansas cow towns, killed an unknown number of men, and toured in Buffalo Bill's Wild West Show—died in Deadwood, shot in the back of the head. Hickok was 39 years old.

Towns such as Deadwood, in the Dakota Territory; Virginia City, Nevada; Leadville, Colorado; and Tombstone, Arizona, demonstrated a new development process in the frontier experience. The farming frontier had developed naturally in a rural setting. On the mining frontier, the germ of a city—the camp—appeared almost simultaneously with the first "strike." Periodicals, the latest fashions, theaters, schools, literary clubs, and lending libraries came quickly to the camps, providing civilized refinements not available on other frontiers. Urbanization also created the need for municipal government, sanitation, and law enforcement.

Mining camps were governed by a simple democracy. Soon after a strike, the miners in the area met to organize a mining "district" and adopted rules governing behavior in it. Rules regulated the size and boundaries of claims, established procedures for settling disputes, and set penalties for crimes. Petty criminals were banished from the district; serious offenders were hanged. In the case of a major dispute, the whole camp gathered, chose legal counsel for both sides, and heard the evidence. If all else failed, miners formed secret vigilance committees to hang a few offenders as a lesson to the rest. Early visitors to the mining country were struck by the way miners, solitary and competitive, joined together, founded a camp, and created a society.

The camps were mostly male, made up of "men who can rough it" and a few "ladies of spirit and energy." In 1870, men outnumbered women in the mining districts by more than two to one; there were few children. Prostitutes followed the camps around the West, and a "respectable" woman was an object of curiosity. Four arrived in Nevada City in 1853, and one observed, "The men stand and gaze at us with mouth and eyes wide open, every time we go out." Some women worked claims, but more often they took jobs as cooks, housekeepers, and seamstresses—for wages considerably higher than in the East.

In most camps, between one-quarter and one-half of the population was foreign born. The lure of gold drew large numbers of Chinese, Chileans, Peruvians, Mexicans, French, Germans, and English. Experienced miners, the Latin Americans brought valuable mining techniques. At least six thousand Mexicans joined the California rush of 1849, and by 1852, there were twenty-five thousand Chinese in California. Painstaking, the Chinese profitably worked claims others had abandoned. In the 1860s, almost one-third of the miners in the West were Chinese.

Hostility often surfaced against foreign miners, particularly the French, Latin Americans, and Chinese. In 1850, California passed a Foreign Miners' Tax that charged foreign miners a $20 monthly licensing fee. As intended, it drove out Mexicans and other foreigners. Riots against Chinese laborers occurred in the 1870s and 1880s in Los Angeles, San Francisco, Seattle, Reno, and Denver. Responding to pressure, Congress passed the Chinese Exclusion Act of 1882, which suspended immigration of Chinese laborers for ten years. The number of Chinese in the United States fell drastically.

By the 1890s, the early mining bonanza was over. All told, the western mines contributed billions of dollars to the economy. They had helped finance the Civil War and provided needed capital for industrialization. The vast boost in silver production from the Comstock Lode changed the relative value of gold and silver, the base of American currency. Bitter disputes over the currency affected politics and led to the famous "battle of the standards" in the presidential election of 1896 (see Chapter 20).

Photographer John C. H. Grabill documented frontier life in Colorado, the Dakota territory, and Wyoming. This 1889 photograph shows three men placer mining at a camp in Rockerville, South Dakota. ❖

The mining frontier populated portions of the West and sped its process of political organization. Nevada, Idaho, and Montana were granted early statehood because of mining. Merchants, editors, lawyers, and ministers moved with the advancing frontier, establishing permanent settlements. Women in the mining camps helped to foster family life and raised the moral tone by campaigning against drinking, gambling, and prostitution. But not all the effects of the mining boom were positive. The industry also left behind painful scars in the form of invaded Indian reservations, pitted hills, and lonely ghost towns.

Gold from the Roots Up: The Cattle Bonanza

"There's gold from the grass roots down," said California Joe, a guide in the gold districts of Dakota in the 1870s, "but there's more gold from the grass roots up." Ranchers began to recognize the potential of the vast grasslands of the West. The Plains were covered with buffalo or grama grass, a wiry variety with short, hard stems. Cattle thrived on it.

For twenty years after 1865, cattle ranching dominated the "open range," a vast fenceless area extending from the Texas Panhandle north into Canada. The techniques of the business came from Mexico. Long before American cowboys moved herds north, their Mexican counterparts, the *vaqueros,* developed the essential techniques of branding, roundups, and roping. The cattle themselves, the famous Texas longhorns, also came from Mexico. Spreading over the grasslands of southern Texas, the longhorns multiplied rapidly. Although their meat was coarse and stringy, they fed a nation hungry for beef at the end of the Civil War.

The problem was getting the beef to eastern markets, and Joseph G. McCoy, a livestock shipper from Illinois, solved it. Looking for a way to market Texas beef, McCoy conceived the idea of taking the cattle to railheads in Kansas. He talked first with the president of the Missouri Pacific, who ordered him out of his office, and then with the head of the Kansas Pacific, who laughed at the idea. The persistent McCoy finally signed a contract in 1867 with the Hannibal and St. Joseph Railroad. Searching for an appropriate rail junction, he settled on the sleepy Kansas town of Abilene, "a very small, dead place," he remembered, with about a dozen log huts and one nearly bankrupt saloon.

In September 1867, McCoy shipped the first train of twenty cars of longhorn cattle. By the end of the year, a thousand carloads had followed, all headed for Chicago markets. In 1870, 300,000 head of Texas cattle reached Abilene, followed the next year—the peak year—by 700,000 head. The Alamo Saloon, crowded with tired cowboys at the end of the drive, now employed seventy-five bartenders, working three 8-hour shifts.

The profits were enormous. Drivers bought cheap Texas steers for $4 a head and sold them for $30 or $40 a head at the northern railhead. The most famous trail

❖ A Look at the Past ❖

Cowboy Clothing

Cowboys hold a special place in American mythology, representing rugged individuals able to survive in the wilderness. They symbolize another element of our nation's history: the variety of people who formed the country. African Americans, Mexican Americans, Anglo-Americans, and others rode the plains. The clothes cowboys wore during the mid-nineteenth century, such as these wool caballeros pants trimmed with gold braid and with flared legs that button down the sides, show the cultural mixing that took place in the West and how people adapted to the demands of the environment. By the end of the nineteenth century, cowboy heroes, such as those in Buffalo Bill's Wild West Show, no longer wore serapes, sashes, short jackets, or pants such as these that shared Spanish and Mexican origins. What does the change in cowboy fashion suggest about attitudes toward Mexicans? Why would it matter that cowboy heroes wore clothes that reflected Anglo origins, rather than Mexican?

was the Chisholm, running from southern Texas through Oklahoma Territory to Ellsworth and Abilene, Kansas, on the Kansas Pacific Railroad. Dodge City, Kansas, became the prime shipping center between 1875 and 1879.

Cowboys pushed steers northward in herds of two to three thousand. Novels and films have portrayed the cowboys as white, but at least a quarter of them were black, and possibly another quarter were Mexicans. A typical crew on the trail north might have eight men, half of them black or Mexican. Most of the trail bosses were white; they earned about $125 a month. James "Jim" Perry, a renowned black cowboy who worked for more than twenty years as a rider, roper, and cook for the XIT ranch, said, "If it weren't for my damned old black face, I'd have been a boss long ago."

Like miners, cattlemen lived beyond the formal reach of the law and so established their own. Before each drive, Charles Goodnight drew up rules governing behavior on the trail. A cowboy who shot another was hanged on the spot. Ranchers adopted rules for cattle ownership, branding, roundups, and drives, and they formed associations to enforce them. The Wyoming Stock Growers' Association, the largest and most formidable, had four hundred members owning two million cattle; its reach extended well beyond Wyoming into Colorado, Nebraska, Montana, and the Dakotas. Throughout this vast territory, the "laws" of the association were often the law of the land.

Hollywood images to the contrary, there was little violence in the booming cow towns. The number of homicides in a year never topped five in any town, and in many years no one was killed. Doc Holliday and William B. "Bat" Masterson never killed anyone. John Wesley Hardin, a legendary teenaged gunman, shot only one man, firing blindly through a hotel room wall to stop him from snoring. Famous western sheriffs had everyday duties. Wild Bill Hickok served as Abilene's street commissioner, and the Wichita city council made its lawmen, including Wyatt Earp, repair streets and sidewalks before each cattle season.

By 1880, more than six million cattle had been driven to northern markets. But the era of the great cattle drive was ending. Farmers were planting wheat on the old buffalo ranges; barbed wire, a recent invention, cut across the trails and divided up the big ranches. Mechanical improvements in slaughtering, refrigerated transportation, and cold storage modernized the industry. Ranchers bred the Texas longhorns with heavier Hereford and Angus bulls, and as the new breeds proved profitable, more and more ranches opened on the northern ranges.

By the mid-1880s, some 4.5 million cattle grazed the High Plains, reminding people of the once great herds of buffalo. Stories of vast profits circulated,

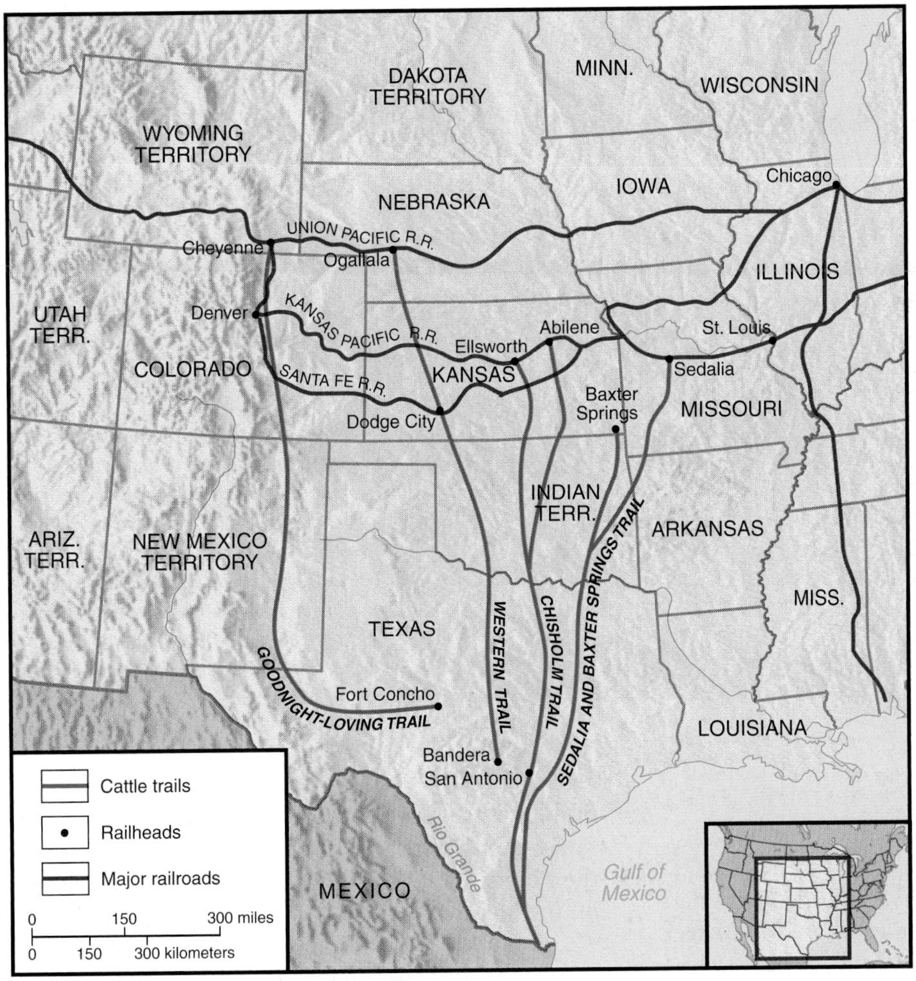

CATTLE TRAILS *Cattle raised in Texas were driven along the cattle trails to the northern railheads, and trains carried them to market.*

attracting outside capital. Large investments transformed ranching into big business, often controlled by absentee owners and subject to new problems.

By 1885, experienced cattle ranchers were growing alarmed. A presidential order that year forced them out of the Indian Territory in Oklahoma, adding 200,000 cattle to the overcrowded northern ranges. The winter of 1885 to 1886 was cold, and the following summer was one of the hottest on record. Water holes dried up; the grass turned brown. Beef prices fell.

The winter of 1886–1887 was one of the worst in western history. Temperatures dropped to 45 degrees below zero, and cattle that once would have saved themselves by drifting ahead of the storms came up against the new barbed wire fences. Herds jammed together, pawing the frozen ground or stripping bark from trees in search of food. Cattle died by the tens of thousands. In the spring of 1887, when the snows thawed, ranchers found stacks of carcasses piled up against the fences.

The melting snows did, however, produce a lush crop of grass for the survivors. The cattle business recovered, but it took different directions. Outside capital, so plentiful in the boom years, dried up. Ranchers began fencing their lands, reducing their herds, and growing hay for winter food. To the dismay of cowboys, mowing machines and hay rakes became as important as chuck wagons and branding irons. "I tell you times have changed," one cowboy said sadly.

The last roundup on the northern ranges took place in 1905. Ranches grew smaller, and some ranchers, at first in the scrub country of the Southwest, then on the Plains themselves, switched to raising sheep. By 1900, there were nearly thirty-eight million sheep west of the Missouri River, far more than there were cattle. In Montana, there were six or seven sheep for each cow, and even Wyoming, the great center of the northern ranches, had more sheep than cows.

Ranchers and sheepherders fought bitterly to control the grazing lands, but they had one problem in common: the troubles ahead. Homesteaders, armed with barbed wire and new strains of wheat, were pushing onto the Plains, and the day of the open range was over.

In the late 1800s, cowboys drove enormous herds of cattle on trails north out of Texas to railheads, where the cattle could be transported by railroad car to major markets such as Chicago. As suggested by this panoramic view of life on the trail, it was no easy task to control two to three thousand steers and the work generally required a crew of several men. ❖

Sodbusters on the Plains: The Farming Bonanza

Like miners and cattle ranchers, millions of farmers moved into the West in the decades after 1870 to seek crop bonanzas and new ways of life. Some realized their dreams; many fought just to survive.

Said a folksong from Greer County, Oklahoma:

> Hurrah for Greer County! The land of the free,
> The land of the bedbug, grasshopper, and flea;
> I'll sing of its praises, I'll tell of its fame,
> While starving to death on my government claim.

Between 1870 and 1900, farmers cultivated more land than ever before in American history. They peopled the Plains from Dakota to Texas, pushed the Indians out of their last sanctuary in Oklahoma, and poured into the basins and foothills of the Rockies. By 1900, the western half of the nation contained almost 30 percent of the population, compared to less than 1 percent just a half century earlier.

Unlike mining, farm settlement often followed predictable patterns, taking population from states east of the settlement line and moving gradually westward. Crossing the Mississippi, farmers settled first in western Iowa, Minnesota, Nebraska, Kansas, Texas, and South Dakota. The movement slumped during the depression of the 1870s, but then a new wave of optimism carried thousands more west. Several years of above average rainfall convinced farmers that the Dakotas, western Nebraska and Kansas, and eastern Colorado were the "rain belt of the Plains." Between 1870 and 1900, the population on the Plains tripled.

In some areas, the newcomers were blacks who had fled the South, fed up with beatings and murders, crop liens, and the Black Codes that institutionalized their subordinate status. In 1879, about six thousand African Americans known as the **Exodusters** left their homes in Louisiana, Mississippi, and Texas to establish new and freer lives in Kansas, the home of John Brown and the Free-Soil campaigns of the 1850s. Once there, they farmed or worked as laborers; women worked in the fields alongside the men or cleaned houses and took in washing to make ends meet. All told, the Exodusters homesteaded 20,000 acres of land, and though they met prejudice, it was not as extreme as they had known at home. "I asked my wife did she know the ground she stands on," said John Solomon Lewis, a Louisianan, soon after arriving. "She said, 'No!' I said it is free ground; and she cried like a child for joy."

Other African Americans moved to Oklahoma, thinking they might establish the first African American state. Whether headed for Oklahoma or Kansas, they picked up and moved in sizable groups that were based on family units; they took with them the customs they had known, and in their new homes they were able, for the first time, to have some measure of self-government.

For blacks and whites alike, farming on the Plains presented new problems. There was little surface water, and wells ranged between 50 and 500 feet deep. Well drillers charged up to $2 a foot. Taking advantage of the steady Plains winds, windmills brought the water to the surface, but they too were expensive, and until 1900, many farmers could not afford them. Lumber for homes and fences was also scarce. Some settlers imported it from distant Wisconsin, but a single homestead of 160 acres cost $1000 to fence, an amount few could pay.

Unable to afford wood, farmers often started out in dreary sod houses. Cut into 3-foot sections, the thick prairie sod was laid like brick, with space left for two windows and a door. Since glass was scarce, cloth hung over the windows; a blanket was hung from the ceiling to make two rooms. Sod houses were small, provided little light and air, and were impossible to keep clean. When it rained, water seeped through the roof. Yet a sod house cost only $2.78 to build.

Outside, the Plains environment sorely tested the men and women who moved there. Neighbors were distant; the land stretched on as far as the eye could see. Always the wind blew. "As long as I live I'll never see such a lonely country," a woman said of the Texas Plains; a Nebraska woman said, "These unbounded prairies have such an air of desolation—and the stillness is very oppressive."

In the winters, savage storms swept the open grasslands. Ice caked on the cattle until their heads were too heavy to hold up. Summertime temperatures stayed near 110 degrees for weeks at a time. Fearsome rainstorms, building in the summer's heat, beat down the young corn and wheat. The summers also brought grasshoppers, arriving without warning, flying in clouds so huge they shut out the sun. The grasshoppers ate everything in sight: crops, clothing, mosquito netting, tree bark, even plow handles. In the summer of 1874, they devastated the whole Plains from Texas to the Dakotas, eating everything "but the mortgage," as one farmer said.

New Farming Methods

Farmers adopted new techniques to meet conditions on the Plains. For one thing, they needed cheap and effective fencing material, and in 1874, Joseph F. Glidden, a farmer from De Kalb, Illinois, provided it with the invention of barbed wire. By 1883, his factory was turning out 600 miles of barbed wire every day, and farmers were buying it faster than it could be produced.

Dry farming, a new technique, helped compensate for the lack of rainfall. By plowing furrows 12 to 14 inches deep and creating a dust mulch to fill the furrow, farmers loosened the soil and slowed evaporation. Wheat farmers imported European varieties of plants that could withstand the harsh Plains winters. Hard-kerneled varieties such as Turkey red wheat from Russia required new milling methods, developed during the 1870s. By 1881, Minneapolis, St. Louis, and Kansas City had become milling centers for the rich "new process" flour.

Disappointed with the failures of Reconstruction and fearful of the violence that surrounded them, many southern blacks migrated to Kansas in the 1870s and 1880s. Comparing their trek to the biblical story of the Israelites' exodus from Egypt, they became known as "Exodusters." ❖

❖ A Look at the Past ❖

Barbed Wire

Barbed wire forever altered land use in the West. Perfected in 1874, barbed wire made effective, economical fencing. Reflecting its importance to western farmers, barbed wire soon came in hundreds of varieties, including decorative versions. Most variations performed equally well, however, making so many designs unnecessary. Why do you think so many types existed?

Farm technology changed long before the Civil War, but later developments improved it. In 1877, James Oliver of Indiana patented a chilled-iron plow with a smooth-surfaced moldboard that did not clog in the thick prairie soils. The spring-tooth harrow (1869) sped soil preparation; the grain drill (1874) opened furrows and scientifically fed seed into the ground. The lister (1880) dug a deep furrow, planted corn at the bottom, and covered the seed—all in one operation.

The first baling press was built in 1866, and the hay loader was patented in 1876. The first successful harvester, the cord binder (1878), cut and tied bundles of grain, enabling two men and a team of horses to harvest 20 acres of wheat a day. Invented earlier, threshers grew larger; employing as many as nine men and ten horses, one machine could thresh 300 bushels of grain a day.

In 1890, more than nine hundred corporations manufactured farm machinery. Scientific agriculture flourished under new discoveries linking soil minerals and plant growth. Samuel Johnson of Yale University published *How Crops Grow* (1868) and *How Crops Feed* (1870), and one of his students pioneered work on nitrogen, the base of many modern fertilizers. The Hatch Act, passed in 1887, supported agricultural experiment stations that spread the discoveries among farmers. Four years later, the stations employed more than 450 persons and distributed more than 300 published reports annually to some 350,000 readers.

In the late 1870s, huge **bonanza farms** rose, run by the new machinery and financed with outside capital. Oliver Dalrymple, the most famous of the bonanza farmers, headed an experiment in North Dakota's Red River Valley in 1875, then moved on to manage the Grandin Bonanza of 61,000 acres, five times the size of Manhattan Island. Dalrymple hired armies of workers, bought machinery by the carload, and planted on a scale that dazzled the West.

The bonanza farms—thanks to their size and machinery—captured the country's imagination. Using 200 pairs of harrows, 155 binders, and 16 threshers, Dalrymple produced 600,000 bushels of wheat in 1881. He and other bonanza managers profited from the economies of scale, buying materials at wholesale prices and receiving rebates from the railroads. Then a period of drought began. Rainfall dropped between 1885 and 1890, and the large-scale growers found it hard to compete with smaller farmers who diversified their crops and cultivated more intensively. Many of the large bonanzas slowly disintegrated, and Dalrymple himself went bankrupt in 1896.

A work crew on the Dalrymple farm in the Red River Valley gathers grain wired into bundles by self-binding harvesters. In 1877, Dalrymple used a hundred workers to harvest his 4000 acres of wheat; by 1884, the number of harvesters employed on the farm had increased to a thousand. ❖

Discontent on the Farm

Touring the South in the 1860s, Oliver H. Kelley, a clerk in the Department of Agriculture, was struck by the drabness of rural life. In 1867, he founded the **National Grange of the Patrons of Husbandry,** known simply as the Grange. The Grange provided social, cultural, and educational activities for its members. Its constitution banned involvement in politics, but Grangers often ignored the rules and supported railroad regulation and other measures.

The Grange grew rapidly during the depression of the 1870s, and by 1875, it had more than 800,000 members in 20,000 local Granges. Most were in the Midwest and South. The Granges set up cooperative stores, grain elevators, warehouses, insurance companies, and farm machinery factories. Many failed, but in the meantime the organization made its mark. Picking up where the Grange left off, farm-oriented groups such as the Farmers' Alliance, with branches in both South and West, began to attract followers.

Like the cattle boom, the farming boom ended sharply after 1887. A severe drought that year cut harvests, and other droughts followed in 1889 and 1894. Thousands of new farmers were wiped out on the western Plains. Between 1888 and 1892, more than half the population of western Kansas left. Farmers grew angry and restless. They complained about declining crop prices, rising railroad rates, and heavy mortgages.

Although many farmers were unhappy, the peopling of the West in those years transformed American agriculture. The states beyond the Mississippi became the garden land of the nation. California sent fruit, wine, and wheat to eastern markets. Under the Mormons, Utah flourished with irrigation. Texas beef stocked the country's tables, and vast wheat fields, stretching to the horizon, covered Minnesota, the

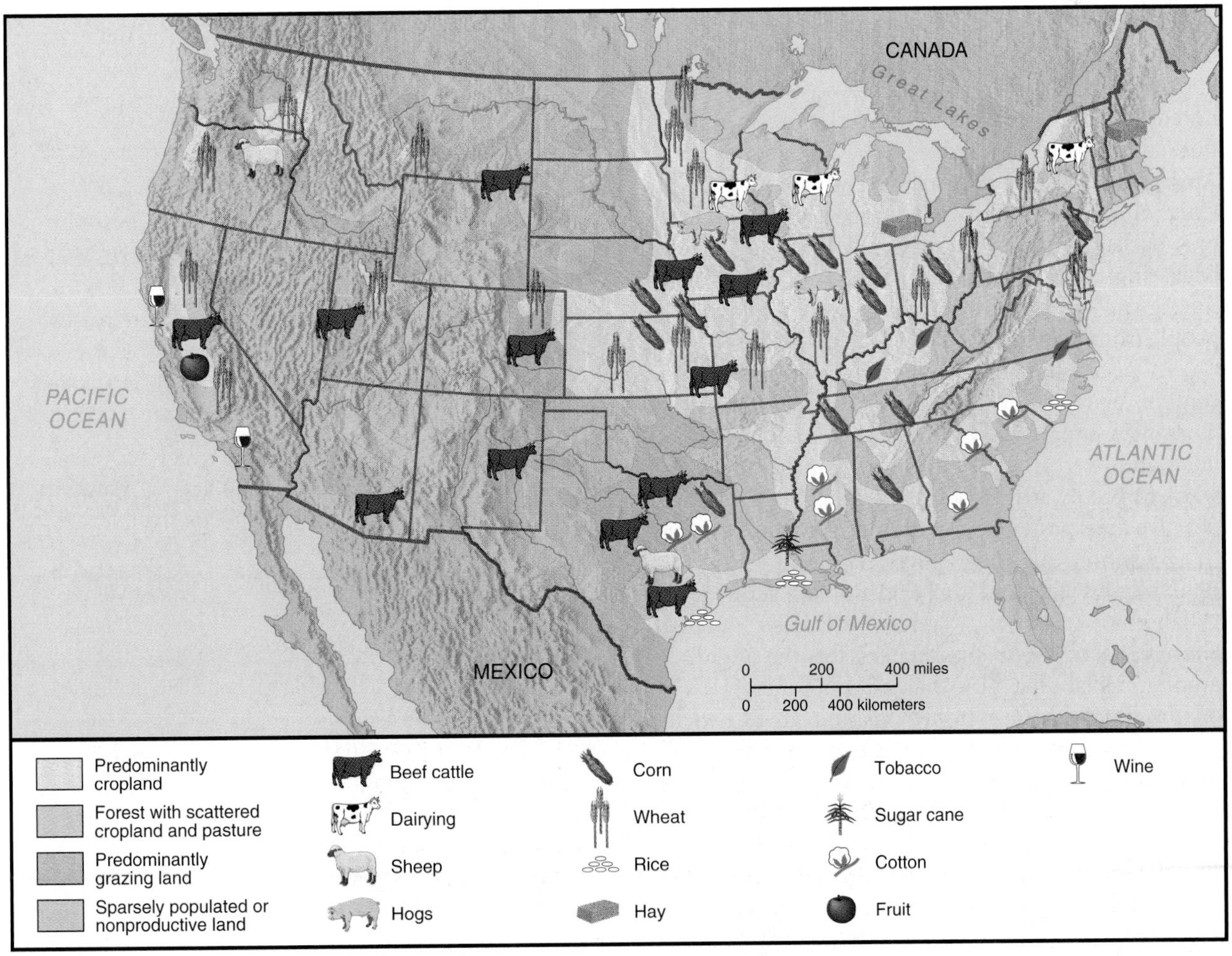

AGRICULTURAL LAND USE IN THE 1880s *New farming technology and new crops enabled more and more land to be put to productive use.* ❖

Dakotas, Montana, and eastern Colorado. All produced more than Americans could consume. By 1890, American farmers were exporting large amounts of wheat and other crops.

Farmers became more commercial and scientific. They needed to know more and work harder. Mail-order houses and rural free delivery diminished their isolation and tied them ever closer to the national future. "This is a new age to the farmer," said a statistician in the Department of Agriculture in 1889. "He is now, more than ever before, a citizen of the world."

The Final Fling

As the West filled in with people, pressure mounted on the president and Congress to open the last Indian territory, Oklahoma, to settlers. In March 1889, Congress acted and forced the Creek and Seminole tribes, who had been moved into Oklahoma in the 1820s, to surrender their rights to the land. With arrangements complete, President Benjamin Harrison announced the opening of the Oklahoma District as of noon, April 22, 1889.

Preparations were feverish all along the frontier. "From all the West," historian Ray Allen Billington noted, "the homeless, the speculators, the adventurers, flocked to the still forbidden land." On the morning of April 22, nearly a hundred thousand people lined the Oklahoma borders; "for miles on end horsemen, wagons, hacks, carriages, bicycles, and a host of vehicles beggaring description stood wheel to wheel awaiting the signal." Fifteen Santa Fe trains were jammed with people from platform to roof.

At noon, the starting flag dropped. Bugles and cannon signaled the opening of the "last" territory. Horsemen lunged forward; overloaded wagons collided and overturned. The trains steamed slowly forward, forced by army troops to keep a pace that would not give their passengers an undue advantage.

By sunset that day, settlers claimed twelve thousand homesteads, and the 1.92 million acres of the Oklahoma District were officially settled. Homesteaders threw up shelters for the night. By evening, Oklahoma City, that morning merely a spot on the prairie with cottonwoods and grass, had ten thousand people; Guthrie to the north had fifteen thousand. Speculators swiftly erected pay toilets, and drinking water cost as much as a beer.

The "Boomers" (those who waited for the signal) and "Sooners" (those who had jumped the gun) reflected the speed of western settlement. "Creation!" a character in Edna Ferber's novel *Cimarron* declared. "Hell! That took six days. This was done in one. It was History made in an hour—and I helped make it."

CHRONOLOGY

1849	Gold Rush to California
1859	More gold and silver discoveries in Colorado and Nevada
1862	Congress passes Homestead Act encouraging western settlement
1864	Nevada admitted to the Union ❖ Colonel John Chivington leads massacre of Indians at Sand Creek, Colorado
1865–1867	Sioux War against white miners and U.S. Army
1866	"Long drive" of cattle touches off cattle bonanzas
1867	Horace Greeley urges Easterners to "Go West, young man" ❖ National Grange of the Patrons of Husbandry (the Grange) founded to enrich farmers' lives
1867–1868	Policy of "small reservations" for Indians adopted
1873	Congress passes Timber Culture Act ❖ Big bonanza discovered on the Comstock Lode in Nevada
1874	Joseph F. Glidden invents barbed wire ❖ Discovery of gold in Dakota Territory sets off Black Hills Gold Rush
1876	Colorado admitted to the Union ❖ Custer and his men defeated and killed by the Sioux at battle of the Little Bighorn (June)
1883	Museum expedition discovers fewer than two hundred buffalo in the West
1886–1887	Severe drought and winter damage cattle and farming bonanzas
1887	Congress passes Dawes Severalty Act, making Indians individual landowners ❖ Hatch Act provides funds for establishment of agricultural experiment stations
1889	Washington, Montana, and the Dakotas admitted to the Union ❖ Oklahoma Territory opened to settlement
1890	Idaho and Wyoming admitted to the Union ❖ Teton Sioux massacred at battle of Wounded Knee, South Dakota (December)
1893	Young historian Frederick Jackson Turner analyzes closing of the frontier
1902	Congress passes National Reclamation Act (the Newlands Act)

Conclusion: The Meaning of the West

Between the Civil War and 1900, the West witnessed one of the greatest migrations in history. With the Native Americans driven into smaller and smaller areas, farms, ranches, mines, and cities took over the vast lands from the Mississippi to the Pacific. The 1890 census noted that for the first time in the country's history, "there can hardly be said to be a frontier line." Picking up the theme, Frederick Jackson Turner, a young history instructor at the University of Wisconsin, examined its importance in an influential 1893 paper, "The Significance of the Frontier in American History."

"The existence of an area of free land," Turner wrote, "its continuous recession, and the advance of American settlement westward, explain American development." It shaped customs and character; gave rise to independence, self-confidence, and individualism; and fostered invention and adaptation. Historians have substantially modified **Turner's thesis** by pointing to frontier conservatism and imitativeness, the influence of varying racial groups, and the persistence of European ideas and institutions. Most recently, they have shown that family and community loomed as large as individualism on the frontier; men, women, and children played very much the same roles as they had back home.

Rejecting Turner almost completely, a group of "new Western historians" has advanced a different and complex view of the West, and one with few heroes and heroines. Emphasizing the region's racial and ethnic diversity, these historians stress the role of women as well as men, trace struggles between economic interests instead of fights between gunslingers, and question the impact of development on the environment. White English-speaking Americans, they suggest, could be said to have conquered the West rather than settled it.

The West, in this view, was not settled by a wave of white migrants moving west across the continent (Turner's "frontier") but by a set of waves—Anglo, Mexican American, African American, Asian American, and others—moving in many directions and interacting with each other and with Native American cultures to produce the modern West. Nor did western history end in 1890 as Turner would have it. Instead, migration, development, and economic exploitation continued into the twentieth century, illustrated in the fact that the number of people who moved to the West after 1900 far exceeded those who had moved there before.

In both the nineteenth and twentieth centuries, there can be no doubt that the image of the frontier and the West influenced American development. Western lands attracted European, Latin American, and Asian immigrants, adding to the society's talent and diversity. The mines, forests, and farms of the West fueled the economy, sent raw materials to eastern factories, and fed the growing cities. Though defeated in warfare, the Native Americans and Mexicans influenced art, architecture, law, and western folklore. The West was the first American empire, and it had a profound impact on the American mind and imagination.

Recommended Reading

The best traditional account of the movement west is Ray Allen Billington, *Westward Expansion* (1967), which also has a first-rate bibliography. Walter Prescott Webb, *The Great Plains* (1931), offers a fascinating analysis of development on the Plains.

For examples of the work of "new Western historians," see Donald Worster, *Rivers of Empire* (1985), a powerful study of the "hydraulic" society, and his *Under Western Skies: Nature and History in the American West* (1992); William Cronon, *Nature's Metropolis: Chicago and the Great West* (1991), a provocative analysis of the relationship of Chicago and the West; Patricia Nelson Limerick, *The Legacy of Conquest* (1987); and Richard White, *"It's Your Misfortune and None of My Own": A History of the American West* (1991).

More recent authors have taken fresh and stimulating looks at older or ignored questions. Robert R. Dykstra, *The Cattle Towns* (1968), examines five Kansas cattle towns, with interesting results. Elliott West discusses the Plains in *The Contested Plains: Indians, Goldseekers, and the Rush to Colorado* (1998). Gregory Nobles, *American Frontiers: Cultural Encounters and Continental Conquest* (1997), is an engaging synthesis of frontier history.

There are a number of insightful recent studies of the environment, including Andrew C. Isenberg, *The Destruction of the Bison: An Environmental History, 1750–1920* (2000), Shepard Krech III, *The Ecological Indian: Myth and History* (1999), Karl Jacoby, *Crimes Against Nature: Squatters, Poachers, Thieves, and the Hidden History of American Conservation* (2001), and Dan L. Flores, *The Natural West: Environmental History in the Great Plains and Rocky Mountains* (2001). Susan Lee Johnson, *Roaring Camp: The Social World of the California Gold Rush* (2000), is a fascinating examination of the gold camps.

On the Native Americans, there are a number of valuable works, including R. Douglas Hurt's excellent *Indian*

Agriculture in America (1987), Janet A. McDonnell, *The Dispossession of the American Indian, 1887–1934* (1991), Robert A. Trennert, Jr., *The Phoenix Indian School* (1988), Scott Riney, *The Rapid City Indian School, 1898–1933* (1999), Paul H. Carlson, *The Plains Indians* (1998), and John William Sayer, *Ghost Dancing the Law: The Wounded Knee Trials* (1997).

Nell Irvin Painter, *Exodusters: Black Migration to Kansas After Reconstruction* (1976), tells the story of the Exodusters, as Monroe Lee Billington does for New Mexico's *Buffalo Soldiers, 1866–1900* (1991). Also see Frank N. Schubert, *Buffalo Soldiers, Braves, and the Brass* (1993).

Julie Roy Jeffrey, *Frontier Women: The Trans-Mississippi West* (1979), Joanna L. Stratton, *Pioneer Women: Voices from the Kansas Frontier* (1981), and Deena J. González, *Refusing the Favor: The Spanish-Mexican Women of Santa Fe, 1820–1880* (1999), are perceptive works on a neglected topic. John Mack Faragher, *Women and Men on the Overland Trail* (1979), and John Phillip Reid, *Law for the Elephant* (1980), examine relationships on the trails west.

For a list of additional titles related to this chapter's topics, please see http://www.ablongman.com/divine.

Suggested Web Sites

Indian Affairs: Laws and Treaties, compiled and edited by Charles J. Kappler (1904)

http://digital.library.okstate.edu/kappler

This digitized text at Oklahoma State University includes preremoval treaties with the Five Civilized Tribes and other tribes.

Native American Documents Project

http://www.csusm.edu/projects/nadp/nadp.htm

California State University at San Marcos has several digital documents relating to Native Americans on this site.

Geronimo

http://odur.let.rug.nl/~usa/B/geronimo/geronixx.htm

This site contains biographical and autobiographical information about the famous Native American who resisted European American domination.

National Museum of the American Indian

http://www.si.edu/nmai

The Smithsonian Institution maintains this site, providing information about the museum. The museum is dedicated to everything about Native Americans.

The Northern Great Plains, 1880–1920: Photographs from the Fred Hultstrand and F. A. Pazandak Photograph Collections

http://memory.loc.gov/ammem/award97/ndfahtml/ngphome.html

This American Memory site from the Library of Congress contains "two collections from the Institute for Regional Studies at North Dakota State University" with "900 photographs of rural and small town life at the turn of the century." Included are "images of sod homes and the people who built them; images of farms and the machinery that made them prosper; and images of one-room schools and the children that were educated in them."

On the Trail in Kansas

http://www.kancoll.org/galtrl.htm

This Kansas Collection site holds several good primary sources with images concerning the Oregon trail and America's early movement westward.

"California as I Saw It": First-Person Narratives of California's Early Years, 1849–1900

http://memory.loc.gov/ammem/cbhtml/cbhome.html

This site is a part of the American Memory series and contains "full texts and illustrations of 190 works documenting the formative era of California's history through eyewitness accounts." It covers the Gold Rush, the interaction of various groups, and the settling of the region.

Home on the Range/Cowboy Heritage

http://history.cc.ukans.edu/heritage/old_west/cowboy.html

This site tells the history of the cattle trails and towns such as Dodge City, with useful text, links, documents, and maps.

The Evolution of the Conservation Movement, 1850–1920

http://memory.loc.gov/ammem/amrvhtml/conshome.html

This American Memory site brings together scores of primary sources and photographs about "the historical formation and cultural foundations of the movement to conserve and protect America's natural heritage."

Heroes and Villains in Kansas

http://www.kancoll.org/galhero.htm

The Kansas Collection Gallery of both famous and little-known people who made up the history of the state.

Chapter 18

The Corliss engine, a "mechanical marvel" at the Centennial Exposition, was a prime example of the giantism so admired by the public. ❖

The Industrial Society

A Machine Culture

In 1876, Americans celebrated their first century of independence. Survivors of a recent civil war, they observed the centenary proudly and rather self-consciously, in song and speech, and above all in a grand Centennial Exposition held in Philadelphia, Pennsylvania.

Spread over nearly 300 acres, in 180 buildings, the exposition focused more on the present than the past. Fairgoers strolled through exhibits of life in colonial times, then hurried off to see the main attractions: machines, inventions, and products of the new industrial era. They saw linoleum, a new, easy-to-clean floor covering. For the first time, they tasted root beer, supplied by a young druggist named Charles Hires, and the exotic banana, wrapped in foil and selling for a dime. They saw their first bicycle, an awkward high-wheeled contraption with solid tires.

A Japanese pavilion generated widespread interest in the culture of Japan. There was also a women's building, the first ever in a major exposition. Inside were displayed paintings and sculpture by women artists, along with rows of textile machinery staffed by female operators.

In the entire exposition, machinery was the focus, and Machinery Hall was the most popular building. Here were the products of an ever improving civilization. Long lines of the curious waited to see the telephone, Alexander Graham Bell's new device. ("My God, it talks!" the emperor of Brazil exclaimed.) Thomas A. Edison displayed several recent inventions, while nearby, whirring machines turned out bricks, chewing tobacco, and other products. Fairgoers saw the first public display of the typewriter, Elisha Otis's new elevator, and the Westinghouse railroad air brake.

But above all, they crowded around the mighty Corliss engine, the focal point of the exposition. A giant steam engine, it dwarfed everything else in Machinery Hall, its twin vertical cylinders towering almost four stories in the air. Alone, it supplied power for the eight thousand other machines, large and small, on the exposition grounds. Poorly designed, the Corliss was soon obsolete, but for the moment it captured the nation's imagination. It symbolized swift movement toward an industrial and urban society. John Greenleaf Whittier, the aging rural poet, likened it to the snake in the Garden of Eden and refused to see it.

AS WHITTIER FEARED, the United States was fast becoming an industrial society. Developments earlier in the century laid the basis, but the most spectacular advances in industrialization came during the three decades after the Civil War. At the start of the war, the country lagged well behind industrializing nations such as Great Britain, France, and Germany. By 1900, it had vaulted far into the lead, with a manufacturing output that exceeded the *combined* output of its three European rivals. Over the same years, cities grew, technology advanced, and farm production rose. Developments in manufacturing, mining, agriculture, transportation, and communications changed society.

OUTLINE

FEATURE ESSAY

In this change, railroads, steel, oil, and other industries, all shaped by the hands of labor, played a leading role. Many Americans eagerly welcomed the new directions. William Dean Howells, a leading novelist, visited the Centennial Exposition and stood in awe before the Corliss. Comparing it to the paintings and sculpture on display, Howells preferred the machine: "It is in these things of iron and steel," he said, "that the national genius most freely speaks."

Industrial Development

American industry owed its remarkable growth to several considerations. It fed on an abundance of natural resources: coal, iron, timber, petroleum, waterpower. An iron manufacturer likened the nation to "a gigantic bowl filled with treasure." Labor was also abundant, drawn from American farm families and the hosts of European immigrants who flocked to American mines, cities, and factories. Nearly eight million immigrants arrived in the 1870s and 1880s; another fifteen million came between 1890 and 1914—large figures for a nation whose total population in 1900 was about seventy-six million people.

The burgeoning population led to expanded markets, which new devices such as the telegraph and telephone helped to exploit. The swiftly growing urban populations devoured goods, and the railroads, spreading pell-mell across the land, linked the cities together and opened a national market. Within its boundaries, the United States had the largest free-trade market in the world, while tariff barriers partially protected its producers from outside competition.

Expansive market and labor conditions buoyed the confidence of investors, European and American, who provided large amounts of capital. Technological progress, so remarkable in these years, doomed some older industries (tallow, for example) but increased productivity in others, such as the kerosene industry, and created entirely new industries as well. Through inventions such as the harvester and the combine, it also helped foster a firm agricultural base, on which industrialization depended.

Eager to promote economic growth, government at all levels—federal, state, and local—gave manufacturers money, land, and other resources. Other benefits, too, flowed from the American system of government: stability, commitment to the concept of private property, and, initially at least, a reluctance to regulate industrial activity. Unlike their European counterparts, American manufacturers faced few legal or social barriers, and their main domestic rivals, the southern planters, had lost political power in the Civil War.

In this atmosphere, entrepreneurs flourished. Taking steps crucial for industrialization, they organized, managed, and assumed the financial risks of the new enterprises. Admirers called them captains of industry; foes labeled them robber barons. To some degree, they were both—creative *and* acquisitive. If sometimes they seemed larger than life, it was because they dealt in concepts, distances, and quantities often unknown to earlier generations.

Industrial growth, it must be remembered, was neither a simple nor steady nor inevitable process. It involved human decisions and brought with it large social benefits and costs. Growth varied from industry to industry and from year to year. It was concentrated in the Northeast, where in 1890, more than 85 percent of America's manufactured goods originated. The more sparsely settled West provided raw materials, while the South, although making major gains in iron, textiles, and tobacco, had to rebuild after wartime devastation. In 1890, the industrial production of the entire South amounted in value to about half that of the state of New York.

Still, industrial development proceeded at an extraordinary pace. Between 1865 and 1914, the real gross national product—the total monetary value of all goods and services produced in a year, with prices held stable—grew at a rate of more than 4 percent a year, increasing about eightfold overall. As Robert Higgs, an economic historian, noted, "Never before had such rapid growth continued for so long."

An Empire on Rails

Genuine revolutions happen rarely, but a major one occurred in the nineteenth century: a revolution in transportation and communications. When the nineteenth century began, people traveled and communicated much as they had for centuries before; when it ended, the railroad, the telegraph, the telephone, and the oceangoing steamship had wrought enormous changes.

The steamship sliced in half the time of the Atlantic crossing and, not dependent on wind and tide, introduced new regularity in the movement of goods and passengers. The telegraph, flashing messages almost instantaneously along miles of wire (400,000 miles of it in the early 1880s), transformed communications, as did the telephone a little later. But the railroad worked the largest changes of all. Along with Bessemer steel, it was the most significant technical innovation of the century.

"Emblem of Motion and Power"

The railroad dramatically affected economic and social life. Economic growth would have occurred without it, of course; canals, inland steamboats, and the country's superb system of interior waterways already provided the outlines of an effective transportation network. But the railroad added significantly to the network and contributed advantages all its own.

Those advantages included more direct routes, greater speed, greater safety and comfort than other modes of land travel, more dependable schedules, a larger volume of traffic, and year-round service. A day's land travel on stagecoach or horseback might cover fifty miles. The railroad covered 50 miles in about an hour, 700 miles in a day. It went where canals and rivers did not go—directly to the loading platforms of great factories or across the arid West. As construction crews pushed tracks onward, vast areas of the continent opened for settlement.

Consequently, American railroads differed from European ones. In Europe, railroads were usually built between cities and towns that already existed; they carried mostly the same goods that earlier forms of transportation had. In the United States, they did that and more: they often created the very towns they then served, and they ended up carrying cattle from Texas, fruit from Florida, and other goods that had never been carried before.

Linking widely separated cities and villages, the railroad ended the relative isolation and self-sufficiency of the country's "island communities." It tied people together, brought in outside products, fostered greater interdependence, and encouraged economic specialization. Under its stimulus, Chicago supplied meat to the nation, Minneapolis supplied grain, and St. Louis, beer. For these and other communities, the railroad made possible a national market and in so doing pointed the way toward mass production and mass consumption, two of the hallmarks of twentieth-century society.

It also pointed the way toward later business development. The railroad, as Alfred D. Chandler, a historian of business, has written, was "the nation's first big business"; it worked out "the modern ways of finance, management, labor relations, competition, and government regulation."

A railroad corporation, far-flung and complex, was a new kind of business. It stretched over thousands of miles, employed thousands of people, dealt with countless customers, and required a scale of organization and decision making unknown in earlier business. Railroad managers never met most customers or even many employees; thus arose new problems in marketing and labor relations. Year by year, railroad companies consumed large quantities of iron, steel, coal, lumber, and glass, stimulating growth and employment in numerous industries.

No wonder, then, that the railroad captured so completely the country's imagination. Walt Whitman, a poet who celebrated American achievement, chanted the locomotive's praises:

Like no form of transportation before it, the railroad could meet the challenge presented by the varied topography of the land west of the Mississippi River—from the Great Plains to the vast deserts, from the deep gorges to the Rocky Mountains. ❖

Thy black cylindric body, golden brass and silvery steel,
. . . .
Thy great protruding head-light fix'd in front,

Thy long, pale, floating vapor-pennants, tinged with delicate purple,
The dense and murky clouds out-belching from thy smoke-stack,
Thy knitted frame, thy springs and valves, the tremulous twinkle of thy wheels,

Thy train of cars behind, obedient, merrily following,
Through gale or calm, now swift, now slack, yet steadily careening;
Type of the modern—emblem of motion and power—pulse of the continent,
. . . .
Fierce-throated beauty!

For nearly a hundred years—the railroad era lasted through the 1940s—children gathered at depots, paused in the fields to wave as the fast express flashed by, listened at night to far-off whistles, and wondered what lay down the tracks. They lived in a world grown smaller.

Building the Empire

When Lee surrendered at Appomattox in 1865, the country already had 35,000 miles of track, and much of the railroad system east of the Mississippi River was in place. Farther west, the rail network stood poised on the edge of settlement. Although southern railroads were in shambles from the war, the United States had nearly as much railroad track as the rest of the world.

After the Civil War, rail construction increased by leaps and bounds. From 35,000 miles in 1865, the network expanded to 93,000 miles in 1880; 166,000 in 1890; and 193,000 in 1900—more than in all Europe, including Russia. Mileage peaked at 254,037 miles in 1916, just before the industry began its long decline into the mid-twentieth century.

To build such an empire took vast amounts of capital—more than $4.5 billion by 1880, before even half of it was complete. American and European investors provided some of the money; government supplied the rest. In all, local governments gave railroad companies about $300 million, and state governments added $228 million more. The federal government loaned nearly $65 million to a half dozen western railroads and donated millions of acres of the public domain. Between 1850 and 1871, some eighty railroads received more than 170 million acres of land.

Almost 90 percent of the federal land grants lay in twenty states west of the Mississippi River. Federal land grants helped build 18,738 miles of track, less than 8 percent of the system. The land was frequently distant and difficult to market. Railroad companies

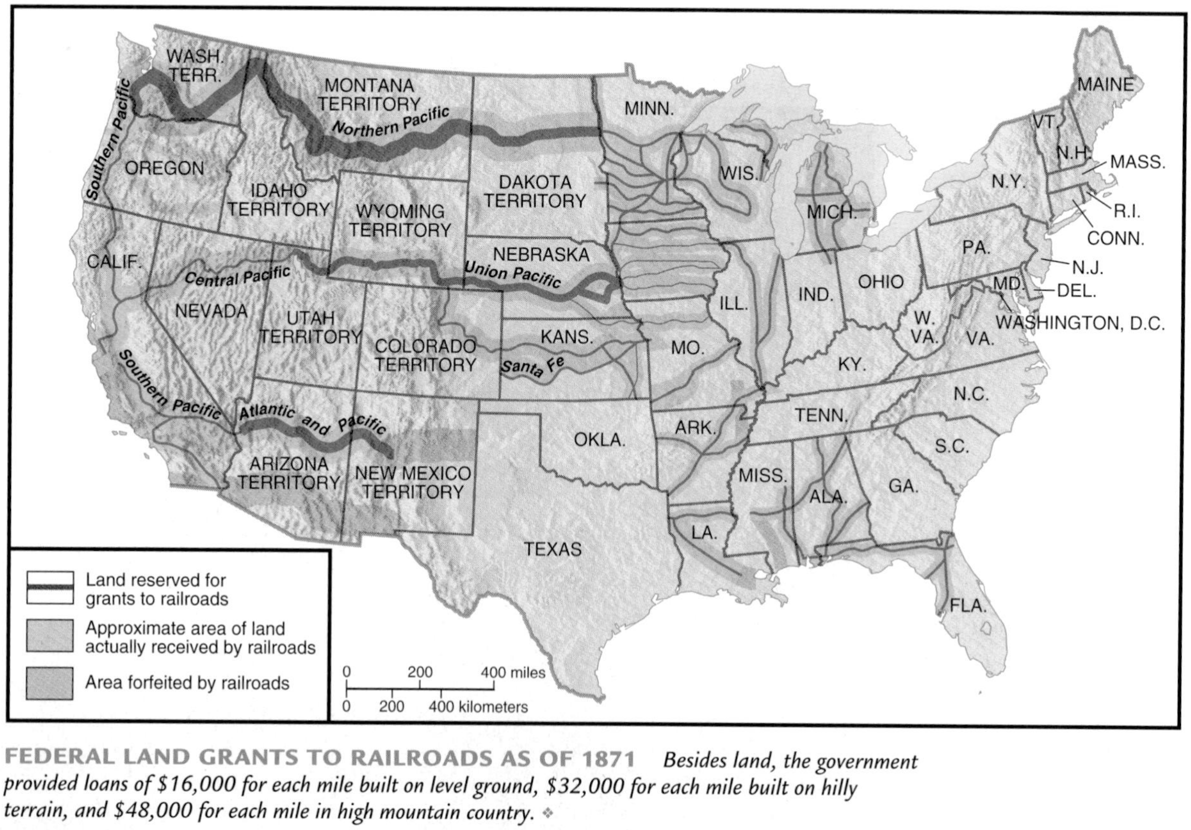

FEDERAL LAND GRANTS TO RAILROADS AS OF 1871 *Besides land, the government provided loans of $16,000 for each mile built on level ground, $32,000 for each mile built on hilly terrain, and $48,000 for each mile in high mountain country.*

RAILROAD CONSTRUCTION, 1830–1920

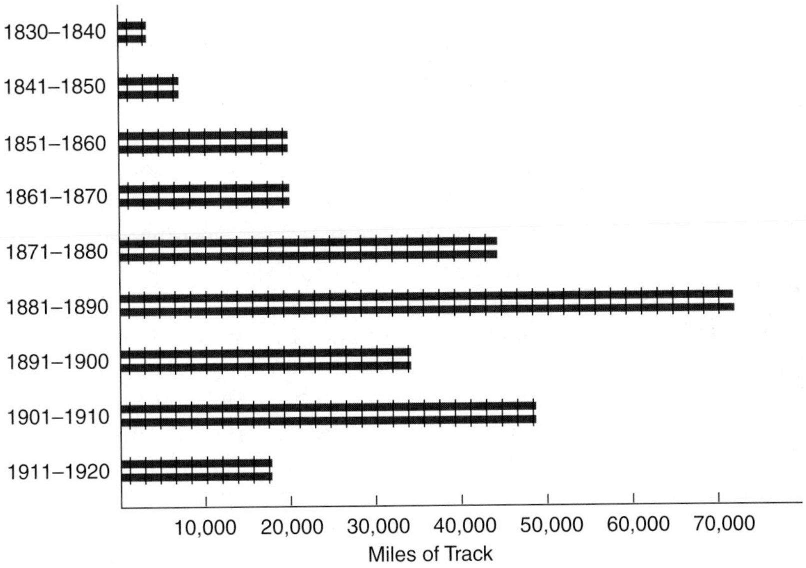

Source: U.S. Bureau of the Census, *Historical Statistics of the United States, Colonial Times to 1970,* Bicentennial Edition, Washington, D.C., 1975.

sometimes sold it to raise cash, but more often they used it as security for bonds or loans.

Beyond doubt, the grants of cash and land promoted waste and corruption. The companies built fast and wastefully, eager to collect the subsidies that went with each mile of track. Wanting quick profits, some owners formed separate construction companies to which they awarded lavish contracts. In this way, the notorious Crédit Mobilier, a construction company controlled by an inner ring on the Union Pacific, enriched its owners in the 1860s, while the Contract and Finance Company did the same on the Central Pacific. The Crédit Mobilier bribed congressmen and state legislators to avoid investigation of its activities. The grants also enabled railroads to build into territories that were pledged to the Indians, thus contributing to the wanton destruction of Indian life.

Yet, on balance, the grants probably worked more benefits than evils. As Congress had hoped, the grants were the lure for railroad building across the rugged, unsettled West, where it would be years before the railroads' revenues would repay their construction. Farmers, ranchers, and merchants poured into the newly opened areas, settling the country and boosting the value of government and private land nearby. The grants seemed necessary in a nation which, unlike Europe, expected private enterprise to build the railroads. In return for government aid, Congress required the railroads to carry government freight, troops, and mail at substantially reduced rates—resulting in savings to the government of almost $1 billion between 1850 and 1945. In no other cases of federal subsidies to carriers—canals, highways, and airlines—did Congress exact specific benefits in return.

Linking the Nation via Trunk Lines

The early railroads may seem to have linked different regions, but in fact they did not. Built with little regard for through traffic, they were designed more to protect local interests than to tap outside markets. Many extended less than fifty miles. To avoid cooperating with other lines, they adopted conflicting schedules, built separate depots, and above all, used different gauges. Gauges, the distance between the rails, ranged from 4 feet $8^{1}/_{2}$ inches, which became the standard gauge, to 6 feet. Without special equipment, trains of one gauge could not run on tracks of another.

The Civil War showed the value of fast long-distance transportation, and after 1865, railroad managers worked to provide it. In a burst of consolidation, the large companies swallowed the small; integrated rail networks became a reality. Railroads also adopted standard schedules, signals, and equipment and finally, in 1886, the standard gauge. In 1866, in a dramatic innovation to speed traffic, railroad companies introduced fast freight lines that pooled cars for service between cities.

In the Northeast, four great **trunk lines** took shape, all intended to link eastern seaports with the rich traffic of the Great Lakes and western rivers. Like a massive river system, trunk lines drew traffic from

Cornelius the "Commodore" Vanderbilt, in this cartoon of the "Modern Colossus of (Rail) Roads," is shown towering over his rail empire and pulling the strings to control its operations. In addition to the New York Central, Vanderbilt gained control of the Hudson River Railroad, the Lake Shore and Michigan Southern Railway, and the Canadian Southern Railway. ❖

dozens of tributaries (feeder lines) and carried it to major markets. The Baltimore and Ohio (B & O), which reached Chicago in 1874, was one; the Erie Railroad, which ran from New York to Chicago, was another. The Erie competed bitterly with the New York Central Railroad, the third trunk line, and its owner, Cornelius Vanderbilt—the "Commodore"—a crusty old multimillionaire from the shipping business.

Nearly seventy years old when he first entered railroading, Vanderbilt wasted no time. In 1867, he took over the New York Central and merged it with other lines to provide a track from New York City to Buffalo and Chicago. When he died in 1877, his Central operated more than 4500 miles of track.

J. Edgar Thomson and Thomas A. Scott built the fourth trunk line, the Pennsylvania Railroad, which initially ran from Philadelphia to Pittsburgh. Restless and energetic, they dreamed of a rail empire stretching through the South and West. An aggressive business leader, Scott expanded the Pennsylvania system to Cincinnati, Indianapolis, St. Louis, and Chicago in 1869; New York City in 1871; and Baltimore and Washington soon thereafter.

In the war-damaged South, consolidation took longer. As Reconstruction waned, northern and European capital rebuilt and integrated the southern lines, especially during the 1880s, when rail construction in the South led the nation. By 1900, the South had five large systems linking its major cities and farming and industrial regions. Four decades after the secession crisis, these systems tied the South into a national transportation network.

Over that rail system, passengers and freight moved in relative speed, comfort, and safety. Automatic couplers (1867), air brakes (1869), refrigerator cars (1867), dining cars, heated cars, electric switches, and stronger locomotives transformed railroad service. George Pullman's lavish sleeping cars became popular. Handsome depots, such as New York's Grand Central and Washington's Union Station, were erected at major terminals. Passenger miles per year increased from 5 billion in 1870 to 16 billion in 1900.

In November 1883, the railroads even changed time. Ending the crazy quilt jumble of local times that caused scheduling difficulties, the American Railway Association divided the country into four time zones and adopted the modern system of standard time. Congress took thirty-five years longer; it adopted standard time in 1918, in the midst of World War I.

Rails Across the Continent

The dream of a transcontinental railroad, linking the Atlantic and Pacific oceans, stretched back many years but had always been lost to sectional quarrels over the route. In 1862 and 1864, with the South out of the picture, Congress moved to build the first transcontinental railroad. It chartered the Union Pacific Railroad Company to build westward from Nebraska and the Central Pacific Railroad Company to build eastward from the Pacific Coast. For each mile built, the two companies received from Congress 20 square miles of land in alternate sections along the track. For each mile, they also received a thirty-year loan of $16,000, $32,000, or $48,000, depending on the difficulty of the terrain over which they built.

Construction began simultaneously at Omaha and Sacramento in 1863, lagged during the war, and moved vigorously ahead after 1865. It became a race, each company vying for land, loans, and potential markets. General Grenville M. Dodge, a tough Union army veteran, served as construction chief for the Union Pacific, while Charles Crocker, a former Sacramento dry goods merchant, led the Central

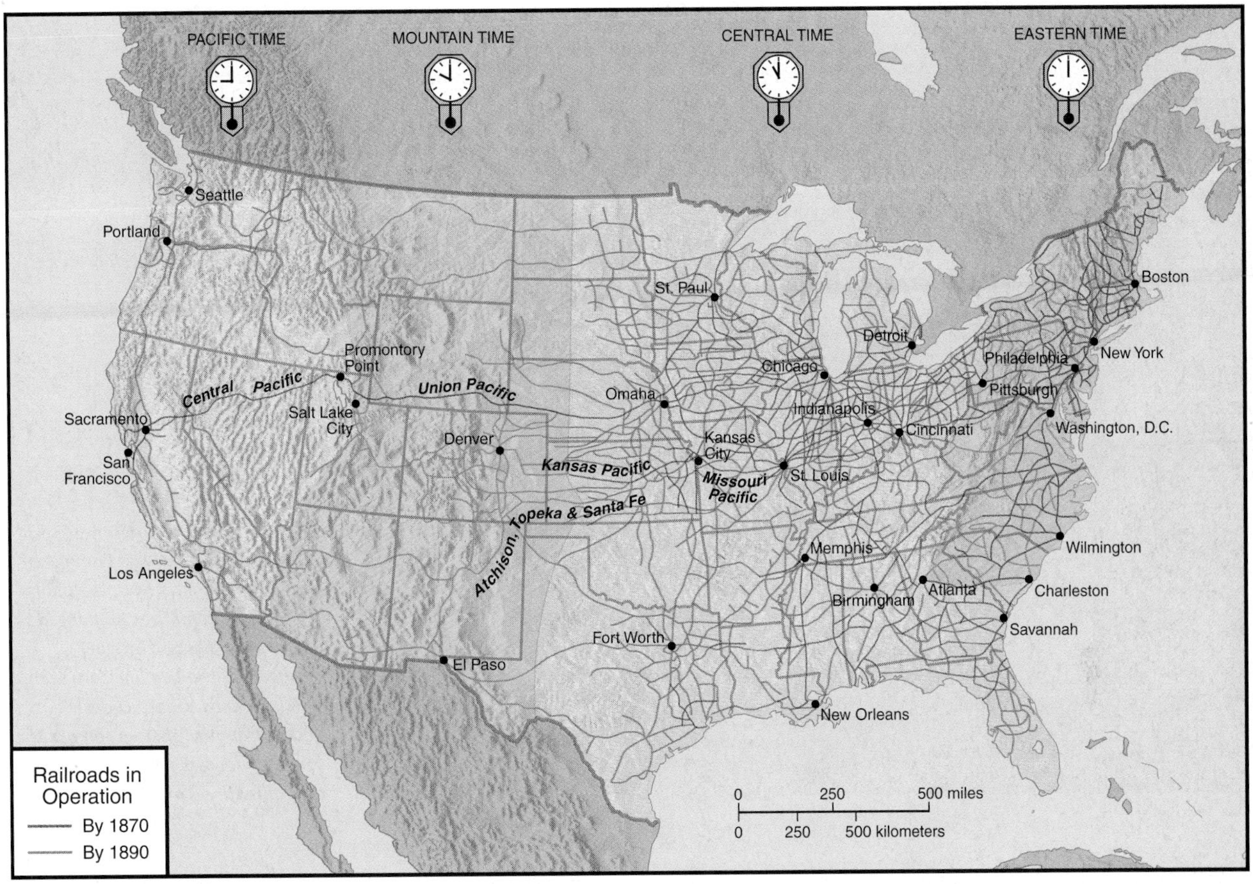

RAILROADS, 1870 AND 1890 *In the last quarter of the nineteenth century, railroads expanded into Texas, the far Southwest, and the Northwest, carrying settlers, businesses, and government to the far-flung areas.* ❖

Pacific crews. Dodge organized an army of ten thousand workers, many of them ex-soldiers and Irish immigrants. Pushing rapidly westward, he encountered frequent attacks from Native Americans defending their lands, but he had the advantage of building over flat prairie.

Crocker faced more trying conditions in the high Sierra Nevada along California's eastern border. After several experiments, he decided that Chinese laborers worked best, and he hired six thousand of them, most brought directly from China. "I built the Central Pacific," Crocker enjoyed boasting, but the Chinese crews in fact did the awesome work. Under the most difficult conditions, they dug, blasted, and pushed their way slowly east.

On May 10, 1869, the two lines met at Promontory, Utah, near the northern tip of the Great Salt Lake. Dodge's crews had built 1086 miles of track, Crocker's 689. The Union Pacific and Central Pacific presidents hammered in a golden spike (both missed it on the first try), and the dreamed-of connection was made. The telegraph flashed the news east and west, setting off wild celebrations. A photograph was taken, but it included none of the Chinese who had worked so hard to build the road; they were all asked to step aside.

The transcontinental railroad symbolized American unity and progress. Along with the Suez Canal, completed the same year, it helped knit the world together. Bret Harte, the exuberant poet of the West, wrote of Promontory:

> What was it the Engines said,
> Pilots touching,—head to head
> Facing on the single track,
> Half a world behind each back?

Three more railroads reached the coast in 1883: the Northern Pacific, running from Minnesota to Oregon; the Atchison, Topeka, and Santa Fe, connecting Kansas City and Los Angeles; and the powerful Southern Pacific, running from San Francisco and Los Angeles to New Orleans. Ten years later James J. Hill's superbly built Great Northern Railway extended from Minneapolis–St. Paul to Seattle, Washington.

By the 1890s, business leaders talked comfortably of railroad systems stretching deep into South America and across the Bering Strait to Asia, Europe, and

After the last spike was hammered in at Promontory, Utah, the pilots of the two locomotives exchanged champagne toasts. The chief engineers of the two lines are seen shaking hands. Conspicuously absent from the photograph are the Chinese laborers who helped build the railroad. ❖

Africa. In an age of progress, anything seemed possible. "The American," said the *Chicago Tribune*, "intelligent and self-reliant, has banished forever the impossible from his philosophy."

Problems of Growth

Overbuilding during the 1870s and 1880s caused serious problems for the railroads. Lines paralleled each other, and where they did not, speculators such as Jay Gould often laid one down to force a rival line to buy it at inflated prices. While many managers worked to improve service, Gould and others bought and sold railroads like toys, watered their stock, and milked their assets. By 1885, almost one-third of railroad stock represented "water," that is, stock distributed in excess of the real value of the assets.

Competition was severe, and managers fought desperately for traffic. They offered special rates and favors: free passes for large shippers; low rates on bulk freight, carload lots, and long hauls; and, above all, rebates—secret, privately negotiated reductions below published rates. Fierce rate wars broke out frequently, convincing managers that ruthless competition helped no one. Rebates made more enemies than friends.

Managers such as Albert Fink, the brilliant vice president of the Louisville & Nashville, tried first to arrange pooling agreements, a way to control competition by sharing traffic. Fink directed the Eastern Trunk Line Association (1877), which divided westbound traffic among the four trunk lines. Similar associations pooled traffic in the South and West, but none survived the intense pressures of competition. Legally unenforceable, pools were handshake agreements among individuals who did not always keep their word. Customers grew adept at bargaining for rebates and other privileges, and railroads rarely felt able to refuse them. In the first six months of 1880, the New York Central alone granted six thousand special rates.

Failing to cooperate, railroad owners next tried to consolidate. Through purchase, lease, and merger, they gobbled up competitors and built "self-sustaining systems" that dominated entire regions. But many of the systems, expensive and unwieldy, collapsed in the Panic of 1893. By mid-1894, a quarter of the railroads were bankrupt. The victims of the panic included such legendary names as the Erie, B & O, Santa Fe, Northern Pacific, and Union Pacific.

Needing money, railroads turned naturally to bankers, who finally imposed order on the industry. J. Pierpont Morgan, head of the New York investment house of J. P. Morgan and Company, took the lead. Massively built, with eyes so piercing they seemed like the headlights of an onrushing train, Morgan was the most powerful figure in American finance. He liked efficiency, combination, and order. He disliked "wasteful" competition. In 1885, during a bruising rate war between the New York Central and the Pennsylvania, Morgan invited the combatants to a conference aboard his palatial steam yacht, *Corsair.* Cruising on Long Island Sound, he arranged a traffic-sharing agreement and collected a million-dollar fee. Bringing peace to an industry could be profitable. It also satisfied Morgan's passion for stability.

After 1893, Morgan and a few other bankers refinanced ailing railroads, and in the process they took control of the industry. Their methods were direct: Fixed costs and debt were ruthlessly cut, new stock was issued to provide capital, rates were stabilized, rebates and competition were eliminated, and control was vested in a "voting trust" of handpicked trustees. Between 1894 and 1898, Morgan reorganized—critics said "Morganized"—the Southern Railway, the Erie, the Northern Pacific, and the B & O. In addition, he took over a half dozen other important railroads. By 1900, he was a dominant figure in American railroading.

As the new century began, the railroads had pioneered the patterns followed by most other industries. Seven giant systems controlled nearly two-thirds of the mileage, and they in turn answered to a few investment banking firms such as the house of Morgan. For good and ill, a national transportation network, centralized and relatively efficient, was now in place.

An Industrial Empire

The new industrial empire was based on a number of dramatic innovations, including steel, oil, and inventions of all kinds that transformed ordinary life. In this process, steel was as important as the railroads. Harder and more durable than other kinds of iron, steel wrought changes in manufacturing, agriculture, transportation, and architecture. It permitted construction of longer bridges, taller buildings, stronger railroad track, deadlier weapons, better plows, heavier machinery, and faster ships. Made in great furnaces by strong men, it symbolized the tough, often brutal nature of industrial society. From the 1870s onward, steel output became the worldwide accepted measure of industrial progress, and nations around the globe vied for leadership.

The Bessemer process, developed in the late 1850s by Henry Bessemer in England and independently by William Kelly in the United States, made increased steel production possible. Both Bessemer and Kelly discovered that a blast of air forced through molten iron burned off carbon and other impurities, resulting in steel of a more uniform and durable quality. The discovery transformed the industry. While earlier methods produced amounts a person could lift, a Bessemer converter handled 5 tons of molten metal at a time. The mass production of steel was now possible.

Carnegie and Steel

Bessemer plants demanded extensive capital investment, abundant raw materials, and sophisticated production techniques. Using chemical and other processes, the plants required research departments, which became critical components of later American industries. Costly to build, they limited entry into the industry to the handful who could afford them.

Great steel districts arose in Pennsylvania, Ohio, and Alabama—in each case around large coal deposits that fueled the huge furnaces. Pittsburgh became the center of the industry, its giant mills employing thousands of workers. Output shot up. In 1874, the United States produced less than half the amount of pig iron produced in Great Britain. By 1890, it took the lead, and in 1900, it produced four times as much as Britain.

Iron ore abounded in the fabulous deposits near Lake Superior, the greatest deposits in the world. In the mines of the Mesabi Range in Minnesota, giant steam shovels loaded ore onto railroad cars for transport to ships on the Great Lakes. Powered lifts, self-loading devices, and other innovations sped the process. "By the turn of the century," historian Peter Temin noted,

INTERNATIONAL STEEL PRODUCTION, 1880–1914

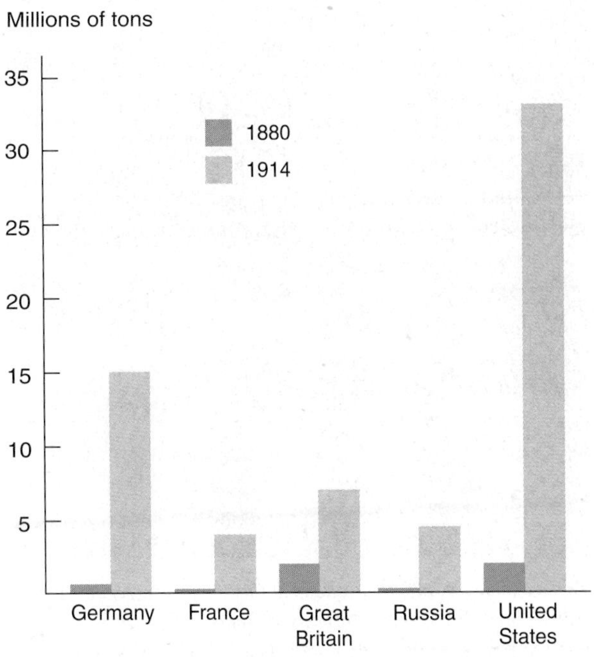

"the transport of Lake ores had become an intricate ballet of large and complex machines."

Like the railroads, steel companies grew larger and larger. In 1880, only nine companies could produce more than 100,000 tons a year. By the early 1890s, several companies exceeded 250,000 tons, and two—including the great Carnegie Steel Company—produced more than 1 million tons a year. As operations expanded, managers needed more complex skills. Product development, marketing, and consumer preferences became important. Competition was fierce, and steel companies, like the railroads, tried secret agreements, pools, and consolidation. During the 1880s and 1890s, they moved toward **vertical integration,** a type of organization in which a single company owns and controls the entire process from the unearthing of the raw materials to the manufacture and sale of the finished product. Such companies combined coal and iron mines, transportation companies, blast furnaces, and rolling mills into integrated networks.

The machinery dwarfs the workers in this colored engraving of steel making using the Bessemer process at Andrew Carnegie's Pittsburgh steel works. Men worked twelve hours a day in the blazing heat and deafening roar of the machines. ❖

Andrew Carnegie emerged as the undisputed master of the industry. Born in Scotland, he came to the United States in 1848 at the age of 12. Settling near Pittsburgh, he went to work as a bobbin boy in a cotton mill, earning $1.20 a week. He soon took a job in a telegraph office, where in 1852 his hard work and skill caught the eye of Thomas A. Scott of the Pennsylvania Railroad. Starting as Scott's personal telegrapher, Carnegie spent a total of twelve years on the Pennsylvania, a training ground for company managers. By 1859, he had become a divisional superintendent. He was 24 years old.

Soon rich from shrewd investments, Carnegie plunged into the steel industry in 1872. On the Monongahela River south of Pittsburgh, he built the giant J. Edgar Thomson Steel Works, named after the president of the Pennsylvania Railroad, his biggest customer. With his warmth and salesmanship, he attracted able partners and subordinates such as Henry Clay Frick and Charles M. Schwab, whom he drove hard and paid well. Although he had written magazine articles defending the rights of workers, Carnegie kept the wages of the laborers in his mills low and disliked unions. With the help of Frick, he crushed a violent strike at his Homestead works in 1892 (see p. 535).

In 1878, he won the steel contract for the Brooklyn Bridge. During the next decade, as city building boomed, he converted the huge Homestead works near Pittsburgh to the manufacture of structural beams and angles, which went into the New York City elevated railway, the first skyscrapers, and the Washington Monument. Carnegie profits mounted: from $2 million in 1888 to $40 million in 1900. That year, Carnegie Steel alone produced more steel than Great Britain. Employing twenty thousand people, it was the largest industrial company in the world.

In 1901, Carnegie sold it. Believing that wealth brought social obligations, he wanted to devote his full time to philanthropy. He found a buyer in J. Pierpont Morgan, who in the late 1890s had put together several steel companies, including Federal Steel, Carnegie's chief rival. Carnegie Steel had blocked Morgan's well-known desire for control, and in mid-1900, when a war loomed between the two interests, Morgan decided to buy Carnegie out. In early January 1901, Morgan told Charles M. Schwab: "Go and find his price." Schwab cornered Carnegie on the golf course; Carnegie listened, and the next day he handed Schwab a note, scribbled in blunt pencil, asking almost a half billion dollars. Morgan glanced at it and said, "I accept this price."

Drawing other companies into the combination, Morgan on March 3, 1901, announced the creation of the United States Steel Corporation. The new firm was capitalized at $1.4 billion, the first billion-dollar company. It absorbed more than 200 other companies, employed 168,000 people, and produced 9 million tons of iron and steel a year. It controlled three-fifths of the country's steel business. Soon there were other giants, including Bethlehem Steel, Republic Steel, and National Steel. As the nineteenth century ended, steel products—rare just thirty years before—had altered the landscape. Huge firms, investment bankers, and professional managers dominated the industry.

John D. Rockefeller, satirized in a 1901 Puck *cartoon, is enthroned on oil, the base of his empire; his crown is girded by other holdings.* ✦

Rockefeller and Oil

Petroleum worked comparable changes in the economic and social landscape, although mostly after 1900. Distilled into oil, it lubricated the machinery of the industrial age. There seemed little use for gasoline (the internal combustion engine had only just been developed), but kerosene, another major distillate, brought inexpensive illumination into almost every home. Whale oil, cottonseed oil, and even tallow candles were expensive to burn; consequently, many people went to bed at nightfall. Kerosene lamps opened the evenings to activity, altering the patterns of life.

Like other changes in these years, the oil boom happened with surprising speed. In the mid-1850s, petroleum was a bothersome, smelly fluid that occasionally rose to the surface of springs and streams. Clever entrepreneurs bottled it in patent medicines; a few scooped up enough to burn. Other entrepreneurs soon found that drilling reached pockets of oil beneath the earth. In 1859, Edwin L. Drake drilled the first oil well near Titusville in northwest Pennsylvania, and the "black gold" fever struck. Chemists soon discovered ways to transform petroleum into lubricating oil, grease, paint, wax, varnish, naphtha, and paraffin. Within a few years, there was a world market in oil.

At first, growth of the oil industry was chaotic. Early drillers and refiners produced for local markets, and since drilling wells and even erecting refineries cost little, competition flourished. Output fluctuated dramatically; prices rose and fell, with devastating effect. Refineries—usually a collection of wooden shacks and tanks—were centered in Cleveland and Pittsburgh, near the original oil-producing regions.

A young merchant from Cleveland named John D. Rockefeller imposed order on the industry. "I had an ambition to build," he later recalled, and beginning in 1863 at the age of 24, he built the Standard Oil Company, soon to become one of the titans of corporate business. Like Morgan, Rockefeller considered competition wasteful, small-scale enterprise inefficient, and consolidation the path of the future. Consolidation "revolutionized the way of doing business all over the world," he said. "The time was ripe for it. It had to come, though all we saw at the moment was the need to save ourselves from wasteful conditions."

Methodically, Rockefeller absorbed or destroyed competitors in Cleveland and elsewhere. As ruthless in his methods as Carnegie, he lacked the steel master's spontaneous charm. He was distant and taciturn, a man of deep religious beliefs who taught Bible classes at Cleveland's Erie Street Baptist Church. Like Carnegie, he demanded efficiency, relentless cost cutting, and the latest technology. He attracted exceptional lieutenants—although, as one said, he could see farther ahead than any of them, "and then see around the corner."

"Nothing in haste, nothing ill-done," Rockefeller often said to himself. "Your future hangs on every day that passes." Paying careful attention to detail, he counted the stoppers in barrels, shortened barrel hoops to save metal, and, in one famous incident, reduced the number of drops of solder on kerosene cans from forty to thirty-nine. In large-scale production, Rockefeller realized, even small reductions meant huge savings. Research uncovered other ways of lowering costs and improving products, and Herman Frasch, a brilliant Standard chemist, solved problem after problem in the refining of oil.

In the end, Rockefeller triumphed over his competitors by marketing products of high quality at the lowest unit cost. But he employed other, less savory methods as well. He threatened rivals and bribed politicians. He employed spies to harass the customers of competing refiners. Above all, he extorted railroad rebates that lowered his transportation costs and undercut competitors. By 1879, he controlled 90 percent of the country's entire oil-refining capacity.

Vertically integrated, Standard Oil owned wells, timberlands, barrel and chemical plants, refineries, warehouses, pipelines, and fleets of tankers and oil cars. Its marketing organization served as the model for the industry. Standard exported oil to Asia, Africa, and South America; its 5-gallon kerosene tin, like Coca-Cola bottles and cans of a later era, was a familiar sight in the most distant parts of the world.

To manage it all, the company developed a new plan of business organization, the **trust,** which had profound significance for American business. In 1881, Samuel T. C. Dodd, Standard's attorney, set up the Standard Oil Trust, with a board of nine trustees empowered "to hold, control, and manage" all Standard's properties. Stockholders exchanged their stock for trust certificates, on which dividends were paid. On January 2, 1882, the first of the modern trusts was born. As Dodd intended, it immediately centralized control of Standard's far-flung empire.

Competition almost disappeared; profits soared. A trust movement swept the country as industries with similar problems—whiskey, lead, and sugar, among others—followed Standard's example. The word *trust* became synonymous with monopoly, amid vehement protests from the public. *Antitrust* became a watchword for a generation of reformers from the 1880s through the era of Woodrow Wilson. But Rockefeller's purpose had been *management* of a monopoly, not monopoly itself, which he had already achieved.

During the 1890s, Rockefeller helped pioneer another form of industrial consolidation, the holding company. Taking advantage of an 1889 New Jersey law that allowed companies to purchase other companies, he moved Standard Oil to New Jersey and bought up his own subsidiaries to form a holding company. The trust, he had learned, was somewhat cumbersome, and it was under attack in Congress and the courts. Holding companies offered the next step in industrial management. They were simply large-scale mergers, in which a central corporate organization purchased the stock of the member companies and established direct formal control.

Other companies followed suit, including American Sugar Refining, the Northern Securities Company, and the National Biscuit Company. Merger followed merger. By 1900, 1 percent of the nation's companies controlled more than one-third of its industrial production. A decade later, a congressional investigation showed that two individuals, Rockefeller and Morgan, between them controlled businesses worth more than $22 billion.

In 1897, Rockefeller retired with a fortune of nearly $900 million, but for Standard Oil and petroleum in general, the most expansive period was yet to come. The great oil pools of Texas and Oklahoma had not yet been discovered. Plastics and other oil-based synthetics were several decades in the future. There were only four usable automobiles in the country, and the day of the gasoline engine, automobile, and airplane lay just ahead.

The Business of Invention

"America has become known the world around as the home of invention," boasted the commissioner of patents in 1892. It had not always been so; until the last third of the nineteenth century, the country had imported most of its technology. Then an extraordinary group of inventors and tinkerers—"specialists in invention," Thomas A. Edison called them—began to study the world around them. Some of their inventions gave rise to new industries; a few actually changed the quality of life.

In the very act of inventing, Edison and others drew on a deeper "invention," a realization that people could mold nature to their own ends. They could create out of "first nature," as one environmental historian has noted, a "second nature," shaped as they wished. (See the Feature Essay, "Chicago's 'Second Nature,'" pp. 526–527.)

The number of patents issued to inventors reflected the trend. During the 1850s, fewer than 2,000 patents were issued each year. By the 1880s and 1890s, the figure reached more than 20,000 a year. Between 1790 and 1860, the U.S. Patent Office issued just 36,000 patents; in the decade of the 1890s alone, it issued more than 200,000.

Some of the inventions transformed communications. In 1866, Cyrus W. Field improved the transatlantic cable linking the telegraph networks of Europe and the United States. By the early 1870s, land and submarine cables ran to Brazil, Japan, and the China coast; in the next two decades, they reached Africa and spread across South America. Diplomats and business leaders could now "talk" to

PATENTS ISSUED, BY DECADE, 1850–1899

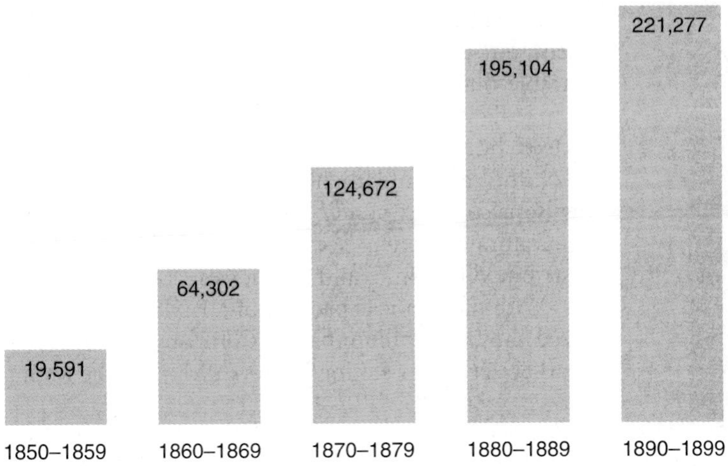

Source: U.S. Bureau of the Census, *Historical Statistics of the United States, Colonial Times to 1970,* Bicentennial Edition, Washington, D.C., 1975.

their counterparts in Berlin or Hong Kong. Even before the telephone, the cables quickened the pace of foreign affairs, revolutionized journalism, and allowed businesses to expand and centralize.

The typewriter (1867), stock ticker (1867), cash register (1879), calculating machine (1887), and adding machine (1888) helped business transactions. High-speed spindles, automatic looms, and electric sewing machines transformed the clothing industry, which for the first time in history turned out ready-made clothes for the masses. In 1890, the Census Bureau first used machines to sort and tabulate data on punched cards, a portent of a new era of information storage and processing.

In 1879, George Eastman patented a process for coating gelatin on photographic dry plates, which led to celluloid film and motion pictures. By 1888, he was marketing the Kodak camera, which weighed 35 ounces, took 100 exposures, and cost $25. Even though early Kodaks had to be returned to the factory, camera and all, for film developing, they revolutionized photography. Now almost anyone could snap a picture.

Other innovations changed the diet. There were new processes for flour, canned meat, vegetables, condensed milk, and even beer (from an offshoot of Louis Pasteur's discoveries about bacteria). Packaged cereals appeared on breakfast tables. Refrigerated railroad cars, ice-cooled, brought fresh fruit from Florida and California to all parts of the country. In the 1870s, Gustavus F. Swift, a Chicago meatpacker, hit on the idea of using the cars to distribute meat nationwide. Setting up "dissembly" factories to butcher meat (Henry Ford later copied them for his famous "assembly" lines), he started an "era of cheap beef," as a newspaper said.

No innovation, however, rivaled the importance of the telephone and the use of electricity for light and power. The telephone was the work of Alexander Graham Bell, a shrewd and genial Scot who settled in Boston in 1871. Interested in the problems of the deaf, Bell experimented with ways to transmit speech electrically, and after several years he had developed electrified metal disks that, much like the human ear, converted sound waves to electrical impulses and back again. On March 10, 1876, he transmitted the first sentence over a telephone: "Mr. Watson, come here; I want you." Later that year, he exhibited the new device to excited crowds at the Centennial Exposition in Philadelphia.

In 1878—the year a telephone was installed in the White House—the first telephone exchange opened in New Haven, Connecticut. Fighting off competitors who challenged the patent, the young Bell Telephone Company dominated the growing industry. By 1895, there were about 310,000 phones; a decade later, there were 10 million—about one for every ten people. American Telephone and Telegraph Company, formed by the Bell interests in 1885, became another of the vast holding companies, consolidating more than a hundred local systems.

If the telephone dissolved communication barriers as old as the human race, Thomas Alva Edison, the "Wizard of Menlo Park," invented processes and products of comparable significance. Born in 1847, Edison had little formal education, although he was an avid reader. Like Carnegie, he went into the new field of

Electric-powered subway systems were an important development in urban mass transportation. The nation's first subway system opened in 1897 in Boston, Massachusetts, allowing commuters to avoid the delays of heavy street traffic via trains that ran on elevated and underground tracks. Here, train cars are shown as they descend into the subway at the Boston Public Garden. ❖

telegraphy. Tinkering in his spare time, he made several important improvements, including a telegraph capable of sending four messages over a single wire. Gathering teams of specialists to work on specific problems, Edison built the first modern research laboratory at Menlo Park, New Jersey. It may have been his most important invention.

The laboratory, Edison promised, would turn out "a minor invention every ten days and a big thing every six months or so." In 1877, it turned out a big thing. Worried about a telephone's high cost, Edison set out to invent a "telephone repeater," which became the phonograph. Those unable to afford a phone, he thought, could record their voices for replay from a central telephone station. Using tin foil wrapped around a grooved, rotating cylinder, he shouted the verses of "Mary Had a Little Lamb" and then listened in awe as the machine played them back. "I was never so taken aback in all my life," he later said. "Everybody was astonished. I was always afraid of things that worked the first time."

In 1896, records made of hard rubber and shellac appeared on the market; the following year, a phonograph sold for $20. In 1904, someone had the idea of recording on both sides of the disk, and the phonograph record in its modern form was born. For the first time in history, people could listen again and again to a favorite symphony or piano solo. The phonograph made human experience repeatable in a way never before possible.

In 1879 came an even larger triumph, the incandescent lamp. Sir Joseph William Swan, an English inventor, had already experimented with the carbon filament, but Edison's task involved more than finding a durable filament. He set out to do nothing less than change light. A trial-and-error inventor, Edison tested sixteen hundred materials before producing, late in 1879, the carbon filament he wanted. Then he had to devise a complex system of conductors, meters, and generators by which electricity could be divided and distributed to homes and businesses.

With the financial backing of J. P. Morgan, he organized the Edison Illuminating Company and built the Pearl Street power station in New York City, the testing

❖ A Look at the Past ❖

Cash Register

Mass-produced goods of every kind flooded markets at the turn of the century. Industrial productivity made the flood possible and consumer spending fueled production. Railroads and free mail delivery after 1896 brought factory-made goods even to consumers who lived in remote, rural locations. In cities, department stores transformed shopping into a pleasurable experience. By the 1880s retailers were investing in cash registers that tallied sales. Previously, merchants recorded sales by hand into daybooks and later, when closed for business, transcribed the sales into a ledger. This wooden model from 1890 registered sales with ceramic balls, which dropped into a labyrinth of tracks to mark daily totals. How did the cash register transform the act of selling goods? Why do you think merchants invested in them?

ground of the new apparatus. On September 4, 1882, as Morgan and others watched, Edison threw a switch and lit the house of Morgan, the stock exchange, the *New York Times,* and a number of other buildings. Amazed, a *Times* reporter marveled that writing stories in the office at night "seemed almost like writing in daylight." Power stations soon opened in Boston, Philadelphia, and Chicago. By 1900, there were 2774 stations, lighting some 2 million electric lights around the country. In a nation alive with light, the habits of centuries changed. A flick of the switch lit homes and factories at any hour of the day or night.

In a rare blunder, Edison based his system on low-voltage direct current, which could be transmitted only about two miles. George Westinghouse, the inventor of the railroad air brake, demonstrated the advantages of high-voltage alternating current for transmission over great distances. In 1886, he formed the Westinghouse Electric Company and with the inventor Nikola Tesla, a Hungarian immigrant, developed an alternating-current motor that could convert electricity into mechanical power. Electricity could light a lamp or illuminate a skyscraper, pull a streetcar or drive an entire railroad, run a sewing machine or power a mammoth assembly line. Transmitted easily over long distances, it freed factories and cities from location near water or coal. Electricity, in short, brought a revolution.

Taking advantage of the new devices, Frank J. Sprague, a young engineer, electrified the Richmond, Virginia, streetcar system in 1887. Other cities quickly followed. Electric-powered subway systems opened in Boston in 1897 and New York City in 1904. Overhead wires and third rails made urban transportation quieter, faster, and cleaner. Buried under pavement or strung from pole to pole, wires of every description—trolley, telephone, and power—marked the birth of the modern city.

❖ A Look at the Past ❖

Typewriter

By the end of the nineteenth century, typewriters became increasingly common in offices. The earliest typewriters worked in a variety of ways and did not even have similar keyboards. By the 1890s, however, the keyboard used today had become standard. The standardized keyboard made it easier for people to learn to type, and also made it possible to type more quickly. The awkward arrangement on the keyboard intentionally slowed typists to prevent keys from jamming as a result of rapid typing. Even though typewriters did not work as quickly as typists could, they offered numerous advantages over pen and ink. What do typewriters suggest about business practices? How do you suppose they affected the amount of paper used in offices? How could typed and printed forms alter the pace of business?

The Sellers

The increased output of the industrial age alone was not enough to ensure huge profits. The products still had to be sold, and that gave rise to a new "science" of marketing. Some business leaders—such as Swift in meatpacking, James B. Duke in tobacco, and Rockefeller in oil—built extensive marketing organizations of their own. Others relied on retailers, merchandising techniques, and advertising, developing a host of methods to convince consumers to buy.

In 1867, businesses spent about $50 million on advertising; in 1900, they spent more than $500 million, and the figure was increasing rapidly. The first advertising agency, N. W. Ayer and Son, of Philadelphia, began to service businesses in the mid-1870s, and it was followed by numerous imitators. The rotary press (1875) churned out newspapers and introduced a new era in newspaper advertising. Woodcuts, halftones, and photoengraving added illustrations to catch the consumer's eye. Brand names became popular, and already Kellogg

Feature Essay

CHICAGO'S "SECOND NATURE"

Chicago's early boosters bragged that nature had given their city everything it needed to be great: a river running through it and a harbor on busy Lake Michigan. What the boosters did not say was that the river was short and shallow—"a sluggish, slimy stream, too lazy to cleanse itself," a visitor noted—or that sand often blocked the entrance to the harbor. To make Chicago work, humans would have to intrude upon nature to change the river and clear the harbor, creating out of "first nature" a "second nature," as environmental historian William Cronon put it.

They did just that. In remaking "first nature," government-financed engineers deepened the river and erected barriers to the sand. Then they turned to another of nature's challenges—the thick, cloying mud that plagued Chicago whenever it rained. Using muscle and jacks, they simply lifted the city a dozen feet out of the mud, producing "second nature" once again.

The city, now raised to working level, next turned to the railroads, the dazzling technological innovation that mastered nature to transform nineteenth-century life. Unlike rivers and canals, railroads could go virtually anywhere, and many of them wound up going to Chicago, which became the main terminal point for trains heading east and west. It was "natural" for them to do so, Chicagoans believed, and they certainly seemed right. By the early 1890s, one-twenty-fifth of all railroad mileage in the world terminated in Chicago.

They terminated there, in part, to drop off and pick up the city's most recent tinkering with nature, the pigs and cows destined to feed the country's growing population. A city that exuded life and growth, Chicago became filled with death, famed for "the Chicago style" of killing pigs. It was, said British writer Rudyard Kipling after visiting the city, a "death factory."

To organize the killing, the giant Union Stockyards opened on Christmas Day, 1865, built just south of the city on a marshy prairie prone to flooding. "Second nature" again took charge. Thirty miles of pipes drained the water from the prairie. The water, carrying with it waste from the stockyards, discharged into the Chicago River, which soon smelled horrific and carried disease. Within the stockyards, 10 miles of troughs dispersed corn and hay among 2000 pens, to feed at any one time 21,000 head of cattle, 75,000 pigs, and 22,000 sheep. Sidetracks allowed animals to be brought into the yards for slaughter and then carried the resulting products out to distant markets.

The river, meanwhile, grew increasingly polluted. Stockyard waste fermented on the bottom, producing large bubbles of methane gas that erupted on the grease-covered surface. Occasionally, the river caught fire. Chicago officials toyed with ways to solve the problem and settled on a most extraordinary idea: Reverse the flow of the river away from Lake Michigan into the Illinois River, a tributary of the Mississippi. Waters from the lake would flush the river and cleanse it—a happy solution for the people of

A view of Chicago's Union Stockyards in 1900. ❖

Chicago, but not so pleasant for those who lived along the Illinois. On a July day in 1871, Chicagoans lined the riverbanks to watch the engineering feat. Helped by pumps and channels, the river suddenly ran "upstream."

Problems remained in the stockyards, however, including how to kill so many animals and keep fresh the marketable remains. Gustavus F. Swift, a butcher from Boston, arrived in 1875 and provided an answer. Drawing on earlier experiments among meat packers in Cincinnati, he hit upon the idea of passing the pigs along on a chain between two lines of stationary workers, each of whom had a specific job in taking apart the carcass. One cut the throat, another made a slit down the body, a third used a saw to cut the breastbone, a fourth tore out the entrails. Others down the chain sliced and chopped.

Without fully knowing it, Swift and rival meat packers such as Philip D. Armour who adopted similar systems were introducing the methods of modern mass production. But instead of Henry Ford's Model T assembly lines, Swift's pigs passed through giant "disassembly" lines, in numbers previously unimagined. By the early 1870s, Chicago meat packers were processing well over a million pigs a year.

Workers dressing beef carcasses for market at the Armour meat packing plant in Chicago. ❖

Killing in such quantities created a problem of its own. For as long as there had been pigs, killing and dressing them had been a seasonal event, confined by nature to the early winter, when cold temperatures would keep the meat from spoiling. While that system worked well with small numbers of pigs, the huge meat packing plants with their many employees could not stand idle for the rest of the year. Swift needed a way to keep the meat cold, and he found it in ice, cut in enormous quantities from area lakes and rivers and stored in insulated warehouses for use during the spring, summer, and fall.

By the 1880s, Swift was buying 450,000 tons of ice a year, and his packing plants never closed. Creating once again a "second nature," he had found a way to make winter last year-round.

He also found a way to carry winter with him. Ice preserved Chicago's slaughtered pigs, to be sure, but the meat still had to get to market, usually over very long distances. Again the solution was ice, this time carried on new-fangled refrigerated railroad cars, developed by Swift himself, who also established icehouses along the tracks so trains could restock the ice and replenish the cold.

Even the very pig itself had moved further and further from its own natural state. In the old days it had become ham, bacon, sausage, and lard, products still recognizable as parts of the original animal. By the 1880s that was no longer true. Dealing with a million pigs a year, Swift and other meat packers found ways to use every part of the animal. Their research laboratories discovered byproducts such as oleomargarine, shoes, fertilizer, buttons, soap, combs, and glue. Lathering up in the bath, few people thought of the pig as the source of their soap.

In a final twist to nature, even nature's skyline changed. Smoke poured from the stockyards, as did the odor of manure that, when the wind was right (or wrong), swept north across the city. Ash from burning bones rained down on the city, "like black snow," one onlooker said. On some days it was hard even to see the river and the harbor. "See that cloud?" a character in a contemporary novel asked, pointing out the train window; "that's Chicago." "There is no sky now," another writer said.

A half-century later, the slaughterhouses had moved west to feedlots on the plains. Brokers on Chicago's Commodity Exchange still trade in hogs and pork belly futures, but those pigs will never see the old Union Stockyards, now a popular tourist attraction. Chicagoans have cleaned up their river; restaurants line the riverbanks and pleasure boats ply the waters.

In their time, the meat packers of Chicago transformed the diet of the United States and, in fact, the world. As early as 1912, Swift and Company had outlets in 400 cities on four continents and employed more than 30,000 people worldwide. The fresh meat products derived from Chicago's "second nature" fed people as never before.

was promising cornflake eaters "Genuine Joy, Genuine Appetite, Genuine Health and therefore Genuine Complexion."

Bringing producer and consumer together, nationwide advertising was the final link in the national market. From roadside signs to newspaper ads, it pervaded American life. "Do you know why we publish the *Ladies' Home Journal?*" the magazine's owner asked an audience of manufacturers. "The editor thinks it is for the benefit of American women. That is an illusion, but a very proper one for him to have. But I will tell you; the real reason, the publisher's reason, is to give you people who manufacture things that American women want and buy a chance to tell them about your products."

R. H. Macy in New York, John Wanamaker in Philadelphia, and Marshall Field in Chicago turned the department store into a national institution. There people could browse (a relatively new concept) and buy. Innovations in pricing, display, and advertising helped customers develop wants they did not know they had. In 1870, Wanamaker took out the first full-page newspaper ad, and Macy, an aggressive advertiser, touted "goods suitable for the millionaire at prices in reach of the millions."

The "chain store"—an American term—spread across the country. The A & P grocery stores, begun in 1859, numbered sixty-seven by 1876, all marked by a familiar red-and-gold facade. By 1915, there were a thousand of them. In 1880, F. W. Woolworth, bored with the family farm, opened the first "Five and Ten Cent Store" in Utica, New York. He had fifty-nine stores in 1900, the year he adopted the bright red storefront and heaping counters to lure customers in and persuade them to buy.

In similar fashion, Sears, Roebuck and Montgomery Ward sold to rural customers through mail-order catalogs—a means of selling that depended on effective transportation and a high level of customer literacy. As a traveler for a dry goods firm, Aaron Montgomery Ward had seen an unfulfilled need of people in the rural West. He started the mail-order trend in 1872, with a one-sheet price list offered from

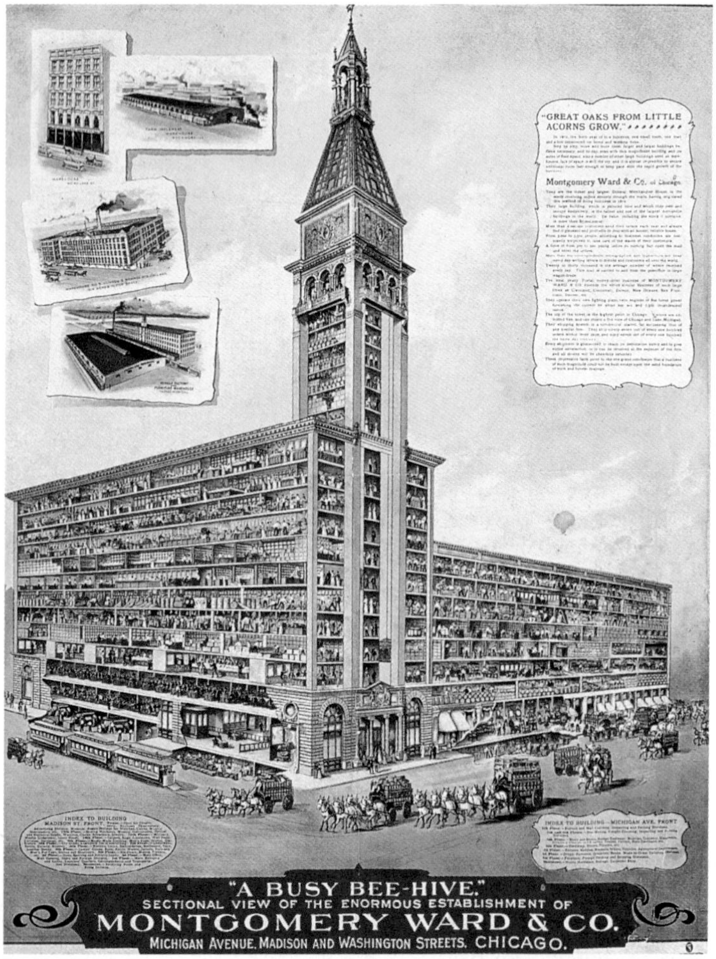

A cutaway view of the "bee-hive" headquarters of mail-order giant Montgomery Ward & Co. of Chicago. By the time Ward moved into this building in 1899, rival retailer Sears, Roebuck & Co. was challenging Ward's mail-order business. ❖

a Chicago loft. By 1884, he offered almost ten thousand items in a catalog of 240 pages.

Richard W. Sears also saw the possibilities in the mail-order business. Starting with watches and jewelry, he gradually expanded his list. In the early 1880s, he moved to Chicago and with Alvah C. Roebuck founded Sears, Roebuck and Company. Sears sold anything and everything, prospering in a business that relied on mutual faith between unseen customers and distant distributors. Sears catalogs, soon more than five hundred pages long, exploited four-color illustration and other new techniques. By the early 1900s, Sears distributed six million catalogs annually.

Advertising, brand names, chain stores, and mail-order houses brought Americans of all varieties into a national market. Even as the country grew, a certain homogeneity of goods bound it together, touching cities and farms, East and West, rich and poor. There was a common language of consumption. The market, some contemporaries thought, also bridged ethnic and other differences. A prominent English economist wrote in 1919, "Widely as the Scandinavians are separated from the Italians, and the native Americans from the Poles, in sentiment, in modes of living, and even in occupations, they are yet purchasers of nearly the same goods. . . . They buy similar clothes, furniture, and implements."

The theory had severe limits; ethnic and racial differences remained entrenched in the society. But Americans *had* become a community of consumers, surrounded by goods unavailable just a few decades before, and able to purchase them. They had learned to make, want, and buy. "Because you see the main thing today is—shopping," Arthur Miller, a twentieth-century playwright, said in *The Price:*

> Years ago a person, he was unhappy, didn't know what to do with himself—he'd go to church, start a revolution—something. Today you're unhappy? Can't figure it out? What is the salvation? Go shopping.

The Wage Earners

Although entrepreneurs were important, it was the labor of millions of men and women that built the new industrial society. In their individual stories, nearly all unrecorded, lay much of the achievement, drama, and pain of these years.

In a number of respects, their lot improved during the last quarter of the nineteenth century. Real wages rose, working conditions improved, and the workers' influence in national affairs increased. Between 1880 and 1914, wages of the average worker rose about $7 a year. Like others, workers also benefited from expanding health and educational services.

Working Men, Working Women, Working Children

Still, life for workers was not easy. Before 1900, most wage earners worked at least ten hours a day, six days a week. If skilled, they earned about 20 cents an hour; if unskilled, just half that. On average, workers earned between $400 and $500 a year. It took about $600 for a family of four to live decently. Construction workers, machinists, government employees, printers, clerical workers, and western miners made more than the average. Eastern coal miners, agricultural workers, garment workers, and unskilled factory hands made considerably less.

There were few holidays or vacations, and there was little respite from the grueling routine. Skilled workers could turn the system to their own ends—New York City cigar makers, for example, paid someone to read to them while they worked—but the unskilled seldom had such luxury. They were too easily replaced. "A bit of advice to you," said a guidebook for immigrant Jews in the 1890s: "do not take a moment's rest. Run, do, work, and keep your own good in mind."

Work was not only grueling; it was very dangerous. Safety standards were low, and accidents were common, more common in fact than in any other

Many children in the late nineteenth century grew up in the nation's factories, working long hours for low wages in often dangerous conditions. This young girl working as a spinner in a textile mill posed for photographer Lewis Hine. ❖

industrial nation in the world at that time. On the railroads, 1 in every 26 workers was injured and 1 in every 399 was killed each year. Thousands suffered from chronic illness, unknowing victims of dust, chemicals, and other pollutants. In the early 1900s, physician Alice Hamilton established a link between jobs and disease, but meanwhile, illness weakened or struck down many a breadwinner.

The breadwinner might be a woman or a child; both worked in increasing numbers. In 1870, about 15 percent of women over the age of 16 were employed for wages; in 1900, 20 percent (5.3 million women) were. Of 303 occupations listed in the 1900 census, women were represented in 296. The textile industry was their largest single employer. Between 1870 and 1900, the number of working children rose nearly 130 percent to 1.8 million. In 1900, 1 out of every 10 girls and 1 out of every 5 boys between the ages of 10 and 15 held jobs. In Paterson, New Jersey, an important industrial city, about half of all boys and girls aged 11 to 14 had jobs.

There were so many children in the labor force that when people spoke of child labor, they often meant boys and girls under the age of 14. Boys were paid little enough, but girls made even less. Girls, it was argued, were headed for marriage; those who worked were just doing so in order to help out their families. "We try to employ girls who are members of families," a box manufacturer said, "for we don't pay the girls a living wage in this trade."

Most working women were young and single. Many began working at 16 or 17, worked a half dozen years or so, married, and quit. In 1900, only 5 percent of all married women were employed outside the home, although African American women were an important exception. Among them, 25 percent of married women worked in 1900, usually on southern farms or as low-paid laundresses or domestic servants. As clerical work expanded, women learned new skills such as typing and stenography. Moving into formerly male occupations, they became secretaries, bookkeepers, typists, telephone operators, and clerks in the new department stores.

A few women—very few—became ministers, lawyers, and doctors. Arabella Mansfield, admitted to the Iowa bar in 1869, was the first woman lawyer in the country. But change was slow, and in the 1880s, some law schools still were refusing to admit women because they "had not the mentality to study law." Among women entering the professions, the overwhelming majority became nurses, schoolteachers, and librarians. In such professions, a process of "feminization" occurred: Women became a majority of the workers, a small number of men took the management roles, and most men left for other jobs, lowering the profession's status.

In most jobs, status and pay were divided unequally between men and women. Many of both sexes thought a woman's place was in the home, "queen of a little house—no matter how humble—where there are children rolling on the floor." When employed in factories, women tended to occupy jobs that were viewed as natural extensions of household activity. They made clothes and textiles, processed food, and made cigars, tobacco, and shoes. In the women's garment industry, which employed large numbers of women, they were the sewers and finishers, doing jobs that paid less; men were the higher-paid cutters and pressers.

In *The Long Day: The Story of a New York Working Girl as Told by Herself* (1906), the "working girl," a young schoolteacher, earned $2.50 a week, paid $1.00 for her room, and had $1.50 for food, clothes, transportation, and any social life. For breakfast, she had bread, butter, and coffee; for lunch, bread and butter;

A typing pool in the audit division of the Metropolitan Life Insurance Company, 1897. As demand for clerical workers grew, women took over many of the secretarial duties formerly performed by men. Despite their prominence in the workplace, however, the women were usually overseen by male supervisors. ❖

for dinner, potato soup, bread, and butter. In Pittsburgh, a worker in a pickle factory said of her day: "I have stood ten hours; I have fitted 1,300 corks; I have hauled and loaded 4,000 jars of pickles. My pay is seventy cents." Exhausted, such workers fell into bed at night and crawled out again at dawn to begin another "long day."

In general, adults earned more than children, the skilled more than the unskilled, native born more than foreign born, Protestants more than Catholics or Jews, and whites more than blacks and Asians. On average, women made a little more than half as much as men, according to contemporary estimates. In some cases, employers defended the differences—the foreign born, for example, might not speak English—but most simply reflected bias against race, creed, or gender. In the industrial society, white, native-born Protestant men—the bulk of the male population—reaped the greatest rewards.

Blacks labored on the fringes, usually in menial occupations. The last hired and first fired, they earned less than other workers at almost every level of skill. On the Pacific Coast, the Chinese—and later the Japanese—lived in enclaves and suffered periodic attacks of discrimination. In 1879, the Workingmen's party of California got a provision in the state constitution forbidding corporations to employ Chinese, and in 1882, Congress passed the **Chinese Exclusion Act,** prohibiting the immigration of Chinese workers for ten years.

Culture of Work

Among almost all groups, industrialization shattered age-old patterns, including work habits and the culture of work, as Herbert G. Gutman, a social historian, noted. It made people adapt "older work routines to new necessities and strained those wedded to premodern patterns of labor." Adaptation was difficult and often demeaning. Virtually everyone went through it, and newcomers repeated the experiences of those who came before.

Men and women fresh from farms were not accustomed to the factory's disciplines. Now they worked indoors rather than out, paced themselves to the clock rather than the movements of the sun, and followed the needs of the market rather than the natural rhythms of the seasons. They had supervisors and hierarchies and strict rules. Piecework determined wages, and always—as Morris Rosenfeld, a clothing presser, wrote—there was the relentless clock:

> The Clock in the workshop,—it rests not a moment;
> It points on, and ticks on: eternity-time;
> Once someone told me the clock had a meaning,
> In pointing and ticking had reason and rhyme.
> At times, when I listen, I hear the clock plainly;
> The reason of old—the old meaning—is gone!
> The maddening pendulum urges me forward
> To labor and still labor on.
> The tick of the clock is the boss in his anger.
> The face of the clock has the eyes of the foe.
> The clock—I shudder—Dost hear how it draws me?
> It calls me "Machine" and it cries [to] me "Sew"!

As industries grew larger, work became more impersonal. Machines displaced skilled artisans, and the unskilled tended the machines for employers they never saw. Workers picked up and left their jobs with startling frequency, and factories drew on a churning, highly mobile labor supply. Historian Stephan Thernstrom, who carefully studied the census records, found that only about half the people recorded in any census still lived in the same community ten years later. "The country had an enormous reservoir of restless and footloose men, who could be lured to new destinations when opportunity beckoned."

Thernstrom and others have also found substantial economic and social mobility. The rags-to-riches stories of Horatio Alger, had always said so, and careers of men such as Andrew Carnegie—the impoverished immigrant boy who made good—seemed to confirm it. The actual record was considerably more limited. Most business leaders in the period came from well-to-do or middle-class families of old American stock. Of 360 iron and steel barons in Pittsburgh, Carnegie's own city, only 5 fit the Carnegie characteristics, and one of those was Carnegie himself. Still, if few workers became steel magnates, many workers made major progress during their lifetimes. Thernstrom discovered that a quarter of the manual laborers rose to middle-class positions, and working-class children were even more likely to move up the ladder. In Boston, about half the Jewish immigrants rose from manual to middle-class jobs, and English, Irish, and Italian immigrants were not far behind.

The chance for advancement played a vital role in American industrial development. It gave workers hope, wedded them to the system, and tempered their response to the appeal of labor unions and working-class agitation. Very few workers rose from rags to riches, but a great many rose to better jobs and higher status.

Labor Unions

Weak throughout the nineteenth century, labor unions never included more than 2 percent of the total labor force or more than 10 percent of industrial workers. To many workers, unions seemed "foreign," radical, and out of step with the American tradition of individual advancement. Craft, ethnic, and other differences fragmented the labor force, and its extraordinary mobility made organization difficult. Employers opposed unions. "I have always had one rule," said an executive of U.S. Steel. "If a worker sticks up his head, hit it."

As the national economy emerged, however, national labor unions gradually took shape. The early unions often represented skilled workers in local areas, but in 1866, William H. Sylvis, a Pennsylvania iron molder, united several unions into a single national organization, the National Labor Union. Like many of the era's labor leaders, Sylvis sought long-range humanitarian reforms, such as the establishment of workers' cooperatives, rather than specific bread-and-butter goals. A talented propagandist, he attracted many members—some 640,000 by 1868—but he died in 1869, and the organization did not long survive him.

The year Sylvis died, Uriah S. Stephens and a group of Philadelphia garment workers founded a far more successful organization, the Noble and Holy Order of the Knights of Labor, known simply as the **Knights of Labor.** A secret fraternal order, it grew slowly through the 1870s, until Terence V. Powderly, the new Grand Master Workman elected in 1879, ended the secrecy and embarked on an aggressive recruitment program. Wanting to unite all labor, the Knights welcomed everyone who "toiled," regardless of skill, creed, sex, or color. Unlike most unions, it organized women workers, and at its peak, it had 60,000 black members.

Harking back to the Jacksonians, the Knights set the "producers" against monopoly and special privilege. As members they excluded only "nonproducers"—bankers, lawyers, liquor dealers, and gamblers. Since employers were "producers," they could join; and since workers and employers had common interests, the Knights maintained that workers should not strike. The order's platform included the eight-hour day and the abolition of child labor, but more often it focused on uplifting, utopian reform. Powderly, the eloquent and idealistic leader, spun dreams of a new era of harmony and cooperation. He wanted to sweep away trusts and end drunkenness. Workers should pool their resources, establish worker-run factories, railroads, and mines, and escape from the wage system. "The aim of the Knights of Labor—properly understood—is to make each man his own employer," Powderly said.

Membership grew steadily—from 42,000 in 1882 to 110,000 in 1885. In March 1885, ignoring Powderly's dislike of strikes, local Knights in St. Louis, Kansas City, and other cities won a victory against Jay Gould's Missouri Pacific Railroad, and membership soared. It soon reached almost 730,000, but neither Powderly nor the union's loose structure could handle the growth. In 1886, the wily Gould struck back, crushing the Knights on the Texas and Pacific Railroad. The defeat punctured the union's growth and revealed the ineffectiveness of its national leaders. Tens of thousands of unskilled laborers, who had recently rushed to join, deserted the ranks. The Haymarket Riot turned public sympathy against unions like the Knights. By 1890, the order had shrunk to 100,000 members, and a few years later, it was virtually defunct.

Women delegates at a national meeting of the Knights of Labor in 1886. Women belonged to separate associations affiliated with local all-male unions. ❖

Even as the Knights waxed and waned, another organization emerged that was to endure. Founded in 1886, the **American Federation of Labor (AFL)** was a loose alliance of national craft unions. It organized only skilled workers along craft lines, avoided politics, and worked for specific practical objectives. "I have my own philosophy and my own dreams," said Samuel Gompers, the founder and longtime president, "but first and foremost I want to increase the workingman's welfare year by year."

Born in a London tenement in 1850, Gompers was a child of the union movement. Settling in New York, he worked as a cigar maker, took an active hand in union activities, and experimented for a time with socialism and working-class politics. As leader of the AFL, he adopted a pragmatic approach to labor's needs. Gompers accepted capitalism and did not argue for fundamental changes in it. For labor he wanted simply a recognized place within the system and a greater share of the rewards.

Unlike Powderly, Gompers and the AFL assumed that most workers would remain workers throughout their lives. The task, then, lay in improving lives in "practical" ways: higher wages, shorter hours, and better working conditions. The AFL offered some attractive assurances to employers. As a trade union, the AFL would use the strike and boycott, but only to achieve limited gains; if treated fairly, the organization would provide a stable labor force. The AFL would not oppose monopolies and trusts, as Gompers said, "so long as we obtain fair wages."

By the 1890s, the AFL was the most important labor group in the country, and Gompers, the guiding spirit, was its president, except for one year, until his death in 1924. Membership expanded from 140,000 in 1886, past 250,000 in 1892, to more than 1 million by 1901. The AFL then included almost one-third of the country's skilled workers. By 1914, it had more than 2 million members. The great majority of workers—skilled and unskilled—remained unorganized, but Gompers and the AFL had become a significant force in national life.

Few unions allowed women to join. The Knights of Labor had a Department of Woman's Work headed by Leonora M. Barry, a shrewd, enthusiastic organizer who established a dozen women's locals and investigated the condition of women's labor. The Knights welcomed housewives because they were "producers." The AFL either ignored or opposed women workers. Only two of its national affiliates—the Cigar Makers' Union and the Typographical Union—accepted women as members; others prohibited them outright, and Gompers himself often complained that women workers undercut the pay scales for men. Working conditions improved after 1900, but even then, unions were largely a man's world. In 1910, when there were 6.3 million women at work, only 125,000 of them were in unions.

The AFL did not expressly forbid black workers from joining, but member unions used high initiation fees, technical examinations, and other means to discourage black membership. The AFL's informal exclusion practices were, all in all, a sorry record, but Gompers defended his policy toward blacks, women, and the unskilled by pointing to the dangers that unions faced. Only by restricting membership, he argued, could the union succeed.

Labor Unrest

Workers used various means to adjust to the factory age. To the dismay of managers and "efficiency" experts, the employees often dictated the pace and quality of their work and set the tone of the workplace. Friends and relatives of newly arrived immigrants found jobs for them, taught them how to deal with factory conditions, and humanized the workplace.

Workers also formed their own institutions to deal with their jobs. Overcoming differences of race or ethnic origin, they often banded together to help each other. They joined social or fraternal organizations, and their unions did more than argue for higher

Violence and fires associated with the great railroad strike of 1877 destroyed railyards across the country. By the end of the strike, which lasted about two weeks, $10 million of railroad property had been reduced to rubble, and more than a hundred people had died. ❖

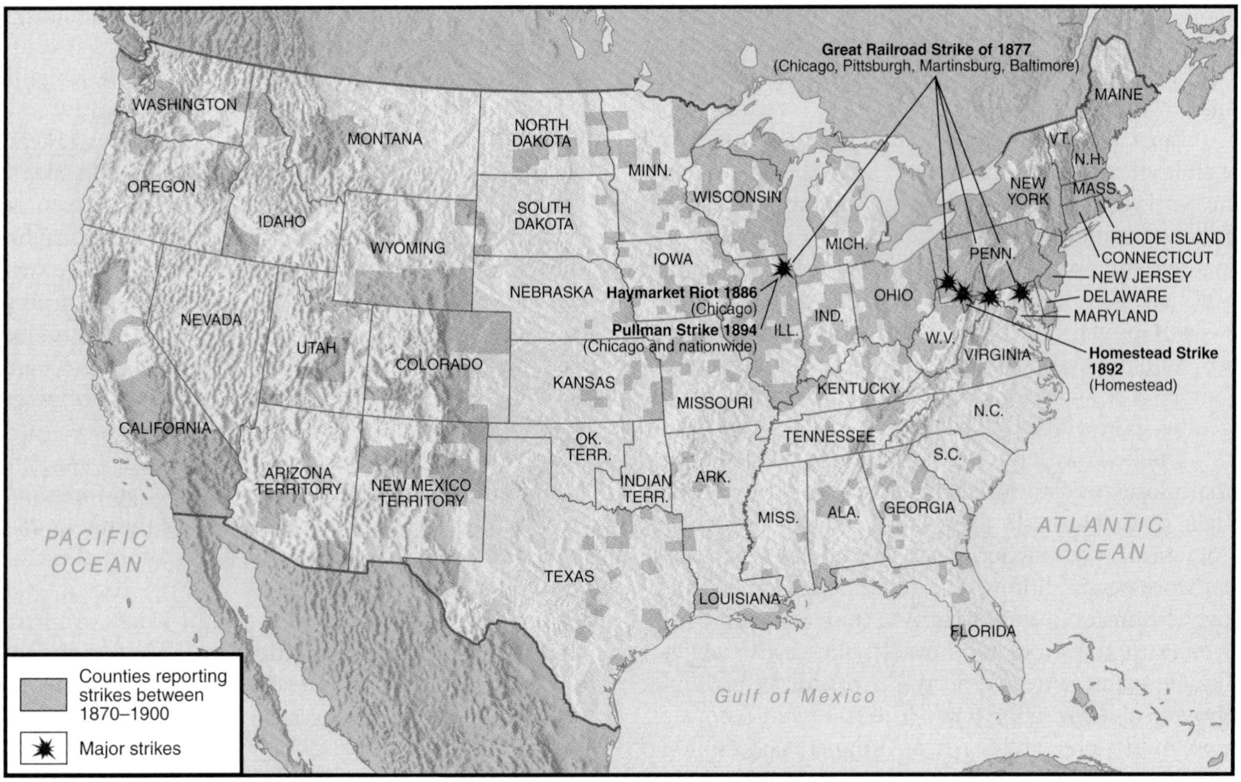

LABOR STRIKES, 1870–1890 *More than 14,000 strikes occurred in the 1880s and early 1890s, involving millions of workers.*

wages. Unions offered companionship, news of job openings, and much needed insurance plans for sickness, accident, or death. Workers went to the union hall to play cards or pool, sing union songs, and hear older workers tell of past labor struggles. Unions provided food for sick members, and there were dances, picnics, and parades. "The night I joined the Cattle Butchers' Union," a young Lithuanian said, "I was led into the room by a negro member. With me were Bohemians, Germans and Poles. . . . We swore to be loyal to our union above everything else except the country, the city and the State—to be faithful to each other—to protect the women workers—to do our best to understand the history of the labor movement, and to do all we could to help it on."

Many employers believed in an "iron law of wages" in which supply and demand, not the welfare of their workers, dictated wages. "If I wanted boiler iron," a steelmaker said, "I would go out on the market and buy where I could get it the cheapest, and if I wanted to employ men I would do the same thing." Wanting a docile labor force, employers fired union members, hired scabs to replace strikers, and used a new weapon, the court injunction, to quell strikes.

The injunction, which forbade workers to interfere with their employers' business, was used to break the great Pullman strike of 1894, and the Supreme Court upheld use of the injunction in *In re Debs* (1895). Court decisions also affected the legal protection offered to workers. In *Holden* v. *Hardy* (1898), the Court upheld a law limiting working hours for miners because their work was dangerous and long hours might increase injuries. In *Lochner* v. *New York* (1905), however, it struck down a law limiting bakery workers to a sixty-hour week and ten-hour day. Because baking was safer than mining, the Court saw no need to interfere with the right of bakers to sell their labor freely. (For a case involving women workers, see "*Muller* v. *Oregon:* Expanding the Definition of Acceptable Evidence," pp. 684–687.)

As employers' attitudes hardened, strikes and violence broke out. The United States had the greatest number of violent confrontations between capital and labor in the industrial world. Between 1880 and 1900, there were more than 23,000 strikes involving 6.6 million workers. The great railroad strike of 1877 paralyzed railroads from West Virginia to California, resulted in the deaths of more than a hundred workers, and required federal troops to suppress it. Another outburst of labor unrest occurred during the mid-1880s; in 1886, the peak year, 610,000 workers were off the job because of strikes and lockouts.

The worst incident took place at Haymarket Square in Chicago, where workers had been campaigning for an eight-hour workday. In early May 1886, police, intervening in a strike at the McCormick Harvester works, shot and killed two workers. The next evening, May 4, labor leaders called a protest meeting at Haymarket Square near downtown Chicago. The meeting was peaceful, even a bit dull. About three thousand people were there; police ordered them to disperse, and someone threw a dynamite bomb that instantly killed one policeman and fatally wounded six others. Police fired into the crowd and killed four people.

The authorities never discovered who threw the bomb, but many Americans—not just business leaders—immediately labeled the incident the **Haymarket Riot** and demanded action against labor "radicalism." Cities strengthened their police forces and armories. In Chicago, donors helped to establish nearby Fort Sheridan and the Great Lakes Naval Training Station to curb social turmoil. Uncertain who threw the bomb, Chicago police rounded up eight anarchists, who were convicted of murder. Although there was no evidence of their guilt, four were hanged, one committed suicide, and three remained in jail until pardoned by the governor in 1893. Linking labor and anarchism in the public mind, the Haymarket Riot weakened the national labor movement.

Violence again broke out in the unsettled conditions of the 1890s. In 1892, federal troops crushed a strike of silver miners in the Coeur d'Alene district of Idaho. That same year, Carnegie and Henry Clay Frick, Carnegie's partner and manager, cut wages nearly 20 percent at the Homestead steel plant. The Amalgamated Iron and Steel Workers, an AFL affiliate, struck, and Frick responded by locking the workers out of the plant. The workers surrounded it, and Frick, furious, hired a small private army of Pinkerton detectives to drive them off. But alert workers spotted the detectives, pinned them down with gunfire, and forced them to surrender. Three detectives and ten workers died in the battle.

A few days later, the Pennsylvania governor ordered the state militia to impose peace at Homestead. On July 23, an anarchist named Alexander Berkman, who was not one of the strikers, walked into Frick's office and shot him twice, then stabbed him several times. Incredibly, Frick survived, watched the police take Berkman away, called in a doctor to bandage his wounds, and stayed in the office until closing time. "I do not think I shall die," he told reporters. "But if I do or not, the company will pursue the same policy and it will win." In late July, the Homestead works reopened under military guard, and in November the strikers gave up.

Events like the **Homestead Strike** troubled many Americans who wondered whether industrialization,

In the rioting that followed the bomb explosion in Haymarket Square in Chicago, seven police officers and four workers died and more than seventy officers were wounded, many of them by fellow police. August Spies, one of the anarchists convicted of murder and sent to the gallows, said at his trial, "Let the world know that in A.D. 1886, in the state of Illinois, eight men were sentenced to death because they believed in a better future; because they had not lost their faith in the ultimate victory of liberty and justice!" (Actually, seven of the agitators were sentenced to death, the eighth to imprisonment.) ❖

for all its benefits, might carry a heavy price in social upheaval, class tensions, and even outright warfare. Most workers did not share in the immense profits of the industrial age, and as the nineteenth century came to a close, there were some who rebelled against the inequity.

Conclusion: Industrialization's Benefits and Costs

In the half century after the Civil War, the United States became an industrial nation—the leading one, in fact, in the world. On one hand, industrialization meant "progress," growth, world power, and in some sense, fulfillment of the American promise of abundance. National wealth grew from $16 billion in 1860 to $88 billion in 1900; wealth per capita more than doubled. For the bulk of the population, the standard of living—a particularly American concept—rose.

But industrialization also meant rapid change, social instability, exploitation of labor, and growing disparity in income between rich and poor. Industry flourished, but control rested in fewer and fewer hands. Maturing quickly, the young system became a new corporate capitalism: giant businesses, interlocking in ownership, managed by a new professional class, and selling an expanding variety of goods in an increasingly controlled market. As goods spread through the society, so did a sharpened, aggressive materialism. Workers felt the strains of the shift to a new social order.

In 1902, a well-to-do New Yorker named Bessie Van Vorst decided to see what it was like to work for a living in a factory. Disguising herself in coarse woolen clothes, a shabby felt hat, a cheap piece of fur, and an old shawl and gloves, she went to Pittsburgh and got a job in a canning factory. She worked ten hours a day, six days a week, including four hours on Saturday afternoons when she and the other women, on their hands and knees, scrubbed the tables, stands, and entire factory floor. For that she earned $4.20 a week, $3 of which went for food alone. "My hands are stiff," she said, "my thumbs almost blistered. . . . Cases are emptied and refilled; bottles are labeled, stamped and rolled away . . . and still there are more cases, more jars, more bottles. Oh! the monotony of it!" The noise around her was deafening; her head grew dazed and weary.

Van Vorst was lucky—when she tired of the life, she could go back to her home in New York. The working men and women around her were not so fortunate. They stayed on the factory floor and, by dint of their labor, created the new industrial society.

Chronology

1859	First oil well drilled near Titusville, Pennsylvania
1866	William Sylvis establishes National Labor Union
1869	Transcontinental railroad completed at Promontory, Utah ❖ Knights of Labor organize
1876	Alexander Graham Bell invents the telephone ❖ Centennial Exposition held in Philadelphia
1877	Railroads cut workers' wages, leading to bloody and violent strike
1879	Thomas A. Edison invents the incandescent lamp
1882	Rockefeller's Standard Oil Company becomes nation's first trust ❖ Edison opens first electric generating station in New York
1883	Railroads introduce standard time zones
1886	Samuel Gompers founds American Federation of Labor (AFL) ❖ Labor protest erupts in violence in Haymarket Riot in Chicago ❖ Railroads adopt standard gauge
1892	Workers strike at Homestead steel plant in Pennsylvania
1893	Economic depression begins
1901	J. P. Morgan announces formation of U.S. Steel Corporation, nation's first billion-dollar company

Recommended Reading

Samuel P. Hays, *The Response to Industrialism: 1885–1914* (1957), is an influential interpretation of the period. Douglass C. North, *Growth and Welfare in the American Past: A New Economic History* (1966), is stimulating. David Montgomery, *The Fall of the House of Labor* (1987), is an outstanding study of labor in the period. Richard Franklin Bensel, *The Political Economy of American Industrialization, 1877–1900* (2000), and Charles Perrow, *Organizing America: Wealth, Power, and the Origins of Corporate Capitalism* (2002), trace the underlying ideas of the new industrialization.

Alfred D. Chandler, *The Visible Hand: The Managerial Revolution in American Business* (1978), Olivier Zunz, *Making America Corporate, 1870–1920* (1990), and JoAnne Yates, *Control Through Communication: The Rise of System in American Management* (1989), are perceptive. The railroad empire is treated in John R. Stilgoe, *Metropolitan Corridor: Railroads and the American Scene* (1983), John

Hoyt Williams, *A Great and Shining Road: The Epic Story of the Transcontinental Railroad* (1988), and John F. Stover, *American Railroads* (1961); its legal implications in, James W. Ely, Jr., *Railroads and American Law* (2001), and Barbara Young Welke, *Recasting American Liberty: Gender, Race, Law, and the Railroad Revolution, 1865–1920* (2001). On the steel industry, see Peter Temin, *Iron and Steel in Nineteenth-Century America* (1964).

Two superb books by Sam Bass Warner, Jr., *Streetcar Suburbs: The Process of Growth in Boston, 1870–1900* (1962), and *The Urban Wilderness: A History of the American City* (1973), examine technology and city development. The wage earner is examined in Herbert G. Gutman, *Work, Culture, and Society in Industrializing America* (1976), and Joshua L. Rosenbloom, *Looking for Work, Searching for Workers: American Labor Markets during Industrialization* (2002). Two books by Stephan Thernstrom, *Poverty and Progress: Social Mobility in the Nineteenth-Century City* (1964) and *The Other Bostonians: Poverty and Progress in the American Metropolis, 1880–1970* (1973), examine mobility. Philip S. Foner, *Women and the American Labor Movement*, 2 vols. (1979), Susan E. Kennedy, *If All We Did Was to Weep at Home* (1979), Barbara Mayer Wertheimer, *We Were There: The Story of Working Women in America* (1977), and Alice Kessler-Harris, *Out to Work: A History of Wage-Earning Women in the United States* (1982), are excellent on the subject of women in the workplace.

For a list of additional titles related to this chapter's topics, please see http://www.ablongman.com/divine.

Suggested Web Sites

Alexander Graham Bell Family Papers at the Library of Congress

http://memory.loc.gov/ammem/bellhtml/bellhome.html
This site contains papers from 1862 to 1939, but includes a chronology, images, selected documents, and interpretive essays about Bell.

The Richest Man in the World: Andrew Carnegie

http://www.pbs.org/wgbh/amex/carnegie/
This American Experience/PBS site provides images and text about Carnegie's life and activities.

The Anarchy Archives at Pitzer University

http://dwardmac.pitzer.edu/Anarchist_Archives/archivehome.html
This archive includes classic anarchist texts, especially information about and graphics of the Haymarket Riot.

John D. Rockefeller and the Standard Oil Company

http://www.micheloud.com/FXM/SO/
This study with accompanying images by François Micheloud tells of the rise of Rockefeller and his mammoth company.

National Refinery Company

http://www.enarco.com/
This positive history of the company reflects the industrial changes of late-nineteenth-century America.

American Labor History

http://www.geocities.com/CollegePark/Quad/6460/AmLabHist/index.html
This site takes a general look at the history of labor in America.

Labor-Management Conflict in American History

http://www.history.ohio-state.edu/projects/laborconflict/
This Ohio State University site includes primary accounts of some of the major events in the history of labor-management conflict in the late nineteenth and early twentieth centuries.

Samuel Gompers Papers at the University of Maryland

http://www.history.umd.edu/Gompers/index.html
This site includes information about the papers project but also has a photo gallery, selected documents, and a brief history of the first president of the American Federation of Labor.

The Strike at Homestead

http://www.history.ohio-state.edu/projects/HomesteadStrike1892/
This site provides a collection of historical documents on the strike and reactions to it.

Chapter 19

During the second half of the nineteenth century, cities of the Midwest drew people and businesses to America's heartland. Milwaukee, shown here in a photograph by William Henry Jackson, was a major center of German immigration. ❖

Toward an Urban Society, 1877–1900

The Overcrowded City

One day around 1900, Harriet Vittum, a settlement house worker in Chicago, went to the aid of a young Polish girl who lived in a nearby slum. The girl, aged 15, had discovered she was pregnant and had taken poison. An ambulance was on the way, and Vittum, told of the poisoning, rushed over to do what she could.

Quickly, she raced up the three flights of stairs to the floor where the girl and her family lived. Pushing open the door, she found the father, several male boarders, and two or three small boys asleep on the kitchen floor. In the next room, the mother was on the floor among several women boarders and one or two small children. Glancing out the window, Vittum saw the wall of another building so close she could reach out and touch it.

There was a third room; in it lay the 15-year-old girl, along with two more small children who were asleep. Looking at the scene, Vittum thought about the girl's life in the crowded tenement. Should she try to save her? Vittum asked herself. Should she even try to bring the girl back "to the misery and hopelessness of the life she was living in that awful place"?

The young girl died, and in later years, Vittum often told her story. It was easy to see why. The girl's life in the slum, the children on the floor, the need to take in boarders to make ends meet, the way the mother and father collapsed at the end of a workday that began long before sunup—all reflected the experiences of millions of people living in the nation's cities.

VITTUM AND PEOPLE LIKE HER were attempting to respond to the overwhelming challenges of the nation's burgeoning cities. People poured into cities in the last part of the nineteenth century, lured by glitter and excitement, by friends and relatives who were already there, and, above all, by the greater opportunities for jobs and higher wages. Between 1860 and 1910, the rural population of the United States almost doubled; the number of people living in cities increased sevenfold.

Little of the increase came from natural growth, since urban families had high rates of infant mortality, a declining fertility rate, and a high death rate from injury and disease. Many of the newcomers came from rural America, and many more came from Europe, Latin America, and Asia. In one of the most significant migrations in American history, thousands of African Americans began in the 1880s to move from the rural South to northern cities. By 1900, there were large black communities in New York, Baltimore, Chicago, Washington, D.C., and other cities. Yet to come was the even greater black migration during World War I.

OUTLINE

FEATURE ESSAY

LAW AND SOCIETY

Two major forces reshaped American society between 1870 and 1920. One was industrialization; the other was urbanization, the headlong rush of people from their rural roots into the modern urban environment. In these years, cities grew upward and outward, attracting millions of newcomers and influencing politics, education, entertainment, and family life. By 1920, they had become the center of American economic, social, and cultural life.

The Lure of the City

William Allen White, later a famous journalist, reflected the country's fascination with the city. He left the small Kansas town of his boyhood in 1891 to go to what he called the "gilded metropolis" of Kansas City. White was 23 years old, and the experience affected him for the rest of his life. He rode the cable cars and used the brand-new telephone—"always with the consciousness that I was tampering with a miracle." He purchased a secondhand dress suit, listened to the music of a sixty-piece orchestra, attended plays, and heard James Whitcomb Riley recite poetry. "Life was certainly one round of joy in Kansas City," White said.

Between 1870 and 1900, the city—like the factory—became a symbol of a new America. Drawn from farms, small towns, and foreign lands, newcomers swelled the population of older cities and created new ones almost overnight. At the beginning of the Civil War, only one-sixth of the American people lived in cities of eight thousand people or more. By 1900, one-third did; by 1920, one-half. "We live in the age of great cities," wrote the Reverend Samuel Lane Loomis in 1887. "Each successive year finds a stronger and more irresistible current sweeping in towards the centers of life."

The current brought growth of an explosive sort. Thousands of years of history had produced only a handful of cities with more than a half million in population. In 1900, the United States had six such cities, including three—New York, Chicago, and Philadelphia—with populations greater than one million.

Skyscrapers and Suburbs

Like so many things in these years, the city was transformed by a revolution in technology. Beginning in the 1880s, the age of steel and glass produced the skyscraper; the streetcar produced the suburbs and new residential patterns.

On the eve of the change, American cities were a crowded jumble of small buildings. Church steeples stood out on the skyline, clearly visible above the roofs of factories and office buildings. Buildings were usually made of masonry, and since the massive walls had to support their own weight, they could be no taller than a dozen or so stories. Steel frames and girders ended that limitation and allowed buildings to soar higher and higher. "Curtain walls," which concealed the steel framework, were no longer load bearing; they

In 1900, Chicago was the most populated U.S. city after New York. The new skyscrapers allowed the city to expand upward, while the elevated rapid transit system enabled the city to sprawl outward into the suburbs. This photograph of Chicago by William Henry Jackson shows the busy sidewalks and elevated track at Wabash Avenue. ❖

were pierced by many windows that let in fresh air and light. Completed in 1885, the Home Insurance Building in Chicago was the country's first metal-frame structure.

To a group of talented Chicago architects, the new trends served as a springboard for innovative forms. The leaders of the movement were John Root and Louis H. Sullivan, both of whom were attracted by the chance to rebuild Chicago after the great fire of 1871. Noting that the fire had fed on fancy exterior ornamentation, Root developed a plain, stripped-down style, bold in mass and form—the keynotes of modern architecture. He had another important insight, too. In an age of business, Root thought, the office tower, more than a church or a government building, symbolized the society, and he designed office buildings that carried out, as he said, "the ideas of modern business life: simplicity, stability, breadth, dignity."

Sullivan had studied at the Massachusetts Institute of Technology (MIT) and in Paris before settling in Chicago. In 1886, at the age of 30, he began work on the Chicago Auditorium, one of the last great masonry buildings. "Then came the flash of imagination which saw the single thing," he later said. "The trick was turned; and there swiftly came into being something new under the sun." Sullivan's skyscrapers, that "flash of imagination," changed the urban skyline.

In the Wainwright Building in St. Louis (1890), the Schiller Building (1892) and the Carson, Pirie, and Scott department store (1899) in Chicago, and the Prudential Building in Buffalo (1895), Sullivan developed the new forms. Architects must discard "books, rules, precedents," he announced; responding to the new, they should design for a building's function. "Form follows function," Sullivan believed, and he passed the idea on to a talented disciple, Frank Lloyd Wright. The modern city should stretch to the sky. A skyscraper "must be every inch a proud and soaring thing, rising in sheer exaltation . . . from bottom to top."

Electric elevators, first used in 1871, carried passengers upward in the new skyscrapers. During the same years, streetcars, another innovation, carried the people outward to expanded boundaries that transformed urban life.

Cities were no longer largely "walking cities," confined to a radius of two or three miles, the distance an individual might walk. Streetcar systems extended the radius and changed the urban map. Cable lines, electric surface lines, and elevated rapid transit brought shoppers and workers into central business districts and sped them home again. Offering a modest five-cent fare with a free transfer, the mass transit systems fostered commuting and widely separated business and residential districts sprang up. The middle class moved farther and farther out to the leafy greenness of the suburbs.

As the middle class moved out of the cities, the immigrants and working class poured in. They took over the older brownstones, row houses, and workers' cottages, turning them, under the sheer weight of numbers, into the slums of the central city. In the cities of the past, classes and occupations had been thrown together; without streetcars and subways, there was no other choice. The streetcar city, sprawling and specialized, became a more fragmented and stratified society with middle-class residential rings surrounding a business and working-class core.

Tenements and the Problems of Overcrowding

In the shadow of the skyscrapers, grimy rows of tenements filled the central city. Exploring them in words and photographs, Jacob Riis described *How the Other Half Lives* (1890):

> Be a little careful, please! The hall is dark and you might stumble. . . . Here where the hall turns and dives into utter darkness is . . . a flight of stairs. You can feel your way, if you cannot see it. Close? Yes! What would you have? All the fresh air that enters these stairs comes from the hall-door that is forever slamming. . . . Here is a door. Listen! That short,

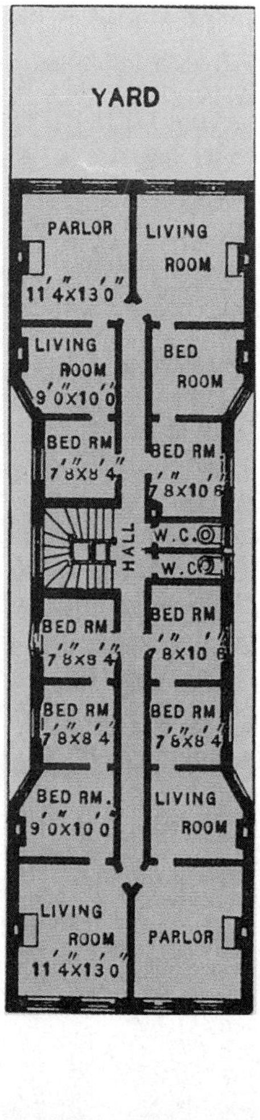

This 1879 dumbbell floor plan was meant to provide four apartments to a floor. However, a whole family might live in each room. Crowded, unsanitary conditions contributed to the spread of tuberculosis, the chief cause of death in the United States until 1909. ❖

The kitchen of a tenement apartment was often a multipurpose room. Here the tenement dwellers prepared and ate their meals; the room might also serve as a workroom, and it might be used as sleeping quarters for one or more members of the family. ❖

> hacking cough, that tiny, helpless wail—what do they mean? . . . The child is dying of measles. With half a chance it might have lived; but it had none. That dark bedroom killed it.

Tenement houses on small city lots crowded people into cramped apartments. In the late 1870s, architect James E. Ware won a competition for tenement design with the "dumbbell tenement." Rising seven or eight stories in height, the dumbbell tenement packed about 30 four-room apartments on a lot only 25 by 100 feet. Between four and sixteen families lived on a floor; two toilets in the hall of each floor served their needs. Narrowed at the middle, the tenement resembled a giant dumbbell in shape. The indented middle created an air shaft between adjoining buildings that provided a little light and ventilation. In case of fire, it also carried flames from one story to the next, making the buildings notorious firetraps. In 1890, nearly half the dwellings in New York City were tenements.

That year, more than 1.4 million people lived on Manhattan Island, one of whose wards had a population density of 334,000 people per square mile. Many people lived in alleys and basements so dark they could not be photographed until flashlight photography was invented in 1887. Exploring the city, William Dean Howells, the prominent author, inhaled "the stenches of the neglected street . . . [and] the yet fouler and dreadfuller poverty smell which breathes from the open doorways."

Howells smelled more than poverty. In the 1870s and 1880s, cities stank. One problem was horse manure, hundreds of tons of it a day in every city. Another was the privy, "a single one of which," said a leading authority on public health, "may render life in a whole neighborhood almost unendurable in the summer."

Baltimore smelled "like a billion polecats," recalled H. L. Mencken, who grew up there. Said one New York City resident, "The stench is something terrible." Another wrote that "the stink is enough to knock you down." In 1880, the Chicago *Times* said that a "solid stink" pervaded the city. "No other word expresses it so well as stink. A stench means something finite. Stink reaches the infinite and becomes sublime in the magnitude of odiousness." In 1892, one neighborhood of Chicago, covering one-third of a square mile, had only three bathtubs.

Cities dumped their wastes into the nearest body of water, then drew drinking water from the same site. Many built modern purified waterworks but could not keep pace with spiraling growth. In 1900, fewer than one in ten city dwellers drank filtered water. Factories, the pride of the era, polluted the urban air. At night, Pittsburgh looked and sounded like "Hell with the lid off," according to contemporary observers. Smoke poured from seventy-three glass factories, forty-one iron and steel mills, and twenty-nine oil refineries. The choking air helped prevent lung diseases and malaria—or so the city's advertising claimed.

Crime was another growing problem. The nation's homicide rate nearly tripled in the 1880s, much of the increase coming in the cities. Slum youths formed street gangs with names such as the Hayes Valley Gang in San Francisco and the Baxter Street Dudes, the Daybreak Boys, and the Alley Gang in New York. After remaining constant for many decades, the suicide rate rose steadily between 1870 and 1900, according to a study of Philadelphia. Alcoholism also rose, especially among men, though recent studies have shown that for working-class men, the urban saloon was as much a gathering spot as it was a place to drink. Nonetheless, a 1905 survey of Chicago counted as many saloons as grocery stores, meat markets, and dry goods stores combined.

Strangers in a New Land

While some of the new city dwellers came from farms and small towns, many more came from abroad. Most came from Europe, where unemployment, food shortages, and increasing threats of war sent millions fleeing across the Atlantic to make a fresh start. Often they knew someone already in the United States, a friend or relative who had written them about prospects for jobs and freer lives in a new land. Italians first came in large numbers to escape an 1887 cholera epidemic in southern Italy; tens of thousands of Jews sought refuge from the anti-Semitic massacres that swept Russia and czarist-ruled Poland after 1880.

All told, the immigration figures were staggering. Between 1877 and 1890, more than 6.3 million people entered the United States. In one year alone, 1882, almost 789,000 people came. By 1890, about 15 percent of the population, 9 million people, were foreign born. (See "Americans by the Numbers: The 1890 Census," pp. 604–605.)

Most newcomers were job seekers. Nearly two-thirds were males, and the majority were between the ages of 15 and 40. Most were unskilled laborers. Most settled on the eastern seaboard. In 1901, the Industrial Relocation Office was established to relieve overcrowding in the eastern cities; opening Galveston, Texas, as a port of entry, it attracted many Russian Jews to Texas and the Southwest. But most immigrants preferred the shorter, more familiar journey to New York. Entering through Ellis Island in New York harbor, as four in every ten immigrants did, most tended to

IMMIGRATION TO THE UNITED STATES, 1870–1900

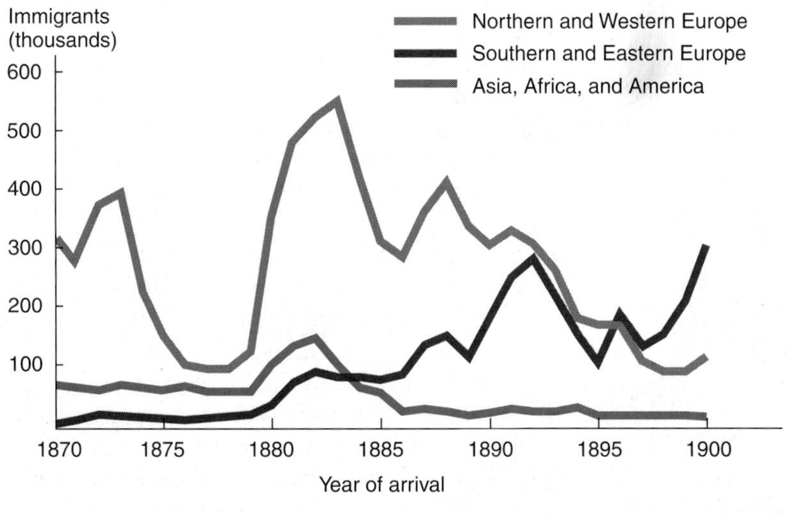

Note: For purposes of classification, "Northern and Western Europe" includes Great Britain, Ireland, Scandinavia, the Netherlands, Belgium, Luxembourg, Switzerland, France, and Germany. "Southern and Eastern Europe" includes Poland, Austria-Hungary, Russia and the Baltic States, Romania, Bulgaria, European Turkey, Italy, Spain, Portugal, and Greece. "Asia, Africa, and America" includes Asian Turkey, China, Japan, India, Canada, the Caribbean, Latin America, and all of Africa.

Source: U.S. Bureau of the Census, *Historical Statistics of the United States, Colonial Times to 1970,* Bicentennial Edition, Washington, DC, 1975.

Feature Essay

Ellis Island

Isle of Hope, Isle of Tears

Ten years after he left Selo, his small Bulgarian village, for the United States, Michael Gurkin returned to tell of the wonders he had seen, including "buildings that scratched the sky," rooms in them that moved up and down, buttons that, pushed, lit a house or a street. Stoyan Christowe, 13, listened intently, caught up in the "Americamania," as he called it, that swept through his village. Soon he was on his way to the new land, his pockets stuffed with walnuts because he was too young to drink the farewell toast.

Unknowingly, he had joined a flood of people who were making their way to the United States. Between 1880 and 1920, a period of just forty years, the remarkable total of 23.5 million immigrants arrived in the country. They came from around the world, though mostly from Europe, driven from their homelands by economic, religious, or other troubles, lured across the ocean by the chance for a better life. They entered the country through several ports, but by far the most—about seven out of every ten—landed in the city of New York.

Until 1892, they landed at a depot known as Castle Garden, a sprawling building on the tip of Manhattan Island. When it could no longer handle the flow, the entry site was moved to Ellis Island, a bank of sand and shells, close to the Statue of Liberty. Contractors erected a wooden structure, which opened in 1892 and burned down five years later. They then put up the current edifice, an imposing red brick building with triple-arch entrances and corner steeples. A small city, it had dormitories, a hospital, a post office, and showers that could bathe eight thousand people a day. It opened in 1900.

The change to Ellis Island represented more than just a shift in site. Entrance at Castle Garden had been fairly informal, since control over immigration still rested largely in the hands of the states. Officials merely registered newcomers, a process that took about thirty seconds.

In 1891, worried about the growing numbers of people who wanted in, Congress acted to bring immigration under federal control. Ellis Island was given tasks Castle Garden had never had, including mandates to keep out people some Americans considered undesirable. It became, one observer said, "the nearest earthly likeness to the Final Day of Judgement, when we have to prove our fitness to enter Heaven."

Many of those who sailed into the harbor, it should be remembered, never passed through the island at all. Arriving in first or second class, they had a fast on-board examination and went ashore, monied enough, it was assumed, not to become wards of the state. But those in third class—"steerage," as it was known—had a very different experience, and they faced it chock full of fear they would fail some test and be sent back home.

The day they docked, in 1910, Christowe and others washed thoroughly, hoping to look clean enough to pass inspection. Crowding the ship's rails, they gazed in wonder at the statue in the harbor, its arm lifted in the air. It was a saint, some guessed; Christopher Columbus, others said. It was a monument to freedom, Christowe was told, with Emma Lazarus's inviting poem at its base, "Give me your tired, your poor, Your huddled masses yearning to breathe free."

Once on the island, those huddled masses were under scrutiny from the moment they landed. Officials watched them climb the stairs, looking for heart problems or lameness.

A view of the landing station at Ellis Island in 1905, where millions of immigrants entered the country. ❖

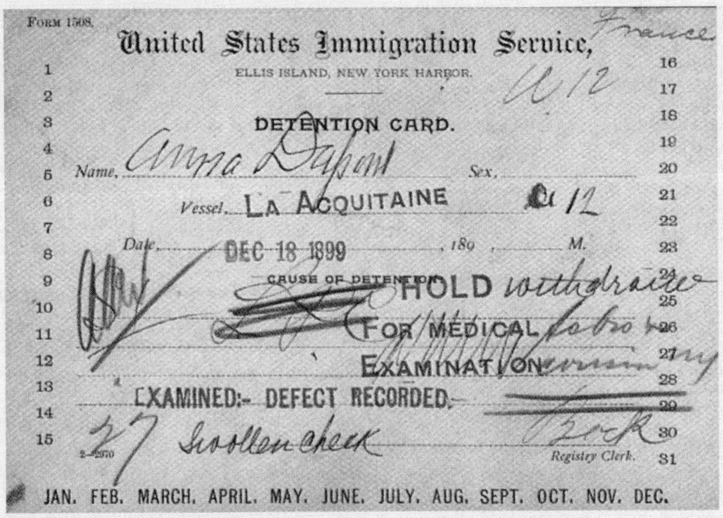
FORM 1508.

United States Immigration Service,

ELLIS ISLAND, NEW YORK HARBOR.

DETENTION CARD.

Name, Anna Dapont Sex,

Vessel, LA ACQUITAINE

Date, DEC 18 1899 , 189 , M.

CAUSE OF DETENTION HOLD FOR MEDICAL EXAMINATION

EXAMINED:- DEFECT RECORDED.

27 Swollen cheek

Registry Clerk.

JAN. FEB. MARCH. APRIL. MAY. JUNE. JULY. AUG. SEPT. OCT. NOV. DEC.

Ellis Island Detention Card for a French immigrant detained because of a "swollen cheek." ❖

Physicians administered the "six-second exam," checking quickly for disabilities or contagious diseases. If anything seemed out of sort, they put a chalk mark on the immigrant's coat calling for closer examination.

The next exam was the most feared of all: a doctor using a tailor's buttonhook to pull back eyelids to look for signs of diseases such as trachoma, a highly contagious bacterial eye infection that could lead to blindness. Most immigrants had never heard of trachoma, nor even knew they had the disease but it alone could strand them in the island's hospital or put them on a boat back home.

No one who went through the exam ever forgot it, as an immigrant poet wrote:

> A stranger receives us
> Harshly and asks: "And your health?"
> He examines us. His look
> Assesses us like dogs.
>
> He studies in depth
> Eyes and mouth. No doubt
> That if he'd probed our hearts
> He would have seen the wound.

Immigrants with chalk marks were herded to the left, while most went to the right, filing by a matron who searched the faces of women for evidence of "loose character." With so many languages among the arrivals, there were few written signs, and officials used metal barricades to guide people along, "like puppets on conveyor-belts," Christowe later recalled.

Last there were the inspectors, seated behind desks, asking name, age, occupation, among dozens of other questions. On a busy day, the inspectors had two minutes to decide the fate of a newcomer. Those who "failed" went before a feared Board of Special Inquiry for final decision. For most immigrants the whole process took less than five hours; many others, held for proof of funds or further examination, spent days in the dormitories or hospital. Despite the harsh rumors, no more than 3 percent in a given year were turned away.

Still, it was becoming harder and harder to get in. People who feared the effect of immigrants on the nation clamored to keep them out. Some worried about the numbers of people who were arriving; others about disease or "radical" political views. Some did not like the shift in immigration after 1890 from largely Protestant northern and western Europe to Catholics, Jews, and others from southern and eastern Europe.

Reflecting such concerns, Congress passed laws to keep certain types of people out. In 1875, it prohibited the entrance of criminals and prostitutes. In 1882, it barred convicts and lunatics and excluded laborers from China, the first measure aimed directly at a racial group. In 1885, it banned the entry of laborers under contract, imported by industries to work at low wages; in 1891, polygamists and people with "loathsome" diseases; in 1903, anarchists. In 1917, it passed, over Woodrow Wilson's veto, a literacy test that required immigrants to read a passage in their native tongue.

The great burst of immigration, halted during World War I, ended with the adoption of restrictive legislation in the 1920s. Ellis Island became more and more a detention center for "radicals" and other people awaiting deportation. Once the gateway to the United States, the famous island had become an exit.

Ellis Island closed in 1954 and in 1965, recognizing its historic importance, the government made it a national monument. It reopened in 1990 as a museum of American immigration, and is so popular it attracts more than two million tourists a year; many of whom retrace the footsteps of their own ancestors who had landed there. Stoyan Christowe's name is in the records. Starting with a miserable job in a railroad yard in St. Louis, he went to college, served in military intelligence during World War II, wrote several books, and became a member of the Vermont legislature.

His experience on Ellis Island blended into the nation's experience. More than 100 million Americans—about four in every ten—trace their ancestry to those who found a new home through its gates.

U.S. inspectors questioned and examined immigrants at Ellis Island. In this photograph from 1905, a woman is shown receiving an eye inspection. ❖

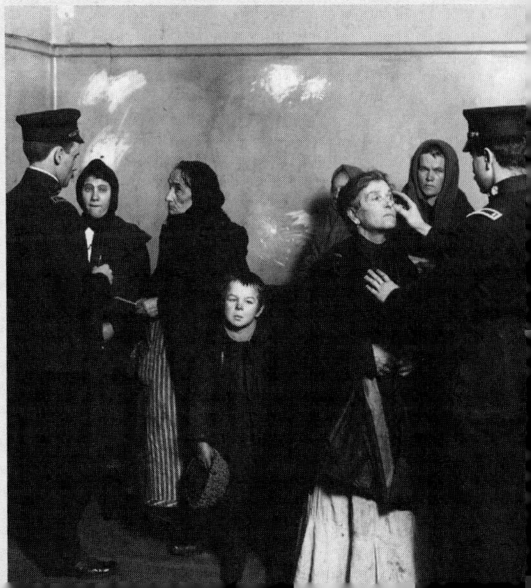

FOREIGN-BORN POPULATION, 1890 *Immigrants tended to settle in regions where jobs were relatively plentiful or conditions were similar to those they had left in their homelands. Cities of the northeast, Midwest, and West offered job opportunities, while land available for cultivation drew immigrant farmers to the plains and prairies of the nation's midsection.*

crowd into northern and eastern cities, settling in areas where others of their nationality or religion lived. (See the Feature Essay, "Ellis Island: Isle of Hope, Isle of Tears," pp. 544–545.)

They were often dazzled by what they saw. They stared at electric lights, indoor plumbing, soda fountains, streetcars, plush train seats for all classes, ice cream, lemons, and bananas. Relatives whisked them off to buy new "American" clothes and showed them the teeming markets, department stores, and Woolworth's new five-and-ten stores. "It seemed quite advanced compared with our home in Khelm," said a Polish girl. "There was a sense of safety and hope that we had never felt in Poland."

Cities had increasingly large foreign-born populations. In 1900, four-fifths of Chicago's population was foreign born or of foreign-born parentage, two-thirds of Boston's, and one-half of Philadelphia's. New York City, where most immigrants arrived and many stayed, had more Italians than lived in Naples, more Germans than lived in Hamburg, and twice as many Irish as lived in Dublin. Four out of five New York City residents in 1890 were of foreign birth or foreign parentage.

Beginning in the 1880s, the sources of immigration shifted dramatically away from northern and western Europe, the chief source of immigration for more than two centuries. More and more immigrants came from southern and eastern Europe: Italy, Greece, Austria-Hungary, Poland, and Russia. Between 1880 and 1910, approximately 8.4 million people came from these lands. The **new immigrants** tended to be Catholics or Jews rather than Protestants. Like their predecessors, most were unskilled rather than skilled, and they often spoke "strange" languages. Most were poor and uneducated; sticking together in close-knit communities, they clung to their native customs, languages, and religions.

More than any previous group, the so-called new immigrants troubled the mainstream society. Could they be assimilated? Did they share "American" values? Such questions preoccupied groups like the American Protective Association, a midwestern anti-Catholic organization that expanded in the 1890s and worked to limit or end immigration. Sneering epithets became part of the national vocabulary: "wop" and "dago" for Italians; "bohunk" for Bohemians, Hungarians, and other Slavs; "greaseball" for Greeks; and "kike" for Jews. "You don't call . . . an Italian a white man?" a congressman asked a railroad construction boss in 1890. "No, sir," the boss replied. "An Italian is a Dago."

Anti-Catholicism and anti-Semitism flared up again, as they had in the 1850s. Edward A. Ross, a prominent sociologist, publicly decried "the lower class of Jews of Eastern Europe [who] reach here [as] moral cripples, their souls warped and dwarfed." In 1889, the head of the Fresh Air Fund, a program that sent New York City children on vacations to the suburbs, noted that "no one asked for Italian children." The Immigration Restriction League, founded in 1894, demanded a literacy test for immigrants from southern and eastern Europe. Congress passed such a law in 1896, but President Cleveland vetoed it.

Immigrants and the City

Industrial capitalism—the world of factories and foremen and grimy machines—tested the immigrants and placed an enormous strain on their families. Many immigrants came from peasant societies where life proceeded according to outdoor routine and age-old tradition. In their new city homes, they found both new freedoms and new confinements, a different language, and a novel set of customs and expectations. Historians have only recently begun to discover the remarkable ways in which they learned to adjust.

Like native-born families, most immigrant families were nuclear in structure—they consisted of two parents and their children. Though variations occurred from group to group, men and women occupied roles similar to those in native families: Men were wage earners, women were housekeepers and mothers. Margaret Byington, who studied steelworkers' homes in Homestead in the early 1900s, learned that the father played a relatively small role in child rearing or managing the family's finances. "His part of the problem is to earn and hers to spend." In Chicago, social reformer Jane Addams discovered that immigrant women made it "a standard of domestic virtue that a man must not touch his pay envelope, but bring it home unopened to his wife."

Although patterns varied among ethnic groups, and between economic classes within ethnic groups, immigrants tended to marry within the group more than did the native born. In one New York community, only 2 percent of French Canadian and 7 percent of Irish workingmen married outside their ethnic group in 1880, compared to almost 40 percent of native-born workingmen. Immigrants also tended to marry at a later age than natives, and they tended to have more children, a fact that worried nativists opposed to immigration.

Immigrants shaped the city as much as it shaped them. Most of them tried to retain their traditional culture for themselves and their children while at the same time adapting to life in their new country. To do this, they spoke their native language, practiced their religious faith, read their own newspapers, and established special parochial or other schools. They observed traditional holidays and formed a myriad of social organizations to maintain ties among members of the group.

Immigrant associations—there were many of them in every city—offered fellowship in a strange land. They helped newcomers find jobs and homes; they provided important services such as unemployment insurance and health insurance. In a Massachusetts textile town, the Irish Benevolent Society said, "We visit our sick, and

In a Puck *cartoon titled "Looking Backward," the shadows of their immigrant origins loom over the rich and powerful who wanted to deny the "new" immigrants from central and southern Europe admission to America. The caption on the cartoon reads, "They would close to the newcomer the bridge that carried them and their fathers over."* ❖

The fiftieth-anniversary issue of the Illinois Staats Zeitung, the Chicago-area German-language newspaper with the largest circulation. There were more than twenty German-language newspapers distributed in Chicago in the 1890s. ❖

bury our dead." Some groups were no larger than a neighborhood; others spread nationwide. In 1914, the Deutsch-Amerikanischer Nationalbund, the largest of the associations, had more than two million members in dozens of cities and towns. Many women belonged to and participated in the work of the immigrant associations; in addition, there were groups exclusively for women, such as the Polish Women's Alliance, the Jednota Ceskyck Dam (Society of Czech Women), and the National Council of Jewish Women.

The Polish National Alliance (PNA), a typical immigrant association, was founded in 1880. Like other organizations, it helped new immigrants on their arrival, offered insurance plans, established libraries and museums, sponsored youth programs, fielded baseball teams, and organized trips back to Poland. Each year, the PNA published a sought-after calendar filled with Polish holidays, information, and proverbs. Extolling Poles' contributions to their new country, it erected monuments to distinguished Americans of Polish descent.

Every major city had dozens of foreign language newspapers, with circulations large and small. The first newspaper published in the Lithuanian language appeared in the United States, not in Lithuania. Eagerly read, the papers not only carried news of events in the homeland but also reported on local ethnic leaders, told readers how to vote and become citizens, and gave practical tips on adjusting to life in the United States. The Swedes, Poles, Czechs, and Germans established ethnic theaters that performed national plays and music. The most famous of these, the Yiddish (Jewish) Theater, started in the 1880s in New York City and lasted more than fifty years.

The church and the school were the most important institutions in every immigrant community. Eastern European Jews established synagogues and religious schools wherever they settled; they taught the Hebrew language and raised their children in a heritage they did not want to leave behind. Among such groups as the Irish and the Poles, the Roman Catholic church provided spiritual and educational guidance. In the parish schools, Polish priests and nuns taught Polish American children about Polish as well as American culture in the Polish language.

Church, school, and fraternal societies shaped the way in which immigrants adjusted to life in America. By preserving language, religion, and heritage, they also shaped the country itself.

The House That Tweed Built

Closely connected with explosive urban growth was the emergence of the powerful city political machine. As cities grew, lines of responsibility in city governments became hopelessly confused, increasing the opportunity for corruption and greed. Burgeoning populations required streets, buildings, and public services; immigrants needed even more services. In this situation, political party machines played an important role.

The machines traded services for votes. Loosely knit, they were headed by a strong, influential leader—the "boss"—who tied together a network of ward and precinct captains, each of whom looked after his local constituents. In New York, "Honest" John Kelly, Richard Croker, and Charles F. Murphy led Tammany Hall, the famous Democratic party organization that dominated city politics from the 1850s to the 1930s. Other bosses included "Hinky Dink" Kenna and "Bathhouse John" Coughlin in Chicago, James McManes in Philadelphia, and Christopher A. Buckley—the notorious "Blind Boss," who used an exceptional memory for voices to make up for failing eyesight—in San Francisco.

William M. Tweed, head of the famed Tweed Ring in New York, provided the model for them all.

❖ A Look at the Past ❖

Political Cartoon

The downfall of "Boss Tweed" was directly attributable to the political cartoons of Thomas Nast who exposed the infamy of Tammany Hall corruption and the Tweed Ring to the reading public. Tweed was reported to have told his henchmen: "Stop them damn pictures. I don't care what the papers write about me. My constituents can't read. But, damn it, they can see pictures." Tweed sent representatives to Nast with offers of a half million dollar bribe if he would quit drawing cartoons, but Nast spent five more years exposing Tweed and his fellow culprits by cartoon until the Boss ended up in prison on corruption charges. This graphic was among that series. Tweed and his cronies point to each other under the caption: "Who Stole the People's Money? Do Tell—'TWAS HIM." Tweed is the large individual with a diamond stud on his shirt on the left.

Nearly six feet tall, weighing almost three hundred pounds, Tweed rose through the ranks of Tammany Hall. He served in turn as city alderman, member of Congress, and New York State assemblyman. A man of culture and warmth, he moved easily between the rough back alleys of New York and the parlors and clubs of the city's elite. Behind the scenes, he headed a ring that plundered New York for tens of millions of dollars.

The New York County Courthouse—"the house that Tweed built"—was his masterpiece. Nestled in City Hall Park in downtown Manhattan, the three-story structure was designed to cost $250,000, but the bills ran a bit higher. Furniture, carpets, and window shades alone came to more than $5.5 million. Three tables and forty chairs cost the city $180,000. Tweed's own quarry supplied the marble; the plumber was paid almost $1.5 million for fixtures. Andrew Garvey, the "prince of plasterers," charged $500,000 for plasterwork, and then $1 million to repair the same work. His total bill came to $2,870,464.06. (The *New York Times* suggested that the six cents be donated to charity.) In the end, the building cost more than $13 million—and in 1872, when Tweed fell, it was still not finished.

The role of the political bosses can be overemphasized. Power structures in the turn-of-the-century city were complex, involving a host of people and institutions. Banks, real estate investors, insurance companies, architects, and engineers, among others, played roles in governing the city. Viewed in retrospect, many city governments were remarkably successful. With populations that in some cases doubled every decade, city governments provided water and sewer lines, built parks and playgrounds, and paved streets. When it was over, Boston had the world's largest public library and New York City had the Brooklyn Bridge and Central Park, two of the finest achievements in city planning and architecture of any era. By the 1890s, New York also had 660 miles of water lines, 464 miles of sewers, and 1800 miles of paved streets, far more than comparable cities in Europe.

Bosses, moreover, differed from city to city. Buckley stayed in power in San Francisco by keeping city tax rates low. "Honest" John Kelly earned his nickname serving as a watchdog over the New York City treasury. Tweed was one of the early backers of the Brooklyn Bridge. Some bosses were plainly corrupt; others believed in *honest graft,* a term Tammany's George Washington Plunkitt coined to describe "legitimate" profits made from advance knowledge of city projects.

Why did voters keep the bosses in power? The answers are complex, but two reasons were skillful political organization and the fact that immigrants and others made up the bosses' constituency. Most immigrants had little experience with democratic government and proved easy prey for well-oiled machines. For the most part, however, the bosses stayed in power because they paid attention to the needs of the least privileged city voters. They offered valued services in an era when neither government nor business lent a hand.

If an immigrant, tired and bewildered after the long crossing, came looking for a job, bosses like Tweed, Plunkitt, or Buckley found him one in city offices or local businesses. If a family's breadwinner died or was injured, the bosses donated food and clothing and saw to it that the family made it through the crisis. If the winter was particularly cold, they provided free coal to heat tenement apartments. They ran picnics for slum children on hot summer days and contributed to hospitals, orphanages, and dozens of worthy neighborhood causes.

Most bosses became wealthy; they were not Robin Hoods who took from the rich to give to the poor. They took for themselves as well. Reformers occasionally ousted them. Tweed fell from power in 1872, "Blind Boss" Buckley in 1891, Croker in 1894. But the reformers rarely stayed in power long. Drawn mainly from the middle and upper classes, they had little understanding of the needs of the poor. Before long, they returned to private concerns, and the bosses, who had known that they would all along, cheerily took power again.

"What tells in holdin' your grip on your district," the engaging Plunkitt once said, "is to go right down among the poor families and help them in the different ways they need help. . . . It's philanthropy, but it's politics, too—mighty good politics. . . . The poor are the most grateful people in the world."

Social and Cultural Change, 1877–1900

The rise of cities and industry between 1877 and the 1890s affected all aspects of American life. Mores changed; family ties loosened. Factories turned out consumer goods, and the newly invented cash register rang up record sales. Public and private educational systems burgeoned, illiteracy declined, life expectancy increased. While many people worked harder and harder just to survive, others found they had a greater amount of leisure time. The roles of women and children changed in a number of ways, and the family took on functions it had not had before. Thanks to advancing technology, news flashed quickly across the oceans, and for the first time in history, people read of the day's events in distant lands when they opened their daily newspapers.

"We are in a period," President Rutherford B. Hayes said in 1878, "when old questions are settled, and the new ones are not yet brought forward." Old questions—questions of racial, social and economic justice, and of federal-state relations—were not settled, but people wanted new directions. Political issues lost the sharp focus of the Civil War and Reconstruction. For men and women of middle age in 1877, the issues of the Union and slavery had been the overriding public concerns throughout their adult lives. Now, with the end of Reconstruction, it seemed time for new concerns.

In 1877, the country had 47 million people. In 1900, it had nearly 76 million. Nine-tenths of the population was white; just under one-tenth was black. There were 66,000 American Indians, 108,000 Chinese, and 148 Japanese. The bulk of the white population, most of whom were Protestant, came from the so-called Anglo-Saxon countries of northern Europe. WASPs—white Anglo-Saxon Protestants—were the dominant members of American society.

Though the rush to the cities was about to begin, most people of 1877 still lived on farms or in small towns. Their lives revolved around the farm, the church, and the general store. In 1880, nearly 75 percent of the population lived in communities of fewer than 2500 people. In 1900, in the midst of city growth, 60 percent still did. The average family in 1880 had three children, dramatically fewer than at the beginning of the century, and life expectancy was about 43 years. By 1900, it had risen to 47 years, a result of improved health care. For blacks and other minorities, who often lived in unsanitary rural areas, life expectancy was substantially lower: 33 years.

In small towns, houses were usually made of wooden shingles or clapboard, set back from unpaved streets. Life was quiet. Many homes had a front porch for summertime sitting. In the backyard there were numerous outbuildings, including one—at the end of a well-worn path—with a distinctive half moon carved in the door. There was a vegetable garden and often a chicken coop or cowshed; families—even in the cities—needed backyard produce to supplement their diets.

Meals tended to be heavy, and so did people. Even breakfast had several courses and could include steak, eggs, fish, potatoes, toast, and coffee. Food prices were

URBAN AND RURAL POPULATION, 1870–1900 (IN MILLIONS)

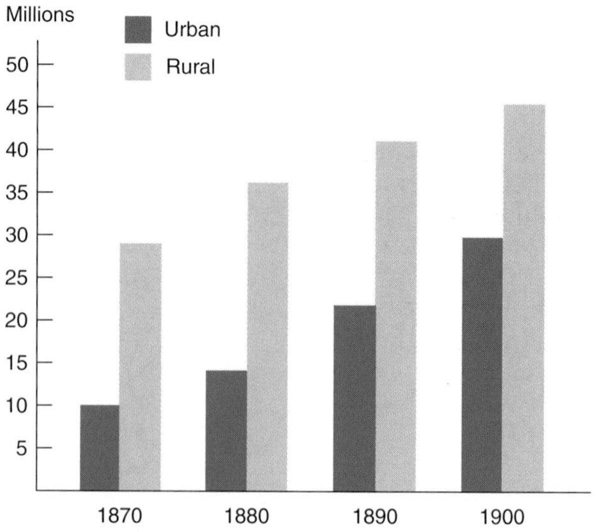

Source: U.S. Bureau of the Census, *Historical Statistics of the United States, Colonial Times to 1970,* Bicentennial Edition, Washington, DC, 1975.

low. Families ate fresh homegrown produce in the summer and "put up" their fruits and vegetables for the long winters. Toward the end of the century, eating habits changed. New packaged breakfast cereals became popular; fresh fruit and vegetables came in on fast trains from Florida and California, and commercially canned food became safer and cheaper. The newfangled icebox, cooled by blocks of ice, kept food fresher and added new treats such as ice cream.

Medical science was in the midst of a major revolution. Louis Pasteur's recent discovery that germs cause infection and disease created the new science of microbiology and led the way to the development of vaccines and other preventive measures. But tuberculosis, typhoid, diphtheria, and pneumonia—all now curable—were still the leading causes of death. Infant mortality declined between 1877 and 1900, but the decline was gradual; a great drop did not come until after 1920.

There were few hospitals and no hospital insurance. Most patients stayed at home, although medical practice, especially surgery, expanded rapidly. Once brutal and dangerous, surgery in these years became relatively safe and painless. Anesthetics—ether and chloroform—eliminated pain, and antiseptic practices helped prevent postoperative infections. Antiseptic practices at childbirth also cut down on puerperal fever, an infection that for centuries had killed many women and newborn infants. The new science of psychology began to explore the mind, hitherto uncharted. William James, a leading American psychologist and philosopher, laid the foundations of modern behavioral psychology, which stressed the importance of the environment on human development.

Victorian fashion ideals for women emphasized elaborate, confining dress styles with a tiny waistline and full skirts that reached to the floor. Throughout the 1890s, as women began to participate in some of the new sports or go to work in factories, stores, or business offices, styles gradually became less restrictive. This 1900 cover of Ladies' Home Journal *shows women wearing tailored jackets and simple pleated skirts hemmed above the ankle playing golf with men.* ❖

Manners and Mores

The code of Victorian morality, its name derived from the British queen who reigned throughout the period, set the tone for the era. The code prescribed strict standards of dress, manners, and sexual behavior. It was both obeyed and disobeyed, and it reflected the tensions of a generation that was undergoing a change in moral standards.

In 1877, children were to be seen and not heard. They spoke when spoken to, listened rather than chattered—or at least that was the rule. Older boys and girls were often chaperoned, although they could always find moments alone. They played post office and spin the bottle; they puffed cigarettes behind the barn. Journalist William Allen White recalled the high jinks of his boyhood. He and his friends smeared their naked bodies with mud and leaped out in full view of passengers on passing trains. Counterbalancing such youthful exuberance was strong pride in virtue and self-control. "Thank heaven I am absolutely pure," Theodore Roosevelt, the future president, wrote in 1880 after proposing to Alice Lee. "I can tell Alice everything I have ever done."

Gentlemen of the middle class dressed in heavy black suits, derby hats, and white shirts with paper collars. Women wore tight corsets, long dark dresses, and black shoes reaching well above the ankles. As with so many things, styles changed dramatically toward the end of the century, spurred in part by new sporting fads such as golf, tennis, and bicycling, which required looser clothing. By the 1890s, a middle-class woman wore a tailored suit or a dark skirt and a blouse, called a shirtwaist, modeled after men's shirts. Her skirts still draped about the ankles, but more and more she removed or loosened the corset, the dread device that squeezed skin and internal organs into fashionable 18-inch waistlines.

Religious and patriotic values were strong. A center of community life, the church often set the tenor for family and social relationships. In the 1880s, eight out of ten church members were Protestants; most of the rest were Roman Catholics. Evangelists such as Dwight L. Moody (a former Chicago shoe salesman) and Ira B. Sankey (an organist and singer) conducted mass revival meetings across the country. Enormously successful, Moody preached to millions and sparked a spiritual awakening on American college campuses.

With slavery abolished, reformers turned their attention to new moral and political issues. One group, known as the **Mugwumps,** worked to end corruption in politics. Drawn mostly from the educated and upper class, they included Thomas Nast, the famous political cartoonist; George William Curtis, editor of *Harper's Weekly;* and E. L. Godkin, editor of the influential *Nation.* Other zealous reformers campaigned for prohibition of the sale of intoxicating liquors, hoping to end the social evils that stemmed from drunkenness. In 1874, women who advocated total abstinence from alcoholic beverages formed the **Women's Christian Temperance Union (WCTU).** Their leader, Frances E. Willard, served as president of the group from 1879 until her death in 1898. By then, the WCTU had 10,000 branches and 500,000 members.

In New York City, Anthony Comstock formed the Society for the Suppression of Vice, which supervised public morality. At his request, Congress passed the Comstock Law (1873) prohibiting the mailing or transporting of "obscene, lewd or lascivious" articles. The law was not successful; within a few years, Comstock reported finding 64,094 "articles for immoral use," 700 pounds of "lead moulds for making obscene matter," 202,679 obscene photographs, and 26 "obscene pictures, framed on walls of saloons."

Leisure and Entertainment

In the 1870s, people tended to rise early. On getting up, they washed from the pitcher and bowl in the bedroom, first breaking the layer of ice if it was winter. After dressing and eating, they went off to work and school. Without large refrigerators, housewives marketed almost daily. In the evening, families gathered in the "second parlor" or living room, where the children did their lessons, played games, sang around the piano, and listened to that day's verse from the Bible.

Popular games included cards, dominoes, backgammon, chess, and checkers. Many homes had a packet of "author cards" that required knowledge of books, authors, and noted quotations. The latest fad was the stereopticon or "magic lantern," which brought three-dimensional life to art, history, and nature. Like author cards and other games, it was instructional as well as entertaining.

The newest outdoor game was croquet, so popular that candles were mounted on the wickets to allow play at night. Croquet was the first outdoor game designed for play by both sexes, and it frequently served as a setting for courtship. Early manuals advised girls how to assume attractive poses while hitting the ball. A popular song of the period told of a pair seated side by side:

> Mallets and balls unheeded lay . . .
> And I thought to myself, is that Croquet?

Sentimental ballads such as "Silver Threads Among the Gold" (1873) remained the most popular musical form, but the insistent syncopated rhythms of ragtime were being heard, reflecting the influence of the new urban culture. By the time the strains of Scott Joplin's "Maple Leaf Rag" (1899) popularized ragtime, critics complained that "a wave of vulgar, filthy and suggestive music has inundated the land." Classical music flour-

The Sells Brothers promised a world of entertainment to the patrons of their circus, which featured—according to this poster—an Australian aviary, an African aquarium, a Roman hippodrome, and an exhibit of trans-Pacific wild beasts. The principal act of the three-ring circus, however, promised to be the spectacular bareback riding of equestrienne Polly Lee. ❖

As early as 1866, Currier and Ives described baseball as the "American National Game." Although we can recognize some similarities between the game portrayed here and the modern game of baseball, there are also some notable differences. For example, the players depicted in the lithograph do not wear any protective gear: The batter wears no batting helmet, the catcher has no face mask or chest protector, and none of the players appear to wear a baseball glove. ❖

ished. The New England Conservatory (1867), the Cincinnati College of Music (1878), and the Metropolitan Opera (1883) were new sources of civic pride; New York, Boston, and Chicago launched first-rate symphony orchestras between 1878 and 1891.

In the hamlets and small towns of America, traveling circuses were enormously popular. Hamlin Garland, an author who grew up in small Iowa villages, recalled how the circus came "trailing clouds of glorified dust and filling our minds with the color of romance. . . . It brought to our ears the latest band pieces and taught us the popular songs. It furnished us with jokes. It relieved our dullness. It gave us something to talk about." Larger circuses, run by entrepreneurs such as P. T. Barnum and James A. Bailey, played the cities, but every town attracted its own smaller version.

Fairs, horse races, balloon ascensions, bicycle tournaments, and football and baseball contests attracted avid fans. The years between 1870 and 1900 saw the rise of organized spectator sports, a trend reflecting both the rise of the city and the new uses of leisure. Baseball's first professional team, the Cincinnati Red Stockings, appeared in 1869, and baseball soon became the preeminent national sport. Fans sang songs about it ("Take Me Out to the Ballgame"), wrote poems about it ("Casey at the Bat"), and made up riddles about it ("What has eighteen feet and catches flies?"). Modern rules were adopted. Umpires were designated to call balls and strikes; catchers wore masks and chest protectors and moved closer to the plate instead of staying back to catch the ball on the bounce. Fielders had to catch the ball on the fly rather than on one bounce in their caps. By 1890, professional baseball teams were drawing crowds of sixty thousand daily. In 1901, the American League was organized, and two years later the Boston Red Sox beat the Pittsburgh Pirates in the first modern World Series.

In 1869, Princeton and Rutgers played the first intercollegiate football game. Soon, other schools picked up the sport, and by the early 1890s, crowds of fifty thousand or more attended the most popular contests. Basketball, invented in 1891, gained a large following. Boxing, a popular topic of conversation in saloons and schoolyards, was outlawed in most states. For a time, championship prizefights were held in secret, with news of the result spread rapidly by word of mouth. Matches were long and bloody, fought with bare knuckles until the invention in the 1880s of the 5-ounce boxing glove. John L. Sullivan, the "Boston Strong Boy" and the era's most popular champion, won the heavyweight title in 1889 in a brutal 75-round victory over the stubborn Jake Kilrain.

As gas and electric lights brightened the night, and streetcars crisscrossed city streets, leisure habits changed. Delighted with the new technology, people took advantage of an increasing variety of things to do. They stayed home less often. New York City's first electric sign—"Manhattan Beach Swept by Ocean

Breezes"—appeared in 1881, and people went out at night filling the streets on their way to the theater, vaudeville shows, and dance halls or just out for an evening stroll.

Changes in Family Life

Under the impact of industrialization and urbanization, family relationships were changing. On the farm, parents and children worked more or less together, and the family was a producing unit. In factories and offices, family members rarely worked together. In working-class families, mothers, fathers, and children separated at dawn and returned, ready for sleep, at dark. Morris Rosenfeld, a clothing presser lamenting that he was unable to spend more time with his son, wrote a poem titled "My Boy":

> I have a little boy at home,
> A pretty little son;
> I think sometimes the world is mine
> In him, my only one. . . .
>
> 'Ere dawn my labor drives me forth;
> Tis night when I am free;
> A stranger am I to my child;
> And stranger my child to me.

Working-class families of the late nineteenth century, like the family of the young Polish girl that Harriet Vittum saw, often lived in complex household units—taking in relatives and boarders to pay the rent. As many as one-third of all households contained people who were not members of the immediate family. Although driven apart by the daily routine, family ties among the working class tended to remain strong, cemented by the need to join forces in order to survive in the industrial economy.

The middle-class wife and children, however, became increasingly isolated from the world of work. Turning inward, the middle-class family became more self-contained. Older children spent more time in adolescence, and periods of formal schooling were lengthier. Families took in fewer apprentices and boarders. By the end of the century, most middle-class offspring continued to live with their parents into their late teens and their twenties, a larger proportion than today.

Fewer middle-class wives participated directly in their husbands' work. As a result, they and their children occupied what contemporaries called a "separate sphere of domesticity," set apart from the masculine sphere of income-producing work. The family home became a "walled garden," a place to retreat from the crass materialism of the outside world. Middle-class fathers began to move their families out of the city to the suburbs, commuting to work on the new streetcars and leaving wives and children at home and school.

The middle-class family had once functioned in part to transmit a craft or skill, arrange marriages, and offer care for dependent kin. Now, as these functions declined, the family took on new emotional and ideological responsibilities. In a society that worried about the weakening hold of other institutions, the family became more and more important as a means of social control. It also placed new burdens on wives.

"In the old days," said a woman in 1907, "a married woman was supposed to be a frump and a bore and a physical wreck. Now you are supposed to keep up intellectually, to look young and well and be fresh and bright and entertaining." Magazines such as the *Ladies' Home Journal,* which started in 1889, glorified motherhood and the home, but its articles and ads featured women as homebound, child-oriented consumers. While society's leaders spoke fondly of the value of homemaking, the status of housewives declined under the factory system, which emphasized money rewards and devalued household labor.

Underlying all these changes was one of the modern world's most important trends, a major decline in fertility rates that lasted from 1800 to 1939. Though blacks, immigrants, and rural dwellers continued to have more children than white native-born city dwellers, the trend affected all classes and races; among white women, the birthrate fell from seven in 1800 to just over four in 1880 to about three in 1900. People everywhere tended to marry later and have fewer children.

Since contraceptive devices were not yet widely used, the decline reflected abstinence and a conscious decision to postpone or limit families. Some women decided to devote greater attention to a smaller number of children, others to pursue their own careers. There was a marked increase in the number of young unmarried women working for wages or attending school, an increase in the number of women delaying marriage or not marrying at all, and a gradual decline in rates of illegitimacy and premarital pregnancy.

In large part, the decline in fertility stemmed from people's responses to the social and economic forces around them, the rise of cities and industry. In a host of individual decisions, they decided to have fewer children, and the result reshaped some of the fundamental attitudes and institutions of American society.

Changing Views: A Growing Assertiveness Among Women

In and out of the family, there was growing recognition of self-sufficient working women, employed in factory, telephone exchange, or business office, who were entering the workforce in increasing numbers. In 1880, 2.6 million women were gainfully employed; in 1890, 4 million. In 1882, the Census Bureau took the first census of working women; most were single and worked out of necessity rather than choice.

Many regarded this "new woman" as a corruption of the ideal vision of the American woman, in which man worshiped "a diviner self than his own," innocent, helpless, and good. Women were to be better than the world around them. They were brought up, said Ida Tarbell, a leading political reformer, "as if wrongdoing were impossible to them."

Views changed, albeit slowly. One important change occurred in the legal codes pertaining to women, particularly in the common law doctrine of *femme couverte.* Under that doctrine, wives were chattel of their husbands; they could not legally control their own earnings, property, or children unless they had drawn up a specific contract before marriage. By 1890, many states had substantially revised the doctrine to allow wives control of their earnings and inherited property. (See "The Legal Rights of Married Women: Reforming the Law of Coverture," pp. 354–357.) In cases of divorce, the new laws also recognized women's rights to custody or joint custody of their children. Although divorce was still far from being socially acceptable, divorce rates more than doubled during the last third of the century. By 1905, one in twelve marriages was ending in divorce.

Susan B. Anthony was a tireless reformer working for abolition, temperance, and women's rights over the course of her long life. After the Civil War she focused her attention on the right for suffrage as an active leader in the National Woman Suffrage Association (1869–1890) and then the National American Woman Suffrage Association (1890–1906). Anthony would spend her life advancing the rights of women. ❖

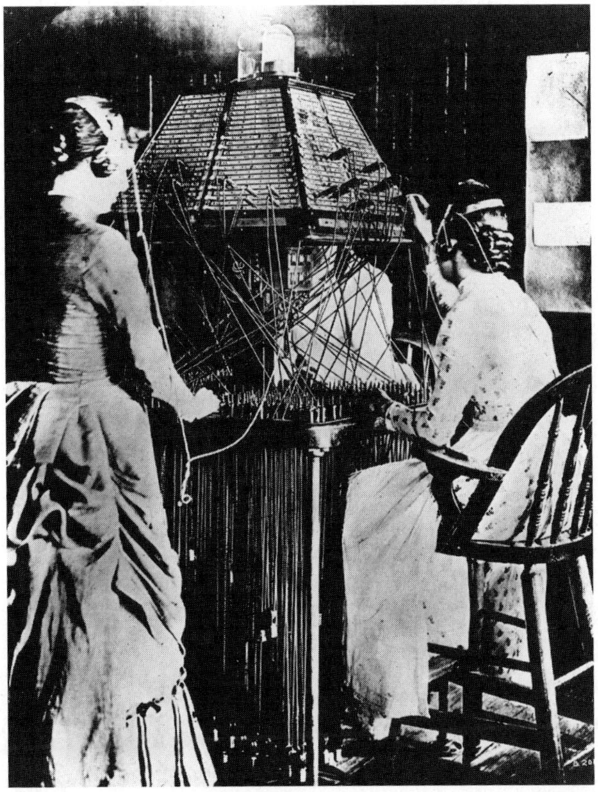

Female operators, called "hello girls," were hired to work telephone switchboards after it was discovered that male operators tended to argue too much with subscribers. As suggested by this photograph of operators working an early switchboard with a tangle of intersecting wires, it was a tough job that required patience. ❖

In the 1870s and 1880s, a growing number of women were asserting their own humanness. They fought for the vote, lobbied for equal pay, and sought self-fulfillment. The new interest in psychology and medicine strengthened their causes. Charlotte Perkins Gilman, author of *Women and Economics* (1898), joined other women in questioning the ideal of womanly "innocence."

Women espoused causes with new fervor. Susan B. Anthony, a veteran of many reform campaigns, tried to vote in the 1872 presidential election and was fined $100, which she refused to pay. In 1890, she helped form the **National American Woman Suffrage Association** to work for the enfranchisement of women. On New York's Lower East Side, the Ladies Anti–Beef Trust Association, which formed to protest increases in the price of meat, established a boycott of butcher shops. When their demands were ignored, the women invaded the shops, poured kerosene on the meat, and set fire to it. "We don't riot," Rebecca Ablowitz told the judge. "But if all we did was to weep at home, nobody would notice it; so we have to do something to help ourselves."

Educating the Masses

Continuing a trend that stretched back a hundred years, childhood was becoming an even more distinct time of life. There was still only a vague concept of adolescence—the special nature of the teenage years—but the role of children was changing. Less and less were children perceived as "little adults," valued for the additional financial gain they might bring into the family. Now children were to grow and learn and be nurtured rather than rushed into adulthood.

As a result, schooling became more important, and American children came closer than ever before to universal education. By 1900, thirty-one states and territories (out of fifty-one) had enacted laws making school attendance compulsory, though most required attendance only until the age of 14. In 1870, there were only 160 public high schools; in 1900, there were 6000. In the same years, public school budgets rose from $63 million to $253 million; illiteracy declined from 20 percent to just over 10 percent of the population. Still, even as late as 1900, the average adult had only five years of schooling.

Educators saw the school as the primary means to train people for life and work in an industrializing society. Hence teachers focused on basic skills—reading and mathematics—and on values—obedience and attentiveness to the clock. Most schools had a highly structured curriculum, built around discipline and routine. In 1892, Joseph Rice, a pediatrician, toured twelve hundred classrooms in thirty-six cities. In a typical classroom, he reported, the atmosphere was "damp and chilly," the teacher strict. "The unkindly spirit of the teacher is strikingly apparent; the pupils being completely subjugated to her will, are silent and motionless." One teacher asked her pupils, "How can you learn anything with your knees and toes out of order?"

Schools, regarded primarily as training grounds for a life of work, stressed conformity and deportment—feet on the floor, hands folded and resting atop the desk. The teacher was drillmaster and disciplinarian as well as instructor. ❖

Many children dropped out of school early, and not just to earn money. Helen Todd, a factory inspector in Chicago, found a group of young girls working in a hot, stuffy attic. When she asked why they were not in school, Tillie Isakowsky, who was 14, said, "School! School is de fiercest t'ing youse kin come up against. Factories ain't no cinch, but schools is worst." A few blocks away, Todd stumbled on a 13-year-old boy hiding in a basement. He cried when she said he would have to go to school, blurting that "they hits ye if yer don't learn, and they hits ye if ye whisper, and they hits ye if ye have string in yer pocket, and they hits ye if yer seat squeaks, and they hits ye if ye don't stan' up in time, and they hits ye if yer late, and they hits ye if ye ferget the page." Curious, Todd asked 500 children whether they would go to school or work in a factory if their families did not need the money—412 preferred the factory.

School began early; boys attended all day, but girls often stayed home after lunch, since it was thought they needed less in the way of learning. On the teacher's command, students stood and recited from *Webster's Spellers* and *McGuffey's Eclectic Readers,* the period's most popular textbooks. The work of William Holmes McGuffey, a professor of languages at Miami University in Ohio, *McGuffey's Eclectic Readers* had been in use since 1836; 100 million copies were sold in the last half of the nineteenth century. Nearly every child read them; they taught not only reading but also ethics, values, and religion. In the *Readers,* boys grew up to be heroes, girls to be mothers, and hard work always meant success:

> Shall birds, and bees, and ants, be wise,
>   While I my moments waste?
> O let me with the morning rise,
>   And to my duty haste.

The South lagged far behind in education. The average family size there was about twice as large as in the North, and a greater proportion of the population lived in isolated rural areas. State and local authorities mandated fewer weeks in the average school year, and many southern states refused to adopt compulsory education laws. Even more important was the effect of Southern Jim Crow laws, passed in the 1890s and after to keep African Americans from voting, serving on juries, and participating in other aspects of Southern life. Southerners used these laws to maintain separate school systems to segregate the races. Supported by the U.S. Supreme Court decision of 1896 in ***Plessy* v. *Ferguson*** (see "The Shaping of Jim Crow," pp. 567–570), segregated schooling added a devastating financial burden to education in the South.

North Carolina and Alabama mandated segregated schools in 1876, South Carolina and Louisiana in 1877, Mississippi in 1878, and Virginia in 1882. A series of Supreme Court decisions in the 1880s and 1890s upheld the concept of segregation. In the ***Civil Rights Cases*** (1883), the Court ruled that the Fourteenth Amendment barred state governments from discriminating on account of race but did not prevent private individuals or organizations from doing so. *Plessy* v. *Ferguson* (1896) established the doctrine of "separate but equal" and upheld a Louisiana law requiring different railroad cars for whites and blacks. The Court applied the doctrine directly to schools in *Cumming* v. *County Board of Education* (1899), which approved the creation of separate schools for whites, even if there were no comparable schools for blacks.

Southern school laws often implied that the schools would be "separate but equal," and they were often separate but rarely equal. Black schools were usually dilapidated, and black teachers were paid considerably less than white teachers. In 1890, only 35 percent of black children attended school in the South; 55 percent of white children did. That year nearly two-thirds of the country's black population was illiterate.

Educational techniques changed after the 1870s. Educators paid more attention to early elementary education, a trend that placed young children in school and helped the growing number of mothers who worked outside the home. The kindergarten movement, started in St. Louis in 1873, spread across the country. In kindergartens, 4- to 6-year-old children learned by playing, not by keeping their knees and toes in order. For older children, social reformers advocated "practical" courses in manual training and homemaking. "We are impatient with the schools which lay all stress on reading and writing," Jane Addams said, for "they fail to give the child any clew to the life about him."

For the first time, education became a field of university study. European theorists such as Johann Friedrich Herbart, a German educator, argued that learning occurred best in an atmosphere of freedom and confidence between teachers and pupils. Teacher training became increasingly professional. Only 10 normal schools, or teacher training institutions, existed in the United States before the Civil War. By 1900, there were 345, and one in every five elementary teachers had graduated from a professional school.

Higher Education

Nearly 150 new colleges and universities opened in the twenty years between 1880 and 1900. The Morrill Land Grant Act of 1862 gave large grants of land to the states for the establishment of colleges to teach "agriculture and the mechanic arts." The act fostered 69 "land-grant" institutions, including the great state universities of Wisconsin, California, Minnesota, and Illinois.

Private philanthropy, born of the large fortunes of the industrial age, also spurred growth in higher education. Leland Stanford gave $24 million to endow Stanford University on his California ranch, and John D. Rockefeller, founder of the Standard Oil Company, gave $34 million to found the University of Chicago. Other industrialists established Cornell (1865), Vanderbilt (1873), and Tulane (1884).

As colleges expanded, their function changed and their curriculum broadened. No longer did they exist primarily to train young men for the ministry. They moved away from the classical curriculum of rhetoric, mathematics, Latin, and Greek toward "reality and practicality," as President David Starr Jordan of Stanford University said. The Massachusetts Institute of Technology (MIT), founded in 1861, focused on science and engineering.

Influenced by the new German universities, which emphasized specialized research, Johns Hopkins University in Baltimore opened the nation's first separate graduate school in 1876. Under President Daniel Coit Gilman, Johns Hopkins stressed the seminar and laboratory as teaching tools, bringing together student and teacher in close association.

Charles W. Eliot, who became president of Harvard in 1869 at the age of 35, moved to end, as an admirer said, the "old fogyism" that marked the institution. Revising the curriculum, Eliot set up the elective system, in which students chose their own courses rather than following a rigidly prescribed curriculum. Lectures and discussions replaced rote recitation, and courses in the natural and social sciences, fine arts, and modern languages multiplied. In the 1890s, Eliot's Harvard moved to the forefront of educational innovation.

Women still had to fight for educational opportunities. Some formed study clubs, an important movement that spread rapidly between 1870 and 1900. Groups such as the Decatur (Illinois) Art Class, the Boston History Class, and the Barnesville (Georgia) Shakespeare Club aimed "to enlarge the mental horizon as well as the knowledge of our members." Club members read Virgil and Chaucer, studied history and architecture, and discussed women's rights. As the Monday Club of Mount Vernon, Ohio, put it:

> In ancient days when Monday came
> We used our clothes to rub,
> And set them boiling on the stove,
> And stir them with a club.
> But, Oh, our Monday Club today

Is quite a different stick;
For we've abandoned household toils
And learned a better trick.
. . . .
And with it, just as Moses did,
We drive the waves apart,
And enter on the promised land
Of learning and of art.

Clubs sprang up almost everywhere there were women: in Caribou, Maine; Tyler, Texas; and Leadville, Colorado—as well as San Francisco, New York, and Boston. Although they were usually small, study clubs sparked a greater interest in education among women and their daughters and contributed to a rapid rise in the number of women entering college in the early 1900s.

Before the Civil War, only three private colleges admitted women to study with men. After the war, educational opportunities increased for women. A number of women's colleges opened, including Vassar (1865), Wellesley (1875), Smith (1875), Bryn Mawr (1885), Barnard (1889), and Radcliffe (1893). The land-grant colleges of the Midwest, open to women from the outset, spurred a nationwide trend toward coeducation, although some physicians, such as Harvard Medical School's Dr. Edward H. Clarke in his popular *Sex in Education* (1873), continued to argue that the strain of learning made women sterile. By 1900, women made up about 40 percent of college students, and four out of five colleges admitted them.

Fewer opportunities existed for African Americans and other minorities. Jane Stanford encouraged the Chinese who had worked on her husband's Central Pacific Railroad to apply to Stanford University, but her policy was unusual. Most colleges did not accept minority students, and only a few applied. W. E. B. Du Bois, the brilliant African American sociologist and civil rights leader, attended Harvard in the late 1880s but found the society of Harvard Yard closed against him. Disdained and disdainful, he "asked no fellowship of my fellow students." Chosen as one of the commencement speakers, Du Bois picked as his topic "Jefferson Davis," treating it, said an onlooker, with "an almost contemptuous fairness."

Black students turned to black colleges such as the Hampton Normal and Industrial Institute in Virginia and the Tuskegee Institute in Alabama. These colleges were often supported by whites who favored manual training for blacks. Booker T. Washington, an ex-slave, put into practice his educational ideas at Tuskegee, which opened in 1881. Washington began Tuskegee with limited funds, four run-down buildings, and only thirty students; by 1900, it was a model industrial and agricultural school. Spread over forty-six buildings, it offered instruction in thirty trades to fourteen hundred students.

A physics lecture at the University of Michigan in the late 1880s or early 1890s. The land-grant university admitted women, but seating in the lecture hall was segregated by gender—although not by race. Notice that both whites and African Americans are seated in the back rows of the men's section. ❖

Booker T. Washington, who served as the first president of Tuskegee Institute, advocated work efficiency and practical skills as keys to advancement for African Americans. Students like these at Tuskegee studied academic subjects and received training in trades and professions. ❖

Washington stressed patience, manual training, and hard work. "The wisest among my race understand," he said in a widely acclaimed speech at the Atlanta Exposition in 1895, "that the agitation of questions of social equality is the extremest folly." Blacks should focus on economic gains; they should go to school, learn skills, and work their way up the ladder. "No race," he said at Atlanta, "can prosper till it learns that there is as much dignity in tilling a field as in writing a poem. It is at the bottom of life we must begin, and not at the top." Southern whites should help out because they would then have "the most patient, faithful, law-abiding, and unresentful people that the world has seen."

Outlined most forcefully in Washington's speech in Atlanta, the philosophy became known as the Atlanta Compromise, and many whites and some blacks welcomed it. Acknowledging white domination, it called for slow progress through self-improvement, not through lawsuits or agitation. Rather than fighting for equal rights, blacks should acquire property and show they were worthy of their rights. But Washington did believe in black equality. Often secretive in his methods, he worked behind the scenes to organize black voters and lobby against harmful laws. In his own way, he bespoke a racial pride that contributed to the rise of black nationalism in the twentieth century.

Du Bois wanted a more aggressive strategy. Born in Massachusetts in 1868, the son of poor parents, he studied at Fisk University in Tennessee and the University of Berlin before he went to Harvard. Unable to find a teaching job in a white college, he took a low-paying research position at the University of Pennsylvania. He had no office but did not need one. Du Bois used the new discipline of sociology, which emphasized factual observation in the field, to study the condition of blacks.

Notebook in hand, he set out to examine crime in Philadelphia's black seventh ward. He interviewed five thousand people, mapped and classified neighborhoods, and produced *The Philadelphia Negro* (1898). The first study of the effect of urban life on blacks, it cited a wealth of statistics, all suggesting that crime in the ward stemmed not from inborn degeneracy but from the environment in which blacks lived. Change the environment, and people would change, too; education was a good way to go about it.

In *The Souls of Black Folk* (1903), Du Bois openly attacked Booker T. Washington and the philosophy of the Atlanta Compromise. He urged African Americans to aspire to professional careers, to fight for the restoration of their civil rights, and, wherever possible, to get a college education. Calling for integrated schools with equal opportunity for all, Du Bois urged blacks to educate their "talented tenth," a highly trained intellectual elite, to lead them.

Du Bois was not alone in promoting careers in the professions. Throughout higher education there was increased emphasis on professional training, particularly in medicine, dentistry, and law. Enrollments swelled, even as standards of admission tightened. The number of medical schools in the country rose from 75 in 1870 to 160 in 1900, and the number of medical students—including more and more women—almost tripled. Schools of nursing grew from only 15 in 1880 to 432 in 1900. Doctors, lawyers, and others became part of a growing middle class that shaped the concerns of the Progressive Era of the early twentieth century.

Although less than 5 percent of the college-age population attended college during the 1877–1890 period, the new trends had great impact. A generation of men and women encountered new ideas that changed their views of themselves and society. Courses never before offered, such as Philosophy II at Harvard, "The

Ethics of Social Reform," which students called "drainage, drunkenness, and divorce," heightened interest in social problems and the need for reform. Some graduating students burned with a desire to cure society's ills. "My life began . . . at Johns Hopkins University," Frederic C. Howe, an influential reformer, recalled. "I came alive, I felt a sense of responsibility to the world, I wanted to change things."

The Stirrings of Reform

When Henry George, one of the era's leading reformers, asked a friend what could be done about the problem of political corruption in American cities, his friend replied: "Nothing! You and I can do nothing at all. . . . We can only wait for evolution. Perhaps in four or five thousand years evolution may have carried men beyond this state of things."

This stress on the slow pace of change reflected the doctrine of **social Darwinism,** based on the writings of English social philosopher Herbert Spencer. In several influential books, Spencer took the evolutionary theories of Charles Darwin and applied Darwinian principles of natural selection to society, combining biology and sociology in a theory of "social selection" that tried to explain human progress. Like animals, society evolved, slowly, by adapting to the environment. The "survival of the fittest"—a term that Spencer, not Darwin, invented—preserved the strong and weeded out the weak. "If they are sufficiently complete to live, they do live, and it is well they should live. If they are not sufficiently complete to live, they die, and it is best they should die."

Social Darwinism had a number of influential followers in the United States, including William Graham Sumner, a professor of political and social science at Yale University. One of the country's best known academic figures, Sumner was forceful and eloquent. In writings such as *What Social Classes Owe to Each Other* (1883) and "The Absurd Effort to Make the World Over" (1894), he argued that government action on behalf of the poor or weak interfered with evolution and sapped the species. Reform tampered with the laws of nature. "It is the greatest folly of which a man can be capable to sit down with a slate and pencil to plan out a new social world," Sumner said.

The influence of social Darwinism on American thinking has been exaggerated, but in the powerful hands of Sumner and others it did influence some journalists, ministers, and policymakers. Between 1877 and the 1890s, however, it came under increasing attack. In fields such as religion, economics, politics, literature, and law, thoughtful people raised questions about established conditions and suggested the need for reform.

Progress and Poverty

Read and reread, passed from hand to hand, Henry George's nationwide best-seller *Progress and Poverty* (1879) led the way to a more critical appraisal of American society in the 1880s and beyond. The book jolted traditional thought. "It was responsible," one historian has said, "for starting along new lines of thinking an amazing number of the men and women" who became leaders of reform.

Born in 1839, the child of a poor Philadelphia family, George had little formal schooling. As a boy he went to sea; he also worked as a prospector, printer, and journalist. Self-educated as an economist, he moved to San Francisco in the late 1850s and began to study "the fierce struggle of our civilized life." Disturbed by the depression of the 1870s and labor upheavals such as the great railroad strikes of 1877, George saw modern society—rich, complex, with material goods hitherto unknown—as sadly flawed.

"The present century," he wrote, "has been marked by a prodigious increase in wealth-producing power. . . . It was natural to expect, and it was expected, that . . . real poverty [would become] a thing of the past." Instead, he argued:

> it becomes no easier for the masses of our people to make a living. On the contrary, it is becoming harder. The wealthy class is becoming more wealthy; but the poorer class is becoming more dependent. The gulf between the employed and the employer is growing wider; social contrasts are becoming sharper; as liveried carriages appear, so do barefooted children.

George proposed a simple solution. Land, he thought, formed the basis of wealth, and a few people could grow wealthy just because the price of their land rose. Since the rise in price did not result from any effort on their part, it represented an "unearned increment," which, George argued, should be taxed for the good of society. A "single tax" on the increment, replacing all other taxes, would help equalize wealth and raise revenue to aid the poor. "Single-tax" clubs sprang up around the country, but George's solution, simplistic and unappealing, had much less impact than his analysis of the problem itself. He raised questions a generation of readers set out to answer.

New Currents in Social Thought

George's emphasis on deprivation in the environment excited a young country lawyer in Ashtabula, Ohio—Clarence Darrow. Unlike the social Darwinists, Darrow was sure that criminals were made and not born. They grew out of "the unjust condition of human life." In the mid-1880s, he left for Chicago and a forty-year career working to convince people that poverty lay at the root of crime. "There is no such thing as crime as the word is generally understood," he told a group of startled prisoners in the Cook County jail. "If every man, woman and child in the world had a chance to make a decent, fair, honest living there would be no jails and no lawyers and no courts."

As Darrow rejected the implications of social Darwinism, in similar fashion Richard T. Ely and a group of young economists poked holes in traditional economic thought. Fresh from graduate study in Germany, Ely in 1884 attacked classical economics for its dogmatism, simple faith in laissez-faire, and reliance on self-interest as a guide for human conduct. The "younger" economics, he said, must no longer be "a tool in the hands of the greedy and the avaricious for keeping down and oppressing the laboring classes. It does not acknowledge laissez-faire as an excuse for doing nothing while people starve."

Accepting a post at Johns Hopkins University, Ely assigned graduate students to study labor conditions in Baltimore and other cities; one of them, John R. Commons, went on to publish a massive four-volume study, *History of Labour in the United States.* In 1885, Ely led a small band of rebels in founding the American Economic Association, which linked economics to social problems and urged government intervention in economic affairs. Social critic Thorstein Veblen saw economic laws as a mask for human greed. In *The Theory of the Leisure Class* (1899), Veblen analyzed the "predatory wealth" and "conspicuous consumption" of the business class.

Edward Bellamy dreamed of a cooperative society in which poverty, greed, and crime no longer existed. A lawyer from western Massachusetts, Bellamy published *Looking Backward, 2000–1887,* in 1887 and became a national reform figure virtually overnight. The novel's protagonist, Julian West, falls asleep in 1887 and awakes in the year 2000. Wide-eyed, he finds himself in a socialist utopia: The government owns the means of production, and citizens share the material rewards. Cooperation, rather than competition, is the watchword.

The world of *Looking Backward* had limits; it was regimented, paternalistic, and filled with the gadgets and material concerns of Bellamy's own day. But it had a dramatic effect on many readers. The book sold at the rate of ten thousand copies a week, and its followers formed Nationalist Clubs to work for its objectives. By 1890, there were such clubs in twenty-seven states, all calling for the nationalization of public utilities and a wider distribution of wealth.

Walter Rauschenbusch, a young Baptist minister, read widely from the writings of Bellamy and George, along with the works of other social reformers. When he took his first church post in Hell's Kitchen, a blighted area of New York City, he soon discovered the weight of the slum environment. "One could hear," he said, "human virtue cracking and crushing all around." In the 1890s, Rauschenbusch became a professor at the Rochester Theological Seminary, and he began to expound on the responsibility of organized religion to advance social justice.

Men sleeping in crowded conditions at the Salvation Army headquarters in New York City, 1897. The Salvation Army's missions for the homeless ministered to the material and spiritual needs of the poor, unemployed, and outcast in the city's slums. ❖

Some Protestant sects stressed individual salvation and a better life in the next world, not in this one. Poverty was evidence of sinfulness; the poor had only themselves to blame. "God has intended the great to be great and the little to be little," said Henry Ward Beecher, the country's best known pastor. Wealth and destitution, suburbs and slums—all formed part of God's plan.

Challenging those traditional doctrines, a number of churches in the 1880s began establishing missions in the city slums. William Dwight Porter Bliss, an Episcopal clergyman, founded the Church of the Carpenter in a working-class district of Boston. Lewis M. Pease worked in the grim Five Points area of New York; Alexander Irvine, a Jewish missionary, lived in a flophouse in the Bowery. Irvine walked his skid row neighborhood every afternoon to lend a hand to those in need. Living among the poor and homeless, the urban missionaries grew impatient with religious doctrines that endorsed the status quo.

Many of the new trends were reflected in an emerging religious philosophy known as the **Social Gospel.** As the name suggests, the Social Gospel focused on society as well as individuals, on improving living conditions as well as saving souls. Sermons in Social Gospel churches called on church members to fulfill their social obligations, and adults met before and after the regular service to discuss social and economic problems. Children were excused from sermons, organized into age groups, and encouraged to make the church a center for social as well as religious activity. Soon churches included dining halls, gymnasiums, and even theaters.

The most active Social Gospel leader was Washington Gladden, a Congregational minister and prolific writer. Linking Christianity to the social and economic environment, Gladden spent a lifetime working for "social salvation." He saw Christianity as a fellowship of love and the church as a social agency. In *Applied Christianity* (1886) and other writings, he denounced competition, urged an "industrial partnership" between employers and employees, and called for efforts to help the poor.

The Settlement Houses

A growing number of social reformers living in the urban slums shared Gladden's concern. Like Tweed and Plunkitt, they appreciated the dependency of the poor; unlike them, they wanted to eradicate the conditions that underlay it. To do so, they formed **settlement houses** in the slums and went to live in them to experience the problems they were trying to solve.

Youthful, idealistic, and mostly middle class, these social workers took as their model Toynbee Hall, founded in 1884 in the slums of East London to provide community services. Stanton Coit, a moody and poetic graduate of Amherst College, was the first American to borrow the settlement house idea; in 1886, he opened the Neighborhood Guild on the Lower East Side of New York. The idea spread swiftly. By 1900, there were more than a hundred settlements in the country; five years later, there were more than two hundred, and by 1910, more than four hundred.

The settlements included Jane Addams's famous Hull House in Chicago (1889), Robert A. Woods's South End House in Boston (1892), and Lillian Wald's Henry Street Settlement in New York (1893). The reformers wanted to bridge the socioeconomic gap between rich and poor and to bring education, culture, and hope to the slums. They sought to create in the heart of the city the values and sense of community of small-town America. Of settlement workers, Wald said in *The House on Henry Street* (1915), "We were to live in a neighborhood . . . identify ourselves with it socially, and, in brief, contribute to it our citizenship."

Many of the settlement workers were women, some of them college graduates, who found that society had little use for their talents and energy. Jane Addams, a graduate of Rockford College in Illinois, opened Hull House on South Halsted Street in the heart of the Chicago slums. Twenty-nine years old, endowed with a forceful and winning personality, she intended "to share the lives of the poor" and humanize the industrial city. "American ideals," she said, "crumbled under the overpowering poverty of the overcrowded city."

Occupying an old, rundown house, Hull House stressed education, offering classes in elementary English and Shakespeare, lectures on ethics and the history of art, and courses in cooking, sewing, and manual skills. A pragmatist, Addams believed in investigating a problem and then doing something to solve it. Noting the lack of medical care in the area, she established an infant welfare clinic and free medical dispensary. Because the tenements lacked bathtubs, she installed showers in the basement of the house and built a bathhouse for the neighbors. Because there was no local library, she opened a reading room. Gradually, Hull House expanded to occupy a dozen buildings sprawling over more than a city block.

Like settlement workers in other cities, Addams and her colleagues studied the immigrants in nearby tenements. Laboriously, they identified the background of every family in a one-third-square-mile area around Hull House. Finding people of eighteen different nationalities, they taught them American history and the English language, yet Addams also

Jane Addams founded Chicago's Hull House in 1889. The settlement house provided recreational and day-care facilities; offered extension classes in academic, vocational, and artistic subjects; and, above all, sought to bring hope to poverty-stricken slum dwellers. ❖

OPENING OF

HULL-HOUSE
PLAY GROUND

Polk Street, Near Halsted

Saturday, May 1st, 1897,
AT 3 O'CLOCK, P. M.

"The air is warm, the skies are clear,
Birds and blossoms all are here,
Come old and young with spirits gay,
To welcome back the charming May."

MUSIC BY THE BRASS BAND

...Kindergarten Games---May Pole Dance...

ALL KINDS OF RACES

encouraged them—through folk festivals and art—to preserve their own heritage.

In Boston, Robert Woods of South End House focused on the problem of school dropouts. He offered manual training, formed clubs to get young people off the streets, and established a cheap restaurant where the hungry could eat. Lillian Wald, the daughter of a middle-class family and herself a graduate nurse, concentrated on providing health care for the poor. In 1898, the first Catholic-run settlement house opened in New York, and in 1900, Bronson House opened in Los Angeles to work in the Mexican American community.

Florence Kelley, an energetic graduate of Cornell University, taught night school one winter in Chicago. Watching children break under the burden of poverty, she devoted her life to the problem of child labor. Convinced of the need for political activism, she worked with Addams and others to push through the Illinois Factory Act of 1893, which mandated an eight-hour day for women in factories and for children under the age of 14.

The settlement house movement had its limits. Hull House, one of the best, attracted two thousand visitors a week, still just a fraction of the seventy thousand people who lived within six blocks. Immigrants sometimes resented the middle-class "strangers" who told them how to live. Dressed always in a brown suit and dark stockings, Harriet Vittum, the head resident of Chicago's Northwestern University Settlement (who told the story of the suicide victim at the beginning of this chapter), was known in the neighborhood as "the police lady in brown." She once stopped a dance because it was too wild, and then watched in disgust as the boys responded by "making vulgar sounds with their lips." Though her attempts to help were sincere, in private Vittum called the people she was trying to help "ignorant foreigners, who live in an atmosphere of low morals . . . surrounded by anarchy and crime."

Although Addams tried to offer a few programs for blacks, most white reformers did not, and after 1900, a number of black reformers opened their own settlements. Like the whites, they offered employment information, medical care, and recreational facilities, along with concerts, lectures, and other educational events. White and black, the settlement workers made important contributions to urban life.

A Crisis in Social Welfare

The depression of 1893 jarred the young settlement workers, many of whom had just begun their work. Addams and the Hull House workers helped form the Chicago Bureau of Charities to coordinate emergency relief. Kelley, recently appointed the chief factory inspector of Illinois, worked even harder to end child labor, and in 1899, she moved to New York City to head the National Consumers League, which marshaled the buying power of women to encourage employers to provide better working conditions.

In cities and towns across the country, traditional methods of helping the needy foundered in the crisis. Churches, Charity Organization Societies, and Community Chests did what they could, but their resources were limited, and they functioned on traditional lines. Many of them still tried to change rather than aid individual families, and people were often reluctant to call on them for help.

Gradually, a new class of professional social workers arose to fill the need. Unlike the church and charity volunteers, these social workers wanted not only to feed the poor but to study their condition and alleviate it. Revealingly, they called themselves "case workers" and daily collected data on the income, housing, jobs, health, and habits of the poor. Prowling tenement districts, they gathered information about the number of rooms, number of occupants, ventilation, and sanitation of the buildings, putting together a fund of useful data.

Studies of the poor popped up everywhere. Walter Wyckoff, a graduate of Princeton University, embarked in 1891 on what he called "an experiment in reality." For eighteen months, he worked as an unskilled laborer in jobs from Connecticut to California. "I am vastly ignorant of the labor problems and am trying to learn by experience," he said as he set out. After working as a ditchdigger, farmhand, and logger, Wyckoff summarized his findings in *The Workers* (1897), a book immediately hailed as a major contribution to sociology.

So many others followed Wyckoff's example that sometimes it seemed the observers outnumbered those being observed. W. E. B. Du Bois did his pioneering study of urban blacks; Lillian Pettengill took a job as a domestic servant to see "the ups and downs of this particular dog-life from the dog's end of the chain." Others became street beggars, miners, lumberjacks, and factory laborers. Bessie and Marie Van Vorst's *The Woman Who Toils: Being the Experiences of Two Gentlewomen as Factory Girls* (1903) studied female workers, as did Helen Campbell's *Women Wage-Earners: Their Past, Their Present and Their Future* (1893), which suggested that the conditions of factory employment prepared women mainly "for the hospital, the workhouse, and the prison."

CHRONOLOGY

1862	Morrill Land Grant gives land to states for establishment of colleges
1869	Rutgers and Princeton play in nation's first intercollegiate football game ❖ Cincinnati Red Stockings, baseball's first professional team, organized
1873	Comstock Law bans obscene articles from U.S. mail ❖ Nation's first kindergarten opens in St. Louis, Missouri
1874	Women's Christian Temperance Union formed to crusade against evils of liquor
1876	Johns Hopkins University opens first separate graduate school
1879	Henry George analyzes problems of urbanizing America in *Progress and Poverty* ❖ Salvation Army arrives in United States
1880	Polish National Alliance formed to help Polish immigrants adjust to life in America
1881	Booker T. Washington opens Tuskegee Institute in Alabama ❖ Dr. John H. Kellogg advises parents to teach their children about sex in *Plain Facts for Old and Young*
1883	Metropolitan Opera opens in New York
1885	Home Insurance Building, country's first metal-frame structure, erected in Chicago ❖ American Economic Association formed to advocate government intervention in economic affairs
1887	Edward Bellamy promotes idea of socialist utopia in *Looking Backward, 2000–1887*
1889	Jane Addams opens Hull House in Chicago
1890	National Woman Suffrage Association and the American Woman Suffrage Association, both formed in 1869, merge to consolidate the women's suffrage movement
1894	Immigration Restriction League formed to limit immigration from southern and eastern Europe
1896	Supreme Court decision in *Plessy* v. *Ferguson* establishes constitutionality of "separate but equal" facilities ❖ John Dewey's Laboratory School for testing and practice of new educational theory opens at University of Chicago

William T. Stead, a prominent British editor, visited the Chicago World's Fair in 1893 and stayed to examine the city. He roamed the flophouses and tenements and dropped in at Hull House to drink hot chocolate and talk over conditions with Jane Addams. Later he wrote an influential book, *If Christ Came to*

Chicago (1894), and in a series of mass meetings during 1893, he called for a civic revival. In response, Chicagoans formed the Civic Federation, a group of forty leaders who aimed to make Chicago "the best governed, the healthiest city in this country." Setting up task forces for philanthropy, moral improvement, and legislation, the new group helped spawn the National Civic Federation (1900), a nationwide organization devoted to reform of urban life.

Conclusion: The Pluralistic Society

"The United States was born in the country and moved to the city," historian Richard Hofstadter said. Much of that movement occurred during the nineteenth century when the United States was the most rapidly urbanizing nation in the Western world. American cities bustled with energy; they absorbed millions of migrants who came from Europe and other distant and not-so-distant parts of the world. That migration, and the urban growth that accompanied it, reshaped American politics and culture.

By 1920, the census showed that, for the first time, most Americans lived in cities. By then, too, almost half the population was descended from people who had arrived after the American Revolution. As European, African, and Asian cultures met in the American city, a culturally pluralistic society emerged. Dozens of nationalities produced a culture whose members considered themselves Polish Americans, African Americans, and Irish Americans. The melting pot sometimes softened distinctions between the various groups, but it only partially blended them into a unified society.

"Ah, Vera," said a character in Israel Zangwill's popular play *The Melting Pot* (1908), "what is the glory of Rome and Jerusalem where all nations and races come to worship and look back, compared with the glory of America, where all races and nations come to labour and look forward!" Critics scorned the play as "romantic claptrap," and indeed it was. But the metaphor of the melting pot clearly depicted a new national image. In the decades after the 1870s a jumble of ethnic and racial groups struggled for a place in society.

That society, it is clear, experienced a crisis between 1870 and 1900. Together, the growth of cities and the rise of industrial capitalism brought jarring change, the exploitation of labor, ethnic and racial tensions, poverty—and, for a few, wealth beyond the imagination. At Homestead, Pullman, and a host of other places, there was open warfare between capital and labor. As reformers struggled to mediate the situation, they turned more and more to state and federal government to look after human welfare, a tendency the Supreme Court stoutly resisted. In the midst of the crisis, the depression of the 1890s struck, adding to the turmoil and straining American institutions. Tracing the changes wrought by waves of urbanization and industrialization, Henry George described the country as "the House of Have and the House of Want," almost in paraphrase of Lincoln's earlier metaphor of the "house divided." The question was, could this house, unlike that one, stand?

Recommended Reading

On urban America, see Sam Bass Warner, Jr., *Streetcar Suburbs* (1962) and *The Urban Wilderness* (1972). William R. Taylor, *In Pursuit of Gotham: Culture and Commerce in New York* (1992), Eric H. Monkkonen, *America Becomes Urban* (1988), Sven Beckert, *The Monied Metropolis: New York City and the Consolidation of the American Bourgeoisie, 1850-1896* (2001), and David Schuyler, *The New Urban Landscape* (1986), are also valuable. See also two books by Jon C. Teaford: *The Unheralded Triumph: City Government in America, 1870–1900* (1984) and *City and Suburb: The Political Fragmentation of Metropolitan America, 1850–1970* (1979).

For family life, see Joseph Kett, *Rites of Passage: Adolescence in America* (1977), Elaine Tyler May, *Great Expectations: Marriage and Divorce in Post-Victorian America* (1980), Steven Mintz, *A Prison of Expectations: The Family in Victorian Culture* (1983), Stephen M. Frank, *Life With Father: Parenthood and Masculinity in the Nineteenth-Century American North* (1998), and Norma Basch, *In the Eyes of the Law: Women, Marriage, and Property in Nineteenth-Century New York* (1982). Karen Lystra, *Searching the Heart: Women, Men, and Romantic Love in Nineteenth-Century America* (1989), is valuable.

Urban reform is examined in Judith Ann Trolander, *Professionalism and Social Change: From the Settlement House Movement to Neighborhood Centers, 1886 to the Present* (1987), Shannon Jackson, *Lines of Activity: Performance, Historiography, Hull-House Domesticity* (2001), Allen F. Davis, *Spearheads for Reform: The Social Settlements and the Progressive Movement, 1890–1914* (1967), and *American Heroine: The Life and Legend of Jane Addams* (1973).

For a list of additional titles related to this chapter's topics, please see http://www.ablongman.com/divine.

Suggested Web Sites

The American Experience: America 1900

http://www.pbs.org/wgbh/amex/1900/

Companion to the PBS documentary, this site includes audio clips of respected historians on the economics, politics, and culture of 1900, a primary source database, a timeline of the year, downloadable software to compile a family tree, and other materials.

Touring Turn-of-the-Century America: Photographs from the Detroit Publishing Company, 1880–1920

http://memory.loc.gov/ammem/detroit/dethome.html

This Library of Congress collection has thousands of photographs from turn-of-the-century America.

World's Columbian Exposition: Idea, Experience, Aftermath

http://xroads.virginia.edu/~MA96/WCE/title.html

This site has a virtual tour of the fair, along with contemporary reactions and modern analysis.

United States History: The Gilded Age (1890) to World War I

http://www.emayzine.com/lectures/Gilded~1.htm

This site consists of a good overview essay of the era.

Frank Lloyd Wright

http://www.prairiestyles.com/wright.htm

This site provides information on Wright's life, work, and influence.

Chapter Three: American Socialists and Reformers

http://www.vineyard.net/vineyard/history/pdgech3.htm

This site includes a fine essay about Edward Bellamy and some of the movements and ideas he inspired.

Jane Addams Hull-House Museum

http://www.uic.edu/jaddams/hull/hull_house.html

This site offers information on Addams, her settlement house programs, and the neighborhoods they served.

African American Perspectives: Pamphlets from the Daniel A. P. Murray Collection, 1818–1907

http://memory.loc.gov/ammem/aap/aaphome.html

This collection includes writings of famous African Americans, including Frederick Douglass, Booker T. Washington, Ida B. Wells-Barnett, Benjamin W. Arnett, Alexander Crummel, and Emanuel Love.

Law and Society

Plessy v. Ferguson

The Shaping of Jim Crow

In a nation of laws, the interpretation of law can profoundly change people's lives. *Plessy* v. *Ferguson* (1896), one of the most important cases ever to reach the Supreme Court, changed the lives of millions of black and white Americans. Interpreting law in a way that lasted for more than a half century, it permitted the segregation of blacks in public facilities throughout the land.

Given the significance of the case, we know surprisingly little about Homer A. Plessy, the man who figured in it. He was young—we know that—and apparently worked as a carpenter in Louisiana. According to the court records, he was "seven-eighths Caucasian," which perhaps was a reason he was chosen to test the constitutionality of a Louisiana law requiring railroad companies to segregate whites and blacks on trains in the state. It seemed a good law to test. Louisiana's own constitution forbade such discrimination; so did the federal **Civil Rights Act of 1875,** which guaranteed blacks "full and equal enjoyment" of public conveyances.

Whatever the details of his life, Plessy lived in a post–Reconstruction South in which racism was widespread but segregation was not. Where segregation did exist, it usually was not enacted into law. During the 1870s and 1880s, blacks and whites often ate together, rode together, and worked together. "I can ride in first-class cars on the railroads and in the streets," a delighted black visitor wrote home from South Carolina in 1885. "I can stop in and drink a glass of soda and be more politely waited upon than in some parts of New England."

That situation changed near the end of the century. The courts often reflect trends in the society, and whites in both North and South in the 1890s had little enthusiasm for civil rights or racial equality. In addition, economic depression heightened racial tensions, and the spread of colonial imperialism in Africa and Asia led to talk about "inferior" people, both at home and abroad. Beginning in the 1870s, the Supreme Court handed down a series of decisions that overturned much Reconstruction legislation, limited federal protection for blacks, and encouraged racial segregation.

In the *Slaughterhouse Cases* of 1873, the Supreme Court narrowed the scope of the Fourteenth Amendment protecting blacks; a decade later, in the *Civil Rights Cases* (1883), it said that Congress could not punish private individuals for acts of racial discrimination. Emboldened by such decisions, southern states passed many segregation laws, including laws requiring railroad companies to separate white and black riders. In the summer of 1890, Louisiana passed "An Act to promote the comfort of passengers" that made railroads in the state provide "equal but separate" cars "for the white and colored races."

Segregationists were delighted. "The Southern whites," a New Orleans newspaper said, had passed the law "in no spirit of hostility to the negroes," but to make sure that "the two races shall live separate and distinct from each other in all things, with separate schools, separate hotels, and separate cars."

New Orleans, more than most southern cities, had a group of talented African American leaders, educated, aggressive, and experienced in politics and the judicial system. Outraged by the new law, they thought first of boycotting the railroads that obeyed it but then decided to contest it in the courts. Led by Louis A. Martinet, a well-known lawyer and physician, and Rodolphe L. Desdunes, an important Reconstruction Republican, they formed the Citizens' Committee to Test the Constitutionality of the Separate Car Law, raised money for the cause, and enlisted the aid of Albion W. Tourgée of New York, a prominent white lawyer, novelist, and longtime crusader for African American rights.

Tourgée did not hesitate to join in the fight, for which he charged no fee. "Submission to such outrages," he angrily wrote his New Orleans friends, tends "only to their multiplication and exaggeration. It is by constant resistance to oppression that the race must ultimately win equality of right."

As a first step, Citizens' Committee members went to various railroad officials to ask for aid in establishing a case that could test the law. Disliking the cost of the extra cars the law forced them to buy, the officials were sympathetic but reluctant. One railroad already refused to enforce the law; officials on two other railroads said it was "a bad and mean one; they would like to get rid of it," but were afraid of public opinion. At last, the East Louisiana Railway agreed to help.

And so on June 7, 1892, to test the law, Homer A. Plessy boarded an East Louisiana Railway train in New Orleans for the 30-mile trip to Covington. He took a seat in the car reserved for whites, refused to move when a conductor asked him to, and was arrested by a detective who was standing by for the occasion. John H. Ferguson, a local judge, ruled against Plessy's argument that the law violated his rights, and Plessy appealed to the State Supreme Court, arguing that the law violated the "equal protection" clause of the Fourteenth Amendment to the Constitution. That Court, too, promptly ruled against him.

Delighted, Louisiana segregationists hoped, as one of their newspapers said, that the two decisions would knock some sense into "the silly negroes who are trying to fight this law. The sooner they drop their so-called 'crusade' against the 'Jim Crow Car,' and stop wasting their money in combating so well-established a principle—the right to separate the races in cars and elsewhere—the better for them."

It took three more years before the United States Supreme Court heard the case. Tourgée himself was pleased with the delay, hoping that time might improve racial feelings in the country and bring popular support to his cause. Those hopes did not bear out, nor did his arguments before the Court.

In an unusual approach, Tourgée began by arguing that Homer A. Plessy, who was light-skinned in color, had been deprived of property without due process of law, contrary to the Fourteenth Amendment. Able to pass for white, he had been identified by the railroad conductor as black. He had been robbed, therefore, of his "property," Tourgée said, the sense of being white, and thus barred from association with white people, who in the United States controlled the avenues to advancement.

"Probably most white persons if given a choice," Tourgée argued, "would prefer death to life in the United States *as colored persons.* Under these conditions, is it possible to conclude that the *reputation of being white* is not property? Indeed, is it not the most valuable sort of property, being the master-key that unlocks the golden door of opportunity?"

The remainder of Tourgée's brief was straightforward, stressing the incompatibility of the separate car law with the intent of the Thirteenth and Fourteenth Amendments, the inequities it fostered, and its basis in claims of white superiority. Unless the Court stopped it now, enforced segregation would soon spread everywhere through life. "Why may [a law] not require all red-headed people to ride in a separate car? Why not require all colored people to walk on one side of the street and the whites on the other?" Why not houses of different color, or clothes, or carriages? Laws might make blacks and whites (or Protestants and Catholics, natives and foreign-born, or anyone else, for that matter) sit on opposite sides of a courtroom or use different playgrounds.

Deciding the case was simple, Tourgée concluded: "Suppose you, the members of the Court, were suddenly ordered into a Jim Crow car of your own. What humiliation, what rage would then fill the judicial mind!"

Finally, on May 18, 1896, the Court handed down its decision in *Plessy* v. *Ferguson.* By a vote of 7 to 1, it decided against Plessy. Upholding the doctrine of "separate but equal," it held that the Louisiana law did not violate Plessy's rights. It did not violate them, the Court said, because the law was "reasonable"; it had been passed "with reference to the established usages, customs and traditions of the people."

It was precisely those usages and customs—race prejudice, in short—that Tourgée had argued against. They were contrary to the Reconstruction amendments to the Constitution, he had argued, but the majority of the Court would have none of it. The authors of those amendments, they said, could not have meant to do away with racial distinctions or institute social equality; that simply could not be done. Laws did not create race prejudice, and they could not change it. Enforced segregation did not label anyone as inferior. "We consider," the Court said, "the underlying fallacy of the plaintiff's argument to consist in the assumption that the enforced separation of the two races stamps the colored race with a badge of inferiority. If this be so, it is not by reason of anything found in the act, but solely because the colored race chooses to put that construction upon it."

There was irony in the Court's vote. Justice Henry Billings Brown, a son of Massachusetts and Michigan, wrote the opinion for the majority, a measure of changing opinion in the North. The single dissenter in the case, Justice John Marshall Harlan of Kentucky, on the other hand, was not only from the South, he had once owned slaves. But accepting the changed requirements of the Reconstruction amendments, he became the "Great Dissenter" in a Court—and a country—fast fleeing its important responsibilities.

Dissenting in *Plessy,* he scoffed at the majority's reasoning. The Louisiana law, he said, was clearly prejudicial, designed to keep blacks from railroad cars occupied by whites, and as such was in clear conflict with both the Thirteenth and Fourteenth Amendments. It was "a badge of servitude," inconsistent with "the equality before the law established by the Constitution. It cannot be justified upon any legal grounds."

"Our Constitution is color-blind, and neither knows nor tolerates classes among citizens. In respect of civil rights, all citizens are equal before the law. The humblest is the peer of the most powerful. The law regards man as man, and takes no account of his surroundings or of his color when his civil rights as guaranteed by the supreme law of the land are involved."

"In my opinion," Harlan concluded, "the judgment this day rendered will, in time, prove to be quite as pernicious as the decision made by this tribunal in the *Dred Scott case.*"

It was.

After Plessy, Jim Crow laws spread swiftly through the South. More and more public conveyances, schools, and restaurants were segregated. Signs saying "Whites only" or "Colored" appeared on entrances and exits, restrooms and water fountains, waiting rooms, and even elevators. In 1905, Georgia passed the first law requiring separate public parks. In 1909, Mobile, Alabama, enacted a curfew requiring blacks to be off the streets by 10 P.M. In 1915, South Carolina forbade blacks and whites to work in the same rooms in textile factories. The Oklahoma legislature required separate telephone booths; New Orleans segregated white and black prostitutes.

The Louisiana segregation law tested by Homer Plessy in 1892 was representative of a growing number of such laws passed in the 1880s and 1890s. *Plessy* v. *Ferguson* served to reinforce policies of racial segregation and eventually resulted in the institution of "separate but equal" facilities, which, like the ones shown here, were often not equal at all. ❖

Atlanta had separate Bibles for black witnesses in the city courts.

Harlan had, in general terms, predicted it all, in words still worth reading today: "The destinies of the two races, in this country, are indissolubly linked together, and the interests of both require that the common government of all shall not permit the seeds of race hate to be planted under the sanction of law. What can more certainly arouse race hate, what more certainly create and perpetuate a feeling of distrust between these races, than state enactments, which, in fact, proceed on the ground that colored citizens are so inferior and degraded that they cannot be allowed to sit in public coaches occupied by white citizens? That, as all will admit, is the real meaning of such legislation as was enacted in Louisiana."

Plessy v. *Ferguson* set a pattern of court-supported segregation that lasted sixty years. Generations of blacks and whites, children and adults alike, were deeply affected—sometimes traumatized—by it. The practice became a major focus of grievance in the growing movement for civil rights during the 1930s and 1940s.

"Justice," Tourgée had written in his original brief, "is pictured blind and her daughter, the Law, ought at least to be color-blind." Harlan had used the same word, "color-blind," a welcome concept to those fighting for civil rights in the 1890s. But history takes interesting and different turns, as does the law, and the word would come up again decades later, in arguments against affirmative action programs that helped African Americans get into colleges and professional schools. (See *Bakke* v. *Regents of the University of California*, pp. 956–959.)

Plessy, by then, was no more. At last, exactly fifty-eight years after the decision had been announced, on May 17, 1954, in the case of *Brown* v. *Board of Education of Topeka* (see Chapter 29), the Supreme Court reversed itself and overturned *Plessy*. Ruling that segregated schools are inherently unequal, the Court's stand toppled segregation of many kinds and changed lives once again.

Questions for Discussion

- What did the majority of the Supreme Court give as its reasons in deciding *Plessy* v. *Ferguson*? What do you think of these reasons? How do you think the majority reflected the climate of their times? What changes in public opinion have occurred since?
- Do you think Tourgée established an effective defense in arguing that the light-skinned Plessy had been deprived of his valuable property, "*the reputation of being white*"? Why or why not?
- What are some of the factors that contributed to increased segregation in the American South, and North, after 1890?

Chapter 20

This campaign card from the 1896 presidential election predicts that Republican candidate William McKinley's protariff, protectionist policy will lead to prosperity and thriving industrialism while Democratic candidate William Jennings Bryan's free trade policy will lead to economic ruin. ❖

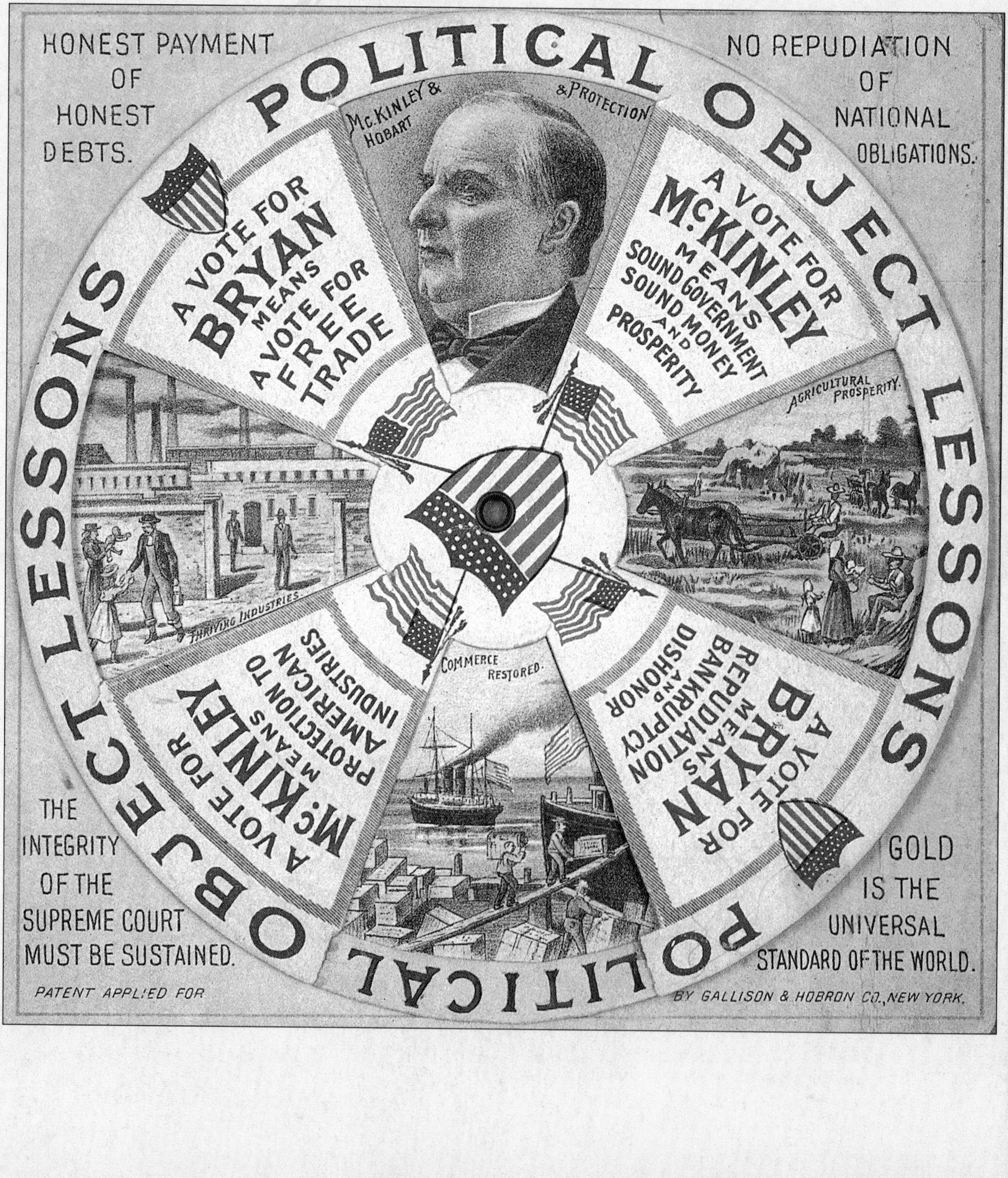

Political Realignments in the 1890s

Hardship and Heartache

In June 1894, Susan Orcutt, a young farm woman from western Kansas, sat down to write the governor of her state a letter. She was desperate. The nation was in the midst of a devastating economic depression, and, like thousands of other people, she had no money and nothing to eat. "I take my Pen In hand to let you know that we are Starving to death," she wrote. Hail had ruined the Orcutts' crops, and none of the household could find work. "My Husband went away to find work and came home last night and told me that we would have to Starve. [H]e has bin in ten countys and did not Get no work. . . . I havent had nothing to Eat today and It is three oclock[.]"

As bad as conditions were on the farms, they were no better in the cities. "There are thousands of homeless and starving men in the streets," reported a journalist in Chicago in the winter of 1893. "I have seen more misery in this last week than I ever saw in my life before." Charity societies and churches tried to help, but they could not handle the huge numbers of people who were in need. The records of the Massachusetts state medical examiner told a grim story:

> K.R., 29 — Suicide by drowning
> Boston — October 2, 1896
> Out of work and despondent for a long while. Body found floating in the Charles [River].
>
> F.S., 29 — Suicide by arsenic
> Boston — January 1, 1896
> Much depressed for several weeks. Loss of employment. At 7:50 A.M. Jan. 1, she called her father and told him she had taken poison and wished to die.
>
> L.M., 38 — Hanging suicide
> E. Boston — October 15, 1895
> Had been out of work for several weeks and was very despondent. Wife went to market at about 11 A.M. and upon returning at about 12 P.M. found him hanging from bedroom door. . . . Slipped noose about his neck and [fell] forward upon it.
>
> R.N., 23 — Suicide by bullet wound of brain
> Boston — June 22, 1896
> Out of work. Mentally depressed. About 3 P.M. June 21 shot himself in right temple. . . . Left a letter explaining that he killed himself to save others the trouble of caring for him.

Lasting until 1897, the depression was the decisive event of the decade. At its height, three million people were unemployed—fully 20 percent of the workforce. The human costs were enormous, even among the well-to-do. "They were for me years of simple Hell," shattering "my whole scheme of life," said Charles Francis Adams, Jr., the descendant of two American presidents. "I was sixty-three years old and a tired man when at last the effects of the 1893 convulsion wore themselves out."

Outline

Feature Essay

LIKE THE GREAT DEPRESSION of the 1930s that gave rise to the New Deal, the depression of the 1890s had profound and lasting effects. Bringing to a head many of the tensions that had been building in the society, it increased rural hostility toward the cities, brought about a bitter fight over the currency, and changed people's thinking about government, unemployment, and reform. There were outbreaks of warfare between capital and labor; farmers demanded a fairer share of economic and social benefits; the "new" immigrants came under fresh attack. The depression of the 1890s changed the course of American history, as did another event of that decade: the war with Spain in 1898.

Under the cruel impact of the depression, ideas changed in many areas, including a stronger impulse toward reform, a larger role for the presidency, and a call for help from many farmers and laborers. One of the most important of these areas was politics. A realignment of the American political system, which had been developing since the end of Reconstruction, finally reached its fruition in the 1890s, establishing new patterns that gave rise to the Progressive Era and lasted well into the twentieth century.

POLITICS OF STALEMATE

Politics was a major fascination of the late nineteenth century, its mass entertainment and favorite sport. Political campaigns were events that involved the whole community, even though in most states men were the only ones who could vote. During the weeks leading up to an election, there were rallies, parades, picnics, and torchlight processions. Millions of Americans read party newspapers, listened to three-hour speeches by party leaders, and in elections turned out in enormous numbers to vote. In the six presidential elections from 1876 to 1896, an average of almost 79 percent of the electorate voted, a higher percentage than voted before or after.

White males made up the bulk of the electorate; until after the turn of the century, women could vote in national elections only in Wyoming, Utah, Idaho, and Colorado. The National Woman Suffrage Association early sued for the vote, but in 1875, the Supreme Court (*Minor* v. *Happersett*) upheld the power of the states to deny this right to women. On several occasions, Congress refused to pass a constitutional amendment for women's suffrage, and between 1870 and 1910, nearly a dozen states defeated referenda to grant women the vote.

Black men were another group kept from the polls. In 1877, Georgia adopted the poll tax to make voters pay an annual tax for the right to vote. The technique, aimed at impoverished blacks, was quickly copied across the South. In 1882, South Carolina adopted the "eight box" law, soon copied elsewhere, that required ballots for separate offices to be placed in separate boxes, a difficult task for illiterate voters.

In 1890, Mississippi required voters to be able to read and interpret the federal Constitution to the satisfaction of registration officials, all of them white. Such literacy tests, which the Supreme Court upheld in the case of *Williams* v. *Mississippi* (1898), excluded poor white voters as well as blacks. In 1898, Louisiana

A delegation of women's rights advocates addressed the judiciary committee of the House of Representatives to present their arguments in favor of woman suffrage. Reading the argument is Victoria Claflin Woodhull, one of the more radical activists in the women's movement. ❖

avoided the problem by adopting the famous "grandfather clause," which used a literacy test to disqualify black voters but permitted men who had failed the test to vote anyway if their fathers and grandfathers had voted before 1867—a time, of course, when no blacks could vote. The number of black voters decreased dramatically. In 1896, there were 130,334 registered black voters in Louisiana; in 1904, there were 1,342.

The Party Deadlock

The 1870s and 1880s were still dominated by the Civil War generation, the unusual group of people who rose to power in the turbulent 1850s. In both the North and South, they had ruled longer than most generations, with a consciousness that the war experience had set them apart. Five of the six presidents elected between 1865 and 1900 had served in the war, as had many civic, business, and religious leaders. In 1890, well over one million veterans of the Union army were still alive, and Confederate veterans numbered in the hundreds of thousands.

Party loyalties—rooted in Civil War traditions, ethnic and religious differences, and perhaps class distinctions—were remarkably strong. Voters clung to their old parties, shifts were infrequent, and there were relatively few "independent" voters. Although linked to the defeated Confederacy, the Democrats revived quickly after the war. In 1874, they gained control of the House of Representatives, which they maintained for all but four of the succeeding twenty years. The Democrats rested on a less sectional base than the Republicans. Identification with civil rights and military rule cut Republican strength in the South, but the Democratic party's principles of states' rights, decentralization, and limited government won supporters everywhere.

While Democrats wanted to keep government local and small, the Republicans pursued policies for the nation as a whole, in which government was an instrument to promote moral progress and material wealth. The Republicans passed the Homestead Act (1862), granted subsidies to the transcontinental railroads, and pushed other measures to encourage economic growth. They enacted legislation and constitutional amendments to protect civil rights. They advocated a high protective tariff as a tool of economic policy, to keep out foreign products while "infant industries" grew.

In national elections, sixteen states, mostly in New England and the North, consistently voted Republican; fourteen states, mostly in the South, consistently voted Democratic. Elections, therefore, depended on a handful of "doubtful" states, which could swing elections either way. These states—New York, New Jersey, Connecticut, Ohio, Indiana, and Illinois—received special attention at election time. Politicians lavished money and time on them; presidential candidates usually came from them. From 1868 to 1912, eight of the nine Republican presidential candidates and six of the seven Democratic candidates came from the "doubtful" states, especially New York and Ohio.

The two parties were evenly matched, and elections were closely fought. In three of the five presidential elections from 1876 to 1892, the victor won by less than 1 percent of the vote; in 1876 and 1888, the losing candidates actually had more popular votes than the winners but lost in the electoral college. Knowing that

❖ A Look at the Past ❖

Ballot Box

Until the 1890s, political parties printed their own ballots, which voters requested in order to cast a ballot. Voters revealed their political decisions simply by obtaining a ballot. Glass ballot boxes such as this one made it possible for others to witness that the voter actually cast the ballot. While today voters make their decisions and cast their votes privately, before 1890 voting was a visible, public act, and political intimidation could and did occur. Why would Americans use such a system? Why did they change to secret balloting at the end of the nineteenth century?

A toy scale pitting the presidential candidates of 1888 (Harrison and Cleveland) against each other invites participation in determining the election outcome. More than a plaything, this scale symbolizes the high level of voter participation during the late nineteenth century when elections hung in balance until the last vote was counted. ❖

small mistakes could lose elections, politicians became extremely cautious. Only twice during these years did one party control both the presidency and the two houses of Congress—the Republicans in 1888 and the Democrats in 1892.

Historians once believed that political leaders accomplished little between 1877 and 1900, but those who saw few achievements were looking in the wrong location. With the impeachment of Andrew Johnson, the authority of the presidency dwindled in relation to congressional strength. For the first time in many years, attention shifted away from Washington itself. North and South, people who were weary of the centralization brought on by war and Reconstruction looked first to state and local governments to deal with the problems of an urban-industrial society.

Experiments in the States

Across the country, state bureaus and commissions were established to regulate the new industrial society. Many of the early commissions were formed to oversee the railroads, at the time the nation's largest businesses. People who shipped goods over the railroads, especially farmers and merchants, wanted to end the policies of rate discrimination and other harmful practices. In 1869, Massachusetts established the first commission to regulate the railroads; by 1900, twenty-eight states had taken such action.

Most of the early commissions were advisory in nature. They collected statistics and published reports on rates and practices—serving, one commissioner said, "as a sort of lens" to focus public attention. Impatient with the results, legislatures in the Midwest and on the Pacific Coast established commissions with greater power to fix rates, outlaw rebates, and investigate rate discrimination. These commissions, experimental in nature, served as models for later policy at the federal level.

Illinois had one of the most thoroughgoing provisions. Responding to local merchants who were upset with existing railroad rate policies, the Illinois state constitution of 1870 declared railroads to be public highways and authorized the legislature to pass laws establishing maximum rates and preventing rate discrimination. In the important case of *Munn* v. *Illinois* (1877), the Supreme Court upheld the Illinois legislation, declaring that private property "affected with the public interest . . . must submit to being controlled by the public for the common good."

But the Court soon weakened that judgment. In the *Wabash* case of 1886 (*Wabash, St. Louis, & Pacific Railway Co.* v. *Illinois*), it narrowed the *Munn* ruling and held that states could not regulate commerce extending beyond their borders. Only Congress could. The *Wabash* decision turned people's attention back to the federal government. It spurred Congress to pass the Interstate Commerce Act (1887), which created the **Interstate Commerce Commission (ICC)** to investigate and oversee railroad activities. The act outlawed rebates and pooling agreements, and the ICC became the prototype of the federal commissions that today regulate many parts of the economy.

Reestablishing Presidential Power

Johnson's impeachment, the scandals of the Grant administrations, and the controversy surrounding the 1876 election weakened the presidency. During the last two decades of the nineteenth century, presidents fought to reassert their authority, and by 1900, under William McKinley, they had succeeded to a remarkable degree. The late 1890s, in fact, marked the birth of the modern powerful presidency.

Rutherford B. Hayes entered the White House with his title clouded by the disputed election of 1876. Opponents called him "His Fraudulency" and "Rutherfraud B. Hayes," but soon he began to reassert the authority of the presidency. Hayes worked for reform in the civil service, placed well-known reformers in high offices, and, ordering the last troops out of South Carolina and Louisiana, ended military Reconstruction. He hoped to revive the Republican party in the South by persuading business-oriented

THE ELECTION OF 1880

Candidate	Party	Popular Vote	Electoral Vote
Garfield	Republican	4,454,416	214
Hancock	Democrat	4,444,952	155
Weaver	Greenback	308,578	0

THE ELECTION OF 1884

Candidate	Party	Popular Vote	Electoral Vote
Cleveland	Democrat	4,874,986	219
Blaine	Republican	4,851,981	182
Butler	Greenback	175,370	0
St. John	Prohibition	150,369	0

ex-Whigs to join a national party that would support their economic interests more effectively than the Democrats did. In this attempt, however, he failed. Committed to the gold standard—the only basis, Hayes thought, of a sound currency—in 1878 he vetoed a bill that called for the partial coinage of silver, but Congress passed this **Bland-Allison Silver Purchase Act** over his veto.

James A. Garfield, a Union army hero and longtime member of Congress, succeeded Hayes. Winning by a handful of votes in 1880, he took office energetically, determined to unite the Republican party (which had been split by personality differences and disagreement over policy toward the tariff and the South), lower the tariff to cut taxes, and assert American economic and strategic interests in Latin America. Ambitious and eloquent, Garfield had looked forward to the presidency, yet within a few weeks he said to friends, "My God! What is there in this place that a man should ever want to get into it?"

Office seekers, hordes of them, evoked Garfield's anguish. Each one wanted a government job, and each one thought nothing of cornering the president on every occasion. The problem of government jobs also provoked a bitter fight with the powerful senator from New York, Roscoe Conkling, who resented some of Garfield's choices. On the verge of victory over Conkling, Garfield planned to leave Washington on July 2, 1881, for a vacation in New England. Walking toward his train, he was shot in the back by Charles J. Guiteau, a deranged lawyer and disappointed office seeker. Suffering through the summer, Garfield died on September 19, 1881, and Vice President Chester A. Arthur—an ally of Senator Conkling—became president.

Arthur was a better president than many had expected. Deftly, he established his independence of Conkling. Conservative in outlook, he reversed Garfield's foreign policy initiatives in Latin America, but he approved the construction of the modern American navy. Arthur worked to lower the tariff, and in 1883, with his backing, Congress passed the **Pendleton Act** to reform the civil service. In part a reaction to Garfield's assassination, the act created a bipartisan Civil Service Commission to administer competitive examinations and appoint officeholders on the basis of merit. Initially, the act affected only about 14,000 of some 100,000 government offices, but it laid the basis for the later expansion of the civil service.

In the election of 1884, Grover Cleveland, the Democratic governor of New York, narrowly defeated Republican nominee, James G. Blaine, largely because of the continuing divisions in the Republican party. The first Democratic president since 1861, Cleveland was slow and ponderous, known for his honesty, stubbornness, and hard work. His term in the White House from 1885 to 1889 reflected the Democratic party's desire to curtail federal activities. Cleveland vetoed more than two-thirds of the bills presented to him, more than all his predecessors combined.

Forthright and sincere, he brought a new respectability to a Democratic party still tainted by its link with secession. Working long into the night, he reviewed veterans' pensions and civil service appointments. He continued Arthur's naval construction program and forced railroad, lumber, and cattle companies to surrender millions of acres of fraudulently occupied

Election of 1888

	Electoral Vote by State	Popular Vote
REPUBLICAN Benjamin Harrison	233	5,439,853
DEMOCRATIC Grover Cleveland	168	5,540,309
MINOR PARTIES	—	396,441
	401	11,376,603

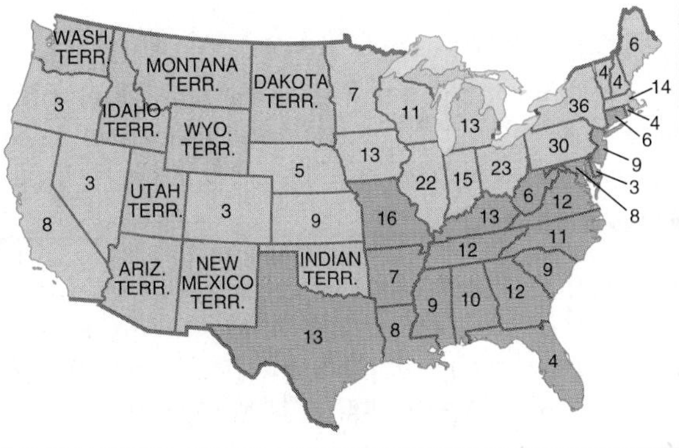

public domain. Late in 1887, he devoted his annual message to an attack on the tariff, "the vicious, inequitable, and illogical source of unnecessary taxation," and committed himself and the Democratic party to lowering the tariff.

The Republicans accused him of undermining American industries, and in 1888, they nominated for the presidency Benjamin Harrison, a defender of the tariff. Cleveland garnered ninety thousand more popular votes than Harrison but won the electoral votes of only two northern states and the South. Harrison won the rest of the North, most of the "doubtful" states, and the election.

Republicans in Power: The Billion-Dollar Congress

Despite Harrison's narrow margin, the election of 1888 was the most sweeping victory for either party in almost twenty years; it gave the Republicans the presidency and both houses of Congress. The Republicans, it seemed, had broken the party stalemate and become the majority party in the country.

Democratic leaders hoped not, and, eager to embarrass the Republicans and block Republican-sponsored laws, the Democrats in Congress used minority tactics, especially the "disappearing quorum" rule, which let members of the House of Representatives join in debate but then refuse to answer the roll call to determine whether a quorum was present.

For two months, the Democrats used the rule to bring Congress to a halt. The Republicans grew angry and impatient. On January 29, 1890, they fell two votes short of a quorum, and speaker of the House Thomas B. Reed, a crusty veteran of Maine politics, made congressional history. "The Chair," he said, "directs the Clerk to record the following names of members present and refusing to vote." Democrats shouted "Czar! Czar!", a title that stuck to Reed for the rest of his life. Tumult continued for days, but in mid-February 1890, the Republicans adopted the Reed rules and proceeded to enact the party's program.

Tariffs, Trusts, and Silver

As if a dam had burst, law after law poured out of the Republican Congress during 1890. The Republicans passed the McKinley Tariff Act, which raised tariff duties about 4 percent, higher than ever before; it also included a novel reciprocity provision that allowed the president to lower duties if other countries did the same. In addition, the act used duties to promote new industries, such as tinplate for packaging the new "canned" foods appearing on grocery store shelves. A Dependent Pensions Act granted pensions to Union army veterans and their widows and children. The pensions were modest—$6 to $12 a month—but the number of pensioners doubled by 1893, when nearly 1 million individuals received about $160 million in pensions.

With little debate, the Republicans and Democrats joined in passing the **Sherman Antitrust Act,** the first federal attempt to regulate big business. As the initial attempt to deal with the problem of trusts and industrial growth, the act shaped all later antitrust policy. It declared illegal "every contract, combination in the form of trust or otherwise, or conspiracy, in restraint of trade or commerce." Penalties for violation were stiff, including fines and imprisonment and the dissolution of guilty trusts. Experimental in nature, the act's terms were often vague and left precise interpretation to later experience and the courts.

One of the most important laws Congress passed, the Sherman Antitrust Act made the United States virtually the only industrial nation to regulate business combinations. It tried to harness big busi-

In this 1886 cartoon illustrating the silver standard versus gold standard controversy, Uncle Sam bicycles to national bankruptcy on an enormous silverite dollar. ❖

ness without harming it. Many members of Congress did not expect the new law to have much effect on businesses, and for a decade, in fact, it did not. The Justice Department rarely filed suit under it, and in the *United States* v. *E. C. Knight Co.* decision (1895), the first judicial interpretation of the law, the Supreme Court severely crippled it. Though the E. C. Knight Co. controlled 98 percent of all sugar refining in the country, the Court drew a sharp distinction between commerce and manufacturing, holding that the company, as a manufacturer, was not subject to the law. But judicial interpretations changed after the turn of the century, and the Sherman Antitrust Act gained fresh power.

Another measure, the **Sherman Silver Purchase Act,** tried to end the troublesome problem presented by silver. As one of the two most commonly used precious metals, silver had once played a large role in currencies around the world, but by the mid-1800s, it had slipped into disuse. With the discovery of the great bonanza mines in Nevada, American silver production quadrupled between 1870 and 1890, glutting the world market and lowering the price of silver. As a result, many European nations decided to demonetize silver in favor of the scarcer metal, gold. The United States kept a limited form of silver coinage with congressional passage of the Bland-Allison Act in 1878.

Support for silver coinage was especially strong in the South and West, where people thought it might inflate the currency, raise wages and crop prices, and challenge the power of the gold-oriented Northeast. Eager to avert the free coinage of silver, which would require the coinage of all silver presented at the U.S. mints, President Harrison and other Republican leaders pressed for a compromise that took shape in the Sherman Silver Purchase Act of 1890.

The act directed the Treasury to purchase 4.5 million ounces of silver a month and to issue legal tender in the form of Treasury notes in payment for it. The act was a compromise; it satisfied both sides. Opponents of silver were pleased that it did not include free coinage. Silverites, on the other hand, were delighted that the monthly purchases would buy up most of the country's silver production. The Treasury notes, moreover, could be cashed for either gold or silver at the bank, a gesture toward a true bimetallic system based on silver and gold.

As a final measure, Republicans in the House courageously passed a federal elections bill to protect the voting rights of blacks in the South. Although restrained in language and intent, it set off a storm of denunciation among the Democrats, who called it a "force bill" that would station army troops in the South. Because of the outcry, the bill failed in the Senate; it was the last major effort until the 1950s to enforce the Fifteenth Amendment to the Constitution.

The 1890 Elections

The Republican Congress of 1890 was one of the most important Congresses in American history. It passed a record number of significant laws that helped shape later policy and asserted the authority of the federal government to a degree the country would not then accept. Sensing the public reaction, the Democrats labeled it the "Billion-Dollar Congress" for spending that much in appropriations and grants.

"This is a billion-dollar country," Speaker Reed replied, but the voters disagreed. The 1890 elections crushed the Republicans, who lost an extraordinary seventy-eight seats in the House. The elections also crushed Republicans in the Midwest, where, again enlarging government authority, they had passed state laws prohibiting the sale of alcoholic beverages, requiring the closing of businesses on Sunday, and mandating the use of English in the public and parochial schools. Roman Catholics, German Lutherans, and other groups resented such laws, which they saw as a direct attack on their religion and personal freedoms, and they angrily deserted the Republicans.

Political veterans went down to defeat, and new leaders vaulted into sudden prominence. Nebraska elected a Democratic governor for the first time in its history. The state of Iowa, once so staunchly Republican that a local leader had predicted that "Iowa will go Democratic when Hell goes Methodist," went Democratic in 1890.

The Rise of the Populist Movement

The elections of 1890 drew attention to a fast-growing movement among farmers that soon came to be known far and wide as populism. The movement had begun rather quietly, in places distant from normal centers of attention, and for a time it went almost unnoticed in the press. But during the summer of 1890, wagonloads of farm families in the South and West converged on campgrounds and picnic areas to socialize and discuss common problems. They came by the thousands, weary of drought, mortgages, and low crop prices. At the campgrounds, they picnicked, talked, and listened to recruiters from an organization called the **National Farmers' Alliance and Industrial Union,** which promised unified action to solve agricultural problems.

Farmers were joining the Alliance at the rate of 1,000 a week; the Kansas Alliance alone claimed

130,000 members in 1890. The summer of 1890 became "that wonderful picnicking, speech-making Alliance summer," a time of fellowship and spirit long remembered by farmers.

The Farm Problem

Farm discontent was a worldwide phenomenon between 1870 and 1900. With the new means of transportation and communication, farmers everywhere were caught up in a complex international market they neither controlled nor entirely understood.

American farmers complained bitterly about declining prices for their products, rising railroad rates for shipping them, and burdensome mortgages. Some of their grievances were valid. Farm profits were certainly low; agriculture in general tends to produce low profits because of the ease of entry into the industry. The prices of farm commodities fell between 1865 and 1890—corn sold at sixty-three cents a bushel in 1881 and twenty-eight cents in 1890—but they did not fall as low as did other commodity prices. Despite the fact that farmers received less for their crops, their purchasing power actually increased.

Neither was the farmers' second grievance—rising railroad rates—entirely justified. Railroad rates actually fell during these years, benefiting shippers of all products. Farm mortgages, the farmers' third grievance, were common because many farmers mortgaged their property to expand their holdings or buy new farm machinery. While certainly burdensome, most mortgages did not bring hardship. They were often short, with a term of four years or less, after which farmers could renegotiate at new rates, and the new machinery the farmers bought enabled them to triple their output and increase their income.

The terms of the farm problem varied from area to area and year to year. New England farmers suffered from overworked land; farmers in western Kansas and Nebraska went broke in a severe drought that followed a period of unusual rainfall. Many southern farmers were trapped in the crop lien system that kept them in debt. They called it the "anaconda" system because of the way it coiled slowly and tightly around them.

A study of farms in the Midwest between 1860 and 1900 suggests that farm income rose substantially in the 1860s, fell during the devastating depression of the 1870s, rose in the 1880s, and remained roughly constant in the 1890s. There were also large variations in farm profits from county to county, again indicating the absence of clear nationwide patterns. Farmers who had good land close to railroad transportation did well; others did not.

Some farmers did have valid grievances, though many understandably tended to exaggerate them. More important, many farmers were sure their condition had declined, and this perception—as bitterly real as any actual fact—sparked a growing anger. Equally upsetting, everyone in the 1870s and 1880s seemed excited about factories, not farms. Farmers had become

SELECTED COMMODITY PRICES

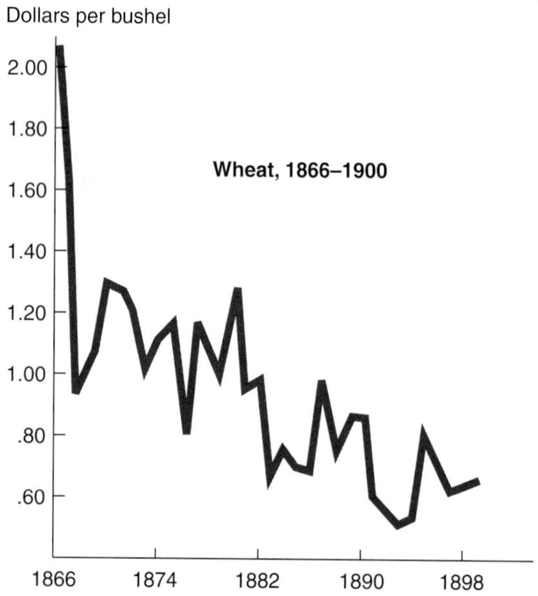

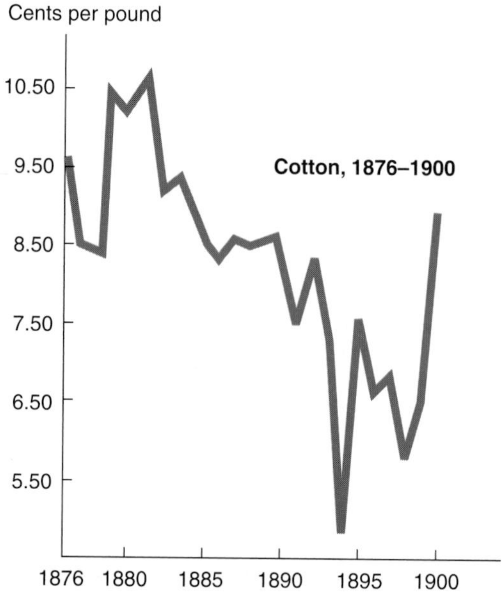

Source: U.S. Bureau of the Census, *Historical Statistics of the United States, Colonial Times to 1970,* Bicentennial Edition, Washington, D.C., 1975.

"hayseeds," a word that first appeared in 1889, and they watched their offspring leave for city lights and new careers. Books such as *The Spider and the Fly: or, Tricks, Traps, and Pitfalls of City Life by One Who Knows* (1873) warned against such a move, but still the children went. A literature of disillusionment emerged, most notably Hamlin Garland's *Son of the Middle Border* (1890) and *Main-Travelled Roads* (1891), which described the drabness of farm life.

The Fast-Growing Farmers' Alliance

Originally a social organization for farmers, the Grange lost many of its members as it turned more and more toward politics in the late 1870s. In its place, a multitude of farm societies sprang into existence. By the end of the 1880s, they had formed into two major organizations: the National Farmers' Alliance, located on the Plains west of the Mississippi and known as the Northwestern Alliance, and the Farmers' Alliance and Industrial Union, based in the South and known as the Southern Alliance.

The Southern Alliance began in Texas in 1875 but did not assume major proportions until Dr. Charles W. Macune, an energetic and farsighted person, took over the leadership in 1886. Rapidly expanding, the Alliance absorbed other agricultural societies. Its agents spread across the South, where farmers were fed up with crop liens, depleted lands, and sharecropping. They "seem like unto ripe fruit," an Alliance organizer said; "you can garner them by a gentle shake of the bush." In 1890, the Southern Alliance claimed more than a million members. It welcomed to membership the farmers' "natural friends"—country doctors, schoolteachers, preachers, and mechanics. It excluded lawyers, bankers, cotton merchants, and warehouse operators.

An effective organization, the Southern Alliance published a newspaper and distributed Alliance material to hundreds of local newspapers, and in five years it sent lecturers to forty-three states and territories where they spoke to two million farm families. It was "the most massive organizing drive by any citizen institution of nineteenth-century America." Like the Grange, the Alliance also established cooperative grain elevators, marketing associations, and retail stores—all designed to bring farmers together to make greater profits. Most of the projects were short-lived, but for a time, between 1886 and 1892, cooperative enterprises blossomed in the South.

Loosely affiliated with the Southern Alliance, a separate Colored Farmers' National Alliance and Cooperative Union enlisted black farmers in the South. Claiming more than 1 million members, it probably had closer to 250,000, but even that figure was sizable in an era when "uppity" blacks faced not merely defeat, but death. In 1891, black cotton pickers struck for higher wages near Memphis, Tennessee. Led by Ben Patterson, a 30-year-old picker, they walked off several plantations, but a posse hunted them down and, following violence on both sides, lynched fifteen strikers, including Patterson. The abortive strike ended the Colored Farmers' Alliance.

This advertisement for Farmer's Delight tobacco from the May 21, 1889, issue of the Progressive Farmer *is an example of the type of products sold through Alliance cooperatives. The Alliance organizations formed cooperatives in an effort to guarantee farmers greater profits by negotiating for better prices for farm products sold in bulk. Farmers could also avoid creditors' fees by buying goods through the cooperatives. However, failure to secure the credit necessary to finance the cooperatives and lack of management experience in operating them doomed the cooperative venture to failure.* ❖

On the Plains, the Northwestern Alliance, a smaller organization, was formed in 1880. Its objectives were similar to those of the Southern Alliance, but it disagreed with the Southerners' emphasis on secrecy, centralized control, and separate organizations for blacks. In 1889, the Southern Alliance changed its name to the National Farmers' Alliance and Industrial Union and persuaded the three strongest state alliances on the Plains—those in North Dakota, South Dakota, and Kansas—to join. Thereafter, the renamed organization dominated the Alliance movement.

The Alliance mainly sponsored social and economic programs, but it turned early to politics. In the West, its leaders rejected both the Republicans and Democrats and organized their own party; in June 1890, Kansas Alliance members formed the first major People's party. The Southern Alliance resisted the idea of a new party for fear it might divide the white vote, thus undercutting white supremacy. The Southerners instead followed leaders such as Benjamin F. Tillman of South Carolina, who wanted to capture control of the dominant Democratic party.

Thomas E. Watson and Leonidas L. Polk, two politically minded Southerners, reflected the high quality of Alliance leadership. Georgia-born, Watson was a talented orator and organizer; he urged Georgia farmers, black and white, to unite against their oppressors. The president of the National Farmers' Alliance, Polk believed in scientific farming and cooperative action. Jeremiah Simpson of Kansas, probably the most able of the western leaders, was reflective and well-read. A follower of reformer Henry George, he pushed for major social and economic change. Also from Kansas, Mary E. Lease—Mary Ellen to her friends, "Mary Yellin" to her opponents—helped head a movement remarkably open to female leadership. A captivating speaker, she made 160 speeches during the summer of 1890, calling on farmers to rise against Wall Street and the industrial East.

Meeting in Ocala, Florida, in 1890, the Alliance adopted the **Ocala Demands,** the platform the organization pushed as long as it existed. First and foremost, the demands called for the creation of a "sub-treasury system," which would allow farmers to store their crops in government warehouses. In return, they could claim Treasury notes for up to 80 percent of the local market value of the crop, a loan to be repaid when the crops were sold. Farmers could thus hold their crops for the best price. The Ocala Demands also urged the free coinage of silver, an end to protective tariffs and national banks, a federal income tax, the direct election of senators by voters instead of state legislatures, and tighter regulation of railroad companies.

The Alliance strategy worked well in the elections of 1890. In Kansas, the Alliance-related People's party, organized just a few months before, elected four congressmen and a U.S. senator. Across the South, the Alliance won victories based on the "Alliance yardstick," a demand that Democratic party candidates pledge support for Alliance measures. Alliance leaders claimed thirty-eight Alliance supporters elected to Congress, with at least a dozen more pledged to Alliance principles.

Populist Mary E. Lease advised farmers to "raise less corn and more hell." She also said, "If one man has not enough to eat three times a day and another man has $25 million, that last man has something that belongs to the first." ❖

The People's Party

After the 1890 elections, Northern Alliance leaders urged the formation of a national third party to promote reform, although the Southerners remained reluctant, still hopeful of capturing control of the Democratic party. Plans for a new party were discussed at Alliance conventions in 1891 and the following year. In July 1892, a convention in Omaha, Nebraska, formed the new **People's (or Populist) party.** Southern Alliance leaders joined in, convinced now that there was no reason to cooperate with the Democrats who exploited Alliance popularity but failed to adopt its reforms.

In the South, some Populists had worked to unite black and white farmers. "They are in the ditch just like we are," a white Texas Populist said. Blacks and whites served on Populist election committees; they spoke from the same platforms, and they ran on the same tickets. Populist sheriffs called blacks for jury duty, an unheard-of practice in the close-of-the-century South. In 1892, a black Populist was threatened with lynching; he took refuge with Tom Watson, and two thousand white farmers, some of whom rode all night to get there, guarded Watson's house until the threat passed.

Election of 1892

	Electoral Vote by State	Popular Vote
DEMOCRATIC* Grover Cleveland	277	5,556,918
REPUBLICAN Benjamin Harrison	145	5,176,108
PEOPLE'S (POPULIST) James B. Weaver	22	1,027,329
MINOR PARTIES	—	264,133
	444	12,024,488

*Electors classed as Democratic were in many states elected on joint Democratic and People's party tickets.

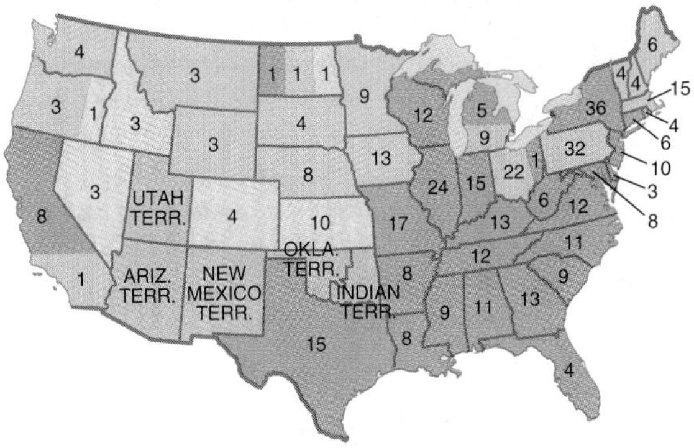

Many of the delegates at the Omaha convention had planned to nominate Leonidas L. Polk for president, but he died suddenly in June, and the convention turned instead to James B. Weaver of Iowa, a former congressman, Union army general, and third-party candidate for president in 1880 (on the Greenback-Labor party ticket). As its platform, the People's party adopted many of the Ocala Demands.

Weaver waged an active campaign but with mixed results. He won 1,029,000 votes, the first third-party presidential candidate ever to attract more than a million. He carried Kansas, Idaho, Nevada, and Colorado, along with portions of North Dakota and Oregon, for a total of twenty-two electoral votes. The Populists elected governors in Kansas and North Dakota, ten congressmen, five senators, and about fifteen hundred members of state legislatures.

Despite the Populists' victories, the election brought disappointment. Southern Democrats used intimidation, fraud, and manipulation to hold down Populist votes. Weaver was held to less than a quarter of the vote in every southern state except Alabama. In most of the country, he lost heavily in urban areas, with the exception of some mining towns in the Far West. He also failed to win over most farmers. In no midwestern state except Kansas and North Dakota did he win as much as 5 percent of the vote.

In the election of 1892, many voters switched parties, but they tended to realign with the Democrats rather than the Populists, whose platform on silver and other issues had relatively little appeal among city dwellers or factory workers. Although the Populists did run candidates in the next three presidential elections, they had reached their peak in 1892. That year, Farmers' Alliance membership dropped for the second year in a row, and the organization, which was once the breeding ground of the People's party, was broken.

While it lived, the Alliance was one of the most powerful protest movements in American history. Catalyzing the feelings of hundreds of thousands of farmers, it attempted to solve specific economic problems while at the same time advancing a larger vision of harmony and community, in which people who cared about each other were rewarded for what they produced.

The Crisis of the Depression

It was economic crisis, however, not harmony and community, that dominated the last decade of the century. Responding to the heady forces of industrialization, the American economy had expanded too rapidly in the 1870s and 1880s. Railroads had overbuilt, gambling on future growth. Companies had grown beyond their markets; farms and businesses had borrowed heavily for expansion.

The Panic of 1893

The mood changed early in 1893. In mid-February, panic suddenly hit the New York stock market. In one day, investors dumped one million shares of a leading company, the Philadelphia and Reading Railroad, and it went bankrupt. Business investment dropped sharply in the railroad and construction industries, touching off the worst economic downturn to that point in the country's history.

Frightened, people hurriedly sold stocks and other assets to buy gold. The overwhelming demand depleted the gold reserve of the U.S. Treasury. Eroding almost daily, in March 1893, the Treasury's reserve slumped toward the $100 million mark, an amount that stood for the government's commitment to maintain the gold standard. On April 22, for the first time since the 1870s, the reserve fell below $100 million.

The news shattered business confidence—the stock market broke. On Wednesday, May 3, railroad and industrial stocks plummeted, and the next day, several major firms went bankrupt. When the market opened on Friday, crowds filled its galleries, anticipating a panic. Within minutes, leading stocks plunged to record lows, and there was pandemonium on the floor and in the streets outside. May 5, 1893, Wall Street's worst day until the Great Crash of 1929, became

Customers line up in front of the Farmers and Mechanics Bank in Minneapolis, Minnesota, in May 1893 to try to withdraw their savings. Many banks had loaned out most of their deposits and kept only a small portion of cash in reserve. When they could not meet depositors' demands for cash withdrawals, banks closed their doors. ❖

"Industrial Black Friday," "a day of terrible strain long remembered on the market."

Afterward, banks cut back on loans. Unable to get capital, businesses failed at an average rate of two dozen a day during the month of May. "The papers are full of failures—banks are breaking all over the country, and there is a tremendous contraction of credits and hoarding of money going on everywhere," an observer noted. On July 26, the Erie Railroad, one of the leading names in railroading history, failed.

August 1893 was the worst month. Across the country, factories and mines shut down. In Orange, New Jersey, Thomas A. Edison, the symbol of the country's ingenuity, laid off 240 employees at the Edison Phonograph Works. On August 15, the Northern Pacific Railroad went bankrupt; the Union Pacific and the Santa Fe soon followed. Some economists estimated unemployment at 2 million people, or nearly 15 percent of the labor force. During 1893, 15,000 business firms and more than 600 banks closed.

The year 1894 was even worse. The gross national product dropped again, and by midyear the number of unemployed stood at 3 million. One out of every five workers was unemployed. "Famine is in our midst," said the head of one city's relief committee. In the summer, a heat wave and drought struck the farm belt west of the Mississippi River, creating conditions unmatched until the devastating Dust Bowl of the 1930s. Corn withered in the fields. In the South, the price of cotton fell below five cents a pound, far under the break-even point.

People became restless and angry. As one newspaper said in 1896: "On every corner stands a man whose fortune in these dull times has made him an ugly critic of everything and everybody." There was even talk of revolution and bloodshed. "Everyone scolds," Henry Adams, the historian, wrote a British friend. "Everyone also knows what ought to be done. Everyone reviles everyone who does not agree with him, and everyone differs, or agrees only in contempt for everyone else. As far as I can see, everyone is right."

Coxey's Army and the Pullman Strike

Some of the unemployed wandered across the country—singly, in small groups, and in small armies. In February 1894, police ejected six hundred unemployed men who stormed the State House in Boston demanding relief. During 1894, there were some fourteen hundred strikes involving more than a half million workers.

On Easter Sunday 1894, an unusual "army" of perhaps three hundred people left Massillon, Ohio. At its head rode "General" Jacob S. Coxey, a mild-looking middle-aged businessman who wanted to put the nation's jobless to work building roads. Coxey wanted Congress to pass the Coxey Good Roads bill, which would authorize the printing of $500 million in paper money to finance road construction. His march to Washington—"a petition in boots," he called it—drew nationwide attention. Forty-three newspaper correspondents accompanied him, reporting every detail of the march.

Other armies sprang up around the country, and all headed for Washington to persuade the government to provide jobs on irrigation, road construction, or other projects. In the West, they commandeered freight trains and headed east. Coxey himself reached Washington on May 1, 1894, after a difficult, tiring

Jacob Coxey (left) and two of his associates in a police station lockup after their arrest for trespassing on the lawn surrounding the U.S. Capitol. On the fiftieth anniversary of his march to Washington, Coxey was permitted to finish the speech that had been interrupted by his arrest in 1894. ❖

march. Police were everywhere, lining the streets and blocking the approaches to the Capitol. Coxey made it to the foot of the Capitol steps, but before he could do anything, the police were on him. He and a companion were clubbed, then arrested for trespassing. A week later, Coxey was sentenced to twenty days in jail.

The armies melted away, but discontent did not. The great **Pullman strike**—one of the largest strikes in the country's history—began just a few days after Coxey's arrest when the employees of the Pullman Palace Car Company, living in a company town just outside Chicago (a town in which everything was owned and meted out by the company), struck to protest wage cuts, continuing high rents, and layoffs. On June 26, 1894, the American Railway Union (ARU) under Eugene V. Debs joined the strike by refusing to handle trains that carried Pullman sleeping cars.

Within hours, the strike paralyzed the western half of the nation. Grain and livestock could not reach markets. Factories shut down for lack of coal. The strike extended into twenty-seven states and territories, tying up the economy and renewing talk of class warfare. In Washington, President Grover Cleveland, who had been reelected to the presidency in 1892, decided to break the strike on the grounds that it obstructed delivery of the mail.

On July 2, he secured a court injunction against the ARU, and he ordered troops to Chicago. When they arrived on the morning of Independence Day, the city was peaceful. Before long, however, violence broke out, and mobs, composed mostly of nonstrikers, overturned freight cars, looted, and burned. Restoring order, the army occupied railroad yards in Illinois, California, and other places. By late July, the strike was over; Debs was jailed for violating the injunction. Many people applauded Cleveland's action, "nominally for the expedition of the mails," a newspaper said, but "really for the preservation of society."

The Pullman strike had far-reaching consequences for the development of the labor movement. Working people resented Cleveland's actions in the strike, particularly as it became apparent that he sided with the railroads. Upholding Debs's sentence in *In re Debs* (1895), the Supreme Court endorsed the use of the injunction in labor disputes, thus giving business and government an effective antilabor weapon that hindered union growth in the 1890s. The strike's failure catapulted Debs into prominence. During his time in jail, he turned to socialism, and after his release, he worked to build the Socialist party of America, which experienced some success after 1900.

The Miners of the Midwest

The plight of coal miners in the Midwest illustrated the personal and social impact of the depression. Even in the best of times, mining was a dirty and dangerous business. One miner in twelve died underground; one in three suffered injury. Mines routinely closed for as long as six months a year, and wages fell with the depression. An Illinois miner earned 97 cents a ton in 1889 and only 80 cents in 1896. A bituminous coal miner made $282 a year.

Midwestern mining was often a family occupation, passed down from father to son. It demanded delicate judgments about when to blast, where to follow a seam, and how to avoid rockfalls. Until 1890, English and Irish immigrants dominated the business. They migrated from mine to mine, and they nearly always lived in flimsy shacks owned by the company. Time and again the miners struck for higher wages—between 1887 and 1894, there were 116 major coal strikes in Illinois, 111 in Ohio.

After 1890, immigration from southern and eastern Europe, hitherto a trickle, became a flood. Italians, Lithuanians, Poles, Slovaks, Magyars, Russians, Bohemians, and Croatians came to the mines to find work. In three years, nearly one thousand Italians settled in Coal City, Illinois; they comprised more than one-third of the population. In other mining towns, Italian and Polish miners soon made up almost half the population.

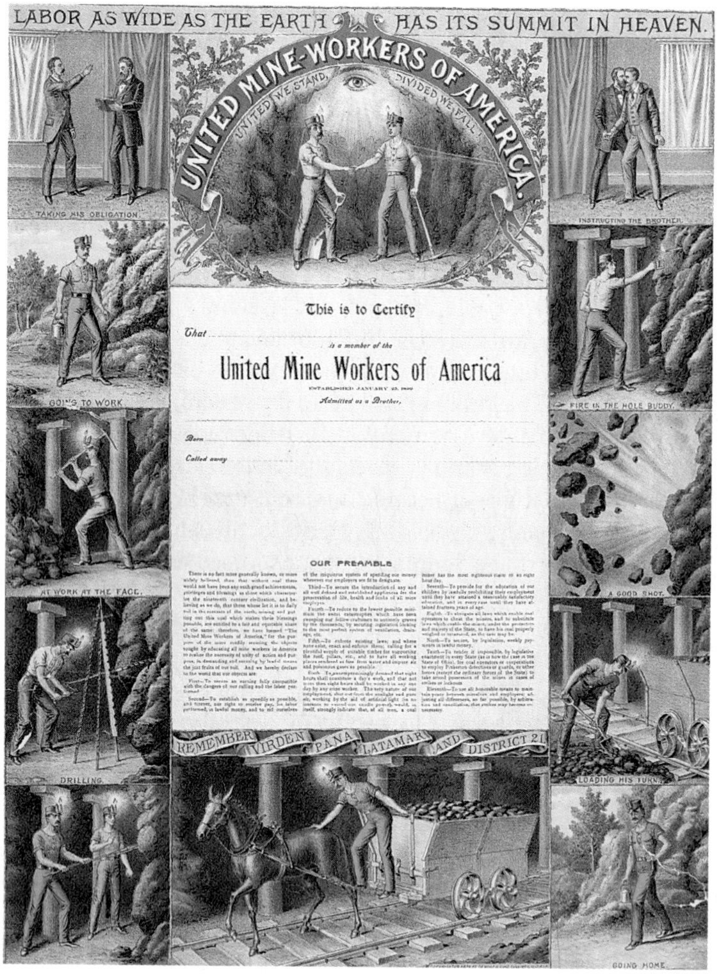

A United Mine Workers certificate of membership illustrates some of the work undertaken by the brother members. The United Mine Workers of America was formed in Columbus, Ohio, in 1890 and sought to provide its members with a safe workplace and fair wages and benefits. Although the union pledged to seek ways to maintain peace between miners and their employers and to make strikes unnecessary, such means as arbitration and conciliation often failed and strikes did occur, many of them violent and destructive. ❖

As the depression deepened, tensions grew between miners and their employers and between "old" miners and the "new." Many "new" miners spoke no English, and often they were "birds of passage," transients who had come to the United States to make money to take back home. Lacking the skills handed down by the "old" miners, they were often blamed for accidents, and they worked longer hours for less pay. At many a tavern after work, "old" miners grumbled about the different-looking newcomers and considered ways to get rid of them.

In April 1894, a wave of wage reductions sparked an explosion of labor unrest in the mines. The United Mine Workers, a struggling union formed just four years earlier, called for a strike of bituminous coal miners, and on April 21, virtually all midwestern and Pennsylvania miners—some 170,000 in all—quit working. The flow of crucial coal slackened; cities faced blackouts; factories closed.

The violence that soon broke out followed a significant pattern. Over the years, the English and Irish miners had built up a set of unspoken understandings with their employers. The "new" miners had not, and they were more prone to violent action to win a strike. The depression hit them especially hard, frustrating their plans to earn money and return home. In many areas, anger and frustration turned the 1894 strikes into outright war.

For nearly two weeks in June 1894, fighting rocked the Illinois, Ohio, and Indiana coalfields. Mobs ignited mine shafts, dynamited coal trains, and defied state militias. While miners of all backgrounds participated in the violence, it often divided "old" miners and "new." In Spring Valley, Illinois, exiled Italian anarchists took over the strike leadership and incited rioting despite the opposition of the "old" miners. Elsewhere, a mine fired by arsonists burned because the "new" miners prevented the "old" ones from extinguishing the blaze.

Shocked by the violence, public opinion shifted against the strikers. The strike ended in a matter of weeks, but its effects lingered. English and Irish miners moved out into other jobs or up into supervisory positions. Jokes and songs poked cruel fun at the "new" immigrants, and the Pennsylvania and Illinois legislatures adopted laws to keep them out of the mines. Thousands of "old" miners voted Populist in 1894—the Populist platform called for restrictions on immigration—in one of the Populists' few successes that year. The United Mine Workers, dominated by the older miners, began in 1896 to urge Congress to stop the "demoralizing effects" of immigration.

Occurring at the same time, the Pullman strike pulled attention away from the crisis in the coalfields, yet the miners' strike involved three times as many workers and provided a revealing glimpse of the tensions within American society. The miners of the Midwest were the first large group of skilled workers seriously affected by the flood of immigrants from southern and eastern Europe. Buffeted by depression, they reflected the social and economic discord that permeated every industry.

A Beleaguered President

Building on the Democratic party's sweeping triumph in the midterm elections of 1890, Grover Cleveland decisively defeated the Populist candidate, James B. Weaver, and the incumbent president, Benjamin Harrison, in 1892. He won by nearly 400,000 votes, a large margin by the standards of the era, and the Democrats increased their strength in the cities and among working-class voters. For the first time since the 1850s, they controlled the White House and both branches of Congress.

The Democrats, it now seemed, had broken the party stalemate, but unfortunately for Cleveland, the Panic of 1893 struck almost as he took office. He was sure that he knew its cause. The Sherman Silver Purchase Act of 1890, he believed, had damaged business confidence, drained the Treasury's gold reserve, and caused the panic. The solution to the depression was equally simple: Repeal the act.

In June 1893, Cleveland summoned Congress into special session. India had just closed its mints to silver, and Mexico was now the only country in the world with free silver coinage. The silverites were on the defensive, although they pleaded for a compromise. Rejecting the pleas, Cleveland pushed the repeal bill through Congress, and on November 1, 1893, he signed it into law. Always sure of himself, he had staked everything on a single measure—a winning strategy if he succeeded, a devastating one if he did not.

Repeal of the Sherman Silver Purchase Act was probably a necessary action. It responded to the realities of international finance, reduced the flight of gold out of the country, and, over the long run, boosted business confidence. Unfortunately, it contracted the currency at a time when inflation might have helped. It did not bring economic revival. The stock market remained listless, businesses continued to close, unemployment spread, and farm prices dropped. "We are hourly expecting the arrival of the benevolent man who is to pay ten cents a pound for cotton," a Virginia newspaper said.

The repeal battle of 1893, discrediting the conservative Cleveland Democrats who had dominated the party since the 1860s, reshaped the politics of the country. It confined the Democratic party largely to the South, helped the Republicans become the majority party in 1894, and strengthened the position of the silver Democrats in their bid for the presidency in 1896. It also focused national attention on the silver issue and thus intensified the silver sentiment Cleveland had intended to dampen. In the end, repeal did not even solve the Treasury's gold problem. By January 1894, the reserve had fallen to $65 million. A year later, it fell to $44.5 million.

In January 1894, Cleveland desperately resorted to a sale of $50 million in gold bonds to replenish the gold reserve. The following November, he again sold bonds, and in February 1895, arousing outrage among many, he agreed to a third bond sale that allowed financier J. Pierpont Morgan and other bankers to reap large profits. A fourth bond sale in January 1896 also failed to stop the drain on the reserve, although it further sharpened the silverites' hatred of President Cleveland.

Still another blow to the morale of the Democrats came in 1894, when they tried to fulfill their long-standing promise to reduce the tariff. Despite all their efforts, the Wilson-Gorman Tariff Act, passed by Congress in August 1894, contained only modest reductions in duties. It reduced the tariff on coal, iron ore, wool, and sugar, ended the McKinley Tariff Act's popular reciprocity agreements with other countries, and moved some duties higher than ever before. It also imposed a small income tax, a provision the Supreme Court overturned in 1895 (*Pollock* v. *Farmer's Loan and Trust Co.*). Very few Democrats, including Cleveland, were pleased with the measure, and the president let it become law without his signature.

Breaking the Party Deadlock

The Democrats were buried in the elections of 1894. Suffering the greatest defeat in congressional history, they lost 113 House seats, while the Republicans gained 117. In twenty-four states, not a single Democrat was elected to Congress. Only one Democrat (Boston's John F. Fitzgerald, the grandfather of President John F. Kennedy) came from all of New England. The Democrats even lost some of the "solid

South," and in the Midwest, a crucial battleground of the 1890s, the party was virtually destroyed.

Wooing labor and the unemployed, the Populists made striking inroads in parts of the South and West, yet their progress was far from enough. In a year in which thousands of voters switched parties, the People's party elected only four senators and four congressmen. Southern Democrats again used fraud and violence to keep the Populists' totals down. In the Midwest, the Populists won double the number of votes they had received in 1892, yet still attracted less than 7 percent of the vote. Across the country, the discontented tended to vote for the Republicans, not the Populists, a discouraging sign for the Populist party.

For millions of people, Grover Cleveland became a scapegoat for the country's economic ills. Fearing attack, he placed new police barracks on the White House grounds. The Democratic party split, and southern and western Democrats deserted him in droves. At Democratic conventions, Cleveland's name evoked jeers. "He is an old bag of beef," Democratic Congressman "Pitchfork" Ben Tillman told a South Carolina audience, "and I am going to go to Washington with a pitchfork and prod him in his old fat ribs."

The elections of 1894 marked the end of the party deadlock that had existed since the 1870s. The Democrats lost, the Populists gained somewhat, and the Republicans became the majority party in the country. In the midst of the depression, the Republican doctrines of activism and national authority, which voters had repudiated in the elections of 1890, became more attractive. This was a development of great significance, because as Americans became more accepting of the use of government power to regulate the economy and safeguard individual welfare, the way lay open to the reforms of the Progressive Era, the New Deal, and beyond.

Changing Attitudes

The depression, brutal and far-reaching, did more than shift political alignments. Across the country, it undermined traditional views and caused people to rethink older ideas about government, the economy, and society. As men and women concluded that established ideas had failed to deal with the depression, they looked for new ones. There was, the president of the University of Wisconsin said, "a general, all-pervasive, restless discontent with the results of current political and economic thought."

In prosperous times, Americans had thought of unemployment as the result of personal failure, affecting primarily the lazy and immoral. "Let us remember," a leading Protestant minister once said, "that there is not a poor person in the United States who was not made poor by his own shortcomings." In the midst of depression, such views were harder to maintain, since everyone knew people who were both worthy and unemployed. Next door, a respected neighbor might be laid off; down the block, an entire factory might be shut down.

People debated issues they had long taken for granted. New and reinvigorated local institutions—discussion clubs, women's clubs, reform societies, university extension centers, church groups, farmers' societies—gave people a place to discuss alternatives to the existing order. Pressures for reform increased, and demand grew for government intervention to help the poor and unemployed.

"Everybody Works But Father"

Women and children had been entering the labor force for years, and the depression accelerated the trend. As husbands and fathers lost their jobs, more and more women and children went to work. Even as late as 1901, well after the depression had ended, a study of working-class families showed that more than half the principal breadwinners were out of work. So many women and children worked that in 1905 there was a popular song titled "Everybody Works But Father."

During the 1890s, the number of working women rose from 4 million to 5.3 million. Trying to make ends meet, they took in boarders and found jobs as laundresses, cleaners, or domestics. Where possible, they worked in offices and factories. Far more black urban women than white worked to supplement their husbands' meager earnings. In New York City in 1900, nearly 60 percent of all black women worked, compared to 27 percent of the foreign-born and 24 percent of native-born white women. Men still dominated business offices, but during the 1890s, more and more employers noted the relative cheapness of female labor. Women telegraph and telephone operators nearly tripled in number during the decade. Women worked as clerks in the new five-and-tens and department stores, and as nurses; in 1900, a half million were teachers. They increasingly entered office work as stenographers and typists, occupations in which they earned between \$6.00 and \$15.00 a week, compared to factory wages of \$1.50 to \$8.00 a week.

The depression also caused an increasing number of children to work. During the 1890s, the number of children employed in southern textile mills jumped more than 160 percent, and boys and girls under 16 years of age made up nearly one-third of the labor force of the mills. Youngsters of 8 and 9 years worked twelve hours a day for pitiful wages. In most cases,

Tiny children peddling newspapers and women domestics serving the rich—their meager earnings were desperately needed. ❖

however, children worked not in factories but in farming and city street trades such as peddling and shoe shining. In 1900, the South had more than half the child laborers in the nation.

Concerned about child labor, middle-class women in 1896 formed the League for the Protection of the Family, which called for compulsory education to get children out of factories and into classrooms. The Mothers Congress of 1896 gave rise to the National Congress of Parents and Teachers, the spawning ground of thousands of local Parent-Teacher Associations. The National Council of Women and the General Federation of Women's Clubs took up similar issues. By the end of the 1890s, the Federation had 150,000 members who worked for various civic reforms in the fields of child welfare, education, and sanitation.

Changing Themes in Literature

The depression also gave point to a growing movement in literature toward realism and naturalism. In the years after the Civil War, literature often reflected the mood of romanticism—sentimental and unrealistic. Walt Whitman called it "ornamental confectionary" and "copious dribble," but it remained popular through the end of the century.

The novels of Horatio Alger, which provided simple lessons about how to get ahead in business and life, continued to attract large numbers of readers. A failed New York minister, Alger published some 130 novels—with titles such as *Sink or Swim, Work and Win,* and *Struggling Upward*—which sold more than 20 million copies. They told of poor youngsters who made their way to the top through hard work, thrift, honesty, and luck. Louisa May Alcott's *Little Women* (1868–1869) related the daily lives of four girls in a New England family, Anna Sewell's *Black Beauty* (1877) charmed readers with the story of an abused horse that found a happy home, and Lew Wallace's *Ben Hur* (1880), one of the era's best-selling books, offered a sweeping epic of life in the Roman empire.

After the 1870s, however, a number of talented authors began to reject romanticism and escapism, turning instead to realism. Determined to portray life as it was, they studied local dialects, wrote regional stories, and emphasized the "true" relationships between people. In doing so, they reflected broader trends in the society, such as industrialism; evolutionary theory, which emphasized the effect of the environment on humans; and the new philosophy of pragmatism, which stressed the relativity of values.

Mark Twain's novel Adventures of Huckleberry Finn, *published in the United States in 1885, was both popular and controversial. Banned by some public libraries shortly after its publication because of Twain's use of dialect and narration from the point of view of an unschooled boy in conflict with conventional society—both shocking by the cultural and literary standards of the day—the novel is still widely read today, and is still considered controversial by some for its portrayal of race relations in the antebellum South.* ❖

Regionalist authors such as Joel Chandler Harris and George Washington Cable depicted life in the South. Hamlin Garland described the grimness of life on the Great Plains, and Sarah Orne Jewett wrote about everyday life in rural New England. Another regionalist, Bret Harte, achieved fame with stories that portrayed the local color of the California mining camps, particularly in his popular tale "The Outcasts of Poker Flat."

Harte was joined by a more talented writer, Mark Twain, who became the country's most outstanding realist author. Growing up along the Mississippi River in Hannibal County, Missouri, the young Samuel Langhorne Clemens observed life around him with a humorous and skeptical eye. Adopting a pen name from the river term "mark twain" (two fathoms), he wrote a number of important works that drew on his own experiences. *Life on the Mississippi* (1883) described his career as a steamboat pilot. *The Adventures of Tom Sawyer* (1876) and *The Adventures of Huckleberry Finn* (1884) gained international prominence. In these books, Twain used dialect and common speech instead of literary language, touching off a major change in American prose style.

William Dean Howells—after Twain, the country's most famous author—came more slowly to the realist approach. At first, he wrote about the happier sides of life, but then he grew worried about the impact of industrialization. *A Traveler from Altruria* (1894), a utopian novel, described an industrial society that consumed lives. The poem "Society" (1895), written in the midst of the depression, compared society to a splendid ball in which men and women danced on flowers covering the bodies of the poor:

> And now and then from out the dreadful floor
> An arm or brow was lifted from the rest,
> As if to strike in madness, or implore
> For mercy; and anon some suffering breast
> Heaved from the mass and sank; and as before
> The revellers above them thronged and prest.

Other writers, the naturalists, became impatient even with realism. Pushing Darwinian theory to its limits, they wrote of a world in which a cruel and merciless environment determined human fate. Often focusing on economic hardship, naturalist writers studied the poor, the lower classes, and the criminal mind; they brought to their writing the social worker's passion for direct and honest experience.

Stephen Crane spent a night in a seven-cent lodging house on the Bowery and in "An Experiment in Misery" captured the smells and sounds of the poor. Crane depicted the carnage of war in *The Red Badge of Courage* (1895) and the impact of poverty in *Maggie: A Girl of the Streets* (1893). His poetry suggested the unimportance of the individual in an uncaring world:

> A man said to the universe
> "Sir, I exist!"
> "However," replied the universe,
> "The fact has not created in me
> A sense of obligation."

Frank Norris assailed the power of big business in two dramatic novels, *The Octopus* (1901) and *The Pit* (1903), both the story of individual futility in the face of the heartless corporations. Norris's *McTeague* (1899) studied the disintegration of character under economic pressure. Jack London, another naturalist author, traced the power of nature over civilized society in novels such as *The Sea Wolf* (1904) and *The Call of the Wild* (1903), his classic tale of a sled dog that

A scene from Stephen Crane's novel Maggie: A Girl of the Streets. *Crane's tale painted a grim picture of life in the tenements of New York City's Bowery as it chronicled the story of slum child Maggie Johnson, victimized and trapped in her squalid, violent world.* ❖

preferred the difficult life of the wilderness to the world of human beings.

Theodore Dreiser, the foremost naturalist writer, grimly portrayed a dark world in which human beings were tossed about by forces beyond their understanding or control. "My own ambition," Dreiser said, "is to represent my world, to conform to the large, truthful lines of life." In his great novel *Sister Carrie* (1901), he followed a young farm girl who took a job in a Chicago shoe factory. He described the exhausting nature of factory work: "Her hands began to ache at the wrists and then in the fingers, and towards the last she seemed one mass of dull, complaining muscle, fixed in an eternal position, and performing a single mechanical movement."

Like other naturalists, Dreiser focused on environment and character. He thought writers should tell the truth about human affairs, not fabricate romance, and *Sister Carrie,* he said, was "not intended as a piece of literary craftsmanship, but was a picture of conditions."

THE PRESIDENTIAL ELECTION OF 1896

The election of 1896 was known as the "battle of the standards" because it focused primarily on the gold and silver standards of money. As an election, it was exciting and decisive. New voting patterns replaced old, a new majority party confirmed its control of the country, and national policy shifted to suit new realities.

The Mystique of Silver

Sentiment for free silver coinage grew swiftly after 1894, dominating the South and West, appearing even in the farming regions of New York and New England. Prosilver literature flooded the country. (See the Feature Essay, "The Wonderful Wizard of Oz," pp. 592–593.) Pamphlets issued by the millions argued silver's virtues.

People wanted quick solutions to the economic crisis. During 1896, unemployment shot up and farm income and prices fell to the lowest point in the decade. "I can remember back as far as 1858," an Iowa hardware dealer said in February 1896, "and I have never seen such hard times as these are." The silverites offered a solution, simple but compelling: the free and independent coinage of silver at the ratio of 16 ounces of silver to every ounce of gold. Free coinage meant that the U.S. mints would coin all the silver offered to them. Independent coinage meant that the country would coin silver regardless of the policies of other nations, nearly all of which were on the gold standard.

It is difficult now to understand the kind of faith the silverites placed in silver as a cure for the depression. But faith it was, and of a sort that some observers compared to religious fervor. Underlying it all was a belief in a quantity theory of money: The silverites believed the amount of money in circulation determined the level of activity in the economy. If money was short, that meant there was a limit on economic activity and ultimately a depression. If the government coined silver as well as gold, that meant more money in circulation, more business for everyone, and thus prosperity. Farm prices would rise; laborers would go back to work. As one silverite said, "It means the reopening of closed factories, the relighting of fires in darkened furnaces; it means hope instead of despair; comfort in place of suffering; life instead of death."

By 1896, silver was also a symbol. It had moral and patriotic dimensions—by going to a silver standard, the United States could assert its independence in the world—and it stood for a wide range of popular grievances. For many, it reflected rural values rather than urban ones, suggested a shift of power

Feature Essay

THE WONDERFUL WIZARD OF OZ

A restless dreamer, Frank Baum tried his hand at several careers before he gained fame and fortune as a writer of children's literature. From 1888 to 1891, he ran a store and newspaper in South Dakota, where he experienced the desolation and grayness that accompanied agrarian discontent. An avid supporter of William Jennings Bryan in the "battle of the standards," Baum wrote what many interpret as an enduring allegory of the silver movement, *The Wonderful Wizard of Oz.* Published in April 1900, it was an immediate success.

The Wicked Witch of the West. ❖

The book opens with a grim description of Kansas:

> When Dorothy stood in the doorway and looked around, she could see nothing but the great gray prairie on every side. Not a tree nor a house broke the broad sweep of flat country that reached the edge of the sky in all directions. The sun had baked the plowed land into a gray mass, with little cracks running through it. Even the grass was not green, for the sun had burned the tops of the long blades until they were the same gray color to be seen everywhere. Once the house had been painted, but the sun blistered the paint and the rains washed it away, and now the house was as dull and gray as everything else.

Kansas had not always seemed that way. After 1854, when the Kansas-Nebraska Act opened to settlement its 50 million acres of grassland, people poured into the state to stake their claims. Many came from the hilly timbered country to the east, and breaking onto the prairie, they saw "a new world, reaching to the far horizon without break of trees or chimney stack; just sky and grass and grass and sky. . . . The hush was so loud. . . . The heavens seemed nearer than ever before and awe and beauty and majesty over all."

In later years, railroads crisscrossed the state, and advertisements touted the fertile soil. Land was plentiful, rainfall somehow seemed to increase each year, crop prices held at levels high enough to pay, new farming implements yielded larger crops, and property values increased.

Yet life on the prairie was never an easy matter. Flat, lonely, and windswept, the land affected people in ways that were hard to describe to the folks back East. When Aunt Em, Dorothy's aunt, came to Kansas to live, she was young and pretty, but the sun and wind soon changed her. "They had taken the sparkle from her eyes and left them a sober gray; they had taken the red from her cheeks and lips, and they were gray also." Like Aunt Em, Uncle Henry never laughed. "He worked hard from morning till night and did not know what joy was."

After 1887, a series of droughts struck Kansas, and as many as three out of four farms were mortgaged in some Kansas counties. Thousands of settlers like Aunt Em and Uncle Henry gave up and retraced their steps East; others trusted in the Farmers' Alliance and pinned their hopes on the free coinage of silver. While gold as a standard of currency symbolized the idle rich of the industrial Northeast, silver stood for the common folk. Added to the currency in the form of silver dollars, it meant more money, higher crop prices, and a return of prosperity.

Or so the supporters of silver coinage believed. In *The Wonderful Wizard of Oz,* read as an allegory, Dorothy (every person) is carried by a cyclone (a victory of the silver forces at the polls) from drought-stricken Kansas to a marvelous land of riches and witches. Unlike dry, gray Kansas, Oz is beautiful, with rippling brooks, stately trees, colorful flowers, and bright-feathered birds. On arrival, Dorothy disposes of one witch, the Wicked Witch of the East (the eastern

Dorothy (wearing silver, not ruby, slippers in the original version) and her friends prepare to "follow the yellow brick road." ❖

money power and those favoring gold), and frees the Munchkins (the common people) from servitude. To return to Kansas, she must first go to the Emerald City (the national capital, greenback-colored).

Dorothy wears magical silver slippers and follows the yellow brick road, thus achieving a proper relationship between the precious metals, silver and gold. Like many of her countrymen, she does not at first recognize the power of the silver slippers, but a kiss from the Good Witch of the North (Northern voters) protects her on the road. Dorothy meets the Scarecrow (the farmer), who has been told he has no brain but actually possesses great common sense (no "hick" or "hayseed," he); the Tin Woodman (the industrial worker), who fears he has become heartless but discovers the spirit of love and cooperation; and the Cowardly Lion (reformers, particularly William Jennings Bryan), who turns out not to be very cowardly at all.

When the four companions reach the Emerald City, they meet the "Great and Terrible" Wizard, who tells them that, to gain his help, they must destroy the Wicked Witch of the West (mortgage companies, heartless nature, and other things opposing progress there). Courageously, they set forth. Dorothy dissolves the witch with a bucket of water (what else for drought-ridden farmers?), but when they return to the Emerald City, they find that the great and powerful Wizard (the money power) is only a charlatan, a manipulator, whose power rests on myth and illusion. "'I thought Oz was a great Head,' said Dorothy. . . . 'And I thought Oz was a terrible Beast,' said the Tin Woodman. 'And I thought Oz was a Ball of Fire,' exclaimed the Lion. 'No; you are all wrong,' said the little man meekly. 'I have been making believe.'"

Dorothy unmasks the wizard, and with the help of Glinda, the Good Witch of the South (support for silver was strong in the South), uses the silver slippers to return home to Kansas. Sadly, the shoes are lost in flight. Back in Oz, the Scarecrow rules the Emerald City (the triumph of the farmers), and the Tin Woodman reigns in the West (industrialism moves West). *Oz* was a familiar abbreviation to those involved in the fight over the ratio of silver to gold—16 ounces to 1.

Baum wanted to write American fairy tales to "bear the stamp of our times and depict the progressive fairies of today." The land of Oz reflected his belief in the American values of freedom and independence, love of family, self-reliance, individualism, and sympathy for the underdog. *Oz,* he said in the original introduction, "aspires to being a modernized fairy tale, in which the wonderment and joy are retained and the heartaches and nightmares are left out."

The *Oz* stories have remained popular, and they still rest on many children's bookshelves. A 1939 film starring Judy Garland as Dorothy, with Ray Bolger as the Scarecrow, Jack Haley as the Tin Woodman, Bert Lahr as the Cowardly Lion, and Frank Morgan as the Wizard, was spectacularly successful. Released in the midst of another depression, the film included songs designed to escape hardship, as Dorothy once had, "somewhere over the rainbow."

away from the Northeast, and spoke for the downtrodden instead of the well-to-do. Silver represented the common people, as the vast literature of the movement showed.

William H. Harvey's *Coin's Financial School* (1894), the most popular of all silver pamphlets, had the eloquent Coin, a wise but unknown youth, tutoring famous people on the currency. Bankers, lawyers, and scholars came to argue for gold, but they left shaken, leaning toward silver. Coin's Financial School sold five thousand copies a day at its peak in 1895, with tens of thousands of copies distributed free by silver organizations. It "is being sold on every railroad train by the newsboys and at every cigar store," a Mississippi congressman said. "It is being read by almost everybody."

Silver was more than just a political or economic issue. It was a social movement, one of the largest in American history, but its life span turned out to be brief. As a mass phenomenon, it flourished between 1894 and 1896, then succumbed to electoral defeat, the return of prosperity, and the onset of fresh concerns. But in its time, the silver movement bespoke a national mood and won millions of followers.

The Republicans and Gold

Scenting victory over the discredited Democrats, numerous Republicans fought for the party's presidential nomination, including "Czar" Thomas B. Reed of the Billion-Dollar Congress. Reed picked up early support but suffered from his reputation for biting wit. William McKinley of Ohio, his chief rival, soon passed him in the race for the nomination.

Able, calm, and affable, McKinley had served in the Union army during the Civil War. In 1876, he won a seat in Congress, where he became the chief sponsor of the tariff act named for him. In the months before the 1896 national convention, Marcus A. Hanna, his campaign manager and trusted friend, built a powerful national organization that featured McKinley as "the advance agent of prosperity," an alluring slogan in a country beset with depression. When the convention met in June, McKinley had the nomination in hand, and he backed a platform that favored the gold standard against the free coinage of silver.

Republicans favoring silver proposed a prosilver platform, but the convention overwhelmingly defeated it. Twenty-three silverite Republicans, far fewer than prosilver forces had hoped, marched out of the convention hall. The remaining delegates waved handkerchiefs and flags and shouted "Good-bye" and "Put them out." Hanna stood on a chair screaming "Go! Go! Go!" William Jennings Bryan, who was there as a special correspondent for a Nebraska newspaper, climbed on a desk to get a better view.

The Democrats and Silver

Silver, meanwhile, had captured large segments of the Democratic party in the South and West. Despite President Cleveland's opposition, more than twenty Democratic state platforms came out for free silver in 1894. Power in the party shifted to the South, where it remained for decades. The party's base narrowed; its outlook increasingly reflected southern views on silver, race, and other issues. In effect, the Democrats became a sectional—no longer a national—party.

The anti-Cleveland Democrats had their issue, but they lacked a leader. Out in Nebraska, Bryan saw the opportunity to take on that role. He was barely 36 years old and had relatively little political experience. But he had spent months wooing support, and he was a captivating public speaker—tall, slender, and handsome, with a resounding voice that, in an era without microphones, projected easily into every corner of an auditorium. Practicing at home before a mirror, he rehearsed his speeches again and again, as his wife, Mary, a bright, sharp, and politically astute woman, listened for errors.

From the outset of the 1896 Democratic convention, the silver Democrats were in charge, and they put together a platform that stunned the Cleveland wing of the party. It demanded the free coinage of silver, attacked Cleveland's actions in the Pullman strike, and censured his sales of gold bonds. On July 9, as delegates debated the platform, Bryan's moment came. Striding to the stage, he stood for an instant, a hand raised for silence, waiting for the applause to die down. He would not contend with the previous speakers, he began, for "this is not a contest between persons. The humblest citizen in all the land, when clad in the armor of a righteous cause, is stronger than all the hosts of error. I come to speak to you in defense of a cause as holy as the cause of liberty—the cause of humanity."

The delegates were captivated. Like a trained choir, they rose, cheered each point, and sat back to listen for more. Easterners, Bryan said, liked to praise businessmen but forgot that plain people—laborers, miners, and farmers—were businessmen, too. Shouts rang through the hall, and delegates pounded on chairs. Savoring each cheer, Bryan defended silver. Then came the famous closing: "Having behind us the producing masses of this nation and the world . . . we will answer their demand for a gold standard by saying to them: 'You shall not press down upon the brow of labor this crown of thorns, you shall not crucify mankind upon a cross of gold.'"

The religious symbolism in Bryan's "Cross of Gold" speech is satirized in this cartoon, but his stirring rhetoric captivated his audience and won him the Democratic presidential nomination for the election of 1896. ❖

Bryan moved his fingers down his temples, suggesting blood trickling from his wounds. He ended with his arms outstretched as on a cross. Letting the silence hang, he dropped his arms, stepped back, then started to his seat. Suddenly, there was pandemonium. Delegates shouted and cheered. When the tumult subsided, they adopted the anti-Cleveland platform, and the next day, Bryan won the presidential nomination.

Campaign and Election

The Democratic convention presented the Populists with a dilemma. The People's party had staked everything on the assumption that neither major party would endorse silver. Now it faced a painful choice: Nominate an independent ticket and risk splitting the silverite forces, or nominate Bryan and give up its separate identity as a party.

The choice was unpleasant, and it shattered the People's party. Meeting late in July, the party's national convention nominated Bryan, but rather than accept the Democratic candidate for vice president, it named Tom Watson instead. The Populists' endorsement probably hurt Bryan as much as it helped. It won him relatively few votes, since many Populists would have voted for him anyway. It also identified him as a Populist, which he was not, allowing the Republicans to accuse him of heading a ragtag army of malcontents. The squabble over Watson seemed to prove that the Democratic-Populist alliance could never stay together long enough to govern.

In August 1896, Bryan set off on a campaign that became an American legend. Much of the conservative Democratic eastern press had deserted him, and he took his campaign directly to the voters, the first presidential candidate in history to do so in a systematic way. By his own count, Bryan traveled 18,009 miles, visited 27 states, and spoke 600 times to a total of some 3 million people. He built skillfully on a new "merchandising" style of campaign in which he worked to educate and persuade voters.

Bryan summoned voters to an older America: a land where farms were as important as factories, where the virtues of rural and religious life outweighed the doubtful lure of the city, where common people still ruled and opportunity existed for all. He drew on the Jeffersonian tradition of rural virtue, distrust of central authority, and abiding faith in the powers of human reason.

Urged to take the stump against Bryan, McKinley replied, "I might just as well put up a trapeze on my front lawn and compete with some professional athlete as go out speaking against Bryan." The Republican candidate let voters come to him. Railroads brought them by the thousands into McKinley's hometown of Canton, Ohio, and he spoke to them from his front porch. Through use of the press, he reached fully as many people as Bryan's more strenuous effort. Appealing to labor, immigrants, well-to-do farmers, businessmen, and the middle class, McKinley defended economic nationalism and the advancing urban-industrial society.

On election day, voter turnout was extraordinarily high, a measure of the intense interest. By nightfall, the

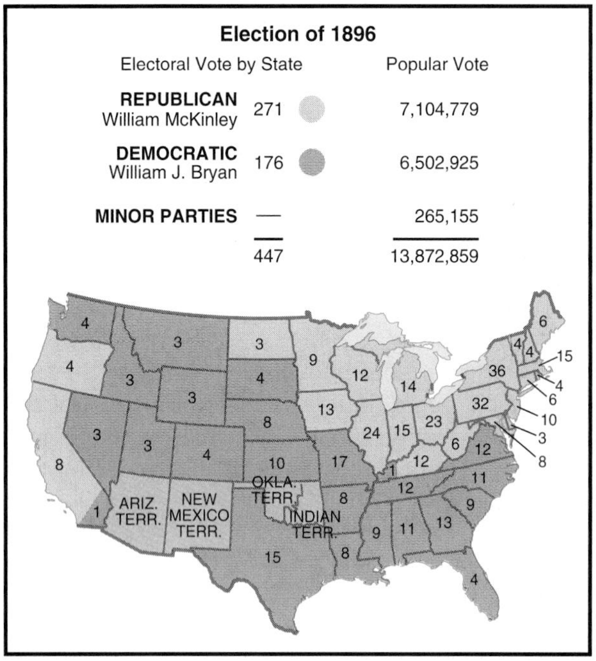

outcome was clear: McKinley won 50 percent of the vote to Bryan's 46 percent. He won the Northeast and Midwest and carried four border states. In the cities, McKinley crushed Bryan.

The election struck down the Populists, whose totals sagged nearly everywhere. Many Populist proposals were later adopted under different leadership. The graduated income tax, crop loans to farmers, the secret ballot, and direct election of U.S. senators all were early Populist ideas. But the People's party never could win over a majority of the voters, and failing that, it vanished after 1896.

The McKinley Administration

The election of 1896 cemented the voter realignment of 1894 and initiated a generation of Republican rule. For more than three decades after 1896, with only a brief Democratic resurgence under Woodrow Wilson, the Republicans remained the country's majority party.

McKinley took office in 1897 under favorable circumstances. To everyone's relief, the economy had begun to revive. The stock market rose, factories once again churned out goods, and farmers prospered. Farm prices climbed sharply during 1897 on bumper crops of wheat, cotton, and corn. Discoveries of gold in Australia and Alaska—together with the development of a new cyanide process for extracting gold from ore—enlarged the world's gold supply, decreased its price, and inflated the currency as the silverites had hoped. For the first time since 1890, the 1897 Treasury statements showed a comfortable gold reserve.

CHRONOLOGY

1876	Mark Twain publishes *The Adventures of Tom Sawyer*
1877	Disputed election of 1876 results in awarding of presidency to Republican Rutherford B. Hayes
1880	Republican James A. Garfield elected president
1881	Garfield assassinated; Vice President Chester A. Arthur becomes president
1884	Democrat Grover Cleveland elected president, defeating Republican James G. Blaine
1887	Cleveland calls for lowering of tariff duties
1888	Republican Benjamin Harrison wins presidential election
1889	National Farmers' Alliance and Industrial Union formed to address problems of farmers
1890	Republican-dominated "Billion-Dollar" Congress enacts McKinley Tariff Act, Sherman Antitrust Act, and Sherman Silver Purchase Act ❖ Farmers' Alliance adopts the Ocala Demands
1892	Democrat Cleveland defeats Republican Harrison for presidency ❖ People's party formed
1893	Financial panic touches off depression lasting until 1897 ❖ Sherman Silver Purchase Act repealed ❖ World Columbian Exposition opens in Chicago
1894	Coxey's army marches on Washington ❖ Pullman employees strike
1896	Republican McKinley defeats William Jennings Bryan, Democratic and Populist candidate, in "battle of the standards"
1897	Gold discovered in Alaska ❖ Dingley Tariff Act raises tariff duties
1900	McKinley reelected, again defeating Bryan ❖ Gold Standard Act establishes gold as standard of currency
1901	McKinley assassinated; Vice President Theodore Roosevelt assumes presidency ❖ Naturalist writer Theodore Dreiser publishes *Sister Carrie*

McKinley and the Republicans basked in the glow. They became the party of progress and prosperity, an image that helped them win victories until another depression hit in the 1930s. McKinley's popularity soared. Open and accessible, in contrast to Cleveland's isolation, he rode the Washington streetcars, walked the streets, and enjoyed looking in department store

The Election of 1900

Candidate	Party	Popular Vote	Electoral Vote
McKinley	Republican	7,207,923	292
Bryan	Democrat	6,358,133	155
Woolley	Prohibition	209,004	0
Debs	Socialist	94,768	0

windows. Cleveland's special police barracks vanished from the White House lawn. McKinley became the first president to ride in an automobile, reaching the speed of 18 miles an hour.

An activist president, he set the policies of the administration. Conscious of the limits of power, he maintained close ties with Congress and worked hard to educate the public on national choices and priorities. McKinley struck new relations with the press and traveled far more than previous presidents. In some ways, he began the modern presidency.

Shortly after taking office, he summoned Congress into special session to revise the tariff. In July 1897, the Dingley Tariff passed the House and Senate. It raised average tariff duties to a record level, and as the final burst of nineteenth-century protectionism, it caused trouble for the Republican party. By the end of the 1890s, consumers, critics, and the Republicans themselves were wondering if the tariff had outlived its usefulness in the maturing American economy.

From the 1860s to the 1890s, the Republicans had built their party on a pledge to *promote* economic growth through the use of state and national power. By 1900, with the industrial system firmly in place, the focus had shifted. The need to *regulate,* to control the effects of industrialism, became a central public concern of the new century. McKinley prodded the Republicans to meet that shift, but he died before his plans matured.

McKinley toyed with the idea of lowering the tariff, but one obstacle always stood in the way: The government needed revenue, and tariff duties were one of the few taxes the public would support. The Spanish-American War of 1898 persuaded people to accept greater federal power and, with it, new forms of taxation. In 1899, McKinley spoke of lowering tariff barriers in a world that technology had made smaller. "God and man have linked the nations together," he said in his last speech at Buffalo, New York, in 1901. "Isolation is no longer possible or desirable."

In 1898 and 1899, the McKinley administration focused on the war with Spain, the peace treaty that followed, and the dawning realization that the war had thrust the United States into a position of world power. In March 1900, Congress passed the **Gold Standard Act,** which declared gold the standard of currency and ended the silver controversy that had dominated the 1890s.

The presidential campaign of 1900 was a replay of the McKinley-Bryan fight of 1896. McKinley's running mate was Theodore Roosevelt, hero of the Spanish-American War and former governor of New York, who was nominated for vice president to capitalize on his popularity and, his enemies hoped, to sidetrack his political career into oblivion. Bryan stressed the issues of imperialism and the trusts; McKinley stressed his record at home and abroad. The result in 1900 was a landslide.

On September 6, 1901, a few months after his second inauguration, McKinley stood in a receiving line at the Pan-American Exposition in Buffalo. Leon Czolgosz, a 28-year-old unemployed laborer and anarchist, moved through the line and, reaching the

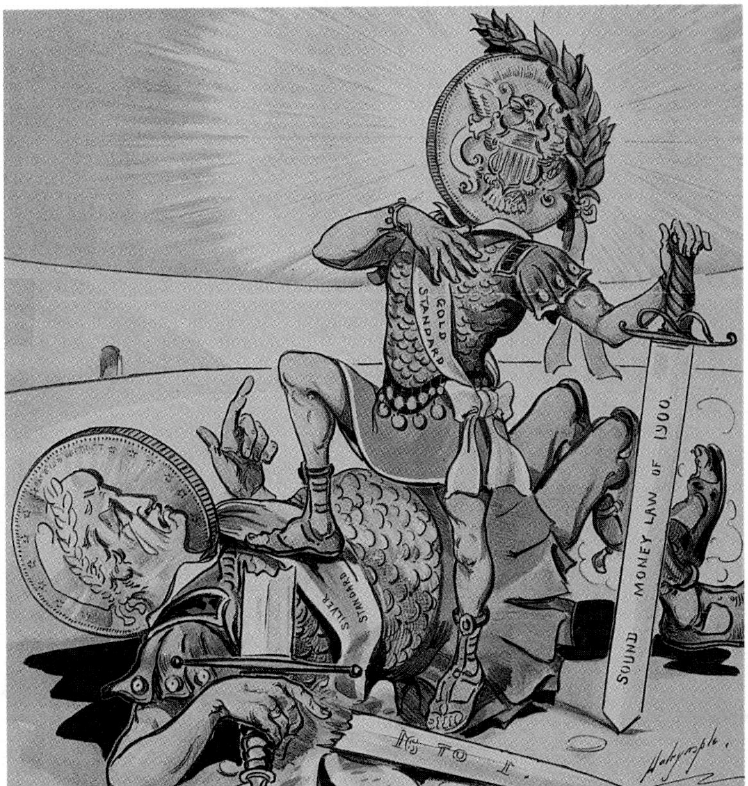

Gold triumphs over silver in this Puck *cartoon referring to the Gold Standard Act of 1900.* ❖

president, shot him. Surgeons probed the wound but could find nothing. A recent discovery called the X ray was on display at the exposition, but it was not used. On September 14, McKinley died, and Vice President Theodore Roosevelt became president. A new century had begun.

Conclusion: A Decade's Dramatic Changes

As the funeral train carried McKinley's body back to Ohio, Mark Hanna, McKinley's old friend and ally, sat slumped in his parlor car. "I told William McKinley it was a mistake to nominate that wild man at Philadelphia," he mourned. "I asked him if he realized what would happen if he should die. Now look, that damned cowboy is president of the United States!"

Hanna's world had changed, and so had the nation's—not so much because "that damned cowboy" was suddenly president, but because events of the 1890s had had powerful effects. In the course of that decade, political patterns shifted, the presidency acquired fresh power, and massive unrest prompted social change. The war with Spain brought a new empire and worldwide responsibilities. Economic hardship posed questions of the most difficult sort about industrialization, urbanization, and the quality of American life. Worried, people embraced new ideas and causes. Reform movements begun in the 1890s flowered in the Progressive Era after 1900.

Technology continued to alter the way Americans lived. In 1896, Henry Ford produced a two-cylinder, four-horsepower car, the first of the famous line that bore his name. In 1899, the first automobile salesroom opened in New York, and some innovative thinkers were already imagining a network of service stations to keep the new cars running. At Kitty Hawk, North Carolina, Wilbur and Orville Wright, two bicycle manufacturers, neared the birth of powered flight.

The realignments that reached their peak in the 1890s seem distant, yet they are not. Important decisions in those years shaped nearly everything that came after them. In character and influence, the 1890s were as much a part of the twentieth century as of the nineteenth and continue to have repercussions into the twenty-first century.

Recommended Reading

The best study of the 1890s depression is Charles Hoffman, *The Depression of the Nineties: An Economic History* (1970). H. Wayne Morgan, *From Hayes to McKinley: National Party Politics, 1877–1896* (1969), Michael E. McGerr, *The Decline of Popular Politics: The American North, 1865–1928* (1986), Mark Lawrence Kornbluh, *Why America Stopped Voting: The Decline of Participatory Democracy and the Emergence of Modern American Politics* (2000), and Richard J. Jensen, *The Winning of the Midwest* (1971) are good on politics. David P. Thelen, *The New Citizenship: Origins of Progressivism in Wisconsin, 1885–1900* (1972), Carl Smith, *Urban Disorder and the Shape of Belief: The Great Chicago Fire, the Haymarket Bomb, and the Model Town of Pullman* (1995), and Douglas W. Steeples and David O. Whitten, *Democracy in Desperation: The Depression of 1893* (1998), stress the impact of the depression on ideas and attitudes. C. Vann Woodward examines the South in *Origins of the New South, 1877–1913* (1951). Also, Michael Perman, *Struggle for Mastery: Disfranchisement in the South, 1888–1908* (2001).

On Populism, see John D. Hicks, *The Populist Revolt* (1931), Lawrence Goodwyn, *Democratic Promise: The Populist Moment in America* (1976), Steven Hahn, *The Roots of Southern Populism* (1983), and Elizabeth Sanders, *Roots of Reform: Farmers, Workers, and the American State, 1877–1917* (1999). Steven W. Usselman, *Regulating Railroad Innovation: Business, Technology, and Politics in America, 1840–1920* (2002), looks at regulatory reform.

For a list of additional titles related to this chapter's topics, please see http://www.ablongman.com/divine.

Suggested Web Sites

World's Columbian Exposition: Idea, Experience, Aftermath

http://xroads.virginia.edu/~MA96/WCE/title.html

This site has a virtual tour of the fair, along with contemporary reactions and modern analysis.

Pullman Links on the Web—Historic Pullman Foundation

http://www.pullmanil.org/links.htm

This page offers several links to sites with Pullman related information, including a section of sites on the Pullman strike and labor history.

Election of 1896

http://jefferson.village.virginia.edu/seminar/unit8/home.htm

This University of Virginia site contains biographical information, images, cartoons, and related links about the pivotal 1896 election.

The Era of William McKinley

http://www.history.ohio-state.edu/projects/mckinley/default.htm

This site contains numerous images from various stages of William McKinley's career along with a brief biographical essay. This Ohio State University site also has a section with an excellent collection of cartoons from the era.

Chapter 21

Return of the Conquerors *by Edward Moran celebrates the triumphant return of America's Great White Fleet. The fleet of 16 white-hulled battleships and supporting craft set off in December 1907 on a 14-month, round-the-world cruise as a dramatic show of America's naval strength.* ❖

Toward Empire

Roosevelt and the Rough Riders

Many Americans regretted the start of the war with Spain that began in April 1898, but many others welcomed it. Many highly respected people believed that nations must fight every now and then to prove their power and test the national spirit.

Theodore Roosevelt, 39 years old in 1898, was one of them. Nations needed to fight in order to survive, he thought. For months, Roosevelt argued strenuously for war with Spain for three reasons: first, on grounds of freeing Cuba and expelling Spain from the hemisphere; second, because of "the benefit done to our people by giving them something to think of which isn't material gain"; and third, because the army and navy needed the practice.

In April 1898, Roosevelt was serving in the important post of assistant secretary of the navy. When war broke out, he quickly resigned to join the army, rejecting the advice of the secretary of the navy, who warned he would only "ride a horse and brush mosquitoes from his neck in the Florida sands." The secretary was wrong—dead wrong—and later had the grace to admit it. "Roosevelt was right," he said. "His going into the Army led straight to the Presidency."

In 1898, officers supplied their own uniforms, and Roosevelt, the son of well-to-do parents, wanted his to be stylish. He wired Brooks Brothers, the expensive New York clothier, for a "regular Lieutenant-Colonel's uniform without yellow on the collar and with leggings," to be ready in a week. Joining a friend, he chose to enlist his own regiment, and after a few telephone calls to friends, and telegrams to the governors of Arizona, New Mexico, and Oklahoma asking for "good shots and good riders," he had more than enough men. The First United States Volunteer Cavalry, an intriguing mixture of Ivy League athletes and western frontiersmen, was born.

Known as the Rough Riders, it included men from the Harvard, Yale, and Princeton clubs of New York City, the Somerset Club of Boston, and New York's exclusive Knickerbocker Club. Former college athletes—football players, tennis players, and track stars—enlisted. Woodbury Kane, a wealthy yachtsman, signed up and promptly volunteered for kitchen duty.

Other volunteers came from the West—natural soldiers, Roosevelt called them, "tall and sinewy, with resolute, weather-beaten faces, and eyes that looked a man straight in the face without flinching." Among the cowboys, hunters, and prospectors, there were Bucky O'Neill, a legendary Arizona sheriff and Indian fighter; a half dozen other sheriffs and Texas Rangers; a large number of Indians; a famous broncobuster; and an ex-marshal of Dodge City, Kansas.

Eager for war, the men trained hard, played harder, and rarely passed up a chance for an intellectual discussion—if Roosevelt's memoir of the war is to be believed. Once, he overheard Bucky O'Neill and a Princeton graduate "discussing Aryan word-roots together, and then sliding off into a review of the novels of Balzac, and a discussion as to how far Balzac could be said to be the founder of the modern realistic school of fiction." Roosevelt himself spent his spare time reading *Superiorité des Anglo-Saxons*, a French work that strove to prove the superiority of English-speaking

Outline

Feature Essay

Colonel Theodore Roosevelt poses in his custom-designed uniform. With surgeon Leonard Wood, Roosevelt organized the First U.S. Volunteer Cavalry—the Rough Riders—for service in the Spanish-American War. ❖

peoples. In such a camp, discipline was lax, and enlisted men got on easily with the officers.

The troops howled with joy when orders came to join the invasion army for Cuba. They won their first victories in Florida, fighting off other regiments to capture a train to take them to the wharf and then seizing the only available troopship to Cuba. The Rough Riders set sail on June 14, 1898, and Lieutenant Colonel Roosevelt, who had performed a war dance for the troops the night before, caught their mood: "We knew not whither we were bound, nor what we were to do; but we believed that the nearing future held for us many chances of death and hardship, of honor and renown. If we failed, we would share the fate of all who fail; but we were sure that we would win, that we should score the first great triumph in a mighty world-movement."

THAT "WORLD-MOVEMENT," ROOSEVELT WAS SURE, would establish the United States as a world power, whose commerce and influence would extend around the globe, particularly in Latin America and Asia. As he hoped, the nation in the 1890s underwent dramatic expansion, building on the foreign policy approaches of administrations from Lincoln to William McKinley. Policymakers fostered business interests abroad, strengthened the navy, and extended American influence into Latin America and the Pacific. Differences over Cuba resulted in a war with Spain that brought new colonies and colonial subjects, establishing for the first time an American overseas empire.

America Looks Outward

The overseas expansion of the 1890s differed in several important respects from earlier expansionist moves of the United States. From its beginning, the American republic had been expanding. After the first landings in Jamestown and Plymouth, settlers pushed westward: into the trans-Appalachian region, the Louisiana Territory, Florida, Texas, California, Arizona, and New Mexico. Most of these lands were contiguous with existing territories of the United States, and most were intended for settlement, usually agricultural.

The expansion of the 1890s was different. It sought to gain island possessions, the bulk of them already thickly populated. The new territories were intended less for settlement than for use as naval bases, trading outposts, or commercial centers on major trade routes. More often than not, they were viewed as colonies, not as states-in-the-making.

Historian Samuel F. Bemis described the overseas expansion of the 1890s as "the great aberration," a time when the country adopted expansionist policies that did not fit with prior experience. Other historians, pointing to expansionist tendencies in thought and foreign policy that surfaced during the last half of the nineteenth century, have found a developing pattern that led naturally to the overseas adventures of the 1890s. In the view of Walter LaFeber, "the United States did not set out on an expansionist path in the late 1890s in a sudden, spur-of-the-moment fashion. The overseas empire that Americans controlled in 1900 was not a break in their history, but a natural culmination."

Catching the Spirit of Empire

Most people in most times in history tend to look at domestic concerns, and Americans in the years following the Civil War were no exception. Among other things, they focused on Reconstruction, the movement westward, and simply making a living. They took seriously the well-remembered advice of George Washington's

❖ A Look at the Past ❖

Battleships

These photos show the two U.S. Navy warships to bear the name of Texas. The first USS *Texas* was laid down in 1889 along with her ill-fated sister ship, the USS *Maine.* Together these two ships represented the beginnings of a rebirth of the U.S. Navy. Built of American steel armor from the Carnegie Steel Company, the ships demonstrated that the United States had become a major industrial and naval power. The USS *Texas* would take revenge against the Spanish navy for the loss of her sister in the battle of Santiago in 1898. The second USS *Texas* was commissioned in 1914 as one of the new dreadnought class of battleships. Serving in both World War I and World War II, it now rests near Houston as a memorial to those who served and died in the two world wars of the twentieth century.

farewell address to "steer clear" of foreign entanglements. Throughout the nineteenth century, Americans enjoyed "free security" without fully appreciating it. Sheltered by two oceans and the British navy, they could enunciate bold policies such as the Monroe Doctrine, which instructed European nations to stay out of the affairs of the Western Hemisphere, while remaining virtually impregnable to foreign attack.

In those circumstances a sense of **isolationism** spread, fostering a desire to stay out of foreign entanglements. Some people even urged abolition of the foreign service, considering it an unnecessary expenditure, a dangerous profession that might lead to involvement in the struggles of the world's great powers. A New York newspaper called it a "relic of medieval, monarchical trumpery," and if not that, it certainly became at times a dumping ground of the spoils system. Presidents named leaders who, though successful in their own fields, had no training in languages or diplomatic relations.

In the 1870s and after, however, Americans began to take an increasing interest in events abroad. There was a growing sense of internationalism, which stemmed in part from the telegraphs, telephones, and undersea cables that kept people better informed about political and economic developments in distant lands. Many Americans continued to be interested in expansion of the country's borders; relatively few were interested in **imperialism**. Expansion meant the kind of growth that had brought California and Oregon into the American system. Imperialism meant the imposition of control over other peoples through annexation, military conquest, or economic domination.

Reasons for Expansion

Several developments in these years combined to shift attention outward across the seas. The end of the frontier, announced officially in the census report of 1890, sparked fears about diminishing opportunities at home. (See the Feature Essay, "Americans by the Numbers: The 1890 Census," pp. 604–605.) Further growth, it seemed to some, must take place abroad, as John A. Kasson, an able and experienced diplomat, said in the *North American Review:* "We are rapidly utilizing the whole of our continental territory. We must turn our eyes abroad, or they will soon look inward upon discontent."

Factories and farms multiplied, producing more goods than the domestic market could consume. Both farmers and industrialists looked for new overseas markets, and the growing volume of exports—including more and more manufactured goods—changed the nature of American trade relations with the world. American exports of merchandise amounted to $393 million in 1870, $858 million in 1890, and $1.4 billion in 1900. In 1898, the United States exported more than it imported, beginning a trend that lasted through the 1960s.

Political leaders such as James G. Blaine began to argue for the vital importance of foreign markets to continued economic growth. Blaine, secretary of state under Garfield and again under Harrison, aggressively sought wider markets in Latin America, Asia, and

Feature Essay

AMERICANS BY THE NUMBERS

The 1890 Census

Censuses measure many things, including their own purposes. In the nation's first census, in 1790, census takers had set out mainly to measure the population, as a way to apportion representatives in Congress. By 1890, one hundred years later, it did that and more, growing into an enormous compilation of numbers covering nearly every aspect of national life. It had become, as a contemporary expert put it, "a leading instrument in the scientific investigation of the social and economic conditions of the nation."

"Scientific" investigation in those years meant the generous use of statistics, a relatively new discipline, and statistics in turn involved the collection and interpretation of massive amounts of data. As recently as 1880, census takers had counted that data by hand, using essentially the same methods people had used in 1790. But it was a slow process at best, futile at worst, and matters looked little different as 1890 dawned. When the new superintendent of the census took charge that year, he found, as he later said, "one clerk and a messenger, and a desk with some white paper on it."

Observing a train conductor punch tickets gave Herman Hollerith the idea for developing a system of punched cards to record census data and an electrical tabulator to read the information. ❖

Fortunately, he found something else as well, a new invention, the brainchild of a young graduate of Columbia University named Herman Hollerith, who had worked with the census in 1880 and had seen its problems firsthand. Experimenting largely on his own, Hollerith devised an ingenious system in which clerks translated data into punched holes in cards, then fed the cards through a machine that used electric current to read the location of the holes. It was a revolution in method—the machine tabulation of data.

Using the Hollerith system, an experienced clerk could tabulate as many as ten thousand cards in a single day and, equally important, calculate all sorts of informative correlations. For the first time, experts could calculate quickly the number of girls between the ages of ten and fifteen working in textile mills in eastern Massachusetts, or the death rate among African Americans raising cotton on tenant farms in Mississippi, or almost anything else they wanted to know. A forerunner of the modern computer industry, Hollerith's system later became part of the International Business Machines Corporation (IBM) and helped begin the information revolution that so influenced the United States into the twenty-first century.

The results were startling. In 1790, 650 census takers had counted nearly 4 million people and printed the results in a booklet of 56 pages. In 1890, 46,804 census takers counted 63 million people and printed the results in 32 large volumes, with 22,000 pages of statistics tracking nearly every aspect of American life.

The new ability to count allowed census takers to ask more questions about more things, which enabled them in turn to respond to the growing desire of government and business to have detailed information about manufacturing, wages, crops, personal debt, mortality, and a host of other matters.

Some of the new questions would not be asked today. Reflecting the era's racial views, the 1890 census called for specific definitions of race, dividing African Americans into black, mu-

Using the tabulating machine invented by Herman Hollerith, a worker operates a presslike device to bring an array of pins into contact with a punch card. As a pin passed through a hole in the punch card, it came into contact with a small cup of mercury to complete a circuit that registered on one of the dials at the top of the electro-mechanical tabulator. To the worker's right is the card sorter. The press/pin/cup device also opened one of the sorter's chutes into which the operator would deposit the punch card. ❖

latto, quadroon, and octoroon, depending on each persons' ancestry. Because some people were worried about the growing number of immigrants in the country, it also wanted to know about place of birth and citizenship, the ability to speak the English language, and differences in birthrates between native- and foreign-born women.

The news, for some, was disturbing. Hollerith's machines turned up the fact that 5,750,000 immigrants had arrived in the United States in the ten years between 1880 and 1890, more than twice as many as in any former decade. Fully a third of the population had parents who were born in another country, a figure quickly pounced upon by those wanting laws that would cut down on immigration.

Out in Madison, Wisconsin, a young historian at the University of Wisconsin studied the new data and noted another important trend as well. From 1790 to 1880, the country had always had "a frontier of settlement," as the superintendent of the census called it, areas of land still awaiting population and development. As of 1890 it did not. Thanks to the rapid spread of population, the "frontier line" had ceased to exist, and no longer would the frontier and the westward movement "have a place in the census reports."

From that official observation, Frederick Jackson Turner, the young historian, drew a rich and powerful interpretation of the nation's history. In an essay entitled "The Significance of the Frontier in American History," published in 1893, he argued that the frontier had made American society what it was. Settling and surviving on the western edge of settlement had sparked innovation, adaptation, and invention; spurred the growth of democratic institutions; and set in place particularly "American" ways of life and thought.

The end of the frontier, Turner wrote, "marks the closing of a great historical movement. Up to our own day American history has been in large degree the history of the colonization of the Great West," but "the frontier has gone, and with its going has closed the first period of American history."

Although "the Turner thesis," as it was quickly known, would later arouse controversy, in the 1890s it became instantly popular, persuading Theodore Roosevelt and others that with the closing of the frontier, a new era had begun in the nation's life. That new era, the 1890 data seemed to make clear, had little to do with frontiers and farms, and everything to do with the growing, bustling world of cities and factories. In 1890, for the first time, more than half the labor force worked in some form of manufacturing, mining, trade, or transportation. People were flocking to the cities to work in the factories and enjoy new opportunities. New York City that year had 1.5 million inhabitants, Philadelphia and Chicago (which had doubled in population during the prior decade) more than a million.

If some people found cause for worry in all the figures, others found reason for hope. With the beginnings of the progressive movement in the late 1890s, reformers drew on the census statistics to study and understand the way people lived, to improve their health, enrich their lives, increase their safety at work, and protect the young and the weak. The census, in short, had become more than ever an instrument with which to monitor the state of society, and in 1902, reflecting that fact, the Census Office at last became a permanent bureau of the government.

Africa, using tariff reciprocity agreements and other measures. To some extent, he and others were also caught up in a worldwide scramble for empire. In the last third of the century, Great Britain, France, and Germany divided up Africa and looked covetously at Asia. The idea of imperialistic expansion was in the air, and the great powers measured their greatness by the colonies they acquired. Inevitably, some Americans—certain business interests and foreign policy strategists, for example—caught the spirit and wanted to enter the international hunt for territory.

Intellectual currents that supported expansion drew on Charles Darwin's theories of evolution. Adherents pointed, for example, to *The Origin of Species,* which mentioned in its subtitle *The Preservation of Favoured Races in the Struggle for Life.* Applied to human and social development, biological concepts seemed to call for the triumph of the fit and the elimination of the unfit. "In this world," said Theodore Roosevelt, who thought of himself as one of the fit, "the nation that has trained itself to a career of unwarlike and isolated ease is bound, in the end, to go down before other nations which have not lost the manly and adventurous qualities."

The "biogenetic law" formulated by German biologist Ernst Haeckel suggested that the development of the race paralleled the development of the individual. Primitive peoples thus were in the arrested stages of childhood or adolescence; they needed supervision and protection. In a similar vein, John Fiske, a popular writer and lecturer, argued for Anglo-Saxon racial superiority, a result of the process of natural selection. The English and Americans, Fiske said, would occupy every land on the globe that was not already "civilized," bringing the advances of commerce and democratic institutions.

Such views were widespread among the lettered and unlettered alike. In Cuba, one of the Rough Riders ushered a visiting Russian prince around the trenches, informing him with ill-considered enthusiasm: "You see, Prince, the great result of this war is that it has united the two branches of Anglo-Saxon people; and now that they are together they can whip the world, Prince! they can whip the world!" Eminent scholars such as John W. Burgess, a professor of political science at Columbia University, argued in similar though more dignified fashion that people of English origin were destined to impose their political institutions on the world.

The career of Josiah Strong, a Congregational minister and fervent expansionist, suggested the strength of the developing ideas. A champion of overseas missionary work, Strong traveled extensively through the West for the Home Missionary Society, and in 1885, drawing on his experiences, he published a book titled *Our Country: Its Possible Future and Its Present Crisis.* An immediate best-seller, the book called on foreign missions to civilize the world under the Anglo-Saxon races. Strong became a national celebrity.

Our Country argued for expanding American trade and dominion. Trade was important, it said, because the desire for material things was one of the hallmarks of civilized people. So was the Christian religion, and by exporting both trade and religion, Americans could civilize and Christianize "inferior" races around the world. As Anglo-Saxons, they were members of a God-favored race destined to lead the world. Anglo-Saxons already owned one-third of the earth, Strong said, and in a famous passage he concluded that they would take more. In "the final competition of races," they would win and "move down upon Mexico, down upon Central and South America, out upon the islands of the sea, over upon Africa and beyond."

Taken together, these developments in social, political, and economic thought prepared Americans for a larger role in the world. The change was gradual, and there was never a day when people awoke with a sudden realization of their interests overseas. But change there was, and by the 1890s, Americans were ready to reach out into the world in a more determined and deliberate fashion than ever before. For almost the first time, they felt the need for a foreign "policy."

Foreign Policy Approaches, 1867–1900

Rarely consistent, American foreign policy in the last half of the nineteenth century took different approaches to different areas of the world. In relation to Europe, seat of the dominant world powers, policymakers promoted trade and tried to avoid diplomatic entanglements. In North and South America, they based policy on the Monroe Doctrine, a recurrent dream of annexing Canada or Mexico, a hope for extensive trade, and Pan-American unity against the nations of the Old World. In the Pacific, they coveted Hawaii and other outposts on the sea-lanes to China.

Secretary of State William Henry Seward, who served from 1861 to 1869, aggressively pushed an expansive foreign policy. "Give me . . . fifty, forty, thirty more years of life," he told a Boston audience in 1867, "and I will give you possession of the American continent and control of the world." Seward, it turned out, had only five more years of life, but he developed a vision of an American empire stretching south into Latin America and west to the shores of Asia. His vision included Canada and Mexico; islands in the Caribbean as strategic bases to protect a canal across the isthmus; and Hawaii and other islands as steppingstones to Asia, which Seward and many others considered a virtually bottomless outlet for farm and manufactured goods.

Seward tried unsuccessfully to negotiate a commercial treaty with Hawaii in 1867, and the same year he annexed the Midway Islands, a small atoll group twelve hundred miles northwest of Hawaii. In 1867, he concluded a treaty with Russia for the purchase of Alaska (which was promptly labeled "Seward's Folly") partly to sandwich western Canada between American territory and lead to its annexation. As the American empire spread, Seward thought, Mexico City would become its capital.

Secretary of State Hamilton Fish, an urbane New Yorker, followed Seward in 1869, serving under President Ulysses S. Grant. An avid expansionist, Grant wanted to extend American influence in the Caribbean and Pacific, though the more conservative Fish often restrained him. They moved first to repair relations with Great Britain. The first business was settlement of the *Alabama* claims—demands that Britain pay the United States for damages to Union ships caused by Confederate vessels which, like the *Alabama,* had been built and outfitted in British shipyards. Negotiating patiently, Fish signed the Treaty of Washington in 1871, providing for arbitration of the *Alabama* issue and other nettlesome controversies. The treaty, one of the landmarks in the peaceful settlement of international disputes, marked a significant step in cementing Anglo-American relations.

Grant and Fish looked most eagerly to Latin America. In 1870, Grant became the first president to proclaim the nontransfer principle—"hereafter no territory on this continent shall be regarded as subject to transfer to a European power." Fish also promoted the independence of Cuba, restive under Spanish rule, while holding off the annexation desired by the more eager Grant. Influenced by speculators, Grant tried to annex Santo Domingo in 1869 but was thwarted by powerful Republicans in the Senate who disliked foreign involvement and feared a subsequent attempt to annex Haiti.

James G. Blaine served briefly as secretary of state under President James Garfield and laid extensive plans to establish closer commercial relations with Latin America. Blaine's successor, Frederick T. Frelinghuysen, changed Blaine's approach but not his strategy. Like Blaine, Frelinghuysen wanted to find Caribbean markets for American goods; he negotiated separate reciprocity treaties with Mexico, Cuba and Puerto Rico, the British West Indies, Santo Domingo, and Colombia. Using these treaties, Frelinghuysen hoped not only to obtain markets for American goods but to bind these countries to American interests.

When Blaine returned to the State Department in 1889 under President Benjamin Harrison, he moved again to expand markets in Latin America. Drawing on earlier ideas, he envisaged a hemispheric system of peaceful intercourse, arbitration of disputes, and expanded trade. He also wanted to annex Hawaii. "I think there are only three places that are of value and not already taken, that are not continental," he wrote in a letter to President Harrison in 1891. "One is Hawaii and the others are Cuba and Puerto Rico." The last two might take a generation to acquire, but "Hawaii may come up for decision at any unexpected hour and I hope we shall be prepared to decide it in the affirmative."

Harrison and Blaine toyed with naval acquisitions in the Caribbean and elsewhere, but in general they focused on Pan-Americanism and tariff reciprocity. Blaine presided over the first Inter-American Conference in Washington on October 2, 1889, where delegates from nineteen American nations negotiated several agreements to promote trade and created the International Bureau of the American Republics, later renamed the Pan-American Union, for the exchange of general information, including political, scientific, and cultural knowledge. The conference, a major step in hemispheric relations, led to later meetings promoting trade and other agreements.

Reciprocity, Harrison and Blaine hoped, would divert Latin American trade from Europe to the United States. Working hard to sell the idea in Congress, Blaine lobbied for a reciprocity provision in the McKinley Tariff Act of 1890, and once that was enacted, he negotiated reciprocity treaties with most Latin American nations. The treaties failed to foster the hoped-for trade because of the depression of the 1890s; nevertheless, they resulted in greater American exports of flour, grain, meat, iron, and machinery. Exports to Cuba jumped by one-third between 1891 and 1893, then dropped precipitously when the 1894 Wilson-Gorman Tariff Act ended reciprocity.

Grover Cleveland, Harrison's successor, also pursued an aggressive policy toward Latin America. In 1895, he brought the United States precariously close to war with Great Britain over a boundary dispute between Venezuela and British Guiana. Cleveland sympathized with Venezuela, and he and Secretary of State Richard Olney urged Britain to arbitrate the dispute. When Britain failed to act, Olney drafted a stiff diplomatic note affirming the Monroe Doctrine and denying European nations the right to meddle in Western Hemisphere affairs.

Four months passed before Lord Salisbury, the British foreign secretary, replied. Rejecting Olney's arguments, he sent two letters, the first bluntly repudiating the Monroe Doctrine as international law.

The second letter, carefully reasoned and sometimes sarcastic, rejected Olney's arguments for the Venezuelan boundary. Enraged, Cleveland defended the Monroe Doctrine, and he asked Congress for authority to appoint a commission to decide the boundary and enforce its decision. "I am fully alive to the responsibility incurred and keenly realize all the consequences that may follow," he told Congress, plainly implying war.

Preoccupied with larger diplomatic problems in Africa and Europe, Britain changed its position. In November 1896, the two countries signed a treaty of arbitration, under which Great Britain and Venezuela divided the disputed territory. Though Cleveland's approach was clumsy—throughout the crisis, for example, he rarely consulted Venezuela—the Venezuelan incident demonstrated a growing determination to exert American power in the Western Hemisphere. Cleveland and Olney had persuaded Great Britain to recognize the United States' dominance, and they had increased American influence in Latin America. The Monroe Doctrine assumed new importance. In averting war, an era of Anglo-American friendship was begun.

The Lure of Hawaii and Samoa

The islands of Hawaii offered a tempting way station to Asian markets. In the early 1800s, they were already called the "Crossroads of the Pacific," and trading ships of many nations stopped there. In 1820, the first American missionaries arrived to convert the islanders to Christianity. Like missionaries elsewhere, they advertised Hawaii's economic and other benefits and attracted new settlers. Their children later came to dominate Hawaiian political and economic life and played an important role in annexation.

After the Civil War, the United States tightened its connections with the islands. The reciprocity treaty of 1875 allowed Hawaiian sugar to enter the United States free of duty and bound the Hawaiian monarchy to make no territorial or economic concessions to other powers. The treaty increased Hawaiian economic dependence on the United States; its political clauses effectively made Hawaii an American protectorate. In 1887, a new treaty reaffirmed these arrangements and granted the United States exclusive use of Pearl Harbor, a magnificent harbor that had early caught the eye of naval strategists.

Following the 1875 treaty, white Hawaiians became more and more influential in the islands' political life. The McKinley Tariff Act of 1890 ended the special status given Hawaiian sugar and at the same time awarded American producers a bounty of two cents a pound. Hawaiian sugar production dropped dramatically, unemployment rose, and property values fell. The following year, the weak King Kalakaua died, bringing to power a strong-willed nationalist, Queen Liliuokalani. Resentful of white minority rule, she decreed a new constitution that gave greater power to native Hawaiians.

The first step toward American annexation of Hawaii came in 1893 when Queen Liliuokalani was removed from the throne. Hawaii was annexed to the United States as a possession in 1898 and became a U.S. territory in 1900. This photograph from ca. 1898 shows the former queen with guests and members of her household at Washington Place, her residence from 1896 until her death in 1917. ❖

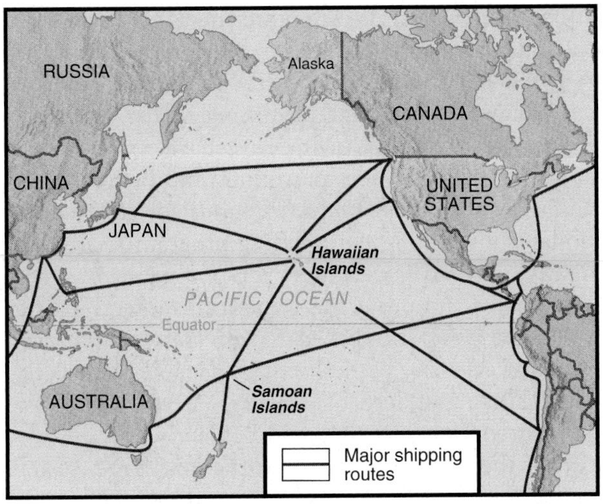

HAWAIIAN ISLANDS *The Hawaiian Islands provided the United States with both a convenient stopping point on the way to Asian markets and a strategic naval station in the Pacific.*

Unhappy, the American residents revolted in early 1893 and called on the United States for help. John L. Stevens, the American minister in Honolulu, sent 150 marines ashore from the cruiser *Boston,* and within three days, the bloodless revolution was over. Queen Liliuokalani surrendered "to the superior force of the United States," and the victorious rebels set up a provisional government. Stevens urged annexation, telling Washington that the "Hawaiian pear is now fully ripe, and this is the golden hour for the United States to pluck it." On February 14, 1893, Harrison's secretary of state, John W. Foster, and delegates of the new government signed a treaty annexing Hawaii to the United States.

But only two weeks remained in Harrison's term, and the Senate refused to ratify the agreement. Five days after taking office, Cleveland withdrew the treaty; he then sent a representative to investigate the cause of the rebellion. The investigation revealed that the Americans' role in it had been improper, and Cleveland decided to restore the queen to her throne. He made the demand, but the provisional government in Hawaii politely refused and instead established the Republic of Hawaii, which the embarrassed Cleveland, unable to do otherwise, recognized.

The debate over Hawaiian annexation, continuing through the 1890s, foreshadowed the later debate over the treaty to end the Spanish-American War. People in favor of annexation pointed to Hawaii's strategic location, argued that Japan or other powers might seize the islands if the United States did not, and suggested that Americans had a responsibility to civilize and Christianize the native Hawaiians. Opponents warned that annexation might lead to a colonial army and colonial problems, the inclusion of a "mongrel" population in the United States, and rule over an area not destined for statehood.

Annexation came swiftly in July 1898 in the midst of excitement over victories in the Spanish-American War. The year before, President William McKinley had sent a treaty of annexation to the Senate, but opposition quickly arose, and the treaty stalled. Japan protested against it, pointing out that Japanese made up a quarter of the Hawaiian population. Japan dispatched a cruiser to Honolulu; the Navy Department sent the battleship *Oregon* and ordered naval forces to take Hawaii if the Japanese made threatening moves.

In 1898, annexationists redoubled arguments about Hawaii's commercial and military importance. McKinley and congressional leaders switched strategies to seek a joint resolution, rather than a treaty, for annexation. A joint resolution required only a majority of both houses, while a treaty needed a two-thirds vote in the Senate. Bolstered by the new strategy, the annexation measure moved quickly through Congress, and McKinley signed it on July 7, 1898. His signature, giving the United States a naval and commercial base in the mid-Pacific, realized a goal held by policymakers since the 1860s.

While annexation of Hawaii represented a step toward China, the Samoan Islands, three thousand miles to the south, offered a strategic location astride the sea-lanes of the South Pacific. Americans showed early interest in Samoa, and in 1872, a naval officer negotiated a treaty granting the United States the use of Pago Pago, a splendid harbor on one of its islands. The Senate rejected the treaty but six years later approved a similar agreement providing for a naval station there. The agreement bound the United States to use its good offices to adjust any disputes between the Samoan chiefs and foreign governments. Great Britain and Germany also secured treaty rights in Samoa, and thereafter the three nations jockeyed for position.

The situation grew tense in 1889, when warships from all three countries gathered in a Samoan harbor. But a sudden typhoon damaged the fleets, and tensions eased. A month later, delegates from Britain, Germany, and the United States met in Berlin to negotiate the problem. Britain and Germany wanted to divide up the islands; Secretary of State Blaine held out for some degree of authority by the indigenous population, with American control over Pago Pago.

The agreement, an uneasy one, ended in 1899 when the United States and Germany divided Samoa and compensated Britain with lands elsewhere in the Pacific. Germany claimed the two larger islands in the chain; the United States kept the harbor at Pago Pago.

The New Navy

Large navies were vital in the scramble for colonies, and in the 1870s the United States had almost no naval power. One of the most powerful fleets in the world during the Civil War, the American navy had fallen into rapid decline. By 1880, there were fewer than two thousand vessels, only forty-eight of which could fire a gun. Ships rotted, and many officers left the service. "It was easy then," said George Dewey, later a hero of the war with Spain, "for an officer to drift along in his grade, losing interest and remaining in the navy only because he was too old to change his occupation."

Conditions changed during the 1880s. A group of rising young officers, steeped in a new naval philosophy, argued for an expanded navy equipped with fast, aggressive fleets capable of fighting battles across the seas. This group had its greatest influence in a special Naval Advisory Board, formed by the secretary of the navy in 1881. Big-navy proponents pointed to the growing fleets of Great Britain, France, and Germany, arguing that the United States needed greater fleet strength to protect its economic and other interests in the Caribbean and Pacific.

This 1881 cartoon depicted "our top heavy navy," a decrepit vessel sinking with idle officers. ✦

In 1883, Congress authorized construction of four steel ships, marking the beginning of the new navy. Experts also worked to improve naval management and the quality of fleet personnel, and between 1885 and 1889, Congress budgeted funds for thirty additional ships. The initial building program focused on lightly armored fast cruisers for raiding enemy merchant ships and protecting American shores, but after 1890, the program shifted to the construction of a seagoing offensive battleship navy capable of challenging the strongest fleets of Europe.

Alfred Thayer Mahan and Benjamin F. Tracy were two of the main forces behind the new navy. Austere and scholarly, Mahan was the era's most influential naval strategist. After graduating from the Naval Academy in 1859, he devoted a lifetime to studying the influence of sea power in history; for more than two decades, he headed the Newport Naval War College, where officers imbibed the latest in strategic thinking. A clear, logical writer, Mahan summarized his beliefs in several major books, including *The Influence of Sea Power upon History, 1660–1783* (1890), and *The Interest of America in Sea Power* (1897).

Mahan's reasoning was simple and, to that generation, persuasive. Industrialism, he argued, produced vast surpluses of agricultural and manufactured goods, for which markets must be found. Markets involved distant ports; reaching them required a large merchant marine and a powerful navy to protect it. Navies, in turn, needed coaling stations and repair yards. Coaling stations meant colonies, and colonies became strategic bases, the foundation of a nation's wealth and power. The bases might serve as markets themselves, but they were more important as steppingstones to other objectives, such as the markets of Latin America and Asia.

Mahan called attention to the worldwide race for power, a race, he warned, the United States could not afford to lose. "All around us now is strife; 'the struggle of life,' 'the race of life' are phrases so familiar that we do not feel their significance till we stop to think about them. Everywhere nation is arrayed against nation; our own no less than others." To compete in the struggle, Mahan argued, the United States must expand. It needed strategic bases, a powerful oceangoing navy, a canal across the isthmus to link the East Coast with the Pacific, and Hawaii as a way station on the route to Asia.

Mahan influenced a generation of policymakers in the United States and Europe; one of them, Benjamin F. Tracy, became Harrison's secretary of the navy in 1889. Tracy organized the Bureau of Construction and Repair to design and build new ships, established the

Naval Reserve in 1891, and ordered construction of the first American submarine in 1893. He also adopted the first heavy rapid-fire guns, smokeless powder, torpedoes, and heavy armor. Above all, Tracy joined with big-navy advocates in Congress to push for a far-ranging battleship fleet capable of attacking distant enemies. He wanted two fleets of battleships, eight ships in the Pacific and twelve in the Atlantic. He got four first-class battleships.

In 1889, when Tracy entered office, the United States ranked twelfth among world navies; in 1893, when he left, it ranked seventh and was climbing rapidly. "The sea," he predicted in 1891, "will be the future seat of empires. And we shall rule it as certainly as the sun doth rise." By the end of the decade, the navy had seventeen steel battleships, six armored cruisers, and many smaller craft. It ranked third in the world.

War with Spain

The war with Spain in 1898 built a mood of national confidence, altered older, more insular patterns of thought, and reshaped the way Americans saw themselves and the world. Its outcome pleased some people but troubled others, who raised questions about war itself, colonies, and subject peoples. The war left a lingering strain of isolationism and antiwar feeling that affected later policy. It also left an American empire, small by European standards, but quite new to the American experience by virtue of its overseas location. When the war ended, American possessions stretched into the Caribbean and deep into the Pacific. American influence went further still, and the United States was recognized as a "world power."

The Spanish-American War established the United States as a dominant force for the twentieth century. It brought America colonies and millions of colonial subjects; it brought the responsibilities of governing an empire and protecting it. For better or worse, it involved the country in other nations' arguments and affairs. The war strengthened the office of the presidency, swept the nation together in a tide of emotion, and confirmed the long-standing belief in the superiority of the New World over the Old. When it was over, Americans looked outward as never before, touched, they were sure, with a special destiny.

They seemed a chosen people, as Mr. Dooley, a character created by humorist Finley Peter Dunne, pointed out to his friend Hennessy over the Archey Road bar. "We're a gr-reat people," said Hennessy, in his rolling Irish brogue. "We ar-re that," replied Mr. Dooley. "We ar-re that. An th' best iv it is we know we ar-re."

A War for Principle

By the 1890s, Cuba and the nearby island of Puerto Rico comprised nearly all that remained of Spain's once vast empire in the New World. Several times, Cuban insurgents had rebelled against Spanish rule, including a decade-long rebellion from 1868 to 1878 (the Ten Years' War) that failed to settle the conflict. The depression of 1893 damaged the Cuban economy,

This print titled "Bohío de Reconcentrados" ("A Reconcentrado Shack") depicts Cubans suffering brutal conditions in one of General Weyler's "reconcentration" camps. Such images appearing in American newspapers and magazines strengthened U.S. sympathy for the Cubans. ❖

and the Wilson-Gorman Tariff of 1894 prostrated it. Duties on sugar, Cuba's lifeblood, were raised 40 percent. With the island's sugar market in ruins, discontent with Spanish rule heightened, and in late February 1895, revolt again broke out.

Recognizing the importance of the nearby United States, Cuban insurgents established a junta in New York City to raise money, buy weapons, and wage a propaganda war to sway American public opinion. Conditions in Cuba were grim. The insurgents pursued a hit-and-run scorched-earth policy to force the Spanish to leave. Spain committed more than 200,000 soldiers; the Spanish commander, who had won with similar tactics in 1878, tried to pin the insurgents in the eastern part of the island where they could be cornered and destroyed.

When this strategy failed, Spain in January 1896 sent a new commander, General Valeriano Weyler y Nicolau. Relentless and brutal, Weyler gave the rebels ten days to lay down their arms. He then put into effect a "reconcentration" policy designed to move the native population into camps and destroy the rebellion's popular base. Herded into fortified areas, Cubans died by the thousands, victims of unsanitary conditions, overcrowding, and disease.

There was a wave of sympathy for the insurgents, stimulated by the newspapers, but so-called **yellow journalism**, sensationalist reporting practiced mainly by a handful of newspapers in New York City that were eager to increase sales, did not cause the war. The conflict stemmed from larger disputes in policies and perceptions between Spain and the United States. Grover Cleveland, under whose administration the rebellion began, preferred Spanish rule to the kind of turmoil that might invite foreign intervention. Opposed to the annexation of Cuba, he issued a proclamation of neutrality and tried to restrain public opinion. In 1896, Congress passed a resolution favoring recognition of Cuban belligerence, but Cleveland ignored it. Instead, he offered to mediate the struggle, an offer Spain declined.

Taking office in March 1897, President McKinley also urged neutrality but leaned slightly toward the insurgents. He immediately sent a trusted aide on a fact-finding mission to Cuba; the aide reported in mid-1897 that Weyler's policy had wrapped Cuba "in the stillness of death and the silence of desolation." The report in hand, McKinley offered to mediate the struggle, but, concerned over the suffering, he protested against Spain's "uncivilized and inhuman" conduct. The United States, he made clear, did not contest Spain's right to fight the rebellion but insisted it be done within humane limits.

Late in 1897, a change in government in Madrid brought a temporary lull in the crisis. The new government recalled Weyler and agreed to offer the Cubans some form of autonomy. It also declared an amnesty for political prisoners and released Americans from Cuban jails. The new initiatives pleased McKinley, though he again warned Spain that it must find a humane end to the rebellion. Then, in January 1898, Spanish army officers led riots in Havana against the new autonomy policy, shaking the president's confidence in Madrid's control over conditions in Cuba.

McKinley ordered the battleship *Maine* to Havana to demonstrate strength and protect American citizens if necessary. On February 9, 1898, the *New York Journal,* a leader of the yellow press, published a letter stolen from Enrique Dupuy de Lôme, the Spanish ambassador in Washington. In the letter, which was private correspondence to a friend, de Lôme called McKinley "weak," "a would-be politician," and "a bidder for the admiration of the crowd." Many Americans were angered by the insult; McKinley himself was more worried about other sections of the letter that revealed Spanish insincerity in the negotiations. De Lôme immediately resigned and went home, but the damage was done.

A few days later, at 9:40 in the evening of February 15, an explosion tore through the hull of the *Maine,* riding at anchor in Havana harbor. The ship, a trim symbol of the new steel navy, sank quickly; 266 lives were lost. McKinley cautioned patience and promised an immediate investigation. Crowds gathered quietly on Capitol Hill and outside the White House, mourning the lost men. Soon there was a new slogan: "Remember the *Maine* and to Hell with Spain!"

The most recent study of the *Maine* incident blames the sinking on an accidental internal explosion, caused perhaps by spontaneous combustion in poorly ventilated coal bunkers. In 1898, Americans blamed it on Spain. Spaniards were hanged in effigy in many communities. Roosevelt, William Jennings Bryan, and others urged war, but McKinley delayed, hopeful that Spain might yet agree to an armistice and perhaps Cuban independence. "I have been through one war; I have seen the dead piled up; and I do not want to see another," he told a White House visitor.

In early March 1898, wanting to be ready for war if it came, McKinley asked Congress for $50 million in emergency defense appropriations, a request Congress promptly approved. The unanimous vote stunned Spain; allowing the president a latitude that was highly unusual for the era, it appropriated the money "for the National defense and for each and every purpose connected therewith to be expended at the discretion of the President." In late March, the report of the investigating board blamed the sinking of the *Maine* on an external (and thus presumably Spanish) explosion. Pressures for war increased.

Lithograph commemorating the sinking of the Maine *in Havana harbor on February 15, 1898, killing 266 men. Coverage of the incident in the "yellow" press encouraged readers to believe that Spanish bombs or torpedoes had sunk the ship.* ❖

On March 27, McKinley cabled Spain his final terms. He asked Spain to declare an armistice, end the reconcentration policy, and—implicitly—move toward Cuban independence. When the Spanish answer came, it conceded some things, but not, in McKinley's judgment, the important ones. Spain offered a suspension of hostilities (but not an armistice) and left the Spanish commander in Cuba to set the length and terms of the suspension. It also revoked the reconcentration policy. But the Spanish response made no mention of a true armistice, McKinley's offer to mediate, or Cuba's independence.

Reluctantly McKinley prepared his war message. It was long and temperate—at seven thousand words even deliberately boring; it suggested the possibility of further negotiations. Congress heard it on April 11, 1898. On April 19, Congress passed a joint resolution declaring Cuba independent and authorizing the president to use the army and navy to expel the Spanish from it. The **Teller Amendment,** offered by Colorado senator Henry M. Teller, pledged that the United States had no intention of annexing the island.

On April 21, Spain severed diplomatic relations. The following day, McKinley proclaimed a blockade of Cuba and called for 125,000 volunteers. On Monday, April 25, Congress passed a declaration of war. Late that afternoon, McKinley signed it.

Some historians have suggested that in leading the country toward war, McKinley was weak and indecisive, a victim of war hysteria in the Congress and the country; others have called him a wily manipulator for war and imperial gains. In truth, he was neither. Throughout the Spanish crisis, McKinley pursued a moderate middle course that sought to end the suffering in Cuba, promote Cuba's independence, and allow Spain time to adjust to the loss of the remnant of empire. He also wanted peace, as did Spain, but in the end, the conflicting national interests of the two countries brought them to war.

"A Splendid Little War"

Ten weeks after the declaration of war, the fighting was over. For Americans, they were ten glorious, dizzying weeks, with victories to fill every headline and slogans to suit every taste. No war can be a happy occasion for those who fight it, but the Spanish-American War came closer than most. Declared in April, it ended in August. Relatively few Americans died, and the quick victory seemed to verify burgeoning American power, though Sherwood Anderson, the author, suggested

A solemn crowd observes the funeral procession of the victims of the USS Maine *as it passes along M Street in Georgetown on the way to Arlington National Cemetery.* ❖

that fighting a weakened Spain was "like robbing an old gypsy woman in a vacant lot at night after a fair." John Hay, soon to be McKinley's secretary of state, called it "a splendid little war."

At the outset, the United States was militarily unprepared. Unlike the navy, the army had not been rebuilt or modernized, and it had shrunk drastically since the day thirty-three years before when Grant's great Civil War army marched sixty abreast, 200,000 strong, down Washington's Pennsylvania Avenue. In 1898, the regular army consisted of only 28,000 officers and men, most of them more experienced in quelling Indian uprisings than fighting large-scale battles. The Indian wars did produce effective small-scale forces, well trained and tightly disciplined, but the army was unquestionably too small for war against Spain.

When McKinley called for 125,000 volunteers, as many as 1 million young Americans responded. Ohio alone had 100,000 volunteers. Keeping the regular army units intact, War Department officials enlisted the volunteers in National Guard units that were then integrated into the national army. Men clamored to join. William Jennings Bryan, a pacifist by temperament, took command of a regiment of Nebraska volunteers; Roosevelt chafed to get to the front; and young Cordell Hull, who became secretary of state in the 1930s, was "wildly eager to leave at once." The secretary of war feared "there is going to be more trouble to satisfy those who are not going than to find those who are willing to go."

In an army inundated with men, problems of equipment and supply quickly appeared. The regulars had the new .30-caliber Krag-Jorgensen rifles, but National Guard units carried Civil War Springfield rifles that used old black-powder cartridges. The cartridges gave off a puff of smoke when fired, neatly marking the troops' position. Spanish troops were better equipped; they had modern Mausers with smokeless powder, which they used to devastating effect. Food was also a problem, as was sickness. The War Department fell behind in supplies and received many complaints about the canned beef it offered the men. Tropical disease felled many soldiers. Scores took ill after landing in Cuba and the Philippines, and it was not uncommon for half a regiment to be unable to answer the bugle call.

Americans then believed that "a foreign war should be fought by the hometown military unit acting as an extension of their community." Soldiers identified with their hometowns, dressed in the local fashion, and thought of themselves as members of a town unit in a national army. The poet Carl Sandburg, 20 years old in 1898, rushed to join the army and called his unit a "living part" of his hometown of Galesburg, Illinois. And the citizens of Galesburg, for their part, took a special interest in Sandburg's unit, in a fashion repeated in countless towns across the country.

Not surprisingly, then, National Guard units mirrored the social patterns of their communities. Since everyone knew each other, there was an easygoing familiarity, tempered by the deference that went with hometown wealth, occupation, education, and length of residence. Enlisted men resented officers who grabbed too much authority, and they expected officers and men to call each other by their first names. Sandburg knew most of the privates in his unit, had worked for his corporal, and had gone to school with the first lieutenant. "Officers and men of the Guard mingle on a plane of beautiful equality," said a visitor to one volunteer camp. "Privates invade the tents of their officers at will, and yell at them half the length of the street."

Each community thought of the hometown unit as its own unit, an extension of itself. In later wars, the government censored news and dominated press relations; there was little censorship in the war with Spain, and the freshest news arrived in the latest letter home. Small-town newspapers printed news of the men and townswomen knit special red or white bellybands of stitched flannel, thought to ward off tropical fevers. Towns sent food, clothing, and occasionally even local doctors to the front. At the close of the war, the Clyde (Ohio) Ladies Society collected funds to provide each member of the town's company a medal struck on behalf of the town.

"Smoked Yankees"

When the invasion force sailed for Cuba, nearly one-fourth of it was African American. In 1898, the regular army included four regiments of African American soldiers, the Twenty-fourth and Twenty-fifth Infantry and the Ninth and Tenth Cavalry. Black regiments had served with distinction in campaigns against the Indians in the West. Most African American troops in fact were posted in the West; no eastern community would accept them. A troop of the Ninth Cavalry was stationed in Virginia in 1891, but whites protested and the troop was ordered back to the West.

When the war broke out, the War Department called for five black volunteer regiments. The army needed men, and military authorities were sure that black men had a natural immunity to the climate and diseases of the tropics. But most state governors refused to accept black volunteers. Only Alabama, Ohio, and Massachusetts mustered in black units in response to McKinley's first call for volunteers. Company L of the Sixth Massachusetts Regiment took part in the invasion of Puerto Rico in July 1898, the only one of the black volunteer units to see action in the Caribbean. African American leaders, among them P. B. S. Pinchback, former acting governor of Louisiana, and George White of North Carolina, the lone African American member of Congress, protested the discrimination. The McKinley administration intervened, and in the end, the volunteer army included more than ten thousand black troops.

Orders quickly went out to the four black regular army regiments in the West to move to camps in the South to prepare for the invasion of Cuba. Crowds and cheers followed the troop trains across the Plains, but as they crossed into Kentucky and Tennessee, the cheering stopped. Welcoming crowds were kept away from the trains, and the troops were hustled onward. Station restaurants refused to serve them; all waiting rooms were segregated. "It mattered not if we were soldiers of the United States, and going to fight for the honor of our country," Sergeant Frank W. Pullen of the Twenty-fourth Infantry wrote; "we were 'niggers' as they called us and treated us with contempt."

Many soldiers were not prepared to put up with the treatment. Those stationed near Chickamauga Park, Tennessee, shot "at some whites who insulted them" and forcibly desegregated the railroad cars on the line into Chattanooga. Troops training near Macon, Georgia, refused to ride in the segregated "trailers" attached to the trolleys, and fights broke out. Discovering a Macon park with a sign saying "Dogs and niggers not allowed," they invaded it and removed

Charge of the 24th and 25th Colored Infantry and Rescue of the Rough Riders at San Juan Hill, July 2, 1898, *colored lithograph by Kurz and Allison, 1899 (right). The twenty-fourth and twenty-fifth Colored Infantry regiments served with exceptional gallantry in the Spanish-American War. Charles Young (above), an 1889 graduate of West Point, was the only African American officer in the army during the Spanish-American War except for a few chaplains.* ❖

the sign. They also chopped down a tree in the park that had been used for lynchings.

More than four thousand black troops training near Tampa and Lakeland, Florida, found segregated saloons, cafes, and drugstores. "Here the Negro is not allowed to purchase over the same counter in some stores as the white man purchases over," Chaplain George W. Prioleau charged. "Why sir, the Negro of this country is a freeman and yet a slave. Talk about fighting and freeing poor Cuba and of Spain's brutality; of Cuba's murdered thousands, and starving reconcentradoes. Is America any better than Spain?"

Near Lakeland, units of the Tenth Cavalry pistol-whipped a drugstore owner who refused to serve a black soldier at the soda fountain. Just before the army's departure for Cuba, the tensions in Tampa erupted in a night of rioting. Drunken white soldiers from an Ohio regiment shot at a black child and black soldiers retaliated. When the night ended, three white and twenty-seven black soldiers were wounded.

When the invasion force sailed a few days later, segregation continued on some of the troopships. Blacks were assigned to the lowest decks, or whites and blacks were placed on different sides of the ship. But the confusion of war often ended the problem, if only temporarily. Blacks took command as white officers died, and Spanish troops soon came to fear the "smoked Yankees," as they called them. Black soldiers played a major role in the Cuban campaign and probably staved off defeat for the Rough Riders at San Juan Hill. In Cuba, they won twenty-six Certificates of Merit and five Congressional Medals of Honor.

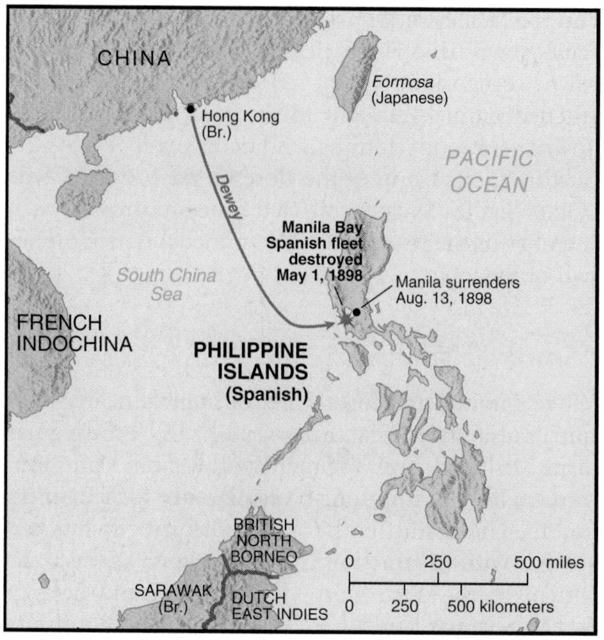

SPANISH-AMERICAN WAR: PACIFIC THEATER
Commodore Dewey, promoted to admiral immediately after the naval victory at Manila Bay, was the first hero of the war.

The Course of the War

Mahan's Naval War College had begun studying strategy for a war with Spain in 1895. By 1898, it had a detailed plan for operations in the Caribbean and Pacific. Naval strategy was simple: Destroy the Spanish fleet, damage Spain's merchant marine, and harry the colonies or the coast of Spain. Planners were excited; two steam-powered armored fleets had yet to meet in battle anywhere in the world. The army's task was more difficult. It had to defend the United States, invade Cuba and probably Puerto Rico, and undertake possible action in far-flung places such as the Philippines or Spain.

Even before war was declared, the secretary of war arranged joint planning between the army and navy. Military intelligence was plentiful, and planners knew the numbers and locations of the Spanish troops. Earlier they had rejected a proposal to send an officer in disguise to map Cuban harbors; such things, they said, were simply not done in peacetime. Still, the War Department's new Military Information Division, a sign of the increasing professionalization of the army, had detailed diagrams of Spanish fortifications in Havana and other points. On the afternoon of April 20, 1898, McKinley summoned the strategists to the White House. To the dismay of those who wanted a more aggressive policy, they decided on a limited strategy: blockading Cuba, sending arms to the insurgents, and annoying the Spanish with small thrusts by the army.

Victories soon changed the strategy. In case of war, long-standing naval plans had called for a holding action against the Spanish base in the Philippines. On May 1, 1898, with the war barely a week old, Commodore George Dewey, commander of the Asiatic Squadron located at Hong Kong, crushed the Spanish fleet in Manila Bay. Suddenly, Manila and the Philippines lay within American grasp. At home, Dewey portraits, songs, and poems blossomed everywhere, and his calm order to the flagship's captain—"You may fire when ready, Gridley"—hung on every tongue. Dewey had two modern cruisers, a gunboat, and a Civil War paddle steamer. He sank eight Spanish warships. Dewey had no troops to attack the Spanish army in Manila, but the War Department, stunned by the speed and size of the victory, quickly raised an expeditionary force. On August 13, 1898, the troops accepted the surrender of Manila, and with it, the Philippines.

McKinley and his aides were worried about Admiral Pascual Cervera's main Spanish fleet, thought to be headed across the Atlantic for an attack on

Florida. On May 13, the navy found Cervera's ships near Martinique in the Caribbean but then lost them again. A few days later, Cervera slipped secretly into the harbor of Santiago de Cuba, a city on the island's southern coast. But a spy in the Havana telegraph office alerted the Americans, and on May 28, a superior American force under Admiral William T. Sampson bottled Cervera up.

In early June, a small force of Marines seized Guantánamo Bay, the great harbor on the south of the island. They established depots for the navy to refuel and pinned down Spanish troops in the area. On June 14, an invasion force of about seventeen thousand men set sail from Tampa. Seven days later, they landed at Daiquiri on Cuba's southeastern coast. All was confusion, but the Spanish offered no resistance. Helped by Cuban insurgents, the Americans immediately pushed west toward Santiago, which they hoped to surround and capture. At first, the advance through the lush tropical countryside was peaceful.

The first battle broke out at Las Guasimas, a crossroads on the Santiago road. After a sharp fight, the Spanish fell back. On July 1, the Rough Riders, troops from the four black regiments, and the other regulars reached the strong fortifications at El Caney and San Juan Hill. Black soldiers of the Twenty-fifth Infantry charged the El Caney blockhouses, surprising the Spanish defenders with Comanche yells. For the better part of a day, the defenders fought stubbornly and held back the army's elite corps. In the confusion of battle, Roosevelt rallied an assortment of infantry and cavalry to take Kettle Hill, adjacent to San Juan Hill.

They charged directly into the Spanish guns, Roosevelt at their head, mounted on a horse, a blue polka-dot handkerchief floating from the brim of his sombrero. "I waved my hat and we went up the hill with a rush," he recalled in his autobiography. Actually, it was not quite so easy. Losses were heavy; eighty-nine Rough Riders were killed or wounded in the attack. Dense foliage concealed the enemy and smokeless powder gave no clue to their position. At nightfall, the surviving Spanish defenders withdrew, and the Americans prepared for the counterattack. "We have won so far at a heavy cost," Roosevelt wrote home, "but the Spaniards fight very hard and charging these entrenchments against modern rifles is terrible. We are within measurable distance of a terrible military disaster."

American troops now occupied the ridges overlooking Santiago. They were weakened by sickness, a fact unknown to the Spanish, who decided the city was lost. The Spanish command in Havana ordered Cervera to run for the open sea, although he knew the attempt to escape was hopeless. On the morning of July 3, Cervera's squadron steamed down the bay and out through the harbor's narrow channel, but the waiting American fleet closed in, and in a few hours every Spanish vessel was destroyed. Two weeks later, Santiago surrendered.

Soon thereafter, army troops, meeting little resistance, occupied Puerto Rico. Cervera had commanded Spain's only battle fleet, and when it sank, Spain was helpless against attacks on the colonies or even its own shores. The war was over. Lasting 113 days, it took relatively few lives, most of them the result of accident, yellow fever, malaria, and typhoid in Cuba. Of the 5500 Americans who died in the war, only 379 were killed in battle. The navy lost one man in the battle at Santiago Bay, and only one to heatstroke in the stunning victory in Manila Bay.

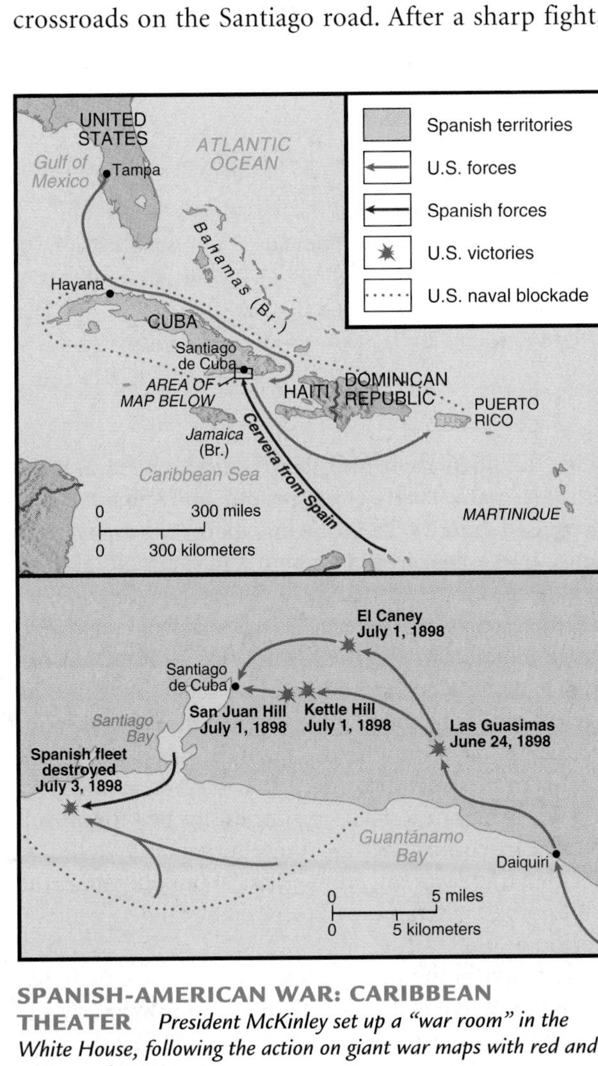

SPANISH-AMERICAN WAR: CARIBBEAN THEATER *President McKinley set up a "war room" in the White House, following the action on giant war maps with red and white marking pins.* ❖

Acquisition of Empire

Late in the afternoon of August 12, 1898, representatives of Spain and the United States met in McKinley's White House office to sign the preliminary instrument of peace. Secretary of State William R. Day beckoned a

❖ A Look at the Past ❖

Cartoon "School Begins"

Uncle Sam teaches a diverse group of students about civilization in this *Puck* cartoon. In the first row, receiving special attention, are recent U.S. acquisitions: Cuba, Puerto Rico, Hawaii, and the Philippines. Carefully examine all the individuals in the cartoon. Who stands outside the classroom and why? How do the students in the first row compare to others in the classroom? Read the message on the chalkboard and consider its meaning. According to this cartoon, how do Americans regard other races and ethnicities? How would Americans define civilization?

presidential aide over to a large globe, remarking, "Let's see what we get by this."

What the United States got was an expansion of its territory and an even larger expansion of its responsibilities. According to the preliminary agreement, Spain granted independence to Cuba, ceded Puerto Rico and the Pacific island of Guam to the United States, and allowed Americans to occupy Manila until the two countries reached final agreement on the Philippines. To McKinley, the Philippines were the problem. Puerto Rico was close to the mainland, and it appealed even to many of the opponents of expansion. Guam was small and unknown; it escaped attention. The Philippines, on the other hand, were huge, sprawling, and thousands of miles from America.

McKinley weighed a number of alternatives for the Philippines, but he liked none of them. He believed he could not give the islands back to Spain; public opinion would not allow it. He might turn them over to another nation, but then they would fall, as he later said, "a golden apple of discord, among the rival powers." Germany, Japan, Great Britain, and Russia had all expressed interest in acquiring them. Germany even sent a large fleet to Manila and laid plans to take the Philippines if the United States let them go.

Rejecting those alternatives, McKinley considered independence for the islands but was soon talked out of it. People who had been there, reflecting the era's racism, told him the Filipinos were not ready for independence. He thought of establishing an American protectorate but discarded the idea, convinced it would bring American responsibilities without full American control. Sifting the alternatives, McKinley decided there was only one practical policy: Annex the Philippines, with an eye to future independence after a period of tutelage.

At first hesitant, American opinion was swinging to the same conclusion. Religious and missionary organizations appealed to McKinley to hold on to the Philippines in order to "Christianize" them. Some merchants and industrialists saw them as the key to the China market and the wealth of Asia. Many Americans simply regarded them as the legitimate fruits of war. In October 1898, representatives of the United States and Spain met in Paris to discuss a peace treaty. Spain agreed to recognize Cuba's independence, assume the Cuban debt, and cede Puerto Rico and Guam to the United States.

Acting on instructions from McKinley, the American representatives demanded the cession of the Philippines. "Grave as are the responsibilities and unforeseen as are the difficulties which are before us, the President can see but one plain path of duty—the acceptance of the archipelago," the instructions said. In return, the United States offered a payment of $20 million. Spain resisted but had little choice, and on December 10, 1898, the American and Spanish representatives signed the **Treaty of Paris.**

The Treaty of Paris Debate

Submitted to the Senate for ratification, the treaty set off a storm of debate throughout the country. Industrialist Andrew Carnegie, reformer Jane Addams, labor leader Samuel Gompers, prominent Republicans such as Thomas B. Reed and John Sherman, Mark Twain, William Dean Howells, and a host of others argued forcefully against annexing the Philippines. Annexation of the Philippines, the anti-imperialists protested over and over again, violated the very principles of independence and self-determination on which the United States was founded.

Some labor leaders feared the importation of cheap labor from new Pacific colonies. Gompers warned about the "half-breeds and semi-barbaric people" who might undercut wages and the union movement. Other anti-imperialists argued against assimilation of different races, "Spanish-Americans," as one said, "with all the mixture of Indian and negro blood, and Malays and other unspeakable Asiatics, by the tens of millions!" Such racial views were also common among those favoring expansion, and the anti-imperialists usually focused on different arguments. If the United States established a tyranny abroad, they were sure, there would soon be tyranny at home. "This nation," declared William Jennings

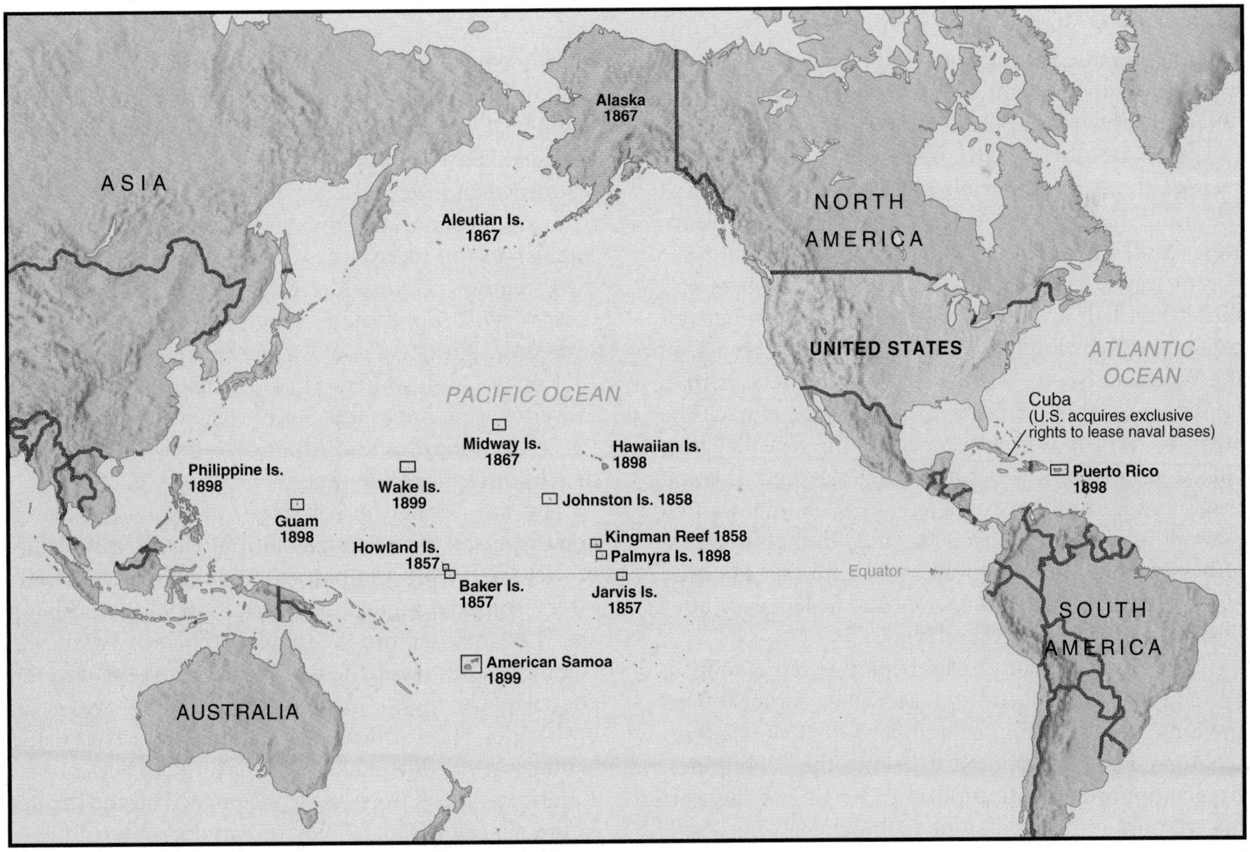

AMERICAN EMPIRE, 1900 *With the Treaty of Paris, the United States gained an expanded colonial empire stretching from the Caribbean to the far Pacific. It embraced Puerto Rico, Alaska, Hawaii, part of Samoa, Guam, the Philippines, and a chain of Pacific islands. The dates on the map refer to the date of U.S. acquisition.*

Bryan, "cannot endure half republic and half colony—half free and half vassal."

Charles Francis Adams, Jr., warned that the possession of colonies meant big armies, government, and debts ("an income tax looms up in the largest possible proportions," he said). Bryan scoffed at the argument that colonies were good for trade, pointing out, "It is not necessary to own people to trade with them." E. L. Godkin, the editor of *The Nation;* George F. Hoar, a leading Republican senator; and many others thought there was no way to reconcile the country's republican ideals with the practice of keeping people under heel abroad. As one of them put it, "Dewey took Manila with the loss of one man—and all our institutions."

William James, the psychologist, said America was about to "puke up its heritage." Unless the Philippines were freed, Americans would rob Filipinos of "the one sacred thing in the world, the spontaneous budding of a national life." To Booker T. Washington, the country had more important things to think about at home, including its treatment of Indians and blacks. Carnegie was so upset that he offered to buy Filipino independence with a personal check for $20 million. He was sure that keeping the Philippines would divert attention from industrial development to foreign adventure, would glorify physical force, and would lead to a war against the Filipinos themselves, in which American soldiers who had signed up "to fight the oppressor" would end up "shooting down the oppressed."

In November 1898, opponents of expansion formed the **Anti-Imperialist League** to fight against the peace treaty. Local leagues sprang up in Boston, New York, Philadelphia, and many other cities; the parent league claimed thirty thousand members and more than half a million "contributors." Membership centered in New England; the cause was less popular in the West and South. It enlisted more Democrats than Republicans, though never a majority of either. The anti-imperialists were weakened by the fact that they lacked a coherent program. Some favored keeping naval bases in the conquered areas. Some wanted Hawaii and Puerto Rico but not the Philippines. Others wanted nothing at all to do with any colonies. Most simply wished that Dewey had sailed away after beating the Spanish at Manila Bay.

The treaty debate in the Senate lasted a month. Pressing hard for ratification, McKinley earlier toured the South to rally support and consulted closely with senators. Though opposed to taking the Philippines, Bryan supported ratification in order to end the war; his support influenced some Democratic votes. Still, on the final weekend before the vote, the treaty was two votes short. That Saturday night, news reached Washington that fighting had broken out between American troops and Filipino insurgents who demanded immediate independence. The news increased pressure to ratify the treaty, which the Senate did on February 6, 1899, with two votes to spare. An amendment promising independence as soon as the Filipinos established a stable government lost by one vote. The United States had a colonial empire.

Guerrilla Warfare in the Philippines

Historians rarely write of the **Philippine-American War,** but it was an important event in American history. The war with Spain was over a few months after it began, but war with the Filipinos lasted more than three years. Four times as many American soldiers fought in the Philippines as in Cuba. For the first time, Americans fought men of a different color in an Asian guerrilla war. The Philippine-American War of 1898–1902 took a heavy toll: 4300 American lives and untold thousands of Filipino lives (estimates range from 50,000 to 200,000).

Emilio Aguinaldo, the Filipino leader, was 29 years old in 1898. An early organizer of the anti-Spanish resistance, he had gone into exile in Hong Kong, from where he welcomed the outbreak of the Spanish-American War. Certain the United States would grant independence, he worked for an American victory. Filipino insurgents helped guide Dewey into Manila Bay, and Dewey himself sent a ship to Hong Kong to bring back Aguinaldo to lead a native uprising against the Spanish. On June 12, 1898, the insurgents proclaimed their independence.

Cooperating with the Americans, they drove the Spanish out of many areas of the islands. In the liberated regions, Aguinaldo established local governments with appointed provincial governors. He waited impatiently for American recognition, but McKinley and others had concluded that the Filipinos were not ready. Soon, warfare broke out between the Filipinos and Americans over the question of Filipino independence.

By late 1899, the American army had defeated and dispersed the organized Filipino army, but claims of victory proved premature. Aguinaldo and his advisers shifted to guerrilla tactics, striking suddenly and then melting into the jungle or friendly native villages. In many areas, the Americans ruled the day, the guerrillas the night. There were terrible atrocities on both sides. The Americans found themselves using brutal, Weyler-like tactics. After any attack on an American patrol, the Americans burned all the houses in the nearest district. They tortured people and executed prisoners. They established protected "zones" and herded Filipinos into them. Seizing or destroying all food outside the zones, they starved many guerrillas into submission.

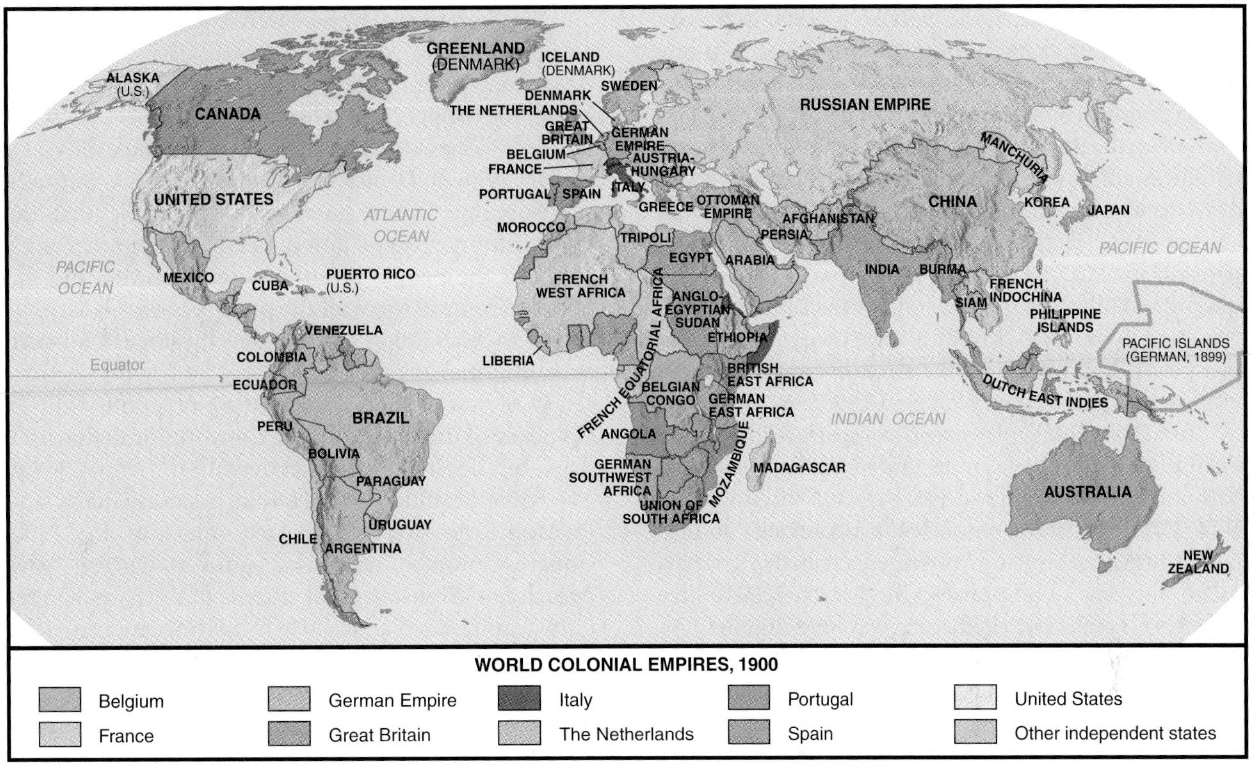

WORLD COLONIAL EMPIRES, 1900 *Events of the nineteenth century increased European hegemony over the world. By 1900, most independent African nations had disappeared and the major European nations had divided the continent among themselves. In the East, the European powers and Japan took advantage of China's internal weakness to gain both trading ports and economic concessions.* ❖

Emilio Aguinaldo (seated, in vest) and his advisors in the Philippines, 1896. Aguinaldo's forces helped the Americans drive Spain out of the Philippines, expecting that the United States would recognize Filipino independence. When the United States failed to do so, Aguinaldo led his forces in warfare against the Americans. ❖

Bryan tried to turn the election of 1900 into a debate over imperialism, but the attempt failed. For one thing, he himself refused to give up the silver issue, which cost him some support among anti-imperialists in the Northeast who were for gold. McKinley, moreover, was able to take advantage of the surging economy, and he could defend expansion as an accomplished fact. "It is no longer a question of expansion with us," he told one audience. "If there is any question at all it is a question of contraction; and who is going to contract?" Riding a wave of patriotism and prosperity, McKinley won the election handily—by an even larger margin than he had in 1896.

In 1900, McKinley sent a special Philippine Commission to the islands under William Howard Taft, a prominent Ohio judge. Directed to establish a civil government, the commission organized municipal administrations and, in stages, created a government for the Philippines. In March 1901, five American soldiers tricked their way into Aguinaldo's camp deep in the mountains and took him prisoner. Back in Manila, he signed a proclamation urging his people to end the fighting. Some guerrillas held out for another year, but to no avail. On July 4, 1901, authority was transferred from the army to Taft, who was named civilian governor of the islands, and his civilian commission. McKinley reaffirmed his purpose to grant the Filipinos self-government as soon as they were deemed ready for it.

Given broad powers, the Taft Commission introduced many changes. New schools provided education and vocational training for Filipinos of all social classes. The Americans built roads and bridges, reformed the judiciary, restructured the tax system, and introduced sanitation and vaccination programs. They established local governments built on Filipino traditions and hierarchies. Taft encouraged Filipino participation in government. During the following decades, other measures broadened Filipino rights. Independence finally came on July 4, 1946, nearly fifty years after Aguinaldo proclaimed it.

Governing the Empire

Ruling the colonies raised new and perplexing questions. How could—and how should—the distant dependencies be governed? Did their inhabitants have the rights of American citizens? Some people contended that acquisition did not automatically incorporate the new possessions into the United States and endow them with constitutional privileges. Others argued that "the Constitution followed the flag," meaning that acquisition made the possessions part of the nation and thus entitled them to all constitutional guarantees. A third group suggested that only the "fundamental" constitutional guarantees of citizenship, the right to vote, and the right to trial by jury were applicable to the new empire. The "formal" privileges of the right to use American currency, the right to be taxed, and the right to run for the presidency did not apply.

In a series of cases between 1901 and 1904 (*De Lima* v. *Bidwell, Dooley* v. *U.S.*, and *Downes* v. *Bidwell*), the Supreme Court asserted the principle that the Constitution did not automatically and immediately apply to the people of an annexed territory and did not confer upon them all the privileges of U.S. citizenship. Instead, Congress could specifically extend such constitutional provisions as it saw fit. "Ye-es," the secretary of war said of the Court's ambiguous rulings, "as near as I can make out the Constitution follows the flag—but doesn't quite catch up with it."

Four dependencies—Hawaii, Alaska, Guam, and Puerto Rico—were organized quickly. In 1900, Congress granted territorial status to Hawaii, gave American citizenship to all citizens of the Hawaiian republic, authorized an elective legislature, and provided for a governor appointed from Washington. A similar measure made Alaska a territory in 1912. Guam and American Samoa were simply placed under the control of naval officers.

Unlike the Filipinos, Puerto Ricans readily accepted the war's outcome, and McKinley early withdrew troops from the island. The **Foraker Act** of 1900 established civil government in Puerto Rico. It organized the island as a territory, made its residents citizens of Puerto Rico (U.S. citizenship was extended to them in 1917), and empowered the president to appoint a governor general and a council to serve as the upper house of the legislature. A lower house of delegates was to be elected.

Cuba proved a trickier matter. McKinley asserted the authority of the United States over conquered territory and promised to govern the island until the Cubans had established a firm and stable government of their own. "I want you to go down there to get the people ready for a republican form of government," he instructed General Leonard Wood, commander of the army in Cuba until 1902. "I leave the details of procedure to you. Give them a good school system, try to straighten out their ports, and put them on their feet as best you can. We want to do all we can for them and to get out of the island as soon as we safely can."

Wood moved quickly to implement the instructions. Early in 1900, he completed a census of the Cuban population, conducted municipal elections, and arranged the election of delegates to a constitutional convention. The convention adopted a constitution modeled on the U.S. Constitution and, at Wood's prodding, included provisions for future relations with the United States. Known as the **Platt Amendment** to the new Cuban Constitution, the provisions stipulated that Cuba should make no treaties with other powers that might impair its independence, acquire no debts it could not pay, and lease naval bases such as Guantánamo Bay to the United States. Most important, the amendment empowered the United States to intervene in Cuba to maintain orderly government.

Between 1898 and 1902, the American military government worked hard for the economic and political revival of the island, though it often demonstrated a paternalistic attitude toward the Cubans themselves. It repaired the damage of the civil war, built roads and schools, and established order in rural areas. A public health campaign headed by Dr. Walter Reed, an army surgeon, wiped out yellow fever. Most troops withdrew at the end of 1899, but a small American occupation force remained until May 1902. When it sailed for home, the Cubans at last had a form of independence, but they were still under the clear domination of their neighbor to the north.

The Open Door

Poised in the Philippines, the United States had become an Asian power on the doorstep of China. Weakened by years of warfare, China in 1898 and 1899 was unable to resist foreign influence. Japan, England, France, Germany, and Russia eyed it covetously, dividing parts of the country into "spheres of influence." They forced China to grant "concessions" that allowed them exclusive rights to develop particular areas and threatened American hopes for extensive trade with the country.

McKinley first outlined a new China policy in September 1898 when he said that Americans sought more trade, "but we seek no advantages in the Orient which are not common to all. Asking only the open door for ourselves, we are ready to accord the open door to others." In September 1899, Secretary of State John Hay addressed identical diplomatic notes to England, Germany, and Russia, and later to France, Japan, and Italy, asking them to join the United States in establishing the **Open Door policy.** This policy urged three agreements: Nations possessing a sphere of influence would respect the rights and privileges of other nations in that sphere; the Chinese government would continue to collect tariff duties in all spheres; and nations would not discriminate against other nations in levying port dues and railroad rates within their respective spheres of influence.

Under the Open Door policy, the United States would retain many commercial advantages it might lose if China was partitioned into spheres of influence. McKinley and Hay also attempted to preserve for the Chinese some semblance of national authority. Great Britain most nearly accepted the principle of the Open Door. Russia declined to approve it, and the other powers, sending evasive replies, stated they would agree only if all the other nations did. Hay turned the situation to American advantage by boldly announcing in March 1900 that all the powers had accepted the Open Door policy.

The policy's first test came just three months later with the outbreak of the Boxer Rebellion in Peking (now Beijing). In June 1900, a secret, intensely nationalistic Chinese society called the Boxers tried to oust all foreigners from their country. Overrunning Peking, they drove foreigners into their legations and penned them up for nearly two months. In the end, the United States joined Britain, Germany, and other powers in sending troops to lift the siege.

In this 1899 cartoon, "Putting His Foot Down" from Puck, *the nations of Europe are getting ready to cut up China to expand their spheres of influence, but Uncle Sam stands firm on American commitments to preserve China's sovereignty.* ❖

Fearing that the rebellion gave some nations, especially Germany and Russia, an excuse to expand their spheres of influence, Hay took quick action to emphasize American policy. In July, he sent off another round of Open Door notes affirming U.S. commitment to equal commercial opportunity and respect for China's independence. While the first Open Door notes had implied recognition of China's continued independence, the second notes explicitly stated the need to preserve it. Together, the two notes comprised the Open Door policy, which became a central element in American policy in the Far East.

To some degree, the policy tried to help China, but it also led to further American meddling in the affairs of another country. Moreover, by committing itself to a policy that Americans were not prepared to defend militarily, the McKinley administration left the opportunity for later controversy with Japan and other expansion-minded powers in the Pacific.

CHRONOLOGY

1867	United States purchases Alaska from Russia ❖ Midway Islands are annexed
1871	Treaty of Washington between United States and Great Britain sets precedent for peaceful settlement of international disputes
1875	Reciprocity treaty with Hawaii binds Hawaii economically and politically to United States
1878	United States acquires naval base in Samoa
1883	Congress approves funds for construction of first modern steel ships; beginning of modern navy
1887	New treaty with Hawaii gives United States exclusive use of Pearl Harbor
1889	First Inter-American Conference meets in Washington, D.C.
1893	American settlers in Hawaii overthrow Queen Liliuokalani; provisional government established
1895	Cuban insurgents rebel against Spanish rule
1898	Battleship *Maine* explodes in Havana harbor (February) ❖ Congress declares war against Spain (April) ❖ Commodore Dewey defeats Spanish fleet at Manila Bay (May) ❖ United States annexes Hawaii (July) ❖ Americans defeat Spanish at El Caney, San Juan Hill (actually Kettle Hill), and Santiago (July) ❖ Spain sues for peace (August) ❖ Treaty of Paris ends Spanish-American War (December)
1899	Congress ratifies Treaty of Paris ❖ United States sends Open Door notes to Britain, Germany, Russia, France, Japan, and Italy ❖ Philippine-American War erupts
1900	Foraker Act establishes civil government in Puerto Rico
1901	Platt Amendment authorizes American intervention in Cuba
1902	Philippine-American War ends with American victory

CONCLUSION: OUTCOME OF THE WAR WITH SPAIN

The war with Spain over, Roosevelt and the Rough Riders sailed for home in mid-August 1898. They sauntered through the streets of New York, the heroes of the city. A few weeks later, Roosevelt bade them farewell. They presented him with a reproduction of Frederick Remington's famed bronze *The Bronco-Buster*, and, close to tears, he told them, "I am proud of this regiment beyond measure." Roosevelt later wrote an account of the war in which he played so central a role that Mr. Dooley suggested, "If I was him, I'd call th' book 'Alone in Cubia.'" By then, Roosevelt was already governor of New York and on his way to the White House.

Other soldiers were also glad to be home, although they were sometimes resentful of the reception they found. "The war is over now," said Winslow Hobson, a black trooper from the Ninth Ohio, "and Roosevelt . . . and others (white of course) have all there is to be gotten out of it." Bravery in Cuba and the Philippines won some recognition for black soldiers, but the war itself set back the cause of civil rights. It spurred talk about "inferior" races, at home and abroad, and united whites in the North and South. "The Negro might as well know it now as later," a black editor said, "the closer the North and South get together by this war, the harder he will have to fight to maintain a footing." A fresh outburst of segregation and lynching occurred during the decade after the war.

McKinley and the Republican party soared to new heights of popularity. Firmly established, the Republican majority dominated politics until 1932. Scandals arose about the canned beef and the conduct of the War Department, but there was none of the sharp sense of deception and betrayal that was to mark the years after World War I. In a little more than a century, the United States had grown from thirteen states stretched along a thin Atlantic coastline into a world power that reached from the Caribbean to the Pacific. As Seward and others had hoped, the nation now dominated its own hemisphere, dealt with European powers on more equal terms, and was a major power in Asia.

Recommended Reading

The best general account of the development of American foreign policy during the last part of the nineteenth century is Walter LaFeber, *The New Empire: An Interpretation of American Expansion, 1860–1898* (1963). William Appleman Williams, *The Tragedy of American Diplomacy* (1959), examines the economic motives for expansion. See also Paul Wolman, *Most Favored Nation: The Republican Revisionists and U.S. Tariff Policy, 1897–1912* (1992) and Laura Wexler, *Tender Violence: Domestic Visions in an Age of U.S. Imperialism* (2000). Lewis L. Gould persuasively reassesses McKinley's diplomacy and wartime leadership in *The Presidency of William McKinley* (1980).

Also helpful are Michael H. Hunt, *Ideology and Foreign Policy* (1987), Tom E. Terrill, *The Tariff, Politics, and American Foreign Policy, 1874–1901* (1973), and Matthew Frye Jacobson, *Barbarian Virtues: The United States Encounters Foreign Peoples at Home and Abroad, 1876–1917* (2000).

Graham A. Cosmas presents a detailed account of military organization and strategy in *An Army for Empire: The United States Army in the Spanish-American War* (1971); Willard B. Gatewood, Jr., offers a fascinating glimpse of the thoughts of some black soldiers in the war in *"Smoked Yankees" and the Struggle for Empire: Letters from Negro Soldiers, 1898–1902* (1971). Ivan Musicant, *Empire by Default: The Spanish-American War and the Dawn of the American Century* (1998), Kristin L. Hoganson, *Fighting for American Manhood: How Gender Politics Provoked the Spanish-American and Philippine-American Wars* (1998), and John L. Offner, *An Unwanted War: The Diplomacy of the United States and Spain over Cuba, 1895–1898* (1992), trace the background to the war with Spain. Brian McAllister Linn, *The Philippine War, 1899–1902* (2000), examines the often forgotten war against the Filipinos. Gerald F. Linderman relates the war to the home front in *The Mirror of War: American Society and the Spanish-American War* (1974).

For a list of additional titles related to this chapter's topics, please see http://www.ablongman.com/divine.

Suggested Web Sites

William McKinley and the Spanish-American War

http://www.history.ohio-state.edu/projects/mckinley/SpanAmWar.htm

Part of Ohio State University's site about William McKinley, this part highlights the Spanish-American War with an essay and photos.

The Spanish-American War in Motion Pictures

http://memory.loc.gov/ammem/sawhtml/sawhome.html

This Library of Congress Web presentation features sixty-eight films of the Spanish American War, the first war to be documented in motion pictures.

The World of 1898: The Spanish-American War

http://www.loc.gov/rr/hispanic/1898/

This Library of Congress site offers resources and documents about the Spanish-American War and the people who participated in or commented about it.

Sentenaryo/Centennial: The Philippine Revolution and Philippine-American War

http://www.boondocksnet.com/centennial/index.html

Jim Zwick organizes primary documents, images, and essays focusing on the Philippines and American involvement.

Anti-Imperialism in the United States, 1898–1935

http://www.boondocksnet.com/ai/ai98-35.html

Jim Zwick edits this extensive site, collating a large number of primary documents about anti-imperialism in America.

The Age of Imperialism

http://www.smplanet.com/imperialism/toc.html

Focusing on the period around the turn of the century, this site puts much information about American imperialism in one place.

Images from the Philippine-United States War

http://historicaltextarchive.com/USA/twenty/filipino.html

The Philippine-American War is one of the least discussed military engagements in American history. This site includes several images from the war.

Theodore Roosevelt Association

http://www.theodoreroosevelt.org/

This site contains much biographical and research information about this famous American.

Chapter 22

Hester Street *(1905), a New York street scene by George Benjamin Luks. Luks was one of a group of artists associated with the Ashcan School, so named because of the artists' preference for painting the realities of modern urban life, including its streets and slums, backyards and bars.*

The Progressive Era

Muckrakers Call for Reform

In 1902, Samuel S. McClure, the shrewd owner of *McClure's Magazine,* sensed something astir in the country that his reporters were not covering. Like *Life, Munsey's,* the *Ladies' Home Journal,* and *Cosmopolitan, McClure's* was reaching more and more people—more than a quarter million readers a month. Americans were snapping up the new popular magazines filled with eye-catching illustrations and up-to-date fiction. Advances in photoengraving during the 1890s dramatically reduced the cost of illustrations; at the same time, income from advertisements rose sharply. By the turn of the century, some magazines earned as much as $60,000 an issue from advertising alone, and publishers could price them as low as 10 cents a copy.

McClure was always chasing new ideas and readers, and in 1902, certain that something was happening in the public mood, he told one of his editors, 36-year-old Lincoln Steffens, a former Wall Street reporter, to find out what it was. "Get out of here, travel, go—somewhere," he said to Steffens. "Buy a railroad ticket, get on a train, and there, where it lands you, there you will learn to edit a magazine."

McClure's, it turned out, had an unpaid bill from the Lackawanna Railroad, and Steffens traveled west. In St. Louis, he came across a young district attorney named Joseph W. Folk who had found a trail of corruption linking politics and some of the city's respected business leaders. Eager for help, Folk did not mind naming names to the visiting editor from New York. "It is good business men that are corrupting our bad politicians," he stressed again and again. "It is the leading citizens that are battening on our city." Steffens's story, "Tweed Days in St. Louis," appeared in the October 1902 issue of *McClure's.*

The November *McClure's* carried the first installment of Ida Tarbell's scathing "History of the Standard Oil Company," and in January 1903, Steffens was back with "The Shame of Minneapolis," another tale of corrupt partnership between business and politics. McClure had what he wanted, and in the January issue he printed an editorial, "Concerning Three Articles in This Number of *McClure's,* and a Coincidence That May Set Us Thinking." Steffens on Minneapolis, Tarbell on Standard Oil, and an article on abuses in labor unions—all, McClure said, on different topics but actually on the same theme: corruption in American life. "Capitalists, workingmen, politicians, citizens—all breaking the law, or letting it be broken."

Readers were enthralled, and articles and books by other **muckrakers**—Theodore Roosevelt coined the unflattering term in 1906 to describe the practice of exposing the corruption of public and prominent figures—spread swiftly. *Collier's* had articles on questionable stock market practices, patent medicines, and the beef trust. Novelist Upton Sinclair tackled the meatpackers in *The Jungle* (1906). In 1904, Steffens collected his McClure's articles in *The Shame of the Cities,* with an introduction expressing confidence that reform was possible, "that our shamelessness is superficial, that beneath it lies a pride which, being real, may save us yet."

Muckraking flourished from 1903 to 1909, and while it did, good writers and bad investigated almost every corner of American life: government, labor unions,

Outline

Feature Essay

At the beginning of the twentieth century magazines enjoyed increasing popularity. McClure's Magazine *pioneered investigative journalism. The cover of the April 1904 edition draws readers not with lively illustrations, but with the best in muckraking, and reveals American interest in corruption. One of the leading muckrakers was Ida Tarbell, whose two-year series on Standard Oil exposed the corrupt practices and deals that had helped create the company.* ❖

big business, Wall Street, health care, the food industry, child labor, women's rights, prostitution, ghetto living, and life insurance. "Time was," Mr. Dooley, the fictional character of humorist Finley Peter Dunne, said to Mr. Hennessy, when magazines

> was very ca'ming to the mind. Angabel an' Alfonso dashin' f'r a marriage license. Prom'nent lady authoresses makin' pomes at the moon. . . . Th' idee ye got fr'm these here publications was that life was wan glad sweet song. . . .
>
> But now whin I pick me fav-rite magazine off th' flure, what do I find? Ivrything has gone wrong. . . . All th' pomes by th' lady authoresses that used to begin: "Oh, moon, how fair!" now begin: "Oh, Ogden Armour, how awful!" . . . Graft ivrywhere. "Graft in th' Insurance Companies," "Graft in Congress," "Graft Be an Old Grafter," "Graft in Its Relations to th' Higher Life.". . .
>
> An' so it goes, Hinnissy . . . till I don't thrust anny man anny more. . . . I used to be nervous about burglars, but now I'm afraid iv a night call fr'm th' prisidint iv th' First National Bank.

AS MCCLURE HAD HOPED, Steffens *had* found something astir in the country, something so important and pervasive that it altered the course of American history in the twentieth century. The muckrakers were a journalistic voice of this larger movement in American society. Called **progressivism,** it lasted from the mid-1890s through World War I. Like muckraking itself, progressivism reflected worry about the state of society, the effects of industrialization and urbanization, social disorder, political corruption, and a host of other issues. With concerns so large, progressivism often had a sense of crisis and urgency, although it was rooted in a spirit of hopefulness and confidence in human progress. For varying reasons, thousands of people became concerned about their society, and, separately and together, they set out to cure some of the ills they saw around them. The efforts of the so-called progressives changed the nation and gave the era its name.

The Changing Face of Industrialism

"Life in the States," an English visitor said in 1900, "is one perpetual whirl of telephones, telegrams, phonographs, electric bells, motors, lifts, and automatic instruments." If not quite as automated as the visitor described, conditions in America were better than just a few years before. Farms and factories were once again prosperous; in 1901, for the first time in years, the economy reached full capacity. Farm prices rose almost 50 percent between 1900 and 1910. Unemployment dropped. "In the United States of today," a Boston newspaper said in 1904, "everyone is middle class. The resort to force, the wild talk of the nineties are over. Everyone is busily, happily getting ahead."

Everyone, of course, was not middle class, nor was everyone getting ahead. "Wild talk" persisted. Many of the problems that had angered people in the 1890s continued into the new century, and millions of Americans still suffered from poverty and disease. Racism sat even more heavily on African Americans in both South and North, and there was increasing hostility against immigrants from southern and eastern Europe and from Mexico and Asia. Yet to some degree the Boston newspaper was right: Economic conditions were better for many people, and as a result, prosperity became one of the keys to understanding the era and the nature of progressive reform.

The start of the new century was another key as well, for it influenced people to take a fresh look at themselves and their times. Excited about beginning the twentieth century, people believed technology and enterprise would shape a better life. Savoring the word *new,* they talked of the new poetry, new cinema, new history, new democracy, new woman, new art, new immigration, new morality, and new city. Magazines picked up the word; there were the *New Republic* and the *New Statesman.* Presidents Theodore Roosevelt and Woodrow Wilson called their political programs the New Nationalism and the New Freedom.

The word *mass* also cropped up frequently. Victors in the recent war with Spain, Americans took pride in teeming cities, burgeoning corporations, and other marks of the mass society. They enjoyed the fruits of mass production, read mass circulation newspapers and magazines, and took mass transit from the growing spiral of suburbs into the central cities.

Behind mass production lay significant changes in the nation's industrial system. Businesses grew at a rapid rate. They were large in the three decades after the Civil War, but in the years between 1895 and 1915, industries became mammoth, employing thousands of workers and equipped with assembly lines to turn out huge quantities of the company's product. Inevitably, changes in management attitudes, business organization, and worker roles influenced the entire society. Inevitably, too, the growth of giant businesses gave rise to a widespread fear of "trusts" and a desire among many progressive reformers to break them up or regulate them.

The Innovative Model T

In the movement toward large-scale business and mass production, the automobile industry was one of those that led the way. In 1895, there were only four cars on the nation's roads; in 1917, there were nearly five million, and the automobile had already helped work a small revolution in industrial methods and social mores.

Mass production of automobiles began in the first years of the century. Using an assembly-line system that foreshadowed later techniques, Ransom E. Olds turned out five thousand Olds runabouts in 1904. But Olds's days of leadership were numbered. In 1903, Henry Ford and a small group of associates formed the Ford Motor Company, the firm that transformed the business.

Henry Ford built his first car in 1896, then produced a number of improved models, each designated by a letter of the alphabet. The Model T debuted in 1908. The "Tin Lizzie" was Ford's "motorcar for the multitudes," affordably priced so that every family could own one. In 1908 Ford's car cost $850, but by the mid-1920s that price was down to $260 for a Ford roadster. The automobile wrought vast changes in American life and in the American landscape as it spawned the development of paved roads, traffic lights, and numerous auto-related businesses. ❖

Ford was 40 years old. He had tried farming and hated it. During the 1890s, he worked as an engineer for Detroit's Edison Company but spent his spare time designing internal combustion engines and automobiles. At first, like many others in the industry, he concentrated on building luxury and racing cars. Racing his own cars, Ford became the "speed demon" of Detroit; in 1904, he set the world's land speed record—more than 90 miles per hour—in the 999, a large red racer that shot flames from the motor.

In 1903, Ford sold the first Ford car. The price was high, and in 1905, Ford raised prices still higher. Sales plummeted. In 1907, he lowered the price; sales and revenues rose. Ford learned an important lesson of the modern economy: A smaller unit profit on a large number of sales meant enormous revenues. Early in 1908, he introduced the Model T, a four-cylinder, 20-horsepower "Tin Lizzie," costing $850, and available only in black. Eleven thousand were sold the first year.

"I am going to democratize the automobile," Ford proclaimed. "When I'm through everybody will be able to afford one, and about everyone will have one." The key was mass production, and after many experiments, Ford copied the techniques of meatpackers who moved animal carcasses along overhead trolleys from station to station. Adapting the process to automobile assembly, Ford in 1913 set up moving assembly lines in his plant in Highland Park, Michigan, that dramatically reduced the time and cost of producing cars. Emphasizing continuous movement, he strove for a nonstop flow from raw material to finished product. In 1914, he sold 248,000 Model T cars.

That year, Ford workers assembled a car in 93 minutes, one-tenth the time it had taken just eight months before. By 1925, the Ford plant turned out 9109 Model T's each day, a new car for every ten seconds of the workday.

While Ford was putting more and more cars on the road, the 1916 Federal Aid Roads Act, a little noticed measure, set the framework for road building in the twentieth century. Removing control from county governments, it required every state desiring federal funds to establish a highway department to plan routes, oversee construction, and maintain roads. In states that had such departments, the federal government paid half the cost of building the roads. Providing for a planned highway system, the act produced a national network of two-lane all-weather intercity roads.

BUSINESS CONSOLIDATIONS (MERGERS), 1895–1905

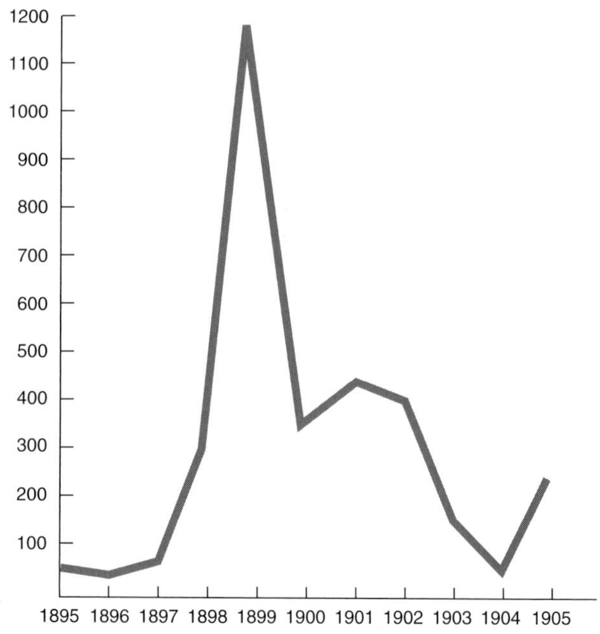

The Burgeoning Trusts

As businesses like Ford's grew, capital and organization became increasingly important, and the result was the formation of a growing number of trusts. Standard Oil started the trend in 1882, but the greatest momentum came two decades later. Between 1898 and 1903, a series of mergers and consolidations swept the economy. Many smaller firms disappeared, swallowed up in giant corporations. By 1904, large-scale combinations of one form or another controlled nearly two-fifths of the capital in manufacturing in the country.

The result was not monopoly but oligopoly—control of a commodity or service by a small number of large, powerful companies. Six great financial groups dominated the railroad industry; a handful of holding companies controlled utilities and steel. Rockefeller's Standard Oil owned about 85 percent of the oil business. Large companies such as Standard Oil and American Tobacco had weathered the depression of the 1890s, and after 1898, financiers and industrialists followed their example and formed the Amalgamated Copper Company, Consolidated Tobacco, U.S. Rubber, and a host of others.

By 1909, just 1 percent of the industrial firms were producing nearly half of all manufactured goods. Giant businesses reached abroad for raw materials and new markets. United Fruit, an empire of plantations and steamships in the Caribbean, exploited opportunities created by victory in the war with Spain. U.S. Steel worked with overseas companies to fix the price of steel rails, an unattainable dream just a few years before. For decades, competition had sent rail prices up and down; now they stayed at $28 a ton, and through the famous "Gary dinners" in which Elbert H. Gary of U.S. Steel brought steel executives from "competing" firms together to set prices, market conditions were fixed for wide areas of the industry.

Though the trend has been overstated, finance capitalists such as J. P. Morgan tended to replace the industrial capitalists of an earlier era. Able to finance the mergers and reorganizations, investment bankers played a greater and greater role in the economy. A multibillion-dollar financial house, J. P. Morgan and Company operated a network of control that ran from New York City to every industrial and financial center in the nation. Like other investment firms, it held directorships in many corporations, creating "interlocking directorates" that allowed it to control many businesses. In 1913, two banking groups—Morgan's and Rockefeller's—held 341 directorships in 112 corporations with an aggregate capital of more than $22 billion.

Massive business growth set off a decade-long debate over what government should do about the trusts. Some critics who believed that the giant companies

As early as 1886, cartoonist Thomas Nast attacked trusts. Here the people's welfare is sinking as the Statue of Liberty is defaced. ❖

were responsible for stifling individual opportunity and raising prices wanted to break them up into small competitive units. Others argued that large-scale business was a mark of the times, and that it produced more goods and better lives.

The debate over the trusts was one of the issues that shaped the Progressive Era, but it was never a simple contest between high-minded reformers and greedy business titans. Some progressives favored big business; others wanted it broken up. Business leaders themselves were divided in their viewpoints, and some welcomed reform-led assaults on giant competitors. As a rule, both progressives and business leaders drew on similar visions of the country: complex, expansive, hopeful, managerially minded, and oriented toward results and efficiency. They both believed in private property and the importance of economic progress. In fact, in working for reform, the progressives often drew on the managerial methods of a business world they sought to regulate.

Managing the Machines

Mass production changed the direction of American industry. Size, system, organization, and marketing became increasingly important. Management focused on speed and product, not on workers. Assembly-line technology changed tasks and, to some extent, values. The goal was no longer to make a unique product that would be better than the one before. "The way to make automobiles," Ford said as early as 1903, "is to make one automobile like another automobile, to make them all alike, to make them come through the factory just alike."

In a development that rivaled assembly lines in importance, businesses established industrial research laboratories where scientists and engineers developed new products. General Electric founded the first one in 1900, housed in a barn. It soon attracted experts who designed improvements in light bulbs, invented the cathode-ray tube, worked on early radio, and even tinkered with atomic theory. Du Pont opened its labs in 1911, Eastman Kodak in 1912, and Standard Oil in 1919. As the source of new ideas and technology, the labs altered life in the twentieth century.

Through all this, business became large-scale, mechanized, and managed. While many shops still employed fewer than a dozen workers, the proportion of such shops shrank. By 1920, close to one-half of all industrial workers toiled in factories employing more than 250 people. More than one-third worked in factories that were part of multiplant companies.

Industries that processed materials—iron and steel, paper, cement, and chemicals—were increasingly automated and operated continuously. In the glass industry, machines ended the domination of highly skilled and well-paid craftspeople. In 1908, Irving W. Colburn invented a machine to manufacture plate glass; the Libbey-Owens-Ford Company bought the patent; and Ford soon had a glassmaking machine from which emerged every day for two years a 3½-mile ribbon of automobile window glass. Eventually, the plant produced almost 2000 miles of glass.

Workers tending such ribbons could not fall behind. Foremen still managed the laborers on the factory floor, but more and more, the rules came down from a central office where trained professional managers supervised production flow. Systematic record keeping, cost accounting, and inventory and production controls became widespread. Workers lost control of the work pace. "If you need to turn out a little more," a manager at Swift and Company said, "you speed up the conveyor a little and the men speed up to keep pace." It worked. For that and other reasons, in the automobile industry, output per worker-hour multiplied an extraordinary four times between 1909 and 1919.

Folkways of the workplace—workers passing job-related knowledge to each other, performing their tasks with little supervision, setting their own pace, and in effect running the shop—began to give way to "scientific" labor management. More than anyone else, Frederick Winslow Taylor, an inventive mechanical engineer, strove to extract maximum efficiency from each worker. "In the past," he believed, "the man has been first; in the future the system must be first."

In his book *The Principles of Scientific Management* (1911), Taylor proposed two major reforms. First, management must take responsibility for job-related knowledge and classify it into "rules, laws, and formulae." Second, management should control the workplace "through *enforced* standardization of methods, *enforced* adoption of the best implements and working conditions, and *enforced* cooperation." Although few factories wholly adopted Taylor's principles, he had great influence, and the doctrines of scientific management spread through American industry.

Workers caught up in the changing industrial system experienced the benefits of efficiency and productivity; in some industries, they earned more. But they suffered important losses as well. Performing repetitive tasks, they seemed part of the machinery, moving to the pace and needs of their mechanical pacesetters. Bored, they might easily lose pride of workmanship, though many workers, it is clear, did not. Efficiency engineers experimented with tools and methods, a process many workers found unsettling. Yet the goal was to establish routine—to work out, as someone said of a garment worker, "one single precise motion each second, 3600 in one hour, and all exactly the same." Praising that worker, the manager said, "She is a sure machine."

Jobs became not only monotonous but dangerous. As machines and assembly lines sped up, boredom or miscalculation could bring disaster. Meat cutters sliced fingers and hands. Illinois steel mills, a magazine said, were "Making Steel and Killing Men"; one mill had forty-six deaths in 1906 alone. Injuries were part of many jobs. "The machines go like mad all day," a garment worker said, "because the faster you work the more money you get. Sometimes in my haste I get my finger caught and the needle goes right through it . . . I bind the finger up with a piece of cotton and go on working."

In March 1911, a fire at the Triangle Shirtwaist Company in New York focused nationwide attention on unsafe working conditions. When the fire started, five hundred men and women, mostly Italians and Jews from eastern Europe, were just finishing their workday. Firefighters arrived within minutes, but they were already too late. Terrified seamstresses raced to the exits to try to escape the flames, but most exit doors were closed, locked by the company to prevent theft and shut out union organizers. Many died in the stampede down the narrow stairways or the single fire escape. Still others, trapped on the building's top stories far above the reach of the fire department's ladders, jumped to their deaths on the street below. One hundred forty-six people died.

A few days later, eighty thousand people marched silently in the rain in a funeral procession up Fifth Avenue. A quarter million people watched. At a mass meeting held to protest factory working conditions, Rose Schneiderman, a dynamic 29-year-old organizer for the Women's Trade Union League, told New York City's civic and religious leaders that they had not done enough, they had not cared. "We have tried you good people of the public and we have found you wanting. . . . Every week I must learn of the untimely death of one of my sister workers. Every

Fire nets were of no avail to the workers at the Triangle Shirtwaist Company who jumped from the upper stories to escape the flames. Speaking to a mass meeting after the fire, labor organizer Rose Schneiderman inveighed against a system that treated human beings as expendable commodities. ❖

year thousands of us are maimed. The life of men and women is so cheap and property is so sacred."

The outcry impelled New York's governor to appoint a State Factory Investigating Commission that recommended laws to shorten the workweek and improve safety in factories and stores.

Society's Masses

Spreading consumer goods through society, mass production not only improved people's lives but sometimes cost lives, too. Tending the machines, as Rose Schneiderman pointed out, took hard, painful labor, often under dangerous conditions. As businesses expanded, they required more and more people, and the labor force increased tremendously to keep up with the demand for workers in the factories, mines, and forests. Women, African Americans, Asian Americans, and Mexican Americans played larger and larger roles. Immigration soared. Between 1901 and 1910, nearly 8.8 million immigrants entered the United States; between 1911 and 1920, another 5.7 million came.

For many of these people, life was harsh, spent in crowded slums and long hours on the job. Fortunately, the massive unemployment of the 1890s was over, and in many skilled trades, such as cigar making, there was plenty of work to go around. Though the economic recovery helped nearly everyone, the less skilled continued to be the less fortunate. Migrant workers, lumberjacks, ore shovelers, and others struggled to find jobs that paid decently.

Under such circumstances, many people fought to make a living, and many, too, fought to improve their lot. Their efforts, along with the efforts of the reform-minded people who came to their aid, became another important hallmark of the Progressive Era.

Better Times on the Farm

While people continued to flee the farms—by 1920, fewer than one-third of all Americans lived on farms, and fewer than one-half lived in rural areas—farmers themselves prospered, the beneficiaries of greater production and expanding urban markets. Rural free delivery, begun in 1893, helped diminish the farmers' sense of isolation and changed farm life. The delivery of mail to the farm door opened that door to a wider world; it exposed farmers to urban thinking, national advertising, and political events. In 1911, more than one billion newspapers and magazines were delivered over RFD routes.

Parcel post (1913) permitted the sending of packages through the U.S. mail. Mail-order houses flourished; rural merchants suffered. Packages went both ways—President Woodrow Wilson's first parcel-post delivery held 8 pounds of New Jersey apples—and within a year, 300 million packages were being mailed annually. While telephones and electricity did not reach most rural areas for decades, better roads, mail-order catalogs, and other innovations knit farmers into the larger society. Early in the new century, Mary E. Lease—who in her Populist days had urged Kansas farmers to raise less corn and more hell—moved to Brooklyn.

Farmers still had problems. Land prices rose with crop prices, and farm tenancy increased, especially in the South. Tenancy grew from one-quarter of all farms in 1880 to more than one-third in 1910. In South Carolina, Georgia, Alabama, and Mississippi, nearly two-thirds of the farms were run by tenant farmers. Many southern tenant farmers were African Americans, and they suffered from farm-bred diseases. In one of the reforms of the Progressive Era, in 1909, the Rockefeller Sanitary Commission, acting on recent scientific discoveries, began a sanitation campaign that eventually wiped out the hookworm disease, and in

IRRIGATION AND CONSERVATION IN THE WEST TO 1917 *To make the arid lands of the western states productive, the state and federal governments regulated the water supply through irrigation projects and the creation of water reservoirs. The federal government also created land reserves.*

1912, the U.S. Public Health Service began work on rural malaria.

In the arid West, irrigation transformed the land as the federal government and private landholders joined to import water from mountain watersheds. The dry lands bloomed, and so did a rural class structure that sharply separated owners from workers. Under the Newlands Act of 1902, the secretary of the interior formed the U.S. Reclamation Service, which gathered a staff of thousands of engineers and technicians, "the largest bureaucracy ever assembled in irrigation history."

Dams and canals channeled water into places such as California's Imperial Valley, and as the water streamed in, cotton, cantaloupes, oranges, tomatoes, lettuce, and a host of other crops streamed out to national markets. By 1920, Idaho, Montana, Utah, Wyoming, Colorado, and Oregon had extensive irrigation systems, all drawing on scarce water supplies; California, the foremost importer of water, had 4.2 million acres under irrigation, many of them picked by migrant workers from Mexico, China, and Japan. The work was backbreaking—and poorly paid. A worker from India called picking asparagus a "ghastly" job, paid at the rate of ten cents a box:

> They gave us miles and miles of asparagus rows. As soon as I had knelt down with my knife and cut out one head and put it in the box, there would be another one sprouting before me. Then I would have to stoop again, and it was continuous picking and stooping that made it a terrible form of exercise. It is walk and bend, bend and walk, from half past four [in the morning] or thereabouts, until seven in the evening.

Women and Children at Work

Women worked in larger and larger numbers. In 1900, more than five million worked—one-fifth of all adult women—and among those aged 14 to 24, the employment rate was almost one-third. Of those employed, single women outnumbered married women by seven to one, yet more than one-third of married women worked. Most women held service jobs. Only a small number held higher-paying jobs as professionals or managers.

In the 1890s, women made up more than one-quarter of medical school graduates. Using a variety of techniques, men gradually squeezed them out, and by the 1920s, only about 5 percent of the graduates were women. Few women taught in colleges and universities, and those who did were expected to resign if they married. In 1906, Harriet Brooks, a promising physicist at Barnard College in New York, became engaged and refused to resign; the dean told her icily that Barnard expected a married woman to "dignify her home-making into a profession, and not assume that she can carry on two full professions at a time."

More women than men graduated from high school, and with professions like medicine and science largely closed to them, they often turned to the new "business schools" that offered training in stenography, typing, and bookkeeping. In 1920, more than one-quarter of all employed women held clerical jobs. Many others taught school.

In 1907 and 1908, investigators studied 22,000 women workers in Pittsburgh; 60 percent of them earned less than $7 a week, a minimum for "decent living." Fewer than 1 percent held skilled jobs; most tended machines, wrapped and labeled, or did handwork that required no particular skill. In New York, many women toiled six days a week as garment workers from eight in the morning to six in the evening, with an extra hour off on Saturdays. They earned $7 to $12 a week, nothing at all during slack season. They had to buy their own needles and thread and pay for electricity and chairs to sit on.

Black women had always worked, and in far larger numbers than their white counterparts. The reason was usually economic; an African American man or woman alone could rarely earn enough to support a family. Unlike many white women, black women tended to remain in the labor force after marriage or the start of a family. They also had less opportunity for job advancement, and in 1920, between one-third and one-half of all African American women who were working were restricted to personal and domestic service jobs.

Critics charged that women's employment endangered the home, threatened their reproductive functions, and even, as one man said, stripped them of "that modest demeanor that lends a charm to their kind." Adding to these fears, the birthrate continued to drop between 1900 and 1920, and the divorce rate soared, in part because working-class men took advantage of the newer moral freedom and deserted their families in growing numbers. By 1916, there was one divorce for every nine marriages as compared to one for twenty-one in 1880.

David Graham Phillips, a novelist troubled by the woman's problem, depicted a husband's oppression of his wife in *The Hungry Heart*, published in 1909. "He kissed her, patted her cheek, went back to his work." When the wife grew restless, the husband knew why: "A few more years'll wash away the smatter she got at college, and this restlessness of hers will yield to nature, and she'll be content and happy in her womanhood. . . . As grandfather often said, it's a dreadful mistake, educating women beyond their sphere." Such views, mild as they were, got Phillips assassinated by a

Japanese immigrants with a Methodist deaconess in the administration buiding of the immigration station at Angel Island, near San Francisco. Quota systems and exclusionary laws severely limited Asian immigration, while other laws placed restrictions on the immigrants, curtailing their right to own or even rent agricultural land. Some Asian immigrants, after months of detention at Angel Island, were refused permission to enter the United States and were forced to return to their homelands. ❖

male median age of 42, their communities were generally dominated by the elderly.

The Chinese American population differed in another respect as well. Unlike other immigrant groups, whose numbers tended to grow, the number of Chinese Americans shrank in these years—from about 125,000 in the early 1880s to just over 60,000 in 1920. After 1910, the U.S. government set up a special immigration facility at Angel Island in San Francisco Bay, but unlike European immigrants who landed at Ellis Island in New York and were quickly sent on, Chinese immigrants were kept for weeks and months, examined and reexamined, before being allowed to cross the narrow band of water to San Francisco. Angel Island remained open until 1940, and a poem carved into the wall of Building 317 showed the feelings of some of those who waited:

> There are tens of thousands of poems composed on
> these walls,
> They are all cries of complaint and sadness.
> The day I am rid of this prison and attain success,
> I must remember that this prison once existed.
> In my daily needs I must be frugal.
> Needless extravagance leads youth to ruin.
> All my compatriots please be mindful.
> Once you have some small gains, return home early.
>
> By One from Xiangshan

Many Japanese also arrived at Angel Island, and though at first fewer in numbers than the Chinese, they developed communities along the Pacific Coast, where they settled mainly on farms. The number of Japanese Americans grew. In 1907, the heaviest year of immigration from Japan, nearly 31,000 Japanese entered the United States; by 1920, there were 111,000 Japanese in the country, nearly three-quarters of them in California.

As the newcomers arrived from Asia, Europe, and Mexico, nativist sentiment, which had criticized earlier waves of immigrants, intensified. Old-stock Americans sneered at their dress and language. Racial theories emphasized the superiority of northern Europeans, and the new "science" of eugenics suggested the need to control the population growth of "inferior" peoples. Hostility toward Catholics and Jews was common but touched other groups as well.

In 1902, Congress enacted a law prohibiting immigration from China. Statutes requiring literacy tests designed to curtail immigration from southern and eastern Europe were vetoed by William Howard Taft in 1913 and by Woodrow Wilson in 1915 and 1917. In 1917, such a measure passed despite Wilson's veto. Other measures tried to limit immigration from Mexico and Japan.

Conflict in the Workplace

Assembly lines, speedups, long hours, and low pay produced a dramatic increase in American industrial output (and profits) after 1900; they also gave rise to numerous strikes and other kinds of labor unrest. Sometimes strikes took place through the action of unions; sometimes workers just decided they had had enough and walked off the job. Whatever the cause, strikes were frequent. In one industry, in one city—the meatpacking industry in Chicago—there were 251 strikes in 1903 alone.

Strikes and absenteeism increased after 1910; labor productivity dropped 10 percent between 1915 and 1918, the first such decline in memory. In many industries, labor turnover became a serious problem; workers changed jobs in droves. Union membership grew. In 1900, only about a million workers—less than 4 percent of the workforce—belonged to unions. By 1920, five million workers belonged, increasing the unionized portion of the workforce to about 13 percent.

As tensions grew between capital and labor, some people in the middle class became fearful that, unless something was done to improve the workers' situation, there might be violence or even revolution. This fear motivated some of the labor-oriented reforms of the Progressive Era. While some reform supporters genuinely wanted to improve labor's lot, others embraced reform because they were afraid of something else.

LABOR UNION MEMBERSHIP, 1897–1920

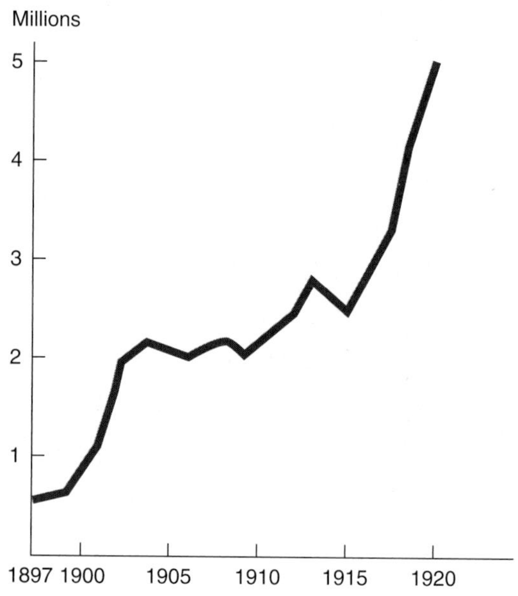

Source: U.S. Bureau of the Census, *Statistical Abstract of the United States: 1982–83* (103rd edition), Washington, D.C., 1982.

Organizing Labor

Samuel Gompers's American Federation of Labor increased from 250,000 members in 1897 to 1.7 million in 1904. By far the largest union organization, it remained devoted to the interests of skilled craftspeople. While it aimed partly at better wages and working conditions, it also sought to limit entry into the crafts and protect worker prerogatives. Within limits, the AFL found acceptance among giant business corporations eager for conservative policies and labor stability.

Of the 8 million female workers in 1910, only 125,000 belonged to unions. Gompers continued to resist organizing them, saying they were too emotional and, as union organizers, "had a way of making serious mistakes." Margaret Dreier Robins, an organizer of proven skill, scoffed at that. "These men died twenty years ago and are just walking around dead!" she protested.

Robins helped found the Women's Trade Union League in 1903. The WTUL led the effort to organize women into trade unions, to lobby for legislation protecting female workers, and to educate the public on the problems and needs of working women. It took in all working women who would join, regardless of skill (although not, at first, African American women), and it won crucial financial support from well-to-do women such as Anne Morgan, daughter of the feared financier J. P. Morgan. Robins's close friend Jane Addams belonged, as did Mary McDowell, the "Angel of the Stockyards," who worked with slaughterhouse workers in Chicago; Julia Lathrop, who tried to improve the lot of wage-earning children; and Dr. Alice Hamilton, a pioneer in American research on the causes of industrial disease.

The WTUL never had many members—a few thousand at most—but its influence extended far beyond its membership. In 1909, it supported the "Uprising of the 20,000," a strike of shirtwaist workers in New York City. When female employees of the Triangle Shirtwaist Company tried to form a union, the company fired them, and they walked out; 20,000 men and women in 500 other shops followed. Strike meetings were conducted in three languages—English, Yiddish, and Italian—and before being forced to go back to work, the strikers won a shorter workweek and a few other gains. Sadly, the Triangle women lost out on another important demand—for unlocked shop doors and safe fire escapes. Their loss proved lethal in the famous Triangle Shirtwaist Company fire of 1911.

The WTUL also backed a strike in 1910 against Hart, Schaffner and Marx, Chicago's largest manufacturer of men's clothing. One day, Annie Shapiro, the 18-year-old daughter of Russian immigrants, was told her wages were being cut from $7 a week to $6.20. That was a large cut, and along with sixteen other young women, Shapiro refused to accept it and walked out. "We had to be recognized as people," she said later. Soon other women walked out, and the revolt spread.

Zoning ordered city development, keeping skyscrapers out of factory districts, factories out of the suburbs. It also had powerful social repercussions. In the South, zoning became a tool to extend racial segregation; in northern cities, it acted against ethnic minorities. Jews in New York, Italians in Boston, Poles in Detroit, African Americans in Chicago—zoning laws held them all at arm's length. Like other migrants, African Americans often preferred to settle together, but zoning also helped put them there. By 1920, ten districts in Chicago were more than three-quarters black. In Los Angeles, Cleveland, Detroit, and Washington, DC, most blacks lived in only two or three wards.

Popular Pastimes

Thanks to changing work rules and mechanization, many Americans enjoyed more leisure time. The average workweek for manufacturing laborers fell from 60 hours in 1890 to 51 in 1920. By the early 1900s, white-collar workers might spend only 8 to 10 hours a day at work and a half day on weekends. Greater leisure time gave more people more opportunity for play and people flocked to places of entertainment. Baseball entrenched itself as the national pastime. Automobiles and streetcars carried growing numbers of fans to ballparks; attendance at major league games doubled between 1903 and 1920. Football also drew fans, although critics attacked the sport's violence and the use of "tramp athletes," nonstudents whom colleges paid to play. In 1905, the worst year, 18 players were killed and 150 seriously injured.

Alarmed, President Theodore Roosevelt—who had once said, "I am the father of three boys [and] if I thought any one of them would weigh a possible broken bone against the glory of being chosen to play on Harvard's football team I would disinherit him"—called a White House conference to clean up college sports. The conference founded the Intercollegiate Athletic Association, which in 1910 became the National Collegiate Athletic Association (NCAA).

Movie theaters opened everywhere. By 1910, there were 10,000 of them, drawing a weekly audience of 10 million people. Admission was usually 5 cents, and movies stressing laughter and pathos appealed to a mass market. In 1915, D. W. Griffith, a talented and creative director—as well as a racist—produced the first movie spectacular: *Birth of a Nation.* Griffith adopted new film techniques, including close-ups, fade-outs, and artistic camera angles, and he staged dramatic battle scenes. (For further discussion of the film, see the Chapter 16 Feature Essay, "Changing Views of Reconstruction," pp. 476–477.)

The "movies" quickly became one of the most popular forms of mass entertainment, and by the 1920s nearly a hundred million Americans were going to the movies each week. Movie theaters sprang up across America, offering patrons a short and inexpensive escape from daily life, such as the popular silent film serial Perils of Pauline *(1914). Viewers flocked to see twenty suspenseful installments in which the heroine evades various attempts on her life, including the abduction shown in this poster for the sixth episode.*

Phonographs brought ready-made entertainment into the home. By 1901, phonograph and record companies included the Victor Talking Machine Company, the Edison Speaking Machine Company, and Columbia Records. Ornate mahogany Victrolas became standard fixtures in middle-class parlors. Early records were usually of vaudeville skits; orchestral recordings began in 1906. In 1919, 2.25 million phonographs were produced; two years later, more than 100 million records were sold.

As record sales grew, families sang less and listened more. Music became a business. In 1909, Congress enacted a copyright law that provided a two-cent royalty on each piece of music on phonograph records or piano rolls. The royalty, small as it was, offered welcome income to composers and publishers, and in 1914, composer Victor Herbert and others formed the American Society of Composers, Authors, and Publishers (ASCAP) to protect musical rights and royalties.

The faster rhythms of syncopated ragtime became the rage, especially after 1911, when Irving Berlin, a Russian immigrant, wrote "Alexander's Ragtime Band." Ragtime set off a nationwide dance craze. Secretaries danced on their lunch hour, the first night-clubs opened, and restaurants and hotels introduced dance floors. Waltzes and polkas gave way to a host of new dances, many with animal names: the fox-trot, bunny hop, turkey trot, snake, and kangaroo dip. Partners were not permitted to dance too close; bouncers tapped them on the shoulder if they got closer than 9 inches. The aging John D. Rockefeller hired a private instructor to teach him the tango; Yale University, however, banned that dance at its 1914 junior prom.

Vaudeville, increasingly popular after 1900, reached maturity around 1915. Drawing on the immigrant experience, it voiced the variety of city life and included skits, songs, comics, acrobats, and magicians. Dances and jokes showed an earthiness new to mass audiences. By 1914, stage runways extended into the crowd; women performers had bared their legs and were beginning to show glimpses of the midriff. Fanny Brice; Ann Pennington, the "shimmy" queen; and Eva Tanguay, who sang "It's All Been Done Before But Not the Way I Do It," starred in Florenz Ziegfeld's Follies, the peak of vaudeville.

In songs like "St. Louis Blues" (1914), W. C. Handy took the black southern folk music of the blues to northern cities. Gertrude "Ma" Rainey, the daughter of minstrels, sang in black vaudeville for nearly thirty-five years. Performing in Chattanooga, Tennessee, about 1910, she came across a 12-year-old orphan, Bessie Smith, who became the "Empress of the Blues." Smith's voice was huge and sweeping. Recording for the Race division of Columbia Records, she made more than eighty records that together sold nearly ten million copies.

Another musical innovation came north from New Orleans. Charles (Buddy) Bolden, a cornetist; Ferdinand "Jelly Roll" Morton, a pianist; and a youngster named Louis Armstrong played an improvisational music that had no formal name. Reaching Chicago, it became "jas," then "jass," and finally "jazz." Jazz jumped, and jazz musicians relied on feeling and mood. A restaurant owner once asked Jelly Roll Morton to play a waltz. "Waltz?" Morton exclaimed. "Man, these people want to dance! And you talking about waltz. This is the Roll you're talking to."

The front jacket cover for Tom Swift and His Undersea Search *by Victor Appleton, one of the pseudonyms used by Edward Stratemeyer. The Stratemeyer Literary Syndicate turned out more than forty volumes about the boy inventor. Stratemeyer and his daughter, Harriet Stratemeyer Adams, also wrote the Nancy Drew mysteries, under the name Carolyn Keene.* ❖

Popular fiction reflected changing interests. Kate Douglas Wiggins's *Rebecca of Sunnybrook Farm* (1903) and Lucy M. Montgomery's *Anne of Green Gables* (1908) showed the continuing popularity of rural themes. Westerns also sold well, but readers turned more and more to detective thrillers with hard-bitten city detectives and science fiction featuring the latest dream in technology. The Tom Swift series, begun in 1910, looked ahead to spaceships, ray guns, and gravity nullifiers.

Edward L. Stratemeyer, the mind behind Tom Swift, brought the techniques of mass production to book writing. In 1906, he formed the Stratemeyer Literary Syndicate, which employed a stable of writers to turn out hundreds of Tom Swift, Rover Boys, and Bobbsey Twins stories for young readers. Burt Standish, another prolific author, took the pen name Gilbert Patten and created the character of Frank Merriwell, wholesome college athlete. As Patten said, "I took the three qualities I most wanted him to represent—frank and merry in nature, well in body and mind—and made the name Frank Merriwell." The Merriwell books sold twenty-five million copies.

Experimentation in the Arts

"There is a state of unrest all over the world in art as in all other things," the director of New York's Metropolitan Museum said in 1908. "It is the same in literature, as in music, in painting, and in sculpture."

Isadora Duncan and Ruth St. Denis transformed the dance. Departing from traditional ballet steps, both women stressed improvisation, emotion, and the human form. "Listen to the music with your soul," Duncan told her students. "Unless your dancing springs from an inner emotion and expresses an idea, it will be meaningless." Draped in flowing robes, she revealed more of her legs than some thought tasteful, and she proclaimed that the "noblest art is the nude." After a triumphant performance with the New York Symphony in 1908, her ideas and techniques swept the country. Duncan died tragically in 1927, her neck broken when her long red scarf caught in the wheel of a racing car.

The lofts and apartments of New York's Greenwich Village attracted artists, writers, and poets interested in experimentation and change. To these artists, the city was the focus of national life and the sign of a new culture. Robert Henri and the realist painters—known to their critics as the **Ashcan School**—relished the city's excitement. They wanted, a friend said, "to paint truth and to paint it with strength and fearlessness and individuality."

To the realists, a painting carried into the future the look of life as it happened. Their paintings depicted street scenes, colorful crowds, and slum children swimming in the river. In paintings such as the *Cliff Dwellers,* George W. Bellows captured the color and excitement of the tenements; John Sloan, one of Henri's most talented students, painted the vitality of ordinary people and familiar scenes.

In 1913, a show at the New York Armory presented sixteen hundred modernist paintings, prints, and sculptures. The work of Picasso, Cézanne, Matisse, Brancusi, Van Gogh, and Gauguin dazed and dazzled American observers. Critics attacked the show as worthless and depraved; a Chicago official wanted it banned from the city because the "idea that people can gaze at this sort of thing without [it] hurting them is all bosh."

George Bellows, Cliff Dwellers *(1913). Bellows's work served as a commentary on contemporary urban life.* ❖

The postimpressionists changed the direction of twentieth-century art and influenced adventuresome American painters. John Marin, Max Weber, Georgia O'Keeffe, Arthur Dove, and other modernists experimented in ways foreign to Henri's realists. Defiantly avant-garde, they shook off convention and experimented with new forms. Using bold colors and abstract patterns, they worked to capture the energy of urban life. "I see great forces at work, great movements," Marin said, "the large buildings and the small buildings, the warring of the great and the small. . . . I can hear the sound of their strife, and there is a great music being played."

There was an extraordinary outburst of poetry. In 1912, Harriet Monroe started the magazine *Poetry* in Chicago, the hotbed of the new poetry; Ezra Pound and Vachel Lindsay, both daring experimenters with ideas and verse, published in the first issue. T. S. Eliot published the classic "Love Song of J. Alfred Prufrock" in *Poetry* in 1915. Attacked bitterly by conservative critics, the poem established Eliot's leadership among a group of poets, many of them living and writing in London, who rejected traditional meter and rhyme as artificial constraints. Eliot, Pound, and Amy Lowell, among others, believed the poet's task was to capture fleeting images in verse.

Others experimenting with new techniques in poetry included Robert Frost (*North of Boston*, 1914), Edgar Lee Masters (*Spoon River Anthology*, 1915), and Carl Sandburg (*Chicago Poems*, 1916). Sandburg's poem "Chicago" celebrated the vitality of the city:

> Come and show me another city with lifted head
> singing so proud to be
> alive and coarse and strong and cunning.
> . . . .
> Fierce as a dog with tongue lapping for action,
> cunning as a savage
> pitted against the wilderness,
> Bareheaded,
> Shoveling,
> Wrecking,
> Planning,
> Building, breaking, rebuilding,
> . . . .
> Bragging and laughing that under his wrist is the
> pulse, and under his
> ribs the heart of the people,
> Laughing!
> Laughing the stormy, husky, brawling laughter of
> Youth, half-naked,
> sweating, proud to be Hog Butcher, Tool
> Maker, Stacker of Wheat,
> Player with Railroads and Freight Handler to
> the Nation.

CHRONOLOGY

1898	Mergers and consolidations begin to sweep the business world, leading to fear of trusts
1903	Ford Motor Company formed ❖ W. E. B. Du Bois calls for justice and equality for African Americans in *The Souls of Black Folk* ❖ Women's Trade Union League (WTUL) formed to organize women workers
1905	Industrial Workers of the World (IWW) established ❖ African American leaders inaugurate the Niagara Movement, advocating integration and equal opportunity for African Americans
1909	Shirtwaist workers in New York City strike in the Uprising of the 20,000 ❖ Campaign by Rockefeller Sanitary Commission wipes out hookworm disease
1910	NAACP founded ❖ Strike at Hart, Schaffner and Marx leads to pioneering collective bargaining agreement ❖ National Collegiate Athletic Association (NCAA) formed
1911	Fire at the Triangle Shirtwaist Company kills 146 people ❖ Irving Berlin popularizes rhythm of ragtime with Alexander's Ragtime Band ❖ Frederick Winslow Taylor publishes *The Principles of Scientific Management*
1912	Harriet Monroe begins publishing magazine *Poetry* ❖ IWW leads strikes in Massachusetts and New Jersey
1913	Ford introduces the moving assembly line in Highland Park, Michigan, plant ❖ Mother's Day becomes national holiday
1915	D. W. Griffith produces the first movie spectacular, *Birth of a Nation* ❖ T. S. Eliot publishes "The Love Song of J. Alfred Prufrock"
1916	Margaret Sanger forms New York Birth Control League ❖ Federal Aid Roads Act creates national road network ❖ New York zoning law sets the pattern for zoning laws across the nation
1917	Congress passes law requiring literacy test for all immigrants
1921	Congress passes the Sheppard-Towner Act to help protect maternal and infant health

Conclusion: A Ferment of Discovery and Reform

Manners and morals change slowly, and many Americans overlooked the importance of the first two decades of the twentieth century. Yet sweeping change was under way; anyone who doubted it could visit a gallery, see a film, listen to music, or read one of the new literary magazines. Garrets and galleries were filled with a breathtaking sense of change. "There was life in all these new things," Marsden Hartley, a modernist painter, recalled. "There was excitement, there was healthy revolt, investigation, discovery, and an utterly new world out of it all."

The ferment of progressivism in city, state, and nation reshaped the country. In a burst of reform, people built playgrounds, restructured taxes, regulated business, won the vote for women, shortened working hours, altered political systems, opened kindergartens, and improved factory safety. They tried to fulfill the national promise of dignity and liberty.

Marsden Hartley, it turned out, had voiced a mood that went well beyond painters and poets. Across society, people in many walks of life were experiencing a similar sense of excitement and discovery. Racism, repression, and labor conflict were present, to be sure, but there was also talk of hope, progress, and change. In politics, science, journalism, education, and a host of other fields, people believed for a time that they could make a difference, and in trying to do so, they became part of the progressive generation.

Recommended Reading

There are several important analyses of the Progressive Era, including Robert H. Wiebe, *The Search for Order, 1877–1920* (1967); Richard Hofstadter, *The Age of Reform* (1955); Samuel P. Hays, *The Response to Industrialism* (1957); and Gabriel Kolko, *The Triumph of Conservatism* (1963). C. Vann Woodward, *Origins of the New South 1877–1913* (1951), is a superb account of developments in the South, along with William A. Link, *The Paradox of Southern Progressivism, 1880–1930* (1992).

George William Shea, *Spoiled Silk: The Red Mayor and the Great Paterson Textile Strike* (2001), and Elliot J. Gorn, *Mother Jones: The Most Dangerous Woman in America* (2001), look at radical labor movements; David I. Macleod, *The Age of the Child: Children in America, 1890–1920* (1998), at children; Nancy C. Unger, *Fighting Bob LaFollette: The Righteous Reformer* (2000), and Patricia A. Schechter, *Ida B. Wells-Barnett and American Reform, 1880–1930* (2001), at specific reformers. Gary Scott Smith, *The Search for Social Salvation: Social Christianity and America, 1880–1925* (2000), and Thomas Winter, *Making Men, Making Class: The YMCA and Workingmen, 1877–1920* (2002), examine the role of religion.

James T. Kloppenberg, *Uncertain Victory: Social Democracy and Progressivism in European and American Thought, 1870–1920* (1986), examines progressivism at home and abroad. C. Vann Woodward, *The Strange Career of Jim Crow* (1955), traces the civil rights setbacks of the Progressive Era.

For a list of additional titles related to this chapter's topics, please see http://www.ablongman.com/divine.

Suggested Web Sites

NAACP Online

http://www.naacp.org/

The National Association for the Advancement of Colored People official Web site explains its mission and includes a primary document explaining the start of the NAACP.

The Evolution of the Conservation Movement, 1850–1920

http://memory.loc.gov/ammem/amrvhtml/conshome.html

This American Memory site brings together scores of primary sources and photographs about "the historical formation and cultural foundations of the movement to conserve and protect America's natural heritage."

The Triangle Shirtwaist Factory Fire, March 25, 1911

http://www.ilr.cornell.edu/trianglefire/

The Kheel Center for Labor-Management Documentation and Archives at Cornell University put together this excellent site composed of oral histories, cartoons, images, and essays.

Labor-Management Conflict in American History

http://www.history.ohio-state.edu/projects/laborconflict/

This site at Ohio State University includes primary accounts of some of the major events in the history of labor-management conflict in the late nineteenth and early twentieth centuries.

Inside an American Factory: The Westinghouse Works, 1904

http://lcweb2.loc.gov/ammem/papr/west/westhome.html

Part of the American Memory Project at the Library of Congress, this site provides a glimpse inside a turn-of-the-century factory.

African American Women Writers of the Nineteenth Century

http://digital.nypl.org/schomburg/writers_aa19/

The New York Public Library's Schomburg Center for Research in Black Culture maintains this site that contains a large number of digital texts by African American women of the nineteenth century.

Touring Turn-of-the-Century America: Photographs from the Detroit Publishing Company, 1880–1920

http://memory.loc.gov/ammem/detroit/dethome.html

This Library of Congress collection has thousands of photographs from turn-of-the-century America.

Bill Haywood Trial (1907)

http://www.law.umkc.edu/faculty/projects/ftrials/haywood/haywood.htm

This site contains images, chronology, court, and official documents maintained by Dr. Doug Linder at University of Missouri–Kansas City Law School.

Margaret Sanger Papers Project

http://www.nyu.edu/projects/sanger/

This site at New York University contains information about Margaret Sanger and digital versions of several of her works.

Scott Joplin, 1868–1817

http://www.lsjunction.com/people/joplin.htm

This site offers information on Joplin and ragtime music.

National Arts and Crafts Archives

http://arts-crafts.com/index.html

This site serves as a guide to materials on the Arts and Crafts movement, which lasted roughly from 1890 to 1929.

Chapter 23

A collage celebrating the career of TR (Theodore Roosevelt)—Rough Rider, assistant secretary of the Navy, builder of the Panama Canal, organizer of the Bull Moose party, and carrier of a "big stick." ❖

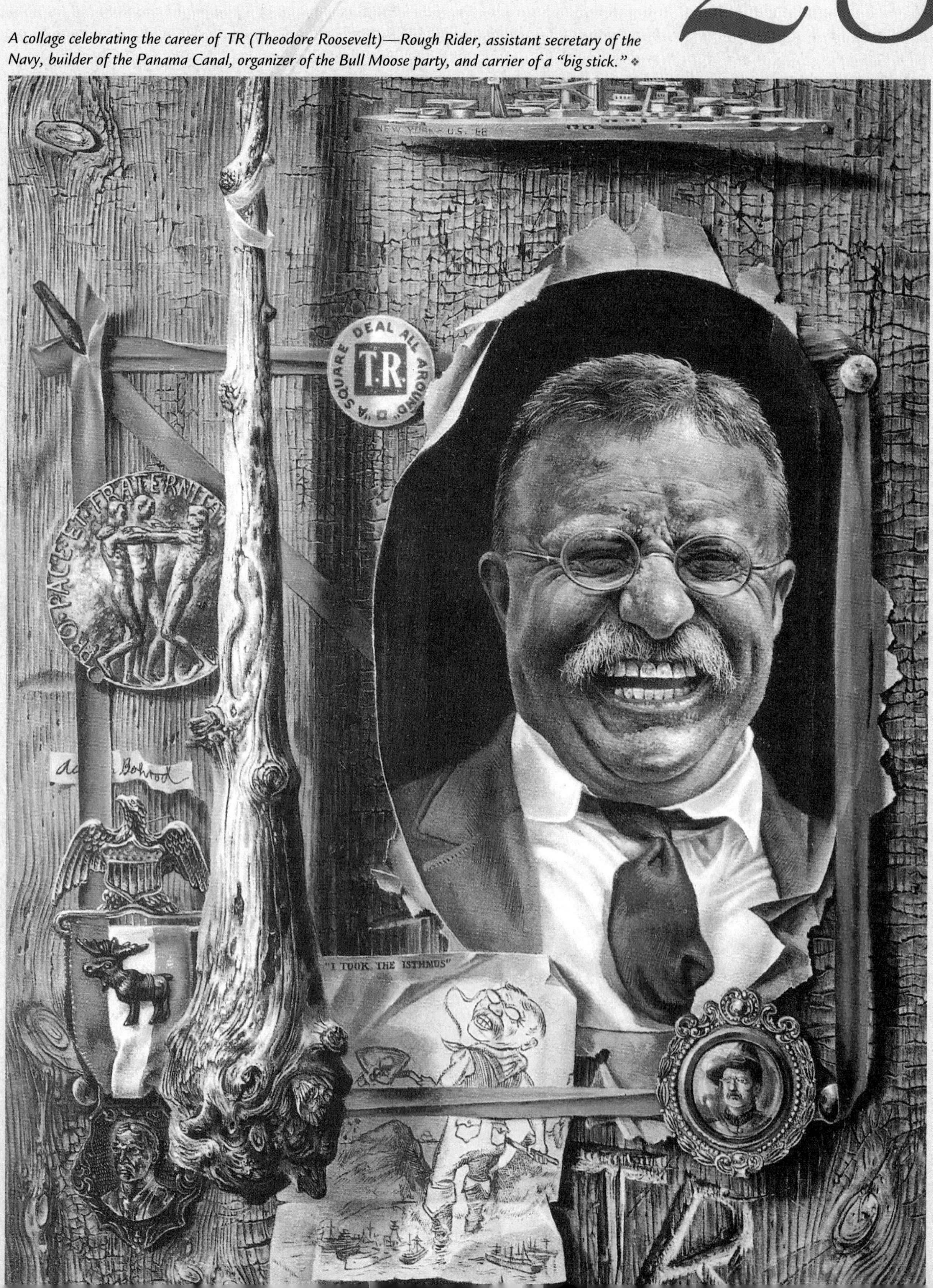

From Roosevelt to Wilson in the Age of Progressivism

The Republicans Split

On a sunny spring morning in 1909, Theodore Roosevelt, wearing the greatcoat of a colonel of the Rough Riders, left New York for a safari in Africa. An ex-president at the age of 50, he had turned over the White House to his chosen successor, William Howard Taft, and was now off for "the joy of wandering through lonely lands, the joy of hunting the mighty and terrible lords" of Africa, "where death broods in the dark and silent depths."

Some of Roosevelt's enemies hoped he would not return. "I trust some lion will do its duty," Wall Street magnate J. P. Morgan said. Always prepared, Roosevelt took nine extra pairs of eyeglasses, and, just in case, several expert hunters accompanied him. When the nearsighted Roosevelt took aim, three others aimed at the same moment. "Mr. Roosevelt had a fairly good idea of the general direction," the safari leader said, "but we couldn't take chances with the life of a former president." Though he had built a reputation as an ardent conservationist, Roosevelt shot nine lions, five elephants, thirteen rhinoceroses, seven hippopotamuses, and assorted other game—acquiring nearly three hundred trophies in all.

It was all good fun, and afterward Roosevelt set off on a tour of Europe. He attended the funeral of the king of England with the crowned heads of Europe, dined with the king and queen of Italy—an experience he likened to "a Jewish wedding on the East Side of New York"—and happily spent five hours reviewing troops of the German empire. Less happily, he followed events back home where, in the judgment of many friends, Taft was not working out as president. Gifford Pinchot, Roosevelt's close companion in the conservation movement, came to Italy to complain personally about Taft, and at almost every stop there were letters waiting for him from other disappointed Republicans.

For his part, Taft was puzzled by it all. Honest and warmhearted, he had intended to continue Roosevelt's policies, even writing Roosevelt that he would "see to it that your judgment in selecting me as your successor and bringing about that succession shall be vindicated." But events turned out differently. The conservative and progressive wings of the Republican party split, and Taft often sided with the conservatives. Among progressive Republicans, Taft's troubles stirred talk of a Roosevelt "back from Elba" movement, akin to Napoleon's return from exile.

Thousands gathered to greet Roosevelt on his return from Europe. He sailed into New York harbor on June 18, 1910, to the sound of naval guns and loud cheers. In characteristic fashion, he had helped make the arrangements: "If there is to be a great crowd, do arrange it so that the whole crowd has a chance to see me and that there is as little disappointment as possible." Greeting Pinchot, one of Taft's leading opponents, with a hearty "Hello, Gifford," Roosevelt slipped away to his home in Oyster Bay, New York, where other friends awaited him.

Outline

Feature Essay

Law and Society

Teddy Roosevelt, with his hunting party in Africa, poses with one of the more than three hundred animals he and his group took down. As president, Roosevelt had supported measures protecting wildlife in the United States, including designating Pelican Island, Florida, as the nation's first wildlife refuge. ❖

He carried with him a touching letter from Taft, received just before he left Europe. "I have had a hard time—I do not know that I have had harder luck than other Presidents, but I do know that thus far I have succeeded far less than have others. I have been conscientiously trying to carry out your policies but my method of doing so has not worked smoothly." Taft invited Teddy to spend a night or two at the White House, but Roosevelt declined, saying that ex-presidents should not visit Washington. Relations between the two friends cooled. "It is hard, very hard," Taft said in 1911, "to see a devoted friendship going to pieces like a rope of sand."

A YEAR LATER, THERE WAS NO longer thought of friendship, only a desperate fight between Taft and Roosevelt for the Republican presidential nomination. Taft won the nomination, but, angry and ambitious, Roosevelt bolted and helped form a new party, the Progressive (or "Bull Moose") party, to unseat Taft and capture the White House. With Taft, Roosevelt, Woodrow Wilson (the Democratic party's candidate), and Socialist party candidate Eugene V. Debs all in the race, the election of 1912 became one of the most exciting in American history.

It was also one of the most important. People were worried about the social and economic effects of urban-industrial growth. The election of 1912 provided a forum for those worries, and, to a degree unusual in American politics, it pitted deeply opposed candidates against one another and outlined differing views of the nation's future. In the spirited battle between Roosevelt and Wilson, it also brought to the forefront some of the currents of progressive reform.

Those currents built on a number of important developments, including the rise of a new professional class, reform movements designed to cure problems in the cities and states, and the activist, achievement-oriented administrations of Roosevelt and Wilson. Together they produced the age of progressivism.

The Spirit of Progressivism

In one way or another, progressivism touched all aspects of society. Politically, it fostered a reform movement that sought cures for the problems of city, state, and nation. Intellectually, it drew on the expertise of the new social sciences and reflected a shift from older absolutes such as religion to newer schools of thought that emphasized relativism and the role of the environment in human development. Culturally, it inspired fresh modes of expression in dance, film, painting, literature, and architecture. Touching individuals in different ways, progressivism became a set of attitudes as well as a definable movement.

Though broad and diverse, progressivism as a whole had a half dozen characteristics that gave it definition. First, the progressives acted out of concern about the effects of industrialization and the conditions of industrial life. While their viewpoints varied, they did not, as a rule, set out to harm big business, but instead sought to humanize and regulate it.

In pursuing these objectives, the progressives displayed a second characteristic: a fundamental optimism about human nature, the possibilities of progress, and the capacity of people to recognize problems and take action to solve them. Progressives believed they could "investigate, educate, and legislate"—learn about a problem, inform people about it, and, with the help of an informed public, find and enforce a solution.

Third, more than many earlier reformers, the progressives were willing to intervene in people's lives, confident that it was their right to do so. They knew best, some of them thought, and as a result, there was an element of coercion in a number of their ideas. Fourth, while progressives preferred if possible to use voluntary means to achieve reform, they tended to turn more and more to the authority of the state and government at all levels in order to put into effect the reforms they wanted.

As a fifth characteristic, many progressives drew on a combination of evangelical Protestantism (which gave them the desire—and, they thought, the duty—to purge the world of sins such as prostitution and drunkenness) and the natural and social sciences (whose theories made them confident that they could understand and control the environment in which people lived). Progressives tended to view the environment as a key to reform, thinking—in the way some economists, sociologists, and other social scientists were suggesting—that if they could change the environment, they could change the individual.

Finally, progressivism was distinctive because it touched virtually the whole nation. Not everyone, of course, was a progressive, and there were many who opposed or ignored the ideas of the movement. There were also those who were untouched by progressive reforms and those whom the movement overlooked. But in one way or another, a remarkable number of people were caught up in it, giving progressivism a national reach and a mass base.

That was one of the features, in fact, that set it off from populism, which had grown mostly in the rural South and West. Progressivism drew support from across society. "The thing that constantly amazed me," said William Allen White, a leading progressive journalist, "was how many people were with us." Progressivism appealed to the expanding middle class, prosperous farmers, and skilled laborers; it also attracted significant support in the business community.

The progressives believed in progress and disliked waste. No single issue or concern united them all. Some progressives wanted to clean up city governments, others to clean up city streets. Some wanted to purify politics or control corporate abuses, others to eradicate poverty or prostitution. Some demanded social justice in the form of women's rights, child labor laws, temperance, and factory safety. They were Democrats, Republicans, Socialists, and independents.

Progressives believed in a better world and in the ability of people to achieve it. They paid to people, as a friend said of social reformer Florence Kelley, "the high compliment of believing that, once they knew the truth, they would act upon it." Progress depended on knowledge. The progressives stressed individual morality and collective action, the scientific method, and the value of expert opinion. Like contemporary business leaders, they valued system, planning, management, and predictability. They wanted not only reform but efficiency. In the introduction to *The Shame of the Cities*, Steffens said that the cure for American ills lay in "good conduct in the individual, simple honesty, courage, and efficiency."

Historians once viewed progressivism as the triumph of one group in society over another. In this view, farmers took on the hated and powerful railroads; upstart reformers challenged the city bosses; business interests fought for favorable legislation; youthful professionals carved out their place in society. Now, historians stress the way progressivism brought people together rather than drove them apart. Disparate groups united in an effort to improve the well-being of many groups in society.

The Rise of the Professions

Progressivism fed on an organizational impulse that encouraged people to join forces, share information, and solve problems. Between 1890 and 1920, a host of national societies and associations took shape—nearly four hundred of them in just three decades. Groups such as the National Child Labor Committee, which lobbied for legislation to regulate the employment and working conditions of children, were formed to attack specific issues. Other groups reflected one of the most significant developments in American society at the turn of the century—the rise of the professions.

Growing rapidly in these years, the professions—law, medicine, religion, business, teaching, and social work—were the source of much of the leadership of the progressive movement. The professions attracted young, educated men and women, who in turn were part of a larger trend: a dramatic increase in the number of individuals working in administrative and professional jobs. In businesses, these people were managers, architects, technicians, and accountants. In city governments, they were experts in everything from education to sanitation. They organized and ran the urban-industrial society.

These professionals formed part of a new middle class whose members did not derive their status from birth or inherited wealth, as had many members of the older middle class. Instead, they moved ahead through education and personal accomplishment and worked to become doctors, lawyers, ministers, and teachers. Proud of their skills, they were ambitious and self-confident, and they thought of themselves as experts who could use their knowledge for the benefit of society. (See the Feature Essay, "Madam C.J. Walker: African American Business Pioneer," pp. 680–681.)

As a way of asserting their status, they formed professional societies to look after their interests and govern entry into their professions. Just a few years before, for example, a doctor had become a doctor simply by stocking up on patent medicines and hanging out a sign. Now doctors began to insist they were part of a medical profession, and they wanted to set educational requirements and minimum standards for practice. In 1901, they reorganized the American Medical Association (AMA) and made it into a modern national professional society. The AMA had 8400 members that year. A decade later, it had more than 70,000, and by 1920, nearly two-thirds of all doctors belonged.

Other groups and professions showed the same pattern. Lawyers formed bar associations, created examining boards, and lobbied for regulations restricting entry into the profession. Teachers organized the National Education Association (1905) and pressed for teacher certification and compulsory education laws. Social workers formed the National Federation of Settlements (1911); business leaders created the National Association of Manufacturers (1895) and the U.S. Chamber of Commerce (1912); and farmers joined the National Farm Bureau Federation to spread information about farming and to try to improve their lot.

Working both as individuals and groups, members of the professions had a major impact on the era, as the career of one of them, Dr. Alice Hamilton, illustrated. Hamilton early decided to devote her life to helping the less fortunate. Choosing medicine, she went to the University of Michigan Medical School, one of a shrinking number of medical schools that admitted women, and then settled in Chicago, where she met Jane Addams and took a room in Hull House. Soon thereafter, she traced a local typhoid epidemic to flies carrying germs from open privies. The study won national acclaim, but Hamilton had already turned her attention to the work-related illnesses she found everywhere around Hull House.

Combining field study with meticulous laboratory techniques, she pioneered research into the causes of lead poisoning and other industrial disease. In 1908, the governor of Illinois appointed her to a commission on occupational diseases; two years later, she headed a statewide survey of industrial poisons. Thanks to her work, in 1911, Illinois passed the first state law providing compensation for industrial disease caused by poisonous fumes and dust. By the end of the 1930s, all the major industrial states had such laws.

One of the new professionals, Hamilton had used her education and skill to broaden knowledge of her subject, change industrial practices, and improve the lives of countless workers. "For me," she said later in a comment characteristic of the progressives, "the satisfaction is that things are better now, and I had some part in it."

The Social-Justice Movement

As Alice Hamilton's career exemplified, progressivism began in the cities during the 1890s. It first took form around settlement workers and others interested in freeing individuals from the crushing impact of cities and factories.

Ministers, intellectuals, social workers, and lawyers joined in a **social-justice movement** that focused national attention on the need for tenement house laws, more stringent child labor legislation, and better working conditions for women. They brought pressure on municipal agencies for more and better parks, playgrounds, day nurseries, schools, and community services. Blending private and public action, settlement leaders turned increasingly to government aid. "Private beneficence," Jane Addams said, "is totally inadequate to deal with the vast numbers of the city's disinherited."

Social-justice reformers were more interested in social cures than individual charity. Unlike earlier reformers, they saw problems as endless and interrelated; individuals became part of a city's larger patterns. With that insight, social-service casework shifted from a focus on an individual's well-being to a scientific analysis of neighborhoods, occupations, and classes.

In the spring of 1900, the Charity Organization Society of New York held a tenement house exhibition that graphically presented the new kind of sociological data. Put together by Lawrence Veiller, a young social worker, the exhibition included more than a thousand photographs, detailed maps of slum districts, statistical tables and charts, and graphic cardboard depictions of tenement blocks. Never before had so much information been pulled together in one place. Veiller correlated data on poverty and disease with housing

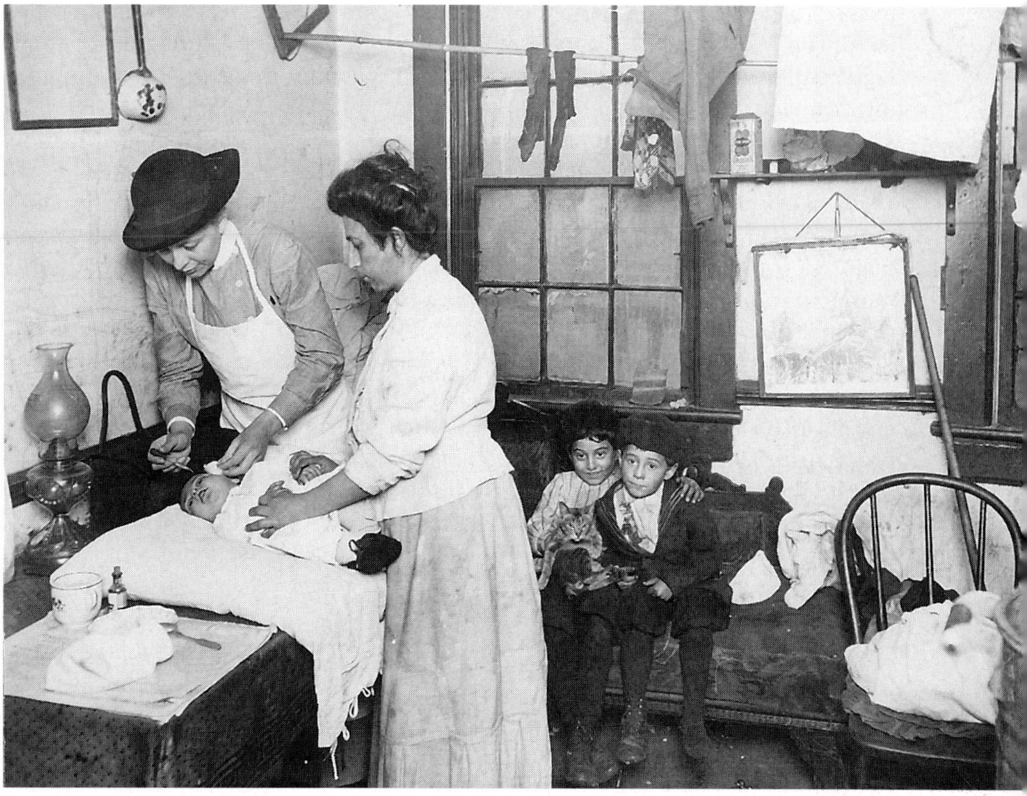

An Infant Welfare Society nurse treats the baby of an immigrant family in Chicago. A host of medical discoveries and improvements in the quality of medical education fostered an interest in public health work among the social-justice reformers. ❖

conditions, and he pointed out that new slums were springing up in more areas of the city. Stirred by the public outcry, Governor Theodore Roosevelt appointed the New York State Tenement House Commission to do something about the problem.

With Veiller's success as a model, study after study analyzed the condition of the poor. Books and pamphlets such as *The Standard of Living Among Working Men's Families in New York City* (1909) contained pages of data on family budgets, women's wages and working conditions, child labor, and other matters. Between 1910 and 1913, the U.S. Commissioner of Labor issued a massive nineteen-volume report on *Conditions of Women and Children Wage-Earners in the United States.*

Social-justice reformers, banding together to work for change, formed the National Conference of Charities and Corrections, which in 1915 became the National Conference of Social Work. Controlled by social workers, the conference reflected the growing professionalization of reform. Through it, social workers discovered each other's efforts, shared methodology, and tried to establish themselves as a separate field within the social sciences. Once content with informal training sessions in a settlement house living room, they now founded complete professional schools at Chicago, Harvard, and other universities. After 1909, they had their own professional magazine, the *Survey,* and instead of piecemeal reforms, they aimed at a comprehensive program of minimum wages, maximum hours, workers' compensation, and widows' pensions.

The Purity Crusade

Working in city neighborhoods, social-justice reformers were often struck by the degree to which alcohol affected the lives of the people they were trying to help. Workers drank away their wages; some men spent more time at the saloon than at home. Drunkenness caused violence, and it angered employers who did not want intoxicated workers on the job. In countless ways, alcohol wasted human resources, the reformers believed, and along with business leaders, ministers, and others, they launched a crusade to remove the evils of drink from American life.

At the head of the crusade was the Women's Christian Temperance Union (WCTU), which had continued to grow since it was founded in the 1870s. By 1911, the WCTU had nearly a quarter of a million members; it was the largest organization of women in American history to that time. In 1893, it was joined by the Anti-Saloon League, and together the groups pressed to abolish alcohol and the places where it was consumed. By 1916, they had succeeded in nineteen states, but as drinking continued elsewhere, they pushed for a nationwide law. In the midst of the moral fervor of World War I, they succeeded, and the Eighteenth Amendment to the Constitution, prohibiting the manufacture, sale, and transportation of intoxicating liquors, took effect in January 1920.

The amendment encountered troubles later in the 1920s as the social atmosphere changed, but at the time it passed, progressives thought Prohibition was a major step toward eliminating social instability and moral wrong. In a similar fashion, some progressive reformers also worked to get rid of prostitution, convinced that poverty and ignorance drove women to the trade. By 1915, nearly every state had banned brothels, and in 1910, Congress passed the Mann Act, which prohibited the interstate transportation of women for immoral purposes. Like the campaign against liquor, the campaign against prostitution reflected the era's desire to purify and elevate, often through the instrument of government action.

Woman Suffrage, Women's Rights

Women played a large role in the social-justice movement. Feminists were particularly active, especially in the political sphere, between 1890 and 1914—feminists were more active then, in fact, than at any other time until the 1960s. Some working-class women pushed for higher wages and better working conditions. College-educated women—five thousand a year graduated after 1900—took up careers in the professions, from which some of them supported reform. From 1890 to 1910, the work of a number of national women's organizations, including the National Council of Jewish Women, the National Congress of Mothers, and the Women's Trade Union League, furthered the aims of the progressive movement.

Excluded from most of these organizations, African American women formed their own groups. The National Association of Colored Women was founded in 1895, fourteen years before the better known male-oriented National Association for the Advancement of Colored People (NAACP). Aimed at social welfare, the women's organization was the first African American social-service agency in the country. At the local level, African American women's clubs established kindergartens, day nurseries, playgrounds, and retirement homes.

From 200,000 members in 1900, the General Federation of Women's Clubs grew to more than 1 million by 1912. The clubs met, as they had before, for coffee and literary conversation, but they also began to look closely at conditions around them. In 1904, Mrs. Sarah P. Decker, the federation's new president, told the national convention, "Ladies, you have chosen me your leader. Well, I have an important piece of news to give you. Dante is dead. He has been dead for several centuries, and I think it is time that we dropped the study of his *Inferno* and turned our attention to our own."

Forming an Industrial Section and a Committee on Legislation for Women and Children, the federation supported reforms to safeguard child and women workers, improve schools, ensure pure food, and beautify the community. Reluctant at first, the federation finally lent support in 1914 to woman suffrage, a cause that dated back to the first women's rights convention in Seneca Falls, New York, in 1848. Divided over tactics since the Civil War, the suffrage movement suffered from disunity, male opposition, indecision over whether to seek action at the state or at the national level, resistance from the Catholic Church, and opposition from liquor interests, who linked the cause to Prohibition.

Women in the social-justice movement needed to influence elected officials—most of them men, whom they could not reach through the vote. Because politics was an avenue for reform, growing numbers of women activists became involved in the suffrage movement. After years of disagreement, the two major suffrage organizations, the National Woman Suffrage Association and the American Woman Suffrage Association, merged in 1890 to form the National American Woman Suffrage Association. The merger opened a new phase of the suffrage movement, characterized by unity and a tightly controlled national organization.

In 1900, Carrie Chapman Catt, a superb organizer, became president of the National American Woman Suffrage Association, which by 1920 had nearly two million members. Catt and Anna Howard Shaw, who became the association's head in 1904, believed in organization and peaceful lobbying to win the vote. Alice Paul and Lucy Burns, founders of the Congressional Union, were more militant; they interrupted public meetings, focused on Congress rather than the states, and in 1917 picketed the White House.

Significantly, Catt, Paul, and others made a major change in the argument for woman suffrage. When the campaign began in the nineteenth century, suffragists had claimed the vote as a natural right, owed to women as much as men. Now, they stressed a pragmatic argument: Since women were more sensitive to moral issues than men, they would use their votes to help create a better society. They would support temperance, clean government, laws to protect workers, and other reforms. This argument attracted many progressives who believed the women's vote would purify politics. In 1918, the House passed a constitutional amendment stating simply that the right to vote shall not be denied "on account of sex." The Senate and enough states followed, and, after three generations of